Lecture Notes in Computer Science 1855
Edited by G. Goos, J. Hartmanis and J. van Leeuwen

Springer
*Berlin
Heidelberg
New York
Barcelona
Hong Kong
London
Milan
Paris
Singapore
Tokyo*

E. Allen Emerson   A. Prasad Sistla (Eds.)

Computer Aided Verification

12th International Conference, CAV 2000
Chicago, IL, USA, July 15-19, 2000
Proceedings

Springer

Series Editors

Gerhard Goos, Karlsruhe University, Germany
Juris Hartmanis, Cornell University, NY, USA
Jan van Leeuwen, Utrecht University, The Netherlands

Volume Editors

E. Allen Emerson
University of Texas, Computer Sciences Department
Taylor Hall 2.124, Austin, TX 78712, USA
E-mail: emerson@cs.utexas.edu

A. Prasad Sistla
University of Illinois at Chicago
Electrical Engineering and Computer Science Department
851 South Morgan Street, Chicago, IL 60607, USA
E-mail: sistla@surya.eecs.uic.edu

Cataloging-in-Publication Data applied for

Die Deutsche Bibliothek - CIP-Einheitsaufnahme

Computer aided verification : 12th international conference ;
proceedings / CAV 2000, Chicago, IL, USA, July 15 - 19, 2000. E. Allen
Emerson ; A. Prasad Sistla (ed.). - Berlin ; Heidelberg ; New York ;
Barcelona ; Hong Kong ; London ; Milan ; Paris ; Singapore ; Tokyo :
Springer, 2000
  (Lecture notes in computer science ; Vol. 1855)
  ISBN 3-540-67770-4

CR Subject Classification (1998): F.3, D.2.4, D.2.2, F.4.1, B.7.2, C.3, I.2.3

ISSN 0302-9743
ISBN 3-540-67770-4 Springer-Verlag Berlin Heidelberg New York

This work is subject to copyright. All rights are reserved, whether the whole or part of the material is
concerned, specifically the rights of translation, reprinting, re-use of illustrations, recitation, broadcasting,
reproduction on microfilms or in any other way, and storage in data banks. Duplication of this publication
or parts thereof is permitted only under the provisions of the German Copyright Law of September 9, 1965,
in its current version, and permission for use must always be obtained from Springer-Verlag. Violations are
liable for prosecution under the German Copyright Law.

Springer-Verlag is a company in the BertelsmannSpringer publishing group.
© Springer-Verlag Berlin Heidelberg 2000
Printed in Germany

Typesetting: Camera-ready by author, data conversion by PTP-Berlin, Stefan Sossna
Printed on acid-free paper   SPIN: 10722167   06/3142   5 4 3 2 1 0

Preface

This volume contains the proceedings of the 12th International Conference on Computer Aided Verification (CAV 2000) held in Chicago, Illinois, USA during 15-19 July 2000.

The CAV conferences are devoted to the advancement of the theory and practice of formal methods for hardware and software verification. The conference covers the spectrum from theoretical foundations to concrete applications, with an emphasis on verification algorithms, methods, and tools together with techniques for their implementation. The conference has traditionally drawn contributions from both researchers and practitioners in academia and industry. This year 91 regular research papers were submitted out of which 35 were accepted, while 14 brief tool papers were submitted, out of which 9 were accepted for presentation. CAV included two invited talks and a panel discussion. CAV also included a tutorial day with two invited tutorials.

Many industrial companies have shown a serious interest in CAV, ranging from using the presented technologies in their business to developing and marketing their own formal verification tools. We are very proud of the support we receive from industry. CAV 2000 was sponsored by a number of generous and forward-looking companies and organizations including: Cadence Design Systems, IBM Research, Intel, Lucent Technologies, Mentor Graphics, the Minerva Center for Verification of Reactive Systems, Siemens, and Synopsys.

The CAV conference was founded by its Steering Committee: Edmund Clarke (CMU), Bob Kurshan (Bell Labs), Amir Pnueli (Weizmann), and Joseph Sifakis (Verimag).

The conference program for this year's CAV 2000 was selected by the program committee: Parosh Abdulla (Uppsala), Rajeev Alur (U. Penn and Bell Labs), Henrik Reif Andersen (ITU Copenhagen), Ed Brinksma (Twente), Randy Bryant (CMU), Werner Damm (Oldenburg), David Dill (Stanford), E. Allen Emerson, co-chair (U. Texas-Austin), Steven German (IBM), Rob Gerth (Intel), Patrice Godefroid (Bell Labs), Ganesh Gopalakrishnan (U. Utah), Mike Gordon (Cambridge), Nicolas Halbwachs (Verimag), Warren Hunt (IBM), Bengt Jonsson (Uppsala), Kim Larsen (Aalborg), Ken McMillan (Cadence), John Mitchell (Stanford), Doron Peled (Bell Labs), Carl Pixley (Motorola), Amir Pnueli (Weizmann), Bill Roscoe (Oxford), Joseph Sifakis (Verimag), A. Prasad Sistla, co-chair (U. Illinois-Chicago), Fabio Somenzi (U. Colorado), and Pierre Wolper (Liege).

We are grateful to the following additional reviewers who aided the reviewing process: Will Adams, Nina Amla, Flemming Andersen, Tamarah Arons, Eugene Asarin, Mohammad Awedh, Adnan Aziz, Clark Barrett, Gerd Behrmann, Wendy Belluomini, Michael Benedikt, Saddek Bensalem, Ritwik Bhattacharya, Tom Bienmueller, Per Bjesse, Roderick Bloem, Juergen Bohn, Bernard Boigelot, Ahmed Bouajjani, Olivier Bournez, Marius Bozga, P. Broadfoot, Udo Brockmeyer, Glenn Bruns, Annette Bunker, Paul Caspi, Prosenjit Chatterjee, Hubert Common, Jordi Cortadella, Sadie Creese, David Cyrluk, Pedro D'Argenio, Satyaki Das, Luca de Alfaro, Willem-P. de Roever, Juergen Dingel, Dan DuVarney, Joost Engelfriet, Kousha Etessami, David Fink, Dana Fisman, Martin Fraenzle, Laurent Fribourg, Malay Ganai, Vijay Garg, Jens Chr. Godskesen, Jeff Golden, M. H. Goldsmith, Guarishankar Govindaraju, Susanne Graf, Radu Grosu, Aarti Gupta, Dilian Gurov, John Havlicek, Nevin Heinze, Holger Hermanns, Thomas Hildebrandt, Pei-Hsin Ho, Holger Hermanns, Ravi Hosabettu, Jae-Young Jang Henrik Hulgaard, Thomas Hune, Hardi Hungar, Anna Ingolfsdottir, Norris Ip, Purushothaman Iyer, Hans Jacobson, Damir Jamsek, Jae-Young Jang, Henrik Ejersbo Jensen, Somesh Jha, Michael Jones, Bernhard Josko, Vineet Kahlon, Joost-Pieter Katoen, Yonit Kesten, Nils Klarlund, Josva Kleist, Kare Jelling Kristoffersen, Andreas Kuehlmann, Robert P. Kurshan, Yassine Lakhnech, Rom Langerak, Salvatore La Torre, Ranko Lazic, Jakob Lichtenberg, Orna Lichtenstein, Jorn Lind-Nielsen, Hans Henrik Løvengreen, Enrico Macii, Angelika Mader, Oded Maler, Pete Manolios, Monica Marcus, Abdelillah Mokkedem, Faron Moller, Jesper Moller, Oliver Möller, In-Ho Moon, Laurent Mounier, Chris Myers, Luay Nakhleh, Kedar Namjoshi, Tom Newcomb, Flemming Nielson, Kasper Overgård Nielsen, Marcus Nilsson, Thomas Noll, David Nowak, Aletta Nylen, Manish Pandey, George Pappas, Atanas Parashkevov, Abelardo Pardo, Catherine Parent-Vigouroux, David Park, Justin Pearson, Paul Pettersson, Nir Piterman, Carlos Puchol, Shaz Qadeer, Stefano Quer, Theis Rauhe, Antoine Rauzy, Kavita Ravi, Judi Romijn, Sitvanit Ruah, Theo Ruys, Jun Sawada, Alper Sen, Peter Sestoft, Ali Sezgin, Elad Shahar, Ofer Shtrichman, Arne Skou, Uli Stern, Kanna Shimizu, Scott D. Stoller, Ian Sutherland, Richard Trefler, Jan Tretmans, Stavros Tripakis, Annti Valmari, Helmut Vieth, Sergei Vorobyov, Bow-Yaw Wang, Farn Wang, Poul F. Williams, Chris Wilson, Hanno Wupper, Jason Yang, Wang Yi, Tsay Yih-Kuen, Sergio Yovine, and Jun Yuan.

Finally, we would like to give our special thanks to John Havlicek for his enormous assistance overall including maintaining the CAV web site, the cav2k account, and in preparing the proceedings. We appreciate the assistance of the UTCS computer support staff, especially John Chambers. We are also most grateful, to Richard Gerber for kindly lending us his "START" conference management software as well as his prompt assistance when a file server error masqueraded as a web server error.

June 2000 E. Allen Emerson and A. Prasad Sistla

Table of Contents

Invited Talks and Tutorials

Keynote Address: Abstraction, Composition, Symmetry, and a Little Deduction: The Remedies to State Explosion 1
   A. Pnueli

Invited Address: Applying Formal Methods to Cryptographic Protocol Analysis 2
   C. Meadows

Invited Tutorial: Boolean Satisfiability Algorithms and Applications in Electronic Design Automation 3
   J. Marques-Silva, K. Sakallah

Invited Tutorial: Verification of Infinite-State and Parameterized Systems . 4
   P.A. Abdulla, B. Jonsson

Regular Papers

An Abstraction Algorithm for the Verification of Generalized C-Slow Designs   5
   J. Baumgartner, A. Tripp, A. Aziz, V. Singhal, F. Andersen

Achieving Scalability in Parallel Reachability Analysis of Very Large Circuits   20
   T. Heyman, D. Geist, O. Grumberg, A. Schuster

An Automata-Theoretic Approach to Reasoning about Infinite-State Systems 36
   O. Kupferman, M.Y. Vardi

Automatic Verification of Parameterized Cache Coherence Protocols 53
   G. Delzanno

Binary Reachability Analysis of Discrete Pushdown Timed Automata 69
   Z. Dang, O.H. Ibarra, T. Bultan, R.A. Kemmerer, J. Su

Boolean Satisfiability with Transitivity Constraints 85
   R.E. Bryant, M.N. Velev

Bounded Model Construction for Monadic Second-Order Logics 99
   A. Ayari, D. Basin

Building Circuits from Relations 113
   J.H. Kukula, T.R. Shiple

Combining Decision Diagrams and SAT Procedures for Efficient Symbolic Model Checking 124
    P.F. Williams, A. Biere, E.M. Clarke, A. Gupta

On the Completeness of Compositional Reasoning 139
    K.S. Namjoshi, R.J. Trefler

Counterexample-Guided Abstraction Refinement 154
    E. Clarke, O. Grumberg, S. Jha, Y. Lu, H. Veith

Decision Procedures for Inductive Boolean Functions Based on Alternating Automata 170
    A. Ayari, D. Basin, F. Klaedtke

Detecting Errors Before Reaching Them 186
    L. de Alfaro, T.A. Henzinger, F.Y.C. Mang

A Discrete Strategy Improvement Algorithm for Solving Parity Games 202
    J. Vöge, M. Jurdziński

Distributing Timed Model Checking – How the Search Order Matters 216
    G. Behrmann, T. Hune, F. Vaandrager

Efficient Algorithms for Model Checking Pushdown Systems 232
    J. Esparza, D. Hansel, P. Rossmanith, S. Schwoon

Efficient Büchi Automata from LTL Formulae 248
    F. Somenzi, R. Bloem

Efficient Detection of Global Properties in Distributed Systems Using Partial-Order Methods 264
    S.D. Stoller, L. Unnikrishnan, Y.A. Liu

Efficient Reachability Analysis of Hierarchical Reactive Machines 280
    R. Alur, R. Grosu, M. McDougall

Formal Verification of VLIW Microprocessors with Speculative Execution . 296
    M.N. Velev

Induction in Compositional Model Checking 312
    K.L. McMillan, S. Qadeer, J.B. Saxe

Liveness and Acceleration in Parameterized Verification 328
    A. Pnueli, E. Shahar

Mechanical Verification of an Ideal Incremental ABR Conformance Algorithm 344
    M. Rusinowitch, S. Stratulat, F. Klay

Model Checking Continuous-Time Markov Chains by Transient Analysis .. 358
  C. Baier, B. Haverkort, H. Hermanns, J.-P. Katoen

Model-Checking for Hybrid Systems by Quotienting and Constraints
Solving 373
  F. Cassez, F. Laroussinie

Prioritized Traversal: Efficient Reachability Analysis for Verification and
Falsification 389
  R. Fraer, G. Kamhi, B. Ziv, M.Y. Vardi, L. Fix

Regular Model Checking 403
  A. Bouajjani, B. Jonsson, M. Nilsson, T. Touili

Symbolic Techniques for Parametric Reasoning about Counter and Clock
Systems 419
  A. Annichini, E. Asarin, A. Bouajjani

Syntactic Program Transformations for Automatic Abstraction 435
  K.S. Namjoshi, R.P. Kurshan

Temporal-Logic Queries 450
  W. Chan

Are Timed Automata Updatable? 464
  P. Bouyer, C. Dufourd, E. Fleury, A. Petit

Tuning SAT Checkers for Bounded Model Checking 480
  O. Shtrichman

Unfoldings of Unbounded Petri Nets 495
  P.A. Abdulla, S.P. Iyer, A. Nylén

Verification Diagrams Revisited: Disjunctive Invariants for Easy
Verification 508
  J. Rushby

Verifying Advanced Microarchitectures that Support Speculation and
Exceptions 521
  R. Hosabettu, G. Gopalakrishnan, M. Srivas

Tool Papers

FoCs: Automatic Generation of Simulation Checkers from Formal
Specifications 538
  Y. Abarbanel, I. Beer, L. Gluhovsky, S. Keidar, Y. Wolfsthal

IF: A Validation Environment for Timed Asynchronous Systems 543
  M. Bozga, J.-C. Fernandez, L. Ghirvu, S. Graf, J.-P. Krimm, L. Mounier

Integrating WS1S with PVS 548
    S. Owre, H. Rueß

PET: An Interactive Software Testing Tool 552
    E. Gunter, R. Kurshan, D. Peled

A Proof-Carrying Code Architecture for Java 557
    C. Colby, P. Lee, G.C. Necula

The STATEMATE Verification Environment – Making It Real 561
    T. Bienmüller, W. Damm, H. Wittke

TAPS: A First-Order Verifier for Cryptographic Protocols 568
    E. Cohen

VINAS-P: A Tool for Trace Theoretic Verification of Timed Asynchronous
Circuits 572
    T. Yoneda

XMC: A Logic-Programming-Based Verification Toolset 576
    C.R. Ramakrishnan, I.V. Ramakrishnan, S.A. Smolka, Y. Dong, X. Du,
    A. Roychoudhury, V.N. Venkatakrishnan

Author Index 581

Keynote Address

Abstraction, Composition, Symmetry, and a Little Deduction: The Remedies to State Explosion

Amir Pnueli

Faculty of Mathematics and Computer Science
The Weizmann Institute of Science
76100 Rehovot, Israel

Abstract. In this talk, we will consider possible remedies to the State Explosion problem, enabling the verification of large designs. All of these require some user interaction and cannot be done in a fully automatic manner. We will explore the tradeoffs and connections between the different approaches, such as deduction and abstraction, searching for the most natural and convenient mode of user interaction, and speculate about useful additional measures of automation which can make the task of user supervision even simpler.

Invited Address:

Applying Formal Methods to Cryptographic Protocol Analysis

Catherine Meadows

Naval Research Laboratory
Washington, DC 20375

Abstract. Protocols using encryption to communicate securely and privately are essential to the protection of our infrastructure. However, since they must be designed to work even under the most hostile conditions, it is not easy to design them correctly. As a matter of fact, it is possible for such protocols to be incorrect even if the cryptographic algorithms they use work perfectly. Thus, over the last few years there has been considerable interest in applying formal methods to the problem of verifying that these protocols are correct. In this talk we give a brief history of this area, and describe some of the emerging issues and new research problems.

Invited Tutorial:

Boolean Satisfiability Algorithms and Applications in Electronic Design Automation

João Marques-Silva[1] and Karem Sakallah[2]

[1] Instituto de Engenharia de Sistemas e Computadores (INESC)
R. Alves Redol, 9
1000-029 Lisboa, Portugal
[2] Electrical Engineering and Computer Science Department
Advanced Computer Architecture Laboratory (ACAL)
The University of Michigan
Ann Arbor, Michigan 48109-2122

Abstract. Boolean Satisfiability (SAT) is often used as the underlying model for a significant and increasing number of applications in Electronic Design Automation (EDA) as well as in many other fields of Computer Science and Engineering. In recent years, new and efficient algorithms for SAT have been developed, allowing much larger problem instances to be solved. SAT "packages" are currently expected to have an impact on EDA applications similar to that of BDD packages since their introduction more than a decade ago. This tutorial paper is aimed at introducing the EDA professional to the Boolean satisfiability problem. Specifically, we highlight the use of SAT models to formulate a number of EDA problems in such diverse areas as test pattern generation, circuit delay computation, logic optimization, combinational equivalence checking, bounded model checking and functional test vector generation, among others. In addition, we provide an overview of the algorithmic techniques commonly used for solving SAT, including those that have seen widespread use in specific EDA applications. We categorize these algorithmic techniques, indicating which have been shown to be best suited for which tasks.

Invited Tutorial:

Verification of Infinite-State and Parameterized Systems

Parosh Aziz Abdulla and Bengt Jonsson

Department of Computer Systems
Uppsala University
Uppsala, Sweden

Abstract. Over the last few years there has been an increasing research effort directed towards the automatic verification of infinite-state systems. There are now verification techniques for many classes of infinite-state systems, including timed and hybrid automata, petri nets, pushdown systems, systems with FIFO channels, systems with a simple treatment of data, etc. In this tutorial, we will cover general verification techniques that have been used for infinite-state and parameterized systems, and try to show their power and limitations. Such techniques are e.g., symbolic model-checking techniques, abstraction, induction over the networks structure, widening, and automata-based techniques. We will focus on linear-time safety and liveness properties.

An Abstraction Algorithm for the Verification of Generalized C-Slow Designs

Jason Baumgartner[1], Anson Tripp[1], Adnan Aziz[2], Vigyan Singhal[3], and Flemming Andersen[1]

[1] IBM Corporation, Austin, Texas 78758, USA,
{jasonb,ajt,fanders}@austin.ibm.com
[2] The University of Texas, Austin, Texas 78712, USA,
adnan@ece.utexas.edu
[3] Tempus Fugit, Inc., Albany, California 94706, USA
vigyan@home.com

Abstract. A c-slow netlist N is one which may be retimed to another netlist N', where the number of latches along each wire of N' is a multiple of c. Leiserson and Saxe [1, page 54] have shown that by increasing c (a process termed *slowdown*) and retiming, any design may be made systolic, thereby dramatically decreasing its cycle time. In this paper we develop a new fully-automated abstraction algorithm applicable to the verification of generalized c-slow flip-flop based netlists; the more generalized topology accepted by our approach allows applicability to a fairly large class of pipelined netlists. This abstraction reduces the number of state variables and divides the diameter of the model by c; intuitively, it folds the state space of the design modulo c. We study the reachable state space of both the original and reduced netlists, and establish a c-slow bisimulation relation between the two. We demonstrate how CTL* model checking may be preserved through the abstraction for a useful fragment of CTL* formulae. Experiments with two components of IBM's Gigahertz Processor demonstrate the effectiveness of this abstraction algorithm.

1 Introduction

Leiserson and Saxe [1,2] have defined a c-slow netlist N as one which is retiming equivalent to another netlist N', where the number of latches along each wire of N' is a multiple of c. Netlist N' may be viewed as having c equivalence classes of latches; latches in class i may only fan out to latches in class $(i+1) \mod c$. Each equivalence class of latches of N' contains data from an independent stream of execution, and data from two or more independent streams may never arrive at any netlist element concurrently. They demonstrate that designs may be made systolic through *slowdown* (increasing c), and how this process dramatically benefits the cycle time of such designs. We have observed at IBM a widespread use of such pipelining through slowdown, for example, in control logic which routes tokens to and from table-based logic (e.g., caches and instruction dispatch logic).

This use has been hand-crafted during the design development, not achieved via a synthesis tool.

The purpose of our research is to develop a sound and complete abstraction algorithm for the verification of a generalized class of flip-flop (FF) based c-slow designs, which eliminates all but one equivalence class of FFs and reduces the diameter of the model by a factor of c. To the best of our knowledge, this paper is the first to exploit the structure of c-slow designs for enhanced verification. Our motivating example was an intricate five-stage pipelined control netlist with feedback, and with an asynchronous interrupt to every stage. This interrupt input prevents the classification of this design as c-slow by the definition in [2], but our generalization of that definition enables us to classify and perform a c-slow abstraction upon this example. Due to its complexity and size, model checking this netlist required enormous computational complexity even after considerable manual abstraction.

Retiming itself is insufficient to achieve the results of c-slow abstraction. Retiming is not guaranteed to reduce the diameter of the model, and does not change the number of latches along a directed cycle. It should also be noted that a good BDD ordering cannot achieve the benefits of this abstraction. For example, assume that we have two netlists, N and N', where N is equivalent to N' except that the FF count along each wire of N' is multiplied by c. One may hypothesize that a BDD ordering which groups the FFs along each wire together may bound the BDD size for the reachable set of N to within a factor of c of that of N'; however, we have found counterexamples to this hypothesis. A better ordering groups all variables of a given class together, as the design could be viewed as comprising c independent machines in parallel. However, such ordering will not reduce the number of state variables nor the diameter of the model.

A related class of research has considered the transformation of level-sensitive latch-based netlists to simpler edge-sensitive FF-based ones. (Refer to [3] for a behavioral definition of these latch types.) Hasteer et al. [4] have shown that multi-phase netlists may be "phase abstracted" to simpler FF-based netlists for sequential hardware equivalence. Baumgartner et al. [5] have taken a similar approach (called "dual-phase abstraction" for a 2-phase design) for model checking. This approach preserves initial values and provides greater reduction in the number of state variables than the phase abstraction from [4] alone. Phase abstraction is fundamentally different than c-slow abstraction. For example, in multi-phase designs, only one class of latches updates at each time-step. Furthermore, the initial values of all but one class of latches will be overwritten before propagation. Therefore, given a FF-based design, these approaches are of no further benefit.

The remainder of the document is organized as follows. Section 2 provides our definition of c-slow netlists, and introduces a 3-slow netlist N. In Section 3 we introduce our abstraction algorithm, as well as the abstracted version of N. We demonstrate the correctness of the abstraction in Section 4. In particular we demonstrate a natural correspondence between the original and abstracted designs which we refer to as a *c-slow bisimulation*, and discuss the effect of the abstraction upon CTL* model checking. In Section 5 we introduce algorithms to determine the maximum c and to translate traces from the abstracted model to traces in the original netlist. We provide experimental results in Section 6, and in Section 7 we summarize and present future work items.

2 C-Slow Netlists

In this section we provide our definition of c-slow netlists, which is a more general definition than that of [2]. We assume that the netlist contains no level-sensitive latches; if it does, phase abstraction [5] should be performed to yield a FF-based netlist. We further assume that the netlist has no gated-clock FFs; if it does, it is at most 1-slow (since an inactive gate mandates that the next state of the FF be equivalent to its present state). Each c-slow netlist N is comprised of c equivalence classes of FFs characterized as follows.

Definition 1. A *c-slow netlist* is one whose gates and FFs may be c-colored such that:

1. Each FF is assigned a color i.
2. All FFs which have FFs of color i in their support have color $(i+1) \bmod c$.
3. All gates which have FFs of color i in their support have color i.

There are several noteworthy points in the above definition. First, since no gate may contain FFs of more than one color in its support, the design may not reason about itself except "modulo c". Intuitively, it is this property which allows us to "fold" the design to a smaller domain of a single coloring of FFs.

Second, the coloring restrictions apply only to FFs and to gates which have FFs in their support. Hence, it is legal for primary inputs to fanout to FFs of multiple colors, which makes our definition more general than that in [2]. This generality has shown great potential in extending the class of netlists to which we may apply the c-slow abstraction; the two design fragments of the Gigahertz Processor from our sample set which were found to be c-slow would not have been classifiable as such without this generality.

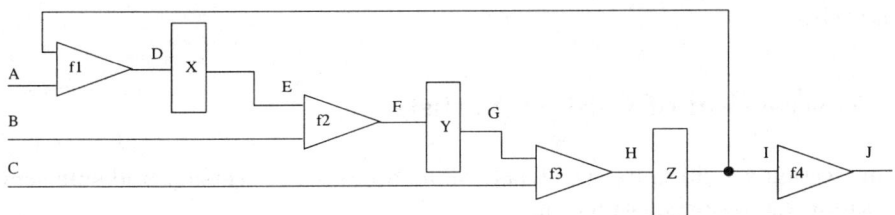

Fig. 1. 3-Stage Netlist N

Consider the generic 3-slow netlist N depicted in Figure 1. We assume that this netlist represents a composition of the design under test and its environment. We also assume that no single input will fan out to FFs of different colors. Later in this section we demonstrate that we may soundly alter netlists which violate this assumption by splitting such inputs into functionally identical yet distinct cones, one per color. All nets may be vectors. We arbitrarily define the color of FFs X as 0, of Y as 1, and of Z as 2.

Consider the first several time-steps of symbolic reachability analysis of N in Table 1 below. The symbolic values a_i, b_i, and c_i represent arbitrary values producible at inputs A, B, and C respectively. The symbol i_j represents the initial value of the FFs of color j.

time	0	1	2	3	4	5
A	a_0	a_1	a_2	a_3	a_4	a_5
B	b_0	b_1	b_2	b_3	b_4	b_5
C	c_0	c_1	c_2	c_3	c_4	c_5
D	$f1(a_0, i_2)$	t_{1_1}	t_{0_2}	$f1(a_3, t_{2_2})$	t_{1_3}	$f1(a_5, t_{0_3})$
E	i_0	$f1(a_0, i_2)$	t_{1_1}	t_{0_2}	$f1(a_3, t_{2_2})$	t_{1_3}
F	$f2(b_0, i_0)$	t_{2_1}	t_{1_2}	$f2(b_3, t_{0_2})$	t_{2_3}	$f2(b_5, t_{1_3})$
G	i_1	$f2(b_0, i_0)$	t_{2_1}	t_{1_2}	$f2(b_3, t_{0_2})$	t_{2_3}
H	$f3(c_0, i_1)$	t_{0_1}	t_{2_2}	$f3(c_3, t_{1_2})$	t_{0_3}	$f3(c_5, t_{2_3})$
I	i_2	$f3(c_0, i_1)$	t_{0_1}	t_{2_2}	$f3(c_3, t_{1_2})$	t_{0_3}
J	$f4(i_2)$	$f4(f3(c_0, i_1))$	$f4(t_{0_1})$	$f4(t_{2_2})$	$f4(f3(c_3, t_{1_2}))$	$f4(t_{0_3})$

$$t_{0_1} = f3(c_1, f2(b_0, i_0)) \quad t_{0_2} = f1(a_2, t_{0_1}) \quad t_{0_3} = f3(c_4, f2(b_3, t_{0_2}))$$
$$t_{1_1} = f1(a_1, f3(c_0, i_1)) \quad t_{1_2} = f2(b_2, t_{1_1}) \quad t_{1_3} = f1(a_4, f3(c_3, t_{1_2}))$$
$$t_{2_1} = f2(b_1, f1(a_0, i_2)) \quad t_{2_2} = f3(c_2, t_{2_1}) \quad t_{2_3} = f2(b_4, f1(a_3, t_{2_2}))$$

Table 1. Reachability Analysis of N

At any instant in time, each signal may only be a function of the value generated by a given "data source" at every c-th cycle. By data source, we refer to inputs and initial values. This observation illustrates the motivation behind this abstraction; our transformation yields a design where each signal may concurrently (nondeterministically) be a function of each data source at each cycle.

3 Abstraction of C-Slow Netlists

In this section we illustrate the structural modifications necessary and sufficient to perform the c-slow abstraction.

The algorithm for performing the abstraction is as follows. Color $c-1$ FFs are abstracted by replacement with a mux selected by a conjunction of a random value with *first_cycle*; the output of this mux passes through a FF, and the initial value of this FF is defined by the value which would appear at its input if *first_cycle* were asserted. Color 0 FFs are abstracted by replacement with a mux which is selected by *first_cycle*. All others are abstracted by replacement with a mux which is selected by a conjunction of a random value with *first_cycle*. If the netlist is a feed-forward pipeline, all variables may be replaced in this last manner, thereby converting the sequential netlist to a combinational one.

Consider netlist N' shown in Figure 2 below, which represents our c-slow abstraction of N. We initialize Z' with the value which would appear at its inputs if *first_cycle* were 1. The new inputs ND and ND' represent unique nondeterministic values. We will utilize one copy of this netlist (with *first_cycle* tied up) to generate the initial values for Z'. This initial value will be utilized in a second copy of this netlist where *first_cycle* is tied down, which is the copy that we will model check. Intuitively, the nondeterministic initial value allows the output of the rightmost mux to take all possible values observable at net I in N during the first c cycles. Thereafter, straightforward reachability analysis will ensure correspondence of N and N'.

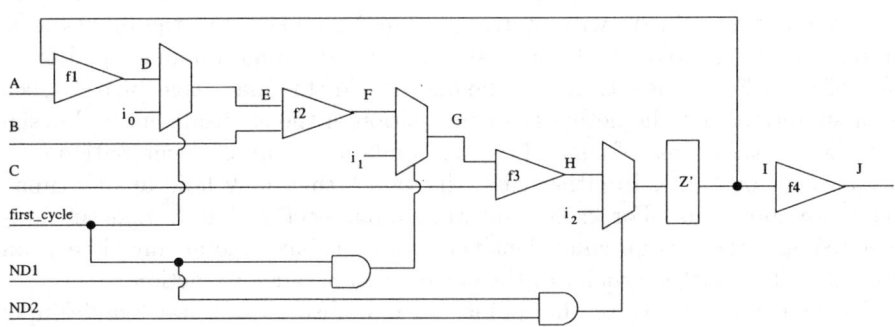

Fig. 2. Abstracted 3-Stage Netlist N'

The first two cycles of symbolic simulation of N' is provided in Table 2. To compensate for the "nondeterministic initial state set" induced by this abstraction, we have split this analysis into three *timeframes*; cycles 0_0 and 1_0 represent the timeframe induced by the first element of the set – that element further being a function only of the initial values of the FFs of color 0, cycles 0_1 and 1_1 induced by the second element, etc. This analysis illustrates the manner in which the design will be treated by the reachability engine.

There are several critical points illustrated by this table. First, the values present at FFs of color $c-1$ in N', at time i along the path induced by initial values of color j, are equivalent to those present upon their correspondents in N at time $3i + j$. This may be inductively expanded by noting that i_j in the above two tables need not correlate to initial values, but to any reachable state.

time	0_0	1_0	0_1	1_1	0_2	1_2
A	a_2	a_5	a_1	a_4	a_0	a_3
B	b_3	b_6	b_2	b_5	b_1	b_4
C	c_4	c_7	c_3	c_6	c_2	c_5
D	t_{0_2}	$f1(a_5, t_{0_3})$	t_{1_1}	t_{1_3}	$f1(a_0, i_2)$	$f1(a_3, t_{2_2})$
E	t_{0_2}	$f1(a_5, t_{0_3})$	t_{1_1}	t_{1_3}	$f1(a_0, i_2)$	$f1(a_3, t_{2_2})$
F	$f2(b_3, t_{0_2})$	t_{0_4}	t_{1_2}	$f2(b_5, t_{1_3})$	t_{2_1}	t_{2_3}
G	$f2(b_3, t_{0_2})$	t_{0_4}	t_{1_2}	$f2(b_5, t_{1_3})$	t_{2_1}	t_{2_3}
H	t_{0_3}	$f3(c_7, t_{0_4})$	$f3(c_3, t_{1_2})$	$f3(c_6, f2(b_5, t_{1_3}))$	t_{2_2}	$f3(c_5, t_{2_3})$
I	t_{0_1}	t_{0_3}	$f3(c_0, i_1)$	$f3(c_3, t_{1_2})$	i_2	t_{2_2}
J	$f4(t_{0_1})$	$f4(t_{0_3})$	$f4(f3(c_0, i_1))$	$f4(f3(c_3, t_{1_2}))$	$f4(i_2)$	$f4(t_{2_2})$

$$t_{0_4} = f2(b_6, f1(a_5, t_{0_3}))$$

Table 2. Reachability Analysis of N'

Another point is that, in order to "align" the values present at FFs of color $c-1$, we have been forced to temporally skew the inputs. For example, comparing any state at time i in N' with state $3i + j$ in N, we see that the inputs which fan out to all but color 0 FFs are skewed forward by an amount equal to the color of the FFs in their transitive fanout. While this may seem bizarre, recall our assumption that the netlist is a composition of the environment and design. Therefore, without loss of generality, the inputs may only be combinational free variables or constants. In either case, the values they may hold at any times i and j are equivalent. For each value that input vector A may take at time i (denoted A_i), there is an equivalent value that A may take at any time j, and vice-versa. This fact is crucial to the correctness of our abstraction.

To further demonstrate this point, we now discuss how we handle inputs which fan out to FFs of multiple colors. We split such "multi-color" input logic cones into a separate cone per color. To illustrate the necessity of this technique, assume that inputs A and B were tied together in N – a single input AB. Thus, values a_i and b_i are identical. Tying these together in N' would violate the correspondence; for example, state t_{3_2} is a function of a_3 and b_4, each being a distinct value producible by input AB. Clearly any state producible in N', where a_3 and b_4 are equivalent, would be producible in N. However, any state in N where a_3 and b_4 differ would be unproducible in N', *unless* we split AB into two functionally equivalent, yet distinct, inputs – one for color 0 and the other for color 1. Such splitting of shared input cones is straightforward, and may be performed automatically in $O(c \cdot nets)$ time. This logic splitting may encompass combinational logical elements, and even logic subcircuits including FFs which themselves are c-slow. The exact theory of such splitting of sequential cones is still under development, though may be visualized by noting that peripheral latches upon multi-color inputs clearly need not limit c.

4 Correctness of Abstraction

In this section we define our notion of correspondence between the original and abstracted netlists, which we term a *c-slow bisimulation* (inspired by Milner's bisimulation relations [6]). We will relate our designs to Kripke structures, which are defined as follows.

Definition 2. A *Kripke structure* $\mathcal{K} = \langle S, S_0, \mathcal{A}, \mathcal{L}, R \rangle$, where S is a set of *states*, $S_0 \subseteq S$ is the set of *initial states*, $\mathcal{A}$ is the set of *atomic propositions*, $\mathcal{L} : S \mapsto 2^{\mathcal{A}}$ is the *labeling function*, and $R \subseteq S \times S$ is the *transition relation*.

Our designs are described as Moore machines (using Moore machines, instead of the more general Mealy machines [7], simplifies the exposition for this paper, though our implementation is able to handle Mealy machines by treating outputs as FFs). We use the following definitions for a Moore machine and its associated structure (similar to Grumberg and Long [8]).

Definition 3. A *Moore machine* $\mathcal{M} = \langle L, S, S_0, I, O, V, \delta, \gamma \rangle$, where L is the set of *state variables (FFs)*, $S = 2^L$ is the set of *states*, $S_0 \subseteq S$ is the set of *initial states*, I is the set of *input variables*, O is the set of *output variables*, $V \subseteq L$ is the set of *property visible FFs*, $\delta \subseteq S \times 2^I \times S$ is the *transition relation*, and $\gamma : S \mapsto 2^O$ is the *output function*.

We uniquely identify each state by a subset of the state variables; intuitively, this subset represents those FFs which evaluate to a 1 at that state. We will define V to be the FFs of color $c - 1$.

Definition 4. The *Kripke structure associated with a Moore machine* $\mathcal{M} = \langle L, S, S_0, I, O, V, \delta, \gamma \rangle$ is denoted by $K(M) = \langle S^K, S_0^K, \mathcal{A}, \mathcal{L}, R \rangle$, where $S^K = 2^{L \cup I}$, $S_0^K = \{s \in S^K : s - I \in S_0\}$, $\mathcal{A} = V$, $\mathcal{L} = S^K \mapsto 2^V$, and $R((s, x), (t, y))$ iff $\delta(s, x, t)$.

Intuitively, we define S_0^K as the subset of S^K which, when projected down to the FFs, is equivalent to S_0. In the sequel we will use M to denote the Moore machine as well as the Kripke structure for the machine.

Definition 5. A *c-transition* of a Kripke structure M is a sequence of c transitions from state s_i to s_{i+c}, where $R(s_j, s_{j+1})$ for all j such that $0 \leq j < c$.

Definition 6. Let M be the Kripke structure of a c-slow machine. We define the *extended initial state set* of M, $S_{init} \subseteq S$, as the set of all states reachable within $c - 1$ time-steps from the initial state of M.

Definition 7. Let M and M' be two Kripke structures. A relation $G \subseteq S \times S'$ is a *c-slow-bisimulation* relation if $G(s, s')$ implies:
 1. $\mathcal{L}(s) = \mathcal{L}'(s')$.

2. for every $t \in S$ such that there exists a $c - transition$ of M from state s to t,, there exists $t' \in S'$ such that $R'(s',t')$ and $G(t,t')$.
3. for every $t' \in S'$ such that $R'(s',t')$, there exists $t \in S$ such that there exists a $c - transition$ of M from state s to t, and $G(t,t')$.

We say that a c-slow-bisimulation exists from M to M' (denoted by $M \prec M'$) iff there exists a c-slow bisimulation relation G such that for all $s \in S_{init}$ and $t' \in S'_0$, there exist $s' \in S'_0$ and $t \in S_{init}$ such that $G(s,s')$ and $G(t,t')$.

An infinite path $\pi = (s_0, s_1, s_2, \ldots)$ is a sequence of states such that any two successive states are related by the transition relation (i.e., $R(s_i, s_{i+1})$). Let π^i denote the suffix path $(s_i, s_{i+1}, s_{i+2}, \ldots)$. We say that a c-slow-bisimulation relation exists between two infinite paths $\pi = (s_0, s_1, s_2, \ldots)$ and $\pi' = (s'_0, s'_1, s'_2, \ldots)$, denoted by $G(\pi, \pi')$, iff for all $i \geq 0$, we have that $G(s_{c \cdot i}, s'_i)$.

Lemma 1. *Let s and s' be states of structures M and M', respectively, such that $G(s,s')$. For each infinite path π starting at s and composed of transitions of M, there exists an infinite path π' starting at s' and composed of transitions of M' such that $G(\pi, \pi')$. Similarly, for each infinite path π' starting at s' and composed of transitions of M', there exists an infinite path π starting at s and composed of transitions of M such that $G(\pi, \pi')$.*

The bisimilarity ensures that the reachable set of the original and abstracted netlists will be equivalent. Thus, properties such as $AG\phi$ and $EF\phi$, where ϕ is a boolean property, are trivially preserved using this abstraction, provided that all formula signals refer to nets of the same color. This may seem limiting: a simple formula such as $AG(latchIn \rightarrow AX(latchOut))$ reasons about two differently colored nets. However, such a formula may be captured by an automaton which transitions upon $latchIn \equiv 1$ to a state where it samples $latchOut$; the new "single-colored" formula asserts that this sampled value $\equiv 1$. Note that such transformations of CTL to automata are commonplace for *on-the-fly* model checking [9].

One approach to transforming properties for this abstraction is to synthesize the original property (for the unabstracted design), and compose it into the model prior to abstraction. The structural abstraction will thereby also abstract the property. Logic synthesis algorithms may need to be tuned for optimal use of the c-slow abstraction. For example, $p \rightarrow AXAXAXq$ may likely be synthesized as a counter (counting the number of cycles which have occurred since p). However, such a direct translation would violate the c-slow topology of the design. We therefore propose a pipelined "one-hot" translation which would, for example, specifically introduce N state variables rather than $\lceil log_2(N) \rceil$ for AX^N, if it is determined that the design has a c-slow topology. Translation of design substructures which violate c-slowness, but may be safely replaced with substructures which do not, is an important topic which is not limited to property automata. We did not implement such a "c-slow-friendly translator" for our experimentation, as our properties were relatively simple and in many cases implemented directly via automata anyway, though we feel that one could be readily automated.

A second approach to abstracting properties is by a dedicated transformation algorithm. Both approaches place substantial constraints upon the fragment of CTL* that our abstraction may handle, as is reflected by the following definition.

Definition 8. A *c-slow reducible* (CSR) subformula ϕ and its *c-slow reduction* $\Omega(\phi)$ are defined inductively as follows.

- every atomic proposition p is a CSR state formula $\phi = p$, and $\Omega(\phi) = p$. (Note that these atomic propositions are limited to the property-visible nets V, which are nets of color $c - 1$.)
- if p is a CSR state formula, so is $\phi = \neg p$, and $\Omega(\phi) = \neg \Omega(p)$.
- if p and q are CSR state formulae, so is $\phi = p \wedge q$, and $\Omega(\phi) = \Omega(p) \wedge \Omega(q)$.
- if p is a CSR path formula, then $\phi = \mathsf{E}p$ is a CSR state formula, and $\Omega(\phi) = \mathsf{E}\Omega(p)$.
- if p is a CSR path formula, then $\phi = \mathsf{A}p$ is a CSR state formula, and $\Omega(\phi) = \mathsf{A}\Omega(p)$.
- each CSR state formula ϕ is also a CSR path formula ϕ.
- if p is a CSR path formula, so is $\phi = \neg p$, and $\Omega(\phi) = \neg \Omega(p)$.
- if p and q are CSR path formulae, so is $\phi = p \wedge q$, and $\Omega(\phi) = \Omega(p) \wedge \Omega(q)$.
- if p is a CSR path formula, so is $\phi = \mathsf{X}^c p$, and $\Omega(\phi) = \mathsf{X}\Omega(p)$. (Note that strings of less than c X operators must be flattened via translation to automata.)

If p is a CSR subformula, then $\phi = AG\ p$ and $\phi = EF\ p$ are CSR state formulae, for which $\Omega(\phi) = AG\ \Omega(p)$ or $\Omega(\phi) = EF\ \Omega(p)$, respectively. These last transformations are not recursively applicable; EF and AG are only applicable as the first tokens in the formula. Furthermore, CSR subformulae are themselves insufficient for model checking using this abstraction; the top-level quantification is necessary to break the dependence on the initial state of the concrete model.

Note that $pU\ q$ is not a CSR formula, since it entails reasoning across consecutive time-steps. However, since the design may only reason about itself modulo c, we have not found it beneficial to use such a property to verify the design. Furthermore, we have found it useful to use a *modulo-c* variant of the U operator for such designs. We define $pU_c\ q$ as true along a path $(s_i, s_{i+1}, ...)$ iff there exists a j such that $s_j \models q$, and for all states at index k where $(j \bmod c) \equiv (k \bmod c)$ and $k < j$, we have that $s_j \models p$. Similar approaches apply to the general use of G and F.

It is noteworthy that every property which we had verified of the designs reported in our experimental results was suitable for *c*-slow abstraction. As per the above discussion, we suspect that all meaningful properties of such netlists will either be directly suitable for *c*-slow abstraction, or may be strengthened to be made suitable.

Theorem 1. *Let s and s' be states of M and M', and $\pi = (s_0, s_1, s_2, ...)$ and $\pi' = (s'_0, s'_1, s'_2, ...)$ be infinite paths of M and M', respectively. If G is a c-slow-bisimulation relation such that $G(s, s')$ and $G(\pi, \pi')$, then*

1. for every c-slow-reducible CTL* state formula ϕ, $s \models \phi$ iff $s' \models \Omega(\phi)$.
2. for every c-slow-reducible CTL* path formula ϕ, $\pi \models \phi$ iff $\pi' \models \Omega(\phi)$.

Proof. The proof is by induction on the length of the formula ϕ. Our induction hypothesis is that Theorem 1 holds for all CTL* formulae ϕ' of length $\leq n$.

Base Case: $n = 0$. There are no CTL* formulae of length 0, hence this base case trivially satisfies the induction hypothesis.

Inductive Step: Let ϕ be an arbitrary CTL* formula of length $n + 1$. We will utilize the induction hypothesis for formulae of length $\leq n$ to prove that Theorem 1 holds for ϕ. There are seven cases to consider.

1. If ϕ is a state formula and an atomic proposition, then $\Omega(\phi) = \phi$. Since s and s' share the same labels, we have that $s \models \phi \Leftrightarrow s' \models \phi \Leftrightarrow s' \models \Omega(\phi)$.
2. If ϕ is a state formula and $\phi = \neg \phi_1$, then $\Omega(\phi) = \neg \Omega(\phi_1)$. Using the induction hypothesis (since the length of ϕ_1 is exactly one less than that of ϕ), we have that $s \models \phi_1 \Leftrightarrow s' \models \Omega(\phi_1)$. Consequently, we have that $s \models \phi \Leftrightarrow s \not\models \phi_1 \Leftrightarrow s' \not\models \Omega(\phi_1) \Leftrightarrow s' \models \Omega(\phi)$.
3. If ϕ is a state formula and $\phi = \phi_1 \wedge \phi_2$, then $\Omega(\phi) = \Omega(\phi_1) \wedge \Omega(\phi_2)$. By definition, we know that $s \models \phi \Leftrightarrow ((s \models \phi_1) \text{ and } (s \models \phi_2))$. Using the induction hypothesis, since the lengths of ϕ_1 and ϕ_2 are strictly less than the length of ϕ, we have that $(s \models \phi_1) \Leftrightarrow s' \models \Omega(\phi_1)$, and also that $(s \models \phi_2) \Leftrightarrow s' \models \Omega(\phi_2)$. Therefore, we have that $s \models \phi \Leftrightarrow (s' \models \Omega(\phi_1) \text{ and } s' \models \Omega(\phi_2)) \Leftrightarrow s' \models \Omega(\phi)$.
4. If $\phi = \mathsf{E}\phi_1$, then $\Omega(\phi) = \mathsf{E}\Omega(\phi_1)$. The relation $s \models \phi$ is true iff there exists an infinite path σ beginning at state s such that $\sigma \models \phi_1$. Consider any σ beginning at s (regardless of whether $\sigma \models \phi_1$), and let σ' be an infinite path beginning at state s' such that $G(\sigma, \sigma')$. Such a σ' must exist by Lemma 1. Using the induction hypothesis, since the length of ϕ_1 is exactly one less than the length of ϕ, we have that $\sigma \models \phi_1 \Leftrightarrow \sigma' \models \Omega(\phi_1)$. This implies that $s \models \phi \Leftrightarrow s' \models \Omega(\phi)$.
5. If $\phi = \mathsf{A}\phi_1$, then $\Omega(\phi) = \mathsf{A}\Omega(\phi_1)$. The expression $s \models \phi$ is true iff for every infinite path σ beginning at state s, we have that $\sigma \models \phi_1$. For every infinite path σ beginning at s, consider the infinite path σ' beginning at state s' such that $G(\sigma, \sigma')$. Such a path must exist by Lemma 1. Applying the induction hypothesis, since the length of ϕ_1 is exactly one less than the length of ϕ, we have that $\sigma \models \phi_1 \Leftrightarrow \sigma' \models \Omega(\phi_1)$. This implies that $s \models \phi \Leftrightarrow s' \models \Omega(\phi)$.
6. Suppose ϕ is a path formula which is also a state formula. Since we have exhausted the possibilities for state formulae in the other cases, we conclude that $\pi \models \phi \Leftrightarrow \pi' \models \Omega(\phi)$.
7. If $\phi = \mathsf{X}^c \phi_1$, then $\Omega(\phi) = \mathsf{X}\Omega(\phi_1)$. Note that expression $\pi \models \phi$ is true iff $\pi^c = (s_c, s_{c+1}, s_{c+2}, \ldots) \models \phi_1$. Since $G(\pi^c, \pi'^1)$, and using the induction hypothesis (since the length of ϕ_1 is less than the length of ϕ), we have that $\pi^c \models \phi_1 \Leftrightarrow \pi'^1 = (s'_1, s'_2, s'_3, \ldots) \models \Omega(\phi_1)$. This is equivalent to $\pi \models \phi \Leftrightarrow \pi' \models \mathsf{X}\Omega(\phi_1)$, and also to $\pi \models \phi \Leftrightarrow \pi' \models \Omega(\phi)$.

Note that one by-product of this abstraction is that it extends the initial state set of M' to encompass all states reachable within $c-1$ time-steps from the initial state of M. The above cases prove preservation of CTL* model checking along each path, and with respect to each state. The necessity of prefixing all c-slow reducible CTL* formulae with EF or AG prevents this extended initial set from becoming visible to properties.

Theorem 2. If N' is a c-slow abstraction of N, then $N \prec N'$.

Proof. Our induction hypothesis is that Theorem 2 holds for all c-slow netlists, where $c \leq n$. If $c < 2$, no c-slow abstraction will be performed.

Base Case: $n = 2$.

As depicted in Figure 3, in this case N has two sets of FFs, where X is color 0, and Z is color 1. The abstraction (used to generate N') is performed as described in Section 3.

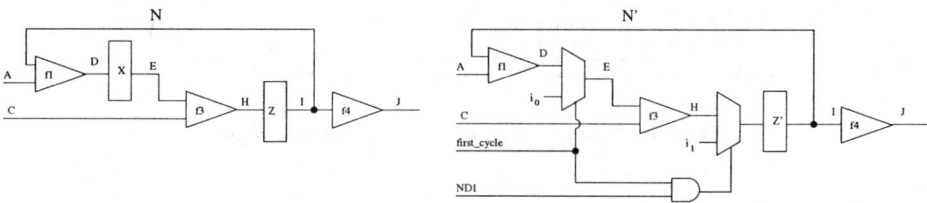

Fig. 3. Original and Abstracted Netlists, N and N', Base Case (C=2)

This proof may be readily completed by enumerating an inductive symbolic simulation for the two netlists (as in Tables 1 and 2), and demonstrating their bisimilarity. This analysis is omitted here due to space constraints.

Inductive Step:

This step shows that if the bisimulation holds for c up to n, then it also holds for $c = n + 1$. The induction relies upon the the addition of "intermediate" colored sets of FFs, which are all replaced with MUXes whose selects are conjunctions of a unique random value (for that color) with *first_cycle*, depicted in Figures 4 and 5 as the "inductive units". A set of zero or more inductive units is depicted as a cloud within these two figures, and used in the obvious manner to bring c (along with the explicitly depicted inductive unit) up to $n + 1$.

This proof also may be completed by an inductive symbolic simulation.

The proof of correctness for feed-forward pipelines is omitted due to space constraints, but follows immediately from the example in the inductive step, by omitting the color 0 and $c - 1$ FFs (and their feedback path).

5 Algorithms

Our algorithm for determining the maximum c is similar to that presented in [2]. We iterate over each FF in the netlist; if unlabeled, it is labeled with an

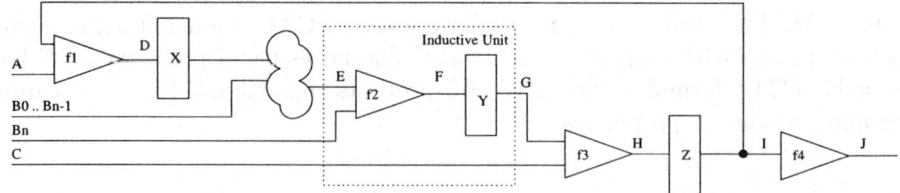

Fig. 4. Unabstracted Netlist N, Inductive Case

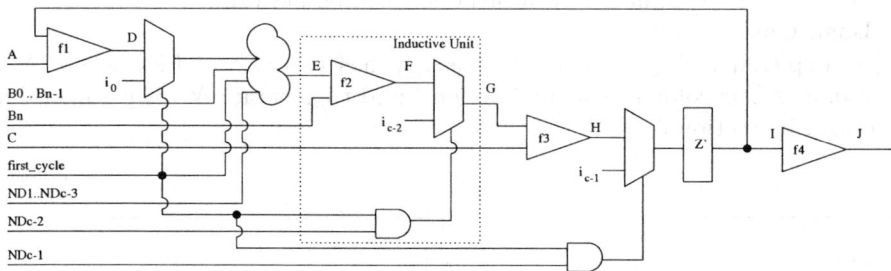

Fig. 5. Abstracted Netlist N', Inductive Case

arbitrary index 0. We next perform a depth-first fanout search from this FF; each time we encounter a FF, we label it with the current index and increment that index for the recursive fanout search from that FF. Once the fanout search is finished, we perform a depth-first fanin search from the original FF; each time we encounter an unlabeled FF, we label it with the current index and decrement that index for the recursive fanin search from that FF. When an already-labeled FF is encountered during a fanin or fanout search, we find the greatest-common divisor of the previous "maximum c" and the difference between the previous index of this FF and the current index. Once completed, this algorithm (which runs in linear time) yields the maximum value of c. If c is equal to 1, no c-slow abstraction may be performed. If c is never updated during coloring, the netlist is a feed-forward pipeline. To obtain the FF colorings, we transform the initial indices modulo c such that the property-visible FFs have color $c - 1$. For feed-forward pipelines, we merely shift the initial indices such that the lowest-numbered ones are equivalent to 0.

Abstraction of the netlist occurs as in Section 3. Rather than introducing $c - 1$ nondeterministic variables (used only for the calculation of initial values), we need only $\lceil log_2(c) \rceil$ variables. This is due to the observation that, if the nondeterministic value conjuncted for the selector of a color i mux is equivalent to 1, then the nondeterministic values conjuncted with the selectors of all color j muxes (where $j < i$) are don't cares. We may utilize this log_2 nondeterministic value to determine the color of the FFs whose initial values will propagate to the remaining FFs. Thus, an abstract initial state may be bound to a unique timeframe of the concrete design. Note that, regardless of the implementation, the same random value must be utilized for all color i muxes to ensure atomicity of the data.

Other than the $\lceil log_2(c) \rceil$ nondeterministic values introduced for initial value generation, the only other variables introduced are due to splitting of input cones. While this may increase the number of inputs of the design by a factor of c, we have found in practice that this increase is quite small – a small fraction of the total number of inputs – and negligible compared to the number of state variables removed. Despite this increase, these split inputs should not cause a serious BDD blowup since they tend to form independent (on a per-color basis) input ports, which a sophisticated BDD ordering may exploit.

5.1 Trace Lifting

We will perform our model checking upon the abstracted netlist N'. However, we must translate the traces obtained to the original netlist N. We have found that the simplest way to perform the translation is to generate a testcase by projecting the trace from N' down to the inputs, and manipulating this testcase for application to N. We perform this generation in two steps: a prefix generation, and a suffix generation.

For suffix generation, if no input splitting occurs, we may merely stutter each input $c-1$ times to convert the testcase. If input splitting does occur, we apply the stuttering technique to all non-split inputs. We define the color of an input as the color of the FFs to which it fans out. For example, if input A drives FFs of color 0 and 2, it will be split into two inputs – A_0 and A_2, of color 0 and 2, respectively. We use the value upon input A_i at cycle j in the abstract trace for the value at time $c \cdot j + i$ of input A in the testcase for N. We fill in any remaining gaps by an arbitrary selection of any legal value; this value does not influence the behavior of interest. The suffix generation accounts for the fact that every transition of the abstract machine correlates to a c-transition of the original machine.

The prefix generation is used to prepend to the suffix trace a path suitable to transition N from an initial state to the first state in the suffix trace (which is an element of S_{init}). Letting nd_init be the value encoded in the log_2 initial value variables in the initial abstract state, the length of the prefix p is equal to $c - 1 - nd\_init$. Generating the prefix backwards (and beginning with $i = 0$), we iteratively prepend the input values (from the *initial value* copy of the netlist) which fan out to color $c - 1 - i$ FFs, then increment i and repeat until $i \equiv p$. For feed-forward pipelines, all trace lifting is performed via prefix generation.

6 Experimental Results

We utilized IBM's model checker, RuleBase [10], to obtain our experimental results. We arbitrarily selected ten components of IBM's Gigahertz Processor which had previously been model checked. Our algorithm identified two of these as being c-slow. The first is a feed-forward pipeline; the second is the five-slow pipeline with feedback mentioned in Section 1. Both were explicitly entered in HDL as c-slow designs – this topology is not the by-product of a synthesis tool. Both had multi-colored inputs, which our generalized topology was able to exploit. Both of these components had been undergoing verification and regression for more than 12 months prior to the development of this abstraction technique. Consequently, the unabstracted variants had very good BDD orderings available. All results were obtained on an IBM RS/6000 Workstation Model 595 with 2 GB main memory. RuleBase was run with the most aggressive automated model reduction techniques it has to offer (including dual-phase abstraction [5]), and with dynamic BDD reordering (Rudell) enabled.

Prior to running the c-slow abstraction algorithm on these netlists, we ran automated scripts which removed scan chain connections between the latches (which unnecessarily limited c), and which cut self-feedback on "operational mode" FFs (into which values are scanned prior to functional use of the netlist, and held during functional use via the self-feedback loop).

We first deployed this abstraction technique on the feed-forward pipeline. The most interesting case was the most complex property against which we verified this design. The unabstracted version had 148 variables, and with our best initial ordering took 409.6 seconds with a maximum of 1410244 allocated BDD nodes. The first run on the abstracted variant (with a random initial ordering) had 53 variables, and took 44.9 seconds with a maximum of 201224 BDD nodes. While this speedup is significant, this comparison is skewed since the unabstracted run benefited from the extensive prior BDD reordering. Re-running the unabstracted experiment with a random initial ordering took 3657.9 seconds, with 2113255 BDD nodes. Re-running the abstracted experiment using the ordering obtained during the first run as the initial ordering took 4.6 seconds with 98396 nodes. Computing the c-slow abstraction took 0.3 seconds.

The next example is the five-slow design. With a good initial ordering, model checking the unabstracted design against one arbitrarily selected formula took 5526.4 seconds, with 251 variables and 3662500 nodes. The first run of the abstracted design (with a random initial ordering) took 381.5 seconds, with 134 variables and 339424 nodes. Re-running the rule twice more (and re-utilizing the calculated BDD orders) yielded a run of 181.1 seconds, 293545 nodes. Model checking the unabstracted design with an random initial ordering took 23692.5 seconds, 7461703 nodes. Computing the c-slow abstraction took 3.2 seconds.

Note that, due to the potential increase in depth of combinational cones entailed by this abstraction, there is a risk of a serious blowup of the transition relation or function. Splitting or conjoining may be utilized to combat such blowup [11]. A reasonable ordering seems fairly important when utilizing this abstraction. One set of experiments were run with reordering off, and a random initial ordering. The results for the feed-forward pipeline were akin to those reported above. However, the five-slow abstracted transition relation was significantly larger than the unabstracted variant given the random ordering, thereby resulting in a much slower execution than on the unabstracted run. With reordering enabled, the results (as reported above) were consistently superior.

7 Conclusions and Future Work

We have developed an efficient algorithm for identifying and abstracting generalized flip-flop based c-slow netlists. Our approach generalizes the definition provided in [2]; this generality allows us to apply our abstraction to a substantial percentage of design components. This abstraction is fully automated, and runs in $O(c \cdot nets)$ time. Our abstraction decreases the number of state variables, and the diameter of the model by c. Our experimental results indicate the substantial benefit of this abstraction in reducing verification time and memory (one to two magnitudes of order improvement), when applicable. We discuss expressibility constraints on CTL* model checking using this abstraction.

Future work items involve efficient techniques for identification of netlist substructures which violate c-slowness, yet may be safely replaced by others which do not. Other work involves extending the class of netlists to which this technique may be applied through the splitting of sequential cones.

References

1. C. E. Leiserson and J. B. Saxe. Optimizing Synchronous Systems. In *Journal of VLSI and Computer Systems*, 1(1):41–67, Spring 1983.
2. C. E. Leiserson and J. B. Saxe. Retiming Synchronous Circuitry. In *Algorithmica*, 6(1):5–35, 1991.
3. S. Mador-Haim and L. Fix. Input Elimination and Abstraction in Model Checking. In *Proc. Conf. on Formal Methods in Computer-Aided Design*, November 1998.
4. G. Hasteer, A. Mathur, and P. Banerjee. Efficient Equivalence Checking of Multi-Phase Designs Using Phase Abstraction and Retiming. In *ACM Transactions on Design Automation of Electronic Systems*, October 1998.
5. J. Baumgartner, T. Heyman, V. Singhal, and A. Aziz. Model Checking the IBM Gigahertz Processor: An Abstraction Algorithm for High-Performance Netlists. In *Proceedings of the Conference on Computer-Aided Verification*, July 1999.
6. R. Milner. *Communication and Concurrency*. Prentice Hall, New York, 1989.
7. Z. Kohavi. *Switching and Finite Automata Theory*. Computer Science Series. McGraw-Hill Book Company, 1970.
8. O. Grumberg and D. E. Long. Module Checking and Modular Verification. In *ACM Transactions on Programming Languages and Systems*, 16(3):843–871, 1994.
9. E. M. Clarke and E. A. Emerson. Design and Synthesis of Synchronization Skeletons Using Branching Time Logic. In *Proc. Workshop on Logic of Programs*, 1981.
10. I. Beer, S. Ben-David, C. Eisner, and A. Landver. RuleBase: an Industry-Oriented Formal Verification Tool. In *Proc. Design Automation Conference*, June 1996.
11. A. J. Hu, G. York, and D. L. Dill. New Techniques for Efficient Verification with Implicitly Conjoined BDDs. In *Proceedings of the Design Automation Conference*, June 1994.

Achieving Scalability in Parallel Reachability Analysis of Very Large Circuits

Tamir Heyman[1], Danny Geist[2], Orna Grumberg[1], and Assaf Schuster[1]

[1] Computer Science Department, Technion, Haifa, Israel
[2] IBM Haifa Research Laboratories, Haifa, Israel

Abstract. This paper presents a scalable method for parallel symbolic reachability analysis on a distributed-memory environment of workstations. Our method makes use of an adaptive partitioning algorithm which achieves high reduction of space requirements. The memory balance is maintained by dynamically repartitioning the state space throughout the computation. A compact BDD representation allows coordination by shipping BDDs from one machine to another, where different variable orders are allowed. The algorithm uses a distributed termination protocol with none of the memory modules preserving a complete image of the set of reachable states. No external storage is used on the disk; rather, we make use of the network which is much faster.
We implemented our method on a standard, loosely-connected environment of workstations, using a high-performance model checker. Our initial performance evaluation using several large circuits shows that our method can handle models that are too large to fit in the memory of a single node. The efficiency of the partitioning algorithm is linear in the number of workstations employed, with a 40-60% efficiency. A corresponding decrease of space requirements is measured throughout the reachability analysis. Our results show that the relatively-slow network does not become a bottleneck, and that computation time is kept reasonably small.

1 Introduction

This paper presents a scalable parallel algorithm for reachability analysis that can handle very large circuits.

Reachability analysis is known to be a key component, and a dominant one, in model checking. In fact, for large classes of properties, model checking is reducible to reachability analysis [3]; most safety properties can be converted into state invariant properties (ones that do not contain any temporal operators) by adding a small state machine (satellite) that keeps track of the temporal changes from the original property. The model checking can be performed "on-the-fly" during reachability analysis. Thus, for safety properties verification is possible if reachability analysis is, and an efficient method for model checking these kind of properties is one where the memory bottleneck is the reachable state space.

There is constant work on finding algorithmic and data structure methods to reduce the memory requirement bottlenecks that arise in reachability analysis.

One of the main approaches to reducing memory requirements is symbolic model checking. This approach uses Binary Decision Diagrams (BDDs) [4] to represent the verified model. However, circuits of a few hundreds of state variables may require many millions of BDD nodes, which often exceeds the computer memory capacity.

There are several proposed solutions to deal with the large memory requirements by using parallel computation. Several papers suggest to replace the BDD with parallelized data structure [11,1]. Stern and Dill [10] show how to parallelize an explicit model checker that does not use symbolic methods. Other papers suggest to reduce the space requirements by partitioning the work to several tasks [5,9,8]. However, these methods do not perform any parallel computation. Rather, they use a single computer to sequentially handle one task at a time, while the other tasks are kept in an external memory. Our work is similar, but we have devised a method to parallelize the computation of the different tasks. Section 7 includes a more detailed comparison with [5] and [8].

Our method parallelizes symbolic reachability analysis on a network of processes with disjoint memory, that communicate via message passing. The state space on which the reachability analysis is performed, is partitioned into *slices*, where each slice is *owned* by one process. The processes perform a standard Breadth First Search (BFS) algorithm on their owned slices. However, the BFS algorithm used by a process can discover states that do not belong to the slice that it owns (called *non-owned* states). When non-owned states are discovered, they are sent to the process that owns them. As a result, a process only requires memory for storing the reachable states it owns, and computing the set of immediate successors for them. As can be seen by the experimental results in Section 6, communication is not the bottleneck. We can thus conclude that usually, the number of non-owned states found by a process is small.

Computation on a single slice usually requires less memory than computation on the whole set. Thus, this method enables the reachability analysis of bigger models than those possible by regular non-parallel reachability analysis. Furthermore, applying computation in parallel reduces execution time (in practice, doing computation sequentially makes partitioning useless because of the large execution time).

Effective slicing should significantly increase the size of the overall state space that can be handled. This is not trivial since low memory requirements of BDDs are based on *sharing* among their parts. Our slicing procedure is therefore designed to avoid as much redundancy as possible in the partitioned slices. This is achieved by using *adaptive* cost function that for each partitioning chooses slices with small redundancy, while making sure that the partition is not trivial. Experimental results show that our slicing procedure results in significantly better slicing than those obtained by fixed cost functions (e.g. [5,8]).

Memory balance is another important factor in making parallel computation effective. Balance obtained by the initial slicing may be destroyed as more reachable states are found by each process. Therefore, balancing is dynamically applied during the computation. Our memory balance procedure maintains approximately equal memory requirement between the processes, during the entire computation.

Our method requires passing BDDs between processes, both for sending non-owned states to their owners and for balancing. For that, we developed a compact and efficient BDD representation as a buffer of bytes. This representation enables different variable orders in the sending and receiving processes.

We implemented our technique on a loosely-connected distributed environment of workstations, embedded it in a powerful model checker RuleBase [2], and tested it by performing reachability analysis on a set of large benchmark circuits. Compared to execution on a single machine with 512MB memory, the parallel execution on 32 machines with 512MB memory uses much less space, and reaches farther when the analysis eventually overflows. Our slicing algorithm achieves linear memory reduction factor with 40-60% efficiency, which is maintained throughout the analysis by the memory balancing protocol. The timing breakdown shows that the communication is not a bottleneck of our approach, even using a relatively slow network.

The rest of the paper is organized as follows: Section 2 describes the main algorithm. Section 3 discusses the slicing procedure and Section 4 suggests several possible optimizations. The way to communicate BDD functions is described in Section 5. Experimental results prove the efficiency of our method in Section 6. Finally, Section 7 concludes with comparison with related works.

2 Parallel Reachability Analysis

Computing the set of reachable states is usually done by applying a Breadth First Search (BFS) starting from the set of initial states. In general, two sets of nodes have to be maintained during the reachability analysis:

1. The set of nodes already reached, called `reachable`. This is the set of reachable states, discovered so far, which becomes the set of reachable state when the exploration ends.
2. The set of reached but not yet developed nodes, called `new`.

The right-hand-side of Figure 1 gives the pseudo-code of the BFS algorithm.

The parallel algorithm is composed of an initial sequential stage, and a parallel stage. In the sequential stage, the reachable states are computed on a single node as long as memory requirements are below a certain threshold. When the threshold is reached, the algorithm described in Section 3 slices the state space into k slices. Then it initiates k processes. Each process is informed of the slice it owns, and of the slices owned by each of the other processes. The process receives its own slice and proceeds to compute the reachable states for that slice in iterative BFS steps.

During a single step each process computes the set `next` of states that are directly reached from the states in its `new` set. The `next` set contains owned as well as non-owned states. Each process splits its `next` set according to the

```
1 mySlice = receive(fromSingle);
2 reachable = receive(fromSingle);
3 new = receive(fromSingle);
4 while (Termination(new)==0) {
5    next = nextStateImage(new);
6    next = sendRecieveAll(next);
7    next = next ∩ mySlice
8    new = next \ reachable;
9    reachable = reachable ∪ next;
}
```
(a) BFS by one process

```
reachable = new = initialStates;
while (new ≠ φ) {
   next = nextStateImage(new);
   new = next \ reachable;
   reachable = reachable ∪ next;
}
```
(b) Sequential BFS

Fig. 1. Breadth First Search

k slices and sends the non-owned states to their corresponding owners. At the same time, it receives states it owns from other processes.

The reachability analysis procedure for one process is presented on the left-hand-side of Figure 1. Lines 1-3 describe the setup stage: the process receives the slice it owns, and the initial sets of states it needs to compute from. The rest of the procedure is a repeated iterative computation until distributed termination detection is reached. Notice that, the main difference between the two procedures in Figure 1 is the modification of the set next in lines 6-7 as the result of communication with the other processes.

The parallel stage requires an extra process called the *coordinator*. This process coordinates the communication between the processes, including exchange of states, dynamic memory balance, and distributed termination detection. However, the information does not go through the coordinator and is exchanged directly between the processes.

In order to exchange non-owned states, each process sends to the coordinator the list of processes it needs to communicate with. The coordinator matches pairs of processes and instructs them to communicate. The pairs exchange states in parallel and then wait for the coordinator, that may match them with other processes. Matching continues until all communication requests are fulfilled. A process which ends its interaction may continue to the next step without waiting for the rest of the processes to complete their interaction.

2.1 Balancing the Memory Requirement

One of the objectives of slicing is to distribute an equal memory requirement amongst the nodes. Initial slicing of the state space is based on the known reachable set at the beginning of the parallel stage. This slicing may become inadequate as more states are discovered during reachability analysis. Therefore the memory requirements of the processes are monitored at each step, and whenever they become unbalanced, a balance procedure is executed. The coordinator matches processes that have a large memory requirement with processes that have a small one. Each pair re-slices the union of their two slices, resulting in a better balanced slicing. The pair uses the same procedure that is used to slice the whole state space (described in Section 3) with $k = 2$. After the balance procedure is completed, the pair informs the new slicing to the other processes.

2.2 Termination Detection

In the sequential algorithm, termination is detected when there are no more undeveloped states i.e., **new** is empty. In the parallel algorithm, each process can only detect when **new** is empty in its slice. However, a process may eventually receive new states even if at some step its **new** set is temporarily empty.

The parallel termination detection procedure starts after the processes exchange all non-owned states. Each process reports to the coordinator whether its **new** set is non-empty. If all the processes report an empty **new** set, the coordinator concludes that termination has been reached and reports this to all the processes.

3 Boolean Function Slicing

Symbolic computation represents all the state sets, and the transition relation as Boolean functions. This representation becomes large when the sets are big. To reduce memory requirements we can partition a set into smaller subsets whose union is the whole set. This partition, or slicing should have smaller memory requirements. Furthermore, the subsets should be disjoint in order to avoid duplication of work when doing reachability analysis. Since sets are represented as Boolean functions, slicing is defined for those functions.

Definition 1. *[Boolean function slicing] [9] Given a Boolean function $f : B^n \to B$, and an integer k, a Boolean function slicing $\chi(f, k)$ of f is a set of k function pairs, $\chi(f, k) = \{(S_1, f_1), \ldots, (S_k, f_k)\}$ that satisfy the following conditions:*

1. S_i and f_i are Boolean functions, for $1 \leq i \leq k$.
2. $S_1 \vee S_2 \vee \ldots \vee S_k \equiv 1$
3. $S_i \wedge S_j \equiv 0$, for $i \neq j$
4. $f_i \equiv S_i \wedge f$, for $1 \leq i \leq k$.

The S_i functions define the slices of the state space and we refer to them as *slices*.

Reducing memory requirements depends on the choice of the slices $S_1, \ldots, S_k$. Specifically, when representing functions as BDDs, the memory requirement of a function f, denoted $|f|$, is defined as the number of BDD nodes of f. Thus slicing a function f into two functions f_1 and f_2 may not necessarily reduce the requirements. BDDs are compressed decision trees where pointers are joined if they refer to the same subtree (see Figure 2 for a BDD example). This causes significant sharing of nodes in the Boolean function (for example node 4 in Figure 2). As a result of this sharing, a poor choice of S_1, S_2 may result in $|f_1| \approx |f|$, and also $|f_2| \approx |f|$.

Finding a good set of slices is a difficult problem. A possible heuristic approach to solving this problem is to find a slicing that minimizes $|f_1|, \ldots, |f_k|$. However as the results of our experiments in Section 6 show, a better approach is to find a slicing that additionally minimizes the sharing of BDD nodes amongst the k functions $f_1, \ldots, f_k$.

3.1 Slicing a Function in Two: SelectVar

Our slicing algorithm, SelectVar, slices a Boolean function (a BDD) into two, using assignment of a BDD variable. The algorithm receives a BDD f, and a threshold δ. It selects one of the BDD variables v and slices f into $f_v = f \wedge v$, and $f_{\bar{v}} = f \wedge \bar{v}$. Figure 2 shows an example of such a slicing where the function f is sliced using variable v_1 into f_1 and f_2.

The cost of such a slicing is defined as:

Definition 2. *[Cost(f,v,α):]*
$$\alpha * \frac{MAX(|f_v|,|f_{\bar{v}}|)}{|f|} + (1-\alpha) * \frac{|f_v|+|f_{\bar{v}}|}{|f|}$$

The $\frac{MAX(|f_v|,|f_{\bar{v}}|)}{|f|}$ factor gives an approximate measure to the reduction achieved by the partition. The $\frac{|f_v|+|f_{\bar{v}}|}{|f|}$ factor gives an approximate measure of the amount of sharing of BDD nodes between f_v and $f_{\bar{v}}$ (e.g., node 4 in Figure 2), and therefore reflects the *redundancy* in the partition.

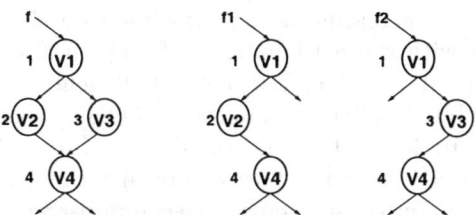

Fig. 2. slicing f into f_1 and f_2

The cost function depends on a choice of $0 \leq \alpha \leq 1$. An $\alpha = 0$ means that the cost function completely ignores the reduction factor, while $\alpha = 1$ means that the cost function completely ignores the redundancy factor. Our algorithm uses a novel approach in which α is adaptive and its value changes in each application of the slicing algorithm, so that the following goals are achieved: **(1)** the size of each slice is below the given threshold δ, and **(2)** redundancy is kept as small as possible.

Initially, the algorithm attempts to find a BDD variable which only minimizes the redundancy factor ($\alpha = 0$), while reducing the memory requirements below the threshold (i.e., $\max(|f_1|,|f_2|) \leq |f| - \delta$). If such a slicing does not exist the algorithm increases α (i.e., allows more redundancy) gradually until $\max(|f_1|,|f_2|) \leq |f| - \delta$ is achieved.

The threshold is used to guarantee that the partition is not trivial, i.e., it is not the case that $|f_1| \approx |f|$ and $|f_2| \approx 0$. If the largest slice is approximately $|f| - \delta$ and the redundancy is small, it is very likely that the other slice is approximately of size δ.

The pseudo code for the algorithm SelectVar(f,δ), is given in Figure 3. We set STEP $= \min(0.1, \frac{1}{k})$ and $\delta = \frac{|f|}{k}$, where k is the number of overall slices we want to achieve.

```
α = Δα = STEP
BestVar = the variable with minimal cost(f,v,α)
while ((max(|f ∧ v|,|f ∧ v̄|) > |f| − δ) ∧ (α <= 1))
    α = α + Δα
    BestVar = the variable with minimal cost(f,v,α)
return BestVar
```

Fig. 3. The pseudo code for the algorithm SelectVar(f,δ).

Note that, even though our algorithm may compute the cost functions for many different α, $|f \wedge v|$ and $|f \wedge \overline{v}|$ are computed only once for each variable v, therefore, computation time is not increased. Furthermore, the computation of $|f \wedge v|$ and $|f \wedge \overline{v}|$ for different variables, v, is done in parallel. Different computers compute the values for the different variables. The values are then sent to a computer that determines the variable with the minimal cost.

Instead of gradually increasing α, it is possible to find the best α by binary search. For a model with a large number of BDD variables, and large k, this improvement is essential in making our method efficient.

Our slicing procedure is different from those of [9,5] in that we use adaptive α, and put a lot of emphasis on obtaining small redundancy. Since cost functions are computed in parallel, we can allow computing them more precisely, thus achieving better fine-tuning of our slicing. The comparison to fixed α as suggested in [9,5] is given in Figure 4.

3.2 Slicing a Function into k Slices

Recall that SelectVar may result in two unbalanced slices that are approximately of sizes $|f| - \delta$ and δ. When we aim at a partition of k slices, we therefore use $\delta = \frac{|f|}{k}$ and repeatedly slice the largest slice, until k slices are obtained. In this way we obtain a balanced partition.

4 Optimizing the SelectVar Procedure

SelectVar(f,δ) selects a state variable v and uses it to split a set f into two sets: $f \wedge v$ and $f \wedge \overline{v}$. Recall that the algorithm attempts to satisfy two conditions;

circuit/method	16 slices		32 slices		65 slices		130 slices	
	mem	red	mem	red	mem	red	mem	red
prolog, 4th step, reachable size is 199,961 BDD nodes								
$\alpha = 1$	8.33	1.38	14.75	1.65	23.26	2.09	37.79	2.69
fixed α	8.33	1.38	14.98	1.65	23.26	2.09	37.76	2.60
adaptive α	10.23	1.34	16.82	1.44	28.54	1.84	43.23	2.34
adaptive α + optimizations	9.89	1.22	16.66	1.44	30.01	1.66	48.87	2.04
s1269, 3rd step, reachable size is 100,170 BDD nodes								
$\alpha = 1$	12.75	1.05	22.45	1.21	36.84	1.42	60.75	1.74
fixed α	12.75	1.04	22.33	1.19	36.16	1.38	61.47	1.66
adaptive α	12.75	1.04	21.40	1.20	36.04	1.38	62.53	1.62
adaptive α + optimizations	12.75	1.02	22.33	1.18	38.53	1.27	70.42	1.41
s3330, 4th step, reachable size is 233,952 BDD nodes								
$\alpha = 1$	6.18	2.17	9.23	2.86	13.46	3.93	19.83	5.35
fixed α	6.18	2.15	9.11	2.82	13.46	3.83	19.83	5.20
adaptive α	6.02	2.16	8.92	2.82	14.00	3.68	19.94	4.72
adaptive α + optimizations	6.17	1.92	9.81	2.40	19.81	3.16	24.16	4.16
s1423, 10th step, reachable size is 175,631 BDD nodes								
$\alpha = 1$	9.87	1.24	16.65	1.37	30.51	1.51	54.59	1.74
fixed α	9.87	1.24	16.65	1.34	31.97	1.47	55.60	1.69
adaptive α	10.64	1.13	19.21	1.21	35.88	1.36	64.76	1.50
adaptive α + optimizations	11.60	1.10	18.24	1.18	38.36	1.23	70.68	1.35
s5378, 7th step, reachable size is 177,105 BDD nodes								
$\alpha = 1$	5.37	2.13	8.96	2.72	13.83	3.43	22.84	4.39
fixed α	5.88	1.95	8.96	2.72	13.83	3.43	25.29	3.84
adaptive α	7.71	1.74	11.81	2.04	19.43	2.63	28.46	3.58
adaptive α + optimizations	8.63	1.56	12.14	2.03	19.94	2.51	30.70	3.26
BIQ, 14th step, reachable size is 203,019 BDD nodes								
$\alpha = 1$	8.06	1.48	13.33	1.67	24.43	1.93	41.12	2.26
fixed α	8.54	1.44	13.60	1.60	26.87	1.86	43.35	2.15
adaptive α	8.54	1.37	16.33	1.50	29.36	1.69	50.00	1.97
adaptive α + optimizations	8.79	1.27	20.11	1.21	37.65	1.24	65.50	1.38
ARB, 5th step, reachable size is 177,105 BDD nodes								
$\alpha = 1$	10.43	1.35	17.15	1.50	28.78	1.72	48.46	1.97
fixed α	9.99	1.31	16.15	1.45	28.77	1.63	51.76	1.83
adaptive α	10.03	1.28	17.46	1.34	32.61	1.46	58.31	1.66
adaptive α + optimizations	10.72	1.08	19.64	1.17	37.03	1.26	71.21	1.27

Fig. 4. Partitioning results measured by two parameters: the redundancy (red) which is the ratio between the overall size of the slices and the original reachable size, and the memory reduction (mem), which is the ratio between the original reachable size and the largest slice in the partition.

that the size of both resulting sets is at most $|f| - \delta$, and that the redundancy is minimized.

The efficiency of this algorithm and its success in meeting the conditions are crucial factors in the efficiency of the whole scheme, especially when the number of processes increases. In this section we observe that the algorithm can be improved in several ways.

The main observation in improving the slicing procedure is that the split of f which meets best the conditions might not be achieved using a single variable. Indeed, it was previously suggested that the algorithm can achieve better results by the choice of a general function g which determines two sets: $f \wedge g$ and $f \wedge \overline{g}$ [9]. However, since there is an exponential number of candidates for g, trying them all will take too much time. In the rest of this section we develop heuristics which help to choose a "good" g while keeping a reasonable complexity for the choice.

We construct g iteratively as follows. Suppose at a certain step we already have g'. We now choose a state variable v and compute the cost $Cost(f, \alpha, g)$ of all the functions of the form $g = g'$ op v. We use the following options: $g' \wedge v$, $\overline{g'} \wedge v$, $g' \otimes v$, $g' \wedge \overline{v}$, $g' \vee v$. Thus, the complexity of computing the cost of all the possibilities at a certain iteration, assuming that we try all state variables, can be as high as five times the number of states variables times the cost of a BDD operation.

In what follows we describe the ways to use the above observation. These are a set of heuristics that we found to be effective (see Table 4). There are several configurable parameters which appear in the description of the heuristics, and which we currently set in our implementation using a trial-and-error methods.

Optimization 1. The general construction of a splitting function g, as described above is called by SelectVar(f, δ) when a splitting variable BestVar which satisfies the conditions is found, we call ImprovingSplit which applies the construction with BestVar as a base function, in an attempt to further improve the cost.

Optimization 2. We choose a small number l of the best variables found so far and send them as inputs to the general construction of the splitting function. This time, we use each variable only once: we start with the best one, add the second best, etc. If any of the $l - 1$ resulting functions meet the conditions – we are done. Else, if the functions are different than those found at the end of the previous iteration of SelectVar, they are added to the existing list of variables. This increases the input to the next iteration of SelectVar by $l - 1$ functions which have high potential of becoming good slicers.

Optimization 3 (Only very small α.) We choose the best splitting variable so far, and iteratively add more variables according to the general construction of the slicing function. However, this time we first select those variables for which the resulting function strictly decreases the size of the slices. Only then, out of those variables selected, we choose the one for which the slicing function achieves a minimal cost.

5 Efficient Transfer of BDDs

As described in Section 2, processes periodically exchange BDDs during reachability analysis. Two utility functions are used. bdd2msg translates a BDD into a more compact msg data and msg2bdd translates the msg data back to a BDD after it has been transferred. The purpose of bdd2msg is to serialize the BDD structure in order for it to be suitable for raw buffer transfer.

BDD nodes represent a boolean function f recursively. The functions 0 and 1 are represented by special BDDs called ZERO, and ONE respectively. Other functions are represented by a node that contains variable identification x, and two pointers, leftPtr and rightPtr, that point to two other BDD nodes that representing $f_{\bar{x}}$ and f_x, respectively. The function f is expressed based on the Shannon expansion: $\bar{x}f_{\bar{x}} + xf_x$.

The msg data is a sequence of records. Each msg record has four fields: An index for that record (symbolic pointer), denoted as Sid. The variable id of the record denoted as Xid. An Sid for the record left son, and an Sid for its right son. The index field indicates the record location in the msg data. The records ZERO, and ONE have special index.

bdd2msg traverses the nodes of BDD f in Depth First Search (DFS) order. It creates the corresponding msg records from the leaves upwards. Every time it creates a new msg record, it increments an index, which serves as the Sid for that record. msg2bdd traverses the msg records sequentially from start to end. It creates the corresponding BDD nodes one by one as it traverses the data. Shannon expansion is used to create the BDD node from the record. Such transformation is possible due to the fact that the Xids remain constant throughout the computation.

Remark: The transferred BDD f is compressed by the restrict operator described in [6], using the slice of the receiving process as the restricting domain.

6 Experimental Results

In this section we report initial performance results of using our approach. We implemented our partitioned BDD and embedded it in an enhanced version of McMillan's SMV [7], due to IBM Haifa Research Laboratory [2].

Our parallel testbed includes 32 RS6000 machines, each consisting of a 225MHz PowerPC processor and 512MB memory. The communication between the nodes consists of a 16Mbit/second token ring. The nodes are non-dedicated; i.e., they are mostly workstations of employees who would often use them (and the network) at the same time that we ran our experiments.

We experimented using five of the largest circuits we found in the benchmarks ISCAS89 +addendum'93. We also used two large examples (BIQ and ARB) which are components in the IBM's Gigahertz processor. Characteristics of the seven circuits are given in Figure 5.

Circuit	# vars	max reachable		max new		peak		fixed point		gc time
		size	step	size	step	size	step	time	steps	
prolog	117	402k	5	578k	5	1,283k	6	1,288	9	113
s1269	55	98k	3	128k	3	3,055k	5	1,371	10	175
s3330	172	839k	6	2,107k	6	4,250k	7	17,777	9	606
s5378	198	524k	25	157k	35	4,058k	19	98,209	44	6,206
s1423	91	3,831k	13	3,691k	13	11,413k	14	4,079	ov(14)	420
BIQ	187	1,744k	22	1,589k	22	8,954k	23	35,495	ov(23)	5,512
ARB	116	1,193k	6	1,183k	6	8,893k	7	3,112	ov(7)	473

Fig. 5. Characteristics of our benchmark suit, taken from ISCAS89+addendum'93, and the IBM's Gigahertz processor. All sizes are given in BDD nodes, and all times in seconds. Max reachable is the maximal (over the steps) set of nodes already reached. Max new is the maximal (over the steps) set of nodes reached but not yet developed. Note that new may be larger than reachable (at any step), since the joint BDD representation of the current-step' new and the previous-step' reachable may reduce in size. The peak is the maximal size at any point during a step. In order to mask the effect of garbage collection (gc) scheduling decisions, the peak is measured after every gc invocation. Fixed point is the number of steps/time it takes to get to fixed point. Ov(x) means memory overflow at step x. The time was measured using an RS6000 machine, consisting of a 225MHz PowerPC processor with 512MB memory.

6.1 Slicing Results

The success of our slicing algorithm is a crucial factor in the efficiency of the parallel execution. This success is indicated by two parameters of the obtained partition: the *redundancy*, which is the ratio between the overall size of the slices and the original reachable size, and the *memory reduction*, which is the ratio between the original reachable size and the largest slice in the partition.

Figure 4 presents the slicing results of reachable sets for four slicing methods. In order to show phenomena which appear only towards large number of slices, results in Figure 4 are given for 16, 32, 64, and 130 slices. The slicing algorithms are invoked when the size of the reachable set exceeds the threshold 100,000 BDD nodes.

The first method selects as a slicing function the variable which achieves the biggest memory reduction. In algorithm SelectVar this corresponds to choosing $\alpha = 1$. The second method is the same as that used in Cabodi et. al. [5]. This corresponds to choosing the splitting variable with the best fixed α. The third method is the one presented in Section 3, adapting α to select the partition with minimal redundancy. The fourth method includes the optimizations described in Section 4, so that splitting is carried using a general function.

The table shows that the average increase in the memory reduction which can be attributed to our optimizations (adapting α and choosing a general splitting function), is 25%, 22%, 18%, and 10% for slicing into 130, 65, 32, and 16 parts, respectively. We conclude that these optimizations become more important as the level of slicing increases. This proves that the key to better slicing when the number of slices increases is to opt for lower duplication, which is the base orientation for our optimizations.

The average memory reduction factor achieved over our benchmark suit for slicing into 130 slices, is more than 55. We expect the results to improve for high slicing levels when a larger threshold is chosen. The reason for that is the threshold per slice, in our experiments $100,000/130 = 750$ which may be too small. On the other hand, efficiency dictates earlier split when the bottleneck is the complexity of the slicing algorithm, or the resources required by the initial sequential stage.

6.2 Parallel Reachability – Space Reduction

We now present the results for reachability analysis of the benchmark suit using our 32 machine testbed. Figures 6 to 12 summarize the memory usage, giving the reachable size and peak usage for every step. Each of the graphs compares the memory usage in the single-machine execution to that of the parallel system. For the parallel system we give both average and highest memory utilization in any of the machines.

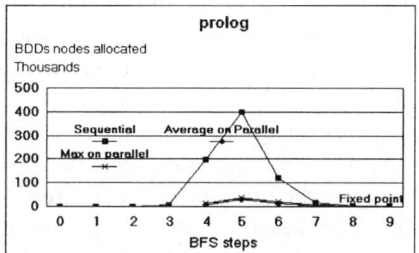 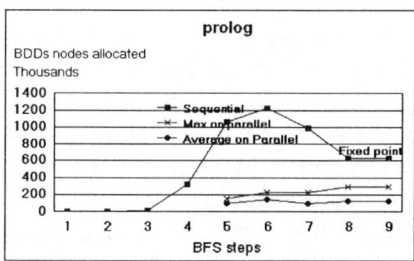

(a) **Size of reachable states set**   (b) **Nodes allocated (peak)**

Fig. 6. Memory utilizations during reachability analysis of prolog.

The graphs show that scalability is obtained due to the performance of the slicing algorithm, which achieves a good memory reduction. The circuits which overflow always reach with the parallel execution to a farther step than when using the single-machine. Figure 11 shows the analysis process for circuit BIQ which safely reaches step 32 with the parallel execution. BIQ reaches only step 22 with the single machine execution.

One of the crucial factors in the success of the parallel reachability scheme is the dynamic memory balancing, which is in charge of maintaining the "accomplishments" of the slicing algorithm. The ratio of worst to average space usage in the graphs indicates that our dynamic load balancing algorithm succeeds to avoid extreme imbalance.

Note that the measures on peak size are subject to the gc scheduling policy, thus the phenomena appearing e.g., in Figure 7, where the reachable set shrinks while the peak remains very high.

6.3 Parallel Reachability – Timing and Communication

Figure 13 gives the timing breakdown for reachability analysis on the benchmark suit. This table provides information regarding the ratio of computation (compute) to communication (exchange) and memory balancing (balance) in our scheme. The table shows that the overall picture is fairly balanced. In other words, the table shows that communication is not a bottleneck in our algorithm, despite the fact that we use a relatively slow network.

7 Comments on Related Work

In this section we discuss the improvements of our algorithm over the reachability analysis algorithms presented in [5,8]. Their algorithms slice the computation, but do not parallelize it. We also summarize the special consideration needed by parallel implementation.

The slicing suggested in [5] is more general than that in [8]. However, as shown in Section 6 above, its effectiveness is limited to a small number of slices. The adaptive α and the general slicing functions used by our algorithm proved scalability and worked well even with 130 slices. Experimental results show that the the impact of our optimizations increases with the level of slicing.

Balancing the memory requirements among slices during computation increases the overall reduction. The algorithm in [8] does not include any balancing. The balancing suggested by [5] constantly increases the number of slices. Our balancing method keeps the number of slices fixed, while successfully maintaining the work balanced. This is important when the network size is fixed.

At the end of each step, [5] and [8] write to the disk the sets `reachable` and `new`, obtained for the slice under consideration. Rather, we send on the network (which is much faster) only the non-owned part of `new`, which is relatively small.

In [8] the authors comment that they believe their algorithm can be parallelized. This, however, is not immediate. In order to exploit the full power of the

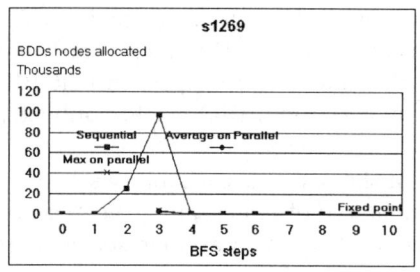
(a) **Size of reachable states set**

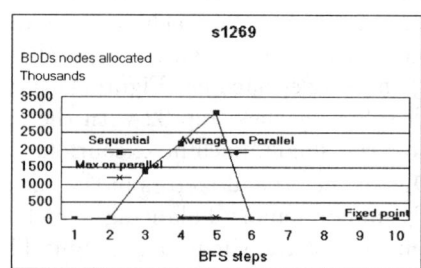
(b) **Nodes allocated (peak)**

Fig. 7. Memory utilizations during reachability analysis of s1269.

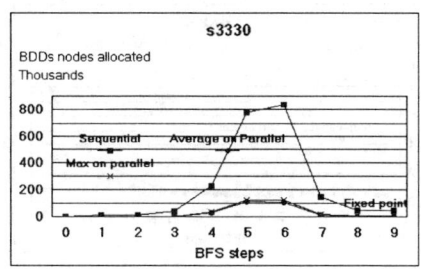
(a) Size of reachable states set

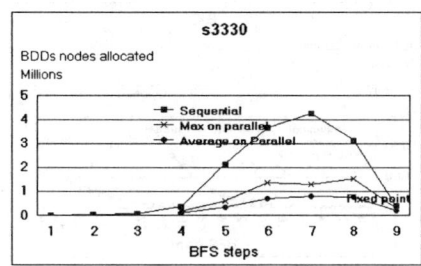
(b) Nodes allocated (peak)

Fig. 8. Memory utilizations during reachability analysis of s3330.

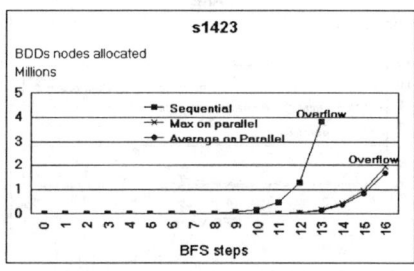
(a) Size of reachable states set

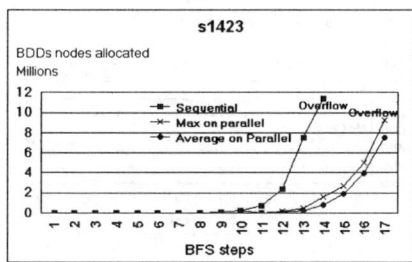
(b) Nodes allocated (peak)

Fig. 9. Memory utilizations during reachability analysis of s1423.

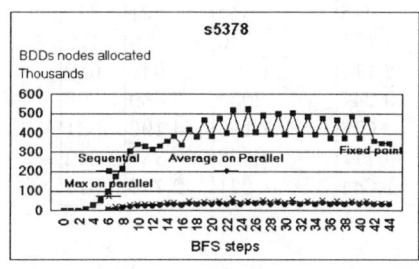
(a) Size of reachable states set

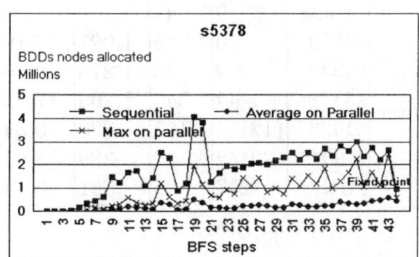
(b) Nodes allocated (peak)

Fig. 10. Memory utilizations during reachability analysis of s5378.

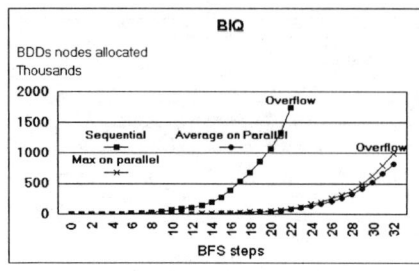
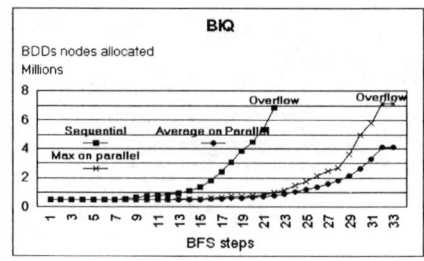

(a) **Size of reachable states set** (b) **Nodes allocated (peak)**

Fig. 11. Memory utilizations during reachability analysis of BIQ.

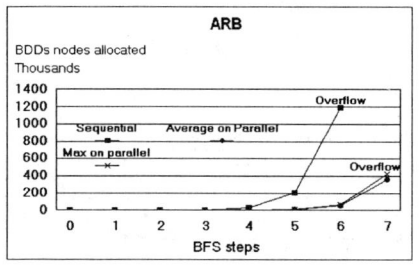
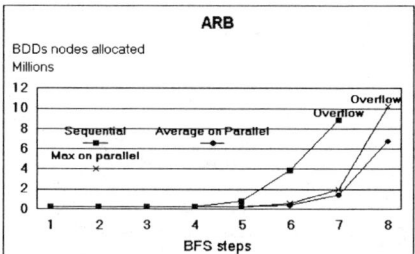

(a) **Size of reachable states set** (b) **Nodes allocated (peak)**

Fig. 12. Memory utilizations during reachability analysis of ARB.

Circuit	steps	seq. stage	slicing	total parallel	compute	exchange non-owned	balance	gc
prolog	9	47	3,289	1,282	478	544	421	371
s1269	10	312	1,091	167	101	46	0	119
s3330	9	28	1,218	9,765	8,113	1,907	646	619
s5378	44	345	1,203	17,224	9,247	2034	5,489	1,698
s1423	(12)14	155	820	5,541	678	186	4,192	681
BIQ	(22)32	50	389	78,515	35,717	4,458	30,881	9,262
ARB	(6)7	26	361	5,137	1,644	231	2,746	515

Fig. 13. Timing data (seconds) for parallel execution on 32×512MB machines. Each of the measures is the worst sample over all the machines. The steps count shows that in the case of overflow we got farther from where the 512MB single-machine experiment gave up (given in brackets). The sequential stage shows the time it took to get to the threshold where slicing is invoked. The total parallel is the total time over all steps, including computing, exchanging non-owned states, memory balancing, and garbage collection time. Note that the total time is the maxima over sums and not the sum over maxima. Note that communication time is counted only in the exchanging non-owned and balancing columns.

parallel machinery, we had to adapt the BFS for asynchronous computation, we coordinated and minimized communications, avoided unnecessary blocking, and employed a distributed termination detection.

Our system uses a powerful model checker, which shows that our scheme integrates nicely with state of the art tools. As a result, we were able to experiment with very large circuits, reaching farther steps. For instance, [5] report overflow in step 4 of s5378, while our system reached fixed point at step 44.

8 Acknowledgement

We would like to thank the SP Hardware Verification group in IBM Poughkeepsie and specifically John Aylward for enabling us to use their 60 nodes IBM SP system in order to perform out experiments.

References

1. S. Basonov. Parallel Implementation of BDD on DSM Systems, 1998. M.Sc. thesis, Computer Science Department, Technion.
2. I. Beer, S. Ben-David, C. Eisner, and A. Landver. Rulebase: an industry-oriented formal verification tool. In *33rd Design Automation Conference*, pages 655–660, 1996.
3. I. Beer, S. Ben-David, and A. Landver. On-the-fly model checking of rctl formulas. In *10th Computer Aided Verification*, pages 184–194, 1998.
4. R. E. Bryant. Graph-based algorithms for boolean function manipulation. *IEEE Transactions on Computers*, C-35(8):677–691, 1986.
5. Gianpiero Cabodi, Paolo Camurati, and Stefano Que. Improved reachability analysis of large fsm. In *Proceedings of the IEEE International Conference on Computer Aided Design*, pages 354–360. IEEE Computer Society Press, June 1996.
6. Olivier Coudert, Jean C. Madre, and Christian Berthet. Verifying Temporal Properties of Sequential Machines Without Building their State Diagrams. In R. Kurshan and E. M. Clarke, editors, *Workshop on Computer Aided Verification, DIMACS*, pages 75–84. American Mathematical Society, Providence, RI, 1990.
7. K. L. McMillan. *Symbolic Model Checking: An Approach to the State Explosion Problem*. Kluwer Academic Publishers, 1993.
8. Adrian A. Narayan, Jain J. Jawahar Isles, Robert K. Brayton, and Alberto L. Sangiovanni-Vincentelli. Reachability analysis using partitioned-robdds. In *Proceedings of the IEEE International Conference on Computer Aided Design*, pages 388–393. IEEE Computer Society Press, June 1997.
9. Adrian A. Narayan, Jain Jawahar, M. Fujita, and A. Sangiovanni-Vincentelli. Partitioned-robdds. In *Proceedings of the IEEE International Conference on Computer Aided Design*, pages 547–554. IEEE Computer Society Press, June 1996.
10. Ulrich Stern and David L. Dill. Parallelizing the murphy verifier. In *Proc. of the 9th International Conference on Computer Aided Verification, LNCS 1254*, pages 256–267. Springer, June 1997.
11. T. Stornetta and F. Brewer. Implementation of an efficient parallel bdd package. In *Design Automation Conference*. IEEE Computer Society Press, 1996.

An Automata-Theoretic Approach to Reasoning about Infinite-State Systems

Orna Kupferman[1] and Moshe Y. Vardi[2]*

[1] Hebrew University, The institute of Computer Science, Jerusalem 91904, Israel
   orna@cs.huji.ac.il, http://www.cs.huji.ac.il/~orna
[2] Rice University, Department of Computer Science, Houston, TX 77251-1892, U.S.A.
   vardi@cs.rice.edu, http://www.cs.rice.edu/~vardi

Abstract. We develop an automata-theoretic framework for reasoning about infinite-state sequential systems. Our framework is based on the observation that states of such systems, which carry a finite but unbounded amount of information, can be viewed as nodes in an infinite tree, and transitions between states can be simulated by finite-state automata. Checking that the system satisfies a temporal property can then be done by an alternating two-way tree automaton that navigates through the tree. As has been the case with finite-state systems, the automata-theoretic framework is quite versatile. We demonstrate it by solving several versions of the model-checking problem for μ-calculus specifications and prefix-recognizable systems, and by solving the realizability and synthesis problems for μ-calculus specifications with respect to prefix-recognizable environments.

1 Introduction

One of the most significant developments in the area of formal design verification is the discovery of algorithmic methods for verifying temporal-logic properties of *finite-state* systems [CES86,LP85,QS81,VW86]. In temporal-logic *model checking*, we verify the correctness of a finite-state system with respect to a desired behavior by checking whether a labeled state-transition graph that models the system satisfies a temporal logic formula that specifies this behavior (for a survey, see [CGP99]). Symbolic methods that enable model checking of very large state spaces, and the great ease of use of fully algorithmic methods, led to industrial acceptance of temporal model checking [BBG+94].

An important research topic over the past decade has been the application of model checking to infinite-state systems. Notable successes in this area has been the application of model checking to real-time and hybrid systems (cf. [HHWT95,LPY97]). Another active thrust of research is the application of model checking to *infinite-state sequential systems*. These are systems in which a state carries a finite, but unbounded, amount of information, e.g., a pushdown store. The origin of this thrust is the important result by Müller and Schupp that the monadic second-order theory of *context-free graphs* is decidable [MS85]. As the complexity involved in that decidability result is nonelementary, researchers sought decidability results of elementary complexity.

---
* Supported in part by NSF grant CCR-9700061, and by a grant from the Intel Corporation.

This started with Burkart and Steffen, who developed an exponential-time algorithm for model-checking formulas in the *alternation-free* μ-calculus with respect to context-free graphs [BS92]. Researchers then went on to extend this result to the μ-calculus, on one hand, and to more general graphs on the other hand, such as *pushdown graphs* [BS99a,Wal96], *regular graphs* [BQ96], and *prefix-recognizable graphs* [Cau96]. The most powerful result so far is an exponential-time algorithm by Burkart for model checking formulas of the μ-calculus with respect to prefix-recognizable graphs [Bur97b]. See also [BCMS00,BE96,BEM97,BS99b,Bur97a,FWW97].

In this paper we develop an automata-theoretic framework for reasoning about infinite-state sequential systems. The automata-theoretic approach uses the theory of automata as a unifying paradigm for system specification, verification, and synthesis [WVS83,EJ91,Kur94,VW94,KVW00]. Automata enables the separation of the logical and the algorithmic aspects of reasoning about systems, yielding clean and asymptotically optimal algorithms. The automata-theoretic framework for reasoning about finite-state systems has proven to be very versatile. Automata are the key to techniques such as on-the-fly verification [GPVW95], and they are useful also for modular verification [KV98], partial-order verification [GW94,WW96], verification of real-time and hybrid systems [HKV96,DW99], and verification of open systems [AHK97,KV99]. Many decision and synthesis problems have automata-based solutions and no other solution for them is known [EJ88,PR89,KV00]. Automata-based methods have been implemented in industrial automated-verification tools (c.f., COSPAN [HHK96] and SPIN [Hol97, VB99]).

The automata-theoretic approach, however, has long been thought to be inapplicable for effective reasoning about infinite-state systems. The reason, essentially, lies in the fact that the automata-theoretic techniques involve constructions in which the state space of the system directly influences the state space of the automaton (e.g., when we take the product of a specification automaton with the graph that models the system). On the other hand, the automata we know to handle have finitely many states. The key insight, which enables us to overcome this difficulty, and which is implicit in all previous decidability results in the area of infinite-state sequential systems, is that in spite of the somewhat misleading terminology (e.g., "context-free graphs" and "pushdown graphs"), the classes of infinite-state graphs for which decidability is known can be described by finite-state automata. This is explained by the fact the the states of the graphs that model these systems can be viewed as nodes in an infinite tree and transitions between states can be expressed by finite-state automata. As a result, automata-theoretic techniques can be used to reason about such systems. In particular, we show that various problems related to the analysis of such systems can be reduced to the emptiness problem for *alternating two-way tree automata*, which was recently shown to be decidable in exponential time [Var98].

We first show how the automata-theoretic framework can be used to solve the μ-calculus model-checking problem with respect to context-free and prefix-recognizable systems. While our framework does not establish new complexity results for model checking of infinite-state sequential systems, it appears to be, like the automata-theoretic framework for finite-state systems, very versatile, and it has further potential applications. We demonstrate it by showing how the μ-calculus model-checking algorithm can be extended to graphs with *regular state properties*, to graphs with *regular fairness constraints*, to μ-calculus with *backwards modalities*, and to checking *realizability* of μ-calculus formulas with respect to infinite-state sequential environments. In each of these problems all we have to demonstrate is a (fairly simple) reduction to the emptiness problem for alternating two-way tree automata; the (exponentially) hard work is then done by the emptiness-checking algorithm.

2 Preliminaries

2.1 Labeled Rewrite Systems

A *labeled transition graph* is quadruple $G = \langle S, Act, \rho, s_0 \rangle$, where S is a (possibly infinite) set of states, Act is a finite set of actions, $\rho \subseteq S \times Act \times S$ is a labeled transition relation, and $s_0 \in S_0$ is an initial state. When $\rho(s, a, s')$, we say that s' is an *a-successor* of s, and s is an *a-predecessor* of s'. For a state $s \in S$, we denote by $G^s = \langle S, Act, \rho, s \rangle$, the graph G with s as its initial state. A *rewrite system* is a quadruple $\mathcal{R} = \langle V, Act, R, x_0 \rangle$, where V is a finite alphabet, Act is a finite set of actions, R maps each action a to a finite set of rewrite rules, to be defined below, and $x_0 \in V^*$ is an initial word. Intuitively, $R(a)$ describes the possible rules that can be applied by taking the action a. We consider here two types of rewrite systems. In a *context-free* rewrite system, each rewrite rule is a pair $\langle A, x \rangle \in V \times V^*$. In a *prefix-recognizable* rewrite system, each rewrite rule is a triple $\langle \alpha, \beta, \gamma \rangle$ of regular expressions over V, each defining a subset of V^*. We refer to rewrite rules in $R(a)$ as *a-rules*.

The rewrite system $\mathcal{R}$ induces the labeled transition graph

$$G_\mathcal{R} = \langle V^*, Act, \rho_\mathcal{R}, x_0 \rangle,$$

where $\langle x, a, y \rangle \in \rho_\mathcal{R}$ if there is a rewrite rule in $R(a)$ whose application on x results in y. Formally, if $\mathcal{R}$ is a context-free rewrite system, then $\rho_\mathcal{R}(A \cdot y, a, x \cdot y)$ if $\langle A, x \rangle \in R(a)$. If $\mathcal{R}$ is a prefix-recognizable system, then $\rho_\mathcal{R}(z \cdot y, a, x \cdot y)$ if there are regular expressions α, β, and γ such that $z \in \alpha$, $y \in \beta$, $x \in \gamma$, and $\langle \alpha, \beta, \gamma \rangle \in R(a)$. A labeled transition graph that is induced by a context-free rewrite system is called a *context-free graph*. A labeled transition system that is induced by a prefix-recognizable rewrite system is called a *prefix-recognizable graph*. Note that in order to apply an a-transition in state x of a context-free graph, we only need to match the first latter of x with the first element of an a-rule. On the other hand, in an application of an a-transition in a prefix-recognizable graph, we should find an a-rule and a partition of x to a prefix that belongs to the first element of the rule and a suffix that belongs to the second element.

Example 1. The context-free rewrite system $\langle \{A, B\}, \{a, b\}, R, A \rangle$, with $R(a) = \{\langle A, AB \rangle\}$ and $R(b) = \{\langle A, \varepsilon \rangle, \langle B, \varepsilon \rangle\}$, induces the labeled transition graph on the right.

$$A \xrightarrow{a} AB \xrightarrow{a} ABB \xrightarrow{a} ABBB\text{-}\text{-}\text{-}$$
$$\downarrow b \quad \downarrow b \quad \downarrow b \quad \downarrow b$$
$$\varepsilon \xleftarrow{b} B \xleftarrow{b} BB \xleftarrow{b} BBB \text{ -}\text{-}\text{-}$$

We define the *size* $|R|$ of R as the space required in order to encode the rewrite rules in R. Thus, in the case of a context-free rewrite system,

$$|R| = \sum_{a \in Act} \sum_{\langle A, x \rangle \in R(a)} |x|,$$

and in a prefix-recognizable rewrite system,

$$|R| = \sum_{a \in Act} \sum_{\langle \alpha,\beta,\gamma \rangle \in R(a)} |\mathcal{U}_\alpha| + |\mathcal{U}_\beta| + |\mathcal{U}_\gamma|,$$

where $|\mathcal{U}_r|$ is the size of a nondeterministic automaton provided for the regular expression r.

2.2 μ-Calculus

The *μ-calculus* is a modal logic augmented with least and greatest fixpoint operators [Koz83]. Given a finite set Act of actions and a finite set Var of variables, a μ-calculus formula (in a positive normal form) over Act and Var is one of the following:

- **true**, **false**, or y for all $y \in Var$;
- $\varphi_1 \wedge \varphi_2$ or $\varphi_1 \vee \varphi_2$, for μ-calculus formulas φ_1 and φ_2;
- $[a]\varphi$ or $\langle a \rangle \varphi$, for $a \in Act$ and a μ-calculus formula φ;
- $\mu y.\varphi$ or $\nu y.\varphi$, for $y \in Var$ and a μ-calculus formula φ.

A *sentence* is a formula that contains no free variables from Var (that is, all the variables are in a scope of some fixed-point operator). We define the semantics of μ-calculus with respect to a labeled transition graph $G = \langle S, Act, \rho, s_0 \rangle$ and a valuation $\mathcal{V} : Var \to 2^S$ for its free variables. Each formula ψ and valuation $\mathcal{V}$ then define a set $\psi^G(\mathcal{V})$ of states of G that satisfy the formula. For a valuation $\mathcal{V}$, a variable $y \in Var$, and a set $S' \subseteq S$, we denote by $\mathcal{V}[y \leftarrow S']$ the valuation obtained from $\mathcal{V}$ by assigning S' to y. The mapping ψ^G is defined inductively as follows:

- $\mathbf{true}^G(\mathcal{V}) = S$ and $\mathbf{false}^G(\mathcal{V}) = \emptyset$;
- For $y \in Var$, we have $y^G(\mathcal{V}) = \mathcal{V}(y)$;
- $(\psi_1 \wedge \psi_2)^G(\mathcal{V}) = \psi_1^G(\mathcal{V}) \cap \psi_2^G(\mathcal{V})$;
- $(\psi_1 \vee \psi_2)^G(\mathcal{V}) = \psi_1^G(\mathcal{V}) \cup \psi_2^G(\mathcal{V})$;
- $([a]\psi)^G(\mathcal{V}) = \{s \in S : \text{for all } s' \text{ such that } R(s,a,s'), \text{ we have } s' \in \psi^G(\mathcal{V})\}$;
- $(\langle a \rangle \psi)^G(\mathcal{V}) = \{s \in S : \text{there is } s' \text{ such that } R(s,a,s') \text{ and } s' \in \psi^G(\mathcal{V})\}$;
- $(\mu y.\psi)^G(\mathcal{V}) = \bigcap \{S' \subseteq S : \psi^G(\mathcal{V}[y \leftarrow S']) \subseteq S'\}$;
- $(\nu y.\psi)^G(\mathcal{V}) = \bigcup \{S' \subseteq S : S' \subseteq \psi^G(\mathcal{V}[y \leftarrow S'])\}$.

Note that ψ^G cares only about the valuation of free variables in ψ. In particular, no valuation is required for a sentence. For a state $s \in S$ and a sentence ψ, we say that ψ holds at s in G, denoted $G, s \models \psi$ iff $s \in \psi^G$. Also, $G \models \psi$ iff $G, s_0 \models \psi$.

2.3 Alternating Two-Way Automata

Given a finite set Υ of directions, an *Υ-tree* is a set $T \subseteq \Upsilon^*$ such that if $\upsilon \cdot x \in T$, where $\upsilon \in \Upsilon$ and $x \in \Upsilon^*$, then also $x \in T$. The elements of T are called *nodes*, and the empty word ε is the *root* of T. For every $\upsilon \in \Upsilon$ and $x \in T$, the node x is the *parent* of $\upsilon \cdot x$. Each node $x \neq \varepsilon$ of T has a *direction* in Υ. The direction of the root is the symbol $\bot$ (we assume that $\bot \notin \Upsilon$). The direction of a node $\upsilon \cdot x$ is υ. We denote by $dir(x)$ the direction of node x. An Υ-tree T is a *full infinite tree* if $T = \Upsilon^*$. A *path* π of a tree T

is a set $\pi \subseteq T$ such that $\varepsilon \in \pi$ and for every $x \in \pi$ there exists a unique $\upsilon \in \Upsilon$ such that $\upsilon \cdot x \in \pi$. Note that our definitions here reverse the standard definitions (e.g., when $\Upsilon = \{0, 1\}$, the successors of the node 0 are 00 and 10 (rather than 00 and 01)[1].

Given two finite sets Υ and Σ, a Σ-labeled Υ-tree is a pair $\langle T, V \rangle$ where T is an Υ-tree and $V : T \to \Sigma$ maps each node of T to a letter in Σ. When Υ and Σ are not important or clear from the context, we call $\langle T, V \rangle$ a labeled tree. We say that an $((\Upsilon \cup \{\bot\}) \times \Sigma)$-labeled Υ-tree $\langle T, V \rangle$ is Υ-exhaustive if for every node $x \in T$, we have $V(x) \in \{dir(x)\} \times \Sigma$.

Alternating automata on infinite trees generalize nondeterministic tree automata and were first introduced in [MS87]. Here we describe alternating *two-way* tree automata. For a finite set X, let $\mathcal{B}^+(X)$ be the set of positive Boolean formulas over X (i.e., boolean formulas built from elements in X using $\wedge$ and $\vee$), where we also allow the formulas **true** and **false**, and, as usual, $\wedge$ has precedence over $\vee$. For a set $Y \subseteq X$ and a formula $\theta \in \mathcal{B}^+(X)$, we say that Y *satisfies* θ iff assigning **true** to elements in Y and assigning **false** to elements in $X \setminus Y$ makes θ true. For a set Υ of directions, the *extension* of Υ is the set $ext(\Upsilon) = \Upsilon \cup \{\varepsilon, \uparrow\}$ (we assume that $\Upsilon \cap \{\varepsilon, \uparrow\} = \emptyset$). An *alternating two-way automaton* over Σ-labeled Υ-trees is a tuple $\mathcal{A} = \langle \Sigma, Q, \delta, q_0, F \rangle$, where Σ is the input alphabet, Q is a finite set of states, $\delta : Q \times \Sigma \to \mathcal{B}^+(ext(\Upsilon) \times Q)$ is the transition function, $q_0 \in Q$ is an initial state, and F specifies the acceptance condition.

A run of an alternating automaton $\mathcal{A}$ over a labeled tree $\langle \Upsilon^*, V \rangle$ is a labeled tree $\langle T_r, r \rangle$ in which every node is labeled by an element of $\Upsilon^* \times Q$. A node in T_r, labeled by (x, q), describes a copy of the automaton that is in the state q and reads the node x of Υ^*. Note that many nodes of T_r can correspond to the same node of Υ^*; there is no one-to-one correspondence between the nodes of the run and the nodes of the tree. The labels of a node and its successors have to satisfy the transition function. Formally, a run $\langle T_r, r \rangle$ is a Σ_r-labeled Γ-tree, for some set Γ of directions, where $\Sigma_r = \Upsilon^* \times Q$ and $\langle T_r, r \rangle$ satisfies the following:

1. $\varepsilon \in T_r$ and $r(\varepsilon) = (\varepsilon, q_0)$.
2. Consider $y \in T_r$ with $r(y) = (x, q)$ and $\delta(q, V(x)) = \theta$. Then there is a (possibly empty) set $S \subseteq ext(\Upsilon) \times Q$, such that S satisfies θ, and for all $\langle c, q' \rangle \in S$, there is $\gamma \in \Gamma$ such that $\gamma \cdot y \in T_r$ and the following hold:
   - If $c \in \Upsilon$, then $r(\gamma \cdot y) = (c \cdot x, q')$.
   - If $c = \varepsilon$, then $r(\gamma \cdot y) = (x, q')$.
   - If $c = \uparrow$, then $x = \upsilon \cdot z$, for some $\upsilon \in \Upsilon$ and $z \in \Upsilon^*$, and $r(\gamma \cdot y) = (z, q')$.

Thus, ε-transitions leave the automaton on the same node of the input tree, and $\uparrow$-transitions take it up to the parent node. Note that the automaton cannot go up the root of the input tree, as whenever $c = \uparrow$, we require that $x \neq \varepsilon$.

A run $\langle T_r, r \rangle$ is *accepting* if all its infinite paths satisfy the acceptance condition. We consider here *parity* acceptance conditions [EJ91]. A parity condition over a state set Q is a finite sequence $F = \{F_1, F_2, \ldots, F_m\}$ of subsets of Q, where $F_1 \subseteq F_2 \subseteq \ldots \subseteq F_m = Q$. The number m of sets is called the *index* of $\mathcal{A}$. Given a run $\langle T_r, r \rangle$ and an infinite path $\pi \subseteq T_r$, let $inf(\pi) \subseteq Q$ be such that $q \in inf(\pi)$ if and only if there are

---

[1] As will get clearer in the sequel, the reason for that is that rewrite rules refer to the prefix of words.

infinitely many $y \in \pi$ for which $r(y) \in \Upsilon^* \times \{q\}$. That is, $inf(\pi)$ contains exactly all the states that appear infinitely often in π. A path π satisfies the condition F if there is an even i for which $inf(\pi) \cap F_i \neq \emptyset$ and $inf(\pi) \cap F_{i-1} = \emptyset$. An automaton accepts a labeled tree if and only if there exists a run that accepts it. We denote by $\mathcal{L}(\mathcal{A})$ the set of all Σ-labeled trees that $\mathcal{A}$ accepts. The automaton $\mathcal{A}$ is *nonempty* iff $\mathcal{L}(\mathcal{A}) \neq \emptyset$.

Theorem 1. *Given an alternating two-way parity tree automaton $\mathcal{A}$ with n states and index k, we can construct an equivalent nondeterministic one-way parity tree automaton whose number of states is exponential in nk and whose index is linear in nk [Var98], and we can check the nonemptiness of $\mathcal{A}$ in time exponential in nk [EJS93].*

2.4 Alternating Automata on Labeled Transition Graphs

Consider a labeled transition graph $G = \langle S, Act, \rho, s_0 \rangle$. For the set Act of actions, let $next(Act) = \{\varepsilon\} \cup \bigcup_{a \in Act}\{[a], \langle a \rangle\}$. An alternating automaton on labeled transition graphs (*graph automaton*, for short) [JW95][2] is a tuple $\mathcal{S} = \langle Act, Q, \delta, q_0, F \rangle$, where Q, q_0, and F are as in alternating two-way automata, Act is a set of actions, and $\delta : Q \to \mathcal{B}^+(next(Act) \times Q)$ is the transition function. Intuitively, when $\mathcal{S}$ is in state q and it reads a state s of G, fulfilling an atom $\langle \langle a \rangle, t \rangle$ (or $\langle a \rangle t$, for short) requires $\mathcal{S}$ to send a copy in state t to some a-successor of s. Similarly, fulfilling an atom $[a]t$ requires $\mathcal{S}$ to send copies in state t to all the a-successors of s. Thus, like symmetric automata [DW99,Wil99], graph automata cannot distinguish between the various a-successors of a state and treat them in an existential or universal way.

Like runs of alternating two-way automata, a run of a graph automaton $\mathcal{S}$ over a labeled transition graph $G = \langle S, Act, \rho, s_0 \rangle$ is a labeled tree in which every node is labeled by an element of $S \times Q$. A node labeled by (s, q), describes a copy of the automaton that is in the state q of $\mathcal{S}$ and reads the state s of G. Formally, a run is a Σ_r-labeled Γ-tree $\langle T_r, r \rangle$, where Γ is an arbitrary set of directions, $\Sigma_r = S \times Q$, and $\langle T_r, r \rangle$ satisfies the following:

1. $\varepsilon \in T_r$ and $r(\varepsilon) = (s_0, q_0)$.
2. Consider $y \in T_r$ with $r(y) = (s, q)$ and $\delta(q) = \theta$. Then there is a (possibly empty) set $S \subseteq next(Act) \times Q$, such that S satisfies θ, and for all $\langle c, q' \rangle \in S$, the following hold:
   - If $c = \varepsilon$, then there is $\gamma \in \Gamma$ such that $\gamma \cdot y \in T_r$ and $r(\gamma \cdot y) = (s, q')$.
   - If $c = [a]$, then for every a-successor s' of s, there is $\gamma \in \Gamma$ such that $\gamma \cdot y \in T_r$ and $r(\gamma \cdot y) = (s', q')$.
   - If $c = \langle a \rangle$, then there is an a-successor s' of s and $\gamma \in \Gamma$ such that $\gamma \cdot y \in T_r$ and $r(\gamma \cdot y) = (s', q')$.

A run $\langle T_r, r \rangle$ is *accepting* if all its infinite paths satisfy the acceptance condition. The graph G is accepted by $\mathcal{S}$ if there is an accepting run on it. We denote by $\mathcal{L}(\mathcal{S})$ the set of all graphs that $\mathcal{S}$ accepts. We denote by $\mathcal{S}^q = \langle Act, Q, \delta, q, F \rangle$ the automaton $\mathcal{S}$ with q as its initial state.

---

[2] The graph automata in [JW95] are different than these defined here, but this is only a technical difference.

We use graph automata as our specification language. We say that a labeled transition graph G satisfies a graph automaton $\mathcal{S}$, denoted $G \models \mathcal{S}$, if $\mathcal{S}$ accepts G. It is shown in [JW95] that graph automata are as expressive as μ-calculus. In particular, we have the following.

Theorem 2. *Given a μ-calculus formula ψ, of length n and alternation depth k, we can construct a graph parity automaton $\mathcal{S}_\psi$ such that $\mathcal{L}(\mathcal{S}_\psi)$ is exactly the set of graphs satisfying ψ. The automaton $\mathcal{S}_\psi$ has n states and index k.*

3 Model Checking of Context-Free Graphs

In this section we present an automata-theoretic approach to model-checking of context-free transition systems. Consider a labeled transition graph $G = \langle V^*, Act, \rho_\mathcal{R}, v_0 \rangle$, induced by a rewrite system $\mathcal{R} = \langle V, Act, R, x_0 \rangle$. Since the state space of G is the full V-tree, we can think of each transition $\langle z, a, z' \rangle \in \rho_\mathcal{R}$ as a "jump" that is activated by the action a from the node z of the V-tree to the node z'. Thus, if $\mathcal{R}$ is a context-free rewrite system and we are at node $A \cdot y$ of the V-tree, an application of the action a takes us to nodes $x \cdot y$, for $\langle A, x \rangle \in R(a)$. Technically, this means that we first move up to the parent y of $A \cdot y$, and then move down along x. Such a navigation through the V-tree can be easily performed by two-way automata.

Theorem 3. *Given a context-free rewrite system $\mathcal{R} = \langle V, Act, R, v_0 \rangle$ and a graph automaton $\mathcal{S} = \langle Act, Q, \delta, q_0, F \rangle$, we can construct an alternating two-way parity automaton $\mathcal{A}$ over $(V \cup \{\bot\})$-labeled V-trees such that $\mathcal{L}(\mathcal{A})$ is not empty iff $G_\mathcal{R}$ satisfies $\mathcal{S}$. The automaton $\mathcal{A}$ has $O(|Q| \cdot |R| \cdot |V|)$ states, and has the same index as $\mathcal{S}$.*

Proof: The automaton $\mathcal{A}$ checks that the input tree is V-exhaustive (that is, each node is labeled by its direction). As such, $\mathcal{A}$ can learn from labels it reads the state in V^* that each node corresponds to. The transition function of $\mathcal{A}$ then consults the rewrite rules in R in order to transform an atom in $next(Act) \times Q$ to a chain of transitions that spread copies of $\mathcal{A}$ to the corresponding nodes of the full V-tree.

We define $\mathcal{A} = \langle V \cup \{\bot\}, Q', \eta, q'_0, F' \rangle$ as follows.

- $Q' = Q \times tails(\mathcal{R}) \times (V \cup \{\bot, \#\})$, where $tails(\mathcal{R}) \subseteq V^*$ is the set of all suffixes of words $x \in V^*$ for which there are $a \in Act$ and $A \in V$ such that $\langle A, x \rangle \in R(a)$. Intuitively, when $\mathcal{A}$ visits a node $x \in V^*$ in state $\langle q, y, A \rangle$, it checks that $G_\mathcal{R}$ with initial state $y \cdot x$ is accepted by $\mathcal{S}^q$. In particular, when $y = \varepsilon$, then $G_\mathcal{R}$ with initial state x (the node currently being visited) needs to be accepted by $\mathcal{S}^q$. In addition, if $A \neq \#$, then $\mathcal{A}$ also checks that $dir(x) = A$. States of the form $\langle q, \varepsilon, A \rangle$ are called *action states*. From these states $\mathcal{A}$ consults δ and R in order to impose new requirements on the exhaustive V-tree. States of the form $\langle q, y, A \rangle$, for $y \in V^+$, are called *navigation states*. From these states $\mathcal{A}$ only navigates downwards y to reach new action states. On its way, $\mathcal{A}$ also checks the V-exhaustiveness of the input tree.
- In order to define $\eta : Q' \times (V \cup \{\bot\}) \to \mathcal{B}^+(ext(V) \times Q')$, we first define the function $apply_R : next(Act) \times Q \times (V \cup \{\bot\}) \to \mathcal{B}^+(ext(V) \times Q')$. Intuitively, $apply_R$ transforms atoms participating in δ, together with a letter $A \in V \cup \{\bot\}$, which stands for the direction of the current node, to a formula that describes the

requirements on $G_\mathcal{R}$ when the rewrite rules in R are applied to words of the form $A \cdot V^*$. For $c \in next(Act)$, $q \in Q$, and $A \in V \cup \{\bot\}$, we define

$$apply_R(c,q,A) = \begin{bmatrix} \langle \varepsilon, (q, \varepsilon, A) \rangle & \text{If } c = \varepsilon. \\ \bigwedge_{\langle A,y \rangle \in R(a)} \langle \uparrow, (q, y, \#) \rangle & \text{If } c = [a]. \\ \bigvee_{\langle A,y \rangle \in R(a)} \langle \uparrow, (q, y, \#) \rangle & \text{If } c = \langle a \rangle. \end{bmatrix}$$

Note that $R(a)$ may contain no pairs in $\{A\} \times V^*$ (that is, the transition relation of $G_\mathcal{R}$ may not be total). In particular, this happens when $A = \bot$ (that is, the state ε of $G_\mathcal{R}$ has no successors). Then, we take empty conjunctions as **true**, and take empty disjunctions as **false**.

In order to understand the function $apply_\mathcal{R}$, consider the case $c = [a]$. When $\mathcal{S}$ reads the state $A \cdot x$ of the input graph, fulfilling the atom $[a]q$ requires $\mathcal{S}$ to send copies in state q to all the a-successors of $A \cdot x$. The automaton $\mathcal{A}$ then sends to the node x copies that check whether all the states $y \cdot x$, with $\rho_\mathcal{R}(A \cdot x, a, y \cdot x)$, are accepted by $\mathcal{S}$ with initial state q.

Now, for a formula $\theta \in \mathcal{B}^+(next(Act) \times Q)$, the formula

$$apply_R(\theta, A) \in \mathcal{B}^+(ext(V) \times Q')$$

is obtained from θ by replacing an atom $\langle c, q \rangle$ by the atom $apply_R(c, q, A)$. We can now define η for all $A \in V \cup \{\bot\}$ as follow.

- $\eta(\langle q, \varepsilon, A \rangle, A) = \eta(\langle q, \varepsilon, \# \rangle, A) = apply_R(\delta(q), A)$.
- $\eta(\langle q, B \cdot y, A \rangle, A) = \eta(\langle q, B \cdot y, \# \rangle, A) = (B, \langle q, y, B \rangle)$.

Thus, in action states, $\mathcal{A}$ reads the direction of the current node and applies the rewrite rules of $\mathcal{R}$ in order to impose new requirements according to δ. In navigation states, $\mathcal{A}$ needs to go downwards $B \cdot y$ and check that the nodes it comes across on its way are labeled by their direction. For that, $\mathcal{A}$ proceeds only with the direction of the current node (maintained as the third element of the state), and sends to direction B a state whose third element is B. Note that since we reach states with $\#$ only with upward transitions, $\mathcal{A}$ visits these states only when it reads nodes x that have already been read by a copy of $\mathcal{A}$ that does check whether x is labeled by its direction.

- $q_0' = \langle q_0, x_0, \bot \rangle$. Thus, in its initial state $\mathcal{A}$ checks that $G_\mathcal{R}$ with initial state x_0 is accepted by $\mathcal{S}$ with initial state q_0. It also checks that the root of the input tree is labeled with $\bot$.
- F' is obtained from F by replacing each set F_i by the set $F_i \times tails(R) \times (V \cup \{\#\})$.

□

Context-free rewrite systems can be viewed as a special case of prefix-recognizable rewrite systems. In the next section we describe how to extend the construction described above to prefix-recognizable graphs, and we also analyze the complexity of the model-checking algorithm that follows for the two types of systems.

4 Model Checking of Prefix-Recognizable Graphs

In this section we extend the construction described in Section 3 to prefix-recognizable transition systems. The idea is similar: two-way automata can navigate through the full

V-tree and simulate transitions in a system induced by a rewrite system by a chain of transitions in the tree. While in context-free transition systems the application of rewrite rules involved one move up the tree and then a chain of moves down, here things are a bit more involved. In order to apply a rewrite rule $\langle \alpha, \beta, \gamma \rangle$, the automaton has to move upwards along a word in α, check that the remaining word leading to the root is in β, and move downwards along a word in γ. As we explain below, $\mathcal{A}$ does so by simulating automata for the regular expressions participating in R.

Theorem 4. *Given a prefix-recognizable rewrite system $\mathcal{R} = \langle V, Act, R, v_0 \rangle$ and a graph automaton $\mathcal{S} = \langle Act, Q, \delta, q_0, F \rangle$, we can construct an alternating two-way parity automaton $\mathcal{A}$ over $(V \cup \{\bot\})$-labeled V-trees such that $\mathcal{L}(\mathcal{A})$ is not empty iff $G_\mathcal{R}$ satisfies $\mathcal{S}$. The automaton $\mathcal{A}$ has $O(|Q| \cdot |R| \cdot |V|)$ states, and has the same index as $\mathcal{S}$.*

Proof: For a regular expression α on V, let $\mathcal{U}_\alpha = \langle V, S_\alpha, M_\alpha, S_\alpha^0, F_\alpha \rangle$ be a nondeterministic word automaton with $\mathcal{L}(\mathcal{U}_\alpha) = \alpha$. Let $\Omega = \{\langle \alpha, \beta, \gamma \rangle : \text{ there is a } a \in Act \text{ such that } \langle \alpha, \beta, \gamma \rangle \in R(a)\}$ be the set of all triples in $R(a)$, for some $a \in Act$, and let $S_\Omega = \bigcup_{\langle \alpha, \beta, \gamma \rangle \in \Omega} S_\alpha \cup S_\beta \cup S_\gamma$ be the union of all the state spaces of the automata associated with regular expressions that participate in R.

As in the case of context-free rewrite systems, $\mathcal{A}$ checks that the input tree is the V-exhaustive tree and then uses its labels in order to learn the state in V^* that each node corresponds to. As there, $\mathcal{A}$ applies to the transition function δ of $\mathcal{S}$ the rewrite rules of $\mathcal{R}$. Here, however, the application of the rewrite rules on atoms of the form $\langle a \rangle q$ and $[a]q$ is more involved, and we describe it below. Assume that $\mathcal{A}$ wants to check whether $\mathcal{S}^q$ accepts $G_\mathcal{R}^x$, and it wants to proceed with an atom $\langle a \rangle q$ in $\delta(t)$. The automaton $\mathcal{A}$ needs to check whether $\mathcal{S}^q$ accepts $G_\mathcal{R}^y$ for some state y reachable from x by applying an a-rule. That is, a state y for which there is $\langle \alpha, \beta, \gamma \rangle \in R(a)$ and partitions $x' \cdot z$ and $y' \cdot z$, of x and y, respectively, such that x' is accepted by $\mathcal{U}_\alpha$, z is accepted by $\mathcal{U}_\beta$, and is y' accepted by $\mathcal{U}_\gamma$. The way $\mathcal{A}$ detects such a state y is the following. From the node x, the automaton $\mathcal{A}$ simulates the automaton $\mathcal{U}_\alpha$ upwards (that is, $\mathcal{A}$ guesses a run of $\mathcal{U}_\alpha$ on the word it reads as it proceeds on direction $\uparrow$ from x towards the root of the V-tree). Suppose that on its way up to the root, $\mathcal{A}$ encounters a state in F_α as it reads the node $z \in V^*$. This means that the word read so far is in α, and can serve as the prefix x' above. If this is indeed the case (and $\mathcal{A}$ may also continue as if a state in F_α has not been encountered; thus guess that the word read so far is not x'), then it is left to check that the word z is accepted by $\mathcal{U}_\beta$, and that there is a state that is obtained from z by prefixing it with a word $y' \in \gamma$ that is accepted by $\mathcal{S}^q$. To check the first condition, $\mathcal{A}$ sends a copy in direction $\uparrow$ that simulates a run of $\mathcal{U}_\beta$, hoping to reach a state in F_β as it reaches the root (that is, $\mathcal{A}$ guesses a run of $\mathcal{U}_\beta$ on the word it reads as it proceeds from z up to the root of the V-tree). To check the second condition, $\mathcal{A}$ simulates the automaton $\mathcal{U}_\gamma$ downwards. A node $y' \cdot z \in V^*$ that $\mathcal{A}$ reads as it encounters a state in F_γ can serve as the state y we are after. The case for an atom $[a]q$ is similar, only that here $\mathcal{A}$ needs to check whether $\mathcal{S}^q$ accepts $G_\mathcal{R}^y$ for all states y reachable from x by applying an a-rule, and thus the choices made by $\mathcal{A}$ for guessing the partition $x' \cdot z$ of x and the prefix y' of y are now treated dually.

In order to follow the above application of rewrite rules, the state space of $\mathcal{A}$ is $Q' = Q \times \Omega \times S_\Omega \times \{0, 1, 2, 3\} \times \{\forall, \exists\} \times (V \cup \{\bot, \#\})$. Thus, a state is a 6-

tuple $q' = \langle q, \langle \alpha, \beta, \gamma \rangle, s, i, b, A \rangle$, where A is the expected direction of the current node (needed in order to check the V-exhaustiveness), $i \in \{0, 1, 2, 3\}$ is the current simulation mode (states in mode 0 are action states, where we apply $\mathcal{R}$ on the transitions in δ, and states in modes 1, 2 and 3 are states where we simulate automata for α, β, and γ, respectively), $b \in \{\forall, \exists\}$ is the simulating mode (depending on whether we are applying $\mathcal{R}$ to an $\langle a \rangle$ or an $[a]$ atom), $\langle \alpha, \beta, \gamma \rangle$ is the rewrite rule in $R(a)$ we are applying, and s is the current state of the simulated automaton[3]. The formal definition of the transition function of $\mathcal{A}$ follows quite straightforwardly from the definition of the state space and the explanation above.

The acceptance condition of $\mathcal{A}$ is the adjustment of F to the new state space. That is, it is obtained from F by replacing each set F_i by the set $F_i \times \Omega \times S_\Omega \times \{0\} \times \{\forall, \exists\} \times (V \cup \{\bot, \#\})$. Considering only action states excludes runs in which the simulation of the automata for the regular expressions continues forever. Indeed, as long as a copy of $\mathcal{A}$ simulates an automaton $\mathcal{U}_\alpha$, $\mathcal{U}_\beta$, or $\mathcal{U}_\gamma$, it stays in simulation mode 1, 2, or 3, respectively. □

The constructions described in Theorems 3 and 4 reduce the model-checking problem to the nonemptiness problem of an alternating two-way parity tree automaton. By Theorem 1, we then have the following.

Theorem 5. *The model-checking problem for a context-free or a prefix recognizable rewrite system* $\mathcal{R} = \langle V, Act, R, v_0 \rangle$ *and a graph automaton* $\mathcal{S} = \langle Act, Q, \delta, q_0, F \rangle$, *can be solved in time exponential in* nk, *where* $n = |Q| \cdot |R| \cdot |V|$ *and k is the index of $\mathcal{S}$.*

Together with Theorem 2, we can conclude with an EXPTIME bound also for the model-checking problem of μ-calculus formulas matching the lower bound in [Wal96]. Note that the fact the same complexity bound holds for both context-free and prefix-recognizable rewrite systems stems from the different definition of $|R|$ in the two cases.

5 Extensions

The automata-theoretic approach offers several extensions to the model-checking setting. We describe some of these extensions below.

5.1 Regular State Properties

The systems we want to reason about often have, in addition to a set of actions, also a set P of *state properties*. In the case of finite-state systems, these are described by a mapping $L : S \to P$ that associates with each state of the labeled transition graph that models the system, the property that is true in it (for simplicity, we assume that exactly one property holds in each state). In our case, of infinite-state graphs induced by rewrite systems, we consider *regular state properties*, where each property $p \in P$ is associated

---

[3] Note that a straightforward representation of Q' results in $O(|Q| \cdot |\Omega| \cdot |R| \cdot |V|)$ states. Since, however, the states of the automata for the regular expressions are disjoint, we can assume that the triple in Ω that each automaton corresponds to is uniquely defined from it.

with a regular expression $[p]$ over V, describing the set of states (words in V^*) in which p holds. Again, we assume that for each $x \in V^*$, there is a single $p \in P$ such that $x \in [p]$.

In order to specify behaviors of labeled transition graphs with regular state properties in P, we consider an extension of graph automata with the alphabet P. The transition function of an extended automaton $\mathcal{S} = \langle P, Act, Q, \delta, q_0, F \rangle$, is $\delta : Q \times P \to \mathcal{B}^+(next(Act) \times Q)$; thus it reads from the input graph both the state properties, in order to know with which transition to proceed, and the actions, in order to know to which successors to proceed. The formal definition of a run of an extended graph automaton on a labeled transition graph with state properties is the straightforward extension of the definition given in Section 2.4 for the graph automata described there. Alternatively, one can consider a μ-calculus with both state properties and actions [Koz83]. Theorem 2 holds also for formulas in such a μ-calculus.

Having our solution to the model-checking problem based on two-way automata, it is simple to extend it to graphs and specifications with state properties. Indeed, whenever the automaton $\mathcal{A}$ from Theorems 3 and 4 reads the state $x \in V^*$ and takes a transition from an action state, it should now also guess the property p that holds in x and proceed according to the transition function of the specification automaton with input letter p. In order to check that the guess $x \in [p]$ is correct, the automaton simulates the word automaton $\mathcal{U}_{[p]}$ upwards, hoping to visit an accepting state when the root is reached. The complexity of the model-checking algorithm stays the same.

5.2 Fairness

The systems we want to reason about are often augmented with *fairness constraints*. Like state properties, we can define a *regular fairness constraint* by a regular expression α, where a computation of the labeled transition graph is fair iff it contains infinitely many states in α (this corresponds to weak fairness; other types of fairness can be defined similarly). It is easy to extend our model-checking algorithm to handle fairness (that is, let the path quantification in the specification range only on fair paths[4]): the automaton $\mathcal{A}$ can guess whether the state currently visited is in α, and then simulate the word automaton $\mathcal{U}_\alpha$ upwards, hoping to visit an accepting state when the root is reached. When $\mathcal{A}$ checks an existential property, it has to make sure that the property is satisfied along a fair path, and it is therefore required to visit infinitely many states in α. When $\mathcal{A}$ checks a universal property, it may guess that a path it follows is not fair, in which case $\mathcal{A}$ eventually always send copies that simulate the automaton for $\neg\alpha$. The complexity of the model-checking algorithm stays the same.

5.3 Backward Modalities

Another extension is the treatment of specifications with *backwards modalities*. While forward modalities express weakest precondition, backward modalities express strongest

---

[4] The exact semantics of *fair graph automata* as well as *fair μ-calculus* is not straightforward, as they enable cycles in which we switch between existential and universal modalities. To make our point here, it is simpler to assume, say, graph automata that correspond to CTL* formulas.

postcondition, and they are very useful for reasoning about the past [LPZ85]. In order to adjust graph automata to backward reasoning, we add to $next(Act)$ the "directions" $\langle a^-\rangle$ and $[a^-]$. This enables the graph automata to move to a-predecessors of the current state. More formally, if a graph automaton reads a state x of the input graph, then fulfilling an atom $\langle a^-\rangle t$ requires $\mathcal{S}$ to send a copy in state t to some a-predecessor of x, and dually for $[a^-]t$. Theorem 2 can then be extended to μ-calculus formulas and graph automata with both forward and backward modalities [Var98].

Extending our solution to graph automata with backward modalities is simple. Consider a node $x \in V^*$ in a prefix-recognizable graph. The a-predecessors of x are states y for which there is a rule $\langle \alpha, \beta, \gamma \rangle \in R(a)$ and partitions $x' \cdot z$ and $y' \cdot z$, of x and y, respectively, such that x' is accepted by $\mathcal{U}_\gamma$, z is accepted by $\mathcal{U}_\beta$, and y' is accepted by $\mathcal{U}_\alpha$. Hence, we can define a mapping R^- such that $\langle \gamma, \beta, \alpha \rangle \in R^-(a)$ iff $\langle \alpha, \beta, \gamma \rangle \in R(a)$, and handle atoms $\langle a^-\rangle t$ and $[a^-]t$ exactly as we handle $\langle a\rangle t$ and $[a]t$, only that for them we apply the rewrite rules in R^- rather than these in R. The complexity of the model-checking algorithm stays the same. Note that the simple solution relies on the fact that the structure of the rewrite rules in a prefix-recognizable rewrite system is symmetric (that is, switching α and γ results in a well-structured rule), which is not the case for context-free rewrite systems[5].

5.4 Global Model Checking

In the full paper we show that in addition to checking whether a system $\mathcal{R}$ satisfies a specification $\mathcal{S}$, we can compute the regular languages of all states satisfying $\mathcal{S}$, thus we solve the *global* model-checking problem. For a rewrite system $\mathcal{R}$ and a regular language L, let $post(L)$, $post^*(L)$, $pre(L)$, and $pre^*(L)$ be the sets of states in $G_\mathcal{R}$ that are immediate sucessors of the states in L, sucessors of the states in L, immediate predecessors of the states in L, and predecessors of the states in L, respectively. The predicates above can be viewed as specifications. Indeed, $post(L) = \langle + \rangle L$, $post^*(L) = \mu y.L \vee \langle + \rangle y$, $pre(L) = \langle - \rangle L$, and $pre^*(L) = \mu y.L \vee \langle - \rangle y$ (in a μ-calculus with state predicates, where $\langle + \rangle$ and $\langle - \rangle$ are the "next" and "previously" modalities). Hence, the algorithm can be used to compute successors and predecessors of regular state sets, and can be viewed as the automata-theoretic approach to the algorithms in [BEM97].

This observation is related to the work in [LS98], where bottom-up automata on finite trees are used in order to recognize sets of terms in Process Algebra. Given a term t, [LS98] shows that it is possible to define $post^*(t)$ as the solution of a regular equation. They conclude that $post*(t)$ is a regular tree language, and similarly for $post(t)$, $pre(t)$, and $pre^*(t)$.

---

[5] Note that this does not mean we cannot model check specifications with backwards modalities in context-free rewrite systems. It just mean that doing so invovles rewrite rules that are no longer context free. Indeed, a rule $\langle A, x \rangle \in R(a)$ in a context-free system corresponds to the rule $\langle A, V^*, x \rangle \in R(a)$ in a prefix recognizable system, inducing the rule $\langle x, V^*, A \rangle \in R^{-1}(a)$.

6 Realizability and Synthesis

Given a rewrite system $\mathcal{R} = \langle V, Act, R, v_0 \rangle$, a *strategy* of $\mathcal{R}$ is a function $f : V^* \to Act$. The function f restricts the graph $G_\mathcal{R}$ so that from a state $x \in V^*$, only $f(x)$-actions are taken. Formally, $\mathcal{R}$ and f together define the graph $G_{\mathcal{R},f} = \langle V^*, Act, \rho, v_0 \rangle$, where $\rho(x, a, y)$ iff $f(x) = a$ and $\rho_\mathcal{R}(x, a, y)$. Given $\mathcal{R}$ and a graph automaton $\mathcal{S} = \langle Act, Q, \delta, q_0, F \rangle$, we say that a strategy f of $\mathcal{R}$ is *winning* for $\mathcal{S}$ iff $G_{\mathcal{R},f}$ satisfies $\mathcal{S}$. Given $\mathcal{R}$ and $\mathcal{S}$, the problem of *realizability* is to determine whether there is a winning strategy of $\mathcal{R}$ for $\mathcal{S}$. The problem of *synthesis* is then to construct such a strategy. The setting described here corresponds to the case where the system needs to satisfy a specification with respect to environments modeled by a rewrite system. Then, at each state, the system chooses the action to proceed with and the environment provides the rules that determine the successors of the state. Branching-time realizability of finite-state systems can be viewed as a special case of our setting here, where for all actions $a \in Act$, we have $R(a) = \{\langle \varepsilon, V^*, A \rangle\}$. Thus, from each state $x \in V^*$, we can apply an a-transitions to all the states $A \cdot x$, for $A \in V$.

The automaton $\mathcal{A}$ from Theorem 4 can be modified to solve the realizability problem and to generate winning strategies. The idea is simple: a strategy $f : V^* \to Act$ can be viewed as an Act-labeled V-tree. Thus, the realizability problem can be viewed as the problem of determining whether we can augment the labels of the V-labeled V-exhaustive tree by elements in Act, and accept the augmented tree in a run of $\mathcal{A}$ in which whenever $\mathcal{A}$ reads an action $a \in Act$, it applies to the transition function of the specification graph automaton only rewrite rules in $R(a)$. Hence the following theorem.

Theorem 6. *Given a prefix-recognizable rewrite system $\mathcal{R} = \langle V, Act, R, v_0 \rangle$ and a graph automaton $\mathcal{S} = \langle Act, Q, \delta, q_0, F \rangle$, we can construct an alternating two-way parity automaton $\mathcal{A}$ over $((V \cup \{\bot\}) \times Act)$-labeled V-trees such that $\mathcal{L}(\mathcal{A})$ contains exactly all the V-exhaustive trees whose projection on Act is a winning strategy of $\mathcal{R}$ for $\mathcal{S}$. The automaton $\mathcal{A}$ has $O(|Q| \cdot |R| \cdot |V|)$ states, and has the same index as $\mathcal{S}$.*

Proof: Exactly as in Theorem 4, only that from an action state we proceed with the rules in $R(a)$, where a is the Act-element of the letter we read. For example, in the case of a context-free rewrite system, we would have, for $c \in next(Act)$, $q \in Q$, $A \in V$, and $a \in Act$ (the new parameter to $apply_\mathcal{R}$, which is read from the input tree),

$$apply_R(c, q, A, a) = \begin{cases} \langle \varepsilon, (q, \varepsilon, A) \rangle & \text{If } c = \varepsilon. \\ \bigwedge_{\langle A,y \rangle \in R(a)} \langle \uparrow, (q, y, \#) \rangle & \text{If } c = [a]. \\ \text{true} & \text{If } c = [b], \text{ for } b \neq a. \\ \bigvee_{\langle A,y \rangle \in R(a)} \langle \uparrow, (q, y, \#) \rangle & \text{If } c = \langle a \rangle. \\ \text{false} & \text{If } c = \langle b \rangle, \text{ for } b \neq a. \end{cases}$$

□

Let $n = |Q| \cdot |R| \cdot |V|$, let k be the index of $\mathcal{S}$, and let $\Sigma = (V \cup \{\bot\}) \times Act$. By Theorem 1, we can transform $\mathcal{A}$ to a nondeterministic one-way parity tree automaton $\mathcal{A}'$ with $2^{O(nk)}$ states and index $O(nk)$. By [Rab69,Eme85], if $\mathcal{A}'$ is nonempty, there exists a Σ-labeled V-tree $\langle V^*, f \rangle$ such that for all $\sigma \in \Sigma$, the set X_σ of nodes $x \in V^*$ for which $f(x) = \sigma$ is a regular set. Moreover, the nonemptiness algorithm of $\mathcal{A}'$, which runs in time exponential in nk, can be easily extended to construct, within the same complexity, a deterministic word automaton $\mathcal{U}_A$ over V such that each state of $\mathcal{U}_A$ is labeled by a letter $\sigma \in \Sigma$, and for all $x \in V^*$, we have $f(x) = \sigma$ iff the state of $\mathcal{U}_A$ that is reached by following the word x is labeled by σ. The automaton $\mathcal{U}_A$ is then the answer to the synthesis problem.

The construction described in Theorems 3 and 4 implies that the realizability and synthesis problem is in EXPTIME. Thus, it is not harder than in the satisfiability problem for the μ-calculus, and it matches the known lower bound [FL79]. Formally, we have the following.

Theorem 7. *The realizability and synthesis problems for a context-free or a prefix recognizable rewrite system* $\mathcal{R} = \langle V, Act, R, v_0 \rangle$ *and a graph automaton* $\mathcal{S} = \langle Act, Q, \delta, q_0, F \rangle$, *can be solved in time exponential in* nk, *where* $n = |Q| \cdot |R| \cdot |V|$, *and* k *is the index of* $\mathcal{S}$.

By Theorem 2, if the specification is given by a μ-calculus formula ψ, the bound is the same, with $n = |\psi| \cdot |R| \cdot |V|$, and k being the alternation depth of ψ.

7 Discussion

The automata-theoretic approach has long been thought to be inapplicable for effective reasoning about infinite-state systems. We showed that infinite-state systems for which decidability is known can be described by finite-state automata, and therefore, the states and transitions of such systems can be viewed as nodes in an infinite tree and transitions between states can be expressed by finite-state automata. As a result, automata-theoretic techniques can be used to reason about such systems. In particular, we showed that various problems related to the analysis of such systems can be reduced to the emptiness problem for alternating two-way tree automata. Our framework achieves the same complexity bounds of known model-checking algorithms, and it enables several extensions, such as treatment of state properties, fairness constraints, backwards modalities, and global model checking. Our framework also provides a solution to the realizability problem.

An interesting open problem is the extension of our framework to the linear paradigm. Since LTL formulas can be translated to automata, a simple extension of our framework to handle specifications in LTL is possible. Nevertheless, since our algorithm involves a translation of a two-way alternating automaton to a nondeterministic automaton, we would end up in a complexity that is at least exponential in the system, which is worst than known polynomial algorithms [EHRS00].

References

[AHK97] R. Alur, T.A. Henzinger, and O. Kupferman. Alternating-time temporal logic. In *Proc. 38th FOCS*, pp. 100–109, October 1997.

[BBG+94] I. Beer, S. Ben-David, D. Geist, R. Gewirtzman, and M. Yoeli. Methodology and system for practical formal verification of reactive hardware. In *Proc. 6th CAV, LNCS* 818, pp. 182–193, June 1994.

[BCMS00] O. Burkart, D. Caucal, F. Moller, and B. Steffen. Verification on infinite structures. Unpublished manuscript, 2000.
[BE96]   O. Burkart and J. Esparza. More infinite results. *Electronic Notes in Theoretical Computer Science*, 6, 1996.
[BEM97]   A. Bouajjani, J. Esparza, and O. Maler. Reachability analysis of pushdown automata: Application to model-checking. In *Proc. 8th CONCUR, LNCS* 1243, pp. 135–150, July 1997.
[BQ96]   O. Burkart and Y.-M. Quemener. Model checking of infinite graphs defined by graph grammers. In *Proc. 1st International workshop on verification of infinite states systems*, volume 6 of *ENTCS*, page 15. Elsevier, 1996.
[BS92]   O. Burkart and B. Steffen. Model checking for context-free processes. In *Proc. 3rd CONCUR, LNCS* 630, pp. 123–137. 1992.
[BS99a]   O. Burkart and B. Steffen. Composition, decomposition and model checking of pushdown processes. *Nordic J. Comut.*, 2:89–125, 1999.
[BS99b]   O. Burkart and B. Steffen. Model checking the full modal μ-calculus for infinite sequential processes. *Theoretical Computer Science*, 221:251–270, 1999.
[Bur97a] O. Burkart. Automatic Verification of Sequential Infinite-State Processes. *LNCS* 1354, 1997.
[Bur97b] O. Burkart. Model checking rationally restricted right closures of recognizable graphs. In *Proc. 2nd International Workshop on Verification of Infinite State Systems*, 1997.
[Cau96]   D. Caucal. On infinite transition graphs having a decidable monadic theory. In *Proc. 23st ICALP, LNCS* 1099, pp. 194–205, 1996.
[CES86]   E.M. Clarke, E.A. Emerson, and A.P. Sistla. Automatic verification of finite-state concurrent systems using temporal logic specifications. *ACM Transactions on Programming Languages and Systems*, 8(2):244–263, January 1986.
[CGP99]   E.M. Clarke, O. Grumberg, and D. Peled. *Model Checking*. MIT Press, 1999.
[DW99]   M. Dickhfer and T. Wilke. Timed alternating tree automata: the automata-theoretic solution to the TCTL model checking problem. In *Proc. 26th ICALP, LNCS* 1644, pp. 281–290, 1999.
[EHRS00] J. Esparza, D. Hansel, P. Rossmanith, and S. Schwoon. Efficient algorithms for model checking pushdown systems. In *Proc. 12th CAV*, 2000.
[EJ88]   E.A. Emerson and C. Jutla. The complexity of tree automata and logics of programs. In *Proc. 29th FOCS*, pp. 328–337, October 1988.
[EJ91]   E.A. Emerson and C. Jutla. Tree automata, μ-calculus and determinacy. In *Proc. 32nd FOCS*, pp. 368–377, October 1991.
[EJS93]   E.A. Emerson, C. Jutla, and A.P. Sistla. On model-checking for fragments of μ-calculus. In *Proc. 5th CAV, LNCS* 697, pp. 385–396, June 1993.
[Eme85]   E.A. Emerson. Automata, tableaux, and temporal logics. In *Proc. Workshop on Logic of Programs, LNCS* 193, pp. 79–87, 1985.
[FL79]   M.J. Fischer and R.E. Ladner. Propositional dynamic logic of regular programs. *Journal of Computer and Systems Sciences*, 18:194–211, 1979.
[FWW97]   A. Finkel, B. Willems, and P. Wolper. A direct symbolic approach to model checking pushdown automata. In *Proc. 2nd International Workshop on Verification of Infinite State Systems*, 1997.
[GPVW95] R. Gerth, D. Peled, M.Y. Vardi, and P. Wolper. Simple on-the-fly automatic verification of linear temporal logic. In *Protocol Specification, Testing, and Verification*, pp. 3–18. Chapman & Hall, August 1995.
[GW94]   P. Godefroid and P. Wolper. A partial approach to model checking. *Information and Computation*, 110(2):305–326, May 1994.

[HHK96]   R.H. Hardin, Z. Har'el, and R.P. Kurshan. COSPAN. In *Computer Aided Verification, Proc. 8th Int. Conference*, LNCS 1102, pp. 423–427, 1996.

[HHWT95] T.A. Henzinger, P.-H Ho, and H. Wong-Toi. A user guide to HYTECH. In *Proc. TACAS*, LNCS 1019, pp. 41–71, 1995.

[HKV96]   T.A. Henzinger, O. Kupferman, and M.Y. Vardi. A space-efficient on-the-fly algorithm for real-time model checking. In *Proc. 7th CONCUR*, LNCS 1119, pp. 514–529, August 1996.

[Hol97]   G.J. Holzmann. The model checker SPIN. *IEEE Trans. on Software Engineering*, 23(5):279–295, May 1997. Special issue on Formal Methods in Software Practice.

[JW95]   D. Janin and I. Walukiewicz. Automata for the modal μ-calculus and related results. In *Proc. 20th MFCS,LNCS*, pp. 552–562, 1995.

[Koz83]   D. Kozen. Results on the propositional μ-calculus. *Theoretical Computer Science*, 27:333–354, 1983.

[Kur94]   R.P. Kurshan. *Computer Aided Verification of Coordinating Processes*. Princeton Univ. Press, 1994.

[KV98]   O. Kupferman and M.Y. Vardi. Modular model checking. In *Proc. Compositionality Workshop*, LNCS 1536, pp. 381–401, 1998.

[KV99]   O. Kupferman and M.Y. Vardi. Robust satisfaction. In *Proc. 10th CONCUR*, LNCS 1664, pp. 383–398, 1999.

[KV00]   O. Kupferman and M.Y. Vardi. Synthesis with incomplete informatio. In *Advances in Temporal Logic*, pp. 109–127. Kluwer Academic Publishers, January 2000.

[KVW00]   O. Kupferman, M.Y. Vardi, and P. Wolper. An automata-theoretic approach to branching-time model checking. *Journal of the ACM*, 47(2), March 2000.

[LP85]   O. Lichtenstein and A. Pnueli. Checking that finite state concurrent programs satisfy their linear specification. In *Proc. 12th POPL*, pp. 97–107, January 1985.

[LPY97]   K. G. Larsen, P. Petterson, and W. Yi. UPPAAL: Status & developments. In *Proc. 9th CAV LNCS* 1254, pp. 456–459, 1997.

[LPZ85]   O. Lichtenstein, A. Pnueli, and L. Zuck. The glory of the past. In *Logics of Programs*, LNCS 193, pp. 196–218, Brooklyn, June 1985.

[LS98]   D. Lugiez and Ph. Schnoebelen. The regular viewpoint on PA-processes. In *Proc. 9th CONCUR*, LNCS 1466, pp. 50–66, September 1998.

[MS85]   D.E. Muller and P.E. Schupp. The theory of ends, pushdown automata, and second-order logic. *Theoretical Computer Science*, 37:51–75, 1985.

[MS87]   D.E. Muller and P.E. Schupp. Alternating automata on infinite trees. *Theoretical Computer Science*, 54:267–276, 1987.

[PR89]   A. Pnueli and R. Rosner. On the synthesis of a reactive module. In *Proc. 16th POPL*, pp. 179–190, January 1989.

[QS81]   J.P. Queille and J. Sifakis. Specification and verification of concurrent systems in Cesar. In *Proc. 5th International Symp. on Programming*, LNCS 137, pp. 337–351, 1981.

[Rab69]   M.O. Rabin. Decidability of second order theories and automata on infinite trees. *Transaction of the AMS*, 141:1–35, 1969.

[Var98]   M.Y. Vardi. Reasoning about the past with two-way automata. In *Proc. 25th ICALP*, LNCS 1443, pp. 628–641, July 1998.

[VB99]   W. Visser and H. Barringer. CTL* model checking for SPIN. In *Software Tools for Technology Transfer*, LNCS, 1999.

[VW86]   M.Y. Vardi and P. Wolper. An automata-theoretic approach to automatic program verification. In *Proc. 1st LICS*, pp. 332–344, June 1986.

[VW94]   M.Y. Vardi and P. Wolper. Reasoning about infinite computations. *Information and Computation*, 115(1):1–37, November 1994.

[Wal96] I. Walukiewicz. On completeness of μ-calculus. In *Proc. 8th CAV*, volume 1102 of *LNCS*, pp. 62–74, 1996.

[Wil99] T. Wilke. CTL$^+$ is exponentially more succinct than CTL. In *Proc. 19th Conference on Foundations of Software Technology and Theoretical Computer Science, LNCS 1738*, pp. 110–121, 1999.

[WVS83] P. Wolper, M.Y. Vardi, and A.P. Sistla. Reasoning about infinite computation paths. In *Proc. 24th FOCS*, pp. 185–194, 1983.

[WW96] B. Willems and P. Wolper. Partial-order methods for model checking: From linear time to branching time. In *Proc. 11th Symp LICS*, pp. 294–303, July 1996.

Automatic Verification of Parameterized Cache Coherence Protocols

Giorgio Delzanno

DISI - University of Genova
via Dodecaneso 35, 16146 Italy
delzanno@disi.unige.it

Abstract. We propose a new method for the verification of *parameterized* cache coherence protocols. Cache coherence protocols are used to maintain data consistency in multiprocessor systems equipped with local fast caches. In our approach we use arithmetic constraints to model possibly infinite sets of global states of a multiprocessor system with many identical caches. In preliminary experiments using symbolic model checkers for *infinite-state* systems based on real arithmetics (HyTech [HHW97] and DMC [DP99]) we have automatically verified *safety* properties for parameterized versions of widely implemented *write-invalidate* and *write-update* cache coherence policies like the Mesi, Berkeley, Illinois, Firefly and Dragon protocols [Han93]. With this application, we show that symbolic model checking tools originally designed for hybrid and concurrent systems can be applied successfully to a new class of *infinite-state* systems of practical interest.

1 Introduction

In a shared-memory multiprocessor system *local caches* are used to reduce memory access latency and network traffic. Each processor is connected to a fast memory backed up by a large (and slower) main memory. This configuration enables processors to work on local copies of main memory blocks, greatly reducing the number of memory accesses that the processor must perform during program execution. Although local caches improve system performance, they introduce the *cache coherence problem*: multiple cached copies of the same block of memory must be consistent at any time during a run of the system. A *cache coherence protocol* ensures the *data consistency* of the system: the value returned by a read must be always the last value written to that location (cf. [AB86, Han93,PD95]). Coherence policies can be described as *finite state machines* that specify the way a single cache reacts to read and write requests. As an example, let us consider a CC-UMA (Uniform-Memory-Access with local Caches model) multiprocessor system, i.e., a system in which all processors have a local cache connected to the main memory via a shared bus. In *write-invalidate* protocols, whenever a processor modifies its cache block a *bus invalidation signal* is sent to all other caches in order to invalidate their content. Instead, in *write-update* protocols a copy of the new data is sent to all caches that share the old data.

Due to the increasing complexity of hardware architectures, the development of *automatic* verification techniques is becoming a major goal to help discovering errors at an early stage of protocol design (see e.g. [CGH+93,MS91]). In particular, one of the main challenges in this area is to develop techniques for validating protocols for *every possible number* of processors (see e.g. [EN98,HQR99,PD95]). In this paper, drawing inspiration from recent works on verification of *parameterized* concurrent systems (e.g. [GS92,EN96,EN98,EN98b,EFM99,LHR97]) we propose a new method for the verification of *parameterized* cache coherence protocols at the *behavior* (specification) level. As mentioned before, in this context a multiprocessor system can be modeled as a collection of many *identical* finite-state machines. As first step, we apply the following *abstraction*: we keep track only of the *number* of caches in every possible protocol state. The resulting abstract protocol can be represented as a transition system with data variables ranging over positive integers. Thus, an abstract protocol can be formally described as an Extended Finite State Machine (EFSM) [CK97]. Via this abstraction, we represent all *symmetric* global states (global state=collection of individual cache states) using a single EFSM-state. We use then arithmetic constraints to implicitly represent (potentially infinite) sets of EFSM-states (tuples of natural numbers). This way, we are able to represent *safety* properties independently from the number of processors, and we reduce the verification problem for parameterized cache coherence protocols to a *reachability problem* for EFSMs. The last problem can be attacked using *general purpose, infinite-state* symbolic model checking methods defined for integers or real arithmetics (see e.g. [BGP97, BW98,Hal93,HHW97,DP99]). Following the general methodology we suggest in [Del00,DP99], we apply efficient tools based on *real* arithmetics (thus, applying a *relaxation* from integers to reals during the analysis) to *automatically* check safety properties like *data-consistency* for *snoopy, write-invalidate* and *write-update* cache coherence protocols for CC-UMA multiprocessors [AB86,Han93,PD97].

More precisely, our contributions are as follows. We first show that parameterized versions of a large class of cache coherence protocols can be formulated in terms of EFSMs. The class of EFSMs we consider is an extension of the broadcast protocols of Emerson and Namjoshi [EN98]. In order to model coherence policies, e.g., like the Illinois protocol, without abstracting away properties that are crucial for their validation (see discussion in Section 5), we need to enforce *global conditions* that cannot be represented using broadcast protocols. To prove the adequacy of this encoding, we relate the EFSM model to the *finite state machine model* of cache coherence protocols proposed by Pong and Dubois [PD95]. Based on this idea, we define a general method for the validation of parameterized coherence protocols. The method is based on invariant checking for the corresponding EFSMs via the *backward reachability* algorithm of [ACJT96]. In contrast to *forward* reachability, the algorithm of [ACJT96] is guaranteed to terminate for the subclass of EFSMs denoting the broadcast protocols of [EN98] under the additional hypothesis that the set of unsafe states is upward-closed [EFM99]. Safety properties can often be modeled as upward-closed sets [AJ99]. We choose a symbolic representation of (potentially infinite) sets of states via *arithmetic constraints*. The constraint operations of *variable elimination, satisfiability* and *entailment test* can be used to implement a symbolic version for the algorithm of [ACJT96]. However, following [DP99], in order to obtain an *efficient* procedure we interpret the above mentioned constraint operations over *reals* instead that over *integers*. This *relaxation* technique is widely-used in integer programming and program analysis. As for other methods handling *global conditions* in parameterized systems (e.g. [ABJN99]) and other methods for infinite-state systems (e.g. [BGP97,BW98,DP99,HHW97]), the resulting procedure is a *semi-algorithm* that must be evaluated on practical examples. We give sufficient conditions for the termination of the resulting procedure. Specifically, we show that the symbolic version of the abstract algorithm of [ACJT96] where sets of states are represented as arithmetic constraints is *robust under the relaxation integer-reals* (it always terminates solving the *control reachability problem* of [AJ99]) whenever: (a) the input EFSM is a broadcast protocol [EN98]; (b) the unsafe states are represented via a special class of constraints that denote upward-closed sets. This result seems to be a new application of general methods for proving the well-structuredness of infinite-state systems [ACJT96,AJ99,FS98]. We use two existing constraint-based model checkers that implement the symbolic backward reachability algorithm described above, namely HyTech [HHW97] (that provides efficient data structures) and DMC [DP99] (that provides built-in accelerations), to check several safety properties for the MESI, University of Illinois, Berkeley RISC, DEC Firefly and Xerox PARC Dragon protocols [AB86,PD95,Han93]. Though the termination of our method is guaranteed only for broadcast protocols, the preliminary results show that it performs well in practice.

To our knowledge, this is the first time that *general purpose* symbolic model checkers for infinite-state systems working over arithmetical domains are used for verification of parameterized cache coherence protocols. With this application, we have shown that techniques developed in the last years for hybrid and concurrent systems can also be applied to a new class of infinite-state systems of practical interest.

The HyTech and DMC code of the protocols together with the results of their analysis and links to download the tools is available on the web at the following address: http://www.disi.unige.it/person/DelzannoG/protocol.html.

2 The Finite State Machine Model

According to [PD95,PD97,EN98], we limit ourselves to consider protocols controlling single memory blocks and single cache lines. Following [PD95], a cache coherence protocol for a multiprocessor system with k local caches $C_1, \ldots, C_k$ can be represented via the following *finite state* machine model.

Local Machine. Each of the caches has the same finite set Q of states. The transitions of cache C_i may be guarded by *global conditions* that depend on the state of the other caches. The global conditions from the perspective of C_i are represented via a predicate f_i. As an example of global condition, let us fix a state $q \in Q$. Then, we could let $f_i = true$ if only if in the current state of the system there exists a cache C_j ($j \neq i$) whose state is equal to q. Formally, the behavior of the cache C_i is represented as a finite system $\langle Q, \Sigma_i, \delta_i, f_i \rangle$, where Q is the set of states, Σ_i is the set of operations causing state transitions, $f_i : Q^k \to \{true, false\}$ is a predicate that represents the global conditions from the perspective of C_i, and δ_i defines the state transition $Q \times \Sigma_i \times \{true, false\} \to Q$. The third component in the domain of δ_i is the guard for the transitions of C_i. As an example, let us fix a state $q \in Q$, and an operation $\sigma \in \Sigma_i$. Then, we could set $\delta_i(q, \sigma, true) = q'$ to express that cache C_i can go from state q to state q' whenever f_i is satisfied in the current global state. The previous definitions allow us to compose the machines of the individual caches $C_1, \ldots, C_k$ into a single global machine $\mathcal{M}_G$.

Global Machine. A global state G of $\mathcal{M}_G$ is defined as the composition of the states of the individual caches. Formally, $\mathcal{M}_G$ is a tuple $\langle Q_G, \Sigma_G, \mathcal{F}, \delta_G \rangle$, where $Q_G = Q^k$, $\Sigma_G = \Sigma_1 \cup \ldots \cup \Sigma_k$, $\mathcal{F}$ is the global characteristic predicate $\langle f_1, \ldots, f_k \rangle$, and $\delta_G : Q_G \times \Sigma_G \to Q_G$. The transition function δ_G is defined as follows. Given a global state $G = \langle q_1, \ldots, q_k \rangle$, $\delta_G(G, \sigma) = \langle q'_1, \ldots, q'_k \rangle$ if and only if $q'_i = \delta_i(q_i, \sigma, f_i(G))$ for $i : 1, \ldots, k$. A run of $\mathcal{M}_G$ is a possibly infinite sequence of global states $G_1, \ldots, G_n \ldots$ where $\delta_G(G_n, \sigma) = G_{n+1}$ for some $\sigma \in \Sigma$. We write $G \xrightarrow{*} G'$ to denote the existence of a run that goes from G to G'.

Terminology. In the rest of the paper we use the state *invalid* to denote either that the cache has no data or that its content has been invalidated. Cache coherence protocols implement the following basic operations from the perspective of cache C_i ($state(C_i) \in Q$ denotes its current state): *Read Miss*, a read request is sent to C_i and $state(C_i) = invalid$; *Read Hit*, a read request is sent to cache C_i and $state(C_i) \neq invalid$; *Write Miss*, a write request is sent to C_i and $state(C_i) = invalid$; *Write Hit*, a write request is sent to C_i and $state(C_i) \neq invalid$. According to the previous definitions, in the next section we give a brief description of a widely implemented *snoopy, write-invalidate* protocol we selected as main case-study.

2.1 The Illinois Protocol

The University of Illinois protocol is a *snoopy* cache, *write-invalidate*, *write-in* coherence policy, originally proposed by Papamarcos and Patel [PP84] (see also [AB86,PD95]). The special feature is that caches can have exclusive copies of data. Bus invalidation signals are sent only for writes to shared data. The memory copy is updated using a write-back policy (*replace* operation). Formally, in addition to *invalid*, caches assume one of the following states: *valid-exclusive*, the cache has an exclusive copy of the data that is consistent with the memory such that a modification of its content requires no bus invalidation signal; *shared*, the cache has a copy of the data consistent with the memory and other caches may have copies of the data; *dirty*, the cache has a modified copy of the data, i.e., the data in main memory are obsolete and the content of the other caches

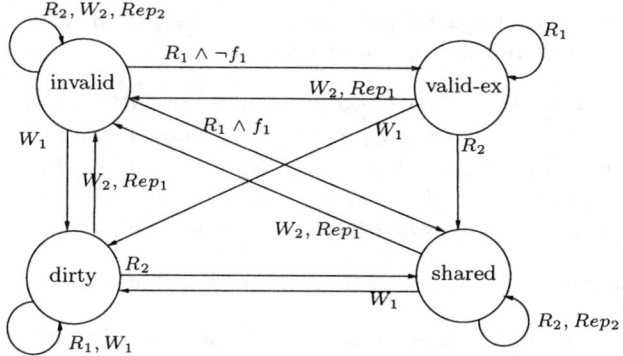

Fig. 1. Illinois protocol for 2 caches viewed from the perspective of cache C_1.

is not valid. The operations are R_i (read), W_i (write), and Rep_i (replace) for $i : 1, \ldots, k$=number of caches. The characteristic predicates f_i in $\mathcal{F}_{ill}$ is used by cache C_i to decide whether or not to move from *invalid* to *valid-exclusive*. Formally, f_i is defined as follows.

$$f_i(\langle q_1, q_2, \ldots, q_k \rangle) \text{ if and only if } \exists j \neq i \text{ such that } q_j \neq invalid$$

The possible transitions from the perspective of cache C_i are as follows.

Read Hit: no coherence action needs to be taken.
Read Miss: if there exists a cache C_j whose state is *dirty* (i.e. $f_i = true$), C_j supplies the missing block to C_i and updates the main memory. Both C_i and C_j end up in state *shared*. If there are *shared* or *valid-exclusive* copies in other caches (i.e. $f_i = true$), C_i gets the missing block from one of the caches and all caches with a copy end up in state *shared*. If there is no cached copy (i.e. $f_i = false$), C_i receives a *valid-exclusive* copy from main memory.
Write Hit: if C_i is in state *dirty*, no action is taken. If C_i is in state *valid-exclusive*, its state changes to *dirty* (note: no invalidation signal is needed). If C_i is in state *shared*, its state changes to *dirty* and all remote copies must be invalidated.
Write Miss: similar to *Read Miss*, except that all remote copies are invalidated and the state of C_i changes to *dirty*.
Replace: if C_i is in state *dirty*, the data are written back to memory.

For $k = 2$, the protocol from the perspective of cache C_1 is shown in Fig. 1.

Safety Properties. In this paper we limit ourselves to verification of *safety* property for data consistency [PD97]. As illustrated before, in the Illinois protocol the state *shared* indicates that a cache has a clean copy consistent with the memory and other caches copies, whereas the state *dirty* indicates that it has the latest and sole copy. Thus, in this example there are two possible sources of data inconsistency:

INV$_1$: a *dirty* cache co-exists with one or more caches in state *shared*;
INV$_2$: there are more than one *dirty* cache.

Thus, all global states that satisfy conditions INV$_1$ or INV$_2$ are *unsafe*. As mentioned before, we are interested in proving the protocol safe for every possible number of caches. For a fixed number of processors k and a given protocol P, let $\mathcal{I}(k)$ be the set of initial global states and $\mathcal{U}(k)$ be the set of unsafe global states. The *parameterized reachability problem* is defined as follows.

$$\exists\, k \geq 1.\ \exists\, G_1 \in \mathcal{I}(k).\ \exists\, G_2 \in \mathcal{U}(k) \text{ such that } G_1 \stackrel{*}{\to} G_2?$$

If the previous statement is true for a given k' than the protocol is not correct, i.e., an unsafe state may be reached for a system configuration with k' caches.

3 EFSMs for Parameterized Cache Coherence Protocols

In order to check parameterized safety properties we apply the following *abstraction*. Let Q be the set of cache states $q_1, \ldots, q_n$, then

we keep track only of the number x_i of processes in every state $q_i \in Q$.

A global state G with k components (k=number of caches) is mapped to a tuple of *positive integers* with n components (n=number of cache states). This way, all *symmetric* global states are clustered together into a single representation. Via this abstraction, we cannot prove properties of individual caches like 'cache i and cache j cannot be in state *dirty* simultaneously'. However, we can still try to prove global properties like 'two different caches cannot be in state *dirty* simultaneously'. This is the kind of properties we are interested in to prove that the protocol will not give inconsistent (wrt. the semantics of states) results. The behavior of an *arbitrary* number of caches can be described *finitely* as a set of linear transformations describing the effect of the actions on the *counters* associated to the states in Q. For this purpose, we model the 'abstract protocol' as a single *Extended Finite State Machine* (EFSM) [CK97], i.e., a finite automaton with data variables (ranging over integers) associated to the locations and with guarded linear transformations associated to the transitions. Formally, let $\mathcal{M}_G$ be the global machine $\langle Q, \Sigma_G, \mathcal{F}, \delta_G \rangle$ associated to a protocol P, and let $Q = \{q_1, \ldots, q_n\}$. We model $\mathcal{M}_G$ as an EFSM with *only one location* and n data variables $\langle x_1, \ldots, x_n \rangle$ ranging over *positive integers*. For simplicity, we will always omit the location. The EFSM-states are tuples of natural numbers $\mathbf{c} = \langle c_1, \ldots, c_n \rangle$, where c_i denotes the number of caches with state $q_i \in Q$ during a run of $\mathcal{M}_G$. The transitions are represented via a collection of *guarded linear transformations* defined over the variables $\mathbf{x} = \langle x_1, \ldots, x_n \rangle$ and $\mathbf{x}' = \langle x'_1, \ldots, x'_n \rangle$ and having the following form

$$G(\mathbf{x}) \to T(\mathbf{x}, \mathbf{x}'),$$

where x_i and x'_i denote the number of caches in state q_i respectively before and after the occurrence of the transition. The guard $G(\mathbf{x})$ may be an arbitrary linear constraint over the variables $\mathbf{x}$. However, in this paper we limit ourselves to constraints defined as $D_1 \cdot \mathbf{x} \geq \mathbf{b} \wedge D_2 \cdot \mathbf{x} = \mathbf{c}$ where D_1 is an $n \times n$ matrix with $0, 1$ coefficients, D_2 is a diagonal $n \times n$-matrix with $0, 1$ coefficients, and $\mathbf{b}$ and $\mathbf{c}$ are vectors of integers. This type of guards allows us to handle both *local* and *global* conditions over the global states of $\mathcal{M}_G$. For instance, consider again the function $\mathcal{F}_{ill}$ of the Illinois protocol. Then, $f_i = false$ for some i can be expressed as $x_1 \geq 1, x_2 = 0, \ldots, x_n = 0$. For the sake of this paper, the transformation $T(\mathbf{x}, \mathbf{x}')$ is defined as $\mathbf{x}' = M \cdot \mathbf{x} + \mathbf{c}$ where M is an $n \times n$-matrix with unit vectors as columns (i.e., there is exactly one non-zero coefficient $= 1$ in each column). This way, we can represent the changes of states of the caches in the system (including the invalidation signals). Since the number of caches is an invariant of the system, we require the transformation to satisfy the condition $x_1' + \ldots + x_n' = x_1 + \ldots + x_n$.

Remark 1. Let us call *additive constraint* a system of *linear inequalities* having the form $D \cdot \mathbf{x} \geq \mathbf{c}$ where D is a matrix with $0, 1$ coefficients, and $\mathbf{c}$ is a vector of positive integers. (Note: an additive constraint can be expressed as a conjunction of atomic formulas $x_{i_1} + \ldots + x_{i_k} \geq c$ where $x_{i_1}, \ldots, x_{i_k}$ are distinct variables from $\mathbf{x}$, and c is a positive integer.) When all guards of an EFSM are restricted to *additive* constraints, we obtain the subclass of *broadcast protocols* introduced in [EN98]. Thus, in broadcast protocols it is not possible to enforce *global* conditions that, e.g, require tests for zero (constants).

We show next some general patterns we use to model protocol actions via guarded transformations.

Internal action. A cache moves from state q_1 to state q_2 ($q_1 \neq q_2$): $x_1' = x_1 - 1, x_2' = x_2 + 1$ with the proviso that $x_1 \geq 1$ is part of $G(\mathbf{x})$.

Rendez-vous. Let us consider the case in which two caches synchronize on a signal. A cache C in state q_1 synchronizes with a cache C' in state q_3, the state of C changes to q_2, the state of C' changes to q_4 (all states are different). We model this transition as $x_1' = x_1 - 1, x_2' = x_2 + 1, x_3' = x_3 - 1, x_4' = x_4 + 1$, with the proviso that $x_1 \geq 1, x_3 \geq 1$ is part of $G(\mathbf{x})$.

Synchronization. All the caches in state $q_1, \ldots, q_m$ go to state q_i, e.g., for $i > m$. We model this transition as $x_1' = 0, \ldots, x_m' = 0, x_i' = x_i + x_1 + \ldots + x_m$. This feature can be used, e.g., to model *bus invalidation signals*.

A run of an EFSM $\mathcal{E}$ is a (possibly infinite) sequence of EFSM-states $\mathbf{c_1}, \ldots, \mathbf{c_i} \ldots$ where $G_r(\mathbf{c_i}) \wedge T_r(\mathbf{c_i}, \mathbf{c_{i+1}}) = true$ for some transitions $G_r \to T_r$ in $\mathcal{E}$. We will denote the existence of a run from $\mathbf{c}$ to $\mathbf{c}'$ as $\mathbf{c} \xrightarrow{*} \mathbf{c}'$ Finally, we define a *predecessor* operator $pre : \mathcal{P}(\mathbb{N}^n) \rightsquigarrow \mathcal{P}(\mathbb{N}^n)$ over *sets* of EFSM-states as follows.

$$pre(S) = \{\mathbf{c} \mid \mathbf{c} \to \mathbf{c}',\ \mathbf{c}' \in S\}.$$

Here $\to$ indicates a one-step EFSM state transition.

(r1) $dirty + shared + exclusive \geq 1 \rightarrow$.

(r2) $invalid \geq 1, dirty = 0, shared = 0, exclusive = 0 \rightarrow$
$invalid' = invalid - 1, exclusive' = exclusive + 1$.

(r3) $invalid \geq 1, dirty \geq 1 \rightarrow$
$invalid' = invalid - 1, dirty' = dirty - 1, shared' = shared + 2$.

(r4) $invalid \geq 1, shared + exclusive \geq 1 \rightarrow$
$invalid' = invalid - 1, shared' = shared + exclusive + 1, exclusive' = 0$.

(r5) $dirty \geq 1 \rightarrow$.

(r6) $exclusive \geq 1 \rightarrow exclusive' = exclusive - 1, dirty' = dirty + 1$.

(r7) $shared \geq 1 \rightarrow$
$shared' = 0, invalid' = invalid + shared - 1, dirty' = dirty + 1$.

(r8) $invalid \geq 1 \rightarrow invalid' = invalid + exclusive + dirty + shared - 1,$
$exclusive' = 0, shared' = 0, dirty' = 1$.

(r9) $dirty \geq 1 \rightarrow dirty' = dirty - 1, invalid' = invalid + 1$.

(r10) $shared \geq 1 \rightarrow shared' = shared - 1, invalid' = invalid + 1$.

(r11) $exclusive \geq 1 \rightarrow exclusive' = exclusive - 1, invalid' = invalid + 1$.

Fig. 2. EFSM for the Illinois Protocol: all variables range over *positive* integers.

3.1 The EFSM for the Illinois Protocol

Let *invalid*, *dirty*, *shared*, and *exclusive* be variables ranging over *positive integers*. The EFSM for the Illinois protocol is shown in Fig. 2. For simplicity, we omit the location and all equalities of the form $x'_i = x_i$. Furthermore, in a rule like '$G \rightarrow$ ' all variables remain unchanged. Rule $r1$ of Fig. 2 represents *read hit* events: since no coherence action is needed, the only precondition is that there exists at least one cache in a valid state, i.e., $dirty + shared + exclusive \geq 1$. Rules $r2 - r4$ correspond to *read miss* events where the global predicate $\mathcal{F}_{ill}$ is expressed via guards containing tests for zero. Specifically, rule $r2$ represents a read miss such that $f_i = false$ for some i, i.e., one cache can move to *valid-exclusive*. The case in which a cache copies its content from a *dirty* cache and the two caches move simultaneously to *shared* is defined via rule $r3$. Rule $r4$ applies whenever the block is copied from a cache in *shared* or *valid-exclusive* state. Rules $r5 - r7$ model *write hits*. Specifically, rule $r5$ models a write in state *dirty* (no action is taken). Rule $r6$ models a write in state *valid-exclusive* where the state changes to *dirty* without bus invalidation signal. Rule $r7$ models a write in state *shared* where the copies in all other caches are invalidated. Note that, in rule $r7$ we implicitly assume that whenever $share \geq 1$ then $dirty = 0$. We will (automatically) prove that this is an invariant of the protocol in Section 5. Rule $r8$ corresponds to a *write miss*: one cache moves to *dirty* and the copies in the other caches are invalidated. Finally, rules $r9 - r11$ model *replacement* events. If the cache is in one of the states *dirty, shared* or *exclusive* its state changes to *invalid*.

4 Protocol Validation = EFSM Invariant Checking

Let P be a protocol with global machine $\mathcal{M}_G$ and states $Q = \{q_1, \ldots, q_n\}$. Given a global state G, we define $\#G$ as the tuple of natural numbers $\mathbf{c} = \langle c_1, \ldots, c_n \rangle$ where $c_i =$*number of caches in G with state* $= q_i$. Now, let $\mathcal{E}_P$ be the EFSM in which a state $\mathbf{c}$ represents the set of global states $\{G \mid \#G = \mathbf{c}\}$, and whose transitions are obtained according to Section 3. The following proposition relates runs in $\mathcal{M}_G$ and runs in $\mathcal{E}_P$.

Proposition 1 (Adequacy of the Encoding). *Let $\mathcal{M}_G$ and $\mathcal{E}_P$ be defined as above. Then, $\mathbf{c} \xrightarrow{*} \mathbf{d}$ in $\mathcal{E}_P$ if and only if there exist two global states G and G', such that $\#G = \mathbf{c}$, $\#G' = \mathbf{d}$ and $G \xrightarrow{*} G'$ in $\mathcal{M}_G$.*

The previous property allows us to reduce the *parameterized reachability* problem for coherence protocols to a *reachability* problem for the corresponding EFSMs. Our approach to attack the second problem is based on the following points.

Symbolic State Representation. In order to represent concisely (possibly infinite) sets of global states independently from the number of caches in the system, we use *linear arithmetic constraints*=systems of linear inequalities as a symbolic representation of sets of EFSM-states. This class of constraints is powerful enough to express *initial* and *unsafe (target)* sets of states for the verification problems we are interested in. For instance, the set of unsafe states of the Illinois protocol where at least 1 cache is in state *shared* and *at least* 1 cache is in state *dirty* can be represented finitely as the constraint $x_{shared} \geq 1 \wedge x_{dirty} \geq 1$. This is a crucial aspect in order to attack the *parameterized reachability problem*. In the rest of the paper we will use the lower-case letters $\varphi, \psi, \ldots$ to denote constraints and the upper-case letter $\Psi, \Phi, \ldots$ to denote *sets* (disjunctions) of constraints. Following [ACJT96], the *denotation* of a constraint φ is defined as $\llbracket \varphi \rrbracket = \{\mathbf{t} \mid \mathbf{t} \in \mathbb{N}^n \text{ satisfies } \varphi\}$. The definition is extended to sets in the natural way. Furthermore, we say that a constraint ψ *entails* a constraint φ, written $\varphi \sqsubseteq \psi$, iff $\llbracket \psi \rrbracket \subseteq \llbracket \varphi \rrbracket$. We define a *symbolic predecessor operator* **sym_pre** over sets of constraints such that $\llbracket \mathbf{sym\_pre}(\Phi) \rrbracket = pre(\llbracket \Phi \rrbracket)$ (*pre* is defined in Section 3). The operator is defined via the satisfiability test and variable elimination over $\mathbb{N}$ (the domain of interpretation of constraints) [BGP97,DP99]. Formally, for a given constraint $\varphi(\mathbf{x}')$ with variables over $\mathbf{x}'$, **sym_pre** is defined as follows

$$\mathbf{sym\_pre}(\varphi(\mathbf{x}')) = \bigcup_{i \in I} \{ \exists \mathbf{x}'.\ G_i(\mathbf{x}) \wedge T_i(\mathbf{x}, \mathbf{x}') \wedge \varphi(\mathbf{x}') \}$$

where $\mathbf{x}$ and $\mathbf{x}'$ range over $\mathbb{N}$, and $G_i(\mathbf{x}) \to T_i(\mathbf{x}, \mathbf{x}')$ is an EFSM transition rule for $i \in I$ (I=index set).

Backward Reachability. We apply a variation of the *backward reachability* algorithm of [ACJT96], where all operations on sets of states are lifted to the constraint-level. The reason we adopt *backward reachability* is due to the result proved in [EFM99]: in contrast to *forward reachability*, the algorithm of [ACJT96] always terminates whenever the input EFSM is a *broadcast protocol* [EN98] and the set of unsafe states is upward-closed. A set $S \subseteq \mathbb{N}^k$ of states is upward-closed whenever for all tuples $\mathbf{t} \in S$: if $\mathbf{t}'$ is greater equal than $\mathbf{t}$ w.r.t. the componentwise ordering of tuples, then $\mathbf{t}' \in S$. As an example, the denotation of the constraint $x_{shared} \geq 1 \land x_{dirty} \geq 1$ (the variables $x_{invalid}$ and $x_{valid-ex}$ are implicitly ≥ 0) is an upward-closed set over $\mathbb{N}^4$. As shown in [DEP99], the result of [EFM99] implies that the symbolic reachability algorithm using *integer constraints* to represent sets of states always terminates on inputs consisting of a broadcast protocol and of constraints that represents upward-closed sets of unsafe states.

Relaxation of Constraint Operations. In order to reduce the complexity of the manipulation of arithmetic constraints, we follow techniques used, e.g., in integer programming and program analysis. Every time we need to solve a system of inequalities $A \cdot \mathbf{x} \leq \mathbf{b}$ we 'relax' the condition that $\mathbf{x}$ must be a vector of positive *integers* and look for a *real* solution of the corresponding linear problem. We apply the *relaxation* to the operations over constraints, i.e., we interpret the *satisfiability* test, *variable elimination*, and *entailment* test (needed to implement the symbolic backward reachability algorithm) over the domain of *reals*. The relaxation allows us to exploit efficient (polynomial) operations over the reals in contrast to potentially exponential operations over the integers. Note that this abstraction is applied *only during* the analysis and not at the semantic level of EFSMs. As we will discuss later, in many cases this method does not lose precision wrt. an analysis over the integers. Formally, given a constraint φ, we define $[\![\varphi]\!]_{\mathbb{R}}$ as the set of real solutions $\{ \mathbf{t} \in \mathbb{R}_+ \mid \mathbf{t} \ satisfies \ \varphi \ \}$. The entailment relation over $\mathbb{R}_+$ is defined then as $\varphi \sqsubseteq_{\mathbb{R}} \psi$ if and only if $[\![\psi]\!]_{\mathbb{R}} \subseteq [\![\varphi]\!]_{\mathbb{R}}$. When we apply the above relaxation to the symbolic predecessor operator, we obtain the new operator $\mathbf{sym\_pre}_{\mathbb{R}}$ defined as follows

$$\mathbf{sym\_pre}_{\mathbb{R}}(\varphi(\mathbf{x}')) = \bigcup_{i \in I} \{ \ \exists \mathbf{x}'. \ G_i(\mathbf{x}) \land T_i(\mathbf{x}, \mathbf{x}') \land \varphi(\mathbf{x}') \ \},$$

where $\mathbf{x}$ and $\mathbf{x}'$ range now over *positive real numbers*, and $\exists_{\mathbb{R}} x.F \equiv \exists x \in \mathbb{R}_+.F$ The symbolic reachability algorithm we obtained is shown in Fig. 3. Note that this is the algorithm for backward reachability implemented in existing symbolic model checkers for hybrid and concurrent systems like HyTech [HHW97] and DMC [DP99]. Each step of the procedure Symb-Reach-over-$\mathbb{R}$ involves only polynomial time cost operations. In fact, $\mathbf{sym\_pre}_{\mathbb{R}}$ can be implemented using satisfiability test over $\mathbb{R}$ (e.g. using the simplex method, 'polynomial' in practical examples) and using Fourier-Motzkin variable elimination (for a fixed number of variables, polynomial in the size of the input constraints). Furthermore, the entailment test $\varphi \sqsubseteq_{\mathbb{R}} \psi$ can be tested in polynomial time. In fact, $\phi \sqsubseteq_{\mathbb{R}} (\psi_1 \land \psi_2)$ holds if and only if $\phi \land \neg \psi_1$ and $\phi \land \neg \psi_2$ are not satisfiable. Thus, the entailment test reduces to a linear (in the size of the input constraints) number of

Proc Symb-Reach-over-$\mathbb{R}(\Phi_o, \Phi_f$: sets of constraints)
　set $\Phi := \Phi_f$ and $\Psi := \emptyset$;
　while $\Phi \neq \emptyset$ do
　　choose $\varphi \in \Phi$ and set $\Phi := \Phi \setminus \{\varphi\}$;
　　if there are <u>no</u> $\psi \in \Psi$ s.t. $\psi \sqsubseteq_\mathbb{R} \varphi$ then
　　　set $\Psi := \Psi \cup \{\varphi\}$ and $\Phi := \Phi \cup \mathbf{sym\_pre}_\mathbb{R}(\varphi)$;
　if $sat_\mathbb{R}(\Phi_o \wedge \Psi)$ then return 'Φ_f is reachable from Φ'_o;
　else return 'Φ_f is not reachable from Φ'_o.

Fig. 3. Symbolic reachability.

satisfiability tests. In contrast, the cost of executing the same operations over $\mathbb{N}$ may be exponential. For instance, in [DEP99] we have shown (via a reduction from the Hitting Set problem) that checking $\varphi \sqsubseteq \psi$ (over $\mathbb{N}$) is already co-NP hard whenever φ and ψ are two instances of the *additive* constraints of Remark 1, Section 3 (i.e., constraints without equalities).

As in other verification methods for infinite-state systems (e.g. for hybrid systems [HHW97], FIFO systems [BW98], and parameterized concurrent programs [ABJN99]), the algorithm is not guaranteed to terminate on every input. This is the price we have to pay in order to model realistic examples. We give next sufficient conditions for the *theoretical* termination of Symb-Reach-over-$\mathbb{R}$. We postpone the evaluation of its *practical* termination to Section 5.

Sufficient Conditions for Termination. As for its companion algorithm defined over the domain of integers, the procedure Symb-Reach-over-$\mathbb{R}$ always terminates, returning exact results, if both the guards of the input EFSM and the unsafe states are expressed via the additive constraints of Remark 1, Section 3. This result proves that, when applied to broadcast protocols, the algorithm of [ACJT96] formulated over constraints is *robust under the relaxation integer-reals* of the constraint operations (*robust*=it always terminates and solves the reachability problem taken into consideration). Formally, we have the following result.

Theorem 1. *Given a broadcast protocol P, Symb-Reach-over-*$\mathbb{R}(\Phi_o, \Phi_f)$ *solves the reachability problem '* $\exists \mathbf{c_0} \in [\![\Phi_0]\!], \exists \mathbf{c_1} \in [\![\Phi_f]\!]$ *such that* $\mathbf{c_0} \xrightarrow{*} \mathbf{c_1}$ *', whenever* Φ_0 *is a set of* additive *constraints (possibly extended with conjunctions of equalities of the form* $x_i = c_i$, $c_i \in \mathbb{N}$*), and* Φ_f *is a set of* additive *constraints.*

Sketch of the proof. Following the methodology of [AJ99,FS98], we need to prove the following lemmas: (1) given an additive constraint φ, we can effectively compute $\mathbf{sym\_pre}_\mathbb{R}(\varphi)$; (2) the class of additive constraints is closed under application of $\mathbf{sym\_pre}_\mathbb{R}$; and, finally, (3) the class of additive constraints equipped with the order $\sqsubseteq_\mathbb{R}$ is a *well-quasi ordering*, i.e., there exist no infinite chains of additive constraints $\varphi_1 \ldots \varphi_i \ldots$ such that $\varphi_j \not\sqsubseteq_\mathbb{R} \varphi_i$ for all $j < i$. Point (1) follows from our definition of $\mathbf{sym\_pre}_\mathbb{R}$, whereas point (2) and (3) are formally proved in [Del00]. For instance, the proof of lemma (2) is based on the following observation. Let $\varphi(\mathbf{x}')$ be an additive constraint and r be a transition $G(\mathbf{x}) \to T(\mathbf{x}, \mathbf{x}')$. Then, we can compute $\mathbf{sym\_pre}_{\mathbb{R}}(\varphi)$ (restricted to r) by replacing all 'primed variables' in φ with the right-hand side of the transformation $T(\mathbf{x}, \mathbf{x}')$, and by conjoining the resulting constraint with the guard $G(\mathbf{x})$. The special form of $T(\mathbf{x}, \mathbf{x}')$ (each variable occurs only once in the right-hand side of assignments) ensures that the resulting constraint is still an additive constraint. As a corollary of lemma (2), it follows that computing symbolically the predecessor of an additive constraint φ over $\mathbb{R}$ and over $\mathbb{N}$ gives the same results (both computations amounts to a replacement by equals). In other words, $\mathbf{sym\_pre}_{\mathbb{R}}$ gives accurate results, i.e., $[\![\mathbf{sym\_pre}_{\mathbb{R}}(\Phi)]\!] = [\![\mathbf{sym\_pre}(\Phi)]\!] = pre([\![\Phi]\!])$. (Note: $[\![\cdot]\!]$ denotes *integer* solutions). □

To our knowledge, this result was not considered in previous works on well structured system [ACJT96,AJ99,FS98]. In the rest of the paper we will discuss some preliminary experimental results.

5 Experimental Results

We have applied HyTech and DMC to automatically verify safety properties for the MESI, Berkeley RISC, Illinois, Xerox PARC Dragon and DEC Firefly protocols [Han93]. The guards we need to model the Dragon and Firefly protocols are more complicated than those of the Illinois protocol. The results of the analysis are shown in Fig. 4. For instance, in the Illinois protocol the parameterized initial configuration is expressed as $\Phi_o = invalid \geq 1$, $exclusive = 0$, $dirty = 0$, $shared = 0$. Similarly, we can represent the potentially *unsafe* states described in Section 2 as follows: $\Phi_1 = invalid \geq 0$, $exclusive \geq 0$, $dirty \geq 1$, $shared \geq 1$ (property INV$_1$) and $\Phi_2 = invalid \geq 0$, $exclusive \geq 0$, $dirty \geq 2$, $shared \geq 0$ (property INV$_2$). We automatically checked both properties using HyTech and DMC (without need of accelerations) as specified in Fig. 4. HyTech execution times are often better (HyTech is based on Halbwachs' efficient *polyhedra* library [Hal93]). However, the HyTech built-in command *reach backward* we use for the analysis does not terminate in two cases (see table). DMC terminates on all examples thanks to a set of built-in *accelerations* [DP99]. Similar techniques (e.g. extrapolation) are described in [HH95,LHR97] but they are not provided by the current version of HyTech. We have tried other experiments using HyTech: *forward* analysis using *parameter* variables (to represent the initial configurations) does not terminate in several examples; approximations based on the *convex hull* (using the built-in *hull* operator applied to intermediate collections of states) returned no interesting results. We have also experimented other type of abstractions. Specifically, we have analyzed the EFSMs obtained by weakening the guards of the original descriptions (e.g. turning tests for zero into inequalities) so as to obtain EFSMs for which our algorithm always terminates. As shown by the 'question marks' in the results for *Abstract Illinois* in Fig. 4, with this abstraction we find *errors* that are not present in the original protocol (in fact, the resulting reachable states are a super-set of those of the Illinois protocol).

Protocol	Unsafe-GS	HyTech-ET[1]	HyTech-NS	DMC-ET[2]	DMC-NS	Safe?
Mesi	D>2	0.77s	3	1.0s	3	yes
	D>1,S>1	0.66s	2	0.6s	2	yes
Berkeley RISC	D>2	0.52s	1	0.3s	1	yes
	D>1,S>1	0.94s	3	1.5s	3	yes
University of Illinois	D>2	1.06s	3	2.0s	3	yes
	D>1,S>1	2.32s	4	10.3s	4	yes
DEC Firefly	D>2	↑	-	28.2s	7	yes
	D>1,S>1	3.01s	4	11.4s	4	yes
Xerox PARC Dragon	D>2	↑	-	84.2s	6	yes
	D>1,S_c>1	5.30s	5	25.1s	5	yes
	D>1,S_d>1	5.26s	5	25s	5	yes
Abstract Illinois	D>2	2.86s	5	16.9s	5	?
	D>1,S>1	8.14s	7	96.3s	7	?

[1] on a Sun-SPARCstation-5 OS 5.6   [2] on a Pentium 133 Linux 2.0.32

Fig. 4. ET=Execution Time; NS=No. Steps (↑=diverges). Unsafe-Global States: D=Dirty, S=Shared, S_c=Shared-Clean, S_d=Shared-Dirty. Abstracted Illinois is obtained by weakening the guards of Illinois.

6 Related Works

Our approach is inspired by the recent work of Emerson and Namjoshi on Parameterized Model Checking [EN96,EN98b], and broadcast protocols [EN98]. As discussed in the paper, broadcast protocols are not general enough to model the *global* conditions required by the protocol we have validated in this paper. The verification technique proposed in [EN98] is an extension of the *coverability graph* for Petri Nets (forward reachability). For broadcast protocols, this construction is not guaranteed to terminate [EFM99]. In contrast, backward reachability always terminates when the target set of states is upward-closed [EFM99]. In [DEP99], the author in collaboration with Esparza and Podelski proposes efficient data structures for representing integer constraints for the verification of broadcast protocols. There exist specialized symbolic state exploration techniques for the analysis of *parameterized* coherence protocols. In [PD95], Pong and Dubois propose the *symbolic state model* (SSM) for the representation of the state-space and the verification of protocols. Specifically, they apply an *abstraction* and represent sets of global states via *repetition* operators to indicate 0,1, or multiple caches in a particular state. In our EFSM-model we keep track of the *exact* number of processes in each state. SSM verification method is based on a *forward* exploration with *ad hoc* expansion and aggregation rules. In [ID99], Norris Ip and Dill have incorporated the repetition operators in Murφ. Murφ automatically checks the soundness of the abstraction based on the repetition operators, verifies the correctness of an abstract state graph of a fixed size using *on_the_fly state enumeration*, and, finally, tries to generalize the results for systems with larger (unbounded) sizes. In contrast, our method is based on general purpose techniques (backward reachability and constraints to represent sets of states) that have been successfully applied to the verification of timed, hybrid and concurrent systems (see e.g. [HHW97,BGP97,DP99]). Being specialized to coherence protocols, SSM can also detect stale write-backs and livelocks. The verification of this type of properties using our method is part of our future works. We are not aware of other applications of infinite-state symbolic model checkers based on arithmetical domains to verification of parameterized cache coherence protocols. Several approaches exist to attack the verification problem of parameterized *concurrent systems*. In [GS92], German and Sistla define an automatic method for verification of parameterized *asynchronous* systems (where processes are model in CCS-style). However, methods that handle *global conditions* like ours (e.g. [ABJN99]) are often semi-algorithms, i.e., they do not guarantee the termination of the analysis. Other methods based on *regular languages* have been proposed in [ABJN99,CGJ97]. Among semi-automatic methods that require the construction of abstractions and invariants we mention [BCG89,CGJ97,HQR99, McM99]. Automated generation of invariants has been studied e.g. in [CGJ97, LHR97]. Automated generation of abstract transition graphs for infinite-state systems has been studied in [GS97]. Symmetry reductions for parameterized systems have been considered, e.g., in [ID99,McM99,PD95].

Finally, in [Del00] the author shows that the method presented in this paper (backward reachability, constraint-based representation, relaxation) can be used as a general methodology to verify properties of parameterized *synchronous systems*.

7 Conclusions

We have proposed a new method for the verification of coherence protocols for any number of processors in the system. We have applied our methods to successfully verify safety properties of several protocols taken from the literature [AB86,Han93,PD95]. This result is obtained using technology originally developed for the verification of hybrid and concurrent systems, namely HyTech [HHW97] and DMC [DP99]. In our approach we propose the following *abstractions*. We 'count' the number of caches in every possible protocol state, so that we get an integer system out of a parameterized protocol; we relax the constraint operations needed to implement the symbolic backard reachability algorithm for the resulting integer system. The abstraction based on the relaxation often gives *accurate* results (e.g. when intermediate results are additive constraints) and allows us to prove all the properties of our examples we were interested in. As discussed in Section 5, with other types of approximation techniques we might abstract away crucial properties of the original protocols. As future works, we plan to extend our method to other classes of coherence protocols (e.g. *directory-based* [Han93]), and properties (e.g., *livelocks*), and to study techniques to provide *error traces* for properties whose verification fails.

Acknowledgements. The author would like to thank Parosh Aziz Abdulla, Howard Wong-Toi, Kedar Namjoshi, Javier Esparza and the anonymous referees for helpful references, suggestions, and encouragement.

References

[ACJT96] P. A. Abdulla, K. Cerāns, B. Jonsson and Y.-K. Tsay. General Decidability Theorems for Infinite-State Systems. In *Proc. 10th IEEE Int. Symp. on Logic in Computer Science*, pages 313–321, 1996.

[ABJN99] P. A. Abdulla, A. Bouajjani, B. Jonsson, and M. Nilsson. Handling Global Conditions in Parameterized System Verification. In *Proc. 11th Int. Conf. on Computer Aided Verification (CAV'99)*, LNCS 1633, pages 134–145, 1999.

[AJ99] P. A. Abdulla, and B. Jonsson. Ensuring Completeness of Symbolic Verification Methods for Infinite-State Systems. To appear in *Theoretical Computer Science*, 1999.

[AB86] P. A. Archibald and J. Baer. Cache Coherence Protocols: Evaluation Using a Multiprocessor Simulation Model. *ACM Transactions on Computer Systems* 4(4): 273–298. 1986.

[BGP97] T. Bultan, R. Gerber, and W. Pugh. Symbolic Model Checking of Infinite-state Systems using Presburger Arithmetics. In *Proc. 9th Conf. on Computer Aided Verification (CAV'97)*, LNCS 1254, pages 400–411, 1997.

[BW98] B. Boigelot and P. Wolper. Verifying Systems with Infinite but Regular State Space. In *Proc. 10th Conf. on Computer Aided Verification (CAV'98)*, LNCS 1427, pages 88–97, 1998.

[BCG89] M. C. Browne, E. M. Clarke, O. Grumberg. Reasoning about Networks with Many Identical Finite State Processes. *Information and Computation* 81(1): 13–31, 1989.

[CK97] K.-T. Cheng and A. S. Krishnakumar. Automatic Generation of Functional Vectors Using the Extended Finite State Machine Model. *ACM Transactions on Design Automation of Electronic Systems* 1(1):57–79, 1996.

[CGH$^+$93] E. M. Clarke, O. Grumberg, H. Hiraishi, S. Jha, D. E. Long, K. L. McMillan, and L. A. Ness. Verification of the Futurebus+cache coherence protocol. In *Proc. 11th Int. Symp. on Computer Hardware Description Languages and their Applications*, 1993.

[CGJ97] E. Clarke, O. Grumberg, and S. Jha. Verifying Parameterized Networks. *TOPLAS* 19(5): 726–750, 1997.

[Del00] G. Delzanno. On Efficient Data Structures for the Verification of Parameterized Synchronous Systems. Tech. Rep. DISI-00-03, Dip. di Informatica e Scienze dell'Informazione, Università di Genova, January 2000.

[DEP99] G. Delzanno, J. Esparza, and A. Podelski. Constraint-based Analysis of Broadcast Protocols. In *Proc. Annual Conf. of the European Association for Computer Science Logic (CSL'99)*, LNCS 1683, pag. 50–66, 1999.

[DP99] G. Delzanno and A. Podelski. Model Checking in CLP. In *Proc. 5th Int. Con. on Tools and Algorithms for the Construction and Analysis of Systems (TACAS'99)*, LNCS 1579, pages 223–239, 1999.

[EN96] E. A. Emerson and K. S. Namjoshi. Automatic Verification of Parameterized Synchronous Systems. In *Proc. 8th Conf. on Computer Aided Verification (CAV'96)*, LNCS 1102, pages 87–98, 1996.

[EN98]   E. A. Emerson and K. S. Namjoshi. On Model Checking for Nondeterministic Infinite-state Systems. In *Proc. of the 13th Annual Symp. on Logic in Computer Science (LICS '98)*, pages 70–80, 1998.

[EN98b]   E. A. Emerson and K. S. Namjoshi. Verification of Parameterized Bus Arbitration Protocol. In *Proc. 10th Conf. on Computer Aided Verification (CAV'98)*, LNCS 1427, pages 452–463, 1998.

[EFM99]   J. Esparza, A. Finkel, and R. Mayr. On the Verification of Broadcast Protocols. In *Proc. 14th Annual Symp. on Logic in Computer Science (LICS'99)*, pages 352–359, 1999.

[FS98]   A. Finkel and P. Schnoebelen. Well-structured transition systems everywhere! Tech. Rep. LSV-98-4, Lab. Spécification et Vérification, ENS de Cachan, April 1998. To appear in *Theoretical Computer Science*.

[GS92]   S. M. German, A. P. Sistla. Reasoning about Systems with Many Processes. *JACM* 39(3): 675–735 (1992)

[GS97]   S. Graf and H. Saïdi. Construction of Abstract State Graphs with PVS. In *Proc. 9th Conf. on Computer Aided Verification (CAV'97)*, LNCS 1254, pages 72–83, 1997.

[Hal93]   N. Halbwachs. Delay Analysis in Synchronous Programs. In *Proc.5th Conf. on Computer-Aided Verification (CAV'93)*, LNCS 697, pages 333–346, 1993.

[Han93]   J. Handy. The Cache Memory Book. Academic Press, 1993.

[HH95]   T. A. Henzinger, P.-H. Ho. A Note on Abstract-interpretation Strategies for Hybrid Automata. In *Proceedings of Hybrid Systems II*, LNCS 999, pages 252–264, 1995.

[HHW97]   T. A. Henzinger, P.-H. Ho, and H. Wong-Toi. HyTech: a Model Checker for Hybrid Systems. In *Proc. 9th Conf. on Computer Aided Verification (CAV'97)*, LNCS 1254, pages 460–463, 1997.

[HQR99]   T. A. Henzinger, S. Qadeer, S. K. Rajamani. Verifying Sequential Consistency on Shared-Memory Multiprocessor Systems. In *Proc. 11th Int. Conf. on Computer Aided Verification (CAV'99)*, LNCS 1633, pages 301–315, 1999.

[ID99]   C. Norris Ip and D. L. Dill. Verifying Systems with Replicated Components in Murphi. *Formal Methods in System Design*, 14(3): 273–310, 1999.

[LHR97]   D. Lesens and N. Halbwachs and P. Raymond. Automatic Verification of Parameterized Linear Networks of Processes. In *Proc. 24th ACM Symposium on Principles of Programming Languages (POPL'97)*, pages 346–357, 1997.

[McM99]   K. L. McMillan. Verification of Infinite State Systems by Compositional Model Checking. In *Proc. Conf. Correct Hardware Design and Verification Methods (CHARME'99)*, LNCS 1703, pages 219–234, 1999.

[MS91]   K. L. McMillan and J. Schwalbe. Formal Verification of the Gigamax Cache Consistency Protocol. In *Proc. Int. Symp. on Shared Memory Multiprocessors*, pages 242–251, 1991.

[PP84]   M. S. Papamarcos, J. H. Patel. A Low-Overhead Coherence Solution for Multiprocessors with Private Cache Memories. In *Proc. Int. Symp. on Computer Architecture (ISCA 84)*, pages 348–354, 1984.

[PD95]   F. Pong, M. Dubois. A New Approach for the Verification of Cache Coherence Protocols. *IEEE Transactions on Parallel and Distributed Systems* 6(8), 1995.

[PD97]   F. Pong, M. Dubois. Verification Techniques for Cache Coherence Protocols. *ACM Computing Surveys* 29(1): 82–126, 1997.

Binary Reachability Analysis of Discrete Pushdown Timed Automata

Zhe Dang*, Oscar H. Ibarra**, Tevfik Bultan***,
Richard A. Kemmerer*, and Jianwen Su**

Department of Computer Science
University of California
Santa Barbara, CA 93106

Abstract. We introduce discrete pushdown timed automata that are timed automata with integer-valued clocks augmented with a pushdown stack. A configuration of a discrete pushdown timed automaton includes a control state, finitely many clock values and a stack word. Using a pure automata-theoretic approach, we show that the binary reachability (i.e., the set of all pairs of configurations (α, β), encoded as strings, such that α can reach β through 0 or more transitions) can be accepted by a nondeterministic pushdown machine augmented with reversal-bounded counters (NPCM). Since discrete timed automata with integer-valued clocks can be treated as discrete pushdown timed automata without the pushdown stack, we can show that the binary reachability of a discrete timed automaton can be accepted by a nondeterministic reversal-bounded multicounter machine. Thus, the binary reachability is Presburger. By using the known fact that the emptiness problem is decidable for reversal-bounded NPCMs, the results can be used to verify a number of properties that can not be expressed by timed temporal logics for discrete timed automata and CTL* for pushdown systems.

1 Introduction

After the introduction of efficient automated verification techniques such as symbolic model-checking [16], finite state machines have been widely used for modeling reactive systems. Due to the limited expressiveness, however, they are not suitable for specifying most infinite state systems. Thus, searching for models to represent more general transition systems and analyzing the decidability of their verification problems such as reachability or model-checking is an important research issue. In this direction, several models have been investigated such as pushdown automata[4,12,17], timed automata[2] (and real-time logics[3,1,14]), and various approximations on multicounter machines[9,7].

---
* This work is supported in part by the Defense Advanced Research Projects Agency (DARPA) and Rome Laboratory, Air Force Materiel Command, USAF, under agreement number F30602-97-1-0207.
** This work is supported in part by NSF grant IRI-9700370.
*** This work is supported in part by NSF grant CCR-9970976.

A pushdown system is a finite state machine augmented by a pushdown stack. On the other hand, a timed automaton can be regarded as a finite state machine with a number of real-valued clocks. All the clocks progress synchronously with rate 1, and a clock can be reset to 0 at some transition. Each transition also comes with an enabling condition in the form of clock constraints (i.e., Boolean combinations of $x \# c$ and $x - y \# c$ where x and y are clocks, c is an integer constant, and $\#$ denotes $>, <$ or $=$. Such constraints are also called regions.). A standard region technique [2] (and more recent techniques[6,18]) can be used to analyze region reachability.

In this paper, we consider integer-valued clocks. We call a timed automaton with integer-valued clocks a *discrete timed automaton*. A strictly more powerful system can be obtained by combining a pushdown system with a discrete timed automaton. That is, a discrete timed automaton is augmented with a pushdown stack (i.e., a discrete pushdown timed automaton). We give a characterization of binary reachability $\leadsto$, defined as the set of pairs of configurations (control state and clock values, plus the stack word if applicable) (α, β) such that α can reach β through 0 or more transitions. Binary reachability characterization is a fundamental step towards developing a model checking algorithm for discrete pushdown timed automata. ¿From classical automata theory, it is known that the binary reachability of pushdown automata is context-free. For timed automata (with either real-valued clocks or integer-valued clocks), the region technique is not enough to give a characterization of the binary reachability. Recently, Comon et. al. [10] showed that the binary reachability of timed automata (with real-valued clocks) is expressible in the additive theory of reals. They show that a timed automaton with real-valued clocks can be flattened into one without nested cycles. Their technique also works for discrete timed automata. However, it is not easy to deduce a characterization of the binary reachability of discrete pushdown timed automata by combining the above results. The reason is, as pointed out in their paper, this flattening destroys the structure of the original automaton. That is, the flattened timed automaton accepts different sequences of transitions, though the binary reachability is still the same. Thus, their approach cannot be used to show the binary reachability of the discrete pushdown timed automata proposed in this paper, since by flattening the sequence of stack operations cannot be maintained. A class of Pushdown Timed Systems (with continuous clocks) was discussed in [5]. However, that paper focuses on region reachability instead of binary reachability.

In this paper, we develop a new automata-theoretic technique to characterize the binary reachability of a discrete pushdown timed automaton. Our technique does not use the region technique [2] nor the flattening technique [10]. Instead, a nondeterministic pushdown multicounter machine (NPCM), which is a nondeterministic pushdown automaton with counters, is used. Obviously, without restricting the counter behaviors, even the halting problem is undecidable, since machines with two counters already have an undecidable halting problem. An NPCM is reversal-bounded if the number of counter reversals (a counter changing mode between nondecreasing and nonincreasing and vice-versa) is bounded by some fixed number independent of the computation. We show that the binary reachability of a discrete pushdown timed automaton can be accepted by a reversal-bounded nondeterministic pushdown multicounter machine. We also discuss the safety analysis problem. That is, given a property P and an initial condition I, which are two sets of configurations of a discrete pushdown timed automaton $\mathcal{A}$, determine whether, starting from a configuration in I, $\mathcal{A}$ can only reach configurations in P. Using the above characterization and the known fact that the emptiness problem for reversal-bounded NPCMs is decidable, we show that the safety analysis problem is decidable for discrete pushdown timed automata, as long as both the safety property and the initial condition are accepted by nondeterministic reversal-bounded multicounter machines.

It is known that Presburger relations can be accepted by reversal-bounded multicounter machines. Therefore, it is immediate that the safety analysis problem is decidable as long as both the safety property and the initial condition are Presburger formulas on clocks. A discrete timed automaton can be treated as a discrete pushdown timed automaton without the pushdown stack. We can show that the binary reachability of a discrete timed automaton can be accepted by a reversal-bounded nondeterministic multicounter machine (i.e., a reversal-bounded NPCM without the pushdown stack). That is, the binary reachability of a discrete timed automaton is Presburger. This result shadows the result in [10] that the binary reachability of a timed automaton with real-valued clocks is expressible in the additive theory of reals, although our approach is totally different.

The characterization of $\leadsto$ for discrete pushdown timed automata will lead us to formulate a model checking procedure for a carefully defined temporal logic. The logic can be used to reason about a class of timed pushdown processes. Due to space limitation, we omit it here. In fact, the binary reachability characterization itself already demonstrates a wide range of safety properties that can be verified for discrete pushdown timed automata. We will show this by investigating a number of examples of properties at the end of the paper.

2 Discrete Pushdown Timed Automata

A timed automaton [2] is a finite state machine augmented with a number of real-valued clocks. All the clocks progress synchronously with rate 1, except a clock can be reset to 0 at some transition. In this paper, we consider integer-valued clocks. A *clock constraint* is a Boolean combination of *atomic clock constraints* in the following form: $x \# c, x-y \# c$ where $\#$ denotes $\leq, \geq, <, >$, or $=$, c is an integer, x, y are integer-valued clocks. Let $\mathcal{L}_X$ be the set of all clock constraints on clocks X. Let $\mathbf{Z}$ be the set of integers with $\mathbf{Z}^+$ for nonnegative integers. Formally, a *discrete timed automaton* $\mathcal{A}$ is a tuple $\langle S, X, E \rangle$ where S is a finite set of *(control) states*. X is a finite set of *clocks* with values in $\mathbf{Z}^+$. $E \subseteq S \times 2^X \times \mathcal{L}_X \times S$ is a finite set of *edges* or *transitions*. Each edge $\langle s, \lambda, l, s' \rangle$ denotes a transition from state s to state s' with *enabling condition* $l \in \mathcal{L}_X$ and a set of clock resets $\lambda \subseteq X$.

Note that λ may be empty. Also note that since each pair of states may have more than one edge between them, $\mathcal{A}$ is, in general, nondeterministic.

The semantics is defined as follows. $\alpha \in S \times (\mathbf{Z}^+)^{|X|}$ is called a *configuration* with α_x being the value of clock x and α_q being the state under this configuration. $\alpha \to^{\langle s, \lambda, l, s' \rangle} \alpha'$ denotes a one-step transition along an edge $\langle s, \lambda, l, s' \rangle$ in $\mathcal{A}$ satisfying

- The state s is set to a new location s', i.e., $\alpha_q = s, \alpha'_q = s'$.
- Each clock changes according to the edge given. If there are no clock resets on the edge, i.e., $\lambda = \emptyset$, then clocks progress by one time unit, i.e., for each $x \in X$, $\alpha'_x = \alpha_x + 1$. If $\lambda \neq \emptyset$, then for each $x \in \lambda$, $\alpha'_x = 0$ while for each $x \notin \lambda$, $\alpha'_x = \alpha_x$.
- The enabling condition is satisfied, that is, $l(\alpha)$ is true.

We simply write $\alpha \to \alpha'$ if α can reach α' by a one-step transition. A *path* $\alpha_0 \cdots \alpha_k$ satisfies $\alpha_i \to \alpha_{i+1}$ for each i. Also write $\alpha \rightsquigarrow^{\mathcal{A}} \beta$ if α reaches β through a path. Given a set P of configurations of $\mathcal{A}$, write the *preimage* $Pre^*(P)$ of P as the set of configurations that can reach a configuration in P, i.e.,

$$Pre^*(P) =_{def} \{\alpha : \text{ for some } \beta \in P, \alpha \rightsquigarrow^{\mathcal{A}} \beta\}.$$

The following figure shows an example of a discrete timed automaton with two clocks x_1 and x_2. The following sequence of configurations is a path: $\langle s_0, x_1 = 0, x_2 = 0 \rangle, \langle s_1, x_1 = 0, x_2 = 0 \rangle, \langle s_0, x_1 = 1, x_2 = 1 \rangle, \langle s_1, x_1 = 1, x_2 = 0 \rangle$.

The above defined $\mathcal{A}$ is a little different from the standard (discrete) timed automaton given in [2]. In that model, each state is assigned with a clock constraint called an *invariant* in which $\mathcal{A}$ can remain in the same control state with all the clocks synchronously progressing with rate 1 as long as the invariant is satisfied. It is easy to see that, when integer-valued clocks are considered, $\mathcal{A}$'s remaining in a state can be replaced by a self-looping transition with the invariant as the enabling condition and without clock resets. Each execution of such a transition causes all the clocks to progress by one time unit. Another difference is that in a standard timed automaton a state transition takes no time, even when the transition has no clock resets. In order to translate a standard timed automaton to our definition, we introduce a dummy clock. Thus, for each state transition t in a standard timed automaton the translated transition t' is exactly the same except the dummy clock is reset in t'. Thus, doing this will ensure that all clock values remain the same when t has no clock resets. Thus, standard

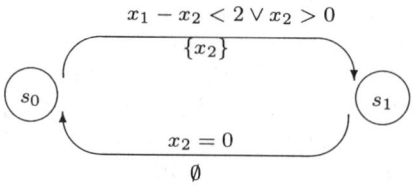

Fig. 1. An example discrete timed automaton

timed automata can be easily transformed into the ones defined above. Since the paper focuses on binary reachability, the ω-language accepted by a timed automaton is irrelevant here. Thus, event labels in a standard timed automaton are not considered in this paper.

Discrete timed automata can be further extended by allowing a pushdown stack. A *discrete pushdown timed automaton* $\mathcal{A}$ is a tuple $\langle \Gamma, S, X, E \rangle$ where Γ is the stack alphabet, and S, X, E are the same as in the definition of a discrete timed automaton except that each edge includes a stack operation. That is, each edge e is in the form of $\langle s, \lambda, (\eta, \eta'), l, s' \rangle$ where $s, s' \in S$, $\lambda \subseteq X$ is the set of clock resets and $l \in \mathcal{L}_X$ is the enabling condition. The stack operation is characterized by a pair (η, η') with $\eta \in \Gamma$ and $\eta' \in \Gamma^*$. That is, replacing the top symbol of the stack η by a word η'. A configuration $\alpha \in (\mathbf{Z}+)^{|X|} \times S \times \Gamma^*$ with $\alpha_w \in \Gamma^*$ indicating the stack content. $\alpha \leadsto^{\mathcal{A}} \beta$ can be similarly defined assuming that the stack contents in α and β are consistent with the sequence of stack operations along the path.

This paper focuses on the characterization of binary reachability $\leadsto^{\mathcal{A}}$ for both discrete timed automata and discrete pushdown timed automata. Before we proceed to show the results, some further definitions are needed.

A *nondeterministic multicounter machine (NCM)* is a nondeterministic machine with a finite set of *(control) states* $Q = \{1, 2, \cdots, |Q|\}$, and a finite number of counters $x_1, \cdots, x_k$ with integer counter values. Each counter can add 1, subtract 1, or stay unchanged. Those counter assignments are called *standard assignments*. M can also test whether a counter is equal to, greater than, or less than an integer constant. Those tests are called *standard tests*.

An NCM can be augmented with a pushdown stack. A *nondeterministic pushdown multicounter machine (NPCM)* M is a nondeterministic machine with a finite set of *(control) states* $Q = \{1, 2, \cdots, |Q|\}$, a pushdown stack with stack alphabet Γ, and a finite number of counters $x_1, \cdots, x_k$ with integer counter values. Both assignments and tests in M are standard. In addition, M can pop the top symbol from the stack or push a word in Γ^* on the top of the stack. It is well-known that counter machines with two counters have undecidable halting problem, and obviously the undecidability holds for machines augmented with a pushdown stack. Thus, we have to restrict the behaviors of the counters. One such restriction is to limit the number of reversals a counter can make. A counter is *n-reversal-bounded* if it changes mode between nondecreasing and nonincreasing at most n times. For instance, the following sequence of a counter values: $0, 0, 1, 1, 2, 2, 3, 3, 4, 4, 3, 2, 1, 1, 1, 1, \cdots$ demonstrates only one counter reversal. A counter is *reversal-bounded* if it is *n-reversal-bounded* for some n. We note that a reversal-bounded M (i.e., each counter in M is reversal-bounded) does not necessarily limit the number of moves or the number of reachable configurations to be finite.

Let $(j, v_1, \cdots, v_k, w)$ denote the *configuration* of M when it is in state $j \in Q$, counter x_i has value $v_i \in \mathbf{Z}$ for $i = 1, 2, \cdots, k$, and the string in the pushdown stack is $w \in \Gamma^*$ with the rightmost symbol being the top of the stack. Each integer counter value v_i can be represented by a unary string 0^{v_i} (1^{v_i}) when v_i

positive (negative). Thus, a configuration $(j, v_1, \cdots, v_k, w)$ can be represented as a string by concatenating the unary representations of each $j, v_1, \cdots, v_k$ as well as the string w with a separator $\# \notin \Gamma$. For instance, (1,2,-2,w) can be represented by $0^1 \# 0^2 \# 1^2 \# w$. Similarly, an integer tuple $(v_1, \cdots, v_k)$ can also be represented by a string. Thus, in this way, a set of configurations and a set of integer tuples can be treated as sets of strings, i.e., a language. It is noticed that a configuration α of a discrete (pushdown) timed automaton $\mathcal{A}$ can be similarly encoded as a string $[\alpha]$.

Note that the above defined M does not have an input tape; in this case it is used as a system specification rather than a language recognizer, in which we are more interested in the behaviors that M generates. When a NPCM (or NCM) M is used as a language recognizer, we attach a separate one-way read-only input tape to the machine and assign a state in Q as the final state. M accepts an input iff it can reach the final state. When M is reversal-bounded, the emptiness problem, i.e., whether M accepts some input, is known to be decidable,

Theorem 1. *The emptiness problem for reversal-bounded nondeterministic pushdown multicounter machines with a one-way input tape is decidable [15].*

It has been shown in [13] that the emptiness problem for reversal-bounded nondeterministic multicounter machines (NCMs) with one-way input is decidable in n^{ck^r} time for some constant c, where n is the size of the machine, k is the number of counters, and r is the reversal-bound on each counter. We believe that a similar bound could be obtained for the case of NPCMs.

Actually, Theorem 1 can be strengthened for the case of NCMs:

Theorem 2. *A set of n-tuples of integers is definable by a Presburger formula iff it can be accepted by a reversal-bounded nondeterministic multicounter machine [15].*

A language is *bounded* if there exist finite words $w_1, \cdots, w_n$ such that each element can be represented as $w_1^* \cdots w_n^*$. A nondeterministic reversal-bounded multicounter machine can be made deterministic on bounded languages.

Theorem 3. *If a bounded language L is accepted by a nondeterministic reversal-bounded multicounter machine, then L can also be accepted by a deterministic reversal-bounded multicounter machine [15].*

For an NPCM M, we can define the *preimage* $Pre^*(P)$ of a set of configurations P similarly to be the set of all predecessors of configurations in P, i.e., $Pre^*(P) = \{t \mid t$ can reach some configuration t' in P in 0 or more moves$\}$. Recently, we have shown [11] that $Pre^*(P)$ can be accepted by a reversal-bounded NPCM assuming that M is reversal-bounded and P is accepted by a reversal-bounded nondeterministic multicounter machine.

Theorem 4. *Let M be a reversal-bounded nondeterministic pushdown multicounter machine. Suppose a set of configurations P is accepted by a reversal-bounded nondeterministic multicounter machine. Then $Pre^*(P)$ with respect to M can be accepted by a reversal-bounded nondeterministic pushdown multicounter machine.*

3 Main Results

Let $\mathcal{A}$ be a discrete pushdown timed automaton with clocks $x_1, \cdots, x_k$. The binary reachability $\leadsto^{\mathcal{A}}$ can be treated as a language $\{[\alpha]\#[\beta]^r : \alpha \leadsto^{\mathcal{A}} \beta\}$ where $[\alpha]$ is the string encoding of configuration α, $[\beta]^r$ is the reverse string encoding of configuration β.[1] The two encodings are separated by a delimiter "#". The main result claims that the binary reachability $\leadsto^{\mathcal{A}}$ can be accepted by a reversal-bounded NPCM using standard tests and assignments. $\mathcal{A}$ itself can be regarded as an NPCM, when we refer to a clock as a counter. However, tests in $\mathcal{A}$ as clock constraints are not standard tests. Furthermore, $\mathcal{A}$ is not reversal-bounded since clocks can be reset for an unbounded number of times.

The proof of the main result proceeds as follows. We first show that $\leadsto^{\mathcal{A}}$ can be accepted by a reversal-bounded NPCM using nonstandard tests and assignments. Then, we show that these nonstandard tests can be made standard. Finally, these nonstandard assignments can be simulated by standard ones. Throughout the two simulations the counters remain reversal-bounded.

First, we show that clocks $x_1, \cdots, x_k$ in $\mathcal{A}$ can be translated into reversal-bounded ones. Let $y_0, y_1, \cdots, y_k$ be another set of clocks such that $x_i = y_0 - y_i$ ($1 \leq i \leq k$). Let $\mathcal{A}'$ be a discrete pushdown timed automaton that is exactly the same as $\mathcal{A}$, except

- $\mathcal{A}'$ has clock y_0 that never resets. Intuitively, the *now-clock* y_0 denotes current time.
- Each y_i with $1 \leq i \leq k$ denotes the (last) time when a reset of clock x_i happens. Thus, each reset of clock x_i on an edge is replaced by updating y_i to the current time, i.e., $y_i := y_0$. If x_i does not reset on an edge, the value of y_i is unchanged. Also, only if there is no clock reset on an edge, add an assignment $y_0 := y_0 + 1$ to the edge to indicate that the now-clock progresses with one time unit. Only these assignments can change y_0.
- the enabling condition on each edge of $\mathcal{A}$ is replaced by substituting x_i with $y_0 - y_i$. Note that the enabling conditions $x_i \# c$ and $x_i - x_j \# c$ become $y_0 - y_i \# c$ and $y_j - y_i \# c$, respectively. Thus, the resulting enabling conditions are Boolean combinations of $y_i - y_j \# c$ with $0 \leq i, j \leq k$ and c being an integer constant.

Counters $y_0, y_1, \cdots, y_k$ in $\mathcal{A}'$ do not reverse. The reason is that assignments that change the counter values are only in the form of: $y_0 := y_0 + 1$ and $y_i := y_0$ for $1 \leq i \leq k$, and there is no way that a counter y_i decreases. For a configuration α of $\mathcal{A}$ and $u \in \mathbf{Z}^+$, write α^u to be a configuration of $\mathcal{A}'$ such that $\alpha^u_{y_0} = u$ (y_0's value is u), and for each $1 \leq i \leq k$, $\alpha^u_{y_i} = u - \alpha_{x_i}$ (y_i is the translation of x_i), and $\alpha^u_w = \alpha_w$ (the stack content is the same). Also write max_α to be the maximal value of clocks α_{x_i} in α (note that, each α_{x_i} is nonnegative by definition). Thus, α^{max_α} is the configuration α^u of $\mathcal{A}'$ with y_0's value being max_α. It follows directly, by induction on the length of a path, that the binary reachability of $\mathcal{A}$ can be characterized by that of $\mathcal{A}'$ as follows.

---
[1] The reason that we use the reverse encoding of β will become apparent in the Proof of Theorem 6.

Theorem 5. *For any pair of configurations α and β of a discrete pushdown timed automaton $\mathcal{A}$, the following holds,*

$\alpha \leadsto^{\mathcal{A}} \beta$ *iff there exist $v \in \mathbf{Z}^+$ with $v \geq max_\alpha$ such that $\alpha^{max_\alpha} \leadsto^{\mathcal{A}'} \beta^v$.*

¿From the above theorem, it suffices for us to investigate the binary reachability of $\mathcal{A}'$. As mentioned above, $\mathcal{A}'$ is an NPCM with reversal-bounded counters $y_0, y_1, \cdots, y_k$. However, instead of standard tests, $\mathcal{A}'$ has tests that check an enabling condition by comparing the difference of two counters against an integer constant. Also the assignments include only $y_0 := y_0 + 1$ and $y_i := y_0$ for $1 \leq i \leq k$ in $\mathcal{A}'$, which are not standard assignments. The following theorem says the nonstandard tests can be made standard.

Theorem 6. *The binary reachability $\leadsto^{\mathcal{A}'}$ of $\mathcal{A}'$ can be accepted by a reversal-bounded NPCM using standard tests and nonstandard assignments that are of the form $y_0 := y_0 + 1$ and $y_i := y_0$ with $1 \leq i \leq k$.*

Proof. We construct the reversal-bounded NPCM as required. Given a pair of string encodings of configurations $\alpha^{\mathcal{A}'}$ and $\beta^{\mathcal{A}'}$ (separated by a delimiter "#" not in the stack alphabet, also recall that the encoding of $\beta^{\mathcal{A}'}$ has the stack word in $\beta^{\mathcal{A}'}$ reversed.) of $\mathcal{A}'$ on M's one-way input tape, M first copies $\alpha^{\mathcal{A}'}$ into its $k+1$ counters $y_0, y_1, \cdots, y_k$ and the stack. Thus, M's input head stops at the beginning of $\beta^{\mathcal{A}'}$. M starts simulating $\mathcal{A}'$ as follows with the stack operations in $\mathcal{A}'$ being exactly simulated on its own stack. Tests in $\mathcal{A}'$ are Boolean combinations of $y_i - y_j \# c$ for $0 \leq i, j \leq k$. Using only standard tests, M cannot directly compare the difference of two counter values against an integer c by storing $y_i - y_j$ in another counter, since each time this "storing" is done it will cause at least a counter reversal, and we don't have a bound on the number of such tests. In the following, we provide a technique to avoid such nonstandard tests. Assume m is one plus the maximal absolute value of all the integer constants that appear in the tests in $\mathcal{A}'$. Denote the finite set $[m] =_{def} \{-m, \cdots, 0, \cdots, m\}$. M uses its finite control to build a finite table. For each pair of counters y_i and y_j with $0 \leq i, j \leq k$, there is a pair of entries a_{ij} and b_{ij}. Each entry can be regarded as finite state control variable with states in $[m]$. Intuitively, a_{ij} is used to record the difference between the values of two counters y_i and y_j. b_{ij} is used to record the "future" value of the difference when a clock assignment $y_i := y_0$ occurs in the future. During the computation of $\mathcal{A}'$, when the difference goes beyond m or below $-m$, a_{ij} stays the same as m or $-m$. M uses $a_{ij} \# c$ to do a test $y_i - y_j \# c$. Doing this is always valid, as we will show later. Thus, M only uses standard tests. Below, "ADD 1" means adding one if the result does not exceed m, otherwise it keeps the same value. "SUBTRACT 1" means subtracting one if the result is not less than $-m$, otherwise it keeps the same value. In the following, we show how to construct the table. When assignment $y_0 := y_0 + 1$ is being executed by $\mathcal{A}'$, M updates the table as follows, for each $0 \leq i, j \leq k$:

- a_{ij} stays the same if $i > 0$ and $j > 0$. That is, the now-clock's progressing does not affect the difference between two non-now-clocks,

- a_{ij} ADD 1 if $i = 0$ and $j > 0$, noticing that y_i is the now-clock and y_j is a non-now-clock (thus it remains unchanged),
- a_{ij} SUBTRACT 1 if $i > 0$ and $j = 0$, noticing that y_j is the now-clock and y_i is a non-now-clock (thus it remains unchanged),
- a_{ij} is always 0 if $i = 0$ and $j = 0$. The difference between two identical now-clocks is always 0.

After updating all a_{ij}, entries b_{ij} are updated as below, for each $0 \leq i, j \leq k$,

- $b_{ij} := a_{0j}$. Thus b_{ij} is the value of $y_i - y_j$ assuming currently there is a jump $y_i := y_0$.

It is noticed that an edge in $\mathcal{A}'$ cannot contain two forms of assignment, i.e., both $y_0 := y_0 + 1$ and $y_i := y_0$. Let $\tau \subseteq \{y_1, \cdots, y_k\}$ denote assignments $y_i := y_0$ for $i \in \tau$ on an edge being executed by $\mathcal{A}'$. M updates the table as follows, for each $0 \leq i, j \leq k$:

- $a_{ij} := 0$ if $i, j \in \tau$, noticing that both y_i and y_j are currently the same value as the now-clock y_0,
- $a_{ij} := b_{ij}$ if $i \in \tau$ and $j \notin \tau$, noticing that y_i currently is the same value of the now-clock y_0 and the difference $y_i - y_j$ is prestored as b_{ij},
- $a_{ij} := -b_{ji}$ if $i \notin \tau$ and $j \in \tau$, noticing that $y_i - y_j = -(y_j - y_i)$,
- a_{ij} stays the same if $i \notin \tau$ and $j \notin \tau$, since clocks outside τ are not changed.

After updating all a_{ij}, entries b_{ij} are updated as follows, for each $0 \leq i, j \leq k$:

- $b_{ij} := 0$ if $i, j \in \tau$, noticing that both y_i and y_j are currently the same value as the now-clock y_0,
- $b_{ij} := a_{0j}$ if $i \in \tau$ and $j \notin \tau$, noticing that y_i currently is the same value as the now-clock y_0,
- $b_{ij} := -a_{0i}$ if $i \notin \tau$ and $j \in \tau$, noticing that y_j currently is set to the now-clock y_0,
- b_{ij} stays the same if $i \notin \tau$ and $j \notin \tau$, noticing that b_{ij} represents $y_0 - y_j$ and in fact the two clocks y_0 and y_j are unchanged after the transition.

The initial values of a_{ij} and b_{ij} can be constructed directly from $\alpha^{\mathcal{A}'}$ as follows, for each $0 \leq i, j \leq k$:

- $a_{ij} := \alpha_{y_i}^{\mathcal{A}'} - \alpha_{y_j}^{\mathcal{A}'}$ if $|\alpha_{y_i}^{\mathcal{A}'} - \alpha_{y_j}^{\mathcal{A}'}| \leq m$,
- $a_{ij} := m$ if $\alpha_{y_i}^{\mathcal{A}'} - \alpha_{y_j}^{\mathcal{A}'} > m$,
- $a_{ij} := -m$ if $\alpha_{y_i}^{\mathcal{A}'} - \alpha_{y_j}^{\mathcal{A}'} < -m$,

and for each $0 \leq i, j \leq k$: $b_{ij} := a_{0j}$.

M then simulates $\mathcal{A}'$ exactly except using $a_{ij}\#c$ for a test $y_i - y_j \#c$ in $\mathcal{A}'$, with $-m < c < m$. Then, we claim that doing this by M is valid,

Claim. Each time after M updates the table by executing a transition, $y_i - y_j \#c$ iff $a_{ij}\#c$, and $y_0 - y_j \#c$ iff $b_{ij}\#c$, for all $0 \leq i, j \leq k$ and for each integer $c \in [m-1]$.

Proof of the Claim. We prove it by induction. Obviously, the Claim holds for the initial values of all clocks y_i (in configuration $\alpha^{\mathcal{A}'}$) and the corresponding entries a_{ij} and b_{ij}, by the choice of m. Suppose that $\mathcal{A}'$ is currently at configuration γ and the Claim holds. Thus, for all $0 \leq i, j \leq k$ and for each integer $c \in [m-1]$, $\gamma_{y_i} - \gamma_{y_j} \#c$ iff $a_{ij}\#c$ and $\gamma_{y_0} - \gamma_{y_j}\#c$ iff $b_{ij}\#c$ hold. Therefore, γ satisfies an enabling condition in $\mathcal{A}'$ iff the entries a_{ij} satisfy the same enabling condition by replacing $y_i - y_j$ with a_{ij}, noticing that m is chosen such that it is greater than the absolute value of any constant in all the enabling conditions in $\mathcal{A}'$. Assume γ satisfies the enabling condition on an edge e and $\mathcal{A}'$ will execute e next. Thus, M, using the entries a_{ij} to test the enabling condition, will also execute the same edge. We use γ' to denote the configuration after executing the edge, and use a'_{ij} and b'_{ij} to denote the table entries after executing the edge. We need to show, for all $0 \leq i, j \leq k$ and for each integer $c \in [m-1]$,

(*) $\gamma'_{y_i} - \gamma'_{y_j}\#c$ iff $a'_{ij}\#c$

and

(**) $\gamma'_{y_0} - \gamma'_{y_j}\#c$ iff $b'_{ij}\#c$

hold. There are two cases to be considered according to the form of the assignment. Suppose the assignment on e is a clock progress $y_0 := y_0 + 1$. After this assignment, $\gamma'_{y_0} = \gamma_{y_0} + 1$ and $\gamma'_{y_i} = \gamma_{y_i}$ for each $1 \leq i \leq k$. On the other hand, according to the updating algorithm above, a'_{ij} are updated for each $0 \leq i, j \leq k$ as follows, depending on the case. There are four subcases:

- If $i > 0$ and $j > 0$, then $\gamma'_{y_i} = \gamma_{y_i}$, $\gamma'_{y_j} = \gamma_{y_j}$, $a'_{ij} = a_{ij}$. The claim (*) holds trivially.
- If $i = 0$ and $j > 0$, then $\gamma'_{y_i} = \gamma_{y_i} + 1$, $\gamma'_{y_j} = \gamma_{y_j}$, $a'_{ij} = a_{ij}$ ADD 1. Since y_0 is the only now-clock, all $\gamma_{y_i} - \gamma_{y_j}$, $\gamma'_{y_i} - \gamma'_{y_j}$, a'_{ij} and a_{ij} are nonnegative. It suffices to show for any $c \geq 0, c \in [m-1]$, the claim holds. In fact, $\gamma'_{y_i} - \gamma'_{y_j}\#c$ iff $\gamma_{y_i} - \gamma_{y_j}\#c - 1$ iff $a_{ij}\#c - 1$ iff $a_{ij} + 1\#c$. Also, $a_{ij} + 1\#c$ iff $a'_{ij}\#c$, by separating the cases for $a_{ij} = m$ and $a_{ij} < m$, and noticing that $c < m$. Thus, (*) holds, i.e., $\gamma'_{y_i} - \gamma'_{y_j}\#c$ iff $a'_{ij}\#c$.
- If $i > 0$ and $j = 0$, similar as above.
- If $i = 0$ and $j = 0$, the Claim (*) holds trivially.

Noticing that under the assignment $y_0 := y_0 + 1$, $b'_{ij} := a'_{0j}$. Thus, (**) can be shown using (*).

When the assignment is in the form of $y_i := y_0$ for $y_i \in \tau \subseteq \{y_1, \cdots, y_k\}$, (note that in this case, the now clock does not progress, i.e., $\gamma'_{y_0} = \gamma_{y_0}$) there are four cases to consider in order to show (*) for all $0 \leq i, j \leq k$,

- If $i, j \in \tau$, then $\gamma'_{y_i} = \gamma'_{y_j} = \gamma_{y_0}$, $a'_{ij} = 0$ and therefore $\gamma'_{y_i} - \gamma'_{y_j} = a'_{ij} = 0$. Thus, the Claim (*) trivially holds.
- If $i \in \tau$ and $j \notin \tau$, then, $\gamma'_{y_i} = \gamma_{y_0}$, $\gamma'_{y_j} = \gamma_{y_j}$, $a'_{ij} = b_{ij}$. Thus, for each $c \in [m-1]$, $\gamma'_{y_i} - \gamma'_{y_j}\#c$ iff $\gamma_{y_0} - \gamma_{y_j}\#c$ iff (induction hypothesis) $b_{ij}\#c$ iff $a'_{ij}\#c$. The Claim (*) holds.
- If $i \notin \tau$ and $j \in \tau$, similar as above.
- If $i \notin \tau$ and $j \notin \tau$, then, $\gamma'_{y_i} = \gamma_{y_i}$, $\gamma'_{y_j} = \gamma_{y_j}$, and $a'_{ij} = a_{ij}$. Thus, the Claim (*) holds trivially.

Now we prove Claim (**) under this assignment for τ. Again, there are four cases to consider:

- If $i, j \in \tau$, then $b'_{ij} = 0$, noticing that $\gamma'_{y_j} = \gamma_{y_0}$ and $\gamma'_{y_0} = \gamma_{y_0}$, Claim (**) holds.
- If $i \in \tau$ and $j \notin \tau$, then, $b'_{ij} = a'_{0j}$. Claim (**) holds directly from Claim (*).
- If $i \notin \tau$ and $j \in \tau$, similar as above.
- If $i \notin \tau$ and $j \notin \tau$, then, $b'_{ij} = b_{ij}$. In fact, $\gamma'_{y_0} = \gamma_{y_0}, \gamma'_{y_j} = \gamma_{y_j}$. Thus, Claim (**) holds directly from the induction hypothesis.

This ends the proof of the Claim. Thus, it is valid for M to use $a_{ij}\#c$ to do each test $y_i - y_j\#c$. At some point, M guesses that it has reached the configuration $\beta^{\mathcal{A}'}$ by comparing the counter values and the stack content with $\beta^{\mathcal{A}'}$ through reading the rest of the input tape. M accepts iff such a comparison succeeds. Clearly M accepts $\leadsto^{\mathcal{A}'}$. There is a slight problem when M compares its own stack content with the one $\beta^{\mathcal{A}'}_w$ on the one-way input tape in $\beta^{\mathcal{A}'}$ by popping the stack. The reason is that popping the stack contents reads the reverse of the stack content. However, recall that the encoding of the stack word $\beta^{\mathcal{A}'}_w$ on the input tape is reversed. Thus, such a comparison can be proceeded. □

Assignments in M constructed in the above proof, in the form of, $y_0 := y_0 + 1$ and $y_i := y_0$ with $1 \leq i \leq k$, are still not standard. We will now show that these assignments can be made standard, while the machine is still reversal-bounded. Let M' be an NPCM that is exactly the same as M. M' simulates M's computation from the configuration $\alpha^{\mathcal{A}'}$. Initially, each $y_i := \alpha^{\mathcal{A}'}_{y_i}$ as we indicated in the above proof. However, each time that M executes an assignment $y_0 := y_0 + 1$, M' increases **all** the counters by 1, i.e., $y_i := y_i + 1$ for each $0 \leq i \leq k$. When M executes an assignment $y_i := y_0$, M' does nothing. The stack operations in M are faithfully simulated by M' on its own stack. For each $1 \leq i \leq k$, at some point, either initially or at the moment $y_i := y_0$ is being executed by M, M' guesses (only once for each i) that y_i has already reached the value given in $\beta^{\mathcal{A}'}$. After such a guess for i, an execution of $y_0 := y_0 + 1$ will not cause $y_i := y_i + 1$ as indicated above (i.e., y_i will no longer be incremented). However, after such a guess for i, a later execution of $y_i := y_0$ in M will cause M' to abort abnormally (without accepting the input). At some point after **all** $1 \leq i \leq k$ have been guessed, M' guesses that it has reached the configuration $\beta^{\mathcal{A}'}$. Then, M' compares its current configuration with the one on the rest of the input tape $\beta^{\mathcal{A}'}$ (recall that the stack word in $\beta^{\mathcal{A}'}$ is reversed on the input tape.). M' accepts iff such a comparison succeeds. Clearly, M' uses only assignments $y_0 := y_0 + 1$ and $y_i := y_i + 1$ for $1 \leq i \leq k$. Thus, M' is also reversal-bounded and accepts $\leadsto^{\mathcal{A}'}$. Therefore,

Theorem 7. *The binary reachability $\leadsto^{\mathcal{A}'}$ of $\mathcal{A}'$ can be accepted by a reversal-bounded NPCM using standard tests and assignments.*

Combining the above theorem with Theorem 5 and noticing that v in Theorem 5 can be guessed, it follows immediately that,

Theorem 8. *The binary reachability of a discrete pushdown timed automaton can be accepted by a reversal-bounded NPCM using standard tests and assignments.*

A discrete timed automaton is a special case of a discrete pushdown timed automaton without the pushdown stack. The above proofs still work for discrete timed automata without considering stack operations. That is,

Theorem 9. *The binary reachability of a discrete timed automaton can be accepted by a reversal-bounded multicounter machine using standard tests and assignments.*

Combining the above theorem and Theorem 2, it is immediate that the binary reachability of a discrete timed automaton is Presburger over clocks. This result shadows the result in [10] that the binary reachability of a timed automaton with real-valued clocks is expressible in the additive theory of reals. However, our proof is totally different from the flattening technique in [10].

4 Verification Results

The importance of the characterization of $\leadsto^{\mathcal{A}}$ for a discrete pushdown timed automaton $\mathcal{A}$ is that the emptiness of reversal-bounded NPCMs is decidable from Theorem 1. In this section, we will formulate a number of properties that can be verified for discrete pushdown timed automata.

We first need some notation. We use $\alpha, \beta \cdots$ to denote variables ranging over configurations. We use $\mathbf{q}, \mathbf{x}, \mathbf{w}$ to denote variables ranging over control states, clock values and stack words respectively. Note that α_{x_i}, α_q and α_w are still used to denote the value of clock x_i, the control state and the stack word of α. We use a count variable $\#_a(\mathbf{w})$ to denote the number of occurrences of a character $a \in \Gamma$ in a stack word variable $\mathbf{w}$. An NPCM-term t is defined as follows:[2]

$$t ::= n \mid \mathbf{q} \mid \mathbf{x} \mid \#_a(\alpha_w) \mid \alpha_{x_i} \mid \alpha_q \mid t - t \mid t + t$$

where n is an integer and $a \in \Gamma$. An NPCM-formula f is defined as follows:

$$f ::= t > 0 \mid t \bmod n = 0 \mid \neg f \mid f \vee f$$

where $n \neq 0$ is an integer[3]. Thus, f is a Presburger formula over control state variables, clock value variables and count variables. Let F be a formula in the following format:

$$\bigvee (f_i \wedge \alpha^i \leadsto \beta^i)$$

---
[2] Control states can be interpreted over a bounded range of integers. In this way, an arithmetic operation on control states is well-defined.
[3] We use $(i, j, \mathbf{w})$ to denote the i-th character of $\mathbf{w}$ is the j-th symbol in Γ. Then, Theorem 10 is still correct when we include (i, j, α_w) as an atomic formula in an NPCM-formula with $i, j \in \mathbf{Z}^+$.

where f_i, α^i and β^i are a number of NPCM-formulas and configuration variables. Write $\exists F$ to be a closed formula such that each free variable in F is existentially quantified. Then, the property $\exists F$ can be verified. [4]

Theorem 10. *The truth value of $\exists F$ with respect to a discrete pushdown timed automaton $\mathcal{A}$ for any NPCM-formula F is decidable.*

Proof. Consider each disjunctive subformula $f_i \wedge \alpha^i \leadsto \beta^i$ in F. Since f_i is Presburger, (the domain of) f_i can be accepted by a NCM M_{f_i} from Theorem 2, and further from Theorem 3, since the domain of f_i can be encoded as a set of integer tuples (thus, bounded), M_{f_i} can be made deterministic. ¿From Theorem 8, we can construct a reversal bounded NPCM accepting (the domain of) $\alpha^i \leadsto \beta^i$. It is obvious that $f_i \wedge \alpha^i \leadsto \beta^i$ can be accepted by a reversal-bounded NPCM M_i by "intersecting" the two machines. Now, F is a union of M_{f_i}. Since reversal-bounded NPCMs are closed under union [15], we can construct a reversal-bounded M to accept F. Since $\exists F = false$ is equivalent to testing the emptiness of M, the theorem follows from Theorem 1. □

Although $\exists F$ cannot be used to specify liveness properties, it can be used to specify many interesting safety properties. For instance, the following property:

"for any configurations α and β with $\alpha \leadsto^{\mathcal{A}} \beta$, clock x_2 in β is the sum of clocks x_1 and x_2 in α, and symbol a appears in β twice as many times as symbol b does in α."

This property can be expressed as, $\forall \alpha \forall \beta (\alpha \leadsto^{\mathcal{A}} \beta \rightarrow (\beta_{x_2} = \alpha_{x_1} + \alpha_{x_2} \wedge \#_a(\beta_w) = 2\#_b(\alpha_w)))$. The negation of this property is equivalent to $\exists F$ for some F. Thus, it can be verified. We also need to point out that

- Even without clocks, $\#_a(\beta_w) = 2\#_b(\alpha_w)$ indicate a nonregular set of stack word pairs. Thus, this property cannot be verified by the model checking procedures for pushdown systems [4,12,17],
- Even without the pushdown stack, $\beta_{x_2} = \alpha_{x_1} + \alpha_{x_2}$ is not a clock region [2]. Thus, the classical region techniques (include [5] for Pushdown Timed Systems) can not verify this property. This is also pointed out in [10].

Note that in an NPCM-formula, the use of a stack word is limited to count the occurrences of a symbol, e.g., $\#_a(\alpha_w)$. In fact we can have the following more general use. Given P and I, two sets of configurations of a discrete pushdown timed automaton $\mathcal{A}$. If, starting from a configuration in I, $\mathcal{A}$ can only reach configurations in P, then P is a *safety property* with respect to the initial condition I. The *safety analysis problem* is whether P is a safety property with respect to the initial condition I, given P and I. The following theorem asserts that the safety analysis problem is decidable for discrete pushdown timed automata,

---

[4] If stack words in α^i and β^i are bounded, i.e., in the form of $w_1^* \cdots w_k^*$ with $w_1, \cdots, w_k$ fixed, then F can be further extended to allow disjunctions *and* conjunctions over $(f_i \wedge \alpha^i \leadsto \beta^i)$ formulas and the following theorem still holds. The reason is that reversal-bounded NPCMs are closed under conjunction when languages are bounded [15].

when both P and I are bounded languages and are accepted by reversal-bounded NCMs.

Theorem 11. *The safety analysis problem is decidable for discrete pushdown timed automata where both the safety property and the initial condition are bounded languages and accepted by reversal-bounded nondeterministic multicounter machines.*

Proof. Let $\mathcal{A}$ be a discrete pushdown timed automaton. Let P and I be accepted by reversal-bounded NCMs M_P and M_I, respectively. Note that P is a safety property with respect to the initial condition I iff $I \cap Pre^*(\neg P) = \emptyset$. That is, if P is a safety property, then, starting from a configuration, $\mathcal{A}$ can not reach a configuration that is in the complement $\neg P$ of P. ¿From Theorem 3, since P and I are bounded, both M_P and M_I can be made deterministic. Thus, $\neg P$ can also be accepted by a reversal-bounded NCM. Therefore, from Theorem 8 and Theorem 4, we can construct a reversal-bounded NPCM M_{Pre^*} accepting $Pre^*(\neg P)$. It is obvious that $I \cap Pre^*(\neg P)$ can also be accepted by a reversal-bounded NPCM M' by "intersecting" M_I and M_{Pre^*}. The theorem follows by noticing that $I \cap Pre^*(\neg P) = \emptyset$, i.e., testing the emptiness of M' is decidable from Theorem 1. □

Thus, from the above theorem, the following property can be verified:

"starting from a configuration α with the stack word $a^n b^{2n}$ for some n, $\mathcal{A}$ can only reach a configuration β satisfying: the clock x_1 in β is the sum of clock x_2 and x_3 in β, and the stack word is $a^n b^{n+2m}$ for some n and m."

The reason is that $a^n b^{2n}$ and $a^n b^{n+2m}$ can be encoded as Presburger tuples (thus bounded). Therefore they can be accepted by reversal-bounded NCMs.

Now let's look at $\mathcal{A}$ without a pushdown stack, i.e., a discrete timed automaton. Obviously, the above two theorems still hold for such $\mathcal{A}$. However, since $\leadsto^{\mathcal{A}}$ now is Presburger from Theorem 9, we can do more. An NCM-term t is defined as follows:

$$t ::= n \mid \mathbf{q} \mid \mathbf{x} \mid \alpha_{x_i} \mid \alpha_q \mid t - t \mid t + t$$

where n is an integer and $a \in \Gamma$. An NCM-formula f is defined as follows:

$$f ::= t > 0 \mid \neg f \mid f \vee f \mid \alpha \leadsto^{\mathcal{A}} \beta \mid \forall \alpha(f) \mid \forall \mathbf{x}(f) \mid \forall \mathbf{q}(f).$$

Thus, f is a Presburger formula over control state variables, clock value variables and configuration variables. Thus, if f is closed (i.e., without free variables), then the truth value of f is decidable since f is Presburger. Thus, a property formulated as a closed NCM-formula can be verified. Even clocks are real values, this is still true from [10]. The following is an example property which can be verified:

"for all configuration α there exists a configuration β such that $\alpha \leadsto^{\mathcal{A}} \beta$ and the clock x_1 in β is the sum of clocks x_1 and x_2 in α."

This property can be written in the following closed NCM-formula,

$$\forall \alpha \exists \beta (\alpha \leadsto^{\mathcal{A}} \beta \wedge \beta_{x_1} = \alpha_{x_1} + \alpha_{x_2}).$$

NCM-formulas can be extended by considering event labels as follows. Consider a discrete timed automata $\mathcal{A}$. Recall that an edge in $\mathcal{A}$ does not have a label. Now we assume that, just as a standard timed automaton, each edge in $\mathcal{A}$ is labeled by a letter in a finite alphabet Γ. Denote $R(\alpha, \beta, \mathbf{n}_\Gamma)$ to be a predicate meaning α can reach β through a path that for each $a \in \Gamma$, the number of occurrence of label a in the path is equal to $\mathbf{n}_a$ with $\mathbf{n}_\Gamma$ being an array of $\mathbf{n}_a$ for $a \in \Gamma$. By introducing a new counter for each $a \in \Gamma$ and increasing the counter whenever M executes a transition labeled by a, we can construct a reversal-bounded NCM M as in the proof of Theorem 9 (and the actual proof is in Theorem 8.). From Theorem 2, we have,

Theorem 12. *R is Presburger.*

Thus, we can add atomic terms $\mathbf{n}_a$ for $a \in \Gamma$ and an atomic formula $R(\alpha, \beta, \mathbf{n}_\Gamma)$ to the above definition of NCM-formulas. Then such closed NCM-formulas can be verified for discrete timed automata with labels. The following is an example property:

"For any configuration α there exists a configuration β such that if the clock x_1 in β is the sum of clocks x_1 and x_2 in α, then α can reach β through a path with the number of transitions labeled by a being twice the number of transitions labeled by b."

This property can be written in a closed NCM-formula,

$$\forall \alpha \exists \beta (\beta_{x_1} = \alpha_{x_1} + \alpha_{x_2} \rightarrow \exists \mathbf{n}_a \exists \mathbf{n}_b (R(\alpha, \beta, \mathbf{n}_a, \mathbf{n}_b) \wedge \mathbf{n}_a = 2\mathbf{n}_b)).$$

Thus, it can be verified.

5 Conclusion

We consider discrete pushdown timed automata that are timed automata with integer-valued clocks augmented with a pushdown stack. Using a pure automata-theoretic approach, we show that the binary reachability can be accepted by a reversal-bounded nondeterministic pushdown multicounter machine. The proof reveals that, by replacing enabling conditions with a finite table, the control part (testing clock constraints) and the clock behaviors (clock progresses and resets) can be separated for a discrete (pushdown) timed automaton, while maintaining the structure of the automaton. By using the known fact that the emptiness problem for reversal-bounded nondeterministic pushdown multicounter machines is decidable, we show a number of properties that can be verified.

Binary reachability characterization is a fundamental step towards a more general model-checking procedure for discrete pushdown timed automata. It is immediate to see that the region reachability in [2] can be similarly formulated by using Theorem 11, as long as stack words are regular. Thus, we can use the idea in [4] as well as in [12] to demonstrate a subset of μ-calculus that has a decidable decision procedure for a class of timed pushdown processes. We plan to investigate this issue in future work. In the future we would also like to investigate the complexity of the verification procedures we have developed in this paper. The techniques in this paper will be used in the implementation of a symbolic model checker for real-time specifications written in the specification language ASTRAL [8].

Thanks to anonymous reviewers for a number of useful suggestions.

References

1. R. Alur, C. Courcoibetis, and D. Dill, "Model-checking in dense real time," *Information and Computation*, **104** (1993) 2-34
2. R. Alur and D. Dill, "Automata for modeling real-time systems," *Theoretical Computer Science*, **126** (1994) 183-236
3. R. Alur, T. A. Henzinger, "A really temporal logic," *J. ACM*, **41** (1994) 181-204
4. A. Bouajjani, J. Esparza, and O. Maler, "Reachability Analysis of Pushdown Automata: Application to Model-Checking,", In *CONCUR'97*, LNCS 1243, pp. 135-150
5. A. Bouajjani, R. Echahed, and R. Robbana, "On the Automatic Verification of Systems with Continuous Variables and Unbounded Discrete Data Structures,", In *Hybrid System II*, LNCS 999, 1995, pp. 64-85
6. G. Behrmann, K. G. Larsen, J. Pearson, C. Weise and W. Yi, "Efficient timed reachability analysis using clock difference diagrams,", In *CAV'99*, LNCS 1633, pp. 341-353
7. B. Boigelot and P. Wolper, "Symbolic verification with periodic sets," In *CAV'94*, LNCS 818, pp. 55-67
8. A. Coen-Porisini, C. Ghezzi and R. Kemmerer, "Specification of real-time systems using ASTRAL," *IEEE Transactions on Software Engineering*, **23** (1997) 572-598
9. H. Comon and Y. Jurski, "Multiple counters automata, safety analysis and Presburger arithmetic," In *CAV'98*, LNCS 1427, pp. 268-279.
10. H. Comon and Y. Jurski, "Timed Automata and the Theory of Real Numbers," In *CONCUR'99*, LNCS 1664, pp. 242-257
11. Z. Dang, O. H. Ibarra, T. Bultan, R. A. Kemmerer, and J. Su "Safety property analysis of reversal-bounded pushdown multicounter machines,", manuscript, 1999
12. A. Finkel, B. Willems and P. Wolper "A direct symbolic approach to model checking pushdown systems," In *INFINITY'97*.
13. E. Gurari and O. Ibarra, "The Complexity of Decision Problems for Finite-Turn Multicounter Machines," *J. Computer and System Sciences*, **22** (1981) 220-229
14. T. A. Henzinger, X. Nicollin, J. Sifakis, and S. Yovine. "Symbolic Model Checking for Real-time Systems," *Information and Computation*, **111** (1994) 193-244
15. O. H. Ibarra, "Reversal-bounded multicounter machines and their decision problems," *J. ACM*, **25** (1978) 116-133
16. K. L. McMillan. "Symbolic model checking - an approach to the state explosion problem," PhD thesis, Carnegie Mellon University, 1992.
17. I. Walukiewicz, "Pushdown processes: games and model checking," In *CAV'96*, LNCS 1102, pp. 62-74
18. F. Wang, "Efficient Data Structure for Fully Symbolic Verification of Real-Time Software Systems ," In *TACAS'00*, to appear.

Boolean Satisfiability with Transitivity Constraints*

Randal E. Bryant[1] and Miroslav N. Velev[2]

[1] Computer Science, Carnegie Mellon University, Pittsburgh, PA
Randy.Bryant@cs.cmu.edu
[2] Electrical and Computer Engineering, Carnegie Mellon University, Pittsburgh, PA
mvelev@ece.cmu.edu

Abstract. We consider a variant of the Boolean satisfiability problem where a subset $\mathcal{E}$ of the propositional variables appearing in formula F_{sat} encode a symmetric, transitive, binary relation over N elements. Each of these *relational* variables, $e_{i,j}$, for $1 \leq i < j \leq N$, expresses whether or not the relation holds between elements i and j. The task is to either find a satisfying assignment to F_{sat} that also satisfies all transitivity constraints over the relational variables (e.g., $e_{1,2} \wedge e_{2,3} \Rightarrow e_{1,3}$), or to prove that no such assignment exists. Solving this satisfiability problem is the final and most difficult step in our decision procedure for a logic of equality with uninterpreted functions. This procedure forms the core of our tool for verifying pipelined microprocessors.

To use a conventional Boolean satisfiability checker, we augment the set of clauses expressing F_{sat} with clauses expressing the transitivity constraints. We consider methods to reduce the number of such clauses based on the sparse structure of the relational variables.

To use Ordered Binary Decision Diagrams (OBDDs), we show that for some sets $\mathcal{E}$, the OBDD representation of the transitivity constraints has exponential size for all possible variable orderings. By considering only those relational variables that occur in the OBDD representation of F_{sat}, our experiments show that we can readily construct an OBDD representation of the relevant transitivity constraints and thus solve the constrained satisfiability problem.

1 Introduction

Consider the following variant of the Boolean satisfiability problem. We are given a Boolean formula F_{sat} over a set of variables $\mathcal{V}$. A subset $\mathcal{E} \subseteq \mathcal{V}$ symbolically encodes a binary, symmetric, transitive relation over N elements. Each of these *relational* variables, $e_{i,j}$, where $1 \leq i < j \leq N$, expresses whether or not the relation holds between elements i and j. Typically, $\mathcal{E}$ will be "sparse," containing much fewer than the $N(N-1)/2$ possible variables. Note that when $e_{i,j} \notin \mathcal{E}$ for some value of i and of j, this does not imply that the relation does not hold between elements i and j. It simply indicates that F_{sat} does not directly depend on the relation between elements i and j.

A *transitivity constraint* is a formula of the form

$$e_{[i_1,i_2]} \wedge e_{[i_2,i_3]} \wedge \cdots \wedge e_{[i_{k-1},i_k]} \Rightarrow e_{[i_1,i_k]} \qquad (1)$$

---
* This research was supported by the Semiconductor Research Corporation, Contract 99-DC-684

where $e_{[i,j]}$ equals $e_{i,j}$ when $i < j$ and equals $e_{j,i}$ when $i > j$. Let $Trans(\mathcal{E})$ denote the set of all transitivity constraints that can be formed from the relational variables. Our task is to find an assignment $\chi: \mathcal{V} \to \{0,1\}$ that satisfies F_{sat}, as well as every constraint in $Trans(\mathcal{E})$. Goel, et al. [GSZAS98] have shown this problem is NP-hard, even when F_{sat} is given as an Ordered Binary Decision Diagram (OBDD) [Bry86]. Normally, Boolean satisfiability is trivial given an OBDD representation of a formula.

We are motivated to solve this problem as part of a tool for verifying pipelined microprocessors [VB99]. Our tool abstracts the operation of the datapath as a set of uninterpreted functions and uninterpreted predicates operating on symbolic data. We prove that a pipelined processor has behavior matching that of an unpipelined reference model using the symbolic flushing technique developed by Burch and Dill [BD94]. The major computational task is to decide the validity of a formula F_{ver} in a logic of equality with uninterpreted functions [BGV99a,BGV99b]. Our decision procedure transforms F_{ver} first by replacing all function application terms with terms over a set of domain variables $\{v_i | 1 \leq i \leq N\}$. Similarly, all predicate applications are replaced by formulas over a set of newly-generated propositional variables. The result is a formula F_{ver}^* containing equations of the form $v_i = v_j$, where $1 \leq i < j \leq N$. Each of these equations is then encoded by introducing a relational variable $e_{i,j}$, similar to the method proposed by Goel et al. [GSZAS98]. The result of the translation is a propositional formula $encf(F_{ver}^*)$ expressing the verification condition over both the relational variables and the propositional variables appearing in F_{ver}^*. Let F_{sat} denote $\neg encf(F_{ver}^*)$, the complement of the formula expressing the translated verification condition. To capture the transitivity of equality, e.g., that $v_i = v_j \wedge v_j = v_k \Rightarrow v_i = v_k$, we have transitivity constraints of the form $e_{[i,j]} \wedge e_{[j,k]} \Rightarrow e_{[i,k]}$. Finding a satisfying assignment to F_{sat} that also satisfies the transitivity constraints will give us a counterexample to the original verification condition F_{ver}. On the other hand, if we can prove that there are no such assignments, then we have proved that F_{ver} is universally valid.

We consider three methods to generate a Boolean formula F_{trans} that encodes the transitivity constraints. The *direct* method enumerates the set of *chord-free* cycles in the undirected graph having an edge (i,j) for each relational variable $e_{i,j} \in \mathcal{E}$. This method avoids introducing additional relational variables but can lead to a formula of exponential size. The *dense* method uses relational variables $e_{i,j}$ for all possible values of i and j such that $1 \leq i < j \leq N$. We can then axiomatize transitivity by forming constraints of the form $e_{[i,j]} \wedge e_{[j,k]} \Rightarrow e_{[i,k]}$ for all distinct values of i, j, and k. This will yield a formula that is cubic in N. The *sparse* method augments $\mathcal{E}$ with additional relational variables to form a set of variables $\mathcal{E}^+$, such that the resulting graph is *chordal* [Rose70]. We then only require transitivity constraints of the form $e_{[i,j]} \wedge e_{[j,k]} \Rightarrow e_{[i,k]}$ such that $e_{[i,j]}, e_{[j,k]}, e_{[i,k]} \in \mathcal{E}^+$. The sparse method is guaranteed to generate a smaller formula than the dense method.

To use a conventional Boolean Satisfiability (SAT) procedure to solve our constrained satisfiability problem, we run the checker over a set of clauses encoding both F_{sat} and F_{trans}. The latest version of the FGRASP SAT checker [M99] was able to complete all of our benchmarks, although the run times increase significantly when transitivity constraints are enforced.

When using Ordered Binary Decision Diagrams to evaluate satisfiability, we could generate OBDD representations of F_{sat} and F_{trans} and use the APPLY algorithm to compute an OBDD representation of their conjunction. From this OBDD, finding satisfying solutions would be trivial. We show that this approach will not be feasible in general, because the OBDD representation of F_{trans} can be intractable. That is, for some sets of relational variables, the OBDD representation of the transitivity constraint formula F_{trans} will be of exponential size regardless of the variable ordering. The NP-completeness result of Goel, et al. shows that the OBDD representation of F_{trans} may be of exponential size using the ordering previously selected for representing F_{sat} as an OBDD. This leaves open the possibility that there could be some other variable ordering that would yield efficient OBDD representations of both F_{sat} and F_{trans}. Our result shows that transitivity constraints can be intrinsically intractable to represent with OBDDs, independent of the structure of F_{sat}.

We present experimental results on the complexity of constructing OBDDs for the transitivity constraints that arise in actual microprocessor verification. Our results show that the OBDDs can indeed be quite large. We consider two techniques to avoid constructing the OBDD representation of all transitivity constraints. The first of these, proposed by Goel et al. [GSZAS98], generates implicants (cubes) of F_{sat} and rejects those that violate the transitivity constraints. Although this method suffices for small benchmarks, we find that the number of implicants generated for our larger benchmarks grows unacceptably large. The second method determines which relational variables actually occur in the OBDD representation of F_{sat}. We can then apply one of our three encoding techniques to generate a Boolean formula for the transitivity constraints over this reduced set of relational variables. The OBDD representation of this formula is generally tractable, even for the larger benchmarks.

Due to space limitations, this paper omits many technical details. More information, including formal proofs, is included in [BV00].

2 Benchmarks

Our benchmarks [VB99] are based on applying our verifier to a set of high-level microprocessor designs. Each is based on the DLX RISC processor described by Hennessy and Patterson [HP96]:

1×DLX-C: is a single-issue, five-stage pipeline capable of fetching up to one new instruction every clock cycle. It implements six instruction types and contains an interlock to stall the instruction following a load by one cycle if it requires the loaded result. This example is comparable to the DLX example first verified by Burch and Dill [BD94].

2×DLX-CA: has a complete first pipeline, capable of executing the six instruction types, and a second pipeline capable of executing arithmetic instructions. This example is comparable to one verified by Burch [Bur96].

2×DLX-CC: has two complete pipelines, i.e., each can execute any of the 6 instruction types.

In all of these examples, the domain variables v_i, with $1 \leq i \leq N$, in F_{ver}^* encode register identifiers. As described in [BGV99a,BGV99b], we can encode the symbolic

Circuit		Domain Variables	Propositional Variables	Equations
1×DLX-C		13	42	27
1×DLX-Ct		13	42	37
2×DLX-CA		25	58	118
2×DLX-CAt		25	58	137
2×DLX-CC		25	70	124
2×DLX-CCt		25	70	143
Buggy	min.	22	56	89
2×DLX-CC	avg.	25	69	124
	max.	25	77	132

Table 1. Microprocessor Verification Benchmarks. Benchmarks with suffix "t" were modified to require enforcing transitivity.

terms representing program data and addresses as distinct values, avoiding the need to have equations among these variables. Equations arise in modeling the read and write operations of the register file, the bypass logic implementing data forwarding, the load interlocks, and the pipeline issue logic.

Our original processor benchmarks do not require enforcing transitivity in order to verify them. In particular, the formula F_{sat} is unsatisfiable in all cases. This implies that the constrained satisfiability problems are unsatisfiable as well. We are nonetheless motivated to study the problem of constrained satisfiability for two reasons. First, other processor designs might rely on transitivity, e.g., due to more sophisticated issue logic. Second, to aid designers in debugging their pipelines, it is essential that we generate counterexamples that satisfy all transitivity constraints. Otherwise the designer will be unable to determine whether the counterexample represents a true bug or a weakness of our verifier.

To create more challenging benchmarks, we generated variants of the circuits that require enforcing transitivity in the verification. For example, the normal forwarding logic in the Execute stage of 1×DLX-C compares the two source registers ESrc1 and ESrc2 of the instruction in the Execute stage to the destination register MDest of the instruction in the memory stage. In the modified circuit, we changed the bypass condition ESrc1 = MDest to be ESrc1 = MDest ∨ (ESrc1 = ESrc2 ∧ ESrc2 = MDest). Given transitivity, these two expressions are equivalent. For each pipeline, we introduced four such modifications to the forwarding logic, with different combinations of source and destination registers. These modified circuits are named 1×DLX-Ct, 2×DLX-CAt, and 2×DLX-CCt.

To study the problem of counterexample generation for buggy circuits, we generated 105 variants of 2×DLX-CC, each containing a small modification to the control logic. Of these, 5 were found to be functionally correct, e.g., because the modification caused the processor to stall unnecessarily, yielding a total of 100 benchmark circuits for counterexample generation.

Table 1 gives some statistics for the benchmarks. The number of domain variables N ranges between 13 and 25, while the number of equations ranges between 27 and 143.

The verification condition formulas F_{ver}^* also contain between 42 and 77 propositional variables expressing the operation of the control logic. These variables plus the relational variables comprise the set of variables $\mathcal{V}$ in the propositional formula F_{sat}. The circuits with modifications that require enforcing transitivity yield formulas containing up to 19 additional equations. The final three lines summarize the complexity of the 100 buggy variants of 2×DLX-CC. We apply a number of simplifications during the generation of formula F_{sat}, and hence small changes in the circuit can yield significant variations in the formula complexity.

3 Graph Formulation

Our definition of $\mathit{Trans}(\mathcal{E})$ (Equation 1) places no restrictions on the length or form of the transitivity constraints, and hence there can be an infinite number. We show that we can construct a graph representation of the relational variables and identify a reduced set of transitivity constraints that, when satisfied, guarantees that all possible transitivity constraints are satisfied. By introducing more relational variables, we can alter this graph structure, further reducing the number of transitivity constraints that must be considered.

For variable set $\mathcal{E}$, define the undirected graph $G(\mathcal{E})$ as containing a vertex i for $1 \leq i \leq N$, and an edge (i,j) for each variable $e_{i,j} \in \mathcal{E}$. For an assignment χ of Boolean values to the relational variables, we will classify edge (i,j) as a *1-edge* when $\chi(e_{i,j}) = 1$, and as a *0-edge* when $\chi(e_{i,j}) = 0$.

A *path* is a sequence of vertices $[i_1, i_2, \ldots, i_k]$ having edges between successive elements, i.e., $1 \leq i_p \leq N$ for all p such that $1 \leq p \leq k$, and (i_p, i_{p+1}) is in $G(\mathcal{E})$ for all p such that $1 \leq p < k$. We consider each edge (i_p, i_{p+1}) for $1 \leq p < k$ to also be part of the path. A *cycle* is a path of the form $[i_1, i_2, \ldots, i_k, i_1]$.

Proposition 1. *An assignment to the variables in $\mathcal{E}$ violates transitivity if and only if some cycle in $G(\mathcal{E})$ contains exactly one 0-edge.*

A path $[i_1, i_2, \ldots, i_k]$ is said to be *acyclic* when $i_p \neq i_q$ for all $1 \leq p < q \leq k$. A cycle $[i_1, i_2, \ldots, i_k, i_1]$ is said to be *simple* when its prefix $[i_1, i_2, \ldots, i_k]$ is acyclic.

Proposition 2. *An assignment to the variables in $\mathcal{E}$ violates transitivity if and only if some simple cycle in $G(\mathcal{E})$ contains exactly one 0-edge.*

Define a *chord* of a simple cycle to be an edge that connects two vertices that are not adjacent in the cycle. More precisely, for a simple cycle $[i_1, i_2, \ldots, i_k, i_1]$, a chord is an edge (i_p, i_q) in $G(\mathcal{E})$ such that $1 \leq p < q \leq k$, that $p+1 < q$, and either $p \neq 1$ or $q \neq k$. A cycle is said to be *chord-free* if it is simple and has no chords.

Proposition 3. *An assignment to the variables in $\mathcal{E}$ violates transitivity if and only if some chord-free cycle in $G(\mathcal{E})$ contains exactly one 0-edge.*

For a set of relational variables $\mathcal{E}$, we define $F_{\text{trans}}(\mathcal{E})$ to be the conjunction of all transitivity constraints generated by enumerating the set of all chord-free cycles in the graph $G(\mathcal{E})$. Each length k cycle $[i_1, i_2, \ldots, i_k, i_1]$ yields k constraints. It is easily proved that an assignment to the relational variables will satisfy all of the transitivity constraints if and only if it satisfies $F_{\text{trans}}(\mathcal{E})$.

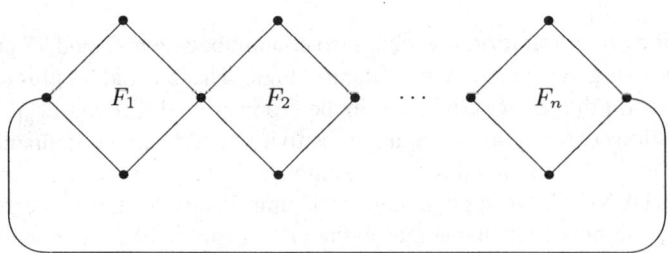

Fig. 1. Class of Graphs with Many Chord-Free Cycles. For a graph with n diamond-shaped faces, there are $2^n + n$ chord-free cycles.

3.1 Enumerating Chord-Free Cycles

To enumerate the chord-free cycles of a graph, we exploit the following properties. An acyclic path $[i_1, i_2, \ldots, i_k]$ is said to have a chord when there is an edge (i_p, i_q) in $G(\mathcal{E})$ such that $1 \leq p < q \leq k$, that $p + 1 < q$, and either $p \neq 1$ or $q \neq k$. We classify a chord-free path as *terminal* when (i_k, i_1) is in $G(\mathcal{E})$, and as *extensible* otherwise.

Proposition 4. *A path $[i_1, i_2, \ldots, i_k]$ is chord-free and terminal if and only if the cycle $[i_1, i_2, \ldots, i_k, i_1]$ is chord-free.*

A *proper prefix* of path $[i_1, i_2, \ldots, i_k]$ is a path $[i_1, i_2, \ldots, i_j]$ such that $1 \leq j < k$.

Proposition 5. *Every proper prefix of a chord-free path is chord-free and extensible.*

Given these properties, we can enumerate the set of all chord-free paths by breadth first expansion. As we enumerate these paths, we also generate C the set of all chord-free cycles. Define P_k to be the set of all extensible, chord-free paths having k vertices, for $1 \leq k \leq N$. As an initial case, we have $P_1 = \{[i] | 1 \leq i \leq n\}$, and we have $C = \emptyset$. At each step we consider all possible extensions to the paths in P_k to generate the set P_{k+1} and to add some cycles of length $k + 1$ to C.

As Figure 1 indicates, there can be an exponential number of chord-free cycles in a graph. In particular, this figure illustrates a family of graphs with $3n + 1$ vertices. Consider the cycles passing through the n diamond-shaped faces as well as the edge along the bottom. For each diamond-shaped face F_i, a cycle can pass through either the upper vertex or the lower vertex. Thus there are 2^n such cycles.

The columns labeled "Direct" in Table 2 show results for enumerating the chord-free cycles for our benchmarks. For each correct microprocessor, we have two graphs: one for which transitivity constraints played no role in the verification, and one (indicated with a "t" at the end of the name) modified to require enforcing transitivity constraints. We summarize the results for the transitivity constraints in our 100 buggy variants of 2×DLX-CC, in terms of the minimum, the average, and the maximum of each measurement. We also show results for five synthetic benchmarks consisting of $n \times n$ planar meshes M_n, with n ranging from 4 to 8, where the mesh for $n = 6$ is illustrated in Figure 2. For all of the circuit benchmarks, the number of cycles, although large, appears to be manageable. Moreover, the cycles have at most 4 edges. The synthetic benchmarks, on

Circuit		Direct			Dense			Sparse		
		Edges	Cycles	Clauses	Edges	Cycles	Clauses	Edges	Cycles	Clauses
1×DLX-C		27	90	360	78	286	858	33	40	120
1×DLX-Ct		37	95	348	78	286	858	42	68	204
2×DLX-CA		118	2,393	9,572	300	2,300	6,900	172	697	2,091
2×DLX-CAt		137	1,974	7,944	300	2,300	6,900	178	695	2,085
2×DLX-CC		124	2,567	10,268	300	2,300	6,900	182	746	2,238
2×DLX-CCt		143	2,136	8,364	300	2,300	6,900	193	858	2,574
Full	min.	89	1,446	6,360	231	1,540	4,620	132	430	1,290
Buggy	avg.	124	2,562	10,270	300	2,300	6,900	182	750	2,244
2×DLX-CC	max.	132	3,216	12,864	299	2,292	6,877	196	885	2,655
M_4		24	24	192	120	560	1,680	42	44	132
M_5		40	229	3,056	300	2,300	6,900	77	98	294
M_6		60	3,436	61,528	630	7,140	21,420	131	208	624
M_7		84	65,772	1,472,184	1,176	18,424	55,272	206	408	1,224
M_8		112	1,743,247	48,559,844	2,016	41,664	124,992	294	662	1,986

Table 2. Cycles in Original and Augmented Benchmark Graphs. Results are given for the three different methods of encoding transitivity constraints.

the other hand, demonstrate the exponential growth predicted as worst case behavior. The number of cycles grows quickly as the meshes grow larger. Furthermore, the cycles can be much longer, causing the number of clauses to grow even more rapidly.

3.2 Adding More Relational Variables

Enumerating the transitivity constraints based on only the variables in $\mathcal{E}$ runs the risk of generating a Boolean formula of exponential size. We can guarantee polynomial growth by considering a larger set of relational variables. In general, let $\mathcal{E}'$ be some set of relational variables such that $\mathcal{E} \subseteq \mathcal{E}'$, and let $F_{\text{trans}}(\mathcal{E}')$ be the transitivity constraint formula generated by enumerating the chord-free cycles in the graph $G(\mathcal{E}')$.

Proposition 6. *If $\mathcal{E}$ is the set of relational variables in F_{sat} and $\mathcal{E} \subseteq \mathcal{E}'$, then:*

$$F_{sat} \wedge F_{trans}(\mathcal{E}) \Leftrightarrow F_{sat} \wedge F_{trans}(\mathcal{E}').$$

Our goal then is to add as few relational variables as possible in order to reduce the size of the transitivity formula. We will continue to use our path enumeration algorithm to generate the transitivity formula.

3.3 Dense Enumeration

For the *dense* enumeration method, let $\mathcal{E}_N$ denote the set of variables $e_{i,j}$ for all values of i and j such that $1 \leq i < j \leq N$. Graph $G(\mathcal{E}_N)$ is a complete, undirected graph. In this graph, any cycle of length greater than three must have a chord. Hence our algorithm will enumerate transitivity constraints of the form $e_{[i,j]} \wedge e_{[j,k]} \Rightarrow e_{[i,k]}$, for all distinct values of i, j, and k. The graph has $N(N-1)$ edges and $N(N-1)(N-2)/6$ chord-free cycles, yielding a total of $N(N-1)(N-2)/2 = O(N^3)$ transitivity constraints.

The columns labeled "Dense" in Table 2 show the complexity of this method for the benchmark circuits. For the smaller graphs 1×DLX-C, 1×DLX-Ct, M_4 and M_5, this method yields more clauses than direct enumeration of the cycles in the original graph. For the larger graphs, however, it yields fewer clauses. The advantage of the dense method is most evident for the mesh graphs, where the cubic complexity is far superior to exponential.

3.4 Sparse Enumeration

We can improve on both of these methods by exploiting the sparse structure of $G(\mathcal{E})$. Like the dense method, we want to introduce additional relational variables to give a set of variables $\mathcal{E}^+$ such that the resulting graph $G(\mathcal{E}^+)$ becomes *chordal* [Rose70]. That is, the graph has the property that every cycle of length greater than three has a chord.

Chordal graphs have been studied extensively in the context of sparse Gaussian elimination. In fact, the problem of finding a minimum set of additional variables to add to our set is identical to the problem of finding an elimination ordering for Gaussian elimination that minimizes the amount of fill-in. Although this problem is NP-complete [Yan81], there are good heuristic solutions. In particular, our implementation proceeds as a series of elimination steps. On each step, we remove some vertex i from the graph. For every pair of distinct, uneliminated vertices j and k such that the graph contains edges (i,j) and (i,k), we add an edge (j,k) if it does not already exist. The original graph plus all of the added edges then forms a chordal graph. To choose which vertex to eliminate on a given step, our implementation uses the simple heuristic of choosing the vertex with minimum degree. If more than one vertex has minimum degree, we choose one that minimizes the number of new edges added.

The columns in Table 2 labeled "Sparse" show the effect of making the benchmark graphs chordal by this method. Observe that this method gives superior results to either of the other two methods. In our implementation we have therefore used the sparse method to generate all of the transitivity constraint formulas.

4 SAT-Based Decision Procedures

We can solve the constrained satisfiability problem using a conventional SAT checker by generating a set of clauses C_{trans} representing $F_{\text{trans}}(\mathcal{E}^+)$ and a set of clauses C_{sat} representing the formula F_{sat}. We then run the checker on the combined clause set $C_{\text{trans}} \cup C_{\text{sat}}$ to find satisfying solutions to $F_{\text{trans}}(\mathcal{E}^+) \wedge F_{\text{sat}}$.

In experimenting with a number of Boolean satisfiability checkers, we have found that FGRASP [MS99] gives the most consistent results. The most recent version can be directed to periodically restart the search using a randomly-generated variable assignment [M99]. This is the first SAT checker we have tested that can complete all of our benchmarks. All of our experiments were conducted on a 336 MHz Sun UltraSPARC II with 1.2GB of primary memory.

As indicated by Table 3, we ran FGRASP on clause sets C_{sat} and $C_{\text{trans}} \cup C_{\text{sat}}$, i.e., both without and with transitivity constraints. For benchmarks 1×DLX-C, 2×DLX-CA, and

Circuit		C_{sat} Satisfiable?	Secs.	$C_{trans} \cup C_{sat}$ Satisfiable?	Secs.	Ratio
1×DLX-C		N	3	N	4	1.4
1×DLX-Ct		Y	1	N	9	N.A.
2×DLX-CA		N	176	N	1,275	7.2
2×DLX-CAt		Y	3	N	896	N.A.
2×DLX-CC		N	5,035	N	9,932	2.0
2×DLX-CCt		Y	4	N	15,003	N.A.
Full	min.	Y	1	Y	1	0.2
Buggy	avg.	Y	125	Y	1,517	2.3
2×DLX-CC	max.	Y	2,186	Y	43,817	69.4

Table 3. Performance of FGRASP on Benchmark Circuits. Results are given both without and with transitivity constraints.

2×DLX-CC, the formula F_{sat} is unsatisfiable. As can be seen, including transitivity constraints increases the run time significantly. For benchmarks 1×DLX-Ct, 2×DLX-CAt, and 2×DLX-CCt, the formula F_{sat} is satisfiable, but only because transitivity is not enforced. When we add the clauses for F_{trans}, the formula becomes unsatisfiable. For the buggy circuits, the run times for C_{sat} range from under 1 second to over 36 minutes. The run times for $C_{trans} \cup C_{sat}$ range from less than one second to over 12 hours. In some cases, adding transitivity constraints actually decreased the CPU time (by as much as a factor of 5), but in most cases the CPU time increased (by as much as a factor of 69). On average (using the geometric mean) adding transitivity constraints increased the CPU time by a factor of 2.3. We therefore conclude that satisfiability checking with transitivity constraints is more difficult than conventional satisfiability checking, but the added complexity is not overwhelming.

5 OBDD-Based Decision Procedures

A simple-minded approach to solving satisfiability with transitivity constraints using OBDDs would be to generate separate OBDD representations of F_{trans} and F_{sat}. We could then use the APPLY operation to generate an OBDD for $F_{trans} \wedge F_{sat}$, and then either find a satisfying assignment or determine that the function is unsatisfiable. We show that for some sets of relational variables $\mathcal{E}$, the OBDD representation of $F_{trans}(\mathcal{E})$ can be too large to represent and manipulate. In our experiments, we use the CUDD OBDD package with variable reordering by sifting.

5.1 Lower Bound on the OBDD Representation of $F_{trans}(\mathcal{E})$

We prove that for some sets $\mathcal{E}$, the OBDD representation of $F_{trans}(\mathcal{E})$ may be of exponential size for all possible variable orderings. As mentioned earlier, the NP-completeness result proved by Goel et al. [GSZAS98] has implications for the complexity of representing $F_{trans}(\mathcal{E})$ as an OBDD. They showed that given an OBDD G_{sat} representing formula F_{sat}, the task of finding a satisfying assignment of F_{sat} that also

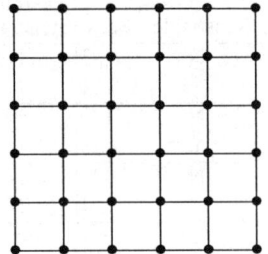

Fig. 2. Mesh Graph M_6

satisfies the transitivity constraints in $Trans(\mathcal{E})$ is NP-complete in the size of G_{sat}. By this, assuming $P \neq NP$, we can infer that the OBDD representation of $F_{\text{trans}}(\mathcal{E})$ may be of exponential size when using the same variable ordering as is used in G_{sat}. Our result extends this lower bound to arbitrary variable orderings and is independent of the P vs. NP problem.

Let M_n denote a planar mesh consisting of a square array of $n \times n$ vertices. For example, Figure 2 shows the graph for $n = 6$. Define $\mathcal{E}_{n \times n}$ to be a set of relational variables corresponding to the edges in M_n. $F_{\text{trans}}(\mathcal{E}_{n \times n})$ is then an encoding of the transitivity constraints for these variables.

Theorem 1. *Any OBDD representation of $F_{trans}(\mathcal{E}_{n \times n})$ must have $\Omega(2^{n/4})$ vertices.*

A complete proof of this theorem is given in [BV00]. We give only a brief sketch here. Being a planar graph, the edges partition the plane into *faces*. The proof first involves a combinatorial argument showing that for any partitioning of the edges into sets A and B, we can identify a set of at least $(n-3)/4$ edge-independent, "split faces," where a split face has some of its edge variables in set A and others in set B. The proof of this property is similar to a proof by Leighton [Lei92, Theorem 1.21] that M_n has a bisection bandwidth of at least n, i.e., one must remove at least n vertices to split the graph into two parts of equal size.

Given this property, for any ordering of the OBDD variables, we can construct a family of $2^{(n-3)/4}$ assignments to the variables in the first half of the ordering that must lead to distinct vertices in the OBDD. That is, the OBDD must encode information about each split face for the variables in the first half of the ordering so that it can correctly deduce the function value given the variables in the last half of the ordering.

Corollary 1. *For any set of relational variables $\mathcal{E}$ such that $\mathcal{E}_{n \times n} \subseteq \mathcal{E}$, any OBDD representation of $F_{trans}(\mathcal{E})$ must contain $\Omega(2^{n/8})$ vertices.*

The extra edges in $\mathcal{E}$ introduce complications, because they create cycles containing edges from different faces. As a result, the lower bound is weaker, because our proof requires that we find a set of vertex-independent, split faces.

Our lower bounds are fairly weak, but this is more a reflection of the difficulty of proving lower bounds. We have found in practice that the OBDD representations of the transitivity constraint functions arising from benchmarks tend to be large relative to those encountered during the evaluation of F_{sat}. For example, although the OBDD representation of $F_{trans}(\mathcal{E}^+)$ for benchmark 1×DLX-Ct is just 2,692 nodes (a function over 42 variables), we have been unable to construct the OBDD representations of this function for either 2×DLX-CAt (178 variables) or 2×DLX-CCt (193 variables) despite running for over 24 hours.

5.2 Enumerating and Eliminating Violations

Goel et al. [GSZAS98] proposed a method that generates implicants (cubes) of the function F_{sat} from its OBDD representation. Each implicant is examined and discarded if it violates a transitivity constraint. In our experiments, we have found this approach works well for the normal, correctly-designed pipelines (i.e., circuits 1×DLX-C, 2×DLX-CA, and 2×DLX-CC) since the formula F_{sat} is unsatisfiable and hence has no implicants. For all 100 of our buggy circuits, the first implicant generated contained no transitivity violation, and hence we did not require additional effort to find a counterexample.

For circuits that do require enforcing transitivity constraints, we have found this approach impractical. For example, in verifying 1×DLX-Ct by this means, we generated 253,216 implicants, requiring a total of 35 seconds of CPU time (vs. 0.1 seconds for 1×DLX-C). For benchmarks 2×DLX-CAt and 2×DLX-CCt, our program ran for over 24 hours without having generated all of the implicants. By contrast, circuits 2×DLX-CA and 2×DLX-CC can be verified in 11 and 29 seconds, respectively. Our implementation could be improved by making sure that we generate only primes that are irredundant and prime. In general, however, we believe that a verifier that generates individual implicants will not be very robust. The complex control logic for a pipeline can lead to formulas F_{sat} containing very large numbers of implicants, even when transitivity plays only a minor role in the correctness of the design.

5.3 Enforcing a Reduced Set of Transitivity Constraints

Circuit		Verts.	Direct			Dense			Sparse		
			Edges	Cycles	Clauses	Edges	Cycles	Clauses	Edges	Cycles	Clauses
1×DLX-Ct		9	18	14	45	36	84	252	20	19	57
2×DLX-CAt		17	44	101	395	136	680	2,040	49	57	171
2×DLX-CCt		17	46	108	417	136	680	2,040	52	66	198
Reduced	min.	3	2	0	0	3	1	3	2	0	0
Buggy	avg.	12	17	19	75	73	303	910	21	14	42
2×DLX-CC	max.	19	52	378	1,512	171	969	2,907	68	140	420

Table 4. Graphs for Reduced Transitivity Constraints. Results are given for the three different methods of encoding transitivity constraints based on the variables in the true support of F_{sat}.

One advantage of OBDDs over other representations of Boolean functions is that we can readily determine the *true support* of the function, i.e., the set of variables on which the function depends. This leads to a strategy of computing an OBDD representation of F_{sat} and intersecting its support with $\mathcal{E}$ to give a set $\hat{\mathcal{E}}$ of relational variables that could potentially lead to transitivity violations. We then augment these variables to make the graph chordal, yielding a set of variables $\hat{\mathcal{E}}^+$ and generate an OBDD representation of $F_{trans}(\hat{\mathcal{E}}^+)$. We compute $F_{sat} \wedge F_{trans}(\hat{\mathcal{E}}^+)$ and, if it is satisfiable, generate a counterexample.

Table 4 shows the complexity of the graphs generated by this method for our benchmark circuits. Comparing these with the full graphs shown in Table 2, we see that we typically reduce the number of relational vertices (i.e., edges) by a factor of 3 for the benchmarks modified to require transitivity and by an even greater factor for the buggy circuit benchmarks. The resulting graphs are also very sparse. For example, we can see that both the direct and sparse methods of encoding transitivity constraints greatly outperform the dense method.

Circuit		F_{sat}	$F_{trans}(\hat{\mathcal{E}}^+)$	$F_{sat} \wedge F_{trans}(\hat{\mathcal{E}}^+)$	CPU Secs.
1×DLX-C		1	1	1	0.2
1×DLX-Ct		530	344	1	2
2×DLX-CA		1	1	1	11
2×DLX-CAt		22,491	10,656	1	109
2×DLX-CC		1	1	1	29
2×DLX-CCt		17,079	7,168	1	441
Reduced	min.	20	1	20	7
Buggy	avg.	3,173	1,483	25,057	107
2×DLX-CC	max.	15,784	93,937	438,870	2,466

Table 5. OBDD-based Verification. Transitivity constraints were generated for a reduced set of variables $\hat{\mathcal{E}}$.

Table 5 shows the complexity of applying the OBDD-based method to all of our benchmarks. The original circuits 1×DLX-C, 2×DLX-CA, and 2×DLX-CC yielded formulas F_{sat} that were unsatisfiable, and hence no transitivity constraints were required. The 3 modified circuits 1×DLX-Ct, 2×DLX-CAt, and 2×DLX-CCt are more interesting. The reduction in the number of relational variables makes it feasible to generate an OBDD representation of the transitivity constraints. Compared to benchmarks 1×DLX-C, 2×DLX-CA, and 2×DLX-CC, we see there is a significant, although tolerable, increase in the computational requirement to verify the modified circuits. This can be attributed to both the more complex control logic and to the need to apply the transitivity constraints.

For the 100 buggy variants of 2×DLX-CC, F_{sat} depends on up to 52 relational variables, with an average of 17. This yielded OBDDs for $F_{trans}(\hat{\mathcal{E}}^+)$ ranging up to 93,937 nodes, with an average of 1,483. The OBDDs for $F_{trans}(\hat{\mathcal{E}}^+) \wedge F_{sat}$ ranged up to 438,870 nodes (average 25,057), showing that adding transitivity constraints does significantly increase the complexity of the OBDD representation. However, this is just one OBDD at the end of a sequence of OBDD operations. In the worst case, imposing transitivity constraints increased the total CPU time by a factor of 2, but on average it only increased by 2%. The memory required to generate F_{sat} ranged from 9.8 to 50.9 MB (average 15.5), but even in the worst case the total memory requirement increased by only 2%.

6 Conclusion

By formulating a graphical interpretation of the relational variables, we have shown that we can generate a set of clauses expressing the transitivity constraints that exploits the sparse structure of the relation. Adding relational variables to make the graph chordal eliminates the theoretical possibility of there being an exponential number of clauses and also works well in practice. A conventional SAT checker can then solve constrained satisfiability problems, although the run times increase significantly compared to unconstrained satisfiability. Our best results were obtained using OBDDs. By considering only the relational variables in the true support of F_{sat}, we can enforce transitivity constraints with only a small increase in CPU time.

References

[Bry86]   R. E. Bryant, "Graph-based algorithms for Boolean function manipulation", *IEEE Transactions on Computers*, Vol. C-35, No. 8 (August, 1986), pp. 677–691.

[BGV99a] R. E. Bryant, S. German, and M. N. Velev, "Exploiting positive equality in a logic of equality with uninterpreted functions," *Computer-Aided Verification (CAV '99)*, N. Halbwachs, and D. Peled *eds.*, LNCS 1633, Springer-Verlag, July, 1999, pp. 470–482.

[BGV99b] R. E. Bryant, S. German, and M. N. Velev, "Processor verification using efficient reductions of the logic of uninterpreted functions to propositional logic," Technical report CMU-CS-99-115, Carnegie Mellon University, 1999. Available as: http://www.cs.cmu.edu/~bryant/pubdir/cmu-cs-99-115.ps.

[BV00]   R. E. Bryant, and M. N. Velev, "Boolean satisfiability with transitivity constraints," Technical report CMU-CS-00-101, Carnegie Mellon University, 2000. Available as:
          http://www.cs.cmu.edu/~bryant/pubdir/cmu-cs-00-101.ps.

[BD94]   J. R. Burch, and D. L. Dill, "Automated verification of pipelined microprocessor control," *Computer-Aided Verification (CAV '94)*, D. L. Dill, *ed.*, LNCS 818, Springer-Verlag, June, 1994, pp. 68–80.

[Bur96]   J. R. Burch, "Techniques for verifying superscalar microprocessors," *33rd Design Automation Conference (DAC '96)*, June, 1996, pp. 552–557.

[GSZAS98] A. Goel, K. Sajid, H. Zhou, A. Aziz, and V. Singhal, "BDD based procedures for a theory of equality with uninterpreted functions," *Computer-Aided Verification (CAV '98)*, A. J. Hu and M. Y. Vardi, *eds.*, LNCS 1427, Springer-Verlag, June, 1998, pp. 244–255.

[HP96]   J. L. Hennessy, and D. A. Patterson, *Computer Architecture: A Quantitative Approach*, 2nd edition Morgan-Kaufmann, San Francisco, 1996.

[Lei92]   F. T. Leighton, *Introduction to Parallel Algorithms and Architectures: Arrays, Trees, and Hypercubes*, Morgan Kaufmann, 1992.

[MS99] J. P. Marques-Silva, and K. A. Sakallah, "GRASP: A search algorithm for propositional satisfiability," *IEEE Transactions on Computers*, Vol. 48, No. 5 (May, 1999), pp. 506–521.

[M99] J. P. Marques-Silva, "The impact of branching heuristics in propositional satisfiability algorithms," *9th Portugese Conference on Artificial Intelligence*, September, 1999.

[Rose70] D. Rose, "Triangulated graphs and the elimination process," *Journal of Mathematical Analysis and Applications*, Vol. 32 (1970), pp. 597–609.

[VB99] M. N. Velev, and R. E. Bryant, "Superscalar processor verification using efficient reductions of the logic of equality with uninterpreted functions," *Correct Hardware Design and Verification Methods (CHARME '99)*, L. Pierre, and T. Kropf, eds., LNCS 1703, Springer-Verlag, September, 1999, pp. 37–53.

[Yan81] M. Yannakakis, "Computing the minimum fill-in is NP-complete," *SIAM Journal of Algebraic and Discrete Mathematics*, Vol. 2 (1981), pp. 77–79.

Bounded Model Construction for Monadic Second-Order Logics

Abdelwaheb Ayari and David Basin

Institut für Informatik, Albert-Ludwigs-Universität Freiburg, Germany.
www.informatik.uni-freiburg.de/~{ayari|basin}

Abstract. The monadic logics M2L-STR and WS1S have been successfully used for verification, although they are nonelementary decidable. Motivated by ideas from bounded model checking, we investigate procedures for bounded model construction for these logics. The problem is, given a formula ϕ and a bound k, does there exist a word model for ϕ of length k. We give a bounded model construction algorithm for M2L-STR that runs in a time exponential in k. For WS1S, we prove a negative result: bounded model construction is as hard as validity checking, *i.e.*, it is nonelementary. From this, negative results for other monadic logics, such as S1S, follow. We present too preliminary tests using a SAT-based implementation of bounded model construction; for certain problem classes it can find counter-examples substantially faster than automata-based decision procedures.

1 Introduction

The monadic logics M2L-STR, WS1S, and S1S are among the most expressive decidable logics known. The logic M2L-STR [11] is a logic on finite words and also appears in the literature (with slight variations) under the names MSO[S] [20] and SOM[+1] [19]. In the early 1960's, Büchi and Elgot gave decision procedures for these logics by exploiting the fact that models can be encoded as words and that the language of models satisfying a formula can be represented by an automaton [5,6,9]. These decision procedures provide nonelementary upper-bounds for these logics, which are also the lower-bounds [16].

Despite their atrocious complexity, the decision procedures for M2L-STR and WS1S have been implemented in numerous tools, *e.g.*, MONA [14], MOSEL [18], MOSEL [12], and the STEP system [15], and have been successfully applied to problems in diverse domains including hardware [2] and protocol [11] verification. Not surprisingly though, many large systems cannot be verified due to state explosion. This is analogous to state explosion in model checking where the state-space is exponential in the number of state variables, except for monadic logics the states in the constructed automaton can be nonelementary in the size of the input formula! For LTL model checking, a way of finessing this problem has recently been proposed: *bounded model checking* [4]. The idea is that one can finitely represent counter-examples (using the idea of a loop, see §4.3), and, by bounding the size of these representations, satisfiability checkers can be used to search for them. This often succeeds in cases where symbolic model checking fails.

Motivated by the bounded model checking approach and the goal of quick generation of counter-examples for falsifiable formulae, we investigate an analogous problem for monadic logics. Namely, given a formula ϕ and a natural number k, determine if ϕ has a word model of length k. Since we are concerned with *constructing* models for formulae, as opposed to *checking* their satisfiability with respect to a given model, we call our problem *bounded model construction* or BMC for short.

We show that for M2L-STR, given a formula ϕ and a natural number k, we can generate a formula in quantified Boolean logic that is satisfiable if and only if ϕ has a word model of length k. The formula generated is polynomial in the size of ϕ and k and can be tested for satisfiability in polynomial space. For generating length k counter-models, this yields a nonelementary improvement over the automata-based decision procedure for M2L-STR. Moreover, we show that the use of SAT-based techniques can have acceptable running times in practice.

We also investigate bounded model construction for other monadic logics and establish negative results. For WS1S we show that BMC is as hard as checking validity, which is nonelementary. This result is somewhat surprising since WS1S has the same expressiveness and complexity as M2L-STR and their decision procedures differ only slightly. Indeed, there has been a recent investigation of the differences of these logics by Klarlund who concluded that WS1S is preferable to M2L-STR due to its simpler semantics and its wider applicability to arithmetic problems [13]. Our results suggests that the issue is not so clear cut and depends on whether error detection through counter-example generation versus full verification is desired, that is, whether one is interested in finding a single model for a formula or computing a description of all models. We also formulate BMC for S1S and several first-order monadic logics and establish similar negative results.

We proceed as follows. In §2 we briefly review quantified Boolean logic and finite automata on words. In §3 we describe the syntax and semantics of M2L-STR and WS1S and their relationship to finite automata. In §4 we present the bounded model construction approach and complexity results. In §5 we present experimental results and in §6 we draw conclusion.

2 Background

Boolean Logic Boolean formulae are built from the constants true and false, variables $x \in \mathcal{V}$, and are closed under the standard connectives. The formulae are interpreted in $\mathbb{B} = \{0, 1\}$. A (Boolean) *substitution* $\sigma : \mathcal{V} \to \mathbb{B}$ is a mapping from variables to truth values that is extended homomorphically to formulae. We say σ *satisfies* ϕ if $\sigma(\phi) = 1$.

Quantified Boolean logic (QBL) extends Boolean logic (BL) by allowing quantification over Boolean variables, *i.e.*, $\forall x. \phi$ and $\exists x. \phi$. A substitution σ

satisfies $\forall x.\,\phi$ if σ satisfies $\phi[\text{true}/x] \wedge \phi[\text{false}/x]$ and dually for $\exists x.\,\phi$. In the remainder of the paper, we write $\sigma \models_{\text{QBL}} \phi$ to denote that σ satisfies ϕ.

QBL is not more expressive than BL, but it is more succinct. The satisfiability problem for Boolean logic is *NP-complete* [8], whereas it is *PSPACE-complete* for QBL [17].

Automata on Words Let Σ denote a finite alphabet. Σ^* (respectively Σ^ω) denotes the set of finite (respectively infinite) words over Σ. A finite automaton $\mathcal{A}$ over Σ is a tuple (S, s_0, Δ, F) where S is a nonempty finite set of states, $s_0 \in S$ is the initial state, $\Delta \subseteq S \times \Sigma \times S$ is a transition relation, and $F \subseteq S$ is a set of final states. A run of $\mathcal{A}$ on a finite word $w = a_1 a_2 \ldots a_n$ (respectively, an infinite word $w = a_1 a_2 \ldots$) is a finite sequences of states $s_0 s_1 \ldots s_n$ (respectively, an infinite sequence of states $s_0 s_1 \ldots$) with $(s_i, a_i, s_{i+1}) \in \Delta$. A finite word is accepted by an automaton if it has a run whose last state is final. To accept infinite words, finite automata are equipped with a *Büchi acceptance condition*, which says that an infinite word is accepted if it has a run in which some final state occurs infinitely often. We will often use the alphabet $\mathbb{B}^n$, with $n \in \mathbb{N}$. Note that $\mathbb{B}^0$ stands for the singleton set $\{()\}$, *i.e.*, the set whose only member is the degenerate tuple "()".

3 Monadic Second-Order Logics on Finite Words

In this section we provide background material on M2L-STR and WS1S. These logics have the same syntax but slightly different semantics. We also explain their relationship to regular languages.

Let $\mathcal{V}_1 = \{x_i \mid i \in \mathbb{N}\}$ be a set of first-order variables and $\mathcal{V}_2 = \{X_i \mid i \in \mathbb{N}\}$ be a set of second-order variables. We will use $n, p, q, \ldots$ as meta-variables ranging over $\mathcal{V}_1$ and we use $X, Y, \ldots$ as meta-variables ranging over $\mathcal{V}_2$.

3.1 Language

Monadic second order (MSO) formulae are formulae in a language of second-order arithmetic specified by the grammar:

$$t ::= 0 \mid p, \qquad\qquad\qquad\qquad p \in \mathcal{V}_1$$
$$\phi ::= \mathsf{s}(t,t) \mid X(t) \mid \neg\phi \mid \phi \vee \phi \mid \exists p.\,\phi \mid \exists X.\,\phi, \qquad p \in \mathcal{V}_1 \text{ and } X \in \mathcal{V}_2$$

Hence terms are built from the constant 0 and first-order variables. Formulae are built from predicates $\mathsf{s}(t,t')$ and $X(t)$ and are closed under disjunction, negation, and quantification over first-order and second-order variables. Other connectives and quantifiers can be defined using standard classical equivalences, *e.g.*, $\forall X.\,\phi \stackrel{def}{=} \neg \exists X.\,\neg \phi$. In other presentations, s is usually a function. We have specified it as a relation for reasons that will become apparent when we give the semantics. In the remainder of this section, formula means MSO-formula.

3.2 Semantics

For X a set, by $\mathcal{F}(X)$ we denote the set of finite subsets of X. A (MSO) substitution σ is a pair of mappings $\sigma = (\sigma_1, \sigma_2)$, with $\sigma_1 : \mathcal{V}_1 \to \mathbb{N}$ and $\sigma_2 : \mathcal{V}_2 \to \mathcal{F}(\mathbb{N})$ and for $x \in \mathcal{V}_1$, $\sigma(x) = \sigma_1(x)$ and for $X \in \mathcal{V}_2$, $\sigma(X) = \sigma_2(X)$. With this in hand, we can now define satisfiability for M2L-STR and WS1S.

The Logic M2L-STR Formulae in M2L-STR are interpreted relative to a natural number $k \in \mathbb{N}$. We will write $[k]$ for the set $\{0, \ldots, k-1\}$ and we call the elements of $[k]$ *positions*. First-order variables are interpreted as positions. The constant 0 denotes the natural number 0 and the symbol s is interpreted as the relation $\{(i,j) \mid j = i+1 \text{ and } i, j \in [k]\}$. Note that $k-1$ has no successor. Second-order variables denote subsets of $[k]$ and the formula $X(t)$ is true when the position denoted by t is in the set denoted by X.

More formally, the semantics of a formula ϕ is defined inductively relative to a substitution σ and a $k \in \mathbb{N}$. In the following, we write σ^k for the pair (σ, k).

Definition 1 *Satisfiability for* M2L-STR

$\sigma^k \models_{M2L} \mathsf{s}(t, t')$, if $\sigma(t') = 1 + \sigma(t)$ and $\sigma(t') \in [k]$
$\sigma^k \models_{M2L} X(t)$, if $\sigma(t) \in \sigma(X)$
$\sigma^k \models_{M2L} \neg \phi$, if $\sigma^k \not\models_{M2L} \phi$
$\sigma^k \models_{M2L} \phi_1 \vee \phi_2$, if $\sigma^k \models_{M2L} \phi_1$ or $\sigma^k \models_{M2L} \phi_2$
$\sigma^k \models_{M2L} \exists p. \phi$, if $(\sigma[i/p])^k \models_{M2L} \phi$, for some $i \in [k]$
$\sigma^k \models_{M2L} \exists X. \phi$, if $(\sigma[M/X])^k \models_{M2L} \phi$, for some $M \subseteq [k]$

If $\sigma^k \models_{M2L} \phi$, we say that σ^k *satisfies*, or is a *model* of, ϕ. We call a formula ϕ *valid*, and we write $\models_{M2L} \phi$, if for every natural number k and substitution σ, σ^k satisfies ϕ.

The Logic WS1S Whereas M2L-STR can be seen as a logic on bounded sets of positions or, as we shall see, finite words, WS1S is best viewed as a logic based on arithmetic. First-order variables range over $\mathbb{N}$ and are not a priori bounded by any natural number. Second-order variables range over finite subsets of the natural numbers, $\mathcal{F}(\mathbb{N})$, and are not restricted to subsets of some $[k]$. Finally, the symbol s is interpreted as the successor relation over $\mathbb{N}$. Formally, we define satisfiability in WS1S, $\sigma \models_{WS1S} \phi$, as follows:

Definition 2 *Satisfiability for* WS1S

$\sigma \models_{WS1S} \mathsf{s}(t, t')$, if $\sigma(t') = 1 + \sigma(t)$
$\sigma \models_{WS1S} X(t)$, if $\sigma(t) \in \sigma(X)$
$\sigma \models_{WS1S} \neg \phi$, if $\sigma \not\models_{WS1S} \phi$
$\sigma \models_{WS1S} \phi_1 \vee \phi_2$, if $\sigma \models_{WS1S} \phi_1$ or $\sigma \models_{WS1S} \phi_2$
$\sigma \models_{WS1S} \exists p. \phi$, if $\sigma[i/p] \models_{WS1S} \phi$, for some $i \in \mathbb{N}$
$\sigma \models_{WS1S} \exists X. \phi$, if $\sigma[M/X] \models_{WS1S} \phi$, for some $M \in \mathcal{F}(\mathbb{N})$

A formula is *valid* in WS1S if it is satisfied by every substitution σ.

Word Models Models in both M2L-STR and WS1S can be encoded as finite words. Let $\phi(\overline{X})$ be a formula, where $\overline{X}$ is the tuple of second-order variables $X_1, \ldots, X_n$ occurring free in ϕ.[1] We encode a M2L-STR model σ^k for ϕ by the word $w_{\sigma^k} \in (\mathbb{B}^n)^k$, such that the length of w_{σ^k} is k and for every position $i \in [k]$, $w_{\sigma^k}(i) = (b_1, \ldots, b_n)$ and for $1 \leq j \leq n$, $b_j = 1$ iff $i \in \sigma(X_j)$. We call w_{σ^k} a *word model* for ϕ and define $\mathcal{L}_{\mathrm{M2L}}(\phi)$ as the set of all M2L-STR word models for ϕ. We shall also write $w \models_{\mathrm{M2L}} \phi$ for $\sigma^k \models_{\mathrm{M2L}} \phi$, where w encodes σ^k.

Similarly, a WS1S model σ for ϕ can be encoded as a finite word w_σ such that $w_\sigma(i) = (b_1, \ldots, b_n)$ where $b_j = 1$ iff $i \in \sigma(X_j)$. We also call w_σ a *word model* for ϕ in WS1S. We define $\mathcal{L}_{\mathrm{WS1S}}(\phi)$ as the set of WS1S word models for ϕ. Note that the encoding of M2L-STR models as words is a bijection, whereas this is not the case for WS1S. In particular, if σ is a WS1S model and w_σ encodes it, then any finite word of the form $w_\sigma aa \cdots a$, where a is $(0, \ldots, 0) \in \mathbb{B}^n$, also encodes σ. We shall also write $w \models_{\mathrm{WS1S}} \phi$ for $\sigma \models_{\mathrm{WS1S}} \phi$, where w encodes σ.

Example Consider the formula $\phi \stackrel{\mathrm{def}}{=} X(0) \wedge \forall p.\, X(p) \leftrightarrow (\exists q.\, \mathsf{s}(p,q) \wedge Y(q))$ and the substitution σ with $\sigma(X) = \{0, 2\}$ and $\sigma(Y) = \{0, 1, 3\}$. σ^4 is a model for ϕ in M2L-STR and σ is a model for ϕ in WS1S. The words w and w' below encode σ^4 and σ, respectively.

w	0	1	2	3
X	1	0	1	0
Y	1	1	0	1

w'	0	1	2	3	4	5
X	1	0	1	0	0	0
Y	1	1	0	1	0	0

As a second example, the formula $\exists X.\, \forall p.\, X(p)$ is valid in M2L-STR, whereas it is unsatisfiable in WS1S.

Connection to Regular Languages We have seen that monadic formulae define sets of word models. Büchi and Elgot proved in [5,9] that the languages formalized by formulae in WS1S and M2L-STR are regular and, conversely, that every regular language is both WS1S and M2L-STR-definable. To show regularity, they proved constructively that, given a formula ϕ, there exists an automaton A_ϕ that accepts all WS1S (respectively, M2L-STR) word models for ϕ. This construction yields a decision procedure: a closed formula is valid in WS1S (respectively, in M2L-STR) iff its corresponding automaton accepts the language $()^*$. This decision procedure (and indeed any decision procedure for these logics) is nonelementary [16,21]: the minimal automaton representing a formula of size n may require space whose lower bound is a stack of exponentials of height n.

As noted previously, in WS1S any word model over $\Sigma = \mathbb{B}^n$ can be suffixed by arbitrarily many $(0, \ldots, 0) \in \mathbb{B}^n$ and the result is again a word model. Hence we explain in which sense regular languages are definable in both monadic logics, as this is not completely straightforward. Let $\Sigma = \{a_1, \ldots, a_n\}$ and let $\theta : \mathbb{B}^n \to$

---

[1] First-order variables can be encoded using second-order variables as we will show in §4.1.

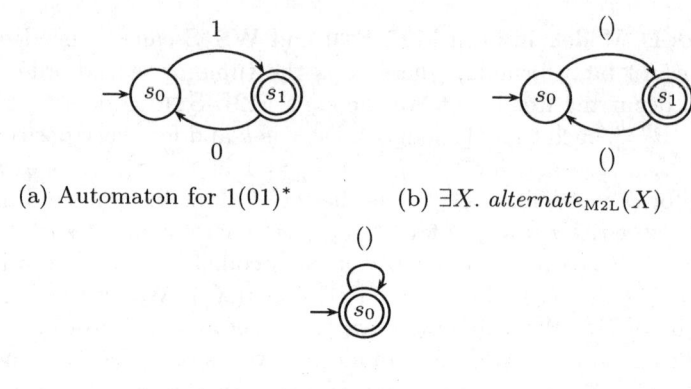

Fig. 1. Automata for Example

Σ be the substitution defined by $\theta(b_1, \ldots, b_n) = a_i$, where $b_j = 1$ iff $j = i$, and let $\sim$ be the congruence relation over $(\mathbb{B}^n)^*$ defined by $u \sim v$ iff $u = x.(0, \ldots, 0)^i$ and $v = x.(0, \ldots, 0)^j$ with $x \in (\mathbb{B}^n)^*$ and $i, j \in \mathbb{N}$. We straightforwardly extend θ to words over $(\mathbb{B}^n)^*$, sets of words, $\sim$-classes, and sets of $\sim$-classes. Now, for a regular language $L \subseteq \Sigma^*$, we can construct formulae $\phi(X_1, \ldots, X_n)$ and $\psi(X_1, \ldots, X_n)$ such that for M2L-STR we have $L = \theta(\mathcal{L}_{\text{M2L}}(\phi(\overline{X})))$ and for WS1S we have $L = \theta(\mathcal{L}_{\text{WS1S}}(\psi(\overline{X}))/\sim)$.

Example Consider the automaton $\mathcal{A}$ depicted in Figure 1(a) that accepts the language $1(01)^* = \{1, 101, 10101, \ldots\}$. This language is defined by the formula[2]

$$\text{alternate}_{\text{M2L}}(X) \stackrel{\text{def}}{=} \exists n. \neg\exists p. \mathsf{s}(n,p) \wedge \tag{1}$$
$$X(0) \wedge X(n) \wedge \tag{2}$$
$$\forall p.\ p < n \rightarrow \exists q.\ \mathsf{s}(p,q) \wedge (X(q) \leftrightarrow \neg X(p)) \tag{3}$$

interpreted in M2L-STR. (1) formalizes that n denotes (the last position) k of Definition 1. (2) states that the first and last positions are in X, and, by (3), the positions in X alternate. Observe that if we existentially quantify the variable X in $\text{alternate}_{\text{M2L}}(X)$, then we obtain a closed formula that is neither valid nor unsatisfiable; its corresponding automaton, given in Figure 1(b), is the same as $\mathcal{A}$ except its transitions are labeled with $() \in \mathbb{B}^0$.

For WS1S we can define the same language with the formula

$$\text{alternate}_{\text{WS1S}}(X) \stackrel{\text{def}}{=} \exists n.\ (\forall p.\ n < p \rightarrow \neg X(p)) \wedge (2) \wedge (3)\ .$$

The only difference is that to state that n is the last position we require that X contains no positions greater than n. The language $\mathcal{L}_{\text{WS1S}}(\text{alternate}_{\text{WS1S}}(X))$

---
[2] The less-than relation $<$ is definable in M2L-STR, WS1S, and S1S (introduced in §4.3).

is $1(01)^*0^*$ and $\mathcal{L}_{\text{ws1s}}(\psi(\overline{X}))/\sim$ is $1(01)^*$. In contrast to M2L-STR, if we existentially quantify the variable X in $alternate_{\text{ws1s}}(X)$, then we obtain a valid formula and its automaton is depicted in Figure 1(c).

4 Bounded Model Construction

In this section we present bounded model construction, which can generate counter-examples for non-theorems nonelementary faster than its automata-theoretic counterpart. We show this for M2L-STR and give negative results, showing the impossibility of such procedures, for other monadic logics.

The problem we analyze is how to generate counter-examples of a given size and do this quickly (elementary!) with respect to the size parameter. We express this in the format of a parameterized complexity problem (cf. [1]). For L either M2L-STR or WS1S, we define:

Definition 3
Bounded Model Construction for L *(*BMC(L)*)*
INSTANCE: *A formula ϕ and a natural number k.*
PARAMETER: *k.*
QUESTION: *Does ϕ have a satisfying word model of length k with respect to* L*? (That is, is there a word w of length k with $w \models_L \phi$?)*

4.1 Bounded Model Construction for M2L-STR

We proceed by defining a family of functions $(\lceil \cdot \rceil_k)_{k \in \mathbb{N}}$ that transforms MSO-formulae into quantified Boolean formulae such that there is word model of length k for ϕ iff $\lceil \phi \rceil_k$ is satisfiable. The size of the resulting formula is polynomial in the size of ϕ and k.

To simplify matters, we reduce MSO to a minimal kernel, called MSO_0, which is as expressive as MSO. The language MSO_0 has the grammar:

$$\phi ::= \text{Succ}(X, Y) \mid X \subseteq Y \mid \neg \phi \mid \phi \vee \phi \mid \exists X.\, \phi, \qquad X, Y \in \mathcal{V}_2 \,.$$

$\text{Succ}(X, Y)$ means that X and Y are singletons $\{p\}$ and $\{q\}$, where $q = p + 1$. The symbol $\subseteq$ denotes the subset relation. Note that first-order variables are omitted and can be encoded as singletons. There is a simple polynomial time translation from MSO formulae into MSO_0 [20].

Translation to QBL Let $k \in \mathbb{N}$ be fixed. We now describe how to calculate the QBL formula $\lceil \phi \rceil_k$ for a MSO_0-formula ϕ. The idea is simple: a set $M \subseteq [k]$ can be represented by k Boolean variables $x_0, \ldots, x_{k-1}$ such that $x_i = 1$ iff $i \in M$. Building on this, we encode relations between finite sets and formulae over these relations.

Let $\mathcal{V}_0 = \{x_j^i \mid i, j \in \mathbb{N}\}$ be a set of Boolean variables and singleton be the proposition

$$\text{singleton}(x_0, \ldots, x_{k-1}) \stackrel{def}{=} \bigvee_{0 \le i \le k-1} (x_i \wedge \bigwedge_{\substack{0 \le j \le k-1 \\ j \ne i}} \neg x_j).$$

The mapping $\lceil . \rceil_k$ is inductively defined as follows:

Definition 4 (Translation)

$\lceil X_m \subseteq X_n \rceil_k = \bigwedge_{0 \le i \le k-1} (x_i^m \to x_i^n)$

$\lceil \text{Succ}(X_m, X_n) \rceil_k = \text{singleton}(x_0^m, \ldots, x_{k-1}^m) \wedge \text{singleton}(x_0^n, \ldots, x_{k-1}^n) \wedge$

$\qquad \bigvee_{0 \le i < k-1} (x_i^m \to x_{i+1}^n)$

$\lceil \phi_1 \vee \phi_2 \rceil_k = \lceil \phi_1 \rceil_k \vee \lceil \phi_2 \rceil_k$

$\lceil \neg \phi \rceil_k = \neg \lceil \phi \rceil_k$

$\lceil \exists X_m . \phi \rceil_k = \exists x_0^m, \ldots, x_{k-1}^m . \lceil \phi \rceil_k$

Definition 5 *For a substitution* $\sigma : \mathcal{V}_2 \to \mathcal{F}(\mathbb{N})$, *we define the Boolean substitution* $\widehat{\sigma} : \mathcal{V}_0 \to \mathbb{B}$, *by* $\widehat{\sigma}(x_i^m) = 1$ *iff* $i \in \sigma(X_m)$.

Lemma 1 *Let σ be a substitution and $k \in \mathbb{N}$. Then $\sigma^k \models_{M2L} \phi$ iff $\widehat{\sigma} \models_{QBL} \lceil \phi \rceil_k$.*

Proof. By induction on the construction of ϕ.

We first establish the claim for atomic formulae. To begin with, $\sigma^k \models_{M2L} X_m \subseteq X_n$ iff for all i, $0 \le i \le k-1$, $i \in \sigma(X_m)$ implies that $i \in \sigma(X_n)$, which is equivalent to $\widehat{\sigma} \models_{QBL} \bigwedge_{0 \le i \le k-1} x_i^m \to x_i^n$. Similarly, if $\sigma^k \models_{M2L} \text{Succ}(X_m, X_n)$, then $\sigma(X_m)$ and $\sigma(X_n)$ are singletons. Moreover, $\sigma(X_m)$ contains a natural number p, with $0 \le p < k-1$, whose successor $p+1$ is in $\sigma(X_n)$. Hence there is some i, where $0 \le i < k-1$, such that $\widehat{\sigma} \models_{QBL} x_i^m \to x_{i+1}^n$, so $\widehat{\sigma} \models_{QBL} \bigvee_{0 \le i < k-1} x_i^m \to x_{i+1}^n$; the converse is argued similarly.

In the inductive step we consider only the case where ϕ is of the form $\exists X_m . \psi$ as the remaining cases are straightforward. By Definition 1, $\sigma^k \models_{M2L} \exists X_m . \psi$ iff there is some set $M \subseteq [k]$ such that $(\sigma[M/X_m])^k \models_{M2L} \psi$. From the induction hypothesis, $(\sigma[M/X_m])^k \models_{M2L} \psi$ iff $\widehat{\delta} \models_{QBL} \lceil \psi \rceil_k$, where $\delta = \sigma[M/X_m]$. Note that $\widehat{\delta} = \widehat{\sigma}[b_0/x_0^m, \ldots, b_{k-1}/x_{k-1}^m]$, where $b_i = 1$ iff $i \in M$, for $0 \le i \le k-1$. Further, $\widehat{\delta} \models_{QBL} \lceil \psi \rceil_k$ iff $\widehat{\sigma} \models_{QBL} \exists x_0^m, \ldots, x_{k-1}^m . \lceil \psi \rceil_k$. Thus $\sigma^k \models_{M2L} \exists X_m . \psi$ iff $\widehat{\sigma} \models_{QBL} \exists x_0^m, \ldots, x_{k-1}^m . \lceil \psi \rceil_k$. □

Observe that given a Boolean substitution τ, it is trivial to define a MSO substitution σ where $\widehat{\sigma} = \tau$, namely by stipulating that $\sigma(X_i) = \{j \mid \tau(x_j^i) = 1\}$. Hence, from the above Lemma we can conclude:

Theorem 1 (Correctness) *Let ϕ be a MSO formula. For $k \in \mathbb{N}$, there exists a MSO substitution σ where $\sigma^k \models_{M2L} \phi$ iff there exists a Boolean substitution τ where $\tau \models_{QBL} \lceil \phi \rceil_k$. Moreover, ϕ is valid in M2L-STR iff for all $k \ge 0$, the QBL formula $\lceil \phi \rceil_k$ is valid.*

We define the size of a formula (in any of the logics we consider) as the number of symbols occurring in its string representation. Exploiting the fact that satisfiability for QBL is PSPACE complete, we prove:

Theorem 2 (Complexity) *BMC(M2L-STR) is PSPACE-complete.*

Proof. Let ϕ and k be a problem instance. The size of $\lceil\phi\rceil_k$ is $O(k^2|\phi|)$. It follows that BMC(M2L-STR) can be reduced in polynomial time to satisfiability in QBL, which establishes membership in PSPACE.

To prove PSPACE-hardness, we show that satisfiability for QBL can be reduced in log-space to BMC(M2L-STR). Let E be a fresh second-order variable and empty be the M2L-STR proposition defined by $\mathsf{empty}(X) \stackrel{def}{=} \forall Y. X \subseteq Y$. We encode each Boolean variable x with a M2L-STR variable X. For a QBL formula ϕ, let $\widetilde{\phi}$ be the M2L-STR formula obtained from ϕ as follows: replace occurrences of Boolean variables x by $X \subseteq E$, and replace the Boolean quantifiers as well as the propositional connectives by the corresponding quantifiers and connectives of M2L-STR. Now, the encoding of ϕ in M2L-STR is the formula $\exists E. \mathsf{empty}(E) \wedge \widetilde{\phi}$. For example, the QBL formula $\forall x\, \exists y.\, x \vee y$ is encoded as $\exists E.\, \mathsf{empty}(E) \wedge \forall X.\, \exists Y.\, X \subseteq E \vee Y \subseteq E$. Under this encoding it is only relevant whether or not a second-order variable is interpreted by the empty set. We immediately conclude that a QBL formula is satisfiable iff its encoding has a word model of length 1. □

4.2 Bounded Model Construction for WS1S

The previously given translation cannot be employed for WS1S. If ϕ is the formula $\exists X_m. \forall X_n. X_n \subseteq X_m$, the translation yields the quantified Boolean formula $\exists x_0^m, \ldots, x_{k-1}^m. \forall x_0^n, \ldots, x_{k-1}^n. \bigwedge_{0 \leq i \leq k-1} x_i^n \rightarrow x_i^m$, which is valid for every k, whereas ϕ is unsatisfiable in WS1S. We now prove that there is no translation that will yield an elementary bounded model construction procedure.

Theorem 3 *BMC(WS1S) is nonelementary.*

Proof. For a closed formula ϕ, $\sigma \models_{\text{WS1S}} \phi$ iff $\sigma' \models_{\text{WS1S}} \phi$ for all substitutions σ and σ', i.e., the satisfiability of a closed formula does not depend on the substitution. Hence, every closed WS1S formula is either valid or unsatisfiable. Equivalently, for ϕ be a closed formula, either $\mathcal{L}_{\text{WS1S}}(\phi) = ()^*$ or $\mathcal{L}_{\text{WS1S}}(\phi) = \emptyset$. Consequently, if a closed formula ϕ has a word model, then $\mathcal{L}_{\text{WS1S}}(\phi) = ()^*$ and therefore ϕ is valid. In other words, computing a word model of any length for ϕ is equivalent to checking ϕ's validity. □

This proof can be easily adapted for other monadic logics. For example, WFO[<] is the first-order fragment of WS1S augmented by the relation <. Meyer showed in [16] that this logic is nonelementary; this result, combined with the above argument, shows that bounded model construction for this logic (BMC(WFO[<])) is also nonelementary.

The reader may wonder what causes these differences. We can gain some insight by comparing semantics. From the semantics of M2L-STR, $\phi(X)$ has a word model of length k iff $\exists X. \phi(X)$ has a word model of length k. This semantic property was employed in the proof of Lemma 1, where in order to use the induction hypothesis we require that the witness set M is a subset of $[k]$. Unfortunately, this property fails for WS1S. As can be seen in Figure 1, existential quantification can change the size of the minimal word model in WS1S. A more dramatic example is the family of formulae (written here with sugared syntax) $\phi_n(X) \stackrel{def}{=} X(n)$, for $n \in \mathbb{N}$. The minimal length word model for $\phi_n(X)$ is n, whereas it is 0 for $\exists X. \phi_n(X)$. In general, to determine if a formula has a small, e.g., length 0, word model, we must consider word models for their subformulae that are non-elementary larger in the worst case.

4.3 Bounded Model Construction for S1S

Here we consider monadic logics over *infinite* words. We start with the logic S1S, which is closely related to WS1S and differs only by allowing infinite subsets of $\mathbb{N}$ as interpretations for second-order variables. A substitution in S1S can be encoded as an infinite word and Büchi showed in [6] that S1S exactly captures the ω-regular languages. In doing so, he provided an effective nonelementary transformation of S1S formulae into *Büchi automata*.

Here we prove a negative result analogous to the previous one: there is no elementary BMC procedure for S1S. This problem must first be properly defined, since bounded model construction is defined above for finite words, and here there are only infinite word models.

We begin with some basic definitions and results for ω-regular languages [20]. From the definition of Büchi acceptance, every nonempty ω-regular language contains an infinite word $w \stackrel{def}{=} uvv\ldots$, for u and v finite words in Σ^*. If uv is of length k, we say the word w *contains* (or *is*) *a lasso of length* k, consisting of a *prefix* u and a *loop* v. Consequently, a S1S formula ϕ is satisfiable iff it has a satisfying word model that is a lasso of length k, for some $k \in \mathbb{N}$.

Using the fact that lassos can be finitely represented, we define an analog of BMC for S1S.

Definition 6
Bounded Model Construction for S1S *(BMC(S1S))*
INSTANCE: *A formula ϕ and a natural number k.*
PARAMETER: *k.*
QUESTION: *Does ϕ have a satisfying lasso of length k in* S1S?

We now prove that no elementary BMC procedure for S1S exists.

Theorem 4 BMC(S1S) *is nonelementary.*

Proof. Our proof uses an embedding of WS1S in S1S. For this, we first show that finiteness is definable in S1S. Let finite and Finite be the following two propositions:

$$\mathsf{finite}(X) \stackrel{def}{=} \exists m.\,\forall p.\, X(p) \to p \leq m \text{ and } \mathsf{Finite}(\phi) \stackrel{def}{=} \bigwedge_{X \in freevars(\phi)} \mathsf{finite}(X).$$

We define an embedding function $[\cdot]$ from WS1S into S1S by $[\phi] = \mathsf{Finite}(\phi) \wedge \lceil \phi \rceil$, where $\lceil \phi \rceil$ is:

$\lceil s(t,t') \rceil = s(t,t') \qquad \lceil X(t) \rceil = X(t) \qquad \lceil \exists p.\,\phi \rceil = \exists p.\,\lceil \phi \rceil$

$\lceil \neg \phi \rceil = \neg \lceil \phi \rceil \qquad \lceil \phi_1 \vee \phi_2 \rceil = \lceil \phi_1 \rceil \vee \lceil \phi_2 \rceil \qquad \lceil \exists X.\,\phi \rceil = \exists X.\,\mathsf{finite}(X) \wedge \lceil \phi \rceil$

We can show by induction over the structure of formulae that $[\cdot]$ preserves satisfiability. Namely, a formula ϕ has a word model of length k in WS1S iff $[\phi]$ has a satisfying lasso of length k in S1S.

The function that assigns to each BMC(WS1S)-instance (ϕ, k) the BMC(S1S)-instance $([\phi], k)$ reduces, in polynomial time, BMC(WS1S) to BMC(S1S). Using Theorem 3, the claim follows. □

Again, we can apply the same proof idea to other monadic logics. Let FO[<] be the first-order fragment of S1S augmented by the less relation <. A similar proof establishes that bounded model construction for FO[<], *i.e.*, BMC(FO[<]), is nonelementary by reducing BMC(WFO[<]) to BMC(FO[<]).

5 Experimental Results

We have implemented bounded model construction for M2L-STR and describe here experimental results. Our system takes as input a natural number and a formula written in a "sugared" version of the syntax of §3.1. It first calculates from the inputs a QBL formula as described in §4.1. Second, it transforms the QBL formula into Boolean logic by eliminating the universal quantifiers (replacing $\forall x.\,\phi$ with $\phi[\text{true}/x] \wedge \phi[\text{false}/x]$) and dropping the remaining existential quantifiers (assuming all bound variables are uniquely named). Third, the resulting Boolean formula is converted into conjunctive normal form. Finally, the result is tested for satisfiability using the SATO system [23], which is an efficient implementation of the Davis-Putnam procedure. Of course, with minor changes other satisfiability checkers could be used.

We used the MONA system [14] for comparison. MONA is an automata-based implementation of decision procedures for the monadic logics M2L-STR, WS1S and their generalizations to trees. MONA compiles a formula into a minimal deterministic automaton, which it represents and manipulates using BDD's. Over the last few years MONA has been continually improved and is now highly optimized (we use version 1.4). For our tests, we used a 450 MHZ Sun Sparc Ultra workstation.

For completeness, we tested examples ranging from those that are easy for MONA to those that are difficult. Table 1 presents tests on several easy examples. In all of these, we find counter-examples (of the same length as MONA's) when they exist. However, for these examples, MONA is much faster.

The first example is a parameterized *n-bit ripple-carry adder*, taken from [2]. The input formula states the equivalence between a structural description of the parameterized adder family (described at the gate level) with a behavioral description, describing how bit-strings are added. We checked this equivalence for $k = 2$, 4, and 6. The second example involves a structural specification of a sequential *D-type flip-flop* circuit, and its behavioral model. The circuit is built from 6 *nand*-gates, each of which has a (unit) time-delay. We tested the correctness of this circuit with respect to a behavioral description proposed by Gordon in [10]. As has been discovered by [2,22], the specification has a subtle bug. Both MONA and our system find a (different) counter-example of length 8. The third example is a buggy mutual exclusion protocol taken from [3]; both systems successfully find a trace showing that the critical sections can be simultaneously accessed.

Next we consider some examples that are difficult for MONA. First, we consider reasoning about two concurrent processes that increment a shared integer variable N by each executing the program: `Load Reg N`, `Add Reg 1`, `Store Reg N`. If we assume an interleaving semantics, it is possible that N is incremented by either 1 or 2. We model the two parallel processes in M2L-STR and assert (incorrectly) that after execution N is incremented by 1. Table 4 gives the results, where we scale the problem by considering registers of different bit-width. For more than 4 bits, MONA runs out of memory as the automata accepting the computations (traces) of the two systems grow exponentially.

Finally, we consider two sequential circuits: a counter and a barrel shifter, which we parameterize in the width of the data-path. Tables 3 and 2 give the results of these experiments for data-paths of various widths. In the first example, the n-bit counter has two selection lines and n data lines. At each point in time the value of the data lines is incremented, reset or unchanged depending on the value of the selection lines. We verify this with respect to an incorrect specification, which asserts that, after eight time units, the data line is always incremented. In our experiments, MONA quickly runs into state explosion problems, whereas even for large data-paths, we can still generate counter-examples quickly. Our procedure finds that, for data-paths between 4 and 40, the short counter-examples have length $k = 8$. The results for the barrel shifter are similar.

6 Conclusion and Future Work

We have explored the possibility of providing more efficient alternatives to counter-example generation than using standard automata-theoretic decision procedures. We have obtained positive results, both in theory and practice, for

Examples	MONA sec	BMC k sec
Ripple-carry adder	0.06	1 0.05
		4 0.30
		6 8.85
Buggy ripple-carry adder	0.11	5 0.82
FlipFlop	0.19	7 0.23
Buggy mutual exclusion	0.20	6 0.58

Table 1. Simple Examples

	MONA		BMC ($k=6$)	
bit	sec	MB	sec	MB
1	0.05	0	0.04	0
4	0.07	0	0.12	0
8	1.00	11	0.39	0
16	abort		1.79	11
32	-		10.00	53

Table 2. Barrel Shifter

	MONA		BMC ($k=8$)	
bit	sec	MB	sec	MB
4	0.15	0	0.16	0
8	0.90	0	0.49	11
12	23.65	67	0.85	22
15	242.17	734	1.25	33
16	abort		1.39	38
24	-		3.14	88
32	-		6.36	167
40	-		11.00	284

Table 3. Counter

$N \leq 2^i$	MONA	BMC ($k=6$)
i	sec	sec
2	0.60	0.49
3	5.48	0.85
4	57.18	1.60
5	abort	3.60
6	-	9.16
7	-	30.85
8	-	105.45

Table 4. Parallel Instruction

M2L-STR, and negative results for WS1S, S1S, WFO[<], and FO[<]. Hence, at least for counter-example generation, M2L-STR is the superior choice.

The theoretical issues seem clear-cut. On the experimental side there is still work to do. In our experiments, most of the time is spent translating QBL formulae into Boolean logic formulae and the resulting normal form calculation. Recent work on testing satisfiability for QBL [7] could offer improvements here; investigating this remains as future work.

References

[1] K. R. Abrahamson, J. A. Ellis, M. R. Fellows, and M. E. Mata. On the complexity of fixed parameter problems (extended abstract). In *30th Annual Symposium on Foundations of Computer Science*. IEEE, 1989.

[2] D. Basin and N. Klarlund. Automata based symbolic reasoning in hardware verification. *The Journal of Formal Methods in Systems Design*, 13(3), November 1998.

[3] M. Ben-Ari. *Principles of Concurrent and Distributed Programming*. Prentice Hall, 1990.

[4] A. Biere, A. Cimatti, E. Clarke, and Y. Zhu. Symbolic model checking without BDDs. In *TACAS'99*, volume 1579 of *LNCS*. Springer, 1999.

[5] J. R. Büchi. Weak second-order arithmetic and finite automata. *Zeitschrift für mathematische Logik und Grundlagen der Mathematik*, 6, 1960.

[6] J. R. Büchi. On a decision method in restricted second-order arithmetic. In *Proc. 1960 Int. Congr. for Logic, Methodology, and Philosophy of Science*. Stanford Univ. Press, 1962.
[7] H. K. Büning, M. Karpinski, and A. Flögel. Resolution for quantified Boolean formulas. *Information and Computation*, 117(1), 1995.
[8] S. A. Cook. The complexity of theorem-proving procedures. In *Third Annual ACM Symposium on Theory of Computing*, pages 151–158, Shaker Heights, Ohio, 3–5 1971 1971.
[9] C. C. Elgot. Decision problems of finite automata design and related arithmetics. *Transactions of the AMS*, 98, 1961.
[10] M. J. Gordon. Why higher-order logic is a good formalism for specifying and verifying hardware. In G. J. Milne and P. A. Subrahmanyam, editors, *Formal Aspects of VLSI Design*. North-Holland, 1986.
[11] J. G. Henriksen, J. Jensen, M. Jørgensen, N. Klarlund, B. Paige, T. Rauhe, and A. Sandholm. Mona: Monadic second-order logic in practice. In *TACAS '95*, volume 1019 of *LNCS*, 1996.
[12] P. Kelb, T. Margaria, M. Mendler, and C. Gsottberger. Mosel: A sound and efficient tool for M2L(Str). In *CAV'97*, volume 1254 of *LNCS*. Springer–Verlag, 1997.
[13] N. Klarlund. A theory of restrictions for logics and automata. In *CAV '99*, volume 1633 of *LNCS*. Springer, 1999.
[14] N. Klarlund and A. Møller. *MONA Version 1.3 User Manual*. BRICS Notes Series NS-98-3 (second revision), Department of Computer Science, University of Aarhus, 1998.
[15] Z. Manna, N. Bjoerner, A. Browne, and E. Chang. STeP: The Stanford Temporal Prover. In *TAPSOFT'95: Theory and Practice of Software Development*, volume 915, 1995.
[16] A. Meyer. Weak monadic second-order theory of successor is not elementary-recursive. In *LOGCOLLOQ: Logic Colloquium*, volume 453. Springer–Verlag, 1975.
[17] A. R. Meyer and L. J. Stockmeyer. Word problems requiring exponential time. In *ACM Symposium on Theory of Computing*, pages 1–9, New York, April 1973. ACM Press.
[18] F. Morawietz and T. Cornell. On the recognizability of relations over a tree definable in a monadic second order tree description language. Research Report SFB 340-Report 85, Sonderforschungsbereich 340 of the Deutsche Forschungsgemeinschaft, 1997.
[19] H. Straubing. *Finite automata, formal logic, and circuit complexity*. Birkhäuser, 1994.
[20] W. Thomas. Automata on infinite objects. In J. van Leeuwen, editor, *Handbook of Theoretical Computer Science*, chapter 4. Elsevier Science Publishers B. V., 1990.
[21] W. Thomas. Languages, automata and logic. In A. Salomaa and G. Rozenberg, editors, *Handbook of Formal Languages*, volume 3, Beyond Words. Springer-Verlag, Berlin, 1997.
[22] A. Wilk and A. Pnueli. Specification and verification of VLSI systems. In *IEEE/ACM International Conference on Computer-Aided Design*, 1989.
[23] H. Zhang. SATO: An efficient propositional prover. In *CADE'97*, volume 1249 of *LNAI*. Springer, 1997.

Building Circuits from Relations

James H. Kukula[1] and Thomas R. Shiple[2]

[1] Synopsys, Inc., Beaverton, OR. kukula@synopsys.com
[2] Synopsys, Inc., Mountain View, CA. shiple@synopsys.com

Abstract. Given a Free BDD for the characteristic function of an input-output relation $T(x, y)$, we show how to construct a combinational logic circuit satisfying that relation. Such relations occur as environmental constraints for module specifications, as parts of a proof strategies, or can be computed from existing circuits, e.g., by formal analysis of combinational cycles. The resulting circuit C can be used for further analysis, e.g. symbolic simulation, or to reformat a circuit as a logic optimization tactic.

The constructed circuit includes supplementary parametric inputs to allow all legal outputs to be generated in the case that T is non-deterministic. The structure of the circuit is isomorphic to that of the BDD for T, and hence is as compact as the BDD. In particular, when T represents a relation between bit vector integer values definable in Presburger arithmetic, the constructed circuit will have a regular bit slice form.

1 Introduction

A general Boolean relation $T(x, y)$ admits multiple interpretations and representations arising in various contexts. We consider the case when the x variables are considered to be inputs presented to some system component, and y are output variables that the system component generates, subject to the constraint that the given x and the generated y must satisfy the T relation. The problem we address is to construct a combinational circuit satisfying the input-output relation represented by a Free Binary Decision Diagram (FBDD). Since an FBDD is a generalization of the more common Ordered BDD (OBDD), such a construction will also work for OBDDs.

The primary context we consider is that of a verification constraint or precondition. In this case, the input variables x encode the state of some module under verification, and the output variables y provide the input stimulus to that module. The set of stimuli to be presented to the module, in general or for a particular verification task, may depend on the current state of the module. For example, Yuan et al. [19] describe a verification methodology where a module's environment is specified as a constraint which can depend on the state of the module. Jain and Gopalakrishnan's methodology [12] also includes "action" constraints which depend on the system state. These constraints are used as a verification tactic rather than a specification of the module's environment. Aagaard et al. [1] also use tactical constraints, but their constraints do not depend on the state of the module and thus are a special case of the more general one we consider.

Input-output relations may arise in other contexts. For example, such a relation may be derived from a combinational logic circuit, summarizing the behavior of the circuit.

In such a case the input-output relation will be complete (for each x at least one y exists that satisfies T) and deterministic (for each x at most one y exists that satisfies T). One can also analyze the context of a subcircuit to construct a nondeterministic input-output relation for the allowable behaviors of the subcircuit which will preserve the overall behavior of the containing complete circuit [18]. Another use of input-output relations is in the analysis of cyclic circuits built of combinational gates. Such circuits may reliably settle their output values to a deterministic function of their inputs despite their cyclic topology. The constructivity analyses of Shiple [17] and Namjoshi et al. [15] generate Boolean relations (output bit by output bit in Shiple's analysis) that represent the combinational function of cyclic circuits, along with checking whether those cyclic circuits are indeed not state holding.

Input-output relations are also used as a means to express the intended function of a machine being designed in high level languages such as SMV [14]. One advantage of using relations for design is the natural representation of non-determinism.

A Boolean relation $T(x, y)$ may be represented in various ways. A OBDD [8] can be used to represent the characteristic function of the relation. A generalization of the OBDD representation is the FBDD [9], where variables may occur in different orders on different paths from root to terminal. Both FBDDs and OBDDs are constrained so that variables occur at most once on any path. The added flexibility of FBDDs permits a much more compact representation for some relations.

Another possible representation is as a multiple output combinational logic circuit with inputs x and outputs y. If the relation T is complete and deterministic then the required values of the outputs are well defined, and can be expressed as the positive cofactors of the bitwise characteristic functions:

$$(\exists_{j \neq i} y_j . T(x, y))|_{y_i}$$

In the general case, a given value of x might be related to multiple y values or to none. One can supplement a circuit with two additional features to allow it to accurately represent a general input-output relation $T(x, y)$. To handle incompleteness, one can add an extra output $v(x) = \exists y . T(x, y)$ to the circuit, indicating whether any y exists that is related to a given input x. To handle non-determinism one can add extra parametric inputs p to the circuit, so that for every output value y that satisfies $T(x, y)$ for a given input x, there is some value of p such that the circuit will generate y when applied to the inputs (x, p).

A multiple output combinational logic circuit provides a broadly applicable represention for T. As Jain and Gopalakrishnan [12], Aagaard et al. [1], and Bertacco et al. [3] point out, symbolic simulation is a powerful technique for exploring the behavior of a circuit. Symbolic simulation can be directly applied to the combinational circuit representation of T. Other state exploration engines such as those based on SAT [4] or ATPG [5] generally accept combinational logic circuits as a problem representation. Logic emulation hardware is another state exploration mechanism for which a combinational logic circuit is an ideal problem representation.

When T represents a constraint on the inputs to some module under verification, the outputs of the circuit we construct for T would be connnected to the inputs of the module, and the composite circuit submitted to state exploration. While the circuit we construct does not reduce the number of input variables compared to the unconstrained circuit, the constraints on the inputs can prevent false error reports that could have occurred if improper input stimuli were allowed to propagate into the module [19]. The constraints may also improve the efficiency of state exploration techniques such as symbolic simulation by reducing BDD sizes [1].

A combinational logic circuit also provides a structure for implementation in digital hardware. In this case, the relation to be implemented should be complete, so the v output should be constant 1 and can be ignored. An implementation will also generally be deterministic. If the input-output relation to be implemented is non-deterministic, the supplementary inputs p in the non-deterministic circuit representation can be connected to arbitrary constants or variable signals to form a deterministic circuit.

Our contribution is an elegant translation procedure that constructs a combinational logic circuit, with inputs x and p and outputs y and v, from a general input-output relation $T(x, y)$ represented as the Free BDD of its characteristic function. The size of the circuit is proportional to the number of nodes in the Free BDD. When the input-output relation is non-deterministic, the supplementary parametric inputs p are used to index all the output y values related to a given input x.

In the remainder of this paper, we will first discuss the details of the construction procedure. We will then demonstrate that the circuit constructed does effectively represent the input-output relation. Next we address the compactness of the circuit. Finally we review related work and conclude.

2 Circuit Construction Procedure

Given an FBDD for an input-output relation $T(x, y)$, we construct a circuit implementing T that has the same top level topology as the FBDD. First we describe the high level structure and signal flow of the circuit. We will then discuss the internal details of each of the modules that compose the circuit.

2.1 High Level Signal Flow

For every node in the BDD for T there is an instantiation of a basic module. The basic modules come in two types, corresponding to the two classes of variables that occur in the BDD. There is an input module that is used in place of BDD nodes labeled by input variables, and an output module used in place of nodes labeled by output variables. The connections between modules are created to match the edges between the corresponding BDD nodes.

We describe the construction process in terms of an example. Suppose we are given the BDD shown in Figure 1. The circuit shown in Figure 2 provides a combinational logic representation for that relation. The inputs to the circuit are at the bottom of the figure, with two main input variables x_1 and x_2, and two supplementary parametric inputs p_1 and p_2. There are many possible ways to parameterize or encode the y in terms of a set of parameters p. In our encoding we use one parameter input bit for each output bit. The outputs are at the top of the figure, with the two main outputs y_1 and y_2 and the supplementary output v.

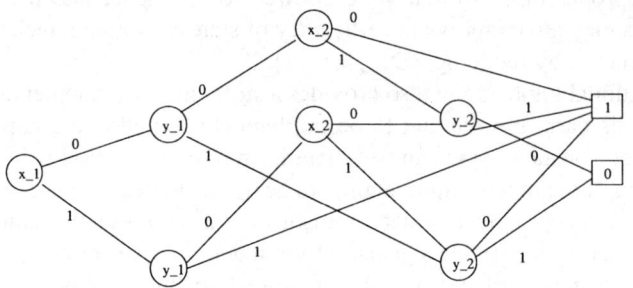

Fig. 1. Binary Decision Diagram Representing Input-Output Relation

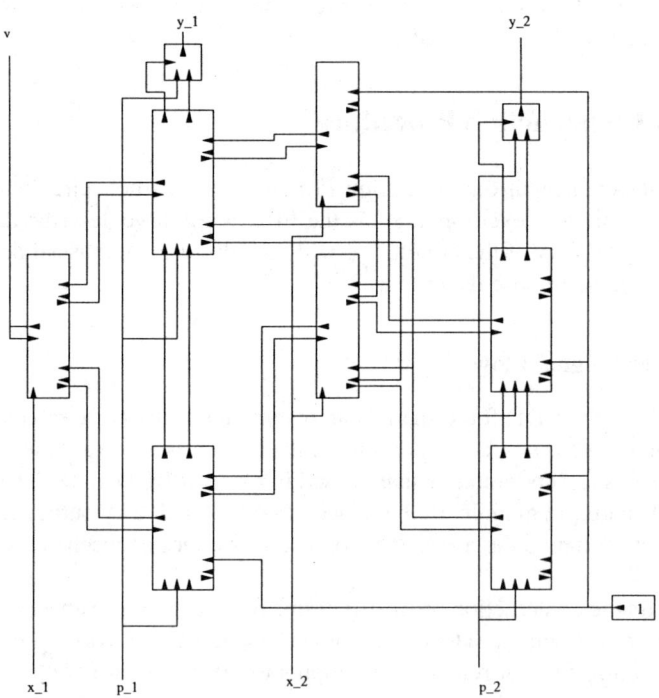

Fig. 2. Circuit Implementing Relation. Disconnected inputs are to be driven by constant 0.

Just as there are seven nodes in the BDD, there are seven major modules in the circuit. In this top level diagram, each connection point on the modules is marked with an arrow to indicate the direction of signal flow. Disconnected inputs are driven by logic value 0. Each edge in the BDD corresponds to two wires in the circuit, one that flows from terminal to root and one that flows from root to terminal.

The overall logic flow in the circuit can be broken into three phases. The first phase flows from the terminal nodes to the root node, the second from the root node back to the terminal nodes, and the third phase across all the nodes labelled by the same variable.

In the first phase, constant 0 and 1 values corresponding to the terminal nodes start to flow toward the root, combining with the circuit inputs x along the way. This terminal-to-root flow results in the v signal which is the auxiliary circuit output, indicating whether any valid circuit outputs are possible for the particular values being presented at the inputs x. In this first phase, each node will receive signals from the modules corresponding to the destination nodes of its two outgoing edges, indicating whether those two nodes have any path to the 1 terminal consistent with the presented values of the primary circuit inputs.

In the second phase, signals propagate from the root to the terminals to activate a single path from root to terminal. This path is steered by the primary circuit inputs and also by the auxiliary inputs. Each node receives a signal that indicates whether any of its incoming edges are active. If an incoming edge is active, then the current node is active and must choose which outgoing edge to activate. If the node is labeled by an input variable, then the node is constrained to choose as directed by the value of that variable. If the node is labeled by an output variable, then the node will choose as directed by the corresponding auxiliary input variable if possible. During the first phase of signal propagation the node received signals from the two destination nodes which indicated which of them had possible paths to the 1 terminal. The node can then use these signal values to be sure to choose a valid value for the primary circuit output signal, one that can form part of an unbroken path from the root of the BDD to the 1 terminal.

In the third phase, the value of the circuit outputs y are computed, based on the activated path. If the activated path includes a node labelled by a particular output bit y_i, then the edge of that node followed by the path will fix the value of the output bit. If the activated path does not include y_i, then the value of the corresponding parametric input p_i is used. The modules substituted for the nodes labelled by a single output variable y_i are connected together in a serial chain. There are two logic signals propagated along this chain. The order of the nodes in the chain is arbitrary. This chain gathers information to compute the value of y_i. For each output variable we also include a single multiplexor to handle the case where the activated path does not include a node labelled by that variable. So in this circuit there are two multiplexors, shown near the top of Figure 2, corresponding to the two output variables y_1 and y_2. If the BDD for an input-output relation doesn't include any nodes at all for a particular output variable, then the value of that output variable is not constrained by the inputs, and can simply be copied directly from the corresponding supplementary parameter variable. In this case no multiplexor is needed.

Another implementation detail arises in handling multiple edges leading to the same destination node. In the circuit we build, this is translated, in part, to a collection of signals whose disjunction drives the module corresponding to the destination node. We implement this here with a chain of OR gates, one in each of the modules corresponding to the sources of the edges which all have the same destination node.

2.2 Input Module

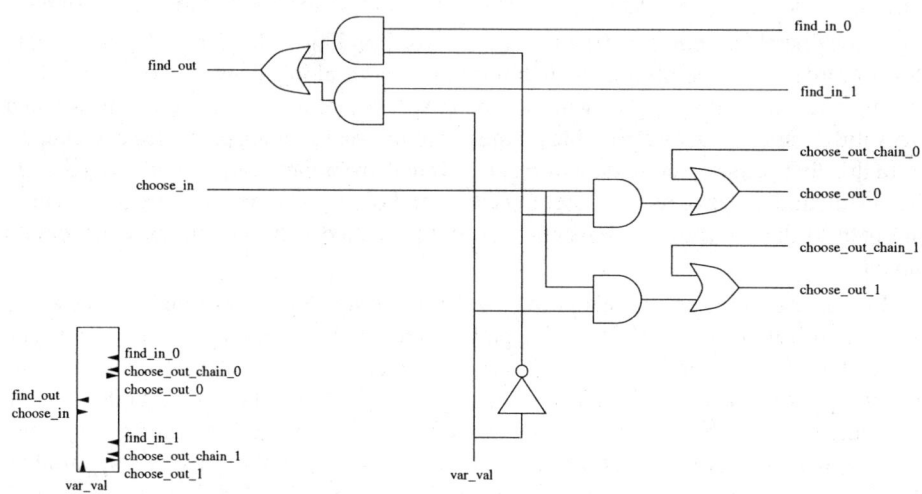

Fig. 3. Module for Input Node

Figure 3 shows the internal details of the module to be substituted for each BDD node labelled with a circuit primary input x_i. The upper part of the circuit is a multiplexor whose data inputs are the signals from the two outgoing edge destination modules. The multiplexor control is the signal x_i. If there is a compatible path to the 1 terminal along the edge labeled by the present value of x_i, then there is a compatible path from this node to the 1 terminal.

The lower part of the circuit steers the active path in the second phase. If this node is marked as active by one of its incoming edges, then it activates one of its destination nodes as chosen by the value of x_i. The OR gates at the outputs work with the other nodes that have edges to the same destination, so that if any of these source nodes activate their edges to that destination, then the activation will reach that node.

2.3 Output Module

Figure 4 shows the module to substitute for a BDD node labelled by a primary output variable y_i. Again the upper part is for the first phase of propagation and the lower part for the second phase. In the first phase the circuit computes the paths through the BDD allowed by the current values of the inputs x before the output values are picked. There is a path to the 1 terminal through this output node compatible with the x inputs if there

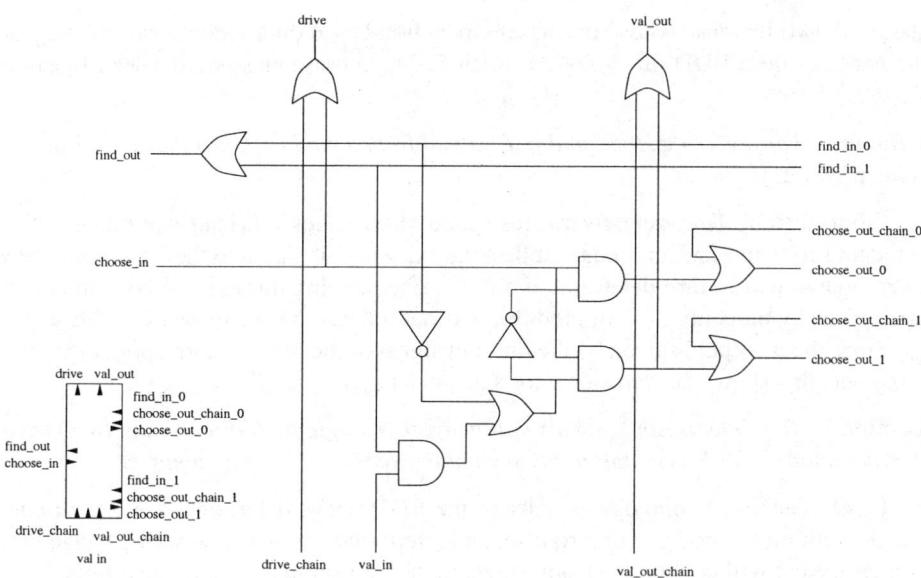

Fig. 4. Module for Output Node

is a path from either of its destination nodes. So a simple OR gate is enough for the first phase.

In the second phase, if an incoming edge to the module is activated then it must choose an outgoing edge to activate. The val_in signal to the module is driven in the top level circuit by the parametric input p_i. If both outgoing edges indicate the existence of paths to the 1 terminal, then the edge suggested by p_i will be activated. If only one edge has a path to the 1 terminal, then that edge will be activated and the p_i value is ignored.

The value for y_i will be computed in the third phase of computation in the circuit. The OR gate at the top right of the diagram works together with all the other nodes labeled by y_i. If any of these nodes has been activated and has chosen the 1 value, then the output should be driven to 1. Otherwise the 0 value should be chosen.

The OR gate at the top left accumulates a value for y_i indicating whether any of the BDD nodes labelled by y_i were activated. This value is then fed to the multiplexor which chooses the final value for y_i. If a node was activated, then the value determined by that node and passed along through the value chain should be chosen. If no node was chosen, this indicates that an edge was activated that skipped over the y_i. In this case its value is unconstrained by the present values of the x inputs, and the value of p_i should be chosen.

3 Circuit Correctness

Let $T_C(\boldsymbol{x}, \boldsymbol{p}, \boldsymbol{y}, v)$ denote the input-output relation of the circuit constructed from the Boolean relation $T(\boldsymbol{x}, \boldsymbol{y})$. In this section we prove that T_C correctly implements T. We start with two lemmas, whose proofs use induction based on a topological ordering of the nodes of the FBDD. Each node n in an FBDD represents some Boolean function $f_n(x, y)$.

Lemma 1. *For a given x, the "find_out" signal from a module n has the value 1 iff, for some y, $f_n(x, y) = 1$.*

Proof (sketch): This is clearly true for a node whose edges both lead to terminal nodes. If the find_in_0 and find_in_1 edges reflect the existence of a path to the 1 terminal, then each module will in turn determine if a path exists flowing through the corresponding node. Thus by induction, for all modules find_out reflects the existence of a path. ∎

Since the v output is given by the find_out signal of the module corresponding to the root node, this shows the value of v for a given x is $\exists y.T(x, y)$.

Lemma 2. *The "choose_in" signals will activate a single path through the BDD from the root node to the 1 terminal, if any such path exists for the given input x.*

Proof (sketch): A topological order of the BDD nodes determines a series of cuts which partition the nodes into a root set and a terminal set, where any BDD edge that crosses the cut will be directed from a node in the root set to a node in the terminal set. We can prove inductively that the number of activated edges crossing any cut is exactly 1 if $\exists y.T(x, y)$, and 0 otherwise. The induction starts with the base case of the cut with all the BDD nodes on the terminal side, where the root edge coming into the root node is activated just in case $\exists y.T(x, y)$ is true. Now we assume that the i'th cut has a single activated edge crossing it, and show that the $i+1$'th cut will also be crossed by a single activated edge. Each node will activate a single outgoing edge if the incoming edge is activated, or neither outgoing edge if the incoming edge is not activated. Thus each node n preserves the number of activated edges crossing the cuts just before and after n. ∎

With these basic properties of the circuit established, we can now prove the correctness of T_C.

Theorem 1. *The input-output relation $T_C(x, p, y, v)$ for the circuit built from the relation $T(x, y)$ satifies:*

$$T(x, y) \Rightarrow T_C(x, y, y, 1)$$
$$T_C(x, p, y, 1) \Rightarrow T(x, y)$$

Proof (sketch): Since any path from root to terminal includes at most one node labelled by any given output variable y_i, then the third phase will propagate to the output y_i the value computed corresponding to the outgoing edge from that node (or the corresponding p_i if no such node is included). Thus

$$T_C(x, p, y, 1) \Rightarrow T(x, y)$$

Since each output module attempts to steer the path to follow the choices suggested by the parametric input p, the path activated will drive the outputs to p if $T(x, y)$ holds. This together with the value of v shows that

$$T(x, y) \Rightarrow T_C(x, y, y, 1)$$

∎

4 Circuit Compactness

Since the circuit constructed by this technique has the same high level topology as the BDD of the input-output relation, its size is proportional to the BDD. The circuit generated is not at all locally optimal. There are many constant inputs to modules, such as the constants corresponding to the BDD terminal nodes and the starting points of the various node chains. There are also disconnected outputs of modules, principally at the last edges of the second pass root-to-terminal propagation, since the activation signal does not have to be propagated to the terminal nodes. These constants and disconnected outputs provide straightforward opportunities for simple local logic optimization, but other more sophisticated techniques could also be applied. As long as the input-output relation's BDD is reasonably compact, the circuit we construct should provide an efficient high level structure and a good starting point for such low level optimization, which could be followed by mapping to a specific technology if the circuit is to be manufactured as digital hardware.

In order to generate a more efficient circuit, before converting the BDD to a circuit one could apply exact [11] or approximate [16] variable reordering techniques to attempt to reduce the size of the BDD. Since the circuit construction procedure we provide here also applies to the Free BDD representation of an input-output relation, one could further reduce the size of the circuit by exploiting the freedom to use different variable orderings on different branches of the diagram [10].

Kukula et al. [13] observe that a relation between radix-encoded integers definable in Presburger arithmetic will have a compact, regularly-structured OBDD so long as the variable ordering interleaves the bits in the order of the encoding weights. In this case the circuit constructed will have a bit slice form, a linear array of repeated instances of a single module. Such a circuit is not only efficient in terms of gate count but also lends itself to an efficient physical layout.

5 Related Work

Brown [7] discusses parametric general solutions for Boolean equations. His method of successive elimination will give the same parametric functions as implemented by the circuit we construct in the special case of an OBDD. Brown's methods deal with general Boolean functions rather than specific circuit implementations or BDD representations, and in particular he does not address the issue of circuit size.

Our construction technique is most closely related to the stimulus generation algorithm of Yuan et al. [19] and the parametric constraint representation of Aagaard et al. [1]. Yuan et al. present an algorithm which generates random stimuli satisfying a constraint, represented as a BDD, which may depend on state variables of the design. Our circuit has a flow very similar to their algorithm. The main differences between their work and ours are that our technique constructs a compact circuit rather than generating a single stimulus instance, and the output value selection of our circuit is controlled by parametric inputs, rather than weighted random numbers as in Yuan et al. The circuit constructed by our technique can be used by a wide variety of downstream tools such as SAT or symbolic simulation.

Aagaard et al. present an algorithm which generates a vector of OBDDs over a set of parametric input variables; the combinations of values of these BDDs span the space of stimulus values which satisfy some constraint. The constraints they deal with do not involve any dependence on state variables in the design, and hence their technique is limited to unary relations. In contrast, we work with the more general problem of binary relations. Another difference is that their algorithm generates a parametric result in the form of OBDDs. Some relations will not admit a tractable parametric representation as a vector of OBDDs. Since we map directly from a Free BDD representation of the input-output relation to a circuit, our technique can be used with a broader range of relations.

Other related work includes synthesis of multiplexor circuits from BDDs [2]. In that work, a multi-rooted BDD defines the vector of output functions to be implemented. Our technique differs, working instead with the input-output relation and also in working with incomplete and/or non-deterministic functions. Synthesis from the input-output relation can result in circuits considerably more compact than those built from the multi-rooted functional BDD used in multiplexor synthesis. Consider the arithmetic function $\max(a, b + c)$, where a, b, and c are n-bit vectors representing integers in the usual radix-2 encoding. Each output bit of this function can be represented by a BDD with size bound $O(n)$, by using an interleaved variable ordering. With n output bits to be represented, the total shared size of the multi-rooted BDD will be quadratic in n unless there is significant node sharing across the multiple outputs. But there is a conflict between the variable orders required by the max and addition functions if nodes are to be shared. With the low-order bits ordered at the top, the max function will give a compact multi-rooted BDD representation, since the high-order bit nodes at the bottom of the BDD can be shared by all the low order nodes. However, efficient multi-rooted representation of addition requires the low order bits at the bottom to be shared by all the high order nodes. Whichever order is chosen, one function or the other will fail to share the nodes at the bottom of the BDD. Thus the entire multi-rooted BDD will end up being quadratic in the bit-width. In contrast to this, the circuit constructed by our technique will grow only linearly with the bit-width since the input-output relation is definable in Presburger arithmetic.

6 Conclusion

We have presented a simple and direct mapping from a Free BDD representing an input-output relation $T(x, y)$ to a compact combinational circuit. This mapping supports both incomplete and non-deterministic relations by means of a supplementary output signal and a set of supplementary parametric inputs. The combinational circuit provides a flexible representation which can be used for verification or synthesis.

The usefulness of the OBDD representation has led to a variety of extensions. We have presented our circuit construction technique in terms of the more general Free BDD representation. Another common extension is to add various attributes to the BDD edges, for example complementation [6]. Edge complementation can reduce BDD size by up to a factor of two. It is quite possible to construct a circuit directly from a BDD with complemented edges, but the modules required grow by about a factor of two, so there doesn't appear to be any advantage. Our next steps in this research will be to investigate other extensions to OBDDs to see which of them can support effective circuit construction techniques.

References

[1] M. Aagaard, R. Jones, and C.-J. Seger. Formal Verification Using Parametric Representation of Boolean Constraints. In *Proc. of the Design Automation Conf.*, pages 402–407, June 1999.
[2] P. Ashar, S. Devadas, and K. Keutzer. Gate-delay-fault Testability Properties of Multiplexor-Based Networks. *Formal Methods in System Design*, 1:93–112, Feb. 1993.
[3] V. Bertacco, M. Damiani, and S. Quer. Cycle-based Symbolic Simulation of Gate-level Synchronous Circuits. In *Proc. of the Design Automation Conf.*, pages 391–396, June 1999.
[4] A. Biere, A. Cimatti, E. Clarke, and Y. Zhu. Symbolic Model Checking without BDDs. In *Tools and Algorithms for the Analysis and Construction of Systems*, 1999.
[5] V. Boppana, S. Rajan, K. Takayama, and M. Fujita. Model Checking Based on Sequential ATPG. In *Proc. of the Computer Aided Verification Conf.*, pages 418–430, July 1999.
[6] K. Brace, R. Rudell, and R. Bryant. Efficient Implementation of a BDD Package. In *Proc. of the Design Automation Conf.*, pages 40–45, June 1990.
[7] F. M. Brown. *Boolean Reasoning*. Kluwer, 1990.
[8] R. Bryant. Graph Based Algorithms for Boolean Function Manipulation. *IEEE Transactions on Computers*, C-35:677–691, Aug. 1986.
[9] J. Gergov and C. Meinel. Efficient Boolean Manipulation with OBDD's Can Be Extended to FBDD's. *IEEE Transactions on Computers*, 43:1197–1209, Oct. 1994.
[10] W. Günther and R. Dreschler. Minimization of Free BDDs. In *Proc. Asia and South Pacific Design Automation Conference*, Jan. 1999.
[11] N. Ishiura, H. Sawada, and S. Yajima. Minimization of Binary Decision Diagrams Based on Exchanges of Variables. In *Proc. Intl. Conf. on Computer-Aided Design*, pages 472–475, Nov. 1991.
[12] P. Jain and G. Gopalakrishnan. Efficient Symbolic Simulation-Based Verification Using the Parametric Form of Boolean Expressions. *IEEE Transactions on Computer-Aided Design*, 13:1005–1015, Aug. 1994.
[13] J. Kukula, T. Shiple, and A. Aziz. Techniques for Implicit State Enumeration of EFSMs. In *Proc. of the Formal Methods in CAD Conf.*, pages 469–482, Nov. 1998.
[14] K. McMillan. *Symbolic Model Checking*. Kluwer, 1993.
[15] K. Namjoshi and R. Kurshan. Efficient Analysis of Cyclic Definitions. In *Proc. of the Computer Aided Verification Conf.*, pages 394–405, July 1999.
[16] R. Rudell. Dynamic Variable Ordering for Ordered Binary Decision Diagrams. In *Proc. Intl. Conf. on Computer-Aided Design*, pages 42–47, Nov. 1993.
[17] T. Shiple. *Formal Analysis of Synchronous Circuits*. PhD Diss., Univ. Calif. Berkeley, 1996.
[18] Y. Watanabe, L. Guerra, and R. Brayton. Permissible Functions for Multioutput Components in Combinational Logic Optimization. *IEEE Transactions on Computer-Aided Design*, 15:732–744, July 1996.
[19] J. Yuan, K. Shultz, C. Pixley, H. Miller, and A. Aziz. Modeling Design Constraints and Biasing in Simulation Using BDDs. In *Proc. Intl. Conf. on Computer-Aided Design*, pages 584–589, Nov. 1999.

Combining Decision Diagrams and SAT Procedures for Efficient Symbolic Model Checking*

Poul F. Williams[1], Armin Biere[2], Edmund M. Clarke[3], and Anubhav Gupta[3]

[1] Department of Information Technology, Technical University of Denmark,
DK-2800 Lyngby, Denmark
`pfw@it.dtu.dk`
[2] Department of Computer Science, Institute of Computer Systems,
ETH Zentrum, 8092 Zürich, Switzerland
`biere@inf.ethz.ch`
[3] School of Computer Science, Carnegie Mellon University,
Pittsburgh, PA 15213, U.S.A.
`{edmund.clarke, anubhav.gupta}@cs.cmu.edu`

Abstract. In this paper we show how to do symbolic model checking using Boolean Expression Diagrams (BEDs), a non-canonical representation for Boolean formulas, instead of Binary Decision Diagrams (BDDs), the traditionally used canonical representation. The method is based on standard fixed point algorithms, combined with BDDs and SAT-solvers to perform satisfiability checking. As a result we are able to model check systems for which standard BDD-based methods fail. For example, we model check a liveness property of a 256 bit shift-and-add multiplier and we are able to find a previously undetected bug in the specification of a 16 bit multiplier. As opposed to Bounded Model Checking (BMC) our method is complete in practice.

Our technique is based on a quantification procedure that allows us to eliminate quantifiers in Quantified Boolean Formulas (QBF). The basic step of this procedure is the *up-one* operation for BEDs. In addition we list a number of important optimizations to reduce the number of basic steps. In particular the optimization rule of *quantification-by-substitution* turned out to be very useful: $\exists x : g \wedge (x \Leftrightarrow f) \equiv g[f/x]$. The rule is used (1) during fixed point iterations, (2) for deciding whether an initial set of states is a subset of another set of states, and finally (3) for iterative squaring.

---

* This research is sponsored in part by the Semiconductor Research Corporation (SRC) under agreement through Contract No. 99-TJ-684 and the National Science Foundation (NSF) under Grant Nos. CCR-9505472 and CCR-9803774. Any opinions, findings, conclusions or recommendations expressed in this material are those of the authors and do not necessarily reflect the views of SRC, NSF, or the United States Government.

1 Introduction

Symbolic model checking has been performed using fixed point iterations for quite some time [11]. The key to the success is the canonical Binary Decision Diagram (BDD) [8] data structure for representing Boolean functions. However, such a representation explodes in size for certain functions. In this paper we show how to do symbolic model checking using Boolean Expression Diagrams (BEDs) [2,3], a non-canonical representation of Boolean functions. The method is theoretically complete as we only change the representation and not the algorithms. Dropping the canonicity requirement has both advantages and disadvantages: Non-canonical data structures are more succinct than canonical ones – sometimes exponentially more. Determining satisfiability of Boolean functions is easy with canonical data structures, but with non-canonical data structures it is hard. We show how to overcome the disadvantages and exploit some of the advantages in symbolic model checking.

As a non-canonical representation, BEDs do not allow for constant time satisfiability checking. Instead we use two different methods for satisfiability checking: (1) SAT-solvers like GRASP [15] and SATO [18], and (2) conversion of BEDs to BDDs. BDDs are canonical and thus satisfiability checking is a constant time operation. We perform symbolic model checking the classical way with fixed point iterations. One of the key elements of our method is the *quantification-by-substitution* rule: $\exists x : g \wedge (x \Leftrightarrow f) \equiv g[f/x]$. The rule is used (1) during fixed point iterations, (2) while deciding whether an initial set of states is a subset of another set of states, and finally (3) while doing iterative squaring.

While complete in the sense that it handles full CTL [13] model checking, our method performs best if the system has few inputs and the transition relation can be written as a conjunction of next-state functions. The reason is that this allows us to fully exploit the *quantification-by-substitution* rule.

Using our method, we can model check a liveness property of a 256 bit shift-and-add multiplier, which requires 256 iterations to reach the fixed point. This should be compared with the 23 bit multipliers that standard BDD methods can handle. In fact, we are able to detect a previously unknown bug in the specification of a 16 bit multiplier. It was generally thought that iterative squaring was of no use in model checking. However, we show that iterative squaring enables us to calculate the reachable set of states for *all* 32 outputs of a 16 bit multiplier faster than without iterative squaring.

Model checking was invented by Clarke, Emerson, and Sistla in the 1980s [13]. Their model checking method required an explicit enumeration of states which limited the size of the systems they could handle. Burch *et al.* [11] showed how to do model checking without enumerating the states. They called this symbolic model checking. The idea is to represent sets of states by characteristic functions. The data structure of Binary Decision Diagrams turns out to be a very efficient representation for characteristic functions. The advantages of BDDs are compactness, canonicity, and ease of manipulation. Since the appearance of BDDs, many other related data structures have been proposed. Bryant gives an overview in [9]. One such data structure is the Boolean Expression Diagram. It is a generalization of BDDs. In this paper we will study BEDs for use in symbolic model checking.

Biere, Clarke et al. have proposed Bounded Model Checking (BMC) as an alternative method to BDD-based model checking [4,5,6]. They unfold the transition relation and look for repeatedly longer and longer counterexamples, and they use SAT-solvers instead of BDDs. BMC is good at finding errors with short counterexamples. The diameter of the system determines the number of unfoldings of the transition relation that are necessary in order to prove the correctness of the circuit. Unfortunately, for many examples the diameter cannot be calculated and the estimates are too rough. In such cases BMC reduces to a partial verification method in practice. Our method does not need the computation of the diameter or approximations of it.

The work most closely related to ours is by Abdulla, Bjesse and Eén. They consider symbolic reachability analysis using SAT-solvers [1]. For representing Boolean functions they use the Reduced Boolean Circuit data structure which closely resembles our Boolean Expression Diagrams. They perform reachability analysis using a fixed point iteration. Both of us make use of the *quantification-by-substitution* rule. They use Stålmarck's patented method [17] to determine satisfiability of Boolean functions. While related, their method and ours differ in a number of ways: In essence, the basic step in their and our quantification algorithm can be computed by the *up-one* [2,3] BED-algorithm. Therefore we think BEDs are the most natural representation in this context. We handle full CTL while they concentrate on reachability (their tool does handle full CTL, but they have only reported reachability results so far). In our method the *quantification-by-substitution* rule is extensively used at three different places and not just during fixed point calculation. We have heuristics for choosing different SAT procedures depending on the expected result of the satisfiability check. Candidates are various SAT-solvers or an explicit BED to BDD conversion. We use SAT-solvers if the formula is expected to be satisfiable and either SAT-solvers or an explicit BED to BDD conversion if the formula is expected to be unsatisfiable. In their work they only use SAT-solvers. BEDs are always locally reduced and we identify further important simplification rules. Finally we make use of iterative squaring.

This paper is organized as follows. In section 2, we review the BED data structure. In section 3, we show how to do model checking using BEDs. In section 4, we give three applications of the *quantification-by-substitution* rule. In section 5, we deal with the size of BEDs. In section 6, we present the experimental results. Finally in section 7, we conclude.

2 Boolean Expression Diagrams

A Boolean Expression Diagram [2,3] is a data structure for representing and manipulating Boolean formulas. In this section we review the data structure.

Definition 1 (Boolean Expression Diagram). *A Boolean Expression Diagram (BED) is a directed acyclic graph* $G = (V, E)$ *with vertex set V and edge set*

E. *The vertex set V contains four types of vertices: terminal, variable, operator, and quantifier vertices.*

- A terminal vertex v has as attribute a value $val(v) \in \{0,1\}$.
- A variable vertex v has as attributes a Boolean variable $var(v)$, and two children $low(v), high(v) \in V$.
- An operator vertex v has as attributes a binary Boolean operator $op(v)$, and two children $low(v), high(v) \in V$.
- A quantifier vertex v has as attributes a quantifier $quant(v) \in \{\exists, \forall\}$, a Boolean variable $var(v)$, and one child $low(v) \in V$.

The edge set E is defined by

$$E = \{(v, low(v)) \mid v \in V \text{ and } v \text{ has the low attribute } \}$$
$$\cup \ \{(v, high(v)) \mid v \in V \text{ and } v \text{ has the high attribute } \}.$$

The relation between a BED and the Boolean function it represents is straightforward. Terminal vertices correspond to the constant functions 0 and 1. Variable vertices have the same semantics as vertices of BDDs and correspond to the *if-then-else* operator $x \to f_1, f_0$ defined as $(x \wedge f_1) \vee (\neg x \wedge f_0)$. Operator vertices correspond to their respective Boolean connectives. Quantifier vertices correspond to the quantification of their associated variable. This leads to the following correspondence between BEDs and Boolean functions:

Definition 2. *A vertex v in a BED denotes a Boolean function f^v defined recursively as:*

- *If v is a terminal vertex, then $f^v = val(v)$.*
- *If v is a variable vertex, then $f^v = var(v) \to f^{high(v)}, f^{low(v)}$.*
- *If v is an operator vertex, then $f^v = f^{low(v)} \ op(v) \ f^{high(v)}$.*
- *If v is a quantifier vertex, then $f^v = quant(v) \ var(v) : f^{low(v)}$.*

The BED data structure is a representation form for formulas in QBF. If we disallow quantifier vertices, we get a representation form for propositional logic. If we disallow both operator and quantifier vertices, we get a BDD. As an example, Figure 1 shows a BED for the formula $\forall b : a \vee (a \wedge b) \Leftrightarrow a$.

There exist algorithms for transforming a BED into a BDD. One such algorithm is *up-one*. It sifts variables one at a time to the root of the BED. Using *up-one* repeatedly to sift all the variables transforms the BED to a BDD. We refer the reader to [2,3,14] for a more detailed description of *up-one* and its applications.

3 Model Checking

In this section, we review the standard model checking algorithm. The system to be verified is represented as a Kripke structure. A Kripke structure M is a tuple (S, I, T, ℓ), with a finite set of states S, a set of initial states $I \subset S$, a

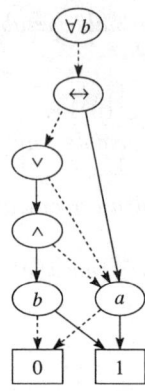

Fig. 1. The BED for $\forall b : a \vee (a \wedge b) \Leftrightarrow a$. All edges are directed downwards; the dashed edges being the low ones.

transition relation $T \subset S \times S$, and a labeling of the states $\ell : S \to \mathcal{P}(\mathcal{A})$ with *atomic propositions* $\mathcal{A}$.

A reactive system consists of a set of states and a set of inputs. The states are encoded as a Boolean vector of state variables $s_1, \ldots, s_n$. The inputs are also encoded as Boolean variables $s_{n+1}, \ldots, s_m$. These together form the state variables of the Kripke structure, $s_1, \ldots, s_m$. The atomic propositions correspond to the state variables. Each state is assumed to be labeled with the variables s_i that are 1 for that state. We use primed variables as next state variables, unprimed variables as current state variables, and we use characteristic functions over the state variables to represent sets. Since the inputs are non-deterministic, they are not constrained by the transition relation. Thus, the transition relation does not contain the primed versions of the input variables.

There are two ways to specify a transition relation in an SMV [16] program: (a) by use of the "TRANS" statement, and (b) by use of the "ASSIGN" statement. In (a) one specifies the transition relation directly as a Boolean expression. In (b) one specifies next-state functions for state variables. Both methods can be used at the same time. We capture this as follows:

$$T(s, s') = t(s, \bar{s}') \wedge \bigwedge_i \tilde{s}'_i \Leftrightarrow f_i(s) \tag{1}$$

where $\bar{s}'$ and $\tilde{s}'$ form a partitioning of $s'_1, \ldots, s'_n$. Here, $t(s, \bar{s}')$ comes from the "TRANS" statements and we call it the relational part, while $\bigwedge_i \tilde{s}'_i \Leftrightarrow f_i(s)$ comes from the "ASSIGN" statements and we call it the functional part. (If a primed variable is restricted by both "TRANS" and "ASSIGN" statements, we place it in the relational part of T.) Our verification method performs best if the transition relation is mainly in functional form.

We use CTL [13] formulas to capture the properties we want to verify. A CTL formula characterizes a set of states, namely the set of states satisfying the formula. This set can be computed by a fixed point iteration. The central part of the fixed point iteration is the computation of relational products. A relational product between the transition relation T and a set of states R is a new set of states. In a *forward* computation, the new set is the set of states reachable in one step from R. We call it the *Image* of R. In a *backward* computation, the new set is the set of states which in one step can reach a state in R. We call it the *PreImage* of R.

The following formulas show how to compute the image and preimage of R:

$$Image_{T,R}(s') = \exists s \ : \ T(s,s') \wedge R(s)$$
$$PreImage_{T,R}(s) = \exists s' \ : \ T(s,s') \wedge R(s')$$

For example, the algorithm in Figure 2 computes the characteristic function for the set of states satisfying the CTL formula "**AG** P" (read: always globally P) using backward iteration. It actually computes "$\neg$**EF** $\neg P$", i.e., it computes the set of states from which there exists a path to a state where P does not hold. The complement set then has the property that P holds along all paths.

AG $P =$
  $R_0 \leftarrow$ characteristic function for
    the set of states *not* satisfying P
  $i \leftarrow -1$
  repeat
    $i \leftarrow i + 1$
    $R_{i+1} \leftarrow R_i \vee PreImage_{T,R_i}(s)$
  until $R_{i+1} \Rightarrow R_i$
  return $\neg R_i$

Fig. 2. The algorithm for computing "**AG** P" using backward iteration. T is the transition relation for the system.

A Kripke structure $M = (S, I, T, \ell)$ satisfies a specification R if and only if I is a subset of R. In terms of characteristic functions this translates to the implication: $I \Rightarrow R$.

3.1 Quantification

The basic step in our quantification algorithm is to eliminate *one* quantified variable by the following rules:

$$\exists x : f \equiv f[0/x] \vee f[1/x] \qquad \forall x : f \equiv f[0/x] \wedge f[1/x]$$

Note that this basic step can easily be computed by performing a $up\text{-}one(f, x)$ BED-operation and then replacing the top level variable vertex by an appropriate operator vertex.

In the worst case, while removing a quantifier from a formula, we double the formula size. Since each *Image/PreImage* computation involves existential quantification of all m state variables, we risk increasing the formula size by a factor of up to 2^m. In this section we present some syntactical transformations which help us to perform the quantifications efficiently.

The most important transformation is the *quantification-by-substitution* rule. It allows us to replace an existential quantification by a substitution:

$$\exists x : g \wedge (x \Leftrightarrow f) \quad \equiv \quad g[f/x] \tag{2}$$

where x does not occur as a free variable in f.

Our verification method performs best when we can exploit the *quantification-by-substitution* rule. Such cases include systems with few inputs and systems with a transition relation that is mainly in functional form. After performing *quantification-by-substitution*, we quantify the remaining state variables (including inputs) using the rules below.

By applying scope reduction rules to a formula, we can push quantifiers down and thus reduce the potential blowup. The scope reduction rules are the following (shown for negation, conjunction and disjunction):

$$\exists x : \neg f \equiv \neg \forall x : f \qquad \forall x : \neg f \equiv \neg \exists x : f$$
$$\exists x : f \vee g \equiv (\exists x : f) \vee (\exists x : g) \qquad \forall x : f \wedge g \equiv (\forall x : f) \wedge (\forall x : g)$$
$$\exists x : f(y) \wedge g(x) \equiv f(y) \wedge (\exists x : g(x)) \qquad \forall x : f(y) \vee g(x) \equiv f(y) \vee (\forall x : g(x))$$

Because BEDs are always reduced, for details see [2,3,14], the quantifiers disappear if they are pushed all the way to the terminals.

3.2 Satisfiability Checking

There are two places where we need to determine whether a Boolean formula represented by a BED is satisfiable. First we need to detect that a fixed point has been reached in the computation of the set of states satisfying a CTL formula. Let R_i be the ith approximation to the fixed point. The fixed point has been reached if $R_{i+1} = R_i$. Using characteristic functions, this translates to $R_{i+1} \Leftrightarrow R_i$. However, depending on the CTL operator, the series of approximations will either be monotonically increasing or monotonically decreasing. It is therefore enough to check set inclusion instead of set equivalence. In the increasing case we check if $R_{i+1} \Rightarrow R_i$ is a tautology. In the decreasing case we check if $R_i \Rightarrow R_{i+1}$ is a tautology. Until we reach the fixed point, these formulas will *not* be tautologies. In other words, the negation of the formulas will be satisfiable. SAT-solvers are good at finding a satisfying variable assignment so we use a SAT-solver here.

Second we need to determine whether the initial set of states I is a subset of the set of states R represented by the CTL specification. In particular we have to check $I \Rightarrow R$ for tautology. There are two cases:

- The specification holds. This means that $I \Rightarrow R$ is a tautology. We could use a SAT-solver to prove that the negation of $I \Rightarrow R$ is not satisfiable. However, it is our experience that most SAT-solvers are not very good at proving non-satisfiability. We can also use BDDs. By using the *up-one* algorithm, we convert the BED for $I \Rightarrow R$ to a BDD.
- The specification does not hold. A proof will be a variable assignment falsifying $I \Rightarrow R$. Or equivalent, a variable assignment satisfying $\neg(I \Rightarrow R)$. SAT-solvers are good at finding such variable assignments.

Of course, we do not know before hand whether the specification holds. A possibility is to run a SAT-solver and a BED to BDD conversion in parallel.

SAT-solvers like GRASP [15] and SATO [18] expect their input to be a propositional formula in conjunctive normal form (CNF). After the elimination of quantifiers, as described in Section 3.1, we still need to convert BEDs into CNF. For this conversion we use the well known technique of introducing new variables for every non-terminal vertex [4].

4 Applications of Quantification-by-Substitution

4.1 PreImage Computation

Consider the *PreImage* computation in section 3. If the transition relation T is written as in equation (1), then we can apply rule (2) directly for the functional part. This can be done in one traversal of the BED. Figure 3 shows the pseudo-code. The algorithm works in a bottom-up way replacing all variables from the functional part of T with their next-state function. Line 4 does the replacing by performing a Shannon expansion of the variable vertex and inserting the next-state function.

```
PreImage(u) =
1:    if u is a terminal then return u
2:    (l, h) ← (PreImage(low(u)), PreImage(high(u)))
3:    if u is a variable vertex with variable from the functional part of T then
4:        return (f_var(u) ∧ h) ∨ (¬f_var(u) ∧ l)
5:    else
6:        return makenode(α(u), l, h)
```

Fig. 3. The algorithm for computing the *PreImage* of u for the functional part of the transition relation: $T_{func} = \bigwedge_i s'_i \Leftrightarrow f_i(s)$. The BED u is assumed to be quantifier-free. The tag $\alpha(u)$ is short for either $var(u)$ or $op(u)$.

4.2 Set Inclusion

We now describe a preprocessing step simplifying $I \Rightarrow R$, i.e., whether the initial set of states is a subset of the states characterized by the specification. The initial set of states I often has the form:

$$I = \bigwedge_i s_i \Leftrightarrow init_i(s)$$

where $init_i(s)$ is the function describing the initial state for the variable s_i. (Note that not all variables have an initial state specified.) In many cases $init_i(s)$ is either a constant or a very simple function, and we can use this fact to simplify $I \Rightarrow R$. Let I be written $I' \wedge (s_i \Leftrightarrow init_i(s))$ and assume $init_i(s)$ does not depend on variable s_i. Recall that $I \Rightarrow R$ is a tautology if and only if $\forall s_i : I \Rightarrow R$ is a tautology:

$$\forall s_i : I \Rightarrow R$$
$$= \forall s_i : \neg\,(I' \wedge (s_i \Leftrightarrow init_i(s)) \wedge \neg R)$$
$$= \neg\exists s_i : I' \wedge (s_i \Leftrightarrow init_i(s)) \wedge \neg R$$
$$= \neg(I' \wedge \neg R)[init_i(s)/s_i]$$
$$= (I' \Rightarrow R)[init_i(s)/s_i]$$

The $[init_i(s)/s_i]$ means a substitution of $init_i(s)$ for s_i. This reduces the number of variables and often simplifies the formula.

4.3 Iterative Squaring

Iterative squaring is a technique for reducing the number of iterations needed to reach the fixed point [10]. During reachability analysis we repeatedly square the transition relation:

$$T^2(s, s') = \exists s'' : T(s, s'') \wedge T(s'', s')$$

Assume that T is written as in equation (1). In general there is no way to square T and keep it in this form – the functional part will disappear. However, if we restrict ourselves to transition relations purely in functional form, squaring can be done easily:

$$T^2(s, s') = \exists s'' : T(s, s'') \wedge T(s'', s')$$
$$= \exists s'' : \left(\bigwedge_i s_i'' \Leftrightarrow f_i(s)\right) \wedge \left(\bigwedge_i s_i' \Leftrightarrow f_i(s'')\right)$$
$$= \bigwedge_i s_i' \Leftrightarrow (f_i(s'')[f(s)/s''])$$

where $[f(s)/s'']$ is a substitution of function $f_j(s)$ for variable s_j'' (for all j). The algorithm is similar to the *PreImage* algorithm in Figure 3.

In this way we can compute $T^{(2^k)}$ in only k steps. $T^{(2^k)}$ is a new transition relation representing all paths in T with a length of *exactly* 2^k. However, it is not possible to represent in functional form the transition relation allowing paths of length *up to* 2^k. As a consequence we cannot combine this form of iterative squaring with, for example, frontier set simplifications.

Consider the algorithm in Figure 2. To use iterative squaring we simply change $PreImage_{T, R_i}(s)$ to $PreImage_{T^{2^i}, R_i}(s)$. As a result, R_i represents the set of states reachable in up to and including $2^i - 1$ steps.

5 BED Simplifications

As we mentioned in section 3.2, transforming a BED to CNF increases the size of the formula as we introduce a new variable for each BED non-terminal vertex. It is therefore vital to keep the size of the BEDs small.

During the conversion of a BED to a BDD, the size may blow up. Even when the final BDD is small (as for a tautology), the intermediate results might be large. In this section we describe a method of keeping the BEDs small.

Keeping the BEDs reduced, as mentioned above, already gives us size reductions due to, for example, constant propagation. But we can reduce the size of the BEDs even more. This can be achieved by increasing the sharing of vertices and by removing local redundancies. In [14] we describe a set of rewriting rules in detail. Here we will just mention some of the ideas:

- Sharing can be increased by disallowing operator vertices which only differ in the order of their children; for example $a \wedge b$ and $b \wedge a$. We fix an ordering $<$ of vertices and only create operator vertices with $low < high$.
- Size can be reduced by eliminating all negations below binary operators since for all binary operators op there exists another operator op' with $op'(x, y) = op(\neg x, y)$.
- Size can be reduced by not using all 16 binary Boolean operators but only a subset of them. We use the set *nand, or, left implication, right implication,* and *bi-implication*. (For clarity, the BED in Figure 1 has not been reduced to this subset.)
- Size can be reduced by exploiting equivalences like the *absorption laws*, for example $a \vee (a \wedge b) = a$, and *distributive laws*, for example $(a \wedge b) \vee (a \wedge c) = a \wedge (b \vee c)$.

We apply all these rewriting rules each time we create a new operator vertex. The rules are important for the performance of *up-one*.

6 Experimental Results

We have constructed a prototype implementation of our proposed model checking method. It performs CTL model checking on SMV programs. For the experiments presented here we use SATO as our SAT-solver. It is worth mentioning that for some examples SATO completes the tasks in seconds where GRASP takes hours. For other examples the reverse is true. We compare our method with the NUSMV model checker [12] and with Bwolen Yang's modified version of SMV[1], both of which are state-of-the-art in BDD-based model checking. Finally we compare reachability results with FIXIT from Adbulla, Bjesse, and Eén [1].

The FIXIT results are taken directly from the paper by Abdulla and his group[2]. All other experiments are run on a Linux computer with a Pentium Pro 200 MHz processor and 1 gigabyte of main memory.

---

[1] http://www.cs.cmu.edu/~bwolen
[2] From personal correspondence with the authors we have learned that they used a 296 MHz Sun UltraSPARC-II for the barrel shifter experiments and a 333 MHz Sun UltraSPARC-IIi for the multiplier experiments.

6.1 Multiplier

This example comes from the BMC-1.0f distribution[3]. It is a 16 × 16 → 32 shift-and-add multiplier. The specification is the c6288 combinational multiplier from the ISCAS'85 benchmark series [7]. For each output bit we verify that we cannot reach a state where the shift-and-add multiplier has finished its computation and the output bits of the two multipliers differ.

The multiplier fits into the category of SMV programs that we handle well. The operands are not modeled as inputs. Instead they are modeled as state variables with an unspecified initial state and the identity function as the next-state function. This lets us use *quantification-by-substitution* for all but the last iteration in the fixed-point calculation. Only in the last iteration do we need to quantify the operands out using the standard quantification methods.

Table 1 shows the runtimes for verifying that the multiplier satisfies the specification. Our BED-based method out-performs both NuSMV and Bwolen

Bit	BED	NuSMV	Bwolen	FixIt
0	2.2	11	9.4	2.9
1	2.3	23	17	3.1
2	2.9	50	33	3.7
3	3.8	130	71	4.8
4	5.2	290	159	6.6
5	7.0	702	383	11
6	9.2	-	1031	20
7	12	-	-	47
8	16	-	-	150
9	31	-	-	544
10	68	-	-	2078
11	352	-	-	8134
12	2201	-	-	30330

Table 1. Runtimes in seconds for verifying the correctness of a 16 bit multiplier. A dash "-" indicates that the verification could not be completed with 800 MB of memory.

Yang's SMV as we are able to model check twice as many outputs as they do. FixIt handles the same number of outputs as our method, however, for the more difficult outputs, our method is faster by an order of magnitude.

For the most difficult output in Table 1, the fixed point iteration accounts for only a fraction of the total runtime for our method. It takes less than a minute and almost no memory to calculate the fixed point. By far the most time is spent in proving $I \Rightarrow R$. SAT-solvers gave poor results, so we converted the BED for $I \Rightarrow R$ to a BDD. The FixIt tool uses a SAT solver to check $I \Rightarrow R$. We expect this is the reason why their runtimes are much longer than ours. However, FixIt does not use much memory, while the memory required for the BED to BDD conversion is quite large. Of course this is expected since the formulas originate from multiplier circuits which are known to be difficult for BDDs. But even though we have to revert to BDDs, we still outperform standard BDD-based model checkers.

We did the experiments in Table 1 without use of iterative squaring to enable fair comparisons. However, iterative squaring speeds up the fixed point calcu-

---
[3] http://www.cs.cmu.edu/~modelcheck

lations. Table 2 shows the runtimes for calculating the fixed points – with and without iterative squaring – for the same model checking problem as above. Note

Bit	Without I.S.	With I.S.
0	2.1	0.9
5	6.8	1.6
10	14	3.7
15	16	8.3
20	37	12
25	19	8.8
30	> 12 hours	6.4

Table 2. Runtimes in seconds for the fixed point calculation in verifying the correctness of the 16 bit shift-and-add multiplier. Results are shown for computations with and without iterative squaring (I.S.). The space requirements are small, i.e., less than 16 MB.

the case for bit 30 where iterative squaring allows us to calculate the fixed point. Without iterative squaring the SAT solver gets stuck. After each iteration the SAT solver looks for new states. With iterative squaring many more new states are added per iteration making it easier for the SAT solver to find a satisfying assignment.

To see how our method handles erroneous designs, we introduced an error in the specification of the multiplier by negating one of the internal nodes (this is marked as "bug D" in the multiplier file in the BMC distribution). We observe that the fixed points are computed in roughly the same amount of CPU time and memory (both with and without iterative squaring). The difference is when we prove $I \Rightarrow R$. Using BED to BDD conversion as with the correct design, we now get poorer results because $I \Rightarrow R$ is *not* a tautology and the final BDD is not necessarily small. However, using a SAT-solver, we get much better results. In many cases, the SAT-solver is able to find a counterexample almost immediately. We are able to model check the first 19 outputs as well as some of the later outputs of the multiplier using less than 16 MB of memory and one minute of CPU time per output. NuSMV and Bwolen Yang's SMV perform as bad as before.

We were able to find a bug in the "correct" specification of the multiplier for the two most significant outputs. Iterative squaring allowed us to quickly compute the fixed points, and SATO instantly found the errors. The total runtimes to find these errors were seven and eight seconds, respectively. It turns out that the two outputs have been swapped. The original net-list for c6288 does not contain information about which gates correspond to which multiplier outputs. However, each gate is numbered and the output numbers seem to be increasing with the the gate numbers – with the exception of the last pair of outputs. This emphasizes the fact that SAT-based methods are good at finding bugs in a system.

We constructed shift-and-add multipliers of different sizes and verified that they always terminate, i.e., we checked "**AF** done". The number of iterations needed to reach the fixed point is equal to the size of the multiplier. This lets us test how well our method handles cases with lots of iterations. Table 3 shows the results. We compare our method with NuSMV and Bwolen Yang's SMV. Our method performs much better as we are both significantly faster and we are able to handle much larger designs. We cannot compare with FIXIT as they did not report results for **AF** properties.

Size	BED	NuSMV	Bwolen
16	1.6	2.2	5.2
18	1.8	18	9.1
20	2.0	90	24
22	2.3	472	104
23	2.7	-	253
24	2.8	-	-
32	3.7	-	-
64	17	-	-
128	119	-	-
256	1185	-	-

Table 3. Runtimes in seconds for verifying that shift-and-add multipliers of different sizes always terminate, i.e., we check "**AF** done". The number of iterations to reach the fixed point is equal to the size of the multiplier.

6.2 Barrel Shifter

This example is a barrel shifter from the BMC-1.0f distribution and like the multiplier, it also falls within the category of systems which we handle well. A barrel shifter consists of two register files. The contents of one of the register files is rotated at each step while the other file stays the same. The width of a register is $\log R$, where R is the size of the register file.

The correctness of the barrel shifter is proven by showing that if two registers from the files have the same contents, then their neighbors are also identical. The set of initial states is restricted to states where this invariant holds. The left part of Table 4 shows the results. The BED and FIXIT methods are both fast, however, the BED method scales better and thus outperforms FIXIT. NuSMV and Bwolen Yang's SMV are both unable to construct the BDD for the transition relation for all but the smallest examples.

We prove liveness for the barrel shifter by showing that a pair of registers in the files will eventually become equal. The number of iterations for the fixed point calculation is equal to the size of the register file. The right part of Table 4 shows the results. We do not compare with FIXIT as no results for this experiment were reported in [1]. As in the previous case, NuSMV and Bwolen Yang's SMV can only handle small examples.

7 Conclusion

We have presented a BED-based CTL model checking method based on the classical fixed point iterations. Quantification is often the Achilles heel in CTL fixed point iterations but by using *quantification-by-substitution* we are in some cases able to deal effectively with it. While our method is complete, it performs best on examples with a low number of inputs and where the transition relation is mainly in functional form. In these situations we can fully exploit the *quantification-by-substitution* rule.

Size	BED	NuSMV	Bwolen	FixIt		Size	BED	NuSMV	Bwolen
2	0.1	0.1	1.0	0.1		2	0.2	0.1	1.0
4	0.3	0.2	2.5	0.1		4	0.5	0.2	2.1
6	0.4	609	-	0.2		6	0.7	521	-
8	0.4	-	-	0.5		8	0.9	-	-
10	0.6	-	-	1.1		10	1.2	-	-
20	1.9	-	-	14		20	3.2	-	-
30	4.0	-	-	52		30	5.9	-	-
40	8.0	-	-	231		40	11	-	-
50	13	-	-	502		50	18	-	-
60	19	-	-	?		60	28	-	-
70	30	-	-	?		70	47	-	-

Table 4. Runtimes in seconds for invariant (left) and liveness (right) checking of the barrel shifter example. A question mark indicates that the runtime for FixIt was not reported in [1]. For the BED method we use SATO for checking satisfiability of $I \Rightarrow R$.

We have shown how the *quantification-by-substitution* rule can also help simplify the final set inclusion problem of model checking and help perform efficient iterative squaring. Our proposed method combines SAT-solvers and BED to BDD conversions to perform satisfiability checking. We use a set of local rewriting rules which helps to keep the size of the BEDs down.

We have demonstrated our method by model checking large shift-and-add multipliers and barrel shifters, and we obtain results superior to standard BDD-based model checking methods. Furthermore, we were able to find a previously undetected bug in the specification of a 16 bit multiplier.

Future work includes investigating two variable ordering problems. One is the variable ordering when converting the BED for $I \Rightarrow R$ to a BDD. The variable ordering is known to be very important in BDD construction, and since we, in some cases, spend much time on converting $I \Rightarrow R$ to a BDD, our method will benefit from a good variable ordering heuristic. The other problem is the order in which we quantify the variables in the *PreImage* computation. This will be interesting especially in cases where we cannot use the *quantification-by-substitution* rule. Finally we are currently investigating how to extend our method to work well for systems with many inputs.

References

[1] P. A. Abdulla, P. Bjesse, and N. Eén. Symbolic reachability analysis based on SAT solvers. In *Tools and Algorithms for the Analysis and Construction of Systems (TACAS)*, 2000.

[2] H. R. Andersen and H. Hulgaard. Boolean expression diagrams. *Information and Computation*. (To appear).

[3] H. R. Andersen and H. Hulgaard. Boolean expression diagrams. In *IEEE Symposium on Logic in Computer Science (LICS)*, July 1997.

[4] A. Biere, A. Cimatti, E. M. Clarke, M. Fujita, and Y. Zhu. Symbolic model checking using SAT procedures instead of BDDs. In *Proc. ACM/IEEE Design Automation Conference (DAC)*, 1999.

[5] A. Biere, A. Cimatti, E. M. Clarke, and Y. Zhu. Symbolic model checking without BDDs. In *Tools and Algorithms for the Analysis and Construction of Systems (TACAS)*, volume 1579 of *Lecture Notes in Computer Science*. Springer-Verlag, 1999.

[6] A. Biere, E. Clarke, R. Raimi, and Y. Zhu. Verifying safety properties of a PowerPC microprocessor using symbolic model checking without BDDs. In *Computer Aided Verification (CAV)*, volume 1633 of *Lecture Notes in Computer Science*. Springer-Verlag, 1999.

[7] F. Brglez and H. Fujiware. A neutral netlist of 10 combinational benchmarks circuits and a target translator in Fortran. In *Special Session International Symposium on Circuits and Systems (ISCAS)*, 1985.

[8] R. E. Bryant. Graph-based algorithms for boolean function manipulation. *IEEE Transactions on Computers*, 35(8):677–691, August 1986.

[9] R. E. Bryant. Binary decision diagrams and beyond: Enabling technologies for formal verification. In *Proc. International Conf. Computer-Aided Design (ICCAD)*, pages 236–243, November 1995.

[10] J. R. Burch, E. M. Clarke, D. E. Long, K. L. MacMillan, and D.L. Dill. Symbolic model checking for sequential circuit verification. *IEEE Transactions on Computer-Aided Design of Integrated Circuits and Systems*, 13(4):401–424, April 1994.

[11] J. R. Burch, E. M. Clarke, K. L. McMillan, D. L. Dill, and L. J. Hwang. Symbolic model checking: 10^{20} states and beyond. *Information and Computation*, 98(2):142–170, June 1992.

[12] A. Cimatti, E.M. Clarke, F. Giunchiglia, and M. Roveri. NuSMV: a new Symbolic Model Verifier. In N. Halbwachs and D. Peled, editors, *Proceedings Eleventh Conference on Computer-Aided Verification (CAV'99)*, volume 1633 of *Lecture Notes in Computer Science*, pages 495–499, Trento, Italy, July 1999. Springer-Verlag.

[13] E. M. Clarke, E. A. Emerson, and A. P. Sistla. Automatic verification of finite-state concurrent systems using temporal logic specifications. *ACM Transactions on Programming Languages and Systems*, 8(2):244–263, April 1986.

[14] H. Hulgaard, P. F. Williams, and H. R. Andersen. Equivalence checking of combinational circuits using boolean expression diagrams. *IEEE Transactions on Computer Aided Design*, July 1999.

[15] J. P. Marques-Silva and K. A. Sakallah. GRASP: A search algorithm for propositional satisfiability. *IEEE Transactions on Computers*, 48, 1999.

[16] K. L. McMillan. *Symbolic Model Checking*. Kluwer Academic Publishers, 1993.

[17] M. Sheeran and G. Stålmarck. A tutorial on Stålmarck's proof procedure for propositional logic. In G. Gopalakrishnan and P. J. Windley, editors, *Proc. Formal Methods in Computer-Aided Design, Second International Conference, FMCAD'98, Palo Alto/CA, USA*, volume 1522 of *Lecture Notes in Computer Science*, pages 82–99, November 1998.

[18] H. Zhang. SATO: An efficient propositional prover. In William McCune, editor, *Proceedings of the 14th International Conference on Automated deduction*, volume 1249 of *Lecture Notes in Artificial Intelligence*, pages 272–275, Berlin, July 1997. Springer-Verlag.

On the Completeness of Compositional Reasoning

Kedar S. Namjoshi[1] and Richard J. Trefler[2]

[1] Bell Laboratories, Lucent Technologies
kedar@research.bell-labs.com
[2] AT&T Labs Research
trefler@research.att.com

Abstract. Several proof rules based on the assume-guarantee paradigm have been proposed for compositional reasoning about concurrent systems. Some of the rules are syntactically circular in nature, in that assumptions and guarantees appear to be circularly dependent. While these rules are sound, we show that several such rules are *incomplete*, i.e., there are true properties of a composition that cannot be deduced using these rules. We present a new sound and complete circular rule. We also show that circular and non-circular rules are closely related. For the circular rules defined here, proofs with circular rules can be efficiently transformed to proofs with non-circular rules and vice versa.

1 Introduction

In his landmark paper [Pnu77], Pnueli advocated the use of temporal logic as a formalism for describing the correct operation of reactive systems [HP85]. To show that a reactive system, M, is correct, one specifies the correctness condition for M as an assertion, f, of temporal logic and applies proof techniques, either automatic [CE81,QS82,CES86] or deductive [Pnu77,MP84], to show that M satisfies f ($M \models f$).

Model checking [CE81,QS82] (*cf.* [CES86] [VW86]) is an automatic technique for showing that $M \models f$. It is efficient, with complexity linear in the size of M ($|M|$) for temporal logics such as Computation Tree Logic (CTL) [CE81] and Linear Temporal Logic (LTL) [Pnu77]. However, when M is given as the parallel composition of n processes, each of size bounded by K, the size of M may be K^n. This *state explosion* problem is one of the main obstacles to the more wide-spread application of model checking.

Compositional reasoning techniques form a promising approach to ameliorating the state explosion problem. To prove that the parallel composition of M_1 with M_2, written as $M_1//M_2$, satisfies the correctness specification h, compositional techniques provide proof rules that justify the above correctness assertion from two proofs done in isolation, the first stating the correctness of M_1 and the second stating the correctness of M_2. For example, the following is a typical rule:

$$\frac{\{f\}M_1\{h\} \quad \{h\}M_2\{g\}}{\{f\}M_1//M_2\{g\}}$$

This rule works as follows. First, show $\{f\}M_1\{h\}$, that is, that M_1 satisfies h under the assumption f. Second, show that $\{h\}M_2\{g\}$. Then the correctness assertion $\{f\}M_1//M_2\{g\}$ may be concluded as a consequence of the soundness of the rule. Such compositional reasoning provides a benefit to the extent that direct reasoning about $M_1//M_2$ has been avoided. In general, however, determining the appropriate auxiliary assertion h may be highly non-trivial.

To ease the difficulty of determining the auxiliary assertions, several so called *circular* proof rules have been proposed. For example, consider the following rule (*cf.* [McM99])

$$\frac{\{f\}M_1\{g_2 \triangleright g_1\} \quad \{f\}M_2\{g_1 \triangleright g_2\}}{\{f\}M_1//M_2\{\mathsf{G}(g_1 \wedge g_2)\}}$$

Several points seem to differentiate this rule from the previous one. Firstly, the form of the postconditions has been restricted to specific operators. The property $q \triangleright p$ (read as "q constrains p") is true of a computation if, for all i, p is true at point i of the computation if q holds at all points $j < i$; this can be expressed in LTL as $\neg(q \mathsf{U} \neg p)$. The property $\mathsf{G}(p)$ (read as "always p") is true of a computation if p holds at all points of the computation. Secondly, in the first sub-goal, $\{f\}M_1\{g_2 \triangleright g_1\}$, g_1 is understood to be the correctness assertion of M_1 while g_2 is a helper assertion. This may be justified by thinking of M_1 as an open system, which interacts with an environment over which it has little control. Thus, the correct operation of M_1 may be dependent on the correct operation of its environment M_2, therefore, g_2 appears as a guarantee of the correct operation of the environment in the proof of the correctness of M_1. The appearance of g_1 in the proof sub-task for M_2 can be similarly justified – hence the use of the word "circular" in the name for such proof rules. The circularity helps to more easily encode the back-and-forth handshake protocols that designers typically use for connecting components of a system.

For any proof system, *soundness* is, of course, the most important property – it should not be possible to deduce false facts. A measure of the quality or usefulness of a proof system is obtained from an investigation into *completeness* – is it possible to deduce *all* true facts using the rules of the system? Existing compositional rules, including the circular ones, are known to be sound.

In this paper, we first investigate the completeness of existing compositional reasoning rules, focusing on rules that are known to be sound for arbitrary linear temporal properties and which have been used successfully to verify large systems. Surprisingly, several such rules turn out to be *incomplete*; that is, there are correctness assertions about $M_1//M_2$ which are true but are not provable from the proof rules. Typically these unprovable assertions are liveness properties, but some rules may also be incomplete for safety properties. The counter-examples for incompleteness are also quite simple, which indicates that the rules may be inadequate for handling many compositions that arise in practice. We propose a new circular reasoning rule similar to the one above and show that it is both sound and complete. The new rule strengthens the previous rule in a manner analogous to strengthening a proof of invariance by introducing auxiliary assertions – to show $\mathsf{G}p$ show $\mathsf{G}(p \wedge h)$. Furthermore, our new rule is backward compatible, in that any proof done using the previous rule is also a proof with the new circular rule.

We then investigate whether circularity is, in itself, essential for reasoning about composed systems. We show that the notion of circularity is a somewhat weak one for LTL properties, in that proofs carried out with circular rules can be efficiently translated to proofs with non-circular rules, and vice-versa.

The paper is organized as follows: Section 2 contains some preliminary definitions; Section 3 gives the details of several different styles of proof rules and develops our new sound and complete circular proof rule; Section 4 discusses the translations between proofs carried out with circular and non-circular rules. Finally, Section 5 contains a brief conclusion and discusses related work.

2 Background

In this section, we define the computational model and provide examples of circular and non-circular rules for compositional reasoning.

2.1 Temporal Logic

LTL was first suggested as a protocol specification language in [Pnu77]. Formulae in the logic define sets of *infinite* sequences. We define LTL formulae w.r.t. a set of *variable* symbols. As in first-order logic, one can construct *terms* over the set of variables using function symbols from a vocabulary $\mathcal{F}$, and *atomic predicates* from terms, using relational symbols from a vocabulary $\mathcal{R}$. We define *atomic predicates* and temporal formulas below. A *predicate* is a boolean combination of atomic predicates.

- For a relational symbol $r \in \mathcal{R}$ of arity n and terms $t_0, \ldots, t_{n-1}$, $r(t_0, \ldots, t_{n-1})$ is an atomic predicate and a formula,
- for formulae f and g, $(f \wedge g)$ and $\neg(f)$ are formulae,
- for formulae f and g, $\mathsf{X}(f), \mathsf{X}^-(f), (f \mathsf{U} g)$, and $(f \mathsf{U}^- g)$ are formulae.

The temporal operators are X (*next-time*), X^- (*previous-time*), U (*until*), and U^- (*since*). Given an interpretation $\mathcal{I}$ (which we assume fixed from now on) for the function and relation symbols, temporal formulae are interpreted w.r.t.

infinite sequences of valuations of the variables. For a set of typed variables W, let a W-*state* be a function mapping each variable in W to a value in its type. The set of W-states is denoted by $\Sigma(W)$. A W-*sequence* σ is an infinite sequence of W-states, which is represented as a function $\sigma : \mathbf{N} \to \Sigma(W)$ ($\mathbf{N}$ is the set of natural numbers). We write $\sigma, i \models f$ to say that the infinite sequence σ *satisfies* the formula f at position i. The *language* of f, denoted by $\mathcal{L}(f)$, is the set $\{\sigma : \sigma, 0 \models f\}$. The satisfaction relation can be defined by induction on the structure of f. First, the value of a term t at location i on σ, denoted as $\sigma_i(t)$, may be defined by induction on the structure of terms. Next, the satisfaction relation for formulas is defined as follows.

- $\sigma, i \models r(t_0, \ldots, t_{n-1})$ iff $(\mathcal{I}(r))(\sigma_i(t_0), \ldots, \sigma_i(t_{n-1}))$ is true.
- $\sigma, i \models \neg(f)$ iff $\sigma, i \models f$ is false; $\sigma, i \models (f \wedge g)$ iff both $\sigma, i \models f$ and $\sigma, i \models g$ are true.
- $\sigma, i \models \mathsf{X}(f)$ iff $\sigma, i+1 \models f$.
- $\sigma, i \models \mathsf{X}^-(f)$ iff $i > 0$ and $\sigma, i-1 \models f$.
- $\sigma, i \models (f \mathrel{\mathsf{U}} g)$ iff there exists j, $j \geq i$, such that $\sigma, j \models g$ and for every k, $i \leq k < j$, $\sigma, k \models f$.
- $\sigma, i \models (f \mathrel{\mathsf{U}^-} g)$ iff there exists j, $j \leq i$, such that $\sigma, j \models g$ and for every k, $j < k \leq i$, $\sigma, k \models f$.

Other connectives can be defined in terms of these basic connectives: $(f \vee g)$ is $\neg(\neg f \wedge \neg g)$, $(f \Rightarrow g)$ is $\neg f \vee g$, $\mathsf{F}g$ ("eventually g") is $(true \mathrel{\mathsf{U}} g)$, $\mathsf{F}^- g$ ("previously g") is $(true \mathrel{\mathsf{U}^-} g)$, $\mathsf{G}f$ ("always f") is $\neg\mathsf{F}(\neg f)$, $(f \mathrel{\mathsf{W}} g)$ ("f holds unless g") is $(\mathsf{G}(f) \vee (f \mathrel{\mathsf{U}} g))$, $\overset{\infty}{\mathsf{F}}p$ ("infinitely often p") is $\mathsf{GF}p$, $\overset{\infty}{\mathsf{G}}p$ ("finitely often $\neg p$") is $\mathsf{FG}p$, and $q \triangleright p$ (read as "q constrains p") is $\neg(q \mathrel{\mathsf{U}} \neg p)$.

Quantified Temporal Logic: The expressive power of temporal logic can be enhanced by allowing variable quantification. The formula $(\exists W : f)$ is true of a V-sequence σ iff there is a $V \cup W$-sequence δ that agrees on the V-variables with σ and which satisfies f. In the finite case, the expressive power of quantified temporal logic is that of ω-regular expressions – see [Tho90] for a survey of these issues.

2.2 Computational Model

We adopt a definition of a process similar to those in [Pnu77,AL95,McM99]. A process is specified by giving an initial condition, a transition condition and a fairness condition over a set of variables.

Definition 0 (Process) *A process is specified by a tuple (V, I, T, F) where*

- V *is a finite, nonempty set of typed variables. We define a set of primed variables V' that is in 1-1 correspondence with V.*
- $I(V)$, *the initial condition, is a predicate on V,*
- $T(V, V')$, *the transition condition, is a predicate on $V \cup V'$, which is left-total.*
- $F(V, V')$, *the fairness condition, is a boolean combination of temporal formulas $\overset{\infty}{\mathsf{F}}(p)$ and $\overset{\infty}{\mathsf{G}}(p)$, for predicates p on $V \cup V'$.*

For W such that $V \subseteq W$, a W-*computation* σ of a process is a W-sequence such that $I(\sigma_0)$, and for each $i \in \mathbf{N}$, $T(\sigma_i, \sigma_{i+1})$. By considering $x' \in V'$ as a term that specifies the value of $x \in V$ in the next state, the set of computations can be defined by the temporal formula $I \wedge \mathsf{G}(T)$, interpreted over W-sequences.

Definition 1 (Language) *For a set of variables W such that $V \subseteq W$, the W-language of a process $M = (V, I, T, F)$, denoted by $\mathcal{L}_W(M)$, is the set of W-computations of M that satisfy the fairness condition F. Thus, $\mathcal{L}_W(M)$ can be expressed by the LTL formula $I \wedge \mathsf{G}(T) \wedge F$, interpreted over W-sequences.*

We define process composition so that the language of a composition $M_1//M_2$ is the *intersection* of the languages of M_1 and M_2. The semantics of most hardware description languages follows this model. In addition, as shown in [AL95], with some reasonable restrictions, it holds also of asynchronous models of computation.

Definition 2 (Process Composition) *The composition of processes $M_1 = (V_1, I_1, T_1, F_1)$ and $M_2 = (V_2, I_2, T_2, F_2)$ is denoted by $M_1//M_2$, and is defined as the process (V, I, T, F) where*

- $V = V_1 \cup V_2$,
- $I = I_1 \wedge I_2$,
- $T = T_1 \wedge T_2$,
- $F = F_1 \wedge F_2$

With this definition of composition, it is possible that T is not left-total even though T_1 and T_2 are left-total. In the rest of the paper, we restrict ourselves to those compositions where T is left-total.

Theorem 0 *For a composition $M = M_1//M_2$ and a set of variables W such that $(V_1 \cup V_2) \subseteq W$, $\mathcal{L}_W(M) = \mathcal{L}_W(M_1) \cap \mathcal{L}_W(M_2)$.* □

Definition 3 (Model Checking) *The model checking question is to determine if a property f defined over a variable set W is true of all computations of a program M with a variable set that is a subset of W; i.e., if $(\forall W : \mathcal{L}_W(M) \Rightarrow f)$ holds.*

2.3 Compositional Reasoning

The model checking question for a composition $M_1//M_2$ may be phrased as $(\forall W : \mathcal{L}_W(M_1//M_2) \Rightarrow f)$, which is equivalent, by Theorem 0, to $(\forall W : \mathcal{L}_W(M_1) \wedge \mathcal{L}_W(M_2) \Rightarrow f)$. Compositional reasoning rules convert this question into two separate model checking questions, one explicitly involving M_1 and the other explicitly involving M_2. This separation is typically required in the proofs of large systems because even the symbolic representation (as BDD's) of the transition relation for $M_1//M_2$ is infeasible.

Assume-guarantee rules for composition attempt to generalize the pre- and post-condition reasoning of Hoare logic [Hoa69]. Informally, a triple $\{f\}M\{g\}$ asserts the property that every computation of M which satisfies the assumption f satisfies the *guarantee* g. Formally, this can be stated as $(\forall W : f \wedge \mathcal{L}_W(M) \Rightarrow g)$. We state below two typical compositional reasoning rules based on the assume-guarantee formulation: the first is syntactically non-circular, while the second is syntactically circular, in that the assumptions of one process form the guarantees of the other and vice-versa.

Definition 4 (Non-circular Reasoning (NC)) *Show $\{f\}M_1//M_2\{g\}$ holds by picking an intermediate property h such that $\{f\}M_1\{h\}$ and $\{h\}M_2\{g\}$ hold.*

Rule **NC** is sound, which can be shown with simple propositional reasoning from the definitions. It is also (trivially) complete; if $\{f\}M_1//M_2\{g\}$ holds, then choosing $h = f \wedge \mathcal{L}_W(M_1)$, one may show $\{f\}M_1\{h\} = (\forall W : f \wedge \mathcal{L}_W(M_1) \Rightarrow f \wedge \mathcal{L}_W(M_1)) =$ true, and $\{h\}M_2\{g\} = (\forall W : f \wedge \mathcal{L}_W(M_1) \wedge \mathcal{L}_W(M_2) \Rightarrow g)$, which is true by the assumption.

The following rule is derived from the application of a property decomposition theorem to compositional reasoning in [McM99] (*cf.* Theorem 1 in [McM99]). Below we make use of the following notation: let $B = \{f_1, \ldots, f_k\}$ be a set of LTL formulae, then the formula B is a shorthand for $(\bigwedge i : f_i)$.

Definition 5 (Syntactically Circular Reasoning (C1)) *Consider the composition $M = (//j : M_j)$. Let $\{g_i\}$ be a set of properties. To show that $\{f\}M\{\mathsf{G}(\bigwedge i : g_i)\}$ holds,*

- *with each i, choose a composition $M(i) = (//k : M_k)$ where k ranges over a strict subset of the process indices,*
- *choose a well founded order $\prec$ and subsets Θ_i and Δ_i of the set of properties $\{g_i\}$, such that if $g_j \in \Theta_i$, then $j \prec i$,*

and show that $\{f\}M(i)\{\Delta_i \triangleright (\neg\Theta_i \vee g_i)\}$ holds for all i.

The requirement that $M(i)$ is a strict sub-composition of M is imposed to prevent trivial applications of this rule with every $M(i)$ equal to M.

3 (In)Complete Proof Rules

We have shown in the previous section that the non-circular rule **NC** is both sound and complete. In this section, we consider the proof rule **C1** and the assume-guarantee rule from [AL95] and show that these circular rules are incomplete, even for *finite-state* processes. Our choice of these rules is guided by two considerations: (i) these rules, unlike many other compositional rules (as discussed in Section 5), are sound for arbitrary linear temporal properties and (ii) they have been used successfully (cf. [McM98]) to verify large systems. We then present a new sound and complete circular rule.

3.1 Incompleteness

To demonstrate that rule **C1** is incomplete, consider the programs below where, informally, M_1 and M_2 juggle four tokens by throwing them back and forth in an circular pattern (the l, r variables indicate left and right "hands", respectively).

program M_1	program M_2
variables l_1, r_1, r_2 : *boolean*	variables l_2, r_2, r_1 : *boolean*
initially $l_1 \wedge r_1$	initially $l_2 \wedge r_2$
transition $(l_1' \equiv r_2) \wedge (r_1' \equiv l_1)$	transition $(l_2' \equiv r_1) \wedge (r_2' \equiv l_2)$

As can be checked easily, the property $\mathsf{G}(l_1 \wedge l_2)$ holds of the composition $M_1//M_2$. Applying the substitution $f = true, g_1 = l_1, g_2 = l_2$ to rule **C1**, we obtain the property $\{true\}M_1//M_2\{\mathsf{G}(l_1 \wedge l_2)\}$. However, as can be checked by enumeration, there is no way to define the well founded order $\prec$, and the subsets Θ_i and Δ_i such that the sub-goals of rule **C1** are satisfied. Intuitively, this is because the next value of l_1 is determined by the current value of r_2, which is unconstrained by the assumptions. Hence, the original property, which is true of the composition, cannot be shown using the proof rule **C1**.

One reason that this rule is incomplete is that it does not permit a choice of auxiliary assertions, as in rule **NC**. If auxiliary assertions were allowed, it is easy to see that the strengthened property $\mathsf{G}(l_1 \wedge r_1 \wedge l_2 \wedge r_2)$ can be shown by properly instantiating rule **C1**. This is similar to the incompleteness of the inductive invariance rule for establishing $\mathsf{G}(p)$; one often needs to strengthen p to $p \wedge h$ and show that this strengthened formula is an inductive invariant. We say more about strengthening in Section 3.2.

The circular proof rule presented in [AL95] is given below. In this rule, $//$ represents asynchronous composition and $\hat{\mathcal{L}}(M)$ is defined so that it is insensitive to stuttering, however, $\hat{\mathcal{L}}(M_1//M_2)$ is defined so that it equals $\hat{\mathcal{L}}(M_1) \wedge \hat{\mathcal{L}}(M_2)$. Although this rule allows the choice of auxiliary assertions E_i, it turns out that it is still incomplete, because of the restricted form of the hypotheses. In the definition below, $C(f)$, for an LTL property f, is the strongest safety property that is weaker than f while f_{+v} asserts that if the formula f should become false then the variable v becomes constant (for more details see [AL95]).

Definition 6 (Circular Rule C2 [AL95]) *To show that $E \wedge \hat{\mathcal{L}}(N_1//N_2) \Rightarrow \hat{\mathcal{L}}(M_1//M_2)$ holds, pick E_i and show that for each i in $\{1, 2\}$ all the following hold.*

- $C(E) \wedge \bigwedge_{j \in \{1,2\}} C(\hat{\mathcal{L}}(M_j)) \Rightarrow E_i$
- $C(E_i)_{+v} \wedge C(\hat{\mathcal{L}}(N_i)) \Rightarrow C(\hat{\mathcal{L}}(M_i))$
- $E_i \wedge \hat{\mathcal{L}}(N_i) \Rightarrow \hat{\mathcal{L}}(M_i)$

Consider the programs M_1, M_2, N_1 and N_2 given below, all of which have initial condition *true* and a weak-fairness condition on the actions a_1, a_2.

program M_1	program M_2
variables x : *boolean*	variables y : *boolean*
transition a_1: $x := true$, b_1: $x := false$	transition a_2: $y := true$, b_2: $y := false$

Thus, the specification programs M_1 and M_2 define the properties $\mathsf{GF}x$ and $\mathsf{GF}y$ respectively. The implementation programs N_1 and N_2 are as follows.

program N_1
variables x, y : boolean
transition a_1: $x := y$

program N_2
variables x, y : boolean
transition a_2: $y := true$, b_2: $y := \neg x \wedge y$

It is easy to check that $E \wedge \hat{\mathcal{L}}(N_1//N_2) \Rightarrow \hat{\mathcal{L}}(M_1//M_2))$ with $E \equiv true$. By a result in [AL95], $C(\hat{\mathcal{L}}(M))$ is just the temporal formula for process M without the fairness condition. Thus, $C(\hat{\mathcal{L}}(M_1)) = true \wedge \mathsf{G}(x' \equiv true \vee x' \equiv false \vee x' \equiv x)$, which simplifies to $true$, as does $C(\hat{\mathcal{L}}(M_2))$. Hence, if the first hypothesis is to hold, both E_1 and E_2 must equal $true$. Therefore, by the third hypothesis, $\hat{\mathcal{L}}(N_1) \Rightarrow \hat{\mathcal{L}}(M_1)$, which is false as N_1 admits computations where x is $false$ at every point. Hence, rule **C2** is incomplete.

3.2 A Sound and Complete Circular Rule

We present a rule that allows the choice of *auxiliary* properties over process interfaces, while retaining the overall style of the proof obligations of rule **C1**. This rule is shown to be sound and complete. For clarity, we restrict the discussion below to the two process case – there is a straightforward generalization to the n process case.

Definition 7 (Circular Reasoning (C3)) *For properties g_1 over V_1 and g_2 over V_2, to show $\{f\}M_1//M_2\{\mathsf{G}(g_1 \wedge g_2)\}$, pick properties h_1 and h_2 for which the following obligations hold.*

1. $\{f\}M_1\{(h_2 \wedge g_2) \triangleright ((h_2 \Rightarrow g_1) \wedge h_1)\}$
2. $\{f\}M_2\{(h_1 \wedge g_1) \triangleright ((h_1 \Rightarrow g_2) \wedge h_2)\}$

Note that an instance of rule **C1** can be obtained from **C3** by making the substitution $h_1 = true, h_2 = true$.

Theorem 1 (Soundness) *Rule C3 is sound.*

Proof. Assume that the hypotheses of the rule hold for some choice of h_1 and h_2. Then the guarantees of both hypotheses are true for any computation of $M_1//M_2$ that satisfies f. Consider any such computation σ, and any point i on σ. Assume inductively that for all points j, $j < i$, the property $(g_1 \wedge h_1 \wedge g_2 \wedge h_2)$ holds. By the first hypothesis of rule **C3**, $(h_2 \Rightarrow g_1) \wedge h_1$ holds at point i, and by the second hypothesis, so does $(h_1 \Rightarrow g_2) \wedge h_2$. Hence, the inductive hypothesis holds at point $i+1$. This shows that $\mathsf{G}(g_1 \wedge h_1 \wedge g_2 \wedge h_2)$ holds of σ, from which it follows that the weaker property $\mathsf{G}(g_1 \wedge g_2)$ also holds of σ. □

Theorem 2 (Completeness) *Rule C3 is complete. Furthermore, if f is defined over the interface variables $V_1 \cap V_2$, it is always possible to choose h_1 and h_2 as properties over $V_1 \cap V_2$.*

Proof. In the following, let $V = V_1 \cup V_2$, and suppose that f is defined over $V_1 \cap V_2$. Suppose that $\{f\}M_1//M_2\{\mathsf{G}(g_1 \wedge g_2)\}$ holds. By definition, this is equivalent to $(\forall V : f \wedge \mathcal{L}_V(M_1) \wedge \mathcal{L}_V(M_2) \Rightarrow \mathsf{G}(g_1 \wedge g_2))$, which is equivalent to

$(\forall V : f \wedge \mathcal{L}_V(M_1) \wedge \mathcal{L}_V(M_2) \Rightarrow \mathsf{G}(g_1))$ and $(\forall V : f \wedge \mathcal{L}_V(M_1) \wedge \mathcal{L}_V(M_2) \Rightarrow \mathsf{G}(g_2))$ both being true. Consider the first property:

$$(\forall V : f \wedge \mathcal{L}_V(M_1) \wedge \mathcal{L}_V(M_2) \Rightarrow \mathsf{G}(g_1)) \tag{1}$$

Let $\alpha_1 = (\exists V \backslash V_2 : f \wedge \mathcal{L}_V(M_1))$ and $\alpha_2 = (\exists V \backslash V_1 : f \wedge \mathcal{L}_V(M_2))$. Define h_1 as $\mathsf{F}^- \alpha_1$ and h_2 as $\mathsf{F}^- \alpha_2$. As M_1 and g_1 are defined over V_1, expression 1 can be re-written as:

$$(\forall V_1 : \mathcal{L}_V(M_1) \wedge \alpha_2 \Rightarrow \mathsf{G}(g_1)) \tag{2}$$

By definition of α_1, it is also true that:

$$(\forall V : f \wedge \mathcal{L}_V(M_1) \Rightarrow \alpha_1) \tag{3}$$

Consider the first hypothesis: $\{f\}M_1\{(h_2 \wedge g_2) \triangleright ((h_2 \Rightarrow g_1) \wedge h_1)\}$, and consider any sequence satisfying $f \wedge \mathcal{L}_V(M_1)$. By equation 3, α_1 is true initially, so $\mathsf{G}(h_1)$ is true. Now consider an arbitrary position i on the sequence such that $(h_2 \wedge g_2)$ holds for all positions j, $j < i$.

case $i = 0$: We have to show that $(h_2 \Rightarrow g_1)$ at position 0. If h_2 is true initially, then α_2 is true initially. By equation 2, g_1 must then be true.

case $i > 0$: As $i > 0$, h_2 holds initially, which implies that α_2 is true initially. By equation 2, $\mathsf{G}(g_1)$ holds at the origin, so that $(h_2 \Rightarrow g_1)$ is true at point i.

Hence, the first hypothesis is true. In a similar manner, one may argue that the second hypothesis is also true; so the rule is complete. Note that the auxiliary assertions h_1 and h_2 are defined over the common interface variables $V_1 \cap V_2$. □

For the first example, which showed the incompleteness of rule **C1**, the following choices for h_1 and h_2 over the common variables $\{r_1, r_2\}$ ensure that the hypotheses of rule **C3** hold: $h_1 = r_1, h_2 = r_2$.

For the second example, which showed the incompleteness of rule **C2**, the property to be satisfied by $N_1//N_2$ may be written as $\mathsf{G}(\mathsf{GF}x \wedge \mathsf{GF}y)$. The following choices for h_1 and h_2 over the common variables x, y ensure that the hypotheses of rule **C3** hold: $h_1 = \mathit{true}, h_2 = \mathsf{GF}y$.

Interestingly[1], if we modify the hypotheses of rule **C3** so that they have the form $\{f\}M_1\{\mathsf{G}(h_1) \wedge (g_2 \wedge h_2) \triangleright (h_2 \Rightarrow g_1)\}$, which is also sound and complete, then these hypotheses may be obtained from rule **C1** for the composition $M_1//M_2$ with the following substitutions: $g_1 = g_1, g_2 = g_2, g_3 = h_1, g_4 = h_2, \Delta_1 = \{g_2, g_4\}, \Theta_1 = \{g_4\}, \Delta_2 = \{g_1, g_3\}, \Theta_2 = \{g_3\}$. The other Θ and Δ variables equal $\emptyset$. We also choose $M(1) = M_1, M(2) = M_2, M(3) = M_1, M(4) = M_2$ and the relation $\prec$: $3 \prec 2, 4 \prec 1$. This shows that modifying rule **C1** by allowing the g_i's to be *augmented with auxiliary assertions* h_i to form $(g_i \wedge h_i)$, results in a sound and complete rule.

---

[1] We thank an anonymous referee for this observation.

4 Translating Proofs

In this section we show how proofs derived using the circular rule **C3** can be translated into proofs using the non-circular rule **NC** and vice-versa. We also discuss some of the consequences of these translations. In the sequel, when W is clear from the context, we will write $(\forall W : f)$ simply as f.

Theorem 3 *(From Circular to Non-Circular) Suppose $\{f\}M_1//M_2\{G(g_1 \wedge g_2)\}$ has been derived from the circular rule **C3**. Then $\{f\}M_1//M_2\{G(g_1 \wedge g_2)\}$ may be derived by application of the rule **NC** by letting the intermediate assertion h equal $f \wedge (g_2 \wedge h_2) \triangleright ((h_2 \Rightarrow g_1) \wedge h_1)$.*

Proof. $\{f\}M_1\{f \wedge (g_2 \wedge h_2) \triangleright ((h_2 \Rightarrow g_1) \wedge h_1)\}$, the first requirement of rule **NC**, follows as a direct result of the first proof obligation from **C3** in the premise. We now show why the second requirement of rule **NC** also holds.

$\quad\quad\{f \wedge (h_2 \wedge g_2) \triangleright ((h_2 \Rightarrow g_1) \wedge h_1)\}M_2\{G(g_1 \wedge g_2)\}$
$\equiv\quad$ (by the definition of $\{f\}M\{g\}$)
$\quad\quad\{f\}M_2\{(h_2 \wedge g_2) \triangleright ((h_2 \Rightarrow g_1) \wedge h_1) \Rightarrow G(g_1 \wedge g_2)\}$
$\Leftarrow\quad$ (by the second proof obligation of rule **C3**)
$\quad\quad(h_1 \wedge g_1) \triangleright ((h_1 \Rightarrow g_2) \wedge h_2) \Rightarrow$
$\quad\quad[(h_2 \wedge g_2) \triangleright ((h_2 \Rightarrow g_1) \wedge h_1) \Rightarrow G(g_1 \wedge g_2)]$
$\equiv\quad$ (re-arranging)
$\quad\quad[(h_1 \wedge g_1) \triangleright ((h_1 \Rightarrow g_2) \wedge h_2)] \wedge [(h_2 \wedge g_2) \triangleright ((h_2 \Rightarrow g_1) \wedge h_1)] \Rightarrow$
$\quad\quad G(g_1 \wedge g_2)$
$\equiv\quad$ (temporal logic (see proof of Theorem 1))
$\quad\quad true$
$\square$

Theorem 4 *(From Non-Circular to Circular) Suppose $\{f\}M_1//M_2\{g\}$ has been derived from the non-circular rule **NC** using the intermediate assumption h. Then the conclusion $\{f\}M_1//M_2\{g\}$ may be derived by application of the rule **C3** using the substitution $h_1 = \mathsf{F}^-h$, $h_2 = true$, $g_1 = true$ and $g_2 = \mathsf{F}^-g$.*

Proof. Firstly, we note that the conclusion of the rule is the desired one. It is straightforward to show that, at the initial point, any computation satisfies GF^-g iff it satisfies g. Therefore, $\{f\}M_1//M_2\{G(g1 \wedge g2)\}$ is equivalent to $\{f\}M_1//M_2\{g\}$.
Consider the first proof obligation.

$\quad\quad\{f\}M_1\{(h_2 \wedge g_2) \triangleright ((h_2 \Rightarrow g_1) \wedge h_1)\}$
$\equiv\quad$ (substituting and simplifying)
$\quad\quad\{f\}M_1\{g_2 \triangleright h_1\}$
$\Leftarrow\quad$ ($\triangleright$ is anti-monotone in its first argument)
$\quad\quad\{f\}M_1\{true \triangleright \mathsf{F}^-(h)\}$
$\equiv\quad$ (as $true \triangleright \mathsf{F}^-(h) \equiv \mathsf{GF}^-(h)$)
$\quad\quad\{f\}M_1\{\mathsf{GF}^-(h)\}$

$\equiv$ (as $\mathsf{GF}^-(p)$ and p are equivalent at the initial point)
$\{f\}M_1\{h\}$
$\equiv$ (by the first premise in the supposition)
true

Now we show that the second premise is also true.

$\{f\}M_2\{(h_1 \wedge g_1) \triangleright ((h_1 \Rightarrow g_2) \wedge h_2)\}$
$\equiv$ (substituting and simplifying)
$\{f\}M_2\{h_1 \triangleright (h_1 \Rightarrow g_2)\}$
(definition of h_1, g_2)
$\equiv$ $\{f\}M_2\{\mathsf{F}^-(h) \triangleright (\mathsf{F}^-(h) \Rightarrow \mathsf{F}^-(g))\}$

This follows by an induction on positions of any sequence satisfying $f \wedge \mathcal{L}(M_2)$. At the initial position, by the second part of **NC**, $(h \Rightarrow g)$ holds, thus, $(\mathsf{F}^-h \Rightarrow \mathsf{F}^-g)$ holds at the initial position. At any other position i, by the assumption F^-h for 0 up to $i-1$, h must be true initially, hence, g is true initially by the second part of **NC**, so that F^-g is true at position i. □

We note that the translations make no use of quantified formulae, which justifies the following corollary.

Corollary 0 *Compositional Rule C3 is complete for linear temporal logic.*

Proof. As in the proof of the previous theorem, one can write a property f as $\mathsf{G}(true \wedge \mathsf{F}^-(f))$ and apply rule **C3**. Since **C3** was shown to be complete for properties of the form $\mathsf{G}(g_1 \wedge g_2)$ it follows that **C3** is sufficient for proving any linear temporal logic property. We note that the proof of Theorem 2, presented above, does make use of quantified temporal properties. This use of quantification is beneficial, in that the properties constructed in the proof of completeness may be restricted to the variables which are mentioned in the interface between M_1 and M_2. However, it is possible to prove Theorem 2 without reference to quantified formulae (this proof has been left out for space reasons) and hence the result follows. □

4.1 The Cost of a Proof

In this section we discuss the computational cost of applying the various rules. The goal is to calculate the cost of translating an instance of the use of one proof rule into the use of another proof rule and to get a measure on the complexity of a proof rule.

Consider the proof obligation $\{f\}M\{g\}$ where f and g are pure LTL formulae (they contain no quantifiers). If such a proof were done by hand then any complexity measure would be, at best, highly subjective. Suppose, on the other hand, that this proof were given to a model checker. The obligation amounts to showing that every W-computation of M that satisfies f also satisfies

g. Typically, this is done as follows [VW86]. First, translate f, M and $\neg g$ into automata A_f, A_M and $A_{\neg g}$, respectively, such that the set of sequences accepted by the automaton is exactly the set of sequences accepted by the corresponding formula. Then $\mathcal{L}(A_f \cap A_M \cap A_{\neg g}) = \emptyset$ iff the set of computations of M which satisfy f all satisfy g. The complexity of the translation is approximately linear in $|M|$ and exponential in the lengths of f and g [VW86] [LPZ85]. This leads to the following definition.

Definition 8 (Proof Cost) *The cost of a proof obligation $\{f\}M\{g\}$, for temporal logic formulae f and g and finite state structure M is $2^{|f|+|g|}|M|$.*

Note that $|q \triangleright p| = |\neg(q \cup \neg(p))|$, which equals $|p|+|q|+3$. Suppose that we have translated a circular proof to a non-circular proof via the method outlined in Theorem 3. Without loss of generality, assume that $|M_1| \leq |M_2|$, $|h_1| \leq |h_2|$ and $|g_1| \leq |g_2|$. The cost, c, of showing the premises of rule **C3**

- $\{f\}M_1\{(h_2 \wedge g_2) \triangleright ((h_2 \Rightarrow g_1) \wedge h_1)\}$ and
- $\{f\}M_2\{(h_1 \wedge g_1) \triangleright ((h_1 \Rightarrow g_2) \wedge h_2)\}$

is bounded by $2^{|f|+3|h_2|+2|g_2|+8}|M_2|$. The cost, nc, of showing the translated premises for rule **NC**

- $\{f\}M_1\{f \wedge (h_2 \wedge g_2) \triangleright ((h_2 \Rightarrow g_1) \wedge h_1)\}$ and
- $\{f \wedge (h_2 \wedge g_2) \triangleright ((h_2 \Rightarrow g_1) \wedge h_1)\}M_2\{\mathsf{G}(g_1 \wedge g_2)\}$

is bounded by $2^{2|f|+3|h_2|+4|g_2|+11}|M_2|$.

So the cost of the circular proof is bounded by $2^{\alpha}|M_2|$, where α is a function linear in the sizes of f, g_i and h_i and the cost of the non-circular proof is bounded by $2^{2\alpha}|M_2|$, so the translation process can be said to be efficient.

Now suppose that we have translated a non-circular proof to a circular proof via the method outlined in Theorem 4. The cost, nc, of showing the premises for rule **NC**

- $\{f\}M_1\{h\}$ and
- $\{h\}M_2\{g\}$

is bounded by $2^{|f|+|h|+|g|+2}|M_2|$. The cost, c of showing the simplified translated premises for rule **C3**

- $\{f\}M_1\{\mathsf{F}^-(g) \triangleright \mathsf{F}^-(h)\}$ and
- $\{f\}M_2\{\mathsf{F}^-(h) \triangleright (\mathsf{F}^-(h) \Rightarrow \mathsf{F}^-(g))\}$

is bounded by $2^{|f|+2|h|+|g|+6}|M_2|$. Hence translating from circular to non-circular is, essentially, efficient.

5 Related Work

There are several proposals for compositional reasoning rules in the literature, but only a few investigations of the completeness of these rules – a good survey of the field appears in the COMPOS97 proceedings [dRLP97]. The earliest proposals for assume-guarantee reasoning are from [Jon81,CM81] – these are concerned with establishing safety properties of networks of processes. Zwiers' book [Zwi89] contains much of the groundwork necessary for reasoning about compositional proof systems. Proofs of the completeness of compositional reasoning systems for safety properties are found in [ZdRvE84][Pan88][PJ91] [dRdBH+99]. Other assume-guarantee rules for safety properties are proposed in [Sta85] [Pnu85] [Kur87] [AH96] [McM97]. More general rules that apply to both safety and liveness properties are proposed in [Pnu85] [Jos87] [CLM89] [GL94] [AL95] [McM99].

We have concentrated on the completeness question for general rules that apply to both safety and liveness properties. As shown in Section 3, the circular rules in [AL95] and the rule **C1** derived from [McM99] are incomplete. The circular rule presented in [HQRT98] for the simulation-based verification paradigm is also incomplete – for lack of space, this proof is left for the full paper. The simplicity of the counter-examples suggests that the incompleteness may indeed impact the verification of systems in practice. We present a new circular rule, which is a modification of rule **C1**, and show it to be sound and complete for all of LTL – in fact it is straightforward to generalize these ideas so that the rule is complete for the ω-regular languages. The proofs carried out using rule **C1**, including that of the Tomasulo algorithm [McM98], can be carried out in exactly the same manner with the new rule. We also investigate whether circularity is, in itself, essential for reasoning about composed systems, and show that for assume-guarantee reasoning in LTL, the notion of circularity is a somewhat weak one, in that proofs carried out with circular rules are efficiently translatable into proofs with non-circular rules, and vice-versa.

The computational complexity of establishing an assume-guarantee triple has been studied extensively in [GL94,KV95,KV97], for various combinations of specification logics. We have considered a different question, that of the complexity of translating between proofs obtained with different compositional rules, whenever this is possible.

There are a number of ways one could choose to strengthen the circular proof rules found in the literature in order to make them complete. We have chosen one in particular, rule **C3**. Our choice was motivated by a desire to remain as close as possible to the spirit of the original circular proof rule - namely, to avoid the "direct" use of $M_1//M_2$ when proving properties about this composition. Specifically, we have decided not to allow the use of temporal implication, $h \Rightarrow g$, as a proof rule [MP95]. Our results show that implication is not necessary in order to obtain a sound and complete rule. Furthermore, rules that include implication may allow the proof of $f \wedge \mathcal{L}_W(M_1) \wedge \mathcal{L}_W(M_2) \Rightarrow g$ to be instantiated directly as an implication without use of the, hopefully, better rules mentioning only M_1 or M_2. That this goal has been, to some extent, mitigated against in our proof of completeness should not come as a surprise in light of the difficulty of the problem.

Acknowledgment: The authors thank Willem-Paul de Roever and the anonymous referees for many interesting and helpful comments.

References

[AH96] R. Alur and T. Henzinger. Reactive modules. In *IEEE LICS*, 1996.

[AL95] M. Abadi and L. Lamport. Conjoining specifications. *ACM Trans. on Programming Languages and Systems (TOPLAS)*, May 1995.

[CE81] E.M. Clarke and E. A. Emerson. Design and synthesis of synchronization skeletons using branching time temporal logic. In *Workshop on Logics of Programs*, volume 131 of *LNCS*. Springer-Verlag, 1981.

[CES86] E.M. Clarke, E.A. Emerson, and A.P. Sistla. Automatic verification of finite-state concurrent systems using temporal logic. *ACM Transactions on Programming Languages and Systems (TOPLAS)*, 8(2), 1986.

[CLM89] E.M. Clarke, D.E. Long, and K.L. McMillan. Compositional model checking. In *IEEE LICS*, 1989.

[CM81] K.M. Chandy and J. Misra. Proofs of networks of processes. *IEEE Transactions on Software Engineering*, 7(4), 1981.

[dRdBH+99] W-P. de Roever, F. de Boer, U. Hannemann, J. Hooman, Y. Lakhnech, M. Poel, and J. Zwiers. *Concurrency Verification: Introduction to Compositional and Noncompositional Proof Methods*. Draft book, 1999.

[dRLP97] W-P. de Roever, H. Langmaack, and A. Pnueli, editors. *Compositionality: The Significant Difference*, volume 1536 of *LNCS*. Springer-Verlag, 1997.

[GL94] O. Grümberg and D.E. Long. Model checking and modular verification. *ACM Trans. on Programming Languages and Systems (TOPLAS)*, 1994.

[Hoa69] C.A.R. Hoare. An axiomatic basis for computer programming. *Communications of the ACM*, 1969.

[HP85] D. Harel and A. Pnueli. On the development of reactive systems. In K. Apt, editor, *Logics and Models of Concurrent Systems*, volume F-13 of *NATO Advanced Summer Institutes*, pages 477–498. Springer-Verlag, 1985.

[HQRT98] T.A. Henzinger, S. Qadeer, S.K. Rajamani, and S. Tasiran. An assume-guarantee rule for checking simulation. In *FMCAD*, volume 1522 of *LNCS*, 1998.

[Jon81] C.B. Jones. *Development methods for computer programs including a notion of interference*. PhD thesis, Oxford University, 1981.

[Jos87] B. Josko. Model checking of CTL formulae under liveness assumptions. In *ICALP*, volume 267 of *LNCS*, 1987.

[Kur87] R.P. Kurshan. Reducibility in analysis of coordination. In *Discrete Event Systems: Models and Applications*, volume 103 of *LNCIS*, 1987.

[KV95] O. Kupferman and M. Vardi. On the complexity of branching modular model checking. In *CONCUR*, volume 962 of *LNCS*, 1995.

[KV97] O. Kupferman and M. Vardi. Module checking revisited. In *CAV*, volume 1254 of *LNCS*, 1997.

[LPZ85]   O. Lichtenstein, A. Pnueli, and L. Zuck. The glory of the past. In *Proc. of the Conf. on Logics of Programs*, 1985.
[McM97]   K.L. McMillan. A compositional rule for hardware design refinement. In *CAV*, volume 1254 of *LNCS*, 1997.
[McM98]   K.L. McMillan. Verification of an implementation of Tomasulo's algorithm by compositional model checking. In *CAV*, volume 1427 of *LNCS*, 1998.
[McM99]   K.L. McMillan. Circular compositional reasoning about liveness. In *CHARME*, volume 1703 of *LNCS*, 1999.
[MP84]   Z. Manna and A. Pnueli. Adequate proof principles for invariance and liveness properties of concurrent programs. *Science of Computer Programming*, 1984.
[MP95]   Z. Manna and A. Pnueli. *Temporal Verification of Reactive Systems: Safety*. Springer-Verlag, 1995.
[Pan88]   P. Pandya. *Compositional Verification of Distributed Programs*. PhD thesis, University of Bombay, 1988.
[PJ91]   P. Pandya and M. Joseph. P-A logic - a compositional proof system for distributed programs. *Distributed Computing*, 1991.
[Pnu77]   A. Pnueli. The temporal logic of programs. In *FOCS*, 1977.
[Pnu85]   A. Pnueli. In transition from global to modular reasoning about programs. In *Logics and Models of Concurrent Systems*, NATO ASI Series, 1985.
[QS82]   J.P. Queille and J. Sifakis. Specification and verification of concurrent systems in CESAR. In *Proc. of the 5th International Symposium on Programming*, volume 137 of *LNCS*, 1982.
[Sta85]   E. Stark. A proof technique for rely/guarantee properties. In *FST&TCS*, volume 206 of *LNCS*, 1985.
[Tho90]   W. Thomas. Automata on infinite objects. In *Handbook of Theoretical Computer Science, Volume B: Formal Models and Semantics*, edited by J. van Leeuwen. Elsevier and MIT Press, 1990.
[VW86]   M. Vardi and P. Wolper. An automata-theoretic approach to automatic program verification. In *IEEE Symposium on Logic in Computer Science*, 1986.
[ZdRvE84]   J. Zwiers, W.P. de Roever, and P. van EmdeBoas. Compositionality and concurrent networks: Soundness and completeness of a proof system. *Technical Report, University of Nijmegen*, 1984.
[Zwi89]   J. Zwiers. *Compositionality, Concurrency and Partial Correctness*, volume 321 of *LNCS*. Springer-Verlag, 1989.

Counterexample-Guided Abstraction Refinement *

Edmund Clarke[1], Orna Grumberg[2], Somesh Jha[1], Yuan Lu[1], and Helmut Veith[1,3]

[1] Carnegie Mellon University, Pittsburgh, USA
[2] Technion, Haifa, Israel
[3] Vienna University of Technology, Austria

Abstract. We present an automatic iterative abstraction-refinement methodology in which the initial abstract model is generated by an automatic analysis of the control structures in the program to be verified. Abstract models may admit erroneous (or "spurious") counterexamples. We devise new symbolic techniques which analyze such counterexamples and refine the abstract model correspondingly. The refinement algorithm keeps the size of the abstract state space small due to the use of abstraction functions which distinguish many degrees of abstraction for each program variable. We describe an implementation of our methodology in NuSMV. Practical experiments including a large Fujitsu IP core design with about 500 latches and 10000 lines of SMV code confirm the effectiveness of our approach.

1 Introduction

The state explosion problem remains a major hurdle in applying model checking to large industrial designs. Abstraction is certainly the most important technique for handling this problem. In fact, it is essential for verifying designs of industrial complexity. Currently, abstraction is typically a manual process, often requiring considerable creativity. In order for model checking to be used more widely in industry, automatic techniques are needed for generating abstractions. In this paper, we describe an automatic abstraction technique for ACTL* specifications which is based on an analysis of the structure of formulas appearing in the program (ACTL* is a fragment of CTL* which only allows universal quantification over paths). In general, our technique computes an upper approximation of the original program. Thus, when a specification is true in the abstract model, it will also be true in the concrete design. However, if the specification is false in the abstract model, the counterexample may be the result of some behavior in the approximation which is not present in the original model. When this happens, it is necessary to refine the abstraction so that the behavior which caused the erroneous counterexample is eliminated. The main contribution of this paper is an efficient automatic refinement technique which uses information obtained from erroneous counterexamples. The refinement algorithm

---

* This research is sponsored by the Semiconductor Research Corporation (SRC) under Contract No. 97-DJ-294, the National Science Foundation (NSF) under Grant No. CCR-9505472, and the Max Kade Foundation. One of the authors is also supported by Austrian Science Fund Project N Z29-INF. Any opinions, findings and conclusions or recommendations expressed in this material are those of the authors and do not necessarily reflect the views of SRC, NSF, or the United States Government.

keeps the size of the abstract state space small due to the use of abstraction functions which distinguish many degrees of abstraction for each program variable. Practical experiments including a large Fujitsu IP core design with about 500 latches and 10000 lines of SMV code confirm the competitiveness of our implementation. Although our current implementation is based on NuSMV, it is in principle not limited to the input language of SMV and can be applied to other languages.

Our paper follows the general framework established by Clarke, Grumberg, and Long [10]. We assume that the reader has some familiarity with that framework. In our methodology, *atomic formulas* are automatically extracted from the program that describes the model. The atomic formulas are similar to the *predicates* used for abstraction by Graf and Saidi [13] and later in [11,20]. However, instead of using the atomic formulas to generate an abstract global transition system, we use them to construct an explicit *abstraction function*. The abstraction function preserves logical relationships among the atomic formulas instead of treating them as independent propositions. The initial abstract model is constructed by adapting the *existential abstraction* techniques proposed in [8, 10] to our framework. Then, a traditional model checker is used to determine whether $ACTL^*$ properties hold in the abstract model. If the answer is yes, then the concrete model also satisfies the property. If the answer is no, then the model checker generates a counterexample. Since the abstract model has more behaviors than the concrete one, the abstract counterexample might not be valid. We say that such a counterexample is *spurious*. Such abstraction techniques are also known as false negative techniques.

In our methodology, we provide a new symbolic algorithm to determine whether an abstract counterexample is spurious. If the counterexample is not spurious, we report it to the user and stop. If the counterexample is spurious, the abstraction function must be refined to eliminate it. In our methodology, we identify the shortest prefix of the abstract counterexample that does not correspond to an actual trace in the concrete model. The last abstract state in this prefix is split into less abstract states so that the spurious counterexample is eliminated. Thus, a more refined abstraction function is obtained. Note that there may be many ways of splitting the abstract state; each determines a different refinement of the abstraction function. It is desirable to obtain the coarsest refinement which eliminates the counterexample because this corresponds to the *smallest* abstract model that is suitable for verification. We prove, however, that finding the coarsest refinement is NP-hard. Because of this, we use a polynomial-time algorithm which gives a suboptimal but sufficiently good refinement of the abstraction function. The applicability of our heuristic algorithm is confirmed by our experiments. Using the refined abstraction function obtained in this manner, a new abstract model is built and the entire process is repeated. Our methodology is complete for the fragment of $ACTL^*$ which has counterexamples that are either paths or loops, i.e., we are guaranteed to either find a valid counterexample or prove that the system satisfies the desired property. In principle, our methodology can be extended to all of $ACTL^*$.

Using counterexamples to refine abstract models has been investigated by a number of other researchers beginning with the *localization reduction* of Kurshan [14]. He models a concurrent system as a composition of L-processes $L_1, \ldots, L_n$ (L-processes are described in detail in [14]). The localization reduction is an iterative technique that starts with a small subset of relevant L-processes that are topologically close to the specification in the *variable dependency graph*. All other program variables are abstracted away with nondeterministic assignments. If the counterexample is found to be spurious, additional variables are added to eliminate the counterexample. The heuristic for selecting these variables also uses information from the variable dependency graph. Note that the localization reduction either leaves a variable unchanged or replaces it by a nondeterministic assignment. A similar approach has been described by Balarin in [2,15]. In our approach, the abstraction functions exploit logical relationships among variables appearing in atomic formulas that occur in the control structure of the program. Moreover, the way we use abstraction functions makes it possible to distinguish many degrees of abstraction for each variable. Therefore, in the refinement step only very small and local changes to the abstraction functions are necessary and the abstract model remains comparatively small.

Another refinement technique has recently been proposed by Lind-Nielson and Andersen [17]. Their model checker uses upper and lower approximations in order to handle all of CTL. Their approximation techniques enable them to avoid rechecking the entire model after each refinement step while guaranteeing completeness. As in [2,14] the variable dependency graph is used both to obtain the initial abstraction and in the refinement process. Variable abstraction is also performed in a similar manner. Therefore, our abstraction-refinement methodology relates to their technique in essentially the same way as it relates to the classical localization reduction.

A number of other papers [16,18,19] have proposed abstraction-refinement techniques for CTL model checking. However, these papers do not use counterexamples to refine the abstraction. We believe that the methods described in these papers are orthogonal to our technique and may even be combined with ours in order to achieve better performance. A recent technique proposed by Govindaraju and Dill [12] may be a starting point in this direction, since it also tries to identify the first spurious state in an abstract counterexample. It randomly chooses a concrete state corresponding to the first spurious state and tries to construct a real counterexample starting with the image of this state under the transition relation. The paper only talks about safety properties and path counterexamples. It does not describe how to check liveness properties with cyclic counterexamples. Furthermore, our method does not use random choice to extend the counterexample; instead it analyzes the cause of the spurious counterexample and uses this information to guide the refinement process. A more detailed comparison with related work will be given in the full version

Summarizing, our technique has a number of advantages over previous work:

- (i) The technique is complete for an important fragment of ACTL*.
- (ii) The initial abstraction and the refinement steps are efficient and entirely automatic. All algorithms are symbolic.
- (iii) In comparison to methods like the localization reduction, we distinguish more degrees of abstraction for each variable. Thus, the changes in the refinement are potentially finer in our approach.
- (iv) The refinement procedure is guaranteed to eliminate spurious counterexamples while keeping the state space of the abstract model small.

We have implemented our new methodology in NuSMV [6] and applied it to a number of benchmark designs [6]. In addition we have used it to debug a large IP core being developed at Fujitsu [1]. The design has about 350 symbolic variables which correspond to about 500 latches. Before using our methodology, we implemented the *cone of influence* reduction [8] in NuSMV to enhance its ability to check large models. Neither our enhanced version of NuSMV nor the recent version of SMV developed by Yang [23] were able to verify the Fujitsu IP core design. However, by using our new technique, we were able to find a subtle error in the design. Our program automatically abstracted 144 symbolic variables and performed three refinement steps. Currently, we are evaluating the methodology on other complex industrial designs.

The paper is organized as follows: Section 2 gives the basic definitions and terminology used throughout the paper. A general overview of our methodology is given in Section 3. Detailed descriptions of our abstraction-refinement algorithms are provided in Section 4. Performance improvements for the implementation are described in Section 5. Experimental results are presented in Section 6. Future research is discussed in Section 7.

2 Preliminaries

A *program* P has a finite set of variables $V = \{v_1, \cdots, v_n\}$, where each variable v_i has an associated finite domain D_{v_i}. The set of all possible states for program P is $D_{v_1} \times \cdots D_{v_n}$ which we denote by D. *Expressions* are built from variables in V, constants in D_{v_i}, and function symbols in the usual way, e.g. $v_1 + 3$. *Atomic formulas* are constructed from expressions and relation symbols, e.g. $v_1 + 3 < 5$. Similarly, *predicates* are composed of atomic formulas using negation ($\neg$), conjunction ($\wedge$), and disjunction ($\vee$). Given a predicate p, $\text{Atoms}(p)$ is the set of atomic formulas occurring in it. Let p be a predicate containing variables from V, and $d = (d_1, \ldots, d_n)$ be an element from D. Then we write $d \models p$ when the predicate obtained by replacing each occurrence of the variable v_i in p by the constant d_i evaluates to true.

Each variable v_i in the program has an associated *transition block*, which defines both the initial value and the transition relation for the variable v_i. An example of a transition block for the variable v_i is shown in Figure 1, where $I_i \subseteq D_{v_i}$ is the initial

$$
\begin{array}{lll}
\textbf{init}(v_i) := I_i; & \textbf{init}(x) := 0; & \textbf{init}(y) := 1; \\
\textbf{next}(v_i) := \textbf{case} & \textbf{next}(x) := \textbf{case} & \textbf{next}(y) := \textbf{case} \\
\quad C_i^1 : A_i^1; & \quad reset = \text{TRUE} : 0; & \quad reset = \text{TRUE} : 0; \\
\quad C_i^2 : A_i^2; & \quad x < y : x + 1; & \quad (x = y) \wedge \neg(y = 2) : y + 1; \\
\quad \cdots : \cdots; & \quad x = y : 0; & \quad (x = y) : 0; \\
\quad C_i^k : A_i^k; & \quad \textbf{else} : x; & \quad \textbf{else} : y; \\
\textbf{esac}; & \textbf{esac}; & \textbf{esac};
\end{array}
$$

Fig. 1. A generic transition block and a typical example

expression for the variable v_i, each condition C_i^j is a predicate, and A_i^j is an expression. The semantics of the transition block is similar to the semantics of the **case** statement in the modeling language of SMV, i.e., find the least j such that in the current state condition C_i^j is true and assign the value of the expression A_i^j to the variable v_i in the next state.

We assume that the specifications are written in a fragment of CTL* called ACTL* (see [10]). Assume that we are given an ACTL* specification φ, and a program P. For each transition block B_i let Atoms(B_i) be the set of atomic formulas that appear in the conditions. Let Atoms(φ) be the set of atomic formulas appearing in the specification φ. Atoms(P) is the set of atomic formulas that appear in the specification or in the conditions of the transition blocks.

Each program P naturally corresponds to a labeled *Kripke structure* $M = (S, I, R, L)$, where $S = D$ is the set of states, $I \subseteq S$ is a set of initial states, $R \subseteq S \times S$ is a transition relation, and $L : S \to 2^{\text{Atoms}(P)}$ is a labelling given by $L(d) = \{f \in \text{Atoms}(P) \mid d \models f\}$. Translating a program into a Kripke structure is straightforward and will not be described here.

An abstraction h for a program P is given by a surjection $h : D \to \widehat{D}$. Notice that the surjection h induces an equivalence relation $\equiv$ on the domain D in the following manner: let d, e be states in D, then

$$d \equiv e \text{ iff } h(d) = h(e).$$

Since an abstraction can be represented either by a surjection h or by an equivalence relation $\equiv$, we sometimes switch between these representations to avoid notational overhead.

Assume that we are given a program P and an abstraction function h for P. The *abstract Kripke structure* $\widehat{M} = (\widehat{S}, \widehat{I}, \widehat{R}, \widehat{L})$ corresponding to the abstraction function h is defined as follows:

1. $\widehat{S}$ is the abstract domain $\widehat{D}$.
2. $\widehat{I}(\widehat{d})$ iff $\exists d(h(d) = \widehat{d} \wedge I(d))$.
3. $\widehat{R}(\widehat{d_1}, \widehat{d_2})$ iff $\exists d_1 \exists d_2 (h(d_1) = \widehat{d_1} \wedge h(d_2) = \widehat{d_2} \wedge R(d_1, d_2))$.
4. $\widehat{L}(\widehat{d}) = \bigcup_{h(d) = \widehat{d}} L(d)$.   (This definition will be justified in Theorem 1.)

This abstraction technique is called *existential abstraction* [8]. An atomic formula f *respects* an abstraction function h if for all d and d' in the domain D, $(d \equiv d') \Rightarrow (d \models f \Leftrightarrow d' \models f)$. Let $\widehat{d}$ be an abstract state. $\widehat{L}(\widehat{d})$ is *consistent*, if all concrete states corresponding to $\widehat{d}$ satisfy all labels in $\widehat{L}(\widehat{d})$, i.e., for all $d \in h^{-1}(\widehat{d})$ it holds that $d \models \bigwedge_{f \in \widehat{L}(\widehat{d})} f$.

Theorem 1. *Let h be an abstraction and φ be an ACTL* specification where the atomic subformulas respect h. Then the following holds: (i) $\widehat{L}(\widehat{d})$ is consistent for all abstract states $\widehat{d}$ in $\widehat{M}$; (ii) $\widehat{M} \models \varphi \Rightarrow M \models \varphi$.*

In other words, correctness of the abstract model implies correctness of the concrete model. On the other hand, if the abstract model invalidates an ACTL* specification, i.e., $\widehat{M} \not\models \varphi$, *the actual model may still satisfy the specification*.

Example 1. Assume that for a traffic light controller (see Figure 2), we want to prove $\psi = \mathbf{AG}\,\mathbf{AF}(state = red)$ using the abstraction function $h(red) = red$ and $h(green) =$

$h(yellow) = go$. It is easy to see that $M \models \psi$ while $\widehat{M} \not\models \psi$. There exists an infinite trace $\langle red, go, go, \dots \rangle$ that invalidates the specification.

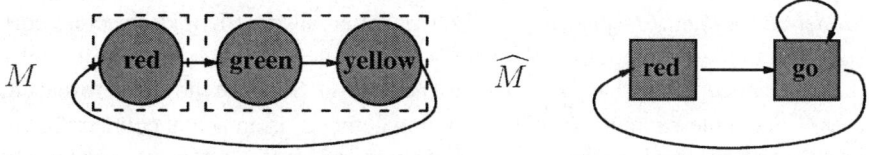

Fig. 2. Abstraction of a Traffic Light.

If an abstract counterexample does not correspond to some concrete counterexample, we call it *spurious*. For example, $\langle red, go, go, \dots \rangle$ in the above example is a spurious counterexample.

When the set of possible states is given as the product $D_1 \times \cdots D_n$ of smaller domains, an abstraction h can be described by surjections $h_i : D_i \to \widehat{D_i}$, such that $h(d_1, \dots, d_n)$ is equal to $(h_1(d_1), \dots, h_n(d_n))$, and $\widehat{D}$ is equal to $\widehat{D_1} \times \cdots \widehat{D_n}$. In this case, we write $h = (h_1, \dots, h_n)$. The equivalence relations $\equiv_i$ corresponding to the individual surjections h_i induce an equivalence relation $\equiv$ over the entire domain $D = D_1 \times \cdots \times D_n$ in the obvious manner:

$$(d_1, \cdots, d_n) \equiv (e_1, \cdots, e_n) \text{ iff } d_1 \equiv_1 e_1 \wedge \cdots \wedge d_n \equiv_n e_n$$

In previous work on existential abstraction [10], abstractions were defined for each variable domain, i.e., D_i in the above paragraph was chosen to be D_{v_i}, where D_{v_i} is the set of possible values for variable v_i. Unfortunately, many abstraction functions h can not be described in this simple manner. For example, let $D = \{0, 1, 2\} \times \{0, 1, 2\}$, and $\widehat{D} = \{0, 1\} \times \{0, 1\}$. Then there are $4^9 = 262144$ functions h from D to $\widehat{D}$. Next, consider $h = (h_1, h_2)$. Since there are $2^3 = 8$ functions from $\{0, 1, 2\}$ to $\{0, 1\}$, there are only 64 functions of this form from D to $\widehat{D}$.

In this paper, we define abstraction functions in a different way. We partition the set V of variables into sets of related variables called *variable clusters* $VC_1, \dots, VC_m$, where each variable cluster VC_i has an associated domain $D_{VC_i} := \prod_{v \in VC_i} D_v$. Consequently, $D = D_{VC_1} \times \cdots D_{VC_m}$. We define abstraction functions as surjections on the domains D_{VC_i}, i.e., D_i in the above paragraph is equal to D_{VC_i}. Thus, the notion of abstraction used in this paper is more general than the one used in [10].

3 Overview

For a program P and an ACTL* formula φ, our goal is to check whether the Kripke structure M corresponding to P satisfies φ. Our methodology consists of the following steps.

1. *Generate the initial abstraction:* We generate an initial abstraction h by examining the transition blocks corresponding to the variables of the program. We consider

the conditions used in the **case** statements and construct variable clusters for variables which interfere with each other via these conditions. Details can be found in Section 4.1.

2. *Model-check the abstract structure:* Let $\widehat{M}$ be the abstract Kripke structure corresponding to the abstraction h. We check whether $\widehat{M} \models \varphi$. If the check is affirmative, then we can conclude that $M \models \varphi$ (see Theorem 1). Suppose the check reveals that there is a counterexample $\widehat{T}$. We ascertain whether $\widehat{T}$ is an actual counterexample, i.e., a counterexample in the unabstracted structure M. If $\widehat{T}$ turns out to be an actual counterexample, we report it to the user, otherwise $\widehat{T}$ is a spurious counterexample, and we proceed to step 3.

3. *Refine the abstraction:* We refine the abstraction function h by partitioning a *single equivalence class* of $\equiv$ so that after the refinement the abstract structure $\widehat{M}$ corresponding to the refined abstraction function does not admit the spurious counterexample $\widehat{T}$. We will discuss partitioning algorithms for this purpose in Section 4.3. After refining the abstraction function, we return to step 2.

4 The Abstraction-Refinement Framework

4.1 Generating the Initial Abstraction

Assume that we are given a program P with n variables $\{v_1, \cdots, v_n\}$. Given an atomic formula f, let $var(f)$ be the set of variables appearing in f, e.g., $var(x = y)$ is $\{x, y\}$. Given a set of atomic formulas U, $var(U)$ equals $\bigcup_{f \in U} var(f)$. In general, for any syntactic entity X, $var(X)$ will be the set of variables appearing in X. We say that two atomic formulas f_1 and f_2 *interfere* iff $var(f_1) \cap var(f_2) \neq \emptyset$. Let $\equiv_I$ be the equivalence relation on $\text{Atoms}(P)$ that is the reflexive, transitive closure of the interference relation. The equivalence class of an atomic formula $f \in \text{Atoms}(P)$ is called the *formula cluster* of f and is denoted by $[f]$. Let f_1 and f_2 be two atomic formulas. Then $var(f_1) \cap var(f_2) \neq \emptyset$ implies that $[f_1] = [f_2]$. In other words, a variable v_i cannot appear in formulas that belong to two different formula clusters. Moreover, the formula clusters induce an equivalence relation $\equiv_V$ on the set of variables V in the following way:

$v_i \equiv_V v_j$ if and only if v_i and v_j appear in atomic formulas that belong to the same formula cluster.

The equivalence classes of $\equiv_V$ are called *variable clusters*. For instance, consider a formula cluster $FC_i = \{v_1 > 3, v_1 = v_2\}$. The corresponding variable cluster is $VC_i = \{v_1, v_2\}$. Let $\{FC_1, \ldots, FC_m\}$ be the set of formula clusters and $\{VC_1, \ldots, VC_m\}$ the set of corresponding variable clusters. We construct the initial abstraction $h = (h_1, \ldots, h_m)$ as follows. For each h_i, we set $D_{VC_i} = \prod_{v \in VC_i} D_v$, i.e., D_{VC_i} is the domain corresponding to the variable cluster VC_i. Since the variable clusters form a partition of the set of variables V, it follows that $D = D_{VC_1} \times \cdots D_{VC_m}$. For each variable cluster $VC_i = \{v_{i_1}, \ldots, v_{i_k}\}$, the corresponding abstraction h_i is defined on D_{VC_i} as follows.

$$h_i(d_1, \cdots, d_k) = h_i(e_1, \cdots, e_k) \text{ iff for all atomic formulas } f \in FC_i,$$
$$(d_1, \cdots, d_k) \models f \Leftrightarrow (e_1, \cdots, e_k) \models f.$$

In other words two values are in the same equivalence class if they cannot be "distinguished" by atomic formulas appearing in the formula cluster FC_i. The following example illustrates how we construct the initial abstraction h.

Example 2. Consider the program P with three variables $x, y \in \{0, 1, 2\}$, and $reset \in$ {TRUE, FALSE} shown in Figure 1. The set of atomic formulas is $\text{Atoms}(P) = \{(reset = \text{TRUE}), (x = y), (x < y), (y = 2)\}$. There are two formula clusters, $FC_1 = \{(x = y), (x < y), (y = 2)\}$ and $FC_2 = \{(reset = \text{TRUE})\}$. The corresponding variable clusters are $\{x, y\}$ and $\{reset\}$, respectively. Consider the formula cluster FC_1. Values $(0, 0)$ and $(1, 1)$ are in the same equivalence class because for all the atomic formulas f in the formula cluster FC_1 it holds that $(0, 0) \models f$ iff $(1, 1) \models f$. It can be shown that the domain $\{0, 1, 2\} \times \{0, 1, 2\}$ is partitioned into a total of five equivalence classes by this criterion. We denote these classes by the natural numbers $0, 1, 2, 3, 4$, and list them below:

$$0 = \{(0, 0), (1, 1)\},$$
$$1 = \{(0, 1)\},$$
$$2 = \{(0, 2), (1, 2)\},$$
$$3 = \{(1, 0), (2, 0), (2, 1)\},$$
$$4 = \{(2, 2)\}$$

The domain {TRUE, FALSE} has two equivalence classes – one containing FALSE and the other TRUE. Therefore, we define two abstraction functions $h_1 : \{0, 1, 2\}^2 \to \{0, 1, 2, 3, 4\}$ and $h_2 : \{\text{TRUE}, \text{FALSE}\} \to \{\text{TRUE}, \text{FALSE}\}$. The first function h_1 is given by $h_1(0, 0) = h_1(1, 1) = 0$, $h_1(0, 1) = 1$, $h_1(0, 2) = h_1(1, 2) = 2$, $h_1(1, 0) = h_1(2, 0) = h_1(2, 1) = 3$, $h_1(2, 2) = 4$. The second function h_2 is just the identity function, i.e., $h_2(reset) = reset$. Given the abstraction functions, we use the standard existential abstraction techniques to compute the abstract model.

4.2 Model Checking the Abstract Model

Given an ACTL* specification φ, an abstraction function h (assume that φ respects h), and a program P with a finite set of variables $V = \{v_1, \cdots, v_n\}$, let $\widehat{M}$ be the abstract Kripke structure corresponding to the abstraction function h. We use standard symbolic model checking procedures to determine whether $\widehat{M}$ satisfies the specification φ. If it does, then by Theorem 1 we can conclude that the original Kripke structure also satisfies φ. Otherwise, assume that the model checker produces a counterexample $\widehat{T}$ corresponding to the abstract model $\widehat{M}$. In the rest of this section, we will focus on counterexamples which are either *(finite) paths* or *loops*.

Identification of Spurious Path Counterexamples First, we will tackle the case when the counterexample $\widehat{T}$ is a path $\langle \widehat{s}_1, \cdots, \widehat{s}_n \rangle$. Given an abstract state $\widehat{s}$, the set of concrete states s such that $h(s) = \widehat{s}$ is denoted by $h^{-1}(\widehat{s})$, i.e., $h^{-1}(\widehat{s}) = \{s | h(s) = \widehat{s}\}$. We extend h^{-1} to sequences in the following way: $h^{-1}(\widehat{T})$ is the set of concrete paths given by the following expression

$$\{\langle s_1, \cdots, s_n \rangle | \bigwedge_{i=1}^{n} h(s_i) = \widehat{s}_i \wedge I(s_1) \wedge \bigwedge_{i=1}^{n-1} R(s_i, s_{i+1})\}.$$

We will occasionally write h_{path}^{-1} to emphasize the fact that h^{-1} is applied to a sequence. Next, we give a *symbolic* algorithm to compute $h^{-1}(\widehat{T})$. Let $S_1 = h^{-1}(\widehat{s}_1) \cap I$ and R be the transition relation corresponding to the unabstracted Kripke structure M. For $1 < i \leq n$, we define S_i in the following manner: $S_i := Img(S_{i-1}, R) \cap h^{-1}(\widehat{s}_i)$. In the definition of S_i, $Img(S_{i-1}, R)$ is the forward image of S_{i-1} with respect to the transition relation R. The sequence of sets S_i is computed symbolically using OBDDs and the standard image computation algorithm. The following lemma establishes the correctness of this procedure.

Lemma 1. *The following are equivalent:*

(i) The path $\widehat{T}$ corresponds to a concrete counterexample.
(ii) The set of concrete paths $h^{-1}(\widehat{T})$ is non-empty.
(iii) For all $1 \leq i \leq n$, $S_i \neq \emptyset$.

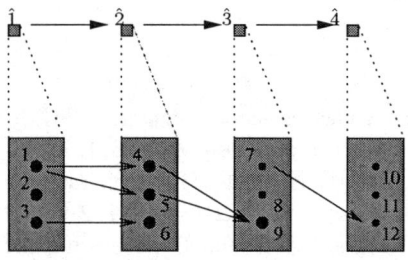

Algorithm SplitPATH
$S := h^{-1}(\widehat{s}_1) \cap I$
$j := 1$
while ($S \neq \emptyset$ and $j < n$) {
    $j := j + 1$
    $S_{\text{prev}} := S$
    $S := Img(S, R) \cap h^{-1}(\widehat{s}_j)$ }
if $S \neq \emptyset$ **then** output counterexample
else output j, S_{prev}

Fig. 3. An abstract counterexample

Fig. 4. SplitPATH checks spurious path.

Example 3. Consider a program with only one variable with domain $D = \{1, \cdots, 12\}$. Assume that the abstraction function h maps $x \in D$ to $\lfloor (x-1)/3 \rfloor + 1$. There are four abstract states corresponding to the equivalence classes $\{1, 2, 3\}, \{4, 5, 6\}, \{7, 8, 9\}$, and $\{10, 11, 12\}$. We call these abstract states $\widehat{1}, \widehat{2}, \widehat{3}$, and $\widehat{4}$. The transitions between states in the concrete model are indicated by the arrows in Figure 3; small dots denote non-reachable states. Suppose that we obtain an abstract counterexample $\widehat{T} = \langle \widehat{1}, \widehat{2}, \widehat{3}, \widehat{4} \rangle$. It is easy to see that $\widehat{T}$ is spurious. Using the terminology of Lemma 1, we have $S_1 = \{1, 2, 3\}$, $S_2 = \{4, 5, 6\}$, $S_3 = \{9\}$, and $S_4 = \emptyset$. Notice that S_4 and therefore $Img(S_3, R)$ are both empty.

It follows from Lemma 1 that if $h^{-1}(\widehat{T})$ is empty (i.e., if the counterexample $\widehat{T}$ is spurious), then there exists a minimal i ($2 \le i \le n$) such that $S_i = \emptyset$. The symbolic Algorithm **SplitPATH** in Figure 4 computes this number and the set of states in S_{i-1}. In this case, we proceed to the refinement step (see Section 4.3). On the other hand, if the conditions stated in Lemma 1 are true, then **SplitPATH** will report a "real" counterexample and we can stop.

Identification of Spurious Loop Counterexamples Now we consider the case when the counterexample $\widehat{T}$ includes a loop, which we write as $\langle \widehat{s_1}, \cdots, \widehat{s_i} \rangle \langle \widehat{s_{i+1}}, \cdots, \widehat{s_n} \rangle^\omega$. The loop starts at the abstract state $\widehat{s_{i+1}}$ and ends at $\widehat{s_n}$. Since this case is more complicated than the path counterexamples, we first present an example in which some of the typical situations occur.

Example 4. We consider a loop $\langle \widehat{s_1} \rangle \langle \widehat{s_2}, \widehat{s_3} \rangle^\omega$ as shown in Figure 5. In order to find out if the abstract loop corresponds to concrete loops, we unwind the counterexample as demonstrated in the figure. There are two situations where cycles occur. In the figure,

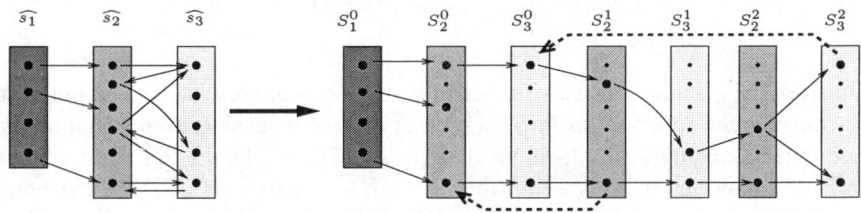

Fig. 5. A loop counterexample, and its unwinding.

for each of these situations, an example cycle (the first one occurring) is indicated by a fat dashed arrow. We make the following important observations: (i) A given abstract loop may correspond to several concrete loops of *different size*. (ii) Each of these loops may start at different stages of the unwinding. (iii) The unwinding eventually becomes periodic (in our case $S_3^0 = S_3^2$), but only after several stages of the unwinding. The size of the period is the least common multiple of the size of the individual loops, and thus, in general *exponential*.

We conclude from the example that a naive algorithm may have exponential time complexity due to an exponential number of loop unwindings. The following surprising result shows that for $\widehat{T} = \langle \widehat{s_1}, \cdots, \widehat{s_i} \rangle \langle \widehat{s_{i+1}}, \cdots, \widehat{s_n} \rangle^\omega$, the number of unwindings can be bounded by $min = \min_{i+1 \le j \le n} |h^{-1}(\widehat{s_j})|$, i.e., the number of unwindings is at most the number of concrete states for any abstract state in the loop. Let $\widehat{T}_{\mathrm{unwind}}$ denote this unwinded loop counterexample, i.e., the finite abstract path $\langle \widehat{s_1}, \ldots, \widehat{s_i} \rangle \langle \widehat{s_{i+1}}, \ldots, \widehat{s_n} \rangle^{min}$. Then the following theorem holds.

Theorem 2. *The following are equivalent: (i) $\widehat{T}$ corresponds to a concrete counterexample. (ii) $h_{\mathrm{path}}^{-1}(\widehat{T}_{\mathrm{unwind}})$ is not empty.*

It can be seen from Example 4 that loop counterexamples are combinatorially more complicated than path counterexamples. Therefore, the proof of Theorem 2 is not immediate; for details, we refer to [7]. We conclude from Theorem 2 that the Algorithm **SplitPATH** can be used to analyze abstract loop counterexamples with minor modifications. For easy reference we shall refer to this algorithm as **SplitLOOP**.

4.3 Refining the Abstraction

First, we will consider the case when the counterexample $\widehat{T} = \langle \widehat{s_1}, \cdots, \widehat{s_n} \rangle$ is a path. Since $\widehat{T}$ does not correspond to a real counterexample, by Lemma 1 (iii) there exists a set $S_i \subseteq h^{-1}(\widehat{s_i})$ with $1 \leq i < n$ such that $Img(S_i, R) \cap h^{-1}(\widehat{s_{i+1}}) = \emptyset$ and S_i is reachable from initial state set $h^{-1}(\widehat{s_1}) \cap I$. Since there is a transition from $\widehat{s_i}$ to $\widehat{s_{i+1}}$ in the abstract model, there is at least one transition from a state in $h^{-1}(\widehat{s_i})$ to a state in $h^{-1}(\widehat{s_{i+1}})$ even though there is no transition from S_i to $h^{-1}(\widehat{s_{i+1}})$. We partition $h^{-1}(\widehat{s_i})$ into three subsets $S_{i,0}, S_{i,1}$, and $S_{i,x}$ as follows (compare Figure 6):

$$S_{i,0} = S_i$$
$$S_{i,1} = \{s \in h^{-1}(\widehat{s_i}) | \exists s' \in h^{-1}(\widehat{s_{i+1}}).R(s, s')\}$$
$$S_{i,x} = h^{-1}(\widehat{s_i}) \setminus (S_{i,0} \cup S_{i,1}).$$

Intuitively, $S_{i,0}$ denotes the set of states in $h^{-1}(\widehat{s_i})$ that are reachable from initial states. $S_{i,1}$ denotes the set of states in $h^{-1}(\widehat{s_i})$ that are not reachable from initial states, but have at least one transition to some state in $h^{-1}(\widehat{s_{i+1}})$. The set $S_{i,1}$ cannot be empty since we know that there is a transition from $h^{-1}(\widehat{s_i})$ to $h^{-1}(\widehat{s_{i+1}})$. $S_{i,x}$ denotes the set of states that are not reachable from initial states, and do not have a transition to a state in $h^{-1}(\widehat{s_{i+1}})$. For illustration, consider again the example in Figure 3. Note that $S_1 = \{1,2,3\}$, $S_2 = \{4,5,6\}$, $S_3 = \{9\}$, and $S_4 = \emptyset$. Using the notation introduced above, we have $S_{3,0} = \{9\}$, $S_{3,1} = \{7\}$, and $S_{3,x} = \{8\}$. Since $S_{i,1}$ is not empty, there is a spurious transition $\widehat{s_i} \to \widehat{s_{i+1}}$. This causes the spurious counterexample $\widehat{T}$. Hence in order to refine the abstraction h so that the new model does not allow $\widehat{T}$, we need a refined abstraction function which separates the two sets $S_{i,0}$ and $S_{i,1}$, i.e., we need an abstraction function, in which no abstract state simultaneously contains states from $S_{i,0}$ and from $S_{i,1}$.

It is natural to describe the needed refinement in terms of equivalence relations: Recall that $h^{-1}(\widehat{s})$ is an equivalence class of $\equiv$ which has the form $E_1 \times \cdots \times E_m$, where each E_i is an equivalence class of $\equiv_i$. Thus, the refinement $\equiv'$ of $\equiv$ is obtained by partitioning the equivalence classes E_j into subclasses, which amounts to refining the equivalence relations $\equiv_j$. The *size of the refinement* is the number of new equivalence classes. Ideally, we would like to find the coarsest refinement that separates the two sets, i.e., the separating refinement with the smallest size. We can show however that this is computationally intractable.

Theorem 3. *(i) The problem of finding the coarsest refinement is NP-hard; (ii) when $S_{i,x} = \emptyset$, the problem can be solved in polynomial time.*

We find that the previously known poblem PARTITION INTO CLIQUES can be reduced to the coarsest refinement problem. The proof is omitted due to space restrictions.

On the other hand, we describe a polynomial time algorithm **PolyRefine** corresponding to case (ii) of Theorem 3 in Figure 7. Let P_j^+, P_j^- be two projection functions, such that for $s = (d_1, \ldots, d_m)$, $P_j^+(s) = d_j$ and $P_j^-(s) = (d_1, \ldots, d_{j-1}, d_{j+1}, \ldots, d_m)$. Then $proj(S_{i,0}, j, a)$ denotes the *projection* set $\{P_j^-(s) | P_j^+(s) = a, s \in S_{i,0}\}$. Intuitively, the condition $proj(S_{i,0}, j, a) \neq proj(S_{i,0}, j, b)$ in the algorithm means that there exists $(d_1, \ldots, d_{j-1}, d_{j+1}, \ldots, d_m) \in proj(S_{i,0}, j, a)$ and $(d_1, \ldots, d_{j-1}, d_{j+1}, \ldots, d_m) \notin proj(S_{i,0}, j, b)$. According to the definition of $proj(S_{i,0}, j, a)$, $s_1 = (d_1, \ldots, d_{j-1}, a, d_{j+1}, \ldots, d_m) \in S_{i,0}$ and $s_2 = (d_1, \ldots, d_{j-1}, b, d_{j+1}, \ldots, d_m) \notin S_{i,0}$, i.e., $s_2 \in S_{i,1}$. Note that s_1 and s_2 are only different at j-th component. Hence, the only way to separate s_1 and s_2 into different equivalence classes is that a and b have to be in different equivalence classes of $\equiv_j'$, i.e., $a \not\equiv_j' b$.

Lemma 2. *When $S_{i,x} = \emptyset$, the relation $\equiv_j'$ computed by **PolyRefine** is an equivalence relation which refines $\equiv_j$ and separates $S_{i,0}$ and $S_{i,1}$. Furthermore, the equivalence relation $\equiv_j'$ is the coarsest refinement of $\equiv_j$.*

Note that in symbolic presentation, the projection operation $proj(S_{i,0}, j, a)$ amounts to computing a generalized cofactor, which can be easily done by standard BDD methods. Given a function $f : D \to \{0, 1\}$, a generalized cofactor of f with respect to $g = (\bigwedge_{k=p}^{q} x_k = d_k)$ is the function $f_g = f(x_1, \ldots, x_{p-1}, d_p, \ldots, d_q, x_{q+1}, \ldots, x_n)$. In other words, f_g is the projection of f with respect to g. Symbolically, the set $S_{i,0}$ is represented by a function $f_{S_{i,0}} : D \to \{0, 1\}$, and therefore, the projection $proj(S_{i,0}, j, a)$ of $S_{i,0}$ to value a of the jth component corresponds to a cofactor of $f_{S_{i,0}}$.

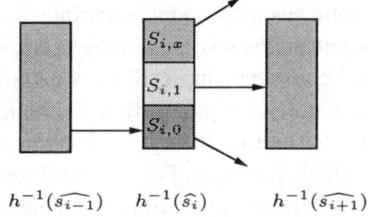

Algorithm PolyRefine
for j := 1 to m {
　　$\equiv_j' := \equiv_j$
　　for every $a, b \in E_j$ {
　　　　if $proj(S_{i,0}, j, a) \neq proj(S_{i,0}, j, b)$
　　　　　　then $\equiv_j' := \equiv_j' \setminus \{(a, b)\}$　　}}

Fig. 6. Three sets $S_{i,0}, S_{i,1}$, and $S_{i,x}$

Fig. 7. The algorithm **PolyRefine**

In our implementation, we use the following heuristics: We merge the states in $S_{i,x}$ into $S_{i,1}$, and use the algorithm **Polyrefine** to find the coarsest refinement that separates the sets $S_{i,0}$ and $S_{i,1} \cup S_{i,x}$. The equivalence relation computed by **PolyRefine** in this manner is not optimal, but it is a correct refinement which separates $S_{i,0}$ and $S_{i,1}$, and eliminates the spurious counterexample. This heuristic has given good results in our practical experiments.

Since according to Theorem 2, the algorithm **SplitLOOP** for loop counterexamples works analogously as **SplitPATH**, the refinement procedure for spurious loop counterexamples works analogously, too. Details are omitted due to space restrictions. Our refinement procedure continues to refine the abstraction function by partitioning equivalence classes until a real counterexample is found, or the $ACTL^*$ property is verified.

The partitioning procedure is guaranteed to terminate since each equivalence class must contain at least one element. Thus, our method is complete.

Theorem 4. *Given a model M and an ACTL* specification φ whose counterexample is either path or loop, our algorithm will find a model $\widehat{M}$ such that $\widehat{M} \models \varphi \Leftrightarrow M \models \varphi$.*

5 Performance Improvements

The symbolic methods described in Section 4 can be directly implemented using BDDs. Our implementation uses additional heuristics which are outlined in this section. For details, we refer to our technical report [7].

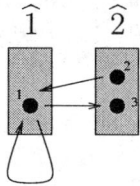

Fig. 8. A spurious loop counterexample $\langle \widehat{1}, \widehat{2} \rangle^\omega$

Two-phase Refinement Algorithms. Consider the spurious loop counterexample $\widehat{T} = \langle \widehat{1}, \widehat{2} \rangle^\omega$ of Figure 8. Although $\widehat{T}$ is spurious, the concrete states involved in the example contain an infinite path $\langle 1, 1, \ldots \rangle$ which is a potential counterexample. Since we know that our method is complete, such cases could be ignored. Due to practical performance considerations, however, we came to the conclusion that the relatively small effort to detect additional counterexamples is justified as a valuable heuristic. For a general loop counterexample $\widehat{T} = \langle \widehat{s}_1, \ldots, \widehat{s}_i \rangle \langle \widehat{s}_{i+1}, \ldots, \widehat{s}_n \rangle^\omega$, we therefore proceed in two phases:
(i) We restrict the model to the state space $S_{\text{local}} := (\bigcup_{1 \leq i \leq n} h^{-1}(\widehat{s}_i))$ of the counterexample and use the standard fixpoint computation for temporal formulas (see e.g. [8]) to check the property on the Kripke structure restricted to S_{local}. If a concrete counterexample is found, then the algorithm terminates.
(ii) If no counterexample is found, we use **SplitLOOP** and **PolyRefine** to compute a refinement as described above.
This two-phase algorithm is slightly slower than the original one if we do not find a concrete counterexample; in many cases however, it can speed up the search for a concrete counterexample. An analogous two phase approach is used for finite path counterexamples.

Approximation. Despite the use of partitioned transition relations it is often infeasible to compute the total transition relation of the model M [8]. Therefore, the abstract model $\widehat{M}$ cannot be computed from M directly. In previous work [2,10], a method which we call *early approximation* has been introduced: first, abstraction is applied to the BDD representation of each transition block and then the BDDs for the partitioned transition relation are built from the already abstracted BDDs for the transition blocks. The disadvantage of early approximation is that it *over-approximates* the abstract model $\widehat{M}$ [9]. In our approach, a heuristic individually determines for each variable cluster VC_i, if early approximation should be applied or if the abstraction function should be applied in an exact manner. Our method has the advantage that it balances overapproximation and memory usage. Moreover, the overall method presented in our paper remains complete with this approximation.

Abstractions For Distant Variables. In addition to the methods of Section 4.1, we completely abstract variables whose distance from the specification in the *variable dependency graph* is greater than a user-defined constant. Note that the variable dependency graph is also used for this purpose in the localization reduction [2,14,17] in a similar way. However, the refinement process of the localization reduction [14] can only turn a completely abstracted variable into a completely unabstracted variable, while our method uses intermediate abstraction functions.

6 Experimental Results

We have implemented our methodology in NuSMV [6] which uses the CUDD package [21] for symbolic representation. We performed two sets of experiments. One set is on five benchmark designs. The other was performed on an industrial design of a multimedia processor from Fujitsu [1]. All the experiments were carried out on a 200MHz PentiumPro PC with 1GB RAM memory using Linux.

The first benchmark designs are publicly available. The PCI example is extracted from [5]. The results for these designs are listed in the table.

Design	#Var	#Prop	NuSMV+COI				NuSMV+ABS			
			#COI	Time	$\|TR\|$	$\|MC\|$	#ABS	Time	$\|TR\|$	$\|MC\|$
gigamax	10(16)	1	0	0.3	8346	1822	9	0.2	13151	816
guidance	40(55)	8	30	35	140409	30467	34-39	30	147823	10670
p-queue	12(37)	1	4	0.5	51651	1155	5	0.4	52472	1114
waterpress	6(21)	4	0-1	273	34838	129595	4	170	38715	3335
PCI bus	50(89)	10	4	2343	121803	926443	12-13	546	160129	350226

In the table, the performance for an enhanced version of NuSMV with cone of influence reduction (**NuSMV + COI**) and our implementation (**NuSMV + ABS**) are compared. #Var and #Prop are properties of the designs: #Var = $x(y)$ means that x is the number of symbolic variables, and y the number of Boolean variables in the design. #Prop is the number of verified properties. The columns #COI and #ABS contain the number of symbolic variables which have been abstracted using the cone of influence reduction (#COI), and our initial abstraction (#ABS). The column "Time" denotes the accumulated running time to verify all #Prop properties of the design. $|TR|$ denotes the maximum number of BDD nodes used for building the transition relation. $|MC|$ denotes the maximum number of *additional* BDD nodes used during the verification of the properties. Thus, $|TR|+|MC|$ is the maximum BDD size during the total model checking process. For the larger examples, we use partitioned transition relations by setting the BDD size limit to 10000.

Although our approach in one case uses 50% more memory than the traditional cone of influence reduction to *build* the abstract transition relation, it requires one magnitude less memory during *model checking*. This is an important achievement since the model checking process is the most difficult task in verifying large designs. More significant improvement is further demonstrated by the Fujitsu IP core design.

The Fujitsu IP core design is a multimedia assist (MMA-ASIC) processor [1]. The design is a system-on-a-chip that consists of a co-processor for multimedia instructions, a graphic display controller, peripheral I/O units, and five bus bridges. The RTL implementation of MM-ASIC is described in about 61,500 lines of Verilog-HDL code. After manual abstraction by engineers from Fujitsu in [22], there still remain about 10,600 lines of code with roughly 500 registers. We translated this abstracted Verilog code into 9,500 lines of SMV code. In [22], the authors verified this design using a "navigated" model checking algorithm in which state traversal is restricted by navigation conditions provided by the user. Therefore, their methodology is not complete, i.e., it may fail to prove the correctness even if the property is true. Moreover, the navigation conditions are usually not automatically generated.

In order to compare our model checker to others, we tried to verify this design using two state-of-the-art model checkers - Yang's SMV [23] and NuSMV [6]. We implemented the cone of influence reduction for NuSMV, but not for Yang's SMV. Both NuSMV+COI and Yang's SMV failed to verify the design. On the other hand, our system abstracted 144 symbolic variables and with three refinement steps, successfully verified the design, and found a bug which has not been discovered before.

7 Conclusion and Future Work

We have presented a novel abstraction refinement methodology for symbolic model checking. The advantages of our methodology have been demonstrated by experimental results. We believe that our technique is general enough to be adapted for other forms of abstraction. There are many interesting avenues for future research. First, we want to find efficient approximation algorithms for the NP-complete separation problem encountered during the refinement step. Moreover, in a recent paper [4], the fragment of ACTL* that admits "trace"-like counterexamples (of a potentially more complicated structure than paths and loops) has been characterized; we plan to extend our refinement algorithm to this language. Since the symbolic methods described in this paper are not tied to representation by BDDs, we will also investigate how they can be applied to recent work on symbolic model checking without BDDs [3]. We are currently applying our technique to verify other large examples.

References

[1] Fujitsu aims media processor at DVD. *MicroProcessor Report*, pages 11–13, 1996.
[2] F. Balarin and A. L. Sangiovanni-Vincentelli. An iterative approach to language containment. In *Computer-Aided Verification*, volume 697 of *LNCS*, pages 29–40, 1993.
[3] A. Biere, A. Cimatti, E. Clarke, M. Fujita, and Y. Zhu. Symbolic model checking using SAT procedures instead of BDDs. In *Design Automation Conference*, pages 317–320, 1999.

[4] F. Buccafurri, T. Eiter, G. Gottlob, and N. Leone. On ACTL formulas having deterministic counterexamples. Technical report, Vienna University of Technology, 1999. available at http://www.kr.tuwien.ac.at/research/reports/index.html.
[5] P. Chauhan, E. Clarke, Y. Lu, and D. Wang. Verifying IP-core based System-On-Chip design. In *IEEE ASIC*, September 1999.
[6] A. Cimatti, E. Clarke, F. Giunchiglia, and M. Roveri. NuSMV: a new symbolic model checker. *Software Tools for Technology Transfer*, 1998.
[7] E. Clarke, O. Grumberg, S. Jha, Y. Lu, and H. Veith. Counterexample-guided abstraction refinement. Technical Report CMU-CS-00-103, Computer Science, Carnegie Mellon University, 2000.
[8] E. Clarke, O. Grumberg, and D. Peled. *Model Checking*. MIT Publishers, 1999.
[9] E. Clarke, S. Jha, Y. Lu, and D. Wang. Abstract BDDs: a technique for using abstraction in model checking. In *Correct Hardware Design and Verification Methods*, volume 1703 of *LNCS*, pages 172–186, 1999.
[10] E. M. Clarke, O. Grumberg, and D. E. Long. Model checking and abstraction. *ACM Transactions on Programming Languages and System (TOPLAS)*, 16(5):1512–1542, September 1994.
[11] S. Das, D. L. Dill, and S. Park. Experience with predicate abstraction. In *Computer-Aided Verification*, volume 1633 of *LNCS*, pages 160–171. Springer Verlag, July 1999.
[12] Shankar G. Govindaraju and David L. Dill. Verification by approximate forward and backward reachability. In *Proceedings of International Conference on Computer-Aided Design*, November 1998.
[13] S. Graf and H. Saidi. Construction of abstract state graphs with PVS. In *Computer-Aided Verification*, volume 1254 of *LNCS*, pages 72–83, June 1997.
[14] R. P. Kurshan. *Computer-Aided Verification of Coordinating Processes*. Princeton University Press, 1994.
[15] Y. Lakhnech. personal communication. 2000.
[16] W. Lee, A. Pardo, J. Jang, G. Hachtel, and F. Somenzi. Tearing based abstraction for CTL model checking. In *Proceedings of the International Conference on Computer-Aided Design*, pages 76–81, November 1996.
[17] J. Lind-Nielsen and H. R. Andersen. Stepwise CTL model checking of state/event systems. In *Computer-Aided Verification*, volume 1633 of *LNCS*, pages 316–327. Springer Verlag, 1999.
[18] A. Pardo. *Automatic Abstraction Techniques for Formal Verification of Digital Systems*. PhD thesis, University of Colorado at Boulder, Dept. of Computer Science, August 1997.
[19] A. Pardo and G.D. Hachtel. Incremental CTL model checking using BDD subsetting. In *Design Automation Conference*, pages 457–462, 1998.
[20] H. Saidi and N. Shankar. Abstract and model checking while you prove. In *Computer-Aided Verification*, number 1633 in LNCS, pages 443–454, July 1999.
[21] F. Somenzi. CUDD: CU decision diagram package. Technical report, University of Colorado at Boulder, 1997.
[22] K. Takayama, T. Satoh, T. Nakata, and F. Hirose. An approach to verify a large scale system-on-chip using symbolic model checking. In *International Conference of Computer Design*, pages 308–313, 1998.
[23] B. Yang et al. A performance study of BDD-based model checking. In *Formal Methods in Computer-Aided Design*, volume 1522 of *LNCS*. Springer Verlag, 1998.

Decision Procedures for Inductive Boolean Functions Based on Alternating Automata

Abdelwaheb Ayari, David Basin, and Felix Klaedtke

Institut für Informatik, Albert-Ludwigs-Universität Freiburg, Germany.

Abstract. We show how alternating automata provide decision procedures for the equivalence of inductively defined Boolean functions that are useful for reasoning about parameterized families of circuits. We use alternating word automata to formalize families of linearly structured circuits and alternating tree automata to formalize families of tree structured circuits. We provide complexity bounds and show how our decision procedures can be implemented using BDDs. In comparison to previous work, our approach is simpler, yields better complexity bounds, and, in the case of tree structured families, is more general.

1 Introduction

Reasoning about parametric system descriptions is important in building scalable systems and generic designs. In hardware verification, the problem arises in verification of parametric combinational circuit families, for example, proving that circuits in one family are equivalent to circuits in another, for every parameter value. Another application of parametric reasoning is in establishing properties of sequential circuits, where time is the parameter considered. In this paper we present a new approach to these problems based on alternating automata on words and trees.

The starting point for our research is the work of Gupta and Fisher [6,7]. They developed a formalism for describing circuit families using one of two kinds of inductively defined Boolean functions. The first, called *Linearly Inductive Boolean Functions*, or LIFs, formalizes families of linearly structured circuits. The second, called *Exponentially Inductive Boolean Functions*, or EIFs, models families of tree structured circuits. As simple examples, consider the linear (serial) and tree structured 4-bit parity circuits described by the following diagrams.

A LIF describing the general case of the linear circuit is given by the following equations. (We will formally introduce slightly different syntax in §3 and §4.)

$$serial\_parity^1(b_1) = b_1$$
$$serial\_parity^n(b_1, \ldots, b_n) = b_n \oplus serial\_parity^{n-1}(b_1, \ldots, b_{n-1}) \qquad \text{for } n > 1 \ .$$

Similarly, an EIF describing the family of tree-structured parity circuits is:

$$tree\_parity^1(b_1) = b_1$$
$$tree\_parity^{2^n}(b_1, \ldots, b_{2^n}) = tree\_parity^{2^{n-1}}(b_1, \ldots, b_{2^{n-1}}) \oplus$$
$$tree\_parity^{2^{n-1}}(b_{2^{n-1}+1}, \ldots, b_{2^n}) \quad \text{for } n \geq 1 \ .$$

Gupta and Fisher developed algorithms to translate these descriptions into novel data-structures that generalize BDDs (roughly speaking, their data-structures have additional pointers between BDDs, which formalize recursion). The resulting data-structures are canonical: different descriptions of the same family are converted into identical data-structures. This yields a decision procedure both for the equivalence of LIFs and for EIFs.

Motivated by their results, we take a different approach. We show how LIFs and EIFs can be translated, respectively, into alternating word and tree automata, whereby the decision problems for LIFs and EIFs are solvable by automata calculations. For LIFs, the translation and decision procedure are quite direct and may be implemented and analyzed using standard algorithms and results for word automata. For EIFs, the situation is more subtle since input is given by trees where only leaves are labeled by data and we are only interested in the equality of complete trees. Here, we decide equality using a procedure that determines whether a tree automaton accepts a complete leaf-labeled tree.

The use of alternating automata has a number of advantages. First, it gives us a simple view of (and leads to simpler formalisms for) LIFs and EIFs based on standard results from automata theory. For example, the expressiveness of these languages trivially falls out of our translations: LIFs describe regular languages on words and EIFs describe regular languages on trees (modulo the subtleties alluded to above). Hence, LIFs and EIFs can formalize any circuit family whose behavior is regular in the language theoretic sense. Second, it provides a handle on the complexity of the problems. For LIFs we show that the equality problem is PSPACE-complete and for EIFs it is in EXPSPACE. The result for LIFs represents a doubly exponential improvement over the previous results of Gupta and Fisher and our results for EIFs, are to our knowledge, the first published bounds for this problem. Finally, the use of alternating automata provides a basis for adapting data-structures recently developed in the MONA project [10]; in their work, as well as ours, BDDs are used to represent automata and can often exponentially compress the representation of the transition function. We show that the use of BDDs to represent alternating automata offers similar advantages and plays an important rôle in the practical use of these techniques.

We proceed as follows. In §2 we provide background material on word and tree automata. In §3 and §4 we formalize LIFs and EIFs and explain our decision procedures. In §5 we make comparisons and in §6 draw conclusions and discuss future work.

2 Background

Boolean Logic The set $B(V)$ of *Boolean formulae (over V)* is built from the constants 0 and 1, variables $v \in V$, and the connectives $\neg$, $\vee$, $\wedge$, $\leftrightarrow$ and $\oplus$. For $\beta \in B(V)$, $\beta[\alpha_1/v_1, \ldots, \alpha_n/v_n]$ denotes the formula where the $v_i \in V$ are simultaneously replaced by the formulae $\alpha_i \in B(V)$.

Boolean formulae are interpreted in the set $\mathbb{B} = \{0,1\}$ of *truth values*. A *substitution* is a function $\sigma : V \to \mathbb{B}$ that is homomorphically extended to $B(V)$. For $\sigma : V \to \mathbb{B}$ and $\beta \in B(V)$ we write $\sigma \models \beta$ if $\sigma(\beta) = 1$. We will sometimes identify a subset M of V with the substitution $\sigma_M : V \to \mathbb{B}$, where $\sigma_M(v) = 1$ iff $v \in M$. For example, for the formula $v_1 \oplus v_2$, we have $\{v_1\} \models v_1 \oplus v_2$ but $\{v_1, v_2\} \not\models v_1 \oplus v_2$.

Words and Trees Σ^* is the set of all words over the alphabet Σ. We write λ for the empty word and Σ^+ for $\Sigma^* \setminus \{\lambda\}$. For $u, v \in \Sigma^*$, $u.v$ denotes concatenation, $|u|$ denotes u's length, and u^R denotes the reversal of u.

A Σ-*labeled tree* (with branching factor $r \in \mathbb{N}$) is a function t where the range of t is Σ and the domain of t, $\mathrm{dom}(t)$ for short, is a finite subset of $\{0, \ldots, r-1\}^*$ where (i) $\mathrm{dom}(t)$ is prefix closed and (ii) if $u.i \in \mathrm{dom}(t)$, then $u.j \in \mathrm{dom}(t)$ for all $j < i$. The elements of $\mathrm{dom}(t)$ are called *nodes* and $\lambda \in \mathrm{dom}(t)$ is called the *root*. The node $u.i \in \mathrm{dom}(t)$ is a *successor* of u. A node is an *inner node* if it has successors and is a *leaf* otherwise. The *height* of t is $|t| = \max(\{0\} \cup \{|u|+1 \mid u \in \mathrm{dom}(t)\})$. The *depth* of a node $u \in \mathrm{dom}(t)$ is the length of u.

A tree is *complete* if all its leaves have the same depth. The *frontier* of t is the word $\mathrm{front}(t) \in \Sigma^*$ where the ith letter is the label of the ith leaf in t (from the left). Σ^{T*} denotes the set of all binary Σ-labeled trees and Σ^{T+} is Σ^{T*} without the empty tree.

Nondeterministic Automata A *nondeterministic word automaton (NWA)* $\mathcal{A}$ is a tuple $(\Sigma, Q, q_0, F, \delta)$, where Σ is a nonempty finite alphabet, Q is a nonempty finite set of states, $q_0 \in Q$ is the initial state, $F \subseteq Q$ is a set of accepting states, and $\delta : Q \times \Sigma \to \mathcal{P}(Q)$ is a transition function. A *run* of $\mathcal{A}$ on a word $w = a_1 \ldots a_n \in \Sigma^*$ is a word $\pi = s_1 \ldots s_{n+1} \in Q^+$ with $s_1 = q_0$ and $s_{i+1} \in \delta(s_i, a_i)$ for $1 \leq i \leq n$. π is *accepting* if $s_{n+1} \in F$. A word w is *accepted* by $\mathcal{A}$ if there is an accepting run of $\mathcal{A}$ on w; $L(\mathcal{A})$ denotes the set of accepted words.

Nondeterministic (top-down, binary) tree automata (NTA) are defined analogously: $\mathcal{A}$ is a tuple $(\Sigma, Q, q_0, F, \delta)$, where Σ, Q, q_0 and F are as before. The transition function is $\delta : Q \times \Sigma \to \mathcal{P}(Q \times Q)$. A *run* of a NTA $\mathcal{A}$ on a tree $t \in \Sigma^{T*}$ is a tree $\pi \in Q^{T+}$, where $\mathrm{dom}(\pi) = \{\lambda\} \cup \{w.b \mid w \in \mathrm{dom}(t) \text{ and } b \in \{0,1\}\}$. Moreover, $\pi(\lambda) = q_0$ and for $w \in \mathrm{dom}(t)$, $(\pi(w.0), \pi(w.1)) \in \delta(\pi(w), t(w))$. The run π is *accepting* if $\pi(w) \in F$ for any leaf $w \in \mathrm{dom}(\pi)$. A tree t is *accepted* by $\mathcal{A}$ if there is an accepting run of $\mathcal{A}$ on t; $L(\mathcal{A})$ denotes the set of accepted trees.

NWAs and NTAs recognize the regular word and tree languages and are effectively closed under intersection, union, complement and projection. For a detailed account of regular word and tree languages see [11] and [4] respectively.

Alternating Automata *Alternating automata* for words were introduced in [2, 3] and for trees in [15]. We use the definition of alternating automata for words from [17] and generalize it to trees. For this we need the notion of the *positive Boolean formulae*: Let $B^+(V)$ be the set of Boolean formulae built from 0, 1, $v \in V$, and the connectives $\vee$ and $\wedge$.

An *alternating word automaton (AWA)* is of the form $\mathcal{A} = (\Sigma, Q, q_0, F, \delta)$ where everything is as before, except for the transition function $\delta : Q \times \Sigma \to B^+(Q)$. The same holds for *alternating tree automata (ATA)* where the only difference is the transition function $\delta : Q \times \Sigma \to B^+(Q \times \{L, R\})$. We write q^X for $(q, X) \in Q \times \{L, R\}$.

We will only define a run for an ATA; the restriction to AWA is straightforward. For an ATA, a *run* π of $\mathcal{A}$ on $t \in \Sigma^{T*}$ is a $Q \times \{0,1\}^*$-labeled tree, with $\pi(\lambda) = (q_0, \lambda)$. Moreover, for each node $w \in \text{dom}(\pi)$, with $\pi(w) = (q, u)$, and for all of the $r \in \mathbb{N}$ successor nodes of w:

$$\{p^L \mid \pi(w.k) = (p, u.0) \text{ for } 0 \leq k < r\} \cup$$
$$\{p^R \mid \pi(w.k) = (p, u.1) \text{ for } 0 \leq k < r\} \models \delta(q, t(u)).$$

π is *accepting* if for every leaf w in π, where $\pi(w) = (p, u.k)$, u is leaf in t and $p \in F$. The *tree language accepted by* $\mathcal{A}$ is $L(\mathcal{A}) = \{t \in \Sigma^{T*} \mid \mathcal{A} \text{ accepts } t\}$. If there exists an accepting run of $\mathcal{A}' = (\Sigma, Q, q, F, \delta)$ for $q \in Q$ on t, then we say that $\mathcal{A}$ *accepts* t *from* q. We use the same terminology for AWAs.

It is straightforward to construct an alternating automaton from a nondeterministic automaton of the same size. Conversely, given an AWA one can construct an equivalent NWA with at most exponentially more states [2,3,17]. The states of the nondeterministic automaton are the interpretations of the Boolean formulae of the alternating automaton's transition function. This construction can be generalized to tree automata. Hence alternation does not increase the expressiveness of word and tree automata but, as we will see, it does enhance their ability to model problems.

3 Linearly Inductive Boolean Functions

3.1 Definition of LIFs

We now define linearly inductive Boolean functions. Our definition differs slightly from [6,7,8], however they are equivalent (see §5).

Syntax Let the two sets $V = \{v_1, \ldots, v_r\}$ and $F = \{f_1, \ldots, f_s\}$ be fixed for the remainder of this paper.

A *LIF formula* (over V and F) is a pair (α, β), with $\alpha \in B(V)$ and $\beta \in B(V \uplus F)$. The formulae α and β formalize the base and step case of a recursive definition. A *LIF system* (over V and F) is a pair (F, η) where F is a set of LIF formulae over V and F and $\eta : \mathsf{F} \to F$. That is, η assigns each $f \in \mathsf{F}$ a LIF formula $(\alpha, \beta) \in \mathsf{F}$. We will write (α_f, β_f) for $\eta(f) = (\alpha, \beta)$ and omit V and F when they are clear from the context.

Semantics Let $\mathcal{S}$ be a LIF system. An *evaluation* of $\mathcal{S}$ on $w = b_1 \ldots b_n \in (\mathbb{B}^r)^+$ is a word $d_1 \ldots d_n \in (\mathbb{B}^s)^+$ such that for $b_i = (a_1^i, \ldots, a_r^i)$, $d_i = (c_1^i, \ldots, c_s^i)$, and $1 \leq k \leq s$:

$$c_k^1 = 1 \quad \text{iff} \quad \{v_l \mid a_l^1 = 1, \text{ for } 1 \leq l \leq r\} \models \alpha_{f_k},$$

and for all i, $1 < i \leq n$,

$$c_k^i = 1 \quad \text{iff} \quad \{v_l \mid a_l^i = 1, \text{ for } 1 \leq l \leq r\} \cup$$
$$\{f_l \mid c_l^{i-1} = 1, \text{ for } 1 \leq l \leq s\} \models \beta_{f_k}.$$

An easy induction over the length of w shows:

Lemma 1. *For $\mathcal{S}$ a LIF system and $w \in (\mathbb{B}^r)^+$, the evaluation of $\mathcal{S}$ on w is uniquely defined.*

Hence $f_k \in \mathsf{F}$ together with $\mathcal{S}$ determine a function $f_k^{\mathcal{S}} : (\mathbb{B}^r)^+ \to \mathbb{B}$. Namely, for $w \in (\mathbb{B}^r)^+$, $f_k^{\mathcal{S}}(w) = c_k^{|w|}$. We call $f_k^{\mathcal{S}}$ the *LIF* of $\mathcal{S}$ and f_k. When $\mathcal{S}$ is clear from the context, we omit it.

Examples We present three simple examples. First, for $V = \{x\}$ and $F = \{serial\_parity\}$, the following LIF system $\mathcal{S}_1$ formalizes the family of linear parity circuits given in the introduction.

$$\alpha_{serial\_parity} = x \qquad \beta_{serial\_parity} = x \oplus serial\_parity$$

In particular, $serial\_parity^{\mathcal{S}_1}$ applied to $b_1 \ldots b_n \in \mathbb{B}^+$ equals $parity^n(b_1, \ldots, b_n)$.

The second LIF system $\mathcal{S}_2$ over $V = \{a, b, cin\}$ and $F = \{sum, carry\}$ formalizes a family of ripple-carry adders.

$$\alpha_{sum} = (a \oplus b) \oplus cin \qquad \beta_{sum} = (a \oplus b) \oplus carry$$
$$\alpha_{carry} = (a \wedge b) \vee ((a \vee b) \wedge cin) \qquad \beta_{carry} = (a \wedge b) \vee ((a \vee b) \wedge carry)$$

Here $sum^{\mathcal{S}_2}$ [respectively $carry^{\mathcal{S}_2}$] represents the adder's nth output bit [respectively carry bit].

The third example shows how to describe a sequential circuit by a LIF system. The LIF system $\mathcal{S}_3$ over $V = \{e\}$ and $F = \{Y_1, Y_2, Y_3\}$ describes a 3-bit counter with an enable bit.

$$\alpha_{Y_1} = 0 \qquad \beta_{Y_1} = (e \wedge \neg Y_1) \vee (\neg e \wedge Y_1)$$
$$\alpha_{Y_2} = 0 \qquad \beta_{Y_2} = (e \wedge (Y_1 \oplus Y_2)) \vee (\neg e \wedge Y_2)$$
$$\alpha_{Y_3} = 0 \qquad \beta_{Y_3} = (e \wedge ((Y_1 \wedge Y_2) \oplus Y_3)) \vee (\neg e \wedge Y_3).$$

$Y_i^{S_3}(w)$, with $w \in \mathbb{B}^+$, is the value of the ith output bit at time $|w|$ of the 3-bit counter, where w encodes the enable input signals.

3.2 Equivalence of LIF Systems and AWAs

A function $g : (\mathbb{B}^r)^+ \to \mathbb{B}$ is *LIF-representable* if there exists a LIF system $\mathcal{S}$ and a $f \in F$, where $g(w) = f^{\mathcal{S}}(w)$ for all $w \in (\mathbb{B}^r)^+$. A language $L \subseteq (\mathbb{B}^r)^+$ is *LIF-representable* if its characteristic function, $g(w) = 1$ iff $w \in L$, is LIF-representable. Gupta and Fisher have shown in [6,9] that any LIF-representable language is regular. They prove that their data-structure for representing a LIF system corresponds to a minimal deterministic automaton that accepts the language $\{w^R \mid f^{\mathcal{S}}(w) = 1, \text{ for } w \in (\mathbb{B}^r)^+\}$.

We present here a simpler proof of regularity by showing that LIF systems directly correspond to AWAs. We also prove a weakened form of the converse: almost all regular languages are LIF-representable. The weakening though is trivial and concerns the empty word, and if we consider languages without the empty word we have an equivalence.[1] Hence, for the remainder of this secction, *we consider only automata (languages) that do not accept (include) the empty word* λ.

For technical reasons we will work with LIF systems in a kind of negation normal form. A Boolean formula $\beta \in B(X)$ is *positive in* $Y \subseteq X$ if negations occur only directly in front of the Boolean variables $v \in X \setminus Y$ and, furthermore, the only connectives allowed are $\neg$, $\wedge$ and $\vee$. A LIF system $\mathcal{S}$ is in *normal form* if β_f is positive in F, for each $f \in F$.

Lemma 2. *Let $\mathcal{S}$ be a LIF system over V and F. Then there is a LIF system $\mathcal{S}'$ over V and $F' = F \uplus \{\overline{f} \mid f \in F\}$ in normal form where, for all $f \in F$ and $w \in (\mathbb{B}^r)^+$, $f^{\mathcal{S}'}(w) = f^{\mathcal{S}}(w)$ and $\overline{f}^{\mathcal{S}'}(w) = 1$ iff $f^{\mathcal{S}}(w) = 0$,*

Proof. Without loss of generality, we assume that for $\beta \in B(X)$ only the connectives $\neg$, $\vee$, and $\wedge$ occur. The other connectives can be eliminated as standard, which may lead to exponentially larger formulae. By $\mathrm{nnf}(\beta)$ we denote the negation normal form of $\beta \in B(X)$.

By using the same idea as [3], it is easy to construct a LIF system $\mathcal{S}'$ by introducing for each $f \in F$ a new variable $\overline{f}$ that "simulates" $\neg f$. Let $\mathcal{S} = (\mathsf{F}, \eta)$. For $f \in F$, with $\eta(f) = (\alpha, \beta)$, the mapping η' of the LIF system $\mathcal{S}'$ is defined by $\eta'(f) = (\alpha, \gamma)$ and $\eta'(\overline{f}) = (\neg \alpha, \overline{\gamma})$ where γ and $\overline{\gamma}$ are obtained from $\mathrm{nnf}(\beta)$, respectively $\mathrm{nnf}(\neg \beta)$, by replacing the sub-formulae $\neg f_i$ by $\overline{f}_i$. □

We now prove that LIF-representable languages and (λ-free) regular languages coincide.

---
[1] We can easily redefine LIFs to define functions over $(\mathbb{B}^r)^*$. However, following Gupta and Fisher we avoid this as the degenerate base case (0 length input) is ill-suited for modeling parametric circuits. Ignoring the empty word is immaterial for our complexity and algorithmic analysis.

Theorem 1. *LIF systems are equivalent to AWAs. In particular:*

i) *Given an AWA $\mathcal{A} = (\mathbb{B}^r, Q, q_0, F, \delta)$, there is a LIF system $\mathcal{S}$ over $V = \{v_1, \ldots, v_r\}$ and Q in normal form such that for all $w \in (\mathbb{B}^r)^+$ and $q \in Q$,*

$$q^{\mathcal{S}}(w) = 1 \quad \text{iff} \quad \mathcal{A} \text{ accepts } w^R \text{ from } q.$$

ii) *Given a LIF system $\mathcal{S}$ in normal form over V and F, there exists an AWA $\mathcal{A}$ with states $F \uplus \{q_{base}, q_{step}\}$ such that for all $w \in (\mathbb{B}^r)^+$ and $f \in F$,*

$$\mathcal{A} \text{ accepts } w \text{ from } f \quad \text{iff} \quad f^{\mathcal{S}}(w^R) = 1.$$

Proof. (i) We encode each $b \in \mathbb{B}^r$ by a formula $\gamma_b \in B(V)$. For example, $(0, 1, 1, 0) \in \mathbb{B}^4$ is encoded as the Boolean formula $\gamma_{(0,1,1,0)} = \neg v_1 \wedge v_2 \wedge v_3 \wedge \neg v_4$. The LIF formula for q in $\mathcal{S}$ is

$$\alpha_q = \bigvee_{b \in \mathbb{B}^r} (\gamma_b \wedge B(q, b)) \qquad \beta_q = \bigvee_{b \in \mathbb{B}^r} (\gamma_b \wedge \delta(q, b))$$

with $B(q, b) = 1$ iff $F \models \delta(q, b)$. Here, the Boolean formula β_q simulates the transition from the state q on a non-final letter of the input word. The final state set F is simulated by the Boolean formula α_q, i.e., $F \models \delta(q, b)$ iff $\{v_i \mid b_i = 1\} \models \alpha_q$.

We prove (i) by induction over the length of $w \in (\mathbb{B}^r)^+$. If $|w| = 1$, then the equivalence follows from the definition of α_q, for any $q \in Q$. Assume (i) is true for the word w, i.e., for each $q_k \in Q$, $\mathcal{A}$ accepts w^R from q_k iff $q_k^{\mathcal{S}}(w) = 1$. Let $u.d$ be an evaluation of $\mathcal{S}$ on w with $d = (c_1, \ldots, c_{|Q|})$. It holds that $q_k^{\mathcal{S}}(w) = 1$ iff $c_k = 1$. We prove (i) for $w.b$ with $b = (a_1, \ldots, a_r)$. As defined, for each $q \in Q$ we have $q^{\mathcal{S}}(w.b) = 1$ iff

$$\{v_l \mid a_l = 1, \text{ for } 1 \leq l \leq r\} \cup \{q_l \mid c_l = 1, \text{ for } 1 \leq l \leq |Q|\} \models \bigvee_{b' \in \mathbb{B}^r} (\gamma_{b'} \wedge \delta(q, b')).$$

By the induction hypothesis, we obtain $\{q_l \mid \mathcal{A} \text{ accepts } w^R \text{ from } q_l, \text{ for } 1 \leq l \leq |Q|\} \models \delta(q_k, b)$. From this we can easily construct an accepting run of $\mathcal{A}$ from q on $(w.b)^R$. The other direction holds by definition of an accepting run.

(ii) For an arbitrary $g \in F$, let $\mathcal{A} = (\mathbb{B}^r, F \uplus \{q_{base}, q_{step}\}, g, \{q_{base}\}, \delta)$ with $\delta(q_{base}, b) = 0$, $\delta(q_{step}, b) = q_{base} \vee q_{step}$, and for $f \in F$

$$\delta(f, (b_1, \ldots, b_r)) = (q_{step} \wedge \beta_f[b_1/v_1, \ldots, b_r/v_r]) \vee \begin{cases} q_{base} & \text{if } \{v_i \mid b_i = 1\} \models \alpha_f \\ 0 & \text{otherwise} \end{cases}$$

Intuitively when $\mathcal{A}$ is in state $f \in F$ and reads $(b_1, \ldots, b_r) \in \mathbb{B}^r$ it guesses if the base case is reached. When this is the case, the next state is q_{base} iff $\{v_i \mid b_i = 1\} \models \alpha_f$. Otherwise, if the base case is not reached, the AWA proceeds according to the step case given by the Boolean formula β_f of the LIF system. The equivalence is proved in a similar way to (i). □

Note that if a LIF formula only uses the connectives $\neg$, $\wedge$ and $\vee$, then, following the proof of Lemma 2, a normal form can be obtained in polynomial time. Moreover, if V is fixed the size, the AWA $\mathcal{A}$ of Theorem 1(ii) can be constructed in polynomial time, since the size of the alphabet $\mathbb{B}^r$ is a constant. However, if we allow V to vary, then the size of the AWA constructed can be exponentially larger than the size of the LIF system, i.e. $|V|+|F|+\sum_{f \in F}(|\alpha_f|+|\beta_f|)$, since the input alphabet of $\mathcal{A}$ is of size $2^{|V|}$.

3.3 Deciding LIF Equality

Given LIF systems $\mathcal{S}$ over V and F, and $\mathcal{T}$ over V and G, and function symbols $f_k \in F$ and $g_l \in G$, the *equality problem for LIFs* is to decide whether $f_k^{\mathcal{S}}(w) = g_l^{\mathcal{T}}(w)$, for all $w \in (\mathbb{B}^r)^+$. We first show that this problem is PSPACE-complete and afterwards show how, using BDDs, the construction in Theorem 1 provides the basis for an efficient implementation.

Theorem 2. *The equality problem for LIFs is PSPACE-complete.*

Proof. We reduce the emptiness problem for AWAs, which is PSPACE-hard [12, 17], to the equality problem for LIFs. Given an AWA $\mathcal{A}$ with initial state q_0, by Theorem 1(i) we can construct an equivalent LIF system $\mathcal{S}$ in polynomial time. Let the LIF system $\mathcal{T}$ be given by the formulae $\alpha_g = 0$ and $\beta_g = 0$. Then $q_0^{\mathcal{S}} = g^{\mathcal{T}}$ iff $L(\mathcal{A}) = \emptyset$.

Theorem 1(ii) cannot be used to show that the problem is in PSPACE because, as explained in the previous section, both the normal form and the size of the two constructed AWAs can be exponentially larger than the size of the LIF instances. Hence, we instead give a direct proof. The following Turing machine $\mathcal{M}$ accepts a problem instance in PSPACE iff a word $w = b_1 \ldots b_n \in (\mathbb{B}^r)^+$ exists with $f_k^{\mathcal{S}}(w) \neq g_l^{\mathcal{T}}(w)$. Let $d_1 \ldots d_n \in (\mathbb{B}^{|F|})^+$ be the evaluation of $\mathcal{S}$ on w and $d'_1 \ldots d'_n \in (\mathbb{B}^{|G|})^+$ be the evaluation of $\mathcal{T}$ on w. $\mathcal{M}$ guesses in the ith step $b_i \in \mathbb{B}^r$ and calculates $d_i = (c_1, \ldots, c_{|F|})$ and $d'_i = (c'_1, \ldots, c'_{|G|})$ of the evaluations. If $c_k \neq c'_l$ then $\mathcal{M}$ accepts the instance and otherwise $\mathcal{M}$ continues with the $(i+1)$th step. Note that for the ith step only d_{i-1} and d'_{i-1} and b_i are required to calculate d_i and d'_i. Hence $\mathcal{M}$ runs in polynomial space, since in the ith step the space $|V|$ is required to store b_i and the space $2(|F|+|G|)$ to store d_{i-1}, d_i, d'_{i-1}, and d'_i. $\mathcal{M}$ needs linear time in the size of the LIF formulae of $\mathcal{S}$ and $\mathcal{T}$ to calculate d_i and d'_i from b_i, d_{i-1} and d'_{i-1}. Since PSPACE is closed under nondeterminism and complementation, the equality problem for LIFs is in PSPACE. □

Although the machinery of alternating automata may appear a bit heavy, it leads to simple translations as there is a direct correspondence between function symbols in a LIF system and states in the corresponding AWA. This would not be possible using nondeterministic automata. Because the emptiness problem for NWAs is LOGSPACE-complete and the equality problem for LIFs is PSPACE-complete, a translation of a LIF system to a nondeterministic automata must, in general, lead to an exponential blow-up in the state space.

INPUT: AWA $\mathcal{A} = (\Sigma, Q, q_0, F, \delta)$
OUTPUT: returns *true* iff $L(\mathcal{A}) = \emptyset$

Current := $\{\{q_0\}\}$;
Processed := $\emptyset$;
while *Current* $\neq \emptyset$ **do begin**
    if *Current* $\cap \mathcal{P}(F) \neq \emptyset$ **then return** *false*;
    else begin
        Processed := *Processed* $\cup$ *Current*;
        Current := $\{T' \subseteq Q \mid T' \models \bigwedge_{q \in T} \delta(q,a)$ for $T \in$ *Current*, $a \in \Sigma\} \setminus$ *Processed*;
    end;
end;
return *true*;

Fig. 1. Decision procedure for the emptiness problem for AWAs.

Implementation In the proof of Theorem 2 we did not use the mapping from LIFs to AWAs given by Theorem 1(ii) due to the possible exponential blow-up when normalizing the LIF system, and the certain exponential blow-up in representing the AWA's alphabet. We describe here how these blow-ups can sometimes be avoided by using BDDs.

The reduction of LIF equality to the emptiness problem for AWAs is straightforward. From the LIF systems $\mathcal{S}$ over V and F, and $\mathcal{T}$ over V and G we construct the LIF system $\widetilde{\mathcal{S}}$ over V and $\{\widetilde{f}\} \uplus F \uplus G$ with the additional LIF formula $\alpha_{\widetilde{f}} = \neg(\alpha_f \leftrightarrow \alpha_g)$ and $\beta_{\widetilde{f}} = \neg(\beta_f \leftrightarrow \beta_g)$. We then normalize $\widetilde{\mathcal{S}}$ and use Theorem 1(ii) to construct the AWA $\mathcal{A}$ with the initial state $\widetilde{f}$. By construction, $L(\mathcal{A}) \neq \emptyset$ iff $\widetilde{f}^{\widetilde{\mathcal{S}}}(w) = 1$ for some $w \in (\mathbb{B}^r)^+$ iff $f^{\mathcal{S}} \neq g^{\mathcal{T}}$.

To decide if an AWA $\mathcal{A} = (\Sigma, Q, q_0, F, \delta)$ accepts the empty language, we construct "on-the-fly" the equivalent NWA $\mathcal{B} = (\Sigma, \mathcal{P}(Q), \{q_0\}, \mathcal{P}(F), \delta')$ with

$$\delta'(T, a) = \{T' \subseteq Q \mid T' \models \bigwedge_{q \in T} \delta(q, a)\},$$

and search for a path from the initial state $\{q_0\}$ of $\mathcal{B}$ to a final state. We do this with a parallel breadth-first search in the state space of $\mathcal{B}$ as described in Figure 1.

To analyze the complexity, observe that the **while**-loop is traversed maximally $2^{|Q|}$-times and the calculation in each iteration requires $O(2^{|Q|}|\Sigma|)$-time. Hence the worst-case running time is $O(2^{2|Q|}|\Sigma|)$. We need two vectors of the length $2^{|Q|}$ to represent the sets *Current* and *Processed*. Hence the required space is the maximum of $O(2^{|Q|})$ and the size of the representation of the AWA $\mathcal{A}$.

It is possible to use BDDs in two places to sometimes achieve an exponential savings in space. First, the sets *Current*, *Processed* $\subseteq \mathcal{P}(Q)$ can be encoded as BDDs where a BDD represents the characteristic function of the set. Second, since the size of $\mathcal{A}$'s alphabet ($\mathbb{B}^r$) is exponential in $|V|$, we use the same idea that Gupta and Fisher employed for their representation of LIFs: we need not

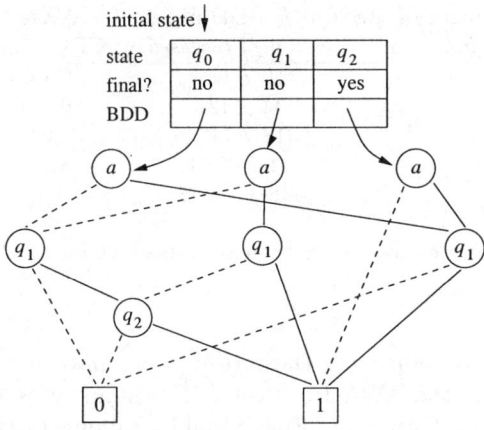

Fig. 2. Representation of an AWA.

explicitly represent the exponentially large alphabet and we can use BDDs to represent the transition function. For example, Figure 2 depicts the representation of the AWA $\mathcal{A} = (\mathbb{B}, \{q_0, q_1, q_2\}, q_0, \{q_2\}, \delta)$ with the transition function

$$\delta(q_0, 0) = q_1 \wedge q_2 \qquad \delta(q_0, 1) = q_1$$
$$\delta(q_1, 0) = q_1 \wedge q_2 \qquad \delta(q_1, 1) = q_1 \vee q_2$$
$$\delta(q_2, 0) = 1 \qquad \delta(q_2, 1) = q_1.$$

The solid [respectively dashed] lines correspond to the variable assignment 1 [respectively 0]. For example, the state q_0 has a pointer to a BDD, where the first node (labeled a) encodes the alphabet; the solid line from this node points to a BDD representing $\delta(q_0, 1) = q_1$ and the dashed line points to a BDD representing $\delta(q_0, 0) = q_1 \wedge q_2$.

We have implemented the emptiness test for AWAs using the CUDD package [16] and have begun preliminary testing and comparison. For the examples given in §3.1, building AWAs for the descriptions given and testing them for emptiness or equivalence with alternative descriptions is very fast: it takes a fraction of a second and most of the time is spent with I/O. We can carry out more ambitious tests by scaling up the sequential 3-bit counter example, namely performing tests on an n-bit counter for different values of n. This example is also interesting as it demonstrates the worst-case performance of our decision procedure since exponential many states of the NWA must be constructed to decide if the AWA describes the empty language.

Table 1 gives empirical results of the required space and time for the emptiness test for the resulting AWAs on a SUN Sparc Ultra with 250MHz. In the rightmost column are the running times on a SUN Sparc Ultra with 300MHz for building the canonical representation in Gupta and Fisher's approach. For large values of n, our approach yields significantly better results, although in both cases the algorithms require exponential time and space. Note that some

n	# BDD nodes of transition function	peak of # BDD nodes of Current/Processed	AWA CPU time	LIF CPU time
2	21	10 / 11	0.1s	0.0s
4	59	34 / 42	0.1s	0.0s
8	189	318 / 717	1.0s	4.0s
10	269	971 / 3063	8.2s	81.0s
12	371	3438 / 13037	71.7s	15241.5s

Table 1. Empirical results of the emptiness test for a n-bit counter

care must be taken in comparing these results: we have not included the time taken in constructing the AWA from the LIF system (it is linear) as this was done by hand. Further, Gupta and Fisher build a canonical representation of the LIF and they have used the older BDD package from David Long.

4 Exponentially Inductive Boolean Functions

The structure of this section parallels that of §3. After defining EIFs, we show how their equality problem can be decided using tree automata. The decision procedure however is not as direct as it is for LIFs. One problem is that inputs to EIFs are words not trees. We solve this by labeling the interior nodes of trees with a dummy symbol. However, the main problem is that the words must be of length 2^n. This restriction cannot be checked by tree automata and we solve this by deciding separately if a tree automaton accepts a complete tree.

4.1 Definitions of EIFs

Syntax An *EIF formula* (over V and F) is a pair (α, β), with $\alpha \in B(V)$ and $\beta \in B(F \times \{L, R\})$. We write f^L [respectively f^R] for the variable (f, L) [respectively (f, R)] in $F \times \{L, R\}$. An *EIF system* (over V and F) is a pair (F, η), where F and η are defined as for a LIF system. Similarly to LIF systems, we write (α_f, β_f) for $\eta(f) = (\alpha, \beta)$.

Semantics Let $\mathcal{S}$ be an EIF system over V and F. An *evaluation* of $\mathcal{S}$ on a word $w = b_1 \ldots b_{2^n} \in (\mathbb{B}^r)^+$ is a complete binary $\mathbb{B}^s$-labeled tree τ with $\text{front}(\tau) = d_1 \ldots d_{2^n} \in (\mathbb{B}^s)^+$ and for $1 \leq k \leq s$:

i) For $b_i = (a_1^i, \ldots, a_r^i)$ and $d_i = (c_1^i, \ldots, c_s^i)$, with $1 \leq i \leq 2^n$,
$$c_k^i = 1 \quad \text{iff} \quad \{v_l \mid a_l^i = 1, \text{ for } 1 \leq l \leq r\} \models \alpha_{f_k}.$$

ii) For each inner node $u \in \text{dom}(\tau)$ with $\tau(u.0) = (c_1', \ldots, c_s')$, $\tau(u.1) = (c_1'', \ldots, c_s'')$, and $\tau(u) = (c_1, \ldots, c_s)$:
$$c_k = 1 \quad \text{iff} \quad \{f_i^L \mid c_l' = 1, \text{ for } 1 \leq l \leq s\} \cup$$
$$\{f_i^R \mid c_l'' = 1, \text{ for } 1 \leq l \leq s\} \models \beta_{f_k}.$$

Let $\Sigma^{2+} = \{w \in \Sigma^* \mid |w| = 2^n,$ for some $n \in \mathbb{N}\}$. As with LIFs, the evaluation τ is uniquely defined; hence $f_k \in F$ and $\mathcal{S}$ together define a function $f_k^{\mathcal{S}} : (\mathbb{B}^r)^{2+} \to \mathbb{B}$. Namely $f_k^{\mathcal{S}}(w) = c_k$, where τ is the unique evaluation of $\mathcal{S}$ on w and $\tau(\lambda) = (c_1, \ldots, c_s)$. *EIF-representable* is defined analogously to LIF-representable.

For example, the tree implementation of the parameterized parity circuit from the introduction is described by the EIF system $\mathcal{S}$ over $V = \{x\}$ and $F = \{tree\_parity\}$ with the EIF formula:

$$\alpha_{tree\_parity} = x \qquad \beta_{tree\_parity} = tree\_parity^L \oplus tree\_parity^R.$$

Here the value of the EIF $tree\_parity^{\mathcal{S}}$ applied to a word $w = b_1 \ldots b_{2^n} \in \mathbb{B}^+$ is the value of the function $parity^{2^n}$ applied to $(b_1, \ldots, b_{2^n})$.

4.2 Equivalence of EIF Systems and ATAs

Using ATAs we can characterize the EIF-representable functions. To interpret a word in the domain of an EIF as a tree, we identify a word $b_1 \ldots b_{2^n} \in \Sigma^*$ with the complete tree $t \in (\Sigma \uplus \{\#\})^{\mathbb{T}^*}$, where front$(t) = b_1 \ldots b_{2^n}$ and all inner nodes are labeled with the dummy symbol $\#$. In the following, $\Sigma_\#$ stands for $\Sigma \uplus \{\#\}$. We call a tree $t \in \Sigma_\#^{\mathbb{T}^*}$ a Σ-*leaf-labeled* tree when (i) if w is a leaf, then $t(w) \in \Sigma$ and (ii) if w is an inner node, then $t(w) = \#$.

Normal forms for EIF systems can be defined and obtained as for LIF systems and the proof of Theorem 1 can, with minor modifications, be generalized to EIFs.

Theorem 3. *EIF systems are equivalent to ATAs if the input trees are restricted to complete, leaf-labeled trees. In particular:*

i) *Let $\mathcal{A} = (\mathbb{B}_\#^r, Q, q_0, F, \delta)$ be an ATA. There is a normal form EIF system $\mathcal{S}$ over $V = \{v_1, \ldots, v_r\}$ and Q, such that for all $q \in Q$ and any complete $\mathbb{B}^r$-leaf-labeled tree $t \in (\mathbb{B}_\#^r)^{\mathbb{T}+}$,*

$$q^{\mathcal{S}}(\text{front}(t)) = 1 \quad \text{iff} \quad \mathcal{A} \text{ accepts } t \text{ from } q.$$

ii) *Let $\mathcal{S}$ be a normal form EIF system over V and F. There is an ATA $\mathcal{A}$ with the state set $F \uplus \{q_{base}, q_{step}\}$, such that $\mathcal{A}$ accepts from $f \in F$ only $\mathbb{B}^r$-leaf-labeled trees, and for any complete $\mathbb{B}^r$-leaf-labeled tree $t \in (\mathbb{B}_\#^r)^{\mathbb{T}+}$,*

$$\mathcal{A} \text{ accepts } t \text{ from } f \quad \text{iff} \quad f^{\mathcal{S}}(\text{front}(t)) = 1.$$

4.3 Deciding EIF Equality

The *equality problem for EIFs* and the *size* of an instance are defined similarly to LIFs. We cannot generalize the decision procedure from §3.3 to EIFs since we are only interested in trees of a restricted form: complete leaf-labeled binary trees. Unfortunately completeness is not a regular property, i.e. one recognizable by tree automata, and hence we cannot reduce the problem to an emptiness problem. Instead, we reduce the problem to the *complete-tree-containment problem (CTCP) for NTAs*, which is to decide whether a given NTA accepts a complete tree.

Theorem 4. *The equality problem for EIFs is in EXPSPACE.*

Proof. Let $\mathcal{S}$ over V and F, and $\mathcal{T}$ over V and G be EIF systems, and let $f \in F$ and $g \in G$ be given. Let $\widetilde{\mathcal{S}}$ be the EIF system over V and $\{\widetilde{f}\} \uplus F \uplus G$ with the additional EIF formula $\alpha_{\widetilde{f}} = \neg(\alpha_f \leftrightarrow \alpha_g)$ and $\beta_{\widetilde{f}} = \neg(\beta_f \leftrightarrow \beta_g)$. We normalize $\widetilde{\mathcal{S}}$, and by Theorem 3(ii) construct an ATA $\mathcal{A}$ with the initial state $\widetilde{f}$, such that $f^{\mathcal{S}} \neq g^{\mathcal{T}}$ iff $\mathcal{A}$ accepts a complete tree. $\mathcal{A}$ has $2|\{\widetilde{f}\} \uplus F \uplus G| + 2$ states and the size of the alphabet $\mathbb{B}_{\#}^{|V|}$ is $2^{|V|} + 1$. From $\mathcal{A}$ we can construct an equivalent NTA $\mathcal{B}$ that has at most $O(2^{2|F|+|G|})$ many states. Hence we have reduced the equality problem for EIFs to CTCP for NTAs. The required space for the reduction is $O(2^{|V|} 2^{2|F|+|G|})$.

We now show that CTCP for NTAs is in PSPACE. For the NTA $\mathcal{A} = (\Sigma, Q, q_0, F, \delta)$ we construct the AWA $\mathcal{A}' = (\{1\}, Q, q_0, F, \delta')$ with $\delta'(q, 1) = \bigvee_{a \in \Sigma} \bigvee_{(p,p') \in \delta(q,a)} (p \wedge p')$. It is easy to prove that $\mathcal{A}$ accepts a complete tree of height h iff $\mathcal{A}'$ accepts a word of length h. From this follows that CTCP for NTAs is in PSPACE because the emptiness problem for AWAs is in PSPACE [12,17]. □

In [13], it is proved that the equality problem for EIFs and CTCP for ATAs (to decide if an ATA accepts a complete tree) are both EXPSPACE-hard. We omit the proof, which is quite technical, due to space limitations.

5 Comparisons and Related Work

Our work was motivated by that of Gupta and Fisher [6,7,8] and we begin by comparing our LIFs and EIFs with theirs, which we will call LIF_0 and EIF_0.

For each $n \geq 1$, a LIF_0 f is given by a Boolean function, called the *n-instance of* f and denoted by f^n, where $f^1 : \mathbb{B}^r \to \mathbb{B}$ and $f^n : \mathbb{B}^{r+s} \to \mathbb{B}$ for $n > 1$ (r is the number of n-instance inputs and s is the number of $(n-1)$-instance function inputs). Further it must hold that for all $m, n > 1$ the m-instance and the n-instance of f are equal, i.e. $f^m = f^n$. By means of the parity function we explain how the value of a LIF_0 is calculated. The n-instances of *serial_parity*^{n} (using their notation) are:

$$serial\_parity^1 = b^1,$$
$$serial\_parity^n = b^n \oplus serial\_parity^{n-1} \qquad \text{for } n > 1.$$

The *value* of the LIF_0 *serial_parity* on the word $b_1 \ldots b_n \in (\mathbb{B}^r)^+$, written as $serial\_parity(b_1, \ldots, b_n)$, is the value of the 1-instance $serial\_parity^1$ applied to b_1 for $n = 1$. For $n > 1$, it is the value of the n-instance $serial\_parity^n$ applied to b_n and $serial\_parity(b_1, \ldots, b_{n-1})$.

The definitions of a "LIF formula" and a "LIF system" correspond to the definition of a "LIF_0". Moreover, the way the "value" of a LIF_0 is calculated corresponds to our definition of "evaluation". Hence both formalisms are equivalent. However, the algorithms, data-structures, and complexity of our approaches are completely different!

Gupta and Fisher formalize LIF_0s using a data-structure based on BDDs where terminal nodes are not just the constants 0 and 1, but also pointers to other BDDs. They then prove that each LIF system has a canonical representation that can be obtained in $O(2^{2^{|F|}} 2^{|V|} + (2^{2^{|F|}})^2)$ time and space in the worst-case. In contrast, we have given a decision procedure (Theorem 2) that requires polynomial space, which is a doubly exponential improvement in space and an exponential improvement in time. Despite its worse space complexity, our algorithm based on BDD-represented AWAs may give better results in practice than our PSPACE decision procedure. This depends on whether the BDDs used require polynomial or exponential space. If the space required is polynomial, then the resulting AWA and its emptiness test require only polynomial space. In the exponential case, as there are only $2|F| + 2$ states, the emptiness test requires $O(2^{|V|+2|F|})$ time and space. This case also represents an exponential improvement over Gupta and Fisher's results, both in time and space.

An EIF_0 f has, like a LIF_0, for each $n \geq 0$, a n-instance function f^{2^n}, where $f^1 : \mathbb{B}^r \to \mathbb{B}$ and, for $n > 0$, f^{2^n} is a Boolean combination of three EIF_0s, e, g and h, i.e. $f^{2^n} : \mathbb{B}^3 \to \mathbb{B}$. Further it must hold that $f^{2^m} = f^{2^n}$ for all $m, n > 0$. The *value* of the EIF_0 f on the word $b_1 \ldots b_{2^n} \in (\mathbb{B}^r)^+$, written as $f(b_1, \ldots, b_{2^n})$, is the value of the 0-instance f^1 applied to b_1 if $n = 0$. For $n > 0$, it is the value of the n-instance f^{2^n} applied to the value of the EIF_0 e of the left half of the word, i.e. $e(b_1, \ldots, b_{2^{n-1}})$, and to the values of the EIF_0s g and h of the right half of the word, i.e. $g(b_{2^{n-1}+1}, \ldots, b_{2^n})$ and $h(b_{2^{n-1}+1}, \ldots, b_{2^n})$.

EIF_0s are strictly less expressive than EIFs. Indeed, since not every Boolean function for the n-instance function of an EIF_0 (for $n > 0$) is allowed, even simple functions cannot be described by an EIF_0, e.g., $F : \mathbb{B}^{2+} \to \mathbb{B}$ with $F(w) = 1$ iff $w = 0000$ or $w = 1100$ or $w = 1011$. The reason is similar to why deterministic top-down tree automata are weaker than nondeterministic top-down tree automata; the restrictions of the n-instance function of an EIF_0 stems from the data-structure proposed for EIF_0s in [6,7] in order to have a canonical representation. On the other hand, it is easy to see that F is EIF-representable.

Our results on the complexity of the equality problem for EIFs are, to our knowledge, the first such results given in the literature. Neither we nor Gupta and Fisher have implemented a decision procedure for the equality problem for EIFs or EIF_0s.

We have seen that LIFs and EIFs can be reduced to word and tree automata. Gupta and Fisher also give in [6,7] an extension of their data-structure for LIF_0s and EIF_0s that handles more than one induction parameter with the restriction that the induction parameters must be mutually independent. We conjecture that it may be possible to develop similar models in our setting based on 2-

dimensional word automata (as described in [5]) and their extension to trees. However, this remains as future work.

There are also similarities between our work and the description of circuits by equations of Brzozowski and Leiss in [2]. A *system of equations* S has the form $X_i = \bigcup_{a \in \Sigma} \{a\}.F_{i,a} \cup \delta_i$ (for $1 \leq i \leq n$) where the $F_{i,a}$ are Boolean functions in the variables X_i, and each δ_i is either $\{\lambda\}$ or $\emptyset$. It is shown in [2] that a solution to S is unique and regular, i.e., if each X_i is interpreted with $L_i \subseteq \Sigma^*$ and the L_i satisfy the equations in S, then the L_i are unique and regular. LIF systems offer advantages in describing parameterized circuits. For example, with LIFs one directly describes the "input ports" using the variables V. In contrast, a system of equations must use the alphabet $\mathbb{B}^r$ and cannot "mix" input pins and the signals of the internal wiring (and the same holds for outputs). Furthermore, descriptions using LIFs cleanly separate the base and step cases of the circuit family, which is not the case with [2].

Finally, note that the use of BDDs to represent word and tree automata, without alternation, is explored in [10,14]. There, BDD-represented automata are used to provide a decision procedures for monadic second-order logics on words and trees. This decision procedure is implemented in the MONA system, and MONA can be used to reason about LIF systems [1]: a LIF system is described by a monadic second-order formula, which MONA translates into a deterministic word automaton. Although this has the advantage of using an existing decision procedure, the complexity can be considerably worse both in theory and in practice. For example, for a 12-bit counter MONA (version 1.3) needs more than an hour to build the automaton and the number of BDD nodes is an order of magnitude larger than what is needed for our emptiness test for AWAs.

6 Conclusions

We have shown that LIFs and EIFs can be understood and analyzed using standard formalisms and results from automata theory. Not only is this conceptually attractive, but we also obtain better results for the decision problem for LIFs and the first complexity results for EIFs. The n-bit counter example in §3.3 indicates that our approach, at least in some cases, is faster in practice. However, an in depth experimental comparison of the procedures remains as future work.

Acknowledgments: The authors thank Aarti Gupta for helpful discussions and kindly providing us with recent timings using her package. We also thank the referees for their suggested improvements.

References

1. D. Basin and N. Klarlund. Automata based symbolic reasoning in hardware verification. *The Journal of Formal Methods in Systems Design*, 13(3):255–288, 1998.
2. J. Brzozowski and E. Leiss. On equations for regular languages, finite automata, and sequential networks. *TCS*, 10(1):19–35, 1980.

3. A. Chandra, D. Kozen, and L. Stockmeyer. Alternation. *Journal of the ACM*, 28(1):114–133, 1981.
4. F. Gécseg and M. Steinby. *Tree Automata*. Akadémiai Kiadó, Budapest, 1984.
5. D. Giammarresi and A. Restivo. Two-dimensional languages. In A. Salomaa and G. Rozenberg, editors, *Handbook of Formal Languages*, volume 3, Beyond Words, chapter 4, pages 215–267. Springer-Verlag, 1997.
6. A. Gupta. *Inductive Boolean Function Manipulation: A Hardware Verification Methodology for Automatic Induction*. PhD thesis, School of Computer Science, Carnegie Mellon University, Pittsburgh, 1994.
7. A. Gupta and A. Fisher. Parametric circuit representation using inductive boolean functions. In *CAV 93*, volume 697 of *LNCS*, pages 15–28, 1993.
8. A. Gupta and A. Fisher. Representation and symbolic manipulation of linearly inductive boolean functions. In *Proc. of the IEEE Internation Conference on Computer-Aided Design*, pages 192–199. IEEE Computer Society, 1993.
9. A. Gupta and A. Fisher. Tradeoffs in canonical sequential representations. In *Proc. of the International Conference on Computer Design*, pages 111–116, 1994.
10. J. Henriksen, J. Jensen, M. Jorgensen, N. Klarlund, B. Paige, T. Rauhe, and A. Sandholm. Mona: Monadic second-order logic in practice. In *TACS 95*, volume 1019 of *LNCS*, pages 89–110, 1996.
11. J. Hopcroft and J. Ullman. *Formal Languages and their Relation to Automata*. Addison-Wesley, 1969.
12. T. Jiang and B. Ravikumar. A note on the space complexity of some decision problems for finite automata. *IPL*, 40(1):25–31, 1991.
13. F. Klaedtke. *Induktive boolesche Funktionen, endliche Automaten und monadische Logik zweiter Stufe*. Master's thesis, Institut für Informatik, Albert-Ludwigs-Universität, Freiburg i. Br., 2000. in German.
14. N. Klarlund. Mona & Fido: The logic-automaton connection in practice. In *CSL 97*, volume 1414 of *LNCS*, pages 311–326, 1998.
15. G. Slutzki. Alternating tree automata. *TCS*, 41(2-3):305–318, 1985.
16. F. Somenzi. *CUDD: CU Decision Diagram Package, Release 2.3.0*. Department of Electrical and Computer Engineering, University of Colorado at Boulder, 1998.
17. M. Vardi. An automata-theoretic approach to linear temporal logic. In *Logics for Concurrency*, volume 1043 of *LNCS*, pages 238–266, 1996.

Detecting Errors Before Reaching Them*

Luca de Alfaro, Thomas A. Henzinger, and Freddy Y.C. Mang

Department of Electrical Engineering and Computer Sciences
University of California at Berkeley, CA 94720-1770, USA
{dealfaro,tah,fmang}@eecs.berkeley.edu

Abstract. Any formal method or tool is almost certainly more often applied in situations where the outcome is failure (a counterexample) rather than success (a correctness proof). We present a method for symbolic model checking that can lead to significant time and memory savings for model-checking runs that fail, while occurring only a small overhead for model-checking runs that succeed. Our method discovers an error as soon as it cannot be prevented, which can be long before it actually occurs; for example, the violation of an invariant may become unpreventable many transitions before the invariant is violated.

The key observation is that "unpreventability" is a local property of a single module: an error is unpreventable in a module state if no environment can prevent it. Therefore, unpreventability is inexpensive to compute for each module, yet can save much work in the state exploration of the global, compound system. Based on different degrees of information available about the environment, we define and implement several notions of "unpreventability," including the standard notion of uncontrollability from discrete-event control. We present experimental results for two examples, a distributed database protocol and a wireless communication protocol.

1 Introduction

It has been argued repeatedly that the main benefit of formal methods is *falsification*, not verification; that formal analysis can only demonstrate the *presence* of errors, not their absence. The fundamental reason for this is, of course, that mathematics can be applied, inherently, only to an abstract formal model of a computing system, not to the actual artifact. Furthermore, even when a formal model is verified, the successful verification attempt is typically preceded by many iterations of unsuccessful verification attempts followed by model revisions. Therefore, in practice, every formal method and tool is much more often applied in situations where the outcome is failure (a counterexample), rather than success (a correctness proof).

Yet most optimizations in formal methods and tools are tuned towards success. For example, consider the use of BDDs and similar data structures in

---

* This research was supported in part by the DARPA (NASA) grant NAG2-1214, the SRC contract 99-TJ-683.003, the MARCO grant 98-DT-660, the DARPA (MARCO) grant MDA972-99-1-0001, and the NSF CAREER award CCR-9501708.

model checking. Because of their canonicity, BDDs are often most effective in applications that involve equivalence checking between complex boolean functions. Successful model checking is such an application: when the set of reachable states is computed by iterating image computations, successful termination is detected by an equivalence check (between the newly explored and the previously explored states). By contrast, when model checking fails, a counterexample is detected before the image iteration terminates, and other data structures, perhaps noncanonical ones, may be more efficient [BCCZ99]. To point out a second example, much ink has been spent discussing whether "forward" or "backward" state exploration is preferable (see, e.g., [HKQ98]). If we expect to find a counterexample, then the answer seems clear but rarely practiced: the simultaneous, dove-tailed iteration of images and pre-images is likely to find the counterexample by looking at fewer states than either unidirectional method. Third, in compositional methods, the emphasis is almost invariably on how to decompose correctness proofs (see, e.g., [HQR98]), not on how to find counterexamples by looking at individual system components instead of their product. In this paper, we address this third issue.

Consider a system with two processes. The first process waits on a binary input from the second process; if the input is 0, it proceeds correctly; if the input is 1, it proceeds for n transitions before entering an error state. Suppose the second process may indeed output 1. By global state exploration (forward or backward), $n + 1$ iterations are necessary to encounter the error and return a counterexample. This is despite the fact that things may go terribly wrong, without chance of recovery, already in the first transition. We propose to instead proceed in two steps. First, we compute on each individual process (i.e., typically on a small state space) the states that are *controllable* to satisfy the requirements. In our example, the initial state is controllable (because the environment may output 0 and avoid an error), but the state following a single 1 input is not (no environment can avoid the error). Second, on the global state space, we restrict search to the controllable states, and report an error as soon as they are left. In our example, the error is reported after a single image (or pre-image) computation on the global state space. (A counterexample can be produced from this and the precomputed controllability information of the first process.) Note that both steps are fully automatic. Moreover, the lower number of global iterations usually translates into lower memory requirements, because BDD size often grows with the number of iterations. Finally, when no counterexample is found, the overhead of our method is mostly in performing step 1, which does not involve the global state space and therefore is usually uncritical.

We present several refinements of this basic idea, and demonstrate the efficiency of the method with two examples, a distributed database protocol and a wireless communication protocol. In the first example, there are two sites that can sell and buy back seats on the same airplane [BGM92]. The protocol aims at ensuring that no more seats are sold than the total available, while enabling the two sites to exchange unsold seats, in case one site wishes to sell more seats than initially allotted. The second example is from the *Two-Chip Intercom* (TCI) project of the Berkeley Wireless Research Center [BWR]. The TCI network is a wireless local network which allows approximately 40 remotes, one for each user, to transmit voice with point-to-point and broadcast communication. The operation of the network is coordinated by a base station, which assigns channels to the users through a TDMA scheme. In both examples, we first found errors that occurred in our initial formulation of the models, and then seeded bugs at random. Our methods succeeded in reducing the number of global image computation steps required for finding the errors, often reducing the maximum number of BDD nodes used in the verification process. The methods are particularly effective when the BDDs representing the controllable states are small in comparison to the BDD representing the set of reachable states.

To explain several fine points about our method, we need to be more formal. To study the controllability of a module P, we consider a game between P and its environment: the moves of P consist in choosing new values for the variables controlled by P; the moves of the environment of P consist in choosing new values for the input variables of P. A state s of P is *controllable with respect to the invariant* $\Box \varphi$ if the environment has a strategy that ensures that φ always holds. Hence, if a state s is not controllable, we know that P from s can reach a $\neg \varphi$-state, regardless of how the environment behaves. The set C_P of controllable states of P can be computed iteratively, using the standard algorithm for solving safety games, which differs from backward reachability only in the definition of the pre-image operator. Symmetrically, we can compute the set C_Q of controllable states of Q w.r.t. $\Box \varphi$. Then, instead of checking that $P \parallel Q$ stays within the invariant $\Box \varphi$, we check whether $P \parallel Q$ stays within the stronger invariant $\Box (C_P \wedge C_Q)$. As soon as $P \parallel Q$ reaches a state s that violates a controllability predicate, say, C_P, by retracing the computation of C_P, taking into account also Q, we can construct a path of $P \parallel Q$ from s to a state t that violates the specification φ. Together with a path from an initial state to s, this provides a counterexample to $\Box \varphi$. While the error occurs only at t, we detect it already at s, as soon as it cannot be prevented. The method can be extended to arbitrary LTL requirements.

The notion of controllability defined above is classical, but it is often not strong enough to enable the early detection of errors. To understand why, consider an invariant that relates a variable x in module P with a variable y in module Q, for example by requiring that $x = y$, and assume that y is an input variable to P. Consider a state s, in which module P is about to change the value of x without synchronizing this change with Q. Intuitively, it seems obvious that such a change can break the invariant, and that the state should not be considered controllable (how can Q possibly know that this is going to happen, and change the value of y correspondingly?). However, according to the classical definition of controllability, the state s is controllable: in fact, the environment has a move (changing the value of y correspondingly) to control P. This example indicates that in order to obtain stronger (and more effective) notions of controllability, we need to compute the set of controllable states by taking into account the real capabilities of the other modules composing the system. We introduce three such stronger notions of controllability: constrained, lazy, and bounded controllability. Our experimental results demonstrate that there is a distinct advantage in using these stronger notions of controllability.

Lazy controllability can be applied to systems in which all the modules are *lazy,* i.e., if the modules always have the option of leaving unchanged the values of the variables they control [AH99]. Thus, laziness models the assumption of speed independence, and is used heavily in the modeling of asynchronous systems. If the environment is lazy, then there is no way of preventing the environment from always choosing its "stutter" move. Hence, we can strengthen the definition of controllability by requiring that the stutter strategy of the environment, rather than an arbitrary strategy, must be able to control. In the above example, the state s of module P is clearly not *lazily controllable,* since a change of x cannot be controlled by leaving y unchanged. *Constrained controllability* is a notion of controllability that can be used also when the system is not lazy. Constrained controllability takes into account, in computing the sets of controllable states, which moves are possible for the environment. To compute the set of *constrainedly controllable states* of a module P, we construct a transition relation that constrains the moves of the environment. This is done by automatically abstracting away from the transition relations of the other modules the variables that are not shared by P. We then define the controllable states by considering a game between P and a so constrained environment. Finally, *bounded controllability* is a notion that can again be applied to any system, and it generalizes both lazy and constrained controllability. It considers environments that have both a set of *unavoidable moves* (such as the lazy move for lazy systems), and *possible moves* (by considering constraints to the moves, similarly to constrained controllability). We also introduce a technique called *iterative strengthening*, which can be used to strengthen any of these notions of controllability. In essence, it is based on the idea that a module, in order to control another module, cannot use a move that would cause it to leave its own set of controllable states.

It is worth noting that the technqiues developed in this paper can also be used in an informal verification environment: after computing the uncontrollability states for each of the components, one can *simulate* the design and check if any of these uncontrollable states can be reached. This is similar to the techniques *retrograde analysis* [JSAA97], or *target enlargement* [YD98] in simulation. The main idea of retrograde analysis and target enlargement is that the set of states that violate the invariants are "enlarged" with their preimages, and hence the chances of hitting this enlarged set is increased. Our techniques not only add modularity in the computation of target enlargemen, they also allow one to detect the violation of *liveness* properties through simulation.

The algorithmic control of reactive systems has been studied extensively before (see, e.g., [RW89,EJ91,Tho95]). However, the use of controllability in automatic verification is relatively new (see, e.g., [KV96,AHK97,AdAHM99]). The work closest to ours is [ASSSV94], where transition systems for components are minimized by taking into account if a state satisfies or violates a given CTL property under all environments. In [Dil88], autofailure captures the concept that no environment can prevent failure and is used to compare the equivalence of asynchronous circuits.

2 Preliminaries

Given a set $\mathcal{V}$ of typed variables, a state s over $\mathcal{V}$ is an assignment for $\mathcal{V}$ that assigns to each $x \in \mathcal{V}$ a value $s[\![x]\!]$. We indicate with $\mathit{States}(\mathcal{V})$ be the set of all states over $\mathcal{V}$, and with $\mathcal{P}(\mathcal{V})$ the set of predicates over $\mathcal{V}$. Furthermore, we denote by $\mathcal{V}' = \{x' \mid x \in \mathcal{V}\}$ the set obtained by priming each variable in $\mathcal{V}$. Given a predicate $H \in \mathcal{P}(\mathcal{V})$, we denote by $H' \in \mathcal{P}(\mathcal{V}')$ the predicate obtained by replacing in H every $x \in \mathcal{V}$ with $x' \in \mathcal{V}'$. A module $P = (\mathcal{C}_P, \mathcal{E}_P, I_P, T_P)$ consists of the following components:

1. A (finite) set $\mathcal{C}_P$ of *controlled variables*, each with finite domain, consisting of the variables whose values can be accessed and modified by P.
2. A (finite) set $\mathcal{E}_P$ of *external variables*, each with finite domain, consisting of the variables whose values can be accessed, but not modified, by P.
3. A *transition predicate* $T_P \in \mathcal{P}(\mathcal{C}_P \cup \mathcal{E}_P \cup \mathcal{C}'_P)$.
4. An *initial predicate* $I_P \in \mathcal{P}(\mathcal{C}_P)$.

We denote by $\mathcal{V}_P = \mathcal{C}_P \cup \mathcal{E}_P$ the set of variables mentioned by the module. Given a state s over $\mathcal{V}_P$, we write $s \models I_P$ if I_P is satisfied under the variable interpretation specified by s. Given two states s, s' over $\mathcal{V}_P$, we write $(s, s') \models T_P$ if predicate T_P is satisfied by the interpretation that assigns to $x \in \mathcal{V}_P$ the value $s[\![x]\!]$, and to $x' \in \mathcal{V}'_P$ the value $s'[\![x]\!]$. A module P is *non-blocking* if the predicate I_P is satisfiable, i.e., if the module has at least one initial state, and if the assertion $\forall \mathcal{V}_P . \exists \mathcal{C}'_P . T_P$ holds, so that every state has a successor.

A *trace* of module P is a finite sequence of states $s_0, s_1, s_2, \ldots s_n \in \mathit{States}(\mathcal{V}_P)$, where $n \geq 0$ and $(s_k, s_{k+1}) \models T_P$ for all $0 \leq k < n$; the trace is *initial* if $s_0 \models I_P$. We denote by $\mathcal{L}(P)$ the set of initial traces of module P. For a module P, we consider specifications expressed by linear-time temporal logic (LTL) formulas whose atomic predicates are in $\mathcal{P}(\mathcal{V}_P)$. As usual, given an LTL formula φ, we write $P \models \varphi$ iff $\sigma \models \varphi$ for all $\sigma \in \mathcal{L}(P)$.

Two modules P and Q are *composable* if $\mathcal{C}_P \cap \mathcal{C}_Q = \emptyset$; in this case, their *parallel composition* $P \parallel Q$ is defined as: $P \parallel Q = (\mathcal{C}_P \cup \mathcal{C}_Q, (\mathcal{E}_P \cup \mathcal{E}_Q) \setminus (\mathcal{C}_P \cup \mathcal{C}_Q), I_P \wedge I_Q, T_P \wedge T_Q)$. Note that composition preserves non-blockingness.

We assume that all predicates are represented in such a way that boolean operations and existential quantification of variables are efficiently computable. Likewise, we assume that satisfiability of all predicates can be checked efficiently. *Binary decision diagrams* (BDDs) provide a suitable representation [Bry86].

Controllability. We can view the interaction between a module P and its environment as a game. At each round of the game, the module P chooses the next values for controlled variables $\mathcal{C}_P$, while the environment chooses the next values for the external variables $\mathcal{E}_P$. Given an LTL specification φ, we say that a state s of P is *controllable* with respect to φ if the environment can ensure that all traces from s satisfy φ. To formalize this definition, we use the notion of *strategy*. A module strategy π for P is a mapping $\pi : States(\mathcal{V}_P)^+ \mapsto States(\mathcal{C}_P)$ that maps each finite sequence $s_0, s_1, \ldots, s_k$ of module states into a state $\pi(s_0, s_1, \ldots, s_k)$ such that $(s_k, \pi(s_0, s_1, \ldots, s_k)) \models T_P$. Similarly, an environment strategy η for P is a mapping $\eta : States(\mathcal{V}_P)^+ \mapsto States(\mathcal{E}_P)$ that maps each finite sequence of module states into a state specifying the next values of the external variables. Given two states s_1 and s_2 over two disjoint sets of variables $\mathcal{V}_1$ and $\mathcal{V}_2$, we denote by $s_1 \bowtie s_2$ the state over $\mathcal{V}_1 \cup \mathcal{V}_2$ that agrees with s_1 and s_2 over the common variables. With this notation, for all $s \in States(\mathcal{V}_P)$ and all module strategies π and environment strategies η, we define $Outcome(s, \pi, \eta) \in States(\mathcal{V}_P)^\omega$ to be the trace $s_0, s_1, s_2, \ldots$ defined by $s_0 = s$ and by $s_{k+1} = \pi(s_0, s_1, \ldots, s_k) \bowtie \eta(s_0, s_1, \ldots, s_k)$. Given an LTL formula φ over $\mathcal{V}_P$, we say that a state $s \in States(\mathcal{V}_P)$ is *controllable with respect to* φ iff there is an environment strategy η such that, for every module strategy π, we have $Outcome(s, \pi, \eta) \models \varphi$. We let $Ctr(P, \varphi)$ be the predicate over $\mathcal{V}_P$ defining the set of states of P controllable with respect to φ.

Roughly, a state of P is controllable w.r.t. φ exactly when there is an environment E for P such that all paths from s in $P \parallel E$ satisfy φ. Since in general E can contain variables not in P, to make the above statement precise we need to introduce the notion of *extension* of a state. Given a state s over $\mathcal{V}$ and a state t over $\mathcal{U}$, with $\mathcal{V} \subseteq \mathcal{U}$, we say that t is an *extension* of s if $s[\![x]\!] = t[\![x]\!]$ for all $x \in \mathcal{V}$. Then, there is module E composable with P such that all paths from extensions of s in $P \parallel E$ satisfy φ iff $s \in Ctr(P, \varphi)$ [AdAHM99].

3 Early Detection of Invariant Violation

Forward and backward state exploration. Given a module R and a predicate φ over $\mathcal{V}_R$, the problem of invariant verification consists in checking whether $R \models \Box\varphi$. We can solve this problem using classic forward or backward state exploration. Forward exploration starts with the set of initial states of R, and iterates a post-image computation, terminating when a state satisfying $\neg\varphi$ has been reached, or when the set of reachable states of R has been computed. In the first case we conclude $R \not\models \Box\varphi$; in the second, $R \models \Box\varphi$. Backward exploration starts with the set $\neg\varphi$ of states violating the invariant, and iterates a pre-image computation, terminating when a state satisfying I_R has been reached, or when the set of all states that can reach $\neg\varphi$ has been computed. Again, in the first case we conclude $R \not\models \Box\varphi$ and in the second $R \models \Box\varphi$. If the answer to the invariant verification question is negative, these algorithms can also construct a counterexample $s_0, \ldots, s_m$ of minimal length leading from $s_0 \models I_R$ to $s_m \models \neg\varphi$, and such that for $0 \le i < m$ we have $(s_i, s_{i+1}) \models T_R$. If our aim is to find counterexamples quickly, an algorithm that alternates forward and backward reachability is likely to explore fewer states than the two unidirectional algorithms. The algorithm alternates post-image computations starting from I_R with pre-image computations starting from $\neg\varphi$, terminating as soon as the post and pre-images intersect, or as soon as a fixpoint is reached. We denote any of these three algorithms (or variations thereof) by $InvCheck(R, \varphi)$. We assume that $InvCheck(R, \varphi)$ returns answer YES or NO, depending on whether $R \models \Box\varphi$ or $R \not\models \Box\varphi$, along with a counterexample in the latter case.

Controllability and early error detection. Given $n > 1$ modules $P_1, P_2, \ldots, P_n$ and a predicate $\varphi \in \mathcal{P}(\bigcup_{i=1}^{n} \mathcal{V}_{P_i})$, the modular version of the invariant verification problem consists in checking whether $P_1 \| \cdots \| P_n \models \Box\varphi$. We can use the notion of controllability to try to detect a violation of the invariant φ in fewer iterations of post or pre-image computation than the forward and backward exploration algorithms described above. The idea is to pre-compute the states of each module $P_1, \ldots, P_n$ that are controllable w.r.t. $\Box\varphi$. We can then detect a violation of the invariant as soon as we reach a state s that is not controllable for some of the modules, rather than waiting until we reach a state actually satisfying $\neg\varphi$. In fact, we know that from s there is a path leading to $\neg\varphi$ in the global system: for this reason, if a state is not controllable for some of the modules, we say that the state is *doomed*.

To implement this idea, let $R = P_1 \| \cdots \| P_n$, and for $1 \leq i \leq n$, let $abs_i(\varphi) = \exists(\mathcal{V}_R \setminus \mathcal{V}_{P_i}) \cdot \varphi$ be an approximation of φ that involves only the variables of P_i; note that $\varphi \to abs_i(\varphi)$. For each $1 \leq i \leq n$, we can compute the set $Ctr(P_i, \Box abs_i(\varphi))$ of controllable states of P_i w.r.t. $\Box abs_i(\varphi)$ using a classical algorithm for safety games. For a module P, the algorithm uses the *uncontrollable predecessor operator* $\text{UPre}_P : \mathcal{P}(\mathcal{V}_P) \mapsto \mathcal{P}(\mathcal{V}_P)$, defined by

$$\text{UPre}_P(X) = \forall \mathcal{E}'_P \cdot \exists \mathcal{C}'_P \cdot (T_P \wedge X') \, .$$

The predicate $\text{UPre}_P(X)$ defines the set of states from which, regardless of the move of the environment, the module P can resolve its internal nondeterminism to make X true. Note that a quantifier switch is required to to compute the uncontrollable predecessors, as opposed to the computations of pre-images and post-images, where where only existential quantification is required. For a module P and an invariant $\Box\varphi$, we can compute the set $Ctr(P, \Box\varphi)$ of controllable states of P with respect to $\Box\varphi$ by letting $U_0 = \neg\varphi$, and for $k > 0$, by letting

$$U_k = \neg\varphi \vee \text{UPre}_P(U_{k-1}), \tag{1}$$

until we have $U_k \equiv U_{k-1}$, at which point we have $Ctr(P, \Box\varphi) = \neg U_k$. For $k \geq 0$ the set U_k consists of the states from which the environment cannot prevent module P from reaching $\neg\varphi$ in at most k steps. Note that for all $1 \leq i \leq n$, the computation of $Ctr(P_i, \Box abs_i(\varphi))$ is carried out on the state space of module P_i, rather than on the (larger) state space of the complete system. We can then solve the invariant checking problem $P_1 \| \cdots \| P_n \models \Box\varphi$ by executing

$$InvCheck\bigl(P_1 \| \cdots \| P_n, \varphi \wedge \bigwedge_{i=0}^{n} Ctr(P_i, \Box abs_i(\varphi))\bigr) \, . \tag{2}$$

It is necessary to conjoin φ to the set of controllable states in the above check, because for $1 \leq i \leq n$, predicate $abs_i(\varphi)$ (and thus, possibly, $Ctr(P_i, \Box abs_i(\varphi))$) may be weaker than φ. If check (2) returns answer YES, then we have immediately that $P_1 \| \cdots \| P_n \models \Box\varphi$. If the check returns answer NO, we can conclude that $P_1 \parallel \cdots \parallel P_n \not\models \Box\varphi$. In this latter case, the check (2) also returns a partial counterexample $s_0, s_1, \ldots, s_m$, with $s_m \not\models Ctr(P_j, \Box\varphi_j)$ for some $1 \leq j \leq n$. If $s_m \models \neg\varphi$, this counterexample is also a counterexample to $\Box\varphi$. Otherwise, to obtain a counterexample $s_0, \ldots, s_m, s_{m+1}, \ldots, s_{m+r}$ with $s_{m+r} \not\models \varphi$, we proceed as follows. Let $U_0, U_1, \ldots, U_k$ be the predicates computed by Algorithm 1 during the computation of $Ctr(P_j, \Box\varphi_j)$; note that $s_m \models U_k$. For $l > 0$, given s_{m+l-1}, we pick s_{m+l} such that $s_{m+l} \models U_{k-l}$ and $(s_{m+l-1}, s_{m+l}) \models \bigwedge_{i=1}^n T_{P_i}$. The process terminates as soon as we reach an l such that $s_{m+l} \models \neg\varphi$: since the implication $U_0 \to \neg\varphi$ holds, this will occur in at most k steps.

4 Lazy and Constrained Controllability

In the previous section, we have used the notion of controllability to compute sets of *doomed states*, from which we know that there is a path violating the invariant. In order to detect errors early, we should compute the largest possible sets of doomed states. To this end, we introduce two notions of controllability that can be stronger than the classical definition of the previous section. The first notion, *lazy controllability*, can be applied to systems that are composed only of *lazy modules*, i.e. of modules that need not react to their inputs. Several communication protocols can be modeled as the composition of lazy modules. The second notion, *constrained controllability*, can be applied to any system.

Lazy controllability. A module is *lazy* if it always has the option of leaving its controlled variables unchanged. Formally, a module P is *lazy* if we have $(s, s) \models T_P$ for every state s over $\mathcal{V}_P$. If all the modules composing the system are lazy, then we can re-examine the notion of controllability described in Section 3 to take into account this fact. Precisely, we defined a state to be controllable w.r.t. an LTL property φ if there is a strategy for the environment to ensure that the resulting trace satisfies φ, regardless of the strategy used by the system. But if the environment is lazy, we must always account for the possibility that the environment plays according to its *lazy strategy*, in which the values of the external variables of the module never change. Hence, if all modules are lazy, there is a second condition that has to be satisfied for a state to be controllable: for every strategy of the module, the lazy environment strategy should lead to a trace that satisfies φ. It is easy to see, however, that this second condition for controllability subsumes the first. We can summarize these considerations with the following definition. For $1 \leq i \leq n$, denote by η^ℓ the lazy environment strategy of module P_i, which leaves the values of the external variables of P_i always unchanged. We say that a state $s \in States(\mathcal{V}_{P_i})$ is *lazily controllable with respect to a LTL formula* ψ iff, for every module strategy π, we have $Outcome(s, \pi, \eta^\ell) \models \varphi$. We let $LCtr(P, \varphi)$ be the predicate over $\mathcal{V}_P$ defining the set of states of P that are lazily controllable with respect to φ.

We can compute for the invariant $\Box\varphi$ the predicate $LCtr(P, \Box\varphi)$ by replacing the operator UPre in Algorithm 1 with the operator $\text{LUPre} : \mathcal{P}(\mathcal{V}_P) \mapsto \mathcal{P}(\mathcal{V}_P)$, the *lazily uncontrollable predecessor operator*, defined by:

$$\text{LUPre}_P(X) = \exists \mathcal{C}'_P \, . \, (T_P \wedge X')[\mathcal{E}_P / \mathcal{E}'_P] \, .$$

where $(T_P \wedge X')[\mathcal{E}_P/\mathcal{E}'_P]$ is obtained from $T_P \wedge X'$ by replacing each variable $x' \in \mathcal{E}'_P$ with $x \in \mathcal{E}_P$. Note that $\text{LUPre}_P X$ computes a superset of $\text{UPre}_P X$, and therefore the set $LCtr(P, \Box\varphi)$ of lazily controllable states is always a subset of the controllable states $Ctr(P, \Box\varphi)$.

Given $n > 1$ lazy modules $P_1, P_2, \ldots, P_n$ and a predicate $\varphi \in \mathcal{P}(\bigcup_{i=1}^n \mathcal{V}_{P_i})$, let $R = P_1 \| \cdots \| P_n$, and for all $1 \leq i \leq n$. We can check whether $P_1 \| \cdots \| P_n \models \Box\varphi$ by executing $InvCheck(R, \varphi \wedge \bigwedge_{i=1}^n LCtr(P_i, \Box abs_i(\varphi)))$. If this check returns answer NO, we can construct a counterexample to $\Box\varphi$ as in Section 3.

Constrained controllability. Consider again $n > 1$ modules $P_1, P_2, \ldots, P_n$, together with a predicate $\varphi \in \mathcal{P}(\bigcup_{i=1}^n \mathcal{V}_{P_i})$. In Section 3, we defined a state to be controllable if it can be controlled by an unconstrained environment, which can update the external variables of the module in an arbitrary way. However, in the system under consideration, the environment of a module P_i is $Q_i = P_1 \| \cdots \| P_{i-1} \| P_{i+1} \| \cdots \| P_n$, for $1 \leq i \leq n$. This environment cannot update the external variables of P_i in an arbitrary way, but is constrained in doing so by the transition predicates of modules P_j, for $1 \leq j \leq n$, $j \neq i$. If we compute the controllability predicate with respect to the most general environment, instead of Q_i, we are giving to the environment in charge of controlling P_i more freedom than it really has. To model this restriction, we can consider games in which the environment of P_i is constrained by a transition predicate over $\mathcal{V}_{P_i} \cup \mathcal{E}'_{P_i}$ that overapproximates the transition predicate of Q_i. We rely on an over-approximation to avoid mentioning all the variables in $\bigcup_{j=1}^n \mathcal{V}_{P_j}$, since this would enlarge the state space on which the controllability predicate is computed.

These considerations motivate the following definitions. Consider a module P together with a transition predicate H over $\mathcal{V}_P \cup \mathcal{E}'_P$. An H-*constrained strategy* for the environment of P is a strategy $\eta : States(\mathcal{V}_P)^+ \mapsto States(\mathcal{E}_P)$ such that, for all $s_0, s_1, \ldots, s_k \in States(\mathcal{V}_P)^+$, we have $(s_k, \eta(s_0, s_1, \ldots, s_k)) \models H$. Given an LTL formula φ over $\mathcal{V}_P$, we say that a state $s \in States(\mathcal{V}_P)$ is H-*controllable* if there is an H-constrained environment strategy η such that, for every module strategy π, we have $Outcome(s, \pi, \eta) \models \varphi$. We let $CCtr(P, \langle\!\langle H \rangle\!\rangle \varphi)$ be the predicate over $\mathcal{V}_P$ defining the set of H-controllable states of P w.r.t. φ.[1] For invariant properties, the predicate $CCtr(P, \langle\!\langle H \rangle\!\rangle \Box\varphi)$ can be computed by replacing in Algorithm 1 the operator UPre with the operator $\text{CUPre}_P[H] : \mathcal{P}(\mathcal{V}_P) \mapsto \mathcal{P}(\mathcal{V}_P)$, defined by:

$$\text{CUPre}_P[H](X) = \forall \mathcal{E}'_P . (H \rightarrow \exists \mathcal{C}'_P . (T_P \wedge X')) .$$

When $H = true$, $\text{CUPre}_P[H](X) = \text{UPre}_P(X)$; for all other stronger predicates H, the H-uncontrollable predecessor operator $\text{CUPre}_P[H](X)$ will be a superset of $\text{UPre}_P(X)$, and therefore the set $CCtr(P, \langle\!\langle H \rangle\!\rangle \varphi)$ of H-controllable states will be a subset of the controllable states $Ctr(P, \Box\varphi)$.

---

[1] If E_H is a module composable with P having transition relation H, the predicate $CCtr(P, \langle\!\langle H \rangle\!\rangle \varphi)$ defines exactly the same set of states as the ATL formula $\langle\!\langle E \rangle\!\rangle \Box\varphi$ interpreted over $P \| E_H$ [AHK97].

Given a system $R = P_1 \| P_2 \| \ldots \| P_n$ and a predicate $\varphi \in \mathcal{P}(\mathcal{V}_R)$, for $1 \leq i \leq n$ we let
$$H_i = \bigwedge_{j \in \{1,\ldots,n\} \setminus \{i\}} \exists \mathcal{U}_j \, . \, \exists \mathcal{U}'_j \, . \, T_{P_j}$$
where $\mathcal{U}_j = \mathcal{V}_{P_j} \setminus \mathcal{V}_{P_i}$. We can then check whether $R \models \Box \varphi$ by executing $InvCheck(R, \varphi \wedge \bigwedge_{i=1}^{n} CCtr(P_i, \langle\!\langle H_i \rangle\!\rangle \Box abs_i(\varphi)))$. If this check returns answer No, we can construct a counterexample proceeding as in Section 3.

5 Experimental Results

We applied our methods for early error detection to two examples: a distributed database protocol and a wireless communication protocol. We implemented all algorithms on top of the model checker MOCHA [AHM+98], which relies on the BDD package and image computation engine provided by VIS [BHSV+96].

Demarcation protocol. The *demarcation protocol* is a distributed protocol for maintaining numerical constraints between distributed copies of a database [BGM92]. We considered an instance of the protocol that manages two sites that sell and buy back seats on the same airplane; each site is modeled by a module. In order to minimize communication, each site maintains a *demarcation* variable indicating the maximum number of seats it can sell autonomously; if the site wishes to sell more seats than this limit, it enters a negotiation phase with the other site. The invariant states that the total number of seats sold is always less than the total available.

In order to estimate the sensitivity of our methods to differences in modeling style, we wrote three models of the demarcation protocol; the models differ in minor details, such as the maximum number of seats that can be sold or bought in a single transaction, or the implementation of the communication channels. In all models, each of the two modules controls over 20 variables, and has 8–10 external variables; the diameter of the set of reachable states is between 80 and 120. We present the number of iterations required for finding errors in the three models using the various notions of controllability in Table 1. Some of the errors occurred in the formulation of the models, others were seeded at random.

Two-chip intercom. The second example is from the *Two-Chip Intercom* (TCI) project of the Berkeley Wireless Research Center [BWR]. TCI is a wireless local network which allows approximately 40 remotes to transmit voice with point-to-point and broadcast communication. The operation of the network is coordinated by a base station, which assigns channels to the remotes through a TDMA scheme. Each remote and base station will be implemented in a two-chip solution, one for the digital component and one for the analog. The TCI protocol involves four layers: the functional layer (UI), the transport layer, the medium access control (MAC) layer and the physical layer. The UI provides an interface between the user and the remote. The transport layer accepts service requests from the UI, defines the corresponding messages to be transmitted across the network, and transmits the messages in packets. The transport layer also accepts and interprets the incoming packets and sends the messages

Error	L	C	R	G
e1	19	19	19	24
e2	31	31	31	36
e3	19	19	19	24
e4	18	23	24	24

(a) Model 1.

Error	L	C	R	G
e1	30	30	35	35
e2	40	40	44	44
e3	28	28	33	33
e4	18	18	25	25

(b) Model 2.

Error	L	C	R	G
e1	14	18	18	18
e2	14	18	18	18
e3	14	18	18	18
e4	12	16	16	16

(c) Model 3.

Table 1. Number of iterations required in global state exploration to find errors in 3 models of the demarcation protocol. The errors are e1,...,e4. The columns are L (lazy controllability), C (constrained controllability), R (regular controllability), and G (traditional global state exploration).

to the UI. The MAC layer implements the TDMA scheme. The protocol stack for a remote is shown in Figure 1(a). Each of these blocks are described by the designers in Esterel and modeled in *Polis* using *Codesign Finite State Machines* [BCG+97].

There are four main services available to a user: *ConnReq*, *AddReq*, *RemReq* and *DiscReq*. To enter the network, a remote sends a connection request, *ConnReq*, together with the id of the remote, to the base station. The base station checks that the remote is not already registered, and that there is a free time-slot for the remote. It then registers the remote, and sends a connection grant back to the the remote. If a remote wishes to leave the network, it sends *DiscReq* to the base station, which unregisters the remote. If two or more remotes want to start a conference, one of them sends *AddReq* to the base station, together with the id's of the remotes with which it wants to communicate. The base station checks that the remotes are all registered, and sends to each of these remotes an acknowledgment and a time-slot assignment for the conference. When a remote wishes to leave the conference, it sends a *RemReq* request to the base station, which reclaims the time slot allocated to the remote.

We consider a TCI network involving one remote and one base station. The invariant states that if a remote believes that it is connected to the network, then the base station has this remote registered. This property involves the functional and transport layers. In our experiment, we model the network in *reactive modules* [AH99] The modules that model the functional and transport layers for both the remote and the base station are translated directly from the corresponding CFSM models; based on the protocol specification, we provide abstractions for the MAC layer and physical layer as well as the channel between the remote and the base station. Due to the semantics of CFSM, the modules are lazy, and therefore, lazy controllability applies. The final model has 83 variables. The number of iterations required to discover the various errors, some incurred during the modeling and some seeded in, are reported in Figure 1(b).

Results on BDD sizes and discussion. In order to isolate the unpredictable effect of dynamic variable ordering on the BDD sizes, we conducted, for each

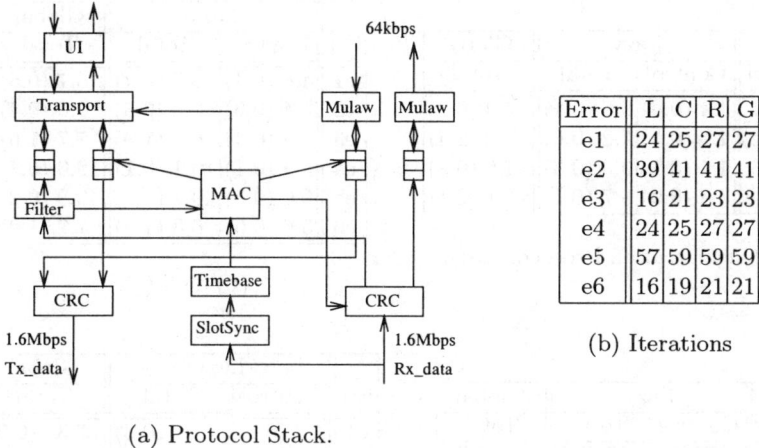

Fig. 1. The TCI protocol stack and the number of iterations of global state exploration to discover the error.

error, two sets of experiments. In the first set of experiments, we turned off dynamic variable ordering, but supplied good initial orders. In the second, dynamic variable ordering was turned on, and a random initial order was given. Since the maximum BDD size is often the limiting factor in formal verification, we give results based on the maximum number of BDD nodes encountered during verification process, taking into account the BDDs composing the controllability predicates, the reachability predicate, and the transition relation of the system under consideration. We only compare our results for the verification using lazy controllability and global state exploration, since these are the most significant comparisons. Due to space constraint, we give results for model 3 of the demarcation protocol as well as the TCI protocol.

Without dynamic variable ordering. For each error, we recorded the maximum number of BDD nodes allocated by the BDD manager encountered during verification process. The results given in Table 2(a) and 2(b) are the averages of four experiment runs, each with a different initial variable order. They show that often the computation of the controllability predicates helps reduce the total amount of required memory by about 10–20%. The reason for this savings can be attributed to the fact that fewer iterations in global state exploration avoids the possible BDD blow-up in subsequent post-image computation.

With dynamic variable ordering. The analysis on BDD performance is more difficult if dynamic variable ordering is used. We present the results in Tables 2(c) and 2(d) which show the averages of nine experiment runs on the same models with dynamic variable ordering on. Dynamic variable ordering tries to minimize the total size of all the BDDs, taking into account the BDDs representing the controllability and the reachability predicates, as well as the BDDs encoding

(a) Demarcation Protocol (Off).

Err	Lazy Control	Lazy Total	Global Total
e1	4.4 (0.8)	6.6 (0.1)	7.9 (0.8)
e2	4.1 (0.1)	7.2 (0.6)	9.2 (2.4)
e3	4.4 (0.1)	9.0 (0.3)	14.6 (0.3)
e4	7.3 (0.9)	8.7 (0.1)	11.1 (2.1)

(b) TCI (Off).

Err	Lazy Control	Lazy Total	Global Total
e1	4.8 (0.4)	6.3 (0.4)	6.7 (0.5)
e2	5.4 (0.6)	8.6 (0.5)	9.0 (0.4)
e3	5.8 (0.4)	6.5 (1.0)	7.7 (1.6)
e4	5.4 (0.1)	10.1 (0.1)	12.0 (0.3)
e5	6.6 (0.5)	40.7 (1.8)	43.8 (0.2)
e6	5.6 (0.6)	6.8 (1.6)	7.7 (1.9)

(c) Demarcation Protocol (On).

Err	Lazy Control	Lazy Total	Global Total
e1	3.0 (0.4)	6.9 (0.7)	7.5 (0.4)
e2	3.5 (1.0)	6.7 (0.4)	8.1 (0.8)
e3	3.6 (0.5)	8.9 (1.3)	12.7 (1.9)
e4	4.4 (0.4)	9.0 (0.9)	11.8 (2.6)

(d) TCI (On).

Err	Lazy Control	Lazy Total	Global Total
e1	4.2 (0.9)	7.2 (0.8)	7.3 (0.9)
e2	3.7 (0.6)	10.1 (2.4)	11.0 (2.3)
e3	4.5 (0.5)	7.4 (1.5)	6.4 (0.6)
e4	3.8 (0.3)	11.4 (2.9)	16.9 (7.4)
e5	4.0 (0.4)	60.2 (19.1)	73.7 (29.8)
e6	4.6 (0.5)	7.9 (0.9)	6.8 (0.9)

Table 2. Average maximum number of BDD nodes required for error detection during the controllability (Control) and reachability computation (Total) phases. Dynamic variable ordering was turned off in (a) and (b), and on in (c) and (d). The results are given for lazy controllability and global state exploration. All data are in thousands of BDD nodes, and the standard deviations are given in parenthesis.

the transition relation of the system. Hence, if the BDDs for the controllability predicates are a sizeable fraction of the other BDDs, their presence slows down the reordering process, and hampers the ability of the reordering process to reduce the size of the BDD of the reachability predicate. Thus, while our methods consistently reduce the number of iterations required in global state exploration to discover the error, occasionally we do not achieve savings in terms of memory requirements.

When the controllability predicates are small compared to the reachability predicate, they do not interfere with the variable ordering algorithm. This observation suggests the following heuristics: one can alternate the iterations in the computation of the controllability and reachability predicates in the following manner. At each iteration, the iteration in the controllability predicate is computed only when its size is smaller than a threshold fraction (say, 50%) of the reachability predicate. Otherwise, reachability iterations are carried out. Another possible heuristics to reduce the size of the BDD representation of the the controllability predicates is to allow approximations: our algorithms remain sound and complete as long as we use over-approximations of the controllability predicates.

6 Bounded Controllability and Iterative Strengthening

Bounded controllability. In lazy controllability, we know that there is a move of the environment that is always enabled (the move that leaves all external variables unchanged); therefore, that move must be able to control the module. In constrained controllability, we are given the set of possible environment moves, and we require that one of those moves is able to control the module. We can combine these two notions in the definition of *bounded controllability*. In bounded controllability, unlike in usual games, the environment may have some degree of insuppressible internal nondeterminism. For each state, we are given a (nonempty) set A of possible environment moves, as in usual games. In addition, we are also given a (possibly empty) set $B \subseteq A$ of moves that the environment can take at its discretion, even if they are not the best moves to control the module. We say that a state is *boundedly controllable* if (a) there is a move in A that can control the state, and (b) all the moves in B can control the state. The name *bounded controllability* is derived from the fact that the sets B and A are the lower and upper bounds of the internal nondeterminism of the controller.

Given a module P, we can specify the lower and upper bounds for the environment nondeterminism using two predicates $H^l, H^u \in \mathcal{P}(\mathcal{V}_P \cup \mathcal{E}'_P)$. We can then define the *bounded uncontrollable predecessor operator* $\text{BUPre}[H^l, H^u] : \mathcal{P}(\mathcal{V}_P) \mapsto \mathcal{P}(\mathcal{V}_P)$ by

$$\text{BUPre}[H^l, H^u](X) = \left[\forall \mathcal{E}'_P.(H^u \to \exists \mathcal{C}'_P.(T_P \wedge X'))\right] \vee \left[\exists \mathcal{E}'_P.(H^l \wedge \exists \mathcal{C}'_P.(T_P \wedge X'))\right].$$

Note that the quantifiers are the duals of the ones in our informal definition, since this operator computes the uncontrollable states, rather than the controllable ones. Note also that in general we cannot eliminate the first disjunct, unless we know that $\exists \mathcal{E}'_P . H^l$ holds at all $s \in States(P)$, as was the case for lazy controllability. By substituting this predecessor operator to UPre in Algorithm 1, given a predicate φ over $\mathcal{V}_P$, we can compute the predicate $BCtr[H^l, H^u](P, \Box\varphi)$ defining the states of P that are boundedly controllable w.r.t. $\Box\varphi$. Given a system $R = P_1 \parallel \cdots \parallel P_n$ and a predicate φ over $\mathcal{V}_R$, we can use bounded controllability to compute a set of doomed states as follows. For each $1 \leq i \leq n$, we let as usual $abs_i(\varphi) = \exists (\mathcal{V}_R \setminus \mathcal{V}_{P_i}) . \varphi$, and we compute the lower and upper bounds by

$$H^l_i = \bigwedge\nolimits_{j \in \{1,\ldots,n\}\setminus\{i\}} \forall \mathcal{U}_{j,i}.\exists \mathcal{U}'_{j,i}.T_{P_j} , \qquad H^u_i = \bigwedge\nolimits_{j \in \{1,\ldots,n\}\setminus\{i\}} \exists \mathcal{U}_{j,i}.\exists \mathcal{U}'_{j,i}.T_{P_j} ,$$

where for $1 \leq j \leq n$, the set $\mathcal{U}_{j,i} = \mathcal{V}_{P_j} \setminus \mathcal{V}_{P_i}$ consists of the variable of P_j not present in P_i. We can then check whether $R \models \Box\varphi$ by executing $InvCheck(R, \varphi \wedge \bigwedge_{i=1}^n BCtr[H^l_i, H^u_i](P_i, \Box abs_i(\varphi)))$. If this check fails, we can construct counterexamples by proceeding as in Section 3.

Iterative strengthening. We can further strengthen the controllability predicates by the process of *iterative strengthening*. This process is based on the following observation. In the system $R = P_1 \| \cdots \| P_n$, in order to control P_i, the environment of P_i must not only take transitions compatible with the transition relation of the modules P_j, for $j \in \{1, \ldots, n\} \setminus \{i\}$, but these modules must also stay in their own sets of controllable states. This suggests that when we compute the controllable states of P_i, we take into account the controllability predicates already computed for the other modules. For $1 \leq i \leq n$, if δ_i is the controllability predicate of module P_i, we can compute the upper bound to the environment nondeterminism by

$$H_i^u(\bar{\delta}) = \bigwedge_{j \in \{1,\ldots,n\} \setminus \{i\}} \exists \mathcal{U}_{j,i} \cdot \exists \mathcal{U}'_{j,i} \cdot (T_{P_j} \wedge \delta_i \wedge \delta'_i) \,,$$

where $\bar{\delta} = \delta_1, \ldots, \delta_n$. For all $1 \leq i \leq n$, we can compute a sequence of increasingly strong controllability predicates by letting $\delta_i^0 = \text{T}$ and, for $k \geq 0$, by $\delta_i^{k+1} = BCtr[H_i^l, H_i^u(\bar{\delta}^k)](P_i, \Box\varphi)$. For all $1 \leq i \leq n$ and all $k \geq 0$, predicate δ_i^{k+1} is at least as strong as δ_i^k. We can terminate the computation at any $k \geq 0$ (reaching a fixpoint is not needed), and we can verify $R \models \Box\varphi$ by executing $InvCheck(R, \varphi \wedge \bigwedge_{i=1}^n \delta_i^k)$. As k increases, so does the cost of computing these predicates. However, this increase may be offset by the faster detection of errors in the global state-exploration phase.

Discussion. The early error detection techniques presented in the previous sections for invariants can be straightforwardly extended to general linear temporal-logic properties. Given a system $R = P_1 \| \cdots \| P_n$ and a general LTL formula ψ over $\mathcal{V}_R$, we first compute for each $1 \leq i \leq n$ the predicate δ_i, defining the controllable states of P_i with respect to ψ. This computation requires the solution of ω-regular games [EJ91,Tho95]; in the solution, we can use the various notions of controllability developed in this paper, such as lazy, constrained, or bounded controllability. Then, we check whether $R \models \psi \wedge \Box(\bigwedge_{i=1}^n \delta_i)$: as before, if a state that falsifies δ_i for some $1 \leq i \leq n$ is entered, we can immediately conclude that $R \not\models \psi$. For certain classes of properties, such as reachability properties, it is convenient to perform this check in two steps, first checking that $R \models \Box(\bigwedge_{i=1}^n \delta_i)$ (enabling early error detection) and then checking that $R \models \psi$.

Acknowledgements. We thank Andreas Kuehlmann for pointing out the connection of this work with target enlargement.

References

[AdAHM99] R. Alur, L. de Alfaro, T.A. Henzinger, and F.Y.C. Mang. Automating modular verification. In *CONCUR 99: Concurrency Theory*, LNCS. Springer-Verlag, 1999.

[AH99] R. Alur and T.A. Henzinger. Reactive modules. *Formal Methods in System Design*, 15(1):7–48, 1999.

[AHK97] R. Alur, T.A. Henzinger, and O. Kupferman. Alternating-time temporal logic. In *Proc. 38th IEEE Symp. Found. of Comp. Sci.*, pages 100–109. IEEE Computer Society Press, 1997.

[AHM+98] R. Alur, T.A. Henzinger, F.Y.C. Mang, S. Qadeer, S.K. Rajamani, and S. Tasiran. Mocha: modularity in model checking. In *CAV 98: Computer Aided Verification*, volume 1427 of *LNCS*, pages 521–525. Springer-Verlag, 1998.

[ASSSV94] A. Aziz, T.R. Shiple, V. Singhal, and Alberto L. Sangiovanni-Vincentelli. Formula-dependent equivalence for CTL model checking. In *CAV 94: Computer Aided Verification*, LNCS. Springer-Verlag, 1994.

[BCCZ99] A. Biere, A. Cimatti, E. Clarke, and Y. Zhu. Symbolic model checking without BDDs. In *Proc. of TACAS: Tools and Algorithms for the Construction and Analysis of Systems*, volume 1579 of *LNCS*, pages 193–207. Springer-Verlag, 1999.

[BCG+97] F. Balarin, M. Chiodo, P. Giusto, H. Hsieh, A. Jurecska, L. Lavagno, C. Passerone, A. Sangiovanni-Vincentelli, E. Sentovich, K. Suzuki, and B. Tabbara. *Hardware-Software Co-Design of Embedded Systems: The Polis Approach*. Kluwer Academic Press, 1997.

[BGM92] D. Barbara and H. Garcia-Molina. The demarcation protocol: a technique for maintaining linear arithmetic constraints in distributed database systems. In *EDBT'92: 3rd International Conference on Extending Database Technology*, volume 580 of *LNCS*, pages 373–388. Springer-Verlag, 1992.

[BHSV+96] R. Brayton, G. Hachtel, A. Sangiovanni-Vincentelli, F. Somenzi, A. Aziz, S. Cheng, S. Edwards, S. Khatri, Y. Kukimoto, A. Pardo, S. Qadeer, R. Ranjan, S. Sarwary, T. Shiple, G. Swamy, and T. Villa. VIS: A system for verification and synthesis. In *CAV 96: Computer Aided Verification*, volume 1102 of *LNCS*, pages 428–432. Springer-Verlag, 1996.

[Bry86] R.E. Bryant. Graph-based algorithms for boolean function manipulation. *IEEE Transactions on Computers*, C-35(8), 1986.

[BWR] Berkeley wireless research center. http://bwrc.eecs.berkeley.edu.

[Dil88] D.L. Dill. *Trace Theory for Automatic Hierarchical Verification of Speed-Independent Circuits*. MIT Press, 1988.

[EJ91] E.A. Emerson and C.S. Jutla. Tree automata, mu-calculus and determinacy (extended abstract). In *32nd Symp. on Foundations of Computer Science (FOCS)*, pages 368–377, 1991.

[HKQ98] T.A. Henzinger, O. Kupferman, and S. Qadeer. From prehistoric to postmodern symbolic model checking. In *CAV 98: Computer Aided Verification*, volume 1427 of *LNCS*, pages 195–206. Springer-Verlag, 1998.

[HQR98] T.A. Henzinger, S. Qadeer, and S.K. Rajamani. You assume, we guarantee: methodology and case studies. In *CAV 98: Computer Aided Verification*, volume 1427 of *LNCS*, pages 440–451. Springer-Verlag, 1998.

[JSAA97] J. Juan, J. Shen, J. Abraham, and A. Aziz. On combining formal and informal verification. In *CAV 97: Computer Aided Verification*, LNCS. Springer-Verlag, 1997.

[KV96] O. Kupferman and M.Y. Vardi. Module checking. In *CAV 96: Computer Aided Verification*, volume 1102 of *LNCS*, pages 75–86. Springer-Verlag, 1996.

[RW89] P.J.G. Ramadge and W.M. Wonham. The control of discrete event systems. *IEEE Transactions on Control Theory*, 77:81–98, 1989.

[Tho95] W. Thomas. On the synthesis of strategies in infinite games. In *Proc. of 12th Annual Symp. on Theor. Asp. of Comp. Sci.*, volume 900 of *LNCS*, pages 1–13. Springer-Verlag, 1995.

[YD98] C.H. Yang and D.L. Dill. Validation with guided search of the state space. In *Design Automation Conference*, June 1998.

A Discrete Strategy Improvement Algorithm for Solving Parity Games
(Extended Abstract)

Jens Vöge[1]* and Marcin Jurdziński[2]**

[1] Lehrstuhl für Informatik VII
RWTH Aachen, D-52056 Aachen, Germany
voege@informatik.rwth-aachen.de

[2] BRICS[1]
Department of Computer Science, University of Århus,
Ny Munkegade Bldg. 540, DK-8000 Århus C, Denmark,
mju@brics.dk

Abstract. A discrete strategy improvement algorithm is given for constructing winning strategies in parity games, thereby providing also a new solution of the model-checking problem for the modal μ-calculus. Known strategy improvement algorithms, as proposed for stochastic games by Hoffman and Karp in 1966, and for discounted payoff games and parity games by Puri in 1995, work with real numbers and require solving linear programming instances involving high precision arithmetic. In the present algorithm for parity games these difficulties are avoided by the use of discrete vertex valuations in which information about the relevance of vertices and certain distances is coded. An efficient implementation is given for a strategy improvement step. Another advantage of the present approach is that it provides a better conceptual understanding and easier analysis of strategy improvement algorithms for parity games. However, so far it is not known whether the present algorithm works in polynomial time. The long standing problem whether parity games can be solved in polynomial time remains open.

1 Introduction

The study of the computational complexity of solving parity games has two main motivations. One is that the problem is polynomial time equivalent to the modal μ-calculus model checking [7,18], and hence better algorithms for parity games may lead to better model checkers, which is a major objective in computer aided verification.

The other motivation is the intriguing status of the problem from the point of view of structural complexity theory. It is one of the few natural problems which

---

* Supported by the Deutsche Forschungsgemeinschaft (DFG), project Th 352/5-3.
** A part of this work was done while the author stayed at Lehrstuhl für Informatik VII, RWTH Aachen, Germany.
[1] Basic Research in Computer Science, Centre of Danish Science Foundation.

is in NP ∩ co-NP [7] (and even in UP ∩ co-UP [9]), and is not known to have a polynomial time algorithm, despite substantial effort of the community (see [7,1, 17,10] and references therein). Other notable examples of such problems include simple stochastic games [3,4], mean payoff games [5,21], and discounted payoff games [21]. There are polynomial time reductions of parity games to mean payoff games [15,9], mean payoff games to discounted payoff games [21], and discounted payoff games to simple stochastic games [21]. Parity games, as the simplest of them all, seem to be the most plausible candidate for trying to find a polynomial time algorithm.

A strategy improvement algorithm has been proposed for solving stochastic games by Hoffman and Karp [8] in 1966. Puri in his PhD thesis [15] has adapted the algorithm for discounted payoff games. Puri also provided a polynomial time reduction of parity games to mean payoff games, and advocated the use of the algorithm for solving parity games, and hence for the modal μ-calculus model checking.

In our opinion Puri's strategy improvement algorithm for parity games has two drawbacks.

- The algorithm uses high precision arithmetic, and needs to solve linear programming instances: both are typically costly operations. An implementation (by the first author) of Puri's algorithm, using a linear programming algorithm of Meggido [12], proved to be prohibitively slow.
- Solving parity games is a discrete, graph theoretic problem, but the crux of the algorithm is manipulation of real numbers, and its analysis is crucially based on continuous methods, such as Banach's fixed point theorem.

The first one makes the algorithm inefficient in practice, the other one obscures understanding of the algorithm.

Our discrete strategy improvement algorithm remedies both above-mentioned shortcomings of Puri's algorithm, while preserving the overall structure of the generic strategy improvement algorithm. We introduce discrete values (such as tuples of vertices, sets of vertices and natural numbers denoting lengths of paths in the game graph) which are being manipulated by the algorithm, instead of their encodings into real numbers. (One can show a precise relationship between behaviour of Puri's and our algorithms; we will treat this issue elsewhere.)

The first advantage of our approach is that instead of solving linear programming instances involving high precision arithmetic, we only need to solve instances of a certain purely discrete problem. Moreover, we develop an algorithm exploiting the structure of instances occurring in this context, i.e., relevance of vertices and certain distance information. In this way we get an efficient implementation of a strategy improvement algorithm with $O(nm)$ running time for one strategy improvement step, where n is the number of vertices, and m is the number of edges in the game graph.

The other advantage is more subjective: we believe that it is easier to analyze the discrete data maintained by our algorithm, rather than its subtle encodings into real numbers involving infinite geometric series [15]. The classical continuous reasoning gives a relatively clean proof of correctness of the algorithm in a more general case of discounted payoff games [15], but we think that in the case of parity games it blurs an intuitive understanding of the underlying discrete structure. However, the long standing open question whether a strategy improvement algorithm works in polynomial time [4] remains unanswered. Nevertheless, we hope that our discrete analysis of the algorithm may help either to find a proof of polynomial time termination, or to come up with a family of examples on which the algorithm requires exponential number of steps. Any of those results would mark a substantial progress in understanding the computational complexity of parity games.

So far, for all families of examples we have considered the strategy improvement algorithm needs only linear number of strategy improvement steps. Notably, a linear number of strategy improvements suffices for several families of difficult examples for which other known algorithms need exponential time.

In this extended abstract, some substantial proofs are omitted, in particular for Lemmas 3 and 5, as well as the detailed correctness proof of the algorithm of Section 4. For a more complete exposition see [19].

Acknowledgement

We are indebted to Wolfgang Thomas for his invaluable advice, support, and encouragement.

2 Preliminaries

A *parity game* is an infinite two-person game played on a finite vertex-colored graph $G = (V_0, V_1, E, c)$ where $V = V_0 \,\dot\cup\, V_1$ is the set of vertices and $E \subseteq V_0 \times V_1 \cup V_1 \times V_0$ the set of edges with $\forall u \in V\ \exists v \in V : uEv$, and $c : V \to \{1, \ldots, d\}$ is a coloring of the vertices. The two players move, in alternation, a token along the graph's edges; player 0 moves the token from vertices in V_0, player 1 from vertices in V_1. A play is an infinite vertex sequence $v_0 v_1 v_2 \ldots$ arising in this way. The decision who wins refers to the coloring c of the game graph: if the largest color which occurs infinitely often in $c(v_0)c(v_1)c(v_2)\ldots$ is even then player 0 wins, otherwise player 1 wins. One says that player 0 (resp. player 1) has a winning strategy from $v \in V$ if starting a play in v, he can force a win for arbitrary choices of player 1 (resp. player 0). By the well-known determinacy of parity games, the vertex set V is divided into the two sets W_0, W_1, called the winning sets, where W_i contains the vertices from which player i has a winning strategy.

Moreover, it is known (see, e.g., [6,14]) that on W_i player i has a memoryless winning strategy, which prescribes the respective next move by a unique edge leaving each vertex in V_i.

In the following we fix the basic notations for games and strategies. Let $G = (V_0, V_1, E, c)$ be a game graph with the vertices $V = V_0 \cup V_1$ and the coloring $c : V \to \{1, \ldots d\}$. Let W_0, W_1 be the winning sets of G.

A strategy for player i ($i = 0, 1$) is a function $\rho : V_i \to V_{1-i}$ such that $vE\rho(v)$ for all $v \in V_i$. A strategy for player i is called a winning strategy on $W \subseteq V$ if player i wins every play starting in W when using that strategy. A *winning strategy* for player i is a winning strategy on the winning set W_i.

We set

$$V_+ = \{v \in V \mid c(v) \text{ is even}\} \text{ and } V_- = \{v \in V \mid c(v) \text{ is odd}\}$$

and we call vertices in V_+ positive and those in V_- negative.

We introduce two orderings of V, the relevance ordering $<$ and the reward ordering $\prec$. The relevance order is a total order extending the pre-order given by the coloring, i.e., such that $c(u) < c(v)$ implies $u < v$. (So higher colors indicate higher relevance.)

By $\inf(\pi)$ we denote the set of vertices occurring infinitely often in the play π. Referring to $<$ over V, we can reformulate the winning condition for player 0 in a play π as

$$\max_<(\inf(\pi)) \in V_+.$$

Another ordering, the reward order $\prec$, indicates the value of a vertex as seen from player 0. The lowest reward originates from the vertex in V_- of highest relevance, the highest from the vertex in V_+ of highest relevance. Formally, we define:

$$u \prec v \iff (u < v \wedge v \in V_+) \vee (v < u \wedge u \in V_-)$$

We extend the reward order $\prec$ to an order on sets of vertices. If $P, Q \in 2^V$ are distinct, the vertex v of highest relevance in the symmetric difference $P \triangle Q$ decides whether $P \prec Q$ or $Q \prec P$: If $v \in V_+$ then the set containing v is taken as the higher one, if $v \in V_-$ then the set not containing v is taken as the higher one. Formally:

$$P \prec Q \iff P \neq Q \wedge \max_<(P \triangle Q) \in Q \triangle V_-$$

Note that we use the same symbol $\prec$ for vertices and for sets of vertices.

We also need a coarser version $\prec_w$ of $\prec$, using a reference vertex w and taking into account only P- and Q-vertices of relevance $\geq w$:

$$P \prec_w Q \iff P \cap \{x \in V \mid x \geq w\} \prec Q \cap \{x \in V \mid x \geq w\},$$

and the corresponding equivalence relation:

$$P \sim_w Q \iff P \preceq_w Q \wedge Q \preceq_w P$$

3 Game Graph Valuations

In this section we present the terminology and main ideas underlying the approximative construction of winning strategies. The plays considered in the sequel are always induced by two given strategies σ and τ for players 0 and 1 respectively. Any such pair σ, τ determines from any vertex a play ending in a loop L. The first Subsection 3.1 introduces certain values called play profiles for such plays. A play profile combines three data: the most relevant vertex of the loop L, the vertices occurring in the play that are more relevant than the most relevant vertex in the loop, and the number of all vertices that are visited before the most relevant vertex of the loop. The order $\prec$ above is extended to play profiles (so that $\prec$-higher play profiles are more advantageous for player 0). An arbitrary assignment of play profile values to the vertices is called a valuation.

Subsection 3.2 gives a certain condition when a valuation originates from a strategy pair (σ, τ) as explained. Such valuations are called locally progressive.

The algorithm will produce successively such locally progressive valuations. In each step, a valuation is constructed from a strategy σ of player 0 and an 'optimal' response strategy τ of player 1. In Subsection 3.3 this notion of optimality is introduced. We show that a valuation which is optimal for both players 0 and 1 represents the desired solution of our problem: a pair of winning strategies for the two players.

The last Subsection 3.4 will explain the nature of an approximation step, from a given valuation φ to a (next) 'response valuation' φ'. One should imagine that player 0 picks edges to vertices with $\prec$-maximal values given by φ, and that player 1 responds as explained above, by a locally progressive valuation φ'. The key lemma says that uniformly φ' will majorize φ (i.e., $\varphi(v) \preceq \varphi'(v)$ for all vertices $v \in V$). This will be the basis for the termination proof because equality $\varphi = \varphi'$ will imply that φ is already optimal for both players.

3.1 Play Profiles

Let $G = (V_0, V_1, E, c)$ be a game graph. Let Π be the set of plays that can be played on this graph. We define the function $w : \Pi \to V$ which computes the most relevant vertex that is visited infinitely often in a play π, i.e., $w(\pi) = \max_{\prec} \inf(\pi)$. Furthermore, we define a function $\alpha : \Pi \to 2^V$ which computes the vertices that are visited before the first occurrence of $w(\pi)$:

$$\alpha(\pi) = \{u \in V \mid \exists i \in \mathbb{N}_0 : \pi_i = u \wedge \forall k \in \mathbb{N}_0 : k \leq i \implies \pi_k \neq w(\pi)\}.$$

We are interested in three characteristic values of a play π:

1. The most relevant vertex u_π that is visited infinitely often: $u_\pi = w(\pi)$.
2. The set of vertices P_π that are more relevant than u_π and visited before the first visit of u_π: $P_\pi = \alpha(\pi) \cap \{v \in V \mid v > w(\pi)\}$.
3. The number of vertices visited before the first visit of u_π: $e_\pi = |\alpha(\pi)|$.

We call such a triple (u_π, P_π, e_π) a *play profile*. It induces an equivalence relation of plays on the given game graph. By definition each profile of a play induced by a pair of strategies belongs to the following set:

$$\mathcal{D} = \{(u, P, e) \in V \times 2^V \times \{0, \ldots, |V| - 1\} \mid \forall v \in P : u < v \wedge |P| \leq e\}.$$

The set $\mathcal{D}$ is divided into profiles of plays that are won by player 0, respectively 1:

$$\mathcal{D}_0 = \{(u,P,e) \in \mathcal{D} \mid u \in V_+\} \text{ and } \mathcal{D}_1 = \{(u,P,e) \in \mathcal{D} \mid u \in V_-\}.$$

We define a linear ordering $\prec$ on $\mathcal{D}$. One play profile is greater than another with respect to this ordering if the plays it describes are 'better' for player 0, respectively smaller if they are better for player 1. Let $(u,P,e), (v,Q,f) \in \mathcal{D}$:

$$(u,P,e) \prec (v,Q,f) \iff \begin{cases} u \prec v \\ \lor \; (u = v \land P \prec Q) \\ \lor \; (u = v \land P = Q \land v \in V_- \land e < f) \\ \lor \; (u = v \land P = Q \land v \in V_+ \land e > f) \end{cases}$$

The idea behind the last two clauses is that in case $u = v$ and $P = Q$ it is more advantageous for player 0 to have a shorter distance to the most relevant vertex v if $v \in V_+$ (case $f < e$), resp. a longer distance if $v \in V_-$ (case $f > e$).

For the subsequent lemmata we need a coarser ordering $\prec_w$ of play profiles:

$$(u,P,e) \prec_w (v,Q,f) \iff u \prec v \lor (u = v \land P \prec_w Q)$$

and a corresponding equivalence relation $\sim_w$:

$$(u,P,e) \sim_w (v,Q,f) \iff u = v \land P \sim_w Q$$

3.2 Valuations

A *valuation* is a function $\varphi : V \to \mathcal{D}$ which labels each vertex with a play profile.

We are interested in valuations where all play profiles $\varphi(v)$ ($v \in V$) are *induced* by the same pair of strategies. An initial vertex v and two strategies σ for player 0 and τ for player 1 determine a unique play $\pi_{v,\sigma,\tau}$. For a pair of strategies (σ, τ) we can define the *valuation induced by* (σ, τ) to be the function φ which maps $v \in V$ to the play profile of $\pi_{v,\sigma,\tau}$. This valuation φ assigns to each vertex the play profile of the play starting in v played with respect to σ and τ. To refer to the components of a play profile $\varphi(v) = (u, P, e)$ we write φ_0, φ_1 and φ_2, where $\varphi_0(v) = u$, $\varphi_1(v) = P$ and $\varphi_2(v) = e$. We call u the most relevant vertex of play profile $\varphi(v)$ (or of v, if φ is clear from the context).

The play profiles in a valuation induced by a strategy pair are related as follows: Let σ, τ be strategies and φ their corresponding valuation. Let $x, y \in V$ be two vertices with $\sigma(x) = y$ or $\tau(x) = y$, i.e., in a play induced by σ and τ a move proceeds from x to y. It follows immediately that $\varphi_0(x) = \varphi_0(y)$. We can distinguish the following cases:

1. Case $x < \varphi_0(x)$: Then $\varphi_1(x) = \varphi_1(y)$ and $\varphi_2(x) = \varphi_2(y) + 1$.
2. Case $x = \varphi_0(x)$: By definition of φ we have: $\varphi_1(x) = \emptyset$ and $\varphi_2(x) = 0$. Furthermore $\varphi_1(y) = \emptyset$, because there are no vertices on the loop through x that are more relevant than x.
3. Case $x > \varphi_0(x)$: Then $\varphi_1(x) = \{x\} \dot\cup \varphi_1(y)$ and $\varphi_2(x) = \varphi_2(y) + 1$.

These conditions define what we call the φ-progress relation $\triangleleft_\varphi$. If an edge leads from x to y then $x \triangleleft_\varphi y$ will mean that the φ-value is correctly updated when passing from x to y in a play. Formally we define for $x, y \in V$, assuming $\varphi(x) = (u, P, e)$, $\varphi(y) = (v, Q, f)$:

$$x \triangleleft_\varphi y \iff u = v \wedge (\quad (x = u \wedge P = Q = \emptyset \quad \wedge e = 0)$$
$$\vee\, (x < u \wedge P = Q \qquad\quad \wedge e = f + 1)$$
$$\vee\, (x > u \wedge P = Q \cup \{x\} \wedge e = f + 1))$$

The following proposition is straightforward.

Proposition 1. *Let φ be a valuation, and let $v \triangleleft_\varphi \sigma(v)$ and $v \triangleleft_\varphi \tau(v)$, for all $v \in V$. Then (σ, τ) induces φ.*

Note that a valuation φ may be induced by several pairs (σ, τ) of strategies so that several plays starting in v with play profile $\varphi(v)$ may exist. We now characterize those valuations which are induced by some strategy pair (σ, τ). A valuation φ is called *locally progressive* if

$$\forall u \in V\; \exists v \in V : uEv \wedge u \triangleleft_\varphi v.$$

The next proposition follows immediately from definitions.

Proposition 2. *Let $G = (V_0, V_1, E, c)$ be a game graph. Let φ be a valuation for G. Then φ is a locally progressive valuation iff there exists a strategy σ for player 0 and a strategy τ for player 1 such that φ is a valuation induced by (σ, τ).*

We call a strategy $\rho : V_i \to V_{1-i}$ ($i \in \{0, 1\}$) *compatible* with the valuation φ if $\forall v \in V_i : v \triangleleft_\varphi \rho(v)$. From Proposition 2 it follows that for a locally progressive valuation φ at least one strategy for each player is compatible with φ.

3.3 Optimal Valuations

A valuation φ is called *optimal* for player 0 if the φ-progress relation $x \triangleleft_\varphi y$ only applies to edges xEy where the value $\varphi(y)$ is $\preceq$-maximal among the E-successors of x (i.e., among the values $\varphi(z)$ with xEz). However, a weaker requirement is made if x is the most relevant vertex associated to x via φ (i.e., $\varphi_0(x) = x$). In this case we discard the distance component φ_2; formally, we replace $\preceq$ by $\preceq_x$. (Recall that $(u, P, e) \prec_x (v, Q, f)$ holds if $u \prec v$ holds, or $u = v$ and $P \prec_x Q$, i.e., e and f are not taken into account.) Formally, φ is called optimal for player 0 if for all $x \in V_0$ and $y \in V_1$ with an edge xEy:

$$x \triangleleft_\varphi y \iff \forall z \in V_1 : xEz \Rightarrow \varphi(z) \preceq \varphi(y) \vee \big(\varphi_0(x) = x \wedge \varphi(z) \preceq_x \varphi(y)\big)$$

In the last case, the vertex y succeeds x in the loop of a play given by a strategy pair (σ, τ) which is compatible with φ; of course, there may be several such y with $x \triangleleft_\varphi y$. Similarly φ is called optimal for player 1 if for all $x \in V_1$ and $y \in V_0$ with an edge xEy:

$$x \triangleleft_\varphi y \iff \forall z \in V_0 : xEz \Rightarrow \varphi(y) \preceq \varphi(z) \vee \big(\varphi_0(x) = x \wedge \varphi(y) \preceq_x \varphi(z)\big)$$

A valuation that is optimal for both players is called optimal valuation.

It is useful to note the following fact: If φ is optimal for player 0, then (since $\preceq_x$ is coarser than $\preceq$) $x \triangleleft_\varphi y$ implies $\varphi(z) \preceq_x \varphi(y)$ for xEz. Similarly if φ is optimal for player 1 then $x \triangleleft_\varphi y$ implies $\varphi(y) \preceq_x \varphi(z)$ for xEz.

The optimal valuations are closely related to the desired solution of a game, namely a pair of winning strategies. Consider a valuation φ which is optimal for player 0, and let W_1 be the set of vertices u whose φ-value $\varphi(u)$ is in $\mathcal{D}_1$ (i.e., the most relevant vertex $\varphi_0(u)$ associated to u is in V_-, signalling a win of player 1). Any strategy for player 1 compatible with φ turns out to be a winning strategy for him on W_1, whatever strategy player 0 chooses *independently* of φ. Applying this symmetrically for both players we shall obtain a pair of winning strategies.

Lemma 1. *Let $G = (V_0, V_1, E, c)$ be a game graph. Let $i \in \{0, 1\}$ and φ be a locally progressive valuation of G which is optimal for player i. Let $W_{1-i} = \{v \in V \mid \varphi(v) \in \mathcal{D}_{1-i}\}$. Then the strategies for player $1 - i$ compatible with φ are winning strategies on W_{1-i} (against an arbitrary strategy of player i).*

Applying this lemma symmetricly for both players leads to the following.

Theorem 1. *Let $G = (V_0, V_1, E, c)$ be a game graph. Let φ be an optimal locally progressive valuation of G. Then all strategies compatible with φ are winning strategies.*

3.4 Improving Valuations

Given two locally progressive valuations φ and φ', we call φ' *improved for player 0 with respect to* φ if

$$\forall x \in V_0 \, \exists y \in V : xEy \wedge x \triangleleft_{\varphi'} y \wedge \forall z \in V_1 : xEz \Rightarrow \varphi(z) \preceq \varphi(y).$$

A locally progressive valuation φ', which is improved for player 0 with respect to φ, can be constructed from a given locally progressive valuation φ by extracting a strategy $\sigma : V_0 \to V_1$ for player 0 that chooses maximal E-successors with respect to φ and constructing a locally progressive valuation φ' such that σ is compatible with φ'.

Lemma 2. *Let $G = (V_0, V_1, E, c)$ be a game graph. Let φ be a locally progressive valuation optimal for player 1 and φ' a locally progressive valuation that is improved for player 0 with respect to φ. Then for all $v \in V$, we have $\varphi(v) \preceq \varphi'(v)$.*

4 The Algorithm

In this section we give an algorithm for constructing an optimal locally progressive valuation for a given parity game graph. This will lead to winning strategies for the game. The algorithm is split into three functions: *main()*, *valuation()*, and *subvaluation()*.

In the function *main()* a sequence of strategies for player 0 is generated and for each of these strategies a locally progressive valuation is computed by calling *valuation()*. This valuation is constructed such that the strategy of player 0 is compatible with it and that it is optimal for player 1. The first strategy for player 0 is chosen randomly. Subsequent strategies for player 0 are chosen such that they are optimal with respect to the previous valuation. The main loop terminates if the strategy chosen for player 0 is the same as in the previous iteration. Finally a strategy for player 1 is extracted from the last computed valuation.

main(G):
1. **for each** $v \in V_0$ {Select initial strategy for player 0.}
2.   **select** $\sigma(v) \in V_1$ **with** $v\, E_G\, \sigma(v)$
3. **repeat**
4. $G_\sigma = (V_0, V_1, E', c)$, where $\forall u, v \in V$:
        $uE'v \iff (\sigma(u) = v \wedge u \in V_0) \vee (uE_G v \wedge u \in V_1)$
5. $\varphi = valuation(G_\sigma)$
6. $\sigma' = \sigma$ {Store σ under name σ'}
7.   **for each** $v \in V_0$ {Optimize σ locally according to φ}
8.   **if** $\varphi(\sigma(v)) \prec \max_{\prec}\{d \in D | \exists v' \in V : v\, E_G\, v' \wedge d = \varphi(v')\}$ **then**
9.   **select** $\sigma(v) \in V_1$
                with $\varphi(\sigma(v)) = \max_{\prec}\{d \in D | \exists v' \in V : v\, E_G\, v' \wedge d = \varphi(v')\}$
10. **until** $\sigma = \sigma'$
11. **for each** $v \in V_1$
12.   **select** $\tau(v) \in V_0$
        with $\varphi(\tau(v)) = \min_{\prec}\{d \in D | \exists v' \in V : v\, E_G\, v' \wedge d = \varphi(v')\}$
13. $W_0 = \{v \in V \mid \varphi_0(v) \in V_+\}$
14. $W_1 = \{v \in V \mid \varphi_0(v) \in V_-\}$
15. **return** W_0, W_1, σ, τ

Fig. 1. This function computes the winning sets and a winning strategy for each player from a given game graph.

In the functions *valuation()* and *subvaluation()*, we use the functions *reach(G, u)*, *minimal_distances(G, u)*, *maximal_distances(G, u)*. The functions work on the graph G and perform a backward search on the graph starting in vertex u.

- The function *reach(G, u)* produces the set of all vertices from which the vertex u can be reached in G (done by a backward depth first search).
- The function *minimal_distances(G, u)* computes a vector $\delta : V_G \to \{0, \ldots, |V_G| - 1\}$ where $\delta(v)$ is the length of the shortest path from v to u (done by a backward breadth first search starting from u).
- The function *maximal_distances(G, u)* yields a vector $\delta : V_G \to \{0, \ldots, |V_G| - 1\}$ where $\delta(v)$ is the length of the longest path from v to u that does not contain u as an intermediate vertex. This is done by a backward search

starting from u where a new vertex is visited if all its successors are visited before. This algorithm only works if every cycle in the graph contains u.

The *valuation(H)*-function produces a locally progressive valuation for the graph H that is optimal for player 1. It does this by splitting the graph into a set of subgraphs for which *subvaluation()* can compute a locally progressive valuation of this kind.

The function searches a loop and then the set of vertices R from which this loop can be reached. Computing the locally progressive valuation for the subgraph induced by R is done by *subvaluation()*. The rest of the graph (i.e., the subgraph induced by $V_H \setminus R$) is recursively treated in the same way.

valuation(H):
1. **for each** $v \in V$ **do**
2. $\quad \varphi(v) = \bot$.
3. **for each** $w \in V$ (ascending order with respect to $\prec$) **do**
4. $\quad$ **if** $\varphi(w) = \bot$ **then**
5. $\quad\quad L = reach(H|_{\{v \in V | v \leq w\}}, w)$
6. $\quad\quad$ **if** $E_H \cap \{w\} \times L \neq \emptyset$ **then**
7. $\quad\quad\quad R = reach(H, w)$
8. $\quad\quad\quad \varphi|_R = subvaluation(H|_R, w)$
9. $\quad\quad\quad E_H = E_H \setminus (R \times (V \setminus R))$
10. **return** φ

Fig. 2. This function computes for graph H a locally progressive valuation that is optimal for player 1.

The algorithm *valuation(H)* is given in Fig. 2. It works as follows:

1. φ is set 'undefined' for all v.
2. In ascending reward order those vertices w are found which belong to a loop L consisting of solely of $\leq$-smaller vertices. Then, for a fixed w, the set R_w of all vertices is determined from which this loop (and hence w) is reachable (excluding vertices which have been used in sets $R_{w'}$ for previously considered w'). The valuation is updated on the set R_w.

The new valuation is determined as follows. By backward depth-first search from w the vertices v in R_w are scanned, and edges leading outside R_w deleted, in order to prohibit entrance to R_w by a later search (from a different w').

In *subvaluation(H)* the role of vertices v in R_w w.r.t. $\prec_w$ is analyzed. We shall have $\varphi_0(v) = w$ for them. One proceeds in decreasing relevance order:

- If u happens to be w, a backward breadth first search is done and only the distance decreasing edges are kept.

- Otherwise one distinguishes whether u is positive or negative. If u is positive, one computes the set $\overline{U}$ of vertices from where w can be reached while avoiding u, and for those v from which a visit to u is unavoidable, add u to $\varphi_1(v)$, and delete edges from v to vertices in $\overline{U}$.
- If u is negative then let U be the set of vertices v, such that u can be visited on a path from v to w. We add u to $\varphi_1(v)$ for all $v \in U$, and we remove edges leading from $U \setminus \{u\}$ to $V \setminus U$.

The function *subvaluation(H)* is given in Fig. 3. It computes the paths to w that have minimal reward with respect to $\prec_w$ and stores for each vertex the resulting path in φ-value. Edges that belong to paths with costs that are not minimal are removed successively.

subvaluation(K, w):
1. **for each** $v \in V_K$ **do**
2. $\quad \varphi_0(v) = w$
3. $\quad \varphi_1(v) = \emptyset$
4. **for each** $u \in \{v \in V_K \mid v > w\}$ (descending order with respect to $<$) **do**
5. $\quad$ **if** $u \in V_+$ **then**
6. $\quad\quad \overline{U} = reach(K|_{V_K \setminus \{u\}}, w)$
7. $\quad\quad$ **for each** $v \in V_K \setminus \overline{U}$ **do**
8. $\quad\quad\quad \varphi_1(v) = \varphi_1(v) \cup \{u\}$
9. $\quad\quad\quad E_K = E_K \setminus ((\overline{U} \cup \{u\}) \times (V \setminus \overline{U}))$
10. $\quad$ **else**
11. $\quad\quad U = reach(K|_{V_K \setminus \{w\}}, u)$
12. $\quad\quad$ **for each** $v \in U$ **do**
13. $\quad\quad\quad \varphi_1(v) = \varphi_1(v) \cup \{u\}$
14. $\quad\quad\quad E_K = E_K \setminus ((U \setminus \{u\}) \times (V \setminus U))$
15. **if** $w \in V_+$ **then**
16. $\quad \varphi_2 = maximal\_distances(K, w)$
17. **else**
18. $\quad \varphi_2 = minimal\_distances(K, w)$
19. **return** φ

Fig. 3. This function computes a locally progressive valuation for a subgraph K with most relevant vertex w.

5 Time Complexity

In the analysis of the running time of a strategy improvement algorithm there are two parameters of major interest:

1. the time needed to perform a single strategy improvement step,
2. the number of strategy improvement steps needed.

We argue that our discrete strategy improvement algorithm for parity games achieves a satisfactory bound on the former parameter. Let n be the number of vertices, and let m be the number of edges in the game graph.

Proposition 3. *A single strategy improvement step, i.e., lines 4.-9. in Figure 1, is carried out in time $O(nm)$.*

A satisfactory analysis of the latter parameter is missing in our work. Despite the long history of strategy improvement algorithms for stochastic and payoff games [8,4,15] very little is known about the number of strategy improvement steps needed. The best upper bounds are exponential [4,15] but to our best knowledge no examples are known which require more than linear number of improvement steps. We believe that our purely discrete description of strategy improvement gives new insights into the behaviour of the algorithm in the special case of parity games. The two long standing questions: whether there is a polynomial time algorithm for solving parity games [7], and, more concretely, whether a strategy improvement algorithm for parity games terminates in polynomial time [4,15], remain open. Below we discuss some disjoint observations we have come up with so far, and some questions which we believe are worth pursuing.

We say that a vertex is *switchable* if the condition in line 8. of the algorithm in Figure 1 is satisfied; we say that a vertex is *switched* in line 9. of Figure 1. Note that switching an arbitrary non-empty subset of the set of switchable vertices in every strategy improvement step gives a correct strategy improvement algorithm for parity games. Therefore, one can view our algorithm as a generic algorithm which can be instantiated to a fully deterministic algorithm by providing a *policy* for choosing the set of vertices to switch in every strategy improvement step. Melekopoglou and Condon [13] exhibit families of examples on which several natural policies switching only one switchable vertex in every strategy improvement step require an exponential number of strategy improvement steps. It is open whether there are families of examples of parity games on which there are policies requiring super-polynomial number of strategy improvement steps. On the other hand, for every parity game and every initial strategy, there *exists* a policy requiring only linear number of strategy improvement steps.

Proposition 4. *For every parity game and initial strategy, there is a policy for which the strategy improvement algorithm switches every vertex at most once, and therefore it terminates after at most n strategy improvement steps.*

This contrasts with an algorithm for solving parity games based on progress measures [10], for which there are families of examples on which every policy requires an exponential number of steps.

Examples of Melekopoglou and Condon [13] are Markov decision processes, i.e., one-player simple stochastic games [3]. It is an open question whether the strategy improvement algorithm using the standard policy, i.e., switching all switchable vertices in every strategy improvement step, works in polynomial time for one-player simple stochastic games [13]. In contrast, our discrete strategy improvement algorithm terminates in polynomial time for one-player parity games.

Proposition 5. *The discrete strategy improvement algorithm terminates after $O(n^3)$ strategy improvement steps for one-player parity games.*

Most algorithms for solving parity games studied in literature have $O\big((n/d)^d\big)$ or $O\big((n/d)^{d/2}\big)$ worst-case running time bounds (see [10] and references therein), where d is the number of different priorities assigned to vertices. The best upper bound we can give at the moment for the number of strategy improvement steps needed by our discrete strategy improvement algorithm is the trivial one, i.e., the number of different strategies for player 0, which can be $2^{\Omega(n)}$.

Proposition 6. *The discrete strategy improvement algorithm terminates after $\prod_{v \in V_0}$ out-deg(v) many strategy improvement steps.*

There is, however, a variation of the strategy improvement algorithm for parity games, for which the number of strategy improvement steps is bounded by $O\big((n/d)^d\big)$.

Proposition 7. *There is a strategy improvement algorithm for parity games which terminates after $O\big((n/d)^d\big)$ improvement steps, and a single strategy improvement step can be performed in $n^{O(1)}$ time.*

Note that in every strategy improvement step the current valuation strictly improves in at least one vertex. We say that a strategy improvement step is *substantial* if in the current valuation the first component of a profile of some vertex strictly improves. Observe that there can be at most $O(n^2)$ substantial strategy improvement steps. It follows that in search for superpolynomial examples one has to manufacture gadgets allowing long sequences of non-substantial strategy improvement steps.

We have collected a little experimental evidence that in practice most improvement steps are non-substantial. There are few interesting scalable families of hard examples of parity games known in literature. Using an implementation of our discrete strategy improvement algorithm due to the first author [16] we have run some experiments on families of examples taken from [2] and from [10], and on a family of examples mentioned in [10] which make Zielonka's version [20] of the McNaughton's algorithm [11] work in exponential time. For all these families only linear number of strategy improvement steps were needed and, interestingly, the number of non-substantial strategy improvement steps was in all cases constant, i.e., not dependent of the size of the game graph.

References

1. A. Browne, E. M. Clarke, S. Jha, D. E. Long, and W. Marrero. An improved algorithm for the evaluation of fixpoint expressions. *Theoretical Computer Science*, 178(1–2):237–255, May 1997.
2. Nils Buhrke, Helmut Lescow, and Jens Vöge. Strategy construction in infinite games with Streett and Rabin chain winning conditions. In Tiziana Margaria and Bernhard Steffen, editors, *Tools and Algorithms for Construction and Analysis of Systems, Second International Workshop, TACAS '96, Proceedings*, volume 1055 of *Lecture Notes in Computer Science*, pages 207–224, Passau, Germany, 27–29 March 1996. Springer.

3. Anne Condon. The complexity of stochastic games. *Information and Computation*, 96:203–224, 1992.
4. Anne Condon. On algorithms for simple stochastic games. In Jin-Yi Cai, editor, *Advances in Computational Complexity Theory*, volume 13 of *DIMACS Series in Discrete Mathematics and Theoretical Computer Science*, pages 51–73. American Mathematical Society, 1993.
5. A. Ehrenfeucht and J. Mycielski. Positional strategies for mean payoff games. *Int. Journal of Game Theory*, 8(2):109–113, 1979.
6. E. A. Emerson and C. S. Jutla. Tree automata, mu-calculus and determinacy (Extended abstract). In *Proceedings of 32nd Annual Symposium on Foundations of Computer Science*, pages 368–377. IEEE Computer Society Press, 1991.
7. E. A. Emerson, C. S. Jutla, and A. P. Sistla. On model-checking for fragments of μ-calculus. In Costas Courcoubetis, editor, *Computer Aided Verification, 5th International Conference, CAV'93*, volume 697 of *LNCS*, pages 385–396, Elounda, Greece, June/July 1993. Springer-Verlag.
8. A. Hoffman and R. Karp. On nonterminating stochastic games. *Management Science*, 12:359–370, 1966.
9. Marcin Jurdziński. Deciding the winner in parity games is in UP ∩ co-UP. *Information Processing Letters*, 68(3):119–124, November 1998.
10. Marcin Jurdziński. Small progress measures for solving parity games. In Horst Reichel and Sophie Tison, editors, *STACS 2000, 17th Annual Symposium on Theoretical Aspects of Computer Science, Proceedings*, volume 1770 of *Lecture Notes in Computer Science*, pages 290–301, Lille, France, February 2000. Springer.
11. Robert McNaughton. Infinite games played on finite graphs. *Annals of Pure and Applied Logic*, 65(2):149–184, 1993.
12. Nimrod Megiddo. Towards a genuinely polynomial algorithm for linear programming. *SIAM Journal on Computing*, 12:347–353, 1983.
13. Mary Melekopoglou and Anne Condon. On the complexity of the policy improvement algorithm for stochastic games. *ORSA (Op. Res. Soc. of America) Journal of Computing*, 6(2):188–192, 1994.
14. A. W. Mostowski. Games with forbidden positions. Technical Report 78, University of Gdańsk, 1991.
15. Anuj Puri. *Theory of Hybrid Systems and Discrete Event Systems*. PhD thesis, Electronics Research Laboratory, College of Engineering, University of California, Berkeley, December 1995. Memorandum No. UCB/ERL M95/113.
16. Dominik Schmitz and Jens Vöge. Implementation of a strategy improvement algorithm for finite-state parity games. manuscipt, unpublished, April 2000.
17. Helmut Seidl. Fast and simple nested fixpoints. *Information Processing Letters*, 59(6):303–308, September 1996.
18. Colin Stirling. Local model checking games (Extended abstract). In Insup Lee and Scott A. Smolka, editors, *CONCUR'95: Concurrency Theory, 6th International Conference*, volume 962 of *LNCS*, pages 1–11. Springer-Verlag, 1995.
19. Jens Vöge and Marcin Jurdziński. A discrete strategy improvement algorithm for solving parity games. Aachener Informatik-Berichte 2000-2, RWTH Aachen, Fachgruppe Informatik, 52056 Aachen, Germany, February 2000.
20. Wiesław Zielonka. Infinite games on finitely coloured graphs with applications to automata on infinite trees. *Theoretical Computer Science*, 200:135–183, 1998.
21. Uri Zwick and Mike Paterson. The complexity of mean payoff games on graphs. *Theoretical Computer Science*, 158:343–359, 1996.

Distributing Timed Model Checking — How the Search Order Matters*

Gerd Behrmann[1], Thomas Hune[2], and Frits Vaandrager[3]

[1] Basic Research in Computer Science, Aalborg University
Frederik Bajersvej 7E, 9220 Aalborg East, Denmark
`behrmann@cs.auc.dk`
[2] Basic Research in Computer Science, Aarhus University
Ny Munkegade, Bygning 540, 8000 Århus C, Denmark
`baris@brics.dk`
[3] Computing Science Institute, University of Nijmegen
P.O. Box 9010, 6500 GL Nijmegen, The Netherlands
`fvaan@cs.kun.nl`

Abstract. In this paper we address the problem of distributing model checking of timed automata. We demonstrate through four real life examples that the combined processing and memory resources of multiprocessor computers can be effectively utilized. The approach assumes a distributed memory model and is applied to both a network of workstations and a symmetric multiprocessor machine. However, certain unexpected phenomena have to be taken into account. We show how in the timed case the search order of the state space is crucial for the effectiveness and scalability of the exploration. An effective heuristic to counter the effect of the search order is provided. Some of the results open up for improvements in the single processor case.

1 Introduction

The technical challenge in model checking is in devising algorithms and data structures that allow one to handle large state spaces. Over the last two decades numerous approaches have been developed that address this problem: symbolic methods such as BDDs, methods that exploit symmetry, partial order reduction techniques, etc [4]. One obvious approach that has been applied successfully by a number of researchers is to parallelize (or distribute) the state space search [1, 15]. Distributed reachability analysis and state-space generation has also been investigated in the related field of performance analysis in the context of stochastic Petri nets [3,8] (see the second paper for further references). Since the state-of-the-art in model checking and performance analysis is still progressing very fast, it does not make sense to develop parallel or distributed tools from scratch. Rather, the goal should be to view parallelization as an orthogonal feature, which can always be easily added when the appropriate hardware is available.

---

* Research supported by Esprit Project 26270, Verification of Hybrid Systems (VHS).

To some extend this goal has been achieved in the work of [3,15,8], all with very similar solutions. Stern and Dill [15], for example, present a simple but elegant approach to parallelize the Murφ tool [5] using the message passing paradigm. In parallel Murφ, the state table, which stores all reached protocol states, is partitioned over the nodes of the parallel machine. Each node maintains a work queue of unexplored states. When a node generates a new state, the *owning* node for this state is calculated with a hash function and the state is sent to this node; this policy implements randomized load balancing. In the case of Murφ, the algorithm of Stern and Dill achieves close to linear speedup. We applied the approach of Stern and Dill to parallelize UPPAAL[11], a model checker for networks of extended timed automata. We experimented with parallel UPPAAL using four existing case studies: DACAPO [13], communication [7] and power-down [6] protocols used in B&O audio/video equipment, and a model of a buscoupler.

In the case of timed automata, the state space is uncountably infinite, and therefore one is forced to work with *symbolic* states, which are finite representations of possibly infinite sets of concrete states. A key problem we had to face in our work is that the number of symbolic states that has to be explored depends on the order in which the state exploration proceeds. In particular, the number of states tends to grow if state space exploration is parallelized. The main contribution of this paper consists an effective heuristic which takes care that the growth of the number of states remains within acceptable bounds. As a result we manage to obtain close to double linear speedups for the B&O protocols and the buscoupler. For the DACAPO example the speedup is not so good, probably because the state space is so small that only a few nodes are involved in the computation at a time. Some of the results open up for improvements in the single processor case.

The rest of this paper is structured as follows: Section 2 reviews the notion of timed automata. Section 3 describes our approach to distributed timed model checking, Section 4 presents experimental results, and Section 5 summarizes some of the conclusions.

2 Model Checking Timed Automata

In this section we briefly review the notion of timed automata that underlies the UPPAAL tool. For a more extensive introduction we refer to [2,10]. For reasons of simplicity and clarity in presentation we have chosen to only give the semantics and exploration algorithms for timed automata. The techniques described in this paper extend easily to networks of timed automata, even when extended with shared variables as is the case in UPPAAL.

Timed automata are finite automata extended with real-valued clocks. Figure 1 depicts a simple two node timed automaton. As can be seen both the locations and edges are labeled with constraints on the clocks. Given a set of clocks C, we use $\mathcal{B}(C)$ to stand for the set of formulas that are conjunctions of atomic constraints of the form $x \bowtie n$ and $x - y \bowtie n$ for $x, y \in C$, $\bowtie \in \{<, \leq, =, \geq, >\}$

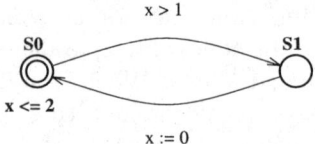

Fig. 1. A simple two state timed automaton with a single clock x.

and n being a natural number. Elements of $\mathcal{B}(C)$ are called clock constraints over C. $P(C)$ denotes the power set of C.

Definition 1. *A timed automaton A over clocks C is a tuple (L, l_0, E, I) where L is a finite set of locations, l_0 is the initial location, $E \subseteq L \times \mathcal{B}(C) \times \mathcal{P}(C) \times L$ is the set of edges, and $I : L \to \mathcal{B}(C)$ assigns invariants to locations. In the case of $(l, g, r, l') \in E$, we write $l \xrightarrow{g,r} l'$.*

Formally, clock values are represented as functions called clock assignments from C to the non-negative reals $\mathbf{R}_{\geq 0}$. We denote by $\mathbf{R}^C$ the set of clock assignments for C. The state space of an automaton A is $L \times \mathbf{R}^C$. The semantics of a timed automaton A is defined as a transition system:

- $(l, u) \to (l, u + d)$ if $u \in I(l)$ and $u + d \in I(l)$
- $(l, u) \to (l', u')$ if there exist g and r s.t. $l \xrightarrow{g,r} l', u \in g$ and $u' = [r \mapsto 0]u$

where for $d \in \mathbf{R}$, $u + d$ maps each clock x in C to the value $u(x) + d$, and $[r \mapsto 0]u$ denotes the assignment for C which maps each clock in r to the value 0 and agrees with u over $C \setminus r$. In short, the first rule describes *delay* and the second *edge* transitions. It is easy to see that the state space is uncountable. However, it is a well-known fact that timed automata have a finite-state symbolic semantics [2] based on countable symbolic states of the form (l, D), where $D \in \mathcal{B}(C)$:

- $(l, D) \to (l, \text{norm}(M, (D \wedge I(l))^\uparrow \wedge I(l)))$
- $(l, D) \to (l', r(g \wedge D \wedge I(l)) \wedge I(l'))$ if $l \xrightarrow{g,r} l'$.

where $D^\uparrow = \{u + d \mid u \in D \wedge d \in \mathbf{R}_{\geq 0}\}$ (the *future* operation), and $r(D) = \{[r \mapsto 0]u \mid u \in D\}$. The function norm $: \mathbf{N} \times \mathcal{B}(C) \to \mathcal{B}(C)$ normalizes the clock constraints with respect to the maximum constant M of the timed automaton. Normalizing the clock constraints guarantees a finite state space. We refer to [2, 10] for an in-depth treatment of the subject.

The state space exploration algorithm is shown in Fig. 2. Central to the algorithm are two data structures: the waiting list, which contains unexplored but reachable symbolic states, and the passed list, which contains all explored symbolic states. An important but in the literature often ignored optimization is to check for state coverage in both lists. Instead of only checking whether a

```
Passed := ∅
Waiting := {(l₀, D₀)}
repeat
    get (l, D) from Waiting
    if D ⊈ D' for all (l, D') ∈ Passed then
        add (l, D) to Passed
        Succ := {(l', D') : (l, D) → (l', D') ∧ D' ≠ ∅}
        for all (l', D') ∈ Succ do
            put (l', D') in Waiting
        od
    end if
until Waiting = ∅
```

Fig. 2. Sequential symbolic state space exploration for timed automata.

symbolic state is already included in the list, UPPAAL searches for states in the list that either cover the new state or is covered by it. In the first case the new state is discarded and in the latter case it replaces the existing state covered by it. We will return to this matter in Section 3.

3 Distributed Model Checking of Timed Automata

The approach we have used for distributing the exploration algorithm is similar to the one presented in [3,15,8]. Each node executes the same algorithm (see Fig. 3) which is a variant of the sequential algorithm shown in Fig. 2. Since we assume a distributed memory model, all variables are local. Each node is assigned a part of the state space according to a distribution function mapping symbolic states to nodes. Whenever a new symbolic state is encountered it is sent to the node responsible for exploring and storing that particular state. Each time a state has been explored and its successors have been sent, all states waiting to be received are received and put into the waiting list. If there are no states in the waiting list, the node waits until a state arrives. Although all nodes run the same algorithm, each node knows its own id and one node is the *master* node. This node is responsible for calculating the initial state and sending it to the owning node, and for deciding when the verification has finished. The verification terminates when there are no more states waiting to be explored in the waiting lists and there are no messages in transit. When the master finds out that the verification is finished it sends a *termination* signal to all the nodes.

3.1 Nondeterminism and Search Orders

When exploring a state space using UPPAAL, one can choose between breadth-first or depth-first search order corresponding to a queue or a stack implementation of the waiting list, respectively. In a distributed search one must still choose

```
PASSED := ∅
WAITING := ∅
repeat
    receive states and place them in WAITING
    get (l, D) from WAITING
    if D ⊈ D' for all (l, D') ∈ PASSED then
        add (l, D) to PASSED
        SUCC := {(l', D') : (l, D) → (l', D') ∧ D' ≠ ∅}
        for all (l', D') ∈ SUCC do
            send (l', D') to h(l')
        od
    end if
until not terminate
```

Fig. 3. The distributed state space exploration algorithm.

whether each node uses a queue or a stack; we will call this "distributed breadth-first" and "distributed depth-first" order, respectively. This only tells in what mode the single nodes run. In general the search order will be nondeterministic and may change from execution to execution.

In a distributed breadth-first search the states are explored in order of arrival at each node. However, the order in which states arrive at a node (enter the waiting list) will differ between executions. Some reasons for this are varying communication delays, and different workloads on the nodes. This means that in general states will not be searched in breadth-first order.

The main difference between a depth-first search and a distributed depth-first search is that in the single processor case only one path is explored at a time while in the distributed case more paths are explored at the same time. This is because all successors of a state are generated and sent to their owning nodes, where the search is continued in parallel. When the waiting list is implemented as a stack small changes of the order in which states arrive may significantly change the search order. Assume two states α and β arrive at a node while it is exploring a state with α arriving last (so α will be on the top of the stack). The successors of α are generated and sent to their owning nodes. One or more of these may go to the node itself which means that they are explored before β (because states are received before a new state is popped from the waiting list), and the same for their successors and so on. It may thus occur that β has to wait a long time before it is explored even though it has arrived at almost the same time as α. Hence small changes in the order of arrival of states may change the search order drastically.

3.2 Why the Search Order Matters

In a distributed state space search the number of states explored (and thereby the work done) may differ from run to run. This is because whether a state is explored or not depends on the states encountered before. As an example, consider two states (l, D) and (l, D') with same location vector l but different time zones satisfying $D \subset D'$. If (l, D) arrives first and is explored before arrival of (l, D'), then (l, D') will also be explored since it is not covered by any state in the passed list (assuming that there are no other states covering it). Since the successors of (l, D') are very likely to have larger time zones than the successors of (l, D) these will also be explored later. However, if (l, D') arrives first and is explored before (l, D) arrives, then (l, D) will not be explored because it is covered by a state in the passed list. This also means that no successors of (l, D) will be generated or explored.

Earlier experiments with the sequential version of UPPAAL showed that breadth-first search is often much faster than depth-first search when generating the complete state space. This comes from the fact that depth-first search order causes higher degree of fragmentation of the zones that breadth-first order, resulting in a higher number of symbolic states being generated.

As noted above, the distributed algorithm neither realizes a strict breadth-first nor depth-first search. When using a queue on each node, the algorithm approximates breadth-first search. In fact, on a single node the search order will be breadth-first. As we increase the number of nodes, chances increase that the nondeterministic nature of the communication causes the ordering within the queue to be such that some states with a large depth (distance from the initial state) are explored before other states with a smaller depth. In cases where breadth-first is actually the optimal search order, increasing the number of nodes is bound to increase the number of symbolic states explored.

Since it seems that breadth-first order in most cases is the optimal search order we propose a heuristic for making a distributed breadth-first order closer to breadth-first order. The heuristic keeps the states in each waiting list ordered by depth, for example by using a priority queue. This guarantees that the state in the waiting list with the smallest depth is explored first. In Section 4, we will demonstrate that this heuristic drastically reduces the rate at which the number of symbolic states increases when the number of nodes grows. In some cases it actually decreases the number of states explored.

3.3 Distribution Functions and Locality

On one hand, a good distribution function should guarantee a uniform work load for the nodes, on the other hand it should reduce communication between nodes. Since these objectives in most cases contradict each other, one has to find a suitable tradeoff. We therefore considered several distribution functions.

As in [15], most of our results are based on using a hash function as the distribution function. However, to make the inclusion checks of the time zones in the waiting and the passed lists possible, states with the same location vector must be mapped to the same node. The hash value of a symbolic state is therefore only based on the location vector and not on the complete state.

One possible hashing function is the one already implemented in UPPAAL and used when states are stored in the passed list. It uniquely maps each state to an integer modulo the size of the hash table. Experiments have shown that it distributes location vectors uniformly. Trying to increase locality of the distribution function, it should be possible to use the fact that transitions only change a small part of the location vector and only some transitions change the integer variables. If we consider a state α and a successor β, we can expect most locations and integer variables in β to be the same as in α. Section 4 reports on experiments where the distribution function only hashes on part of the location vector or only on the integer variables.

Some experiments with model specific distribution functions were done, but it was extremely difficult to even approach the performance of the generic distribution functions. Finding effective model specific distribution functions requires much work and a thorough understanding of the given model.

Within UPPAAL the techniques described in [12] for reducing memory consumption by only storing loop entry points in the passed list are quite important for verifying large models. The idea is to keep a single state from every static loop (which are simple to compute). This guarantees termination while giving considerable reductions in memory consumption for some models. UPPAAL implements two variations of this techniques. The most aggressive one is described in [12] which only stores loop entry points. While reducing memory consumption this technique may increase the number of states explored, since certain states are explored more than once. A less aggressive approach is to also store all non-committed states (in which no automaton is in a committed location) in the passed list. Experiments show that this is a good compromise between space and speed.

We propose using this technique to increase locality in the exploration. Since non loop entry points are not stored on the passed list they might as well be explored by the node which computed the state in the first place instead of sending it to another node, thereby increasing locality. Consider, for example, a state α and its successor β. If β is not a loop entry point and therefore is not going to be stored on the passed list, we may as well explore β on the same node as α. Section 4 reports on experiments with this technique.

3.4 Generating Shortest Traces

An important feature of a model checker is its ability to provide good debugging information in case a certain property is not satisfied. For a failed invariant property this is commonly a trace to the state violating the invariant. Providing a short trace increases the value of a trace. One of the features of UPPAAL is that when the algorithm from Fig. 2 is used with a breadth-first search order, the trace to the error state is the shortest possible, since all states that can be reached with a shorter trace have been explored before. It would be nice to have this feature also in a distributed version of the tool. However, as described above, the order of a distributed state space search is non-deterministic, and this may lead to non-minimal traces. Fortunately, with little extra computational effort a shortest trace can be found regardless of the search order. The idea is to record for each symbolic state its "depth", i.e., the length of the shortest trace leading to this state. When a violating state is found the algorithm does not stop, but instead continues to search for violating states that can be reached with a shorter trace. We need to make sure that the inclusion checks performed on the waiting and passed lists do not discard potential violating states. When a new state (l, D) is added to the waiting or passed list, we normally compare it to every state (l, D') on the list, and if an inclusion exists we keep the larger of the two states. In order not to discard potential traces, we add the restriction that a state is only replaced/discarded if it does not have a smaller depth than the state it is compared to. The same idea is used for the decision whether or not to explore a state when looking it up in the passed list: we only decide not to explore a state if its clock constraints are included in the clock constraints of another state with the same location vector *and* at the same time does not have a smaller depth than the state it is included in. The corresponding line in the algorithm changes to:

if $D \not\subseteq D'$ **or** depth(l, D) < depth(l, D') **for all** $(l, D') \in$ PASSED **then**

With these changes the algorithm in Fig. 3 can find shortest traces independently of the ordering used on the waiting list. As described above we have implemented a heuristic which approximates breadth-first search. In Section 4, we demonstrate that when using this heuristic the extra cost for finding the shortest trace is minor and we keep good speedups.

4 Experimental Results

For implementing communication between nodes we have used the *Message Passing Interface* (MPI) [14]. This facilitates porting and running the program on different kinds of machines and architectures. We have conducted experiments on a Sun Enterprise 10000 with 24 333Mhz processors, which has a shared memory architecture, and on a Linux Beowulf cluster of 10 450Mhz Pentium III CPUs.

4.1 Nondeterminism and Search Orders

One of the first examples the distributed UPPAAL was tried on, was a model of a batch plant [9] constructed to verify schedulability of a production process. The verification, which on one processor took several hours, surprisingly took less than five minutes on 16 nodes. This super linear speedup came as a surprise to us. Verifying schedulability in this model means searching for a state where all batches have been processed. For this particular model we had previously identified depth-first search as the fastest strategy on one node, and therefore we used a distributed depth-first search. In this particular model, the verification benefited from the nondeterministic search order. The distributed depth-first search did not find the same state as the verification on a single processor, and in fact the number of states searched was not the same in the two cases. It should be possible to achieve a similar effect with the sequential algorithm by introducing randomness into the search order. First experiments with using a kind of random depth-first search have been promising.

Because of this property of checking for a particular state (or a set of states), we have in the remaining experiments chosen to generate the complete state space of the given system using a distributed breadth-first search. Generating the complete state space reduces the impact of the nondeterministic search order because one cannot find a "lucky" path which finds the state searched for quickly. This makes the results from different runs comparable.

4.2 Speedup Gained

We have chosen to focus our experiments around four UPPAAL examples: the start-up algorithm of the DACAPO [13] protocol which is quite small but had some interesting behavior as will be discussed later; a communication protocol used in B&O audio/video equipment (CP)[7]; a power-down protocol also used in B&O audio/video equipment (PD)[6]; and a model of a buscoupler (which thus far has not been published). The reason not to look further at the model of the batch plant is that the state space was too big to be generated completely. All other known UPPAAL examples were also tried, but these were so small that the complete state space can be generated in a matter of seconds using a few processors, and were therefore considered too small to be of interest.

The examples were run on the Sun Enterprise on 1, 2, 3, 4, 5, 8, 11, 14, 17, 20 and 23 nodes; and on the Beowulf on 1 to 10 nodes to the extend it was possible (only the DACAPO model could be run on a single node because of memory usage). Since the search order (and thereby the work done) is non-deterministic we repeated one experiment several times. The observed running times[1] and number of states generated varied less than 3%. Running the experiments only once therefore seemed reasonable.

When generating the complete state space for a number of examples using distributed breadth-first search a general pattern occurred. In most cases the number of states generated increased with the number of nodes, and in all cases the smallest number of states was generated using one node. It therefore seems that in most cases breadth-first is *close to* the optimal search order for generating the complete state space. In most cases the increase in the number of states was minor (less than 10%), but for a few examples the increase was substantial. In the DACAPO example the number of states more than doubled — from 45000 states to more than 110000 states using 17 nodes (see Table 1).

To counter this effect, we applied the heuristic described in Section 3.2 and used a priority queue to order the states waiting on each node such that the states with the shortest path to the initial state is searched first. Not only did this counter the increase in the number of states, it actually decreased the number of states generated in some cases. This shows that there is still room for improvement with respect to the search order even when using a single processor. Table 1 and 2 show the effect of applying the heuristic to our examples. As can

---

[1] When talking about the running time we always consider the time of the slowest node.

Table 1. States generated with (Priority) and without (FIFO) use of heuristic on Sun Enterprise.

#	States							
	DACAPO		CP		Buscoupler		PD	
	FIFO	Priority	FIFO	Priority	FIFO	Priority	FIFO	Priority
1	45001	44925	3466548	3010244	6502 804	6436543	7992048	7992098
2	45754	44863	5505161	3027728	8042882	6199274	8004165	8003477
3	69141	45267	5472878	3070491	8064519	6243785	8001670	7997859
4	62541	45177	5454067	3086016	8123748	6171125	8004717	8004439
5	78008	45667	5583368	3077890	8651090	6481067	8002412	7998607
8	77396	46510	5452888	3113378	8359647	6185288	8004898	8004898
11	84598	46318	5642463	3059169	8968257	6184329	8004888	8004892
14	108344	49741	5653134	3102709	8914300	6278855	8004888	8004888
17	110634	52247	5270822	3082967	9049252	6243571	8001813	7996979
20	98266	47573	5449055	3111333	9271401	6251283	8004881	8004880
23	104945	52457	5535724	3065916	9146026	6103629	8004714	8004651

Table 2. States generated with (Priority) and without (FIFO) use of heuristic on Beowulf.

#	States							
	DACAPO		IR		Buscoupler		PD	
	noorder	order	noorder	order	noorder	order	noorder	order
1	45858	45748	N/A	N/A	N/A	N/A	N/A	N/A
2	48441	46899	N/A	3028368	N/A	N/A	N/A	N/A
3	74882	47671	5605882	3053837	N/A	N/A	N/A	N/A
4	62398	47640	5533159	3058230	15832617	12794520	9473496	9409935
5	79899	47678	5454676	3060070	16637609	13603603	9432828	9287527
6	92678	49438	5684749	3133769	20443824	13896789	9511548	9482742
7	97065	49739	5702856	3074131	20329057	13797531	9513477	9441041
8	97662	50477	5358514	3106414	22430748	14442925	9527173	9488775
9	92642	49284	5449403	3071827	21086691	14455201	9535657	9515920
10	92400	48821	5532205	3060705	20704595	15507978	9526732	9500000

be seen from the tables, the heuristic performs well in three of the four examples and in the PD example it has no effect. We also tried to use a distributed depth-first search order, and to 'reverse' the heuristic to first explore the states with the longest path to the initial state during distributed depth-first search. In both cases the number of states generated was increased substantially. Therefore these search orders were discarded for the remaining experiments.

An important question is of course how well the distribution of the search scales in terms of number of nodes. Tables 3 and 4 show the running times in seconds for the different examples on the Sun Enterprise and the Beowulf, respectively. When running on the Sun Enterprise we were able to generate the complete state space on a single node for all the examples. We can therefore calculate the speedup with respect to running on a single node. The speedups we have calculated are normalized with respect to the number of states explored, to clarify the effect of the distribution. The speedup for i nodes is calculated as

$$\frac{time\ on\ one\ node/states\ on\ one\ node}{time\ on\ i\ nodes/states\ on\ i\ nodes}$$

where *time on one node* is the time for generating the complete state space using the distributed version running on one node, and *time on i nodes* is the time of the slowest node when running on i nodes.

Table 3. Run time with (Priority) and without (FIFO) use of heuristic on Sun Enterprise.

#	Run time							
	DACAPO		CP		Buscoupler		PD	
	FIFO	Priority	FIFO	Priority	FIFO	Priority	FIFO	Priority
1	8.6	9.0	804.0	732.0	2338.6	2213.8	3362.8	3195.4
2	5.2	5.0	725.8	351.6	1506.5	861.4	1507.1	1101.2
3	5.4	3.7	446.4	238.6	773.0	559.4	943.0	649.8
4	3.9	2.9	317.9	175.2	596.4	413.4	713.4	467.6
5	4.0	2.5	266.9	142.0	501.2	342.5	453.5	373.1
8	2.8	2.1	152.8	86.8	283.0	202.3	231.6	226.9
11	2.6	1.9	121.7	65.3	221.4	148.0	159.9	161.4
14	2.7	2.0	95.5	53.9	172.2	118.0	127.3	133.4
17	2.7	2.1	74.2	43.1	145.2	97.7	106.9	102.4
20	2.4	2.3	66.5	38.8	127.6	83.6	93.0	92.1
23	2.2	2.4	60.2	34.3	112.4	72.7	76.9	79.6

For the DACAPO example the speedup decreases from being linear already in the case of 5 nodes. However, it only takes 2.5 seconds to generate the complete states space using 5 nodes. Since the states space is small not all nodes can be kept busy and relatively much time is spent to start and close down the exploration. Therefore, a poor speedup was to be expected. For the CP example

Table 4. Run time with (Priority) and without (FIFO) use of heuristic on Beowulf.

#	Run time							
	DACAPO		CP		Buscoupler		PD	
	FIFO	Priority	FIFO	Priority	FIFO	Priority	FIFO	Priority
1	3.88	4.15	N/A	N/A	N/A	N/A	N/A	N/A
2	3.20	3.16	N/A	682.57	N/A	N/A	N/A	N/A
3	3.49	2.37	934.44	349.86	N/A	N/A	N/A	N/A
4	2.88	2.02	540.19	218.94	1060.09	799.69	616.85	541.89
5	2.71	1.64	390.02	169.93	836.09	646.02	413.45	401.30
6	2.62	1.52	337.79	144.50	1796.23	563.08	453.20	377.39
7	2.55	2.47	285.30	124.69	811.78	476.69	343.49	315.69
8	2.51	1.39	200.50	97.84	782.28	440.87	283.07	274.41
9	2.23	1.38	178.75	87.38	619.84	394.91	244.72	242.16
10	2.00	1.19	173.07	82.44	536.74	387.27	214.03	217.98

the speedup is close to linear. However, for the buscoupler and the PD examples the speedup is super linear, which is surprising since the speedup has been normalized with respect to the total number of states. Figure 4 shows the graphs for the speedups of the CP and buscoupler examples. We are not sure about the reason for these super linear speedups. For the Sun Enterprise machine, accessing main memory is considered to be a bottleneck. When the number of nodes used in an exploration increases so does the amount of cache available (each node has 4Mb of cache). Since UPPAAL spends much time looking up states in the passed and waiting lists, faster access to larger parts of these lists may increase the speed substantially. This conjecture is supported by the fact that the examples with the largest number of states (and therefore most accesses to the passed and waiting lists) gain the largest speedup. The same kind of super linear speedups were not encountered by Stern and Dill [15]. As mentioned in their paper, Murφ has implemented a wide range of techniques for minimizing the state space. This means that, compared to UPPAAL, Murφ spends less time on looking up states and accessing memory, and therefore Murφ does not gain the same speedup from the larger cache.

On the Beowulf it was in most cases not possible to generate the complete state space using only one processor. We have therefore chosen to present the amount of work done, where work for i nodes is defined as *the time on i nodes* times i divided by *the number of states on i nodes*, to normalize with respect to the number of node generated. A horizontal then corresponds to a linear speedup. As expected the line for the DACAPO example increases, so we do not have a linear speedup. The speedup looks better for the CP on the Beowulf example but since we do not have the time on one node (this could not complete due to memory shortage) it is hard to judge whether the work is approaching the work in one node or really is decreasing below that. The same is the case for the buscoupler and the PD example. Figure 5 shows the work for the CP and buscoupler examples. One interesting point to notice is that for six nodes without the heuristic the buscoupler performs very poorly (we have no explanation for this behavior).

The explanations we suggest for the super linear speedups we encounter on the Beowulf are the same as for the Sun Enterprise: access to a larger amount of local (cache) memory.

4.3 Distribution Functions and Locality

In most of the experiments, states are distributed evenly among nodes using the hash function from UPPAAL. However, for small models we observed that some nodes explore twice as many states as others because some location vectors have more reachable symbolic states than others, which means that some nodes have more states allocated than others. Counting the number of different location vectors on the different nodes, the distribution again looks uniform. This effect does not show up in larger models.

We ran experiments for different distribution functions: a function hashing on the discrete part of a state (D0), a function hashing on the complete state (D1), a function hashing on the integer variables (D2), and a function hashing on every second location (D3). We also ran experiments for different settings of the state space reduction technique described in Section 3.3, where only states that are actually stored in the passed list are mapped to different nodes: storing all states (S0), storing non-committed or loop entry points (S1), and storing only loop entry points (S2). Table 5 shows for the buscoupler and the power-down models the percentage of states explored on the same node they were generated on. These experiments were run on the Sun Enterprise with 8 CPUs, but similar results were obtained using the Beowulf cluster.

Table 5. Percent of locally explored states for different distribution and storage policies for the buscoupler model (left) and the power-down protocol (right) when verified on a Sun Enterprise using 8 nodes.

Bus	D0	D1	D2	D3
S0	14%	n/a	52%	42%
S1	36%	n/a	60%	58%
S2	55%	n/a	62%	62%

PD	D0	D1	D2	D3
S0	4%	n/a	76%	22%
S1	34%	n/a	76%	48%
S2	60%	n/a	78%	86%

For the buscoupler with D0 and S0 we almost obtain the expected uniform distribution ($100\%/8 = 12.5\%$). This was not the case for the power-down model although the total load on the nodes was uniform. None of the D1 experiments terminated within a reasonable time frame. This was expected since much fewer inclusion checks can succeed with this distribution function and hence a much higher number of symbolic states will be generated. Both S1/S2 and D2/D3 improve locality. What cannot be seen is that both S1 and S2 increase the number of states generated (for the buscoupler to such an extend that S2 is actually slower than S0). D2 is surprisingly uniform while increasing locality, but the load distribution of D3 was observed to be highly non-uniform, resulting in poor performance. For the buscoupler D2 and S1 turned out to be the fastest combination. For the power-down model D2 and S2 turned out to be the fastest combination.

4.4 Generating Shortest Traces

For the buscoupler system we tried the version finding the shortest trace on four different properties (finding a particular state not generating the complete state space) on the Sun Enterprise. The speedups are displayed in Fig. 6. As for the DACAPO system the speedup for properties one and two suffer from too few states being explored. The speedup for properties three and four are much better but here more states are searched to find the state satisfying the property. So we can conclude that also the version finding shortest trace scales quite well, as long as sufficiently many states need to be generated.

5 Conclusions

This paper demonstrates the feasibility of distributed model checking of timed automata. A side effect of the distribution was an altered search order, which in turn increased the number of symbolic states generated when exploring the reachable state space. We have proposed explicit ordering of the states in the waiting list as an effective heuristic to improve the scalability of the approach. In addition we propose an algorithm for finding shortest traces that performs well in a distributed model checker.

In several cases we obtained super linear speedups. We have suggested some explanations, but more work is needed to clarify the observed phenomena. Importantly, some of our results suggests possible improvements to the sequential state space exploration algorithm for timed automata.

References

1. S. Aggarwal, R. Alonso, and C. Courcoubetis. Distributed reachability analysis for protocol verification environments. In *Discrete Event Systems: Models and Applications. IIASA Conference*, pages 40–56, 1987.
2. R. Alur and D. L. Dill. A theory of timed automata. *Theoretical Computer Science*, 126:183–235, 1994.
3. S. Caselli, G. Conte, and P. Marenzoni. Parallel state space exploration for GSPN models. In G. De Michelis and M. Diaz, editors, *Proceedings 16th Int. Conf. on Application and Theory of Petri Nets,* Turin, Italy, volume 935 of *Lecture Notes in Computer Science*, pages 181–200. Springer-Verlag, June 1995.
4. E.M. Clarke, O. Grumberg, and D. Peled. *Model Checking*. MIT Press, Cambridge, Massachusetts, 1999.
5. D. L. Dill. The murφ verification system. In *Conference on Computer-Aided Verification*, LNCS, pages 390–393. Springer-Verlag, July 1996.

6. K. Havelund, K. Larsen, and A. Skou. Formal verification of a power controller using the real-time model checker UPPAAL. In Joost-Pieter Katoen, editor, *Formal Methods for Real-Time and Probabilistic Systems, 5th International AMAST Workshop, ARTS'99*, volume 1601 of *Lecture Notes in Computer Science*, pages 277–298. Springer-Verlag, 1999.

7. K. Havelund, A. Skou, K. G. Larsen, and K. Lund. Formal modelling and analysis of an audio/video protocol: An industrial case study using UPPAAL. In *Proc. of the 18th IEEE Real-Time Systems Symposium*, pages 2–13, December 1997. San Francisco, California, USA.

8. B.R. Haverkort, A. Bell, and H.C. Bohnenkamp. On the efficient sequential and distributed generation of very large Markov chains from stochastic Petri nets. In *Proceedings of the 8th International Workshop on Petri Nets and Performance Models (PNPM'99)*, Zaragoza, Spain, pages 12–21. IEEE Computer Society Press, 1999.

9. T. Hune, K. G. Larsen, and P. Pettersson. Guided synthesis of control programs using UPPAAL. In *Proc. of the International Workshop on Distributed Systems, Verification and Validation*, April 2000. Taipei, Taiwan.

10. K.J. Kristoffersen, F. Laroussinie, K.G. Larsen, P. Pettersson, and W. Yi. A compositional proof of a real-time mutual exclusion protocol. In M. Bidoit and M. Dauchet, editors, *Proceedings TAPSOFT'97: Theory and Practice of Software Development*, Lille, France, volume 1214 of *Lecture Notes in Computer Science*, pages 565–579. Springer-Verlag, April 1997.

11. K. G. Larsen, P. Pettersson, and W. Yi. UPPAAL in a nutshell. *Int. Journal on Software Tools for Technology Transfer*, 1(1–2):134–152, October 1997.

12. Fredrik Larsson, Kim G. Larsen, Paul Pettersson, and Wang Yi. Efficient Verification of Real-Time Systems: Compact Data Structures and State-Space Reduction. In *Proc. of the 18th IEEE Real-Time Systems Symposium*, pages 14–24. IEEE Computer Society Press, December 1997.

13. H. Lönn and P. Pettersson. Formal verification of a TDMA protocol startup mechanism. In *Proc. of the Pacific Rim Int. Symp. on Fault-Tolerant Systems*, pages 235–242, December 1997.

14. M. Snir, S.W. Otto, S. Huss-Lederman, D. Walker, and J.J. Dongarra. *MPI:The Complete Reference*. MIT Press, Cambridge, Massachusetts, 1996.

15. U. Stern and D. L. Dill. Parallelizing the Murφ verifier. In Orna Grumberg, editor, *Computer Aided Verification, 9th International Conference*, volume 1254 of *LNCS*, pages 256–67. Springer-Verlag, June 1997. Haifa, Isreal, June 22-25.

A Results

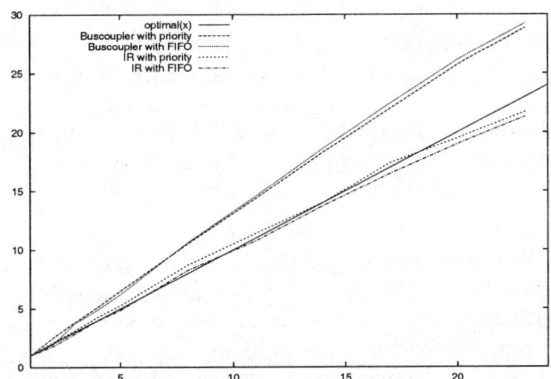

Fig. 4. Speedup for CP and buscoupler on Sun Enterprise

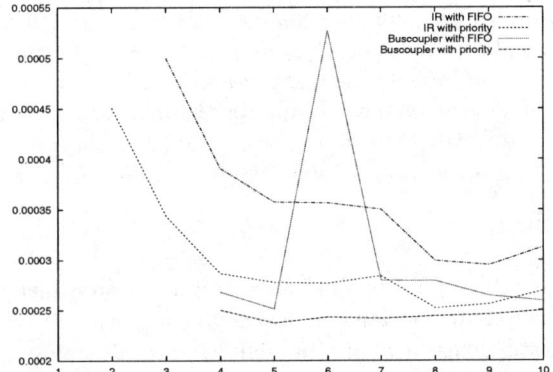

Fig. 5. Work for CP and buscoupler on Beowulf

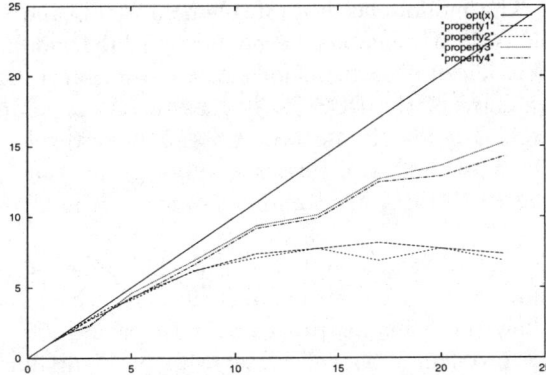

Fig. 6. Speedup for finding shortest trace in Buscoupler model.

Efficient Algorithms for Model Checking Pushdown Systems

Javier Esparza, David Hansel, Peter Rossmanith, and Stefan Schwoon

Technische Universität München, Arcisstr. 21, 80290 München, Germany
{esparza,hanseld,rossmani,schwoon}@in.tum.de

Abstract. We study model checking problems for pushdown systems and linear time logics. We show that the global model checking problem (computing the set of configurations, reachable or not, that violate the formula) can be solved in $O(g_\mathcal{P} g_\mathcal{P}{}^3 g_\mathcal{B} g_\mathcal{B}{}^3)$ time and $O(g_\mathcal{P} g_\mathcal{P}{}^2 g_\mathcal{B} g_\mathcal{B}{}^2)$ space, where $g_\mathcal{P} g_\mathcal{P}$ and $g_\mathcal{B} g_\mathcal{B}$ are the size of the pushdown system and the size of a Büchi automaton for the negation of the formula. The global model checking problem for reachable configurations can be solved in $O(g_\mathcal{P} g_\mathcal{P}{}^4 g_\mathcal{B} g_\mathcal{B}{}^3)$ time and $O(g_\mathcal{P} g_\mathcal{P}{}^4 g_\mathcal{B} g_\mathcal{B}{}^2)$ space. In the case of pushdown systems with constant number of control states (relevant for our application), the complexity becomes $O(g_\mathcal{P} g_\mathcal{P} g_\mathcal{B} g_\mathcal{B}{}^3)$ time and $O(g_\mathcal{P} g_\mathcal{P} g_\mathcal{B} g_\mathcal{B}{}^2)$ space and $O(g_\mathcal{P} g_\mathcal{P}{}^2 g_\mathcal{B} g_\mathcal{B}{}^3)$ time and $O(g_\mathcal{P} g_\mathcal{P}{}^2 g_\mathcal{B} g_\mathcal{B}{}^2)$ space, respectively. We show applications of these results in the area of program analysis and present some experimental results.

1 Introduction

Pushdown systems (PDSs) are pushdown automata seen under a different light: We are not interested in the languages they recognise, but in the transition system they generate. These are infinite transition systems having configurations of the form (control state, stack content) as states.

PDSs have already been investigated by the verification community. Model checking algorithms for both linear and branching time logics have been proposed in [1,2,3,7,11]. The model checking problem for CTL and the mu-calculus is known to be DEXPTIME-complete even for a fixed formula [1,11]. On the contrary, the model checking problem for LTL or the linear time mu-calculus is polynomial in the size of the PDS [1,7]. This makes linear time logics particularly interesting for PDSs. It must be observed, however, that the model checking problem for branching time logics is only exponential in the number of control states of the PDS; for a fixed number of states the algorithms of [2,11] are polynomial.

Inspired by the work of Steffen and others on the connection between model checking and dataflow analysis (see for instance [9]), it has been recently observed that relevant dataflow problems for programs with procedures (so-called interprocedural dataflow problems), as well as security problems for Java programs can be reduced to different variants of the model checking problem for PDSs and LTL [5,6,8]. Motivated by this application, we revisit the model checking problem for linear time logics. We follow the symbolic approach of [1], in which infinite sets of configurations are finitely represented by multi-automata. We obtain an efficient implementation of the algorithm of [1], which was described there as 'polynomial', without further details. Our algorithm has the same time complexity and better space complexity than the algorithm of [7]. This better space complexity turns out to be important for our intended applications to dataflow analysis.

The paper is structured as follows. Sections 2 and 3 contain basic definitions, and recall some results of [1]. The 'abstract' solution of [1] to the model-checking problem is described and refined in Sections 4 to 6. In Section 7 we provide an efficient implementation for this solution. Applications and experimental results are presented in Section 9.

All proofs and some constructions have been omitted due to lack of space. They can all be found in the technical report version of this paper [4].

2 Pushdown Systems and $\mathcal{P}$-Automata

A pushdown system is a triplet $\mathcal{P} = (P, \Gamma, \Delta)$ where P is a finite set of *control locations*, Γ is a finite *stack alphabet*, and $\Delta \subseteq (P \times \Gamma) \times (P \times \Gamma^*)$ is a finite set of *transition rules*. If $((q, \gamma), (q', w)) \in \Delta$ then we write $\langle q, \gamma \rangle \hookrightarrow \langle q', w \rangle$ (we reserve $\rightarrow$ to denote the transition relations of finite automata).

Notice that pushdown systems have no input alphabet. We do not use them as language acceptors but are rather interested in the behaviours they generate.

A *configuration* of $\mathcal{P}$ is a pair $\langle p, w \rangle$ where $p \in P$ is a control location and $w \in \Gamma^*$ is a *stack content*. The set of all configurations is denoted by $\mathcal{C}$.

If $\langle q, \gamma \rangle \hookrightarrow \langle q', w \rangle$, then for every $v \in \Gamma^*$ the configuration $\langle q, \gamma v \rangle$ is an *immediate predecessor* of $\langle q', wv \rangle$, and $\langle q', wv \rangle$ an *immediate successor* of $\langle q, \gamma v \rangle$. The *reachability relation* $\Rightarrow$ is the reflexive and transitive closure of the immediate successor relation; the transitive closure is denoted by $\stackrel{+}{\Rightarrow}$. A *run* of $\mathcal{P}$ is a maximal sequence of configurations such that for each two consecutive configurations $c_i c_{i+1}$, c_{i+1} is an immediate successor of c_i.

The predecessor function $pre: 2^{\mathcal{C}} \rightarrow 2^{\mathcal{C}}$ of $\mathcal{P}$ is defined as follows: c belongs to $pre(C)$ if some immediate successor of c belongs to C. The reflexive and transitive closure of pre is denoted by pre^*. Clearly, $pre^*(C) = \{c \in \mathcal{C} \mid \exists c' \in C.\ c \Rightarrow c'\}$. Similarly, we define $post(C)$ as the set of immediate successors of elements in C and $post^*$ as the reflexive and transitive closure of $post$.

2.1 $\mathcal{P}$-Automata

Given a pushdown system $\mathcal{P} = (P, \Gamma, \Delta)$, we use so-called $\mathcal{P}$-*automata* in order to represent sets of configurations of $\mathcal{P}$. A $\mathcal{P}$-automaton uses Γ as alphabet, and P as set of initial states (we consider automata with possibly many initial states). Formally, a $\mathcal{P}$-automaton is an automaton $\mathcal{A} = (\Gamma, Q, \delta, P, F)$ where Q is the finite set of states, $\delta \subseteq Q \times \Gamma \times Q$ is the set of *transitions*, P is the set of initial states and $F \subseteq Q$ the set of *final states*. We define the *transition relation* $\to \subseteq Q \times \Gamma^* \times Q$ as the smallest relation satisfying:

- $q \xrightarrow{\varepsilon} q$ for every $q \in Q$,
- if $(q, \gamma, q') \in \delta$ then $q \xrightarrow{\gamma} q'$, and
- if $q \xrightarrow{w} q''$ and $q'' \xrightarrow{\gamma} q'$ then $q \xrightarrow{w\gamma} q'$.

All the automata used in this paper are $\mathcal{P}$-automata, and so we drop the $\mathcal{P}$ from now on. An automaton *accepts* or *recognises* a configuration $\langle p, w \rangle$ if $p \xrightarrow{w} q$ for some $p \in P$, $q \in F$. The set of configurations recognised by an automaton $\mathcal{A}$ is denoted by $Conf(\mathcal{A})$. A set of configurations of $\mathcal{P}$ is *regular* if it is recognized by some automaton.

Notation In the paper, we use the symbols p, p', p'' etc., eventually with indices, to denote initial states of an automaton (i.e., the elements of P). Non-initial states are denoted by s, s', s'' etc., and arbitrary states, initial or not, by q, q', q''.

3 Model-Checking Problems for Linear Time Logics

In this section we define the problems we study, as well as the automata-theoretic approach.

Let *Prop* be a finite set of atomic propositions, and let $\Sigma = 2^{Prop}$. It is well known that the semantics of properties expressed in linear time temporal logics like LTL or the linear-time μ-calculus are ω-regular sets over the alphabet Σ, and there exist well-known algorithms which construct Büchi automata recognizing these sets. This is all we need to know about these logics in this paper in order to give model-checking algorithms for pushdown systems.

Let $\mathcal{P} = (P, \Gamma, \Delta)$ be a pushdown system, and let $\Lambda \colon (P \times \Gamma) \to \Sigma$ be a labelling function, which intuitively associates to a pair $\langle p, \gamma \rangle$ the set of propositions that are true of it. We extend this mapping to arbitrary configurations: $\langle p, \gamma w \rangle$ satisfies an atomic proposition if $\langle p, \gamma \rangle$ does.[1]

Given a formula φ of such an ω-regular logic we wish to solve these problems:

- The global model-checking problem: compute the set of configurations, reachable or not, that violate φ.
- The global model-checking problem for reachable configurations: compute the set of reachable configurations that violate φ.

Our solution to these problems uses the automata-theoretic approach. We start by constructing a Büchi automaton $\mathcal{B} = (\Sigma, Q, \delta, q_0, F)$ corresponding to the negation of φ. The product of $\mathcal{P}$ and $\mathcal{B}$ yields a Büchi pushdown system $\mathcal{BP} = ((P \times Q), \Gamma, \Delta', G)$, where

- $\langle (p, q), \gamma \rangle \hookrightarrow \langle (p', q'), w \rangle \in \Delta'$ if $\langle p, \gamma \rangle \hookrightarrow \langle p', w \rangle$, $q \xrightarrow{\sigma} q'$, and $\sigma \subseteq \Lambda(\langle p, \gamma \rangle)$.
- $(p, q) \in G$ if $q \in F$.

---

[1] We could also define $\Lambda \colon P \to \Sigma$, but our definition is more general, and it is also the one we need for our applications.

The global model checking problem reduces to the *accepting run problem*:

> Compute the set $\mathcal{C}_a$ of configurations c of $\mathcal{BP}$ such that $\mathcal{BP}$ has an accepting run starting from c (i.e., a run which visits infinitely often configurations with control locations in G).

Notice that the emptiness problem of Büchi pushdown systems (whether the initial configuration has an accepting run) also reduces to the accepting run problem; it suffices to check if the initial configuration belongs to the set $\mathcal{C}_a$. The following proposition characterises the configurations from which there are accepting runs.

Definition 1. *Let $\mathcal{BP} = (P, \Gamma, \Delta, G)$ be a Büchi pushdown system.*

The relation $\stackrel{r}{\Longrightarrow}$ between configurations of $\mathcal{BP}$ is defined as follows: $c \stackrel{r}{\Longrightarrow} c'$ if $c \Rightarrow \langle g, u \rangle \stackrel{+}{\Longrightarrow} c'$ for some configuration $\langle g, u \rangle$ with $g \in G$.

The head *of a transition rule $\langle p, \gamma \rangle \hookrightarrow \langle p', w \rangle$ is the configuration $\langle p, \gamma \rangle$. A head $\langle p, \gamma \rangle$ is* repeating *if there exists $v \in \Gamma^*$ such that $\langle p, \gamma \rangle \stackrel{r}{\Longrightarrow} \langle p, \gamma v \rangle$. The sets of heads and repeating heads of $\mathcal{BP}$ are denoted by H and R, respectively.*

Proposition 1. [1] *Let c be a configuration of a Büchi pushdown system $\mathcal{BP} = (P, \Gamma, \Delta, G)$ and let $R\Gamma^*$ denote the set $\{ \langle p, \gamma w \rangle \mid \langle p, \gamma \rangle \in R, w \in \Gamma^* \}$. $\mathcal{BP}$ has an accepting run starting from c if and only if $c \in pre^*(R\Gamma^*)$.*

Proposition 1 reduces the global model-checking problem to computing the set $pre^*(R\Gamma^*)$; the global model-checking problem for reachable configurations reduces to computing $post^*(\{c\}) \cap pre^*(R\Gamma^*)$ for a given initial configuration c.

In the next sections we present a solution to these problems. We first recall the algorithm of [1] that computes $pre^*(C)$ for an arbitrary regular language C (observe that $R\Gamma^*$ is regular since R is finite). Then we present a new algorithm for computing R, obtained by modifying the algorithm for $pre^*(C)$. We also present an algorithm for computing $post^*(C)$ which is needed to solve the model-checking problem for reachable configurations.

4 Computing $pre^*(C)$ for a Regular Language C

Our input is an automaton $\mathcal{A}$ accepting C. Without loss of generality, we assume that $\mathcal{A}$ has no transition leading to an initial state. We compute $pre^*(C)$ as the language accepted by an automaton $\mathcal{A}_{pre^*}$ obtained from $\mathcal{A}$ by means of a saturation procedure. The procedure adds new transitions to $\mathcal{A}$, but no new states. New transitions are added according to the following *saturation rule*:

> If $\langle p, \gamma \rangle \hookrightarrow \langle p', w \rangle$ and $p' \stackrel{w}{\longrightarrow} q$ in the current automaton, add a transition (p, γ, q).

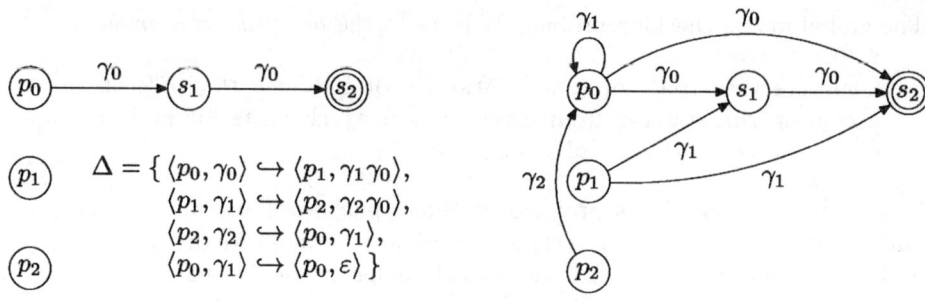

Fig. 1. The automata $\mathcal{A}$ (left) and $\mathcal{A}_{pre^*}$ (right)

Notice that all new transitions start at initial states. Let us illustrate the procedure by an example. Let $\mathcal{P} = (P, \Gamma, \Delta)$ be a pushdown system with $P = \{p_0, p_1, p_2\}$ and Δ as shown in in the left half of Figure 1. Let $\mathcal{A}$ be the automaton that accepts the set $C = \{\langle p_0, \gamma_0 \gamma_0 \rangle\}$, also shown in the figure. The result of the algorithm is shown in the right half of Figure 1.

The saturation procedure eventually reaches a fixpoint because the number of possible new transitions is finite. Correctness was proved in [1].

5   Computing the Set R of Repeating Heads

We provide an algorithm more efficient than that of [1]. The problem of finding the repeating heads in a Büchi pushdown system is reduced to a graph-theoretic problem. More precisely, given a Büchi pushdown system $\mathcal{BP} = (P, \Gamma, \Delta, G)$ we construct a head reachability graph $\mathcal{G} = ((P \times \Gamma), E)$ whose nodes are the heads of $\mathcal{BP}$. The set of edges $E \subseteq (P \times \Gamma) \times \{0, 1\} \times (P \times \Gamma)$ generates the reachability relation between heads. Define $G(p) = 1$ if $p \in G$ and $G(p) = 0$ otherwise. E consists of exactly the following edges:

If $\langle p, \gamma \rangle \hookrightarrow \langle p'', v_1 \gamma' v_2 \rangle$ and $\langle p'', v_1 \rangle \Rightarrow \langle p', \varepsilon \rangle$, then $((p, \gamma), G(p), (p', \gamma')) \in E$.
If, moreover, $\langle p'', v_1 \rangle \stackrel{r}{\Longrightarrow} \langle p', \varepsilon \rangle$, then $((p, \gamma), 1, (p', \gamma')) \in E$.

The reachability relation $\rightarrow \subset (P \times \Gamma) \times \{0, 1\} \times (P \times \Gamma)$ is then defined as the smallest relation satisfying

- $(p, \gamma) \stackrel{0}{\rightarrow} (p, \gamma)$ for every $(p, \gamma) \in (P \times \Gamma)$.
- If $((p, \gamma), b, (p', \gamma')) \in E$, then $(p, \gamma) \stackrel{b}{\rightarrow} (p', \gamma')$.
- If $((p, \gamma), b, (p', \gamma')) \in E$ and $(p', \gamma') \stackrel{b'}{\rightarrow} (p'', \gamma'')$, then $(p, \gamma) \stackrel{b \vee b'}{\longrightarrow} (p'', \gamma'')$.

Once the graph is constructed, R can be computed by exploiting the fact that some head $\langle p, \gamma \rangle$ is repeating if and only if (p, γ) is part of a strongly connected component of $\mathcal{G}$ which has an internal 1-labelled edge. The instances for which $\langle p, v \rangle \stackrel{r}{\Longrightarrow} \langle p', \varepsilon \rangle$ holds can be found with a small modification of the algorithm for pre^*.

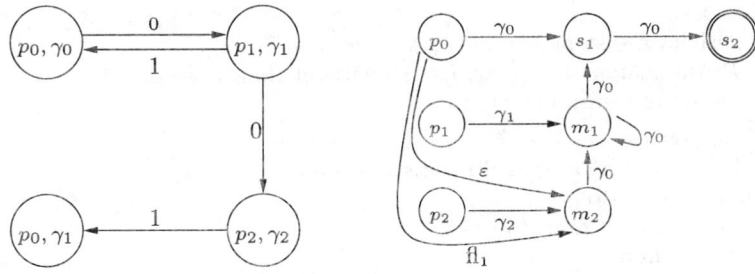

Fig. 2. Left: The graph $\mathcal{G}$. Right: $\mathcal{A}_{post^*}$

Let $\mathcal{BP} = (P, \Gamma, \Delta, G)$ be a Büchi pushdown system with P, Γ and Δ as in the previous example and $G = \{p_2\}$. The left part of Figure 2 shows the graph $\mathcal{G}$.

6 Computing $post^*(C)$ for a Regular Set C

We provide a solution for the case in which each transition rule $\langle p, \gamma \rangle \hookrightarrow \langle p', w \rangle$ of Δ satisfies $|w| \leq 2$. This restriction is not essential; our solution can easily be extended to the general case. Moreover, any pushdown system can be transformed into an equivalent one in this form, and the pushdown systems in the application discussed in Section 9 directly satisfy this condition.

Our input is an automaton $\mathcal{A}$ accepting C. Without loss of generality, we assume that $\mathcal{A}$ has no transition leading to an initial state. We compute $post^*(C)$ as the language accepted by an automaton $\mathcal{A}_{post^*}$ with ϵ-moves. We denote the relation $(\xrightarrow{\epsilon})^* \xrightarrow{\gamma} (\xrightarrow{\epsilon})^*$ by $\xRightarrow{\gamma}$. $\mathcal{A}_{post^*}$ is obtained from $\mathcal{A}$ in two stages:

- Add to $\mathcal{A}$ a new state r for each transition rule $r \in \Delta$ of the form $\langle p, \gamma \rangle \hookrightarrow \langle p', \gamma' \gamma'' \rangle$, and a transition (p', γ', r).
- Add new transitions to $\mathcal{A}$ according to the following saturation rules:

> If $\langle p, \gamma \rangle \hookrightarrow \langle p', \epsilon \rangle \in \Delta$ and $p \xRightarrow{\gamma} q$ in the current automaton, add a transition (p', ϵ, q).
>
> If $\langle p, \gamma \rangle \hookrightarrow \langle p', \gamma' \rangle \in \Delta$ and $p \xRightarrow{\gamma} q$ in the current automaton, add a transition (p', γ', q).
>
> If $r = \langle p, \gamma \rangle \hookrightarrow \langle p', \gamma' \gamma'' \rangle \in \Delta$ and $p \xRightarrow{\gamma} q$ in the current automaton, add a transition (r, γ'', q).

Consider again the pushdown system $\mathcal{P}$ and the automaton $\mathcal{A}$ from Figure 1. Then the automaton shown in the right part of Figure 2 is the result of the algorithm above and accepts $post^*(\{\langle p_0, \gamma_0 \gamma_0 \rangle\})$.

Algorithm 1
Input: a pushdown system $\mathcal{P} = (P, \Gamma, \Delta)$ in normal form;
       a $\mathcal{P}$-Automaton $\mathcal{A} = (\Gamma, Q, \delta, P, F)$ without transitions into P
Output: the set of transitions of $\mathcal{A}_{pre^*}$

```
1   rel ← ∅;  trans ← δ;  Δ' ← ∅;
2   for all ⟨p, γ⟩ ↪ ⟨p', ε⟩ ∈ Δ do trans ← trans ∪ {(p, γ, p')};
3   while trans ≠ ∅ do
4      pop t = (q, γ, q') from trans;
5      if t ∉ rel then
6         rel ← rel ∪ {t};
7         for all ⟨p₁, γ₁⟩ ↪ ⟨q, γ⟩ ∈ (Δ ∪ Δ') do
8            trans ← trans ∪ {(p₁, γ₁, q')};
9         for all ⟨p₁, γ₁⟩ ↪ ⟨q, γγ₂⟩ ∈ Δ do
10           Δ' ← Δ' ∪ {⟨p₁, γ₁⟩ ↪ ⟨q', γ₂⟩};
11           for all (q', γ₂, q'') ∈ rel do
12              trans ← trans ∪ {(p₁, γ₁, q'')};
13  return rel
```

7 Efficient Algorithms

In this section we present efficient implementations of the abstract algorithms given in sections 4 through 6. We restrict ourselves to pushdown systems which satisfy $|w| \leq 2$ for every rule $\langle p, \gamma \rangle \hookrightarrow \langle p', w \rangle$; any pushdown system can be put into such a normal form with linear size increase.

7.1 Computing $pre^*(C)$

Given an automaton $\mathcal{A}$ accepting the set of configurations C, we compute $pre^*(C)$ by constructing the automaton $\mathcal{A}_{pre^*}$.

Algorithm 1 computes the transitions of $\mathcal{A}_{pre^*}$, implementing the saturation rule from section 4. The sets rel and $trans$ contain the transitions that are known to belong to $\mathcal{A}_{pre^*}$; rel contains the transitions that have already been examined. No transition is examined more than once.

The idea of the algorithm is to avoid unnecessary operations. When we have a rule $\langle p, \gamma \rangle \hookrightarrow \langle p', \gamma'\gamma'' \rangle$, we look out for pairs of transitions $t_1 = (p', \gamma', q')$ and $t_2 = (q', \gamma'', q'')$ (where q', q'' are arbitrary states) so that we may insert (p, γ, q'') – but we don't know in which order such transitions appear in $trans$. If every time we see a transition like t_2 we check the existence of t_1, many checks might be negative and waste time to no avail. However, once we see t_1 we know that all subsequent transitions (q', γ'', q'') must lead to (p, γ, q''). It so happens that the introduction of an extra rule $\langle p, \gamma \rangle \hookrightarrow \langle q', \gamma'' \rangle$ is enough to take care of just these cases. We collect these extra rules in a set called Δ'; this notation should make it clear that the pushdown system itself is not changed. Δ' is merely needed for the computation and can be thrown away afterwards.

For a better illustration, consider again the example shown in Figure 1.

The initialisation phase evaluates the ε-rules and adds (p_0, γ_1, p_0). When the latter is taken from $trans$, the rule $\langle p_2, \gamma_2 \rangle \hookrightarrow \langle p_0, \gamma_1 \rangle$ is evaluated and

(p_2, γ_2, p_0) is added. This, in combination with (p_0, γ_0, s_1) and the rule $\langle p_1, \gamma_1 \rangle \hookrightarrow \langle p_2, \gamma_2\gamma_0 \rangle$, leads to (p_1, γ_1, s_1), and Δ' now contains $\langle p_1, \gamma_1 \rangle \hookrightarrow \langle p_0, \gamma_0 \rangle$. We now have $p_1 \xrightarrow{\gamma_1} s_1 \xrightarrow{\gamma_0} s_2$, so the next step adds (p_0, γ_0, s_2), and Δ' is extended by $\langle p_0, \gamma_0 \rangle \hookrightarrow \langle s_1, \gamma_0 \rangle$. Because of Δ', (p_0, γ_0, s_2) leads to (p_1, γ_1, s_2). Finally, Δ' is extended by $\langle p_0, \gamma_0 \rangle \hookrightarrow \langle s_2, \gamma_0 \rangle$, but no other transitions can be added and the algorithm terminates.

Theorem 1. *Let $\mathcal{P} = (P, \Gamma, \Delta)$ be a pushdown system and $\mathcal{A} = (\Gamma, Q, \delta, P, F)$ be an automaton. There exists an automaton $\mathcal{A}_{pre^*}$ recognising $pre^*(Conf(\mathcal{A}))$. Moreover, $\mathcal{A}_{pre^*}$ can be constructed in $O(n_Q^2 n_\Delta)$ time and $O(n_Q n_\Delta + n_\delta)$ space, where $n_Q = |Q|$, $n_\delta = |\delta|$, and $n_\Delta = |\Delta|$.*

Observe that a naive implementation of the abstract procedure of section 4 leads to an $O(n_\mathcal{P}^2 n_\mathcal{A}^3)$ time and $O(n_\mathcal{P} n_\mathcal{A})$ space algorithm, where $n_\mathcal{P} = |P| + |\Delta|$, and $n_\mathcal{A} = |Q| + |\delta|$.

7.2 Computing the Set of Repeating Heads

Given a Büchi pushdown system (P, Γ, Δ, G) we want to compute the set R introduced in section 3, i.e. the set of transition heads $\langle p, \gamma \rangle$ that satisfy $\langle p, \gamma \rangle \xRightarrow{r} \langle p, \gamma v \rangle$ for some $v \in \Gamma^*$.

Algorithm 2 runs in two phases. In the first phase, the cases for which $\langle p, w \rangle \Rightarrow \langle p', \varepsilon \rangle$ holds are computed. To this end, we employ the algorithm for pre^* on the set $\{ \langle p, \varepsilon \rangle \mid p \in P \}$. Then every resulting transition (p, γ, p') signifies that $\langle p, \gamma \rangle \Rightarrow \langle p', \varepsilon \rangle$ holds.

However, we also need the information whether $\langle p, \gamma \rangle \xRightarrow{r} \langle p', \varepsilon \rangle$ holds. To this end, we enrich the automaton's alphabet; instead of transitions of the form (p, γ, p') we now have transitions $(p, [\gamma, b], p')$ where b is a boolean. The meaning of a transition $(p, [\gamma, 1], p')$ should be that $\langle p, \gamma \rangle \xRightarrow{r} \langle p', \varepsilon \rangle$.

The second phase of the algorithm constructs the graph $\mathcal{G}$ using the results of the first phase. Finally, Tarjan's algorithm [10] can be used to find the strongly connected components of $\mathcal{G}$ and thus to determine the repeating heads.

In the example from Figure 2, the components of $\mathcal{G}$ are $\{(p_0, \gamma_0), (p_1, \gamma_1)\}$, $\{(p_0, \gamma_1)\}$, and $\{(p_2, \gamma_2)\}$. Of these, the first one has an internal 1-edge, meaning that $\langle p_0, \gamma_0 \rangle$ and $\langle p_1, \gamma_1 \rangle$ are the repeating heads of this example.

Theorem 2. *Let $\mathcal{BP} = (P, \Gamma, \Delta, G)$ be a Büchi pushdown system. The set of repeating heads R can be computed in $O(n_P^2 n_\Delta)$ time and $O(n_P n_\Delta)$ space, where $n_P = |P|$ and $n_\Delta = |\Delta|$.*

A direct implementation of the procedure of [1] for computing the repeating heads leads to $O(n_{\mathcal{BP}}^5)$ time and $O(n_{\mathcal{BP}}^2)$ space, where $n_{\mathcal{BP}} = |P| + |\Delta|$.

7.3 Computing $post^*(C)$

Given a regular set of configurations C, we want to compute $post^*(C)$, i.e. the set of successors of C. Without loss of generality, we assume that $\mathcal{A}$ has no ε-transitions.

Algorithm 2
Input: a Büchi pushdown system $\mathcal{BP} = (P, \Gamma, \Delta, G)$ in normal form
Output: the set of repeating heads in $\mathcal{BP}$

1 $rel \leftarrow \emptyset$; $trans \leftarrow \emptyset$; $\Delta' \leftarrow \emptyset$;
2 **for all** $\langle p, \gamma \rangle \hookrightarrow \langle p', \varepsilon \rangle \in \Delta$ **do**
3    $trans \leftarrow trans \cup \{(p, [\gamma, G(p)], p')\}$;
4 **while** $trans \neq \emptyset$ **do**
5   pop $t = (p, [\gamma, b], p')$ from $trans$;
6   **if** $t \notin rel$ **then**
7      $rel \leftarrow rel \cup \{t\}$;
8   **for all** $\langle p_1, \gamma_1 \rangle \hookrightarrow \langle p, \gamma \rangle \in \Delta$ **do**
9        $trans \leftarrow trans \cup \{(p_1, [\gamma_1, b \vee G(p_1)], p')\}$;
10   **for all** $\langle p_1, \gamma_1 \rangle \xhookrightarrow{b'} \langle p, \gamma \rangle \in \Delta'$ **do**
11       $trans \leftarrow trans \cup \{(p_1, [\gamma_1, b \vee b'], p')\}$;
12   **for all** $\langle p_1, \gamma_1 \rangle \hookrightarrow \langle p, \gamma \gamma_2 \rangle \in \Delta$ **do**
13       $\Delta' \leftarrow \Delta' \cup \{\langle p_1, \gamma_1 \rangle \xhookrightarrow{b \vee G(p_1)} \langle p', \gamma_2 \rangle\}$;
14   **for all** $(p', [\gamma_2, b'], p'') \in rel$ **do**
15         $trans \leftarrow trans \cup \{(p_1, [\gamma_1, b \vee b' \vee G(p_1)], p'')\}$;
16
17 $R \leftarrow \emptyset$; $E \leftarrow \emptyset$;
18 **for all** $\langle p, \gamma \rangle \hookrightarrow \langle p', \gamma' \rangle \in \Delta$ **do** $E \leftarrow E \cup \{((p, \gamma), G(p), (p', \gamma'))\}$;
19 **for all** $\langle p, \gamma \rangle \xhookrightarrow{b} \langle p', \gamma' \rangle \in \Delta'$ **do** $E \leftarrow E \cup \{((p, \gamma), b, (p', \gamma'))\}$;
20 **for all** $\langle p, \gamma \rangle \hookrightarrow \langle p', \gamma' \gamma'' \rangle \in \Delta$ **do** $E \leftarrow E \cup \{((p, \gamma), G(p), (p', \gamma'))\}$;
21 find strongly connected components in $\mathcal{G} = ((P \times \Gamma), E)$;
22 **for all** components C **do**
23   **if** C has a 1-edge **then** $R \leftarrow R \cup C$;
24 **return** R

Algorithm 3 calculates the transitions of $\mathcal{A}_{post^*}$, implementing the saturation rule from section 6. The approach is in some ways similar to the solution for pre^*; again we use $trans$ and rel to store the transitions that we need to examine. Note that transitions from states outside of P go directly to rel since these states cannot occur in rules.

The algorithm is very straightforward. We start by including the transitions of $\mathcal{A}$; then, for every transition that is known to belong to $\mathcal{A}_{post^*}$, we find its successors. A noteworthy difference to the algorithm in section 6 is the treatment of ε-moves: ε-transitions are eliminated and simulated with non-ε-transitions; we maintain the sets $eps(q)$ for every state q with the meaning that whenever there should be an ε-transition going from p to q, $eps(q)$ contains p.

Again, consider the example in Figure 2. In that example, m_1 is the node associated with the rule $\langle p_0, \gamma_0 \rangle \hookrightarrow \langle p_1, \gamma_1 \gamma_0 \rangle$, and m_2 is associated with $\langle p_1, \gamma_1 \rangle \hookrightarrow \langle p_2, \gamma_2 \gamma_0 \rangle$. The transitions (p_1, γ_1, m_1) and (m_1, γ_0, s_1) are a consequence of (p_0, γ_0, s_1); the former leads to (p_2, γ_2, m_2) and (m_2, γ_0, m_1) and, in turn, to (p_0, γ_1, m_2). Because of $\langle p_0, \gamma_1 \rangle \hookrightarrow \langle p_0, \varepsilon \rangle$, we now need to simulate an ε-move from p_0 to m_2. This is done by making copies of all the transitions that leave m_2; in this example, (m_2, γ_0, m_1) is copied and changed to (p_0, γ_0, m_1). The latter

Algorithm 3
Input: a pushdown system $\mathcal{P} = (P, \Gamma, \Delta)$ in normal form;
    a $\mathcal{P}$-Automaton $\mathcal{A} = (\Gamma, Q, \delta, P, F)$ without transitions into P
Output: the automaton $\mathcal{A}_{post^*}$

1 $trans \leftarrow \delta \cap (P \times \Gamma \times Q)$;
2 $rel \leftarrow \delta \setminus trans$; $Q' \leftarrow Q$; $F' \leftarrow F$;
3 **for all** $r = \langle p, \gamma \rangle \hookrightarrow \langle p', \gamma_1 \gamma_2 \rangle \in \Delta$ **do**
4      $Q' \leftarrow Q' \cup \{q_r\}$;
5      $trans \leftarrow trans \cup \{(p', \gamma_1, q_r)\}$;
6 **for all** $q \in Q'$ **do** $eps(q) \leftarrow \emptyset$;
7 **while** $trans \neq \emptyset$ **do**
8   pop $t = (p, \gamma, q)$ from $trans$;
9   **if** $t \notin rel$ **then**
10         $rel \leftarrow rel \cup \{t\}$;
11   **for all** $\langle p, \gamma \rangle \hookrightarrow \langle p', \varepsilon \rangle \in \Delta$ **do**
12   **if** $p' \notin eps(q)$ **then**
13                 $eps(q) \leftarrow eps(q) \cup \{p'\}$;
14   **for all** $(q, \gamma', q') \in rel$ **do**
15                     $trans \leftarrow trans \cup \{(p', \gamma', q')\}$;
16   **if** $q \in F'$ **then** $F' \leftarrow F' \cup \{p'\}$;
17   **for all** $\langle p, \gamma \rangle \hookrightarrow \langle p', \gamma_1 \rangle \in \Delta$ **do**
18             $trans \leftarrow trans \cup \{(p', \gamma_1, q')\}$;
19   **for all** $r = \langle p, \gamma \rangle \hookrightarrow \langle p', \gamma_1 \gamma_2 \rangle \in \Delta$ **do**
20             $rel \leftarrow rel \cup \{(q_r, \gamma_2, q)\}$;
21   **for all** $p'' \in eps(q_r)$ **do**
22                 $trans \leftarrow trans \cup \{(p'', \gamma_2, q)\}$;
23 **return** (Γ, Q', rel, P, F')

finally leads to (p_1, γ_1, m_1) and (m_1, γ_0, m_1). Figure 3 shows the result, similar to Figure 2 but with the ε-transition resolved.

Theorem 3. *Let $\mathcal{P} = (P, \Gamma, \Delta)$ be a pushdown system, and $\mathcal{A} = (\Gamma, Q, \delta, P, F)$ be an automaton. There exists an automaton $\mathcal{A}_{post^*}$ recognising $post^*(Conf(\mathcal{A}))$. Moreover, $\mathcal{A}_{post^*}$ can be constructed in $O(n_P n_\Delta (n_Q + n_\Delta) + n_P n_\delta)$ time and space, where $n_P = |P|$, $n_\Delta = |\Delta|$, $n_Q = |Q|$, and $n_\delta = |\delta|$.*

In [7] the same problem was considered (with different restrictions on the rules in the pushdown system). The complexity of the $post^*$ computation for the initial configuration was given as $O(n_\mathcal{P}^3)$ where $n_\mathcal{P}$ translates to $n_P + n_\Delta$. An extension to compute $post^*(C)$ for arbitrary regular sets C is also proposed. The different restrictions on the pushdown rules make a more detailed comparison difficult, but it is safe to say that our algorithm is at least as good as the one in [7]. Also, we give an explicit bound for the computation of $post^*$ for arbitrary regular sets of configurations.

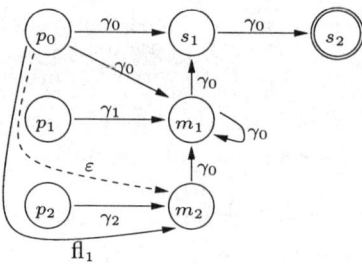

Fig. 3. $\mathcal{A}_{post^*}$ as computed by Algorithm 3.

8 The Model-Checking Problem

Using the results from the previous section we can now compute the complexity of the problems presented in section 3. The following steps are necessary to solve the global model-checking problem for a given formula φ:

- Construct the Büchi automaton $\mathcal{B} = (\Sigma, Q, \delta, q_0, F)$ corresponding to $\neg\varphi$.
- Compute $\mathcal{BP}$ as the product of $\mathcal{B}$ and the pushdown system $\mathcal{P} = (P, \Gamma, \Delta)$.
- Compute the set of repeating heads R of $\mathcal{BP}$.
- Construct an automaton $\mathcal{A}$ accepting $R\Gamma^*$. $\mathcal{A}$ has one final state r and contains transitions (p, γ, r) for every $\langle p, \gamma \rangle \in R$ and (r, γ, r) for every $\gamma \in \Gamma$.
- Compute $\mathcal{A}_{pre^*}$. A configuration $\langle p, w \rangle$ violates φ exactly if $\langle (p, q_0), w \rangle$ is accepted by $\mathcal{A}_{pre^*}$.

The dominant factors in these computations are the time needed to compute the repeating heads, and the space needed to store $\mathcal{A}_{pre^*}$.

Theorem 4. *Let $g_\mathcal{P}$ denote the size of $\mathcal{P}$ and $g_\mathcal{B}$ the size of $\mathcal{B}$. The global model-checking problem can be solved in $O(g_\mathcal{P}^3 g_\mathcal{B}^3)$ time and $O(g_\mathcal{P}^2 g_\mathcal{B}^2)$ space.*

In [7] an algorithm is presented for deciding if the initial configuration satisfies a given LTL property. (The problem of obtaining a representation for the set of configurations violating the property is not discussed.) The algorithm takes cubic time but also cubic space in the size of the pushdown system. More precisely, it is based on a saturation routine which requires $\Theta(g_\mathcal{P}^3 g_\mathcal{B}^3)$ space. Observe that the space consumption is Θ, and not O. Our solution implies therefore an improvement in the space complexity without losses in time. To solve the problem for reachable configurations we need these additional steps:

- Rename the states (p, q_0) into p for all $p \in P$ and take P as the new set of initial states.
- Compute $post^*$ for the initial configuration of $\mathcal{P}$.
- Compute the intersection of $\mathcal{A}_{pre^*}$ and $\mathcal{A}_{post^*}$. The resulting automaton $\mathcal{A}_i$ accepts the set of reachable configurations violating φ.

Theorem 5. *The global model-checking problem for reachable configurations can be solved in $O(g_\mathcal{P}^4 g_\mathcal{B}^3)$ time and $O(g_\mathcal{P}^4 g_\mathcal{B}^2)$ space.*

9 Application

As an application, we use pushdown systems to model sequential programs with procedures (written in C or Java, for instance). We concentrate on the control flow and abstract away information about data. The model establishes a relation between the control states of a program and the configurations of the corresponding pushdown system.

The model is constructed in two steps. In the first step, we represent the program by a system of flow graphs, one for each procedure. The nodes of a flow graph correspond to control points in the procedure, and its edges are annotated with statements, e.g. calls to other procedures. Control flow is interpreted non-deterministically since we abstract from the values of variables.

Given a system of flow graphs with a set N of control points, we construct a pushdown system with N as its stack alphabet. More precisely, a configuration $\langle p, nw \rangle$, $w \in N^*$ represents the situation that execution is currently at control point n where w represents the return addresses of the calling procedures. Pushdown systems of this kind need only one single control state (called p in the following). The transition rules of such a pushdown system are:

- $\langle p, n \rangle \hookrightarrow \langle p, n' \rangle$ if control passes from n to n' without a procedure call.
- $\langle p, n \rangle \hookrightarrow \langle p, f_0 n' \rangle$ if an edge between point n and n' contains a call to procedure f, assuming that f_0 is f's entry point. n' can be seen as the return address of that call.
- $\langle p, n \rangle \hookrightarrow \langle p, \varepsilon \rangle$ if an edge leaving n contains a return statement.

Let us examine how the special structure of these systems affects the complexity of the model-checking problem. Under the assumption that the number of control states is one (or, more generally, constant), the number of states in the Büchi pushdown system $\mathcal{BP}$ only depends on the formula, and we get the following results:

Theorem 6. *If the number of control states in $\mathcal{P}$ is constant, the global model-checking problem can be solved in $O(g_\mathcal{P} g_\mathcal{B}{}^3)$ time and $O(g_\mathcal{P} g_\mathcal{B}{}^2)$ space, and the problem for reachable configurations in $O(g_\mathcal{P}{}^2 g_\mathcal{B}{}^3)$ time and $O(g_\mathcal{P}{}^2 g_\mathcal{B}{}^2)$ space.*

9.1 A Small Example

As an example, consider the program in Figure 4. This program controls a plotter, creating random bar graphs via the commands *go_up*, *go_right*, and *go_down*. Among the correctness properties is the requirement that an upward movement should never be immediately followed by a downward movement and vice versa which we shall verify in the following.

The left side of Figure 5 displays the set of flow graphs created from the original program. Calls to external functions are treated as ordinary statements. (In this example we assume that the *go...* functions are external.) The procedure *main* ends in an infinite loop which ensures that all executions are infinite. The right side shows the resulting pushdown system. The initial configuration is $\langle p, main_0 \rangle$. The desired properties can be expressed as follows:

$$\mathbf{G}(up \to (\neg down \ \mathbf{U} \ right)) \quad \text{and} \quad \mathbf{G}(down \to (\neg up \ \mathbf{U} \ right))$$

where the atomic proposition *up* is true of configurations $\langle p, m_7 w \rangle$ and $\langle p, s_2 w \rangle$, i.e. those that correspond to program points in which *go_up* will be the next statement. Similarly, *down* is true of configurations with m_9 or s_5 as the topmost stack symbol, and *right* is true of m_4. Analysis of the program with our methods yields that both properties are fulfilled.

9.2 Experimental Results

Apart from the example, we solved the global model-checking problem on a series of randomly generated flow graphs. These flow graphs model programs with procedures. The structure of each statement was decided randomly; the average proportion of sequences, branches and loops was 0.6 : 0.2 : 0.2 (these numbers were taken from the literature). After generating one flow graph for each procedure we connected them by inserting procedure calls, making sure that each procedure was indeed reachable from the start. The formulas we checked were of the form $\mathbf{G}(n \to \mathbf{F}n')$, where n and n' were random control states.

Table 1 lists the execution times in seconds for programs with an average of 20 resp. 40 lines per procedure. One fifth of the statements in these programs contained a procedure call. Results are given for programs with recursive and mutual procedure calls. The table lists the times needed to compute the sets of repeating heads, *pre**, and the total time for the model-checking which includes several other tasks. In fact, in our experiments the majority of time was spent reading the pushdown system and computing the product with a Büchi automaton. Also, memory usage is given. All computations were carried out on an Ultrasparc 60 with sufficient amount of memory.

Obviously, these experiments can only give a rough impression of what the execution times would be like when analysing real programs. However, these experiments already constitute 'stress tests', i.e. their construction is based on

```
void m() {
    double d = drand48();
    if (d < 0.66) {
        s(); go_right();
        if (d < 0.33) m();
    } else {
        go_up(); m(); go_down();
    }
}

void s() {
    if (drand48() < 0.5) return;
    go_up(); m(); go_down();
}

main() {
    srand48(time(NULL));
    s();
}
```

Fig. 4. An example program.

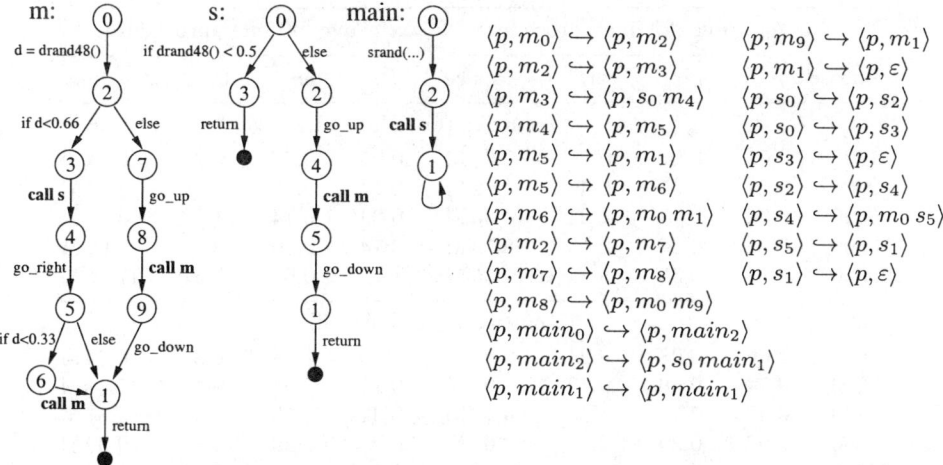

Fig. 5. Flowgraph of the program in Figure 4 (left) and associated PDS (right)

certain exaggerated assumptions which affect execution times negatively. For instance, the number of procedure calls is very high, and with mutual calls we allowed every procedure to call every other procedure (which greatly increases the time needed to find repeating heads). We have run preliminary experiments with three real programs of ten to thirty thousand lines, and the time for the model-checking was never more than a few seconds even for the largest program.

10 Conclusions

We have presented detailed algorithms for model-checking linear time logics on pushdown systems. The global model-checking problem can be solved in $O(g_\mathcal{P}{}^3 g_\mathcal{B}{}^3)$ time and $O(g_\mathcal{P}{}^2 g_\mathcal{B}{}^2)$ space. In the case of pushdown systems with one single control state the problem can be solved in $O(g_\mathcal{P} g_\mathcal{B}{}^3)$ time and $O(g_\mathcal{P} g_\mathcal{B}{}^2)$ space. Our results improve on [7], where the model-checking problem (i.e., deciding if an initial configuration satisfies a property, without computing the set of configurations violating the property) was solved in $O(n^3)$ time but also $O(n^3)$ space in the size of the pushdown system.

Our work needs to be carefully compared to that on branching time logics. For arbitrary pushdown systems, linear time logics can be checked in polynomial time in the size of the system, while checking CTL provably requires exponential time. However, in the case of pushdown systems with one single control state, a modal mu-calculus formula of alternation depth k can be checked in time $O(n^k)$ [3,11], where n is the size of the system. In this case, linear time formulas can be checked in $O(n)$ time, and so we obtain linear complexity in the size of the system for both linear time logics and for the alternation-free mu-calculus.

The information provided by the branching-time and linear-time algorithms is different. Walukiewicz's algorithm [11] only says whether the initial configuration satisfies the property or not. The algorithm of Burkart and Steffen [2,3]

	avg. 20 lines/procedure				avg. 40 lines/procedure			
lines	RH	pre^*	total	space	RH	pre^*	total	space
	recursive procedure calls								
1000	0.05	0.02	0.23	0.91 M	0.05	0.02	0.20	0.84 M
2000	0.12	0.05	0.46	1.82 M	0.14	0.05	0.48	1.84 M
5000	0.36	0.13	1.23	4.46 M	0.34	0.14	1.20	4.29 M
10000	0.76	0.26	2.55	8.79 M	0.74	0.30	2.52	8.62 M
20000	1.64	0.55	5.43	17.56 M	1.75	0.64	5.57	17.69 M
	mutual procedure calls								
1000	0.06	0.03	0.24	0.97 M	0.05	0.03	0.22	0.90 M
2000	0.14	0.06	0.49	1.91 M	0.14	0.08	0.49	1.87 M
5000	0.43	0.18	1.35	4.72 M	0.42	0.18	1.32	4.67 M
10000	0.97	0.39	2.91	9.68 M	0.95	0.39	2.84	9.39 M
20000	2.10	0.81	6.21	19.27 M	2.08	0.84	6.15	18.93 M

Table 1. Results for programs with recursive and mutual procedure calls

returns a set of *predicate transformers*, one for each stack symbol; the predicate transformer for the symbol X shows which formulas hold for a stack content $X\alpha$ as a function of the formulas that hold in α.[2] Essentially, this allows to determine for each symbol X if there exists some stack content of the form $X\alpha$ that violates the formula, but doesn't tell which these stack contents are. Finally, our algorithm returns a finite representation of the set of configurations that violate the formula.

Whether one needs all the information provided by our algorithm or not depends on the application. For certain dataflow analysis problems we wish to compute the set of control locations p such that some reachable configuration $\langle p, w \rangle$ violates the property. This information can be efficiently computed by the algorithm of [2,3]. Sometimes we may need more. For instance, in [8] an approach is presented to the verification of control flow based security properties. Systems are modelled by pushdown automata, and security properties as properties that all reachable configurations should satisfy. It is necessary to determine which configurations violate the security property to modify the system accordingly. The model checking algorithm of [2,3] seems to be inadequate in this case. It may be possible to modify the algorithm in order to obtain an automata representation of the configurations that violate the formula. This is surely an interesting research question.

---

[2] Not for arbitrary formulas, but only for those in the closure of the original formula to be checked.

References

1. A. Bouajjani, J. Esparza, and O. Maler. Reachability analysis of pushdown automata: Application to model-checking. In *Proceedings of CONCUR '97*, LNCS 1243, pages 135–150, 1997.
2. O. Burkart and B. Steffen. Composition, decomposition and model checking of pushdown processes. *Nordic Journal of Computing*, 2(2):89–125, 1995.
3. O. Burkart and B. Steffen. Model–checking the full–modal mu–calculus for infinite sequential processes. In *Proceedings of ICALP'97, Bologna*, LNCS 1256, pages 419–429, 1997.
4. J. Esparza, D. Hansel, P. Rossmanith, and S. Schwoon. Efficient algorithms for model checking pushdown systems. Technical Report TUM-I0002, Technische Universität München, Department of Computer Science, Feb. 2000.
5. J. Esparza and J. Knoop. An automata-theoretic approach to interprocedural dataflow analysis. In *Proceedings of TACAS '99*, LNCS 1578, pages 14 – 30, 1999.
6. J. Esparza and A. Podelski. Efficient algorithms for pre* and post* on interprocedural parallel flow graphs. In *Proceedings of POPL '00*, 2000.
7. A. Finkel, B. Willems, and P. Wolper. A direct symbolic approach to model checking pushdown systems. *Electronic Notes in Theoretical Computer Science*, 9, 1997.
8. T. Jensen, D. Le Métayer, and T. Thorn. Verification of control flow based security properties. Technical Report 1210, IRISA, 1998.
9. D. Schmidt and B. Steffen. Program analysis as model checking of abstract interpretations. In *Proceedings of SAS'98, Pisa*, LNCS 1503, pages 351–380, 1998.
10. R. E. Tarjan. Depth first search and linear graph algorithms. In *SICOMP 1*, pages 146–160, 1972.
11. I. Walukiewicz. Pushdown Processes: Games and Model Checking. In *CAV'96*. LNCS 1102, 1996.

Efficient Büchi Automata from LTL Formulae*

Fabio Somenzi and Roderick Bloem

Department of Electrical and Computer Engineering
University of Colorado, Boulder, CO, 80309-0425
{Fabio,Roderick.Bloem}@Colorado.EDU

Abstract. We present an algorithm to generate small Büchi automata for LTL formulae. We describe a heuristic approach consisting of three phases: rewriting of the formula, an optimized translation procedure, and simplification of the resulting automaton. We present a translation procedure that is optimal within a certain class of translation procedures. The simplification algorithm can be used for Büchi automata in general. It reduces the number of states and transitions, as well as the number and size of the accepting sets—possibly reducing the strength of the resulting automaton. This leads to more efficient model checking of linear-time logic formulae. We compare our method to previous work, and show that it is significantly more efficient for both random formulae, and formulae in common use and from the literature.

1 Introduction

The standard approach to LTL model checking [18,14] consists of translating the negation of a given LTL formula into a Büchi automaton, and checking the product of the property automaton and the model for language emptiness. The quality of the translation affects the resources required by the model checking experiment. This motivates the search for algorithms that generate efficient automata, i.e., automata with few states, few transitions, and simple acceptance conditions.

The initial approaches to translation of LTL formulae were not designed to yield small automata. The process of [18] always yields the worst-case result of $O(2^n)$ states, where n is the length of the formula. The approach of [11] was the first to produce automata that were not necessarily of worst-case size. In [9], a more efficient algorithm was proposed that works on-the-fly. A further improvement over this algorithm, based on syntactic simplification, was discussed in [5].

We present an approach to the generation of Büchi automata from LTL formulae that extends the work of [9,5] in three ways:

1. It applies rewriting rules to the formula before translation.
2. It reduces the number of states generated by the translation by applying boolean optimization techniques.
3. It simplifies both the transition structure and the acceptance conditions of the resulting Büchi automaton.

---
* This work was supported in part by SRC contract 98-DJ-620 and NSF grant CCR-99-71195.

The last phase of our algorithm is independent of LTL, and can be applied whenever one is interested in simplifying a Büchi automaton. Our algorithm is not designed to work on-the-fly, since the automata generated by the algorithm are typically much smaller than the model.

Both explicit and implicit model checking algorithms benefit from the simplification of the Büchi automata. Explicit techniques check emptiness of the product automata in time proportional to the size of the property automaton. Symbolic algorithms need, in general, a number of symbolic operations that is quadratic in the size of the property automaton [4,12]. We can hence expect appreciable speedups in emptiness checks using either technique if we can reduce the size of the automaton significantly.

The *strength* of a Büchi automaton [13,2] relates to the complexity of the procedure required to symbolically model check the corresponding property. For a *strong* automaton, an emptiness check requires the computation of a μ-calculus formula of alternation depth 2, which takes a number of preimage computations quadratic in the size of the automaton. A *weak* automaton requires an alternation-free greatest fixpoint computation, and hence only linearly many preimage computations. Finally, a *terminal* automaton only requires reachability analysis, and is therefore amenable to on-the-fly model checking. Our procedure tends to produce results of lesser strength than results of previous algorithms.

We compare our technique to those of [9] and [5]. The comparison is based on both random formulae, and a set of formulae that are either in common use or found in the literature. In both cases, it is significantly more efficient in terms of number of states, transitions, acceptance conditions, and strength of the resulting automaton.

Etessami and Holzmann [8] have independently developed a similar approach. In their approach, like ours, rewriting is followed by translation and simulation-based optimization. Etessami and Holzmann perform rewriting using a set of rules that is incomparable to ours. They do not expand on the translation stage. In the minimization stage backward simulation is not employed. Their technique is geared towards non-generalized automata.

The flow of this paper is as follows. Section 2 presents the preliminaries. Section 3 covers rewriting of the LTL formulae. Section 4 describes how boolean optimization can be used to make the translation into automata more efficient. Then, Sections 5 and 6 describe the simplification of the automaton by deleting arcs and states, and pruning acceptance conditions. Finally, Section 7 presents the experimental results, and Section 8 concludes the paper.

2 Preliminaries

There are several variants of Büchi automata. We adopt automata with multiple acceptance conditions and with labels on the states (as opposed to labels on the arcs) as in [9].

Definition 1. *A labeled, generalized Büchi automaton is a six-tuple*

$$\mathcal{A} = \langle Q, Q_0, \delta, \mathcal{F}, D, \mathcal{L} \rangle,$$

where Q is the finite set of states, $Q_0 \subseteq Q$ is the set of initial states, $\delta : Q \to 2^Q$ is the transition relation, $\mathcal{F} \subseteq 2^Q$ is the set of acceptance conditions (or fair sets), D is a finite domain, and $\mathcal{L} : Q \to 2^D$ is the labeling function.

A run of $\mathcal{A}$ is an infinite sequence $\rho = \rho_0, \rho_1, \ldots$ over Q, such that $\rho_0 \in Q_0$, and for all $i \geq 0$, $\rho_{i+1} \in \delta(\rho_i)$. A run ρ is accepting if for each $F_i \in \mathcal{F}$ there exists $q_j \in F_i$ that appears infinitely often in ρ.

The automaton accepts an infinite word $\sigma = \sigma_0, \sigma_1, \ldots$ in D^ω if there exists an accepting run ρ such that, for all $i \geq 0$, $\sigma_i \in \mathcal{L}(\rho_i)$. The language of $\mathcal{A}$, denoted by $L(\mathcal{A})$, is the subset of D^ω accepted by $\mathcal{A}$.

We write $\mathcal{A}^q$ for the labeled, generalized Büchi automaton $\langle Q, \{q\}, \delta, \mathcal{F}, D, \mathcal{L} \rangle$.

Notice that with labels on the states we must allow multiple initial states. Multiple acceptance conditions, although not strictly necessary, simplify the translation. We will refer to a labeled generalized Büchi automaton simply as a Büchi automaton.

The temporal logic LTL is obtained from propositional logic by adding three temporal operators: U (until), R (releases, the dual of U), and X (next). The familiar G and F are defined as abbreviations, as are **T** (true) and **F** (false). Translation of an LTL formula φ into a Büchi automaton is accomplished by application of expansion rules also known as *tableau rules*:

$$\psi_1 \,\mathsf{U}\, \psi_2 = \psi_2 \vee (\psi_1 \wedge \mathsf{X}(\psi_1 \,\mathsf{U}\, \psi_2)) \;, \qquad \psi_1 \,\mathsf{R}\, \psi_2 = \psi_2 \wedge (\psi_1 \vee \mathsf{X}(\psi_1 \,\mathsf{R}\, \psi_2)) \;.$$

The rules are applied to φ until the resulting expression is a propositional formula in terms of *elementary subformulae* of φ. An elementary formula is a constant, an atomic proposition, or a formula starting with X. The expanded formula, put in disjunctive normal form (DNF), is an *elementary cover* of φ. Each term of the cover identifies a state of the automaton. The atomic propositions and their negations in the term define the *label* of the state, that is, the conditions that the input word must satisfy in that state. The remaining elementary subformulae of the term form the *next part* of the term; they are LTL formulae that identify the obligations that must be fulfilled to obtain an accepting run; they determine the transitions out of the state as well as the acceptance conditions.

The expansion process is applied to the next part of each state, creating new covers until no new obligations are produced. In this way, a *closed* set of elementary covers is obtained. The set is closed in the sense that there is an elementary cover in the set for the next part of each term of each cover in the set. The automaton is obtained by connecting each state to the states in the cover for its next part. The states in the elementary cover of φ are the initial states. Acceptance conditions are added to the automaton for each elementary subformula of the form $\mathsf{X}(\psi_1 \,\mathsf{U}\, \psi_2)$. The acceptance condition contains all the states s such that the label of s does not imply $\psi_1 \,\mathsf{U}\, \psi_2$ or the label of s implies ψ_2.

3 Rewriting the Formula

The first step towards an efficient translation is rewriting, a cheap, simple, and effective way to minimize result of the translation. Prior to generation of the Büchi automaton, a formula is put in positive normal form. Then we use the following identities and their duals to rewrite the formula, always replacing the left-hand side by the right-hand side.

$$\varphi \leq \psi \Rightarrow (\varphi \wedge \psi) \equiv \varphi$$
$$\varphi \leq \neg\psi \Rightarrow (\varphi \wedge \psi) \equiv \mathbf{F}$$
$$(\mathsf{X}\varphi) \cup (\mathsf{X}\psi) \equiv \mathsf{X}(\varphi \cup \psi)$$
$$(\varphi \mathsf{R}\psi) \wedge (\varphi \mathsf{R} r) \equiv \varphi \mathsf{R}(\psi \wedge r)$$
$$(\varphi \mathsf{R} r) \vee (\psi \mathsf{R} r) \equiv (\varphi \vee \psi) \mathsf{R} r$$
$$(\mathsf{X}\varphi) \wedge (\mathsf{X}\psi) \equiv \mathsf{X}(\varphi \wedge \psi)$$
$$\mathsf{X}\mathbf{T} \equiv \mathbf{T}$$
$$\varphi \cup \mathbf{F} \equiv \mathbf{F}$$
$$\varphi \leq \psi \Rightarrow (\varphi \cup \psi) \equiv \psi$$
$$\neg\psi \leq \varphi \Rightarrow (\varphi \cup \psi) \equiv (\mathbf{T} \cup \psi)$$

$$\mathsf{GF}\varphi \vee \mathsf{GF}\psi \equiv \mathsf{GF}(\varphi \vee \psi)$$
$$\mathsf{FX}\varphi \equiv \mathsf{XF}\varphi$$
$$\varphi \leq \psi \Rightarrow \varphi \cup (\psi \cup r) \equiv \psi \cup r$$
$$\mathsf{GGF}\varphi \equiv \mathsf{GF}\varphi$$
$$\mathsf{FGF}\varphi \equiv \mathsf{GF}\varphi$$
$$\mathsf{XGF}\varphi \equiv \mathsf{GF}\varphi$$
$$\mathsf{F}(\varphi \wedge \mathsf{GF}\psi) \equiv (\mathsf{F}\varphi) \wedge (\mathsf{GF}\psi)$$
$$\mathsf{G}(\varphi \vee \mathsf{GF}\psi) \equiv (\mathsf{G}\varphi) \vee (\mathsf{GF}\psi)$$
$$\mathsf{X}(\varphi \wedge \mathsf{GF}\psi) \equiv (\mathsf{X}\varphi) \wedge (\mathsf{GF}\psi)$$
$$\mathsf{X}(\varphi \vee \mathsf{GF}\psi) \equiv (\mathsf{X}\varphi) \vee (\mathsf{GF}\psi)$$

The rewriting rules have been chosen to eliminate redundancies and to reduce the size of the resulting automaton. Checking for $\varphi \leq \psi$ is hard in general. Hence, we just look for simple cases that can be detected by purely syntactic means. We use the following set of rules and their duals.

$$\varphi \leq \varphi$$
$$\varphi \leq \mathbf{T}$$
$$(\varphi \leq \psi) \wedge (\varphi \leq \chi) \Rightarrow \varphi \leq (\psi \wedge \chi)$$
$$(\varphi \leq \chi) \vee (\psi \leq \chi) \Rightarrow (\varphi \wedge \psi) \leq \chi.$$

$$\chi \leq \psi \Rightarrow \chi \leq (\varphi \cup \psi)$$
$$(\varphi \leq \chi) \wedge (\psi \leq \chi) \Rightarrow (\varphi \cup \psi) \leq \chi$$
$$(\varphi \leq \chi) \wedge (\psi \leq s) \Rightarrow (\varphi \cup \psi) \leq (\chi \cup s)$$

The first two rules are the terminal cases of a recursive procedure in which one applies the remaining ones to decompose the problem.

Example 1. The rewriting rules transform the formula $(\mathsf{X} p \cup \mathsf{X} q) \vee \neg \mathsf{X} (p \cup q)$ into $\mathbf{T}$. The automaton produced by our algorithm when rewriting is disabled is shown in Figure 1. The optimal automaton obviously has only one state with a self-loop.

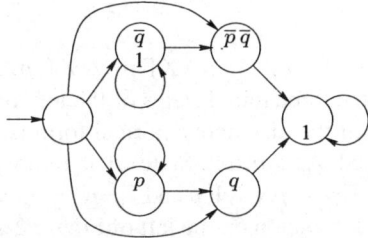

Fig. 1. Sub-optimal automaton for $(\mathsf{X} p \cup \mathsf{X} q) \vee \neg \mathsf{X} (p \cup q)$. Each node is annotated with its label, (first line), and the fair sets to which it belongs (second line). In the label, an overline indicates negation, and concatenation indicates conjunction.

4 Reducing the Number of States via Boolean Optimization

The LTL formula produced by rewriting is the input to the second phase of the procedure, which produces a closed set of elementary covers and constructs the Büchi automaton from it. We refer to the covers in this set as the elementary covers of the automaton. An

LTL formula has infinitely many elementary covers; which one is chosen affects the size of the resulting automaton by directly affecting what states are added to the automaton, and by determining what covers will belong to the closed set.

By regarding each elementary formula as a literal, one can apply boolean optimization techniques to minimize the cost of the elementary covers. (In this case, the implication tests required to compute the fair sets must also be carried out with boolean techniques.) However, the best result is not always obtained by computing a minimum cost cover for each formula. The following example illustrates this case.

Example 2. Consider translating the LTL formula $\varphi = \mathsf{F}\, p \wedge \mathsf{F}\, \neg p$ into a Büchi automaton. The algorithm of [5] produces the automaton on the left of Figure 2. Applying the

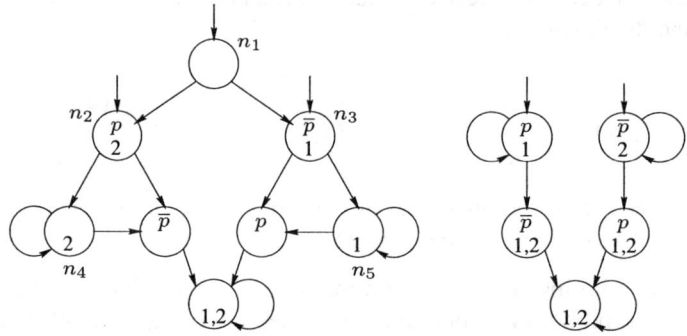

Fig. 2. Büchi automata for $\mathsf{F}\, p \wedge \mathsf{F}\, \neg p$: without (left) and with (right) boolean optimization.

tableau rules to φ yields $(p \wedge \mathsf{X}\, \mathsf{F}\, \neg p) \vee (\neg p \wedge \mathsf{X}\, \mathsf{F}\, p) \vee (\mathsf{X}\, \mathsf{F}\, p \wedge \mathsf{X}\, \mathsf{F}\, \neg p)$. The three terms of this cover correspond to the three initial states of the left automaton of Figure 2 (n_1, n_2, and n_3). The third term of the disjunctive normal form is the consensus of the first two; hence, it can be dropped. As a result, State n1 is removed. Applying the tableau rules to $\mathsf{F}\, p$ and $\mathsf{F}\, \neg p$ yields $\mathsf{F}\, p = p \vee \mathsf{X}\, \mathsf{F}\, p$ and $\mathsf{F}\, \neg p = \neg p \vee \mathsf{X}\, \mathsf{F}\, \neg p$, from which the remaining five states of the automaton on the left of Figure 2 are produced. Notice, however, that the alternative expansion $\mathsf{F}\, p = p \vee (\neg p \wedge \mathsf{X}\, \mathsf{F}\, p)$, $\mathsf{F}\, \neg p = \neg p \vee (p \wedge \mathsf{X}\, \mathsf{F}\, \neg p)$, though it requires more literals, prevents the creation of States n_4 and n_5, leading to the automaton on the right of Figure 2.

We can formulate the choice of the optimum covers as a 0-1 ILP as follows. We define one set of formulae $\Phi(\psi_0)$, and a set of terms $\Gamma(\psi_0)$ such that the automaton for ψ_0 will be obtained from elementary covers for a subset of the formulae in $\Phi(\psi_0)$, and will have states corresponding to a subset of $\Gamma(\psi_0)$. We then impose constraints that guarantee that the automaton will recognize exactly the models of the LTL formula.

Definition 2. *For an LTL formula φ, let $E(\varphi)$ be the expansion of φ in terms of elementary subformulae. Let $M(\varphi)$ be the set of minterms of $E(\varphi)$, and $P(\varphi)$ be the set of prime implicants of $E(\varphi)$. Finally, for γ a term of an elementary cover, let $N(\gamma) = \bigwedge \{\psi : \mathsf{X}\, \psi \text{ is a literal of } \gamma\}$ be its next part.*

The sets $\Phi(\psi_0)$ and $\Gamma(\psi_0)$ are the smallest sets that satisfy the following constraints:

$$\psi_0 \in \Phi(\psi_0) \ , \qquad \Psi \subseteq \Phi(\psi_0) \Rightarrow P(\bigwedge \Psi) \subseteq \Gamma(\psi_0) \ ,$$
$$\gamma \in \Gamma(\psi_0) \Rightarrow N(\gamma) \in \Phi(\psi_0) \ .$$

We associate 0-1 variables to the elements of $\Phi(\psi_0)$ and $\Gamma(\psi_0)$ as follows: $y_i = 1$ if and only if an elementary cover of ψ_i is a cover of the automaton; $x_i = 1$ if and only if γ_i is a state of the automaton. We then search for $\min \sum x_i$, subject to:

$$y_0 \wedge \bigwedge_{\psi_i \in \Phi} (\neg y_i \vee \bigwedge_{\mu_j \in M(\psi_i)} \bigvee_{\gamma_k \in \Gamma} (x_k \wedge [\mu_j \leq \gamma_k \leq \psi_i])) \wedge \bigwedge_{\gamma_i \in \Gamma} (\neg x_i \vee y_{I(N(\gamma_i))}) \ ,$$

where $I(\psi_j) = j$. The intuition behind this formulation is that constructing the automaton corresponds to finding DNF formulae for a set of boolean functions. (Each function is an elementary cover for some LTL formula.) It is well known that the solution consists of prime implicants of intersections of subsets of the functions in the set [15]. A function needs to be in the set if it is the expansion of the given LTL formula, or if it is the expansion of the next part of a term in the elementary cover chosen for a function that is in the set. This situation gives rise to *closure* constraints analogous to those found in the minimization of incompletely specified finite state machines [10]. Notice that we do not guarantee the optimum Büchi automaton for the given LTL formula (cf. Example 5 in Section 6); rather, we guarantee that no closed set of elementary covers can be found that has fewer terms, and such that each elementary cover can be generated from the formula it covers by exclusive application of the tableau rules and the laws of boolean algebra. Note that prior research on translation algorithms has focused on this class of algorithms.

Example 3. Continuing Example 2, let $\psi_0 = \mathsf{F} p \wedge \mathsf{F} \neg p$. We find:

$$\begin{array}{lll}
\psi_0 = \mathsf{F} p \wedge \mathsf{F} \neg p \Rightarrow & \gamma_0 = p \wedge \mathsf{X} \mathsf{F} \neg p, & \gamma_1 = \neg p \wedge \mathsf{X} \mathsf{F} p, \quad \gamma_2 = \mathsf{X} \mathsf{F} p \wedge \mathsf{X} \mathsf{F} \neg p \\
\psi_1 = \mathsf{F} p \Rightarrow & \gamma_3 = p, & \gamma_4 = \mathsf{X} \mathsf{F} p \\
\psi_2 = \mathsf{F} \neg p \Rightarrow & \gamma_5 = \neg p, & \gamma_6 = \mathsf{X} \mathsf{F} \neg p.
\end{array}$$

Since $\psi_0 = \psi_1 \wedge \psi_2$, no further formulae and terms are generated by considering subsets of $\Phi(\psi_0)$. The minterms of the formulae in $\Phi(\psi_0)$ are:

$$\begin{aligned}
M(\psi_0) = \{ & p \wedge \mathsf{X} \mathsf{F} p \wedge \mathsf{X} \mathsf{F} \neg p, p \wedge \neg \mathsf{X} \mathsf{F} p \wedge \mathsf{X} \mathsf{F} \neg p, \\
& \neg p \wedge \mathsf{X} \mathsf{F} p \wedge \mathsf{X} \mathsf{F} \neg p, \neg p \wedge \mathsf{X} \mathsf{F} p \wedge \neg \mathsf{X} \mathsf{F} \neg p \} \\
M(\psi_1) = \{ & p \wedge \mathsf{X} \mathsf{F} p \wedge \mathsf{X} \mathsf{F} \neg p, p \wedge \mathsf{X} \mathsf{F} p \wedge \neg \mathsf{X} \mathsf{F} \neg p, p \wedge \neg \mathsf{X} \mathsf{F} p \wedge \mathsf{X} \mathsf{F} \neg p, \\
& p \wedge \neg \mathsf{X} \mathsf{F} p \wedge \neg \mathsf{X} \mathsf{F} \neg p, \neg p \wedge \mathsf{X} \mathsf{F} p \wedge \mathsf{X} \mathsf{F} \neg p, \neg p \wedge \mathsf{X} \mathsf{F} p \wedge \neg \mathsf{X} \mathsf{F} \neg p \} \\
M(\psi_2) = \{ & \neg p \wedge \mathsf{X} \mathsf{F} p \wedge \mathsf{X} \mathsf{F} \neg p, \neg p \wedge \mathsf{X} \mathsf{F} p \wedge \neg \mathsf{X} \mathsf{F} \neg p, \neg p \wedge \neg \mathsf{X} \mathsf{F} p \wedge \mathsf{X} \mathsf{F} \neg p, \\
& \neg p \wedge \neg \mathsf{X} \mathsf{F} p \wedge \neg \mathsf{X} \mathsf{F} \neg p, p \wedge \mathsf{X} \mathsf{F} p \wedge \mathsf{X} \mathsf{F} \neg p, p \wedge \neg \mathsf{X} \mathsf{F} p \wedge \mathsf{X} \mathsf{F} \neg p \} \ .
\end{aligned}$$

The constraint is:

$y_0 \wedge$
$[\neg y_0 \vee (x_0 \vee x_2) \wedge x_0 \wedge (x_1 \vee x_2) \wedge x_1] \wedge$
$[\neg y_1 \vee (x_0 \vee x_2 \vee x_3 \vee x_4) \wedge (x_3 \vee x_4) \wedge (x_0 \vee x_3) \wedge x_3 \wedge (x_1 \vee x_2 \vee x_4) \wedge (x_1 \vee x_4)] \wedge$
$[\neg y_2 \vee (x_1 \vee x_2 \vee x_5 \vee x_6) \wedge (x_1 \vee x_5) \wedge (x_5 \vee x_6) \wedge x_5 \wedge (x_0 \vee x_2 \vee x_6) \wedge (x_0 \vee x_6)] \wedge$
$(\neg x_0 \vee y_2) \wedge (\neg x_1 \vee y_1) \wedge (\neg x_2 \vee y_0) \wedge (\neg x_4 \vee y_1) \wedge (\neg x_6 \vee y_2)$,

which simplifies to $y_0 \wedge y_1 \wedge y_2 \wedge x_0 \wedge x_1 \wedge x_3 \wedge x_5$. The feasible assignment that minimizes $\sum_{0 \leq i \leq 6} x_i$ is: $y_0 = y_1 = y_2 = x_0 = x_1 = x_3 = x_5 = 1$, $x_2 = x_4 = x_6 = 0$. This assignment corresponds to the solution found in Example 2. The fifth state of Figure 2 is required because $N(p) = N(\neg p) = \mathbf{T}$.

Solving the 0-1 ILP exactly is expensive, and, as we just observed, only guarantees optimality within a class of algorithms; therefore, we adopt a heuristic approach. In choosing the elementary cover for a formula, we first obtain a prime and irredundant cover from the one produced by the approach of [5]. Then, we look for existing states that imply the new terms. If we find a state that exactly matches a new term, we do not need to create a new state for the latter. If we find an existing state that implies the new term, we try to *reduce* [3] the new term to the existing one. That is, we check whether the replacement of the new term by the existing one changes the function represented by the cover. For instance, in Example 2, the initial cover for $\mathsf{F}\, p$, $p \vee \mathsf{X}\,\mathsf{F}\, p$, is reduced to $p \vee (\neg p \wedge \mathsf{X}\,\mathsf{F}\, p)$, because the second term already appears in the cover for φ.

If, on the other hand, we find a term that is implied by the new term, we check whether it can be reduced to the new term in all covers in which it already appears. We impose the constraint that the reduction only add atomic propositions or their negations. This constraint leaves the next part of the reduced term unchanged, and does not invalidate the covers obtained up to that point.

5 Simplifying Büchi Automata Using Simulations

The Büchi automata produced by our translation algorithm are not necessarily optimal. In this section we examine criteria that allow us to remove states from an automaton, while retaining its language. The techniques presented in this section can be used to simplify arbitrary Büchi automata. They do not always find the smallest possible Büchi automaton. Rather, they minimize the number of states and transitions heuristically. We deal with the simplification of the acceptance conditions in Section 6.

Our results derive from the notions of direct and reverse simulation. Direct simulation relations for Büchi automata have been studied in [6], and used in [1] for state-space minimization. Raimi [17] uses both direct and reverse simulations to minimize the state space, but does not take fairness into account.

In Subsection 5.3, we contrast simulation with language containment. Intuitively, simulation takes care of correspondence of acceptance conditions, which is one of the reasons why it is stronger than language containment. We show that this means that the conditions under which we can use simulation to reduce the number of states are more general than the conditions under which we can use language containment.

It is clear that we can remove all states that are not reachable from at least one initial state. Such states are not produced by the translation procedure, but they do occur as a result of other optimizations. It is equally obvious that we can remove any state q with $\mathcal{L}(q) = \emptyset$ or $\delta(q) = \emptyset$.

Definition 3. *A* direct simulation relation *over the states of a Büchi automaton $\mathcal{A}$ is any relation $\preceq \subseteq Q \times Q$ that satisfies the following property:*

$$p \preceq q \text{ implies } \begin{cases} \mathcal{L}(p) \subseteq \mathcal{L}(q) \ , \ F \in \mathcal{F} \Rightarrow [p \in F \Rightarrow q \in F] \\ s \in \delta(p) \Rightarrow \exists t \in \delta(q) : s \preceq t \ . \end{cases}$$

The largest direct simulation relation is denoted by $\preceq_D$. If both $p \preceq_D q$ and $q \preceq_D p$, then p and q are direct-simulation equivalent *($p \simeq_D q$).*

A reverse simulation relation *over the states of $\mathcal{A}$ is any relation $\preceq \subseteq Q \times Q$ that satisfies the following property:*

$$p \preceq q \text{ implies } \begin{cases} \mathcal{L}(p) \subseteq \mathcal{L}(q) \ , \ p \in Q_0 \Rightarrow q \in Q_0 \ , \ F \in \mathcal{F} \Rightarrow [p \in F \Rightarrow q \in F] \\ s \in \delta^{-1}(p) \Rightarrow \exists t \in \delta^{-1}(q) : s \preceq t \ . \end{cases}$$

The largest reverse simulation relation is denoted by $\preceq_R$. If both $p \preceq_R q$ and $q \preceq_R p$, then p and q are reverse-simulation equivalent *($p \simeq_R q$).*

The largest direct and reverse simulation relations can be found in polynomial time as the greatest fixpoints of the recursive definitions. Our definition of direct simulation corresponds to that of *BSR-aa* of [6]. If $p \preceq_D q$ in $\mathcal{A}$, then $L(\mathcal{A}^p) \subseteq L(\mathcal{A}^q)$ [16,6].

5.1 Direct Simulation

A simulation relation between two states may allow us to remove a transition without disturbing the simulation relation.

Theorem 1. *Let $\mathcal{A}$ be a Büchi automaton. For $p, q \in Q$, $p \neq q$, assume that $p \preceq_D q$. Let $\mathcal{M} = \langle Q, Q_{0M}, \delta_M, \mathcal{F}, D, \mathcal{L} \rangle$, where $Q_{0M} = Q_0 \setminus \{p\}$ if $q \in Q_0$, and $Q_{0M} = Q_0$ otherwise, and δ_M is defined as follows:*

$$\delta_M(s) = \begin{cases} \delta(s) \setminus \{p\} & \text{if } q \in \delta(s), \\ \delta(s) & \text{otherwise.} \end{cases}$$

Then for all $s, t \in Q$, $s \preceq_D t$ in $\mathcal{A}$ if and only if $s \preceq_D t$ in $\mathcal{M}$. Also, any state in $\mathcal{A}$ is simulation-equivalent to the state of the same name in $\mathcal{M}$.

Proof. (Sketch.) For the first statement, one can prove that the largest simulation relation on $\mathcal{A}$ is a simulation relation on $\mathcal{M}$, using Definition 3 and transitivity of $\preceq_D$. In the same manner, one can prove that the largest simulation relation on $\mathcal{M}$ is a simulation relation on $\mathcal{A}$. This proves that $s \preceq_D t$ in $\mathcal{A}$ if and only if $s \preceq_D t$ in $\mathcal{M}$. The second statement can also be proved by direct application of Definition 3. □

The following corollary holds because simulation implies language equivalence.

Corollary 1. *Let $\mathcal{A}$ and $\mathcal{M}$ be as in Theorem 1. Then, $L(\mathcal{A}) = L(\mathcal{M})$.*

Theorem 1 obviously works in both directions. Hence, we can also add an arc from r to p if $q \in \delta(r)$ and $p \preceq_D q$. Repeated application of this transformation gives us the following corollary, which implies that we can remove one of any two simulation-equivalent states.

Corollary 2. *Let $\mathcal{A}$ be a Büchi automaton. Let $p, q \in Q$, $p \neq q$, and assume that $p \simeq_D q$. Let $\mathcal{M} = \langle Q, Q_{0M}, \delta_M, \mathcal{F}, D, \mathcal{L} \rangle$, where $Q_{0M} = (Q_0 \setminus \{p\}) \cup \{q\}$ if $p \in Q_0$, and $Q_{0M} = Q_0$ otherwise, and δ_M coincides with δ, except that, for all s, if $p \in \delta(s)$, $\delta_M(s) = (\delta(s) \setminus \{p\}) \cup \{q\}$. Then $L(\mathcal{A}) = L(\mathcal{M})$, and for all $s, t \in Q$, we have $s \preceq_D t$ in $\mathcal{A}$ if and only if $s \preceq_D t$ in $\mathcal{M}$.*

5.2 Reverse Simulation

In this subsection, we present techniques similar to the one in the last subsection, but pertaining to reverse similarity.

Theorem 2. *Let $\mathcal{A}$ be a Büchi automaton. For $p, q \in Q$, $p \neq q$, assume that $p \preceq_R q$. Let $\mathcal{M} = \langle Q, Q_0, \delta_M, \mathcal{F}, D, \mathcal{L} \rangle$, where δ_M coincides with δ, except that $\delta_M(p) = \delta(p) \setminus \delta(q)$. Then for all $s, t \in Q$, $s \preceq_R t$ in $\mathcal{A}$ if and only if $s \preceq_R t$ in $\mathcal{M}$, and any state in $\mathcal{A}$ is reverse-simulation equivalent to the state of the same name in $\mathcal{M}$.*

Corollary 3. *Let $\mathcal{A}$ and $\mathcal{M}$ be as in Theorem 2. Then, $L(\mathcal{A}) = L(\mathcal{M})$.*

Proof. (Sketch.) For any accepting run ρ of $\mathcal{A}$, we can construct an accepting run ρ' of $\mathcal{M}$. We can do this because for every i, we can choose a state ρ_i' in $\mathcal{M}$ such that $\rho_i \preceq_R \rho_i'$, $\rho_i' \in Q_0$ for $i = 0$, and $\rho_i' \in \delta(\rho_{i-1}')$ for $i > 0$. □

In analogy to direct simulation, we only need to retain one state in every reverse-similarity equivalence class.

Corollary 4. *Let $\mathcal{A}$ be a Büchi automaton. Let $p, q \in Q$, $p \neq q$, and assume that $p \simeq_R q$. Let $\mathcal{M} = \langle Q, Q_0, \delta_M, \mathcal{F}, D, \mathcal{L} \rangle$, where $\delta_M(p) = \emptyset$, $\delta_M(q) = \delta(p) \cup \delta(q)$, and $\delta_M(s) = \delta(s)$ for $s \notin \{p, q\}$. Then $L(\mathcal{A}) = L(\mathcal{M})$, and for all $s, t \in Q$ we have $s \preceq_R t$ in $\mathcal{A}$ if an only if $s \preceq_R t$ in $\mathcal{M}$.*

5.3 Language Containment

In this section we consider the more general case of language containment, and contrast it with simulation relations. The techniques in this section are not used in the algorithm, since language inclusion can not be checked easily, and because the minimization requires stricter conditions in the case of language containment. Indeed, we cannot simply substitute $L(\mathcal{A}^p) \subseteq L(\mathcal{A}^q)$ for $p \preceq_D q$ in Theorem 1 as evidenced by the following example.

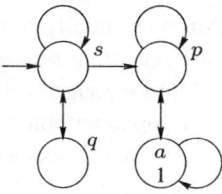

Fig. 3. Automaton showing that $L(\mathcal{A}^p) = L(\mathcal{A}^q)$ is not sufficient to allow simplification.

Example 4. Consider the automaton of Figure 3. The languages $L(\mathcal{A}^p)$ and $L(\mathcal{A}^q)$ are the same (they correspond to the formula G F a). State s is a common predecessor of p and q. However, we cannot remove the arc from s to p without making the language of the automaton empty. The problem is that the accepting runs starting at q must use the arc that we want to remove in order to reach the accepting state. Notice that q does not direct simulate p.

The next theorem is analogous to Corollary 1 for direct simulation. It allows us to remove an arc from a state r to a successor p if r has another successor q with $L(\mathcal{A}^p) \subseteq L(\mathcal{A}^q)$. We impose a condition sufficient to guarantee that the $L(\mathcal{A}^q)$ is not changed by removal of the arc.

Theorem 3. *Let $\mathcal{A}$ be a Büchi automaton. For $p, q \in Q$, $p \neq q$, assume that $L(\mathcal{A}^p) \subseteq L(\mathcal{A}^q)$. Let $\mathcal{M} = \langle Q, Q_{0M}, \delta_M, \mathcal{F}, D, \mathcal{L}\rangle$, where $Q_{0M} = Q_0 \setminus \{p\}$ if $q \in Q_0$, and $Q_{0M} = Q_0$ otherwise, and δ_M coincides with δ, except that for all $r \in Q$ such that $q \in \delta(r)$ and r is not reachable from q, $\delta_M(r) = \delta(r) \setminus \{p\}$. Then $L(\mathcal{A}) = L(\mathcal{M})$.*

By repeated application of Theorem 3, we can also prove that we can merge two language-equivalent states p and q, as long as q cannot reach any predecessors of p, in analogy to Corollary 2.

6 Pruning the Fair Sets

The automata produced by the algorithm of Section 4 have as many accepting conditions as there are *until* subformulae in the LTL formula. In this section we show how to shrink some fair sets or drop them altogether. Simplifying the fair sets has several benefits. First of all, it may lead to a reduction in strength of the resulting automaton. (For instance, if the automaton is reduced to *terminal*, model checking requires a simple reachability analysis.) Even if the strength of the automaton is not reduced, fewer, smaller fair sets usually lead to faster convergence of the language emptiness check. Simplifying the acceptance conditions may also enable further reductions in the number of states or transitions. Finally, the resulting automaton is often easier to understand.

The pruning of the fair sets is based on the analysis of the strongly connected components (SCCs) of the state graph.

Definition 4. *An SCC of a Büchi automaton $\mathcal{A}$ is fair if it is non-trivial and it intersects all fair sets. Let Θ_A be the union of all fair SCCs of $\mathcal{A}$; Θ_A is called the* final *set of $\mathcal{A}$.*

Every accepting run of an automaton is eventually contained in a fair SCC. Hence, states not in Θ_A can be removed from the accepting sets. Furthermore, states with no paths to Θ_A can be removed altogether: their language is empty. Fair sets that contain Θ_A, or that include another fair set, can be dropped without changing the language accepted by the automaton. It is not uncommon for one fair sets to become included in another once a few states are dropped from it, as a consequence, for instance, of the application of the following results.

When one fair set is contained in another we can remove states from the latter if they do not appear in the former. We can extend this result by focusing on a single SCC.

Theorem 4. *Let $\mathcal{A} = \langle Q, Q_0, \delta, \mathcal{F}, D, \mathcal{L} \rangle$ be a Büchi automaton and let γ be an SCC of $\mathcal{A}$. Suppose that there exist $F, F' \in \mathcal{F}$ such that $F \cap \gamma \subseteq F' \cap \gamma$. Let $\mathcal{M} = \langle Q, Q_0, \delta, \mathcal{F}_M, D, \mathcal{L} \rangle$, where*

$$\mathcal{F}_M = (\mathcal{F} \setminus \{F'\}) \cup \{F'_M\}, \text{ with}$$
$$F'_M = F' \setminus (\gamma \setminus F).$$

Then $L(\mathcal{A}) = L(\mathcal{M})$.

The next theorem, which shows that a state can be removed from a fair set if there is a suitable 'detour', will be followed by an example.

Theorem 5. *Let $\mathcal{A} = \langle Q, Q_0, \delta, \mathcal{F}, D, \mathcal{L} \rangle$ be a Büchi automaton. Let F be a fair set in $\mathcal{F}$, and p, q distinct states in F such that $\mathcal{L}(p) \subseteq \mathcal{L}(q)$, $\delta(p) \subseteq \delta(q)$, and $\delta^{-1}(p) \subseteq \delta^{-1}(q)$. Let $\mathcal{M} = \langle Q, Q_0, \delta, \mathcal{F}_M, D, \mathcal{L} \rangle$, where $\mathcal{F}_M = (\mathcal{F} \setminus \{F\}) \cup \{F \setminus \{p\}\}$. Then $L(\mathcal{A}) = L(\mathcal{M})$.*

Example 5. Two automata for G (F $p \wedge$ F q) are shown in Figure 4. Theorem 5 applies to

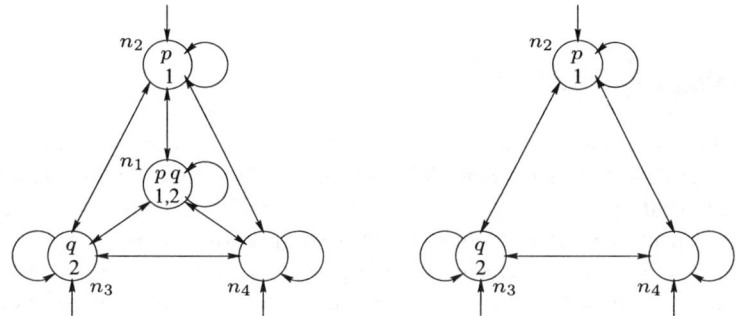

Fig. 4. Büchi automata for G (F $p \wedge$ F q) illustrating the application of Theorem 5.

State n_1 of the automaton on the left. After its removal from the two fair sets, State n_1 can be merged with State n_4. The resulting automaton is shown on the right of Figure 4. It is worth pointing out that the automaton on the left is constructed from a minimum cost elementary cover of G (F p ∧ F q). Since there is no elementary cover with fewer than four terms, there is no way to generate the three-state solution by direct application of the translation algorithm of Section 4.

Definition 5. *Let $p \preceq_r q$ be like $p \preceq_R q$, but without the condition on the fair sets.*

Theorem 6. *Let $\mathcal{A} = \langle Q, Q_0, \delta, \mathcal{F}, D, \mathcal{L} \rangle$ be a Büchi automaton. Let $\gamma \subseteq Q$ be an SCC, and $q \in \gamma$ a state. Suppose that for all $p \in \gamma$ we have $p \preceq_r q$, $\delta(p) \subseteq \delta(q)$, and $q \in \delta(p)$. Let $\mathcal{M} = \langle Q, Q_0, \delta_M, \mathcal{F}, D, \mathcal{L} \rangle$ with $\delta_M(s) = \delta(s) \setminus (\gamma \setminus \{q\})$ for $s \in \gamma$, $s \neq q$, and $\delta_M(s) = \delta(s)$ otherwise. Then, $L(\mathcal{A}) = L(\mathcal{M})$.*

Proof. Clearly, $L(\mathcal{A}) \supseteq L(\mathcal{M})$. Let ρ be an accepting run for $\sigma \in D^\omega$ in $\mathcal{A}$. If ρ does not go through γ, it is also an accepting run for σ in $\mathcal{M}$. If ρ enters and exits γ, let (s, p) be the last arc of ρ before it leaves γ. If $s \notin \gamma$, ρ does not use any arc internal to γ. Hence, it is also an accepting run for σ in $\mathcal{M}$. If $s \in \gamma$, $s \preceq_r q$. (This is not changed by the removal of arcs internal to γ.) Hence, there is a run ρ_M in $\mathcal{M}$ that reaches q when ρ reaches s, goes to p (also a successor of q) next, and then continues identical to ρ.

If ρ dwells in γ forever (inf$(\rho) \subseteq \gamma$), γ is a fair SCC (it intersects all fair sets). For each $F_i \in \mathcal{F}$, choose $s_i \in (F_i \cap \text{inf}(\rho))$. We can build a run ρ_M such that every occurrence of s_i is followed by an occurrence of $s_{(i+1) \bmod |\mathcal{F}|}$. This can be done by going from s_i to q, waiting in q until ρ goes to $s_{(i+1) \bmod |\mathcal{F}|}$, and then going to that state. We may "skip a beat" if $s_{(i+1) \bmod |\mathcal{F}|}$ follows immediately s_i in ρ, but we shall just take the next occurrence of $s_{(i+1) \bmod |\mathcal{F}|}$. Since $p \preceq_r q$ for all $p \in \gamma$, $\mathcal{L}(p) \subseteq \mathcal{L}(q)$; hence, ρ_M accepts σ. □

Thanks to Theorem 6 we can remove the arcs out of States n_2 and n_3 in the right automaton of Figure 4, except those going to State n_4. It is also possible to remove n_2 and n_3 from the set of initial states, though this is not covered by the theorem.

The next result is based on the observation that, in determining what states of an SCC should belong to a fair set, we can ignore the arcs out of the SCC.

Theorem 7. *Let $\mathcal{A} = \langle Q, Q_0, \delta, \mathcal{F}, D, \mathcal{L} \rangle$ be a Büchi automaton. Let γ be an SCC of $\mathcal{A}$, and p a state in γ such that, when the arcs out of γ are removed, $q \in \gamma$ implies $q \preceq_D p$ and $q \preceq_r p$. Let $\mathcal{M} = \langle Q, Q_0, \delta, \mathcal{F}_M, D, \mathcal{L} \rangle$, where $\mathcal{F}_M = \{F \setminus \{p\} | F \in \mathcal{F}\}$. Then $L(\mathcal{A}) = L(\mathcal{M})$.*

If every cycle through a state p visits a fair set in some other state, we do not need to include p in that fair set.

Theorem 8. *Let $\mathcal{A} = \langle Q, Q_0, \delta, \mathcal{F}, D, \mathcal{L} \rangle$ be a Büchi automaton. Let $F \in \mathcal{F}$, and p a state in F such that every cycle through p intersects F in a state different from p. Let $\mathcal{M} = \langle Q, Q_0, \delta, \mathcal{F}_M, D, \mathcal{L} \rangle$, where $\mathcal{F}_M = (\mathcal{F} \setminus F) \cup \{F \setminus \{p\}\}$. Then $L(\mathcal{A}) = L(\mathcal{M})$.*

After application of the results presented in this section, a Büchi automaton may still have multiple fair sets. It is well-known that we can always reduce the number of acceptance conditions to one by introducing a counter. This is not usually done because the algorithm of Emerson and Lei [7] deals with multiple acceptance conditions. However, for weak and terminal automata, we do not need to resort to the counter to reduce the number of fair sets to one.

Definition 6. *A Büchi automaton is* weak *if and only if for each SCC* γ, *either for each fair set* F, $\gamma \subset F$, *or there exists a fair set* F *such that* $\gamma \cap F = \emptyset$. *A Büchi automaton is* terminal *if and only if it is weak, there is no arc from a fair SCC to a non-fair SCC, and for every state s in a fair SCC,* $\bigcup \{\mathcal{L}(t) : t \in \delta(s)\} = D$.

Theorem 9. *Let* $\mathcal{A} = \langle Q, Q_0, \delta, \mathcal{F}, D, \mathcal{L} \rangle$ *be a weak (generalized) Büchi automaton. Let* $\mathcal{M} = \langle Q, Q_0, \delta, \{\Theta_A\}, D, \mathcal{L} \rangle$. *Then* $L(\mathcal{A}) = L(\mathcal{M})$.

States that are not in Θ_A can be added to fair sets as long as Θ_A is not changed by the addition. In particular, states in trivial SCCs are "don't care" states when it comes to checking the conditions on $\mathcal{F}$ in Definition 3.

The automaton simplification procedure prunes the fair sets a first time before applying simulation-based simplification, because smaller fair sets tend to produce larger simulation relations. The simulation-based techniques may break up SCCs because they remove arcs. Hence, pruning is performed a second time after they are applied. This can be iterated until a fixpoint is reached, but the benefits are minor and the extra CPU time comparatively large.

7 Experimental Results

In this section we report the results obtained with a translator from LTL to Büchi automata named *Wring* and based on the results discussed thus far. *Wring* is written in Perl. Based on our experience, we estimate that speed could be increased by at least an order of magnitude by coding the algorithms in C. However, CPU times are modest, and even a relatively slow implementation is more than adequate.

Table 1 shows a comparison to the algorithms analyzed in [5] on common formulae and formulae found in the literature. It should be noted that the outcomes of the translation algorithms depend on the order in which sub-formulae are examined. Hence, different implementations may produce different results. Rewriting of the formula (see Section 3) is most effective in detecting tautologies and contradictions. The transformations discussed in Section 6 are quite effective in reducing the number of fair sets.

Table 2 shows results for randomly generated formulae [5], showing the effects of each of the three major extensions that we propose. It should be noted that working on simpler formulae and smaller automata offsets most of the additional cost of minimization. One can see from Table 2 that the reduction in transitions and fair sets corresponds to an increase in the number of terminal automata. Though we do not present a detailed analysis of the dependence of the results on the statistics of the formulae (number of nodes, number of atomic propositions, and percentage of temporal operators), we have observed the same trends reported in [5].

8 Conclusions and Future Work

We have presented a heuristic algorithm for the generation of small Büchi automata from LTL formulae. It works in three stages: rewriting of the formula, boolean optimization

Table 1. Comparison to our implementation of the algorithms analyzed in [5]. For each formula and each method, the numbers of states, transitions, and accepting conditions are given. The letters in the accepting sets columns indicate whether the automata are strong (s), weak (w), or terminal (t).

Formula	GPVW st.	GPVW tran.	GPVW acc.	GPVW+ st.	GPVW+ tran.	GPVW+ acc.	LTL2AUT st.	LTL2AUT tran.	LTL2AUT acc.	Wring st.	Wring tran.	Wring acc.
$p \cup q$	3	4	1t	3	4	1t	3	4	1t	3	4	1t
$p \cup (q \cup r)$	6	10	2t	6	10	2t	4	7	2t	4	7	1t
$\neg(p \cup (q \cup r))$	7	15	0w	7	15	0w	7	15	0w	6	10	0w
$GFp \to GFq$	9	15	2s	5	8	2s	5	11	2s	4	7	1s
$Fp \cup Gq$	8	15	2w	8	15	2w	6	17	2w	3	4	1w
$Gp \cup q$	5	6	1w	5	6	1w	5	6	1w	5	6	1w
$\neg(FFp \leftrightarrow Fp)$	12	16	2t	1	1	2t	1	1	2t	0	0	0t
$\neg(GFp \to GFq)$	10	28	2s	6	16	2s	6	24	2s	3	6	1s
$\neg(GFp \leftrightarrow GFq)$	20	56	4s	12	32	4s	12	48	4s	5	11	1s
$p R (p \vee q)$	5	11	0w	5	11	0w	4	8	0w	3	4	0w
$(X(p) \cup X(q)) \vee \neg X(p \cup q)$	9	13	1w	9	13	1w	9	13	1w	1	1	0t
$(X(p) \cup q) \vee \neg X(p \cup (p \wedge q))$	10	21	1w	10	21	1w	9	17	1w	7	12	1w
$G(p \to Fq) \wedge ((X(p) \cup q) \vee \neg X(p \cup (p \wedge q)))$	29	149	2s	23	118	2s	17	56	2s	10	23	1s
$G(p \to Fq) \wedge ((X(p) \cup X(q)) \vee \neg X(p \cup q))$	26	93	2s	24	78	2s	20	51	2s	3	8	1s
$G(p \to Fq)$	5	17	1s	5	17	1s	3	8	1s	3	8	1s
$\neg G(p \to X(q R r))$	5	8	2w	5	8	2w	5	8	2w	5	8	1t
$\neg(GFp \vee FGq)$	10	28	2s	6	16	2s	6	24	2s	3	6	1s
$G(Fp \wedge Fq)$	4	16	2s	4	16	2s	8	40	2s	3	9	2s
$Fp \wedge F \neg p$	11	21	2t	8	14	2t	8	14	2t	5	7	1t
$(X(q) \wedge r) R X(((s \cup p) R r) \cup (s R r))$	130	1013	2s	78	483	2s	64	378	2s	8	13	1w
$(G(q \vee GFp) \wedge G(r \vee GF \neg p)) \vee Gq \vee Gr$	33	320	2s	23	234	2s	14	71	2s	4	6	2s
$(G(q \vee FGp) \wedge G(r \vee FG \neg p)) \vee Gq \vee Gr$	51	368	2w	29	170	2w	10	29	2w	2	2	0w
$\neg((G(q \vee GFp) \wedge G(r \vee GF \neg p)) \vee Gq \vee Gr)$	132	428	6w	106	310	6w	64	230	6w	11	26	1w
$\neg((G(q \vee FGp) \wedge G(r \vee FG \neg p)) \vee Gq \vee Gr)$	114	478	6s	78	288	6s	66	289	6s	21	32	1s
$G(q \vee XGp) \wedge G(r \vee XG \neg p)$	16	40	0w	12	28	0w	10	20	0w	5	7	0w
$G(q \vee (Xp \wedge X \neg p))$	2	2	0w	1	1	0w	1	1	0w	1	1	0w
$(p \cup p) \vee (q \cup p)$	9	13	2t	5	7	2t	5	7	2t	3	3	1t
Total	681	3204	51	484	1940	51	372	1397	51	122	231	22

Table 2. Results for 1000 random formulae with parse graphs of 15 nodes, using 3 atomic propositions, and uniform distribution of the operators ($\vee, \wedge, X, U, R$) for the internal nodes. In the designation of the method, 'r' stands for rewriting, 'b' stands for boolean optimization, and 's' stands for automaton simplification. Method Wring is equivalent to LTL2AUT+rbs. The experiments were run on an IBM Intellistation with a 400 MHz Pentium II CPU.

Method	states	transitions	fair sets	initial states	weak	terminal	CPU time (s)
GPVW	34216	137565	1555	4388	743	87	1195.0
GPVW+	29231	114146	1555	4246	745	95	1016.1
LTL2AUT	19424	62370	1555	3803	718	136	640.5
LTL2AUT+r	9430	25722	747	2117	511	374	209.7
LTL2AUT+b	13213	29573	1555	3161	738	162	1047.4
LTL2AUT+s	6063	11300	637	1628	362	552	1229.8
LTL2AUT+rb	7632	16124	747	1998	532	385	439.9
LTL2AUT+rs	5800	10624	491	1569	382	531	527.6
LTL2AUT+bs	5834	10525	620	1553	354	568	1292.2
Wring	5648	10053	492	1535	390	537	631.4

to reduce the number of states in the translation procedure, and simplification of the automaton. Rewriting is a cheap, simple, and effective technique to shrink the formula and reduce redundancy. The boolean optimization technique that we have presented yields the smallest translation of any procedure in its class. We do not know of any translation procedures that do not fall within this class, its most important characteristic being the use of the given expansion functions. Since the optimal algorithm is expensive, we have implemented a heuristic approximation. Finally, the simplification step uses direct and reverse simulation to minimize the number of states and transitions in the formula, and it prunes the acceptance conditions to make the emptiness check easier.

We have shown that our algorithm outperforms previously published algorithms on both random formulae, and formulae in common use and from the literature.

We are investigating weaker relations that allow for state minimization, and can still be computed efficiently. In particular, we are working on combinations of direct and reverse simulation, and simulation with less strict conditions on the acceptance conditions such as *BSR-lc* of [6]. Another area of investigation is the use of semantic information about the literals in the simplification of elementary covers. For symbolic model checking, the automata must be given binary encodings. A careful choice of the state encodings and the use of don't care conditions derived from simulation relations and from the analysis of the SCCs of the graph should help reduce the cost of the language emptiness check.

Acknowledgment

The authors thank Kavita Ravi for stimulating discussions on language containment and for her many comments on various drafts of this manuscript.

References

[1] A. Aziz, V. Singhal, G. M. Swamy, and R. K. Brayton. Minimizing interacting finite state machines. In *Proceedings of the International Conference on Computer Design*, pages 255–261, Cambridge, MA, October 1994.

[2] R. Bloem, K. Ravi, and F. Somenzi. Efficient decision procedures for model checking of linear time logic properties. In N. Halbwachs and D. Peled, editors, *Eleventh Conference on Computer Aided Verification (CAV'99)*, pages 222–235. Springer-Verlag, Berlin, 1999. LNCS 1633.

[3] R. K. Brayton, G. D. Hachtel, C. T. McMullen, and A. Sangiovanni-Vincentelli. *Logic Minimization Algorithms for VLSI Synthesis*. Kluwer Academic Publishers, Boston, Massachusetts, 1984.

[4] J. R. Burch, E. M. Clarke, K. L. McMillan, D. L. Dill, and L. J. Hwang. Symbolic model checking: 10^{20} states and beyond. *Information and Computation*, 98:142–170, 1992.

[5] M. Daniele, F. Giunchiglia, and M. Y. Vardi. Improved automata generation for linear time temporal logic. In N. Halbwachs and D. Peled, editors, *Eleventh Conference on Computer Aided Verification (CAV'99)*, pages 249–260. Springer-Verlag, Berlin, 1999. LNCS 1633.

[6] D. L. Dill, A. J. Hu, and H. Wong-Toi. Checking for language inclusion using simulation relations. In K. G. Larsen and A. Skou, editors, *Third Workshop on Computer Aided Verification (CAV'91)*, pages 255–265. Springer, Berlin, July 1991. LNCS 575.

[7] E. A. Emerson and C.-L. Lei. Efficient model checking in fragments of the propositional mu-calculus. In *Proceedings of the First Annual Symposium of Logic in Computer Science*, pages 267–278, June 1986.

[8] K. Etessami and G. Holzmann. Optimizing Büchi automata. Submitted for publication, 2000.

[9] R. Gerth, D. Peled, M. Y. Vardi, and P. Wolper. Simple on-the-fly automatic verification of linear temporal logic. In *Protocol Specification, Testing, and Verification*, pages 3–18. Chapman & Hall, 1995.

[10] A. Grasselli and F. Luccio. A method for minimizing the number of internal states in incompletely specified sequential networks. *IEEE Transactions on Electronic Computers*, EC-14(3):350–359, June 1965.

[11] Y. Kesten, Z. Manna, H. McGuire, and A. Pnueli. Checking that finite-state concurrent programs satisfy their linear specification. In *Proceedings of the 11th ACM Symposium on Principles of Programming Languages*, pages 97–107, 1984.

[12] Y. Kesten, A. Pnueli, and L.-o. Raviv. Algorithmic verification of linear temporal logic specifications. In *International Colloquium on Automata, Languages, and Programming (ICALP-98)*, pages 1–16, Berlin, 1998. Springer. LNCS 1443.

[13] O. Kupferman and M. Y. Vardi. Freedom, weakness, and determinism: From linear-time to branching-time. In *Proc. 13th IEEE Symposium on Logic in Computer Science*, June 1998.

[14] O. Lichtenstein and A. Pnueli. Checking that finite state concurrent programs satisfy their linear specification. In *Proceedings of the Twelfth Annual ACM Symposium on Principles of Programming Languages*, New Orleans, January 1985.

[15] E. J. McCluskey, Jr. Minimization of boolean functions. *Bell Syst. Technical Journal*, 35:1417–1444, November 1956.

[16] R. Milner. An algebraic definition of simulation between programs. *Proc. 2nd Int. Joint Conf. on Artificial Intelligence*, pages 481–489, 1971.

[17] R. S. Raimi. *Environment Modeling and Efficient State Reachability Checking*. PhD thesis, University of Texas at Austin, 1999.

[18] P. Wolper, M. Y. Vardi, and A. P. Sistla. Reasoning about infinite computation paths. In *Proceedings of the 24th IEEE Symposyium on Foundations of Computer Science*, pages 185–194, 1983.

Efficient Detection of Global Properties in Distributed Systems Using Partial-Order Methods*

Scott D. Stoller, Leena Unnikrishnan, and Yanhong A. Liu

Computer Science Dept., Indiana University, Bloomington, IN 47405-7104 USA

Abstract. A new approach is presented for detecting whether a particular computation of an asynchronous distributed system satisfies **Poss** Φ (read "possibly Φ"), meaning the system could have passed through a global state satisfying predicate Φ, or **Def** Φ (read "definitely Φ"), meaning the system definitely passed through a global state satisfying Φ. Detection can be done easily by straightforward state-space search; this is essentially what Cooper and Marzullo proposed. We show that the persistent-set technique, a well-known partial-order method for optimizing state-space search, provides efficient detection. This approach achieves the same worst-case asymptotic time complexity as two special-purpose detection algorithms of Garg and Waldecker that detect **Poss** Φ and **Def** Φ for a restricted but important class of predicates. For **Poss** Φ, our approach applies to arbitrary predicates and thus is more general than Garg and Waldecker's algorithm. We apply our algorithm for **Poss** Φ to two examples, achieving a speedup of over 700 in one example and over 70 in the other, compared to unoptimized state-space search.

1 Introduction

Detecting global properties (*i.e.*, predicates on global states) in distributed systems is useful for monitoring and debugging. For example, when testing a distributed mutual exclusion algorithm, it is useful to monitor the system to detect concurrent accesses to the critical sections. A system that performs leader election may be monitored to ensure that processes agree on the current leader. A system that dynamically partitions and re-partitions a large dataset among a set of processors may be monitored to ensure that each portion of the dataset is assigned to exactly one processor.

An *asynchronous* distributed system is characterized by lack of synchronized clocks and lack of bounds on processor speed and network latency. In such a system, no process can determine in general the order in which events on different processors actually occurred. Therefore, no process can determine in general the

---

* The authors gratefully acknowledge the support of NSF under Grants CCR-9876058 and CCR-9711253 and the support of ONR under Grants N00014-99-1-0358 and N00014-99-1-0132. Email: {stoller,lunnikri,liu}@cs.indiana.edu Web: http://www.cs.indiana.edu/~{stoller,lunnikri,liu}/

sequence of global states through which the system passed. This leads to an obvious difficulty for detecting whether a global property held.

Cooper and Marzullo's solution to this difficulty involves two modalities, which we denote by **Poss** (read "possibly") and **Def** (read "definitely") [CM91]. These modalities are based on logical time as embodied in the *happened-before* relation, a partial order that reflects causal dependencies [Lam78]. A history of an asynchronous distributed system can be approximated by a *computation*, which comprises the local computation of each process together with the happened-before relation. Happened-before is useful for detection algorithms because, using vector clocks [Fid88,Mat89,SW89], it can be determined by processes in the system.

Happened-before is not a total order, so it does not uniquely determine the history. But it does restrict the possibilities. Histories *consistent* with a computation c are those sequences of the events in c that correspond to total orders containing the happened-before relation. A *consistent global state* (CGS) of a computation c is a global state that appears in some history consistent with c. A computation c satisfies **Poss** Φ iff, in *some* history consistent with c, the system passes through a global state satisfying Φ. A computation c satisfies **Def** Φ iff, in *all* histories consistent with c, the system passes through a global state satisfying Φ.

Cooper and Marzullo give centralized algorithms for detecting **Poss** Φ and **Def** Φ [CM91]. A stub at each process reports the local states of that process to a central monitor. The monitor incrementally constructs a lattice whose elements correspond to CGSs of the computation. **Poss** Φ and **Def** Φ are evaluated by straightforward traversals of the lattice. In a system of N processes, the worst-case number of CGSs, which can occur in computations containing little communication, is $\Theta(S^N)$, where S is the maximum number of steps taken by a single process. Any detection algorithm that enumerates all CGSs—like the algorithms in [CM91,MN91,JMN95,AV94]—has time complexity that is at least linear in the number of CGSs. This time complexity can be prohibitive. This motivated the development of efficient algorithms for detecting restricted classes of predicates [TG93,GW94,GW96,CG98]. The algorithms of Garg and Waldecker are classic examples of this approach. A predicate is *n-local* if it depends on the local states of at most n processes. In [GW94] and [GW96], Garg and Waldecker give efficient algorithms that detect **Poss** Φ and **Def** Φ, respectively, for predicates Φ that are conjunctions of 1-local predicates. Those two algorithms are presented as two independent works, with little relationship to each other or to existing techniques.

This paper shows that efficient detection of global predicates can be done using a well-known partial-order method. *Partial-order methods* are optimized state-space search algorithms that try to avoid exploring multiple interleavings of independent transitions [PPH97]. This approach achieves the same worst-case asymptotic time complexity as the two aforementioned algorithms of Garg and Waldecker, assuming weak vector clocks [MN91], which are updated only by events that can change the truth value of Φ and by receive events by which a process first learns of some event that can change the truth value of Φ, are used with our algorithm. Specifically, we show that persistent-sct selective search [God96] can be used to detect **Poss** Φ or **Def** Φ for conjunctions of 1-local predicates with time complexity $O(N^2 S)$. In some non-worst cases, Garg and Waldecker's algorithms may be faster than ours by up to a factor of N, because their algorithms also incorporate an idea, not captured by partial-order methods, by which the algorithm ignores local states of a process that do not satisfy the 1-local predicate associated with that process. For details, see [SUL99].

Our method for detecting **Def** Φ handles only conjunctions of 1-local predicates. Our method for detecting **Poss** Φ handles arbitrary predicates and thus is more general than Garg and Waldecker's algorithm. Furthermore, our method is asymptotically faster than Cooper and Marzullo's algorithm for some classes of systems to which Garg and Waldecker's algorithm does not apply. For some other classes of systems, although our method has the same asymptotic worst-case complexity as Cooper and Marzullo's algorithm, we expect our method to be significantly faster in practice; this is typical of general experience with partial-order methods. Our algorithm for detecting **Poss** Φ can be further optimized to sometimes explore sequences of transitions in a single step. This can provide significant speedup, even reducing the asymptotic time and space complexities for certain classes of systems.

We give simple specialized algorithms PS_{Poss} and PS_{Def} for computing persistent sets for detection of **Poss** Φ and **Def** Φ, respectively. These algorithms exploit the structure of the problem in order to efficiently compute small persistent sets. One could instead use a general-purpose algorithm for computing persistent sets, such as the conditional stubborn set algorithm (CSSA) [God96, Section 4.7], which is based on Valmari's work on stubborn sets [Val97]. When CSSA is used for detecting **Poss** Φ, it is either ineffective (*i.e.*, it returns the set of all enabled transitions) or slower than PS_{Poss} by a factor of S (and possibly by some factors of N) in the worst case, depending on how it is applied. The cheaper algorithms for computing persistent sets in [God96] are ineffective for detecting **Poss** Φ. When CSSA (or any of the other algorithms in [God96]) is used for detecting **Def** Φ, it is ineffective. Detailed justifications of these claims appear in [SUL99].

For simplicity, we present algorithms for *off-line* property detection, in which the detection algorithm is run after the distributed computation has terminated. Our approach can also be applied to *on-line* property detection, in which a monitor runs concurrently with the system being monitored.

Property detection is a special case of model-checking of temporal logics interpreted over partially-ordered sets of global configurations, as described in [AMP98,Wal98]. Those papers do not discuss in detail the use of partial-order methods to avoid exploring all global states and do not characterize classes of global predicates for which partial-order methods reduce the worst-case asymptotic time complexity. Alur *et al.* give a decision procedure for the logic ISTL$^\diamond$. **Poss** Φ is expressible in ISTL$^\diamond$ as $\exists \Diamond \Phi$. **Def** Φ is expressible in ISTL as $\neg \exists \Box \neg \Phi$ but appears not to be directly expressible in ISTL$^\diamond$.

An avenue for future work is to try to extend this approach to efficient analysis of message sequence charts [MPS98,AY99].

2 Background on Property Detection

A local state of a process is a mapping from identifiers to values. Thus, $s(v)$ denotes the value of variable v in local state s. A *history* of a single process is represented as a sequence of that process's states. Let $[m..n]$ denote the set of integers from m to n, inclusive. We use integers $[1..N]$ as process names.

In the distributed computing literature, the most common representation of a *computation* c of an asynchronous distributed system is a collection of histories $c[1], \ldots, c[N]$, one for each constituent process, together with a *happened-before* relation $\to$ on local states [GW94]. For a sequence h, let $h[k]$ denote the kth element of h (i.e., we use 1-based indexing), and let $|h|$ denote the length of h. Intuitively, a local state s_1 happened-before a local state s_2 if s_1 finished before s_2 started. Formally, $\to$ is the smallest transitive relation on the local states in c such that

1. $\forall i \in [1..N], k \in [1..|c[i]|-1] : c[i][k] \to c[i][k+1])$.
2. For all local states s_1 and s_2 in c, if the event immediately following s_1 is the sending of a message and the event immediately preceding s_2 is the reception of that message, then $s_1 \to s_2$.

We always use S to denote the maximum number of local states per process, i.e., $\max(|c[1]|, \ldots, |c[N]|)$.

Each process has a distinguished variable vt such that for each local state s, $s(vt)$ is a *vector timestamp* [Mat89], i.e., an array of N natural numbers such that $s(vt)[i]$ is the number of local states of process i that happened-before s. Vector timestamps capture the happened-before relation. Specifically, for all local states s_1 and s_2, $s_1 \to s_2$ iff $(\forall i \in [1..N] : s_1(vt)[i] \leq s_2(vt)[i])$. Two local states s_1 and s_2 of a computation are *concurrent*, denoted $s_1 \parallel s_2$, iff neither happened-before the other: $s_1 \parallel s_2 = s_1 \not\to s_2 \land s_2 \not\to s_1$.

A *global state* s of a computation c is an array of N local states such that, for each process i, $s[i]$ appears in $c[i]$. A global state is *consistent* iff its constituent local states are pairwise concurrent. Intuitively, consistency means that the system could have passed through that global state during the computation.

Concurrency of two local states can be tested in constant time using vector timestamps by exploiting the following theorem [FR94]: for a local state s_1 of process i_1 and a local state s_2 of process i_2, $s_1 \parallel s_2$ iff $s_2(vt)[i_2] \geq s_1(vt)[i_2] \land s_1(vt)[i_1] \geq s_2(vt)[i_1]$. Thus, a global state s is consistent iff $(\forall i, j \in [1..N] : s[i](vt)[i] \geq s[j](vt)[i])$.

A computation c satisfies $\textbf{Poss}\,\Phi$, denoted $c \models \textbf{Poss}\,\Phi$, iff there exists a CGS of c that satisfies Φ.

Introduce a partial order $\prec_G$ on global states: $s_1 \preceq_G s_2 = (\forall i \in [1..N] : s_1[i] = s_2[i] \lor s_1[i] \to s_2[i])$. A *history consistent with* a computation c is a finite or infinite sequence σ of consistent global states of c such that, with respect to

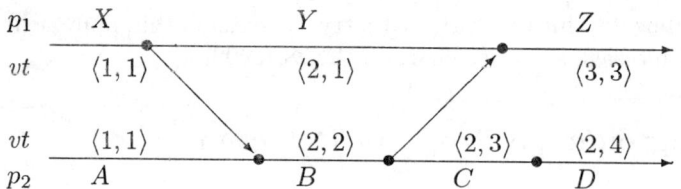

Fig. 1. Computation c_0.

$\preceq_G$: (i) $\sigma[1]$ is minimal; (ii) for all $k \in [1..|\sigma|-1]$, $\sigma[k+1]$ is an immediate successor[1] of $\sigma[k]$; and (iii) if σ is finite, then $\sigma[|\sigma|]$ is maximal.

A computation c satisfies **Def** Φ, denoted $c \models$ **Def** Φ, iff every history consistent with c contains a global state satisfying Φ.

Example. Consider the computation c_0 shown in Figure 1. Horizontal lines correspond to processes; diagonal lines, to messages. Dots represent events. Each process has a variable vt containing the vector time. Variable p_i contains the rest of process i's local state. Let s_{k_1,k_2} denote the global state comprising the k_1'th local state of process 1 and the k_2'th local state of process 2. The CGSs of c_0 are $\{s_{1,1}, s_{2,1}, s_{2,2}, s_{2,3}, s_{3,3}, s_{2,4}, s_{3,4}\}$. Some properties of this computation are: $c_0 \models$ **Poss** $(p_1 = Y \wedge p_2 = D)$, $c_0 \models$ **Def** $(p_1 = Y \wedge p_2 = B)$, $c_0 \not\models$ **Def** $(p_1 = Y \wedge p_2 = D)$, and $c_0 \not\models$ **Poss** $(p_1 = X \wedge p_2 = B)$.

3 Background on Partial-Order Methods

The material in this section is paraphrased from [God96]. Beware! The system model in this section differs from the model of distributed computations in the previous section. For example, "state" has different meanings in the two models. Sections 4 and 5 give mappings from the former model to the latter.

A concurrent system is a collection of finite-state automata that interact via shared variables (more generally, shared objects). More formally, a *concurrent system* is a tuple $\langle \mathcal{P}, \mathcal{O}, \mathcal{T}, s_{init} \rangle$, where

- $\mathcal{P}$ is a set $\{P_1, \ldots, P_N\}$ of processes. A *process* is a finite set of control points.
- $\mathcal{O}$ is a set of shared variables.
- $\mathcal{T}$ is a set of transitions. A *transition* is a tuple $\langle L_1, G, C, L_2 \rangle$, where: L_1 is a set of control points, at most one from each process; L_2 is a set of control points of the same processes as L_1, and with at most one control point from each process; G is a guard, *i.e.*, a boolean-valued expression over the shared variables; and C is a command, *i.e.*, a sequence of operations that update the shared variables.
- s_{init} is the initial state of the system.

---

[1] For a reflexive or irreflexive partial order $\langle S, \prec \rangle$ and elements $x \in S$ and $y \in S$, y is an *immediate successor* of x iff $x \neq y \wedge x \prec y \wedge \neg(\exists z \in S \setminus \{x,y\} : x \prec z \wedge z \prec y)$.

A (global) state is a tuple $\langle L, V \rangle$, where L is a collection of control points, one from each process, and V is a collection of values, one for each shared variable. For a state s and a shared variable v, we abuse notation and write $s(v)$ to denote the value of v in s (the same notation is used in Section 2 but with a different definition of "state"). Similarly, for a state s and a predicate ϕ, we write $s(\phi)$ to denote the value of ϕ in s. A transition $\langle L_1, G, C, L_2 \rangle$ is *enabled* in state $\langle L, V \rangle$ if $L_1 \subseteq L$ and G evaluates to true using the values in V. Let $enabled(s)$ denote the set of transitions enabled in s. If a transition $\langle L_1, G, C, L_2 \rangle$ is enabled in state $s = \langle L, V \rangle$, then it can be executed in s, leading to the state $\langle (L \setminus L_1) \cup L_2, C(V) \rangle$, where $C(V)$ represents the new values obtained by using the operations in C to update the values in V. We write $s \xrightarrow{t} s'$ to indicate that transition t is enabled in state s and executing t in s leads to state s'.

An *execution* of a concurrent system is a finite or infinite sequence $s_1 \xrightarrow{t_1} s_2 \xrightarrow{t_2} s_3 \cdots$ such that $s_1 = s_{init}$ and for all i, $s_i \xrightarrow{t_i} s_{i+1}$. A state is *reachable* (in a system) if it appears in some execution (of that system).

Suppose we wish to find all the "deadlocks" of a system. Following Godefroid (but deviating from standard usage), a *deadlock* is a state in which no transitions are enabled. Clearly, all reachable deadlocks can be identified by exploring all reachable states. This involves explicitly considering all possible execution orderings of transitions, even if some transitions are "independent" (*i.e.*, executing them in any order leads to the same state; formal definition appears in Appendix). Exploring one interleaving of independent transitions is sufficient for finding deadlocks. This does cause fewer intermediate states (*i.e.*, states in which some but not all of the independent transitions have been executed) to be explored, but it does not affect reachability of deadlocks, because the intermediate states cannot be deadlocks, because some of the independent transitions are enabled in those states. Partial-order methods attempt to eliminate exploration of multiple interleavings of independent transitions, thereby saving time and space.

A set T of transitions enabled in a state s is persistent in s if, for every sequence of transitions starting from s and not containing any transitions in T, all transitions in that sequence are independent with all transitions in T. Formally, a set $T \subseteq enabled(s)$ is *persistent* in s iff, for all nonempty sequences of transitions $s_1 \xrightarrow{t_1} s_2 \xrightarrow{t_2} s_3 \cdots \xrightarrow{t_{n-1}} s_n \xrightarrow{t_n} s_{n+1}$, if $s_1 = s$ and $(\forall i \in [1..n] : t_i \notin T)$, then t_n is independent in s_n with all transitions in T. As shown in [God96], in order to find all reachable deadlocks, it suffices to explore from each state s a set of transitions that is persistent in s. State-space search algorithms that do this are called *persistent-set selective search* (PSSS). Note that $enabled(s)$ is trivially persistent in s. To save time and space, small persistent sets should be used.

4 Detecting Poss Φ

Given a computation c and a predicate Φ, we construct a concurrent system whose executions correspond to histories consistent with c, express $c \models \mathbf{Poss}\,\Phi$

as a question about reachable deadlocks of that system, and use PSSS to answer that question. The system has one transition for each pair of consecutive local states in c, plus a transition t_0 whose guard is Φ. t_0 disables all transitions, so it always leads to a deadlock.

Each process has a distinct control point corresponding to each of its local states. The control point corresponding to the k'th local state of process i is denoted $\ell_{i,k}$. Thus, for $i \in [1..N]$, process i is $P_i = \bigcup_{k=1..|c[i]|}\{\ell_{i,k}\}$. We introduce a new process, called process 0, that monitors Φ. Process 0 has a single transition t_0, which changes the control point of process 0 from $\ell_{0,nd}$ (mnemonic for "not detected") to $\ell_{0,d}$ ("detected"). Thus, process 0 is $P_0 = \{\ell_{0,nd}, \ell_{0,d}\}$. The set of processes is $\mathcal{P} = \bigcup_{i=0..N}\{P_i\}$. Initially, process 0 is at control point $\ell_{0,nd}$, and for $i > 0$, process i is at control point $\ell_{i,1}$.

The local state of process i is stored in a shared variable p_i. The initial value of p_i is $c[i][1]$. For convenience, the index of the current local state of process i is stored in a shared variable τ_i. The initial value of τ_i is 1, and τ_i is incremented by each transition of process i. Whenever process i is at control point $\ell_{i,k}$, τ_i equals k. The set of shared variables is $\mathcal{O} = \bigcup_{i=1..N}\{p_i, \tau_i\}$.

Transition $t_{i,k}$ takes process i from its k'th local state to its $(k+1)$'th local state. $t_{i,k}$ is enabled when process i is at control point $\ell_{i,k}$, process 0 is at control point $\ell_{0,nd}$, τ_i equals k, and the $(k+1)$'th local state of process i is concurrent with the current local states of the other processes. The set of transitions is $\mathcal{T} = \{t_0\} \cup \bigcup_{i=1..N, k=1..|c[i]|-1}\{t_{i,k}\}$, where $t_0 = \langle\{\ell_{0,nd}\}, \Phi(p_1, \ldots, p_N), \text{skip}, \{\ell_{0,d}\}\rangle$ and

$$t_{i,k} = \langle\{\ell_{i,k}, \ell_{0,nd}\}, \tag{1}$$
$$\tau_i = k \wedge (\forall j \in [1..N] \setminus \{i\} : c[j][\tau_j](vt)[j] \geq c[i][k+1](vt)[j]),$$
$$p_i := c[i][k+1]; \ \tau_i := k+1,$$
$$\{\ell_{i,k+1}, \ell_{0,nd}\}\rangle$$

The guard can be simplified by noting that $c[i][\tau_i](vt)[i]$ always equals τ_i. It is easy to show that $\ell_{0,d}$ is reachable iff a state satisfying Φ is reachable, and that all states containing $\ell_{0,d}$ are deadlocks. Thus, $c \models \mathbf{Poss}\,\Phi$ iff a deadlock containing $\ell_{0,d}$ is reachable.

Example. The transitions of the concurrent system corresponding to c_0 of Figure 1 are t_0 and

$$\begin{aligned}
t_{1,1} &= \langle\{\ell_{1,1}, \ell_{0,nd}\}, \tau_1 = 1 \wedge \tau_2 \geq 1, p_1 := Y; \tau_1 := 2, \{\ell_{1,2}, \ell_{0,nd}\}\rangle \\
t_{1,2} &= \langle\{\ell_{1,2}, \ell_{0,nd}\}, \tau_1 = 2 \wedge \tau_2 \geq 3, p_1 := Z; \tau_1 := 3, \{\ell_{1,3}, \ell_{0,nd}\}\rangle \\
t_{2,1} &= \langle\{\ell_{2,1}, \ell_{0,nd}\}, \tau_2 = 1 \wedge \tau_1 \geq 2, p_2 := B; \tau_2 := 2, \{\ell_{2,2}, \ell_{0,nd}\}\rangle \quad (2)\\
t_{2,2} &= \langle\{\ell_{2,2}, \ell_{0,nd}\}, \tau_2 = 2 \wedge \tau_1 \geq 2, p_2 := C; \tau_2 := 3, \{\ell_{2,3}, \ell_{0,nd}\}\rangle \\
t_{2,3} &= \langle\{\ell_{2,3}, \ell_{0,nd}\}, \tau_2 = 3 \wedge \tau_1 \geq 2, p_2 := D; \tau_2 := 4, \{\ell_{2,4}, \ell_{0,nd}\}\rangle
\end{aligned}$$

An alternative is to construct a transition system similar to the one above but in which both occurrences of $\ell_{0,nd}$ in $t_{i,k}$ are deleted. As before, $c \models \mathbf{Poss}\,\Phi$ iff $\ell_{0,d}$ is reachable (or, equivalently, t_0 is reachable), but now, states containing $\ell_{0,d}$ are not necessarily deadlocks. PSSS can be used to determine reachability of control points (or transitions), provided the dependency relation is weakly uniform [God96, Section 6.3]. Showing that the dependency relation is weakly uniform requires more effort than including $\ell_{0,nd}$ in $t_{i,k}$ and has no benefit: we obtain essentially the same detection algorithm either way.

We give a simple algorithm PS_{Poss} that efficiently computes a small persistent set in a state s by exploiting the structure of Φ. Without loss of generality, we write Φ as a conjunction: $\Phi = \bigwedge_{i=1..n} \phi_i$, with $n \geq 1$. The *support* of a formula ϕ, denoted $supp(\phi)$, is the set of processes on whose local states ϕ depends. Suppose Φ is true in s. Then $\text{PS}_{\text{Poss}}(s)$ returns $enabled(s)$. When such a state is reached, there is no need to try to find a small persistent set, because we can immediately halt the search and return "$c \models \textbf{Poss}\,\Phi$". We return "$c \not\models \textbf{Poss}\,\Phi$" if the selective search terminates without encountering a state satisfying Φ; by construction, this is equivalent to unreachability of deadlocks containing $\ell_{0,d}$. Suppose Φ is false in s. The handling of this case is based on the following theorem, a proof of which appears in the Appendix.

Theorem 1. *Suppose Φ is false in s. Let T be a subset of $enabled(s)$ such that, for all sequences of transitions starting from s and staying outside T, Φ remains false; more precisely, for all sequences of transitions $s_1 \xrightarrow{t_1} s_2 \xrightarrow{t_2} \cdots s_n \xrightarrow{t_n} s_{n+1}$, if $s_1 = s$ and $(\forall i \in [1..n] : t_i \notin T)$, then Φ is false in s_{n+1}. Then T is persistent in s.*

To construct such a set T, choose some conjunct ϕ of Φ that is false in s. Clearly, Φ cannot become true until ϕ does, and ϕ cannot become true until the next transition of some process in $supp(\phi)$ is executed. Note that the next transition of process i must be $t_{i,s(\tau_i)}$. Thus, for each process i in $supp(\phi)$, if process i is not in its final state (*i.e.*, $s(\tau_i) < |c[i]|$), and if the next transition $t_{i,s(\tau_i)}$ of process i is enabled, then add $t_{i,s(\tau_i)}$ to T, otherwise find some enabled transition t that must execute before $t_{i,s(\tau_i)}$, and add t to T. To find such a t, we introduce the *wait-for graph* $WF(s)$, which has nodes $[1..N]$, and has an edge from i to j if the next transition of process j must execute before the next transition of process i, *i.e.*, if $s(\tau_j) < c[i][s(\tau_i)+1](vt)[j]$ (we call this a wait-for graph because of its similarity to the wait-for graphs used for deadlock detection [SG98, Section 7.6.1]). Such a transition t can be found by starting at node i in $WF(s)$, following any path until a node j with no outedges is reached, and taking t to be $t_{j,s(\tau_j)}$. The case in which $t_{i,s(\tau_i)}$ is enabled is a special case of this construction, corresponding to a path of length zero, which implies $i = j$. Pseudo-code appears in Figure 2.

The wait-for graph can be incrementally maintained in $O(N)$ time per transition. Let $d = \max(|supp(\phi_1)|, \ldots, |supp(\phi_n)|)$. $\text{PS}_{\text{Poss}}(s)$ returns a set of size at most d if Φ is false in s. Computing $\text{PS}_{\text{Poss}}(s)$ takes $O(Nd)$ time, because the algorithm follows at most d paths of length at most N in the wait-for graph. Thus, the overall time complexity of the search is $O(NdN_e)$, where N_e is the number of states explored by the algorithm.

Suppose Φ is a conjunction of 1-local predicates. Then PS_{Poss} returns sets of size at most 1, except when Φ is true in s, in which case the search is halted immediately, as described above. Thus, at most one transition is explored from

if (Φ holds in s) $\vee$ $enabled(s) = \emptyset$ **then return** $enabled(s)$
else choose some conjunct ϕ of Φ such that ϕ is false in s;
  $T := \emptyset$;
  for all i in $supp(\phi)$ such that $s(\tau_i) < |c[i]|$
    start at node i in $WF(s)$;
    follow any path until a node j with no outedges is reached;
    insert $t_{j,s(\tau_j)}$ in T;
  return T

Fig. 2. Algorithm $\text{PS}_{\text{Poss}}(s)$.

each state. Also, the system has a unique initial state. Thus, the algorithm explores one linear sequence of transitions. Each transition in $\mathcal{T}$ appears at most once in that sequence, because t_0 disables all transitions, and each transition $t_{i,k}$ permanently disables itself. $|\mathcal{T}|$ is $O(NS)$, so N_e is also $O(NS)$, so the overall time complexity is $O(N^2S)$.

Example. In evaluation of $c_0 \models \textbf{Poss}\,(p_1 = X \wedge p_2 = B)$, $t_{1,1}$, $t_{2,1}$, and $t_{2,2}$ are executed. In the resulting state $s_{2,3}$, $\text{PS}_{\text{Poss}}(s_{2,3})$ may return $\{t_{1,2}\}$ or $\{t_{2,3}\}$, causing $s_{2,4}$ or $s_{3,3}$, respectively, to be never visited.

Example. Consider evaluation of $c \models \textbf{Poss}\,\phi_1(p_1) \wedge \phi_2(p_2, p_3)$, for predicates ϕ_1 and ϕ_2 such that ϕ_1 is true in most states of process 1, and ϕ_2 is true in at most $O(S)$ consistent states of processes 2 and 3. PSSS does not explore transitions of process 1 in states where ϕ_2 is false and ϕ_1 is true, so its worst-case running time for such systems is $\Theta(S^2)$. Garg and Waldecker's algorithm [GW94] is inapplicable, because ϕ_2 is not 1-local. The worst-case running time of Cooper and Marzullo's algorithm [CM91] for such systems is $\Theta(S^3)$.

Exploring Sequences of Transitions. The following optimization can be used to reduce the number of explored states and transitions. In the **else** branch of PS_{Poss}, if the next transition of process i is not enabled, and if process i is not waiting for any other process in $supp(\phi)$, then insert in T a minimum-length sequence w of transitions that ends with a transition of process i. For details and an example, see [SUL99].

On-line Detection. For simplicity, the above presentation considers off-line property detection. Our approach can also be applied to on-line property detection. Local states arrive at the monitor one at a time. For each process, the local states of that process arrive in the order they occurred. However, there is no constraint on the relative arrival order of local states of different processes. For on-line detection of **Poss** Φ, detection must be announced as soon as local states comprising a CGS satisfying Φ have arrived. This is easily achieved by modifying the selective search algorithm to explore transitions as they become available: there is no need for the selective search to proceed in depth-first order, so the stack can be replaced with a "to-do set", and in each iteration, any element of that set can be selected. This does not affect the time or space complexity of the algorithm.

5 Detecting Def Φ

As in Section 4, we construct a concurrent system whose executions correspond to histories consistent with c, express $c \models \mathbf{Def}\,\Phi$ as a question about reachable deadlocks of that system, and use PSSS to answer that question. The construction in Section 4 for **Poss** is similar to well-known constructions for reducing safety properties to deadlock detection [God96], but our construction for **Def** seems novel. The transitions are similar to those in (1), except the guard of each transition is augmented to check whether the transition would truthify Φ; if so, the transition is disabled. If $s_{init}(\Phi)$ holds, then $c \models \mathbf{Def}\,\Phi$, and no search is performed. Thus, in a search, Φ is false in all reachable states. If the final state (i.e., the state satisfying $\bigwedge_{i=1..N} \tau_i = |c[i]|$) is reachable, then each sequence of transitions from s_{init} to the final state corresponds to a history consistent with c and in which Φ never holds, so $c \not\models \mathbf{Def}\,\Phi$.

The processes are the same as in Section 4, except with process 0 omitted. Thus, $\mathcal{P} = \bigcup_{i=1..N}\{P_i\}$, where $P_i = \bigcup_{k=1..|c[i]|}\{\ell_{i,k}\}$. The shared variables are the same as in Section 4. Thus, $\mathcal{O} = \bigcup_{i=1..N}\{p_i, \tau_i\}$. The initial state is the same as in Section 4, except with the control point for process 0 omitted. The transitions are $\mathcal{T} = \bigcup_{i=1..N, k=1..|c[i]|-1}\{t_{i,k}\}$, where

$$t_{i,k} = \langle \{\ell_{i,k}\}, \qquad (3)$$
$$\tau_i = k \wedge (\forall j \in [1..N] \setminus \{i\} : c[j][\tau_j](vt)[j] \geq c[i][k+1](vt)[j])$$
$$\wedge \neg \Phi(p_1, \ldots, p_{i-1}, c[i][\tau_i+1], p_{i+1}, \ldots, p[N]),$$
$$p_i := c[i][k+1]; \tau_i := k+1,$$
$$\{\ell_{i,k+1}\}\rangle$$

It is easy to show that $c \not\models \mathbf{Def}\,\Phi$ iff Φ is false in s_{init} and the final state is a reachable deadlock.

Example. The transitions of the concurrent system corresponding to computation c_0 of Figure 1 and the predicate $(p_1 = Y \wedge p_2 = D)$ are

$$\begin{aligned}
t_{1,1} &= \langle \{\ell_{1,1}\},\ \tau_1 = 1\ \wedge\ \tau_2 \geq 1\ \wedge\ p_2 \neq D,\ p_1 := Y;\ \tau_1 := 2,\ \{\ell_{1,2}\}\rangle \\
t_{1,2} &= \langle \{\ell_{1,2}\},\ \tau_1 = 2\ \wedge\ \tau_2 \geq 3,\ p_1 := Z;\ \tau_1 := 3,\ \{\ell_{1,3}\}\rangle \\
t_{2,1} &= \langle \{\ell_{2,1}\},\ \tau_2 = 1\ \wedge\ \tau_1 \geq 2,\ p_2 := B;\ \tau_2 := 2,\ \{\ell_{2,2}\}\rangle \qquad (4)\\
t_{2,2} &= \langle \{\ell_{2,2}\},\ \tau_2 = 2\ \wedge\ \tau_1 \geq 2,\ p_2 := C;\ \tau_2 := 3,\ \{\ell_{2,3}\}\rangle \\
t_{2,3} &= \langle \{\ell_{2,3}\},\ \tau_2 = 3\ \wedge\ \tau_1 \geq 2\ \wedge\ p_1 \neq Y,\ p_2 := D;\ \tau_2 := 4,\ \{\ell_{2,4}\}\rangle
\end{aligned}$$

Our algorithm PS$_{\mathbf{Def}}$ for computing persistent sets of such concurrent systems applies when Φ is a conjunction of 1-local predicates: $\Phi = \bigwedge_{i=1..N} \phi_i$, where $supp(\phi_i) = \{i\}$. Pseudo-code for PS$_{\mathbf{Def}}$ appears in Figure 3, where

$$stayfalse(i,k) = \neg c[i][k](\phi_i) \wedge \neg c[i][k+1](\phi_i). \qquad (5)$$

> **if** $enabled(s) = \emptyset$ **then return** $enabled(s)$
> **else** choose some $i \in [1..N]$ such that $stayfalse(i, s(\tau_i))$;
>   start at node i in $WF(s)$;
>   follow any path until a node j with no outedges is reached;
>   **return** $\{t_{j,s(\tau_j)}\}$

Fig. 3. Algorithm $\text{PS}_{\textbf{Def}}(s)$.

Theorem 2. $\text{PS}_{\textbf{Def}}(s)$ *is well-defined and is persistent in s.*

Proof: To show that $\text{PS}_{\textbf{Def}}(s)$ is well-defined, we show that the following formulas hold in the **else** branch:

$$(\exists i \in [1..N] : stayfalse(i, s(\tau_i))) \tag{6}$$

$$t_{j,s(\tau_j)} \in enabled(s). \tag{7}$$

Proofs that these formulas hold and that $\text{PS}_{\textbf{Def}}(s)$ is persistent in s appear in the Appendix. □

The worst-case time complexity of $\text{PS}_{\textbf{Def}}$ is the same as $\text{PS}_{\textbf{Poss}}$ for conjunctions of 1-local predicates, namely $O(N)$. Thus, the overall time complexity of the search is $O(NN_e)$, where N_e is the number of states explored by the algorithm. By the same reasoning as for $\text{PS}_{\textbf{Poss}}$, N_e is $O(NS)$. Thus, the overall time complexity is $O(N^2S)$.

Example. In evaluation of $c_0 \models \textbf{Def}\ (p_1 = Y \wedge p_2 = D)$, $t_{1,1}$, $t_{2,1}$, and $t_{2,2}$ are executed. In the resulting state $s_{2,3}$, $t_{2,3}$ is disabled by its guard (executing $t_{2,3}$ would truthify Φ), so $\text{PS}_{\textbf{Def}}(s_{2,3})$ returns $\{t_{1,2}\}$.

On-line Detection. For on-line detection of **Def** Φ, detection must be announced as soon as all histories consistent with the known prefix of the computation contain a CGS satisfying Φ. As for on-line detection of **Poss** Φ, this is easily achieved by modifying the selective search algorithm to explore transitions as they become available, *i.e.*, by replacing the stack with a "to-do set". The algorithm announces that **Def** Φ holds whenever the "to-do set" becomes empty.

6 Examples

We implemented our algorithm for detecting **Poss** Φ in Java and applied it to two examples.

In the first example, called database partitioning, a database is partitioned among processes 2 through N, while process 1 assigns task to these processes based on the current partition. Each process $i \in [1..N]$ has a variable $partn_i$ containing the current partition. A process $i \in [2..N]$ can suggest a new partition at any time by setting variable chg_i to true and broadcasting a message containing the proposed partition and an appropriate version number. A recipient of this message accepts the proposed partition if its own version of the partition has a smaller version number or if its own version of the partition has the same version number and was proposed by a process i' with $i' > i$. An invariant I_{db} that should be maintained is: if no process is changing the partition, then all processes agree on the partition.

$$I_{db} = (\bigwedge_{i \in [2..N]} \neg chg_i) \Rightarrow \bigwedge_{i,j \in [1..N], i \neq j} partn_i = partn_j \qquad (8)$$

The second example, called primary-secondary, concerns an algorithm designed to ensure that the system always contains a pair of processes that will act together as primary and secondary (*e.g.*, for servicing requests). This is expressed by the invariant

$$I_{pr} = \bigvee_{i,j \in [1..N], i \neq j} isPrimary_i \wedge isSecondary_j \wedge secondary_i = j \wedge primary_j = i. \qquad (9)$$

Initially, process 1 is the primary and process 2 is the secondary. At any time, the primary may choose a new primary as its successor by first informing the secondary of its intention, waiting for an acknowledgment, and then multicasting to the other processes a request for volunteers to be the new primary. It chooses the first volunteer whose reply it receives and sends a message to that process stating that it is the new primary. The new primary sends a message to the current secondary which updates its state to reflect the change and then sends a message to the old primary stating that it can stop being the primary. The secondary can choose a new secondary using a similar protocol. The secondary must wait for an acknowledgment from the primary before multicasting the request for volunteers; however, if the secondary receives instead a message that the primary is searching for a successor, the secondary aborts its current attempt to find a successor, waits until it receives a message from the new primary, and then re-starts the protocol.

We implemented a simulator that generates computations of these protocols, and we used state-space search to detect possible violations of the given invariant in those computations, *i.e.*, to detect **Poss** $\neg I_{db}$ or **Poss** $\neg I_{pr}$. To apply PS$_{\mathbf{Poss}}$, we write both predicates as conjunctions. For $\neg I_{db}$, we rewrite the implication $P \Rightarrow Q$ as $\neg P \vee Q$ and then use DeMorgan's Law (applied to the outermost negation and the disjunction). For $\neg I_{pr}$, we simply use DeMorgan's Law. The simulator accepts N and S as arguments and halts when some process has executed $S - 1$ events. Message latencies and other delays are selected randomly from the distribution $1 + \exp(1)$, where $\exp(x)$ is the exponential distribution with mean x. The search optionally uses sleep sets, as described in [God96], as a further optimization. Sleep sets help eliminate redundancy caused by exploring multiple interleavings of independent transitions in a persistent set. Sleep sets are particularly effective for **Poss** Φ because, if Φ does not hold in s, then transitions in PS$_{\mathbf{Poss}}(s)$ are pairwise independent.

Search was done using four levels of optimization: no optimization, persistent sets only, sleep sets only ([God96, Fig. 5.2] with PS = *enabled*), and both persistent sets and sleep sets ([God96, Fig. 5.2] with PS = PS$_{\mathbf{Poss}}$).

Data collected by fixing the value of N at 3 or 5 and varying S in the range [2..80] indicate that in all cases, N_T and N_S are linear in S. This is because both examples involve global synchronizations, which ensure that a new local state of any process is not concurrent with any very old local state of any process.

The following table contains measurements for the database partitioning example with $N = 5$ and $S = 80$ and for the primary-secondary example with $N = 9$ and $S = 60$. Using both persistent sets and sleep sets reduced N_T (and, roughly, the running time) by factors of 775 and 72, respectively, for the two examples.

Example	No optimization		Sleep		Persistent		Persis. + Sleep	
	N_T	N_S	N_T	N_S	N_T	N_S	N_T	N_S
database partition	343170	88281	88280	88281	640	545	443	444
primary-secondary	3878663	752035	752034	752035	91874	61773	53585	53586

To help determine the dependence of N_T on N, we graphed $\ln N_T$ vs. N and fit a line to it; this corresponds to equations of the form $N_T = e^{aN+b}$. The results are graphed in Figure 4. The dependence on S is linear, so using different values of S in different cases does not affect the dependence on N (i.e., it affects b but not a). In one case, namely, the database partitioning example with both persistent sets and sleep sets, the polynomial $N_T = bN^{1.54}$ yields a better fit than an exponential for the measured region of $N = [3..8]$. The dependence of N_S on N is similar.

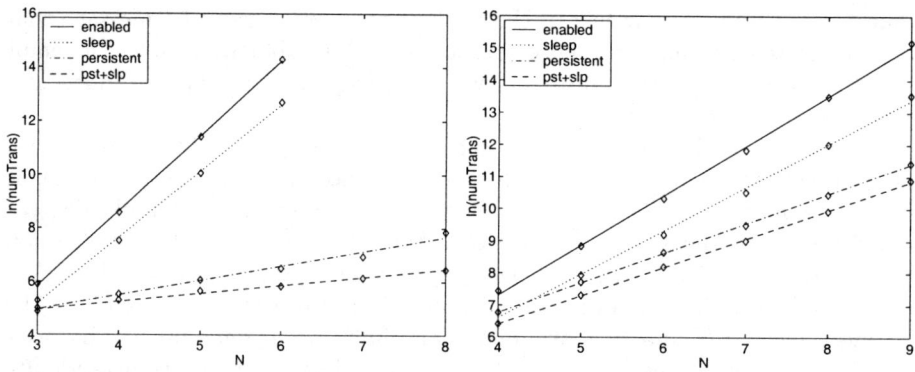

Fig. 4. Datapoints and fitted curves for $\ln N_T$ vs. N for all four levels of optimization. Left: Database partitioning example with $S = 25$ for the two searches not using persistent sets and $S = 50$ for the two searches using persistent sets. Right: Primary-secondary example with $S = 60$.

Garg and Waldecker's algorithm for detecting **Poss** Φ for conjunctions of 1-local predicates [GW94] is not applicable to the database partitioning example, because $\neg I_{db}$ contains clauses like $partn_i \neq partn_j$ which are not 1-local. Their algorithm can be applied to the primary-secondary example by putting $\neg I_{pr}$ in disjunctive normal form (DNF) and detecting each disjunct separately. $\neg I_{pr}$ is compactly expressed in conjunctive normal form. Putting $\neg I_{pr}$ in DNF causes an exponential blowup in the size of the formula. This leads to an exponential factor in the time complexity of applying their algorithm to this problem.

References

[AMP98] Rajeev Alur, Ken McMillan, and Doron Peled. Deciding global partial-order properties. In *Proc. 25th International Colloquium on Automata, Languages, and Programming (ICALP)*, volume 1443 of *Lecture Notes in Computer Science*, pages 41–52. Springer-Verlag, 1998.

[AV94] Sridhar Alagar and S. Venkatesan. Techniques to tackle state explosion in global predicate detection. In *Proc. International Conference on Parallel and Distributed Systems*, pages 412–417, December 1994.

[AY99] Rajeev Alur and Mihalis Yannakakis. Model checking of message sequence charts. In *Proc. 10th Int'l. Conference on Concurrency Theory (CONCUR)*, volume 1664 of *Lecture Notes in Computer Science*, pages 114–129, 1999.

[CG98] Craig M. Chase and Vijay K. Garg. Detection of global predicates: Techniques and their limitations. *Distributed Computing*, 11(4):169–189, 1998.

[CM91] Robert Cooper and Keith Marzullo. Consistent detection of global predicates. In *Proc. ACM/ONR Workshop on Parallel and Distributed Debugging, 1991*. ACM SIGPLAN Notices 26(12):167-174, Dec. 1991.

[Fid88] C. Fidge. Timestamps in message-passing systems that preserve the partial ordering. In *Proceedings of the 11th Australian Computer Science Conference*, pages 56–66, 1988.

[FR94] Eddy Fromentin and Michel Raynal. Local states in distributed computations: A few relations and formulas. *Operating Systems Review*, 28(2), April 1994.

[God96] Patrice Godefroid. *Partial-Order Methods for the Verification of Concurrent Systems*, volume 1032 of *Lecture Notes in Computer Science*. Springer-Verlag, 1996.

[GW94] Vijay K. Garg and Brian Waldecker. Detection of weak unstable predicates in distributed programs. *IEEE Transactions on Parallel and Distributed Systems*, 5(3):299–307, 1994.

[GW96] Vijay K. Garg and Brian Waldecker. Detection of strong unstable predicates in distributed programs. *IEEE Transactions on Parallel and Distributed Systems*, 7(12):1323–1333, 1996.

[JMN95] R. Jegou, R. Medina, and L. Nourine. Linear space algorithm for on-line detection of global predicates. In J. Desel, editor, *Proc. Int'l Workshop on Structures in Concurrency Theory (STRICT '95)*. Springer, 1995.

[Lam78] Leslie Lamport. Time, clocks, and the ordering of events in a distributed system. *Communications of the ACM*, 21(7):558–564, 1978.

[Mat89] Friedemann Mattern. Virtual time and global states of distributed systems. In M. Corsnard, editor, *Proc. International Workshop on Parallel and Distributed Algorithms*, pages 120–131. North-Holland, 1989.

[MN91] Keith Marzullo and Gil Neiger. Detection of global state predicates. In *Proc. 5th Int'l. Workshop on Distributed Algorithms (WDAG)*, volume 579 of *Lecture Notes in Computer Science*, pages 254–272. Springer, 1991.

[MPS98]   Anca Muscholl, Doron Peled, and Zhendong Su. Deciding properties of message sequence charts. In *FoSSaCS '98*, volume 1378 of *Lecture Notes in Computer Science*, pages 226–242, 1998.

[PPH97]   Doron Peled, Vaughan R. Pratt, and Gerard J. Holzmann, editors. *Proc. Workshop on Partial Order Methods in Verification*, volume 29 of *DIMACS Series*. American Mathematical Society, 1997.

[SG98]   Abraham Silberschatz and Peter B. Galvin. *Operating System Concepts*. Addison Wesley, 5th edition, 1998.

[SUL99]   Scott D. Stoller, Leena Unnikrishnan, and Yanhong A. Liu. Efficient detection of global properties in distributed systems using partial-order methods. Technical Report 523, Computer Science Dept., Indiana University, 1999.

[SW89]   A. Prasad Sistla and Jennifer Welch. Efficient distributed recovery using message logging. In *Proc. Eighth ACM Symposium on Principles of Distributed Computing*. ACM SIGOPS-SIGACT, 1989.

[TG93]   Alexander I. Tomlinson and Vijay K. Garg. Detecting relational global predicates in distributed systems. In *Proc. ACM/ONR Workshop on Parallel and Distributed Debugging*, 1993. ACM SIGPLAN Notices 28(12), December 1993.

[Val97]   Antti Valmari. Stubborn set methods for process algebras. In Peled et al. [PPH97], pages 213–231.

[Wal98]   Igor Walukiewicz. Difficult configurations - on the complexity of *ltrl*. In *Proc. 25th International Colloquium on Automata, Languages, and Programming (ICALP)*, volume 1443 of *Lecture Notes in Computer Science*, pages 140–151. Springer-Verlag, 1998.

Appendix: Selected Definitions and Proofs

Definition of Independence [God96]. Transitions t_1 and t_2 are *independent* in a state s if

1. Independent transitions can neither disable nor enabled each other, *i.e.*,
   (a) if $t_1 \in enabled(s)$ and $s \xrightarrow{t_1} s'$, then $t_2 \in enabled(s)$ iff $t_2 \in enabled(s')$;
   (b) condition (a) with t_1 and t_2 interchanged holds; and
2. Enabled independent transitions commute, *i.e.*, if $\{t_1, t_2\} \subseteq enabled(s)$, then there is a unique state s' such that $s \xrightarrow{t_1} s_1 \xrightarrow{t_2} s'$ and $s \xrightarrow{t_2} s_2 \xrightarrow{t_1} s'$.

Proof of Theorem 1: It suffices to show that for each transition t in T, t is independent with t_n in s_n. Φ is false in s, so $t_0 \notin enabled(s)$, so t is $t_{i,k}$, as defined in (1), for some i and k. Note that $t_n \neq t_0$, because by hypothesis, Φ is false in s_n. The transitions of each process occur in the order they are numbered, and $t_{i,k} \in enabled(s)$, so the next transition of process i that is executed after state s is $t_{i,k}$; in other words, from state s, no transition of process i can occur before $t_{i,k}$ does. Since $t_{i,k} \in T$ and $(\forall i \in [1..n] : t_i \notin T)$, it follows that t_n is a transition of some process i' with $i' \neq i \wedge i' \neq 0$. From the structure of the system, it is easy to show that, once $t_{i,k}$ has become enabled, such a transition t_n cannot enable or disable $t_{i,k}$ and commutes with $t_{i,k}$ when both are enabled. Thus, $t_{i,k}$ and t_n are independent in s_n. □

Proof of Theorem 2: First we show that (6) holds in the **else** branch. In that branch, $enabled(s) \neq \emptyset$, so $enabled(s)$ contains some transition $t_{j,s(\tau_j)}$. Let $s \stackrel{t_{j,s(\tau_j)}}{\rightarrow} s'$. Suppose ϕ_j is true in s'. The guard of $t_{j,s(\tau_j)}$ implies that Φ is false in s', so there exists $i \neq j$ such that ϕ_i is false in s'. A transition of process j does not change the local state of process i, so $s(p_i) = s'(p_i)$, so ϕ_i is false in s, so $stayfalse(i, s(\tau_i))$ holds.

Suppose ϕ_j is false in s'. If ϕ_j is false in s, then $stayfalse(j, s(\tau_j))$ holds. Otherwise, suppose ϕ_j is true in s. Since s is reachable, Φ is false in s, so there exists $i \neq j$ such that ϕ_i is false in s. Note that $s(p_i) = s'(p_i)$, so ϕ_i is false in s', so $stayfalse(i, s(\tau_i))$ holds.

Now we show that (7) holds in the **else** branch. By (6), $stayfalse(i, s(\tau_i))$ holds for some i. Let j be the node with no outedges that was selected by the algorithm. If suffices to show that executing $t_{j,s(\tau_j)}$ from state s would not cause Φ to become true. If $i = j$, then this follows immediately from the second conjunct in $stayfalse(i, s(\tau_i))$. If $i \neq j$, then this follows immediately from the first conjunct in $stayfalse(i, s(\tau_i))$ and the fact that $t_{j,s(\tau_j)}$ does not change the local state of process i. Note that, in both cases, ϕ_i is false in s'.

Finally, we show that $\text{PS}_{\textbf{Def}}(s)$ is persistent in s. This is trivial if $enabled(s) = \emptyset$. Suppose $enabled(s) \neq \emptyset$, so $stayfalse(i, s(\tau_i))$ holds. Let $\{t_{j,s(\tau_j)}\} = \text{PS}_{\textbf{Def}}(s)$. Let $s_1 \stackrel{t_1}{\rightarrow} s_2 \stackrel{t_2}{\rightarrow} s_3 \cdots \stackrel{t_{n-1}}{\rightarrow} s_n \stackrel{t_n}{\rightarrow} s_{n+1}$ such that $s_1 = s$ and $(\forall k \in [1..n] : t_k \neq t)$. It suffices to show that t_n and $t_{j,s(\tau_j)}$ are independent in s_n. As noted at the end of the previous paragraph, executing $t_{j,s(\tau_j)}$ in s leaves ϕ_i false. $t_1, \ldots, t_n$ are not transitions of process i, because the next transition of process i cannot occur before $t_{j,s(\tau_j)}$ occurs (this follows from the choice of j and the definition of wait-for graph). Thus,

$$(\forall k \in [1..n+1] : s_k(p_i) = s(p_i) \land \text{ executing } t_{j,s(\tau_j)} \text{ in } s_k \text{ leaves } \phi_i \text{ false}). \quad (10)$$

Consider the requirements in the definition of independence.

(1a) Suppose $t_{j,s(\tau_j)} \in enabled(s_n)$. Let $s_n \stackrel{t_{j,s(\tau_j)}}{\rightarrow} s'$. By hypothesis, $t_n \in enabled(s_n)$, so we need to show that $t_n \in enabled(s')$. Since t_n is enabled in s_n, it suffices to show that executing t_n in s' leaves Φ false. By (10), executing $t_{j,s(\tau_j)}$ in s_n leaves ϕ_i false, and t_n is not a transition of process i, so executing t_n in s' leaves ϕ_i false.

(1b) Suppose $t_n \in enabled(s_n)$. Recall that $s_n \stackrel{t_n}{\rightarrow} s_{n+1}$. We need to show that $t_{j,s(\tau_j)} \in enabled(s_n)$ iff $t_{j,s(\tau_j)} \in enabled(s_{n+1})$. $t_{j,s(\tau_j)}$ is enabled in s, and by (10), executing $t_{j,s(\tau_j)}$ in s_n or in s_{n+1} leaves ϕ_i and hence Φ false. It follows that $t_{j,s(\tau_j)}$ is enabled in both s_n and s_{n+1}.

(2) It is easy to show that $t_{j,s(\tau_j)}$ and t_n commute.

Thus, t_n and $t_{j,s(\tau_j)}$ are independent in s_n, and $\text{PS}_{\textbf{Def}}(s)$ is persistent in s. □

Efficient Reachability Analysis of Hierarchical Reactive Machines

R. Alur, R. Grosu, and M. McDougall

Department of Computer and Information Science
University of Pennsylvania
alur,grosu,mmcdouga@cis.upenn.edu
www.cis.upenn.edu/~alur,grosu,mmcdouga

Abstract. Hierarchical state machines is a popular visual formalism for software specifications. To apply automated analysis to such specifications, the traditional approach is to compile them to existing model checkers. Aimed at exploiting the modular structure more effectively, our approach is to develop algorithms that work directly on the hierarchical structure. First, we report on an implementation of a visual hierarchical language with modular features such as nested modes, variable scoping, mode reuse, exceptions, group transitions, and history. Then, we identify a variety of heuristics to exploit these modular features during reachability analysis. We report on an enumerative as well as a symbolic checker, and case studies.

1 Introduction

Recent advances in formal verification have led to powerful design tools for hardware (see [CK96] for a survey), and subsequently, have brought a lot of hope of their application to reactive programming. The most successful verification technique has been *model checking* [CE81,QS82]. In model checking, the system is described by a state-machine model, and is analyzed by an algorithm that explores the reachable state-space of the model. The state-of-the-art model checkers (e.g. SPIN [Hol97] and SMV [McM93]) employ a variety of heuristics for efficient search, but are typically unable to analyze models with more than hundred state variables, and thus, *scalability* still remains a challenge. A promising approach to address scalability is to exploit the modularity of design. Modern software engineering methodologies such as UML [BJR97] exhibit two kinds of modular structures, *architectural* and *behavioral*. Architectural modularity means that a system is composed of subsystems using the operations of parallel composition and hiding of variables. The input languages of standard model checkers (e.g., S/R in Cospan [AKS83] or Reactive modules in Mocha [AH99]) support architectural modularity, but provide no support for modular description of the behaviors of individual components. In this paper, we focus on exploiting the *behavioral hierarchy* for efficient model checking.

The notion of behavioral hierarchy was popularized by the introduction of STATECHARTS [Har87], and exists in many related modeling formalisms such as

MODECHARTS [JM87] and RSML [LHHR94]. It is a central component of various object-oriented software development methodologies developed in recent years, such as ROOM [SGW94], and the Unified Modeling Language (UML [BJR97]). Such hierarchic specifications have many powerful primitives such as exceptions, group transitions, and history, which facilitate modular descriptions of complex behavior. The conventional approach to analyze such specifications is to compile them into input languages of existing model checkers. For instance, Chan et al [CAB+98] have analyzed RSML specifications using SMV, and Leue et al have developed a hierarchical and visual front-end to SPIN. While the structure of the source language is exploited to some extent (e.g., [CAB+98] reports heuristics for variable ordering based on hierarchical structure, and [BLA+99] reports a way of avoiding repeated search in same context), compilation into a *flat* target language loses the input structure. In terms of theoretical results concerning the analysis of such descriptions, verifying linear properties of sequential hierarchical machines can be done efficiently without flattening [AY98], but in presence of concurrency, hierarchy causes an exponential blow-up [AKY99].

The input language to our model checker is based on *hierarchic reactive modules* [AG00]. This choice was motivated by the fact that, unlike STATECHARTS and other languages, in hierarchic reactive modules, the notion of hierarchy is *semantic* with an observational trace-based semantics and a notion of refinement with assume-guarantee rules. Furthermore, hierarchic reactive modules support *extended* state machines where the communication is via shared variables. The first contribution of this paper is a concrete implementation of hierarchic reactive modules. Our implementation is *visual* consistent with modern software design tools, and is in Java. The central component of the description is a *mode*. The attributes of a mode include global variables used to share data with its environment, local variables, well-defined entry and exit points, and submodes that are connected with each other by transitions. The transitions are labeled with guarded commands that access the variables according to the the natural scoping rules. Note that the transitions can connect to a mode only at its entry/exit points, as in ROOM, but unlike STATECHARTS. This choice is important in viewing the mode as a black box whose internal structure is not visible from outside. The mode has a *default exit* point, and transitions leaving the default exit are applicable at all control points within the mode and its submodes. The default exit retains the history, and the state upon exit is automatically restored by transitions entering the default entry point. Thus, a transition from default exit to entry models a group transition applicable to all control points inside. While defining the operational semantics of modes, we follow the standard paradigm in which transitions are executed repeatedly until there are no more enabled transitions. Our language distinguishes between a mode *definition* and a mode *reference*, and this allows sharing and reuse.

Our model checker checks invariants by reachability analysis of the input model. The model is parsed into an internal representation that directly reflects the hierarchical structure, and the analysis algorithms, symbolic and enumerative, attempt to exploit it in different ways:

Transition indexing. The transition relation is maintained indexed by the modes and their control points. In the enumerative setting, this is beneficial for quick access to potentially enabled transitions, and also due to shared mode definitions. In the symbolic setting, this provides a generalization of the traditional *conjunctively partitioned* representation [McM93].

State-space representation. In the enumerative setting, states are represented as *stacks* of vectors rather than vectors, and this is useful in handling priorities of transitions. In symbolic search, we maintain the state-space as a forest of binary decision diagrams indexed by control points. The resulting search has, consequently, a mixture of enumerative and symbolic strategies.

Typing. Each mode explicitly declares the variables that it reads and writes, thus, providing different types for different transitions. This information is used in symbolic search for heuristics such as early quantification.

Variable scoping. The pool of variables is not global. For instance, the state can consist of variables x and y in one mode, and x and z in another. This information, available statically, is exploited by both the searches. This optimization is possible due to the encapsulation provided by our language.

Note that the above heuristics are quite natural to the hierarchical representation, and has advantages with respect to the flat representation of the same model. Another advantage of the language is that the granularity of steps of interacting components can be controlled as desired. This is because a *macro-step* of a mode corresponds to executing its *micro-steps* repeatedly until there are no more enabled transitions, and parallel composition corresponds to interleaving macro-steps.

We have implemented an enumerative checker based on depth-first search, and a symbolic search that uses BDD packages from VIS [BHSV+96]. We report on two case studies. As a first example, we modeled the tcp protocol. Our visual interface allowed a direct mapping of the block-diagram description from [PD96], and our enumerative checker found a deadlock bug in that description. Second, we constructed an example that is illustrative of nesting and sharing of modes, and scoping of variables. The performance of both enumerative and symbolic checkers is significantly superior compared to the respective traditional checks.

2 Modeling Language

Modes A *mode* has a refined control structure given by a hierarchical state machine. It basically consists of a set of *submode instances* connected by *transitions* such that at each moment of time *only one* of the submode instances *is active*. A submode instance has an associated mode and we require that the modes form an *acyclic* graph with respect to this association. For example, the mode M in Figure 1 contains two submode instances, m and n pointing to the mode N. By distinguishing between modes and instances we may control the degree of *sharing* of submodes. Sharing is highly desirable because submode instances (on the same hierarchy level) are never simultaneously active in a mode. Note that a mode resembles an *or* state in STATECHARTS but it has more powerful structuring mechanisms.

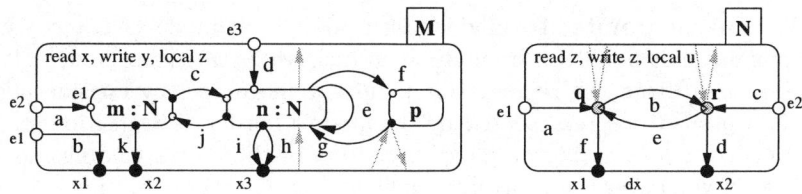

Fig. 1. Mode diagrams

Variables and scoping A mode may have *global* as well as *local variables*. The set of global variables is used to share data with the mode's environment. The global variables are classified into *read* and *write variables*. The *local variables* of a mode are accessible only by its transitions and submodes. The local and write variables are called *controlled variables*. Thus, the scoping rules for variables are as in standard structured programming languages. For example, the mode M in Figure 1 has the global read variable x, the global write variable y and the local variable z. Similarly, the mode N has the global read-write variable z and the local variable u.

The transitions of a mode may refer only to the declared global and local variables of that mode and only according to the declared read/write permission. For example, the transitions a,b,c,d,e,f,g,h,i,j and k of the mode M may refer only to the variables x, y and z. Moreover, they may read only x and z and write y and z. The global and local variables of a mode may be shared between submode instances if the associated submodes declare them as global (the set of global variables of a submode has to be included in the set of global and local variables of its parent mode). For example, the value of the variable z in Figure 1 is shared between the submode instances m and n. However, the value of the local variable u is not shared between m and n.

Control points and transitions To obtain a modular language, we require the modes to have well defined *control points* classified into entry points (marked as white bullets) and exit points (marked as black bullets). For example, the mode M in Figure 1 has the entry points e1,e2, e3 and the exit points x1,x2,x3. Similarly, the mode N has the entry points e1,e2 and the exit points x1,x2. The transitions connect the control points of a mode and of its submode instances to each other. For example, in Figure 1 the transition a connects the entry point e2 of the mode M with the entry point e1 of the submode instance m. The name of the control points of a transition are attributes and our drawing tool allows to optionally show or hide them to avoid cluttering.

According to the points they connect, we classify the transitions into *entry*, *internal* and *exit* transitions. For example, in Figure 1, a,d are *entry* transitions, h,i,k are *exit* transitions, b is an *entry/exit* transition and c,e,f,g,j are *internal* transitions. These transitions have different types. Entry transitions initialize the controlled variables by reading only the global variables. Exit transitions read the global and local variables and write only the global variables. The internal transitions read the global and the local variables and write the controlled variables.

Default control points To model preemption each mode (instance) has a special, default exit point dx. In mode diagrams, we distinguish the default exit point of a mode from the regular exit points of the mode, by considering the default exit point to be represented by the mode's border. A transition starting at dx is called a *preempting* or *group transition* of the corresponding mode. It may be taken whenever the control is inside the mode and no internal transition is enabled. For example, in Figure 1, the transition f is a group transition for the submode n. If the current control point is q inside the submode instance n and neither the transition b nor the transition f is enabled, then the control is transferred to the default exit point dx. If one of e or f is enabled and taken then it acts as a preemption for n. Hence, inner transitions have a higher priority than the group transitions, i.e., we use *weak preemption*. This priority scheme facilitates a modular semantics. As shown in Figure 1, the transfer of control to the default exit point may be understood as a *default exit transition* from an exit point x of a submode to the default exit point dx that is enabled if and only if, all the explicit outgoing transitions from x are disabled. We exploit this intuition in the symbolic checker.

History and closure To allow history retention, we use a special default entry point de. As with the default exit points, in mode diagrams the default entry point of a mode is considered to be represented by the mode's border. A transition entering the default entry point of a mode either restores the values of all local variables along with the position of the control or initializes the controlled variables according to the read variables. The choice depends on whether the last exit from the mode was along the default exit point or not. This information is implicitly stored in the constructor of the state passed along the default entry point. For example, both transitions e and g in Figure 1, enter the default entry point de of n. The transition e is called a *self* group transition. A self group transition like e or more generally a self loop like f,p,g may be understood as an interrupt handling routine. While a self loop may be arbitrarily complex, a self transition may do simple things like counting the number of occurrences of an event (e.g., clock events). Again, the transfer of control from the default entry point de of a mode to one of its internal points x may be understood as a *default entry transition* that is taken when the value of the local history variable coincides with x. If x was a default exit point $n.dx$ of a submode n then, as shown in Figure 1, the default entry transition is directed to $n.de$. The reason is that in this case, the control was blocked somewhere inside of n and default entry transitions originating in $n.de$ will restore this control. A mode with added default entry and exit transitions is called *closed*. Note that the closure is a semantic concept. The user is not required to draw the implicit default entry and exit transitions. Moreover, he can override the defaults by defining explicit transitions from and to the default entry and exit points.

Operational semantics: macro-steps In Figure 1, the execution of a mode, say n, starts when the environment transfers the control to one of its entry points e1 or e2. The execution of n terminates either by transferring the control back to the environment along the exit points x1 or x2 or by "getting stuck" in q or r as all transitions starting from these leaf modes are disabled. In this case the control is implicitly transferred to M along the default exit point n.dx. Then, if the transitions e and f are enabled, one of them is nondeterministically chosen and the execution continues with n and respectively with p. If both transitions are disabled the execution of M terminates by passing the control implicitly to its environment at the default exit M.dx. Thus, the transitions within a mode have a higher priority compared to the group transitions of the enclosing modes.

Intuitively, a round of the machine associated to a mode starts when the environment passes the updated state along a mode's entry point and ends when the state is passed to the environment along a mode's exit point. All the internal steps (the *micro steps*) are hidden. We call a round also a *macro step*. Note that the macro step of a mode is obtained by alternating its closed transitions and the macro steps of the submodes.

Semantics The execution of a mode may be best understood as a game, i.e., as an alternation of moves, between the mode and its environment. In a *mode move*, the mode gets the state from the environment along its entry points. It then keeps executing until it gives the state back to the environment along one of its exit points. In an *environment move*, the environment gets the state along one of the mode's exit points. Then it may update any variable except the mode's local ones. Finally, it gives the state back to the mode along one of its entry points. An *execution* of a mode M is a sequence of macro steps of the mode. Given such an execution, the corresponding *trace* is obtained by projecting the states in the execution to the set of global variables. The *denotational semantics* of a mode M consists of its control points, global variables, and the set of its traces.

Parallel composition by interleaving A mode having only two points, the default entry and the default exit, is called a mode in *top level form*. These modes can be used to explicitly model all the parallel composition operators found in the theory of reactive systems [AG00]. For simplicity we consider in this paper only the *interleaving semantics* of parallel composition. In this semantics, a round (macro step) of a composed mode is a round of one of its submodes. The choice between the submodes is arbitrary. We can easily model this composition, by overriding the default entry transions of the submodes if these are in top level form. Note also that, the state of the supermode is given, as expected, as a tuple of the states of the submodes.

3 Search Algorithms

3.1 Enumerative Search

The enumerative search algorithm takes as input a set of top-level modes and a set of global variables that these modes can read and modify. We are also given an invariant that we want this system to satisfy. The invariant is a boolean

Mode Diagram

```
┌─────────────────────────────────────┐
│ a : int                             │
│  ┌─────────────┐   ┌─────────────┐  │
│  │ x : bool    │   │ u : bool    │  │
│  │ y : bool    │   │             │  │
│  │     M1      │   │     M3      │  │
│  └─────────────┘   └─────────────┘  │
│                  M2                 │
└─────────────────────────────────────┘
```

Some Possible States

```
┌──────────┐   ┌──────────┐   ┌──────────┐
│ x= true  │   │          │   │          │
│ y= false │   │          │   │ u= true  │
│ a = 3    │   │ a = 3    │   │ a = 3    │
└──────────┘   └──────────┘   └──────────┘
     s1             s2             s3
```

Fig. 2. Local variables conserve state size

expression defined on the global variables. For the enumerative search we assume that each of the top-level modes is sequential; each top-level mode represents a single thread of execution. These top-level modes are run concurrently by interleaving their macro-steps. A state of the system consists of the values of all the global variables and the state of each of the top-level modes. In each round one of the modes may modify the variables and change its own internal state yielding a new state. The set of states of the system can therefore be viewed as a directed graph where, if s and t are states of the system, (s,t) is an edge in the graph if and only if s yields t after one round of execution.

Searching all states is straightforward; beginning from an initial state we perform a depth-first search on the graph. For each state we encounter during the search we check that the desired invariant holds. If the invariant doesn't hold for some state then the depth-first search algorithm supplies us with a path in the graph from the initial state to the state which violates the invariant. This path forms a counter-example which is returned to the user.

The set of states that have been visited is stored in a hash table so that we can check if a given state is in the set in constant time. The set of successors of a state is computed by examining the modes. The hierarchical structure of the modes is retained throughout the search. This structure allows us to optimize the search in a number of ways.

Transition Indexing To determine if there is an edge from a state s to a state t we need to examine all the possible sequences of micro-steps that are enabled in s. Each micro-step corresponds to a transition from the active control point to a destination point (which becomes the active point in the next micro-step). In the mode representation transitions are indexed by their starting points. If we want to find all enabled transitions we only need to examine those that start from the active point.

Local Variables Modes have local variables which are only visible to submodes. The internal state of a mode can be stored as a stack of sets of variables. This stack resembles the control stack present during the execution of a program in C or Java. Each element of the stack contains the variables that are local to the corresponding level in the mode hierarchy.

Since local variables of a mode are available only to the submodes of that mode the size of a mode's state is smaller than a system where all variables are global. Figure 2 shows a simple mode diagram and three possible states of the mode. Modes $M1$ and $M3$ are submodes of $M2$. States $s1, s2$ and $s3$ are the respective possible states when $M1, M2$ and $M3$ are active. If $M1$ is active the x, y and a variables are in scope and therefore must be present in the state $s1$, The variable u is not in scope if $M1$ is active and therefore it is not present in state $s1$. If $M2$ is active then x, y and u are not scope and not present in $s2$. Similarly, $s3$ does not contain the x and y variables. This means the total size of the state of a mode is proportional to the depth of the hierarchy.

State Sharing The stack structure of a mode's state also allows us to conserve memory by sharing parts of the state. Two states which are distinct may nevertheless contain some stack elements which are identical. We can construct the states in such a way that the equivalent elements of the stack are actually the same piece of memory.

For example, states s and t have two levels of hierarchy corresponding to local and global variables. If all the global variables have the same values in s and t then both s and t can refer to the same piece of memory for storing the values of the global variables.

State Hashing The tool gives the user the option of storing a hash of a state instead of the entire state. Since the hashed version of a state occupies less memory than the state itself we can search more states before we run out of memory. The problem with this technique is that the enumerative search will skip states whose hashes happen to be the same as previously visited states. As a result the enumerative search may falsely conclude that an invariant is true for all states. On the other hand, any counter-example that is found *is* valid. By varying the amount of information lost through hashing we can balance the need for accuracy with the need to search large state spaces. The SPIN modelchecker uses this hashing technique [Hol91] for states which have a fixed number of variables. However, our tool must hash states which vary in size and structure (because of the local variables).

3.2 Symbolic Search

Similarly to the enumerative search algorithm, the symbolic search algorithm takes as input a set of top-level modes and a set of variables that these modes can read and modify and an invariant that we want this system to satisfy. However, in contrast to the enumerative search we do not need to assume that the top-level modes are sequential. The reason is that a state in this case is not a stack, but rather a map (or context) of variables to their values. This context varies *dynamically*, depending on the currently accessible variables.

In order to perform the symbolic search for a hierarchic mode we could proceed as follows. (1) Obtain a flat transition relation associated to the hierarchic mode. (2) Represent the reached states and the transition relation by ordered multi-valued binary decision diagrams (mdds). (3) Apply the classic symbolic search algorithm. This is the current model checking technology.

We argue however, that such a flat representation is not desirable. The main reason is its inefficient use of memory. One can do much better by keeping the above mdds in a decomposed way, as suggested by the modular structure. In particular, a natural decomposition is obtained by keeping and manipulating the control points outside the mdds.

Reached set representation. Keeping the control points outside the state allows us to *partition* the state space in regions, each containing all states with the same control point. This decomposition has not only the advantage that any partition may be considerably smaller than the entire set but also that it is very intuitive. It is the way mode diagrams, and in general extended state machines, are drawn. Hence, we represent the *reached state space* by a mapping of the currently reached control points to their associated reached region mdd. The *region mdd* of a control point is minimized by considering only the variables visible at that control point. This takes advantage of the natural scoping of variables in a hierarchic mode.

Update relation representation. The update relation of a hierarchic mode d is not flattened. It is kept in d by annotating each transition of d with the mdd corresponding to the transition. This has the following advantages. First, all instances of d at the same level of the hierarchy and connected only at their regular points may share these transitions. The reason is that their local variables are never simultaneously active. Second, working with scoped transition relations and knowing the set of variables U updated by a transition t (broadly speaking working with typed transition relations) we may compute the image $image(R, t)$ of a region R in an optimal way as $(\exists U.R \wedge t)[U/U']$ and not as $(\exists V.R \wedge t \wedge id_{V \setminus U}))[V/V']$ where V is the set of all variables and $id_{V \setminus U}$ is the conjunction of all relations $x' = x$ with $x \in V \setminus U$. The second, more inefficient representation is to our knowledge the way the image is computed in all current model checkers. Moreover, while the internal and default transitions have this optimized form, the entry and exit transitions allow even further optimization via quantification of variables that are no longer needed.

> **Entry transitions.** $image(R, t) = (\exists (U \setminus V_l).R \wedge t)[U/U']$ because R and t is not allowed to reference the unprimed local variables in V_l.
> **Exit transitions.** $image(R, t) = (\exists (U \cup V_l).R \wedge t)[U/U']$ because t is not allowed to reference the primed local variables in V_l' and the unprimed local variables in V_l are hidden.

Variable ordering The variable ordering is naturally suggested by the partial ordering between modes. Considering that variable names are made disjoint by prefixing them with the names of the submode instances along the path to the referencing submode instance, then the ordering is nothing but the lexicographic ordering of the prefixed names. This ordering makes sure that variables defined at the same level in the mode hierarchy are grouped together.

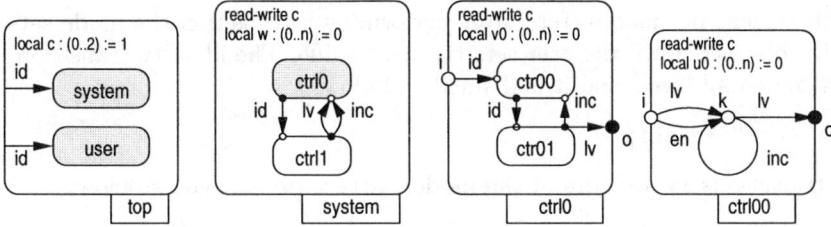

Fig. 3. A generic hierarchic example

Initialization. The initial state is a mapping of the history variables to a special, bottom value. Passing this state along the default entry point of the top-level mode, all the way down in the mode hierarchy, assures the selection of an initialization transition that updates the local variables according to their initialization statement in the mode diagram. The initial reached set maps the default entry point of the top level mode to this state.

Image computation. The main loop of the image computation algorithm is as usual. It starts with the initial *macro onion ring* (the initial reached set) and computes in each iteration (macro-step) a new macro onion ring by applying the image computation to the current macro onion and (the update relation of) the top level mode. The algorithm terminates either if the new macro onion ring is empty or if its intersection with the target region (containing the "bad" states) is nonempty.

The image computation of the next macro onion ring is the secondary loop. It starts with a *micro onion ring* having only one control point: the pair consisting of the default entry point of the top level mode and the macro onion ring mdd. Each micro step computes a new onion ring by applying the image computation to all points in the current micro onion ring and for each point to all outgoing transitions in a breadth first way. A destination point is added to the new micro onion ring if the difference between the computed mdd and the mdd associated to that point in the reached set is not empty. The mdd in the reached set is updated accordingly. The loop terminates when the new micro onion ring contains again only one control point, the default exit point of the top level mode and its associated mdd. The new macro onion ring is then the difference between the set of states corresponding to this mdd and the reached set associated to the top level default entry point.

Generic hierarchic system. In Figure 3 we show a generic hicrarchic system with three levels of nesting. The mode user nondeterministically sets a control variable c to 1 or 2 meaning increment and respectively leave. The mode system consists of the nested modes $ctrl_0$ and $ctrl_1$, that are further decomposed in the modes $ctrl_{00}$, $ctrl_{01}$ and $ctrl_{10}$, $ctrl_{11}$, respectively. Each has a local variable ranging between zero and a maximum value n that is incremented when c is 1 and the value of the local variable is less than n. When c is 2 or when c is one and the local variable reached n the mode is left. To ensure only one increment per macro-step, after performing a transition the mode sets c to 0. This blocks it until the user sets the next value. The identity transition id is the same on all levels and it is defined as follows:

```
id ≜   true -> skip
```

The transitions lv and inc of the mode system are defined as below:

```
lv  ≜   c = 2 | (c = 1 & w = n) -> c := 0; w := 0;
inc ≜   c = 1 & w < n           -> c := 0; w := w + 1;
```

Except the local variable to be tested and incremented, the transition inc has the same definition in all modes. The exit transition lv has a simpler body in the submodes. For example in mode $ctrl_{00}$:

```
lv ≜   c = 2 | (c = 1 & u₀ = n) -> skip
```

Finally, the entry transitions en and lv of the leaf modes have the same definition modulo the local variable. For example, in mode $ctrl_{00}$:

```
lv ≜   c = 2   -> skip
en ≜   c != 2  -> c := 0; u₀ := 0;
```

The mdd associated to the point k of the mode $ctrl_{00}$ is a boolean relation $R_{ctrl_{00}.k}(c, w, v_0, u_0)$. Similarly, the mdds associated to the exit point o of the modes $ctrl_{00}$ and $ctrl_0$ are boolean relations $R_{ctrl_{00}.o}(c, w, v_0)$ and $R_{ctrl_0.o}(c, w)$ respectively. Note that variables are not quantified out at the default exit points because we have to remember their value. Additionally, at these points we have to save the active submode information. Hence, the mdds associated to the default exit points dx of the modes $ctrl_{00}$ and $ctrl_0$ are boolean relations $R_{ctrl_{00}.dx}(c, w, v_0, u_0)$ and $R_{ctrl_0.dx}(c, w, v_0, u_0, h_0)$ respectively. The history variable h_0 is 0 if the active submode is $ctrl_{00}$ and 1 if the active submode is $ctrl_{01}$.

The mdd associated to a transition is a relation constructed, as usual, by considering primed variables for the next state values. For example, the transition inc of the mode $ctrl_{00}$ is defined by the relation

$$inc(c, c', u_0, u_0') \triangleq c = 1 \land u_0 < n \land c' = 0 \land u_0' = u_0 + 1$$

The image of the region $R_{ctrl_{00}.k}$ under the transition inc is computed as below:

$$(\exists c, u_0.\ R_{ctrl_{00}.k}(c, w, v_0, u_0) \land inc(c, c', u_0, u_0'))\ [c, u_0/c', u_0']$$

Lacking typing information, most model checkers use the more complex relation:

$$(\exists c, w, v_0, u_0.\ R_{ctrl_{00}.k}(c, w, v_0, u_0) \land inc(c, c', u_0, u_0') \land$$
$$w' = w \land v_0' = v_0)\ [c, w, v_0, u_0/c', w', v_0', u_0']$$

The exit transition lv of the mode $ctrl_{00}$ is defined by the following relation:

$$lv(c, u_0) \triangleq c = 2 \lor (c = 1 \land u_0 = n)$$

The image of the region $R_{ctrl_{00}.k}$ under this transition is computed as below:

$$\exists u_0.\ R_{ctrl_{00}.k}(c, w, v_0, u_0) \land lv(c, u_0)$$

It quantifies out the local variable u_0. It is here where we obtain considerable savings compared to classic model checkers. The image of the region $R_{ctrl_{00}.i}$ under the entry transition:

$$en(c, c', u'_0) \doteq c \neq 2 \land c' = 0 \land u'_0 = 0$$

does not quantify out the local variable u_0 even if u_0 was updated, because the transition is not allowed to used the unprimed value of u_0.

$$(\exists c.\ R_{ctrl_{00}.i}(c, w, v_0) \land lv(c, c', u'_0))\ [c, u_0/c', u'_0]$$

The ordering of the unprimed variables in the generic hierarchic system is defined as follows: $c < w < v_0 < u_0 < u_1 < v_1 < u_2 < u_3$.

4 Experimental Results

Mutual Exclusion Our smallest non-trivial experiment involved Peterson's algorithm for two party mutual exclusion [Pet81]. We implemented the algorithm using three modes that run concurrently. Modes p_1 and p_2 represented the two parties that want to use the shared resource. A special mode called *clock* was used to toggle a variable *tick* that the other modes consume whenever a step of the algorithm is executed. This use of a *tick* variable ensures that each macro-step of a mode corresponds to exactly one step of the algorithm that we are modeling. Once the *tick* variable is consumed a mode is blocked until the next macro-step. This technique allows a programmer to control the number of micro-steps that occur within one macro-step. Our tool performed an enumerative search of all possible executions. The search revealed that the model has 276 distinct states, all of which preserve mutual exclusion. The tool also verified that the algorithm is free of deadlock by checking that each state of the model leads to at least one successor state. Both searches took about 4 seconds to complete on an Intel Celeron 333 mhz.

TCP The Transmission Control Protocol (TCP) is a popular network protocol used to ensure reliable transmission of data. TCP connections are created when a client opens a connection with a server. Once a connection is opened the client and server exchange data until one party decides to close the connection. When a connection is opened or closed the client and server exchange special messages and enter a series of states.

TCP is designed to work even if some messages get lost or duplicated. It is also designed to work if both parties simultaneously decide to close a connection. A desirable property of protocol like TCP is that it cannot lead to deadlock; it should be impossible for both client and server to be waiting for the other to send a message.

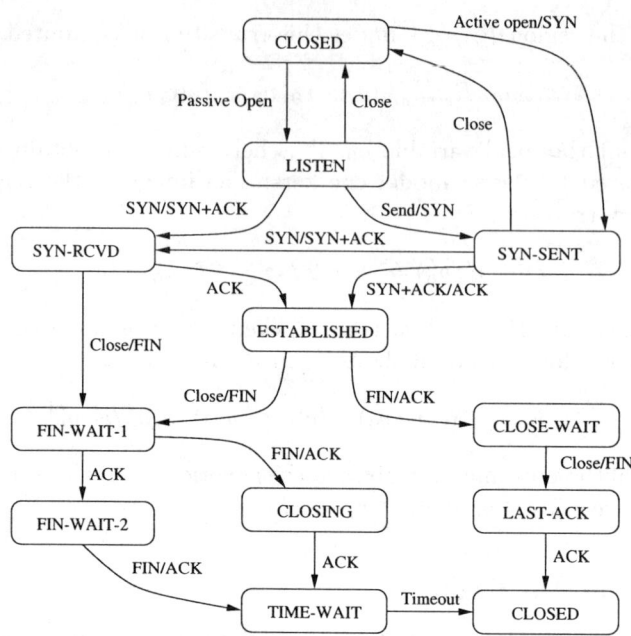

Fig. 4. TCP state-transition diagram

There is a concise description of the messages and states of TCP in [PD96] which is reproduced in Figure 4. This description is given as a state-transition diagram which makes it very easy to model it as a mode in our tool. We set out to verify that the TCP protocol, as described in [PD96], is free of deadlock under certain assumptions.

In our first experiment we simulated a client and server opening and closing a TCP connection. In our model we assumed that the network never lost or duplicated a message. We also assumed the client and server both had a one cell queue for storing incoming messages; if a party received a second message before it had a chance to process the first message then the first message would be lost. Our tool performed an enumerative search of possible execution sequences and discovered a bug in the description of TCP after searching 2277 states. If both parties decide simultaneously to close the connection while in the *established* state then they will both send *FIN* messages. One of the parties, say the client, will receive the *FIN* message and respond by sending an *ACK* message and entering the *closing* state. If this *ACK* arrives at the server before the other *FIN* is processed the second *FIN* will get lost. When the *ACK* is read the server will move to the *fin-wait-2* state. Now the protocol is deadlocked; the client is waiting for an *ACK* message while the server is waiting for a *FIN* message.

For our second experiment we modified the model so that the client and server had queues that could hold two messages instead of one. A message would only get lost if a third message arrived before the first was processed. Our tool found a deadlock state in this model after searching 3535 states. Once again the deadlock occurs after both client and server decide simultaneously to close the connection. In this case, however, the server decides to close the connection *before* it has been established. This can lead to a state where the server's queue gets filled and a message gets dropped. The deadlock occurs when the server is in the *fin-wait-2* state and the client is in the *closing* state, which is the same deadlock state that we saw in the first TCP experiment.

Both experiments were performed using an Intel Celeron 333mhz machine. The first experiment ran for 74 seconds and the second experiment ran for 138 seconds.

Generic hierarchic system The hierarchical structure of the example in Figure 3 makes it a good candidate for the state sharing optimization described in Section 3.1. The three levels of local variables allow memory to be re-used when storing states; if some levels are identical in two distinct states the enumerative search algorithm makes an effort to share the memory used to store the levels that both states have in common.

Each state contains a set of objects called *environments*. Each environment keeps track of one level of the hierarchy. An enumerative search of this example found 3049 distinct states in 138 seconds. These states contained 14879 environment objects, but because of state sharing only 8103 environment objects needed to be allocated. The technique yields a 45% reduction in the number of objects needed to store the set of visited states.

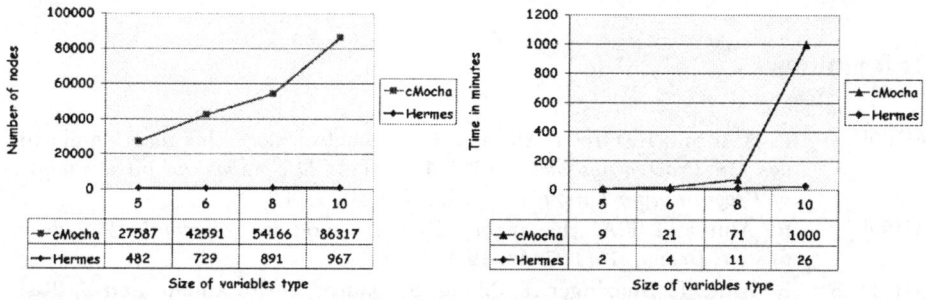

The symbolic search takes advantage of the existential quantification of local variables at all regular exit points. This leads, as shown in Figure 4, to a significant saving both in space (total number of nodes in the mdd pool) and time (for the reachability check) compared to the (C version) of the Mocha model checker [AHM+98]. The comparison was done for different values for n.

Since the concurrency is in this example only on the top level and all the variables (excepting c) are local, one can heavily share the transition relations. In fact, only the modes ctr0 and ctr00 are necessary and all references may point to these modes. As expected, using this sharing, we obtained the same results with respect to the reached set.

5 Conclusions

We have reported on an implementation of a visual hierarchical language for modeling reactive systems, and enumerative and symbolic checkers that work directly on the hierarchical representation attempting to exploit the modularity. While hierarchical specifications seem more convenient to express complex requirements, in terms of the efficiency of analysis, two questions are of interest. First, given a verification problem, should one use a hierarchical notation hoping for tractable analysis? We don't have adequate experimental evidence yet to answer this. In fact, given that the modeling languages of different tools differ so much, and different tools implement many different heuristics, parameters of a scientific comparison are unclear. Second, if the input specification is hierarchical, should one use the proposed solution over compilation into a non-hierarchical checker? Even though experimental data is small so far, we believe that there is adequate conceptual evidence suggesting a positive answer. A lot of work remains to be done to optimize the two checkers, and apply them to more and substantial examples.

Acknowledgments This work was partially supported by NSF CAREER award CCR97-34115, by DARPA/NASA grant NAG2-1214, by SRC contract 99-TJ-688, by Bell Laboratories, Lucent Technologies, by Alfred P. Sloan Faculty Fellowship, and by DARPA/ITO MARS program. The implementation of our enumerative and symbolic model checker uses components from Mocha, and the help of all members of the Mocha team is greatfully acknowledged.

References

[AG00] R. Alur and R. Grosu. Modular refinement of hierarchic reactive machines. In *Proceedings of the 27th Annual ACM Symposium on Principles of Programming Languages*, pages 390–402, 2000.

[AH99] R. Alur and T.A. Henzinger. Reactive modules. *Formal Methods in System Design*, 15(1):7–48, 1999.

[AHM+98] R. Alur, T. Henzinger, F. Mang, S. Qadeer, S. Rajamani, and S. Tasiran. MOCHA: Modularity in model checking. In *Proceedings of the 10th International Conference on Computer Aided Verification*, LNCS 1427, pages 516–520. Springer-Verlag, 1998.

[AKS83] S. Aggarwal, R.P. Kurshan, and D. Sharma. A language for the specification and analysis of protocols. In *IFIP Protocol Specification, Testing, and Verification III*, pages 35–50, 1983.

[AKY99] R. Alur, S. Kannan, and M. Yannakakis. Communicating hierarchical state machines. In *Automata, Languages and Programming, 26th International Colloquium*, pages 169–178. 1999.

[AY98] R. Alur and M. Yannakakis. Model checking of hierarchical state machines. In *Proceedings of the Sixth ACM Symposium on Foundations of Software Engineering*, pages 175–188. 1998.

[BHSV+96] R. Brayton, G. Hachtel, A. Sangiovanni-Vincentell, F. Somenzi, A. Aziz, S. Cheng, S. Edwards, S. Khatri, Y. Kukimoto, A. Pardo, S. Qadeer, R. Ranjan, S. Sarwary, T. Shiple, G. Swamy, and T. Villa. VIS: A system for verification and synthesis. In *Proceedings of the Eighth Conference on Computer Aided Verification*, LNCS 1102, pages 428–432. 1996.

[BJR97] G. Booch, I. Jacobson, and J. Rumbaugh. *Unified Modeling Language User Guide*. Addison Wesley, 1997.

[BLA+99] G. Behrmann, K. Larsen, H. Andersen, H. Hulgaard, and J. Lind-Nielsen. Verification of hierarchical state/event systems using reusability and compositionality. In *TACAS '99: Fifth International Conference on Tools and Algorithms for the Construction and Analysis of Software*, 1999.

[CAB+98] W. Chan, R. Anderson, P. Beame, S. Burns, F. Modugno, D. Notkin, and J. Reese. Model checking large software specifications. *IEEE Transactions on Software Engineering*, 24(7):498–519, 1998.

[CE81] E.M. Clarke and E.A. Emerson. Design and synthesis of synchronization skeletons using branching time temporal logic. In *Proc. Workshop on Logic of Programs*, LNCS 131, pages 52–71. Springer-Verlag, 1981.

[CK96] E.M. Clarke and R.P. Kurshan. Computer-aided verification. *IEEE Spectrum*, 33(6):61–67, 1996.

[Har87] D. Harel. Statecharts: A visual formalism for complex systems. *Science of Computer Programming*, 8:231–274, 1987.

[Hol91] G.J. Holzmann. *Design and Validation of Computer Protocols*. Prentice-Hall, 1991.

[Hol97] G.J. Holzmann. The model checker SPIN. *IEEE Trans. on Software Engineering*, 23(5):279–295, 1997.

[JM87] F. Jahanian and A.K. Mok. A graph-theoretic approach for timing analysis and its implementation. *IEEE Transactions on Computers*, C-36(8):961–975, 1987.

[LHHR94] N.G. Leveson, M. Heimdahl, H. Hildreth, and J.D. Reese. Requirements specification for process control systems. *IEEE Transactions on Software Engineerings*, 20(9), 1994.

[McM93] K. McMillan. *Symbolic model checking: an approach to the state explosion problem*. Kluwer Academic Publishers, 1993.

[PD96] L. Peterson and B. Davie. *Computer Networks: A Systems Approach*. Morgan Kaufmann, 1996.

[Pet81] G. Peterson. Myths about the mutual exclusion problem. *Information Processing Letters*, 12(3), 1981.

[QS82] J.P. Queille and J. Sifakis. Specification and verification of concurrent programs in CESAR. In *Proceedings of the Fifth International Symposium on Programming*, LNCS 137, pages 195–220. Springer-Verlag, 1982.

[SGW94] B. Selic, G. Gullekson, and P.T. Ward. *Real-time object oriented modeling and design*. J. Wiley, 1994.

Formal Verification of VLIW Microprocessors with Speculative Execution[1]

Miroslav N. Velev

mvelev@ece.cmu.edu
http://www.ece.cmu.edu/~mvelev
Department of Electrical and Computer Engineering
Carnegie Mellon University, Pittsburgh, PA 15213, U.S.A.

Abstract. This is a study of the formal verification of a VLIW microprocessor that imitates the Intel Itanium [9][12][17] in features such as predicated execution, register remapping, advanced and speculative loads, and branch prediction. The formal verification is done with the Burch and Dill flushing technique [5] by exploiting the properties of Positive Equality [3][4]. The contributions include an extensive use of conservative approximations in abstracting portions of the processor and a framework for decomposition of the Boolean evaluation of the correctness formula. The conservative approximations are applied automatically when abstracting a memory whose forwarding logic is not affected by stalling conditions that preserve the correctness of the memory semantics for the same memory. These techniques allow a reduction of more than a factor of 4 in the CPU time for the formal verification of the most complex processor model examined relative to the monolithic evaluation of the correctness formula for a version of the same processor where conservative approximations are not applied.

1 Introduction

VLIW architectures have been adopted recently by microprocessor design companies in an effort to increase the instruction parallelism and achieve higher instructions-per-cycle counts. The goal of this work is to make the Burch and Dill flushing technique [5] scale efficiently and with a high degree of automation for the formal verification of VLIW processors with speculative execution. The speculative features considered include predicated execution, register remapping, advanced and speculative loads, and branch prediction—all of them found in the Intel Itanium [9][12][17], to be fabricated in the summer of 2000.

The focus of this work is on efficient and automatic scaling that is clearly impossible with theorem-proving approaches, as demonstrated by Sawada and Hunt [16] and Hosabettu et al. [11]. The former approach was applied to a superscalar processor and required the proofs of around 4,000 lemmas that could be defined only after months, if not a year, of manual work by an expert. The latter work examined the formal verification of a single-issue pipelined and a dual-issue superscalar processors, each of which was formally verified after a month of manual work, with the complexity of the manual intervention increasing with the complexity of the verified design. Clearly, methods that require months of manual work in order to detect a bug will be impractical for the formal verification of wide VLIW designs with many parallel pipelines and specu-

---

1. This research was supported by the SRC under contract 99-DC-684

lative features that will be fine-tuned constantly during aggressive time-to-market design cycles.

The most complex VLIW processor examined in this paper has 9 parallel execution pipelines, all the speculative features listed above, including branch prediction and multicycle functional units of arbitrary latency. Its exhaustive binary simulation would require more than 2^{609} sequences of 5 VLIW instructions each. However, the proposed techniques allow that processor to be formally verified in less than 8 hours of CPU time on a 336 MHz SUN4.

2 Background

In this work, the logic of Equality with Uninterpreted Functions and Memories (EUFM) [5] is used in order to define abstract models for both the implementation and the specification processors. The syntax of EUFM includes terms and formulas. A term can be an Uninterpreted Function (UF) applied on a list of argument terms, a domain variable, or an *ITE* operator selecting between two argument terms based on a controlling formula, such that *ITE(formula, term1, term2)* will evaluate to *term1* when *formula* = **true** and to *term2* when *formula* = **false**. A formula can be an Uninterpreted Predicate (UP) applied on a list of argument terms, a propositional variable, an *ITE* operator selecting between two argument formulas based on a controlling formula, or an equation (equality comparison) of two terms. Formulas can be negated and connected by Boolean connectives. The syntax for terms can be extended to model memories by means of the functions *read* and *write*, where *read* takes 2 argument terms serving as memory and address, respectively, while *write* takes 3 argument terms serving as memory, address, and data. Both functions return a term. Also, they can be viewed as a special class of (partially interpreted) uninterpreted functions in that they are defined to satisfy the forwarding property of the memory semantics, namely that *read(write(mem, aw, d), ar)* = *ITE(ar = aw, d, read(mem, ar))*, in addition to the property of functional consistency. Versions of *read* and *write* that extend the syntax for formulas can be defined similarly, such that the version of *read* will return a formula and the version of *write* will take a formula as its third argument. Both terms and formulas are called expressions.

UFs and UPs are used to abstract away the implementation details of functional units by replacing them with "black boxes" that satisfy no particular properties other than that of *functional consistency*—the same combinations of values to the inputs of the UF (or UP) produce the same output value. Three possible ways to impose the property of functional consistency of UFs and UPs are Ackermann constraints [1], nested *ITE*s [3][4][19], and "pushing-to-the-leaves" [19].

The correctness criterion is based on the flushing technique [5] and is expressed by an EUFM formula of the form

$$m_{1,0} \wedge m_{2,0} \cdots \wedge m_{n,0} \ \vee \ m_{1,1} \wedge m_{2,1} \cdots \wedge m_{n,1} \ \vee \ldots \vee \ m_{1,k} \wedge m_{2,k} \cdots \wedge m_{n,k}, \qquad (1)$$

where n is the number of user-visible state elements in the implementation processor, k is the maximum number of instructions that the processor can fetch in a clock cycle, and $m_{i,j}$, $1 \leq i \leq n$, $0 \leq j \leq k$, is an EUFM formula expressing the condition that user-visible state element i is updated by the first j instructions from the ones fetched in a single clock cycle. (See the electronic version of [19] for a detailed discussion.) The EUFM formulas $m_{1,j}, m_{2,j}, ..., m_{n,j}, 0 \leq j \leq k$, are conjuncted in order to ensure that the user-visible state elements are updated in "sync" by the same number of instructions. The correctness criterion expresses a safety property that the processor completes between 0 and k of the newly fetched k instructions.

In our previous work [19] we developed a completely automatic tool that exploits the properties of Positive Equality [3][4], the e_{ij} encoding [8], and a number of conservative approximations in order to translate the correctness EUFM formula (1) to a propositional formula. The implementation processor is *verified*, i.e., is correct, if the propositional formula obtained from (1) after replacing each $m_{i,j}$ with its corresponding propositional formula $f_{i,j}$, obtained after the translation, evaluates to **true**. This evaluation can be done with either BDDs [2] or SAT-checkers. Our previous research [19] showed that BDDs are unmatched by SAT-checkers in the verification of correct processors. However, we found that SAT-checkers can very quickly generate counter-examples for buggy designs.

Positive Equality allows the identification of two types of terms in the structure of an EUFM formula—those which appear only in positive equations and are called *p-terms*, and those which can appear in both positive and negative equations and are called *g-terms* (for general terms). A *positive equation* is never negated (or appears under an even number of negations) and is not part of the controlling formula for an *ITE* operator. A *negative equation* appears under an odd number of negations or as part of the controlling formula for an *ITE* operator. The computational efficiency from exploiting Positive Equality is due to a theorem which states that the truth of an EUFM formula under a maximally diverse interpretation of the p-terms implies the truth of the formula under any interpretation. The classification of p-terms vs. g-terms is done before UFs and UPs are eliminated by nested *ITE*s, such that if an UF is classified as a p-term (g-term), the new domain variables generated for its elimination are also considered to be p-terms (g-terms). After the UFs and the UPs are eliminated, a maximally diverse interpretation is one where: the equality comparison of two syntactically identical (i.e., exactly the same) domain variables evaluates to **true**; the equality comparison of a p-term domain variable with a syntactically distinct domain variable evaluates to **false**; and the equality comparison of a g-term domain variable with a syntactically distinct g-term domain variable could evaluate to either **true** or **false** and can be encoded with a dedicated Boolean variable—an e_{ij} variable [8].

In order to fully exploit the benefits of Positive Equality, the designer of an abstract processor model must use a set of suitable abstractions and conservative approximations. For example, an equality comparison of two data operands, as used to determine the condition to take a branch-on-equal instruction, must be abstracted with an UP in both the implementation and the specification, so that the data operand terms will not appear in negated equations but only as arguments to UPs and UFs and hence will be classified as p-terms. Similarly, a Finite State Machine (FSM) model of a memory has to be employed for abstracting the Data Memory in order for the addresses, which are produced by the ALU and also serve as data operands, to be classified as p-terms. In the FSM abstraction of a memory, the present memory state is a term that is stored in a latch. Reads are modeled with an UF f_r that depends on the present memory state and the address, while producing a term for the read data. Writes are modeled with an UF f_u that depends on the present memory state, the address, and a data term, producing a term for the new memory state, which is to be stored in the latch. The result is that data values produced by the Register File, the ALU, and the Data Memory can be classified as p-terms, while only the register identifiers, whose equations control forwarding and stalling conditions that can be negated, are classified as g-terms.

We will refer to a transformation on the implementation and specification processors as a *conservative approximation* if it omits some properties, making the new processor models more general than the original ones. Note that the same transformation is applied to both the implementation and the specification processors. However, if the more general model of the implementation is verified against the more general model of the specification, so would be the detailed implementation against the detailed specification, whose additional properties were not necessary for the verification.

Proposition 1. *The FSM model of a memory is a conservative approximation of a memory.*

Proof. If a processor is verified with the FSM model of a memory where the update function f_u and the read function f_r are completely arbitrary uninterpreted functions that do not satisfy the forwarding property of the memory semantics, then the processor will be verified for any implementation of f_u and f_r, including $f_u \equiv$ *write* and $f_r \equiv$ *read*. ∎

3 VLIW Architecture Verified

The goal of this paper is to formally verify the VLIW processor shown in Fig. 1. On every clock cycle, the Fetch Engine produces a packet of 9 instructions that are already matched with one of 9 functional units: 4 integer (Int FU), 2 floating-point (FP FU), and 3 branch-address (BA FU). There are no data dependencies among the instructions in a packet, as guaranteed by the compiler. Any number of instructions in a packet can be valid, i.e., can have the potential to modify user-visible state. Data values are stored in 4 register files—Integer (Int), Floating-Point (FP), Branch-Address (BA), and Predicate (Pred). A location in the Predicate Register File contains a single bit of data. Every instruction is predicated with a qualifying predicate register, such that the result of the instruction is written to user-visible state only if the qualifying predicate register has a value of 1. The predication is done at compile time.

A Current Frame Marker register (CFM) is used to remap the register identifiers for accessing the Integer, Floating-Point, and Predicate Register Files. The CFM can be modified by every instruction in a packet. Two of the Integer Functional Units can generate addresses for accessing the Data Memory that is used for storing both integer and floating-point values. An Advanced Load Address Table (ALAT) is used as hardware support for advanced and speculative loads—a compile-time speculation. Every data address accessed by an advanced/speculative load is stored in the ALAT and is evicted from there by subsequent store instructions overwriting the same address. Special instructions check if an address, that was accessed by an advanced/speculative load, is still in the ALAT. If not, these instructions perform a branch to code where the load will be repeated non-speculatively together with any computations that have been performed on the incorrect speculative data. Both the CFM and the ALAT are user-visible state elements. A Branch Predictor supplies the Fetch Engine with one prediction on every clock cycle.

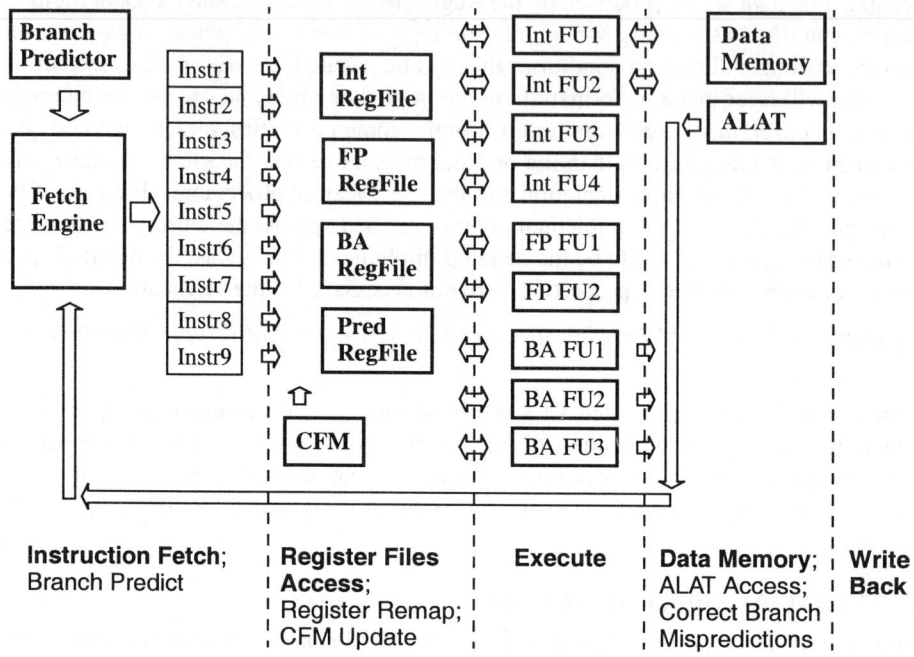

Fig. 1. Block diagram of the VLIW architecture that is formally verified.

The Predicate Register File can be updated with predicate values computed by each of the 4 integer and 2 floating-point functional units. A predicate result depends on the instruction Opcode, the integer or floating-point data operands, respectively, and the value of a source predicate register. The Predicate Register File contents can be overwritten entirely or partially with the value of a data operand, as determined by an instruction Opcode for those 6 functional units. Note that each predicate value consists of a single bit, so that the contents of the Predicate Register File is the concatenation of these bits for all predicate register identifiers. The Predicate Register File contents can be moved to a destination integer register by each of the 4 integer functional units.

Integer values from the Integer Register File can be converted to floating-point values and written to a destination in the Floating-Point Register File by each of the two floating-point functional units. These functional units can similarly convert a floating-point value to an integer one, which gets written to a destination in the Integer Register File. The floating-point functional units also perform floating-point computations on 2 floating-point operands. The 2 floating-point ALUs, the Instruction Memory, and the Data Memory can each have a multicycle and possibly data-dependent latency for producing a result.

The value of a register in the Branch-Address Register File can be transferred to a destination in the Integer Register File by each of the 4 integer functional units. Furthermore, the integer functional units can perform computations for which one of the operands is supplied by the Branch-Address Register File, the other by the Integer Register File, with the result being written to a destination in the Branch-Address Register File. The values in that register file are used by the 3 branch-address functional units for computing of branch target addresses, which also depend on the PC of the VLIW instruction packet and the instruction Opcode for the corresponding functional unit. A branch is taken if its qualifying predicate evaluates to 1.

The VLIW processor that is formally verified has 5 pipeline stages (see Fig. 1): Fetch, Register-Files-Access, Execution, Data-Memory-Access, and Write-Back. The Fetch Engine is implemented as a Program Counter (PC) that accesses a read-only Instruction Memory in order to produce a VLIW packet of 9 instructions. Forwarding is employed in the Execution stage in order to avoid read-after-write hazards for data values read from each of the 4 register files by supplying the latest data to be written to the corresponding source register by the instructions in the Data-Memory-Access and Write-Back stages. However, forwarding is not possible for integer and floating-point values loaded from the Data Memory and used by an instruction in the next packet. In such cases, the hazards are avoided by stalling the entire packet of the dependent instruction(s) in the Register-Files-Access stage and inserting a bubble packet in the Execution stage. Testing a qualifying predicate register for being 1 is done in the Execution stage after forwarding the most recent update for that predicate register.

The updates of the CFM are done speculatively in the Register-Files-Access stage in order not to delay the execution of the instructions in subsequent packets. However, the original value of the CFM is carried down the pipeline together with the packet that modified it. Should that packet be squashed in a later pipeline stage, then its modification of the CFM should not have been done and the original CFM value is restored.

Accounting for all control bits that affect the updating of user-visible state and for all possible forwarding and stalling conditions, an exhaustive binary simulation need consider 2^{609} sequences of 5 VLIW instruction packets each, based on the Burch and Dill flushing technique. This number increases significantly when also considering possible mispredictions or correct predictions of branches, and single-/multi- cycle latencies of the multicycle functional units and memories.

4 Discussion

The above VLIW architecture imitates the Intel Itanium [9][17] in that it has the same numbers and types of execution pipelines, as well as features such as predicated execution, register remapping, advanced and speculative loads, and branch prediction. A further similarity is that the Instruction Memory, the two Floating-Point ALUs, and the Data Memory can each take single or multiple cycles in order to produce their results. The processor also has the same register files as the Itanium, as well as the same capabilities to move data between them. However, two differences should be mentioned.

First, the Register-Files-Access stage is distributed across 3 pipeline stages in the Intel Itanium [9]. While these 3 stages are very simple, their modeling as separate stages resulted in an order of magnitude increase in the CPU time for the formal verification. This was due to an increase in the number of e_{ij} Boolean variables encoding equalities (see Sect. 2) between the then much larger numbers of source and destination register identifiers for accessing the Integer and Floating-Point Register Files. However, the single Register-Files-Access stage can be viewed as an unpipelined implementation of these 3 stages in the Itanium. It will be the focus of our future research to prove the correctness of a superpipelining transformation that splits that single stage into 3 stages. Alternatively, one can prove the correctness of unpipelining the 3 stages into a single stage. Unpipelining has been previously used for merging stages in a pipelined processor [13] in order to reduce the formal verification complexity, although that was possible only after extensive manual intervention for defining induction hypotheses correlating the signals in the two design versions.

Second, the Itanium Fetch Engine also occupies 3 pipeline stages, the last of which dispatches instructions to the 9 functional units. However, the Fetch stage of the architecture in Fig. 1 can be viewed as an abstraction of a 3-stage Fetch Engine in that it has the same communication mechanism with the Execution Engine (the last 4 stages in Fig. 1) as the Fetch Engine in the Itanium. Namely, the Fetch stage will provide the Execution Engine with the same group of inputs on the next clock cycle if it is stalled by the Execution Engine in the present clock cycle. The refinement of the single Fetch stage into a detailed model of the Itanium Fetch Engine will be the focus of our future research.

On the other hand, the VLIW architecture verified is comparable to, if not more complex than, the StarCore [10] by Motorola and Lucent. The StarCore is a VLIW processor that also has a 5-stage pipeline, consisting of exactly the same stages. It supports predicated execution. However, it has 6 instructions per VLIW packet, does not implement register remapping, does not support floating-point computations (so that it does not have a Floating-Point Register File), does not execute advanced and speculative loads, and does not have branch prediction.

5 Exploiting Conservative Approximations

The CFM and the ALAT were abstracted with finite state machines (FSMs), similar to the Data Memory (see Sect. 2). In the case of the CFM, shown in Fig. 2, the first instruction in a packet modifies the present state via an UF that depends on the CFM present state and the Opcode of the instruction. Each subsequent instruction similarly modifies the latest CFM state obtained after the updates by the preceding instructions in the packet. The final modified CFM state is written to the CFM latch only if the instruction packet is valid. In the case of the ALAT, each valid load or store instruction modifies the present state. The modification is done by an UF that depends on the present state of the ALAT, the instruction Opcode, and the address for the Data Memory access. In this way, an arbitrary update is modeled, including the actual update that takes place only if the Opcode designates an advanced/speculative load or a store instruction. The special check instructions, that check whether the address of an advanced/speculative load has been evicted from the ALAT, are modeled with an UP that depends on the present ALAT state, the instruction Opcode, and the checked address. That UP produces a Boolean signal indicating whether to take a branch to an address provided in the instruction encoding in order to redo the speculative computations done with possibly incorrect data. Because the UFs used in the abstraction of the CFM and the ALAT do not model any actual properties of these units, the FSM models of the CFM and the ALAT are conservative approximations (see Proposition 1). Note that the ALAT is part of the user-visible state and is used in the non-pipelined specification as it provides support for static compile-time speculation—advanced and speculative loads—as opposed to dynamic run-time speculation that is done only in the implementation processor.

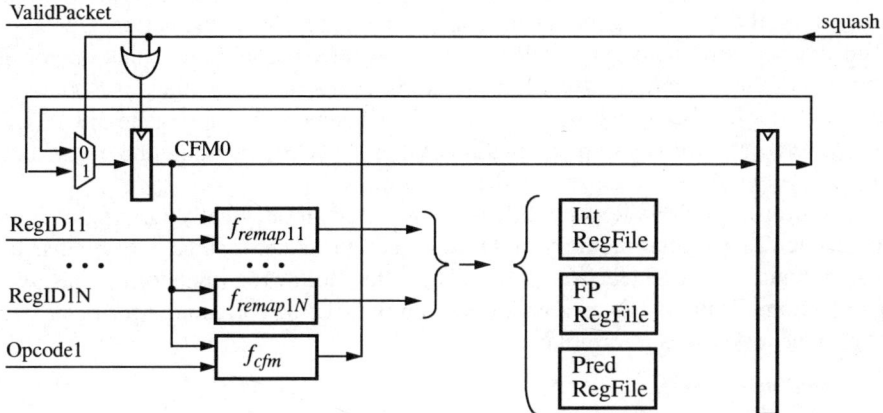

Fig. 2. Abstraction of the CFM. Uninterpreted functions $f_{remap11}, ..., f_{remap1N}$ abstract the functional units that remap register ids provided in an instruction encoding into new register ids to be used for accessing a register file. The updates of the CFM are abstracted with UF f_{cfm}. The original value CFM0 is restored if the packet is squashed in a later stage. The remapping and updating UFs are shown for only one instruction. Register remapping is a compile-time optimization.

The Predicate Register File was also abstracted with an FSM, as shown in Fig. 3. The latest updated state of the entire Predicate Register File is available in the Execution stage, because the VLIW architecture is defined to be able to transfer the entire contents of the Predicate Register File to a destination in the Integer Register File.

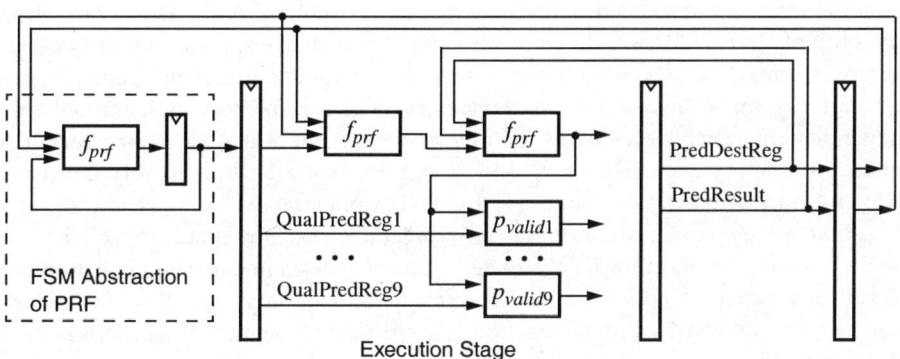

Fig. 3. Abstraction of the Predicate Register File (PRF). Uninterpreted function f_{prf} abstracts the updating of the PRF in both the FSM model of this register file and its forwarding logic. Each predicate result in flight gets reflected on the latest PRF state by one application of f_{prf}. Uninterpreted predicates $p_{valid1}, ..., p_{valid9}$ abstract the testing of a qualifying predicate register for being 1.

Each level of forwarding logic for the Predicate Register File is abstracted with an application of the same UF that is used to update the state of that register file in its FSM abstraction. The value of a qualifying predicate register identifier is tested for being **true/false** by means of an UP that depends on the latest Predicate Register File state and the qualifying predicate register identifier. Thus, an arbitrary predicate is modeled, including the actual multiplexor selecting the predicate bit at the location specified by the qualifying predicate register identifier. The instruction Opcode is included as an extra input to that UP in order to achieve partial functional non-consistency [18] of the UP across different instructions. Including extra inputs is a conservative approximation, because if the processor is verified with the more general UP (UF), it would be correct for any implementation of that UP (UF), including the original one where the output does not depend on the extra inputs.

The Branch-Address Register File was abstracted automatically. Originally, it was implemented as a regular memory in the Register-Files-Access stage with regular forwarding logic in the Execution stage. Then, the following transformations were applied automatically by the evaluation tool on the EUFM correctness formula, starting from the leaves of the formula:

$$read(m, a) \rightarrow f_r(m, a) \tag{2}$$

$$write(m, a, d) \rightarrow f_u(m, a, d) \tag{3}$$

$$ITE(e \wedge (ar = aw), d, f_r(m, ar)) \rightarrow f_r(ITE(e, f_u(m, aw, d), m), ar) \tag{4}$$

Transformations (2) and (3) are the same as those used in the abstraction of the Data Memory, described in Sect. 2. Transformation (4) occurs in the cases when one level of forwarding logic is used to update the data read from address ar of the previous state m for the memory, where function $read$ is already abstracted with UF f_r. Accounting for the forwarding property of the memory semantics that was satisfied before function $read$ was abstracted with UF f_r, the left handside of (4) is equivalent to a read from address ar of the state of memory m after a write to address aw with data d is done under the condition that formula e is **true**. On the right handside of (4), functions $read$ and $write$ are again abstracted with f_r and f_u after accounting for the forwarding property. Multiple levels of forwarding are abstracted by recursive applications of (4), starting from the leaves of the correctness formula. Uninterpreted functions f_u and f_r can be automatically made unique for every memory, where a memory is identified by a unique domain variable serving as the memory argument at the leaves of a term that represents memory state. Hence, f_u and f_r will no longer be functionally consistent across memories—yet another conservative approximation.

After all memories are automatically abstracted as presented above, the tool checks if an address term for an abstracted memory is used in a negated equation outside the abstracted memories, i.e., is a g-term. If so, then the abstractions for all such memories are undone. Hence, abstraction is performed automatically only for a memory whose addresses are p-terms outside the memory and the forwarding logic for it. From Proposition 1, it follows that such an abstraction is a conservative approximation. The fact that address terms of abstracted memories are used only as p-terms outside the abstracted memories avoids false negatives that might result when a (negated) equation of two address terms will imply that a write to one of the addresses will (not) affect a read from the other address in the equation when that read is performed later—a property that is lost in the abstraction with UFs. In the examined architecture, the Integer and Floating-Point Register Files end up having g-term addresses after abstraction because of the stalling logic that enforces a load interlock avoiding the data hazard when a load provides data for an immediately following dependent instruction. Hence, only the Branch-Address Register File, that is not affected by load interlocks, is abstracted automatically. The Data Memory was abstracted manually with an FSM in order to define its UFs for reading and updating to have the Opcode as an extra input in order to model byte-level memory accesses, as well as to achieve partial functional non-consistency. However, if the Opcode is not used as an extra input and the Data Memory is defined as a regular memory, then the algorithm will automatically achieve conservative approximation of the Data Memory by applying transformations (2) and (3) only.

Note that the abstraction of the Branch-Address and Predicate Register Files helps avoid the introduction of e_{ij} Boolean variables that would have been required otherwise in order to encode the equality comparisons of branch-address and predicate register identifiers, respectively, as would have been needed by unabstracted memories and forwarding logic.

An UF was used as a "translation box" for the new PC value before it is written to the PC latch, similar to our previous work [20]. That UF models an arbitrary modification of the new PC values. Therefore, this transformation is a conservative approximation in that if a processor is verified with a translation box, it would be correct for any implementation of that UF, including the identity function that simply connects the input to the output—the case before inserting the translation box. However, that UF results in common subexpression substitution, reducing the complexity of the PC values, and hence of the final equality comparisons for the state of the PC as used in the correctness formula.

6 Decomposing the Computation of the Correctness Criterion

The problem that was encountered in formally verifying variants of the VLIW architecture presented in Sect. 3 is that the monolithic evaluation of the propositional formula obtained from (1) does not scale well with increasing the design complexity. The solution is to propose a framework for decomposing the monolithic evaluation into a set of simpler evaluations, each of which depends on a subset of the propositional formulas $f_{i,j}$ obtained after the translation of the EUFM formulas $m_{i,j}$ in (1) to propositional logic. Furthermore, these simpler evaluations are not dependent on each other, so that they can be performed in parallel. Some terminology first.

A *literal* is an instance of a Boolean variable or its complement. Any Boolean function that depends on n Boolean variables can be expresses as a sum of products (disjunction of conjuncts) of n literals, called the *minterms* of the function. Equivalently, a Boolean function can be interpreted as the set of its minterms. Then, the disjunction and the conjunction of two Boolean functions are the union and intersection of their minterm sets, respectively. Stating that $a \subseteq b$, where a and b are two Boolean functions, is equivalent to say that the set of minterms of b includes the minterms of a, while $a \subset b$ means that b includes extra minterms in addition to the minterms of a. We will say that the $k+1$ Boolean functions, $b_0, b_1, ..., b_k$, form a base, if they cover the entire Boolean space, i.e., $b_0 \vee b_1 \vee ... \vee b_k \equiv$ **true**, and are pair-wise disjoint, i.e., $b_i \wedge b_j \equiv$ **false** for all $i \neq j$, $0 \leq i, j \leq k$. We will refer to functions b_i, $0 \leq i \leq k$, that form a base as *base functions*. The definition of base functions is identical to that of disjoint window functions in Partitioned-ROBDDs [14].

Proposition 2. *If the Boolean functions $b_0, b_1, ..., b_k$ form a base, and $b_0 \wedge a_0 \vee b_1 \wedge a_1 \vee ... \vee b_i \wedge a_i \vee ... \vee b_k \wedge a_k \equiv$ **true**, where a_i, $0 \leq i \leq k$, are Boolean functions, then $b_i \subseteq a_i$ for all i, $0 \leq i \leq k$.*

Proof. The proposition is proved by contradiction. Let $b_j \not\subseteq a_j$ for some j, $0 \leq j \leq k$. Then a_j does not contain at least one minterm of b_j, so that $b_j \wedge a_j \subset b_j$ since the conjunction of two Boolean functions can be interpreted as the intersection of their minterm sets. Furthermore, since $b_i \wedge a_i \subseteq b_i$ for $i \neq j$, $0 \leq i \leq k$, it follows that $b_0 \wedge a_0 \vee b_1 \wedge a_1 \vee ... \vee b_j \wedge a_j \vee ... \vee b_k \wedge a_k \subseteq b_0 \vee b_1 \vee ... \vee b_j \wedge a_j \vee ... \vee b_k \subset b_0 \vee b_1 \vee ... \vee b_j \vee ... \vee b_k \equiv$ **true**. Hence, $b_0 \wedge a_0 \vee b_1 \wedge a_1 \vee ... \vee b_i \wedge a_i \vee ... \vee b_k \wedge a_k \not\equiv$ **true**, which is a contradiction to the assumption in the proposition. □

Proposition 3. *If the Boolean functions $b_0, b_1, ..., b_k$ form a base, and $b_0 \vee ... \vee b_{i-1} \vee a_i \vee b_{i+1} \vee ... \vee b_k \equiv$ **true**, $0 \leq i \leq k$, (i.e., replacing one b_i with a Boolean function a_i does not change the value of the disjunction) then $b_i \subseteq a_i$.*

Proof. The proposition is proved by contradiction. Let $b_i \not\subseteq a_i$. Then a_i does not contain at least one minterm of b_i and since that minterm is not contained in any other b_j, $j \neq i$, $0 \leq j \leq k$, as the base functions are pair-wise disjoint, it follows that $b_0 \vee ... \vee b_{i-1} \vee a_i \vee b_{i+1} \vee ... \vee b_k \subset b_0 \vee ... \vee b_{i-1} \vee b_i \vee b_{i+1} \vee ... \vee b_k \equiv$ **true**. Therefore, $b_0 \vee ... \vee b_{i-1} \vee a_i \vee b_{i+1} \vee ... \vee b_k \not\equiv$ **true**, which is a contradiction to the assumption in the proposition. □

Proposition 4. *If the Boolean functions $b_0, b_1, ..., b_k$ form a base, and $b_i \subseteq a_i$, for some i, $0 \leq i \leq k$, where a_i is a Boolean function, then $b_0 \vee ... \vee b_{i-1} \vee b_i \wedge a_i \vee b_{i+1} \vee ... \vee b_k \equiv$ **true**.*

Proof. If $b_i \subseteq a_i$ then $b_i \wedge a_i \equiv b_i$. Therefore, $b_0 \vee ... \vee b_{i-1} \vee b_i \wedge a_i \vee b_{i+1} \vee ... \vee b_k \equiv b_0 \vee ... \vee b_{i-1} \vee b_i \vee b_{i+1} \vee ... \vee b_k \equiv$ **true**. □

Propositions 2 – 4 allow us to decompose the evaluation of the propositional formula for the correctness criterion. First, we have to find a set of Boolean functions $b_0, b_1, ..., b_k$ that form a base, where each b_i is selected as the conjunction of a subset of the Boolean functions $f_{1,i}, f_{2,i}, ..., f_{n,i}$, which are conjuncted together in the propositional translation of (1). Then, for each $f_{j,i}$, $1 \leq j \leq n$, not used in forming b_i, we have to prove that its set of minterms is a superset of the minterms of b_i by using either Proposition 2 or Proposition 3. Then, by Proposition 4, we can compose the results, proving that the monolithic Boolean formula for the processor correctness evaluates to **true** without actually evaluating it.

As an example, let's consider a pipelined processor that can fetch either 0 or 1 new instructions on every clock cycle and that has 3 user-visible state elements—PC, Data Memory (DM), and Register File (RF). In order for the processor to be correct, we will have to prove that a Boolean formula of the form $PC_0 \wedge RF_0 \wedge DM_0 \vee PC_1 \wedge RF_1 \wedge DM_1$ evaluates to **true**. However, instead of evaluating the monolithic Boolean formula, we can prove that PC_0 and PC_1 form a base, i.e., $PC_0 \vee PC_1 \equiv$ **true** and $PC_0 \wedge PC_1 \equiv$ **false**. Additionally, we can prove that, for example:

1. $PC_0 \wedge DM_0 \vee PC_1 \wedge DM_1 \equiv$ **true**, which implies that $PC_0 \subseteq DM_0$ and $PC_1 \subseteq DM_1$ by Proposition 2;
2. $RF_0 \vee PC_1 \equiv$ **true**, which implies that $PC_0 \subseteq RF_0$ by Proposition 3; and,
3. $PC_0 \vee RF_1 \equiv$ **true**, which implies that $PC_1 \subseteq RF_1$ by Proposition 3.

Then, by Proposition 4, it follows that:

$$PC_0 \wedge RF_0 \wedge DM_0 \vee PC_1 \wedge RF_1 \wedge DM_1 \equiv \textbf{true.}$$

If computing resources are available, we can run a redundant set of computations in parallel, i.e., using multiple sets of Boolean functions as bases, and exploiting both propositions 2 and 3. Note that Proposition 2 can be applied in a version where only one of the base functions b_i, $0 \le i \le k$, is conjuncted with a Boolean function a_i by setting $a_j =$ **true** for all $j \ne i$, $0 \le j \le k$. Also note that both propositions 2 and 3 hold when a_i, $0 \le i \le k$, is the conjunction of several Boolean functions. Furthermore, we can use both BDDs and SAT-checkers. All computations that are still running can be stopped as soon as enough containment properties have been proved, so that they can be composed by Proposition 4 in order to imply that the monolithic Boolean formula for the correctness criterion will evaluate to **true**. Additionally, the simpler Boolean computations will speed up the generation of counterexamples for buggy designs.

Note that the proposed decomposition of the Boolean evaluation of the correctness formula does not require much expertise and can be done automatically. Namely, the Boolean functions that form a base can be selected automatically by choosing such $f_{i,j}$ from the propositional translation of (1) that have the smallest number of Boolean variables before their BDD is built or, alternatively, the smallest number of nodes in their EUFM representation. The base functions serve as automatic case-splitting expressions. In his work, Burch had to manually identify 28 case-splitting expressions [6]. He also had to manually decompose the commutative diagram for the correctness criterion into three diagrams. That decomposition required the intervention of an expert user, and was sufficiently subtle to warrant publication of its correctness proof as a separate paper [21].

7 Modeling Multicycle Functional Units and Branch Prediction

Multicycle functional units are abstracted with "place holders" [20], where an UF abstracts the function of the unit, while a new Boolean variable is produced by a generator of arbitrary values on every clock cycle in order to express the completion of the multicycle computation in the present cycle. Under this scheme, however, a multicycle computation will never finish under the assignments where the Boolean variables expressing completion evaluate to **false**. This is avoided by forcing the completion signal to **true** during the flushing of the processor, based on the observation [6] that the logic of the processor can be modified during flushing as all it does is completing the instructions in flight. A mistake in this modification can only result in a false negative.

The correct semantics of the multicycle functional unit is modeled in the non-pipelined specification only by the UF used to abstract the functionality. The place holder for a multicycle memory is defined similarly, except that a regular memory or an FSM abstraction of a memory is used instead of the UF.

The Branch Predictor in the implementation processor is abstracted with a generator of arbitrary values [20], producing arbitrary predictions for both the taken/not-taken direction (represented with a new Boolean variable) and the target (a new domain variable) of a branch. What is verified is that if the implementation processor updates speculatively the PC according to a branch prediction made in an early stage of the pipeline and the prediction is incorrect as determined when the actual direction and target become available, then the processor has mechanisms to correct the misprediction. The non-pipelined specification does not include a Branch Predictor, which is not part of the user-visible state and is irrelevant for defining the correct instruction semantics. Note that if an implementation processor is verified with completely arbitrary predictions for the direction and target of a branch, that processor will be correct for any actual implementation of the Branch Predictor.

8 Experimental Results

The base benchmark, **9×VLIW**, implements all of the features of the VLIW architecture presented in Sect. 3 except for branch prediction and multicycle functional units. Conservative approximations were used for modeling the Predicate Register File, the CFM, and the ALAT (see Sect. 5). The Branch-Address Register File was abstracted automatically, as described in Sect. 5. In order to measure the benefit of using conservative approximations, 9×VLIW was formally verified with unabstracted Branch-Address Register File that was left as a regular memory with regular forwarding logic—**9×VLIW.uBARF**. The base benchmark was extended with branch prediction in order to create **9×VLIW-BP**, which was then extended with multicycle functional units—the Instruction Memory, the 2 floating-point ALUs, and the Data Memory—in order to build **9×VLIW-BP-MC**. These models were verified against the same non-pipelined VLIW specification, whose semantics was defined in terms of VLIW instruction packets. Because of that, there was no need to impose constraints that the instructions in a packet do not have data dependencies between each other.

The VLIW implementation processors were described in 3,200 – 3,700 lines of our HDL that supports the constructs of the logic of EUFM, while the non-pipelined VLIW specification processor was described in 730 lines of the same HDL. This HDL is very similar to Verilog, so that the abstract description of the implementation processor can be viewed as a level in a hierarchical Verilog description of the processor. At that level, functional units and memories are left as modules (black boxes), while the control logic that glues these modules together is described entirely in terms of logic gates, equality comparators, and multiplexors (the constructs of EUFM). Then, based on information provided in the description and identifying whether a module is either a single-cycle or multicycle functional unit or memory, each of the modules can be automatically replaced by an UF, or an abstract memory, or a place holder for a multicycle functional unit or memory. Similarly, modules like the ALAT (see Sect. 5) can be automatically replaced with an FSM-based abstraction. Hence, the abstract description of the implementation processor can be generated automatically.

The results are presented in Table 1. The experiments were performed on a 336 MHz Sun4 with 1.2 GB of memory. The Colorado University BDD package [7] and the sifting BDD variable reordering heuristic [15] were used to evaluate the final propositional formulas. Burch's controlled flushing [6] was employed for all of the designs.

Processor	Correctness Computation		BDD Variables			Max. BDD Nodes $\times 10^6$	Memory [MB]	CPU Time [h]	CPU Time Ratio
			e_{ij}	Other	Total				
9×VLIW.uBARF	monolithic		1,816	236	2,052	4.8	122	13.68	2.6
	decomposed	sufficient	1,176	174	1,350	2.9	77	5.28	
		max.	1,194	170	1,364	3.3	90		
9×VLIW	monolithic		1,468	236	1,704	1.6	53	6.26	3.58
	decomposed	sufficient	1,176	174	1,350	1.2	45	1.75	
		max.	1,194	170	1,364	1.9	57		
9×VLIW-BP	monolithic		1,886	246	2,132	1.8	59	9.45	3.72
	decomposed	sufficient	1,191	175	1,366	1.3	43	2.54	
		max.	1,209	175	1,384	9.0	200		
9×VLIW-BP-MC	monolithic		2,356	259	2,615	6.8	163	31.57	3.97
	decomposed	sufficient	1,469	214	1,683	2.5	74	7.96	
		max.	1,469	214	1,683	4.2	97		

Table 1. BDD-based Boolean evaluation of the correctness formula. The BDD and memory statistics for the decomposed computations are reported as: "sufficient"—the maximum in each category across the computations that were sufficient to prove that the monolithic Boolean formula is a tautology; "max."—the maximum in each category across all computations run. The CPU time reported for the decomposed computations is the minimum that was required for proving a sufficient set of Boolean containment properties that would imply the monolithic Boolean correctness formula is a tautology.

Decomposition of the Boolean evaluation of the correctness formula accelerated almost 4 times the verification of the most complex benchmark, 9×VLIW-BP-MC. Furthermore, the CPU time ratio would have been much higher than 3.97 if it were calculated relative to the CPU time for the monolithic verification of a version of that processor where conservative approximations are not used to abstract the Branch-Address and Predicate Register Files and their forwarding logic. Indeed, the CPU time ratio for the monolithic verification of 9×VLIW.uBARF (where only the Branch-Address Register File is not abstracted) vs. the CPU time for the decomposed verification of 9×VLIW is 7.86. Note that with faster new computers, the CPU times for the formal verification will decrease, while the CPU time ratio of monolithic vs. decomposed computation can be expected to stay relatively constant for the same benchmarks.

Although decomposition always reduced the number of BDD variables—with up to 35%, compared to the monolithic evaluation—some of the simpler computations required almost 5 times as many BDD nodes and more than 3 times as much memory as the monolithic computation. This was due to differences in the structures of the evaluated Boolean formulas, some of which proved to be difficult for the sifting dynamic BDD variable reordering heuristic. However, the computations that were sufficient to prove that the monolithic formula is a tautology always required fewer resources than the monolithic computation.

The examined processors had 8 user-visible state elements: PC; 4 register files—Integer, Floating-Point, Predicate, and Branch-Address; CFM; ALAT; and Data Memory. The Boolean formulas that form a base were selected to be the ones from the equality comparisons for the state of the CFM, which has a relatively simple updating logic (see Sect. 5). Proving that these functions form a base took between 6 seconds in the case of 9×VLIW and 54 seconds in the case of 9×VLIW-BP-MC, while the number of BDD nodes varied between 10,622 and 52,372, and the number of BDD variables was between 255 and 411.

The relatively simple Boolean formulas formed from the equality comparisons for the state of the ALAT were used in order to perturb the structure of the evaluated Boolean formulas. Specifically, instead of proving only that $CFM_i \subseteq f_i$ for some i (i.e., the base function CFM_i is contained in f_i), where f_i is the Boolean formula formed from the equality comparison for the state of some user-visible state element, a simultaneous proof was run for $CFM_i \subseteq f_i \wedge ALAT_i$. This strategy resulted in additional Boolean formulas with slightly different structure, without a significant increase in the number of Boolean variables. Note that the number of Boolean variables in a formula is not indicative of the time that it would take to build the BDD for the formula. Sometimes the structural variations helped the sifting heuristic for dynamic BDD variable reordering to speed up the BDD-based evaluation. Applied only for Proposition 2, this strategy reduced the formal verification time for 9×VLIW-BP-MC with around half an hour—from 8.44 hours, that would have been required otherwise, to 7.96 hours.

Decompositions based on Proposition 2 usually required less time to prove the same containment properties, compared to decompositions with Proposition 3. However, Proposition 2 alone would have required 9.64 hours in order to prove a sufficient set of containment properties for the most complex model, 9×VLIW-BP-MC. Given sufficient computing resources, a winning approach will be to run a large set of computations in parallel, exploiting different structural variations in the Boolean formulas in order to achieve a performance gain for the BDD variable reordering heuristic.

9 Conclusions

A VLIW microprocessor was formally verified. Its Execution Engine imitates that of the Intel Itanium [9][16], while its Fetch Engine is simpler. The modeled features are comparable to, if not more complex than, those of the StarCore [10] microprocessor by Motorola and Lucent. Efficient formal verification was possible after an extensive use of conservative approximations—some of them applied automatically—in defining the abstract implementation and specification processors, in addition to exploiting a decomposed Boolean evaluation of the correctness formula.

Acknowledgments

The author thanks his advisor, Prof. Randy Bryant, for comments on the paper.

References

[1] W. Ackermann, *Solvable Cases of the Decision Problem*, North-Holland, Amsterdam, 1954.
[2] R.E. Bryant, "Symbolic Boolean Manipulation with Ordered Binary-Decision Diagrams," ACM Computing Surveys, Vol. 24, No. 3 (September 1992), pp. 293-318.
[3] R.E. Bryant, S. German, and M.N. Velev, "Exploiting Positive Equality in a Logic of Equality with Uninterpreted Functions,"[2] *Computer-Aided Verification (CAV'99)*, N. Halbwachs and D. Peled, eds., LNCS 1633, Springer-Verlag, June 1999, pp. 470-482.
[4] R.E. Bryant, S. German, and M.N. Velev, "Processor Verification Using Efficient Reductions of the Logic of Uninterpreted Functions to Propositional Logic,"[2] Technical Report CMU-CS-99-115, Carnegie Mellon University, 1999.
[5] J.R. Burch, and D.L. Dill, "Automated Verification of Pipelined Microprocessor Control," *Computer-Aided Verification (CAV'94)*, D.L. Dill, ed., LNCS 818, Springer-Verlag, June 1994, pp. 68-80.
[6] J.R. Burch, "Techniques for Verifying Superscalar Microprocessors," *33rd Design Automation Conference (DAC'96)*, June 1996, pp. 552-557.
[7] CUDD-2.3.0, http://vlsi.colorado.edu/~fabio.
[8] A. Goel, K. Sajid, H. Zhou, A. Aziz, and V. Singhal, "BDD Based Procedures for a Theory of Equality with Uninterpreted Functions," *Computer-Aided Verification (CAV'98)*, A.J. Hu and M.Y. Vardi, eds., LNCS 1427, Springer-Verlag, June 1998, pp. 244-255.
[9] L. Gwennap, "Merced Shows Innovative Design," Microprocessor Report, Vol. 13, No. 13 (October 6, 1999), pp. 1-10.
[10] T.R. Halfhill, "StarCore Reveals Its First DSP," Microprocessor Report, Vol. 13, No. 6 (May 10, 1999), pp. 13-16.
[11] R. Hosabettu, M. Srivas, and G. Gopalakrishnan, "Decomposing the Proof of Correctness of Pipelined Microprocessors," *Computer-Aided Verification (CAV'98)*, A.J. Hu and M.Y. Vardi, eds., LNCS 1427, Springer-Verlag, June 1998, pp. 122-134.
[12] *IA-64 Application Developer's Architecture Guide*,[3] Intel Corporation, May 1999.
[13] J.R. Levitt, *Formal Verification Techniques for Digital Systems*, Ph.D. Thesis, Department of Electrical Engineering, Stanford University, December 1998.
[14] A. Narayan, J. Jain, M. Fujita, and A. Sangiovanni-Vincentelli, "Partitioned ROBDDs—A Compact, Canonical and Efficient Manipulable Representation for Boolean Functions," *International Conference on Computer-Aided Design (ICCAD'96)*, November 1996, pp. 547-554.
[15] R. Rudell, "Dynamic Variable Ordering for Ordered Binary Decision Diagrams," *International Conference on Computer-Aided Design (ICCAD'93)*, November 1993, pp. 42-47.
[16] J. Sawada, and W.A. Hunt, Jr., "Processor Verification with Precise Exceptions and Speculative Execution," *Computer-Aided Verification (CAV'98)*, A.J. Hu and M.Y. Vardi, eds., LNCS 1427, Springer-Verlag, June 1998, pp. 135-146.
[17] H. Sharangpani, "Intel Itanium Processor Michroarchitecture Overview,"[3] *Microprocessor Forum*, October 1999.
[18] M.N. Velev, and R.E. Bryant, "Exploiting Positive Equality and Partial Non-Consistency in the Formal Verification of Pipelined Microprocessors,"[2] *36th Design Automation Conference (DAC '99)*, June 1999, pp. 397-401.
[19] M.N. Velev, and R.E. Bryant, "Superscalar Processor Verification Using Efficient Reductions of the Logic of Equality with Uninterpreted Functions to Propositional Logic,"[2] *Correct Hardware Design and Verification Methods (CHARME '99)*, L. Pierre and T. Kropf, eds., LNCS 1703, Springer-Verlag, September 1999, pp. 37-53.
[20] M.N. Velev, and R.E. Bryant, "Formal Verification of Superscalar Microprocessors with Multicycle Functional Units, Exceptions, and Branch Prediction,"[2] *37th Design Automation Conference (DAC '00)*, June 2000.
[21] P.J. Windley, and J.R. Burch, "Mechanically Checking a Lemma Used in an Automatic Verification Tool," *Formal Methods in Computer-Aided Design (FMCAD'96)*, M. Srivas and A. Camilleri, eds., LNCS 1166, Springer-Verlag, November 1996, pp. 362-376.

---

2. Available from: http://www.ece.cmu.edu/~mvelev
3. Available from: http://developer.intel.com/design/ia-64/architecture.htm

Induction in Compositional Model Checking

Kenneth L. McMillan[1], Shaz Qadeer[2], and James B. Saxe[2]

[1] Cadence Berkeley Labs
[2] Compaq Systems Research Center

Abstract. This paper describes a technique of inductive proof based on model checking. It differs from previous techniques that combine induction and model checking in that the proof is fully mechanically checked and temporal variables (process identifiers, for example) may be natural numbers. To prove $\forall n.\varphi(n)$ inductively, the predicate $\varphi(n-1) \Rightarrow \varphi(n)$ must be proved for all values of the parameter n. Its proof for a fixed n uses a conservative abstraction that partitions the natural numbers into a finite number of intervals. This renders the model finite. Further, the abstractions for different values of n fall into a finite number of isomorphism classes. Thus, an inductive proof of $\forall n.\varphi(n)$ can be obtained by checking a finite number of formulas on finite models. The method is integrated with a compositional proof system based on the SMV model checker. It is illustrated by examples, including the N-process "bakery" mutual exclusion algorithm.

1 Introduction

In verifying concurrent or reactive systems, we are often called upon to reason about ordered sets. For example, a packet router may be required to deliver a sequence of packets in order, or a set of processes may be ordered by a linear or grid topology. In such cases, it is convenient to reason by induction. For example, we show that if packet $i-1$ is delivered correctly, then so is packet i, or that if a ring arbiter with $n-1$ processes is live, then so is a ring with n processes. Indeed, inductive proof may be necessary if the ordered set is unbounded.

For an ordered set of finite state processes, it is natural to consider using model checking to prove the inductive step. This was proposed a decade ago by Kurshan and McMillan [KM89] and by Wolper and Lovinfosse [WL89]. They considered a class of finite-state processes constructed inductively, and an inductive invariant over this class also expressed as a finite-state process. To prove the invariant, it suffices to check the inductive step of the proof for a finite number of instances of the induction parameter. This task can be carried out by finite-state methods. However, no mechanical method was proposed to check the validity of this "meta-proof", or to automatically generate the required instances of the induction step. Further the technique was limited to finite state invariants. This limitation can be observed, for example, in the work of Henzinger, Qadeer and Rajamani [HQR99], who constructed an inductive proof of a cache coherence protocol. The method cannot be applied to protocols that exchange process identifiers (a very common case in practice) because these are not "finite state".

Here, we extend induction *via* model checking beyond finite state invariants, to problems that have not generally been considered amenable to solution by model checking. Our proof method uses a general induction scheme that allows mutual induction over multiple induction parameters. Models for appropriate instances of the induction parameters are generated automatically, and all proof steps are mechanically checked. We illustrate these advantages by examples, including a proof of safety and liveness of a version of the N-process "bakery" mutual exclusion algorithm [Lam74].

Our technique has been integrated into the SMV proof assistant, a proof system based on a first order temporal logic [McM97,McM98,McM99].[1] Both the system to be verified and the specification are expressed in temporal logic, though with a great deal of "syntactic sugar". Inductive proofs are reduced to finite state subgoals in the following way. To prove a predicate $\forall n.\varphi(n)$ inductively, we need to prove $\varphi(n-1) \Rightarrow \varphi(n)$ for all values of the parameter n ($\varphi(-1)$ is defined to be true). In general, $\varphi(n)$ may also refer to some fixed constants such as zero, the number of processes, sizes of arrays, etc. To make the problem finite-state for a particular value of n, we abstract the natural numbers to a finite set of intervals. Typically, the values $n-1$, n, and the fixed constants of interest are represented by singleton intervals, while each interval between these values becomes a single abstract value. We observe that the abstractions for values of n satisfying the same inequality relationships over the given terms (*e.g.*, $0 < n-1 < n$) are isomorphic. Thus it is sufficient to enumerate the feasible inequality relationships (which we call "inequality classes") and verify one representative value of n from each. Thus, we reduce the problem to a finite number of finite-state subgoals.

Related work This work builds on the techniques developed by McMillan [McM98,McM99] —temporal case splitting, reduction of cases by symmetry and data type reduction— to reduce proof goals to a finite collection of finite-state subgoals that can be discharged by model checking. The idea of using model checking to prove an inductive step has also been used by Rajan, Shankar and Srivas in the PVS system [RSS95]. They embedded the mu-calculus in PVS, using model checking to verify formulas on finite abstract models. These abstractions, however, were constructed manually, and their soundness was proved with user assistance. Here, the abstractions are constructed automatically and are correct by construction. The user specifies at most a set of constants to be used in an abstract type, although often a suitable set can be inferred automatically. Another approach to model checking within a theorem prover is *predicate abstraction*, in which the state of the abstract model is defined by the truth values of a set of predicates on the concrete model (*e.g.*, [SG97]). Once suitable predicates are chosen, decision procedures can construct the abstract model. However, a suitable set of predicates must still be chosen, manually or heuristically. Saïdi and Shankar used such a method in PVS [ORS92] to verify a two-process mutual exclusion algorithm, similar to our N-process example [SS99]. Only safety (*i.e.*,

---

[1] SMV can be obtained from http://www-cad.eecs.berkeley.edu/~kenmcmil/smv.

mutual exclusion) was proved however, and the two-process case does not require induction (except over time). Bensalem, Lakhnech and Owre also report an abstraction technique in PVS that has been used to prove safety in the two-process case [BLO98]. Das, Dill and Park [DDP99] have extended predicate abstraction to deal with parameterized systems by using predicates that involve quantifiers, but they have also considered only safety proofs, not requiring induction. Here, we prove N-process liveness, by induction over a lexical order. We note further that unlike predicate abstraction, which in general requires a high-complexity decision procedure, the present method generates abstract models in linear time.

2 Type Reductions for Ordered Sets

We now consider the abstraction technique used in SMV to support induction. We begin with the notion of an ordered set type, or *ordset*. This is a data type isomorphic to the natural numbers $\{0, 1, \ldots\}$. We would like to prove a proposition of the form $\forall i.\ p(i)$, where p is a temporal property and i ranges over an ordset type T. There are two complications in proving this fact using model checking. First, p may refer to variables of infinite type T, hence the state space is not finite. Second, $p(i)$ must be proved for infinitely many values of i. An abstraction of the type T to a finite set can solve both of these problems, in that it makes the state space finite, and also reduces the values of i to a finite number of equivalence classes.

As observed in [McM98], if values of type T were used in a symmetric way, then it would suffice to check only one fixed value of i. However, this rules out expressions such as $x + 1$ or $x < y$, where x and y are of type T. Since precisely such expressions are needed for proofs by induction over T, we cannot rely on this kind of symmetry argument. We can, however, induce a symmetry by abstracting the type T relative to the value of i. Suppose we fix a value of i. We may then abstract the type T to a set of three values: i itself, an abstract symbol representing the semi-closed interval $[0, i)$, and an abstract symbol representing the open interval (i, ∞). Using a suitable abstract interpretation of each operator in the logic, we obtain a conservative abstraction: if $p(i)$ is true in the abstract (finite) model, then it is true in the concrete (infinite) model.

Abstract operators The abstract operators operate on subsets of the abstract type. We use $\perp$ to refer to the set of all abstract values. As an example, consider the *successor* operation on x, denoted $x + 1$, where x is of type T. The successor of a number in the interval $[0, i)$ might be another value in $[0, i)$, or it might be i, since $[0, i)$ contains $i - 1$. The abstraction does not provide enough information to determine which is the answer. Thus, we say $\{[0, i)\} + 1 = \{[0, i), i\}$. The successor of i is $i + 1$, which must be in the interval (i, ∞). Thus, $\{i\} + 1 = \{(i, \infty)\}$. Further, $x + 1$ for any value of x in (i, ∞) is also in (i, ∞). Thus, in the abstraction, $\{(i, \infty)\} + 1 = \{(i, \infty)\}$. When operating on non-singleton sets of abstract values, we simply define the operator so that it is linear with respect to set union. That is, for example, $(x \cup y) + 1 = (x+1) \cup (y+1)$.

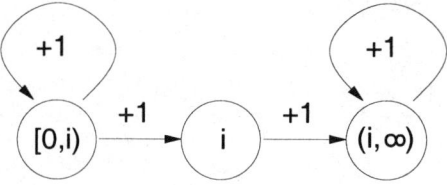

Fig. 1. Abstraction of the natural numbers

=	$[0,i)$	i	(i,∞)
$[0,i)$	$\{0,1\}$	0	0
i	0	1	0
(i,∞)	0	0	$\{0,1\}$

<	$[0,i)$	i	(i,∞)
$[0,i)$	$\{0,1\}$	1	1
i	0	0	1
(i,∞)	0	0	$\{0,1\}$

Fig. 2. Truth tables for abstract comparison operations

This abstract model of type T is depicted in figure 1. As we increment a value of type T, it stays in the interval $[0,i)$ for some arbitrary amount of time, then shifts to i, then stays forever in the interval (i,∞). Note that this model is finite, and homomorphic to the natural numbers, where each number maps to itself, or the interval that contains it (in the extreme case $i = 0$, note that no value maps into the interval $[0,i)$, but the homomorphism still holds). Note that some of the abstract operators are too abstract to be truly useful. For example, we abstract $x + y$ to be simply $\bot$, and any operator on mixed types yields $\bot$.

Now consider the operators $x = y$ and $x < y$ over type T. Figure 2 shows suitable abstract truth tables for these operators. For example, any value in $[0,i)$ is less than i, so $\{[0,i)\} < \{i\}$ is true. Therefore, we let $\{[0,i)\} < \{i\}$ equal $\{1\}$. On the other hand, if both x and y are in $[0,i)$, then $x < y$ may be either true or false, depending on the choice of x and y. Thus, let $\{[0,i)\} < \{[0,i)\}$ equal $\{0,1\}$. By suitable abstract definitions of all the operators in the logic, we maintain a homomorphism from the concrete to the abstract model. Thus, if the abstract model satisfies $p(i)$, then the concrete one does.

Equivalence classes of abstractions This abstraction solves the problem of non-finiteness of the model, but it still leaves us with an infinite set of values of i to check. Note, however, that the abstraction of type T has been chosen so that the abstract models for all values of i are isomorphic. Thus, if we denote by M_i the abstract model for parameter value i, then for any two values x and y of type T, M_x satisfies $p(x)$ exactly when M_y satisfies $p(y)$. It therefore suffices to verify that M_i satisfies $p(i)$ for just one fixed value of i to infer $\forall i.\ p(i)$. Of course, the abstract model may yield a false negative. However, we know at least that all values of i will give the same truth value.

Now, suppose that we have more than one parameter to deal with. For example, we may want to prove $\forall i, j.p(i,j)$, where i and j range over type T. In this case, we introduce more than one concrete value into the abstract type. We do

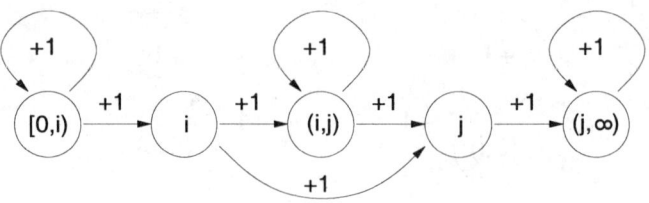

Fig. 3. Abstraction with two parameters

not, however, expect all the abstract models to be isomorphic. Rather, we must distinguish three cases: $i < j$, $i = j$ and $j < i$. In the first case, for example, we can abstract the type T to the set

$$\{[0, i), i, (i, j), j, (j, \infty)\}.$$

The abstract model of type T would then be as pictured in figure 3. Note in particular that the value of $i + 1$ here can be either (i, j) or j. This is because the the interval (i, j) can be either empty or non-empty, and both cases must be accounted for. The case where $j < i$ is the same, with the roles of i and j reversed, and the case $i = j$ is the same as for the simpler problem above (figure 1). Within each of these three classes, the abstract models are all isomorphic. This schema can be extended to any number of parameters. However, the number of equivalence classes increases exponentially with the number of parameters. In general, we must consider as a separate class each feasible theory of inequality over the given parameters.

Introduction of fixed constants Generally, proofs by induction refer to one or more fixed constants. For example, the base case (typically 0) often occurs as a constant in the formula p, and other constants may occur as well, as for example the upper bound of an array. Note that in the above system, constants must be abstracted to $\bot$, otherwise the isomorphism between cases is lost. However, it is possible to treat fixed constants in the same way as parameters in the abstract model. The only difference is that certain inequality classes may be vacuous. For example, suppose that we wish to prove $\forall i.\ p(i)$, and the formula $p(i)$ contains the constant 0. We have three classes to consider here: $i = 0$, $i < 0$ and $0 < i$. However, since i ranges over the natural numbers, the case $i < 0$ is infeasible, thus we have only two feasible cases to check. Note that the number of values in the abstract type may sometimes be reduced when fixed constants are involved. For example, for the case where $0 < i$, we could abstract the type T to the set $\{[0, 0), 0, (0, i), i, (i, \infty)\}$. Since the interval $[0, 0)$ is empty, it can be dropped from the abstraction.

In a proof by induction over the parameter i, it is clearly important to be able to refer to the value $i - 1$. That is, the formula $p(i)$ that we wish to prove is typically of the form $q(i - 1) \Rightarrow q(i)$. If the formula $i - 1$ yielded an abstract constant, the proof would be unlikely to succeed. However, we can also include terms of the form $i + c$, where c is a fixed value, in the abstraction without

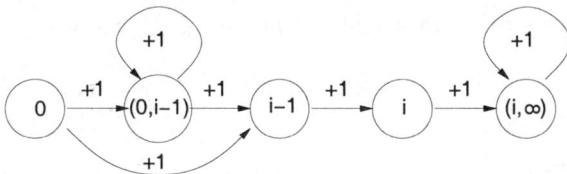

Fig. 4. Abstract type for induction proof

breaking the isomorphism. It is simply a matter of enumerating all the feasible inequality relations and eliminating the interval constants that are necessarily empty. For example, suppose we choose to an abstraction using the terms 0, i and $i - 1$. There are three feasible inequality relations among these terms:

$$i - 1 < 0 = i$$
$$0 = i - 1 < i$$
$$0 < i - 1 < i$$

In the case $0 < i - 1 < i$, for example, the intervals $[0, 0)$ and $(i - 1, i)$ are necessarily empty. Thus, we abstract the type T to the set $\{0, (0, i - 1), i - 1, i, (i, \infty)\}$, as shown in figure 4. To prove $p(i)$, we need only choose one value of i satisfying each inequality relation (for example, $i = 0, 1, 2$) as all values satisfying a given relation yield isomorphic abstractions.

Example To see how this abstraction technique can be used in an inductive proof, suppose we have a counter that starts at 0 and increments at each time step by one. This can be represented by the following temporal formula ϕ:

$$(x = 0) \wedge G(x' = x + 1).$$

Here, assume x to be a variable of type T. We would like to prove that for all i in T, eventually $x = i$. That is, $\forall i. q(i)$, where $q(i)$ is $F(x = i)$. By induction, it is sufficient to prove $\forall i.\ p(i)$, where

$$p(i) \equiv (\phi \wedge q(i - 1)) \Rightarrow q(i)$$

(assuming we take $q(-1)$ to be equivalent to true). Using the above abstraction (containing the values 0, $i - 1$ and i) we have three values of i to check, each with a different abstraction of T. For example, the case $i = 2$ falls in the class $0 < i - 1 < i$ (fig 4). Note that if $x = i - 1$, then in this abstraction x must be i at the next time. Thus, if $F(x = i - 1)$, then $F(x = i)$, which is exactly what we want to prove. Since this is true in the abstract model, it must be true in the concrete model. The reader might want to consider the other two cases ($i = 0, 1$), and confirm that our property holds under these abstractions as well. This suffices to prove $p(i)$ for all i, since all of the remaining values of i yield abstractions isomorphic to the case $i = 2$.

Here is how this problem would be entered in the SMV system:

init$(x) := 0$;
next$(x) := x + 1$;

forall(i **in** T) {
    $q[i]$: **assert F** $(x = i)$;
    using $q[i$-$1]$ **prove** $q[i]$;
}

The system automatically chooses the values $0, i - 1, i$ for the abstraction of type T (though this can be chosen manually as well). The three feasible equality relations among these constants are enumerated automatically, and one representative value of i from each relation is chosen. The induction step is then verified by model checking for each corresponding abstraction of type T (this is possible because all are finite). SMV then reports that the property q has been proved. How SMV recognizes that the induction itself is valid is the subject of the next section.

3 Induction Principle

While the above technique allows us to prove that $q(i-1)$ implies $q(i)$, for all i, it does not tell us that this in fact implies $q(i)$ for all i. For this we need an induction rule in the system. While precisely this rule could easily be added to the system, we will consider here a more general scheme, that allows mutual induction over multiple induction parameters. This will be illustrated in section 5 using the "bakery" mutual exclusion algorithm.

To present this, we must first consider how a proof is represented in the SMV system. A proof is a graph, in which the nodes are properties and an edge from property p to property q indicates that p is used to prove q. Proof edges are suggested to the prover by a statement like the following:

using p **prove** q;

The proof graph must be well founded, *i.e.*, have no infinite backward paths. A parameterized property is considered to be equivalent to the set of its ground instances. Thus, for example, the property

forall(i **in** T) $q[i]$: **assert F**$(x = i)$;

is considered to be a shorthand for the infinite set of properties

$q[0]$: **assert F**$(x = 0)$; $q[1]$: **assert F**$(x = 1)$; ...

Similarly, a parameterized proof graph statement, such as

forall(i **in** T) **using** $q[i$-$1]$ **prove** $q[i]$;

is considered to be equivalent to the infinite set of statements:

using $q[-1]$ **prove** $q[0]$; **using** $q[0]$ **prove** $q[1]$; ...

Note, $q[-1]$ is considered to be equivalent to "true". In the case of finitely bounded parameters, SMV can simply construct the proof graph consisting of all of the ground instances and check that there are no cycles. However, for infinite types this is clearly not possible, and for large types it is impractical. Instead, an abstract proof graph is constructed, in which the nodes are parameterized properties and an arc exists between two such properties when there is an arc between any ground instances of the properties. This graph is homomorphic to the graph of ground instances, thus well-foundedness of the former is a sufficient (but not necessary) condition for well-foundedness of the latter.

Unfortunately, this does not allow for inductive proofs. That is, the statement

forall(i **in** T) **using** $q[i\text{-}1]$ **prove** $q[i]$;

implies an edge from $q[i]$ to itself in the abstract proof graph, and hence a cycle. We need an abstraction of the proof graph that preserves well foundedness of inductive proofs. We can obtain this based on the following observation: an infinite path in a graph either is a *simple path* (with no repeated nodes), or it contains a cycle. Thus, if we can prove that every node in the graph is neither on a cycle, nor the root of an infinite simple (backward) path, we know the graph is well founded. The key is that we can show this using a *different* abstraction for each node.

That is, let $G = (V, E)$ be the (possibly infinite) proof graph on the set ground instances V, let $P = \{P_1, \ldots, P_n\}$ be a *finite* partition of V, where each P_i is the set of ground instances of property p_i, and for each instance $v \in V$, let $H_v = (V_v, E_v)$ be a *finite* graph (the abstract proof graph for v), such that there is a homomorphism $h_v : V \to V_v$ from G to H_v.

Theorem 1. *If there is an infinite backward path in G, then for some $1 \leq j \leq n$ and $v \in P_j$,*

- $h_v(v)$ *is on a cycle in H_v, or*
- *there is a backward path in H_v from $h_v(v)$ to some $w \in V_v$ such that for infinitely many $w' \in P_j$, $h_v(w') = w$.*

Proof. Let $\sigma = s_0, s_1, \ldots$ be an infinite backward path in G. This path uses either a finite or an infinite subset of V. In the first case, let v be some repeated element of σ. There is a cycle in G containing v, hence a cycle in H_v containing $h_v(v)$ (since h_v is a homomorphism from G to H_v). In the second case, σ must use an infinite number of elements of some P_j. Let v be some element of P_j on σ, and let σ' be the tail of σ beginning with v. Since V_v is finite, it follows that h_v maps an infinite number of elements $w' \in P_j$ of σ' to some $w \in V_v$. □

By the theorem, it suffices to check each ground instance of a property in one abstract proof graph, verifying that its image in the abstract graph is neither on a cycle, nor on a backward path to an node abstracting an infinite set of

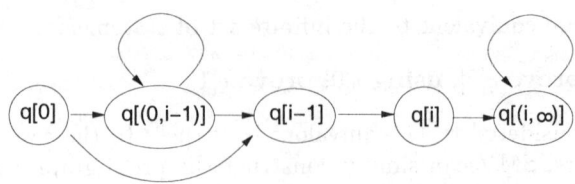

Fig. 5. An abstract proof graph

instances of the same property. In practice, we can use the same abstraction of the natural numbers to generate the abstract proof graph H_v that we use to verify instance v. This means that the abstract proof graphs within an inequality class are isomorphic, hence we need only check one representative of each class.

Example Consider our proof from the previous section. There are three cases of feasible inequality relations to consider. In the case $0 < i-1 < i$, we abstract type T to the set $\{0, (0, i-1), i-1, i, (i, \infty)\}$. Substituting these abstract values into the proof graph statement, we obtain the abstract proof graph of figure 5. We must check two properties of this graph:

1. The node $q[i]$ is not on a cycle.
2. No backward path rooted at $q[i]$ reaches an instance of q containing an infinite interval.

Since the abstract graphs are isomorphic for all values of i satisfying $0 < i-1 < i$, we need check only one instance in this class (say, $i = 2$). In fact, we can verify the above properties for one representative of each inequality class, so we conclude that the proof graph is acyclic.

On the other hand, suppose we had written instead:

forall(i in T) **using** $q[i+1]$ **prove** $q[i]$;

In the abstract proof graph, we would find a backward path $q[i]$, $q[i+1]$, $q[(i+1, \infty)]$. Since the last of these contains an infinite interval, we reject this graph. In fact, there is an infinite backward chain in the proof, so the proof is not valid.

Using this technique, we can handle more general induction schema than the simple example above. For example, we can use mutual induction over two invariants:

... **using** $p[i]$ **prove** $q[i]$;
... **using** $q[i\text{-}1]$ **prove** $p[i]$;

Or, we can use induction simultaneously over two parameters:

... **using** $p[i\text{-}1][j]$, $p[i][j\text{-}1]$ **prove** $p[i][j]$;

(here, imagine a grid in which each cell is proved using its neighbors to the left and below). In section 5, we will see an example of induction over multiple parameters.

4 A FIFO Buffer

As a simple example of proof by induction using model checking, we verify a hardware implementation of a FIFO buffer. We can decompose this problem into two parts. The first is to show that each data item output by the FIFO is correct, and the second is to show that the data items are output in the correct order. This separation is done by tagging each data item with an index number indicating its order at the input. Since only the ordering problem requires induction, we consider only that part of the proof here.

The input *inp* and output *out* of our FIFO have three fields: *valid*, a boolean indicating valid data at the interface, *data*, the actual data item, and *idx*, the index number of the data item. To specify ordering at either interface, we simply introduce a counter *cnt* that counts the number of items received or transmitted thus far. If there is valid data at the interface, we specify that the index of that data is equal to *cnt*. This counter ranges over an *ordset* type called *INDEX*.

$cnt : INDEX$;
init(cnt) := 0;
if($valid$) **next**(cnt) := $cnt + 1$;

ordered: **assert G** ($valid \Rightarrow idx = cnt$);

We create an instance of this specification for both input and output of the FIFO, and would like to prove that the property *ordered* at the input implies *ordered* at the output.

Let us implement the FIFO as a circular buffer, with a large number of entries (say, 1024) so that it is too large to verify temporal properties of it directly by model checking. To solve this problem, we need to abstract the type of buffer addresses as well. Thus, we create another *ordset* type and declare the type of buffer addresses *ADDR* to be the subrange $0\ldots 1023$ of this type. Note that there are two fixed constants of this type that appear in the code: 0 and 1023. For example, to increment the head pointer in the circular buffer, the following code is used:

next($head$) := ($head = 1023$) ? 0 : $head + 1$;

Now, we can prove the *ordered* property at the output by induction on the value of *cnt*. We prove that if the last item output was numbered $i-1$, then the current one is numbered i. The natural abstraction needed to prove this would use the values 0, $i-1$ and i (we need 0, since the initial value must be zero). In fact, SMV chooses this abstraction by default. Note that if the item indexed i gets stored in address j of the circular buffer, then item $i-1$ must have been stored at address $j-1$ mod 1024. Thus, if we analyze cases on j, we only have to consider two addresses in the array to prove the inductive step. To do the case analysis in SMV, we say:

forall(i **in** $INDEX$) **forall**(j **in** $ADDR$)
   subcase $out.ordered[i][j]$ **of** $out.ordered$
     for $out.cnt = i \wedge tail = j$;

The property $ordered[i][j]$ says that, if the current cnt at the output is i, and the current value of the tail pointer (i.e., the address of the current output) is j, then the current index at the output must be cnt. Now, we use induction over i in the following way:

> **forall**(i **in** *INDEX*) **forall**(j **in** *ADDR*)
>   **using** $ADDR \Rightarrow \{0, j\text{-}1, j, 1023\}$, $inp.ordered$, $out.ordered[i\text{-}1]$
>   **prove** $out.ordered[i][j]$;

In the abstracted models, there are maximally four elements in the buffer, the remainder being abstracted to $\bot$. With this abstraction, the buffer implementation can be model checked without difficulty. Note, we are not actually using induction over the type *ADDR* here. We are simply using the ordered set abstraction to make the model checking of a 1024 element buffer tractable. The use of this abstraction does increase the number of cases that must be checked, however. We must check three cases of i times five cases of j (the additional fixed constant of type *ADDR* increases the number of feasible ordering relations) for a total of fifteen. Nonetheless, all of these cases can be verified by SMV in less than two seconds.

We can also prove our buffer implementation for arbitrary depth by using an uninterpreted constant to represent the buffer depth. This would be of secondary interest in hardware verification, however, where resources are fixed and finite.

5 Bakery Mutual Exclusion Algorithm

Leslie Lamport's "bakery" algorithm [Lam74] is a mutual exclusion algorithm for a set of N processes, each running a program with two parts, a *critical section* and a *noncritical section*. We have adapted from Lamport's original presentation with minor changes for the present exposition.[2] For each process i, the algorithm uses a boolean variable $choosing[i]$, natural number variables $number[i]$ and $max[i]$, and a variable $count[i]$ that ranges over process id's $1, \ldots, N$. We denote the type of natural numbers by NAT, and the type of process id's by PID. These can all be read and written by process i. In addition, $choosing[i]$, and $number[i]$ are readable, but not writable by other processes. Each process i starts execution in its noncritical section with $choosing[i]$ and $number[i]$ initially equal to 0. The following pseudo-code (not SMV input) gives the program for process i:

```
L1:     {noncritical section; nondeterministically goto L1 or L2;}
L2:     choosing[i] := 1;
L3:     {count[i] := 1; max[i] := 0;}
L4:         max[i] := maximum(max[i], number[count[i]]);
L5:         if count[i] < N then {count[i] := count[i]+1; goto L4;}
```

---

[2] The proof described here disregards two important features of the algorithm: the non-atomicity of reads and writes, and the possibility of crashes. SMV files for this version and the general algorithm can be found at
      http://www-cad.eecs.berkeley.edu/~kenmcmil/bakery.html.

L6: $number[i] := max[i]+1$;
L7: $choosing[i] := 0$;
L8: $count[i] := 1$;
L9:   **if** $choosing[count[i]] = 1$ **then goto** L9;
L10:   **if** $number[count[i]] \neq 0$ **and**
        $(number[count[i]] < number[i]$ **or**
        $(number[count[i]] = number[i]$ **and** $count[i] <$ i$))$
        then goto L10;
L11:   **if** $count[i] <$ N **then** $\{count[i] := count[i]+1;$ **goto** L9;$\}$
L12:   critical section;
L13: $\{number[i] := 0;$ **goto** L1;$\}$

In lines L3–L6, process i chooses a positive number $number[i]$; the ordered pair $(number[i], i)$ serves as process i's "ticket" to enter the critical section. In lines L8–L11, process i loops over all processes j, waiting at L9 until process j is not in the act of choosing a ticket, and waiting at L10 until process j either does not have a ticket $(number[j] = 0)$ or has a ticket that is greater (in lexicographic order) than process i's ticket.

The algorithm has two key properties. First, it ensures *safety*: no two processes can ever be in the critical section (at L12) at the same time. Second, it guarantees *liveness* under an assumption of *fairness*: if every process continues to execute instructions (the fairness assumption), then any process that reaches L2 eventually gets to the critical section (the liveness guarantee). The fairness assumption includes the assumption that a process in the critical section will eventually leave the critical section. However, as indicated by the pseudo-code "nondeterministically goto L1 or L2", a process may remain in the noncritical section forever (and this does not interfere with the liveness of any other process).

To encode the bakery algorithm in SMV we introduce some additional variables. For each process i the variable $pc[i]$ (i's "program counter") ranges over the values $\{L1, L2, \ldots, L13\}$ and designates the next line to be executed by process i. The variable act takes on an arbitrary value in the range $1, \ldots, N$ at each time step and designates the process that executes a line at that time step. Thus the action taken at any time step depends on the value of $pc[act]$:

switch $(pc[act])$ {
  $L1$: { **next**$(pc[act]) := \{L1, L2\};$ }
  $L2$: { **next**$(choosing[act]) := 1;$ **next**$(pc[act]) := L3;$ }
  ...
  $L13$: { **next**$(number[act]) := 0;$ **next**$(pc[act]) := L1;$ } }

The code also includes initial conditions for the processes (not shown here) and the fairness condition:

forall (i **in** *PID*) $fair[i]$: **assert** $\mathbf{G}(\mathbf{F}(act = i))$;

The safety and liveness properties of the algorithm can now be defined as follows:

```
forall (i in PID) forall (j in PID) {
    safe[i][j]: assert G(i ≠ j ⇒ ¬(pc[i] = L12 ∧ pc[j] = L12));
    live[i]: assert G(pc[i] = L2 ⇒ F(pc[i] = L12)); }
```

In the limited remaining space, we concentrate on sketching the liveness proof, which is more interesting and difficult than the safety proof. The liveness property is easily proved using the following two lemmas, the first saying that any process that starts the loop in lines L3–L5 eventually completes it, and the second saying the same for the loop in lines L8–L11:

```
forall (i in PID) {
    reaches_L6[i]: assert G(pc[i] = L3 ⇒ F(pc[i] = L6));
    reaches_L12[i]: assert G(pc[i] = L8 ⇒ F(pc[i] = L12));
    using reaches_L6[i], reaches_L12[i], fair[i] prove live[i]; }
```

Note that the proof of *live[i]* relies on the fairness assumption *fair[i]* to ensure that process i eventually gets from L2 to L3 and from L6 to L8. Of course, the assumption of fairness is also essential for the proofs of the lemmas *reaches_L6* and *reaches_L12*.

To prove that the loop in L3–L5 terminates (once it is started), we use a helper lemma, stating that the j-th iteration is eventually completed, for any process id i. The helper lemma is proved by straightforward induction: eventual completion of the j-th iteration follows from completion of the $(j-1)$-th iteration, together with the fairness assumption. Completion of the entire loop then follows from fairness and completion of the last iteration. Here is the SMV code:

```
forall (i in PID) forall (j in PID) {
    reaches_L5[i][j]: assert G(pc[i] = L3 ⇒ F(pc[i] = L5 ∧ count[i] = j));
    using reaches_L5[i][j-1], fair[i] prove reaches_L5[i][j];
    using reaches_L5[i][N], fair[i] prove reaches_L6[i]; }
```

The termination proof for the loop in lines L8–L11 (that is, for the lemma *reaches_L12*) is more difficult in that it involves induction not only over iterations of the loop, but also over tickets. To prove that a process i completes the loop, we use the induction hypothesis that any process j with a lower ticket eventually reaches (and by fairness, eventually leaves) the critical section, and so cannot cause process i to wait forever at L10. We use the following three lemmas:

```
forall (n in NAT) forall (i in PID) forall (j in PID) {
    reaches_L11[n][i][j]:
        assert G(pc[i] = L8 ∧ number[i] = n ⇒ F(pc[i] = L11 ∧ count[i] = j));
    lower_number_reaches_L12[n][j]:
        assert G(number[j] < n ∧ pc[j] = L8 ⇒ F(pc[j] = L12));
    lower_pid_reaches_L12[n][i][j]:
        assert G(number[j] = n ∧ j < i ∧ pc[j] = L8 ⇒ F(pc[j] = L12)); }
```

The first states that a process with ticket (n, i) eventually completes the j-th iteration of the loop. The other two together state the induction hypothesis that any process j with a ticket lexicographically less than (n,i) eventually completes the entire loop. We prove these three lemmas by mutual induction, over three parameters n, i and j, where (n,i) is the ticket and j is the value of the loop counter. For example, induction over j can be seen in the SMV command to prove $reaches\_L11$:

using $fair[i]$, $fair[j]$, $reaches\_L11[n][i][j\text{-}1]$,
$lower\_pid\_reaches\_L12[n][i][j]$, $lower\_number\_reaches\_L12[n][j]$,
$reaches\_L6[j]$, $NAT \Rightarrow \{0,n\}$, ...
prove $reaches\_L11[n][i][j]$;

To prove that process i eventually finishes waiting for process j, we assume that if process j has a lower ticket it will eventually reach $L12$. The next time around the loop, process j must choose a larger ticket. Note we also need $reaches\_L6$, to ensure that process j cannot make process i wait forever at $L9$. By writing $NAT \to \{0,n\}$, we specify that the abstraction for type NAT keep 0 as a distinguished value, lest we get an abstraction too coarse to model the interaction of the assignment at $L13$ with the test at line $L10$.

We omit here the similar, but simpler, proofs of the other two lemmas, which contain the inductive steps over n and i respectively. We remark simply that the three lemmas are mutually dependent, and that well-foundedness of the entire mutual induction is automatically checked by SMV, as described in section 3. We also omit the command to prove that $reaches\_L12$ follows from $lower\_number\_reaches\_L12$.

Note that we could have combined lemma $lower\_number\_reaches\_L12$ and lemma $lower\_pid\_reaches\_L12$ (or even these two and $reaches\_L11$) into a single lemma. However, the proof would then have involved temporal case-splitting over four (or more) variables at once, rather than three. Increasing the number of simultaneous case splits increases the number of concrete values in the abstract types, thus making the proof inefficient in two ways. First, the resulting finer abstractions tend to be individually more costly to model-check. Second, more distinct abstractions must be checked in order to check a representative of every equivalence class. In general, it is desirable to structure proofs so that the abstractions used are as coarse as possible (but no coarser).

6 Conclusion

By using an appropriate parameterized abstraction of the natural numbers, we can reduce a proof by induction over the natural numbers to a finite number of finite state verification problems. This is because, on the one hand, each abstracted type is finite, and on the other hand, the infinite set of abstractions falls into a finite number of isomorphism classes. As a result, we can check proofs by model checking that would ordinarily be considered to be only in the domain of theorem provers. The advantage is that, in a proof by model checking, we need not consider the details of the control of a system, since these are handled by state enumeration. This technique has been implemented in the SMV proof assistant, and integrated with a variety of techniques for reducing infinite state problems to finite state problems.

This technique is more general than previous techniques that use model checking as part of an induction proof [KM89,WL89] in that variables may range over unbounded types, and the proof is fully mechanically checked. Further, a novel induction scheme based on proof graph abstractions makes it possible to do fairly complex proofs using mutual induction over multiple variables, without explicit recourse to an induction rule, as the induction scheme is inferred by analyzing the abstract proof graphs.

The method is not fully automated, in that it relies on the user to supply inductive properties, which may have to be stronger than the property being proved. Note, however, that it is not required to provide an inductive *temporal* invariant, since the model checker can, in effect, compute the strongest invariants of the abstract models. Since linear temporal logic with natural number variables is undecidable (by a trivial reduction from termination of a two-counter machine), the method described here is necessarily incomplete.

A practical problem with the method is that the number of cases (*i.e.*, feasible inequality relations) expands very rapidly with the number of parameters and fixed constants of a given type. Thus, in the proof of the bakery algorithm, for example, considerable care had to be used to minimize the number of parameters in the lemmas. Clearly, techniques of reducing this case explosion (perhaps using weaker abstractions) would make the technique easier to apply.

Finally, we note that the proof of the bakery algorithm, which relies substantially on properties of the natural numbers, was more difficult than proofs of considerably more complex systems (*e.g.* [McM99]) that are control dominated. Nevertheless, we think this example shows that model checking can be used to advantage even in an area where finite control plays a relatively small part. This suggests that there may be many areas in which model checking can be applied that previously have not been considered amenable to finite state methods.

References

[BLO98] S. Bensalem, Y. Lakhnech, and S. Owre. Computing abstractions of infinite state systems compositionally and automatically. In A.J. Hu and M.Y. Vardi, editors, *Computer Aided Verification (CAV'98)*, volume 1427 of *LNCS*, pages 319–331. Springer-Verlag, 1998.

[DDP99] S. Das, D.L. Dill, and S. Park. Experience with predicate abstraction. In N. Halbwachs and D. Peled, editors, *Computer Aided Verification (CAV'99)*, volume 1633 of *LNCS*, pages 160–171. Springer-Verlag, 1999.

[HQR99] T. A. Henzinger, S. Qadeer, and S. K. Rajamani. Verifying sequential consistency on shared-memory multiprocessor systems. In N. Halbwachs and D. Peled, editors, *Computer Aided Verification (CAV'99)*, volume 1633 of *LNCS*, pages 301–315. Springer-Verlag, 1999.

[KM89] R. Kurshan and K. L. McMillan. A structural induction theorem for processes. In *Proceedings of the 8th Annual ACM Symposium on Principles of Distributed Computing*, pages 239–247, 1989.

[Lam74]   L. Lamport. A new solution of Dijkstra's concurrent programming problem. *Comm. ACM*, 17:453–455, August 1974.
[McM97]   K. L. McMillan. A compositional rule for hardware design refinement. In O. Grumberg, editor, *Computer Aided Verification (CAV'97)*, volume 1254 of *LNCS*, pages 24–35. Springer-Verlag, 1997.
[McM98]   K. L. McMillan. Verification of an implementation of Tomasulo's algorithm by compositional model checking. In A. J. Hu and M. Y. Vardi, editors, *Computer Aided Verification (CAV'98)*, volume 1427 of *LNCS*, pages 110–121. Springer-Verlag, 1998.
[McM99]   K. L. McMillan. Verification of infinite state systems by compositional model checking. In L. Pierre and T. Kropf, editors, *Correct Hardware Design and Verification Methods (CHARME'99)*, volume 1703 of *LNCS*, pages 219–233. Springer-Verlag, 1999.
[ORS92]   S. Owre, J.M. Rushby, and N. Shankar. PVS: A prototype verification system. In D. Kapur, editor, *Computer Aided Deduction (CADE'92)*, volume 607 of *LNAI*, pages 748–752. Springer-Verlag, 1992.
[RSS95]   S. Rajan, N. Shankar, and M. K. Srivas. An integration of model checking with automated proof checking. In P. Wolper, editor, *Computer Aided Verification (CAV'95)*, volume 939 of *LNCS*, pages 84–97. Springer-Verlag, 1995.
[SG97]   H. Saïdi and S. Graf. Construction of abstract state graphs with PVS. In O. Grumberg, editor, *Computer Aided Verification (CAV'97)*, volume 1254 of *LNCS*, pages 72–83. Springer-Verlag, 1997.
[SS99]   H. Saïdi and N. Shankar. Abstract and model check while you prove. In N. Halbwachs and D. Peled, editors, *Computer Aided Verification (CAV'99)*, volume 1633 of *LNCS*, pages 443–454. Springer-Verlag, 1999.
[WL89]   P. Wolper and V. Lovinfosse. Verifying properties of large sets of processes with network invariants. In *Workshop on Automatic Verification Methods for Finite State Systems*, volume 407 of *LNCS*, pages 68–80. Springer-Verlag, 1989.

Liveness and Acceleration in Parameterized Verification*

Amir Pnueli and Elad Shahar

Dept. of Computer Science and Applied Mathematics
Weizmann Institute of Science, Rehovot, Israel
{Amir,Elad}@wisdom.weizmann.ac.il

Abstract. The paper considers the problem of *uniform verification* of *parameterized systems* by symbolic model checking, using formulas in FS1S (a syntactic variant of the 2nd order logic WS1S) for the symbolic representation of sets of states. The technical difficulty addressed in this work is that, in many cases, standard model-checking computations fail to converge.

Using the tool TLV[P], we formulated a general approach to the *acceleration* of the transition relations, allowing an unbounded number of different processes to change their local state (or interact with their neighbor) in a single step. We demonstrate that this acceleration process solves the difficulty and enables an efficient symbolic model-checking of many parameterized systems such as mutual-exclusion and token-passing protocols for any value of N, the parameter specifying the size of the system.

Most previous approaches to the uniform verification of parameterized systems, only considered *safety properties* of such systems. In this paper, we present an approach to the verification of *iveness* properties and demonstrate its application to prove accessibility properties of the considered protocols.

Keywords: Symbolic model checking; Parametric systems; Acceleration; Liveness; Regular expressions; WS1S

1 Introduction

The problem of uniform verification of parameterized systems is one of the most thoroughly researched problems in computer-aided verification. The problem seems particularly elusive in the case of systems that consist of regularly connected finite-state processes (a process network). Such a system can be model checked for any given configuration, but this does not provide a conclusive evidence for the question of *uniform verification*, i.e., showing that the system is correct for *all* possible configurations. In [KMM+97], we proposed an approach to the uniform verification of parameterized systems based on symbolic model

---
* This research was supported in part by the Minerva Center for Verification of Reactive Systems, a gift from Intel, and a grant from the U.S.-Israel bi-national science foundation.

checking in which the assertional language used to represent sets of reachable global states is that of a regular expressions over a finite alphabet which represents the local state of each of the processes in the system. As a trivial illustrative example, consider a parameterized system $S(N)$ consisting of N processes arranged in a linear array. Assume that the local state of each process can be represented by the two values 0 and 1, where the state of a process $P[i]$ is 1 iff $P[i]$ currently has the token which is passed around.

The initial global state (to which we refer as a *configuration*) can be described by the regular expression $I = 10^*$ representing the global state in which the leftmost process has the token. Note that even though every instance of the system $S(N)$ has a unique initial configuration, the expression 10^* represents the infinite set of initial configurations obtained by considering the infinitely many different values of N.

The transition relation of this parameterized system can be represented by the binary rewrite rule given by $10 \rightarrow 01$. This rewrite rules states that a single step of the system applied to a configuration represented by a word w may locate the substring 10 within w and replace it by the substring 01. Obviously, such a step represents the transmission of a token from a process with a token to its right neighbor, provided the neighbor is not currently in possession of a token.

To represent such rewrite rules in the most general context, [KMM+97] suggested to use a finite-state *transducer* which is an automaton reading a string of pairs of letters, one representing the pre-transition configuration and the other representing the post-transition configuration. Using the standard notation of unprimed and primed values to respectively represent these two configurations, the transducer corresponding to the above transmission transition can again be represented by the following regular expression:

$$T = (00' + 11')^* (10') (01') (00' + 11')^*$$

Given a finite-state transducer T representing the transition relation and a regular expression E representing a set of configurations, it is not difficult to compute the set of T-postimages or T-preimages of the configurations in E which is guaranteed to be another regular expression. For example the T-postimage of 10^* is the regular expression 010^*. We denote by $E \diamond T$ and $T \diamond E$ the T-postimages (T-successor) and T-preimages (T-predecessor) of E, respectively.

To perform symbolic model checking we usually need the iterated versions of these two operators computed as follows:

$$E \diamond T^* = E + E \diamond T + (E \diamond T) \diamond T + ((E \diamond T) \diamond T) \diamond T + \cdots$$
$$T^* \diamond E = E + T \diamond E + T \diamond (T \diamond E) + T \diamond (T \diamond (T \diamond E)) + \cdots$$

Now, if φ is a regular expression representing a property we wish to prove an invariant of the system, then $S(N) \models \varphi$ for every N iff

$$(I \diamond T^*) \cap \overline{\varphi} = \emptyset \quad \text{or} \quad (T^* \diamond \overline{\varphi}) \cap I = \emptyset,$$

where $\overline{\varphi}$ denotes the complement of φ. The first clause corresponds to *forward exploration* starting from the initial condition I while the second clause corresponds to *backwards exploration* starting from the set of states violating the property φ.

The difficulty specific to regular model checking of parameterized systems is that, unlike BDD-based model checking of finite-state systems, the computation of either $I \diamond T^*$ or $T^* \diamond \overline{\varphi}$ may fail to terminate. In fact, theoretical considerations predict that there will be cases in which these computations cannot terminate. Termination of the computation of $I \diamond T^*$ implies that the set of strings encoding reachable configurations is a regular language, and it is easy to construct systems in which the set of reachable configurations forms a context-free language.

However, experience with these methods shows that there are many cases in which the set of reachable configurations is regular yet the straightforward computation of $I \diamond T^*$ fails to converge. Assume that we wish to establish for the above example system the invariance of the property $\varphi = 0^*10^*$, claiming that all reachable configurations contains precisely one token. To apply backwards exploration, we first compute the set of violating configurations, given by $\overline{\varphi} = 0^* + (0+1)^*1(0+1)^*1(0+1)^*$. The computation of $T^* \diamond \overline{\varphi}$ terminates in one step, yielding $T^* \diamond \overline{\varphi} = \overline{\varphi} = 0^* + (0+1)^*1(0+1)^*1(0+1)^*$ which, obviously, has an empty intersection with $I = 10^*$, establishing that φ is an invariant of the considered system.

On the other hand, the computation of the forward exploration according to $I \diamond T^*$ fails to terminate, yielding the following infinite sequence of approximations:

$10^* + 010^* + 0010^* + 00010^* + \cdots$

The source of the problem was identified in [ABJN99] as stemming from the fact that the transition relation T represents a step in which only one process (or a pair of contiguous processes) makes a move. The remedy proposed by this paper is to use the notion of an *accelerated transition* in which several (unbounded many) processes can make a move at the same step. For example, the accelerated version of the transition relation $T = (00' + 11')^* (10') (01') (00' + 11')^*$ can be computed to be

$$T_a = (00' + 11')^* (10') (00')^* (01') (00' + 11')^*$$

Applying the accelerated transition in a forward exploration terminates now in a single step and yields $I \diamond T_a^* = 0^*10^*$.

The work in [ABJN99] proposes a "speed-up" (acceleration) operation which transforms a single-process transition relation presented by a transducer T into an accelerated transducer T_a which represents the effect of many processors taking an action in the same step, under certain conditions restricting the dependency of a single-process action on the local states of the other processes. The analysis there is based on a language-theoretic representation of the assertions and the representation of transition relations by finite-state transducers. Using such acceleration techniques, [ABJN99] managed to verify fully automatically various parameterized protocols such as the Bakery and Ticket algorithms by Lamport, Burn's protocol, Dijkstra's and Szymanski's algorithms for mutual exclusion.

The methods of [ABJN99] could only accelerate elementary transitions which only modified the local state of one process at a time. This made them inapplicable to the representation of systems which included synchronous message passing, such as the binary transformation $10 \to 01$ appearing in our example system. This drawback has been recently corrected in [JN00] which presents a speed-up operation which can be applied to elementary transitions that modify several contiguous processes at the same time.

The work presented here improves upon the results of [ABJN99] and [JN00] in several directions. To start with, our presentation framework uses the logic FS1S (a syntactic variant of WS1S, the weak second-order monadic theory of one successor [Tho90]) to present sets of configurations, e.g. the initial condition and the properties, as well as the transition relation. This uniform presentation by a powerful logic enables us to formulate several acceleration schemes still within the same language. Furthermore, the soundness of the transducer-based acceleration schemes of [ABJN99] and [JN00] depends on particular assumptions that the transition relation has to satisfy, such as a particular forms of left- and right-contexts, These have to be checked whenever one wants to apply the acceleration schemes of [ABJN99] and [JN00] to a particular transition relation. In our case, the acceleration is always sound and could never lead to false positive. In the worse case, they will not produce a useful acceleration and the process will continue to diverge even after the acceleration.

Using our acceleration schemes which are applicable to unary and binary elementary transitions in an unrestricted way, we managed to verify the protocols considered in [ABJN99] in a very efficient manner, and consider some additional protocols which use synchronous communication, such as a token-passing protocol for mutual exclusion and the distributed termination detection algorithm of [DFvG83].

However, the most important contribution of this paper is the extension of the regular model checking method to include verification of *liveness* properties, while all previous efforts concentrated on the parameterized verification of safety properties. Using these extensions, we managed to verify the property of accessibility for some of the protocols considered above.

Related Work

There are several results on algorithmic verification of parameterized systems [SG92,AJ98,CGJ95]. In most of these works the transitions are guarded by local conditions involving the local states of a fixed (unparameterized) number of processes, in contrast with the general global dependency which is allowed in [KMM+97,ABJN99,JN00]. The notions of speed-ups and acceleration of transitions were considered in [BG96,BGWW97,BH97,ABJ98]. However, the accelerations considered there only condensed several moves of a fixed number of processes, while in our case (and in [ABJN99,JN00]) we consider speed-ups obtained by performing actions of an unbounded number of different processes, sequentially or in parallel. Previous attempts to verify parameterized protocols such as

Burn's protocol [JL98] and Szymanski's algorithm [GZ98,MAB+94,MP90] relied on abstraction functions or lemmas provided by the user. Other approaches to uniform parameterized verification are based on induction, where the user supplies the induction hypothesis either in the form of an assertion or in the form of a network invariant [CGJ95,KM89,WL89].

A recent work which has a significant overlap with our work has been presented by Bodeveix and Filali in [BF00]. Similarly to our approach, they advantageously employ the expressive power of WS1S to present explicit formulas which capture various acceleration schemes. They report about a tool FMONA which is a high-level macro-processor for MONA [HJJ+96]. The main differences between their work and ours are that, at this point, they do not consider liveness. Also, on the technical level, unlike the TLV[P] tool which we use for the verification reported in this paper, the FMONA tool does not seem to support a programming layer in which algorithms such as model-checking for safety and liveness can be programmed. As a result, if one wants to iterate the application of a transition relation to a set of states until it converges, it is necessary to provide an a priori bound n on how many iterations are necessary and to invoke the FMONA macro processor which will expand the appropriate iteration into a pure MONA code of size linear in n.

2 The Logic FS1S

We use the logic FS1S, (*finitary second-order theory of one successor*) as a specification language for sets of global states of parameterized systems. This logic is derived from the *weak second order logic of one successor* [Tho90] and also resembles the language M2L used in MONA [HJJ+96]. The main difference between WS1S and FS1S is that, in FS1S, we assume the existence of a special variable M which provides an upper bound to the size of all arrays. We found the use of this common upper bound to be of much help in the description of circular architectures such as rings. This is only a matter of convenience, because, it is always possible to introduce M as a second-order variable of WS1S and postulate its upper-bound properties. It is well known that FS1S (as well as WS1S) has the expressive power of regular expressions, as well as finite automata which are the representation underlying our implementation. Following is a brief definition of the logic.

Syntax

We assume a *signature* $\Xi : \{\Sigma_1, \ldots, \Sigma_k\}$ consisting of a finite set of finite alphabets. The *vocabulary* consists of *position variables* $p_1, p_2, \ldots$ and, for each $\Sigma_i \in \Xi$, a set of Σ_i-*array variables* $X_i, Y_i, Z_i, \ldots$. The special position variable M denotes the upper bound on the length of all arrays and all position variables.

- Position (First-order) terms:
  The constant 1 and any position variable p_i are position terms. If t is a position term then so is $t + 1$.
- Letter terms:

- Every $a \in \Sigma_i$ is a Σ_i-term.
- If X is a Σ_i-array variable and t is a position term, then $X[t]$ is a Σ_i-term.
- Atomic Formulas:
  - $t_1 \sim t_2$, where t_1 and t_2 are position terms and $\sim \in \{=, <\}$.
  - $x = y$, where x and y are Σ_i-terms for some $\Sigma_i \in \Xi$.
- Formulas:
  - An atomic formula is a formula.
  - Let φ and ψ be formulas. Then $\neg\varphi$, $\varphi \vee \psi$, $\exists p : \varphi$, $\exists X : \varphi$ are formulas, where p is a position variable and X is an array variable.

For example, assume that Π is an array over the alphabet $\Sigma_1 = \{N, T, C\}$ intended to represent the control location of a process in a process-array $P[1], \ldots, P[M]$. Similarly, assume that tok is a Boolean array (special case of $\Sigma_2 = \{0, 1\}$) intended to represent the fact that process $P[i]$ currently has the token. Then, the WS1S-formula

$$\Theta : \quad \forall i : (\Pi[i] = N) \wedge tok[1] \wedge \forall j \neq 1 : \neg tok[j]$$

characterizes the set of initial configurations in which all processes are in their initial control location N and only the leftmost process (process $P[1]$) has the token.

We refer the reader to [KMM+97] for the definition of the semantics of FS1S.

3 The Logic FS1S is Adequate

In this section we demonstrate the use of FS1S for expressing the constituents of a parameterized system. As a running example, we will use program MUX of Fig. 1 which implements mutual exclusion by synchronous communication.

The body of the program is a variable-size parallel composition of processes $P[1], \ldots, P[M]$. Each process $P[i]$ has two local state variables: a local boolean variable tok whose initial value is 1 (*true*) for $i = 1$ and 0 (*false*) for all other processes, and a control variable Π ranging over the set of locations $\{N, T, C\}$ (the noncritical section, the trying section, and the critical section, respectively). Process $P[i]$ sends the boolean value 1 on channel $\alpha[i \oplus_M 1]$ to its right neighbor ($i \oplus_M 1$ is addition modulo M) and reads into variable tok a (true) boolean value from its left neighbor on channel $\alpha[i]$. As seen in the program, process $P[i]$ can enter its critical section only if $P[i].tok = 1$.

As our computational model we use the model of *fair discrete systems* consisting of a set X of *state variables*, an *initial condition* Θ, a *transition relation* ρ, a set $\mathcal{J}$ of *justice (weak fairness)* requirements, and a set $\mathcal{C}$ of *compassion (strong fairness)* requirements. We proceed to show how these constituents can be specified in FS1S for system MUX.

The State Variables: We define the type

$$state = \textbf{record of } \langle \Pi : \{N, T, C\}, tok : \textbf{boolean} \rangle$$

and the array variable

$$X : \textbf{array } 1..M \textbf{ of } state.$$

Note that this is equivalent to the definition of two arrays, the array $\Pi[1..M]$ and the Boolean array $tok[1..M]$. Therefore, we will often abbreviate $X[i].\Pi$ and

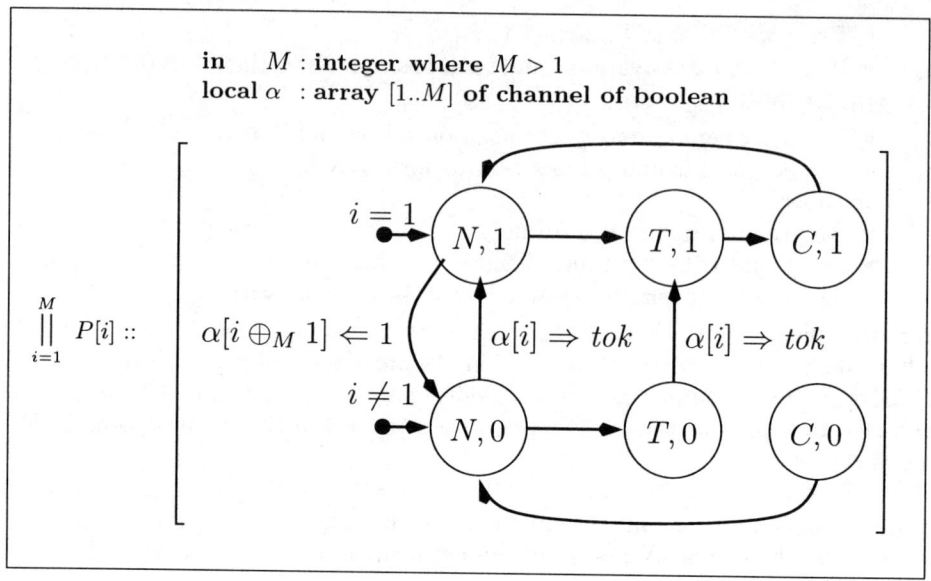

Fig. 1. Parameterized Program MUX.

$X[j].tok$ to $\Pi[i]$ and $tok[j]$ respectively. On the other hand, we write $X[i] = X[j]$ as an abbreviation for $(X[i].\Pi = X[j].\Pi) \land (X[i].tok = X[j].tok)$ and $\exists X : \varphi$ as an abbreviation for $\exists X.\Pi : \exists X.tok : \varphi$.

The Initial Condition: The initial condition can be given by the FS1S formula

$$\Theta: \quad (\forall i : \Pi[i] = N) \land tok[1] \land \forall i \neq 1 : \neg tok[i]$$

The Transition Relation: The transition relation can be formed as the disjunction of three types of elementary transitions. Using the abbreviation $presX(j) = X'[j] = X[j]$, these can be expressed as follows:

$idle \qquad : \forall j : presX(j)$

$\rho_1(X, X', i) : idle \lor (\forall j \neq i : presX(j)) \land$
$$\begin{pmatrix} (\Pi[i] = N) \land (\Pi'[i] = T) \land (tok'[i] = tok[i]) \\ \lor (\Pi[i] = C) \land (\Pi'[i] = N) \land (tok'[i] = tok[i]) \\ \lor (\Pi[i] = T) \land (\Pi'[i] = C) \land (tok'[i] = tok[i] = 1) \end{pmatrix}$$

$\rho_2(X, X', i) : idle \lor (\forall j \notin \{i, i \oplus_M 1\} : presX(j))$
$\land \ (\Pi[i] = N) \land \quad tok[i] \quad \land \ (\Pi[i \oplus_M 1] \in \{N, T\}) \qquad \land \ \neg tok[i \oplus_M 1]$
$\land \ (\Pi'[i] = N) \land \neg tok'[i] \land \ (\Pi'[i \oplus_M 1] = \Pi[i \oplus_M 1]) \land \quad tok'[i \oplus_M 1]$

Subtransition *idle* represents the case that the system does not change it's state. Subtransition $\rho_1(X, X', i)$ is a *unary transition* in which a single process $P[i]$ takes a local action that can only modify the local state of $P[i]$. All other processes retain their local state. Finally, subtransition $\rho_1(X, X', i)$ corresponds to a *binary transition* in which process $P[i]$ sends the token to process $P[i \oplus_M 1]$. Only the two involved processes change their local states.

We can now define the global transition relation by taking

$$\rho(X, X') = idle \ \vee \ (\exists i : \rho_1(X, X', i) \ \vee \ \rho_2(X, X', i)).$$

However, as explained in the introduction, this single-action transition can be used in few cases for backwards exploration model checking but will often fail to converge when used in a forward exploration model checking.

We defer the specification of the justice and compassion requirements of system MUX to Section 5 in which we discuss the verification of liveness properties, where the fairness requirements become relevant.

3.1 Model Checking

Having obtained the FS1S representation of the transition relation $\rho(X, X')$ of a system such as MUX, there are several symbolic model checking tasks we can perform. For an FS1S formula $\varphi(X)$ representing a set of configurations, we can compute the ρ-successor and ρ-predecessor of φ by the following expressions:

$$\varphi \diamond \rho = unprime(\exists X : \varphi(X) \ \wedge \ \rho(X, X'))$$
$$\rho \diamond \varphi = \exists V : \rho(X, V) \ \wedge \ \varphi(V),$$

where *unprime* is a substitution operation which transforms each occurrence of $X'[k]$ into $X[k]$, and V is an auxiliary array variable of type *state*.

Note that $\rho \diamond \varphi$ computes the set of states satisfying $\mathbf{EX}\varphi$ from which, by iteration and boolean operations, we can compute $\mathbf{EF}\varphi$ and $\mathbf{AG}\varphi$, provided the iteration converges.

4 Acceleration

Acceleration condenses a potentially unbounded number of applications of transitions into a single transition, by defining a single "accelerated transition relation". It is up to the user to observe that acceleration is required and select the appropriate accelerations schemes to be applied. Since all accelerations are sound, there is no danger (except loss of time) in applying all the acceleration schemes which are available at a particular implementation. Since the verification problem for parameterized system is, in general, undecidable [AK86], there is no chance of accumulating a "complete" set of acceleration schemes. The best we can hope for is the assembly of a large set of schemes which can cover many of the useful examples.

To handle most of the cases in which regular model checking with single-action transition relation failed to terminate, we found it necessary to consider three types of acceleration which we will now present.

4.1 Local Acceleration

In this mode of acceleration, we allow several actions to be taken in succession by the same process $P[i]$. Given a unary transition relation $\rho_1(X, X', i)$, we can compute its locally accelerated version by the repeated composition

$$\rho_1^\alpha \;=\; \rho_1 \;\vee\; \rho_1 \diamond \rho_1 \;\vee\; (\rho_1 \diamond \rho_1) \diamond \rho_1 \;\vee\; ((\rho_1 \diamond \rho_1) \diamond \rho_1) \diamond \rho_1 \;\vee\; \cdots,$$

where the composition $\rho_a \diamond \rho_b$ is defined by

$$\rho_{a;b}(X, X', i) \;=\; (\exists V : \rho_a(X, V, i) \wedge \rho_b(V, X', i)).$$

For example, applying local acceleration to the unary transition relation $\rho_1(X, X', i)$ of program MUX, we obtain (after some manual simplification) the following accelerated unary transition:

$$\rho_1^\alpha(X, X', i) \;=\; \left(\begin{array}{l} \Pi[i] \in \{N, T, C\} \;\wedge\; tok[i]' = tok[i] \\ \wedge\; \forall j \neq i : (\Pi'[j] = \Pi[j] \;\wedge\; tok'[j] = tok[j]) \\ \wedge\; \left(\begin{array}{l} \Pi[i]' = \Pi[i] \\ \vee\; tok[i] = 0 \;\wedge\; \Pi'[i] \in \{N, T\} \\ \vee\; tok[i] = 1 \;\wedge\; \Pi'[i] \in \{N, T, C\} \end{array} \right) \end{array} \right)$$

4.2 Global Acceleration of Unary Transitions

Next, we consider the acceleration of a unary transition on which each of a set of processes takes a single action. Assume as before that the unary transition relation of process $P[i]$ is given by $\rho_1(X, X', i)$, and that $idle \to \rho_1$. The following formula expressing this acceleration uses the auxiliary *state*-array variables T and V.

$$\rho_1^g(X, X') \;=\; \forall i \left(\begin{array}{l} X'[i] = X[i] \\ \vee\; \exists T, V \left[\begin{array}{l} \forall j \left[\begin{array}{l} T[j] = \text{if } j < i \text{ then } X'[j] \text{ else } X[j] \\ V[j] = \text{if } j \leq i \text{ then } X'[j] \text{ else } X[j] \end{array} \right] \\ \wedge\; \rho_1(T, V, i) \end{array} \right] \end{array} \right)$$

This accelerated transition applies $\rho_1(X, X', i)$ to processes $P[1], \ldots, P[M]$ in sequential order. Every activated process $P[i]$ may non-deterministically choose to idle (which is one of the options allowed by ρ_1) or change its local state according to ρ_1. For process $P[i]$ we require that, after all processes $P[1], P[2], \ldots, P[i-1]$ have taken their actions, we reach a configuration from which $P[i]$ can take its action. This is done by forming the two arrays T and V. where V represents the configuration prior to $P[i]$'s action and V represents the configuration resulting from $P[i]$'s action.

For example, applying global acceleration to the accelerated unary transition relation $\rho_1^\alpha(X, X', i)$ of program MUX, we obtain (after some manual simplification to improve readability) the following accelerated unary transition:

$$\rho_1^g(X, X') \;=\; \forall i \left(\begin{array}{l} \Pi[i] \in \{N, T, C\} \;\wedge\; tok[i]' = tok[i] \\ \wedge\; \left(\begin{array}{l} \Pi[i]' = \Pi[i] \\ \vee\; tok[i] = 0 \;\wedge\; \Pi'[i] \in \{N, T\} \\ \vee\; tok[i] = 1 \;\wedge\; \Pi'[i] \in \{N, T, C\} \end{array} \right) \end{array} \right)$$

Note that the acceleration scheme presented here proceeds from left to right. It is straightforward to define an acceleration scheme which proceeds from right to left.

4.3 Global Acceleration of Binary Transitions

Finally, let us consider the acceleration of a binary transition, such as $\rho_2(X, X', i)$ previously presented for program MUX.

Unlike the acceleration of unary transitions, where the local state of each process changed at most once, in the case of binary acceleration some processes may change their local state twice. For example, they may change their state once when they receive the token from their left neighbor and then once more when they send the token to their right neighbor. Thus the acceleration of a binary token-passing transition may in one step move the token from process $P[i]$ to process $P[j]$ for an arbitrary $j > i$. To accommodate the phenomenon that some processes may change their values twice, we employ an additional *state*-array W to save the sequence of intermediate local states for these processes.

Let $\rho_2(X, X', i)$ be a binary transition which may affect at most the components $X[i]$ and $X[i \oplus_M 1]$. Without loss of generality, assume that $idle \to \rho_2$. The formula $\rho_2^g(X, X')$, expressing the global acceleration of $\rho_2(X, X', i)$ is given by

$$\exists W \left(\begin{array}{l} W[1] = X[1] \ \land \ W[M] = X'[M] \\ \land \ \forall i < M \ \exists T, V \left(\forall j \land \left(\begin{array}{l} T[j] = \left[\begin{array}{l} \text{case} \\ \quad j = i : W[j] \\ \quad j < i : X'[j] \\ \quad 1 \quad\ \ : X[j] \\ \text{esac} \end{array} \right] \\ V[j] = \left[\begin{array}{l} \text{case} \\ \quad j = i+1 : W[j] \\ \quad j \leq i \quad\ \ : X'[j] \\ \quad 1 \qquad\ \ : X[j] \\ \text{esac} \end{array} \right] \end{array} \right) \\ \land \ \rho_2(T, V, i) \end{array} \right) \right)$$

As we can see, in the binary acceleration case, we sequentially apply the binary transition ρ_2 to processes $P[1], \ldots P[M-1]$, where any of them may nondeterministically choose to take the idling transition. In the general case, each of the processes $P[2], \ldots, P[M-1]$ may change their local states at most twice, while processes $P[1]$ and $P[M]$ may change their local state at most once. We use the auxiliary array W to store the intermediate value of the local state of all processes.

Note that this acceleration scheme does not apply ρ_2 to process $P[M]$. When we compute the total transition relation we add $\rho_2(X, X', M)$ as an additional explicit disjunct.

These acceleration schemes were successfully applied to program MUX and transformed the regular model checking procedure based on forward exploration from a divergent process into an efficiently convergent one, requiring no more than 4 iterations to converge in a matter of few seconds. More details about these computations are presented in Section 6.

5 Liveness

All of the previous results for the uniform algorithmic verification of parameterized systems concentrated on proofs of safety properties. Here we present an approach to the verification of liveness properties, using regular symbolic model checking. The main problem with parameterized verification of liveness properties is not so much that the property to be proven is more complex, but that we have to take into account an unbounded number of fairness assumptions, several for each process, and that these requirements are also parameterized. To appreciate the problem, let us specify the fairness requirements associated with program MUX which, for the sake of simplicity of presentation, we restricted to justice (weak fairness) only.

5.1 Justice Requirements for Program MUX

There are three justice requirements associated with each process of program MUX. Respectively, they require that the process will never get stuck at location C, that it will never get stuck at location T while the process has the token, and that the process will not retain the token forever while it's right neighbor is continuously ready to receive it. In the computational model of *fair discrete systems*, justice requirements are presented as a set of assertions $\mathcal{J} = \{J_1, \ldots, J_k\}$, with the requirement that a computation should infinitely often visit states satisfying J_j for each $j = 1, \ldots, k$. In the parameterized case, each justice requirement is also parameterized by a process index i, and the requirement should be extended to cover all $i \in [1..M]$.

For program MUX, the justice requirements are given by

$$J_1[i] : \neg(\Pi[i] = C)$$
$$J_2[i] : \neg((\Pi[i] = T) \wedge tok[i])$$
$$J_3[i] : \neg(tok[i] \wedge (\Pi[i \oplus_M 1] \in \{N, T\}))$$

In theory, one may try to verify a liveness property "every p is eventually followed by q" of a parameterized system using the standard symbolic model-checking algorithm. The core of this algorithm is the computation of the set of states lying on a fair $\neg q$-path. This computation can be succinctly described by the following fix-point formula:

$$\mathbf{E}_f \mathbf{G} \neg q \;\; = \;\; \nu Y(\neg q \;\wedge\; \rho \diamond Y \;\wedge\; \forall i : (\bigwedge_j ((\rho \wedge \neg q)^* \diamond (Y \wedge J_j[i]))))$$

Unfortunately, this computation seldom converges, even if we use an accelerated version of the transition relation. This is certainly the case for program MUX.

5.2 Detecting Bad Cycles

Since the systems we analyze are finite-state (for every value of their parameter), it is obvious that the formula $\mathbf{E}_f \mathbf{G} \neg q$ characterizes the states from which there exists a $(\neg q)$-path leading to a fair $(\neg q)$-cycle, where the cycle being fair means that it visits at least once a J_j-state, for each $j = 1, \ldots, k$. Denoting by G the set of states that participate in a fair $(\neg q)$-cycle, an equivalent requirement is that each $s \in G$ has a successor in G and that, for each $s \in G$ and each $j = 1, \ldots, k$, there exists a cycle from s to itself which visits on the way some J_j-state.

Assume that $\rho(X, X')$ represents the total transition relation of the parameterized system, after all accelerations. The following algorithm computes the set of states participating in a fair $(\neg q)$-cycle:

1. $\varphi_1 := (\Theta \diamond \rho^*) \wedge \neg q$
2. $\rho_1 := \rho \wedge \varphi_1 \wedge (\forall i : U'[i] = U[i])$
3. $\varphi_2 := \varphi_1 \wedge (\forall i : U[i] = X[i])$
4. $\varphi_3 := \varphi_2 \wedge \rho_1^* \diamond (\rho_1 \diamond \varphi_2)$
5. **for** $j := 1, \ldots, k$ **do**
6. $\quad \varphi_3 := \varphi_3 \wedge (\forall i : \rho_1^* \diamond (J_j[i] \wedge \varphi_1 \wedge (\rho_1^* \diamond \varphi_2)))$
7. $\varphi_4 := (\exists U : \varphi_3)$

Line 1 places in φ_1 the set of $(\neg q)$-states which are reachable. Line 2 places in ρ_1 a version of ρ restricted to move only within φ_1-states and to preserve a set of variables called U, which is a newly introduced copy of the state variables. Line 3 adds to the sets of states the interpretation of the auxiliary variables U and places in φ_2 the subset of φ_1-states in which the interpretations of X and U agree. Line 4 places in φ_3 the set of φ_2-states from which there exists a non-empty ρ_1-path leading to another φ_2-state.

To see this, consider a state s_1 belonging to φ_3, and let s_2 be the φ_2-state reached at the end of the non-empty ρ_1-path. Since s_2 is a φ_2-state, we know that $s_2[U] = s_2[X]$, i.e. the interpretation of U in s_2 is identical to the interpretation of X in s_2. Since any ρ_1-path preserves the interpretation of U, we also have that s_1 and s_2 agree on the interpretation of U, i.e., $s_1[U] = s_2[U]$. Since s_1 is also a φ_2-state, it follows that $s_1[X] = s_1[U]$. Consequently, we have that $s_1[X] = s_1[U] = s_2[X] = s_2[U]$ which implies that s_1 and s_2 are identical states and, therefore, s_1 participates in a non-empty φ_1-cycle.

Following a similar argument, the iterations at line 6 retain at φ_3 only the φ_2-states which reside on a cycle containing a $J_j[i]$ state for each j and each i. The cycles may be different for different values of j and i, but they can always be combined into a very big cycle which contains them all, and may revisit the originating state many times.

It follows that, when (and if) the algorithm terminates, φ_4 contains the states which reside on a non-empty fair $(\neg q)$-cycle.

The algorithm presented above can, in principle, be used also for conventional (non-parametric) symbolic model checking of liveness properties. However it is not advisable to do so, because the algorithm is highly inefficient in the conventional context due to the introduction of the auxiliary copy U of the state variables.

Normally, assertions of states and transitions relations are specified as having the types $\varphi : V \to \{0,1\}$ and $\rho : V \times V' \to \{0,1\}$. When adding an additional copy of the state variables we obtain assertions: $\varphi : V \times U \to \{0,1\}$ and $\rho : V \times U \times V' \times U' \to \{0,1\}$.

Note that all the work on acceleration actually computes $\rho \diamond \rho$ separately from its application to any assertion φ. This kind of computation is usually avoided whenever possible. For example, in symbolic backwards exploration, it is more efficient to compute $\rho \diamond (\rho \diamond \varphi)$ rather than $(\rho \diamond \rho) \diamond \varphi$.

For these reasons the additional copy of the state variables excises a heavy penalty, as is evident from the performance figures presented in Table 1 of Section 6. However, in the parameterized context, this is the only fully automatic algorithm we managed to successfully use for the verification of liveness properties.

5.3 Liveness Using Pseudo Cycles

Realizing the heavy price one has to pay for a full second copy of the state variables, we developed another approach which replaces the notion of a cycle by a *pseudo cycle*. Assume that the set of reachable states is partitioned by a partition Π into a set of disjoint classes. A pseudo-cycle, relative to the partition Π, is a path which begins and ends in two states belonging to the same class. Note, that when the partition Π is the finest possible, that is, each class containing a single state, then the notions of a pseudo-cycle and a cycle coincide.

To use this approach, the user has to provide a parameterized assertion $E(i)$, which defines the partition, consisting of a class for each value of i. The pseudo-cycle method is guaranteed to be sound but may produce false negatives due to its approximative nature.

The following is the improved algorithm for finding fair $(\neg q)$-pseudo-cycles:

1. $\varphi_1 := (\Theta \diamond \rho^*) \wedge \neg q$
2. $\rho_1 := \rho \wedge \varphi_1$
3. $\varphi_2 := \varphi_1 \wedge E(i)$
4. $\varphi_3 := \varphi_2 \wedge \rho_1^* \diamond (\rho_1 \diamond \varphi_2)$
5. **for** $j := 1, \ldots, k$ **do**
6. $\quad \varphi_3 := \varphi_3 \wedge (\forall i : \rho_1^* \diamond (J_j[i] \wedge \varphi_1 \wedge (\rho_1^* \diamond \varphi_2)))$

Let $E(i)$ be an assertion such that $\varphi_1 \to E(i)$. $E(i)$ should be such that it partitions the space of $(\neg q)$-reachable states. This partition corresponds to the set of state classes we use in order to find pseudo cycles.

The improved algorithm is similar to the original one, except for lines 2,3, in which we omitted the references to U, and line 7 which is omitted entirely. Instead, line 3 includes a conjunct of $E(i)$. The original constraint on line 3, $(\forall i : U[i] = X[i])$, uses U to form the finest partition, where each partition class contains only a single state.

It is clear that if there exists a real fair $\neg q$-cycle, then the improved algorithm will find it. Therefore, if the algorithm declares that there are no bad pseudo-cycles, this implies that, in particular there are no bad cycles, which establishes the soundness of the algorithm when it is used to deduce the absence of any bad cycles.

6 Results

In table 1, we present the results of our regular uniform verification applied to several well-known algorithms. The results do not include the computations of the accelerated transitions. It is obvious that the verification of safety properties is significantly more efficient than the verification of liveness properties.

Algorithm	Safety		Liveness		Improved Liveness	
	Time	Iterations	Time	Iterations	Time	Iterations
Token ring	0.4	3	53	40	9.2	32
Szymanski	0.2	8	–	–	–	–
Termination detection	5.6	9	–	–	–	–
Dining philosophers	0.6	3	–	–	–	–

Table 1. Experimental results (times in seconds)

7 Conclusions

In this paper we presented several significant extensions to the state-of-the art in uniform verification of parameterized systems. We demonstrated the expressive power of the logic FS1S as an efficient vehicle for expressing both the system constituents as well as the meta-operations of acceleration. We presented several acceleration schemes that lead to a very efficient regular model checking of safety parameterized properties. Finally, we presented the first approach to the uniform verification of liveness properties of parameterized systems using the FS1S framework and the TLV[P] tool.

References

[ABJ98]   P.A. Abdulla, A. Bouajjani, and B. Jonsson. On-the-fly analysis of systems with unbounded, lossy FIFO channels. In A.J. Hu and M.Y. Vardi, editors, *Proc. 10th Intl. Conference on Computer Aided Verification (CAV'98)*, volume 1427 of *Lect. Notes in Comp. Sci.*, pages 305–318. Springer-Verlag, 1998.

[ABJN99] P.A. Abdulla, A. Bouajjani, B. Jonsson, and M. Nilsson. Handling global conditions in parametrized system verification. In N. Halbwachs and D. Peled, editors, *Proc. 11st Intl. Conference on Computer Aided Verification (CAV'99)*, volume 1633 of *Lect. Notes in Comp. Sci.*, pages 134–145. Springer-Verlag, 1999.

[AJ98]   P.A. Abdulla and B. Jonsson. Verifying networks of timed processes. In B. Steffen, editor, *4th Intl. Conf. TACAS'98*, volume 1384 of *Lect. Notes in Comp. Sci.*, pages 298–312. Springer-Verlag, 1998.

[AK86]   K. R. Apt and D. Kozen. Limits for automatic program verification of finite-state concurrent systems. *Information Processing Letters*, 22(6), 1986.

[BF00]   J-P. Bodeveix and M. Filali. Experimenting acceleration methods for the validation of infinite state systems. In *International Workshop on Distributed System Validation and Verification (DSVV'2000)*, Taipei, Taiwan, April 2000.

[BG96]   B. Boigelot and P. Godefroid. Symbolic verification of coomunication protocols with infinite state spaces using QDDs. In R. Alur and T. Henzinger, editors, *Proc. 8th Intl. Conference on Computer Aided Verification (CAV'96)*, volume 1102 of *Lect. Notes in Comp. Sci.*, pages 1–12. Springer-Verlag, 1996.

[BGWW97] B. Boigelot, P. Godefroid, B. Willems, and P. Wolper. The power of QDDs. In *Proc. of the Fourth International Static Analysis Symposium*, Lect. Notes in Comp. Sci. Springer-Verlag, 1997.

[BH97]   A. Bouajjani and P. Habermehl. Symbolic reachability analysis of FIFO-channel systems with non-regular sets of configurations. In *Proc. 24th Int. Colloq. Aut. Lang. Prog.*, volume 1256 of *Lect. Notes in Comp. Sci.* Springer-Verlag, 1997.

[CGJ95]   E.M. Clarke, O. Grumberg, and S. Jha. Verifying parametrized networks using abstraction and regular languages. In *6th International Conference on Concurrency Theory (CONCUR'95)*, pages 395–407, Philadelphia, PA, August 1995.

[DFvG83] E.W. Dijkstra, W.H.J. Feijen, and A.J.M van Gasteren. Derivation of a termination detection algorithm for distributed computations. *Info. Proc. Lett.*, 16(5):217–219, 1983.

[GZ98]   E.P. Gribomont and G. Zenner. Automated verification of szymanski's algorithm. In B. Steffen, editor, *4th Intl. Conf. TACAS'98*, volume 1384 of *Lect. Notes in Comp. Sci.*, pages 424–438. Springer-Verlag, 1998.

[HJJ+96] J.G. Henriksen, J. Jensen, M. Jørgensen, N. Klarlund, B. Paige, T. Rauhe, and A. Sandholm. Mona: Monadic second-order logic in practice. In *Tools and Algorithms for the Construction and Analysis of Systems, First International Workshop, TACAS '95, LNCS 1019*, 1996. Also available through http://www.brics.dk/klarlund/Mona/main.html.

[JL98]   E. Jensen and N.A. Lynch. A proof of burn's n-process mutual exclusion algorithm using abstraction. In B. Steffen, editor, *4th Intl. Conf. TACAS'98*, volume 1384 of *Lect. Notes in Comp. Sci.*, pages 409–423. Springer-Verlag, 1998.

[JN00]   B. Jonsson and M. Nilsson. Transitive closures of regular relations for verifying infinite-state systems. In S. Graf, editor, *Proceedings of TACAS'00*, Lect. Notes in Comp. Sci., 2000. To Appear.

[KM89]   R.P. Kurshan and K. McMillan. A structural induction theorem for processes. In P. Rudnicki, editor, *Proceedings of the 8th Annual Symposium on Principles of Distributed Computing*, pages 239–248, Edmonton, AB, Canada, August 1989. ACM Press.

[KMM+97]   Y. Kesten, O. Maler, M. Marcus, A. Pnueli, and E. Shahar. Symbolic model checking with rich assertional languages. In O. Grumberg, editor, *Proc. 9th Intl. Conference on Computer Aided Verification (CAV'97)*, Lect. Notes in Comp. Sci., pages 424–435. Springer-Verlag, 1997.

[MAB+94]   Z. Manna, A. Anuchitanukul, N. Bjørner, A. Browne, E. Chang, M. Colón, L. De Alfaro, H. Devarajan, H. Sipma, and T.E. Uribe. STeP: The Stanford Temporal Prover. Technical Report STAN-CS-TR-94-1518, Dept. of Comp. Sci., Stanford University, Stanford, California, 1994.

[MP90]   Z. Manna and A. Pnueli. An exercise in the verification of multi – process programs. In W.H.J. Feijen, A.J.M van Gasteren, D. Gries, and J. Misra, editors, *Beauty is Our Business*, pages 289–301. Springer-Verlag, 1990.

[SG92]   A.P. Sistla and S.M. German. Reasoning about systems with many processes. *J. ACM*, 39:675–735, 1992.

[Tho90]   W. Thomas. Automata on infinite objects. *Handbook of theoretical computer science*, pages 165–191, 1990.

[WL89]   P. Wolper and V. Lovinfosse. Verifying properties of large sets of processes with network invariants. In J. Sifakis, editor, *Automatic Verification Methods for Finite State Systems*, volume 407 of *Lect. Notes in Comp. Sci.*, pages 68–80. Springer-Verlag, 1989.

Mechanical Verification of an Ideal Incremental *ABR* Conformance Algorithm ⋆

Michaël Rusinowitch[1], Sorin Stratulat[2], and Francis Klay[3]

[1] LORIA-INRIA
[2] LORIA-Université Henri Poincaré
54506 VANDŒUVRE-LES-NANCY CEDEX, FRANCE
email:rusi,stratula@loria.fr
[3] France Telecom CNET DTL/MSV, Technopole Anticipa
2 av. Pierre Marzin, 22307, Lannion, France
email:Francis.Klay@cnet.francetelecom.fr

Abstract. The Available Bit Rate protocol (ABR) for ATM networks is well-adapted to data traffic by providing minimum rate guarantees and low cell loss to the ABR source end system. An ABR conformance algorithm for controlling the source rates through an interface has been defined by ATM Forum and a more efficient version of it has been designed in [13]. We present in this work the first complete mechanical verification of the equivalence between these two algorithms. The proof is involved and has been supported by the PVS theorem-prover. It has required many lemmas, case analysis and induction reasoning for the manipulation of unbounded scheduling lists. Some ABR conformance protocols have been verified in previous works. However these protocols are approximations of the one we consider here. For instance, the algorithms mechanically proved in [10] and [5] consider scheduling lists with only two elements.

Introduction

The Available Bit Rate protocol (ABR) for ATM networks is well-adapted to data traffic by providing minimum rate guarantees and low cell loss to the ABR source end system. The protocol relies on a contract between the operator who ensures a minimum rate and the source who must respect a rate that is dynamically allocated to him, according to the resources available in the networks. Due to its flexibility the ABR service admits elaborated traffic management mechanisms. To avoid congestion the operator should control in real-time that the actual rate consumed by every ABR application is consistent with the allowed rate. Several algorithms for this conformance control have been proposed and discussed in standardization committees.

⋆ Supported by CNET CTI 96 1B 008 and Action de Recherche Coopérative INRIA PRESYSA

It is essential for an operator to give evidence that the conformance control of the service he proposes does not jeopardize the quality of service (QoS) provided by the ATM network. For such a task formal validation through mathematical arguments is required. However conformance control verification often involves complex case analysis or inductions. This has motivated some operators to employ automated verification tools such as proof-assistants or model-checkers to process these proof obligations.

The algorithm Acr that has been defined by ATM Forum is considered to give the optimal conformance control, in that it computes the minimal allowed rate among the other algorithms. An algorithm (B') for computing an approximation of the optimal control has been designed by C. Rabadan from France-Telecom [12]. It is more efficient since the next two rates to be controlled are scheduled and are updated when receiving RM-cells. This incremental algorithm has been generalized in [13] to the scheduling of an arbitrary number of rates in the future. Our goal here is to derive a mechanical proof that this ideal incremental algorithm is indeed equivalent to the reference algorithm Acr. By this we mean that every step in the equivalence proof has been verified mechanically. The theorem prover we use is PVS [11]. Although PVS is interactive and operates under the direct control of the user it is capable of large autonomous deduction steps by appealing to decision procedures for arithmetics, to rewriting and induction.

Related works Some ABR conformance protocols have been automatically verified in previous works. However all these protocols are approximations of Acr. In particular unlike our case they assume a bound on the number of rates to be scheduled. For instance Algorithm B' of C. Rabadan [12] admits scheduling lists with only two elements. It has been proved recently in [10]. This proof is based on the calculus of weakest preconditions [6] (inductive invariants) and has been completely formalized with the COQ proof-assistant [2]. According to [10] the correctness proof of Algorithm B' *has been a key argument in the standardization process of ABR*. Several proof techniques have been experimented in the FORMA project (http://www-verimag.imag.fr) for the validation of ABR protocols. But the model checking approaches have been hindered by the numerical parameters of the algorithm. L. Fribourg has also obtained good results with extended timed automata [7]. A successful proof of protocol B' with the parameterized temporized automata of Hytech [8] has been reported in [5].

Layout of the paper We first describe the principle of ABR Conformance in Section 1. Then we introduce the algorithms Acr and Acr1 for controlling the ABR Conformance in Section 2 and 3 respectively. The rest of the paper is devoted to the equivalence proof of these two algorithms. We first introduce some key properties in Section 4, then an overview of the proof in Section 5. Since the PVS proof is too complex to be presented in extenso we give a skeleton that follows closely the mechanical proof. We comment about the mechanical proof in Section 6. For the interested reader, the full PVS specification and proof scripts can be found at http://www.loria.fr/~stratula/abr.

1 ABR Conformance Control

ATM (Asynchronous Transfer Mode) technology allows networks to transmit on the same media various applications whose needs are different in term of data-flow rate or quality of services. ATM is a connection-oriented technology since users should declare service requirements and traffic parameters to all intermediates switches when initializing connections. They also may agree to control these parameters on demand. In order to guarantee QoS a traffic contract specifying a traffic mode is negotiated when the connection is set up. Traffic management should ensure that users get their desired QoS although traffic demand is constantly varying. In other words traffic management should ensure that all contracts are met.

In order to solve the critical issue of *congestion control* the effective rate of cells emitted by user applications is controlled by a *conformance algorithm* called GCRA (Generic Control of Cell Rate Algorithm). Among the possible traffic modes, Constant Bit Rate (CBR) and Variable Bit Rate (VBR) were designed mainly for traffic like voice and video. The Available Bit Rate (ABR) service class is especially adapted for standard data traffic, where timing constraints are not tight. Target applications for ABR are email, WWW, file transfer and variable quality video and voice. The principle of ABR is to divide the available bandwidth[1] fairly among active traffic sources so that the network should provide each user with the best rate that is compatible with the current traffic (best-effort service principle). In ABR connections the allowed cell rate (ACR) is determined by the network from load information and may vary during the same connection. The network informs periodically the user about the new rate he can apply by sending back to him *Resource Management (RM)* cells. Hence the source rate is dynamically adjusted according to the available resources of the network by a *feedback control loop* (see Fig. 1). Since the allocated rate varies during a connection with ABR mode, the conformance control is performed by a dynamic GCRA (DGCRA).

Several ABR conformance algorithms have been proposed to the normalization committees. Algorithm Acr [4] can be viewed as a reference for defining the control of the user data-flow in the case of ABR. Each time a data cell arrives from the ABR terminal into the control interface Algorithm Acr computes the rate that should be applied to this cell. The computational cost induced by Acr has been considered too high and there were several proposals to improve it.

For instance it was noticed that the rate change is only determined by the departure of RM-cells leaving the control interface towards the ABR terminal (called *backward RM-cells*) and these RM-cells are much less frequent than data cells. Hence there is much improvement in scheduling rate changes in advance when receiving backward RM-cells in the interface. This is the motivation for

---

[1] left-over by CBR,VBR, e.g.

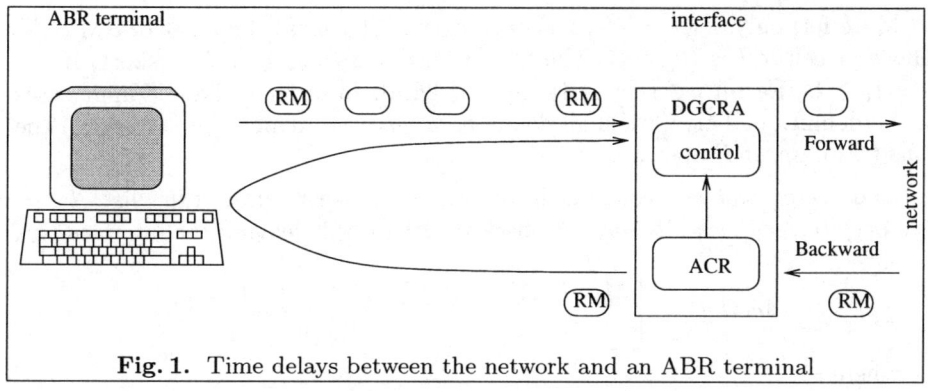

Fig. 1. Time delays between the network and an ABR terminal

the so-called incremental algorithm Acr1 which has been designed to maintain a list of planned rates. This list is updated each time the interface receives a new backward RM-cell. Also controlling the rates with the scheduling list of Acr1 seems to be less expensive than computing the maximum of a list of rates with Acr.

2 Data-Flow Control Definition with ABR (Algorithm Acr)

We shall give the data-flow control definition called here Acr. It has been first introduced in ATM Forum by [4] and since then it has been considered as a reference for the other algorithms.

The principle of the algorithm Acr running in the interface is to manage the list of backward RM-cells received from the network (Fig. 1) in order to determine the rate that has to be controlled at some instant. We shall associate with each RM-cell a couple (t, er) where t is the time when the backward RM-cell leaves the interface (where conformance control is performed) towards the ABR terminal and er is the new rate imposed by the network to the ABR terminal. For our discussion we identify a cell with its associated couple. By convention we call *time* (resp. *rate*) of c the first (resp. second) component of a cell c. The control device receives the new expected rate value before the ABR terminal. Hence due to the transmission delays in the networks, the control device should apply at time t a value received at time $t - \tau$ where τ represents a propagation delay equal to the time taken by an RM-cell to go from the interface to the ABR terminal and back to the interface. However the propagation times in the network may vary according to the traffic load. In order to take into account variations of these delays, the ITU-T has proposed that the rate to be controlled at time t is computed as the maximum among the rates received by the interface within a temporal window limited by $t - \tau_2$ and $t - \tau_3$ and the rate received just before or at $t - \tau_2$. The *window parameters* τ_2, τ_3 satisfy $\tau_2 > \tau_3$. They have been negotiated during the establishment of the traffic contract.

More formally, let $l = [(t_1, er_1), (t_2, er_2), \ldots, (t_n, er_n)]$ be a list of RM-cells. The *first cell* of l is (t_1, er_1). The list l is *time-decreasing* (t.d. in short) if $i < j \Rightarrow t_i \geq t_j$, for all $i \in [1..n-1]$ and $j \in [2..n]$. In order to handle limit cases in the definitions below we shall define $t_0 = +\infty$. We denote by $\cdot$ (resp. @) the *cons* (resp. *append*) operator on lists.

The rate to be controlled at time t w.r.t. the t.d. list $l = [(t_1, er_1), (t_2, er_2), \ldots, (t_n, er_n)]$ of backward RM-cells leaving the interface is:

$$Acr(l,t) = \begin{cases} MaxEr(Wind(l,t)) & \text{if } Wind(l,t) \neq \emptyset, \\ 0 & \text{otherwise} \end{cases}$$

where

$$Wind(l,t) = \{(t_i, er_i) \in l | \ (t - \tau_2 < t_i \leq t - \tau_3) \text{ or } (t_i \leq t - \tau_2 < t_{i-1})\}$$
$$MaxEr(s) = max\{er|(t, er) \in s\}$$

For instance, with this rate control policy the end user can benefit at time $t + \tau_3$ from a rate increase received on a backward cell at time t by the interface, that is, as soon as possible. On the other hand a rate decrease will be taken into account only at time $t + \tau_2$, that is, as late as possible. Hence this is a policy in favour of the user and based on worst-case situations. It can be noticed that for a fixed list l, $Acr(l,t)$ is decreasing on t after $t + \tau_3$ since the window is (non strictly) decreasing for the inclusion relation.

3 Incremental Conformance Checking (Algorithm Acr1)

We now introduce an ideal incremental algorithm Acr1 for conformance control. Unlike Acr the algorithm Acr1 computes a list of rates to be controlled in the future. Hence it maintains a list $Prog(l)$ of cells (l is as above) (t_j, er_j) containing a future rate er_j to be controlled together with the time t_j it comes into effect. Similar to l, $Prog(l)$ will be sorted in decreasing order on time. This list is updated when receiving a backward RM-cell. An important gain over Acr is due to the fact that the RM-cells are much less frequent than the data cells. The ratio of RM-cells to all cells recommended by the ATM Forum[2] is 1/32. Let us assume that the list $Prog(l)$ is constructed. We shall prove later that it is time-decreasing as l. Then the rate to be controlled at time t is:

$$Acr1(l,t) = Prog(l)_t$$

where p_t is a function that computes by extrapolation the rate at time t from a list of scheduled rates p. This function simply extracts from p the first rate value that is scheduled at or immediately before the time t. This rate is the one to be controlled at t. Formally:

---

[2] ATM Forum Traffic Management Specification Version 4.0. ftp://ftp.atmforum.com/pub/approved-specs/af-tm-0056.000.ps

$$p_t = \begin{cases} er_i & \text{if there exists a cell } (t_i, er_i) \in p \text{ such that } t \geq t_i \text{ and} \\ & \text{there is no cell } (t_j, er_j) \in p \text{ with } t \geq t_j, i > j \text{ and } i,j \in [1..n] \\ 0 & \text{otherwise} \end{cases}$$

We now describe how the list $Prog(l)$ is updated. A list l' is a *prefix* of a list l if there exists a list l'' such that $l = l'@l''$. Given a list l' and a time t we denote by $l'_{>_\tau t}$ the maximal prefix of l' containing cells with time greater than t. Similarly we define $l'_{\leq_\rho er}$ as the maximal prefix of l' containing cells with rate less or equal than er. This gives the following recursive definition of $Prog(l)$:

$$Prog((t, er) \cdot l) = \begin{cases} \text{if} & er \geq Prog(l)_{t+\tau_3} \text{ then } (t + \tau_3, er) \cdot l' \\ & \text{where } Prog(l) = Prog(l)_{>_\tau t+\tau_3}@l'. \\ \text{else if } Prog(l)_{\leq_\rho er} \text{ is empty then } (t + \tau_2, er) \cdot Prog(l) \\ \text{else } (t', er) \cdot l'' \\ & \text{where } Prog(l) = Prog(l)_{\leq_\rho er}@l'' \\ & \text{and } Prog(l)_{\leq_\rho er} = L@[(t', er')] \end{cases}$$

$Prog(l)$ is by definition the empty list when l is the empty list.

Our goal in the remaining of the paper is to show that the incremental algorithm Acr1 delivers the same rate values as the reference algorithm Acr, i.e.

$$\forall t \; \forall l \quad Acr1(l, t) = Acr(l, t)$$

4 Two Key Properties

Two properties were used abundantly in the main proof. The first one `time_dec` states that $Prog(l)$ is sorted in decreasing order on its time components. The second one `rate_inc` specifies a prefix of $Prog(l)$ that is sorted in increasing order on its rate component. Both assume that l is time-decreasing (t.d.). We denote by $Timel(l)$ the time of its first cell (0 if l is empty).

Property 1 (time_dec) *Given a t.d. cell list l the list $Prog(l)$ is also t.d..*

Proof. By induction on l. When l is empty $Prog(l)$ is empty hence t.d.. Assume by induction hypothesis that for any t.d. list l_1 of length less or equal than the length of l, $Prog(l_1)$ is t.d.. Let us prove that $Prog((t, er) \cdot l)$ is t.d. when $t \geq Timel(l)$. We perform a case analysis guided by the definition of $Prog$ from Section 3. Note that any sublist of a t.d. list is also t.d..

1. assume that $er \geq Prog(l)_{t+\tau_3}$. Let l' be such that $Prog(l) = Prog(l)_{>_\tau t+\tau_3}@l'$. Then $Prog((t, er) \cdot l)$ is equal to $(t + \tau_3, er) \cdot l'$ which is t.d. since $t + \tau_3 \geq Timel(l')$ and l' is t.d..

2. otherwise, let $Prog(l) = Prog(l)_{\leq_\rho er}@l''$. If $Prog(l)_{\leq_\rho er}$ is empty then the list $(t + \tau_2, er) \cdot Prog(l)$ is t.d. because $t + \tau_2 \geq Timel(Prog(l))$. This can be deduced from (i) the time-decreasing property of $(t, er) \cdot l$, and (ii) the fact that for any nonempty t.d. list $L = (\bar{t}, \bar{e}) \cdot L'$ we have $\bar{t} + \tau_2 \geq Timel(Prog(L))$. (This can be proved by a simple induction on L.)

If $Prog(l)_{\leq_\rho er}$ is a nonempty list of the form $L''@[(t', er')]$ then $(t', er) \cdot l''$ is a t.d. list as it can be deduced from the time-decreasing property of $Prog(l)$. □

We denote by $l_{\frown t}$ the maximal prefix l' of l such that the time of any cell from l' except possibly the last one is greater than t. We remark that for any nonempty t.d. list l, the prefix $l_{\frown t}$ and l have the same first cell. We say that a cell list $l = [(t_1, er_1), (t_2, er_2), \ldots, (t_n, er_n)]$ is *strictly rate-increasing* (s.r.i. in short) if the rate-values of its cells are strictly increasing: $i < j \Rightarrow er_i < er_j$, for all $i, j \in [1..n]$. We can observe that given an s.r.i. list l and two time values $t > t'$ we have $l_t \leq l_{t'}$.

Property 2 (rate_inc) *Given a t.d. cell list l the prefix $Prog(l)_{\frown Timel(l) + \tau_3}$ of $Prog(l)$ is s.r.i..*

Proof. By induction on l. If l is empty then $Prog(l)$ is empty hence s.r.i.. Otherwise by induction hypothesis we assume that $Prog(l)_{\frown Timel(l) + \tau_3}$ is s.r.i.. If $t \geq Timel(l)$ we will prove that $Prog((t, er) \cdot l)_{\frown t + \tau_3}$ is also s.r.i. by case analysis according to the definition of $Prog$.

1. if $er \geq Prog(l)_{t + \tau_3}$ then $Prog((t, er) \cdot l) = (t + \tau_3, er) \cdot l'$ where l' is such that $Prog(l) = Prog(l)_{>_\tau t + \tau_3}@l'$. It results that $Prog((t, er) \cdot l)_{\frown t + \tau_3} = [(t + \tau_3, er)]$ which is s.r.i..
2. otherwise let l'' be such that $Prog(l) = Prog(l)_{\leq_\rho er}@l''$:

2.1. if $Prog(l)_{\leq_\rho er}$ is empty then $Prog((t, er) \cdot l) = (t + \tau_2, er) \cdot Prog(l)$. We have $Prog((t, er) \cdot l)_{\frown t + \tau_3} = (t + \tau_2, er) \cdot Prog(l)_{\frown t + \tau_3}$. Moreover, $Prog(l)_{\frown t + \tau_3}$ is a prefix of $Prog(l)_{\frown Timel(l) + \tau_3}$ because $t \geq Timel(l)$. By consequence $(t + \tau_2, er) \cdot Prog(l)_{\frown t + \tau_3}$ is s.r.i..

2.2. otherwise $Prog(l)_{\leq_\rho er} = L@[(t', er')]$ for some L and $Prog((t, er) \cdot l) = (t', er) \cdot l''$. If l'' is empty, $Prog((t, er) \cdot l)_{\frown t + \tau_3}$ consists of the unique cell (t', er') and is obviously s.r.i. Since l'' is a sublist of $Prog(l)$ the list $l''_{\frown t + \tau_3}$ is a sublist of $Prog(l)_{\frown t + \tau_3}$. Therefore it is s.r.i.. Moreover er is less than the rate of the first cell of l'' (or $l''_{\frown t + \tau_3}$) when l'' is not empty. We conclude that $Prog((t, er) \cdot l)_{\frown t + \tau_3} = (t', er) \cdot l'''_{\frown t + \tau_3}$ is s.r.i.. □

5 The Main Proof

We will employ the following notations. Assume that x is a cell, $Time(x)$ its time, $Er(x)$ its rate and τ_2, τ_3 the two window parameters. The model checking approaches with MEC [1] and UPPAAL [3] had to assign values to these parameters in order to proceed. Here we only assume all over the proof that $\tau_2 > \tau_3$

without any further mention of this hypothesis. We introduce $T_2(x)$ to denote $Time(x) + \tau_2$ and $T_3(x)$ to denote $Time(x) + \tau_3$. The predicate $\mathcal{S}^{\geq \tau}(l)$, resp. $\mathcal{S}^{<\rho}(l)$, is true if l is t.d., resp. s.r.i.. We will omit the quantifier prefixes of the formulas since all the variables are considered as universally quantified.

The proof of the conjecture $Acr1(l,t) = Acr(l,t)$ is immediate if we prove the *main lemma* $P(l)$, where:

$$P(l): \quad \mathcal{S}^{\geq \tau}(l) \Rightarrow Prog(l)_t = MaxEr(Wind(l,t))$$

We apply an induction on the length of l. When l is empty, the proof is immediate, by expanding the definitions of $Prog$, $MaxEr$ and $Wind$. In the step case, we suppose $P(l)$ and we try to prove $P(a' \cdot l)$. More precisely, we should prove that $Prog(a' \cdot l)_t = MaxEr(Wind(a' \cdot l, t))$ follows from $\mathcal{S}^{\geq \tau}(a' \cdot l)$. From the hypothesis $\mathcal{S}^{\geq \tau}(a' \cdot l)$ we deduce $\mathcal{S}^{\geq \tau}(l)$ since l is a sublist of $(a' \cdot l)$. Hence, we can assume that $Prog(l)_t = MaxEr(Wind(l,t))$. The arguments for proving the step case are also based on the following property depending on the induction hypothesis:

Property 3 The list $Prog(l)_{\frown T_3(a')}$ is s.r.i..

Proof. From Property 2 we have $\mathcal{S}^{\geq \tau}(l) \Rightarrow \mathcal{S}^{<\rho}(Prog(l)_{\frown (Timel(l)+\tau_3)})$. Together with the hypothesis $\mathcal{S}^{\geq \tau}(l)$, we deduce $\mathcal{S}^{<\rho}(Prog(l)_{\frown (Timel(l)+\tau_3)})$. We also have $Time(a') \geq Timel(l)$ since
$\mathcal{S}^{\geq \tau}(a' \cdot l)$ and by consequence $Prog(l)_{\frown T_3(a')}$ is a prefix of $Prog(l)_{\frown (Timel(l)+\tau_3)}$. Hence $Prog(l)_{\frown T_3(a')}$ is s.r.i.. □

By T_m we denote $Prog(l)_t$. Then $t \geq T_m$ and no cell from the list $Prog(l)$ has its time in the interval $(T_m, t]$. Let $I_{a'}$ be the time of the first cell of $Prog(a \cdot l)$. We have the following facts about $I_{a'}$.

1. $I_{a'} \in \{T_2(t'), T_3(t') \mid t'$ is the time of an $(a' \cdot l)$ cell$\}$, as can be easily proved by induction on l.

2. $I_{a'} \in [T_3(a'), T_2(a')]$. Since $a' \cdot l$ is t.d., from the first fact it results that $I_{a'} \leq T_2(a')$. Moreover from the definition of $Prog$: (i) if $Er(a') < Acr1(l, T_3(a'))$ then the prefix $Prog(l)_{\leq_\rho Er(a')}$ contains only cells with rates $\leq Er(a')$ which therefore occur at a time $> T_3(a')$. If $Prog(l)_{\leq_\rho Er(a')}$ is empty, then $I_{a'} = T_2(a')$, otherwise $I_{a'}$ is the time of the last cell of it. By consequence, $I_{a'} > T_3(a')$. (ii) if $Er(a') \geq Acr1(l, T_3(a'))$ then $I_{a'} = T_3(a')$.

The domain where $I_{a'}$ can take its value for each case is included in the hachured time interval of the corresponding figure. From the definition of $Prog$, it can be shown that the rate of the first cell of $Prog(a' \cdot l)$ is $Er(a')$. Hence $Prog(a' \cdot l) = (I_{a'}, Er(a')) \cdot L''$ for some list L''.

We perform a case analysis according to the position of t w.r.t. the values $T_2(a')$ and $T_3(a')$:

1. If $T_2(a') \leq t$ (see Fig. 2) then $Acr1(a' \cdot l, t) = Acr(a' \cdot l, t)(= Er(a'))$ because
   - $MaxEr(Wind(a' \cdot l, t)) = Er(a')$ since $Wind(a' \cdot l, t) = [a']$.
   - $Prog(a' \cdot l)_t = Er(a')$ because $(I_{a'}, Er(a'))$ is the first cell of $Prog(a' \cdot l)$ and $I_{a'} \leq T_2(a') \leq t$.

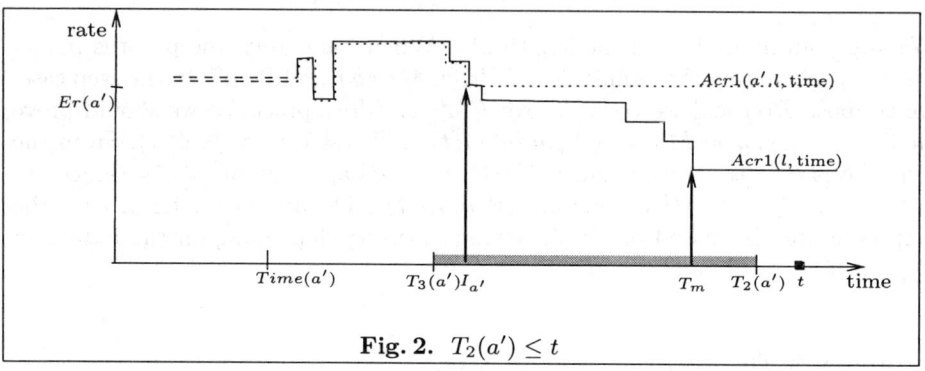

Fig. 2. $T_2(a') \leq t$

2. If $T_3(a') > t$ (see Fig. 3) then
   - a' is not member of $Wind(a' \cdot l, t)$. Therefore, $Acr(a' \cdot l, t) = Acr(l, t)$, and
   - $Acr1(a' \cdot l, t) = Acr1(l, t)$ because $I_{a'} \in [T_3(a'), T_2(a')]$.

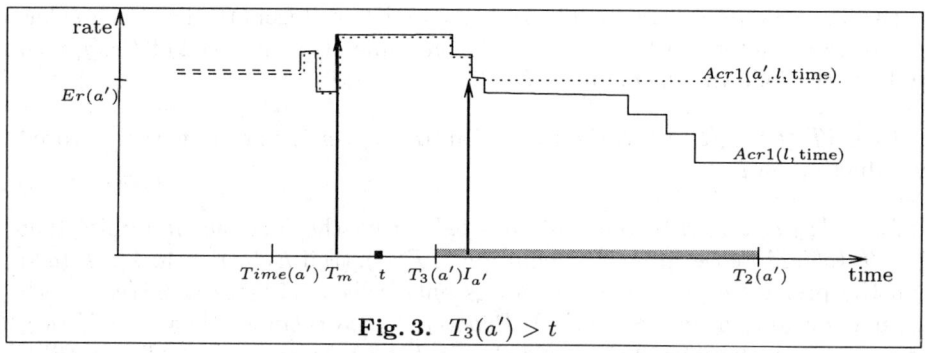

Fig. 3. $T_3(a') > t$

By the induction hypothesis $Acr1(l, t) = Acr(l, t)$. It results that $Acr1(a' \cdot l, t) = Acr(a' \cdot l, t)$.

3. If $T_2(a') > t \geq T_3(a')$ we deduce that $a' \in Wind(a' \cdot l, t)$, by definition of Wind.

3.1. If $Wind(l,t)$ is empty then the list l is also empty. Otherwise, the first cell of l belongs to $Wind(l,t)$. Then $Prog([a']) = [(Er(a'), T_3(a'))]$ since $t \geq T_3(a')$ and $Wind([a'],t) = [a']$. Therefore $Acr1([a'],t) = Acr([a'],t) = Er(a')$.

3.2. If $Wind(l,t)$ is nonempty, let ER_m be the value of the maximal rate of the $Wind(l,t)$ cells. According to the induction hypothesis $Acr(l,t) = Acr1(l,t)$. Thus the rate of the $Prog(l)$ cell situated at T_m equals ER_m.

In order to schedule $Er(a')$, we perform a case analysis according to the definition of $Prog$:

3.2.1. If the condition

$$Acr1(l, T_3(a')) \leq Er(a') \qquad (Cond.1)$$

is true (see Fig. 4), then $I_{a'} = T_3(a')$. Moreover $(I_{a'}, Er(a'))$ is the first cell of $Prog(a' \cdot l)$. Then $Acr1(a' \cdot l, t) = Er(a')$ because $T_3(a') \leq t$.

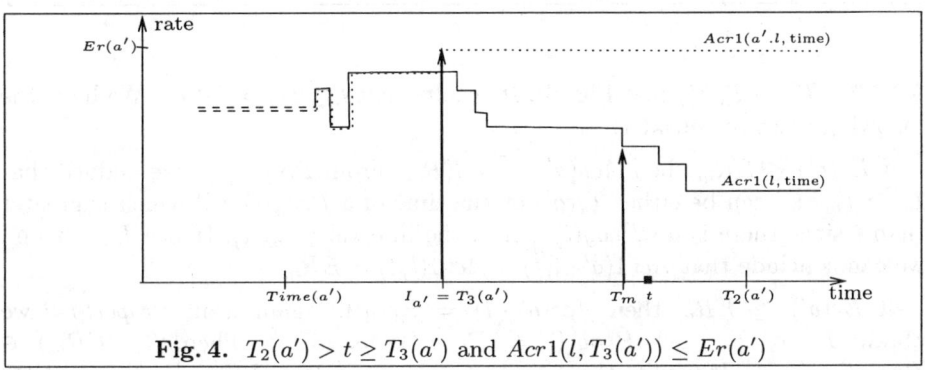

Fig. 4. $T_2(a') > t \geq T_3(a')$ and $Acr1(l, T_3(a')) \leq Er(a')$

It remains to prove that $Acr(a' \cdot l, t)$ also equals $Er(a')$ or equivalently $ER_m \leq Er(a')$.

Again from $T_3(a') \leq t$ together with the fact that the sublist $Prog(l)_{\frown T_3(a')}$ is s.r.i. according to *Property 3* we deduce $Acr1(l,t) \leq Acr1(l, T_3(a'))$. Therefore by the condition $Cond.1$ and the induction hypothesis we have $ER_m \leq Er(a')$.

3.2.2. If the condition

$$Acr1(l, T_3(a')) > Er(a') \qquad (Cond.2)$$

is true we know that $I_{a'} > T_3(a')$. We distinguish the following cases:

3.2.2.1 $T_m \leq T_3(a')$ (see Fig. 5). Since $T_3(a') \leq t$ it results that $t \geq T_3(a') \geq T_m$. By the definition of T_m, no cell of $Prog(l)$ has its time in the interval $(T_m, t]$. Hence $Acr1(l, T_3(a')) = ER_m$. On the one hand by the condition $Cond.2$ we have $ER_m > Er(a')$. Consequently $Acr(a' \cdot l, t) = ER_m$. On the other hand the instant $I_{a'}$ can be either $T_2(a')$ or the time of a $Prog(l)$ cell. $T_2(a')$ also cannot be inside the interval $(T_m, t]$ since $T_2(a') > t$. If $I_{a'} = T_2(a')$ then $I_{a'} > t$. Assume now that $I_{a'}$ is the time of a $Prog(l)$ cell. Since $I_{a'} > T_3(a')$, $t \geq T_3(a') \geq T_m$ and there is no $Prog(l)$ cell located in the interval $(T_m, t]$ we deduce that $I_{a'} > t$. Therefore $Acr1(a' \cdot l, t)$ is also equal to ER_m.

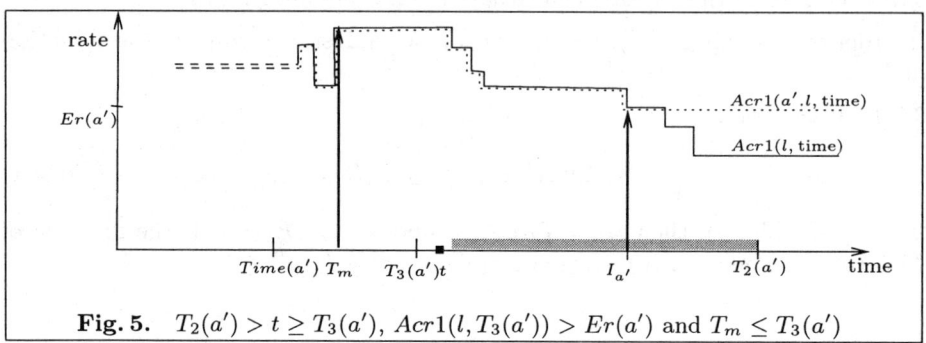

Fig. 5. $T_2(a') > t \geq T_3(a')$, $Acr1(l, T_3(a')) > Er(a')$ and $T_m \leq T_3(a')$

3.2.2.2. $T_m > T_3(a')$ (see Fig. 6). It results that $t \geq T_m > T_3(a')$. We have the following cases to consider:

– if $Er(a') < ER_m$ then $Acr(a' \cdot l) = ER_m$. From *Property 3* we deduce that $I_{a'} \geq T_m$. $I_{a'}$ can be either $T_2(a')$ or the time of a $Prog(l)$ cell which is greater than t since there is no $Prog(l)$ cell in the interval $(T_m, t]$. Hence $I_{a'} > t$ and we can conclude that $Acr1(a' \cdot l, t) = Acr1(l, t) = ER_m$.

– if $Er(a') \geq ER_m$ then $Acr(a' \cdot l) = Er(a')$. Again from *Property 3* we obtain $I_{a'} \leq T_m$. Let $Prog(l) = Prog(l)_{\leq_\rho Er(a')} @ l'''$. Then $(T_m, ER_m) \in Prog(l)_{\leq_\rho Er(a')}$. It results that $Acr1(a' \cdot l, t) = Acr1(a' \cdot l, T_m) = (I_{a'}, Er(a')) \cdot l'''_t = Er(a')$.

6   Comments on the Mechanical Proof

The equivalence theorem has been successfully developed within PVS [11] environment. PVS provides an expressive specification language that builds on classical typed higher-order logic with mechanisms for defining abstract datatypes. Hence the specification of the algorithms already given in functional style was relatively easy. In this work we deliberately restricted ourselves to first-order features of the language since our final goal is to prove the equivalence theorem with a first-order prover in a more automatic way, i.e. with less input from the user.

The first difficult proof step we encountered was to show that if a list of cells l is time-decreasing then its associated scheduling list $Prog(l)$ is also time-decreasing: this property is expressed by Property 1. We have tried to apply

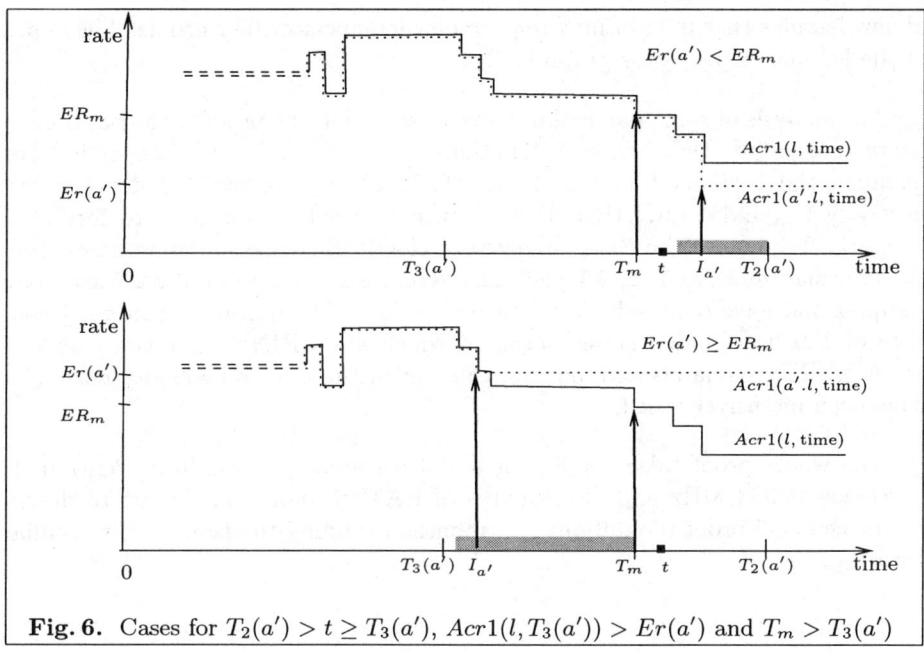

Fig. 6. Cases for $T_2(a') > t \geq T_3(a')$, $Acr1(l, T_3(a')) > Er(a')$ and $T_m > T_3(a')$

induction on the length of the list but it failed because the scheduling list in the induction conclusion is not a sublist of the one in the induction hypothesis. Therefore, the direct application of the induction hypothesis was impossible. After a closer analysis, we discovered that auxiliary lemmas concerning time properties of cell lists were needed. However the initial functions were not sufficient to express them. Hence an important decision was to enrich the initial specification with auxiliary functions such as Time1.

The formal verification of time_dec follows closely the semi-formal proof from Section 5. By the rules ASSERT and GRIND, the theorem prover PVS applies its decision procedures to perform arithmetic reasoning, employs congruence closure for equality reasoning, installs theories and rewrite rules along with all the definitions relevant to the goal in order to prove the trivial cases, to simplify complex expressions and definitions, and to perform matching. In detail, the formal proof of time_dec requires 32 user-steps in PVS, 6 of which are ASSERT, 5 are GRIND and 4 are LEMMA, which introduce instances of previously proved lemmas as new formulas.

The proof of main_conj, which codes the main lemma, is the most complex that was elaborated for this specification. It follows the skeleton of the semi-formal proof described in Section 5. We have applied an INDUCT rule to perform induction on the length of the cell list. The basic case was completed by a GRIND operation. However, the proof of the step case has needed 27 invocations of lemmas and for 6 times the application of the CASE rule, to perform case reasoning. The analysis of each particular case was a source for the development of new lemmas that in turn may require new lemmas for their proofs. The depth of the lemmas dependency graph is 7.

The analysis of some particular cases presented in the proof of the `main_conj` lemma suggested other auxiliary functions to express additional properties. For instance, the auxiliary functions `ListUpTo(l,t)` and `SortedE(l)` denoted respectively $l_{\frown t}$ and $\mathcal{S}^{<_\rho}(l)$ that have been introduced in Section 4 to formalize Property 2. Some of the cases follow very closely the corresponding cases from the informal proof, as 1, 2, 3.1 and 3.2.1. The cases 3.2.2.1 and 3.2.2.2 are more complex and have required 17 lemma invocations. The proof of `main_conj` consists of 120 user-guided steps, seven of which are GRIND operations and 29 are ASSERT commands and indicate that the arithmetic and equality reasoning have been intensively used.

The whole proof takes 78.97s on a PC featured with an Intel Pentium II processor at 333 MHz and 128 Mbytes of RAM memory. The effort to design the mechanical proof took about two months including the time to get familiar with PVS.

7 Conclusions and Perspectives

Our objective was to derive the first mechanical proof of an ideal incremental ABR conformance algorithm. A proof by hand of the algorithm has been designed before [13]. However this kind of manual proofs is not fully convincing in general since limit cases or apparently trivial arguments are often omitted and they may be source of mistakes. In this respect our machine proof gives more evidence of the correctness of the algorithm since every single step has been verified by PVS.

On the one hand, the specification of the algorithm as a recursive function in PVS was relatively easy. The proof we obtained on the other hand was rather involved. It has required about 80 intermediate lemmas and the introduction of auxiliary definitions. We feel that there is space for optimization and many inference steps can possibly be simplified. It is also our plan to search for a proof with more automated tools. We expect to derive entirely automatic proofs for many lemmas. In another direction we also think about using higher-order specification and reasoning techniques to derive a proof that is more synthetic and therefore easier to grasp. Finally we should prove that by limiting the size of the scheduling lists the ideal ABR conformance algorithm indeed reduces to approximate algorithms such as B'.

Acknowledgements: We thank Laurent Fribourg, Bernhard Gramlich and Jean-François Monin for interesting discussions and remarks about this work.

References

1. A. Arnold. MEC: A system for constructing and analysing transition systems. In J. Sifakis, editor, *Proceedings of the International Workshop on Automatic Verification Methods for Finite State Systems*, number 407 in LNCS, pages 117–132. Springer Verlag, 1990.
2. B. Barras, S. Boutin, C. Cornes, J. Courant, J.C. Filliatre, E. Giménez, H. Herbelin, G. Huet, C. Muñoz, C. Murthy, C. Parent, C. Paulin, A. Saïbi, and B. Werner. The Coq Proof Assistant Reference Manual – Version V6.1. Technical Report 0203, INRIA, August 1997.
3. J. Bengtsson, K. G. Larsen, F. Larsson, P. Pettersson, and Wang Yi. UPPAAL: a tool suite for the automatic verification of real-time systems. In R. Alur, T. A. Henzinger, and E.D. Sontag, editors, *Hybrid Systems III*, number 1066 in LNCS, pages 232–243, 1996.
4. A. Berger, F. Bonomi, and K. Fendick. Proposed TM baseline text on an ABR conformance definition. Technical Report 95-0212R1, ATM Forum Traffic Management Group, 1995.
5. B. Bérard and L. Fribourg. Automated verification of a parametric real-time program: the ABR conformance protocol. In *Proc. 11th Int. Conf. Computer Aided Verification (CAV'99)*, number 1633 in LNCS, pages 96–107, Trento, Italy, July 1999.
6. E. W. Dijkstra. *A Discipline of Programming*. Prentice-Hall, Englewood Cliffs, NJ, 1976.
7. L. Fribourg. A closed-form evaluation for extended timed automata. Technical Report LSV-98-2, Lab. Specification and Verification, ENS de Cachan, Cachan, March, France 1998. 17 pages.
8. T.A. Henzinger, P.H. Ho, and H. Wong-Toi. HYTECH: A model checker for hybrid systems. In *CAV'97*, number 1254 in LNCS, pages 460–463. Springer-Verlag, 1997.
9. R. Jain. Congestion control and traffic management in ATM networks: Recent advances and a survey. *Computer Networks and ISDN Systems*, 28:1723–1738, 1996. ftp://ftp.netlab.ohio-state.edu/pub/jain/papers/cnis/index.html.
10. J.F. Monin and F. Klay. Correctness proof of the standardized algorithm for ABR conformance. In J. Wing, J. Woodcock, and J. Davies, editors, *Formal Methods (FM) '99*, number 1709 in LNCS, pages 662–681. Springer Verlag, 1999.
11. S. Owre, J. M. Rushby, and N. Shankar. PVS: A prototype verification system. In D. Kapur, editor, *11th International Conference on Automated Deduction (CADE)*, volume 607 of *Lecture Notes in Artificial Intelligence*, pages 748–752. Springer Verlag, 1992.
12. C. Rabadan. L'ABR et sa conformité. Technical report, NT DAC/ARP/034, CNET, 1997.
13. C. Rabadan and F. Klay. Un nouvel algorithme de contrôle de conformité pour la capacité de transfert "Available Bit Rate". Technical Report NT/CNET/5476, CNET, 1997.

Model Checking Continuous-Time Markov Chains by Transient Analysis

Christel Baier[1], Boudewijn Haverkort[2],
Holger Hermanns[3], and Joost-Pieter Katoen[3,*]

[1] Institut für Informatik I, University of Bonn
Römerstraße 164, D-53117 Bonn, Germany
[2] Dept. of Computer Science, RWTH Aachen
Ahornstraße 55, D-52056 Aachen, Germany
[3] Dept. of Computer Science, University of Twente
P.O. Box 217, 7500 AE Enschede, The Netherlands
*katoen@cs.utwente.nl,
Tel.: +31-53-4895675, fax: +31-53-4893247,

Abstract. The verification of continuous-time Markov chains (CTMCs) against continuous stochastic logic (**CSL**) [3,6], a stochastic branching-time temporal logic, is considered. **CSL** facilitates among others the specification of steady-state properties and the specification of probabilistic timing properties of the form $\mathcal{P}_{\bowtie p}(\Phi_1 \mathcal{U}^I \Phi_2)$, for state formulas Φ_1 and Φ_2, comparison operator $\bowtie$, probability p, and real interval I. The main result of this paper is that model checking probabilistic timing properties can be reduced to the problem of computing transient state probabilities for CTMCs. This allows us to verify such properties by using efficient techniques for transient analysis of CTMCs such as uniformisation. A second result is that a variant of ordinary lumping equivalence (i.e., bisimulation), a well-known notion for aggregating CTMCs, preserves the validity of all **CSL**-formulas.

1 Introduction

Continuous-time Markov chains (CTMCs) have been widely used to determine important system performance and reliability characteristics. To mention just a few applications, these models have been used to quantify the throughput of production lines, to determine the mean time between failure in safety-critical systems, or to identify bottlenecks in communication networks. Due to the rapidly increasing size and complexity of systems, obtaining such models in a direct way becomes more and more cumbersome and error-prone. An effective solution to this problem is to generate CTMCs from higher-level specifications, like queueing networks, stochastic Petri nets [1], or stochastic process algebras [20,24].

Although these approaches have shown to be rather valuable — several (industrial) case studies have been carried out and mature tool-support is available

[19,21] — the specification of the measure of interest is mostly done informally. The analysis of the CTMC most often boils down to the determination of *steady-state* and *transient state probabilities*. Steady-state probabilities refer to the system behaviour on the "long run" while the transient probabilities consider the system at a fixed time instant t.

In [3] measures of interest of CTMCs are specified in a branching-time logic **CSL** (*continuous stochastic logic*) that includes a **TCTL**-like time-bounded until operator $\mathcal{U}^I$, where I is a time-interval, and a probabilistic operator $\mathcal{P}_{\bowtie p}(\cdot)$ to reason about the probabilities of timing properties. As in the logic **PCTL** [17], a probabilistic variant of **CTL** interpreted over DTMCs, the operator $\mathcal{P}_{\bowtie p}(\varphi)$ replaces the usual **CTL** path quantifiers $\forall$ and $\exists$ and refers to the probability for the event specified by the path formula φ. The subscript $\bowtie p$ (where $\bowtie$ is a comparison operator and $p \in [0,1]$) specifies a lower or upper bound for the "allowed" probabilities. The combination of the probabilistic operator with the temporal operator $\Diamond^{[t,t]}$ (which can be derived from the time-bounded until operator) analyses the quantitative behaviour at time instant t and can be used to reason about transient probabilities. For instance, $\mathcal{P}_{\leq 0.001}(\Diamond^{[4,4]} error)$ asserts that the probability for a system error at time instant 4 is at most 10^{-3}.

In [6], **CSL** was extended by the usual next step and until operator and by a novel steady-state operator, e.g. the formula $\mathcal{S}_{\geq 0.98}(up)$ asserts that the steady-state probability for the system "being up" is at least 0.98. Moreover, [6] presented a model checking algorithm for the extended version of **CSL** that uses a variant of multi-terminal BDDs [12,4]; thus, obtaining a single framework that combines the traditional approach of steady-state and transient analysis of CTMCs with the symbolic BDD-based model checking approach for temporal logics.

While [6] focuses on model checking with techniques that have been proven to be very efficient for non-stochastic systems, viz. BDDs, in this paper we investigate the complementary question and present a **CSL** model checking algorithm that operates with well-understood efficient techniques for analyzing CTMCs, namely *transient analysis* of CTMCs represented by sparse matrices. The main difficulty is the treatment of $\mathcal{P}_{\bowtie p}(\varphi)$ applied to a path formula φ of the form $\Phi_1 \mathcal{U}^I \Phi_2$.[1] Our main result states that, for a given CTMC $\mathcal{M}$ and state s in $\mathcal{M}$, the measure $Prob^{\mathcal{M}}(s, \varphi)$ for the event that φ holds when the system starts in state s, can be calculated by means of a transient analysis of the CTMC $\mathcal{M}'$, which can easily be derived from $\mathcal{M}$. This allows us to adopt efficient techniques for performing transient analysis of CTMCs, like *uniformisation* [15,16, 25,27], for model checking probabilistic timing properties. In addition, we show that (ordinary) lumping-equivalence — a notion on Markov chains to aggregate state spaces [10,24] that can be viewed as a continuous variant of probabilistic bisimulation [26] — preserves the validity of all **CSL**-formulas. This allows us to switch from the original state space to the (possibly much smaller) quotient

---

[1] The steady-state operator and the probabilistic operator applied to next step or (unbounded) until require essentially matrix operations like multiplication and solving linear equation systems that can be treated by standard tools for sparse matrices.

space under lumping equivalence. Using this property, we indicate how the state space for checking probabilistic timing properties on the derived CTMC $\mathcal{M}'$ can be obtained.

Organisation of the paper. Section 2 introduces CTMCs and **CSL**. Section 3 presents a reduction of the model checking problem for time-bounded until to a transient analysis on CTMCs. Section 4 discusses lumping equivalence and preservation of **CSL**-properties. Section 5 reports on the checking of properties on a large plain-old telephone system [21]. Section 6 concludes the paper.

2 CTMCs and CSL

In this section, we briefly recall the basic concepts of CTMCs [28] and the logic **CSL** [3,6]. We slightly depart from the standard notations for CTMCs and consider a CTMC as an ordinary transition system (Kripke structure) where the edges are equipped with probabilistic timing information. Let AP be a fixed, finite set of atomic propositions.

CTMCs. A (labelled) CTMC $\mathcal{M}$ is a tuple $(S, \mathbf{R}, L)$ where S is a finite set of *states*, $\mathbf{R} : S \times S \to \mathbb{R}_{\geqslant 0}$ the *rate matrix*[2], and $L : S \to 2^{AP}$ the *labelling* function which assigns to each state $s \in S$ the set $L(s)$ of atomic propositions $a \in AP$ that are valid in s. A state s is called *absorbing* iff $\mathbf{R}(s, s') = 0$ for all states s'. We assume that for any state s, AP contains an atomic proposition a_s which is characteristic for s, i.e., $a_s \in L(s)$ and $a_s \notin L(s')$ for any $s' \neq s$.

Intuitively, $\mathbf{R}(s, s') > 0$ iff there is a transition from s to s'; $1 - e^{-\mathbf{R}(s,s') \cdot t}$ is the probability that the transition $s \to s'$ can be triggered within t time units. Thus, the delay of transition $s \to s'$ is governed by an exponential distribution with rate $\mathbf{R}(s, s')$. If $\mathbf{R}(s, s') > 0$ for more than one state s', a competition between the transitions originating in s exists, known as the *race condition*. The probability to move from non-absorbing state s to a particular state s' within t time units, i.e., $s \to s'$ wins the race, is given by

$$\mathbf{P}(s, s', t) = \frac{\mathbf{R}(s, s')}{\mathbf{E}(s)} \cdot \left(1 - e^{-\mathbf{E}(s) \cdot t}\right)$$

where $\mathbf{E}(s) = \sum_{s' \in S} \mathbf{R}(s, s')$ denotes the *total rate* at which any transition emanating from state s is taken. More precisely, $\mathbf{E}(s)$ specifies that the probability of leaving s within t time-units is $1 - e^{-\mathbf{E}(s) \cdot t}$, due to the fact that the minimum of exponential distributions (competing in a race) is characterised by the sum of their rates. Consequently, the probability of moving from a non-absorbing state s to s' by a single transition, denoted $\mathbf{P}(s, s')$, is determined by the probability that the delay of going from s to s' finishes before the delays of other outgoing

---

[2] We do not set $\mathbf{R}(s, s) = -\sum_{s' \neq s} \mathbf{R}(s, s')$, as is usual for CTMCs. In our setting, self-loops at a state s are possible and can be modelled by $\mathbf{R}(s, s) > 0$. The inclusion of self-loops does neither alter the transient nor the steady-state behaviour of the CTMC, but allows the usual interpretation of linear-time temporal operators like next step and unbounded or time-bounded until.

edges from s; formally, $\mathbf{P}(s,s') = \mathbf{R}(s,s')/\mathbf{E}(s)$. For an absorbing state s, the total rate $\mathbf{E}(s)$ is 0. (In this case, we have $\mathbf{P}(s,s') = 0$ for any state s'.)

The initial state probabilities of $\mathcal{M} = (S, \mathbf{R}, L)$ are given by an *initial distribution* $\alpha : S \to [0,1]$ with $\sum_{s \in S} \alpha(s) = 1$. In case we have a unique initial state s, the initial distribution is denoted α_s^1, where $\alpha_s^1(s) = 1$ and $\alpha^1(s') = 0$ for any $s' \neq s$.

Example 1. As a running example we address a *triple modular redundant system* (TMR) taken from [18], a fault-tolerant computer system consisting of three processors and a single (majority) voter that we model by a CTMC where state $s_{i,j}$ models that i processors and j voters are operational. Initially all components are functioning correctly (i.e., $\alpha = \alpha_{s_{3,1}}^1$). The failure rate of a processor is λ and of the voter ν failures per hour (fph). The expected repair time of a processor is $1/\mu$ and of the voter $1/\delta$ hours. The system is operational if at least two processors and the voter are functioning correctly. If the voter fails, the entire system is assumed to have failed, and after a repair (with rate δ) the system is assumed to start "as good as new". The details of the CTMC are:

$$\mathbf{R} = \begin{pmatrix} 0 & 3\lambda & 0 & 0 & \nu \\ \mu & 0 & 2\lambda & 0 & \nu \\ 0 & \mu & 0 & \lambda & \nu \\ 0 & 0 & \mu & 0 & \nu \\ \delta & 0 & 0 & 0 & 0 \end{pmatrix} \text{ and } \mathbf{E} = \begin{pmatrix} 3\lambda + \nu \\ 2\lambda + \mu + \nu \\ \lambda + \mu + \nu \\ \mu + \nu \\ \delta \end{pmatrix}$$

We have e.g., $\mathbf{P}(s_{2,1}, s_{3,1}) = \mu/(\mu + 2\lambda + \nu)$ and $\mathbf{P}(s_{0,1}, s_{0,0}) = \nu/(\mu + \nu)$. ∎

Paths. A *path* σ is a finite or infinite sequence $s_0, t_0, s_1, t_1, s_2, t_2, \ldots$ with, for $i \in \mathbb{N}$, $s_i \in S$ and $t_i \in \mathbb{R}_{>0}$ such that $\mathbf{R}(s_i, s_{i+1}) > 0$, if σ is infinite. For an infinite path σ and $i \in \mathbb{N}$ let $\sigma[i] = s_i$, the i-th state of σ, and $\delta(\sigma, i) = t_i$, the time spent in s_i. For $t \in \mathbb{R}_{\geq 0}$ and i the smallest index i with $t \leq \sum_{j=0}^{i} t_j$ let $\sigma@t = \sigma[i]$, the state of σ at time t. If σ is finite and ends in s_l, we require that s_l is absorbing, and $\mathbf{R}(s_i, s_{i+1}) > 0$ for all $i < l$. For finite σ, $\sigma[i]$ and $\delta(\sigma, i)$ are defined for $i \leq l$ in the above way, whereas $\delta(\sigma, l) = \infty$, and $\sigma@t = s_l$ for $t > \sum_{j=0}^{l-1} t_j$. Let *Path* denote the set of paths in $\mathcal{M}$, *Path(s)* the set of paths starting in s.

Borel space. An initial distribution α yields a probability measure $\Pr_\alpha$ on paths as follows. Let $s_0, \ldots, s_k \in S$ with $\mathbf{R}(s_i, s_{i+1}) > 0$, $(0 \leq i < k)$, and $I_0, \ldots, I_{k-1}$ non-empty intervals in $\mathbb{R}_{\geq 0}$. Then, $C(s_0, I_0, \ldots, I_{k-1}, s_k)$ denotes the *cylinder set* consisting of all paths $\sigma \in Path(s_0)$ such that $\sigma[i] = s_i$ $(i \leq k)$, and $\delta(\sigma, i) \in I_i$ $(i < k)$. Let $\mathcal{F}(Path)$ be the smallest σ-algebra on *Path* which contains all sets $C(s, I_0, \ldots, I_{k-1}, s_k)$ where $s_0, \ldots, s_k$ ranges over all state-sequences with $s = s_0$, $\mathbf{R}(s_i, s_{i+1}) > 0$ $(0 \leq i < k)$, and $I_0, \ldots, I_{k-1}$ ranges over all sequences of non-empty intervals in $\mathbb{R}_{\geq 0}$. The probability measure $\Pr_\alpha$ on

$\mathcal{F}(Path)$ is the unique measure defined by induction on k by $\Pr_\alpha(C(s_0)) = \alpha(s_0)$ and for $k \geqslant 0$:

$$\Pr_\alpha(C(s_0,\ldots,s_k,I',s')) = \Pr_\alpha(C(s_0,\ldots,s_k)) \cdot \mathbf{P}(s_k,s') \cdot \left(e^{-\mathbf{E}(s_k)\cdot a} - e^{-\mathbf{E}(s_k)\cdot b}\right)$$

where $a = \inf I'$ and $b = \sup I'$. (For $b = \infty$ and $\lambda > 0$ let $e^{-\lambda \cdot \infty} = 0$.)

Remark 1. For an infinite path $\sigma = s_0, t_0, s_1, t_1, \ldots$ we do not assume *time divergence*. Although $\sum_{j \geqslant 0} t_j$ might converge, in which case σ represents an "unrealistic" computation where infinitely many transitions are taken in a finite amount of time, the probability measure of such non-time-divergent paths is 0 (independent of α). This allows a lazy treatment of the notation $\sigma @ t$ in the description of measurable sets of paths for which we just refer to the probability measure. ∎

Steady state and transient probabilities. For a CTMC two major types of state probabilities are distinguished: steady-state probabilities where the system is considered "on the long run" i.e., when an equilibrium has been reached, and transient probabilities where the system is considered at a given time instant t. Formally, the transient probability

$$\pi^{\mathcal{M}}(\alpha, s', t) = \Pr_\alpha\{\sigma \in Path \mid \sigma @ t = s'\}$$

stands for the probability to be in state s' at time t given the initial distribution α. Steady-state probabilities are defined as $\pi^{\mathcal{M}}(\alpha, s') = \lim_{t \to \infty} \pi^{\mathcal{M}}(\alpha, s', t)$. This limit always exists for finite CTMCs. For $S' \subseteq S$, let $\pi^{\mathcal{M}}(\alpha, S') = \sum_{s' \in S'} \pi^{\mathcal{M}}(\alpha, s')$ denote the steady-state probability for S' given α, i.e.,

$$\pi^{\mathcal{M}}(\alpha, S') = \lim_{t \to \infty} \Pr_\alpha\{\sigma \in Path \mid \sigma @ t \in S'\}.$$

We let $\pi^{\mathcal{M}}(\alpha, \varnothing) = 0$. We often omit the superscript $\mathcal{M}$ if the CTMC $\mathcal{M}$ is clear from the context. In case of a unique initial state s, i.e., $\alpha = \alpha_s^1$, we write $\Pr_s$ for $\Pr_\alpha$, $\pi(s, s', t)$ for $\pi(\alpha, s', t)$, and $\pi(s, s')$ for $\pi(\alpha, s')$.

Syntax of CSL. CSL is a branching-time temporal logic where the state-formulas are interpreted over states of a CTMC [3,6]. As in [6] we consider the extension of **CSL** of [3] with $\mathcal{S}_{\bowtie p}(\cdot)$ to reason about steady-state probabilities. We generalise **CSL** as defined in [6] with a time-bounded until operator that is parametrized by an arbitrary time-interval I. Let $a \in AP$, $p \in [0,1]$ and $\bowtie \in \{\leqslant, \geqslant\}$. The state-formulas of **CSL** are defined by:

$$\Phi ::= \text{tt} \;\big|\; a \;\big|\; \Phi \wedge \Phi \;\big|\; \neg \Phi \;\big|\; \mathcal{S}_{\bowtie p}(\Phi) \;\big|\; \mathcal{P}_{\bowtie p}(\varphi)$$

where, for interval $I \subseteq \mathbb{R}_{\geqslant 0}$, path-formulas are defined by:

$$\varphi ::= X\Phi \;\big|\; \Phi \mathcal{U} \Phi \;\big|\; \Phi \mathcal{U}^I \Phi.$$

The other boolean connectives are derived in the usual way, i.e. ff $= \neg$tt, $\Phi_1 \vee \Phi_2 = \neg(\neg\Phi_1 \wedge \neg\Phi_2)$, and $\Phi_1 \rightarrow \Phi_2 = \neg\Phi_1 \vee \Phi_2$. The meaning of $\mathcal{U}$ ("until") and $\mathcal{X}$ ("next step") is standard. The temporal operator $\mathcal{U}^I$ is the timed variant of $\mathcal{U}$; $\Phi_1 \mathcal{U}^I \Phi_2$ asserts that Φ_2 will be satisfied at some time instant in the interval I and that at all preceding time instants Φ_1 holds. $\mathcal{S}_{\bowtie p}(\Phi)$ asserts that the steady-state probability for a Φ-state falls in the interval $I_{\bowtie p} = \{q \in [0,1] \mid q \bowtie p\}$. $\mathcal{P}_{\bowtie p}(\varphi)$ asserts that the probability measure of the paths satisfying φ meets the bound given by $\bowtie p$.

Temporal operators like $\Diamond$, $\Box$ and their real-time variants $\Diamond^I$ or $\Box^I$ can be derived, e.g. $\mathcal{P}_{\bowtie p}(\Diamond^I \Phi) = \mathcal{P}_{\bowtie p}(\text{tt}\,\mathcal{U}^I \Phi)$ and $\mathcal{P}_{\geq p}(\Box \Phi) = \mathcal{P}_{\leq 1-p}(\Diamond \neg \Phi)$.

Example 2. Let $AP = \{\, up_i \mid 0 \leq i < 4\,\} \cup \{\,down\,\}$ and consider the CTMC of Example 1. $\mathcal{P}_{\leq 10^{-5}}(\Diamond^{[0,10]} down)$ denotes that the probability of a failure of the voter within the next 10 hours is at most 10^{-5}; the formula $\mathcal{S}_{\geq 0.99}(up_3 \vee up_2)$ asserts that with 0.99 probability the system is operational, when the system is in equilibrium. ■

Semantics of CSL. The state-formulas are interpreted over the states of a CTMC. Let $\mathcal{M} = (S, \mathbf{R}, L)$ with labels in AP. The definition of the satisfaction relation $\models\, \subseteq S \times \mathbf{CSL}$ is as follows. Let $Sat(\Phi) = \{\, s \in S \mid s \models \Phi\,\}$.

$$\begin{array}{ll}
s \models \text{tt} & \text{for all } s \in S \\
s \models a & \text{iff } a \in L(s) \\
s \models \neg \Phi & \text{iff } s \not\models \Phi
\end{array} \qquad \begin{array}{ll}
s \models \Phi_1 \wedge \Phi_2 & \text{iff } s \models \Phi_i, i=1,2 \\
s \models \mathcal{S}_{\bowtie p}(\Phi) & \text{iff } \pi(s, Sat(\Phi)) \in I_{\bowtie p} \\
s \models \mathcal{P}_{\bowtie p}(\varphi) & \text{iff } Prob^{\mathcal{M}}(s, \varphi) \in I_{\bowtie p}.
\end{array}$$

Here, $Prob^{\mathcal{M}}(s,\varphi)$ denotes the probability measure of all paths $\sigma \in Path$ satisfying φ when the system starts in state s, i.e., $Prob^{\mathcal{M}}(s,\varphi) = \Pr_s\{\sigma \in Path \mid \sigma \models \varphi\}$.[3] The satisfaction relation for the path-formulas is defined as:

$$\begin{array}{ll}
\sigma \models X\Phi & \text{iff } \sigma[1] \text{ is defined and } \sigma[1] \models \Phi \\
\sigma \models \Phi_1 \mathcal{U} \Phi_2 & \text{iff } \exists k \geq 0.\ (\sigma[k] \models \Phi_2 \wedge \forall 0 \leq i < k.\ \sigma[i] \models \Phi_1) \\
\sigma \models \Phi_1 \mathcal{U}^I \Phi_2 & \text{iff } \exists t \in I.\ (\sigma@t \models \Phi_2 \wedge \forall u \in [0,t[.\ \sigma@u \models \Phi_1)
\end{array}$$

We note that for $I = \emptyset$ the formula $\Phi_1 \mathcal{U}^I \Phi_2$ is not satisfiable and that $\Phi_1 \mathcal{U} \Phi_2$ can be interpreted as an abbreviation of $\Phi_1 \mathcal{U}^{[0,\infty)} \Phi_2$.

Remark 2. Although **CSL** does not contain an explicit transient state operator, it is possible to reason about transient state probabilities as we have: $\pi(s,s',t) = Prob(s,\Diamond^{[t,t]} a_{s'})$. Thus, whereas the steady-state operator $\mathcal{S}_{\bowtie p}(\Phi)$ cannot be derived from the other operators, a transient-state operator $\mathcal{T}_{\bowtie p}^{@t}(\Phi) = \mathcal{P}_{\bowtie p}(\Diamond^{[t,t]} \Phi)$ can be defined. It states that the probability for a Φ-state at time point t meets the bound $\bowtie p$. ■

3 Model Checking $\mathcal{U}^I$ by Transient Analysis

In [6], we presented a **CSL** model checking algorithm that essentially relies on the following ideas. The steady-state operator requires the computation of steady-state probabilities which can be obtained by a graph analysis and by solving

---

[3] The fact that the set $\{\,\sigma \in Path \mid \sigma \models \varphi\,\}$ is measurable can be easily verified.

a linear equation system. The basis for calculating the probabilities $Prob(s, \varphi)$ are the following results. For the temporal operators next X and until $\mathcal{U}$ (that abstract from the amount of time spent in states but just refer to the states that are passed in an execution), we have the same characterizations for the values $Prob(s, X\Phi)$ and $Prob(s, \Phi_1 \mathcal{U} \Phi_2)$ as in the case of DTMCs [17]:

$$Prob(s, X\Phi) = \sum_{s' \models \Phi} \mathbf{P}(s, s') \quad \text{and}$$

$$Prob(s, \Phi_1 \mathcal{U} \Phi_2) = \begin{cases} 1 & \text{if } s \models \Phi_2 \\ \sum_{s' \in S} \mathbf{P}(s, s') \cdot Prob(s', \Phi_1 \mathcal{U} \Phi_2) & \text{if } s \models \Phi_1 \wedge \neg \Phi_2 \\ 0 & \text{otherwise.} \end{cases}$$

This amounts to matrix/vector-multiplication for next and solving a linear equation system for until.

For the time-bounded until operator, [6] suggested an iterative method which relies on the observation that the function $(s, t, t') \mapsto Prob(s, \Phi_1 \mathcal{U}^{[t,t']} \Phi_2)$ can be characterized as the least fixed point of a higher-order operator Ω where $\Omega(F)$ is defined by means of Volterra integrals. This fixed-point characterization then serves as a basis for an iterative method that uses numerical integration techniques. First experiments in a non-symbolic setting have shown that this approach can be rather time-consuming and that numerical stability is hard to achieve [22]. [6] suggested a symbolic approach by combining (MT)BDD-techniques [9,12,4] with an operator for solving integrals by quadrature formulas. Here, we propose an alternative strategy that reduces the model checking problem for the time-bounded until operator to the problem of calculating transient probabilities in CTMCs. This observation allows us to implement **CSL** model checking on the basis of well-established transient analysis techniques for CTMCs (see below).

Four correctness-preserving transformations. We first observe that it suffices to consider time bounds specified by compact intervals, since:

$$Prob(s, \Phi_1 \mathcal{U}^I \Phi_2) = Prob(s, \Phi_1 \mathcal{U}^{cl(I)} \Phi_2)$$

where $cl(I)$ denotes the closure of I. Secondly, unbounded time intervals $[t, \infty)$ can be treated by combining time-bounded until and unbounded until, since:

$$Prob(s, \Phi_1 \mathcal{U}^{[t,\infty)} \Phi_2) = \sum_{s' \in S} Prob(s, \Phi_1 \mathcal{U}^{[t,t]} a_{s'}) \cdot Prob(s', \Phi_1 \mathcal{U} \Phi_2).$$

In the sequel, we treat 4 types of time-bounded until-formulas with a compact interval I and show how they all can be reduced to instances of two simple base cases. For CTMC $\mathcal{M} = (S, \mathbf{R}, L)$ and **CSL**-state formula Φ let CTMC $\mathcal{M}[\Phi]$ result from $\mathcal{M}$ by making all Φ-states in $\mathcal{M}$ absorbing; i.e., $\mathcal{M}[\Phi] = (S, \mathbf{R}', L)$ where $\mathbf{R}'(s, s') = \mathbf{R}(s, s')$ if $s \not\models \Phi$ and 0 otherwise. Note that $\mathcal{M}[\Phi_1][\Phi_2] = \mathcal{M}[\Phi_1 \vee \Phi_2]$.

Case A: Bounded until for absorbing Φ_2-states. Let $\varphi = \Phi_1 \mathcal{U}^{[0,t]} \Phi_2$ and assume that all Φ_2-states are absorbing, i.e., once a Φ_2-state is reached it will not be left anymore. We first observe that once a $(\neg \Phi_1 \wedge \neg \Phi_2)$-state is reached, φ will be invalid, regardless of the future evolution of the system. As a result, we may switch from $\mathcal{M}$ to $\mathcal{M}[\neg\Phi_1 \wedge \neg\Phi_2]$ and consider the property on the obtained CTMC. The assumption that all Φ_2-states are absorbing allows us to conclude that φ is satisfied once a Φ_2-state is reached at time t. Thus,

Lemma 1. *If all Φ_2-states are absorbing in $\mathcal{M}$ (i.e., $\mathcal{M} = \mathcal{M}[\Phi_2]$) then:*

$$Prob^{\mathcal{M}}(s, \Phi_1 \mathcal{U}^{[0,t]} \Phi_2) = Prob^{\mathcal{M}'}(s, \Diamond^{[t,t]} \Phi_2) = \sum_{s'' \models \Phi_2} \pi^{\mathcal{M}'}(s, s'', t)$$

for $\mathcal{M}' = \mathcal{M}[\neg\Phi_1 \wedge \neg\Phi_2]$.

Case B: Point-interval until for $\Phi_2 \to \Phi_1$. Let $\varphi = \Phi_1 \mathcal{U}^{[t,t]} \Phi_2$ and assume $\Phi_2 \to \Phi_1$. Note that such implication holds in case of $\Diamond$-properties. With the same motivation as for the previous case, we make $(\neg\Phi_1 \wedge \neg\Phi_2)$-states absorbing. Since $\Phi_2 \to \Phi_1$ it follows that $Prob(s, \varphi)$ equals the probability to be in a Φ_2-state at time t in the obtained CTMC:

Lemma 2. *If $\Phi_2 \to \Phi_1$ we have for any CTMC $\mathcal{M}$:*

$$Prob^{\mathcal{M}}(s, \Phi_1 \mathcal{U}^{[t,t]} \Phi_2) = Prob^{\mathcal{M}'}(s, \Diamond^{[t,t]} \Phi_2) = \sum_{s'' \models \Phi_2} \pi^{\mathcal{M}'}(s, s'', t).$$

for $\mathcal{M}' = \mathcal{M}[\neg\Phi_1 \wedge \neg\Phi_2]$.

Case C: Bounded until. Let $\varphi = \Phi_1 \mathcal{U}^{[0,t]} \Phi_2$ and consider an arbitrary CTMC $\mathcal{M}$. This property is fulfilled if a Φ_2-state is reached before (or at) time t via some Φ_1-path. Once such Φ_2-state has been reached, the future behaviour of the CTMC is irrelevant for the validity of φ. Accordingly, the Φ_2-states can be safely made absorbing without affecting the validity of φ. As a result, it suffices to consider the probability of being in a Φ_2-state at time t for $\mathcal{M}[\Phi_2]$, thus reducing to the case in Lemma 1. As $\mathcal{M}[\Phi_2][\neg\Phi_1 \wedge \neg\Phi_2] = \mathcal{M}[\neg\Phi_1 \vee \Phi_2]$ we obtain:

Theorem 1. *For any CTMC $\mathcal{M}$:*

$$Prob^{\mathcal{M}}(s, \Phi_1 \mathcal{U}^{[0,t]} \Phi_2) = Prob^{\mathcal{M}[\Phi_2]}(s, \Phi_1 \mathcal{U}^{[0,t]} \Phi_2)$$
$$= \sum_{s'' \models \Phi_2} \pi^{\mathcal{M}[\neg\Phi_1 \vee \Phi_2]}(s, s'', t).$$

Case D: Interval-until. Let $\varphi = \Phi_1 \mathcal{U}^{[t,t']} \Phi_2$ with $0 < t \leqslant t'$ and let $\mathcal{M}$ be an arbitrary CTMC[4]. We first observe that for any path σ with $\sigma \models \varphi$: (i) Φ_1 continuously holds in the interval $[0, t]$ (i.e., $\sigma \models \Box^{[0,t]}\Phi_1$), in particular, $s' = \sigma@t$ is a Φ_1-state, and (ii) $\sigma' \in Path(s')$, the suffix of σ that starts at time t, fulfills the path formula $\Phi_1 \mathcal{U}^{[0,t'-t]}\Phi_2$.[5] Let the intermediate state $s' \in Sat(\Phi_1)$ and consider the set $\Sigma(s')$ of paths $\sigma \in Path(s)$ where $\sigma@t = s'$ and $\sigma \models \varphi$. Then

---
[4] Note that $Prob(s, \Phi_1 \mathcal{U}^{[t,t']}\Phi_2) \neq Prob(s, \Phi_1 \mathcal{U}^{[0,t']}\Phi_2) - Prob(s, \Phi_1 \mathcal{U}^{[0,t]}\Phi_2)$.
[5] Formally, σ' is the unique path with $\sigma'@x = \sigma@(t+x)$ for any positive real x.

$\mathrm{Pr}_s(\Sigma(s'))$ equals $Prob(s, \Phi_1\, \mathcal{U}^{[t,t]}\, a_{s'})$ times $Prob(s', \Phi_1\, \mathcal{U}^{[0,t'-t]}\, \Phi_2)$. As the sets $\Sigma(s')$ for $s' \in Sat(\Phi_1)$ are pairwise disjoint we obtain:

$$Prob(s, \Phi_1\, \mathcal{U}^{[t,t']}\, \Phi_2) = \sum_{s' \models \Phi_1} Prob(s, \Phi_1\, \mathcal{U}^{[t,t]}\, a_{s'}) \cdot Prob(s', \Phi_1\, \mathcal{U}^{[0,t'-t]}\, \Phi_2).$$

To compute the probabilities $Prob(s, \Phi_1\, \mathcal{U}^{[t,t]}\, a_{s'})$ for $s' \models \Phi_1$ we use Lemma 2, i.e., we switch from $\mathcal{M}$ to $\mathcal{M}_1 = \mathcal{M}[\neg\Phi_1]$ and compute the transient probabilities for any Φ_1-state s' at time t in $\mathcal{M}_1$. The probabilities $Prob(s', \Phi_1\, \mathcal{U}^{[0,t'-t]}\, \Phi_2)$ can be obtained as in Theorem 1. This yields the following result:

Theorem 2. *For any CTMC $\mathcal{M}$ and $0 < t \leq t'$:*

$$Prob^{\mathcal{M}}(s, \Phi_1\, \mathcal{U}^{[t,t']}\, \Phi_2) = \sum_{s' \models \Phi_1} \sum_{s'' \models \Phi_2} \pi^{\mathcal{M}[\neg\Phi_1]}(s, s', t) \cdot \pi^{\mathcal{M}[\neg\Phi_1 \vee \Phi_2]}(s', s'', t'-t).$$

With Theorem 2 we can calculate the values $Prob^{\mathcal{M}}(s, \varphi)$, using one of the following two methods. Let $\mathcal{M}_2 = \mathcal{M}[\neg\Phi_1 \vee \Phi_2]$. Either we calculate the matrices

$$\mathbf{A} = (\pi^{\mathcal{M}_1}(s, s', t))_{s \in S, s' \in Sat(\Phi_1)},$$
$$\mathbf{B} = (\pi^{\mathcal{M}_2}(s', s'', t'-t))_{s' \in Sat(\Phi_1), s'' \in Sat(\Phi_2)}$$

and then take the product $\mathbf{A} \cdot \mathbf{B}$. Or, we first calculate the distributions α_s for $s \in S$, given by $\alpha_s(s') = \pi^{\mathcal{M}_1}(s, s', t)$ and then compute $Prob^{\mathcal{M}}(s, \varphi) = \sum_{s'' \models \Phi_2} \pi^{\mathcal{M}_2}(\alpha_s, s'', t'-t)$. This alternative is based on the observation

$$\sum_{s' \models \Phi_1} \alpha_s(s') \cdot \pi^{\mathcal{M}_2}(s', s'', t'-t) = \pi^{\mathcal{M}_2}(\alpha_s, s'', t'-t)$$

for any Φ_2-state s''.[6]

Example 3. Consider our TMR with initial distribution $\alpha = \alpha^1_{s_{3,1}}$ and let $\Phi = \mathcal{P}_{\geq 0.15}(\Phi_1\, \mathcal{U}^{[3,7]}\, \Phi_2)$ for $\Phi_1 = up_3 \vee up_2$ and $\Phi_2 = up_2 \vee up_1$. According to Theorem 2 model checking Φ boils down to first computing the transient probabilities at time 3, i.e., $\alpha_2 = (\pi^{\mathcal{M}_1}(s_{3,1}, 3))_{s \in S}$ in CTMC $\mathcal{M}_1$ of Fig. 1(a) where all $\neg\Phi_1$-states are made absorbing. We obtain $\alpha_2 = (0.968, 0.0272, 0.011, 0, 0.003)$ with a precision of $\varepsilon = 10^{-6}$ for $\lambda = 0.01$, $\nu = 0.001$, $\mu = 1.0$ and $\delta = 0.2$. In the second phase, we compute the transient probabilities at time 4 in CTMC $\mathcal{M}_2$ of Fig. 1(b) starting from initial distribution α_2, i.e., computing $\sum_{s'' \models up_2} \pi^{\mathcal{M}_2}(\alpha_2, s'', 4) \approx 0.1365$. Thus, the property Φ is violated.

Uniformisation. Based on the general principle of uniformisation [25], efficient techniques to compute transient state probabilities for CTMCs have been proposed [16,15]. With uniformisation, the transient probabilities of a CTMC are

---

[6] For both alternatives, in the worst case, for any state s, we need a transient analysis in $\mathcal{M}_1$ (with initial state s) and $\mathcal{M}_2$ (with initial distribution α_s). The second alternative might be preferable if there are only a few different distributions α_s.

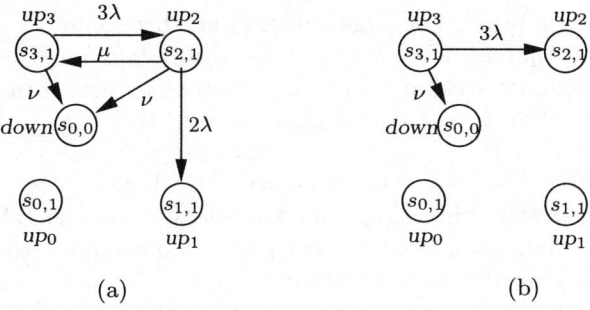

Fig. 1. CTMCs to be analysed for checking $\mathcal{P}_{\geqslant 0.15}((up_3 \vee up_2)\, \mathcal{U}^{[3,7]} (up_2 \vee up_1))$

computed via a so-called *uniformised DTMC* which characterises the CTMC at state transition epochs.

Denoting with $\underline{\pi}(\alpha, t)$ the vector of state probabilities at time t, i.e., $\underline{\pi}(\alpha, t) = (\pi(\alpha, s_1, t), \cdots, \pi(\alpha, s_N, t))$ (with $N = |S|$ the number of states), the Chapman-Kolmogorov differential equations characterise the transient behaviour: $\underline{\pi}'(\alpha, t) = \underline{\pi}(\alpha, t) \cdot \mathbf{Q}$, where $\mathbf{Q} = \mathbf{R} - diag(\mathbf{E})$. A formal solution is then given by the Taylor-series expansion:

$$\underline{\pi}(\alpha, t) = \alpha \cdot e^{\mathbf{Q} \cdot t} = \alpha \cdot \sum_{i=0}^{\infty} \frac{(\mathbf{Q} \cdot t)^i}{i!}.$$

This solution, however, should not be used as the basis for a numerical algorithm since: (i) it suffers from numerical instability due to the fact that $\mathbf{Q}$ contains both positive and negative entries; (ii) the matrix powers will become less and less sparse for large i, thus requiring $\mathcal{O}(N^2)$ storage; (iii) it is difficult to find a proper truncation criterion for the infinite summation.

Instead, by choosing $q = \max_i\{\mathbf{E}(s_i)\}$, we construct the uniformised DTMC with transition probability matrix $\mathbf{P} = \mathbf{I} + \mathbf{Q}/q$. By the choice of q, $\mathbf{P}$ is a stochastic matrix. Substituting $\mathbf{Q} = q(\mathbf{P} - \mathbf{I})$ in the above solution, we obtain

$$\underline{\pi}(\alpha, t) = \alpha \cdot \sum_{i=0}^{\infty} e^{-q \cdot t} \frac{(q \cdot t)^i}{i!} \mathbf{P}^i,$$

which can be rewritten as

$$\underline{\pi}(\alpha, t) = \sum_{i=0}^{\infty} PP(i) \cdot \underline{\pi}_i,$$

where $PP(i) = e^{-q \cdot t} \frac{(q \cdot t)^i}{i!}$ is the i-th Poisson probability with parameter qt, and $\underline{\pi}_i = \underline{\pi}_{i-1} \mathbf{P}$ and $\underline{\pi}_0 = \alpha$. The Poisson probabilities can be computed in a stable way with the algorithm of Fox and Glynn [14]. There is no need to compute explicit powers of the matrix $\mathbf{P}$. Furthermore, since the terms in the summation are all between 0 and 1, the number of terms to be taken given a required accuracy, can be computed a priori. For large values of qt, this number is of order $\mathcal{O}(qt)$. Notice, however, that for large values of qt, the DTMC described by $\mathbf{P}$ might even have reached steady-state, so that a further reduction in computational complexity is reached. For further details, see [28,18].

Regarding storage complexity, we note that we require $\mathcal{O}(3N)$ storage for the probability vectors and $\mathcal{O}(\eta N)$ for the matrix $\mathbf{P}$, where η denotes the (average) number of transitions originating from a single state in the DTMC (typically $\eta << N$). Regarding computational complexity, to compute $\underline{\pi}(\alpha, t)$ we require the sum of $\mathcal{O}(qt)$ vectors, each of which is the result of a matrix-vector multiplication. Given a sparse implementation of the latter, we require $\mathcal{O}(\eta N)$ scalar multiplications for that, so that we have an overall computational complexity of $\mathcal{O}(qt \cdot \eta N)$.

4 Abstraction with Bisimulation (Lumping) Equivalence

In this section, we discuss some techniques to reduce the state space of a CTMC. These techniques are mainly based on the observation that (a slight variant of) ordinary *lumping equivalence* (i.e., bisimulation) preserves all **CSL**-formulas. This result is in the spirit of [8] where bisimilar states of an ordinary transition system are shown to satisfy the same **CTL**-formulas. Similar results have been established for many types of transition systems and branching-time logics; e.g., in the probabilistic setting, [2] shows that probabilistic bisimulation on DTMCs preserves **PCTL** [17]. Our result below can be considered as the continuous version of that result. Let $\mathcal{M} = (S, \mathbf{R}, L)$ be a CTMC, F a set of **CSL**-formulas, and $L_F : S \to 2^F$ a labelling defined by $L_F(s) = \{\, \Phi \in F \mid s \models \Phi \,\}$.

Definition 1. *An F-bisimulation on $\mathcal{M} = (S, \mathbf{R}, L)$ is an equivalence R on S such that whenever $(s, s') \in R$ then $L_F(s) = L_F(s')$ and $\mathbf{R}(s, C) = \mathbf{R}(s', C)$ for all $C \in S/R$. States s and s' are F-bisimilar iff there exists an F-bisimulation R that contains (s, s').*

Here, S/R denotes the quotient space and $\mathbf{R}(s, C)$ abbreviates $\sum_{s' \in C} \mathbf{R}(s, s')$. F-bisimulation is a slight variant of Markovian bisimulation (which is defined on CTMCs with action-labelled transitions) on CTMCs with labelled states. Markovian bisimulation coincides with (ordinary) lumping equivalence [11], a well-known notion to aggregate CTMCs.

For $s \in S$, let $[s]_R$ denote the equivalence class of s under R. For $\mathcal{M} = (S, \mathbf{R}, L)$ we define the CTMC $\mathcal{M}/R = (S/R, \mathbf{R}_R, L_R)$ with $\mathbf{R}_R([s]_R, C) = \mathbf{R}(s, C)$ and $L_R([s]_R) = L_F(s)$. That is, $\mathcal{M}/R$ results from $\mathcal{M}$ by building the quotient space under R and labelling states with F (rather than AP). $\mathcal{M}/R$ can be computed by a modified version of the partition refinement algorithm for ordinary bisimulation without an increase of the worst case complexity [23]. Let $\mathbf{CSL}_F$ denote the smallest set of **CSL**-formulas that includes F and that is closed under all **CSL**-operators. In the following we write $\models_\mathcal{M}$ for the satisfaction relation $\models$ (on **CSL**) on $\mathcal{M}$.

Theorem 3. *Let R be an F-bisimulation on $\mathcal{M}$ and s a state in $\mathcal{M}$. Then:*

(a) For all $\mathbf{CSL}_F$-formulas Φ: $s \models_\mathcal{M} \Phi$ iff $[s]_R \models_{\mathcal{M}/R} \Phi$
(b) For all $\mathbf{CSL}_F$ path-formulas φ: $Prob^\mathcal{M}(s, \varphi) = Prob^{\mathcal{M}/R}([s]_R, \varphi)$.

In particular, F-bisimilar states satisfy the same $\mathbf{CSL}_F$ formulas.

Proof. Straightforward by structural induction on Φ and φ.

Theorem 3 allows to verify **CSL**-formulas on the possibly much smaller $\mathcal{M}/R$ rather than on $\mathcal{M}$, for AP-bisimulation R.

In addition, we can exploit the above result to our transformations of the previous section by using the following observation. ¿From Theorem 3(b) and Remark 2 it follows:

$$\sum_{s' \models_\mathcal{M} \Phi} \pi^\mathcal{M}(s, s', t) = \sum_{S' \models_{\mathcal{M}/R} \Phi} \pi^{\mathcal{M}/R}([s]_R, S', t) \qquad (1)$$

for any $\mathbf{CSL}_F$ formula Φ and F-bisimulation R. This observation allows us to simplify the CTMCs $\mathcal{M}[\ldots]$ that occur in the cases A–D of our model checking procedure presented in the previous section in the following way. For cases C and D, we compute the transient probabilities for Φ_2-states in the CTMC $\mathcal{M}' = \mathcal{M}[\neg\Phi_1 \vee \Phi_2]$. Let $F = \{\neg\Phi_1 \wedge \neg\Phi_2, \Phi_2\}$ and R be the smallest equivalence on the state space S of $\mathcal{M}'$ that identifies all Φ_2-states and all $(\neg\Phi_1 \wedge \neg\Phi_2)$-states. Clearly, R is an F-bisimulation on $\mathcal{M}'$. The state space of $\mathcal{M}'/R$ is

$$S/R = Sat(\Phi_1 \wedge \neg\Phi_2) \cup [Sat(\Phi_2)]_R \cup [Sat(\neg\Phi_1 \wedge \neg\Phi_2)]_R$$

Since Φ_2 is a $\mathbf{CSL}_F$-formula, equation (1) yields

$$\sum_{s'' \models \Phi_2} \pi^{\mathcal{M}'}(s, s'', t) = \pi^{\mathcal{M}'/R}(s, [Sat(\Phi_2)]_R, t)$$

for any state $s \in Sat(\Phi_1 \wedge \neg\Phi_2)$. Similar arguments are applicable to case A and B. As a result, the sets $[Sat(\neg\Phi_1 \wedge \neg\Phi_2)]_R$ and $[Sat(\Phi_2)]_R$ in cases A–D can be considered as single states. This may yield a substantial reduction of the state space of the CTMC under consideration. ¿From a computational point of view, the switch from $\mathcal{M}$ to the modified $\mathcal{M}[\ldots]/R$ is quite simple as we just collapse certain states into a single absorbing state. The generator matrix $\mathbf{R}_R$ for $\mathcal{M}[\ldots]/R$ can be obtained by simple manipulations of the generator matrix $\mathbf{R}$ for $\mathcal{M}$ (matrix multiplication).

Example 4. According to the above observations, in the CTMC of Fig. 1(a) we may aggregate states $[Sat(\Phi_1)]_R = \{s_{0,1}, s_{0,0}, s_{1,1}\}$ into a single state. This new state is reachable from $s_{3,1}$ with rate ν and from $s_{2,1}$ with rate $2\lambda+\nu$. In the CTMC of Fig. 1(b) we may collapse $[Sat(\Phi_2)]_R = \{s_{2,1}, s_{1,1}\}$ and $[Sat(\neg\Phi_1 \wedge \neg\Phi_2)]_R = \{s_{0,0}, s_{0,1}\}$ into single states.

5 Model Checking a Telephone System

In this section, we report on model checking the stochastic behaviour of an instance of the plain-old telephone system (POTS), where two users concurrently try to get connected to each other. In [21], we have shown how a formal specification of the POTS (in LOTOS) can be augmented with stochastic timing constraints, leading to a model of more than 10^7 states. We aggregated this model compositionally using appropriate stochastic extensions of (strong and weak) bisimulation [23], to come up with a lumped CTMC $\mathcal{M}$ of 720 states. Here we model check the resulting CTMC using transient analysis. In short, the following atomic propositions are used: *conn* characterises states where both partners are connected to each other, and conversation is running. *fed_up* characterises states where either of the user is hooking the phone because he is apparently out of luck, unable to reach his conversation partner. Our basic time unit is 1 minute. The following properties are checked:

- $\mathcal{P}_{\bowtie p}(\Diamond^{[0,t]} conn)$, the probability of being connected within t minutes.
- $\mathcal{P}_{\bowtie p}(\Diamond^{[t,t]} conn)$, the probability of being connected after exactly t minutes.
- $\mathcal{P}_{\bowtie p}(\Diamond^{[100,100+t]} conn)$, the probability of being connected at some time between 100 and 100+t minutes.
- $\mathcal{P}_{\bowtie p}(\neg fed\_up\, \mathcal{U}^{[t,100+t]} conn)$, the probability of a running conversation between t and $100 + t$ minutes, without failing to get connected beforehand.

Note that only the first property can be checked with the current implementation [22] of the non-symbolic model checking algorithm based on numerical integration [6]. We do not instantiate p, as the execution times and computed probabilities will be the same for all $p \in\,]0,1[$. Statistics of the computation time needed to check these formulas globally, i.e., for all states, are depicted in Table 1. They have been obtained by means of a trial implementation of the uniformisation method written in C, running on a 300 MHz SUN Ultra 5 workstation with 256 MB memory under the Solaris 2.6 operating system. (In all cases reported below, the memory requirements are less than 20 MB.)

t	$\mathcal{P}_{\bowtie p}(\Diamond^{[0,t]} conn)$		$\mathcal{P}_{\bowtie p}(\Diamond^{[t,t]} conn)$		$\mathcal{P}_{\bowtie p}(\Diamond^{[100,100+t]} conn)$		$\mathcal{P}_{\bowtie p}(\neg fed\_up\, \mathcal{U}^{[t,100+t]} conn)$	
	MV-mult.	time	MV-mult.	time	MV-mult.	time	MV-mult.	time
0.1	59	7.75	138	41.91	15,325	3,549.70	5,234	351.75
1	102	10.75	267	75.04	15,368	3,552.69	5,349	378.05
10	583	38.40	1,714	416.38	15,848	3,580.27	6,795	747.21
100	5,081	303.33	15,265	3,541.84	20,347	3,845.27	20,347	3,956.01
1000	8,901	619.51	39,155	8,835.01	24,167	4,161.41	151,815	34,405.14
10000	8,901	624.68	39,155	8,902.41	24,167	4,166.52	151,815	34,567.23

Table 1. Computation time (in *sec*) and number of matrix-vector multiplications (times 10^3) needed for checking **CSL** properties by means of uniformisation

From these statistics, we draw the following conclusions. (1) We observe a roughly linear dependency between the time bound t and the run-time of uniformisation, due to the fact that the (precomputed) number of iterations needed by uniformisation is $\mathcal{O}(t)$. (2) The number of iterations needed for $t \geqslant 1000$ is constant, due to the fact that our algorithm has a built-in steady-state detection.

In other words, the chain at time 1000 is already behaving close to equilibrium, up to a truncation error ε (set to 10^{-6} in all experiments). For time-bounds larger than 1000, transient analysis could in fact be replaced by a (much cheaper) steady-state analysis. (3) The times needed to check $\mathcal{P}_{\bowtie p}(\Diamond^{[t,t]} conn)$ are approximately one order of magnitude higher than those needed for $\mathcal{P}_{\bowtie p}(\Diamond^{[0,t]} conn)$. This is a consequence of the fact that the pruning of transitions in $\mathcal{M}[conn]$ (cf. Theorem 1) leads to a CTMC containing mutually unreachable parts, and for each state we perform transient analysis only on the reachable (lumped) CTMC. On average, this chain has only 62 states, explaining the order of magnitude difference. Note that according to Lemma 2, transient analysis can take the original chain (with 720 states) *unchanged* to check $\mathcal{P}_{\bowtie p}(\Diamond^{[t,t]} conn)$, since $conn \to$ tt. The two rightmost formulas involve more than one (iterative) transient solution, on different lumped CTMCs (cf. Theorem 2). Their time consumption is mainly determined by the size of the lower time bound (an observation that does not hold in general).

6 Concluding Remarks

The main result of this paper is that the verification problem for probabilistic timing properties, i.e., **CSL**-formulas of the form $\mathcal{P}_{\bowtie p}(\Phi_1 \mathcal{U}^I \Phi_2)$, is reducible to a transient analysis of CTMCs. Thus, efficient techniques for transient analysis, such as uniformisation, can be adopted for model checking these formulas. In addition, we showed that a slight variant of (ordinary) lumpability on CTMCs preserves all **CSL**-formulas. We illustrated these results by analysing a plain-old telephone system. Future work includes the adaption of partial uniformisation [27] to our setting (thus allowing a partial search of the state space) and considering a symbolic variant of our presented approach using multi-terminal BDDs [4,12] in order to compare this approach with the symbolic (numerical integration) approach in [6]. The extension of our approach towards Markov reward models is reported in [7].

References

[1] M. Ajmone Marsan, G. Balbo, G. Conte, S. Donatelli, and G. Franceschinis. *Modelling with Generalized Stochastic Petri Nets*. John Wiley & Sons, 1995.
[2] A. Aziz, V. Singhal, F. Balarin, R. Brayton and A. Sangiovanni-Vincentelli. It usually works: the temporal logic of stochastic systems. In *CAV*, LNCS 939, pp. 155–165, 1995.
[3] A. Aziz, K. Sanwal, V. Singhal and R. Brayton. Verifying continuous time Markov chains. In *CAV*, LNCS 1102, pp. 269–276, 1996.
[4] I. Bahar, E. Frohm, C. Gaona, G. Hachtel, E. Macii, A. Padro and F. Somenzi. Algebraic decision diagrams and their applications. *Form. Meth. in Syst. Design*, **10**(2/3): 171–206, 1997.
[5] C. Baier. On algorithmic verification methods for probabilistic systems. Habilitation thesis, Univ. of Mannheim, 1999.

[6] C. Baier, J.-P. Katoen and H. Hermanns. Approximate symbolic model checking of continuous-time Markov chains. In *CONCUR*, LNCS 1664, pp. 146–162, 1999.
[7] C. Baier, B. Haverkort, H. Hermanns and J.-P. Katoen. On the logical characterisation of performability properties. In *ICALP*, LNCS, 2000 (to appear).
[8] M. Brown, E. Clarke, O. Grumberg. Characterizing finite Kripke structures in propositional temporal logic. *Th. Comp. Sc.*, **59**: 115–131, 1988.
[9] R. Bryant. Graph-based algorithms for boolean function manipulation. *IEEE Trans. on Comp.*, **C-35**(8): 677–691, 1986.
[10] P. Buchholz. Exact and ordinary lumpability in finite Markov chains. *J. of Appl. Prob.*, **31**: 59–75, 1994.
[11] P. Buchholz. Markovian process algebra. Tech. Rep. 500, Fachbereich Informatik, Univ. of Dortmund, 1994.
[12] E. Clarke, M. Fujita, P. McGeer, J. Yang and X. Zhao. Multi-terminal binary decision diagrams: an efficient data structure for matrix representation. In *Proc. IEEE Int. Workshop on Logic Synthesis*, pp. 1–15, 1993.
[13] C. Courcoubetis and M. Yannakakis. Verifying temporal properties of finite-state probabilistic programs. In *Proc. IEEE Symp. on Found. of Comp. Sc.*, pp. 338–345, 1988.
[14] B.L. Fox and P.W. Glynn. Computing Poisson probabilities. *Comm. of the ACM* **31**(4): 440–445, 1988.
[15] W.K. Grassmann. Finding transient solutions in Markovian event systems through randomization. In W.J. Stewart, ed, *Num. Sol. of Markov Chains*, pp. 357–371, Marcel Dekker, 1991.
[16] D. Gross and D.R. Miller. The randomization technique as a modeling tool and solution procedure for transient Markov chains. *Oper. Res.* **32**(2): 343–361, 1984.
[17] H. Hansson and B. Jonsson. A logic for reasoning about time and reliability. *Form. Asp. of Comp.* **6**: 512–535, 1994.
[18] B.R. Haverkort. *Performance of Computer Communication Systems: A Model-Based Approach*. John Wiley & Sons, 1998.
[19] B.R. Haverkort and I. Niemegeers. Performability modelling tools and techniques. *Perf. Ev.*, **25**: 17–40, 1996.
[20] H. Hermanns, U. Herzog and J.-P. Katoen. Process algebra for performance evaluation. *Th. Comp. Sc.*, 2000 (to appear).
[21] H. Hermanns and J.-P. Katoen. Automated compositional Markov chain generation for a plain-old telephone system. *Sci. of Comp. Programming*, **36**(1): 97–127, 2000.
[22] H. Hermanns, J.-P. Katoen, J. Meyer-Kayser and M. Siegle. A Markov chain model checker. In *TACAS*, LNCS 1785, pp. 347–362, 2000.
[23] H. Hermanns and M. Siegle. Bisimulation algorithms for stochastic process algebras and their BDD-based implementation. In *ARTS*, LNCS 1601, pp. 244–265, 1999.
[24] J. Hillston. *A Compositional Approach to Performance Modelling*. Cambridge University Press, 1996.
[25] A. Jensen. Markov chains as an aid in the study of Markov processes. *Skand. Aktuarietidskrift* **3**: 87–91, 1953.
[26] K.G. Larsen and A. Skou. Bisimulation through probabilistic testing. *Inf. and Comp.*, **94**(1): 1–28, 1992.
[27] A.P.A. van Moorsel and B.R. Haverkort. Probabilistic evaluation for the analytical solution of large Markov models. *Microelectron. and Reliab.* **36**(6): 733–755, 1996.
[28] W.J. Stewart. *Introduction to the Numerical Solution of Markov Chains*. Princeton Univ. Press, 1994.

Model-Checking for Hybrid Systems by Quotienting and Constraints Solving

Franck Cassez[1] and François Laroussinie[2]

[1] IRCCyN, EC Nantes & CNRS UMR 6597, France,
Franck.Cassez@irccyn.ec-nantes.fr
[2] LSV, ENS de Cachan & CNRS UMR 8643, France,
Francois.Laroussinie@lsv.ens-cachan.fr

Abstract. In this paper we present a semi-algorithm to do compositional model-checking for hybrid systems. We first define a modal logic L_ν^h which is expressively complete for linear hybrid automata. We then show that it is possible to extend the result on compositional model-checking for parallel compositions of finite automata and networks of timed automata to linear hybrid automata. Finally we present some results obtained with an extension of the tool CMC to handle a subclass of hybrid automata (the stopwatch automata).

1 Introduction

Model checking for timed and hybrid systems. Model-checking algorithms for finite-state automata have been extended to *timed automata* [ACD93] and tools like KRONOS [Yov97] or UPPAAL [LPY97] have been used successfully also for verifying many industrial applications [BGK+96,MY96]. Hybrid systems [ACH+95] are a strong extension of timed automata and model-checking (or reachability) is undecidable [HKPV98] for these models. Nevertheless semi-algorithms have been implemented in tools like HyTech [HHWT97].

Heuristics for model-checking. In the timed verification area, model-checking is decidable but its complexity is high (PSPACE-complete or EXPTIME-complete) [ACD93,AL99]. A lot of works deal with heuristics to overcome this complexity blow-up (symbolic approaches [HNSY94], efficient and compact data structures [BLP+99], on-the-fly algorithms [BTY97] etc). From a practical point of view it is interesting to have different methods to verify a system: an approach can be very efficient over some classes of systems while another one works well for other classes. This last point is crucial for hybrid systems as model-checking is undecidable: for instance the so-called *forward* and *backward* reachability analysis algorithms [ACH+95,AHH96] are complementary.

Compositional Model-Checking. An alternative method to standard model-checking is *compositional model-checking* [And95,LL95,LPY95]. Given a system $S = (H_1 | \cdots | H_n)$ and a property φ, the method consists in building a *quotient* formula φ/H_n s.t. $(H_1|\cdots|H_n) \models \varphi$ iff $(H_1|\cdots|H_{n-1}) \models \varphi/H_n$. Some simplification techniques can be applied in order to keep a small size for φ/H_n. By quotienting every component of the system one after the other, the remaining problem (if the last formula is not reduced to tt nor ff by simplifications) is to check a quotient property φ' on the *nil* process which is an automaton that cannot do any action. Figure 1 describes the two steps of the method.

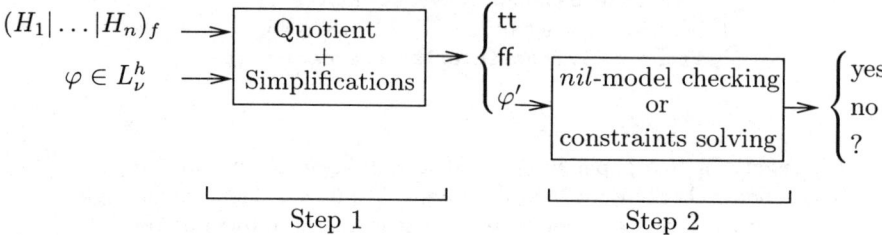

Fig. 1. Compositional Model Checking overview.

Our contribution. We propose here a compositional algorithm for linear hybrid automata. First we introduce a new modal logics L_ν^h (a kind of hybrid μ-calculus) which uses variables. L_ν^h allows us to express many kinds of properties, in particular it can be used to do compositional model-checking. Then we present reduction strategies to simplify L_ν^h formulas. When H_i's are hybrid automata, the two steps of the compositional method may not terminate (they require to compute fixed points over polyhedras), but it is possible to use abstractions for the first step in such a way that (1) termination is ensured and (2) $S \models \varphi \Leftrightarrow nil \models \varphi/S$ still holds. Then any problem $(H_1|\ldots|H_n) \models \varphi$ can be reduced to a *nil*-model-checking problem. Moreover we will see that this last step can be seen as a kind of constraints solving problem. Finally we present results obtained with a prototype HCMC which deals with hybrid automata where the slopes of variables belong to $\{0,1\}$.

2 Hybrid Automata

Notations. Let V and V' be two finite sets of variables with $V \cap V' = \emptyset$. A *valuation* is a mapping from a set V of variables into $\mathbb{R}$. For two valuations $v \in \mathbb{R}^V$, $v' \in \mathbb{R}^{V'}$, we define the valuation $v.v' \in \mathbb{R}^{V \cup V'}$ by $(v.v')(x) = v(x)$ if $x \in V$ and $(v.v')(x) = v'(x)$ if $x \in V'$. If $|V| = n$, a valuation v can be interpreted as a vector $\bar{v}$ of $\mathbb{R}^n$. We also recall the following useful definitions:

- A linear expression over V is of the form $a + \sum_i a_i v_i$ with $a, a_i \in \mathbb{Z}, v_i \in V$. The set of *linear constraints* $\mathcal{C}(V)$ over V is the set of formulas built using boolean connectives over expressions of the form $e_1 \bowtie e_2$ where e_1 and e_2 are linear expressions and $\bowtie$ belongs to $\{=, <, >, \leq, \geq\}$. Given a valuation v and a linear constraint γ, the boolean value $\gamma(v)$ describes whether γ is satisfied by v or not.

- A *linear assignment* over V is of the form $\bar{v} := A.\bar{v} + b$ where A is a $n \times n$ matrix with coefficients in $\mathbb{Z}$ and b is a vector of $\mathbb{Z}^n$. We denote an assignment α by a pair (A, b) and write $\bar{v} := \alpha(\bar{v})$ for $\bar{v} := A.\bar{v} + b$. $\mathcal{L}(V)$ is the set of linear assignments.
- A *continuous change* of variables is defined w.r.t. an element d of $\mathbb{Z}^V$ (hereafter referred to as the activity vector or direction) corresponding to the first derivative of each variable: given $t \in \mathbb{R}_{\geq 0}$, the valuation $v + d.t$ is defined by $(v + d.t)(x) = v(x) + d(x).t$.

We will need a particular property on subsets of $\mathbb{R}^n$ we refer to as d-strongly connection for some $d \in \mathbb{Z}^n$: A region $r \subseteq \mathbb{R}^n$ is d-strongly connected iff $\forall v, v' \in r$ $v' = v + d.t$ (for some $t \in \mathbb{R}_{\geq 0}$) implies $\forall 0 \leq t' \leq t, v + d.t' \in r$. This means that if one can go from one point in r to another also in r following the direction d then all the intermediate points along the path are in r. If $\mathsf{Future}(r, d)$ (resp. $\mathsf{Past}(r, d)$) denotes the future (resp. past) extension of r in direction d, then r is d-strongly connected is equivalent to $r = \mathsf{Future}(r, d) \cap \mathsf{Past}(r, d)$ (then this condition can be effectively checked for).

The model. Hybrid automata [ACH+95,AHH96,Hen96] are used to model systems which combine *discrete* and *continuous* evolutions.

Definition 1 (Hybrid automaton) *A hybrid automaton H is a 7-tuple $(N, l_0, V, A, E, Act, Inv)$ where:*

- *N is a finite set of* locations,
- *$l_0 \in N$ is the* initial location,
- *V is a finite set of real-valued* variables,
- *A is a finite set of* actions,
- *$E \subseteq N \times \mathcal{C}(V) \times A \times \mathcal{L}(V) \times N$ is a finite set of* edges; *$e = \langle l, \gamma, a, \alpha, l' \rangle \in E$ represents an edge from the location l to the location l' with the guard γ, the label a and the linear assignment α.*
- *$Act \in (\mathbb{Z}^V)^N$ assigns an* activity *vector for V to any location. $Act(l)(x)$ represents the first derivative of x in location l.*
- *$Inv \in \mathcal{C}(V)^N$ assigns an* invariant *to any location. We require that for any l, $Inv(l)$ is $Act(l)$-strongly connected.* □

Example 1. As a running example we will use the scheduler given in [AHH96] and depicted[1] on Figures 2 and 3. This scheduler *Sched* (Figure 3) can handle two types of tasks: type T_1 and type T_2. Priority is given to tasks of type T_2 and in case a task of type T_1 is currently running it is preempted: then measuring the execution time of tasks of type T_1 requires the use of a stopwatch y_1. We also use a stopwatch y_2 to measure the execution time of tasks of type T_2 (although it is not necessary as tasks of type T_2 cannot be preempted.) Obviously, y_i will

---
[1] The automata are designed using the GasTeX package available at http://www.liafa.jussieu.fr/~gastin/gastex.

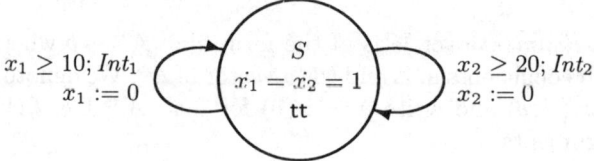

Fig. 2. Automaton of the environment: Env

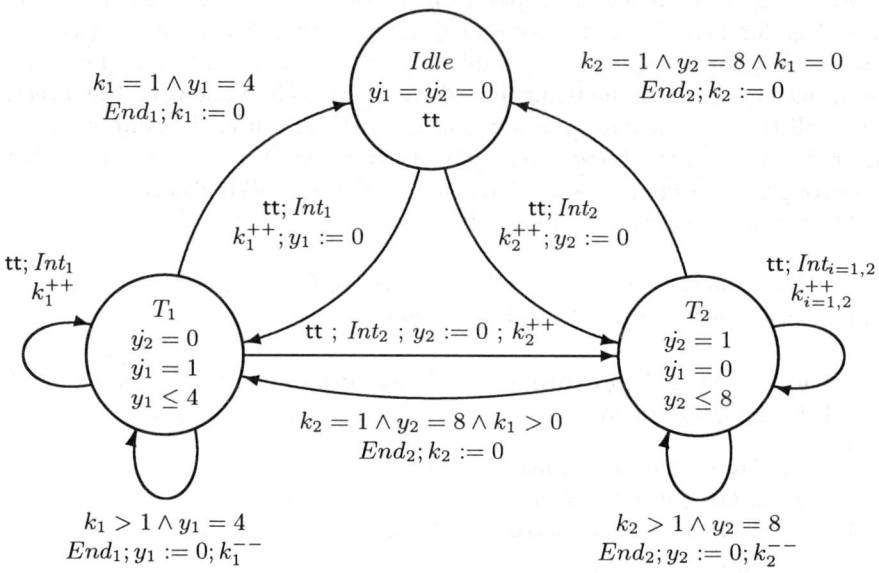

Fig. 3. Automaton of the scheduler: $Sched$

be running at rate 1 in location T_i and 0 otherwise. Tasks of type T_1 take 4 time units and 8 time units for T_2. The initial state of $Sched$ is $Idle$.

The number of pending and running tasks of type i is given by the integers[2] k_i (integers are implemented as stopwatch with slope 0 in every location). The arrivals (events Int_1 and Int_2) of the tasks are described by the (timed) automaton Env (Figure 2). This automaton specifies that the interval between two consecutive arrivals of tasks of type T_1 (resp. T_2) is more than 10 (resp. 20) time units. □

Semantics of hybrid automata. The semantics of a hybrid automaton is given by an (infinite) transition system. At any time, the *configuration* of the system is a pair (l, v) where l is a location and v a valuation. The configuration can

---
[2] On the figures, k_i^{++} stands for $k_i := k_i + 1$ and k_i^{--} for $k_i := k_i - 1$.

change in two different ways: **a discrete change** can occur when a transition in E is enabled in the configuration (l, v), and **a continuous change** can occur according to the evolution law of the variables (given by $Act(l)$) and as long as the invariant $Inv(l)$ remains true. The initial configuration of the hybrid automaton is (l_0, v_0) with $v_0 = \{0\}^V$ (i.e. $v_0(x) = 0 \ \forall x \in V$).

Definition 2 (Semantics of a hybrid automaton) *The semantics of a hybrid automaton $H = (N, l_0, V, A, E, Act, Inv)$ is a labeled transition system $S_H = (Q, q_0, \rightarrow)$ with $Q = N \times \mathbb{R}^V$, $q_0 = (l_0, v_0)$ is the initial state ($v_0(x) = 0, \forall x \in V$) and $\rightarrow$ is defined by:*

$$\langle l, v \rangle \xrightarrow{a} \langle l', v' \rangle \quad \text{iff} \ \exists (l, \gamma, a, \alpha, l') \in E \ \text{s.t.} \ \begin{cases} \gamma(v) = \text{tt}, \ v' = \alpha(v) \text{ and} \\ Inv(l')(v') = \text{tt} \end{cases}$$

$$\langle l, v \rangle \xrightarrow{\epsilon(t)} \langle l', v' \rangle \ \text{iff} \ \begin{cases} l = l' \quad v' = v + Act(l).t \text{ and} \\ \forall 0 \leq t' \leq t, \ Inv(l)(v + Act(l).t') = \text{tt} \end{cases}$$

A run *of a hybrid automata H is a path in S_H.* □

Remark 1. Due to the $Act(l)$-connectedness, the condition

$$\forall 0 \leq t' \leq t, \ Inv(l)(v + Act(l).t') = \text{tt}$$

is equivalent to $Inv(l)(v + Act(l).t) = \text{tt}$ whenever $Inv(l)(v) = \text{tt}$.

Parallel composition of hybrid automata. It is convenient to describe a system as a parallel composition of hybrid automata. To this end, we use the classical composition notion based on a *synchronization function* à la Arnold-Nivat [Arn94]. Let $H_1, \ldots, H_n$ be n hybrid automata with $H_i = (N_i, l_{i,0}, V_i, A, E_i, Act_i, Inv_i)$. A *synchronization function* f is a partial function from $(A \cup \{\bullet\})^n \hookrightarrow A$ where $\bullet$ is a special symbol used when an automaton is not involved in a step of the global system. Note that f is a synchronization function with renaming. We denote by $(H_1|\ldots|H_n)_f$ the parallel composition of the H_i's w.r.t. f. The configurations of $(H_1|\ldots|H_n)_f$ are pairs $(\bar{l}, v)$ with $\bar{l} = (l_1, \ldots, l_n) \in N_1 \times \ldots \times N_n$ and $v = v_1 \cdots v_n$ with[3] $v_i \in \mathbb{R}^{V_i}$ (we assume that all sets V_i of variables are disjoint.) Then the semantics of a synchronized product is also a transition system: the synchronized product can do a discrete transition if all the components agree to and time can progress in the synchronized product also if all the components agree to. This is formalized by the following definition:

Definition 3 (Parallel composition of hybrid automata) *Let $H_1, H_2, \ldots, H_n$ be n hybrid automata with $H_i = (N_i, l_{i,0}, V_i, A, E_i, Act_i, Inv_i)$, and f a (partial) synchronization function $(A \cup \{\bullet\})^n \hookrightarrow A$. The semantics of $(H_1|\ldots|H_n)_f$ is a labeled transition system $S = (Q, q_0, \rightarrow)$ with $Q = N_1 \times \ldots \times N_n \times \mathbb{R}^V$, q_0 is the initial state $((l_{1,0}, \ldots, l_{n,0}), v_0)$ and $\rightarrow$ is defined by:*

---
[3] v_i is the restriction of v to V_i.

- $(\bar{l}, v) \xrightarrow{b} (\bar{l'}, v')$ iff there exists $(a_1, \ldots, a_n) \in (A \cup \{\bullet\})^n$ s.t. $f(a_1, \ldots, a_n) = b$ and for any i we have:
  . If $a_i = \bullet$, then $l'_i = l_i$ and $v'_i = v_i$,
  . If $a_i \in A$, then $\langle l_i, v_i \rangle \xrightarrow{a_i} \langle l'_i, v'_i \rangle$.
- $(\bar{l}, v) \xrightarrow{\epsilon(t)} (\bar{l}, v')$ iff $\forall i \in [1..n]$, we have $\langle l_i, v_i \rangle \xrightarrow{\epsilon(t)} \langle l_i, v'_i \rangle$ □

Example 2. The synchronization function f for the parallel composition ($Sched \mid Env$) of the scheduler and the environment of example 1 is given by:

$$f(Int_i, Int_i) = Int_i \quad \text{and} \quad f(End_i, \bullet) = End_i$$

for any i in $\{1, 2\}$.

3 L_ν^h: A Modal Logic for Hybrid Automata

3.1 Syntax of L_ν^h

We use a fixed point logic L_ν^h to specify the properties of hybrid automata. This logic is an extension (with variables) of the logic L_ν presented in [LL95]. It allows only maximal fixed points and consequently the specification of safety properties (this includes time-bounded liveness properties).

Definition 4 (L_ν^h: L_ν for hybrid systems) *Let K be a finite set of variables, Id a set of identifiers, and A an alphabet of actions. The set of L_ν^h formulas over K, A and Id is defined inductively by:*

$$L_\nu^h \ni \varphi, \psi \ ::= \ \varphi \vee \psi \mid \varphi \wedge \psi \mid \langle a \rangle \varphi \mid [a]\varphi \mid \langle \delta_d \rangle \varphi \mid [\delta_d]\varphi \mid Z \mid \alpha \text{ in } \varphi \mid \gamma$$

where $a \in A$, $\alpha \in \mathcal{L}(K)$, $\gamma \in \mathcal{C}(K)$, $d \in \mathbb{Z}^K$ and $Z \in \mathsf{Id}$. □

3.2 Semantics of L_ν^h

It is straightforward to define the tt and ff operators and moreover implication $\varphi \Rightarrow \psi$ whenever no identifier occurs in φ (for example, $c \Rightarrow \varphi$ with $c \in \mathcal{C}(K)$) since this fragment is closed under negation. The meaning of identifiers is given by a declaration $\mathcal{D} : \mathsf{Id} \to L_\nu^h$.

Given a parallel composition S of hybrid automata, we interpret L_ν^h formula w.r.t. extended states $(\bar{l}, v, u)$ where $(\bar{l}, v)$ is a state of S and u is valuation for K variables (namely formula variables). Intuitively $\langle a \rangle$ (resp. $[a]$) denotes the existential (resp. universal) quantification over a-transitions, $\langle \delta_d \rangle$ (resp. $[\delta_d]$) denotes the existential (resp. universal) quantification over continuous transitions of S w.r.t. the direction d for the variables of K. The α in φ formula means that after the change of formula variables according to α ($\alpha \in \mathcal{L}(K)$), the new extended state verifies φ. The linear constraint γ over K variables holds for $(\bar{l}, v, u)$ whenever $\gamma(u) = $ tt. Finally Z holds for an an extended state, if it belongs to the largest solution of the equation $Z = \mathcal{D}(Z)$. For formula of the type $x := 0$ in φ we simply write x in φ. Moreover when no formula variable occur in a formula, we write $\langle \delta \rangle$ (resp. $[\delta]$) instead of $\langle \delta_\emptyset \rangle$ (resp. $[\delta_\emptyset]$). Formally the semantics of L_ν^h is given in Table 1.

$\langle \bar{l}, v, u \rangle \models_{\mathcal{D}} \varphi \wedge \phi$ iff $\langle \bar{l}, v, u \rangle \models_{\mathcal{D}} \varphi$ and $\langle \bar{l}, v, u \rangle \models_{\mathcal{D}} \phi$

$\langle \bar{l}, v, u \rangle \models_{\mathcal{D}} \varphi \vee \phi$ iff $\langle \bar{l}, v, u \rangle \models_{\mathcal{D}} \varphi$ or $\langle \bar{l}, v, u \rangle \models_{\mathcal{D}} \phi$

$\langle \bar{l}, v, u \rangle \models_{\mathcal{D}} \langle a \rangle \varphi$ iff $\exists \langle \bar{l'}, v', u \rangle$ s.t. $\langle \bar{l}, v \rangle \xrightarrow{a} \langle \bar{l'}, v' \rangle$ and $\langle \bar{l'}, v', u \rangle \models_{\mathcal{D}} \varphi$

$\langle \bar{l}, v, u \rangle \models_{\mathcal{D}} [a] \varphi$ iff $\forall \langle \bar{l'}, v', u \rangle, \langle \bar{l}, v \rangle \xrightarrow{a} \langle \bar{l'}, v' \rangle$ implies $\langle \bar{l'}, v', u \rangle \models_{\mathcal{D}} \varphi$

$\langle \bar{l}, v, u \rangle \models_{\mathcal{D}} \langle \delta_d \rangle \varphi$ iff $\exists t \in \mathbb{R}^{\geq 0}$ s.t. $\langle \bar{l}, v \rangle \xrightarrow{\epsilon(t)} \langle \bar{l}, v + Act(\bar{l}).t \rangle$ and
$\langle \bar{l}, v + Act(\bar{l}).t, u + d.t \rangle \models_{\mathcal{D}} \varphi$

$\langle \bar{l}, v, u \rangle \models_{\mathcal{D}} [\delta_d] \varphi$ iff $\forall t \in \mathbb{R}^{\geq 0}, \langle \bar{l}, v \rangle \xrightarrow{\epsilon(t)} \langle \bar{l}, v + Act(\bar{l}).t \rangle$ implies
$\langle \bar{l}, v + Act(\bar{l}).t, u + d.t \rangle \models_{\mathcal{D}} \varphi$

$\langle \bar{l}, v, u \rangle \models_{\mathcal{D}} \gamma$ iff $\gamma(u) = \text{tt}$

$\langle \bar{l}, v, u \rangle \models_{\mathcal{D}} \alpha$ in φ iff $\langle \bar{l}, v, \alpha(u) \rangle \models_{\mathcal{D}} \varphi$

$\langle \bar{l}, v, u \rangle \models_{\mathcal{D}} Z$ iff $\langle \bar{l}, v, u \rangle$ belongs to the maximal solution of $Z = \mathcal{D}(Z)$

Table 1. Semantics of the modal logic L_ν^h

3.3 Examples of L_ν^h Formulas

As L_ν^h is a conservative extension of L_ν, we can derive classical temporal operators as in the examples below:

- To express that the action error is never performed, we can use the following equation:

$$X \stackrel{def}{=} \bigwedge_{a \in A} [a]X \wedge [\text{error}]\text{ff} \wedge [\delta]X$$

We denote this formula by $\mathsf{ALWAYS}_\mathcal{A}([\text{error}]\text{ff})$. In this example there is no formula variable and the $[\delta]$ deals only with continuous transitions [4] of the system S which is being specified.

- To express that the number of a-transitions is less than 100 along any run, we can use the formula: $x := 0$ in X with X defined by:

$$X \stackrel{def}{=} (x \leq 100) \wedge \bigwedge_{b \in \mathcal{A} \setminus \{a\}} [b]X \wedge [a](x := x+1 \text{ in } X) \wedge [\delta_{\{\dot{x}=0\}}]X$$

In this case, x is just a discrete formula variable.

- More generally $\mathsf{ALWAYS}_{\mathcal{A},E}(\varphi)$ with $\mathcal{A} \subseteq A$ and $E \subseteq \mathbb{Z}^K$ a finite set of directions for K variables, states that φ holds from any reachable state using actions transition in $\mathcal{A}$ and delay transitions with derivatives in E for K variables. $\mathsf{ALWAYS}_{\mathcal{A},E}(\varphi)$ can be defined with the following equation:

$$X \stackrel{def}{=} \varphi \wedge \bigwedge_{b \in \mathcal{A}} [b]X \wedge \bigwedge_{e \in E} [\delta_e]X$$

---

[4] the operator does not contain the evolution law of automata variables since they only depend on the system.

- In the same manner, the weak until operator $\varphi_1 \text{Until}_{\mathcal{A},E}\, \varphi_2$ is defined as the largest fixed point of:

$$X \stackrel{def}{=} \varphi_2 \vee (\varphi_1 \wedge \bigwedge_{b \in \mathcal{A}} [b]X \wedge \bigwedge_{e \in E} [\delta_e]X)$$

- As for timed automata, the following fixed point equation interpreted over a parallel composition of two hybrid automata (without invariant [5] H_1 and H_2 with the synchronization function $f(a, \bullet) = a_1$ and $f(\bullet, a) = a_2$ for any $a \in A$, expresses the (strong) bisimilarity of H_1 and H_2:

$$X \stackrel{def}{=} \bigwedge_{a \in A} [a_1]\langle a_2 \rangle X \wedge \bigwedge_{a \in A} [a_2]\langle a_1 \rangle X \wedge [\delta]X$$

Example 3. We want to specify on our scheduling system that a task of type T_2 never waits: as a new arrival of a task T_2 will preempt a running T_1 task, this amounts to check that $k_2 \leq 1$ as k_2 gives the number of pending and running T_2 tasks; we would also like to prove that at most one task of type T_1 may be pending i.e. $k_1 \leq 2$. We express the previous property as a reachability property of an error transition. Let $Sched'$ be the hybrid automaton obtained from $Sched$ by adding error-transitions $\langle l, (k_1 > 2 \vee k_2 > 1), \text{error}, \emptyset, l\rangle$ for $l \in \{Idle, T_1, T_2\}$. It remains to check that error-transitions can not be fired i.e. $(Env|Sched')_{f'} \models \text{ALWAYS}_{\mathcal{A}}([\text{error}]\text{ff})$ that is:

$$X \stackrel{def}{=} [Int_1]X \wedge [Int_2]X \wedge [End_1]X \wedge [End_2]X \wedge [\text{error}]\text{ff} \wedge [\delta]X$$

□

4 Compositional Verification of Hybrid Automata

4.1 Quotient Construction

Given a hybrid system $(H_1 \mid \cdots \mid H_n)_f$ and a L_ν^h formula φ, we want to build a formula $\varphi/_f H_n$ s.t. $(H_1 \mid \cdots \mid H_n)_f \models \varphi$ iff $(H_1 \mid \cdots \mid H_{n-1}) \models \varphi/_f H_n$. The definition of the quotient construction is given in Table 2. Note that it is easier to define it w.r.t. a binary synchronization function between $(H_1 \mid \cdots \mid H_{n-1})$ and H_n but it is straightforward to decompose $(H_1 \mid \cdots \mid H_n)_f$ in such a manner.

For the no-action label, the conventions are the following: $\langle \bullet \rangle \varphi \equiv [\bullet]\varphi \equiv \varphi$. Note that the variables in V_n become formula variables in the quotient formula; this entails that the operators $\langle \delta_d \rangle$ and $[\delta_d]$ occurring in $\varphi/_f H_n$ deal with $K \cup V_n$. Moreover given $d \in \mathbb{Z}^K$ and $d' \in \mathbb{Z}^{V_n}$, $d.d'$ denotes the corresponding integer activity vector over $K \cup V_n$. Finally note that the quotienting of identifiers may increase [6] the number of fixed point equations in $\mathcal{D}'$; in the worst case, the size of $\mathcal{D}'$ is $|\mathcal{D}|.|N|$ where $|N|$ is the number of locations of the quotiented automaton. This will motivate the use of reduction methods. Now we have:

---

[5] The case of automata with invariant can be handled by a more complex formula based on the same idea.
[6] A new Z^l identifier can be added to $\mathcal{D}'$ for any location l and any $Z \in \text{Id}$.

This computation of sets $S_{X_i}^j$ is done by a forward propagation of linear constraint, the sub-formulas (α in φ), ($[\delta_d]\varphi$) and ($\gamma \Rightarrow \varphi$) are seen as *predicate transformers*.

Figure 4 shows the final value of S_{X_0}, S_{X_1} and S_{X_2}. Therefore the constraint $(x_2 \geq x_1-3)$ in X_2 can be reduced to tt since $S_{X_2} \subseteq [\![x_2 \geq x_1-3]\!]$. Then trivial equation elimination allows us to reduce X_2 (resp. X_1) to tt. Finally we can simplify X_0 to $\langle b \rangle (x_1 := 0 \text{ in } X_0) \wedge [\delta_{(1,1)}] X_0$.

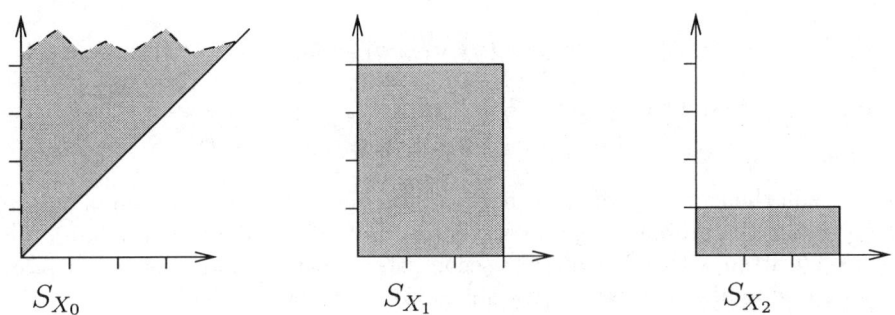

Fig. 4. Example of hitzones computation.

Of course, the computation of S_ξ is based on operations over polyhedra and may not terminate (contrary to other simplifications). Nevertheless it is possible to use coarser over-approximation of the S_ξ's to ensure termination, this clearly leads to less efficient simplifications (i.e. allowing less atomic constraints reductions).

Sharing variables. In the definitions of L_ν^h and H_i, we assume that the variables sets V_i and K are disjoint. This hypothesis is important only if hitzone simplification is applied because this reduction assumes that transitions of automata which have not yet been quotiented do not modify the value of formula variables (for ex. the sub-formula $(x < 10) \wedge \langle a \rangle (x > 10)$ is reduced to ff because it is assumed that x is not updated by performing the a-transition). If we do not apply the hitzone simplification, automata variables can be used inside the formula and variables can even be shared between several automata. In these cases, the hitzone reduction can only be applied after the quotienting of the last automaton that uses the shared variables (i.e. when all the control part they are concerned with is present in the quotient formula).

Nil-model-checking and constraints solving. Let φ' be $\varphi/H_n/\ldots/H_1$. Note that φ' expresses a property over *nil* and then we can assume [9] that no $\langle a \rangle$ and no $[a]$ occur in φ'. In fact, deciding whether φ' holds for *nil* requires to compute the fixed point of equations $X_i = \mathcal{D}'(X_i)$ where $\mathcal{D}'$ is the definition of identifiers occurring in φ'. But an extended configuration of *nil* is just an $|K'|$-tuple of real

---
[9] For *nil* process, we have $\langle a \rangle \varphi \equiv$ ff and $[a]\varphi \equiv$ tt.

numbers and then $nil \models \varphi'$ can be seen as a constraints problem over sets of $|K'|$-tuple of real numbers. For example, $nil \models X_0$ with the following declaration:

$$X_0 \stackrel{def}{=} \left[(x_2 = 1) \Rightarrow (x_2 := 0 \text{ in } X_1)\right] \wedge (x_1 < 1 \vee x_1 > 1) \wedge [\delta_{(0,1)}](x_2 \leq 1 \Rightarrow X_0)$$
$$X_1 \stackrel{def}{=} \left[(x_2 = 1) \Rightarrow (x_2 := 0 \text{ in } X_0)\right] \wedge [\delta_{(1,1)}](x_2 \leq 1 \Rightarrow X_1)$$

is equivalent to the problem of deciding [10] whether $(0,0) \in S_0$ where S_0 and S_1 ($\subseteq \mathbb{R} \times \mathbb{R}$) are defined as the maximal sets verifying:

If $(x_1, x_2) \in S_0$ Then $(x_2 = 1 \Rightarrow (x_1, 0) \in S_1)$ and $(x_1 < 1 \vee x_1 > 1)$ and
$(\forall t \geq 0, x_2 + t \leq 1 \Rightarrow (x_1, x_2 + t) \in S_0)$
If $(x_1, x_2) \in S_1$ Then $(x_2 = 1 \Rightarrow (x_1, 0) \in S_0)$ and
$(\forall t \geq 0, x_2 + t \leq 1 \Rightarrow (x_1 + t, x_2 + t) \in S_1)$

Therefore in the compositional verification, the first step deals with an high level description of the problem (a parallel composition of hybrid automata and a specification written with L_ν^h) while the second step treats a more basic description and could be analyzed by a constraints solver over real numbers.

In [ACH+95] reachability problems of the form "is it possible to reach a configuration verifying φ_0 ?" (where φ_0 is an atomic constraint) are reduced to a fixed point computation of an equation system which encodes the behavior of the hybrid system. In fact if we apply our quotient technique over the reachability formula ALWAYS($\neg \varphi_0$), we obtain the same kind of equations (it can be smaller thanks to the simplification step), and then the compositional method can be seen as an extension of the previous results over hybrid system since it deals with any kind of property which can be expressed with alternation-free modal μ-calculus.

5 Hybrid CMC and Examples

Hybrid CMC . We extended CMC (a tool implementing the compositional method for timed automata [LL98]) in order to handle a subclass of hybrid systems where variables have slopes in $\{0, 1\}$. Moreover we use classical constraints of TA (viz. $x \bowtie m$ or $x - y \bowtie m$) and assignments are of the form $x := y + m$ or $x := m$. The same restrictions apply to the modal logic handled by HCMC. This subclass of hybrid system remains very expressive (model checking is clearly undecidable) and allows to model a large variety of systems [BF99a].

Given an hybrid system and a modal specification, HCMC allows us to build the simplified quotient formula. Moreover there is a procedure to (try to) solve nil model-checking problems. We use a DBM-like data structure to represent constraints over variables in the algorithms [Dil89]. This choice motivates the restriction to slopes in $\{0, 1\}$ (other slopes would require extended forms of constraints) but even in this framework some operations (like $\text{Future}(d, z) = \{v + d.t \mid v \in$

---

[10] Here the answer is " no ".

$z, t \in \mathbb{R}\}$) can only be approximated. These abstractions ensures termination of the two steps (simplifications and *nil* model-checking algorithm) of the compositional approach. However the problem being undecidable, an answer not in {yes, no} may occur. This third result corresponds to cases where the abstractions used for the second step are too large to be able to conclude. The prototype HCMC is available at the web address: http://www.lsv.ens-cachan.fr/~fl.

Examples. The current version of HCMC has been applied over several examples. Here are the results:

- The scheduler described in Example 1 has been successfully verified: the quotienting of the formula in Example 3 by the two components is directly reduced to tt by the simplifications.
- We applied the method over a verification problem for two Petri Nets considered in the MARS project [11] and verified by HyTech (following the method of [BF99b]). Here the problem consists in verifying that a place always contains less than 2 tokens. The verification succeeds in every case (either directly after the first step, or after the *nil* model-checking computation).
- We have tried to verify the ABR protocol. We adapted the model used in [BF99a] for HyTech to HCMC. Here the first step gave a specification with 25 equations but the second step couldn't conclude due to approximations.

6 Conclusion and Future Work

In this paper we have extended the compositional model-checking method defined in [LL95] for timed automata to hybrid automata. Our work is two fold:

1. on the theoretical aspects we have proven that it is possible to do compositional model-checking for hybrid automata; we have defined the logic L_ν^h, i.e. an extension of modal μ-calculus, so that this logic can express many properties for specification of reactive systems and is expressively complete for linear hybrid automata.
2. we have implemented a prototype tool HCMC to handle verification of hybrid automata where variables have slopes in $\{0, 1\}$.

As described in section 5, our method consists in two distinct steps: quotienting and then constraints solving. Our current implementation uses DBMs as a data structure to represent the regions of $\mathbb{R}^n$. Obviously we are only able to manipulate over-approximation of the actual regions of our hybrid automata.

If this is no harm for step 1 as we only miss some simplifications, it is a real impediment for step 2: if the approximation is too coarse we are not able to prove some properties.

Our future work will consist in extending HCMC in order to deal with integer slopes without approximations (this could be done by using a tool like HyTech

---
[11] http://www.loria.fr/~xie/Mars.html

and a polyhedra library to do the final *nil*-model-checking and simplifications or a constraints solver over the reals). We can also easily extend our logic and algorithm to cope with slopes within integers intervals i.e. $\dot{x} \in [l, u]$ so that we will be able to use HCMC on real-life examples and compare the performances with other related tools.

Acknowledgment

The authors would like to thank Béatrice Bérard, Kim Guldstrand Larsen and the anonymous referees for their useful comments on this work.

References

[ACD93] R. Alur, C. Courcoubetis, and D.L. Dill. Model-checking in dense real-time. *Information and Computation*, 104(1):2–34, 1993.

[ACH+95] R. Alur, C. Courcoubetis, N. Halbwachs, T. Henzinger, P. Ho, X. Nicollin, A. Olivero, J. Sifakis, and S. Yovine. The algorithmic analysis of hybrid systems. *Theoretical Computer Science B*, 137, January 1995.

[AHH96] R. Alur, T. A. Henziger, and P. H. Ho. Automatic symbolic verification of embedded systems. *IEEE Transactions On Software Engineering*, 22(3):181–201, March 1996.

[AL99] L. Aceto and F. Laroussinie. Is your model checker on time ? In *Proc. 24th Int. Symp. Math. Found. Comp. Sci. (MFCS'99), Szklarska Poreba, Poland, Sep. 1999*, volume 1672 of *Lecture Notes in Computer Science*, pages 125–136. Springer, 1999.

[And95] H. R. Andersen. Partial Model Checking. In *Proc. of LICS'95*, 1995.

[Arn94] André Arnold. *Finite Transition System*. Prentice Hall, 1994.

[BF99a] B. Bérard and L. Fribourg. Automated verification of a parametric real-time program: the ABR conformance protocol. In *Proc. 11th Int. Conf. Computer Aided Verification (CAV'99), Trento, Italy, July 1999*, volume 1633 of *Lecture Notes in Computer Science*, pages 96–107. Springer, 1999.

[BF99b] B. Bérard and L. Fribourg. Reachability analysis of (timed) Petri nets using real arithmetic. In *Proc. 10th Int. Conf. Concurrency Theory (CONCUR'99), Eindhoven, The Netherlands, Aug. 1999*, volume 1664 of *Lecture Notes in Computer Science*, pages 178–193. Springer, 1999.

[BGK+96] J. Bengtsson, W. O. David Griffioen, K. J. Kristoffersen, K. G. Larsen, F. Larsson, P. Pettersson, and W. Yi. Verification of an audio protocol with bus collision using uppaal. In *Proc. of the 8th International Conference on Computer-Aided Verification, LNCS 1102*, pages 244–256, 1996.

[BLP+99] G. Behrmann, K. G. Larsen, J. Pearson, C. Weise, and W. Yi. Efficient timed reachability analysis using clock difference diagrams. In *11th Computer-Aided Verification*, Trento, Italy, July 1999.

[BTY97] A. Bouajjani, S. Tripakis, and S. Yovine. On-the-Fly Symbolic Model Checking for Real-Time Systems. In *Proc. of the 18th IEEE Real-Time Systems Symposium, RTSS'97*. IEEE Computer Society Press, December 1997.

[Dil89]   D.L. Dill. Timing assumptions and verification of finite-state concurrent systems. In *Proc. Workshop Automatic Verification Methods for Finite State Systems, Grenoble, LNCS 407*, 1989.

[Hen96]   T. A. Henzinger. The theory of hybrid automata. In *Proceedings, 11th Annual IEEE Symposium on Logic in Computer Science*, pages 278–292, New Brunswick, New Jersey, 27–30 July 1996. IEEE Computer Society Press.

[HHWT97]   T. A. Henzinger, P. H. Ho, and H. Wong-Toi. HYTECH: A model checker for hybrid systems. *Lecture Notes in Computer Science*, 1254:460–??, 1997.

[HKPV98]   T. A. Henzinger, P. W. Kopke, A. Puri, and P. Varaiya. What's decidable about hybrid automata? *Journal of Computer and System Sciences*, 57(1):94–124, August 1998.

[HNSY94]   T. A. Henzinger, X. Nicollin, J. Sifakis, and S. Yovine. Symbolic model checking for real-time systems. *Information and Computation*, 111(2):193–244, 1994.

[KVW98]   O. Kupferman, M. Y. Vardi, and P. Wolper. An automata-theoretic approach to branching-time model checking, 1998. Full version of the CAV'94 paper, accepted for publication in J. ACM.

[LL95]   F. Laroussinie and K.G. Larsen. Compositional Model-Checking of Real Time Systems. In *Proc. CONCUR'95, Philadelphia, USA, LNCS 962*, pages 27–41. Springer-Verlag, August 1995.

[LL98]   F. Laroussinie and K. G. Larsen. CMC: A tool for compositional model-checking of real-time systems. In *Proc. IFIP Joint Int. Conf. Formal Description Techniques & Protocol Specification, Testing, and Verification (FORTE-PSTV'98)*, pages 439–456. Kluwer Academic Publishers, 1998.

[LPY95]   K. G. Larsen, P. Pettersson, and W. Yi. Compositional and symbolic model-checking of real-time systems. In *Proc. of the 16th IEEE Real-Time Systems Symposium, RTSS'95*, 1995.

[LPY97]   K. G. Larsen, P. Pettersson, and W. Yi. UPPAAL in a Nutshell. *Journal of Software Tools for Technology Transfer*, 1(1/2):134–152, October 1997.

[MY96]   O. Maler and S. Yovine. Hardware timing verification using KRONOS. In *Proc. 7th Israeli Conference on Computer Systems and Software Engineering*, Herzliya, Israel, June 1996.

[Yov97]   S. Yovine. Kronos: A Verification Tool for real-Time Systems. *Journal of Software Tools for Technology Transfer*, 1(1/2):123–133, October 1997.

A Proof of Theorem 1

For simplicity we restrict the proof to the case of two hybrid automata H_1 and H_2 and a synchronization function f. The proof is carried out by induction on the formula of L_ν^h. For all inductive definitions except $[\delta_d]\varphi$ and its dual $\langle\delta_d\rangle\varphi$ the induction steps are exactly the same as for timed automata (see [LL95]). We here focus on the case of the rule $[\delta_d]\varphi$ (the case $\langle\delta_d\rangle\varphi$ works in the same manner) involving continuous evolution as this case involves the main difference between hybrid and timed automata: the rates of the variables are values of $\mathbb{Z}$ and not always 1.

Proof (Rule $[\delta_d]\varphi$.). Let $\langle (l_1, l_2), v_1.v_2 \rangle$ be a configuration of $(H_1|H_2)_f$. Given a $t \geq 0$, v'_1 (resp. v'_2) will denote $v_1 + Act(l_1).t$ (resp. $v_2 + Act(l_2).t$) and given an activity vector d, u' will denote $u + d.t$.

$\Rightarrow$. Assume $\langle (l_1, l_2), v_1.v_2, u \rangle \models_{\mathcal{D}} [\delta_d]\varphi$ and $Inv(l_2)(v_2) = \text{tt}$. Then by definition of L_ν^h semantics (Table 1), we have:

$$\forall t \geq 0, \langle (l_1, l_2), v_1.v_2 \rangle \xrightarrow{\epsilon(t)} \langle (l_1, l_2), v'_1.v'_2 \rangle \text{ implies } \langle (l_1, l_2), v'_1.v'_2, u' \rangle \models_{\mathcal{D}} \varphi$$

We have to show: $\langle l_1, v_1, v_2.u \rangle \models_{\mathcal{D}'} [\delta_{d.Act(l_2)}](Inv(l_2) \Rightarrow \varphi/_f l_2)$.

Let $t \geq 0$ s.t. $\langle l_1, v_1 \rangle \xrightarrow{\epsilon(t)} \langle l_1, v'_1 \rangle$, there are two cases:

- $Inv(l_2)(v'_2) = \text{ff}$: therefore $(Inv(l_2) \Rightarrow \varphi/_f l_2)$ holds for $\langle l_1, v'_1, v'_2.u' \rangle$,
- $Inv(l_2)(v'_2) = \text{tt}$: therefore there exists $\langle (l_1, l_2), v_1.v_2 \rangle \xrightarrow{\epsilon(t)} \langle (l_1, l_2), v'_1.v'_2 \rangle$ because $Inv(l_2)(v_2) = Inv(l_2)(v'_2) = \text{tt}$ and $Inv(l_2)$ is $Act(l_2)$-strongly connected. Moreover $\langle (l_1, l_2), v'_1.v'_2, u' \rangle \models_{\mathcal{D}} \varphi$ entails that $(\varphi/_f l_2)$ holds for $\langle l_1, v'_1, v'_2.u' \rangle$ because we have the induction hypothesis:

$$\langle (l_1, l_2), v'_1.v'_2, u' \rangle \models_{\mathcal{D}} \varphi \Leftrightarrow \langle l_1, v'_1, v'_2.u' \rangle \models_{\mathcal{D}'} \varphi/_f l_2$$

Then we have: $\langle l_1, v'_1, v'_2.u' \rangle \models_{\mathcal{D}'} (Inv(l_2) \Rightarrow \varphi/_f l_2)$.

Therefore we have: $\langle l_1, v_1, v_2.u \rangle \models_{\mathcal{D}'} [\delta_{d.Act(l_2)}](Inv(l_2) \Rightarrow \varphi/_f l_2)$.

$\Leftarrow$. Assume $\langle l_1, v_1, v_2.u \rangle \models_{\mathcal{D}'} [\delta_{d.Act(l_2)}](Inv(l_2) \Rightarrow \varphi/_f l_2)$.
We want to show $\langle (l_1, l_2), v_1.v_2, u \rangle \models_{\mathcal{D}} [\delta_d]\varphi$.
Let $t \geq 0$ s.t. $\langle (l_1, l_2), v_1.v_2 \rangle \xrightarrow{\epsilon(t)} \langle (l_1, l_2), v'_1.v'_2 \rangle$. This entails that there exists $\langle l_1, v_1 \rangle \xrightarrow{\epsilon(t)} \langle l_1, v'_1 \rangle$ and then $\langle l_1, v'_1, v'_2.u' \rangle \models_{\mathcal{D}'} (Inv(l_2) \Rightarrow \varphi/_f l_2)$. Moreover we know $Inv(l_2)(v'_2) = Inv(l_2)(v_2) = \text{tt}$ and then we have $\langle l_1, v'_1, v'_2.u' \rangle \models_{\mathcal{D}'} (\varphi/_f l_2)$. Therefore by i.h. we obtain: $\langle (l_1, l_2), v'_1.v'_2, u' \rangle \models_{\mathcal{D}} \varphi$.
Then we have: $\langle (l_1, l_2), v_1.v_2, u \rangle \models_{\mathcal{D}} [\delta_d]\varphi$.

□

Prioritized Traversal: Efficient Reachability Analysis for Verification and Falsification

Ranan Fraer[1], Gila Kamhi[1], Barukh Ziv[1], Moshe Y. Vardi[2]*, Limor Fix[1]

[1]Logic and Validation Technology, Intel Corporation, Haifa, Israel
{rananf, gkamhi, zbarukh, lfix}@iil.intel.com,

[2]Dept. of Computer Science, Rice University
vardi@cs.rice.edu

Abstract. Our experience with semi-exhaustive verification shows a severe degradation in usability for the corner-case bugs, where the tuning effort becomes much higher and recovery from dead-ends is more and more difficult. Moreover, when there are no bugs at all, shifting semi-exhaustive traversal to exhaustive traversal is very expensive, if not impossible. This makes the output of semi-exhaustive verification on non-buggy designs very ambiguous. Furthermore, since after the design fixes each falsification task needs to converge to full verification, there is a strong need for an algorithm that can handle efficiently both verification and falsification. We address these shortcomings with an enhanced reachability algorithm that is more robust in detecting corner-case bugs and that can potentially converge to exhaustive reachability. Our approach is similar to that of Cabodi et al. in partitioning the frontiers during the traversal, but differs in two respects. First, our partitioning algorithm trades quality for time resulting in a significantly faster traversal. Second, the subfrontiers are processed according to some priority function resulting in a mixed BFS/DFS traversal. It is this last feature that makes our algorithm suitable for both falsification and verification.

1 Introduction

Functional RTL validation is addressed today by two complementary technologies. The more traditional one, *simulation*, has high capacity but covers only a tiny fraction out of all the possible behaviors of the design. On the contrary, *formal verification* guarantees full coverage of the entire state space but is severely limited in terms of capacity. A number of hybrid approaches that combine the strengths of the two validation technologies have emerged lately. One of them is *semi-exhaustive verification* [1,3,4,5,9] that aims at exploring a more significant fraction of the state space within the same memory and time limits. While maintaining high coverage, similar to exhaustive verification, this technique is reaching more buggy states, in less time and with smaller memory consumption. In this family we can include several heuristics, like the *high-density reachability* [1], and *saturated simulation* [4,5].

---

* Work partially supported by NSF grant CCR-9700061 and a grant from Intel Corporation.

We have run extensive experiments using the high-density reachability on a rich set of industrial designs, and we have reported encouraging results [15]. As opposed to previous studies, where semi-exhaustive algorithms are evaluated on the basis of their state space coverage, our results show these algorithms to be highly effective in bug finding too. We have identified two classes of problems where semi-exhaustive verification is particularly beneficial:

- *Dense bugs*: Designs characterized by a high density of buggy states. The exhaustive verification usually finds these bugs too, but the semi-exhaustive one reaches the buggy states much faster.
- *Corner-case bugs*: Designs characterized by sparsely distributed bugs in the state space such that the exhaustive verification blows up long before reaching them. These bugs are now within the reach of semi-exhaustive algorithms that can go deeper in the state space, while keeping the memory consumption under control.

Nevertheless, the corner-case bugs require a much higher tuning effort. Experience shows that often only a specific subsetting heuristic and a particular threshold are leading the semi-exhaustive algorithm to a buggy state, and very small variations of this "golden" setting are bound to fail. Failure here means getting stuck in a *dead-end*, where no more new states are found, and yet we are not sure if all the reachable states have been covered. The dead-end recovery algorithm of [11] addresses this problem by using the *scrap* states (the non-dense subsets, ignored by previous subsettings) to regenerate the traversal. The scrap states are partitioned as well, similarly to [11]. However, we had little success with this algorithm, as the BDDs of the scrap partitions gets larger and larger and more difficult to use.

For the same reason, shifting from semi-exhaustive traversal to an exhaustive one is very expensive, and often impossible. This makes the semi-exhaustive approach unsuitable for verification tasks (where there are no bugs at all). The ability to address both verification and falsification problems is important in an industrial context, since after the design fixes each falsification task needs to converge to full verification. Moreover, a significant problem in industrial-size projects is to ensure that the process of fixing one design problem does not introduce another. In the context of conventional testing this is checked through regression testing [19]. If consecutive test suites check N properties, a failure in one property may require re-testing all the previous suites, once a fix has been made. Efficient regression testing, clearly, requires an algorithm powerful both for verification and falsification.

To overcome the above drawbacks in the semi-exhaustive approach, we introduce in this paper an enhanced reachability analysis that is efficient both for falsification and verification and that is less sensitive to tuning. For falsification, we still want to use the mixed BFS/DFS strategy that is at the core of the semi-exhaustive approach. As for verification, we replace the dense/non-dense partitioning of [1] with a balanced partitioning as in Cabodi et al. [13]. As noted above, the density criterion is unsuitable for verification, due to the difficulty of exploring the non-dense part of the state space.

So our approach follows the lines of Cabodi et al. [13], producing at each step a set of balanced partitions instead of one dense partition, but differs in two respects. First, our partitioning algorithm trades quality for time resulting in a significantly faster traversal. The partitioning is based as in [13] on selecting a splitting variable. We have witnessed that the selection of the splitting variable can be very expensive computationally and significantly increase the overall traversal time. Therefore, we make use of a new heuristics to select only a subset of the variables as candidates for the splitting as opposed to [13] where all the variables are involved in the selection process. Although the new partitioning algorithm may generate less balanced partitions, it is faster than the original and reduces the overall traversal time.

Second, while [13] does a strict breadth-first search as in the classic reachability, we make use of a mixed breadth-first /depth-first traversal controlled by a prioritized queue of partitions. We check the correctness of the invariant properties *on-the-fly* during the reachability analysis. The mixed approach, in addition to enjoying the benefits reported by Cabodi et al. for balanced decomposition (i.e., low peak memory requirement and drastic CPU-time and capacity improvement), makes the search more robust in case of falsification, by getting faster to the bugs. On-the-fly verification [16] clearly reduces the time required to get to the bugs. Experiments on Intel designs show a marked improvement on the existing exact and partial reachability techniques.

The paper starts with a summary of related work in Section 2. Section 3 introduces the new prioritized traversal as well as the fast splitting algorithm. In Section 4 we report experimental results comparing prioritized traversal to existing traversal algorithms and the new splitting algorithm to the original one. We conclude in Section 5 by summarizing the contributions of this work.

2 Related Work

Semi-exhaustive verification addresses the concerns of practicing verifiers by shifting the focus from verification to *falsification*. Rather than ensuring the absence of bugs, it turns the verification tool into an effective bug hunter. This hybrid approach aims at improving over both simulation and formal verification in terms of state space coverage and capacity respectively.

Our usage of semi-exhaustive verification follows the lines of [1,3,5,9], being based on subsetting the frontiers during state space exploration, whenever these frontiers reach a given threshold by making use of various under-approximation techniques.

The effectiveness of the semi-exhaustive verification is clearly very sensitive to the nature of the algorithm employed for subsetting the frontiers. A large number of BDD subsetting algorithms have been proposed lately in the model checking literature. Each of them is necessarily a heuristic, attempting to optimize different criteria of the chosen subset. An important class of heuristics takes the *density* of the BDDs as the criterion to be optimized, where density is defined as the ratio of states represented by the BDD to the size of the BDD. This relates to the observation that large BDDs are needed for representing sparse sets of states (as it is the case for the frontiers). Removing the isolated states can lead to significant reductions in the size of the BDDs.

Ravi and Somenzi [1] have introduced the first algorithms for extracting dense BDD subsets, *Heavy-Branch* (HB) and *Short-Path* (SP). Independently, Shiple proposed in his thesis [8] the algorithm *Under-Approx* (UA) that also optimizes the subset according to the density criterion. Recently, Ravi et al. [9] proposed *Remap-Under-Approx* (RUA) as a combination of UA with more traditional BDD minimization algorithms like *Constrain* and *Restrict* [10]. A combined algorithm is

Compress (COM) [9], which applies first SP with the given threshold and then RUA with a threshold of 0 to increase the density of the result. Although more expensive, the combination of the two algorithms is supposed to produce better results.

The *Saturation* (SAT) algorithm [3,5] is based on a different idea. Rather than keeping as *many* states as possible, it attempts to preserve the *interesting* states. In the context of [3,5] the control states are defined as the interesting ones. The heuristic makes sure to *saturate* the subset with respect to the control states, i.e. that each possible assignment to the control variables is represented exactly once in the subset. In terms of BDDs, this is implemented by Lin and Newton's *Cproject* operator [12].

Previous studies [1,3,5,9] advocate the merits of dense frontier subsetting techniques on the basis of their coverage of the reachable state space and the density of the approximated frontiers. We have evaluated in [15] the effectiveness of these techniques for bug hunting and confirmed their usefulness in the fast detection of design or specification errors. However, a major shortcoming of these techniques is the difficulty, and in many cases the inability, to provide formal guarantees of correctness, in case no bug is found. In other words, these techniques, although useful for *falsification,* are not practical for *verification.* Furthermore, these techniques suffer from high tuning effort in case they are used to find the corner-case bugs.

Our approach is closely related to the work of Cabodi et al. [13], which considers as a key goal the good decomposition of state sets. They adopt a technique aimed at producing balanced partitions with a possibly minimum overall BDD size. This size is often slightly larger than the original one, but this drawback is largely overcome by the benefits derived from partitioned storage and computations. We have observed that the balanced partitioning approach is very effective in reducing peak memory requirements and it can drastically decrease the overall BDD size. From our experience, the benefits of balanced partitioning over dense subsetting is that it requires less tuning effort and it can much more easily and efficiently converge to exact reachability. On the other hand, the BDD splitting algorithm used in [13] may be computationally very expensive. For average designs the time spent in BDD splitting may outweigh the overall benefits of balanced partitioning. Cabodi et al. make use of a partitioned breadth-first search. For falsification we have observed the mixed breadth-first/depth-first approach to be much more effective. The enhanced reachability analysis that we propose enjoys the benefits of balanced partitioning and addresses its shortcomings.

Finally, the work of Narayan et al. [14] on partitioned ROBDDs takes a more radical approach where all the BDDs in the systems (not just the frontier and the reachable states) are subject to partitioning. Moreover, different partitions can be reordered with different variable orders. This approach can cope better with the BDD explosion problem, but it involves significant effort in maintaining the coherency of the infrastructure where several BDD variable orders coexist simultaneously.

3 Improved Reachability Search

A finite state machine is an abstract model describing the behavior of a sequential circuit. A completely specified FSM M is a 5-tuple $M = (I, S, \delta, \lambda, S_o)$, where I is the input alphabet, S is the state space, δ is the transition relation contained in S x I x S, and $S_o \subseteq S$ is the initial state set. BDDs are used to represent and manipulate functions and state sets, by means of their *characteristic functions*. In the rest of paper, we make no distinction between BDDs and set of states.

3.1 Invariant Verification

A common verification problem for hardware designs is to determine if every state reachable from a designated set of initial states lies within a specified set of "good states" (referred to as the *invariant*). This problem is variously known as *invariant verification*, or *assertion checking*. Invariant verification can be performed by computing all states reachable from the initial states and checking that they all lie in the invariant. This reduces the invariant verification problem to the one of traversing the state transition graph of the design, where the successors of a state are computed according to the transition relation of the model. Moreover, traversing the state graph in a breadth-first order makes possible to work on sets of states that are symbolically represented as BDDs [6]. This is an instance of the general technique of *symbolic model checking* [7].

Given an invariant *inv* and an initial set of states S_o, *reachability analysis* starts with the BDD for S_o, and uses BDD functions to iterate up to a fixed point, which is the set of all the states reachable from S_o using the *Img* operator. If the set of reachable states R is contained in *inv*, then the invariant is verified to be true, otherwise the invariant is not satisfied by the model and a counter-example needs to be generated.

The primary limitation of this classic traversal algorithm is that the BDDs encountered at each iteration F, commonly referred as *frontiers*, and R, referred as *reachable states*, can grow very large leading to a blow-up in memory or to a verification time-out. Moreover, it may be impossible to perform image computation because of the BDDs involved in the intermediate computations.

Subsetting traversal introduced by Ravi and Somenzi [1] and *Partitioned traversal* proposed by Cabodi et al. [13] (Figure 1) tackle these shortcomings of the classic traversal by decomposing state sets when they become too large to be represented as a monolithic BDD or when image computation is too expensive.

Subsetting traversal keeps the size of the frontiers under control by computing the image computation only on a dense subset of the frontier, each time the size of the current frontier reaches a given threshold. When no new states are produced, the sub-traversal may have reached the actual fixed-point (the one that would be obtained during pure BFS traversal) or a *dead-end*, which arises from having discarded some states during the process of subsetting. Theoretically, termination could be checked by computing the image of current reached set of states (as in Figure 1). In practice, this is rarely feasible, given the size of the BDD representing the reachable states. A dead-end resolution algorithm was proposed in [11] that keeps the *scrap* states (ignored by previous subsettings) in a partitioned form to regenerate the traversal. However, we had little success with this algorithm, as the BDDs of the scrap partitions (the non-dense part of the state space) get larger and larger and more difficult to use.

SUBSETTING_TRAVERSAL (δ S_o th)	PARTITIONED_TRAVERSAL (δ S_o th)
$R = F = S_o$;	$R_p = F_p = S_o$;
while $(F \neq \emptyset)$ {	while $(N_p \neq \emptyset)$ {
$\quad F = IMG(\delta\, F) - R$;	$\quad T_p = \{IMG(\delta\, f) \mid f \in F_p\}$;
$\quad R = R \cup F$;	$\quad F_p = SET\_DIFF\,(T_p, R_p)$;
$\quad$ if $(F = \emptyset)$ // check if dead-end	$\quad R_p = SET\_UNION\,(F_p, R_p)$;
$\quad\quad F = Img(\delta\, R) - R$;	$\quad F_p = RE\_PARTITION(F_p, th)$;
$\quad$ if $(size(F) > th)$	$\quad R_p = RE\_PARTITION(R_p, th)$;
$\quad\quad F = subset\,(F)$;	}
}	

Figure 1. Subsetting traversal [1] and Partitioned Traversal [13]

Partitioned traversal is a BFS one, just like the classic algorithm, except that it keeps the frontier F as a set of partitions F_p, and the reachable states R as a set of partitions R_p. The T_p sets are the results of image computation for each of the subfrontiers F_p, which may be either re-combined or partitioned again. This is done by functions like SET_DIFF, SET_UNION, and RE_PARTITION that work on partitioned sets. The intuition behind this approach is to overcome the complexity issue of large frontiers by splitting the frontiers to balanced partitions with minimum overall size and decrease peak BDD size by performing the image computation on the partitions of the frontier. One advantage of partitioned traversal over subsetting traversal is that it can more easily converge to exhaustive reachability. During the whole computation, all the partitions are preserved and image computation is performed on all the partitions. The computation never gets into dead-ends and consequently there is no need to perform image computation on the reached states. On the other hand, a major drawback of this approach is the time spent in selecting the BDD variable to split the frontier to balanced partitions. Moreover, if this traversal is used for falsification purposes, since the reachable states are computed still in a BFS fashion, it is time consuming to get to deep bugs.

Our approach is related to both [1] and [13]. As [13] it aims at generating balanced partitions instead of dense subsets, since we have experienced that balanced partitioning requires less tuning effort than dense subsetting and makes it easy to converge to full verification. Similarly to [1], we make use of a mixed breadth-first/depth-first search strategy in order to reach the deep bugs faster. Moreover, we propose a fast splitting algorithm that reduces the overall traversal time.

Consequently, our approach enjoys the benefits of both subsetting and partitioned traversal, while addressing the shortcomings of the two approaches: unsuitability of subsetting traversal for full verification, inefficiency of partitioned traversal for falsification and performance penalty induced by the splitting algorithm in partitioned traversal.

3.2 Fast Frontier Splitting

Cabodi et al. [13] proposed a BDD splitting algorithm based on single variable selection, that aims at producing balanced partitions with minimum overall BDD size. The algorithm is based on a procedure estimating the size of the cofactors with respect to a given variable. The cost of splitting a BDD with variable v is computed making use of the estimated node counts. The cost function calculates the potential of a variable v to generate balanced BDDs with minimum overall BDD size. The main drawback of this approach is that the estimated node counts may be quite inaccurate, resulting in unbalanced partitions. The estimations are computed without considering the reductions and sub-tree sharing. Therefore, in [18] an enhanced procedure was proposed. The enhanced algorithm takes into consideration the sharing factor while estimating the size of the cofactors with respect to a given variable. This refinement yields very precise estimates but is much slower than the original one.

Moreover, both algorithms estimate the size of the BDD representing f constrained either by v or $\sim v$ for each variable v in the true support of f. The cofactor size estimation for each variable in the support is computationally very expensive, and therefore, is a major drawback of the partitioned reachability analysis.

Our frontier splitting algorithm aims at achieving a good time/accuracy trade-off. We still want to use the accurate cofactor estimation of [18], but only on a subset of the variables. Therefore, we propose a two-stage algorithm[†]. The first stage prioritizes the variables according to their splitting quality. The second stage calculates accurate cofactor size estimations as in [18] for the subset of variables chosen to be the best candidates at the first stage. The performance improvement is mainly due to the accurate cofactor size estimation of only a subset of the variables. Additionally, the first stage of the algorithm, which prioritizes the variables with respect to their splitting quality is quite fast. This first stage is comparable to the function counting the nodes of a BDD, so its time complexity is linear in the size of the BDD. Therefore, we get a significant performance gain that outweighs the degradation in splitting quality, as testified by the results in Section 4.

In order to prioritize the variables with respect to their splitting quality, we estimate the size of every sub-function f in a BDD (i.e., the size of the sub-DAG under every BDD node), which we refer to as $c[f]$. Clearly, $c[f] \leq c[f_0] + c[f_1] + 1$, and the equality holds only when there is no sharing between f_0 and f_1. Using a DFS traversal of the BDD representing the function f, the exact $c[f]$ may be calculated as $c[f] = c'[f_0] + c'[f_1] + 1$, where $c'[f_0]$ and $c'[f_1]$ are the number of unvisited nodes encountered during the traversal of f_0 and f_1, respectively. If f_0 is traversed first, then $c'[f_0] = c[f_0]$ and $c'[f_1] \leq c[f_1]$, since there may be node sharing between f_0 and f_1. Similarly, $c'[f_1] = c[f_1]$ and $c'[f_0] \leq c[f_0]$ if f_1 is traversed first. Therefore, the value of $c'[f_0]$ is different if the traversal starts from F_0 or F_1. The maximum of the two values gives an accurate estimate for $c[f_0]$). The same holds for $c[f_1]$.

Based on these facts, we make two traversals on the BDD of F, where at the first traversal we expand the 0-edge of every node f of F, while at the second pass the 1-edge is expanded first. At each pass, $c[f]$ is updated such that its final value is the maximum value resulting from the two traversals. Note that the resulting $c[f]$ is only an estimate of the real size of f. To measure the splitting quality of each variable v in the support of F, we make use of the estimate sizes of sub-functions in F. We

---

[†] We would like to thank one of the reviewers for pointing us to a more recent paper of Cabodi et al. [17] proposing similar improvements to the splitting algorithm. However, their estimation of cofactor sizes is based on computing different metrics during the DFS traversal of the BDD.

experimented with several cost functions and we have found the following one to be satisfying:

$$COST(v) = \frac{w \cdot \sum_{f: \text{var}(f)=v} \frac{\text{abs}(c[f_v] - c[f_{\bar{v}}])}{\max(c[f_v], c[f_{\bar{v}}])} + (1-w) \cdot \sum_{f: \text{var}(f)=v} \frac{c[f_v] + c[f_{\bar{v}}] + 1}{c[f]}}{\text{card}(\{f \mid \text{var}(f) = v\})}$$

where var(f) is the root variable of the sub-BDD f, so the summations in the nominator are done over all the BDD nodes f that are at the level of the variable v. The denominator is simply the number of all the nodes at the level of v. The first term in the nominator represents the balance between the cofactors, and the second term is the node sharing. The weight w of the balancing term was empirically determined to be 0.4.

We then proceed to the second stage, where variables are prioritized in increasing order of their COST(v), and an accurate estimation of cofactors' sizes is calculated on the best N variables using the size estimation algorithm in [18]. The variable with the minimum larger cofactor, that is $\min(\max(|f_v|,|f_{\neg v}|))$, is chosen as the splitting variable v. We experienced that calculating an accurate estimate to a small set of variables (for instance, $N = 15$) is sufficient to get to a nearly optimal splitting.

3.3 On-the-Fly Verification

We have incorporated on-the-fly verification of the invariants [16] to our reachability algorithms. Instead of checking the invariant only after all reachable states are computed, this check is performed after each computation of a new frontier. This feature is critical for falsification problems, where the different algorithms are evaluated with respect to their success in bug finding. This should be contrasted with previous work ([1,11,13]) where the evaluation is strictly based on the number of reached states.

3.4 Prioritized Traversal

Figure 2 shows the pseudo-code for the prioritized traversal. The set of states that satisfy the invariant is represented by *inv*. Prioritized traversal can be performed with a transition relation δ in monolithic or partitioned form. The results in Section 4 are obtained when a partitioned transition relation is used.

R represents the set of states reached so far, initially equal to the set of initial states S_0. *Fqueue* is the prioritized queue of the frontiers that have yet to be processed. Initially *Fqueue* contains just the set S_0. As long as the queue is not empty, we pop its first element F, compute its image and reinsert the result into *Fqueue* according to the priority function. Whenever a new frontier F is inserted into the queue, if its size exceeds the threshold th, F is completely partitioned (i.e., decomposed until the size of all its sub-partitions are below th) making use of the splitting algorithm explained in Section 3.2. The new partitions are inserted in the queue in the order imposed by the *priority function*. We have experimented with several priority functions (*minimum_size, density, frontier_age*). Our experience, as can be observed from the results reported in Section 4, shows that *minimum_size* is the most efficient and the least sensitive priority function. At each fixed-point iteration step, the correctness of the invariant is checked. The traversal ends if the invariant is falsified during the reachability analysis.

PRIORITIZED_TRAVERSAL
(δS_o, th, prio_func)
$R = S_o$;
INVARIANT_CHECK(*So*, *inv*);
INSERT(*So*, *Fqueue*, *th*, *prio_func*);
While (*Fqueue* ≠ []) {
  F = POP (*Fqueue*);
  F = IMG(δ, F) - R;
  $R = R \cup F$;
  INVARIANT_CHECK(*F*, *inv*);
  INSERT(*F*, *Fqueue*, *th*, *prio_func*);
}
	INSERT(*F*, *Fqueue*, *th*, *prio_func*)
	  if (size(*F*) > *th*) {
	    F_p = COMPLETE_PARTITION(*F th*);
	    Foreach $f \in F_p$
	      insert *f* in *Fqueue* using *prio_func*;
	  }
	  else if ($F \neq \emptyset$)
	    insert *f* in *Fqueue* using *prio_func*;
	
	INVARIANT_CHECK(*F*, *inv*)
	  if ($F \not\subset inv$) report the bug and exit;

Figure 2. Prioritized traversal

Prioritized traversal is a mixed BFS/DFS traversal, which can be converged to full DFS or BFS by inserting the new frontiers always to the top or the bottom of the queue. Therefore, as a search traversal, it subsumes the partitioned traversal introduced by Cabodi et al. [13]. Note that our approach, unlike [13], does not repartition the reachable states and the frontiers at each step. We estimate the repartitioning to be very expensive, and we avoid using a partitioned SET_DIFF (Figure 1) to detect the fixpoint.

4 Experimental Results

The results reported in this section come to support our main claims about the advantages of the new algorithms proposed in this paper. Section 4.1 compares our fast splitting algorithm against the one in [18] by measuring the impact of the time/quality tradeoff on the overall performance. Section 4.2 compares prioritized traversal with classic, subsetting and partitioned traversal on a set of verification and falsification problems. While these problems can be handled by most of the algorithms, our data shows that prioritized traversal behaves consistently well all over the spectrum. It is the only algorithm that is robust for both verification and falsification. Finally, section 4.3 reports successful results of prioritized traversal on a number of challenging testcases (both verification and falsification) that no other algorithm can handle. This emphasizes the capacity improvement of our new algorithm.

4.1 Comparing Splitting Algorithms

For the purpose of this experiment we have run prioritized traversal using two different BDD splitting algorithms: the one implemented in [18] denoted by SPLIT below, and our fast splitting algorithm denoted by SPLIT+. Running the two algorithms on four full verification tasks (requiring exact reachability) allowed us to compare the impact of the splitting algorithms on the overall traversal time. Table 1 describes the number or variables of each circuit (latches and inputs), the threshold that triggers frontier partitioning, as well as the time (seconds) and memory (Mb) for the complete traversal.

ckt	ckt1		ckt2		ckt3		ckt4	
vars	81 lat/101 inp		79 lat/80 inp		136 lat /73 inp		129 lat /82 inp	
thresh	50000 nodes		100000 nodes		100000 nodes		100000 nodes	
Trials	time	mem	time	mem	time	mem	time	mem
SPLIT	327	169	368	91	3880	219	3522	190
SPLIT+	244	169	309	98	2840	219	2359	185

Table 1. Impact of splitting algorithms on overall traversal time

While the *speed* of the splitting algorithm obviously affects the traversal time, so does the *accuracy* of the splitting. Indeed, a poor split requires additional splitting steps and increases the number of iterations of the traversal. In this respect, the speed of SPLIT+ compensates its occasional loss in accuracy, causing it to perform systematically better than SPLIT.

Even more convincing is to compare the two algorithms on a few specific partitioning problems. In Table 2 we pick three representative cases and report the sizes of the initial BDD and of the two partitions resulting from the split, as well as the time required by the split. SPLIT+ is consistently 8-10X faster than SPLIT, without a significant loss in accuracy, although occasionally it can produce a poor decomposition (as seen in the first line of Table 2).

	SPLIT		SPLIT+	
Initial BDD	Partitions (BDD nodes)	Time	Partitions (BDD nodes)	Time
331520	224731 / 215579	98.83	63834 / 268414	8.86
100096	52527 / 52435	31.13	54293 / 47042	4.86
105003	53321 / 53312	27.96	53321 / 53312	2.81

Table 2. Comparing splitting algorithm on specific partitioning problems

4.2 Robustness for Both Verification and Falsification

In this section, we selected for the purpose of evaluation several real-life verification and falsification problems that can be handled by all the algorithms: classic reachability (CLS), subsetting traversal using the Shortest Paths heuristic (SUB), partitioned traversal (PART) and prioritized traversal (PRIO). The point that we want to make here is that PRIO behaves consistently well all over the spectrum. It is the only algorithm that is efficient and robust for both verification and falsification. As opposed to [13], our implementation of PART does not re-partition the frontiers and reachable states.

As for PRIO, the priority queue is sorted by BDD size (the smallest frontiers are traversed first). This setting was uniformly a good choice, but different priority functions perform better on different examples, which justifies the need for a general priority queue mechanism. Also, the results obtained with the different priority functions, and for each of them several thresholds have been consistently good, which supports our claim about the robustness of this approach. The results for other priority functions are not included here, due to space constraints.

ckt	ckt1		ckt2		ckt3		ckt4	
vars	81 lat/101 inp		79 lat/80 inp		136 lat /73 inp		129 lat /82 inp	
thresh	50000 nodes		100000 nodes		100000 nodes		100000 nodes	
	time	mem	time	mem	time	mem	time	mem
CLS	174	169	253	92	2923	265	2271	224
SUB	2763	245	568	108	Out	Out	Out	Out
PART	299	169	457	95	3844	219	2550	190
PRIO	244	169	309	98	2840	219	2359	185

Table 3. Performance comparison on verification problems

Let us look first at the verification results in Table 3 (ckt 1–4). We notice that CLS is still the fastest algorithm. However, PRIO comes close behind – for larger examples, it is only 10-20% slower and occasionally it beats the classic algorithm (as seen for ckt3). Also, PRIO has lower memory consumption and this trend gets more emphasized as we lower the threshold or run more challenging examples. This is similar to the time/memory trade-off observed in the usage of partitioned transition relations [20] compared to monolithic ones.

PART takes more time to complete these examples, we suspect that PRIO wins over PART due to its mixed BFS/DFS nature that allows to reach deeper states faster and converge in less iterations. As for SUB, its dead-end resolution algorithm rarely succeeds to converge to full reachability and when it does is much slower than both PRIO and PART. This is due to the unbalanced partitioning used in SUB – the dense partition is explored first, but when it comes to traversing the non-dense one we are dealing with increasingly larger BDDs and a rapid degradation in performance.

Table 4 reports falsification results on three buggy test cases (ckts 5–7). The time and memory data are measured only until the bug is encountered, due to the use of "on-the-fly" verification. As opposed to previous evaluations [1,13] of subsetting traversal that aimed at high state coverage, our evaluation criteria measures the efficiency and robustness of the different algorithms with respect to bug finding.

ckt	ckt5		ckt6		ckt7	
vars	195 lat/67 inp		129 lat/54 inp		136 lat /73 inp	
thresh	50000 nodes		50000 nodes		100000 nodes	
	time	mem	time	mem	time	mem
CLS	944	234	1307	344	4655	494
SUB	Out	Out	810	220	Out	Out
PART	1262	155	1012	227	5650	210
PRIO	470	128	540	157	1600	210

Table 4. Performance comparison on falsification problems

PRIO is clearly faster than both CLS and PART, again due to its mixed BFS/DFS nature. It is no surprise that PART is even slower than CLS, since both do a BFS traversal only that PART does it slower and with lower memory consumption (just as noticed in Table 3). When comparing performance, there is no a priori winner between PRIO and SUB, but PRIO is definitely more robust. When SUB's approximations miss the closest bugs, it is harder and harder to recover from dead-ends and to encounter the buggy states ignored previously. This is why SUB requires a high tuning effort – often only the combination of a specific subsetting heuristic and a specific threshold succeeds in finding the bug. By contrast, the usage of balanced partitioning in PRIO allows it to explore more states and eventually hit the bug. Different priority queues or different thresholds have a smaller impact on the chances of finding the bug, although they may affect the time required for it.

4.3 Capacity Improvement

One of the main benefits of PRIO is the capacity improvement over CLS, SUB and PART. This can be noted in Table 5 for both verification (ckt 8-10) and falsification problems (ckt 11-12). Both SUB and PART were run with the best tuning (i.e. different thresholds, approximation heuristics) and SUB actually succeeded to handle the two falsification problems, but only with a very specific configuration: the RUA approximation [9] and a threshold of 400000 nodes.

ckt	Verification						Falsification			
	ckt8		ckt9		ckt10		ckt11		ckt12	
# vars	90 lat /104 inp		145 lat/55 inp		139 lat /41 inp		129 lat /82 inp		71 lat /58 inp	
thresh	50000 nodes		50000 nodes		20000 nodes		100000 nodes		50000 nodes	
	time	mem	time	time	time	mem	time	mem	time	mem
CLS	Out	Out	Out	Out	Out	Out	Out	Out	Out	Out
SUB	Out	Out	Out	Out	Out	Out	2236*	41	2763*	59
PART	Out	Out	Out	Out	Out	Out	Out	Out	Out	Out
PRIO	14768	851	54324	237	86522	228	512	48	739	63

Table 5. Capacity comparison on verification and falsification problems

These results only confirm the trend noticed in section 4.2. While CLS had a slight edge for average verification problems, for the difficult examples PRIO has better chances for success than both SUB and PART. All the arguments mentioned above still apply here: PRIO wins against SUB due to the balanced partitioning, and is better than PART due to its mixed BFS/DFS strategy.

5 Conclusions

The ability of the same algorithm to address both verification and falsification problems is critical in an industrial context. The prioritized traversal proposed here achieves this goal by combining the best features of subsetting traversal [1] and partitioned traversal [13]. As in [1], the mixed BFS/DFS strategy makes the algorithm efficient for falsification problems. As in [13], using balancing instead of density as the partitioning criterion makes partitioned traversal suitable for verification problems. The results reported on Intel designs show a marked improvement on existing exact and partial traversal techniques.

Another important contribution of this paper is the fast splitting algorithm. As it addresses the general BDD decomposition problem, we suspect that such an algorithm might be useful for many other applications relying on BDD technology. In the specific context of partitioned traversal the speed of the algorithm outweighs the loss in the quality of the partitions, resulting in a significant reduction of the overall traversal time.

Also it is worthwhile to note that the usage of prioritized traversal is not limited to reachability analysis and invariant checking. It can be easily adapted to other least-fixpoint computations, like the evaluation of CTL formulas of type EU or EF. Since the evaluation of such formulas involves a backward traversal of the state space, one only has to replace the image operator with the pre-image one in order to get the corresponding dual algorithm.

6 References

[1] K.Ravi, F. Somenzi, "High Density Reachability Analysis", in Proceedings of ICCAD'95
[2] M.Ganai, A Aziz, "Efficient Coverage Directed State Space Search", in Proceedings of IWLS'98
[3] J. Yuan, J.Shen, J.Abraham, and A.Aziz, "On Combining Formal and Informal Verification", in Proceedings of CAV'97
[4] C.Yang, D.Dill, "Validation with Guided Search of the State Space", In Proceedings of DAC'98
[5] A.Aziz, J.Kukula, T. Shiple, "Hybrid Verification Using Saturated Simulation", In Proceedings of DAC'98
[6] R.Bryant, "Graph-based Algorithms for Boolean Function Manipulations", IEEE Transactions on Computers,C-35:677-691, August 1986.
[7] K.L. McMillan. "Symbolic Model Checking", Kluwer 1993.
[8] T.R. Shiple "Formal Analysis of Synchronous Circuits". PhD thesis, University of California at Berkeley, 1996.
[9] K. Ravi, K.L. McMillan, T.R. Shiple, F. Somenzi "Approximation and Decomposition of Binary Decision Diagrams", in Proceedings of DAC'98.
[10] O. Coudert, J. Madre "A Unified Framework for the Formal Verification of Sequential Circuits", in Proceedings of ICCAD'90.
[11] K.Ravi, F. Somenzi, "Efficient Fixpoint Computation for Invariant Checking", In Proceedings of ICCD'99, pp. 467-474.
[12] B. Lin, R. Newton "Implicit Manipulation of Equivalence Classes Using Binary Decision Diagrams" in Proceedings of ICCD'91.
[13] G.Cabodi, P.Camurati, S.Quer. "Improved Reachability Analysis of Large Finite State Machines" in Proceedings of ICCAD'96.
[14] A.Narayan, J.Jain, M.Fujita, A.Sangiovanni-Vincentelli. "Partitioned ROBDDs – A Compact, Canonical and Efficiently Manipulable Representation for Boolean Functions" in Proceedings of ICCAD'96.
[15] R.Fraer, G.Kamhi, L.Fix, M.Vardi. "Evaluating Semi-Exhaustive Verification Techniques for Bug Hunting" in Proceedings of SMC'99.
[16] I.Beer, S. Ben-David, A.Landver. "On-the-Fly Model Checking" of RCTL Formulas", in Proceedings of CAV'98.
[17] G. Cabodi, P. Camurati, S. Quer, "Improving the Efficiency of BDD-Based Operators by Means of Partitioning," IEEE Transactions on CAD, pp. 545-556, May 1999.
[18] F.Somenzi, " CUDD : CU Decision Diagram Package – Release 2.3.0", Technical Report, Dept. Electrical and Computer Engineering, University of Colorado, Boulder
[19] R. H. Hardin, R. P. Kurshan, K. L. McMillan, J. A. Reeds and N. J. A. Sloane, "Efficient Regression Verification", Int'l Workshop on Discrete Event Systems (WODES '96), 19-21 August, Edinburgh, IEE, London, 1996, pp. 147-150.
[20] J. R. Burch, E. M. Clarke, D. E. Long, K. L. McMillan, D. L. Dill, "Symbolic Model Checking for Sequential Circuit Verification", IEEE Transactions on Computer-Aided Designs of Integrated Circuits and Systems, 401-424 Vol.13, No. 4, April 1994.

Regular Model Checking

Ahmed Bouajjani[1], Bengt Jonsson[2], Marcus Nilsson*[2], and Tayssir Touili[1]

[1] LIAFA, Univ. Paris 7, Case 7014, 2 place Jussieu, 75251 Paris Cedex 05, France
{Ahmed.Bouajjani,Tayssir.Touili}@liafa.jussieu.fr
[2] Dept. of Computer Systems, P.O. Box 325, S-751 05 Uppsala, Sweden
{bengt, marcusn}@docs.uu.se

Abstract. We present *regular model checking*, a framework for algorithmic verification of infinite-state systems with, e.g., queues, stacks, integers, or a parameterized linear topology. States are represented by strings over a finite alphabet and the transition relation by a regular length-preserving relation on strings. Major problems in the verification of parameterized and infinite-state systems are to compute the set of states that are reachable from some set of initial states, and to compute the transitive closure of the transition relation. We present two complementary techniques for these problems. One is a direct automata-theoretic construction, and the other is based on widening. Both techniques are incomplete in general, but we give sufficient conditions under which they work. We also present a method for verifying ω-regular properties of parameterized systems, by computation of the transitive closure of a transition relation.

1 Introduction

This paper presents *regular model checking*, intended as a uniform paradigm for algorithmic verification of several classes of parameterized and infinite-state systems. Regular model checking considers systems whose states can be represented as finite strings of arbitrary length over a finite alphabet. This includes parameterized systems consisting of an arbitrary number of homogeneous finite-state processes connected in a linear or ring-formed topology, and systems that operate on queues, stacks, integers, and other data structures that can be represented by sequences of symbols.

Regular model checking can be seen as symbolic model checking, in which regular sets words over a finite alphabet is used as a symbolic representation of sets of states, and in which regular length-preserving relations between words, usually in the form of finite-state transducers, represent transition relations. This framework has been advocated by, e.g., Kesten et al. [KMM+97] and by Boigelot and Wolper [WB98], as a uniform framework for analyzing several classes of parameterized and infinite-state systems, where automata-theoretic algorithms

---

* supported in part by the ASTEC competence center, and by the Swedish Board for Industrial and Technical Development (NUTEK)

for manipulation of regular sets can be exploited. Such algorithms have been implemented, e.g., in the Mona [HJJ+96] and MoSel [KMMG97] packages.

A major problem in regular model checking is that the standard iteration-based methods, used for finite-state systems (e.g., [BCMD92]), to compute, e.g., the set of reachable states, are guaranteed to terminate only if there is a bound on the distance (in number of transitions) from the initial configurations to any reachable configuration. An analogous observation holds if we perform a reachability backwards, from a set of "unsafe" configurations, as in [KMM+97]. In general, a parameterized or infinite-state system does not have such a bound. To explore the entire state-space, one must therefore be able to calculate the effect of arbitrarily long sequences of transitions. For instance, consider a transition of a parameterized system in which a process passes a token to its neighbor. The effect of an arbitrarily long sequence of such transitions will be to pass the token to any other process through an arbitrary sequence of neighbors.

The problem of calculating the effect of arbitrarily long sequences of transitions has been addressed for certain classes of systems, e.g., systems with unbounded FIFO channels [BG96,BGWW97,BH97,ABJ98], systems with pushdown stacks [BEM97,Cau92,FWW97], systems with counters [BW94,CJ98], and certain classes of parameterized systems [ABJN99]. A more uniform calculation of the *transitive closure* of a transition relation was presented in our previous work [JN00] for the case that the transition relation satisfies a condition of *bounded local depth*. This construction was used to verify safety properties of several parameterized algorithms and algorithms that operate on unbounded FIFO channels or on counters.

In this paper, we develop the regular model checking paradigm further. We give a simple and uniform presentation of the program model, which is simpler than that used in [JN00]. The main part of the paper considers the problem of calculating the set of configurations reachable from a set of initial configurations via a transition relation, and the problem of computing the transitive closure of a transition relation. We present two complementary techniques to attack these problems:

- The first technique is an automata-theoretic construction, which uses the standard subset-construction and minimization techniques from automata theory. The construction succeeds if the resulting automaton is finite-state. It generalizes the transitive closure construction in [JN00].
- The second technique is based on computing fixpoints using widening, in the spirit of [CC77]. We propose exact widening techniques for regular languages and show how to use them for reachability analysis and for computing transitive closures.

As another main contribution, we show how to verify *liveness properties* (or, more generally, ω-regular properties). When applied to parameterized systems, our method allows to prove, e.g., absence of starvation in resource allocation algorithms. In general, it allows to prove a liveness property, given an arbitrary number of *parameterized fairness requirements*. For instance, in a parameterized algorithm there is typically a fairness requirement associated with each process.

Our method is based on a reduction of the model-checking problem of ω-regular properties to the problem of finding fair loops, which can be detected after having computed the transitive closure of a transition relation.

Both the automata-theoretic and the widening-based techniques presented in this paper have been implemented and experimented on several examples of parameterized and infinite-state systems, including different parameterized algorithms for mutual exclusion (e.g., the Bakery algorithm by Lamport, Burns protocol, Dijkstra algorithm), unbounded FIFO-channel systems (e.g., Alternating-bit protocol), and counter systems (e.g., Sliding Window protocol with unbounded sequence numbers).

Outline In the next section, we present the framework of regular model checking, and define the verification problems that are considered in the paper. In Section 3 we present an automata-theoretic construction for computing the transitive closure of a transition relation. The construction can also be used to compute reachability sets. Sect. 4 presents widening techniques for the same problem. A method for model checking of ω-regular properties is given in Sect. 5, and concluding remarks are given in Sect, 6.

Related Work Previous work on the general aspects of regular model checking, and on analyzing classes of systems, e.g., pushdown systems, parameterized systems, systems with FIFO channels, or with counters, has already been mentioned earlier in the introduction. The acceleration techniques presented in this paper are able to emulate the acceleration operations for FIFO channels reported in [BG96].

Widening techniques have been introduced in [CC77] in order to speed up the computation of fixpoints in the framework of abstract interpretation. Many works have proposed widening operators for different kinds of systems, e.g., widening operators defined on representations based on convex polyhedra for use in the analysis of systems operating on integers or reals (e.g., [CH78,Hal93]), or widening operators on automata [LHR97]. All these techniques compute upper approximations of the desired fixpoint.

Other researchers, e.g., [FO97,Sis97], use regular sets in a deductive framework, where basic manipulations on regular sets are performed automatically. These methods are based on proving an invariant given by the user or by some invariant generation technique, but are not fully automatic. In [FO97], the authors show how to check that a given regular set is the reachability set of special kind of relations. We use their result to prove that our widening technique is exact. However, they do not provide any technique to find automatically the fixpoint.

2 Preliminaries

2.1 Model

We introduce the program model used in regular model checking.

Let Σ be a finite alphabet. As usual, Σ^* is the set of finite words over Σ. A relation R on Σ^* is *regular* and *length-preserving* if w and w' are of equal length whenever $(w, w') \in R$, and the set $\{(a_1, a_1') \cdots (a_n, a_n') : (a_1 \cdots a_n, a_1' \cdots a_n') \in R\}$ is a regular subset of $(\Sigma \times \Sigma)^*$. In the following, we will implicitly understand that a regular relation is also length-preserving. A regular relation can be conveniently recognized by a finite-state transducer over $(\Sigma \times \Sigma)$.

Definition 1. A *program* is a triple $\mathcal{P} = \langle \Sigma, \phi_I, R \rangle$ where

Σ is a finite alphabet,
ϕ_I is a regular set over Σ, denoting a set of *initial configurations*, and
R is a regular relation on Σ^*, sometimes called the *transition relation*. □

A *configuration* w of a program $\mathcal{P}$ is a word $a_1 a_2 \cdots a_n$ over Σ. We denote by $R_{id} = \{(w, w') : w = w'\}$ the identity relation on configurations. Regular relations can be composed to yield new regular relations. For two regular relations R and R', their union $R \cup R'$, intersection $R \cap R'$, sequential (or relational) composition $R \circ R'$, and concatenation $R \cdot R'$ are regular.

2.2 Modeling Parameterized and Infinite-State Systems

We give two examples of different classes of systems that can be modeled in the framework of the preceding subsection. More examples can be found in [JN00].

Parameterized Systems. Consider a parameterized system consisting of an arbitrary number of homogeneous finite-state processes connected in a linear topology. A configuration of this system can be represented by a word over an alphabet consisting of the set of states for each process, where the length of the word equals the number of processes. A particular example of such a system is an array of processes that pass a token from the left to the right. Each process can be in one of two states, $\bot$ or t, where $\bot$ denotes that the process does not have the token, and t denotes that the process has the token. We model this system as the program $\mathcal{P} = \langle \Sigma, \phi_I, R \rangle$ where

- $\Sigma = \{\bot, t\}$ is the set of states of a process,
- $\phi_I = t\bot^*$ is the set of initial configurations, in which the leftmost process has the token, and
- $R = (\bot, \bot)^* \cdot (t, \bot) \cdot (\bot, t) \cdot (\bot, \bot)^* \ \cup \ (\bot, \bot)^* \cdot ((\bot, \bot) \cup (t, t)) \cdot (\bot, \bot)^*$
  is the union of two relations, of which the first denotes the passing of the token from a process to its right neighbor, and the second denotes an idling computation step. Note that the transition relation is implicitly constrained by the invariant that there is exactly one token in the system.

Systems Communicating over Unbounded FIFO Channels As another example, consider systems of finite-state processes that communicate over unbounded FIFO channels. Assume for simplicity that there is only one FIFO channel, containing a sequence of messages in the finite set $\mathcal{M}$. Let Q be the finite set of combinations of control states of the processes. A configuration of this system can be modeled as a word of the form

$$q \perp\perp \cdots \perp\ m_1 m_2 \cdots m_n\ \perp\perp \cdots \perp$$

where $q \in Q$ is the current control state, and $m_1 m_2 \cdots m_n$ is the sequence of messages in the channel. In order to allow messages to be added to and removed from the channel, we add an arbitrary amount of "padding symbols" $\perp$ before and after the sequence of messages. Thus, we can model this system as the program $\mathcal{P} = \langle \Sigma, \phi_I, R \rangle$, where

- $\Sigma = Q \cup \mathcal{M} \cup \{\perp\}$,
- ϕ_I is the regular set $q_i \perp^*$ of configurations with no message in the channel, and the initial control state q_i,
- R is the union of several relations: one for each operation in the system. An operation which sends a message $m \in \mathcal{M}$ while making a transition from control state q to q' is modeled by the relation

$$(q, q') \cdot (\perp, \perp)^* \cdot (R_{id} \cap \mathcal{M}^2)^* \cdot (\perp, m) \cdot (\perp, \perp)^*$$

Receive operations are modeled in a similar way.

2.3 Verification

Let R be a regular relation. We use R^+ to denote the transitive closure of R, and R^* to denote the reflexive and transitive closure of R, and R^{-1} to denote the inverse of R. For a regular set ϕ of configurations, $R(\phi)$ denotes the image $\{w' : \exists w \in \phi.(w, w') \in R\}$ of ϕ under R.

In this paper, we will consider two verification problems:

- *Computing Reachability Sets:* Given a regular set ϕ of configurations and a regular relation R, compute the reachability set $R^*(\phi)$. This can be used for checking whether some configuration in a set ϕ_F is reachable from a set ϕ_I of initial configurations, either by checking whether $\phi_F \cap R^*(\phi_I) = \emptyset$ (forward reachability analysis), or whether $\phi_I \cap (R^{-1})^*(\phi_F) = \emptyset$ (backward reachability analysis). If R is a union $R_1 \cup \cdots \cup R_k$ of several regular relations, then one can also compute the set of reachable configurations stepwise, by repeatedly extending the set ϕ of currently reached configurations by $R_i^*(\phi)$ for some i.
- *Computing Transitive Closure:* Given a regular relation R, compute its transitive closure R^+. The transitive closure can be used for finding loops of parameterized systems. The relation $R^+ \cap R_{id}$ represents the identity relation on the set of configurations that can reach themselves via a non-empty sequence of computation steps. To obtain the loops that can actually occur in an execution, we intersect this set with the set of reachable configurations, computed as a reachability set. The transitive closure can also be used for computing the reachability set.

A straight-forward approach to computing $R^*(\phi)$ is to compute a sequence of unions $\cup_{i=0}^{n} R^i(\phi)$ for $n = 1, 2, 3, \ldots$ until a fixpoint is reached, i.e., $\cup_{i=0}^{n} R^i(\phi) = \cup_{i=0}^{n+1} R^i(\phi)$ for some n. This approach is guaranteed to terminate for finite-state systems [BCMD92], but in general not for parameterized and infinite-state systems, as observed, e.g., in [ABJN99]. The analogous observation holds for the approach of computing R^+ through the sequence of unions $\cup_{i=1}^{n} R^i$ for $n = 1, 2, 3, \ldots$ until convergence.

We present two complementary techniques which are applicable to both of the above problems.

- A direct automata-theoretic construction for computing $R^*(\phi)$ or R^+, which is based on the transducer for R. It is presented in Section 3.
- A technique based on widening, in the spirit of [CC77] is presented in Section 4. The technique is based on observing successive approximations to $R^*(\phi)$, and trying to guess automatically the limit. The guess can always be checked to be an upper-approximation, and to be *exact* under some conditions. The technique can also be applied to the computation of R^*, by viewing it as a regular set over $\Sigma \times \Sigma$.

3 Automata Theoretic Construction of the Transitive Closure

In this section, we present a technique for computing R^+, which attempts to compute a minimal deterministic transducer that recognizes R^+ using the standard subset-construction and minimization techniques from elementary automata theory. The technique can also, with obvious modifications, be used for computing $R^*(\phi)$. We will here concentrate on the transitive closure construction, and only briefly summarize the reachability set construction at the end of this section.

Our transitive closure construction is not guaranteed to terminate, in particular if R^+ is not regular. However, if R has bounded *local depth*, a concept introduced in [JN00], a slightly modified version of our construction will yield a finite transducer.

3.1 The Transducer Construction

For the remainder of this section, let R be a regular relation on Σ, represented as a finite-state transducer $R = \langle Q, q_0, \delta, F \rangle$ where Q is the set of states, q_0 is the initial state, $\delta : (Q \times (\Sigma \times \Sigma)) \mapsto 2^Q$ is the transition function, and $F \subseteq Q$ is the set of accepting states. For each pair (w, w') in R^+, there is a sequence $w^0, w^1, \ldots, w^m$ of configurations such that $w = w^0$, $w' = w^m$ and $(w^{i-1}, w^i) \in R$ for $0 < i \leq m$. Let w^i be the word $a_1^i a_2^i \cdots a_n^i$ of length n. Then $(w^{i-1}, w^i) \in R$ means that there is a run $q_0^i q_1^i \cdots q_n^i$ of R which accepts the word

$(a_1^{i-1}, a_1^i) (a_2^{i-1}, a_2^i) \cdots (a_n^{i-1}, a_n^i)$. Let us organize these runs into a matrix of form:

$$q_0^1 \xrightarrow{(a_1^0, a_1^1)} q_1^1 \xrightarrow{(a_2^0, a_2^1)} q_2^1 \cdots q_{n-1}^1 \xrightarrow{(a_n^0, a_n^1)} q_n^1$$
$$q_0^2 \xrightarrow{(a_1^1, a_1^2)} q_1^2 \xrightarrow{(a_2^1, a_2^2)} q_2^2 \cdots q_{n-1}^2 \xrightarrow{(a_n^1, a_n^2)} q_n^2$$
$$\vdots \quad \vdots \quad \vdots$$
$$q_0^m \xrightarrow{(a_1^{m-1}, a_1^m)} q_1^m \xrightarrow{(a_2^{m-1}, a_2^m)} q_2^m \cdots q_{n-1}^m \xrightarrow{(a_n^{m-1}, a_n^m)} q_n^m$$

with m rows, where each row shows a run of the transducer R with n transitions.

The first step in our construction of R^+ is to regard the above matrix as a single run of another transducer, whose states are columns (i.e., sequences) of form $q^1 q^2 \cdots q^m$ for $m \geq 1$, and whose transitions represent the relationship between adjacent columns in a matrix of the above form. More precisely, define the *column transducer for* R^+ as the tuple $\langle Q^+, q_0^+, \Delta, F^+ \rangle$ where

- Q^+ is the set of non-empty sequences of states of R,
- q_0^+ is the set of non-empty sequences of initial states of R,
- $\Delta : (Q^+ \times (\Sigma \times \Sigma)) \mapsto 2^{Q^+}$ is defined as follows: for any columns $r^1 r^2 \cdots r^m$ and $q^1 q^2 \cdots q^m$, and pair (a, a'), we have $r^1 r^2 \cdots r^m \in \Delta(q^1 q^2 \cdots q^m, (a, a'))$ iff there are $a^0, a^1, \ldots, a^m$ with $a = a^0$ and $a' = a^m$ such that $r^i \in \delta(q^i, (a^{i-1}, a^i))$ for $1 \leq i \leq m$.

It is not difficult to show that the column transducer for R^+ accepts exactly the relation R^+. The only problem is that it has infinitely many states. We will therefore determinize it using the standard subset-construction, in the hope of decreasing the number of states. Let x, y range over columns and X, Y over sets of columns. The subset construction applied to the column transducer for R^+ yields the automaton, $\langle 2^{Q^+}, q_0^+, \wp\Delta, \mathcal{F} \rangle$ whose states are sets of columns of states of R, whose initial state is the set q_0^+ of columns of initial states, whose set $\mathcal{F}$ of accepting states is the set of states with at least one column in F^+, and whose transition function $\wp\Delta$ is the lifting of Δ to sets: $\wp\Delta(X, (a, a')) = \bigcup_{x \in X} \Delta(x, (a, a'))$. We note that for each pair (a, a'), the relation $\{(x, y) : y \in \Delta(x, (a, a'))\}$ is regular, so that a transducer which implements the function $\wp\Delta$ can be constructed directly from the definition of Δ. It follows that if X is a regular set of columns, then $\wp\Delta(X)$ is also a regular set of columns, which can be constructed by composing the automaton for X with that for $\wp\Delta$ and projecting onto the "next column".

In most cases, the subset construction does not yield a finite automaton. We therefore try to make it smaller by identifying equivalent sets of columns during the construction (cf. the minimization of deterministic finite automata). For a set X of columns (i.e., a state in the subset-automaton), let suff(X) denote the set of suffixes of X, i.e., the set of words $\pi \in (\Sigma \times \Sigma)^*$ such that $\wp\Delta(X, \pi) \in \mathcal{F}$. Two sets X, Y of columns are *equivalent* if suff(X) = suff(Y). We employ a simple (and incomplete) technique to detect equivalent sets, based on *saturation*. The basic idea is to extend (saturate) each set X of columns by additional columns

x such that $\mathsf{suff}(\{x\}) \subseteq \mathsf{suff}(X)$. Hopefully, two equivalent sets of columns will become identical after saturation, in which case they will identified during the subset construction.

Let us present the saturation rule. A state q in the original transducer R is a *copying state* if $\mathsf{suff}(\{q\}) \subseteq R_{id}$, i.e., if its suffixes only perform copying of words. We use the following saturation rule:.

- if $xy \in X$ or if $xqqy \in X$, where x and y are (possibly empty) columns and q is a copying state, then add xqy to X.

It is not difficult to see that $\mathsf{suff}(\{xqy\}) \subseteq \mathsf{suff}(\{xy\})$ and that $\mathsf{suff}(\{xqy\}) \subseteq \mathsf{suff}(\{xqqy\})$, implying the soundness of the saturation rule. Let $\lceil X \rceil$ denote the saturation of X, i.e., the least set of columns containing X which is closed under the above rule. To saturate a regular set of columns is an easy operation on the automaton which represents the set.

It follows from the above construction that the transducer obtained after saturation recognizes R^+. We summarize the discussion in the following theorem.

Theorem 1. *Let $R = \langle Q, q_0, \delta, F \rangle$ be a finite-state transducer. Then the deterministic (possibly infinite-state) transducer $\langle \mathcal{Q}, \lceil q_0^+ \rceil, \tilde{\Delta}, \tilde{\mathcal{F}} \rangle$, where*

- $\mathcal{Q} \subseteq 2^{Q^+}$ *is the set of saturated regular subsets of Q^+,*
- $\tilde{\Delta} : (\mathcal{Q} \times (\Sigma \times \Sigma)) \mapsto \mathcal{Q}$ *is defined by $\tilde{\Delta}(X, (a, a')) = \lceil \wp \Delta(X, (a, a')) \rceil$,*
- $\tilde{\mathcal{F}}$ *are the sets with at least one sequence in F^+.*

accepts the relation R^+. □

It follows that if the set set of reachable states in the above automaton is finite, then R^+ is regular. We can then, using standard techniques, obtain a minimal deterministic finite-state transducer which recognizes R^+.

3.2 A Sufficient Condition for Termination

In [JN00], it was shown that R^+ is regular under some sufficient conditions on a regular relation R. We will restate these conditions and note that the construction given in the previous section, with slight modifications, will terminate under these conditions. It should be noted that these conditions are merely sufficient conditions for regularity, and that there are many other situations in which our construction of R^+ yields a finite-state transducer.

Let R be of the form $\phi_L \cdot R_l \cdot \phi_R$ where

- $\phi_L \subseteq R_{id}$ is a *left context*, i.e., it copies a regular language which can be accepted by a deterministic finite automaton which has a unique accepting state, and which has no transitions from an accepting to a non-accepting state,
- R_l is any regular relation,
- $\phi_R \subseteq R_{id}$ is a *right context*, i.e., the mirror image of some left context.

We say that R has *local depth* k if for each $(w, w') \in R^+$ there is a sequence $w = w^0, w^1, \ldots, w^m = w'$ such that for each $1 \leq i \leq m$ we can find indices l_i and u_i such that

- $(a_1^{i-1} a_2^{i-1} \cdots a_{l_i-1}^{i-1}, a_1^i a_2^i \cdots a_{l_i-1}^i) \in \phi_L$,
- $(a_{u_i+1}^{i-1} a_{u_i+2}^{i-1} \cdots a_n^{i-1}, a_{u_i+1}^i a_{u_i+2}^i \cdots a_n^i) \in \phi_R$, and
- $(a_{l_i}^{i-1} a_{l_i+1}^{i-1} \cdots a_{u_i}^{i-1}, a_{l_i}^i a_{l_i+1}^i \cdots a_{u_i}^i) \in R_l$.

where $w^i = a_1^i a_2^i \cdots a_n^i$ and such that for each position p (with $1 \leq p \leq n$), there are at most k indices i with $1 \leq i \leq m$ such that $l_i \leq p \leq u_i$. Intuitively, the decomposition of R into $\phi_L \cdot R_l \cdot \phi_R$ serves to structure R as a local rewriting R_l in a "context", represented by ϕ_L and ϕ_R. A relation with local depth k never needs to rewrite any element of a word more than k times to relate two words.

Theorem 2. *[JN00] If R has local depth k, for any k, the transitive closure R^+ is regular and can be recognized by a transducer of size exponential in k.* □

The proof of the above theorem divides the set of columns into a finite set of equivalence classes. We will try to apply the same reasoning to the saturated columns in the construction of Theorem 1.

Let a *copied state* be a state whose prefixes are a subset of the identity relation, in analogy with copying states. The key of the proof is the observation that all sets X of columns generated in the subset construction satisfy the following closure property:

- if $xqy \in X$, where x and y are (possibly empty) columns and q is a copied state, then $xzy \in X$ for any $z \in q^*$.

It can be shown that the saturated columns corresponding to sequences of configurations satisfying the conditions of local depth k is built up from sets of the form

$$X_0 q_0 X_1 q_1 \cdots X_{n-1} q_{n-1} X_n$$

with $n \leq k$ and where each q_i with $0 \leq i < n$ is a state in the transducer for R_l and each X_i with $0 \leq i \leq n$ is one of the following sets, where q_L is a copied state and q_R is a copying state:

1. q_R^* 2. $(q_L + q_R)^*$ 3. $(q_L + q_R)^* q_R (q_L + q_R)^*$
4. $q_R(q_L + q_R)^*$ 5. $(q_L + q_R)^* q_R$ 6. $q_R(q_L + q_R)^* q_R$ 7. q_R^+

To obtain the termination result, we therefore restrict the columns in the construction to have up to k states from the transducer for R_l. The conditions on R ensure that it is enough to consider such columns.

3.3 Computing Reachable Configurations

We will finally sketch the modifications for computing instead the set $R^*(\phi)$, where ϕ is a regular set of configurations. Assume that ϕ is recognized by a finite automaton. In the construction of Section 3.1, a run of ϕ will replace the transducer run in the first row of the matrix, with the obvious modifications.

The end result, corresponding to Theorem 1, is a (possibly infinite-state) automaton that recognizes $R^*(\phi)$, with the starting state $\lceil p_0 q_0^* \rceil$, where p_0 is the starting state of an automaton that recognizes ϕ and q_0 is the starting state of a transducer for R.

4 Widening Based Techniques

We present in this section techniques for computing the effect of iterating a regular relation. These techniques are based on using *exact widening* operations in order to speed up the calculation of a regular fixpoint.

Roughly speaking, our techniques consist in (1) guessing automatically the image of iterating a relation starting from some given regular set, and (2) deciding whether this guess is correct.

The guessing technique we use consists in, given a relation R and a set ϕ, comparing the sets ϕ and $R(\phi)$ in order to detect some "growth" (e.g., $R(\phi) = \phi \cdot \Lambda$ for some regular Λ), and then extrapolate by guessing that each application of R will have the same effect (e.g., we guess that the limit could be $\phi \cdot \Lambda^*$). Then, we apply a simple fixpoint test which ensures (in general) that the guessed set is an upper approximation of the set $R^*(\phi)$. This means that using our widening techniques we can capture in one step (at least) all the reachable configurations from ϕ by R^*. Moreover, we show that under some conditions on R, the fixpoint test allows in fact to *decide* the *exactness* of our guess (i.e., that the guessed set in precisely $R^*(\phi)$).

4.1 Widening on Regular Sets

Widening is applied during the iterative construction of the set of reachable configurations in order to help termination. Given a set of configurations $\phi \subseteq \Sigma^*$ and a relation R, a widening step consists in guessing the result of iterating R starting from ϕ by comparing ϕ with $R(\phi)$ (in general, this guess can be made by considering the sets $R^i(\phi)$ up to some finite bound k). Once this guess is made, the obtained set is added to the computed set of configurations and the exploration of the configuration space is continued.

Let $\phi \subseteq \Sigma^*$ and let R be a regular relation on Σ^*. Our widening principle consists in checking whether there are regular sets ϕ_1, ϕ_2, and Λ such that the following two conditions are satisfied

C1: $\phi = \phi_1 \cdot \phi_2$ and $R(\phi) = \phi_1 \cdot \Lambda \cdot \phi_2$,
C2: $\phi_1 \cdot \Lambda^* \cdot \phi_2 = R(\phi_1 \cdot \Lambda^* \cdot \phi_2) \cup \phi$.

and, if C1 and C2 hold, in adding $\phi_1 \cdot \Lambda^* \cdot \phi_2$ to the computed set of configurations.

Intuitively, condition C1 means that the effect of applying R to ϕ is to "add" Λ between ϕ_1 and ϕ_2. Notice that when ϕ_1 or ϕ_2 is equal to $\{\epsilon\}$, this corresponds respectively to the case where a growth occurs to the left or to the right of ϕ. Condition C2 implies that $R^*(\phi) \subseteq \phi_1 \cdot \Lambda^* \cdot \phi_2$. Indeed, C2 means that $\phi_1 \cdot \Lambda^* \cdot \phi_2$ is a fixpoint of $\mathcal{F} = \lambda X. \phi \cup R(X)$ and $R^*(\phi)$ is the least fixpoint of $\mathcal{F}$. Hence, by adding $\phi_1 \cdot \Lambda^* \cdot \phi_2$ to the computed set of configurations, we capture at least all the reachable configurations from ϕ by iterating R.

The inclusion $\phi_1 \cdot \Lambda^* \cdot \phi_2 \subseteq R^*(\phi)$ is not guaranteed in general by C2 (for any kind of relation R). Nevertheless, we show in the next section that for a large class of relations, condition C2 *guarantees* the *exactness* of our technique, i.e., it computes exactly the set $R^*(\phi)$.

The application of the widening principle depends on the quality of the "automatic guessing" part which is implicit in C1. Given two regular sets ϕ and $\phi' = R(\phi)$, we have to *find* regular sets ϕ_1, ϕ_2 and Λ such that C1 holds, and check that for these sets the condition C2 also holds. We use techniques on automata allowing to extract from ϕ and ϕ' these sets. Roughly speaking, these techniques consist in finding cuts in the automata of ϕ and ϕ' that delimit ϕ_1, ϕ_2 and Λ. To reduce the number of choices to examine, we adopt a heuristic which consists in considering cuts at entering vertices to strongly connected components. This heuristic behaves well because almost always the automata we need are of simple forms (e.g., their loops are only self-loops) and the Λ is very often a nonempty word (or a sum of nonempty words $w_1 + \cdots + w_n$), or a set of the form $w \cdot \Lambda'$ or $\Lambda' \cdot w$ where w is a nonempty word.

4.2 Simple Rewriting Relations

We introduce in this section a class of relations for which it can be shown that our widening technique is exact.

A regular relation R is *unary* if it is a subset of $\Sigma \times \Sigma$. A unary relation is *acyclic* if there is no $a \in \Sigma$ such that $(a, a) \in R^+$. A regular relation R is *binary* if it is a subset of $\Sigma^2 \times \Sigma^2$. A binary relation R is a *permutation* if it is a set of pairs of form (ab, ba) where $a, b \in \Sigma$ and $a \neq b$. A permutation is *antisymmetric* if there are no $a, b \in \Sigma$ such that both $(ab, ba) \in R$ and $(ba, ab) \in R$.

A regular relation is defined to be *simple* if it is a finite union of relations of form $\phi_L \cdot R_l \cdot \phi_R$, such that

1. In each sub-relation of form $\phi_L \cdot R_l \cdot \phi_R$, the "contexts" ϕ_L and ϕ_R are regular subsets of R_{id}, and R_l is either unary or binary,
2. The union of all unary R_l's is acyclic,
3. The union of all binary R_l's is antisymmetric.

The class of simple relations is noncomparable with the class of relations of bounded local depth. We can now prove the following theorem, stating that conditions C1 and C2 give an exact guess for simple relations.

Theorem 3. *If R is a simple relation, and if there are regular sets ϕ_1, ϕ_2, and Λ such that conditions C1 and C2 are satisfied, then $R^*(\phi) = \phi_1 \cdot \Lambda^* \cdot \phi_2$.*

To prove this theorem, we need to introduce the notion of *nœtherian* relations. We say that a relation R is *nœtherian* if for every word $w \in \Sigma^*$, there is no infinite sequence $w_0, w_1, w_2, \ldots$ such that $w_0 = w$ and for every $i \geq 0$, $(w_i, w_{i+1}) \in R$ (i.e., no word can be rewritten an infinite number of times). Notice that a length preserving relation R is nœtherian if and only if $R_{id} \cap R^+ = \emptyset$. We can prove the following fact:

Proposition 1. *For every simple relation R, both R and R^{-1} are nœtherian.*

Then, Theorem 3 can be deduced from Proposition 1 and the following result by Fribourg and Olsen on nœtherian relations:

Proposition 2 ([FO97]). *Let R be a relation. If R^{-1} is nœtherian, then for every $\phi, \phi' \subseteq \Sigma^*$, $\phi' = R(\phi') \cup \phi$ if and only if $\phi' = R^*(\phi)$.*

4.3 Constructing Transitive Closures

Given a length preserving relation R, widening can also be used to compute the transitive closure of R. Indeed, R can be seen as a language over $\Sigma \times \Sigma$ and R^+ can be computed as the limit of the sequence $(R^i)_{i>0}$. Our procedure starts from R and computes iteratively the sets R^i for increasing i's. Each step consists in applying the operation $\lambda X. R \circ X$. During this iterative computation, widening operations can be applied in order to jump to the limit. Now, from the definition of nœtherian relations, it is easy to see that:

Lemma 1. *For every nœtherian relation R, the relation $\{((w, w_1), (w, w_2)) : w_2 \in R(w_1)\}$ is nœtherian.*

From Lemma 1 and Proposition 1, we deduce that our widening technique is also *exact* when computing the transitive closure of a simple relation R, starting from R and applying iteratively $\lambda X. R \circ X$. Notice that R^* can be computed in the same manner, starting from R_{id} instead of R.

4.4 Example

We have applied our widening-based techniques to several examples of parameterized systems including the mutual exclusion protocols of Szymanski, Burns, Dijkstra, the Bakery protocol of Lamport, as well as the Token passing protocol. All these examples can be modeled as simple relations, and our procedure terminates for all of them and computes the exact set of reachable configurations. Moreover, our techniques allow also to construct the transitive closures of the relations modeling these systems.

We show here the application of our techniques on the example of the token passing protocol described in section 2.2. It is easy to see that the relation R in this model is indeed simple.

First, let us consider the problem of computing the reachability set. Our procedure starts from the initial set of configurations $\phi_I = t\bot^*$ and computes the set $R(\phi_I) = \bot t\bot^*$. At this point, it checks that condition C1 holds since $R(t\bot^*) = \Lambda \cdot t\bot^*$ where $\Lambda = \bot$. Then, it checks that condition C2 also holds:

$$R(\bot^* t\bot^*) \cup t\bot^* = \bot^* \bot t\bot^* \cup t\bot^* = \bot^* t\bot^*$$

Hence, we can apply an exact widening step by adding $\bot^* t\bot^*$ to the set of reachable configurations. By doing this, our procedure terminates (since no new configurations can be added) and we get the result:

$$R^*(t\bot^*) = \bot^* t\bot^*$$

Now, let us consider the problem of constructing the relation R^+. Our procedure starts from the relation

$$R = (\bot, \bot)^* \cdot (t, \bot) \cdot (\bot, t) \cdot (\bot, \bot)^*$$

(We omit here the part of the relation corresponding to idle transitions.) The first step is to compute R^2 which is:

$$R^2 = (\bot, \bot)^* \cdot (t, \bot) \cdot (\bot, \bot) \cdot (\bot, t) \cdot (\bot, \bot)^*$$

Then, it can be checked that C1 holds because $R = \phi_1 \cdot \phi_2$ and $R^2 = \phi_1 \cdot \Lambda \cdot \phi_2$ with $\phi_1 = (\bot, \bot)^* \cdot (t, \bot)$, $\phi_2 = (\bot, t) \cdot (\bot, \bot)^*$, and $\Lambda = (\bot, \bot)$. It can also be checked that C2 holds:

$$(R \circ (\phi_1 \cdot (\bot, \bot)^* \cdot \phi_2)) \cup R = \phi_1 \cdot (\bot, \bot)^* \cdot (\bot, \bot) \cdot \phi_2 \cup \phi_1 \cdot \phi_2$$
$$= \phi_1 \cdot (\bot, \bot)^* \cdot \phi_2$$

and hence, our procedure gives the result:

$$R^+ = (\bot, \bot)^* \cdot (t, \bot) \cdot (\bot, \bot)^* \cdot (\bot, t) \cdot (\bot, \bot)^*$$

5 Model Checking of ω-Regular Properties

In this section we will show how to reduce the problem of verifying a property specified by a Büchi automaton to the problem of computing the transitive closure. A related technique is presented by Pnueli and Shahar [PS00]. Our technique is based on the observation that the problem of detecting infinite sequences reduces to that of detecting loops. This is true because the transition relation is length preserving which implies that each state, which is a word of a certain length, can only reach a finite set of states. For a program $\mathcal{P} = \langle \Sigma, \phi_I, R \rangle$, we can check for loops by checking the emptiness of the set

$$R^*(\phi_I) \cap R^+ \cap R_{id}$$

We can use this idea to verify that a program satisfies an ω-regular property under a set of fairness requirements, as follows. We use the standard technique [VW86] of encoding the negation of the property to be checked as a Büchi automaton. We also encode each fairness constraint as a Büchi automaton. Actually, we can handle parameterized fairness requirements, using the position as the parameter: simply associate one Büchi automaton with each position in the word, which expresses the fairness constraint for that position. Now construct the product of the program with the Büchi automaton for the negation of the property, and the Büchi automata for the fairness requirements. We must now check whether this product has a reachable "fair loop" in which each Büchi automaton visits an accepting state.

To check for fair loops, we first construct the set of reachable configurations of the product. Then, for each Büchi automaton, we add an observer. This is a bit which can be initialized to *false* in a reachable state and thereafter detects whether the Büchi automaton has visited some accepting state during a sequence of transitions. More precisely, the transition relation is extended so that it sets an observer bit to *true* whenever the corresponding Büchi automaton reaches an accepting state; an observer bit can never become *false* after being set to true.

Let R_{aug} be the so constructed transition relation containing both Büchi automata and their observer bits. Fair loops can now be detected by checking whether R_{aug}^+ relates a reachable state with all observer bits being *false* with the same reachable state but with all observer bits being *true*.

We illustrate this method by verifying a liveness property for the token array system, given in Sect. 2.2, extended with fairness constraints. We will verify that every process eventually gets the token. The negation of this property is "some process never gets the token", which can be expressed by a Büchi automaton accepting an infinite sequence of states of a process where the token is never obtained, i.e., an infinite sequence of the symbol $\bot$. We encode this automaton by adding one boolean variable r which is true at the position at which the Büchi automaton reads symbols and by constraining the transition relation and the set of initial configurations so that

- r is true at exactly one position in the word,
- the truth value of r never changes in any position, and
- the token is never passed to the position where r holds.

We also impose for each process the fairness constraint that "the process may not hold the token indefinitely". For each position, this fairness constraint can be expressed by the Büchi automaton

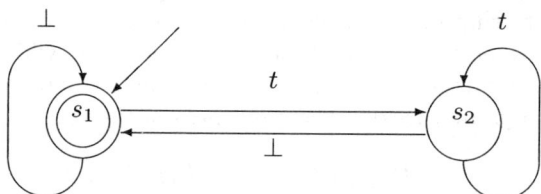

These Büchi automata, one for each position in the word, are encoded by an extra variable s, initialized to s_1 and ranging over the set of automaton states $\{s_1, s_2\}$. The transition relation is extended so that the variable s simulates the state of the above automaton. Let $\hat{\mathcal{P}} = \langle \hat{\Sigma}, \hat{\phi}_I, \hat{R} \rangle$ denote the resulting program obtained by adding the variables r and s as described above.

Finally, a boolean observer s_{obs} is added to each position and the transition relation is changed so that s_{obs} becomes true when s becomes the accepting state s_1. Let R_{aug} be the resulting transition relation.

Let the variable $\hat{a}$ range over $\hat{\Sigma}$, the alphabet of the program $\hat{\mathcal{P}}$. We can now check for *fair* infinite runs that violate the original property ("every process eventually gets the token") by checking emptiness of the set

$$\hat{R}^*(\hat{\phi}_I) \cap R_{aug}^+ \cap (\hat{a} = \hat{a}' \wedge \neg s_{obs} \wedge s'_{obs})^*$$

Note that the set $\hat{R}^*(\hat{\phi}_I)$ can be computed as a reachability set. We have applied the construction given in Sect. 3 to construct a transducer for R_{aug}^+ successfully in our implementation.

6 Conclusions

We have presented *regular model checking*, a framework for algorithmic verification of parameterized and infinite-state systems. To solve verification problems in this framework, we need to reason about the effect of iterating regular relations an unbounded number of times. It is well-known that the verification of safety properties reduces to reachability analysis. Moreover, the verification problem of any ω-regular properties, including liveness properties, can be reduced to the construction of the transitive closure of a regular length-preserving relation.

We have investigated properties of transitive closures, which lead to the development of new techniques for the construction of transitive closures. We have also presented widening-based techniques for constructing transitive closures and for reachability analysis. These techniques can be combined for computing sets of reachable configurations and transitive closures during verification.

Acknowledgments We are grateful to Amir Pnueli for fruitful discussions. Collaboration was supported by a travel grant from the ARTES network for real time research and graduate education in Sweden.

References

[ABJ98]   Parosh Aziz Abdulla, Ahmed Bouajjani, and Bengt Jonsson. On-the-fly analysis of systems with unbounded, lossy fifo channels. In *Proc. 10th CAV*, volume 1427 of *LNCS*, pages 305–318, 1998.

[ABJN99] Parosh Aziz Abdulla, Ahmed Bouajjani, Bengt Jonsson, and Marcus Nilsson. Handling global conditions in parameterized system verification. In *Proc. 11th CAV*, volume 1633 of *LNCS*, pages 134–145, 1999.

[BCMD92] J.R. Burch, E.M. Clarke, K.L. McMillan, and D.L. Dill. Symbolic model checking: 10^{20} states and beyond. *Information and Computation*, 98:142–170, 1992.

[BEM97]   A. Bouajjani, J. Esparza, and O. Maler. Reachability Analysis of Pushdown Automata: Application to Model Checking. In *Proc. CONCUR '97*. LNCS 1243, 1997.

[BG96]   B. Boigelot and P. Godefroid. Symbolic verification of communication protocols with infinite state spaces using QDDs. In Alur and Henzinger, editors, *Proc. 8th CAV*, volume 1102 of *LNCS*, pages 1–12. Springer Verlag, 1996.

[BGWW97] B. Boigelot, P. Godefroid, B. Willems, and P. Wolper. The power of QDDs. In *Proc. of the Fourth International Static Analysis Symposium*, LNCS. Springer Verlag, 1997.

[BH97]   A. Bouajjani and P. Habermehl. Symbolic reachability analysis of fifo-channel systems with nonregular sets of configurations. In *Proc. ICALP '97*, volume 1256 of *LNCS*, 1997.

[BW94] B. Boigelot and P. Wolper. Symbolic verification with periodic sets. In *Proc. 6th CAV*, volume 818 of *LNCS*, pages 55–67. Springer Verlag, 1994.

[Cau92] Didier Caucal. On the regular structure of prefix rewriting. *Theoretical Computer Science*, 106(1):61–86, Nov. 1992.

[CC77] P. Cousot and R. Cousot. Abstract interpretation: A unified model for static analysis of programs by construction or approximation of fixpoints. In *Proc. 4th POPL*, pages 238–252, 1977.

[CH78] Patrick Cousot and Nicholas Halbwachs. Automatic discovery of linear restraints among variables of a program. In *POPL'78*. ACM, 1978.

[CJ98] H. Comon and Y. Jurski. Multiple counters automata, safety analysis and presburger arithmetic. In *CAV'98*. LNCS 1427, 1998.

[FO97] L. Fribourg and H. Olsén. Reachability sets of parametrized rings as regular languages. In *Proc. 2nd INFINITY'97*, volume 9 of *Electronical Notes in Theoretical Computer Science*. Elsevier Science Publishers, July 1997.

[FWW97] A. Finkel, B. Willems, , and P. Wolper. A direct symbolic approach to model checking pushdown systems (extended abstract). In *Proc. Infinity'97, Electronic Notes in Theoretical Computer Science*, Bologna, Aug. 1997.

[Hal93] N. Halbwachs. Delay Analysis in Synchronous Programs. In *CAV'93*. LNCS 697, 1993.

[HJJ+96] J.G. Henriksen, J. Jensen, M. Jørgensen, N. Klarlund, B. Paige, T. Rauhe, and A. Sandholm. Mona: Monadic second-order logic in practice. In *Proc. TACAS '95, 1th TACAS*, volume 1019 of *LNCS*, 1996.

[JN00] Bengt Jonsson and Marcus Nilsson. Transitive closures of regular relations for verifying infinite-state systems. In *Proc. TACAS '00, 6th TACAS*, LNCS, 2000. to appear.

[KMM+97] Y. Kesten, O. Maler, M. Marcus, A. Pnueli, and E. Shahar. Symbolic model checking with rich assertional languages. In O. Grumberg, editor, *Proc. 9th CAV*, volume 1254, pages 424–435, Haifa, Israel, 1997. Springer Verlag.

[KMMG97] P. Kelb, T. Margaria, M. Mendler, and C. Gsottberger. Mosel: A flexible toolset for monadic second–order logic. In *Proc. TACAS '97, Enschede (NL)*, volume 1217 of *LNCS (LNCS)*, pages 183–202, Heidelberg, Germany, March 1997. Springer–Verlag.

[LHR97] D. Lesens, N. Halbwachs, and P. Raymond. Automatic verification of parameterized linear networks of processes. In *24th POPL*, Paris, January 1997.

[PS00] A. Pnueli and E. Shahar. Liveness and acceleration in parameterized verification. In *Proc. 12th CAV*, 2000. In this Volume.

[Sis97] A. Prasad Sistla. Parametrized verification of linear networks using automata as invariants. In O. Grumberg, editor, *Proc. 9th CAV*, volume 1254 of *LNCS*, pages 412–423, Haifa, Israel, 1997. Springer Verlag.

[VW86] M. Y. Vardi and P. Wolper. An automata-theoretic approach to automatic program verification. In *Proc. 1st LICS*, pages 332–344, June 1986.

[WB98] Pierre Wolper and Bernard Boigelot. Verifying systems with infinite but regular state spaces. In *Proc. 10th CAV*, volume 1427 of *LNCS*, pages 88–97, Vancouver, July 1998. Springer Verlag.

Symbolic Techniques for Parametric Reasoning about Counter and Clock Systems

Aurore Annichini[1], Eugene Asarin[1], and Ahmed Bouajjani[2]

[1] VERIMAG, Centre Equation, 2 av. de Vignate, 38610 Gières, France.
{Aurore.Annichini,Eugene.Asarin}@imag.fr

[2] LIAFA, Univ. of Paris 7, Case 7014, 2 place Jussieu, 75251 Paris Cedex 5, France.
abou@liafa.jussieu.fr

Abstract. We address the problem of automatic analysis of parametric counter and clock automata. We propose a semi-algorithmic approach based on using (1) expressive symbolic representation structures called Parametric DBM's, and (2) accurate extrapolation techniques allowing to speed up the reachability analysis and help its termination. The techniques we propose consist in guessing automatically the effect of iterating a control loop an arbitray number of times, and in checking that this guess is exact. Our approach can deal uniformly with systems that generate linear or nonlinear sets of configurations. We have implemented our techniques and experimented them on nontrivial examples such as a parametric timed version of the Bounded Retransmission Protocol.

1 Introduction

Counter automata and clock automata (timed automata) are widely used models of both hardware and software systems. A lot of effort has been devoted to the design of analysis techniques for these models (see e.g., [AD94,HNSY92,Hal93, BW94,BGL98,CJ98]). While the verification problem is undecidable in general for counter automata, this problem is decidable for timed automata [AD94], and there are model-checking algorithms and efficient verification tools for them [DOTY96,LPY97].

In this paper, we address the problem of analysing *parametric* counter and timed automata, i.e., models with counters and/or clocks that can be compared with parameters defined lower and upper bounds on their possible values. These parameters may range over infinite domains and are in general related by a set of constraints. We are interested in reasoning in a parametric way about the behaviours of a system: *verify* that the system satisfies some property for *all* possible values of the parameters, or *find* constraints on the parameters defining the set of all possible values for which the system satisfies a property. These two problems, i.e., parametric verification and parameter synthesis, can be solved (in the case of safety properties) as reachability problems in parametric models. Unfortunately, classical timed automata, where clocks can only be compared to constants, do not allow such a *parametric reasoning*. Moreover, it has been shown that for parametric timed automata, the reachability problem is undecidable [AHV93].

In this paper, we propose a semi-algorithmic approach that allows to deal with parametric counter and timed systems. We define new symbolic representations for use in their reachability analysis, and provide powerful and accurate techniques for computing representations of their sets of reachable configurations. The representation structures we define are extensions of the Difference Bound Matrices that are commonly used for representing reachability sets of (nonparametric) timed automata [Dil89,ACD+92,Yov98]. Our structures, called Parametric DBM's (PDBM's) encode constraints on counters and/or clocks expressing the fact that their values (and their differences) range in *parametric bound intervals*, i.e., the bounds of these intervals depend from the parameters. PDBM's are coupled with a set of constraints on the parameters. Such Constrained PDBM's allow to represent linear as well as nonlinear sets of configurations. We show in the paper how the basic manipulation operations on DBM's can be lifted to the parametric case, and then, we address the problem of computing the set of reachable configurations using Constrained PDBM's.

The main contribution of the paper is the definition of accurate extrapolation techniques that allow to speed up the computation of the reachability set and help the termination of the analysis. Our extrapolation technique consists in *guessing* automatically the effect of iterating a control loop (a loop in the control graph of the model) an arbitrary number of times, and *checking*, also automatically, that this guess is *exact*. More precisely, we can decide the exactness in the linear case and a subclass of the nonlinear case which can be reduced to the linear one. Hence, our extrapolation technique allows to generate automatically the *exact* set of reachable configurations. Furthermore, the extrapolation principle we propose is simple and uniform for counter and clock systems, which allows to consider systems with both kinds of variables. Another feature of our techniques is that they allow the automatic analysis of systems that generate *nonlinear* sets of configurations, which is beyond the scope of the existing algorithmic analysis techniques and tools.

We have implemented a package on Constrained PDBM's as well as a reachability analysis procedure based on our extrapolation techniques. We have experimented our prototype on nontrivial examples including systems generating linear sets of reachable configurations, as well as systems generating nonlinear sets of constraints. In all these examples, our analysis procedure terminates and generates the exact set of reachable configurations. These experiments show that our approach is powerful and accurate. In particular, we have been able to verify automatically a parametric timed version of the Bounded Retransmission Protocol (BRP) [HSV94]. The model we consider is a parametric timed counter system where parameters are constrained by nonlinear formulas (defined in [DKRT97]).

Outline: In Section 2, we give some basic definitions and introduce the kind of constraints and operations we use in our models. In Section 3, we introduce the parametric counter and timed systems. In Section 4, we introduce the PDBM's and the basic operations we consider on these structures. In Section 5, we define extrapolation techniques and show their use in reachability analysis. In Section 6, we discuss the current status of our implementation and experiments.

Related Work: The (semi-)algorithmic symbolic approach have been used for counter automata and timed systems in many works such as [CH78,HNSY92, Hal93,BW94,HHWT95,BGL98,BGP98,CJ98]. However, none of the existing works can deal with systems with nonlinear sets of reachable configurations.

Our extrapolation techniques have the same motivation as the widening operations [CH78,BGP98] used in the framework of abstract interpretation [CC77], and the techniques based on the use of meta-transitions [BW94,CJ98]. The aim of all these techniques is to speed up the computation of the reachable configurations and help the termination of the analysis. However, the existing widening techniques compute upper approximations using convex polyhedra. Our techniques are more accurate since they compute the exact effect of iterating an operation (control loop) an arbitrary number of times. Hence, our techniques are similar from this point of view to the techniques based on computing meta-transitions such as [BW94]. Compared with the technique of [BW94] for instance, our technique can sometimes detect "periodicities" more efficiently because it takes into account the set of configurations under consideration.

Furthermore, our extrapolation techniques are based on a principle of *guessing* the effect of the iterations which is in the same spirit as the principle of widening. But our principle differs technically from it and also differs from widening because we can check that our guess is exact. The principle of checking the exactness of a guess has been used in [FO97] in the context of system on strings. However, the techniques in [FO97] are different from ours, and [FO97] does not address the question of making a guess.

The problem of verifying the BRP has been addressed by several researchers [HSV94,GdP96,Mat96,DKRT97]. However these work either provide manual proofs, or use finite-state model-checking on abstract versions of the protocol or for particular instances of its parameters. In [AAB99a,AAB+99b] we have verified automatically an infinite-state version of the protocol with unbounded queues. However, we have considered in that work an abstraction of the clocks and counters and we have ignored the timing aspects that are addressed in this paper. In [DKRT97] the constraints that must be satisfied by the parameters are investigated. Then, their automatic verification using Uppaal is done only for a finite set of particular values satisfying these constraints. As far as we know, our work is the first one which allows to check automatically that these (nonlinear) constraints indeed allow the BRP to meet its specifications.

2 Preliminaries

Let $\mathcal{X}$ be a set of variables and let x range over $\mathcal{X}$. The set of *arithmetical terms* over $\mathcal{X}$, denoted $AT(\mathcal{X})$, is defined by the grammar:

$$t ::= 0 \mid 1 \mid x \mid t - t \mid t + t \mid t * t$$

The set of *first-order arithmetical formulas* over $\mathcal{X}$, denoted $FO(\mathcal{X})$, is defined by the grammar:

$$\phi ::= t \leq t \mid \neg \phi \mid \phi \vee \phi \mid \exists x.\ \phi \mid Is\_int(t)$$

Formulas are interpreted over the set of reals. The predicate Is_int expresses the constraint that a term has an integer value.

The fragment of $FO(\mathcal{X})$ of formulas without the Is_int predicate is called the *first-order arithmetics of reals* and denoted $RFO(\mathcal{X})$. The fragment of $FO(\mathcal{X})$ of formulas without multiplication ($*$) is called the *linear arithmetics* and is denoted $LFO(\mathcal{X})$. It is well-known that the problem of satisfiability in $FO(\mathcal{X})$ is undecidable, whereas it is decidable for both fragments $RFO(\mathcal{X})$ and $LFO(\mathcal{X})$.

Let $\mathcal{P}$ be a set of *parameters*. Then, a *simple parametric constraint* is a conjunction of formulas of the form $x \prec t$ or $x - y \prec t$, where $x, y \in \mathcal{X}$, $\prec \in \{<, \leq\}$, and $t \in AT(\mathcal{P})$. We denote by $SC(\mathcal{X}, \mathcal{P})$ the set of simple parametric constraints.

Each simple parametric constraint defines a family of convex polyhedra with parametric bounds. These polyhedra are of a special kind called *zones* in the timed automata literature. Notice that if all the bounds in a simple constraint are parameter-free terms (i.e., they represent constant values), then this constraint defines a unique convex polyhedron (zone).

We consider *simple operations* on variables corresponding to special kinds of assignments. We allow assignments of variables that are either of the form $x := y + t$ or of the form $x := t$, where $x, y \in \mathcal{X}$ are variables (x and y may be the same variable), and $t \in AT(\mathcal{P})$.

3 Parametric Timed Counter Systems

A Parametric Timed System (PTS) is a tuple $\mathcal{T} = (Q, C, P, I, \delta)$ where

- Q is a finite set of *control states*,
- $C = \{c_1, \ldots, c_n\}$ is a finite set of *clocks*,
- P is a finite set of *parameters*,
- $I : Q \to SC(C, P)$ is a function associating *invariants* with control states,
- δ is a finite set of *transitions* of the form (q_1, g, sop, q_2) where $q_1, q_2 \in Q$, $g \in SC(C, P)$ is a *guard*, and sop is a simple operation over C.

Clocks and parameters range over a set $\mathbb{D}$ which can be either the set of positive reals $\mathbb{R}^{\geq 0}$ (dense-time model) or the set of positive integers $\mathbb{N}$ (discrete-time model). Parameters can be seen as variables that are not modified by the system (they keep their initial values all the time). A configuration of $\mathcal{T}$ is a triplet $\langle q, \nu, \gamma \rangle$ where $q \in Q$, $\nu : C \to \mathbb{D}$ is a valuation of the clocks, and $\gamma : P \to \mathbb{D}$ is a valuation of the parameters.

Given a transition $\tau = (q_1, g, sop, q_2) \in \delta$, we define a transition relation $\to_\tau$ between configurations: $\langle q_1, \nu_1, \gamma_1 \rangle \to_\tau \langle q_2, \nu_2, \gamma_2 \rangle$ iff $(\nu_1, \gamma) \models g$ and $\nu_2 = sop(\nu_1)$. We also define a time-transition relation $\leadsto$ between configurations:

$\langle q_1, \nu_1, \gamma_1 \rangle \rightsquigarrow \langle q_2, \nu_2, \gamma_2 \rangle$ iff $q_1 = q_2$ and $\exists r \in \mathbb{D}.\ \nu_2 = \nu_1 + r$ and $\forall r' \leq r.\ (\nu_1 + r', \gamma) \models I(q_1)$.

Let $\tau \in \delta$ and let Σ be set of configurations. Then, we define $post_\tau(\Sigma)$ to be the set $\{\sigma\ :\ \exists \sigma' \in \Sigma.\ \sigma' \rightsquigarrow \circ \rightarrow_\tau \circ \rightsquigarrow \sigma\}$, and $post(\Sigma) = \bigcup_{\tau \in \delta} post_\tau(\Sigma)$. Given a sequence of transitions $\theta = \tau_1, \ldots, \tau_n$, we define $post_\theta = post_{\tau_n} \circ \cdots \circ post_{\tau_1}$.

A Parametric Counter System (PCS) is a tuple $\mathcal{C} = (Q, X, P, \delta)$ where X is a set of integer valued variables (counters), and Q, P, and δ are defined in the same manner as for PTS's (substitute C by X in the definition of δ).

A configuration of $\mathcal{C}$ is a triplet $\langle q, \nu, \gamma \rangle$ where $q \in Q$, $\nu : X \to \mathbb{N}$, and $\gamma : P \to \mathbb{N}$. Given a transition $\tau \in \delta$, we define a relation $\to_\tau$ in the same manner as for PTS's. The function $post_\tau$ here is defined without considering time-transitions.

We can define also parametric models $\mathcal{M} = (Q, C, X, P, I, \delta)$ having both counters and clocks by a straightforward extension of the definitions of the PTS's and PCS's. We do not allow comparisons between clocks and counters in the guards and the invariants. We call these models Parametric Timed Counter Systems (PTCS's).

4 Symbolic Representation Structures

4.1 Parametric Difference Bound Matrices

To simplify the presentation, we consider here only the case of PTS's. The treatment of counters is analogous since we have the same kind of guards and operations on counters as on clocks. We introduce representation structures for sets of configurations of PTS's that are extensions of the Difference Bound Matrices used for representing reachability sets of (nonparametric) timed automata.

Let $\mathcal{T} = (Q, C, P, I, \delta)$ be a PTS, let $C = \{c_1, \ldots, c_n\}$ be the set its clocks, and let c_0 be an additional clock whose value is always equal to 0. Then, any simple parametric constraint can be represented by a $(n+1) \times (n+1)$ matrix M of elements in $AT(P) \times \{<, \leq\}$, where each entry $M(i, j) = (t, \prec)$ encodes the constraint $c_i - c_j \prec t$. We call such a matrix M a *Parametric Difference Bound Matrix* (PDBM).

A *parameter constraint* is a *quantifier-free* formula in $FO(P)$. A *Constrained PDBM* is a pair (M, Φ) where M is a PDBM and Φ is a parameter constraint. A *symbolic configuration* is a pair $(q, (M, \Phi))$ where $q \in Q$ is a control state, and (M, Φ) is a Constrained PDBM representing a set of clock and parameter values.

4.2 Basic Operations on Constrained PDBM's

We define operations for manipulating Constrained PDBM's by lifting all the standard operations on DBM's [Dil89,ACD+92,Yov98] to the parametric case. The operations that are worth discussing are: transformation into a canonical form (which is also used for emptyness check), intersection (used with guards and invariants when computing sets of successors), and inclusion test.

Canonical form Different constrained PDBM's can represent the same parametric set of configurations due to the fact that some of the bounds may not be tight enough. For instance, consider the constrained PDBM corresponding to the set of constraints:

$$S = (0 \leq x \leq p_2 \wedge 0 \leq y \leq p_1 \wedge 0 \leq x - y \leq 0, 0 \leq p_1 < p_2)$$

It can be seen that if the upper bound on x (i.e., p_2) is replaced by p_1, then we obtain another representation of the same parametric set of configurations as S. This representation corresponds to the *canonical form* of S.

We recall that in the nonparametric case, canonical forms of DBM's are constructed using the Floyd Warshall algorithm which computes the minimum path between all pairs of entries. In the parametric case we consider here, we follow the same principle by running a *symbolic* Floyd Warshall algorithm. During its execution, this algorithm needs to determine minimums between terms built from those appearing in the original matrix. (We omit here the technical discussion about how to deal with strict vs. nonstrict inequalities.) For that, the algorithm assumes each of the two possible cases and check their consistency w.r.t. the parameter constraints: given two terms t_1 and t_2, it considers the case where $min(t_1, t_2) = t_1$ (resp. $min(t_1, t_2) = t_2$) and adds $t_1 < t_2$ (resp. $t_1 \geq t_2$) in the parameter constraints, and then it delivers the consistent cases among these two, may be both of them. (We address below the decidability of this consistency check.)

For instance, the canonical form of S can be easily computed in this manner; the case splitting gives two cases but one of them is inconsistent ($p_1 \geq p_2$). However, if we remove $p_1 < p_2$ from S, we obtain two constrained PDBM's corresponding to each of the possible cases ($p_1 < p_2$ or $p_1 \geq p_2$). Notice that the construction of canonical forms allows also to test the emptyness of constrained PDBM's.

Now, in order to check the consistency of each of the possible cases when computing the minimum between two terms, we have to test the satisfiability of formulas ϕ of the form

$$\Phi(P) \wedge t_1 \prec t_2$$

where $\prec \in \{<, \leq\}$ and Φ is a parameter constraint. If Φ is in $LFO(P)$ (linear constraint) or in $RFO(P)$ (all parameters are reals), then this test is decidable.

If Φ is a nonlinear formula of $FO(P)$ mixing integer and real parameters, this test is of course undecidable. Nevertheless, we still can test *safely* the satisfiability of ϕ in $RFO(P)$ (i.e., we check the satisfiability of ϕ under the assumption that all the parameters are reals). If ϕ in not satisfiable in $RFO(P)$, we are sure that it is not satisfiable for its original interpretation in $FO(P)$. However, ϕ could be satisfiable in $RFO(P)$ whereas there are no integer valuations of P satisfying it. Hence, by interpreting formulas of $FO(P)$ in $RFO(P)$, we consider *upper approximations* of the sets of possible configurations.

Intersection Given two constrained PDBM's $S_1 = (M_1, \Phi_1)$ and $S_2 = (M_2, \Phi_2)$, the intersection of S_1 and S_2 is represented in general by a *set* of constrained

PDBM's. Roughly speaking, the construction consists in computing for every i and j, the minimum between the two *terms* $M_1(i,j)$ and $M_2(i,j)$, under the parameter constraints $\Phi_1 \wedge \Phi_2$. This is done by case splitting and checking the consistency of each case, as in the construction of canonical representations explained above.

Again, checking the consistency of the different cases produced by case splitting is decidable if the parameter constraints are in $LFO(P)$ or $RFO(P)$. Hence, in this case the construction of the intersection is exact. In the general case, checking satisfiability in $RFO(P)$ instead of $FO(P)$ is a safe consistency test that yields an upper approximation of the intersection.

Test of inclusion Let $S_1 = (M_1, \Phi_1)$ and $S_2 = (M_2, \Phi_2)$ be two canonical constrained PDBM's. The inclusion of S_1 in S_2 can be expressed by the following formula ψ:

$$\forall P.\ \Phi_1(P) \wedge \Phi(P) \Rightarrow M_1 \leq M_2$$

The validity of ψ is decidable if it is in $LFO(P)$ or in $RFO(P)$. Otherwise, we have a safe test of inclusion by checking the validity of ψ in $RFO(P)$. Indeed, if ψ is valid $RFO(P)$, then it is also valid in $FO(P)$ and hence, if our inclusion test answer positively, we are sure that it is true. However, if ψ is not valid, it does not mean that S_1 is not included in S_2.

5 Reachability Analysis

5.1 Building Symbolic Reachability Graphs

Let $\mathcal{T}$ be a PTCS. We present a procedure which, given a symbolic configuration S, computes a representation of the set $post^*(S)$. For that, starting from S, we construct a symbolic reachability graph where each vertex is a symbolic configuration and edges correspond to transitions of $\mathcal{T}$. The vertices of the symbolic graph are treated according to a depth-first traversal. The construction stops when each symbolic configuration that can be generated is covered by (included in) some symbolic configuration that has been already computed. During this construction, we use extrapolation in order to help termination.

Our extrapolation technique is based on guessing automatically the effect of iterating an arbitrary number of times a control loop (cycle in the control graph of $\mathcal{T}$), starting from a given symbolic configuration, and checking that this guess is exact (does not introduce nonreachable configuarations). Informally, we can present our extrapolation principle as follows: Let S be a symbolic constraint and let θ be a control loop, and suppose that the difference (in a sense which will be defined later) between $post_\theta(S)$ and S, say Δ, is equal to the difference between $post_\theta^2(S)$ and $post_\theta(S)$. Then, we suspect that the effect of iterating θ will be to add at each step the same Δ to the original set, i.e., after n iterations, the set of reachable configurations will be roughly $S + n\Delta$ (the precise set is given below). Roughly speaking, our technique consists in guessing that a control loop

θ (which is may be a composition of several simple loops) defines a periodic operation starting from a *particular* set of configurations. In many cases, our guess is exact. Moreover, the exactness of the effect obtained by extrapolation can be expressed as an arithmetical formula (we discuss later the decidability issue of this check).

Notice that our extrapolation technique introduces new parameters (n) corresponding to numbers of iterations of control loops. In order to deal with sets represented by means of such variables, we have to extend our symbolic representations and introduce *open* constrained PDBM's.

Let us call *iteration parameters* these auxiliary variables and let N be the set of such variables. In order to deal with sets represented using iteration variables we have to extend our symbolic representation and introduce *open* PDBM's.

5.2 Open Constrained PDBM's

Let N be a (countable) set of *iteration variables*. An *open* PDBM is a PDBM such that its elements are terms are in $AT(P \cup N) \times \{<, \leq\}$. We extend also the definitions of Constrained PDBM's and symbolic configurations by considering that the terms appearing in parameter constraints are in $AT(P \cup N)$.

Now, let us see how to extend the operations on PDBM to open PDBM's. The construction of canonical forms as well as intersection can be done as previously. The problematic operation if the test of inclusion. Indeed, given two canonical constrained open PDBM's $S_1 = (M_1, \Phi_1)$ and $S_2 = (M_2, \Phi_2)$, the inclusion of S_1 in S_2 can be expressed by the formula ψ:

$$\forall P. \forall N. (Is\_int(N) \wedge \Phi_1(P, N) \Rightarrow \exists N'. Is\_int(N') \wedge \Phi_2(P, N') \wedge M_1(N) \leq M_2(N'))$$

When ψ is a linear formula (a *LFO* formula), the validity of ψ is decidable, and hence, the inclusion problem between constrained open PDBM's is decidable in this case.

Another interesting case is what we call the *half-linear case* which corresponds to the following situation: using quantifier elimination, the obtained formula from ψ after eliminating all the *real valued* parameters in P is a *linear* formula on $N \cup N'$. The validity of this formula can be checked since *LFO* on integers (Presburger arithmetics) is decidable. The elimination of the real valued parameters can be done automatically using the techniques of quantifier elimination in *RFO* (we do not need to assume that N and N' are sets of integer variables).

Using this technique, we can deal with significant cases of systems generating nonlinear sets of configurations. For instance, in the analysis of the Bounded Retransmission Protocol, all the inclusion tests are half-linear.

Beyond the class of half-linear systems, the test of inclusion is undecidable. Nevertheless, even in this general case, it is possible to have a *safe* test of inclusion. However, we cannot adopt the naive approach which consists in checking the validity of ψ in *RFO* since ψ has an alternation of universal and existential quantification. Then, the solution we propose is to define a formula ψ' in RFO which is "reasonably" stronger than ψ. This formula is:

$$\forall P. \forall N. \Phi_1(P, N) \Rightarrow$$
$$\exists N'. \forall N''. \bigwedge_{i=1}^{|N'|} |N'_i - N''_i| \leq \frac{1}{2} \Rightarrow \Phi_2(P, N'') \wedge M_1(N) \leq M_2(N'')$$

The idea is to require that for every real vector N, there is a real vector N' such that $M_1 \leq M_2$ holds for all the real vectors N'' in a neighborhood of N' which contains at least one integer vector. Thus, if ψ' holds, necessarily ψ holds too.

5.3 Extrapolation

We present hereafter our extrapolation principle. We need first to introduce some notations.

Let $\mathcal{T} = (Q, C, X, P, I, \delta)$ be a PTCS. A *control loop* is a cycle in the graph (Q, δ), i.e., a path $(q_1, g_1, sop_1, q'_1) \ldots (q_n, g_n, sop_n, q'_n)$ such that $q_1 = q'_n$ and $\forall i \in \{1, \ldots, n-1\}, q'_i = q_{i+1}$.

Given an open PDBM M (resp. symbolic constraint $S = (M, \Phi)$), we denote by $Iter(M)$ (resp. $Iter(S)$) the set of iteration variables appearing in M (resp. in M or Φ). Let $S = (M, \Phi)$ be a constrained PDBM. Given $n \in N$ such that $n \notin Iter(S)$, we denote by $S\uparrow_n$ the constrained PDBM $(M, \Phi \wedge n \geq 0)$. Given a PDBM M' such that $Iter(M') \subseteq Iter(S)$, we denote by $S + M'$ the symbolic constraint $(M + M', \Phi)$.

Now, let θ be a control loop and let (q, S) be a symbolic configuration, where $S = (M, \Phi)$ is a constrained PDBM. Then, suppose we have computed $S_1 = (M_1, \Phi_1)$ and $S_2 = (M_2, \Phi_2)$ such that $(q, S_1) = post_\theta(q, S)$ and $(q, S_2) = post_\theta(q, S_1)$. Let $\Delta = M_1 - M$ and $\Delta' = M_2 - M_1$. Our extrapolation principle consists in checking whether the two following conditions hold:

C1: $\forall P. \forall N. Is\_int(N) \wedge \Phi_2(P, N) \Rightarrow \Delta = \Delta'$,
C2: $\forall n \geq 0. post_\theta^2(q, S\uparrow_n + n\Delta) = post_\theta(q, S\uparrow_n + (n+1)\Delta)$,

and, if C1 and C2 hold, in adding $post_\theta(q, S\uparrow_n + n\Delta)$ to the computed set of reachable configurations, and the edge $(q, S_1) \xrightarrow{\theta^*} post_\theta(q, S\uparrow_n + n\Delta)$ to the symbolic graph.

Condition C1 says that the effect of θ after two iterations is to add Δ at each step. Notice that we check the equality of the two matrices $M_2 - M_1$ and $M_1 - M$ under the constraint Φ_2. This constraint is stronger than Φ_1 which is itself stronger than Φ due to the fact that each application of θ may introduce but never remove parameter constraints. Condition C2 allows to check that each application of θ has an effect of adding Δ, provided the guards and the invariants in θ are satisfied. In order to take into account the guards and invariants, we compute the effect after $n+1$ iterations of θ as the $post_\theta$-image of $(q, S\uparrow_n + n\Delta)$. We can prove, by straightforward inductions, the following fact:

Lemma 1 *Let θ be a control loop, let (q, S) be a symbolic configuration, and let Δ be a PDBM. Then, the two following formulas are equivalent:*

1. $\forall n \geq 0.\ post_\theta^2(q, S\uparrow_n + n\Delta) = post_\theta(q, S\uparrow_n + (n+1)\Delta)$,
2. $\forall n \geq 0.\ post_\theta^{n+1}(q, S) = post_\theta(q, S\uparrow_n + n\Delta)$.

By Lemma 1, we can deduce that when it can be applyed, our extrapolation principle is exact (it computes precisely the set $post_\theta^{n+1}(q, S)$, for any $n \geq 0$).

Both conditions C1 and C2 correspond to arithmetical formulas. These conditions are of course decidable in the linear case, and they are also decidable in the half-linear case, i.e., after elimination of the real-valued parameters in P, the obtained formula is linear. Hence, we have an *exact* extrapolation technique in these case.

In the general (nonlinear) case, the test of exactness C2 is actually not relevant, since we can only compute upper-approximations of the reachability set in this case. So, the extrapolation principle we apply in this case is a *weak extrapolation principle* which consists in checking condition C1 only.

Actually, even in the linear and half-linear cases, it is often not necessary to check the condition C2. It can be observed that the *weak extrapolation principle*, even if it not guaranteed to compute the exact reachability set (it computes and upper-approximation of it in general), it is more accurate than existing widening operators [CH78,Hal93] since it allows to capture periodicities (see the examples in Section 5.1). We have used this principle to analyse several examples of parametric counter and timed systems and in all these cases, our procedure was able to compute the *exact* set of reachable configurations. In fact, we can prove that for an important class of systems, the weak extrapolation principle is exact. This class includes many of the usual examples encountered in the literature (Bakery algorithm, lift controler, etc). For lack of space, we omit addressing this issue in this version of the paper.

5.4 Examples

Let us illustrate the use of our reachability analysis techniques on small examples.

A simple linear system: Let us consider first a very simple *counter* system which is described in Figure 1. In this example, x is counter and T is a parameter.

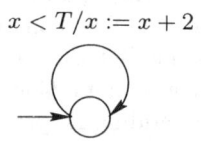

Fig. 1. Linear counter system

We suppose that the initial value of x is 0 and that T is not contrained. So, the initial symbolic configuration is $(0, true)$. The first execution of the unique transition θ of the system creates the edge:

$$(0, true) \xrightarrow{\theta} (2, 0 < T)$$

since x is incremented by 2, and before that (when its value was 0), it was compared to T. The second iteration creates the edge

$$(2, 0 < T) \xrightarrow{\theta} (4, 2 < T)$$

At this point, we can check that condition C1 holds since the effect of the first and second iteration of θ is to add the same value 2 to x. Then, by the weak extrapolation principle, the following edge is created

$$(2, 0 < T) \xrightarrow{\theta^*} post_\theta((0, 0 \leq n) + 2n) = post_\theta(2n, 0 \leq n)$$
$$= (2n + 2, 0 \leq n \wedge 2n < T)$$

Notice that the application of θ to the symbolic configuration $(2n, n \geq 0)$ allowed to generate the constraint $2n < T$ relating n with T. This illustrates how guards (and also invariants in the case of timed systems) are taken into account in the extrapolation technique.

It can be easily checked that condition C2 also holds. Indeed, we have

$$post_\theta^2(2n, 0 \leq n) = (2n + 4, 0 \leq n \wedge 2n + 2 < T) = post_\theta(2n + 2, 0 \leq n)$$

and thus, we are sure that our extrapolation is exact.

It worths noting that our extrapolation principle can generate periodic sets whereas classical widening techniques [CH78,Hal93] will not.

A simple half-linear system: Now, let us consider the parametric timed automaton given in Figure 2, where c and c' are real-valued clocks, and T and T' are real-valued parameters. Let us assume that the initial configuration is

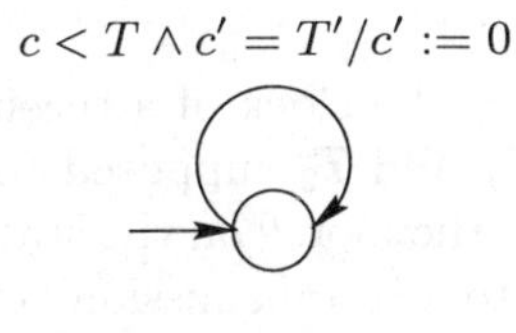

$$c < T \wedge c' = T'/c' := 0$$

Fig. 2. Half-linear clock system

$(c = 0, c' = 0, 0 \leq T \wedge 0 \leq T')$. Then, the first application of the transition θ of the system gives:

$$(0, 0, 0 \leq T \wedge 0 \leq T') \xrightarrow{\theta} (T', 0, 0 < T \wedge 0 \leq T')$$

and the second iteration gives:

$$(T', 0, 0 < T \wedge 0 \leq T') \xrightarrow{\theta} (2T', 0, 0 \leq T' < T)$$

Then, the condition C1 of our extrapolation principle holds with $\Delta(c) = T'$ and $\Delta(c') = 0$. Following the weak extrapolation principle, we create a θ^*-edge from $(T', 0, 0 < T \wedge 0 \leq T')$ to $post_\theta(n * T', 0, 0 \leq n \wedge 0 \leq T \wedge 0 \leq T')$ wich is equal to:

$$((n+1) * T', 0, 0 \leq n \wedge 0 \leq T' \wedge n * T' < T)$$

The generated symbolic configuration is nonlinear, but still, all decision problems we need on it are decidable due to the fact that they are half-linear. For instance, after generating this symbolic configuration, we need to check for its emptyness by deciding whether the parameter constraints are satisfiable. This is very simple in this example because after eliminating the parameters T and T' (supposed to be real valued), we get a trivial linear constraint on n which is $n \geq 0$. It can also be seen that in this case, the condition C2 (exactness of the extrapolation) can be done straigthforwardly.

A complex half-linear system: We consider here an example which is inspired from the model of the Bounded Retransmission Protocol. It consists of a systems with two clocks c_1 and c_2 and a counter x (see Figure 3). Intuitively, c_1 represents

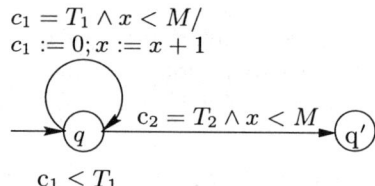

Fig. 3. The Nonlinear Kernel of the BRP

the clock of a sender and c_2 the clock of a receiver. These clocks are compared with parametric bounds T_1 and T_2 supposed to be real values. The counter x counts the number of times the loop θ on the state q is performed. The transition θ corresponds in the BRP to a retransmission action by the sender. The number of these retransmissions is bounded by M which is an integer parameter. We assume that the parameters T_1, T_2, and M are related by a nonlinear constraint

$$T_2 > M * T_1$$

which means that the timeout of the receiver is at least M (the maximum number of retransmissions) times the timeout of the sender. The question is whether the state q_1 (considered as a bad state) is reachable under the constraint above.

Roughly speaking, this correponds to a property of synchronisation between the sender and receiver in the BRP: The timeout of the receiver should not expire before the sender has finished all his possible retransmissions. Notice that the constraint above is not precisely the one considered on the timeouts in the BRP [DKRT97], but our aim here is just to show simply and faitfuly the main problems that appear in the analysis of a complex system such as the BRP.

Let us compute the reachability set starting from the initial configuration:

$$0 \leq c_1 \leq T_1 \wedge 0 \leq c_2 \leq T_1 \wedge c_1 - c_2 = 0 \wedge x = 0,$$
$$0 \leq T_1 \wedge 0 \leq T_2 \wedge 0 \leq M \wedge T_2 > M * T_1$$

The two first applications of θ give successively

$$0 \leq c_1 \leq T_1 \wedge T_1 \leq c_2 \leq 2T_1 \wedge c_1 - c_2 = T_1 \wedge x = 1,$$
$$0 \leq T_1 \wedge 0 \leq T_2 \wedge 0 < M \wedge T_2 > M * T_1$$

and

$$0 \leq c_1 \leq T_1 \wedge 2T_1 \leq c_2 \leq 3T_1 \wedge c_1 - c_2 = 2T_1 \wedge x = 2,$$
$$0 \leq T_1 \wedge 0 \leq T_2 \wedge 1 < M \wedge T_2 > M * T_1$$

At this point, it can be checked that the extrapolation condition C1 holds with $\Delta(c_1) = 0$, $\Delta(c_2) = T_1$, $\Delta(c_1 - c_2) = T_1$, and $\Delta(x) = 1$. (Notice that, in general, the differences between lowers bounds and upper bounds could be different, and thus, Δ may correspond to nondeterministic increasings represented by intervals instead of precise values as in this example and the previous ones.) Then, by the weak extrapolation principle we can create the configuration:

$$0 \leq c_1 \leq T_1 \wedge (n+1) * T_1 \leq c_2 \leq (n+2) * T_1$$
$$\wedge\ c_1 - c_2 = (n+1) * T_1 \wedge x = n+1,$$
$$0 \leq n \wedge 0 \leq T_1 \wedge 0 \leq T_2 \wedge n < M \wedge T_2 > M * T_1$$

The transition to the state q_1 is executable if the following set of parameter constraints (obtained by intersection with the guard) is satisfiable:

$$0 \leq n \wedge 0 \leq T_1 \wedge 0 \leq T_2 \wedge n+1 < M \wedge (n+1)*T_1 \leq T_2 \leq (n+2)*T_1 \wedge T_2 > M*T_1$$

The formula above is actually half-linear because after the elimination of the real parameter T_2 we obtain the constraint

$$0 \leq n \wedge 0 \leq T_1 \wedge n+1 < M \wedge (n+2) * T_1 > M * T_1$$

and after the elimination of T_1 we obtain the formula:

$$0 \leq n \wedge n+1 < M \wedge M < n+2$$

This formula is a linear constraint on integer variables, and thus its satisfiability can be decided. Clearly the formula above is unsatisfiable since there is no integers strictly between two successive integers. Hence, we conclude that q_1 is not reachable.

Notice that we have omitted here the test of condition C2. Actually, this test can also be decided as a half-linear satisfiability problem.

6 Implementation and Experiments

We have implemented a package of Constrained PDBM's containing all the basic manipulation operations. Our current implementation uses the tool REDLOG/REDUCE [DS97,DSW98] for quantification elimination and deciding satisfiability in RFO, and uses the tool OMEGA [BGP97] for deciding satisfiability in Presburger arithmetics. In the nonparametric case, our package behaves as a DBM package: all operations involving only constants are done without case splitting (used for comparing parametric terms) and without invoking REDLOG or OMEGA).

Based on this package, we have implemented a procedure for reachability analysis using extrapolation. This procedure computes, when it terminates, a symbolic graph of a given PTCS starting from a given symbolic configuration. We have applied our procedure to several examples including counter and timed systems that generate linear constraints such as:

- the Bakery algorithm for mutual exclusion with unbounded ticket counters (0.82 sec with Omega as constraint solver) and two processes,
- the timed parametric Fisher's mutual exclusion protocol (169.64 sec., Omega) with two processes,
- the parametric lift controler of [Val89] where the number of floors is a parameter (286.32 sec, Omega),

as well as complex systems generating *nonlinear constraints* relating clocks and counters. Indeed, we have applied our techniques to analyse the Bounded Retransmission Protocol which involves a nontrivial parametric reasoning on both counters and clocks ($\sim$ 91 mn, Redlog/Reduce). We have considered for this example the modelisation given in [DKRT97]. Our reachability analysis procedure has been able to construct a symbolic graph corresponding to the partition of the set of reachable configurations according to control states. This symbolic graph represents a finite abstraction of the original infinite-state model. After projection on external actions and minimisation (using the CADP toolbox [FGK+96]), we got a finite model with 7 states on which the safety properties of the BRP has been automatically checked.

The analysis of linear systems such as the Bakery algorithm and the lift controler has been already done by other researchers using different techniques such as widening [BGP97,BGL98] or the computation of meta-transitions [BW94]. Our experiments show that our techniques are powerful enough to deal with all these cases as well as, and in a uniform way, with systems generating nonlinear constraints that are beyond the scope of the existing methods and tools. In all the cases we considered, our procedure was able to compute the *exact* set of reachable configurations.

7 Conclusion

We have introduced an extrapolation principle for analysing systems with counters and clocks based on the use of Parametric DBM's. Our approach is an extension of the existing methods on timed automata to the case of systems with parametric constraints. An interesting feature of our techniques is that they can be applied uniformly to nonparametric or to parametric systems, to linear systems or to nonlinear ones (which are beyond the scope of the known techniques and tools). Moreover, our techniques are accurate and generate exact reachability sets for a wide class of systems.

We have implemented our techniques in a tool prototype using Redlog/Reduce and Omega as constraint solvers. The experiments we have done with our prototype show that our approach is powerful and effective. In particular, we have been able to verify automatically a parametric timed version of the Bounded Retransmission Protocol. Future work includes studying other symbolic representations and associated extrapolation techniques, and identifying classes of arithmetical constraints that can be handled efficiently. In particular, it would be interesting to investigate parametric extensions of structures like CDD's [LPWY99] and DDD's [MLAH99].

Finally, let us mention that in this paper we have addressed only *forward* reachability analysis. Actually, the techniques we have developed can also be used for *backward* analysis as well.

References

[AAB99a]   P. Abdulla, A. Annichini, and A. Bouajjani. Symbolic Verification of Lossy Channel Systems: Application to the Bounded Retransmission Protocol. In *TACAS'99*. LNCS 1579, 1999.

[AAB+99b] P.A. Abdulla, A. Annichini, S. Bensalem, A. Bouajjani, and Y. Lakhnech P. Habermehl. Verification of Infinite-State Systems by Combining Abstraction and Reachability Analysis. In *11th Intern. Conf. on Computer Aided Verification (CAV'99)*. LNCS 1633, 1999.

[ACD+92]   R. Alur, C. Courcoubetis, D. Dill, N. Halbwachs, and H. Wong-Toi. An implementation of three algorithms for timing verification based on automata emptiness. In *RTSS'92*. IEEE, 1992.

[AD94]   R. Alur and D. Dill. A Theory of Timed Automata. *TCS*, 126, 1994.

[AHV93]   R. Alur, T.A. Henzinger, and M.Y. Vardi. Parametric real-time reasoning. In *Proceedings of the 25th Annual Symposium on Theory of Computing*, pages 592–601. ACM Press, 1993.

[BGL98]   Tevfik Bultan, Richard Gerber, and Christopher League. Verifying systems with integer constraints and Boolean predicates: A composite approach. In *Proc. of the Intern. Symp. on Software Testing and Analysis*. ACM Press, 1998.

[BGP97]   T. Bultan, R. Gerber, and W. Pugh. Symbolic model checking of infinite state systems using Presburger arithmetic. *LNCS*, 1254, 1997.

[BGP98]   Tevfik Bultan, Richard Gerber, and William Pugh. Model checking concurrent systems with unbounded integer variables: Symbolic representations, approximations and experimental results. Tech. Rep. CS-TR-3870, University of Maryland, College Park, 1998.

[BW94]   B. Boigelot and P. Wolper. Symbolic Verification with Periodic Sets. *Lecture Notes in Computer Science*, 818:55–67, 1994.

[CC77] P. Cousot and R. Cousot. Static Determination of Dynamic Properties of Recursive Procedures. In *IFIP Conf. on Formal Description of Programming Concepts*. North-Holland Pub., 1977.

[CH78] Patrick Cousot and Nicholas Halbwachs. Automatic discovery of linear restraints among variables of a program. In *POPL'78*. ACM, 1978.

[CJ98] H. Comon and Y. Jurski. Multiple counters automata, safety analysis and presburger arithmetic. In *CAV'98*. LNCS 1427, 1998.

[Dil89] D. Dill. Timing assumptions and verification of finite-state concurrent systems. In *CAV'89*. LNCS 407, 1989.

[DKRT97] P. D'Argenio, J-P. Katoen, T. Ruys, and G.J. Tretmans. The Bounded Retransmission Protocol must be on Time. In *TACAS'97*. LNCS 1217, 1997.

[DOTY96] C. Daws, A. Olivero, S. Tripakis, and S. Yovine. The Tool KRONOS. In *Hybrid Systems III, Verification and Control*. LNCS 1066, 1996.

[DS97] A. Dolzmann and T. Sturm. Redlog: Computer algebra meets computer logic. *ACM SIGSAM Bulletin*, 31(2):2–9, 1997.

[DSW98] A. Dolzmann, T. Sturm, and V. Weispfenning. A new approach for automatic theorem proving in real geometry. *Automated Reasoning*, 21(3):357–380, 1998.

[FGK+96] J-C. Fernandez, H. Garavel, A. Kerbrat, R. Mateescu, L. Mounier, and M. Sighireanu. CADP: A Protocol Validation and Verification Toolbox. In *CAV'96*. LNCS 1102, 1996.

[FO97] L. Fribourg and H. Olsen. Reachability sets of parametrized rings as regular languages. In *Infinity'97*. volume 9 of Electronical Notes in Theoretical Computer Science. Elsevier Science, 1997.

[GdP96] J-F. Groote and J. Van de Pol. A Bounded Retransmission Protocol for Large Data Packets. In *AMAST'96*. LNCS 1101, 1996.

[Hal93] N. Halbwachs. Delay Analysis in Synchronous Programs. In *CAV'93*. LNCS 697, 1993.

[HHWT95] T. Henzinger, P.H. Ho, and H. Wong-Toi. A User Guide to HyTech. In *TACAS'95*. LNCS 1019, 1995.

[HNSY92] T.A. Henzinger, X. Nicollin, J. Sifakis, and S. Yovine. Symbolic Model-Checking for Real-Time Systems. In *LICS'92*. IEEE, 1992.

[HSV94] L. Helmink, M.P.A. Sellink, and F. Vaandrager. Proof checking a Data Link Protocol. In *Types for Proofs and Programs*. LNCS 806, 1994.

[LPWY99] K. Larsen, J. Pearson, C. Weise, and W. Yi. Efficient timed reachability analysis using clock difference diagrams. In *CAV'99*. LNCS 1633, 1999.

[LPY97] K.G. Larsen, P. Pettersson, and W. Yi. UPPAAL: Status and Developments. In *CAV'97*. LNCS, 1997.

[Mat96] R. Mateescu. Formal Description and Analysis of a Bounded Retransmission Protocol. Technical report no. 2965, INRIA, 1996.

[MLAH99] J. Moller, J. Lichtenberg, H.R. Andersen, and H. Hulgaard. Difference decision diagrams. Tech. rep it-tr-1999-023, Department of Information Technology, Technical University of Denmark, 1999.

[Val89] A. Valmari. State generation with induction. In *Scandinavian Conference on Artificial Intelligence*, 1989.

[Yov98] S. Yovine. Model-checking timed automata. *Embedded Systems, LNCS*, 1998.

Syntactic Program Transformations for Automatic Abstraction

Kedar S. Namjoshi and Robert P. Kurshan

Bell Laboratories, Lucent Technologies
{kedar,k}@research.bell-labs.com
http://cm.bell-labs.com/cm/cs/who/{kedar,k}

Abstract. We present an algorithm that constructs a finite state "abstract" program from a given, possibly infinite state, "concrete" program by means of a *syntactic* program transformation. Starting with an initial set of predicates from a specification, the algorithm iteratively computes the predicates required for the abstraction relative to that specification. These predicates are represented by boolean variables in the abstract program. We show that the method is *sound*, in that the abstract program is always guaranteed to simulate the original. We also show that the method is *complete*, in that, if the concrete program has a finite abstraction with respect to simulation (bisimulation) equivalence, the algorithm can produce a finite simulation-equivalent (bisimulation-equivalent) abstract program. Syntactic abstraction has two key advantages: it can be applied to infinite state programs or programs with large data paths, and it permits the effective application of other reduction methods for model checking. We show that our method generalizes several known algorithms for analyzing syntactically restricted, data-insensitive programs.

1 Introduction

Model Checking [CE81,QS82] is a fully automatic method for checking that a finite state program satisfies a propositional temporal specification. It has proved to be quite useful for the analysis of concurrent hardware and software systems; there are several academic and commercial model checking tools. The main obstacle to the wider application of model checking is the exponential growth in the size of the state space with increasing program size: current tools are typically limited to programs with a few hundred boolean state variables. There are two main approaches to ameliorating this state-explosion problem: *compositional verification*, where one manually constructs a proof outline that exploits the compositional structure of the program, while model-checking sufficiently small components, and *abstraction*, where one constructs a smaller *abstract* program in a manner which ensures that the specification holds for the original program if it holds for the abstract program.

Abstraction is often carried out manually and justified only informally. For large programs, such manual abstraction is error-prone and often infeasible. Our focus in this paper, therefore, is on automating the abstraction process. We present an algorithm that constructs a *finite state* "abstract" program from a given, possibly infinite state, "concrete" program by means of a *syntactic* program transformation. The abstract program represents predicates of the concrete program by boolean variables. Starting with the atomic predicates from a specification or statement of a property that is to be verified, the algorithm iteratively computes the predicates required for the abstraction relative to that specification, as well as the necessary updates to the corresponding boolean variables. This is achieved by a syntactic analysis that does not construct the explicit transition graph either of the original or of the abstract program, each of which may be too large to compute.

We show that the algorithm is *sound*, in that the abstract program is always guaranteed to be a conservative approximation of (i.e., simulates) the original, with respect to the set of specification predicates, AP. Under certain conditions, the algorithm produces an *exact* (i.e., bisimular) abstraction of the original program. The soundness result implies that a temporal property in $ACTL^*$ over AP holds for the original program if it holds for the abstraction. For an exact abstraction, this is true for properties written in the full μ–calculus. We also show that the algorithm is *complete* in the sense that, if the state transition graph of the original program has a finite simulation (bisimulation) quotient, then the algorithm can produce a finite simulation-equivalent (bisimulation-equivalent) abstract program.

Syntactic abstraction has several advantages:

- The algorithm produces an implicit (syntactic) description of the abstract program. Hence, other methods for model checking, such as symbolic (BDD-based) model checking and partial-order reduction, can be applied to the abstract program.
- It supports the abstraction of *data-insensitive* programs with large or infinite data paths. Our method generalizes several earlier algorithms for analyzing data-insensitive programs and may also be used in other cases, such as symmetric programs, where large reductions can be achieved through bisimulation minimization.
- It can often be substantially more efficient than the symbolic minimization algorithms of [BFH90,LY92,HHK95] as, unlike these methods, our algorithm does not construct the explicit transition graph of the minimized system, which could be quite large.
- For programs with bounded non-determinacy, our algorithm is able to construct abstractions without the manual application of theorem-provers, as proposed for other predicate abstraction methods (cf. [GS97,BLO98]).

The paper is structured as follows. In Section 2, we provide some background on simulation, bisimulation, temporal logic and model checking. We describe the basic algorithm in Section 3 and prove the soundness and completeness claims. In Section 4, we present some useful extensions to the basic algorithm. In Section 5, we describe several applications of the algorithm. Section 6 concludes the paper with a discussion of related work.

2 Background

We provide some background on abstraction and model checking, and present a simple program syntax on which the analyses of the algorithm are defined.

2.1 Labeled Transition Systems

The state transition graph of a program is represented by a *Transition System* (TS, for short) [Kel76] which is a tuple (S, Δ, I, AP, L), where
- S is the set of *states*,
- $\Delta \subseteq S \times S$, is the (left-total) transition relation. We write $s \longrightarrow t$ instead of $(s,t) \in \Delta$ for clarity.
- $I \subseteq S$ is the set of initial states,
- AP is the set of atomic propositions, and
- $L : S \to 2^{AP}$ is the state labeling function, which maps each state to the set of atomic propositions that hold at that state.

A *computation* σ of the TS is an infinite sequence of states such that $\sigma_0 \in I$, and for each i, $\sigma_i \longrightarrow \sigma_{i+1}$. A TS is often constrained by a fairness condition, expressed as a boolean combination of basic fairness conditions "infinitely often p", where p is a set of state pairs [1]. A *fair computation* of the TS is a computation that satisfies the fairness condition, where the basic fairness formula above is satisfied iff transitions from p appear infinitely often on the sequence.

2.2 The µ-Calculus

The µ-calculus [Koz83] is a branching-time temporal logic, where formulas are built from atomic propositions, boolean connectives, the least-fixpoint operator, and the modality $\langle\rangle\phi$ ("there is a successor satisfying ϕ"). For a state s in a TS M and a µ-calculus formula ϕ over the atomic propositions of M, we write $M, s \models \phi$ to mean that "ϕ is true at state s in model M". The sub-logic $A\mu$ consists of those µ-calculus formulae where every $\langle\rangle$ operator is under an odd number of negations. It is possible [EL86] to encode a number of temporal logics, including *CTL*, *CTL** [CES86,EH86] and *LTL* [Pnu77] into the µ-calculus.

2.3 Simulation and Bisimulation

The correctness of any abstraction method is determined by the nature of the relationship between the concrete and the abstract program. A typical relationship is that the abstract program is able to match every computation of the concrete program. This is formalized in the definitions below.

Definition 0 (Simulation Relation) [Mil71] *A relation $R \subseteq S \times S$ is a simulation relation on a TS $M = (S, \Delta, I, AP, L)$ iff for any $(s,t) \in R$, $L(s) = L(t)$ and for any u such that $s \longrightarrow u$, there exists v such that $t \longrightarrow v$ and $(u,v) \in R$.*

---
[1] The usual unconditional, weak and strong fairness conditions can be written as boolean combinations of basic fairness conditions.

Definition 1 (Bisimulation Relation) [Par81] *A relation R is a bisimulation on TS M iff R is symmetric and a simulation relation on M.*

State t *simulates* a state s iff (s,t) is in the greatest simulation, which exists as simulations are closed under arbitrary union. States s and t are *simulation-equivalent* (written as $s \sim t$) iff they simulate each other. States s and t are *bisimular* in M (written as $s \approx t$) iff (s,t) is contained in the greatest bisimulation relation on M. The connection between model checking and these notions of program equivalence is as follows.

Theorem 0 *For a TS M and states s,t in M,*

1. (cf.[GL94]) *For any $A\mu$ formula f on AP, if t simulates s then $M,t \models f$ implies $M,s \models f$.*
2. (cf. [BCG88]) *For any μ-calculus formula f on AP, if $s \approx t$ then $M,s \models f$ iff $M,t \models f$.* □

As $\sim$ ($\approx$) is an equivalence relation, it induces a *quotient* TS whose states are the equivalence classes of M w.r.t. $\sim$ ($\approx$), the initial set of states is the equivalence classes of the initial states of M, and there is a transition (C,a,D) iff $(\exists s,t : s \in C \wedge t \in D : s \xrightarrow{a} t)$.

2.4 Program Syntax

Our algorithms transform one program text to another. For our purposes, instead of specifying a particular program syntax, it suffices to consider a program as being defined on a set of variables, and being specified once an initial condition, a transition relation and a fairness constraint are defined. These are specified syntactically as *predicates*: a predicate is a quantifier-free formula of a first-order logic. The relation symbols form the *atomic* predicates. Some relation and function symbols may have fixed interpretations, for instance $=, \leq, +$.

Definition 2 (Program) *A program is specified by a tuple (X, I, T, F), where*

- *X is a finite, non-empty set of variables. Each variable x has an associated domain of values, $dom(x)$.*
- *$I(X)$ is the initial condition, specified as a predicate on X.*
- *$T(X, X')$ is the transition relation, specified as a predicate on $X \cup X'$, where X' is a set of "next-state" variables that is in 1-1 correspondence with X.*
- *$F(X, X')$ is the fairness condition, specified as a boolean combination of the basic fairness condition "infinitely-often p", for a predicate p over $X \cup X'$.*

The semantics of such a program is given by a TS defined as follows. The state space is the Cartesian product of the domains of the variables. The value of an expression e in state s is denoted by $e(s)$; this can be defined by induction on the expression syntax. An initial state is one for which the initial state predicate evaluates to *true*. The transition relation is defined as follows: there is a transition

$s \longrightarrow t$ iff $T(s,t)$ is true. The state labeling function L is defined by: for each atomic predicate P, $P \in L(s)$ iff $P(s) = true$. The fairness condition of the fair TS is obtained in a straightforward manner from the condition F.

We develop our algorithm under the assumption that the set of predicates is effectively closed under the application of the "weakest liberal precondition" transformer [Dij75], denoted by $wlp(P)$ (in terms of the μ-calculus, $wlp(P) = \neg\langle\rangle(\neg P)$).

Typical programming constructs can be rewritten into the program syntax presented above. For example, a guarded command [Dij75], which has the form $g(X) \hookrightarrow U := e(X)$, defines the transition relation $(g(X) \wedge (\bigwedge i : x_i \in U : x'_i = e_i(X)) \wedge (\bigwedge i : x_i \in X \backslash U : x'_i = x_i)$. For guarded commands, $wlp(P)$ can be calculated by simple substitution as $(g(X) \Rightarrow P[U \leftarrow e(X)])$, where $P[U \leftarrow e(X)]$ is the predicate obtained by replacing each occurrence of $x_i \in U$ by e_i in P, for all i. Programs with external, non-deterministic inputs can be defined by partitioning the set of variables X into the input variables Y, which are unconstrained, and state variables Z, whose next-state values are constrained by the transition relation. Using the syntax $[Y] : g(X) \hookrightarrow U := e(X)$ for describing such transitions, $wlp(P)$ is given by $(\forall Y :: g(X) \Rightarrow P[U \leftarrow e(X)])$. In this case, it may be necessary to use a quantifier-elimination procedure, such as that for Presburger arithmetic, to re-write $wlp(P)$ as a predicate.

3 The Abstraction Algorithm

We motivate and describe our algorithm for the simpler case of programs that exhibit *bounded* non-determinism. For such programs, the transition relation $T(X, X')$ is equivalent to a bounded disjunction $(\bigvee i :: T_i(X, X'))$, where each T_i is *deterministic*, i.e., for any state s, there is at most one state t such that $T_i(s,t)$ holds. We assume that the transition relation is given in this form and refer to each T_i as an *action*. The key property that we exploit is that for a deterministic action a, wlp_a distributes over all boolean operators [2].

We do not consider fairness conditions in this section. The extensions needed to handle fairness and unbounded nondeterminism are described in Section 4. The results established here carry over, essentially unchanged, to the general case.

3.1 A Motivating Example: the 2-Process Bakery Protocol

Consider the 2-process "Bakery" mutual exclusion protocol [Lam74] presented in Figure 1 as a finite collection of guarded commands. The specification of mutual exclusion in CTL is $\mathsf{AG}(\neg(st_1 = C \wedge st_2 = C))$. To verify this property, an abstraction of the protocol needs to preserve at least the atomic predicates $st_1 = C$ and $st_2 = C$, as well as those in the initial condition: $st_1 = N$, $st_2 = N$, $y_1 = 0$, $y_2 = 0$. We may choose to retain the variables st_1, st_2, as they have

---
[2] In the case of negation, $wlp_a(\neg P) \equiv wlp_a(false) \vee \neg wlp_a(P)$

```
var st₁, st₂ : {N, W, C}
(* N="Non-critical", W="Waiting", C="Critical" *)
var y₁, y₂ : natural
initially (st₁ = N) ∧ (y₁ = 0) ∧ (st₂ = N) ∧ (y₂ = 0)

action wait₁       st₁ = N ↪ st₁, y₁ := W, y₂ + 1
action enter₁      st₁ = W ∧ (y₂ = 0 ∨ y₁ ≤ y₂) ↪ st₁ := C
action release₁    st₁ = C ↪ st₁, y₁ := N, 0

action wait₂       st₂ = N ↪ st₂, y₂ := W, y₁ + 1
action enter₂      st₂ = W ∧ (y₁ = 0 ∨ y₂ < y₁) ↪ st₂ := C
action release₂    st₂ = C ↪ st₁, y₂ := N, 0
```

Fig. 1. The 2-process Bakery mutual exclusion algorithm.

small finite domains, but we would want to abstract y_1, y_2, as they have infinite domains, retaining only those predicates on y_1, y_2 which are necessary to preserve the control flow of the protocol. We do so by introducing auxiliary boolean variables b_1 and b_2 which represent $y_1 = 0$ and $y_2 = 0$, respectively. The initial condition can now be expressed as $(st_1 = N) \wedge b_1 \wedge (st_2 = N) \wedge b_2$.

To preserve the correspondence between b_1 and $y_1 = 0$, we need to compute an update to b_1 for each action. For a deterministic action a, b_1 is true after an update to y_1 exactly if $wlp_a(y_1 = 0)$ is true before the update. For the action $wait_1$, the syntactic wlp calculation yields $((st_1 = N) \Rightarrow (y_2 + 1 = 0))$. Now, however, we have a new predicate $(y_2 + 1 = 0)$, which can be simplified to *false*, as y_2 is a natural number. Hence, the modified action is:

action $wait_1$ $st_1 = N \hookrightarrow st_1, y_1, b_1 := W, y_2 + 1, (st_1 = N \Rightarrow false)$

We may simplify this further by replacing occurrences of the guard expression by *true* in the assignment, to get:

action $wait_1$ $st_1 = N \hookrightarrow st_1, y_1, b_1 := W, y_2 + 1, false$

The result of $wlp_{enter_1}(y_1 = 0)$ is $((st_1 = W \wedge (y_2 = 0 \vee y_1 \leq y_2)) \Rightarrow (y_1 = 0))$. In this case, we have a new atomic predicate, $y_1 \leq y_2$, which must therefore be tracked by a new boolean variable, b_3. Repeating the steps above, we get:

action $enter_1$ $st_1 = W \wedge (b_2 \vee b_3) \hookrightarrow st_1, b_1 := C, b_1$

This iterative process of computing weakest preconditions and collecting new predicates terminates for our example program; i.e., after a finite number of iterations, no new predicates are generated. Hence, it suffices to consider only these predicates to verify the property. As the auxiliary boolean variables track the predicates exactly, the infinite-domain variables y_1 and y_2 are unnecessary and can be removed, resulting in the *finite-state* abstraction shown in Figure 2, which is *bisimulation-equivalent* to the original with respect to the initial predicate set $\{st_1 = C, st_2 = C\}$. From Theorem 0, the mutual exclusion property is true of the original program if and only if it is true of the abstraction.

```
var st₁, st₂ : {N, W, C}
(* N="Non-critical", W="Waiting", C="Critical" *)
var b₁, b₂, b₃ : boolean
(* b₁ = (y₁ = 0), b₂ = (y₂ = 0), b₃ = (y₁ ≤ y₂) *)
initially (st₁ = N) ∧ b₁ ∧ (st₂ = N) ∧ b₂ ∧ b₃

action wait₁         st₁ = N ↪ st₁, b₁, b₂, b₃ := W, false, b₂, false
action enter₁        st₁ = W ∧ (b₂ ∨ b₃) ↪ st₁, b₁, b₂, b₃ := C, b₁, b₂, b₃
action release₁      st₁ = C ↪ st₁, b₁, b₂, b₃ := N, true, b₂, true

action wait₂         st₂ = N ↪ st₂, b₁, b₂, b₃ := W, b₁, false, true
action enter₂        st₂ = W ∧ (b₁ ∨ ¬b₃) ↪ st₂, b₁, b₂, b₃ := C, b₁, b₂, b₃
action release₂      st₂ = C ↪ st₁, b₁, b₂, b₃ := N, b₁, true, b₁
```

Fig. 2. Abstraction of the 2-process Bakery mutual exclusion algorithm.

3.2 The Algorithm

The Bakery example introduced the key ingredients of our algorithm: starting from the atomic predicates in the specification formula, predicates of the original program are represented by boolean variables in the abstraction, exact updates for these boolean variables are computed by a syntactic *wlp* computation, possibly introducing new predicates to be examined, and simplifications are performed to avoid introducing new predicates that are syntactically distinct but semantically identical to predicates generated earlier. The algorithm is presented in its entirety in Figure 3.

The algorithm maintains a correspondence table, C, which relates syntactic atomic predicates to corresponding boolean variables. The algorithm also maintains two sets of atomic predicates: *oldPred*, which consists of those predicates for which *wlp* has been calculated, and *newPred*, which consists of the unexamined predicates. Initially (step 1), *oldPred* is empty, and *newPred* contains the atomic predicates of the specification formula, the initial condition, and the actions. In each iteration (steps 2a-2c), *wlp* is calculated for each predicate in *newPred* and the result is massaged (described below) to extract new predicates, for which new boolean variables are introduced. In steps 3, the abstract transition relation is defined by updating each boolean variable with the expression formed by massaging *wlp* for the corresponding predicate.

Although the process of generating new predicates terminates for the Bakery example, in general, it may not terminate. To ensure termination, we iterate this process for K steps, where K is a parameter to the algorithm. After K iterations, however, the predicates in *newPred* have not been processed by a *wlp* computation. Boolean *input* variables are introduced for these predicates, which are constrained by Φ to valuations that are consistent relative to their corresponding predicates. Similarly, Ψ constrains the initial values of boolean variables corresponding to the predicates in *oldPred*. In the definition of $T_\mathcal{A}$, the

wlp operator is applied only to predicates from $oldPred$, so the result is in terms of $oldPred \cup newPred$ and gets massaged into an expression on X_A.

It is not necessary to add Φ and Ψ to obtain a program that is a conservative approximation; these are needed only to establish the completeness results. If the atomic predicates come from a class with quantifier elimination (such as Presburger arithmetic), Φ and Ψ can be computed syntactically. In general, the computability of Φ and Ψ is equivalent to the decidability of satisfiability for predicates – in the worst case, Φ (similarly, Ψ) can be computed by checking the predicate in the scope of the $(\exists X)$ quantifier for satisfiability for each valuation of the boolean free variables. The decidability of this satisfiability question is also assumed for the symbolic minimization algorithms [BFH90,LY92,HHK95].

The massaging step ($massage : (e, C) \mapsto (\bar{e}, newC, fP)$) simplifies the expression e and replaces atomic predicates by corresponding boolean variables, defining new boolean variables for predicates not already in C. These new predicates are collected in fP, and C is updated to $newC$ by adding the new predicate-variable correspondences. The resulting expression is denoted by $\bar{e}$. We also use this notation to let $\bar{S}$ represent the set of boolean variables corresponding to the atomic predicates in set S. The simplifications accelerate the convergence of the algorithm and are thus necessary in practice, but not in theory, as shown in Theorems 3 and 4. Examples of simplification rules are: $((\text{if } c \text{ then } e \text{ else } f) \leq g) = \text{if } c \text{ then } (e \leq g) \text{ else } (f \leq g)$, $(true \wedge x) = true$, $(x = x) = true$, $(x + y) \leq (x + z) = (y \leq z)$, $(\text{if } c \text{ then } e \text{ else } c) = (c \wedge e)$. For example, if the expression e is $(\text{if } x = u \text{ then } y \text{ else } x) = u$ and the current correspondence table is $\{(x = u, b)\}$, the massaging step produces the new table $\{(x = u, b), (y = u, c)\}$ and the massaged expression $\bar{e} = (b \wedge c)$.

There are several interesting claims that can be made about the algorithm, despite its simplicity. The algorithm is *sound*, in that the abstract program is guaranteed to simulate the original, with respect to the initial set of atomic predicates, AP. A more interesting fact is that the algorithm is also *complete*, in that, if the TS of the original program has a finite simulation (bisimulation) quotient, then iterating the main loop (step 2) of the algorithm sufficiently many times (i.e., with a large enough value for K) results in an abstract program whose TS is simulation-equivalent (bisimulation-equivalent) to the original with respect to AP. These propositions are stated precisely below. Due to space limitations, we present only a sketch of the proof. We use the following notation: for an abstract state t (which is always defined over $\overline{oldPred}$), $\uparrow t$ (read as "up t") denotes the set of concrete states that agree with t on the valuations of the atomic predicates in $oldPred$; precisely, $\uparrow t = \{s | (\forall P : P \in oldPred : P(s) \equiv \overline{P}(t))\}$. Let $\mathcal{A}$ be the TS of the abstract program, and $\mathcal{C}$ the TS of the concrete program.

Lemma 0 (Invariance Lemma) *For every state t of $\mathcal{A}$, $\uparrow t$ is a non-empty set of concrete states.*

Proof Sketch. The formula Ψ ensures this for initial states, while Φ and the wlp computation ensure that the invariant holds. □

> 1. The initial set of atomic predicates consists of those in the specification formula, the initial condition of the program, and the transition relation. This forms the set of unexamined predicates, *newPred*. The set *oldPred*, of already examined predicates is initially empty. The initial correspondence table C is empty.
> 2. While *newPred* is non-empty, and the iteration bound K is not reached,
>   a) Initialize *freshPred* to the empty set
>   b) For each predicate P in *newPred* and each action a, compute $(\overline{e}, C, fP) := massage(wlp_a(P), C)$, and add the predicates in fP to *freshPred*.
>   c) Compute *newPred*, *oldPred* := *freshPred*, *oldPred* ∪ *newPred*.
> 3. The abstract program (X_A, I_A, T_A, F_A) is formed as follows.
>   - $X_A = b \cup c$, where b is the set of boolean variables corresponding to *oldPred*, and c is the set of boolean variables corresponding to *newPred*.
>   - $I_A(b)$ is defined as $massage(I, C) \wedge \Psi$, where $\Psi = (\exists X :: I(X) \wedge (\bigwedge i : P_i \in oldPred : b_i \equiv P_i(X)))$.
>   - $T_A(bc, b'c')$ is defined as $(\bigvee a :: \Phi \wedge (\bigwedge i : P_i \in oldPred : b'_i \equiv massage(wlp_a(P_i), C)))$, where $\Phi = (\exists X :: (\bigwedge i : Q_i \in newPred : c_i \equiv Q_i(X)))$.
>   - As we are not considering fairness, both F and F_A are *true*.

Fig. 3. The abstraction algorithm

Theorem 1 (Simulation Theorem) *The finite state abstract program simulates the concrete program w.r.t. the set of predicates AP.*

Proof Sketch. The claim is proved by showing that the relation R defined by $(s, t) \in R$ iff $s \in \uparrow t$ is a simulation relation from $\mathcal{C}$ to $\mathcal{A}$. As $AP \subseteq oldPred$, this relation preserves the values of the predicates in AP. □

Theorem 2 (Bisimulation Theorem) *If newPred = ∅ on termination of step 2 of the abstraction algorithm, then the finite state abstract program is bisimulation-equivalent to the concrete program w.r.t. the set of predicates AP.*

Proof Sketch. If *newPred* = ∅ upon termination then, for each atomic predicate P in *oldPred* and each action a of the concrete program, $wlp_a(P)$ is a predicate over *oldPred*. As each action a is deterministic, for each predicate P, the transition $\overline{P}' = massage(wlp_a(P), C)$ (step 3) exactly captures the change to P after execution of action a. Let B be the relation on the disjoint union of the abstract and concrete programs defined by $(s, t) \in B$ iff $s \in \uparrow t \vee t \in \uparrow s$. The claim is proved by showing that B is a bisimulation, under the condition *newPred* = ∅. □

Theorem 3 (Bisimulation Completeness) *If the concrete program has a finite reachable bisimulation quotient, there is an appropriate choice for the iteration bound K such that the abstract program produced by the algorithm is bisimulation-equivalent to the concrete program w.r.t. AP.*

Proof Sketch. Suppose that the concrete program has a finite reachable bisimulation quotient. By the results in [BFH90,LY92], the states of this quotient can be calculated as a finite partition Π by a symbolic partition refinement algorithm. The classes of Π are defined by boolean combinations of a finite set of atomic predicates, $\mathcal{P}$, that includes AP. The minimization algorithm computes the formulae defining these classes by repeated wlp computations. As wlp distributes over all boolean operators, these wlp computations may be rewritten to apply wlp only to atomic predicates, which is what our algorithm does. Since the unexamined predicate set $newPred$ is obtained through wlp computations in a *breadth-first* manner, the algorithm eventually generates every predicate necessary for describing the classes of Π. Let K be the least iteration after which $\mathcal{P} \subseteq oldPred$ holds.

While the classes of the quotient can be described using a finite number of atomic predicates, our algorithm considers each predicate individually, not as part of a class formula. Hence, it is possible for our algorithm to generate new predicates (even semantically new predicates) beyond the Kth iteration. If $newPred$ is empty after K iterations, the claim follows by Theorem 2. Otherwise, define the relation R by $(s,t) \in R$ iff the concrete state s and the set of concrete states $\uparrow t$ are both included in the same class of Π. As the extra predicates in $oldPred \backslash \mathcal{P}$ are unnecessary, the relation B defined by sBt iff $(sRt \vee tRs)$ can be shown to be a bisimulation between $\mathcal{C}$ and $\mathcal{A}$. As $AP \subseteq oldPred$, this bisimulation preserves the predicates in AP. □

Theorem 4 (Simulation Completeness) *If the concrete program has a finite simulation quotient, there is an appropriate choice for the iteration bound K such that the abstract program produced by the algorithm is simulation-equivalent to the concrete program w.r.t. AP.*

Proof Sketch. There is a partition refinement algorithm [HHK95] to compute the greatest simulation relation that also employs wlp computations in a manner similar to the bisimulation minimization algorithms. The claim then follows from arguments similar to those in the proof of Theorem 3. □

4 Extensions to the Algorithm

4.1 Retaining a Set of Finite-Domain Control Variables

The algorithm can be easily modified to retain a set of finite-domain control variables V while abstracting out the rest $(X \backslash V)$. We assume that V is closed under next-state dependencies; formally that, for any predicate $P(V)$, $wlp_a(P(V))$ does not introduce any atomic predicates over $X \backslash V$ other than those already present in the action a. During the massaging process, atomic predicates over V are *not* replaced with corresponding boolean variables. After step 2 terminates, the concrete program transitions for the V-variables are massaged and copied over to the abstract program. This modification was used in the Bakery example to retain the variables st_1, st_2. It is particularly useful when data variables are to be abstracted while retaining control variables.

4.2 Handling Fairness

There are two ways in which fairness may be specified. In the first type, one may specify fairness constraints on the actions of the program. Since the abstract program is strongly similar (bisimular) to the original, $A\mu$ (μ) properties over fair computations that hold in the abstract program also hold of the original. If fairness is specified instead by constraints on program states, we can add the atomic predicates from these constraints to *newPred* in step 1 of the algorithm and, in step 3, massage the fairness conditions to get the corresponding conditions for the abstract program.

4.3 Abstracting Programs with Unbounded Nondeterminacy

We presented our algorithm for programs with bounded non-determinacy, which was exploited by considering each deterministic action individually. For transition relations that exhibit unbounded nondeterminacy, this partitioning is not possible, so we adopt a slightly different strategy. The key idea is to replace the computation (in step 2) of *wlp* for individual predicates with a computation of *wlp* for all clauses formed out of *oldPred* ∪ *newPred* (a clause is disjunction of literals, where each literal is an atomic predicate or its negation). This algorithm is both *sound* and *complete*, in the sense used earlier; however, it is probably impractical as an exponential number of clauses is generated in each iteration of step 2. We present below a simpler algorithm which is sound but not complete; however, as shown in the next section, it generalizes existing algorithms for data-insensitive programs.

Consider a partitioning of the transition relation into actions of the form $[W]$: $g(V, W) \hookrightarrow V := e(V, W)$, where W is a set of unbounded input variables, and V is a set of state variables. Hence, $wlp_a(P(V))$ is $(\forall W :: wlp_a^V(P))$, where $wlp_a^V(P)$ is $g(V, W) \Rightarrow P(W, e(V, W))$. The expression $wlp_a^V(P)$ may contain two types of predicates: state predicates over V and "mixed" predicates over $V \cup W$. Step 2 of the original algorithm is replaced with the following.

1. Compute $wlp_a^V(P)$ repeatedly with only the state predicates in *newPred* until no new state predicates are generated or the iteration bound K is reached.
2. If the iteration bound K is reached, proceed as before. Otherwise, define a boolean *input* variable c_i for each mixed predicate P_i in *newPred* ∪ *oldPred*, and compute $F = (\exists W :: (\bigwedge_i :: c_i = P_i(W, V)))$, which is the condition for a *c*-valuation to be consistent. Quantifier-elimination results in a definition of F as a predicate on $V \cup \{c_i\}$. If there are new state predicates in F, add those to *newPred* and return to the first step, otherwise conjoin $massage(F, C)$ to the abstract transition relation.

Theorem 5 *(i) The modified algorithm always produces a conservative abstraction. (ii) If the algorithm terminates at step 2 with newPred = ∅, the abstract program is bisimular to the concrete program w.r.t. AP.*□

5 Applications

From the completeness results, our method can be applied to any program that has a finite quotient relative to the atomic predicates in the specification. Specific types of programs are particularly amenable to the application of this algorithm.

5.1 Data-Insensitive Programs

We define *data-insensitive* programs as those that have a finite simulation quotient that preserves the values of all control variables. Hence, the control-flow is dependent on only a finite number of data predicates. Several papers describe restrictions on program syntax to ensure data-insensitivity, and provide abstraction algorithms which replace data domains by small finite domains, keeping the program actions unchanged [Wol86,HB95,ID96,Laz99]. This is justified by showing a bisimulation between the large- and small-domain instances.

Our program transformation method terminates for each of the above classes of programs. For instance, in [ID96], the only atomic predicate is $=$, and every assignment has the form $X := Y$. As there are n^2 distinct atomic equality predicates over the n variables $x_i \in X$, our algorithm terminates in at most n^2 steps, creating a bisimulation-equivalent abstraction by Theorem 5. The transformation of [ID96] replaces each data domain with $[0 \ldots n]$, hence the abstract state is represented by $n * \log(n)$ bits. In contrast, if only a few combinations of equality predicates are necessary, our method will result in states representable with fewer than $n * \log(n)$ bits [3]. One may also show the following theorem.

Theorem 6 *For programs without unbounded inputs where assignments are of the form $X := Y$, our abstraction algorithm terminates with a bisimulation-equivalent abstract program.*

Our algorithm also terminates for showing that the program below has an infinite computation, which is not possible to show with a finite domain method (cf. [HB95]). Thus, our algorithm is strictly more powerful than the finite-domain methods.

var x : **natural**
initially $x = 0$
action $a[i : \mathbf{natural}]$ $\quad (x < i) \hookrightarrow x := i$

5.2 Symmetric Programs

Bisimulation reductions for semantically symmetric programs have been proposed in [ES93,CFJ93]. It is computationally difficult, however, to implement such reductions symbolically (i.e., with BDD's) [CFJ93]. Hence, [ET99] consider syntactically symmetric programs, defined using symmetric predicates such as

---

[3] A similar tradeoff occurs in finite-domain [PRSS99] vs. predicate abstraction [SGZ+98] approaches to verifying combinational circuits over integer variables.

($\forall i :: P(i)$). The reduction of such a program with n processes, each with k local states, is obtained by introducing k variables $\{x_i\}$, each with a domain of $[0 \ldots n]$. By considering symmetric predicates to be atomic, our algorithm can be applied to such programs. In the worst case, it may produce all predicates of the form $x_i \geq l$ for each $l \in [0 \ldots n]$, requiring $k * (n+1)$ (correlated) boolean variables, but with a $poly(n)$ size BDD for each action. On the other hand, as our algorithm calculates only those predicates necessary for the reduction, it may also produce a program with fewer than the $k * \log(n)$ bits required by [ET99].

6 Related Work and Conclusions

Among related work, [GS97,CABN97,BLO98,CU98] also propose predicate abstraction methods. [CABN97] performs a simple syntactic transformation, but requires the use of a constraint solver during the model checking process. The methods of [GS97,BLO98,CU98] utilize general-purpose theorem proving to compute the abstract program, which is defined over boolean variables that correspond to an *a priori fixed* set of predicates. If the verification fails on the abstract program, the set of predicates is refined heuristically, and the abstraction process is repeated. In contrast, our algorithm, which has the same initial choice of predicates, both refines the set of predicates and computes the abstract program *automatically*, in a manner that is shown to be both sound and complete.

The papers [Wol86,ID96,HB95,Laz99] present algorithms for abstracting syntactically restricted programs. As shown in the previous section, our algorithm can be applied with guaranteed termination to these classes of programs, and is more generally applicable.

The symbolic minimization algorithms in [BFH90,LY92,HHK95] produce an *explicit* abstract transition system, which can be quite large and may preclude the effective application of symbolic model checking and partial order reduction methods. In contrast, our algorithm produces an *implicit* program description in the same syntax as the original program, which can then be analyzed using any model checking method. Our completeness results guarantee that our algorithm can find an equivalent finite abstract program, if one exists, given an appropriate termination bound.

The deductive model checking algorithm of [SUM99] produces an abstraction relative to a *LTL* specification by a process of iterative refinement which, however, requires significant human intervention. In [KP00], it is shown that finite state abstractions exist for programs that satisfy *LTL* properties; the completeness proof is non-constructive in general but partly utilizes predicate abstraction. Other automatic abstraction methods [DGG93,CGL94] apply only to finite state systems. Other semi-algorithms [HGD95,KMM+97,BGP97,BDG+98] directly model check infinite state systems without computing an abstract program. The algorithm in [GS92] for model checking a special type of parameterized system relies on a trace equivalent abstraction.

We have hand-simulated our algorithm for a simple data transfer protocol that transmits natural numbers with 0 representing null data. The correctness property is that data that is sent is eventually received. The abstracted protocol is verified by COSPAN using less resources (time, space) than the verification of the original protocol with data domain size 1. We are currently developing a prototype implementation to experiment with larger examples.

References

[BCG88] M. C. Browne, E. M. Clarke, and O. Grümberg. Characterizing finite Kripke structures in Propositional Temporal Logic. *Theoretical Computer Science*, 59, 1988.

[BDG+98] J. Bohn, W. Damm, O. Grumberg, H. Hungar, and K. Laster. First-order-CTL model checking. In *FST&TCS*, volume 1530 of *LNCS*, 1998.

[BFH90] A. Bouajjani, J-C. Fernandez, and N. Halbwachs. Minimal model generation. In *CAV*, volume 531 of *LNCS*, 1990. Full version in *Science of Computer Programming*, vol. 18, 1992.

[BGP97] T. Bultan, R. Gerber, and W. Pugh. Symbolic model checking of infinite state systems using Presburger arithmetic. In *CAV*, volume 1254 of *LNCS*, 1997.

[BLO98] S. Bensalem, Y. Lakhnech, and S. Owre. Computing abstractions of infinite state systems compositionally and automatically. In *CAV*, volume 1427 of *LNCS*, 1998.

[CABN97] W. Chan, R. Anderson, P. Beame, and D. Notkin. Combining constraint solving and symbolic model checking for a class of systems with non-linear constraints. In *CAV*, volume 1254 of *LNCS*, 1997.

[CE81] E.M. Clarke and E. A. Emerson. Design and synthesis of synchronization skeletons using branching time temporal logic. In *Workshop on Logics of Programs*, volume 131 of *LNCS*, 1981.

[CES86] E.M. Clarke, E.A. Emerson, and A.P. Sistla. Automatic verification of finite-state concurrent systems using temporal logic. *TOPLAS*, 8(2), 1986.

[CFJ93] E.M. Clarke, T. Filkorn, and S. Jha. Exploiting symmetry in temporal logic model checking. In *CAV*, volume 697 of *LNCS*, 1993.

[CGL94] E.M. Clarke, O. Grumberg, and D. Long. Model checking and abstraction. *TOPLAS*, 1994.

[CU98] M.A. Colon and T.E. Uribe. Generating finite-state abstractions of reactive systems using decision procedures. In *CAV*, volume 1427 of *LNCS*, 1998.

[DGG93] D. Dams, R. Gerth, and O. Grumberg. Generation of reduced models for checking fragments of CTL. In *CAV*, volume 697 of *LNCS*, 1993.

[Dij75] E.W. Dijkstra. Guarded commands, nondeterminacy, and formal derivation of programs. In *C.ACM*, volume 18, 1975.

[EH86] E.A. Emerson and J. Halpern. "Sometimes" and "Not Never" revisited: On branching versus linear time temporal logic. *J.ACM*, 33, 1986.

[EL86] E.A. Emerson and C-L. Lei. Efficient model checking in fragments of the propositional mu-calculus (extended abstract). In *LICS*, 1986.

[ES93] E.A. Emerson and A.P. Sistla. Symmetry and model checking. In *CAV*, number 697 in LNCS, 1993.

[ET99] E.A. Emerson and R.J. Trefler. From asymmetry to full symmetry: New techniques for symmetry reduction in model checking. In *CHARME*, volume LNCS, 1999.

[GL94]   O. Grumberg and D. Long. Model checking and modular verification. *TOPLAS*, 16, 1994.
[GS92]   S. German and A.P. Sistla. Reasoning about systems with many processes. *J.ACM*, 1992.
[GS97]   S. Graf and H. Saidi. Construction of abstract state graphs with PVS. In *CAV*, volume 1254 of *LNCS*, 1997.
[HB95]   R. Hojati and R.K. Brayton. Automatic datapath abstraction of hardware systems. In *CAV*, volume 939 of *LNCS*, 1995.
[HGD95]   H. Hungar, O. Grumberg, and W. Damm. What if model checking must be truly symbolic. In *CHARME*, volume 987 of *LNCS*, 1995.
[HHK95]   M.R. Henzinger, T.A. Henzinger, and P. W. Kopke. Computing simulations on finite and infinite graphs. In *IEEE FOCS*, 1995.
[ID96]   C.N. Ip and D.L. Dill. Better verification through symmetry. *Formal Methods in System Design*, 1996.
[Kel76]   R. M. Keller. Formal verification of parallel programs. *C.ACM*, 1976.
[KMM+97]   Y. Kesten, O. Maler, M. Marcus, A. Pnueli, and E. Shahar. Symbolic model checking with rich assertional languages. In *CAV*, volume 1254 of *LNCS*, 1997.
[Koz83]   D. Kozen. Results on the propositional mu-calculus. *Theoretical Computer Science*, 1983.
[KP00]   Y. Kesten and A. Pnueli. Verification by augmented finitary abstraction. *Information and Computation (to appear)*, 2000. Earlier version at MFCS 1998, published in LNCS 1450.
[Lam74]   L. Lamport. A new solution of Dijkstra's concurrent programming problem. *C.ACM*, August 1974.
[Laz99]   R.S. Lazić. *A Semantic Study of Data Independence with Applications to Model Checking*. PhD thesis, Oxford University, 1999.
[LY92]   D. Lee and M. Yannakakis. Online minimization of transition systems. In *STOC*, 1992.
[Mil71]   R. Milner. An algebraic definition of simulation between programs. In *2nd IJCAI*, 1971.
[Par81]   D. Park. Concurrency and automata on infinite sequences. In *Theoretical Computer Science: 5th GI-Conference, Karlsruhe*, volume 104 of *LNCS*, 1981.
[Pnu77]   A. Pnueli. The temporal logic of programs. In *FOCS*, 1977.
[PRSS99]   A. Pnueli, Y. Rodeh, O. Shtrichman, and M. Siegel. Deciding equality formulas by small domains instantiations. In *CAV*, volume 1633 of *LNCS*, 1999.
[QS82]   J.P. Queille and J. Sifakis. Specification and verification of concurrent systems in CESAR. In *Proc. of the 5th International Symposium on Programming*, volume 137 of *LNCS*, 1982.
[SGZ+98]   K. Sajid, A. Goel, H. Zhou, A. Aziz, S. Barber, and V. Singhal. Bdd-based procedures for a theory of equality with uninterpreted functions. In *CAV*, volume 1427 of *LNCS*, 1998.
[SUM99]   H. Sipma, T. Uribe, and Z. Manna. Deductive model checking. *Formal Methods in System Design*, 15, 1999. Earlier version at CAV 1996, published in LNCS 1102.
[Wol86]   P. Wolper. Expressing interesting properties of programs in propositional temporal logic. In *POPL*, 1986.

Temporal-Logic Queries

William Chan*

Abstract. This paper introduces temporal-logic queries for model understanding and model checking. A temporal-logic query is a temporal-logic formula in which a placeholder appears exactly once. Given a model, the semantics of a query is a proposition that can replace the placeholder to result in a formula that holds in the model and is as strong as possible. The author defines a class of CTL queries that can be evaluated in linear time, and show how they can be used to help the user understand the system behaviors and obtain more feedback in model checking.

1 Introduction

Although model *checking* was proposed as a verification (or falsification) technique [3], we find it valuable for model *understanding*: The user hypothesizes a behavior of the system, expresses it as a temporal-logic formula, and attempts to use the model checker to validate the hypothesis. The process is iterated while the user gains knowledge about the system. In our opinion, this use of model checking has not been emphasized enough in the literature. To further help the user understand system behaviors, in this paper we introduce temporal-logic queries and use a technique similar to symbolic model checking to *infer* temporal properties as opposed to merely checking them.

This work was partly motivated by the recent interest in deriving invariants of software for comprehension, documentation, or evolution [6, 10, 12]. Inferring invariants is not a new idea, but the traditional objective is to assist in theorem proving [e.g., 2]. We believe that inferring properties is particularly useful for software models, which, unlike hardware, often lack explicit correctness criteria.

Let us first consider inferring invariants. Observe that when the reachable state space can be computed symbolically, we in fact obtain the *strongest invariant* of the system. Although this invariant contains a tremendous amount of useful information, it is likely to be too complex for the user to understand. But note that most interesting invariants in practice involve only a small number of atomic propositions. So, one way to extract useful information from the reachable states is to project its symbolic representation onto a small subset of atomic propositions, thereby deriving a weaker, but more comprehensible, invariant. (In fact, in version 2.5 of CMU's SMV model checker, a user can select a subset of atomic propositions on which to project the reachable states.) We have found situations in which insightful information can be obtained even if we project the reachable states on only singleton sets or pairs of atomic propositions.

---

* William Chan did this research in the Department of Computer Science and Engineering at the University of Washington. On 26 November 1999, one week after successfully defending his doctoral dissertation, William Chan died in an automobile accident. For requests concerning this paper, please contact Paul Beame, Department of Computer Science and Engineering, University of Washington, Seattle, WA 98195, beame@cs.washington.edu

Inferring invariants is a special case of evaluating temporal-logic queries. A query is a formula in which a special symbol ?, called a placeholder, appears exactly once. An example CTL query is AG?. The semantics of a query is a proposition p such that replacing ? with p in the query results in a formula that holds in a given model and is as strong as possible. Therefore, the query AG? evaluates to the strongest p that makes AGp hold; in other words, it represents the strongest invariant. More complex examples include AG($req \to$ A$((? \lor$ AG$\neg ack)$W$ack))$, which asks what is true between the receipt of a request and the transmission of an acknowledgement, and AF($startup\_complete \lor$ AG?), which roughly asks, what is eventually always true in the case that the startup operation cannot be completed.

As it turns out, however, not every query is meaningful. For example, in most models, the desired proposition defined above cannot be found for the query AF?. Indeed, we show that identifying the "valid" queries is intractable (EXPTIME-complete for CTL queries), so we resort to a conservative approach: We define a class of CTL queries that are guaranteed to be valid, and furthermore can be evaluated in time linear in the size of the model and in the length of the query. That is, the asymptotic worst-case time complexity is the same as that of CTL model checking. Though syntactically quite restricted, the class contains interesting queries such as the two examples given above.

In addition to deriving temporal properties based on a given pattern, the technique can also be used to provide more feedback to the user in model checking, such as providing a partial explanation when the property checked holds, and diagnostic information when it does not. Suppose we would like to check the invariant AG($x \lor y$). We can evaluate the query AG?. Assume that after projecting the strongest invariant on x and y, we obtain AG($x \land y$) as an inferred formula. Note that this formula is stronger than the one we wanted to check. Not only can we conclude that AG($x \lor y$) holds, we can also inform the user of the stronger property. This information can either serve as an explanation of the verification result ($x \lor y$ is an invariant because $x \land y$ is), or as an indication that the checked property is in a sense vacuously true. Furthermore, in case a formula is falsified, apart from obtaining a counterexample, the user can pose queries to acquire more feedback. For example, if AG($req \to$ AFack) is false, that is, a request is not always followed by an acknowledgement, we can ask what can guarantee an acknowledgement, AG(? $\to$ AFack).

The rest of the paper is organized as follows. We review CTL model checking in Section 2, Section 3 gives the main technical results, while Section 4 explains how to simplify a proposition so the user can understand it. Section 5 describes some initial experience of the technique. We conclude in Section 6 with some discussion of future work.

2 Background

This section gives an overview of CTL model checking [3]. Note that, to facilitate our definition of CTL queries, our formulation of CTL is non-standard.

A *model* is a tuple $\langle Q, Q_0, \Delta, X, L \rangle$, where Q is a finite set of *states*, $Q_0 \subseteq Q$ is the set of *initial states*, $\Delta \subseteq Q \times Q$ is the *transition relation*, X is a finite set of *atomic propositions*, and the function $L \colon Q \to \mathcal{P}(X)$ maps each state to a set of atomic propositions that are true at the state. The transition relation Δ is assumed to be total; that is, for every $q \in Q$, there exists a *successor* $q' \in Q$ with $\langle q, q' \rangle \in \Delta$. A *path* is an infinite sequence of states in which each consecutive pair of states belongs to Δ. A state is *reachable* if it appears on some path starting from some initial state.

Properties about a model can be specified in the Computation Tree Logic (CTL). CTL formulas consists of atomic propositions, Boolean operators, path quantifiers, and temporal operators. Formally,

- any atomic proposition and *true* are CTL formulas, and
- if ϕ and ψ are CTL formulas, then $\neg\phi$, $\phi \vee \psi$, $\mathsf{AX}\phi$, $\mathsf{A}\,(\phi\,\mathring{\mathsf{W}}\,\psi)$, and $\mathsf{A}\,(\phi\,\mathsf{U}\,\psi)$ are also CTL formulas.

As usual, A is the universal path quantifier, X is the *next-time* operator, and U is the *strong until* operator. We call the operator $\mathring{\mathsf{W}}$ the *overlapping weak until* operator, which is like the dual of U, that is, $\phi\,\mathring{\mathsf{W}}\,\psi \equiv \neg(\neg\psi\,\mathsf{U}\,\neg\phi)$.[1] Intuitively, $\mathsf{X}\phi$ means that ϕ is true in the next state, $\phi\,\mathsf{U}\,\psi$ means that ϕ remains true until ψ becomes true, and $\phi\,\mathring{\mathsf{W}}\,\psi$ means that either ϕ is true forever, or ϕ remains true until both ϕ and ψ become true. A formula is *propositional* (or, simply, abusing terminology, a *proposition*) if it does not contain temporal operators X, $\mathring{\mathsf{W}}$, or, U.

Assume a fixed model M. We write $q \models \phi$ if the CTL formula ϕ is true at state q. The truth value of a CTL formula at a state q_0 is then defined as follows (x is any atomic proposition, and ϕ and ψ are CTL formulas): 1. $q_0 \models \mathit{true}$. 2. $q_0 \models x$ iff $x \in L(q_0)$. 3. $q_0 \models \neg\phi$ iff it is not the case that $q_0 \models \phi$. 4. $q_0 \models \phi \vee \psi$ iff either $q_0 \models \phi$ or $q_0 \models \psi$. 5. $q_0 \models \mathsf{AX}\phi$ iff $q_1 \models \phi$ for every q_1 with $(q_0, q_1) \in \Delta$. 6. $q_0 \models \mathsf{A}\,(\phi\,\mathsf{U}\,\psi)$ iff for every path $q_0, q_1, q_2, \ldots$, there exists an $i \geq 0$ with $q_i \models \psi$, and $q_j \models \phi$ for all $j < i$. 7. $q_0 \models \mathsf{A}\,(\phi\,\mathring{\mathsf{W}}\,\psi)$ iff for every path $q_0, q_1, q_2, \ldots$, for all $i \geq 0$, if $q_j \models \neg\psi$ for all $j < i$, then $q_i \models \phi$.

We write $S \models \phi$ if $q \models \phi$ for each $q \in S$. We say that M satisfies ϕ, written $M \models \phi$, if ϕ is true at every initial state of M. The CTL *model-checking* problem is, given a model and a CTL formula, determine whether the model satisfies the formula. A formula is *valid* if it is satisfied by every model. As usual, we write $\phi \Rightarrow \psi$ if $(\neg\phi) \vee \psi$ is valid, and write $\phi \Leftrightarrow \psi$ if $\phi \Rightarrow \psi$ and $\psi \Rightarrow \phi$. Note that if we have $\phi \Rightarrow \psi$ and $M \models \phi$, then we also have $M \models \psi$.

We define the usual abbreviations *false* $\equiv \neg\mathit{true}$, $\phi \rightarrow \psi \equiv (\neg\phi) \vee \psi$, and $\phi \wedge \psi \equiv \neg(\neg\phi \vee \neg\psi)$, as well as

$$\mathsf{AG}\phi \equiv \mathsf{A}\,(\phi\,\mathring{\mathsf{W}}\,\mathit{false}) \qquad \mathsf{AF}\phi \equiv \mathsf{A}\,(\mathit{true}\,\mathsf{U}\,\phi).$$

The operator G is the *global* operator, and F is the *future* operator. For symmetry, we also define the *weak until* operator W and the *overlapping strong until* operator $\mathring{\mathsf{U}}$:

$$\mathsf{A}\,(\phi\,\mathsf{W}\,\psi) \equiv \mathsf{A}\,(\phi \vee \psi\,\mathring{\mathsf{W}}\,\psi) \qquad \mathsf{A}\,(\phi\,\mathring{\mathsf{U}}\,\psi) \equiv \mathsf{A}\,(\phi\,\mathsf{U}\,\phi \wedge \psi).$$

---

[1] In other words, the operator $\mathring{\mathsf{W}}$ is the same as the so-called "release" operator V with the operands swapped: $\phi\,\mathring{\mathsf{W}}\,\psi \equiv \psi\,\mathsf{V}\,\phi$ [9]. Our definition of CTL might remind the reader of the sublogic ACTL. We are actually defining the full CTL here because we allow negating arbitrary formulas. We do not explicitly define the existential fragment because it is not needed in this paper.

In addition it can be shown that

$$\mathsf{A}\,(\phi\,\mathring{\mathsf{W}}\,\psi) \Leftrightarrow \mathsf{A}\,(\phi\,\mathsf{W}\,\phi \wedge \psi) \qquad \mathsf{A}\,(\phi\,\mathsf{U}\,\psi) \Leftrightarrow \mathsf{A}\,(\phi\,\mathsf{W}\,\psi) \wedge \mathsf{AF}\psi.$$

To summarize the different versions of until operators, intuitively $\phi\,\mathcal{U}\,\psi$ means that ϕ remains true until ψ is true if $\mathcal{U} \in \{\mathsf{W}, \mathsf{U}\}$, and until both ϕ and ψ are true if $\mathcal{U} \in \{\mathring{\mathsf{W}}, \mathring{\mathsf{U}}\}$. If $\mathcal{U} \in \{\mathsf{W}, \mathring{\mathsf{W}}\}$, we also allow ψ to never hold provided ϕ is true forever.

For any CTL formula ϕ, let $[\![\phi]\!]$ denote the set of states in which ϕ is true. The model-checking problem is then equivalent to determining whether the set of initial states is a subset of $[\![\phi]\!]$. For any atomic proposition x, the set $[\![x]\!]$ is easy to find. For any state set S, define $pre_\forall(S)$ as

$$pre_\forall(S) = \{\, q \in Q \mid \forall q'.\ \text{if}\ \langle q, q'\rangle \in \Delta\ \text{then}\ q' \in S\,\},$$

the set of states with every successor in S. The following equations hold for any CTL formulas ϕ and ψ:

$$[\![\neg\phi]\!] = Q \setminus [\![\phi]\!] \qquad [\![\mathsf{A}\,(\phi\,\mathsf{U}\,\psi)]\!] = \mu Z.\,([\![\psi]\!] \cup ([\![\phi]\!] \cap pre_\forall(Z)))$$
$$[\![\phi \vee \psi]\!] = [\![\phi]\!] \cup [\![\psi]\!] \qquad [\![\mathsf{A}\,(\phi\,\mathring{\mathsf{W}}\,\psi)]\!] = \nu Z.\,([\![\phi]\!] \cap ([\![\psi]\!] \cup pre_\forall(Z)))$$
$$[\![\mathsf{AX}\phi]\!] = pre_\forall([\![\phi]\!])$$

where μ and ν are respectively the least fixed-point and greatest fixed-point operators. It can be shown that $pre_\forall$ and these fixed points can be computed in time linear in the size of the model, which is denoted $|M|$ and defined as $|Q| + |\Delta|$. This suggests a model-checking algorithm that given ϕ, recursively converts the subformulas of ϕ to sets of states in an inside-out manner. The algorithm thus runs in time linear in the size of the model and in the length of the formula. Because the formula is evaluated by computing predecessors of states, we say that the algorithm is based on *backward traversals*.

3 CTL Queries

The *placeholder* is a special symbol ?. A *CTL query* is a string in which the placeholder appears exactly once, and for any CTL formula ϕ, substituting ϕ for ? results in a CTL formula. A query is *positive* if the placeholder appears under an even number of negations; otherwise, it is *negative*. For example, the query AG? is positive, while AG(? $\to$ AF*ack*) is negative. We use $\gamma(p)$ to denote the result of replacing the placeholder with p in the query γ.

For any query γ and any formulas ϕ and ψ, we write $\phi \Rightarrow^\gamma \psi$ for $\phi \Rightarrow \psi$ if γ is positive, and for $\psi \Rightarrow \phi$ if γ is negative. Intuitively, the lemma below shows that, if we view a query as a function that maps formulas to formulas, then depending on the polarity of the query, the function is either monotonically increasing or monotonically decreasing.

Lemma 1. *For all formulas ϕ and ψ and every query γ, if $\phi \Rightarrow \psi$, then $\gamma(\phi) \Rightarrow^\gamma \gamma(\psi)$.*

Proof Idea. Apply structural induction. Note that the truth of this lemma relies on the fact that we do not allow bi-implication $\leftrightarrow$ in CTL queries. □

If we have $M \models \gamma(p)$ for some proposition p, we say that p is a *solution* to γ in M. We write $\gamma(\top)$ and $\gamma(\bot)$ for $\gamma(\textit{true})$ and $\gamma(\textit{false})$ respectively if γ is positive, and $\gamma(\textit{false})$ and $\gamma(\textit{true})$ respectively otherwise. Checking whether a given query has a solution in a given model can be reduced to model checking.

Lemma 2. *For every query γ and every model M, we have 1. γ has a solution in M if and only if $M \models \gamma(\top)$, and 2. every proposition is a solution to γ in M if and only if $M \models \gamma(\bot)$.*

Proof. The *if* direction of 1 and the *only-if* direction of 2 are trivial. For the rest of the proof: Consider any proposition p. Because $\textit{false} \Rightarrow p \Rightarrow \textit{true}$, Lemma 1 implies $\gamma(\textit{false}) \Rightarrow^\gamma \gamma(p) \Rightarrow^\gamma \gamma(\textit{true})$, or $\gamma(\bot) \Rightarrow \gamma(p) \Rightarrow \gamma(\top)$. Therefore, if $M \models \gamma(\bot)$, then $M \models \gamma(p)$, proving the *if* direction of 2. Also, if $M \models \gamma(p)$, then $M \models \gamma(\top)$, proving the *only-if* direction of 1. □

3.1 Exact Solutions and Valid Queries

Finding an arbitrary solution to a query is not very interesting; finding all solutions does not seem useful either, because there are likely to be too many of them. Instead, we would like to find a single solution that summarizes all solutions. We say that a solution s to γ in M is *exact* if for every solution p, we have $s \Rightarrow^\gamma p$. (It is not hard to see from Lemma 1 that, if s is exact, then p is a solution *if and only if* $s \Rightarrow^\gamma p$.) Solving a query means finding an exact solution to a given query in a given model.

Note that not every query has an exact solution in a model. Consider the query AF?. Suppose x and y are solutions. Note that $x \wedge y$ is not necessarily a solution because x and y may hold at different states on the paths. In this case the query has no exact solutions in the model. We say that a query is *valid* if it has an exact solution in every model.

For any query γ and any formulas ϕ and ψ, we write $\phi \wedge^\gamma \psi$ for $\phi \wedge \psi$ if γ is positive, and for $\phi \vee \psi$ if γ is negative. We say that γ is *distributive over conjunction*, if for any propositions p_1 and p_2, we have $(\gamma(p_1) \wedge \gamma(p_2)) \leftrightarrow \gamma(p_1 \wedge^\gamma p_2)$.

Lemma 3. *A query is valid if and only if it has a solution in every model and is distributive over conjunction.*

Proof. Fix any CTL query γ. For the *if* direction: Consider any model M. Let P be the non-empty set of solutions of γ in M, and let s be $\bigwedge^\gamma P$, which we claim is an exact solution. By the definition of P, we know that $M \models \bigwedge_{r \in P} \gamma(r)$. By distributivity, the formula is equivalent to $\gamma(s)$, and therefore s is a solution. Clearly, we have $s \Rightarrow^\gamma r$ for every $r \in P$, so s is exact.

For the *only-if* direction: We only need to show that assuming γ is valid, it is distributive over conjunction. That is, we want to show that for any model M, we have $M \models (\gamma(p_1) \wedge \gamma(p_2)) \leftrightarrow \gamma(p_1 \wedge^\gamma p_2)$ for all propositions p_1 and p_2. For the $\leftarrow$ direction: Because we have $p_1 \wedge^\gamma p_2 \Rightarrow^\gamma p_1$, by Lemma 1, we have $\gamma(p_1 \wedge^\gamma p_2) \Rightarrow \gamma(p_1)$, which implies $M \models \gamma(p_1 \wedge^\gamma p_2) \to \gamma(p_1)$. The argument for p_2 is symmetric. For the $\to$ direction: If M does not satisfy $\gamma(p_1) \wedge \gamma(p_2)$, we are done. Otherwise, let s be an exact solution to γ in M. By definition, we have $s \Rightarrow^\gamma p_1$ and $s \Rightarrow^\gamma p_2$, and therefore $s \Rightarrow^\gamma (p_1 \wedge^\gamma p_2)$. Lemma 1 now implies that $\gamma(s) \Rightarrow \gamma(p_1 \wedge^\gamma p_2)$. Since by definition $M \models \gamma(s)$, we also have $M \models \gamma(p_1 \wedge^\gamma p_2)$. □

Unfortunately, identifying valid queries is hard in general.

Theorem 1. *Determining whether a given CTL query is valid is complete for EXPTIME.*

Proof. We show that the problem of identifying queries that always admit exact solutions and are distributive over conjunction is equivalent to CTL formula validity, which is complete for EXPTIME [5, 7]. For a reduction to CTL validity: By Lemma 2, a CTL query γ always has an exact solution if and only if the formula $\phi_1 = \gamma(\top)$ is valid, and, by definition, γ is distributive if and only if the formula $\phi_2 = (\gamma(x_1) \wedge \gamma(x_2)) \leftrightarrow \gamma(x_1 \wedge^\gamma x_2)$ is valid, where x_1 and x_2 are atomic propositions not appearing in γ. So we simply check whether the formula $\phi_1 \wedge \phi_2$ is valid. To reduce from CTL validity, observe that a CTL formula ϕ is valid if and only if for an atomic proposition x not appearing in ϕ, the query $\mathsf{A}\,(x \vee \phi\,\mathsf{W}\,?)$ always has a solution and is distributive over conjunction. □

We can solve a valid query using a naïve approach: Enumerate the exponentially many possible assignments to the atomic propositions. More explicitly, given a set X of atomic propositions, an *assignment* is a proposition of the form

$$\bigwedge_{x \in Y} x \wedge \bigwedge_{x \in X \setminus Y} \neg x$$

for some $Y \subseteq X$. A *satisfying assignment* of a proposition p is an assignment a with $a \Rightarrow p$. Note that every proposition is equivalent to the disjunction of its satisfying assignments. If γ is a positive query and P is the set of every proposition $\neg p$ such that p is an assignment and $\neg p$ is a solution to γ, then it can be shown that $\bigwedge P$ is an exact solution. If γ is negative, it can be shown that $\bigvee P'$ is an exact solution, where P' is the set of every assignment p that is a solution to γ.

Lemma 4. *Given a valid CTL query γ and a model M with atomic propositions X, solving γ in M can be done in time $O(|M|\,|\gamma|\,2^{|X|})$.*

Proof. We assume γ is positive; the case when γ is negative is similar. Let s denote $\bigwedge P$, where P is defined above. We claim that s is an exact solution. It is a solution by the definition of P and the distributivity of γ. To see that it is exact, we want to show $s \Rightarrow r$ for every solution r. We are done if r is a tautology. Otherwise, let A be the non-empty set of all satisfying assignments of $\neg r$. Notice that r is equivalent to $\bigwedge_{a \in A} \neg a$. Consider any $a \in A$. By definition, we have $a \Rightarrow \neg r$, or $r \Rightarrow \neg a$. Because r is a solution, by Lemma 1, $\neg a$ is also a solution. So by the definition of P, we have $\neg a \in P$, and therefore $s \Rightarrow \neg a$, for every $a \in A$. Hence, we have $s \Rightarrow \bigwedge_{a \in A} \neg a$, or equivalently, $s \Rightarrow r$.

Computing P amounts to solving $2^{|X|}$ model-checking problems, each of which takes time $O(|M|\,|\gamma|)$, so the total running time is $O(|M|\,|\gamma|\,2^{|X|})$. □

A time complexity exponential in the number of atomic propositions is hardly desirable. But notice that only backward traversals are used. We now show how, using mixed forward and backward traversals, the exponential factor can be removed for a subclass of valid queries.

3.2 CTL^v Queries

Although valid queries are hard to identify, we can syntactically define classes of queries that are guaranteed to be valid. Intuitively, there are two major cases in which a query is not distributive over conjunction. The first case is when the placeholder appears within the scope of a temporal operator that is under an odd number of negations, such as ¬AG?. These queries are concerned about what happens on *some* paths. If ϕ_1 and ϕ_2 are true on some paths, we do not know whether $\phi_1 \wedge \phi_2$ holds on any path. (We do know that $\phi_1 \vee \phi_2$ is true on some paths, but this is not sufficient.) The second case is when the placeholder appears on the right hand side of untils, e.g., AF?. Such queries ask what will eventually happen. Even if ϕ_1 and ϕ_2 eventually hold, they may not hold in the same states along the paths. There are many exceptions to the second case, however, such as $A(\phi W \neg \phi \wedge ?)$ and AFAG?. Our strategy is to define a class of queries that excludes these known problems while allowing for the exceptions.

We first define two additional until operators, the *disjoint weak until* $\overline{W}$ and the *disjoint strong until* $\overline{U}$, as

$$A(\phi \overline{W} \psi) \equiv A(\phi W \neg \phi \wedge \psi) \qquad A(\phi \overline{U} \psi) \equiv A(\phi U \neg \phi \wedge \psi)$$

Formally, we define the class of *CTL^v queries* as the smallest set of queries satisfying the following:

- ? and ¬? are CTL^v queries.
- If ϕ is a CTL formula and γ is a CTL^v query, then $\phi \vee \gamma$, AXγ, $A(\gamma \mathring{W} \phi)$, and $A(\phi \overline{W} \gamma)$ are also CTL^v queries.
- A persistence query is also a CTL^v query.

The class of *persistence queries* is defined as follows:

- If γ is a CTL^v query, then AGγ is a persistence query.
- If γ is a persistence query and ϕ is a CTL formula, then $\phi \vee \gamma$, AXγ, $A(\phi W \gamma)$, and $A(\phi U \gamma)$ are persistence queries.

Two queries γ_1 and γ_2 are equivalent, written $\gamma_1 \Leftrightarrow \gamma_2$, if we have $\gamma_1(\phi) \Leftrightarrow \gamma_2(\phi)$ for every ϕ. Additional CTL^v queries are allowed using these equivalences:

$$\gamma \vee \phi \Leftrightarrow \phi \vee \gamma \qquad AG\gamma \Leftrightarrow A(\gamma \mathring{W} \textit{false})$$
$$AF\gamma \Leftrightarrow A(\textit{true} \, U \, \gamma) \qquad A(\gamma W \phi) \Leftrightarrow A(\phi \vee \gamma \mathring{W} \phi).$$

In other words, in CTL^v queries: 1. Negations can only be applied to the placeholder or to CTL formulas. 2. The placeholder cannot appear on either side of $\mathring{U}$ or $\overline{U}$, on the left hand side of $\overline{W}$ or U, or on the right hand side of $\mathring{W}$. 3. If the placeholder appears on the right hand side of W or U, then there must be an AG between the placeholder and the until. The first restriction on negation is to avoid querying existentially about paths. The second restriction on untils is to ensure that we do not have any eventuality obligation (which may not be fulfillable in every model). The third restriction rules out queries like AF? but allows valid queries like AFAG?.

Note that $\overline{W}$ and $\overline{U}$ are not monotone with respect to the left operand. But since we do not allow the placeholder to appear on their left hand side, this is not a problem and Lemma 1 still holds.

Examples of queries in this class include $A\,(\neg shutdown\,\overline{W}\,?)$: what is true when the first shutdown occurs; $AG(shutdown \to AG?)$: what is invariably true after shutdown; $AG(? \to AFack)$: what is true before an acknowledgement is sent; $AG(? \to \neg AFack)$: what is true so that an acknowledgement may never be sent; $AFAG?$: what is the set of persistent states, or, roughly, the set of states within which the system eventually stays; and the more complex examples given in Section 1. Note that the notion of persistence here is that of the branching time, which seems less useful than the linear-time notion. We will come back to this issue in Section 6.

Not only are these queries guaranteed to be valid, they can be efficiently solved by mixing forward and backward traversals, i.e., by applying $pre_\forall$ and $post_\exists$, where

$$post_\exists(S) = \{\, q' \in Q \mid \exists q.\, \langle q, q' \rangle \in \Delta \text{ and } q \in S \,\},$$

the set of successors of states in S. For any CTL formula ϕ, the set R_ϕ is defined as

$$R_\phi = \mu Z.\, ((S \cup post_\exists(Z)) \cap \llbracket \phi \rrbracket),$$

or the set of states reachable from S going through only the states that satisfy ϕ. Figure 1 shows a procedure $Solve$ that takes a CTL^v query and a state set, and returns a state set.

$$
\begin{aligned}
Solve(?,\, S) &= S \\
Solve(\neg?,\, S) &= Q \setminus S \\
Solve(\phi \vee \gamma,\, S) &= Solve(\gamma,\, S \setminus \llbracket \phi \rrbracket) \\
Solve(\mathsf{AX}\gamma,\, S) &= Solve(\gamma,\, post_\exists(S)) \\
Solve(\mathsf{A}\,(\gamma\,\mathring{W}\,\phi),\, S) &= Solve(\gamma,\, S \cup R_{\neg\phi} \cup post_\exists(R_{\neg\phi})) \\
Solve(\mathsf{A}\,(\phi\,\overline{W}\,\gamma),\, S) &= Solve(\gamma,\, (S \cup post_\exists(R_\phi)) \setminus \llbracket \phi \rrbracket) \\
Solve(\mathsf{A}\,(\phi\,\mathsf{W}\,\gamma),\, S) &= Solve(\gamma,\, B) \\
&\quad \text{where } R = R_{\phi \wedge \neg\gamma(\bot)} \\
&\quad B = (S \cup post_\exists(R)) \setminus (\llbracket \phi \rrbracket \cup \llbracket \gamma(\bot) \rrbracket) \\
Solve(\mathsf{A}\,(\phi\,\mathsf{U}\,\gamma),\, S) &= Solve(\gamma,\, B \cup C) \\
&\quad \text{where } C = \nu Z.\,(R \cap post_\exists(Z)) \\
&\quad R \text{ and } B \text{ are the same as above}
\end{aligned}
$$

Fig. 1: Solving CTL^v queries (γ is any CTL^v query, ϕ is any CTL formula, and $S \subseteq Q$ is any state set)

The idea is that if γ is any CTL^v query, M is any model with initial states Q_0, and S is the result of $Solve(\gamma, Q_0)$, then the *characteristic function* of S, namely

$$\bigvee_{q \in S} \left(\bigwedge_{x \in L(q)} x \wedge \bigwedge_{x \in X \setminus L(q)} \neg x \right),$$

is an exact solution to γ in M. The procedure *Solve* runs in time linear in the size of the model and linear in the length of the query.

4 Simplification

Recall that our motivation is to help the user understand the system behaviors. Although an exact solution gives complete information, it is likely to be too complex to comprehend. In this section, we suggest a strategy to cope with the problem by decomposing a proposition into a set of conjuncts (for positive queries) or disjuncts (for negative queries) using projection and don't-care minimization. Decomposition is not a new problem in symbolic model checking, but the usual objective is to produce a small number of small, balanced conjuncts or disjuncts to reduce the time or space for the fixed-point computation [e.g., 11]. Our purpose, rather, is to decompose a proposition into a possibly large number of "simple" pieces.

Without loss of generality, we assume positive queries in this section; disjunctive decomposition for negative queries can then be dealt with using DeMorgan's Law. Our conjunctive decomposition is a conservative approximation in the sense that the conjunction obtained may be weaker than the given proposition. Indeed, our method bears some resemblance to the technique of overlapping projections for approximate traversals [8].

Let $\exists \overline{Y}. p$ denote the result of projecting the proposition p onto a set Y of atomic propositions. For any symbolic state-set representation for model checking, an implementation of projection is usually available because it is most likely used to implement $pre_\forall$ and $post_\exists$.

For any propositions p and c, let $p \downarrow c$ be any proposition with $p \wedge c \Leftrightarrow (p \downarrow c) \wedge c$. Intuitively, the proposition $\neg c$ represents a don't-care condition. Typically, an implementation of the operation tries to choose a result that minimizes the representation of $p \downarrow c$, and we assume that a minimized representation is also simpler to human users. For BDDs, many operators can be used for this purpose, such as *restrict* [4]. For a set C of propositions, let $p \downarrow C$ be any proposition with $p \wedge (\bigwedge C) \Leftrightarrow (p \downarrow C) \wedge (\bigwedge C)$. In our implementation, we perform $p \downarrow C$ simply by computing $p \downarrow \bigwedge C$ using *restrict*, although there are other possibilities.

Figure 2 shows a greedy algorithm for approximate conjunctive decomposition. We use $atoms(s)$ to denote the set of atomic propositions appearing in s. With increasing j up to the given k, the algorithm finds nontrivial propositions that are weaker than s and contains only j atomic propositions. Redundant information in the result is reduced by simplifying a candidate conjunct using other conjuncts already computed. The algorithm runs in time exponential in k. However, this is not a serious problem in practice, because the result will be too complicated to understand for large k anyway. In our preliminary experience, we have only used $k \leq 4$.

To reduce noise from the output, before we run the decomposition algorithm, it helps to project the proposition s onto the set of atomic propositions which the user is truly

```
{Input: proposition s
    and k with 0 < k ≤ |atoms(s)| }
C := ∅
for j := 1 to k
    for each Y ⊆ atoms(s) with |Y| = j
        r := (∃Ȳ. s) ↓ C
        if r ⇎ true and r ⇎ s
            C := C ∪ {r}
        fi
    end
end
{Output: C with s ⇒ ⋀C}
```

Fig. 2: Approximate conjunctive decomposition of a proposition

interested in. One way to find out these interesting atomic propositions is to examine the temporal-logic formulas to be checked. Sometimes the number of relevant atomic propositions might appear large, but the user may only want to derive properties of a restricted form. For example, if a subset of the atomic propositions contains x_0, x_1, ..., x_n, the user may not be interested in each of them individually, but only in their disjunction. In this case, we can create a new atomic proposition d and compute

$$s \wedge (d \leftrightarrow (x_0 \vee x_1 \vee \cdots \vee x_n)).$$

We then project out $x_0, x_1, \ldots, x_n$, and use the result as an input to the decomposition algorithm.

A final remark is that, for simplicity, we have been focusing on only atomic propositions in our discussion. However, a model is often specified as a high-level program with some of its variables ranging over finite domains. In this case, several atomic propositions are used to encode a single source-level variable. When we perform projection and decomposition, we actually operate on these source-level variables instead of the atomic propositions to obtain more meaningful results.

5 Applications

In addition to allowing the user to infer properties based on a given pattern, temporal-logic queries also suggest an alternative model-checking algorithm. Given a model M and a formula ϕ, instead of determining $M \models \phi$ using the standard backward traversals, we can find a query γ with $\phi \Leftrightarrow \gamma(p)$ for some proposition p, and then compute its exact solution s in M. We have $M \models \phi$ if and only if $s \Rightarrow^\gamma p$. This gives a model-checking algorithm with mixed forward and backward traversals. An advantage of this over the conventional approach is that, in case ϕ does not hold, the formula $\gamma(s)$ gives insights into why ϕ fails. As an example, suppose that we check AG$((x \wedge y) \rightarrow$ AF$ack)$ by evaluating AG(? $\rightarrow$ AFack), and obtain $x \wedge y \wedge z$ as an exact solution. This tells us that the formula does not hold because, apart from x and y, the condition z is also necessary for *ack* to occur.

Furthermore, the approach can be used for detecting a particular form of vacuity [1]. Let $\hat{s}$ be $\overline{\exists atoms(p).\, s}$, that is, the projection of s on to the atomic propositions appearing in p. Because $\hat{s}$ is the strongest (or weakest, for negative queries) of the solutions that involve only the atomic propositions in $atoms(p)$, we have $M \models \phi$ if and only if $\hat{s} \Rightarrow^\gamma p$. However, if we have $\hat{s} \Rightarrow^\gamma p$ but $\hat{s} \not\Leftarrow p$, we may say that ϕ trivially holds because the stronger formula $\gamma(\hat{s})$ also holds. For the previous example, if we obtain x after projecting the exact solution to $\mathsf{AG}(? \to \mathsf{AF}ack)$ on x and y, we know that y is not needed to produce ack and that the original formula holds vacuously. Or the user may suspect that $\mathsf{AG}(x \to y)$ holds, and can verify this using model checking to learn more about the model.

In the rest of this section, we report on some initial experience of applying temporal-logic queries to two SMV models. We found that the technique is most useful when unexpected properties are inferred.

5.1 A Cache Consistency Protocol

We applied our algorithm to an abstract model of a cache consistency protocol that comes with CMU's SMV 2.5.3 distribution.[2] The model has 3408 reachable states. Among other components, it consists of three processors p_0, p_1, and p_2. The temporal-logic properties specified in the program are concerned with the propositions $p_0.readable$, $p_0.writable$, $p_1.readable$, and $p_1.writable$. For example, an invariant listed is

$$\mathsf{AG}\neg(p_0.writable \land p_1.writable). \tag{1}$$

That is, p_0 and p_1 are never simultaneously writable. Note that no properties listed in the code are about p_2. Its correctness was probably assumed by the symmetries in the code.

We asked the query $\mathsf{AG}?$, and projected the exact solution obtained onto $p_i.readable$ and $p_i.writable$ for $i \in \{0, 1, 2\}$. Using the conjunctive decomposition algorithm in Figure 2 with $k = 4$, the following invariants, in addition to Formula (1) above, were inferred:

$$\mathsf{AG}\neg p_2.writable \tag{2}$$
$$\mathsf{AG}\neg p_2.readable \tag{3}$$
$$\mathsf{AG}(p_0.writable \to p_0.readable) \tag{4}$$
$$\mathsf{AG}(p_1.writable \to p_1.readable) \tag{5}$$

Formulas (4) and (5) are evident from the code. However, Formulas (2) and (3) are surprising. They indicate that p_2 is never readable nor writable, and therefore p_2 is not symmetric to p_0 or p_1. Upon closer examination of the code, we found a typo in the SMV program that caused p_2's faulty behaviors. We fixed the error, and, as expected, inferred that Formulas (2) and (3) no longer hold, and that the model satisfies

---
[2] File `gigamax.smv` in `http://www.cs.cmu.edu/˜modelcheck/smv/smv.r2.5.3.1d.tar.gz`

$\mathsf{AG}(p_i.writable \to p_i.readable)$ and $\mathsf{AG}\neg(p_i.writable \land p_j.writable)$ for every distinct $i, j \in \{0, 1, 2\}$. In addition, we also discovered

$$\mathsf{AG}((p_i.readable \land p_j.readable) \to \neg p_k.writable) \tag{6}$$

for every distinct $i, j, k \in \{0, 1, 2\}$. It says that if any two of the processors are readable, then the remaining one cannot be writable. This is not a natural property that one would expect from every cache consistency protocol.

5.2 A Shuttle Digital Autopilot

Another example that we looked at was an SMV model of the "shuttle digital autopilot engines out (3E/O) contingency guidance requirements" in the NuSMV 1.1 distribution.[3] There are 70 source-level variables and over 10^{14} reachable states.

One of the properties listed in the SMV program is

$$\mathsf{AG}(\neg cg.idle \to \mathsf{AF}\, cg.finished), \tag{7}$$

which says that the component cg eventually terminates after it is started. We evaluated the query $\mathsf{AG}(?\to \mathsf{AF}(cg.finished))$, and projected the exact solution on all singleton sets of variables. In addition to the formula above, we also inferred the following two properties:[4]

$$\mathsf{AG}(\neg cs.idle \to \mathsf{AF}\, cg.finished) \tag{8}$$
$$\mathsf{AG}(\neg start\_guide \to \mathsf{AF}\, cg.finished). \tag{9}$$

Formula (9) is easy to see from the SMV program and is not very interesting. Formula (8), however, does not seem obvious; it says that after the component cs is started, cg will eventually finish. Given Formulas (7) and (8), it is natural to ask whether there is any causality relationship between $\neg cg.idle$ and $\neg cs.idle$. So we checked the formulas

$$\mathsf{AG}(\neg cs.idle \to \mathsf{AF}\neg cg.idle) \tag{10}$$
$$\mathsf{AG}(\neg cg.idle \to \mathsf{AF}\neg cs.idle) \tag{11}$$

and found that the first formula holds while the second does not. Note how this process of model checking and evaluating queries in tandem allowed us to discover relationships between the two components cs and cg.

Another formula listed is

$$\mathsf{AG}((cg.idle \lor cg.finished) \to \neg\mathsf{AG}((cg.idle \lor cg.finished) \lor \mathsf{AG}\neg cg.finished)). \tag{12}$$

We evaluated the query $\mathsf{AG}(? \to \neg\mathsf{AG}((cg.idle \lor cg.finished) \lor \mathsf{AG}\neg cg.finished))$, and, to our surprise, obtained $true$ as the exact solution. This indicates that the stronger formula

$$\mathsf{AG}\neg\mathsf{AG}((cg.idle \lor cg.finished) \lor \mathsf{AG}\neg cg.finished) \tag{13}$$

---
[3] The SMV model was written by Sergey Berezin.
   http://afrodite.itc.it:1024/~nusmv/examples/guidance/guidance.smv
[4] What we call $cs.idle$ here corresponds to cs.step = undef in the SMV program.

holds, and that Formula (12) is in a sense vacuously true.

As our last example, $cs.r$ is an enumerated-type variable with a range of size six. Comments in the SMV program suggest checking the six formulas of the form

$$\neg \mathsf{AG}(cs.r \neq c) \tag{14}$$

for every c in the range of $cs.r$, to ensure that the variable may take on any value in its range. We instead asked only one query AG?, and, after projecting the exact solution on $cs.r$, obtained *true*. This implies that there are no constraints on $cs.r$ in the reachable states, and therefore it may take on any of its possible values.

6 Future Work

One interesting direction for future work is to extend the results to Linear Temporal Logic (LTL). All of our definitions extend to LTL in a straightforward way, and Lemmas 1–3 hold for LTL queries as well. The proof of Theorem 1 can be trivially modified for LTL queries, so it can be easily seen that determining whether an LTL query is valid is equivalent to determining LTL formula validity, which is complete for PSPACE. An advantage of LTL queries over CTL queries is the expressiveness. For example, if the CTL formula $\mathsf{AG}(req \to \mathsf{AF}ack)$ does not hold (or equivalently, the LTL formula $\mathsf{G}(req \to \mathsf{F}ack)$ does not hold), the user can ask the LTL query

$$\mathsf{G}(req \to \mathsf{F}(ack \vee \mathsf{G}?))$$

to find out what is eventually always true if a request is never followed by an acknowledgement. This in essence gives a summary of all the counterexamples to the formula above. Note that the similar CTL query

$$\mathsf{AG}(req \to \mathsf{AF}(ack \vee \mathsf{AG}?))$$

is much weaker. However, in general, it is not obvious how to evaluate valid LTL queries.

Bibliography

[1] I. Beer, S. Ben-David, C. Eisner, and Y. Rodeh. Efficient detection of vacuity in ACTL formulas. In O. Grumberg, editor, *Computer Aided Verification, 9th International Conference, CAV'97 Proceedings*, volume 1254 of *Lecture Notes in Computer Science*, pages 279–290, Haifa, Israel, June 1997. Springer-Verlag.

[2] S. Bensalem and Y. Lakhnech. Automatic generation of invariants. *Formal Methods in System Design*, 15(1):75–92, July 1999.

[3] E. M. Clarke, E. A. Emerson, and A. P. Sistla. Automatic verification of finite-state concurrent systems using temporal logic specifications. *ACM Transactions on Programming Languages and Systems*, 8(2):244–263, April 1986.

[4] O. Coudert, C. Berthet, and J. C. Madre. Verification of synchronous sequential machines based on symbolic execution. In J. Sifakis, editor, *Automatic Verification Methods for Finite State Systems: International Workshop Proceedings*, volume 407 of *Lecture Notes in Computer Science*, pages 365–373, Grenoble, France, June 1989. Springer-Verlag.

[5] E. A. Emerson and J. Y. Halpern. Decision procedures and expressiveness in the temporal logic of branching time. *Journal of Computer and Systems Sciences*, 30:1–21, 1985.
[6] M. Ernst, J. Cockrell, W. G. Griswold, and D. Notkin. Dynamically discovering likely program invariants to support program evolution. In ICSE99, editor, *Proceedings of the 1999 International Conference on Software Engineering: ICSE 99*, pages 213–224, Los Angeles, USA, May 1999. ACM.
[7] M. J. Fischer and R. E. Ladner. Propositional dynamic logic of regular programs. *Journal of Computer and Systems Sciences*, 18:194–211, 1979.
[8] S. G. Govindaraju, D. L. Dill, A. J. Hu, and M. A. Horowitz. Approximate reachability with BDDs using overlapping projections. In *35th Design Automation Conference, Proceedings 1998*, pages 451–456, San Francisco, USA, June 1998. ACM.
[9] O. Grumberg and D. E. Long. Model checking and modular verification. *ACM Transactions on Programming Languages and Systems*, 16(3):843–871, May 1994.
[10] R. Jeffords and C. Heitmeyer. Automatic generation of state invariants from requirements specifications. In FSE6, editor, *Proceedings of the ACM SIGSOFT 6th International Symposium on the Foundations of Software Engineering: FSE-6*, pages 56–69, Lake Buena Vista, Florida, USA, November 1998.
[11] K. Ravi, K. L. McMillan, T. R. Shiple, and F. Somenzi. Approximation and decomposition of binary decision diagrams. In *35th Design Automation Conference, Proceedings 1998*, pages 445–450, San Francisco, USA, June 1998. ACM.
[12] M. Vaziri and G. Holzmann. Automatic invariant deduction in Spin. In J.-C. Gregoire, G. J. Holzmann, and D. A. Peled, editors, *The SPIN Verification System: The 4th International Workshop*, Paris, France, November 1998.

Are Timed Automata Updatable?

Patricia Bouyer, Catherine Dufourd,
Emmanuel Fleury, and Antoine Petit*

LSV, CNRS UMR 8643, ENS de Cachan,
61 Av. du Président Wilson,
94235 Cachan Cedex, France
{ bouyer, dufourd, fleury, petit}@lsv.ens-cachan.fr

Abstract. In classical timed automata, as defined by ALUR and DILL [AD90,AD94] and since widely studied, the only operation allowed to modify the clocks is the reset operation. For instance, a clock can neither be set to a non-null constant value, nor be set to the value of another clock nor, in a non-deterministic way, to some value lower or higher than a given constant. In this paper we study in details such updates.
We characterize in a thin way the frontier between decidability and undecidability. Our main contributions are the following :

- We exhibit many classes of updates for which emptiness is undecidable. These classes depend on the clock constraints that are used – diagonal-free or not – whereas it is well known that these two kinds of constraints are equivalent for classical timed automata.
- We propose a generalization of the region automaton proposed by ALUR and DILL, allowing to handle larger classes of updates. The complexity of the decision procedure remains PSPACE-complete.

1 Introduction

Since their introduction by ALUR and DILL [AD90,AD94], timed automata are one of the most studied models for real-time systems. Numerous works have been devoted to the "theoretical" comprehension of timed automata and their extensions (among a lot of them, see [ACD+92], [AHV93], [AFH94], [ACH94], [Wil94], [HKWT95], [BD00], [BDGP98]) and several model-checkers are now available (HYTECH[1] [HHWT95,HHWT97], KRONOS[2] [Yov97], UPPAAL[3] [LPY97]). These works have allowed to treat a lot of case studies (see the web pages of the tools) and it is precisely one of them – the ABR protocol [BF99,BFKM99] – which has motivated the present work. Indeed, the most simple and natural modelization of the ABR protocol uses updates which are not allowed in classical timed automata, where the only authorized operations on clocks are resets. Therefore we

---

* This work has been partly supported by the french project RNRT "Calife"
[1] http://www-cad.eecs.berkeley.edu/~tah/HyTech/
[2] http://www-verimag.imag.fr/TEMPORISE/kronos/
[3] http://www.docs.uu.se/docs/rtmv/uppaal

have considered updates constructed from simple updates of one of the following forms:

$x :\sim c \mid x :\sim y + c$, where x, y are clocks, $c \in \mathbb{Q}_+$, and $\sim \in \{<, \leq, =, \neq, \geq, >\}$

More precisely, we have studied the (un)decidability of the emptiness problem for the extended timed automata constructed with such updates. We call these new automata *updatable timed automata*. We have characterized in a thin way the frontier between classes of updatable timed automata for which emptiness is decidable or not. Our main results are the following :

- We exhibit many classes of updates for which emptiness is undecidable. A surprising result is that these classes depend on the clock constraints that are used – diagonal-free (*i.e.* where the only allowed comparisons are between a clock and a constant) or not (where the difference of two clocks can also be compared with a constant). This point makes an important difference with "classical" timed automata for which it is well known that these two kinds of constraints are equivalent.
- We propose a generalization of the region automaton proposed by ALUR and DILL, which allows to handle large classes of updates. We thus construct an (untimed) automaton which recognizes the untimed language of the considered timed automaton. The complexity of this decision procedure remains PSPACE-complete.

    Note that these decidable classes are not more powerful than classical timed automata in the sense that for any updatable timed automaton of such a class, a classical timed automaton (with ε−transitions) recognizing the same language – and even most often bisimilar – can be effectively constructed. But in most cases, an exponential blow-up seems unavoidable and thus a transformation into a classical timed automaton can not be used to obtain an efficient decision procedure. These constructions of equivalent automata are available in [BDFP00b].

The paper is organized as follows. In section 2, we present basic definitions of clock constraints, updates and updatable timed automata, generalizing classical definitions of ALUR and DILL. The emptiness problem is briefly introduced in section 3. Section 4 is devoted to our undecidability results. In section 5, we propose a generalization of the region automaton defined by ALUR and DILL. We then use this procedure in sections 6 (resp. 7) to exhibit large classes of updatable timed automata using diagonal-free clock constraints (resp. arbitrary clock constraints) for which emptiness is decidable. A short conclusion summarizes our results.

For lack of space, this paper does not contain proofs which can be found in [BDFP00a].

2 About Updatable Timed Automata

In this section, we briefly recall some basic definitions before introducing an extension of the timed automata, initially defined by ALUR and DILL [AD90,AD94].

2.1 Timed Words and Clocks

If Z is any set, let Z^* (resp. Z^ω) be the set of *finite* (resp. *infinite*) sequences of elements in Z. And let $Z^\infty = Z^* \cup Z^\omega$.

In this paper, we consider $\mathbb{T}$ as time domain, $\mathbb{Q}_+$ as the set of non-negative rational and Σ as a finite set of *actions*. A *time sequence* over $\mathbb{T}$ is a finite or infinite non decreasing sequence $\tau = (t_i)_{i \geq 1} \in \mathbb{T}^\infty$. A *timed word* $\omega = (a_i, t_i)_{i \geq 1}$ is an element of $(\Sigma \times \mathbb{T})^\infty$, also written as a pair $\omega = (\sigma, \tau)$, where $\sigma = (a_i)_{i \geq 1}$ is a word in Σ^∞ and $\tau = (t_i)_{i \geq 1}$ a time sequence in $\mathbb{T}^\infty$ of same length.

We consider an at most countable set $\mathbb{X}$ of variables, called *clocks*. A clock valuation over $\mathbb{X}$ is a mapping $v : \mathbb{X} \to \mathbb{T}$ that assigns to each clock a time value. The set of all clock valuations over $\mathbb{X}$ is denoted $\mathbb{T}^\mathbb{X}$. Let $t \in \mathbb{T}$, the valuation $v + t$ is defined by $(v + t)(x) = v(x) + t, \forall x \in \mathbb{X}$.

2.2 Clock Constraints

Given a subset of clocks $X \subseteq \mathbb{X}$, we introduce two sets of clock constraints over X. The most general one, denoted by $\mathcal{C}(X)$, is defined by the following grammar:

$$\varphi ::= x \sim c \mid x - y \sim c \mid \varphi \wedge \varphi \mid \neg \varphi \mid true$$
$$\text{where } x, y \in X, \ c \in \mathbb{Q}_+, \ \sim \in \{<, \leq, =, \neq, \geq, >\}$$

We will also use the proper subset of *diagonal-free* constraints, denoted by $\mathcal{C}_{df}(X)$, where the comparison between two clocks is not allowed. This set is defined by the grammar:

$$\varphi ::= x \sim c \mid \varphi \wedge \varphi \mid \neg \varphi \mid true,$$
$$\text{where } x \in X, \ c \in \mathbb{Q}_+ \text{ and } \sim \in \{<, \leq, =, \neq, \geq, >\}$$

We write $v \models \varphi$ when the clock valuation v satisfies the clock constraint φ.

2.3 Updates

An *update* is a function from $\mathbb{T}^\mathbb{X}$ to $\mathcal{P}(\mathbb{T}^\mathbb{X})$ which assigns to each valuation a set of valuations. In this work, we restrict ourselves to local updates which are defined in the following way.

A *simple update* over a clock z has one of the two following forms:

$$up ::= z :\sim c \mid z :\sim y + d$$
$$\text{where } c \in \mathbb{Q}_+, \ d \in \mathbb{Q}, \ y \in \mathbb{X} \text{ and } \sim \in \{<, \leq, =, \neq, \geq, >\}$$

Let v be a valuation and up be a simple update over z. A valuation v' is in $up(v)$ if $v'(y) = v(y)$ for any clock $y \neq z$ and if $v'(z)$ verifies:

$$\begin{cases} v'(z) \sim c & \text{if } up = z :\sim c \\ v'(z) \sim v(y) + d & \text{if } up = z :\sim y + d \end{cases}$$

A *local update* over a set of clocks X is a collection $up = (up_i)_{1 \leq i \leq k}$ of simple updates, where each up_i is a simple update over some clock $x_i \in X$ (note that it could happen that $x_i = x_j$ for some $i \neq j$). Let $v, v' \in \mathbb{T}^n$ be two clock valuations. We have $v' \in up(v)$ if and only if, for any i, the clock valuation v'' defined by

$$\begin{cases} v''(x_i) = v'(x_i) \\ v''(y) = v(y) \end{cases} \text{for any } y \neq x_i$$

verifies $v'' \in up_i(v)$. The terminology *local* comes from the fact that $v'(x)$ depends on x only and not on the other values $v'(y)$.

Example 1. If we take the local update $(x :> y, x :< 7)$, then it means that the value $v'(x)$ must verify : $v'(x) > v(y) \wedge v'(x) < 7$. Note that $up(v)$ may be empty. For instance, the local update $(x :< 1, x :> 1)$ leads to an empty set.

For any subset X of $\mathbb{X}$, $\mathcal{U}(X)$ is the set of local updates which are collections of simple updates over clocks of X. In the following, we need to distinguish the following subsets of $\mathcal{U}(X)$:

- $\mathcal{U}_0(X)$ is the set of reset updates. A reset update up is an update such that for every clock valuations v, v' with $v' \in up(v)$ and any clock $x \in X$, either $v'(x) = v(x)$ or $v'(x) = 0$.
- $\mathcal{U}_{cst}(X)$ is the set of constant updates. A constant update up is an update such that for every clock valuations v, v' with $v' \in up(v)$ and any clock $x \in X$, either $v'(x) = v(x)$ or $v'(x)$ is a rational constant independent of $v(x)$.

2.4 Updatable Timed Automata

An *updatable timed automaton* over $\mathbb{T}$ is a tuple $\mathcal{A} = (\Sigma, Q, T, I, F, R, X)$, where Σ is a finite alphabet of actions, Q is a finite set of states, $X \subseteq \mathbb{X}$ is a finite set of clocks, $T \subseteq Q \times [\mathcal{C}(X) \times \Sigma \times \mathcal{U}(X)] \times Q$ is a finite set of transitions, $I \subseteq Q$ is the subset of initial states, $F \subseteq Q$ is the subset of final states, $R \subseteq Q$ is the subset of repeated states.

Let $\mathcal{C} \subseteq \mathcal{C}(\mathbb{X})$ be a subset of clock constraints and $\mathcal{U} \subseteq \mathcal{U}(\mathbb{X})$ be a subset of updates, the class $Aut(\mathcal{C}, \mathcal{U})$ is the set of all timed automata whose transitions only use clock constraints of $\mathcal{C}$ and updates of $\mathcal{U}$. The usual class of timed automata, defined in [AD90], is the family $Aut(\mathcal{C}_{df}(\mathbb{X}), \mathcal{U}_0(\mathbb{X}))$.

A *path* in $\mathcal{A}$ is a finite or an infinite sequence of consecutive transitions:

$$P = q_0 \xrightarrow{\varphi_1, a_1, up_1} q_1 \xrightarrow{\varphi_2, a_2, up_2} q_2 \ldots, \text{ where } (q_{i-1}, \varphi_i, a_i, up_i, q_i) \in T, \forall i > 0$$

The path is said to be *accepting* if it starts in an initial state ($q_0 \in I$) and *either* it is finite and it ends in an final state, *or* it is infinite and passes infinitely often through a repeated state. A *run* of the automaton through the path P is a sequence of the form:

$$\langle q_0, v_0 \rangle \xrightarrow[t_1]{\varphi_1, a_1, up_1} \langle q_1, v_1 \rangle \xrightarrow[t_2]{\varphi_2, a_2, up_2} \langle q_2, v_2 \rangle \ldots$$

where $\tau = (t_i)_{i\geq 1}$ is a time sequence and $(v_i)_{i\geq 0}$ are clock valuations such that:

$$\begin{cases} v_0(x) = 0, \ \forall x \in \mathbb{X} \\ v_{i-1} + (t_i - t_{i-1}) \models \varphi_i \\ v_i \in up_i\,(v_{i-1} + (t_i - t_{i-1})) \end{cases}$$

Remark that any set $up_i(v_{i-1} + (t_i - t_{i-1}))$ of a run is non empty.
The label of the run is the timed word $w = (a_1, t_1)(a_2, t_2)\ldots$ If the path P is accepting then the timed word w is said to be accepted by the timed automaton. The set of all timed words accepted by $\mathcal{A}$ over the time domain $\mathbb{T}$ is denoted by $L(\mathcal{A}, \mathbb{T})$, or simply $L(\mathcal{A})$.

Remark 1. A "folklore" result on timed automata states that the families $Aut(\mathcal{C}(\mathbb{X}), \mathcal{U}_0(\mathbb{X}))$ and $Aut(\mathcal{C}_{df}(\mathbb{X}), \mathcal{U}_0(\mathbb{X}))$ are language-equivalent. This is because any classical timed automaton (using reset updates only) can be transformed into a diagonal-free classical timed automaton recognizing the same language (see [BDGP98] for a proof). Another "folklore" result states that constant updates are not more powerful than reset updates *i.e.* the families $Aut(\mathcal{C}(\mathbb{X}), \mathcal{U}_{cst}(\mathbb{X}))$ and $Aut(\mathcal{C}(\mathbb{X}), \mathcal{U}_0(\mathbb{X}))$ are language-equivalent.

3 The Emptiness Problem

For verification purposes, a fundamental question about timed automata is to decide whether the accepted language is empty. This problem is called the *emptiness problem*. To simplify, we will say that a class of timed automata is *decidable* if the emptiness problem is decidable for this class. The following result, due to ALUR and DILL [AD90], is one of the most important about timed automata.

Theorem 1. *The class $Aut(\mathcal{C}(\mathbb{X}), \mathcal{U}_0(\mathbb{X}))$ is decidable.*

The principle of the proof is the following. Let $\mathcal{A}$ be an automaton of $Aut(\mathcal{C}(\mathbb{X}), \mathcal{U}_0(\mathbb{X}))$, then a Büchi automaton (often called the *region automaton* of $\mathcal{A}$) which recognizes the *untimed language* UNTIME($L(\mathcal{A})$) of $L(\mathcal{A})$ is effectively constructible. The untimed language of $\mathcal{A}$ is defined as follows : UNTIME($L(\mathcal{A})$) = $\{\sigma \in \Sigma^\infty \mid$ there exists a time sequence τ such that $(\sigma, \tau) \in L(\mathcal{A})\}$.
The emptiness of $L(\mathcal{A})$ is obviously equivalent to the emptiness of UNTIME($L(\mathcal{A})$) and since the emptiness of a Büchi automaton on words is decidable [HU79], the result follows. In fact, the result is more precise: testing emptiness of a timed automaton is PSPACE-complete (see [AD94] for the proofs).

Remark 2. From [AD94] (Lemma 4.1) it suffices to prove the theorem above for timed automata where all constants appearing in clock constraints are integers (and not arbitrary rationals). Indeed, for any timed automaton $\mathcal{A}$, there exists some positive integer δ such that for any constant c of a clock constraint of $\mathcal{A}$, $\delta.c$ is an integer. Let $\mathcal{A}'$ be the timed automaton obtained from $\mathcal{A}$ by replacing each constant c by $\delta \cdot c$, then it is immediate to verify that $L(\mathcal{A}')$ is empty if and only if $L(\mathcal{A})$ is empty.

4 Undecidable Classes of Updatable Timed Automata

In this section we exhibit some important classes of updatable timed automata which are undecidable. All the proofs are reductions of the emptiness problem for counter machines.

4.1 Two Counters Machine

Recall that a two counters machine is a finite set of instructions over two counters (x and y). There are two types of instructions over counters:

- *incrementation instruction* of counter $i \in \{x, y\}$:

$$p : i := i + 1; \text{ goto } q \text{ (where } p \text{ and } q \text{ are instruction labels)}$$

- *decrementation (or zero-testing) instruction* of counter $i \in \{x, y\}$:

$$p : \text{ if } i > 0 \begin{cases} \text{then } i := i - 1; \text{ goto } q \\ \text{else goto } q' \end{cases}$$

The machine starts at instruction labelled by s_0 with $x = y = 0$ and stops at a special instruction HALT labelled by s_f.

Theorem 2. *The emptiness problem of two counters machine is undecidable [Min67].*

4.2 Diagonal-Free Automata with Updates $x := x - 1$

We consider here a diagonal-free constraints class.

Proposition 1. *Let $\mathcal{U}$ be a set of updates containing both $\{x := x - 1 \mid x \in \mathbb{X}\}$ and $\mathcal{U}_0(\mathbb{X})$. Then the class $Aut(\mathcal{C}_{df}(\mathbb{X}), \mathcal{U})$ is undecidable.*

Sketch of proof. We simulate a two counters machine $\mathcal{M}$ with an updatable timed automaton $\mathcal{A}_\mathcal{M} = (\Sigma, Q, T, I, F, R, X)$ with $X = \{x, y, z\}$, $\Sigma = \{a\}$ (for convenience reasons labels are omitted in the proof) and equipped with updates $x := x - 1$ and $y := y - 1$. Clocks x and y simulate the two counters.

Simulation of an increment appears on Figure 1. Counter x is implicitly incremented by letting the time run during 1 unit of time (this is controlled with the test $z = 1$). Then the other counter y is decremented with the $y := y - 1$ update.

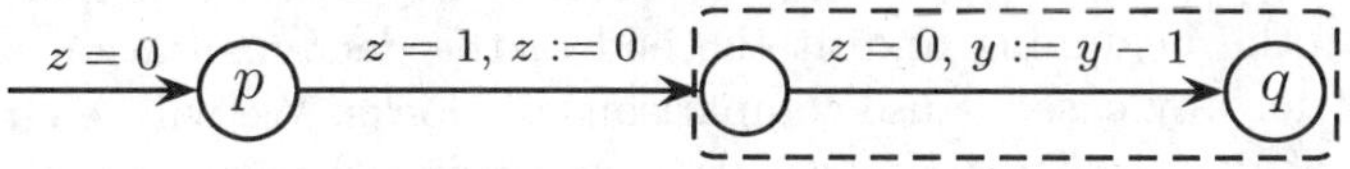

Fig. 1. *Simulation of a incrementation operation over counter x.*

Simulation of a decrement appears on Figure 2. Counter x is either decremented using the $x := x - 1$ update if $x \geq 1$, or unchanged otherwise.

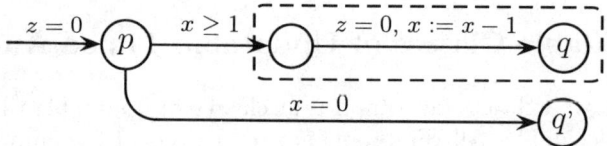

Fig. 2. *Simulation of a decrementation operation on the counter x.*

Remark that we never compare two clocks but only use guards of the form $i \sim c$ with $i \in \{x, y, z\}$ and $c \in \{0, 1\}$.
To complete the definition of $\mathcal{A}_\mathcal{M}$, we set $I = \{s_0\}$ and $F = \{s_f\}$. The language of $\mathcal{M}$ is empty if and only if the language of $\mathcal{A}_\mathcal{M}$ is empty and this implies undecidability of emptiness problem for the class $Aut(\mathcal{C}_{df}(\mathbb{X}), \mathcal{U})$.

4.3 Automata with Updates $x := x + 1$ or $x :> 0$ or $x :> y$ or $x :< y$

Surprisingly, classes of arbitrary timed automata with special updates are undecidable.

Proposition 2. *Let $\mathcal{U}$ be a set of updates containing $\mathcal{U}_0(\mathbb{X})$ and (1) $\{x := x + 1 \mid x \in \mathbb{X}\}$ or (2) $\{x :> 0 \mid x \in \mathbb{X}\}$ or (3) $\{x :> y \mid x, y \in \mathbb{X}\}$ or (4) $\{x :< y \mid x, y \in \mathbb{X}\}$, then the class $Aut(\mathcal{C}(\mathbb{X}), \mathcal{U})$ is undecidable.*

Sketch of proof. The proofs are four variations of the construction given for proposition 1. The idea is to replace every transition labelled with updates $x := x - 1$ or $y := y - 1$ (framed with dashed lines on pictures) by a small automaton involving the other kinds of updates only. The counter machine will be now simulated by an updatable timed automaton with four clocks $\{w, x, y, z\}$. We show how to simulate an $x := x - 1$ in any of the four cases :

(1) Firstly clock w is reset, then update $w := w + 1$ is performed until $x - w = 1$ (recall that x simulates a counter and that we are interested to its integer values). Secondly, clock x is reset and update $x := x + 1$ is performed until $x = w$.
(2) A $w :> 0$ is guessed, followed by a test $x - w = 1$. Then a $x :> 0$ is guessed, followed by a test $x = w$.
(3) Clock w is reset, $w :> w$ is guessed and test $x - w = 1$ is made. Then clock x is reset, $x :> x$ is guessed and test $x = w$ is made.
(4) A $w :< x$ is guessed, followed by test $x - w = 1$. Then a $x :< x$ is guessed, followed by a test $x = w$.

In the four cases, operations are made instantaneously with the help of test $z = 0$ performed at the beginning and at the end of the decrementation simulation. Remark that for any case we use comparisons of clocks. We will see in section 6 that classes of diagonal-free timed automata equipped with any of these four updates are decidable.

Let us end the current section with a result about *mixed updates*. Updates of the kind $y + c \leq: x :\leq z + d$ (with $c, d \in \mathbb{N}$) can simulate clock comparisons. In fact, in order to simulate a test $x - w = 1$, it suffices to guess a $w + 1 \leq: z' :\leq x$

followed by a $x \leq: z' :\leq w+1$. Both guesses have solutions if and only if $[w+1;x] = [x;w+1] = \{x\}$ if and only if $(x-w=1)$. In conclusion, we cannot mix different kinds of updates anyhow, while keeping diagonal-free automata decidable:

Proposition 3. *Let $\mathcal{U}$ be a set of updates containing $\mathcal{U}_0(\mathbb{X})$ and $\{x + c \leq: y :\leq z + d \mid x, y, z \in \mathbb{X}, \ c, c' \in \mathbb{N}\}$. Then the class $Aut(\mathcal{C}_{df}(\mathbb{X}), \mathcal{U})$ is undecidable.*

5 Construction of an Abstract Region Automaton

We want to check emptiness of the timed language accepted by some timed automaton. To this aim, we will use a technique based on the original construction of the region automaton ([AD94]).

5.1 Construction of a Region Graph

Let $X \subset \mathbb{X}$ be a finite set of clocks. A *family of regions* over X is a couple $(\mathcal{R}, \text{Succ})$ where $\mathcal{R}$ is a finite set of regions (*i.e.* of subsets of $\mathbb{T}^X$) and the *successor function* $\text{Succ} : \mathcal{R} \to \mathcal{R}$ verifies that for any region $R \in \mathcal{R}$ the following holds:

- for each $v \in R$, there exists $t \in \mathbb{T}$ such that $v + t \in \text{Succ}(R)$ and for every $0 \leq t' \leq t$, $v + t' \in (R \cup \text{Succ}(R))$
- if $v \in R$, then for all $t \in \mathbb{T}$, $v + t \in \text{Succ}^*(R)$

Let $\mathcal{U} \subset \mathcal{U}(X)$ be a finite set of updates. Each update $up \in \mathcal{U}$ induces naturally a function $\widehat{up} : \mathcal{R} \to \mathcal{P}(\mathcal{R})$ which maps each region R into the set $\{R' \in \mathcal{R} \mid up(R) \cap R' \neq \emptyset\}$. The set of regions $\mathcal{R}$ is *compatible* with $\mathcal{U}$ if for all $up \in \mathcal{U}$ and for all $R, R' \in \mathcal{R}$:

$$R' \in \widehat{up}(R) \iff \forall v \in R, \exists v' \in R' \text{ such that } v' \in up(v)$$

Then, the *region graph* associated with $(\mathcal{R}, \text{Succ}, \mathcal{U})$ is a graph whose set of nodes is $\mathcal{R}$ and whose vertices are of two distinct types:

$$R \longrightarrow R' \quad \text{if } R' = \text{Succ}(R)$$
$$R \Longrightarrow_{up} R' \quad \text{if } R' \in \widehat{up}(R)$$

Let $\mathcal{C} \subset \mathcal{C}(X)$ be a finite set of clock constraints. The set of regions $\mathcal{R}$ is *compatible* with $\mathcal{C}$ if for all $\varphi \in \mathcal{C}$ and for all $R \in \mathcal{R}$: either $R \subseteq \varphi$ or $R \subseteq \neg\varphi$.

5.2 Construction of the Region Automaton

Let $\mathcal{A}$ be a timed automaton in $Aut(\mathcal{C}, \mathcal{U})$. Let $(\mathcal{R}, \text{Succ})$ be a family of regions such that $\mathcal{R}$ is compatible with $\mathcal{C}$ and $\mathcal{U}$. We define the *region automaton* $\Gamma_{\mathcal{R}, \text{Succ}}(\mathcal{A})$ associated with $\mathcal{A}$ and $(\mathcal{R}, \text{Succ})$, as the finite (untimed) automaton defined as follows:

- Its set of locations is $Q \times \mathcal{R}$; its initial locations are $(q_0, \mathbf{0})$ where q_0 is initial and $\mathbf{0}$ is the region where all clocks are equal to zero; its repeated locations are (r, R) where r is repeated in $\mathcal{A}$ and R is any region; its final locations are (f, R) where f is final in $\mathcal{A}$ and R is any region.
- Its transitions are defined by:
  · $(q, R) \xrightarrow{\varepsilon} (q, R')$ if $R \to R'$ is a transition of the region graph,
  · $(q, R) \xrightarrow{a} (q', R')$ if there exists a transition (q, φ, a, up, q') in $\mathcal{A}$ such that $R \subseteq \varphi$ and $R \Longrightarrow_{up} R'$ is a transition of the region graph.

Theorem 3. *Let $\mathcal{A}$ be a timed automaton in $\mathrm{Aut}(\mathcal{C}, \mathcal{U})$ where $\mathcal{C}$ (resp. $\mathcal{U}$) is a finite set of clock constraints (resp. of updates). Let $(\mathcal{R}, \mathtt{Succ})$ be a family of regions such that $\mathcal{R}$ is compatible with $\mathcal{C}$ and $\mathcal{U}$. Then the automaton $\Gamma_{\mathcal{R}, \mathtt{Succ}}(\mathcal{A})$ accepts the language $\mathrm{UNTIME}(L(\mathcal{A}))$.*

Assume we can encode a region in a polynomial space, then we can decide the emptiness of the language in polynomial space. It suffices to guess an accepted run in the automaton by remembering only the two current successive configurations of the region automaton (this is the same proof than in [AD94]).

We will now study some classes of timed automata, and consider particular regions which verify the conditions required by the region automaton. This will lead us to some decidability results using the above construction.

6 Considering Diagonal-Free Updatable Timed Automata

Definition of the Regions We Consider - We consider a finite set of clocks $X \subset \mathbb{X}$. We associate an integer constant c_x to each clock $x \in X$, and we define the set of intervals:

$$\mathcal{I}_x = \{[c] \mid 0 \leq c \leq c_x\} \cup \{]c; c+1[\mid 0 \leq c < c_x\} \cup \{]c_x; +\infty[\}$$

Let α be a tuple $(({I}_x)_{x \in X}, \prec)$ where:

- $\forall x \in X, I_x \in \mathcal{I}_x$
- $\prec$ is a total preorder on $X_0 = \{x \in X \mid I_x$ is an interval of the form $]c; c+1[\}$

The *region* (defined by) α is thus

$$R(\alpha) = \left\{ v \in \mathbb{T}^X \;\middle|\; \begin{array}{l} \forall x \in X, v(x) \in I_x \\ \forall x, y \in X_0, \text{ the following holds} \\ x \prec y \iff \mathtt{frac}(v(x)) \leq \mathtt{frac}(v(y)) \end{array} \right\}$$

The set of all regions defined in such a way will be denoted by $\mathcal{R}_{(c_x)_{x \in X}}$.

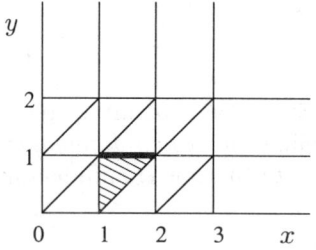

Example 2. As an example, assume we have only two clocks x and y with the constants $c_x = 3$ and $c_y = 2$. Then, the set of regions associated with those constants is described in the figure beside. The hashed region is defined by the following: $I_x =]1; 2[$, $I_y =]0; 1[$ and the preorder $\prec$ is defined by $x \prec y$ and $y \not\prec x$.

We obtain immediately the following proposition:

Proposition 4. *Let $\mathcal{C} \subseteq \mathcal{C}_{df}(X)$ be such that for any clock constraint $x \sim c$ of $\mathcal{C}$, it holds $c \leq c_x$. Then the set of regions $\mathcal{R}_{(c_x)_{x \in X}}$ is compatible with $\mathcal{C}$.*

Note that the result does not hold for any set of constraints included in $\mathcal{C}(X)$. For example, the region $(]1; +\infty[\times]1; +\infty[, \emptyset)$ is neither included in $x - y \leq 1$ nor in $x - y > 1$.

Computation of the successor function - Let $R = ((I_x)_{x \in X}, \prec)$ be a region. We set $Z = \{x \in X \mid I_x \text{ is of the form } [c]\}$. Then the region $\text{Succ}(R) = ((I'_x)_{x \in X}, \prec')$ is defined as follows, distinguishing two cases:

1. If $Z \neq \emptyset$, then
   - $I'_x = \begin{cases} I_x & \text{if } x \notin Z \\ ]c, c+1[& \text{if } I_x = [c] \text{ with } c \neq c_x \\ ]c_x, \infty[& \text{if } I_x = [c_x] \end{cases}$
   - $x \prec' y$ if $(x \prec y)$ or $I_x = [c]$ with $c \neq c_x$ and I'_y has the form $]d, d+1[$

2. If $Z = \emptyset$, let M be the set of maximal elements of $\prec$. Then
   - $I'_x = \begin{cases} I_x & \text{if } x \notin M \\ [c+1] & \text{if } x \in M \text{ and } I_x =]c, c+1[\end{cases}$
   - $\prec'$ is the restriction of $\prec$ to $\{x \in X \mid I'_x \text{ has the form }]d, d+1[\}$

Taking the previous example, the successor of the gray region is defined by $I_x =]1; 2[$ and $I_y = [1]$ (drawn as the thick line).

We will now define a suitable set of updates compatible with the regions.

What about the updates ? - We consider now a **local** update $up = (up_x)_{x \in X}$ over a finite set of clocks $X \subset \mathbb{X}$ such that for any clock x, up_x is in one of the four following subsets of $\mathcal{U}(X)$, each of them being given by an abstract grammar:

- $det_x ::= x := c \mid x := z + d$ with $c \in \mathbb{N}$, $d \in \mathbb{Z}$ and $z \in X$.
- $inf_x ::= x :\triangleleft c \mid x :\triangleleft z + d \mid inf_x \wedge inf_x$ with $\triangleleft \in \{<, \leq\}$, $c \in \mathbb{N}$, $d \in \mathbb{Z}$ and $z \in X$.
- $sup_x ::= x :\triangleright c \mid x :\triangleright z + d \mid sup_x \wedge sup_x$ with $\triangleright \in \{>, \geq\}$, $c \in \mathbb{N}$, $d \in \mathbb{Z}$ and $z \in X$.
- $int_x ::= x :\in (c; d) \mid x :\in (c; z+d) \mid x :\in (z+c; d) \mid x :\in (z+c; z+d)$ where (and) are either [or], z is a clock and c, d are in $\mathbb{Z}$.

Let us denote by $\mathcal{U}_1(X)$ this set of local updates. As in the case of simple updates, we will give a necessary and sufficient condition for R' to be in $\widehat{up}(R)$ when R, R' are regions and up is a local update.

Case of simple updates - We will first prove that for any **simple** update up, $\mathcal{R}_{(c_x)_{x \in X}}$ is compatible with up. To this aim, we construct the regions belonging to $\widehat{up}(R)$ by giving a necessary and sufficient condition for a given region R' to be in $\widehat{up}(R)$.

Assume that $R = ((I_x)_{x \in X}, \prec)$ where $\prec$ is a total preorder on X_0 and that up is a simple update over z, then the region $R' = ((I'_x)_{x \in X}, \prec')$ (where $\prec'$ is a total preorder on X'_0) is in $\widehat{up}(R)$ if and only if $I'_x = I_x$ for all $x \neq z$ and :

if $up = z :\sim c$ with $c \in \mathbb{N}$: I'_z can be any interval of $\mathcal{I}_z$ which intersects $\{\gamma \mid \gamma \sim c\}$ and
  - either I'_z has the form $[d]$ or $]c_z; +\infty[$, $X'_0 = X_0 \setminus \{z\}$ and $\prec' = \prec \cap (X'_0 \times X'_0)$.
  - either I'_z has the form $]d; d+1[$, $X'_0 = X_0 \cup \{z\}$ and $\prec'$ is any total preorder which coincides with $\prec$ on $X_0 \setminus \{z\}$.

if $up = z :\sim y + c$ with $c \in \mathbb{Z}$: we assume in this case that $c_z \leq c_y + c$. Thus if I_y is any interval in $\mathcal{I}_y$ then $I_y + c$ is included in an interval of $\mathcal{I}_z$ (in particular, whenever I_y is non bounded then $I_y + c$ is non bounded, which is essential in order to prove the compatibility).

I'_z can be any interval of $\mathcal{I}_z$ such that there exists $\alpha \in I'_z$, $\beta \in I_y$ with $\alpha \sim \beta + c$ and
  - either I'_z has the form $[d]$ or $]c_z; +\infty[$, $X'_0 = X_0 \setminus \{z\}$ and $\prec' = \prec \cap (X'_0 \times X'_0)$.
  - either I'_z has the form $]d; d+1[$, $X'_0 = X_0 \cup \{z\}$ and
    - If $y \notin X_0$, $\prec'$ is any total preorder on X'_0 which coincides with $\prec$ on $X_0 \setminus \{z\}$.
    - If $y \in X_0$, then:
      • either $I_y + c \neq I'_z$ and $\prec'$ is any total preorder on X'_0 which coincides with $\prec$ on $X_0 \setminus \{z\}$
      • either $I_y + c = I'_z$ and $\prec'$ is any total preorder on X'_0 which coincides with $\prec$ in $X_0 \setminus \{z\}$ and verifies:
        · $z \prec' y$ and $y \prec' z$ if $\sim$ is $=$
        · $z \prec' y$ and $y \not\prec' z$ if $\sim$ is $<$
        · $z \prec' y$ if $\sim$ is $\leq$
        · $y \prec' z$ if $\sim$ is $\geq$
        · $z \not\prec' y$ and $y \prec' t$ if $\sim$ is $>$
        · ($z \prec' y$ and $y \not\prec' z$) or ($z \not\prec' y$ and $y \prec' z$) if $\sim$ is $\neq$

From this construction, it is easy to verify that $\mathcal{R}_{(c_x)_{x \in X}}$ is compatible with any simple update.

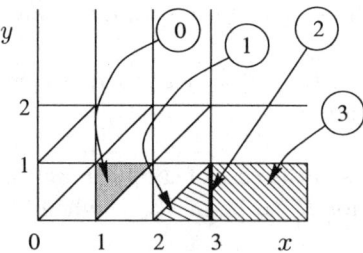

Example 3. We take the regions described in the figure beside. We want to compute the updating successors of the region 0 by the update $x :> y+2$. The three updating successors are drawn in the figure beside. Their equations are:
- Region 1: $I'_x =]2; 3[$, $I'_y =]0; 1[$ and $y \prec' x$
- Region 2: $I'_x = [3]$, $I'_y =]0; 1[$
- Region 3: $I'_x =]3; +\infty[$, $I'_y =]0; 1[$

Remark 3. Note that the fact that updates of the form $z := z-1$ (even used with diagonal-free constraints only) lead to undecidability of emptiness (Section 4), is not in contradiction with our construction. This is because we can not assume that $c_z \leq c_z - 1$.

Case of local updates - We will use the semantics of the local updates from section 2.3 to compute the updating successors of a region. Assume that $R = ((I_x)_{x \in X}, \prec)$ and that $up = (up_x)_{x \in X}$ is a local update over X then $R' = ((I'_x)_{x \in X}, \prec') \in \widehat{up}(R)$ if and only if there exists a total preorder $\prec''$ on a subset of $X \cup X'$ (where X' is a disjoint copy of X) verifying

$$y \prec'' z \iff y \prec z \text{ for all } y, z \in X$$
$$y' \prec'' z' \iff y \prec' z \text{ for all } y, z \in X$$

and such that, for any simple update up_i appearing in up_x, the region $R_i = ((I_{i,x})_{x \in X}, \prec_i)$ defined by

$$I_{i,x} = \begin{cases} I_x & \text{if } x \neq x_i \\ I'_x & \text{otherwise} \end{cases} \quad \text{and} \quad \begin{aligned} &\cdot y \prec_i z \iff y \prec z \text{ for } y, z \neq x_i \\ &\cdot x_i \prec_i z \iff x'_i \prec'' z \text{ for } z \neq x_i \\ &\cdot z \prec_i x_i \iff z \prec'' x'_i \text{ for } z \neq x_i \end{aligned}$$

belongs to $\widehat{up_i}(R)$.

Assume now that $\mathcal{U}$ is a set of updates included in $\mathcal{U}_1(X)$. It is then technical, but without difficulties, to show that under the following hypothesis:

- for each simple update $y :\sim z+c$ which is part of some local update of $\mathcal{U}$, condition $c_y \leq c_z + c$ holds

the family of regions $(\mathcal{R}_{(c_x)_{x \in X}}, \mathsf{Succ})$ is compatible with $\mathcal{U}$. In fact, the set $X \cup X'$ and the preorder $\prec''$ both encode the original and the updating regions. This construction allows us to obtain the desired result for local updates.

Remark 4. In our definition of $\mathcal{U}_1(X)$, we considered restricted set of local updates. Without such a restriction, it can happen that no such preorder $\prec''$ exists. For example, let us take the local update $x :> y \land x :< z$ and the region R defined by $I_x = [0]$, $I_y = I_z =]0;1[$, $z \prec y$ and $y \not\prec z$. Then the preorder $\prec''$ should verify the following : $y \prec'' x'$, $x' \prec'' z$, $z \prec'' y$ and $y \not\prec z$, but this leads to a contradiction. There is no such problem for the local updates from $\mathcal{U}_1(X)$, as we only impose to each clock x' to have a value greater than or lower than some other clock values.

For the while, we have only considered updates with integer constants but an immediate generalization of Remark 2 allows to treat updates with any rational constants. We have therefore proved the following theorem:

Theorem 4. *Let $\mathcal{C} \subseteq \mathcal{C}_{df}(X)$ be a set of diagonal-free clock constraints. Let $\mathcal{U} \subseteq \mathcal{U}_1(X)$ be a set of updates. Let $(c_x)_{x \in X}$ be a family of constants such that for each clock constraint $y \sim c$ of $\mathcal{C}$, condition $c \leq c_y$ holds and for each update $z :\sim y + c$ of $\mathcal{U}$, condition $c_z \leq c_y + c$ holds. Then the family of regions $(\mathcal{R}_{(c_x)_{x \in X}}, \mathsf{Succ})$ is compatible with $\mathcal{C}$ and $\mathcal{U}$.*

Remark 5. Obviously, it is not always the case that there exists a family of integer constants such that for each update $y :\sim z+c$ of $\mathcal{U}$, condition $c_y \leq c_z + c$ holds. Nevertheless:

- It is the case when all the constants c appearing in updates $y :\sim z + c$ are non-negative.
- In the general case, the existence of such a family is decidable thanks to results on systems on linear Diophantine inequations [Dom91].

For any couple $(\mathcal{C},\mathcal{U})$ verifying the hypotheses of theorem 4, by applying theorem 3, the family $Aut(\mathcal{C},\mathcal{U})$ is decidable. Moreover, since we can encode a region in polynomial space, testing emptiness is PSPACE, and even PSPACE-complete (since it is the case for classical timed automata).

Remark 6. The p-automata used in [BF99] to modelize the ABR protocol can be easily transformed into updatable timed automata from a class which fulfills the hypotheses of theorem 4. Their emptiness is then decidable.

7 Considering Arbitrary Updatable Timed Automata

In this section, we allow arbitrary clock constraints. We thus need to define a bit more complicated set of regions. To this purpose we consider for each pair y, z of clocks (taken in $X \subset \mathbb{X}$ a finite set of clocks), two constants $d_{y,z}^- \leq d_{y,z}^+$ and we define

$$\mathcal{J}_{y,z} = \{]-\infty; d_{y,z}^-[\} \cup \{[d] \mid d_{y,z}^- \leq d \leq d_{y,z}^+\} \cup$$
$$\{]d; d+1[\mid d_{y,z}^- \leq d < d_{y,z}^+\} \cup \{]d_{y,z}^+; +\infty[\}$$

The region defined by a tuple $((I_x)_{x \in X}, (\mathcal{J}_{x,y})_{x,y \in X}, \prec)$ where

- $\forall x \in X, I_x \in \mathcal{I}_x$
- if $\mathcal{X}_\infty$ denotes the set $\{(y,z) \in X^2 \mid I_y \text{ or } I_z \text{ is non bounded}\}$, then $\forall (y,z) \in \mathcal{X}_\infty, \mathcal{J}_{y,z} \in \mathcal{J}_{y,z}$
- $\prec$ is a total preorder on $X_0 = \{x \in X \mid I_x \text{ is an interval of the form }]c,c+1[\}$

is the following subset of $\mathbb{T}^X$:

$$\left\{ v \in \mathbb{T}^X \;\middle|\; \begin{array}{l} \forall x \in X, v(x) \in I_x \\ \forall x, y \in X_0, \text{ it holds} \\ \quad x \prec y \iff \texttt{frac}(v(x)) \leq \texttt{frac}(v(y)) \\ \forall y, z \in \mathcal{X}_\infty, v(y) - v(z) \in \mathcal{J}_{y,z} \end{array} \right\}$$

In fact, we do not have to keep in mind the values $d^-_{*,*}$ as y and z play symmetrical roles and $d^-_{y,z}$ is equal to $-d^+_{z,y}$, thus we set $d_{y,z} = d^+_{y,z}$. The set of all regions defined in such a way will be denoted by $\mathcal{R}_{(c_y)_{x \in X}, (d_{y,z})_{y,z \in X}}$.

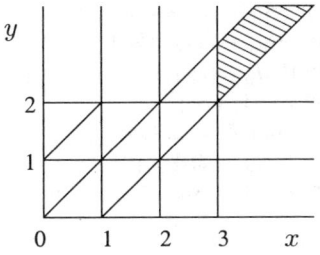

Example 4. Assume that we have only two clocks x and y and that the maximal constants are $c_x = 3$ and $c_y = 2$, with clocks constraints $x-y \sim 0$ and $x-y \sim 1$. Then, the set of regions associated with those constants is described in the figure beside. The gray region is defined by $I_x =]3; +\infty[$, $I_y =]2; +\infty[$ and $-1 < y - x < 0$ (*i.e.* $J_{y,x}$ is $]-1; 0[$).

The region $\text{Succ}(R)$ can be defined in a way similar to the one used in the diagonal-free case. We also have to notice that this set of regions is compatible with the clock constraints we consider.

Indeed we define the set $\mathcal{U}_2(X)$ of local updates $up = (up_x)_{x \in X}$ where for each clock x, up_x is one of the following simple updates:

$$x := c \mid x := y \mid x :< c \mid x :\leq c$$

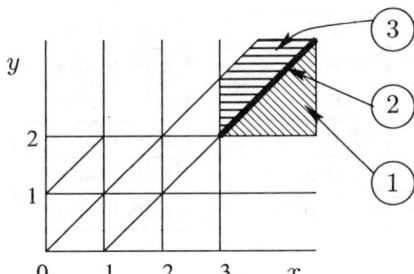

From the undecidability results of Section 4, we have to restrict the used updates if we want to preserve decidability. For example, if we consider the update $y := y+1$ and the regions described in the figure beside, the images of the region 1 are the regions 1, 2 and 3. But we can not reach region 1 (resp. 2, resp. 3) from any point of region 1. Thus, this set of regions does not seem to be compatible with the update $y := y + 1$.

By constructions similar to the ones of Section 6, we obtain the following theorem:

Theorem 5. *Let $\mathcal{C} \subseteq \mathcal{C}(X)$ be a set of clock constraints. Let $\mathcal{U} \subseteq \mathcal{U}_2(X)$ be a set of updates. Let $(c_x)_{x \in X}$ and $(d_{y,z})_{y,z \in X}$ be families of constants such that*
- *for each clock constraint $y \sim c$ of $\mathcal{C}$, condition $c \leq c_y$ holds,*
- *for each clock constraint $x - y \sim c$, condition $c \leq d_{x,y}$ holds,*
- *for each update $y :< c$ or $y :\leq c$ or $y := c$, it holds $c \leq c_y$, and for each clock z, condition $c_z \geq c + d_{y,z}$ holds,*
- *for each update $y := z$, condition $c_y \leq c_z$ holds*

Then the family of regions $(\mathcal{R}_{(c_x)_{x \in X}, (d_{y,z})_{y,z \in X}}, \text{Succ})$ is compatible with $\mathcal{C}$ and $\mathcal{U}$.

Thus, the class $Aut(\mathcal{C}, \mathcal{U})$ is decidable, and as in the previous case, testing emptiness of updatable timed automata is PSPACE-complete (unlike the case of diagonal-free updates, the previous system of Diophantine equations always has a solution).

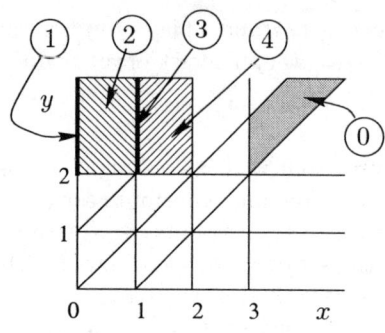

Example 5. We take the regions we used before. We want to compute the updating successors of the region 0 by the update $x :< 2$. The four updating successors are drawn in the figure beside. Their equations are:
- Region 1: $I'_x = [0]$ and $I'_y =]2; +\infty[$
- Region 2: $I'_x =]0; 1[$, $I'_y =]2; +\infty[$
  and $J_{y,x} =]1; +\infty[$
- Region 3: $I'_x = [1]$ and $I'_y =]2; +\infty[$
- Region 4: $I'_x =]1; 2[$, $I'_y =]2; +\infty[$
  and $J_{y,x} =]1; +\infty[$

8 Conclusion

The main results of this paper about the emptiness problem are summarized in the following table:

$\mathcal{U}_0(\mathbb{X}) \cup \cdots$	$\mathcal{C}_{df}(\mathbb{X})$	$\mathcal{C}(\mathbb{X})$
$\emptyset$	PSPACE	PSPACE
$\{x := c \mid x \in \mathbb{X}\} \cup \{x := y \mid x, y \in \mathbb{X}\}$	PSPACE	PSPACE
$\{x :< c \mid x \in \mathbb{X}, c \in \mathbb{Q}^+\}$	PSPACE	PSPACE
$\{x := x + 1 \mid x \in \mathbb{X}\}$	PSPACE	Undecidable
$\{x :> c \mid x \in \mathbb{X}, c \in \mathbb{Q}^+\}$	PSPACE	Undecidable
$\{x :> y \mid x, y \in \mathbb{X}\}$	PSPACE	Undecidable
$\{x :< y \mid x, y \in \mathbb{X}\}$	PSPACE	Undecidable
$\{x :\sim y + c \mid x, y \in \mathbb{X}, c \in \mathbb{Q}^+\}$	PSPACE	Undecidable
$\{x := x - 1 \mid x \in \mathbb{X}\}$	Undecidable	Undecidable

One of the surprising facts of our study is that the frontier between what is decidable and not depends on the diagonal constraints (except for the $x := x - 1$ update), whereas it is well-known that diagonal constraints do not increase the expressive power of classical timed automata.

Note that, as mentioned before, the decidable classes are not more powerful than classical timed automata in the sense that for any updatable timed automaton of such a class, a classical timed automaton (with ε-transitions) recognizing the same language – and even most often bisimilar – can be effectively constructed [BDFP00b]. However, in most cases an exponential blow-up seems unavoidable. This means that transforming updatable timed automata into classical timed automata cannot constitute an efficient strategy to solve the emptiness problem.

In the existing model-checkers, time is represented through data structures like DBM (Difference Bounded Matrix) or CDD (Clock Difference Diagrams). An interesting and natural question is to study how such structures can be used to deal with updatable timed automata.

Acknowledgements: We thank Béatrice Bérard for helpful discussions.

References

[ACD+92] R. Alur, C. Courcoubetis, D.L. Dill, N. Halbwachs, and H. Wong-Toi. Minimization of timed transition systems. In *Proc. of CONCUR'92*, LNCS 630, 1992.

[ACH94] R. Alur, C. Courcoubetis, and T.A. Henzinger. The observational power of clocks. In *Proc. of CONCUR'94*, LNCS 836, pages 162–177, 1994.

[AD90] R. Alur and D.L. Dill. Automata for modeling real-time systems. In *Proc. of ICALP'90*, LNCS 443, pages 322–335, 1990.

[AD94] R. Alur and D.L. Dill. A theory of timed automata. *Theorical Computer Science*, 126:183–235, 1994.

[AFH94] R. Alur, L Fix, and T.A. Henzinger. A determinizable class of timed automata. In *Proc. of CAV'94*, LNCS 818, pages 1–13, 1994.

[AHV93] R. Alur, T.A. Henzinger, and M. Vardi. Parametric real-time reasoning. In *Proc. of ACM Symposium on Theory of Computing*, pages 592–601, 1993.

[BD00] B. Bérard and C. Dufourd. Timed automata and additive clock constraints. To appear in IPL, 2000.

[BDFP00a] P. Bouyer, C. Dufourd, E. Fleury, and A. Petit. Are timed automata updatable ? Research Report LSV-00-3, LSV, ENS de Cachan, 2000.

[BDFP00b] P. Bouyer, C. Dufourd, E. Fleury, and A. Petit. Expressiveness of updatable timed automata. Research report, LSV, ENS de Cachan, 2000. Submitted to MFCS'2000.

[BDGP98] B. Bérard, V. Diekert, P. Gastin, and A. Petit. Characterization of the expressive power of silent transitions in timed automata. *Fundamenta Informaticae*, pages 145–182, 1998.

[BF99] B. Bérard and L. Fribourg. Automatic verification of a parametric realtime program : the ABR conformance protocol. In *Proc. of CAV'99*, LNCS 1633, 1999.

[BFKM99] B. Bérard, L. Fribourg, F. Klay, and J.F. Monin. A compared study of two correctness proofs for the standardized algorithm of ABR conformance. Research Report LSV-99-7, LSV, ENS de Cachan, 1999.

[Dom91] E. Domenjoud. Solving systems of linear diophantine equations : an algebraic approach. In *Proc. of MFCS'91*, LNCS 520, pages 141–150, 1991.

[HHWT95] T.A. Henzinger, P. Ho, and H. Wong-Toi. A user guide to HYTECH. In *Proc. of TACAS'95*, LNCS 1019, pages 41–71, 1995.

[HHWT97] T.A. Henzinger, P. Ho, and H. Wong-Toi. Hytech: A model checker for hybrid systems. In *Software Tools for Technology Transfer*, pages 110–122, 1997.

[HKWT95] T.A. Henzinger, P.W. Kopke, and H. Wong-Ti. The expressive power of clocks. In *Proc. of ICALP'95*, LNCS 944, pages 335–346, 1995.

[HU79] J.E. Hopcroft and J.D. Ullman. *Introduction to automata theory, languages and computation*. Addison Wesley, 1979.

[LPY97] Kim G. Larsen, Paul Pettersson, and Wang Yi. UPPAAL in a Nutshell. *Int. Journal on Software Tools for Technology Transfer*, 1:134–152, 1997.

[Min67] M. Minsky. *Computation: finite and infinite machines*. Prentice Hall Int., 1967.

[Wil94] T. Wilke. Specifying timed state sequences in powerful decidable logics and timed automata. In *Proc. of Formal Techniques in Real-Time and Fault-Tolerant Systems*, LNCS 863, 1994.

[Yov97] S. Yovine. A verification tool for real-time systems. *Springer International Journal of Software Tools for Technology Transfer*, 1, October 1997.

Tuning SAT Checkers for Bounded Model Checking

Ofer Shtrichman

The Minerva Center for Verification of Reactive Systems, at the Dep. of Computer Science and Applied Mathematics, The Weizmann Institute of Science, Israel; and IBM Haifa Research Lab
ofers@summer.weizmann.ac.il

Abstract. Bounded Model Checking based on SAT methods has recently been introduced as a complementary technique to BDD-based Symbolic Model Checking. The basic idea is to search for a counter example in executions whose length is bounded by some integer k. The BMC problem can be efficiently reduced to a propositional satisfiability problem, and can therefore be solved by SAT methods rather than BDDs. SAT procedures are based on general-purpose heuristics that are designed for any propositional formula. We show that the unique characteristics of BMC formulas can be exploited for a variety of optimizations in the SAT checking procedure. Experiments with these optimizations on real designs proved their efficiency in many of the hard test cases, comparing to both the standard SAT procedure and a BDD-based model checker.

1 Introduction

The use of SAT methods for Symbolic Model Checking has recently been introduced in the framework of Bounded Model Checking [4]. The basic idea is to search for a counter example in executions whose length is bounded by some integer k. The BMC problem can be efficiently reduced to a propositional satisfiability problem, and can therefore be solved by SAT methods rather than BDDs. SAT procedures do not suffer from the potential space explosion of BDDs and can handle propositional satisfiability problems with thousands of variables. The first experiments with this idea showed that if k is small enough, or if the model has certain characteristics, it outperforms BDD-based techniques [5].

SAT procedures are based on general-purpose heuristics that are designed for any propositional formula. In this paper we will show that the unique characteristics of BMC formulas can be exploited for a variety of optimizations in the SAT checking procedure. These optimizations were implemented on top of CMU's BMC [4][1] and the SAT checker Grasp [11,12], without making use of features that are unique to either one of them.

---

[1] We distinguish between the tool BMC and the method BMC.

We benchmarked the various optimizations, and also compared them to results achieved by RuleBase, IBM's BDD-based Model Checker [1,2]. RuleBase is considered one of the strongest verification tools on the market, and includes most of the reductions and BDD optimizations that have been published in recent years. The benchmark's database included 13 randomly selected 'real-life' designs from IBM's internal benchmark set. Instances trivially solved by RuleBase are typically not included in this set, a fact which clearly creates a statistical bias in the results. Thus, although we will show that in 10 out of the 13 cases the improved SAT procedure outperformed RuleBase, we can not conclude from this that in general it is a better method. However, we can conclude that many of the (BDD-based model checking) hard problems can easily be solved by the improved SAT procedure. A practical conclusion is therefore that the best strategy would be to run several engines in parallel, and then present the user with the fastest result.

Our results are compatible with [5] in the sense that their experiment also showed a clear advantage of SAT when k is small, and when the design has specific characteristics that make BDDs inefficient. We found it hard to predict which design can easily be solved by BMC, because the results are not strictly monotonic in k or the size of the design. We have one design that could not be solved with BMC although there was a known bug in cycle 14, and another design which was trivially solved, although it included a bug only in cycle 38. The SAT instance corresponding to the second design was 5 times larger than the first one, in terms of number of variables and clauses. We also found that increasing k in a *given design* can speed up the search. This can be explained, perhaps, by the fact that increasing k can cause an increase in the ratio of satisfying to unsatisfying assignments.

The rest of this paper is organized as follows: in the next two sections we describe in more detail the theory and practice of BMC and SAT. In Section 4 we describe various BMC-specific optimizations that we applied to the SAT procedure. In sections 5 and 6 we list our experimental results, and our conclusions from them.

2 BMC - The Tool and the Generated Formulas

The general structure of an **AG**p formula, as generated in BMC, is the following:

$$\varphi: \quad I_0 \wedge \bigwedge_{i=0}^{k-1} \rho(i, i+1) \wedge (\bigvee_{i=0}^{k} \sim P_i) \tag{1}$$

where I_0 is the initial state, $\rho(i, i+1)$ is the transition between cycles i and $i+1$, and P_i is the property in cycle i. Thus, this formula can be satisfied iff for some i ($i \leq k$) there exists a reachable state in cycle i which contradicts the property P_i. Focusing on potential bugs in a specific cycle can be formulated by simply restricting the disjunction over P_i to the appropriate cycle. BMC takes an SMV - compatible model and generates a propositional SAT instance according to Equation (1). The size of the generated formula is linear in k, and indeed empirical results show that k strongly affects the performance. As a second step, BMC transforms the formula to CNF. To avoid the potential exponential growth of the formula associated with this translation, it adds auxiliary variables, and performs various optimizations.

Every ACTL* formula (the subset of CTL* that contain only universal path quantifiers) can be reduced to a SAT instance, under bounded semantics [4]. While all safety properties can be expressed in the form of **AG**p [3], to handle temporal operators such as **AF**p, BMC adds to φ the disjunction $\bigvee_{i=0..k-1} \rho(k,i)$, thus capturing the possibility of a loop in the state transition graph. Fairness is handled by changing the loop condition to include at least one state which preserves the fairness condition.

3 SAT Checkers and Grasp

In this section we briefly outline the principles followed by modern propositional SAT-checkers, and in particular those that Grasp (Generic seaRch Algorithm for the Satisfiability Problem) is based on. Our description follows closely the one in [11].

Most of the modern SAT-checkers are variations of the well known Davis-Putnam procedure [7]. The procedure is based on a backtracking search algorithm that, at each node in the search tree, chooses an *assignment* (i.e. both a variable and a Boolean value, which determines the next subtree to be traversed) and prunes subsequent searches by iteratively applying the unit clause rule. Iterated application of the unit clause rule is commonly referred to as Boolean Constraint Propagation (BCP). The procedure backtracks once a clause is found to be unsatisfiable, until either a satisfying assignment is found or the search tree is fully explored. The latter case implies that the formula is unsatisfiable.

A more generic description of a SAT algorithm was introduced in [11]. A simplified version of this algorithm is shown in Fig. 1.

At each *decision level d* in the search, a variable assignment $V_d = \{T, F\}$ is selected with the Decide() function. If all the variables are already decided (indicated by ALL-DECIDED), it implies that a satisfying assignment has been found, and SAT returns SATISFIABLE. Otherwise, the *implied assignments* are identified with the Deduce() function, which in most cases corresponds to a straightforward BCP. If this process terminates with no conflict, the procedure is called recursively with a higher decision level. Otherwise, Diagnose() analyzes the conflict and decides on the next step. First, it identifies those assignments that led to the conflict. Then it checks if the assignment to V_d is one of them. If the answer is yes, it implies that the value assigned to V_d should be swapped and the deduction process in line l_3 is repeated. If the swapped assignment also fails, it means that V_d is not responsible for the conflict. In this case Diagnose() will indicate that the procedure should BACK-TRACK to a lower decision level β (β is a global variable that can only be changed by Diagnose()). The procedure

```
// Input arg: Current decision level d
// Return value:
//    SAT():      {SATISFIABLE, UNSATISFIABLE}
//    Decide():   {DECISION, ALL-DECIDED}
//    Deduce():   {OK, CONFLICT}
//    Diagnose():{SWAP, BACK-TRACK}

SAT (d)
    {
$l_1$:      if (Decide (d) == ALL-DECIDED) return SATISFIABLE;
$l_2$:      while (TRUE) {
$l_3$:          if (Deduce(d) != CONFLICT) {
$l_4$:              if (SAT (d+1) == SATISFIABLE) return SATISFIABLE;
$l_5$:              else if ($\beta < d$ || d == 0) // $\beta$ is calculated in Diagnose()
$l_6$:                  { Erase (d); return UNSATISFIABLE; }
            }
$l_7$:          if (Diagnose (d) == BACK-TRACK) return UNSATISFIABLE;
        }
    }
```

Fig. 1. Generic backtrack search SAT algorithm

will then backtrack $d - \beta$ times, each time Erase()-ing the current decision and its implied assignments, in line l_6.

Different SAT procedures can be modeled by this generic algorithm. For example, the Davis-Putnam procedure can be emulated with the above algorithm by implementing BCP and the pure literal rule in deduce(), and implementing chronological backtracking (i.e. $\beta = d-1$) in diagnose(). Modern SAT checkers include *Non-chronological Backtracking* search strategies (i.e. $\beta = d - j, j \geq 1$). Hence, irrelevant assignments can be skipped over during the search. The analysis of conflicts can also be used for adding new constraints (called *conflict clauses*) on the search. These constraints prevent the repetition of assignments that lead to conflicts. This way the search procedure backtracks immediately if a 'bad' assignment is repeated. For example, if Diagnose() concludes that the assignment $x = T, y = F, z = F$ inevitably leads to a conflict, it adds the conflict clause $\pi = (\sim x \vee y \vee z)$ to φ.

From the large number of decide() strategies suggested over the years, experiments with Grasp have demonstrated that the Dynamic Largest Individual Sum (DLIS) has the best average results [10]. DLIS is a rather straightforward strategy: it chooses an assignment that leads to the largest number of satisfied clauses. In this research we only experimented with DLIS, although different problem domains may be most efficiently solved with different strategies.

4 Satisfiability Checking of BMC Formulas

In this section we describe various BMC-specific optimizations that have been implemented on top of Grasp. Many of the optimizations deal with familiar issues that are typically associated with BDDs: variable ordering, direction of traversal (backward Vs. forward), first subtree to traverse, etc.

4.1 Constraints Replication

The almost symmetric structure of Equation (1) can be used for pruning the search tree when verifying **AG**p formulas. In the following discussion let us first ignore I_0, and assume that φ is fully symmetric.

Conflict clauses, as explained in Section 3, are used for pruning the search tree by disallowing a conflicting sequence (i.e. an assignment that leads to an unsatisfied clause) to be assigned more than once. We will use the alleged symmetry in order to add *replicated clauses*, which are new clauses that are symmetric to the original conflict clause. Each of these clauses can be seen as a *constraint* on the state-space which, on the one hand preserves the satisfiability of the formula and, on the other hand, prunes the search tree.

Let us illustrate this concept by an example. Suppose that deduce() concluded that the assignment $x_4 = T, y_7 = F, z_5 = F$ always leads to a conflict (the subscript number in our notation is the cycle index that the variable refers to). In this case it will add the conflict clause $\pi = (\sim x_4 \vee y_7 \vee z_5)$ to φ. We claim that the symmetry of Equation (1) implies that, for example, the assignment $x_3 = T, y_6 = F, z_4 = F$ will also lead to a conflict, and we can therefore add the *replicated clause* $\pi = (\sim x_3 \vee y_6 \vee z_4)$ to φ. Let us now generalize this analysis. Let δ be the difference between the largest and lowest index of the variables in π (in our case $\delta = 7 - 4 = 3$). For all $0 \leq i \leq k - \delta$, the assignment $x_i = T, y_{i+3} = F, z_{i+1} = F$ will also result in a conflict and we can therefore add the replicated clause $m_i = (\sim x_i \vee y_{i+3} \vee z_{i+1})$.

Yet, φ is not fully symmetric. φ is not fully symmetric because of I_0 and because of the Bounded Cone of Influence reduction [5] [2]. The BCOI reduction eliminates variables that are not affecting the property up to cycle k. It can eliminate, for example, x_i for $k - 3 \leq i \leq k$ and y_j for $k - 5 \leq j \leq k$. Consequently cycle $k - 5$ will not be symmetric anymore to cycle $k - 3$ in φ. Typically variables are eliminated only from the right hand side, i.e., if a variable x_k is not eliminated, than for all $i < k$, x_i is also not eliminated. In the following discussion we concentrate on this typical case. Minor adjustments are needed for the general case.

There are two options to handle the asymmetry caused by the BCOI reduction. One option is to restrict the replicated clauses to $0 < i < k - \delta - \Delta$, where

---

[2] This is in addition to several other manipulations that BMC performs on φ which are easy to overcome, and will not be listed here.

Δ is the number of cycles affected by the BCOI reduction. Another option is to add replicated clauses as long as all their variables are contained in the BCOI.

The second option can be formalized as follows. Let C be the set of variables in the conflict clause. For a variable $\sigma \in C$, denote by $k_\sigma \leq k$ the highest index s.t. σ_{k_σ} is a variable in φ (without the BCOI reduction, $k_\sigma = k$ for all variables) and by i_σ the index of σ in C. Also, let $min_C = min\{i_\sigma\}$ and $\psi = min\{(k_\sigma - i_\sigma)\}$ for all $\sigma \in C$. Intuitively, ψ is the maximum number of clauses we can add to the 'right' (i.e. with a higher index) of the conflict clause. We now add replicated clauses s.t. the variable σ for which $i_\sigma = min_c$ ranges from 0 to $min_C + \psi$.

Example 1. For the conflict clause $\pi = (\sim x_4 \vee y_7 \vee z_5)$, we have $C = \{x_4, y_7, z_5\}$ and $min_C = 4$. Suppose that $k_x = 5, k_y = 10$ and $k_z = 7$. Also, suppose that $k = 10$ and $\Delta = 5$ (since $k_x = 5$, Δ has to be greater or equal to $(10 - 5) = 5$). According to the first option, x will range from 0 to $(10 - 5 - (7 - 4)) = 2$. Thus, the replicated clauses will be $(\sim x_0 \vee y_3 \vee z_1)...(\sim x_2 \vee y_5 \vee z_3)$. According to the second option, we calculate $\psi = min((5 - 4), (10 - 7), (7 - 5)) = 1$, and therefore x will range from 0 to $(4 + 1) = 5$. Thus, this time the right most clause will be $(\sim x_5 \vee y_8 \vee z_6)$. □

Example 1 demonstrates that the second option allows for more replicated clauses to be added, and is therefore preferable.

The influence of I_0 is not bounded, and can propagate up to cycle k. Therefore a simple restriction on the replicated clauses is insufficient. A somewhat 'brute-force' solution is to simulate an assignment for every potential replicated clause, (i.e. assign values that satisfy the complement of m_i) and check if it leads to a conflict. The overhead of this option is rather small, since it only requires to assign $|m_i|$ variables and then deduce() once. If this results in a conflict, we can add m_i to the formula. However, the addition of wrong clauses can only lead to false positives, and therefore we can skip the simulation and refer to constraint replication as an under approximation method (this also implies that for the purpose of faster falsification, many other under approximation heuristics can be implemented by adding clauses to φ). Hence, we can first skip the simulation, and only if the formula is unsatisfiable, run it again with simulation.

The overhead of adding and simulating the replicated clauses is small in comparison to its benefit. In all the test cases we examined, as will be shown in Section 5, the replicated clauses accelerated the search, although not dramatically.

4.2 Static Ordering

The variable ordering followed by dynamic decide() procedures (such as the previously mentioned DLIS strategy) is constructed according to various 'greedy' criteria, which do not utilize our knowledge of φ's structure. A typical scenario when using these procedures, in the context of BMC formulas, is that large sets of clauses associated with distant cycles are being satisfied independently, until they 'collide', i.e. it is discovered that the assignments that satisfied them contradict each other. Fig. 2 demonstrates this scenario, by showing two distant sets of assigned variables (around the 5th and 20th cycles), that grow independently until at some point they collide. Similarly, they can collide with the constraints imposed by the initial state I_0 or the negation of the property in cycle k. To resolve this conflict, it may be necessary to go back hundreds of variables up the decision tree. We claim that this phenomena can potentially be avoided by guiding the search according to the (k-unfolding of the) Variable Dependency Graph (VDG). This way conflicts will be resolved on a more 'local' level, and consequently less time will be wasted in backtracking.

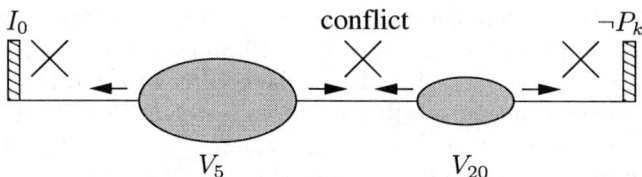

Fig. 2. With default dynamic ordering strategies, it is common that distant sets of variables are assigned values independently. We refer the reader to a technical report [9], where we show snapshots of the number of variables from each cycle that are assigned a value at a given moment. These charts prove that this phenomena indeed occur when using these strategies.

The most natural way to implement such a strategy is to predetermine a *static* order, following either a forward or a backward Breadth - First Search (BFS) on VDG. Indeed, our experiments have shown that in most cases this strategy speeds up the search.

Ordering strategies. We now investigate variations of the BFS strategy. Let us first assume that we are looking for a counter example in a particular cycle k. In this case a strict backward traversal may spend a significant amount of time in paths which include unreachable states. This fact will be revealed only when the search reaches $\overline{I_0}$ (we denote the set of variables in a sub-formula ψ by $\overline{\psi}$), which is placed last in the suggested order. Enforcing a static *forward* traversal, on the other hand, may result in a prolonged search through legal paths (i.e. paths that preserve the property), that will be revealed only when $\overline{P_k}$ is decided (these are the two 'walls' in Fig. 2). A similar dilemma is associated with BDD-based techniques (see for example [6] and [8]). It seems that the (unknown) ratio between the number of paths that go through unreachable states and the number of legal paths is crucial for determining the most efficient direction of traversal in both methodologies.

The strict backward or forward BFS causes the constraints, either on the first or the k-th cycle, to be considered only in a very 'deep' decision level, and the number of backtracks will consequently be very high, sometimes higher than the default dynamic strategies. Another problem with straight BFS results from the very large number of variables in each cycle. Typically there are hundreds or even thousands of variables in each cycle. It creates a large gap between each variable and its immediate neighbors in VDG, and therefore conflicts are not resolved as locally as we would like to.

These two observations indicate that the straightforward BFS solution should be altered. On the one hand, we should keep a small distance between $\overline{P_0}$ and $\overline{P_k}$, and on the other hand we should follow VDG as close as possible. This strategy can be achieved, for example, by triggering the BFS with a set S of small number of variables from each cycle. As a minimum, it has to include $\overline{P_k}$ (otherwise not all the variables will be covered by the search). Different strategies can be applied for choosing the variables from the other cycles. For example, we can choose $\overline{P_i}$ for all i.[3]

When we generalize our analysis and assume that we are looking for a counter example in the range $0..k$, the set $S := \bigcup_{0 \leq i \leq k} \overline{P_i}$ is the smallest initial set which enables the BFS procedure to cover the full set of variables in a single path. Initial sets smaller than S will require more than one path. This will split the set of variables of each cycle into a larger number of small sets, and consequently create a big gap between them (i.e. between each node and its siblings on the graph). If two such distant siblings are assigned values which together contradict their parent node, then the backtrack 'jump' will be large. Increasing S, on the other hand, will create a large gap between neighboring variables on VDG (i.e. between a node and its sons on the graph). This tradeoff indicates that a single optimal heuristic for all designs probably does not exist, and that only experiments can help us to fine-tune S.

There are, of course, numerous other possible ordering strategies. Like BDDs, on the one hand it has a crucial influence on the procedure efficiency, and on the other hand, an ordering heuristic which is optimal for all designs is hard to find.

Unsatisfiable instances. A major consideration in designing SAT solvers, is their efficiency in solving unsatisfiable instances. Although the various optimizations (e.g. conflicting clauses, non-chronological backtracking) are helpful in these cases as much as they are with satisfiable instances, while satisfiable instances can be solved fast by a good 'guess' of assignments, an instance can be proven to be unsatisfiable only after an exhaustive exploration of the state-space.

We now show that the order imposed by the previously suggested backward BFS is particularly good for unsatisfiable BMC-formulas. In the following discussion we denote φ's sub-formulas $\bigvee_{i=0..k} \sim P_i$ and $\bigwedge_{i=0}^{k-1} \rho(i, i+1)$ by P and ρ respectively.

Let us assume that the property holds up to cycle k, and consequently φ is unsatisfiable. Since the transition relation ρ is consistent [4], a contradiction in φ will not be found before the first variables from $\overline{P}$ are decided. Yet, since

---

[3] This is not always possible because for $i < k$, $\overline{P_i}$ might be removed by the BCOI reduction.

[4] Inconsistent transition relations can occur, but typically can also be trivially detected.

typically $|\overline{P}| \ll |\overline{\rho}|$, it is possible that the search will backtrack on ρ's variables for a very long time before it reaches $\overline{P}$. Thus, by forcing the search to begin with $\overline{P}$, we may be able to avoid this scenario. However, starting from $\overline{P}$ is not necessarily enough, because this way we only shift the problem to the variables that define $\overline{P}$. It is clear that a BFS backwards on the dependency graph, from the property variables to the initial state is a generalization of this idea and should therefore speed up the proof of unsatisfiability.

4.3 Choosing the Next Branch in the Search Tree

The proposed static ordering does not specify the Boolean value given to each variable. This is in contrast to the dynamic approach where this decision is implicit. Here are four heuristics that we examined:

1. *Dynamic decision.* The value is chosen according to one of the dynamic Decide() strategies, which are originally meant for deciding both on the variable and its value. For example, the DLIS strategy chooses the value that satisfies the largest number of clauses.
2. *Constant, or random decision.* The most primitive decision strategy is to constantly assign either '0' or '1' to the chosen variable, or alternatively, to choose this value randomly. As several experiments have shown in the past [10], choosing a random or a constant value is not apriori inferior to dynamic decision strategies as one might expect. Any dynamic decision strategy can lead to the 'wrong side of the tree', i.e. can cause the search to focus on an unsatisfiable sub-tree. Apparently constant or random decisions in many cases avoid this path and consequently speed up the search.
3. *Searching for a flat counter example.* Analysis of bugs in real designs, leads to the observation that most of them can be reached by computations which are mostly 'flat', i.e. computations where the frequency in which the majority of the variables swap their values is low. This phenomenon can be exploited when 'guessing' the next subtree to be traversed. Suppose that the Decide() function chose to assign a variable x_i for some $0 \leq i \leq k$. Let x_l and x_r be the left and right closest neighboring variables of x_i that are already assigned a value at this point (if no such variable exists, we will say that x_l, or x_r, is equal to $\bot$). To construct a flat counter example, if $x_l = x_r$ we will assign x_i their common value. The following simple procedure generalizes this principle:

    ```
    l = largest number s.t. l < i and x_l is assigned.
    r = smallest number s.t. r > i and x_r is assigned.
    if x_l ≠ ⊥
         if (x_l = x_r || x_r =⊥) return x_l; else return {T,F};
    else
         if (x_r ≠⊥) return x_r; else return {T,F};
    ```

    The non-deterministic choice can be replaced by one of the heuristics that were suggested above (e.g. dynamic, constant).

4. *Repeating previous assignments.* When the search engine backtracks from decision level d to β, all the assignments that are either decide()d or deduce()d between these two levels are undone by erase(). We claim that repeating previous assignments can reduce the number of backtracks. This is because we know that all assignments between levels $\beta + 1$ and d do not contradict one another nor do they contradict the assignments with decision level lower than β (otherwise the procedure would backtrack before level d). In order to decide on each variable's value for the first time, this strategy should be combined with one of the strategies that were described before.

4.4 A Combined Dynamic and Static Variable Ordering

The static ordering can be combined in various ways with the more traditional dynamic procedures. We have implemented two such strategies:

1. *Two phase ordering.* The static traversal is used for the first max_s variables, and then the variables are Decide()-d dynamically.
2. *Sliding window.* Variables are chosen dynamically from a small set of variables, corresponding to a 'window' which progresses along the static order that we chose. Let $V : v_1..v_n$ be the static variable ordering, and let $V' : v'_1..v'_k$ be the (ordered) subset of V's variables that are currently not assigned a value. Let $1 \leq w \leq k$ be an arbitrary number denoting the *window* size. In each step, a variable is dynamically chosen from the set of variables that are within the borders of the window $[v'_1 - v'_w]$. Note that the two extreme ends of w, namely $w = 1$ and $w = k$, correspond to the pure static and dynamic orderings, respectively.

4.5 Restricting Decide() to Dominating Variables

While φ typically contains tens of thousands of variables, not more than 10%-20% of them are the actual model's variables. The other 80% are auxiliary variables that were added to φ in order to generate a compact CNF formula. It is clear that the model's variables are sufficient for deciding the satisfiability of the formula, and therefore it should be enough to decide() only them (however, if the formula has more than one satisfying assignment, some of the auxiliary variables should be assigned too). The same argument can be applied to a much smaller set of variables: the inputs. The input variables are typically less than 5% of the total number of variables, and can determine alone the satisfiability of the formula[5]. Thus, if we restrict Decide() to one of these small sets, we potentially reduce the depth of the decision tree, on the expense of more deduce() operations.

---

[5] Here we assume that all non-deterministic assignments are replaced by conditional assignments, where the 'guard' of the condition is a new input variable.

5 Experimental Results

The Benchmark included 13 designs, on a 'one property per design' base. The properties were proven in the past to be false, and the cycle in which they fail was known as well. Thus, the Benchmark focuses on a narrow view of the problem: the time it takes to find a bug in cycle k, when k is pre-known. The iterative process of finding k is, of course, time consuming, which might be more significant than any small time gap between BMC and regular model checking.

The results presented in Fig. 3 summarize some of the more interesting configurations which we experimented with. In Fig. 4 we present more information regarding the SAT instance of each case study (the no. of variables and clauses) as well as some other Grasp configurations which were generally less successful. The right-most column in this figure includes the time it takes to prove that there is no bug up to cycle $k-1$, with the **SM** configuration. These figures are important for evaluating the potential performance differences between satisfiable and unsatisfiable instances.

We present results achieved by RuleBase under two different configurations. **RB1** is the default configuration, with dynamic reordering. **RB2** is the same configuration without reordering, but the initial order is taken from the order that was calculated with **RB1**. These two configurations represent a typical scenario of Model-Checking with RuleBase. Each time reordering is activated, the initial order is potentially improved and saved in a special order file for future runs. Thus, **RB2** results can be further improved.

RuleBase results are compared with various configurations of Grasp, where the first one is simply the default configuration without any of the suggested optimizations.

The following table summarizes the various configurations, where the left part refers to Fig. 3 and the right part to Fig. 4:

	Grasp	+R	+SM	+SMF	+SMR	+SMP	+SMD	+W_i
Ordering:	Dyn	Dyn	Stat	Stat	Stat	Stat	Stat	Win i
Value:	Dyn	Dyn	1	Flat	1	Prev	Dyn	Dyn
Variable set:	All	All	Model	Model	Model	Model	Model	Model
Replication:	No	Yes	No	No	Yes	No	No	No

The *Stat* ordering refers to the static order suggested in Section 4.2, whereas *Dyn* is the default dynamic decision strategy adopted by Grasp (DLIS). The *Win i* refers to a combined dynamic and static ordering, where variables within a window of size i are selected dynamically, as explained in Section 4.4. The '1', *Flat* and *Prev* default values refer to the constant, flat and previous values suggested in Section 4.3 (in **+SMP** we combined the *Prev* strategy with the default value '1'). The *Model* variable set refers to a restriction on decide() to model variables only, as described in Section 4.5. The Replication refers to constraint replication and simulation, as explained in Section 4.1. All configurations include the flag '+g60', which restricts the size of the conflict clauses (and consequently also the size of the replicated clauses) to 60 literals. Other than very few cases, all the other possible configurations did not perform better than those that are presented.

The test cases in the figure below are separated into two sets: the 10 designs in the first set demonstrate better results for the optimized SAT procedure, and the 3 designs in the second set demonstrate an advantage to the BDD-based procedure. Both sets are sorted according to the **RB1** results.

Design #	K	RB1	RB2	Grasp	+R	+SM	+SMF	+SMP	+SMR
1	18	7	6	282	115	**3**	57	29	4.1
2	5	70	8	1.1	1.1	0.8	1.1	**0.7**	0.9
3	14	597	375	76	52	**3**	2069	**3**	**3**
4	24	690	261	510	225	**12**	27	**12**	**12**
5	12	803	184	24	24	**2**	**2**	**2**	3
6	22	*	356	*	*	18	**16**	38	18
7	9	*	2671	10	10	2	**1.8**	1.9	2
8	35	*	*	6317	2870	**20**	338	101	74
9	38	*	*	9035	*	**25**	277	126	96
10	31	*	*	*	9910	312	**22**	64	330
11	32	152	**60**	*	*	*	*	*	*
12	31	1419	**1126**	*	*	*	*	*	*
13	14	*	**3626**	*	*	*	*	*	*

Fig. 3. Results table (Sec.). Best results are bold-faced. Asterisks (*) represent run times exceeding 10,000 sec.

Remarks for Figures 3 and 4

1. The time required by BMC to generate the formula is not included in the results. BMC generates the formula typically in one or two minutes for the large models, and several seconds for the small ones. While generating the formula, the improved BMC generate several files which are needed for performing the various optimizations.
2. RuleBase supports multiple engines. The presented results were achieved by the 'classic' SMV-based engine. Yet, a new BDD-based engine that was recently added to RuleBase (January 2000), performs significantly better on some of these designs. This engine is based on sophisticated under and over approximation methods that were not yet published.
3. When comparing RuleBase results to BMC results, one should remember that the former has undergone years of development and optimizations, which the latter did not yet enjoy. The various optimizations that have been presented in this paper can be further improved and tuned. Various combinations of the dynamic and static orderings are possible, and it is expected that more industrial experience will help in fine tuning them. The

Design #	vars	clauses	+SM	+SMD	+W$_{50}$	+W$_{100}$	+W$_{200}$	+SM ($k-1$)
1	9685	55870	3	36	46	46	51	20
2	3628	14468	0.8	0.7	0.7	0.7	0.8	0.4
3	14930	72106	3	1216	8	3	17	934
4	28161	139716	12	26	31	42	61	26
5	9396	41207	2	3	2	3	3	1
6	51654	368367	18	243	111	418	950	28
7	8710	39774	2	1.8	2.5	1.9	2.8	1.3
8	58074	294821	20	123	163	86	105	30
9	63624	326999	25	136	164	153	181	230
10	61088	334861	312	125	70	107	223	1061
11	32109	150027	*	*	*	*	*	*
12	39598	19477	*	*	*	*	*	*
13	13215	6572	*	*	*	*	*	*

Fig. 4. Other, less successful configurations

implementation of the SAT checker Grasp can also be much improved even without changing the search strategy. It was observed by [10] that an efficient implementation can be more significant than the decision strategy.[6]

6 Conclusions

1. Neither BDD techniques nor SAT techniques are dominant. Yet, in most (10 out of 13) cases the optimized SAT procedure performs significantly better. As was stated before, only significant differences in performance are meaningful, because normally k is not pre-known. Such differences exist in 8 of the 10 cases.
2. The **SM**, **SMP** and **SMR** strategies are better in all cases compared to the default procedure adopted by Grasp. The **SM** strategy seems to be the best one.
3. The static ordering apparently has a stronger impact on the results than the strategy for choosing the next subtree. This can be explained by the fact that wrong choices of values are corrected 'locally' when the variable ordering follows the dependency graph, as was explained before. Surprisingly, the constant decision 'TRUE', which is the most primitive strategy, proved to be the most efficient (in another experiment we tried to solve design #10, which is the only one that is solved significantly better by other configurations, with a constant decision 'FALSE'. It was solved in about 3 seconds, faster than all other configurations). The 'flat' decision strategy performed better only in three cases. The 'Prev' decision was better than 'flat' in 6 designs, but only once better than the simple constant decision. Yet, it seems to be

---

[6] In [4], SATO [13] was used rather than Grasp. Although in some cases it is faster than Grasp, it is restricted in the number of variables it can handle, and seems to be less stable.

more stable in achieving fast results than both of them. As for the sliding window strategy, Fig. 4 shows that in most cases increasing the window size only slows down the search. The surprising success of the constant decision strategy can perhaps be attributed to its zero overhead. It can also indicate that most bugs in hardware designs can be revealed when the majority of the signals are 'on'. Only further experiments can clarify if this is a general pattern or an attribute of the specific designs that were examined in the benchmark.

4. Constraint replication (+simulation) requires a small overhead, which does not seem to be worthwhile when used in combination with static ordering. Yet, it speeds up the standard search based on dynamic ordering.

   This can be explained by the inherent difference between dynamic and static orderings: suppose that the assignment $x_1 = T$ and $y_{20} = F$ leads to a conflict, and suppose that their associated decision levels were 10 and 110 respectively when the conflict clause $(\neg x_1 \vee y_{20})$ was added to φ. In static ordering, the decision level for each variable remains constant. As a result, even if the search backtracks to a decision level lower than 10, the conflict clause will not be effective until the search once again arrives at decision level 110. In dynamic ordering, on the other hand, there is a chance that these two variables will be decided much closer to each other, and therefore the clause will prune the search tree earlier.

   Another reason for the difference is related to the typical sizes of backtracking in each of the methods. Since conflicts are resolved on a more 'local' level in the **SM** strategy, conflict clauses (either the original ones or the replicated clauses) are made of variables which are relatively close to each other in terms of their associated decision level. Therefore the non-chronological backtracking 'jump' caused by these clauses is relatively small.

5. Both SAT methods and BDD based methods do not have a single dominant configuration. BDDs can run with or without reordering, with or without conjunctive partitioning, etc. As for SAT methods, all the optimizations described in Section 4 can be activated separately, and indeed, as the results table demonstrate, different designs are solved better with different configurations. Given this state of affairs, the most efficient solution, as was mentioned in the introduction, would be to run several engines in parallel and present the user with the fastest solution. This architecture will not only enable the users to run SAT and BDD based tools in parallel, but also to run these tools under different configurations in the same time, which will obviously speed up the process of model checking.

Acknowledgments I would like to thank Armin Biere and Joao Marques-Silva for making `BMC` and `Grasp` publicly available, respectively, and for their most helpful assistance in figuring them out.

References

[1] I. Beer, S. Ben-David, C. Eisner, D. Geist, L. Gluhovsky, T. Heyman, A. Landver, P. Paanah, Y. Rodeh, G. Ronin, and Y. Wolfsthal. RuleBase: Model checking at IBM. In Orna Grumberg, editor, *Proc. 9th Intl. Conference on Computer Aided Verification (CAV'97)*, volume 1254 of *Lect. Notes in Comp. Sci.*, pages 480–483. Springer-Verlag, 1997.

[2] I. Beer, S. Ben-David, C. Eisner, and A. Landver. RuleBase: An industry oriented formal verification tool. In *Proc. Design Automation Conference 96 (DAC96)*, 1996.

[3] I. Beer, S. Ben-David, and A. Landver. On-the-fly model checking of RCTL formulas. In A.J. Hu and M.Y. Vardi, editors, *Proc. 10th Intl. Conference on Computer Aided Verification (CAV'98)*, volume 1427 of *Lect. Notes in Comp. Sci.*, pages 184–194. Springer-Verlag, 1998.

[4] A. Biere, A. Cimatti, E. Clarke, and Y. Zhu. Symbolic model checking without BDDs. In *Proceedings of the Workshop on Tools and Algorithms for the Construction and Analysis of Systems (TACAS99)*, Lect. Notes in Comp. Sci. Springer-Verlag, 1999.

[5] A. Biere, E. Clarke, R. Raimi, and Y. Zhu. Verifying safety properties of a power pc^{TM} microprocessor using symbolic model checking without bdds. In N. Halbwachs and D. Peled, editors, *Proc. 11st Intl. Conference on Computer Aided Verification (CAV'99)*, Lect. Notes in Comp. Sci. Springer-Verlag, 1999.

[6] Wililiam Chan, Richard Anderson, Paul Beame, and David Notkin. Improving efficiency of symbolic model checking for state-based system requirements. In *International Symposium on Software Testing and Analysis (ISSTA98)*, Lect. Notes in Comp. Sci. Springer-Verlag, 1998.

[7] M. Davis and H. Putnam. A computing procedure for quantification theory. *J. ACM*, 7:201–215, 1960.

[8] H. Iwashita, T. Nakata, and F. Hirose. Ctl model checking based on forward state traversal. In *IEEE/ACM International conference on Computer Aided Design*, pages 82–87, November 1996.

[9] Ofer Shtrichman. Tuning sat checkers for bounded model checking – experiments with static and dynamic orderings. Technical report, Weizmann Institute, 2000. can be downloaded from www.weizmann.ac.il/~ofers.

[10] J.P.M Silva. The impact of branching heuristics in propositional satisfiability algorithms. In *9th Portuguese Conference on Artificial Intelligence (EPIA)*, 1999.

[11] J.P.M Silva and K. A. Sakallah. GRASP - a new search algorithm for satisfyability. Technical Report TR-CSE-292996, Univerisity of Michigan, 1996.

[12] J.P.M Silva and K. A. Sakallah. GRASP: A search algorithm for propositional satisfiability. *IEEE Transactions on Computers*, 48:506–516, 1999.

[13] H. Zhang. SATO: An efficient propositional prover. In *International Conference on Automated Deduction (CADE-97)*, 1997.

Unfoldings of Unbounded Petri Nets

Parosh Aziz Abdulla[1], S. Purushothaman Iyer[2], and Aletta Nylén[1]

[1] Dept. of Computer Systems
P.O. Box 325
Uppsala University
S-751 05 Uppsala, Sweden
{parosh,aletta}@docs.uu.se
[2] Dept of Computer Science
NC State University
Raleigh, NC 27695-7534
purush@csc.ncsu.edu

Abstract. Net unfoldings have attracted much attention as a powerful technique for combating state space explosion in model checking. The method has been applied to verification of 1-safe (finite) Petri nets, and more recently also to other classes of finite-state systems such as synchronous products of finite transition systems. We show how unfoldings can be extended to the context of infinite-state systems. More precisely, we apply unfoldings to get an efficient symbolic algorithm for checking safety properties of unbounded Petri nets. We demonstrate the advantages of our method by a number of experimental results.

1 Introduction

Model Checking has had a great impact as an efficient method for algorithmic verification of finite-state systems. A limiting factor in its application is the *state space explosion* problem, which occurs since the number of states grows exponentially with the number of components inside the system. Therefore, much effort has been spent on developing techniques for reducing the effect of state space explosion in practical applications. One such a technique is that of *partial orders* which is based on the observation that not all interleavings of a given set of independent actions need to be explored during model checking. Several criteria for independency has been given, e.g., *stubborn sets* [Val90], *persistent sets* [GW93] or *ample sets* [Pel93]. A method which has drawn considerable attention recently is that of *unfoldings* [McM95,ERV96,ER99]. Unfoldings are *occurrence nets*: unrollings of Petri nets that preserve their semantics. Although unfoldings are usually infinite, it is observed in [McM95] that we can always construct a finite initial prefix of the unfolding which captures its entire behaviour, and which in many cases is much smaller than the state space of the system. Unfoldings have been applied to n-safe (i.e., finite-state) Petri nets, and more recently to other classes of finite-state systems such as synchronous products of finite transition systems [LB99,ER99]

In a parallel development, there has been numerous efforts, to extend the applicability of model checking to the domain of infinite-state systems. This has resulted in several highly nontrivial algorithms for verification of timed automata, lossy channel systems, (unbounded) Petri nets, broadcast protocols, relational automata, parametrized systems, etc. These methods operate on symbolic representations, called *constraints* each of which may represent an infinite set of states. However, in a manner similar to finite-state verification, many of these algorithms suffer from a *constraint explosion* problem limiting their efficiency in practical applications. As the interest in the area of infinite-state systems increases, it will be important to design tools which limit the impact of constraint explosion. With this in mind, we have considered [AKP97,AJKP98] a refinement of the ample set construction and applied it to infinite-state systems such as Petri nets and lossy channel systems.

In this paper, we show how the unfolding technique can be made to work in the context of infinite state systems. More precisely, we present an unfolding algorithm for symbolic verification of unbounded Petri nets. We adapt an algorithm described in [AČJYK96] for backward reachability analysis which can be used to verify general classes of safety properties. Instead of working on individual markings (configurations) of the net (as is the case with the previous approaches [McM95,ERV96,ER99,LB99]) we let our unfolding algorithm operate on constraints each of which may represent an (infinite) upward closed set of markings. We start from a constraint describing a set of "final" markings, typically undesirable configurations which we do not want to occur during the execution of the net. ¿From the set of final markings we unroll the net backwards, generating a *Reverse Occurrence Net (RON)*. In order to achieve termination we present an algorithm to compute a postfix of the RON, which gives a complete characterization of the set of markings from which we can reach a final marking. Using concepts from the theory of well quasi-orderings we show that the postfix is always finite. In fact, our method offers the same advantages over the algorithm in [AČJYK96], as those offered by the algorithms of [McM95,ERV96] in the context of finite-state systems.

Based on the algorithm, we have implemented a prototype, whose results on a number of simple examples are encouraging.

Outline In the next section we give some preliminaries on Petri nets. In Section 3 we introduce Reverse Occurrence Nets (RONs). In Section 4 we describe the unfolding algorithm. In Section 5 we describe how to compute a finite postfix of the unfolding. In Section 6 we report some experimental results. Finally, in Section 7 we give some conclusions and directions for future research.

2 Preliminaries

Let $\mathbb{N}$ be the set of natural of numbers. For $a, b \in \mathbb{N}$, we define $a \ominus b$ to be equal to $a - b$ if $a \geq b$, and equal to 0 otherwise. A *bag* over a set A is a mapping from A to $\mathbb{N}$. Relations and operations on bags such as $\leq, +, -, \ominus$, etc, are defined as usual. Sometimes, we write bags as tuples, so (a, b, a) represents a bag B with

$B(a) = 2$, $B(b) = 1$, and $B(d) = 0$ if $d \neq a, b$. A set A of bags is said to be *upward closed* if $B_1 \in A$ and $B_1 \leq B_2$ imply $B_2 \in A$. The *upward closure* of a bag A is the set $\{A' \mid A \leq A'\}$. We may interpret a set S as a bag with $S(a) = 1$ if $a \in S$ and $S(a) = 0$ if $a \notin S$. We use $|S|$ to denote the size of the set S. In this paper, we shall use the terminology of [ERV96] as much as possible.

A *net* is a triple (S, T, F) where S is a finite set of *places*, T is a finite set of *transitions*, and $F \subseteq (S \times T) \cup (T \times S)$ is the *flow relation*. By a *node* we mean a place or a transition. The preset ${}^\bullet x$ of a node x is the set $\{y \mid (y, x) \in F\}$. The postset $x^\bullet$ is similarly defined. A *marking* M is a bag over S. We say that a transition t is *enabled* in a marking M if ${}^\bullet t \leq M$. We define a transition relation on the set of markings, where $M_1 \longrightarrow M_2$ if there is $t \in T$ which is enabled in M_1 and $M_2 = M_1 - {}^\bullet t + t^\bullet$. We let $\stackrel{*}{\longrightarrow}$ denote the reflexive transitive closure of $\longrightarrow$. We say that a marking M_2 is *coverable* from a marking M_1 if $M_1 \stackrel{*}{\longrightarrow} M_2'$, for some $M_2' \geq M_2$. A *net system* is a tuple $N = (S, T, F, M_{init}, M_{fin})$, where (S, T, F) is a net and M_{init}, M_{fin} are markings, called the *initial* and the *final* marking of N respectively. In this paper, we consider the *coverability problem* defined as follows.

Instance A net system $(S, T, F, M_{init}, M_{fin})$.

Question Is M_{fin} coverable from M_{init}?

Using standard methods [VW86,GW93], we can reduce the problem of checking safety properties for Petri nets to the coverability problem.

To solve the coverability problem, we perform a backward reachability analysis. We define a *backward* transition relation [AČJYK96], such that, for markings M_1 and M_2 and a transition t, we have $M_2 \leadsto_t M_1$ if $M_1 = (M_2 \ominus t^\bullet) + {}^\bullet t$. We let $\leadsto = \bigcup_{t \in T} \leadsto_t$, and let $M \stackrel{k}{\leadsto} M'$ denote that $M = M_0 \leadsto M_1 \leadsto \cdots M_k = M'$, for markings $M_0, \ldots, M_k$. We define $\stackrel{*}{\leadsto}$ to be the reflexive transitive closure of $\leadsto$. Observe that, for each marking M_2 and transition t, there is a marking M_1 with $M_2 \leadsto_t M_1$, i.e., transitions are always enabled with respect to $\leadsto$. The following lemma relates the forward and backward transition relations.

Lemma 1.
1. If $M_1 \longrightarrow M_2$ and $M_2' \leq M_2$ then there is $M_1' \leq M_1$ such that $M_2' \leadsto M_1'$.
2. If $M_2 \leadsto M_1$ and $M_1' \geq M_1$ then there is M_2' such that $M_2' \geq M_2$ and $M_1' \longrightarrow M_2'$.

3 Reverse Occurrence Nets

In this section we introduce *Reverse Occurrence Nets (RONs)*. A RON corresponds to "unrolling" a net *backwards*. Formally, a *RON* R is a net $(\mathsf{C}, \mathsf{E}, \mathsf{F})$ satisfying the following three conditions

(i) $|c^\bullet| \leq 1$ for each $c \in \mathsf{C}$.
(ii) there is no infinite sequence of the form $c_1 \mathsf{F} e_1 \mathsf{F} c_2 \mathsf{F} \cdots$. This condition implies that there are no cycles in the RON, and that there is a set $\max(\mathsf{F})$ of nodes which are maximal with respect to F.
(iii) $\max(\mathsf{F}) \subseteq \mathsf{C}$.

In a RON, the places and transitions are usually called *conditions* and *events* respectively. A set of events $E \subseteq \mathsf{E}$ is considered to be a *configuration* if $e \in E$ and $e\mathsf{F}^* e'$ imply $e' \in E$.

Remark 1. In [McM95,ERV96], a configuration E is upward closed in the sense that if an event e belongs to E, then all events above e (with respect to F) also belong to E. In our case, configurations are downward closed. Furthermore, in [McM95,ERV96], configurations are required to be *conflict free*, i.e., for all events $e_1, e_2 \in E$ we have ${}^\bullet e_1 \cap {}^\bullet e_2 = \emptyset$. Notice that this property is always satisfied by our configurations, since we demand that $|c^\bullet| \leq 1$ for each condition.

Consider a net system $N = (S, T, F, M_{init}, M_{fin})$ and a RON $(\mathsf{C}, \mathsf{E}, \mathsf{F})$, and let $\mu : \mathsf{C} \cup \mathsf{E} \to S \cup T$ such that $\mu(c) \in S$ if $c \in \mathsf{C}$ and $\mu(e) \in T$ if $e \in \mathsf{E}$. For $C \subseteq \mathsf{C}$, we define $\#C$ to be a marking such that, for each place s, the value of $\#C(s)$ is equal to the size of the set $\{c \in C \mid \mu(c) = s\}$. In other words $\#C(s)$ is the number of conditions in C labeled with s. We say that $(\mathsf{C}, \mathsf{E}, \mathsf{F}, \mu)$ is a *(backward) unfolding* of N if the following two conditions are satisfied: (i) $\#\max(\mathsf{F}) = M_{fin}$, i.e., the set of conditions which are maximal with respect to F correspond to the final marking; and (ii) μ preserves F, viz., if $(x, y) \in \mathsf{F}$ then $(\mu(x), \mu(y)) \in F$.

For a configuration E, we define $Cut(E)$ to be the set

$$(\{{}^\bullet e \mid e \in E\} \cup \max(\mathsf{F})) - \{e^\bullet \mid e \in E\}$$

We define the marking $mark(E) = \#(Cut(E))$.

In Figure 1, we show a net system N with seven places, $s_1, \ldots, s_7$, and four transitions, $t_1, \ldots, t_4$. We also show an unfolding[1] U of N, assuming a final marking (s_1, s_7). Examples of configurations in U are $E_1 = \{e_2, e_4\}$ with $mark(E_1) = (s_1, s_2, s_3)$, and $E_2 = \{e_1, e_2, e_3, e_4\}$ with $mark(E_2) = (s_1, s_2, s_2, s_3)$.

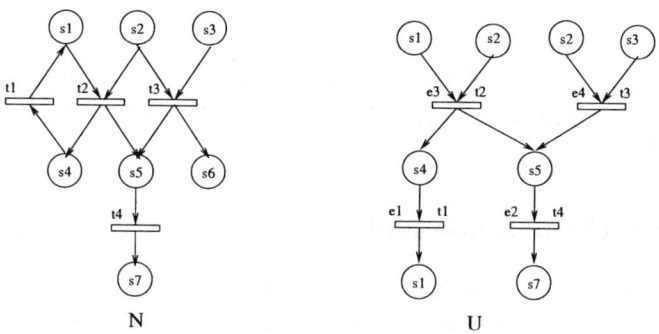

Fig. 1. A net system and one of its unfoldings

---

[1] To increase readability, we show both names and labels of events in the figure, while we omit name of conditions.

4 An Unfolding Algorithm

We present an algorithm (Figure 2) which, for a given net system

$$N = (S, T, F, M_{init}, M_{fin}) ,$$

generates an unfolding of N in an incremental manner. In a manner similar to [ERV96], an unfolding $U = (\mathsf{C}, \mathsf{E}, \mathsf{F}, \mu)$ is represented as a list of objects corresponding to conditions and events in the underlying RON. An event e is represented as an object (C, t) where t is the label $\mu(e)$ of e and C is its set $e^\bullet$ of post-conditions. A condition c is represented by an object (e, s) where s is the label $\mu(c)$ of c, and e is its (single) post-event $c^\bullet$. We observe the flow relation F and the labeling function μ are included in the encoding.

Consider a set of conditions C of U to be t-enabled provided there exists a configuration E such that $C \subseteq Cut(E)$ and $0 < \#C \le t^\bullet$, i.e., there is a configuration E such that $C \subseteq Cut(E)$ and all the conditions in C are in the postset of t. Furthermore, consider C to be maximally t-enabled provided there is no other set C' such that $C \subset C' \subseteq Cut(E)$ and C' is t-enabled. We will write $\mathsf{ME}_t(C)$ to denote that C is maximally t-enabled. We define $Xtnd(U)$ to be the set of events by which U can be extended and is formally defined as follows:

$$Xtnd(U) = \{(C, t) \mid \mathsf{ME}_t(C) \text{ and } (C, t) \notin U\}$$

Observe that the definition implies that there are no redundancies in the unfolding. In other words we will not have two different events both having the same label and the same postcondition.

The unfolding algorithm is shown in Figure 2. It maintains two variables, namely the current unfolding U (initialized to the final marking M_{fin}), and a set X of events by which the unfolding can be extended. The algorithm proceeds by considering the events in X in turn (this procedure is fair in the sense that each event added to X will eventually be considered). At each iteration an event in X is picked and moved to U. Furthermore, the possible extensions of the new unfolding are computed, using the function $Xtnd$, and added to X. Notice that the algorithm does not necessarily terminate.

The unfolding algorithm gives a symbolic representation of upward closed sets from which M_{fin} is coverable. More precisely (Theorem 1), the upward closure of the markings appearing in U, gives exactly the set of markings from which M_{fin} is coverable. Notice that each event in the unfolding corresponds to a step in the backward unrolling of the net. The efficiency we gain through applying unfoldings on upward closed sets, as compared to the standard symbolic algorithm based on the backward transition relation $\rightsquigarrow$, can be explained in a manner similar to the finite state case [McM95,ERV96]; namely the addition of a set of concurrent events to the unfolding corresponds to an exponential number of applications of the $\rightsquigarrow$ relation.

In the sequel we let U^i denote the value of the variable U after i iterations of the loop. The following lemmas (the proof of which can be found in the appendix) relate unfoldings with the backward transition relation $\rightsquigarrow$.

Input: net system $N = (S, T, F, M_{init}, M_{fin})$, where $M_{fin} = (s_1, \ldots, s_n)$.
var U: unfolding of N; X: set of events.
begin
    $U := (s_1, \emptyset), \ldots, (s_m, \emptyset)$
    $X := Xtnd(U)$
    while $(X \neq \emptyset)$ **do**
        Pick and delete $e = (C, t)$ from X
        Add (C, t) to U and also add $\forall s \in {}^{\bullet}t$ a new condition (s, e) to U
        $X := X \cup Xtnd(U)$
end

Fig. 2. Unfolding Algorithm

Lemma 2. *If $M_{fin} \overset{k}{\leadsto} M$ then there is an ℓ and a configuration E in U^ℓ such that $mark(E) \leq M$*

We now present the lemma in the other direction which shows that the marking associated with every configuration in an unfolding is backwards reachable.

Lemma 3. *For each ℓ and configuration E in U^ℓ, there is a marking M such that $M \leq mark(E)$ and $M_{fin} \overset{*}{\leadsto} M$.*

¿From Lemma 1, Lemma 2, and Lemma 3 we get the following theorem.

Theorem 1. *M_{fin} is coverable from a marking M if and only if there is an ℓ and a configuration E in U^ℓ such that $mark(E) \leq M$.*

Notice that as a special case we can take M in Theorem 1 to be equal to M_{init}.

5 Termination

In this section we show how to compute finite postfixes of unfoldings. We define special types of events which we call *cut-off points*. In Theorem 2 we show that cut-off points do not add any markings to the upward closed sets characterized by the unfolding. This means that, in the unfolding algorithm (Figure 2) we can safely discard all cut-off points, without ever adding them to the unfolding U. Furthermore, we use concepts from the theory of well quasi-orderings (Theorem 2) to show that, if all cut-off points are discarded, then the variable X in the unfolding algorithm eventually becomes empty implying termination of the algorithm. We start with some definitions and auxiliary lemmas.

We assume a net system N and an unfolding U of N. For an event, we use $e{\downarrow}$ to denote the configuration $\{e' \mid eF^*e'\}$. For configurations E_1 and E_2, we use $E_1 \prec E_2$ to denote that $|E_1| < |E_2|$ and $mark(E_1) \leq mark(E_2)$. For an event e, we say that e is a *cutoff point* in U if there is a configuration E in U such that $E \prec e{\downarrow}$.

We recall from the previous section that U^i denotes the value of the variable U in the unfolding algorithm, after i iterations of the loop. In order to prove the cutoff theorem we need the following lemma (the proof of which can be found in the appendix).

Lemma 4. *Consider configurations E_1, E_2, and E_2' in U^k where $E_1 \prec E_2$ and $E_2 \subseteq E_2'$. There is an ℓ and a configuration E_1' in U^ℓ such that $E_1' \prec E_2'$.*

Now we are ready to show in the following theorem that cutoff points can be discarded safely.

Theorem 2. *For each k and configuration E_2 in U^k, there is an ℓ and configuration E_1 in U^ℓ where $mark(E_1) \leq mark(E_2)$ and E_1 does not contain any cutoff points.*

Proof. We use induction on $|E_2|$. The base case is trivial. If E_2 does not contain any cutoff points, then the proof is trivial. Otherwise let e_2 be a cutoff point in E_2. Clearly, $e_2{\downarrow} \subseteq E_2$. Since e_2 is a cut-off point, we know that there is a configuration E in U^k such that $E \prec e_2{\downarrow}$. By Lemma 4 there is an ℓ and a configuration E_1 in U^ℓ such that $E_1 \prec E_2$, i.e., $|E_1| < |E_2|$ and $mark(E_1) \leq mark(E_2)$. The claim follows by induction hypothesis.

To prove termination of the unfolding algorithm, we use the fact that markings are well quasi-ordered (consequence of Dickson's lemma [Dic13]), i.e., for any infinite sequence $M_0, M_1, \ldots$ of markings, there are i and j with $i < j$ and $M_i \leq M_j$.

Theorem 3. *The unfolding algorithm terminates if all cut-off points are discarded.*

Proof. Suppose that the algorithm does not terminate. Since all nodes are finitely branching we have an infinite sequence $e_0, e_1, e_2, \ldots$, of events where $e_{i+1} F c_i F e_i$, for some condition c_i. Notice that $|e_j{\downarrow}| > |e_i{\downarrow}|$, whenever $j > i$. By Dickson's lemma, it follows that there are i and j with $i < j$ and $mark(e_i{\downarrow}) \leq mark(e_j{\downarrow})$. This implies that e_j is a cut-off point, which is a contradiction.

Remark Theorem 1, Theorem 2, and Theorem 3 give a complete terminating procedure for checking coverability in unbounded Petri nets: use the unfolding algorithm discarding all cutoff points. The final marking M_{fin} is coverable from the initial marking M_{init} iff a configuration E appears in the unfolding with $mark(E) \leq M_{init}$.

6 Experimental Results

In this section we report on some of the issues that we had to solve in implementing the unfolding algorithm. While our implementation borrows ideas from [McM95,ERV96], there are several issues that are peculiar to our backward reachability. To wit, they are:

- **Implementation of $Xtnd$:** The abstract algorithm (presented in Section 4) implies that $Xtnd$ is computed in every iteration. However, in the implementation a queue of possible sets of conditions that could be the postset of a

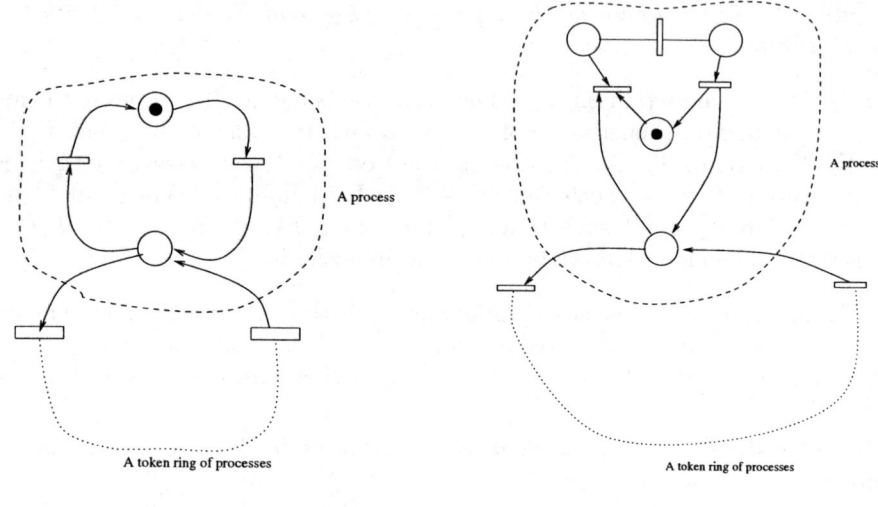

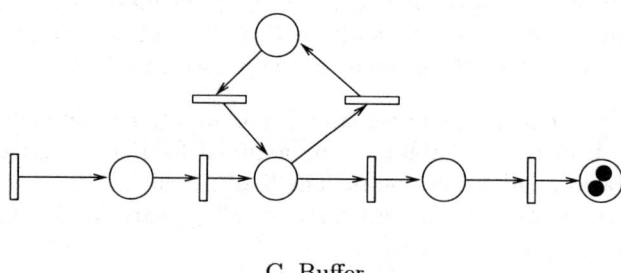

Fig. 3. Examples of nets considered

(potential) event are maintained. As new conditions are generated we check whether these new conditions can be added to already existing (partial) sets of post-conditions to form larger sets of postconditions. By doing so we reduce a seemingly combinatorial problem to a depth-first search on the unfolding.
- **Checking termination:** As a new event e is generated we calcluate $|e\downarrow|$ and $mark(e\downarrow)$. We compare this information against $mark(e'\downarrow)$ and $|mark(e'\downarrow)|$ for all events e' currently in the unfolding. While our definition of a cut-off event calls for comparing against all configurations in the unfolding, our implemention is sound, though not effecient (as otherwise, by Dickson's Lemma there would be sequence of events e_i such that $e_i\downarrow \prec e_{i+1}\downarrow$).

Given that the hypothesis of our paper is

for nets with a great deal of concurrency the storage required to build (reverse) occurence nets would be smaller than implementations that consider all interleavings

we compute (a) the maximum number of markings that need to be maintained for the traditional backward analysis [AJ98] and (b) the total number of nodes generated by the unfolding algorithm. Given that the storage requirements of a node is bounded by the storage required for a marking, comparing the number of markings from backwards analysis against the total number of nodes in an unfolding is appropriate.

We now report on the results of our experimentation. In Figure 3 we present two versions of token-rings and a buffer. A process in a token ring can be active when it has a token. We considered several experiments with varying numbers of tokens available in the ring and varying numbers of processes. For the buffer example we varied the number of tokens available. The result of our experimentation is reported in Figure 4, where we provide the time taken in seconds and the number of nodes/markings using unfoldings and backward analysis. As can be seen these results do support our hypothesis that when there is a lot of concurrency in a net then unfoldings would require lesser amount of storage than traditional backward analysis (which considers all possible interleavings).

7 Conclusions and Future Work

We have shown how to extend the technique of unfoldings in order to obtain an efficient implementation of a symbolic algorithm for verification of unbounded Petri nets. In contrast to earlier approaches, the algorithm operates over an infinite-state space, using constraints to characterize upward closed sets of markings. Since our algorithm relies on a small set of properties of Petri nets which are shared by other computation models, we believe that our approach can be lifted to a more general setting. In particular we aim to develop a theory of unfoldings for *well-structured systems* [AČJYK96,FS98] a framework which has been applied for verification of several types of infinite-state systems such as timed

Token Ring				
# Proc	# Tokens	Rev. Occ. Net		Backward Analysis	
		# nodes	Time in 10^{-2} secs	# nodes	Time in 10^{-2} secs
4	1	15	3	46	1
4	2	30	13	124	10
4	3	45	29	320	100
4	4	60	60	744	747
4	5	75	105	1573	4344
4	6	90	167	3055	21049
4	7	105	265	5672	84682
4	8	120	357	9976	295815
4	2	30	13	124	10
8	2	62	78	504	334
12	2	94	263	1096	3010
16	2	126	658	1912	14820
20	2	158	1379	2952	52892

A. Experimentation on Token Ring

Token Ring 2				
# Proc	# Tokens	Rev. Occ. Net		Backward Analysis	
		# nodes	Time in 10^{-2} secs	# nodes	Time in 10^{-2} secs
4	1	18	5	97	4
4	2	36	210	458	176
4	3	54	52	1973	4161
8	2	68	108	2112	8724
12	2	100	324	4896	90622
16	2	132	777	*	*

B. Experimentation on Token Ring, Version 2

Buffer				
# Tokens	# RON nodes	Time in 10^{-2} secs (RON)	# Bkwrd nodes	Time in 10^{-2} secs (Bkwrd)
5	50	28	215	39
10	100	177	1367	2591
15	150	549	4898	53507
20	200	1289	*	*

C. Experimentation with buffer

Note:* denotes non-termination after a reasonable amount of time.

Fig. 4. Result of experimentation

automata, broadcast protocols, lossy channels systems, relational automata, etc. This would allow us to extract common concepts, and provide a guideline for developing unfolding algorithms for these classes of systems. Another important direction of future research is the design of efficient data structures for implementation of the unfolding algorithm, and to carry out experiments to study the performance of the algorithm on more advanced examples. We hope to adapt, to our context, reasoning techniques for unfoldings, based on integer programming and constraints, that have been considered in the literature [MR97,Hel99].

Acknowledgements

We wish to thank Javier Esparza and Stefan Römer for patiently answering our questions about unfoldings and their implementations.

This work is supported in part by ARO under grant P-38682-MA, by STINT– The Swedish Foundation for International Cooperation in Research and Higher Education, and by TFR– The Swedish Research Council for Engineering Sciences.

References

[AČJYK96] Parosh Aziz Abdulla, Karlis Čerāns, Bengt Jonsson, and Tsay Yih-Kuen. General decidability theorems for infinite-state systems. In *Proc.* 11th *IEEE Int. Symp. on Logic in Computer Science*, pages 313–321, 1996.

[AJ98] Parosh Aziz Abdulla and Bengt Jonsson. Ensuring completeness of symbolic verification methods for infinite-state systems, 1998. To appear in the journal of Theoretical Computer Science.

[AJKP98] Parosh Aziz Abdulla, Bengt Jonsson, Mats Kindahl, and Doron Peled. A general approach to partial order reductions in symbolic verification. In *Proc.* 10th *Int. Conf. on Computer Aided Verification*, volume 1427 of *Lecture Notes in Computer Science*, pages 379–390, 1998.

[AKP97] Parosh Aziz Abdulla, Mats Kindahl, and Doron Peled. An improved search strategy for Lossy Channel Systems. In Tadanori Mizuno, Nori Shiratori, Teruo Hegashino, and Atsushi Togashi, editors, *FORTE X / PSTV XVII '97*, pages 251–264. Chapman and Hall, 1997.

[Dic13] L. E. Dickson. Finiteness of the odd perfect and primitive abundant numbers with n distinct prime factors. *Amer. J. Math.*, 35:413–422, 1913.

[ER99] J. Esparza and S. Römer. An unfolding algorithm for synchronous products of transition systems. In *Proc. CONCUR '99*, 9th *Int. Conf. on Concurrency Theory*, volume 1664 of *Lecture Notes in Computer Science*, pages 2–20. Springer Verlag, 1999.

[ERV96] J. Esparza, S. Römer, and W. Vogler. An improvement of McMillan's unfolding algorithm. In *Proc. TACAS '96*, 2th *Int. Conf. on Tools and Algorithms for the Construction and Analysis of Systems*, volume 1055 of *Lecture Notes in Computer Science*, pages 87–106. Springer Verlag, 1996.

[FS98] A. Finkel and Ph. Schnoebelen. Well-structured transition systems everywhere. Technical Report LSV-98-4, Ecole Normale Supérieure de Cachan, April 1998.

[GW93]   P. Godefroid and P. Wolper. Using partial orders for the efficient verification of deadlock freedom and safety properties. *Formal Methods in System Design*, 2(2):149–164, 1993.

[Hel99]   K. Heljanko. Using logic programs with stable model semantics to solve deadlock and reachability problems for 1-safe Petri nets. *Fundamenta Informaticae*, 37:247–268, 1999.

[LB99]   R. Langerak and E. Brinksma. A complete finite prefix for process algebra. In *Proc. 11th Int. Conf. on Computer Aided Verification*, volume 1633 of *Lecture Notes in Computer Science*, pages 184–195. Springer Verlag, 1999.

[McM95]   K.L. McMillan. A technique of a state space search based on unfolding. *Formal Methods in System Design*, 6(1):45–65, 1995.

[MR97]   S. Melzer and S. Römer. Deadlock checking using net unfoldings. In *Proc. 9th Int. Conf. on Computer Aided Verification*, 1997.

[Pel93]   D. Peled. All from one, one for all, on model-checking using representatives. In *Proc. 5th Int. Conf. on Computer Aided Verification*, volume 697 of *Lecture Notes in Computer Science*, pages 409–423. Springer-Verlag, 1993.

[Val90]   A. Valmari. Stubborn sets for reduced state space generation. In *Advances in Petri Nets*, volume 483 of *Lecture Notes in Computer Science*, pages 491–515. Springer-Verlag, 1990.

[VW86]   M. Y. Vardi and P. Wolper. An automata-theoretic approach to automatic program verification. In *Proc. 1st IEEE Int. Symp. on Logic in Computer Science*, pages 332–344, June 1986.

A   Proof of Lemmas

Proof of Lemma 2 By induction on k.

Base case: Follows from the first step of the algorithm (initializing the value of U).

Induction case: Suppose that $M_{fin} \stackrel{k}{\leadsto} M' \leadsto_t M$. By the induction hypothesis there is an ℓ' and a configuration E' in $U^{\ell'}$ such that $mark(E') \leq M'$. Let C_1 be a maximal subset of $Cut(E')$ such that $\#C_1 \leq t^\bullet$.

There are two cases.

(1) if C_1 is empty. We define $E = E'$. We show that $mark(E)(s) \leq M(s)$ for each place s. We have two subcases.

(1a) if $s \notin t^\bullet$, then $mark(E)(s) = mark(E')(s) \leq mark(E')(s) + {}^\bullet t(s) \leq M'(s) + {}^\bullet t(s) = M(s)$.

(1b) if $s \in t^\bullet$ then we know by maximality of C_1 that $mark(E')(s) = 0$, and hence $mark(E)(s) = mark(E')(s) \leq M(s)$.

(2) if C_1 is not empty. Notice that $\mathsf{ME}_t(C_1)$ holds. Given that our algorithm is fair in selecting transitions that are backward firable, an event $e = (C_1, t)$ will be chosen and added at some point ℓ. We define $E = E' \cup \{e\}$. Clearly, E is a configuration in U^ℓ. Observe that $mark(E) = (mark(E') \ominus t^\bullet) + {}^\bullet t$. This means that $mark(E) = (mark(E') \ominus t^\bullet) + {}^\bullet t \leq (M'(s) \ominus t^\bullet) + {}^\bullet t = M$.   □

Proof of Lemma 3 By induction on ℓ.

Base case: Follows from the first step of the algorithm (initializing the value of U).

Induction case: Suppose that in step $\ell + 1$ we add an event $e = (C, t)$ (together with its preset) to U^ℓ. Take any configuration E in $U^{\ell+1}$. If $e \notin E$ then we know that E is also a configuration in U^ℓ, implying the result by induction hypothesis. Hence, we can assume that $E = E' \cup \{e\}$ where E' is a configuration in U^ℓ. By the induction hypothesis we know that there is a marking M' such that $M' \leq mark(E')$ and $M_{fin} \stackrel{*}{\rightsquigarrow} M'$. We define $M = (M' \ominus t^\bullet) + {}^\bullet t$. Clearly $M' \rightsquigarrow M$ and hence $M_{fin} \stackrel{*}{\rightsquigarrow} M$. Observe that $mark(E) = (mark(E') \ominus t^\bullet) + {}^\bullet t$. This means that $mark(E) = (mark(E') \ominus t^\bullet) + {}^\bullet t \geq (M'(s) \ominus t^\bullet) + {}^\bullet t = M$. □

Proof of Lemma 4 We show the claim for a configuration $E_2' = E_2 \cup \{e_2\}$ where $e_2 \notin E_2$. The result follows using induction on $|E_2'| - |E_2|$. Let e_2 be of the form (C_2, t). We know that $mark(E_2') = (mark(E_2) \ominus t^\bullet) + {}^\bullet t$. We define C_1 to be a maximal subset of $Cut(E_1)$ such that $\#C_1 \leq t^\bullet$.

There are two cases

1. If C_1 is empty we define $E_1' = E_1$. We have $|E_1'| = |E_1| < |E_2| < |E_2'|$. We show that $mark(E_1')(s) \leq mark(E_2')(s)$ for each place s. There are two subcases.

1a. if $s \notin t^\bullet$. We have $mark(E_2')(s) = mark(E_2)(s) + {}^\bullet t(s) \geq mark(E_1)(s) + {}^\bullet t(s) \geq mark(E_1)(s) = mark(E_1')(s)$.

1b. if $s \in t^\bullet$. By maximality of C_1 we know that $mark(E_1)(s) = 0$. This means that $mark(E_2')(s) = (mark(E_2)(s) \ominus {}^\bullet t(s)) + {}^\bullet t(s) \geq {}^\bullet t(s) \geq mark(E_1)(s) = mark(E_1')(s)$.

2. If C_1 is not empty then by fairness of the algorithm in selecting transitions that are backward firable, an event $e_1 = (C_1, t)$ will be chosen and added at some point ℓ. We define $E_1' = E_1 \cup \{e_1\}$. It is clear that E_1' is a configuration in U^ℓ. We have $|E_1'| = |E_1| + 1 < |E_2| + 1 \leq |E_2'|$. We know that $mark(E_1') = (mark(E_1) \ominus t^\bullet) + {}^\bullet t$. this means that $mark(E_2') = (mark(E_2) \ominus {}^\bullet t) + {}^\bullet t \geq (mark(E_1) \ominus {}^\bullet t) + {}^\bullet t = mark(E_1')(s)$. □

Verification Diagrams Revisited: Disjunctive Invariants for Easy Verification[*]

John Rushby

Computer Science Laboratory
SRI International
333 Ravenswood Avenue
Menlo Park, CA 94025, USA
rushby@csl.sri.com

Abstract. I describe a systematic method for deductive verification of safety properties of concurrent programs. The method has much in common with the "verification diagrams" of Manna and Pnueli [17], but derives from different intuitions. It is based on the idea of strengthening a putative safety property into a disjunction of "configurations" that can easily be proved to be inductive. Transitions among the configurations have a natural diagrammatic representation that conveys insight into the operation of the program. The method lends itself to mechanization and is illustrated using a simplified version of an example that had defeated previous attempts at deductive verification.

1 Introduction

In 1997, Shmuel Katz, Patrick Lincoln and I presented an algorithm for Group Membership together with a detailed, but informal proof of its correctness [14]. Shortly thereafter, our colleague Shankar and, independently, Sadie Creese and Bill Roscoe of Oxford University, noted that the algorithm is flawed when the number of nonfaulty processors is three. Model checking a downscaled instance can be effective in finding bugs (that is how Creese and Roscoe found the problem in our algorithm [8]), but true assurance for a potentially infinite-state n-process algorithm such as this seems to require (mechanically checked) deductive methods—either direct proof or justification of an abstraction that can be verified by algorithmic means. Over the next year or so, Katz, Lincoln and I each made several attempts to formalize and mechanically verify a corrected version of the algorithm using the PVS verification system [19]. On each occasion, we were defeated by the number and complexity of the auxiliary invariants needed, and by the "case explosion" that bedevils deductive approaches to formal verification.

Eventually, I stumbled upon the method presented in this paper and completed the verification in April 1999 [23]. This new method made the verification not merely possible, but easy, and it provides a visual representation that conveys considerable insight into the operation of the algorithm. Holger Pfeifer of the University of Ulm was subsequently able to use the method to verify a related but much more complicated group

---

[*] This research was supported by DARPA through USAF Rome Laboratory Contract F30602-96-C-0204 and USAF Electronic Systems Center Contract F19628-96-C-0006, and by the National Science Foundation contract CCR-9509931.

membership algorithm [21] used in the Time Triggered Architecture for critical real-time control [15]

I later discovered that my method has much in common with the "verification diagrams" introduced by Manna and Pnueli [17], and subsequently generalized by Manna and several colleagues [5,7,10,16]. However, the intuition that led to my method is rather different than that for verification diagrams, as is the way I approach its mechanization. I hope that by revisiting these methods from a slightly different perspective, I will help others to see their value and to investigate their application to new problems.

I describe my method in the next section and present an example of its application in the one after that. The final section compares the method with verification diagrams and with other techniques and provides conclusions and suggestions for further work.

2 The Method

Concurrent systems are modeled as nondeterministic automata over possibly infinite sets of states. Given set of states S, initiality predicate I on S, and transition relation T on S, a predicate P on S is *inductive* for $S = (S, I, T)$ if

$$I(s) \supset P(s)^1 \tag{1}$$

and

$$P(s) \land T(s,t) \supset P(t). \tag{2}$$

The *reachable states* are those characterized by the smallest (ordered by implication) inductive predicate R on S. A predicate G is an *invariant* or *safety property* if it is larger than R (i.e., includes all reachable states). The focus here is on safety (as opposed to liveness) properties, so we do not need to be concerned with the acceptance criterion on the automaton S.

The deductive method for verifying safety properties attempts to establish that a predicate G is invariant by showing that it is inductive—i.e., we attempt to prove the verification conditions (1) and (2) with G substituted for P. The problem, of course, is that many safety properties are not inductive, and must be strengthened (i.e., replaced by a smaller property) to make them so. Typically, this is done by conjoining additional predicates in an incremental fashion, so that G is replaced by

$$G_\land^i = G \land G_1 \land \cdots \land G_i \tag{3}$$

until an inductive $G_\land^m$ is found. This process can be made systematic, but is always tedious. In one well-known example, 57 such strengthenings were required to verify a communications protocol [12]; each G_{i+1} was discovered by inspecting a failed proof for inductiveness of $G_\land^i$, and the process consumed several weeks.

Some improvements can be made in this process: static analysis [4] and automated calculations of (approximations to) fixpoints of weakest preconditions or strongest

---

[1] Formulas are implicitly universally quantified in their free variables; the horseshoe symbol $\supset$ denotes logical implication.

postconditions [5] can discover many useful invariants that can be used to seed the process as $G_1, \ldots, G_i$. Nonetheless, the transformation of a desired safety property into a provably inductive invariant remains the most difficult and costly element in deductive verification, and systematic methods are sorely needed.

The method proposed here is based on strengthening a desired safety property with a *disjunction* of additional predicates, rather than the *conjunction* appearing in (3). That is, we construct

$$G_\vee^m = G \wedge (G_1 \vee \cdots \vee G_m)$$

instead of $G_\wedge^m$. Obviously, this can be rewritten as follows

$$G_\vee^m = (G \wedge G_1) \vee \cdots \vee (G \wedge G_m).$$

Rather than form each disjunct as a conjunction $(G \wedge G_i)$, it is generally preferable to use

$$G_\vee^m = G_1' \vee \cdots \vee G_m' \qquad (4)$$

and then prove $G_i' \supset G$ for each G_i'. The subexpressions G_i' are referred to as *configurations*, and the indices i as *configuration indices*.

Observe that in the construction of $G_\wedge^m$, each G_i must be an invariant (the very property we are trying to establish), and that the inadequacy of $G_\wedge^i$ only becomes apparent through failure of the attempted proof of its inductiveness—and proof of the putative inductiveness of $G_\wedge^{i+1}$ must then start over.[2] In contrast, the configurations used in construction of $G_\vee^m$ need not themselves be invariants, and can be discovered in a rather systematic manner. To see this, first suppose that $G_\vee^m$ is inductive, and consider the proof obligations needed to establish this fact. Instantiating (2) with $G_\vee^m$ of (4) and case-splitting across the configurations, we will need to prove a verification condition of the following form for each configuration index i:

$$G_i'(s) \wedge T(s,t) \supset G_1'(t) \vee \cdots \vee G_m'(t).$$

We can further case-split on the right of the implication by introducing predicates $C_{i,j}(s)$ called *transition conditions* such that, for each configuration index i

$$\forall s \in S : \bigvee_j C_{i,j}(s) \qquad (5)$$

(here j ranges over the indices of the transition conditions for configuration G_i') and

$$G_i'(s) \wedge T(s,t) \wedge C_{i,j}(s) \supset G_j'(t) \qquad (6)$$

for each transition condition $C_{i,j}$ of each configuration G_i'. Note that some of the $C_{i,j}$ may be identically *false* (so that the proof obligation (6) is vacuously true for this case) and that it is not necessary that the $C_{i,j}$ for different j be disjoint.

This construction can be represented in a diagrammatic form called a *configuration diagram* such as that shown several pages ahead in Figure 1. Here, each vertex represents

---

[2] PVS attempts to lessen the amount of rework that must be performed in this situation by allowing conjectures to be modified during the course of a proof; such proofs are marked provisional until a final "clean" verification is completed.

a configuration and is labeled with the name of the corresponding formula G'_i and each arc represents a non-*false* transition condition and is labeled with a phrase that suggests the corresponding predicate. To verify the diagram, we need to show that the initiality predicate implies some disjunction of configurations

$$I(s) \supset G'_1(s) \vee \cdots \vee G'_m(s) \tag{7}$$

(typically there is just a single *starting configuration*), that each configuration implies the desired safety property

$$G'_1(s) \vee \cdots \vee G'_m(s) \supset G(s), \tag{8}$$

that the disjunction of the transition conditions leaving each configuration is *true* (i.e., (5)), and that the transition relation indeed relates the configurations in the manner shown in the diagram (i.e., the verification conditions (6)). Notice that this is just a new way of organizing a traditional deductive invariance proof (i.e., the proof obligations (5)–(8) imply (1) and (2) with G substituted for P). And although a configuration diagram has some of the character of an abstraction, its verification involves only the original model, and no new verification principles are involved.

The previous discussion assumed we already had a configuration diagram; in practice, the diagram is constructed incrementally in the course of the proof. To construct a configuration diagram, we start by inventing a starting configuration and checking that it is implied by the initiality predicate and implies the safety property (i.e., proof obligations (7) and (8)). Then, by contemplation of the algorithm (the guard predicates and other case-splits in the specification are good guides here), we invent some transition conditions for the starting configuration and check that their disjunction is true (i.e., proof obligation (5)). For each transition condition, we symbolically simulate a step of the algorithm from the starting configuration, under that condition. The result of symbolic simulation becomes a new configuration (and implicitly discharges proof obligation (6) for that case)—unless we recognize it as a variant of an existing configuration, in which case we must explicitly discharge proof obligation (6) by proving that the result of symbolic simulation implies the existing configuration concerned (sometimes it may be necessary to generalize an existing configuration, in which case we will need to revisit previously-proved proof obligations involving this configuration to ensure that they are preserved by the generalization). We also check that each new or generalized configuration implies the safety property (i.e., proof obligation (8)). This process is repeated for each transition condition and each new configuration until the diagram is closed. The creative steps are the selection of transition conditions, and recognition of new configurations as variants of existing ones. Neither of these is hard, given an informal understanding of the algorithm being verified, and the resulting diagram not only verifies the desired safety property (once all its proof obligations are discharged), but it also serves to explain the operation of the algorithm in a very effective way. Bugs in the algorithm, or unfortunate choices of configurations or of transition conditions, will be manifested as difficulty in closing the diagram (typically, the result of a symbolic simulation step will not imply the expected configuration). As with most deductive methods, it can be tricky to distinguish between these causes of failure.

3 An Example: Group Membership

A simplified version of the group membership algorithm mentioned earlier [14] will serve as an example. There are n processors numbered $0, 1, \ldots, n-1$ connected to a broadcast bus; a distributed clock synchronization algorithm (not discussed here) provides a global clock that ticks off "slots" $0, 1, 2, \ldots$ In slot i it is the turn of processor $i \bmod n$ to broadcast. The broadcast contains a message, not considered here, and the ack bit of the broadcasting processor, which is described below. Processors may be faulty or nonfaulty; those that are faulty may be *send-faulty*, *receive-faulty*, or both. A processor that is send-faulty will fail to send its broadcast message in its first slot after it becomes faulty; thereafter it may or may not broadcast in its slots. A processor that is receive-faulty will fail to receive the first broadcast from a nonfaulty processor after it becomes faulty; thereafter it may or may not receive broadcasts. Notice that faults affect only communications: a faulty processor still executes the algorithm correctly; additional elements in the full protocol suite ensure that other kinds of faults are manifested as "fail silence," which appears to the algorithm described here as a combined send- and receive-fault in the processor concerned.

Each processor maintains a *membership set* which contains all and only the processors that it believes to be nonfaulty. Processors broadcast in their slots only if they are in their own membership sets. The goal of the algorithm is to maintain accurate membership sets: all nonfaulty processors should have the same membership sets (this is the *agreement* property) and those membership sets should contain all the nonfaulty processors and at most one faulty one (this is the *validity* property; it is necessary to allow one faulty processor in the membership because it takes time to diagnose a fault). These safety properties must be ensured subject to the *fault arrival hypothesis* that faults do not arrive closer than n slots apart. Initially all processors are nonfaulty, their membership sets contain all processors, and their ack bits are *true*.

The algorithm is a synchronous one: in each slot one processor broadcasts and all the other processors expect to receive its message, provided the broadcaster is in their membership sets. Receivers set their ack bits to *true* in each slot iff they receive an expected message. In addition, they remove the broadcaster from their membership sets if they fail to receive an expected message (on the interim assumption that the broadcaster must have been send-faulty). A receiver that subsequently receives a message carrying ack *false* when its own ack is also *false* knows that it made the correct decision in this case (since the current broadcaster also missed the previous expected message), but one that receives ack *true* realizes that it must have been receive-faulty (since the current broadcaster did receive the message) and removes itself from its own membership; a receiver that fails to receive an expected message when its ack bit is *false* also removes itself from its own membership (because it has missed two expected messages in a row, which is consistent with the fault arrival hypothesis only if that processor is itself receive-faulty); a receiver that receives a message with ack *false* when its own ack bit is *true* removes the broadcaster from its membership (since the broadcaster must have been receive-faulty on the previous broadcast). Processors that remove themselves from their own membership remain silent when it is their turn to broadcast—thereby communicating their self-diagnosed receive-faultiness to the other processors.

Formally, we let mem(p) and ack(p) denote the membership set and ack bit of processor p. Note that processor p has access to its own mem and ack, and can also read the value of ack(b), where $b = i \mod n$ and i is the current slot number, because this is sent in the message broadcast in that slot.

Initiality predicate: mem(p) = $\{0, 1, \ldots, n-1\}$, ack(p) = $true$.[3]

The algorithm is specified by two lists of guarded commands: one for the broadcaster and one for the receivers. Primes denote the updated values of the state variables. The current slot is i and the current broadcaster is b, where $b = i \mod n$.

Broadcaster: Processor b executes the appropriate guarded command from the following list.

(a) $b \in$ mem(b) $\quad\quad\quad\quad\quad\to$ mem(b)$'$ = mem(b), $\quad\quad$ ack(b)$'$ = $true$
otherwise $\quad\quad\quad\quad\quad\to$ no change.

Receiver: Each processor $p \neq b$ executes the appropriate guarded command from the following list:

The guards (b)–(g) apply when $b \in$ mem(p) $\wedge$ $p \in$ mem(p).

(b) ack(p) $\wedge$ no msg rcvd $\to$ mem(p)$'$ = mem(p) $- \{b\}$, ack(p)$'$ = $false$
(c) ack(p) $\wedge$ ack(b) $\quad\quad\to$ mem(p)$'$ = mem(p), $\quad\quad\quad\,$ ack(p)$'$ = $true$[4]
(d) ack(p) $\wedge$ ¬ack(b) $\quad\,\to$ mem(p)$'$ = mem(p) $- \{b\}$, ack(p)$'$ = $true$
(e) ¬ack(p) $\wedge$ no msg rcvd $\to$ mem(p)$'$ = mem(p) $- \{p\}$
(f) ¬ack(p) $\wedge$ ¬ack(b) $\quad\to$ mem(p)$'$ = mem(p), $\quad\quad\quad\,$ ack(p)$'$ = $true$
(g) ¬ack(p) $\wedge$ ack(b) $\quad\,\to$ mem(p)$'$ = mem(p) $- \{p\}$
otherwise $\quad\quad\quad\quad\quad\quad\to$ no change.

The environment can perform only a single action: it can cause a new fault to arrive—provided no other fault has arrived "recently." Characterization of "recently" is considered below. We let the_mem denote the current set of nonfaulty processors, so that the following specifies arrival of a fault in a previously nonfaulty processor x.

Fault Arrival: $\exists x \in$ the_mem : the_mem$'$ = the_mem $- \{x\}$

The desired safety properties are specified as follows.

Agreement: $p \in$ the_mem $\wedge$ $q \in$ the_mem $\supset$ mem(p) = mem(q)

Validity: $p \in$ the_mem $\supset$ mem(p) = the_mem $\vee$ $\exists x :$ mem(p) = the_mem $\cup \{x\}$

The first says that all nonfaulty processors p and q have the same membership sets; the second says that the membership set of a nonfaulty processor p contains all nonfaulty processors, and possibly one faulty one.

The starting configuration is the following: all nonfaulty processors have their ack bits $true$ and their membership sets contain just the nonfaulty processors.

---
[3] I use the redundant $= true$ because some find that form easier to read.
[4] This case could be absorbed into the "otherwise" clause with no change to the algorithm; however, the structure of the algorithm seems clearer written this way.

Stable: $p \in \text{the\_mem} \supset \text{mem}(p) = \text{the\_mem} \land \text{ack}(p) = \textit{true}$

It is natural to consider two transition conditions from this configuration: one where a new fault arrives, and one where it does not. In the latter case, the broadcaster will leave its state unchanged (no matter whether its executes command (a) or its "otherwise" case), and the receivers will execute either their command (c) or their "otherwise" case, and leave their states unchanged. The overall effect is to remain in the *stable* configuration. In the case that a new fault arrives, the same transitions as above will be executed but some previously nonfaulty processor x will become faulty, leading to the following configuration.

Latent(x): $x \notin \text{the\_mem}$
$\land\, p \in \text{the\_mem} \cup \{x\} \supset \text{mem}(p) = \text{the\_mem} \cup \{x\} \land \text{ack}(p) = \textit{true}$

There are two transition conditions from *latent(x)*: one where x is the broadcaster in the next slot, and one where it is a receiver.

In the former case, x will execute its command (a) while all nonfaulty receivers will note the absence of an expected message and execute their commands (b), leading to the following configuration.

Excluded$_1$(x): $x \notin \text{the\_mem} \land \text{mem}(x) = \text{the\_mem} \cup \{x\} \land \text{ack}(x) = \textit{true}$
$\land\, p \in \text{the\_mem} \supset \text{mem}(p) = \text{the\_mem} \land \text{ack}(p) = \textit{false}$

In the latter case, a nonfaulty broadcaster will transmit[5] and its message will be received by all nonfaulty receivers, but missed by x, leading to the following configuration.

Missed_rcv(x): $x \notin \text{the\_mem} \land \text{mem}(x) = \text{the\_mem} \cup \{x\} - \{b\} \land \text{ack}(x) = \textit{false}$
$\land\, p \in \text{the\_mem} \supset \text{mem}(p) = \text{the\_mem} \cup \{x\} \land \text{ack}(p) = \textit{true}$

There are four transition conditions from *missed_rcv(x)*: one where the next broadcaster is x and it fails to broadcast; one where x does broadcast; one where the next broadcaster is already faulty; and an "otherwise" case. The first of these is similar to the transition from *latent(x)* to *excluded$_1$(x)* and leads to the following configuration.

Excluded$_2$(x): $x \notin \text{the\_mem} \land \text{mem}(x) = \text{the\_mem} \cup \{x\} - \{b\} \land \text{ack}(x) = \textit{true}$
$\land\, p \in \text{the\_mem} \supset \text{mem}(p) = \text{the\_mem} \land \text{ack}(p) = \textit{false}$

We recognize that *excluded$_1$(x)* and *excluded$_2$(x)* should each be generalized to yield the following common configuration.

Excluded(x): $p \in \text{the\_mem} \supset \text{mem}(p) = \text{the\_mem} \land \text{ack}(p) = \textit{false}$

In the case where x does broadcast, it will do so with ack *false*, causing nonfaulty processors to execute their commands (d) and leading directly to the *stable* configuration.

---

[5] Treatment of the case that the next broadcaster is an already-faulty one depends on how fault "arrivals" are axiomatized: in one treatment, a fault is not considered to arrive until it can be manifested (thereby excluding this case); the other treatment will produce a self-loop on *latent(x)* in this case. These details are a standard complication in verification of fault-tolerant algorithms and are not significant here.

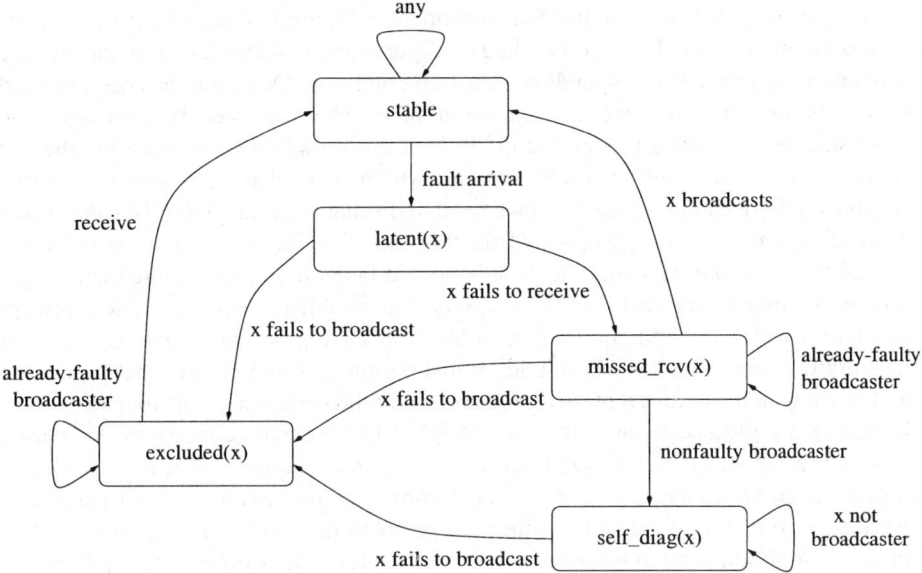

Fig. 1. Configuration Diagram for the Group Membership Example

The case where the next broadcaster is already faulty causes all nonfaulty processors and processor x to leave their states unchanged (since that broadcaster will not be in their membership sets), thereby producing a loop on *missed_rcv*(x). The remaining case (a broadcast by a nonfaulty processor, executing its command (a)) will cause nonfaulty receivers to execute their commands (c), while x will either miss the broadcast (executing its command (e)), or will discover the *true* ack bit on the received message and recognize its previous error (executing its command (g)); in either case, x will exclude itself from its own membership, leading to the following configuration.

Self_diag(x): $x \notin \text{the\_mem} \land x \notin \text{mem}(x)$
$\land\, p \in \text{the\_mem} \supset \text{mem}(p) = \text{the\_mem} \cup \{x\} \land \text{ack}(p) = true$

The transition conditions from this new configuration are those where x is the broadcaster, and those where it is not. In the former case, x will fail to broadcast (since it is not in its own membership), causing nonfaulty processors to execute their commands (b) and leading to the configuration *excluded*(x). The other case will cause them to execute their commands (c), or their "otherwise" cases, producing a self-loop on the configuration *self_diag*(x).

The only transitions that remain to be considered are those from configuration *excluded*(x). The transition conditions here are the case where the next broadcaster is already faulty, and that where it is not. The former produces a self-loop on this configuration, while the latter causes all nonfaulty receivers to execute their commands (f) while the broadcaster executes its command (a), leading to a transition to configuration *stable*.

It is easy to see that the initiality predicate implies the *stable* configuration and that all configurations imply the desired safety properties, and so we have now completed construction and verification of the diagram shown in Figure 1. The labels in the vertices of this diagram indicate the corresponding configuration, while the labels on the arcs are intended to suggest the corresponding transition condition. One detail has been glossed over in this construction, however: what about the cases where a new fault arrives while we are still dealing with a previous fault? In fact, this possibility is excluded in the full axiomatization of the fault arrival hypothesis, which states that faults may only arrive when the configuration is *stable* (we then need to discharge trivial proof obligations that all the other configurations are disjoint from this one). We connect this axiomatization of the fault arrival hypothesis with the "real" one that faults must arrive more than n slots apart by proving a bounded liveness property that establishes that the system always returns to a *stable* configuration within n slots of leaving it. This proof requires that configurations are embellished with additional parameters and clauses that remember the slots on which certain events occurred and count the numbers of self-loop iterations. The details are glossed because they are peripheral to the main concern of this paper; they are present in the mechanized verification of this example using PVS, which is available at http://www.csl.sri.com/~rushby/cav00.html and in a paper that describes verification of the full membership protocol [23]. (The full algorithm differs from the simplified version given here in that all faulty processors eventually diagnose their faults and exclude themselves from their own membership; its proof is about four times as long as that presented here).[6]

4 Discussion, Comparison, and Conclusion

The flawed verification of the full membership algorithm in [14] strengthens the desired safety properties, *agreement* and *validity*, with six additional invariants in an attempt to obtain a conjunction that is inductive. Five of these additional invariants are quite complicated, such as the following.

> "If a receive fault occurred to processor p less than n steps ago, then either p is not the broadcaster or ack(p) is *false* while all nonfaulty q have ack(q) = *true*, or p is not in its own membership set."

The informal proof of inductiveness of the conjoined invariants is long and arduous, and it must be flawed because the algorithm has a bug in the $n = 3$ case. This proof resisted several determined attempts to correct and formalize it in PVS. In contrast, the approach presented here led to a straightforward mechanized verification of a corrected version of the algorithm.[7] Furthermore, as I hope the example has demonstrated, this approach is naturally incremental, develops understanding of the target algorithm, and yields a diagram that helps convey that understanding to others. In fact, the diagram (or at least its outline) can usually be constructed quite easily using informal reasoning, and then serves as a guide for the mechanized proof.

---

[6] The algorithm presented here is fairly obvious; there is a similarly obvious solution to the full problem (with self-diagnosis) that uses two ack bits per message; this clarifies the contribution of [14], which is to achieve full self-diagnosis with only one ack bit per message.

[7] The verification was completed on a Toshiba Libretto palmtop computer of decidedly modest performance (75 MHz Pentium with 32 MB of memory).

This approach is strongly related to the verification diagrams and their associated methods introduced by Manna and Pnueli [17]. These were subsequently extended and generalized by Manna with Bjørner, Browne, de Alfaro, Sipma, and Uribe [5,7,10,16]. However, these later methods mostly concern fairness and liveness properties, or extensions for deductive model checking and hybrid systems, and so I prefer to compare my approach with the original verification diagrams. These comprise a set of vertices labeled with formulas and a set of arcs labeled with transitions that correspond to the configurations and transition conditions, respectively, of my method. However, there are small differences between the corresponding notions. First, it appears that verification diagrams have a finite number of vertices, whereas configurations can be finite or infinite in number. The example presented in the previous section is a parameterized system with an unbounded parameter n, and most of the configurations are parameterized by an individual x selected from the set $\{0, 1, \ldots, n\}$, yielding an arbitrarily large number of configurations; Skolemization (selection of an arbitrary representative) reduces the number of proof obligations to a finite number. Second, the arcs in verification diagrams are associated with transitions, whereas those in my approach are associated with predicates. It is quite possible that this difference is a natural manifestation of the different examples we have undertaken: those performed with verification diagrams have been asynchronous systems (where each system transition corresponds to a transition by *some* component), whereas I have been concerned with synchronous systems (where each system transition corresponds to simultaneous transitions by *all* components). Thus, in asynchronous systems the transitions suggest a natural analysis by cases, whereas in synchronous systems (especially those, as here, without explicit control) the case analysis must be consciously imposed by selection of suitable transition conditions.

Mechanized support for verification diagrams is provided in STeP [18]: the user proposes a diagram and the system generates the necessary verification conditions. PVS provides no special support for my approach, but its standard mechanisms are adequate because the approach ultimately yields a conventional inductive invariance proof that is checked by PVS in the usual way. As illustrated in the example, the configuration diagram can be constructed incrementally: starting from an existing configuration, the user proposes a transition condition and then symbolically simulates a step of the algorithm (mechanized in PVS by rewriting and simplification); the result either suggests a new configuration or corresponds to (possibly a generalization of) an existing one. Enhancements to PVS that would better support this activity are primarily improvements in symbolic simulation (e.g., faster rewriting and better simplification).

The key to any inductive invariance proof is to find a partitioning of the state space and a way to organize the case analysis so that the overall proof effort is manageable. The method of disjunctive invariants is a systematic way to do this that seems effective for some problem domains. Other recent methods provide comparably systematic constructions for verifications based on simulation arguments: the *aggregation method* of Park and Dill [20] and the *completion functions* of Hosabettu, Gopalakrishnan and Srivas [13] greatly simplify construction of the abstraction functions used in verifying cache protocols and processor pipelines, respectively.

Other methods with some similarity to the approach proposed here are those based on abstractions: typically the idea is to construct an abstraction of the original system that preserves the properties of interest and that has some special form (e.g., finite state) that allows very efficient analysis (e.g., model checking). Methods based on *predicate abstraction* [24] seem very promising [1,3,9,25]. A configuration diagram can be considered an abstraction of the original state machine and it is plausible that it could be generated automatically by predicate abstraction on the predicates that characterize its configurations and transition conditions. However, it is difficult to see how the user could obtain sufficient insight to propose these predicates without constructing most of the configuration diagram beforehand, and it is also questionable whether fully automated theorem proving can construct sufficiently precise abstractions of these fairly difficult examples using current technology.

Such an abstracted system would still have n processes and further reduction would be needed to obtain a finite-state system that could be model checked. Creese and Roscoe [8] do exactly this for the algorithm of [14] using a technique based on a suitable notion of data independence [22]. They use a clever generalization to make the processes of algorithm independent of how they are numbered and are thereby able to establish the abstracted n-process case by an induction whose cases can be discharged by model checking with FDR. This is an attractive approach with much promise, but formal and mechanized justification for the abstraction of the original algorithm still seems quite difficult (Creese and Roscoe provide a rigorous but informal argument).[8]

In summary, the approach presented here is one of a growing number of methods for verifying properties of certain classes of algorithms in a systematic manner. Circumstances in which this approach seems most effective are those where the algorithm concerned naturally progresses through different phases: these give rise to distinct disjuncts G'_i in a disjunctive invariant $G_\vee^m$ but are correspondingly hard to unify within a conjunctive invariant $G_\wedge^m$. Besides those examples already mentioned, the approach has been used successfully by Holger Pfeifer to verify another group membership algorithm [21]: the very tricky and industrially significant algorithm used in the Time Triggered Architecture for safety-critical distributed real-time control [15].

The most immediate targets for further research are empirical and, perhaps, theoretical investigations into the general utility of these approaches. The targets of my approach have all been synchronous group membership algorithms, while the verification diagrams of Manna et al. seem not to have been applied to any hard examples (the verification in STeP of an interesting Leader Election algorithm [6] did not use diagrammatic methods). If practical experience with a variety of different problem types shows the approach to have sufficient utility, then it will be worth investigating provision of direct mechanical support.

Acknowledgments

I am grateful for useful criticisms and suggestions made by the anonymous referees and by my colleagues Jean-Christophe Filliâtre, Patrick Lincoln, Ursula Martin, Holger Pfeifer, N. Shankar, and M. Srivas, and also for feedback received from talks on this material at NASA Langley, SRI, and Stanford.

---

[8] Verification by abstraction of the communications protocol example mentioned earlier required 45 of the 57 auxiliary invariants used in the direct proof [12].

References

Papers on formal methods and automated verification by SRI authors can generally be found at http://www.csl.sri.com/fm-papers.html.

[1] Parosh Aziz Abdulla, Aurore Annichini, Saddek Bensalem, Ahmed Bouajjani, Peter Habermehl, and Yassine Lakhnech. Verification of infinite-state systems by combining abstraction and reachability analysis. In Halbwachs and Peled [11], pages 146–159.

[2] Rajeev Alur and Thomas A. Henzinger, editors. *Computer-Aided Verification, CAV '96*, Volume 1102 of Springer-Verlag *Lecture Notes in Computer Science*, New Brunswick, NJ, July/August 1996.

[3] Saddek Bensalem, Yassine Lakhnech, and Sam Owre. Computing abstractions of infinite state systems compositionally and automatically. In Alan J. Hu and Moshe Y. Vardi, editors, *Computer-Aided Verification, CAV '98*, Volume 1427 of Springer-Verlag *Lecture Notes in Computer Science*, pages 319–331, Vancouver, Canada, June 1998.

[4] Saddek Bensalem, Yassine Lakhnech, and Hassen Saïdi. Powerful techniques for the automatic generation of invariants. In Alur and Henzinger [2], pages 323–335.

[5] Nikolaj Bjørner, I. Anca Browne, and Zohar Manna. Automatic generation of invariants and intermediate assertions. *Theoretical Computer Science*, 173(1):49–87, 1997.

[6] Nikolaj Bjørner, Uri Lerner, and Zohar Manna. Deductive verification of parameterized fault-tolerant systems: A case study. In *Second International Conference on Temporal Logic, ICTL'97*, Manchester, England, July 1997.

[7] I. Anca Browne, Zohar Manna, and Henny Sipma. Generalized temporal verification diagrams. In *15th Conference on the Foundations of Software Technology and Theoretical Computer Science*, Volume 1026 of Springer-Verlag *Lecture Notes in Computer Science*, pages 484–498, Bangalore, India, December 1995.

[8] S. J. Creese and A. W. Roscoe. TTP: A case study in combining induction and data independence. Technical Report PRG-TR-1-99, Oxford University Computing Laboratory, Oxford, England, 1999.

[9] Satyaki Das, David L. Dill, and Seungjoon Park. Experience with predicate abstraction. In Halbwachs and Peled [11], pages 160–171.

[10] Luca de Alfaro, Zohar Manna, Henny B. Sipma, and Tomás E. Uribe. Visual verification of reactive systems. In Ed Brinksma, editor, *Tools and Algorithms for the Construction and Analysis of Systems (TACAS '97)*, Volume 1217 of Springer-Verlag *Lecture Notes in Computer Science*, pages 334–350, Enschede, The Netherlands, April 1997.

[11] Nicolas Halbwachs and Doron Peled, editors. *Computer-Aided Verification, CAV '99*, Volume 1633 of Springer-Verlag *Lecture Notes in Computer Science*, Trento, Italy, July 1999.

[12] Klaus Havelund and N. Shankar. Experiments in theorem proving and model checking for protocol verification. In *Formal Methods Europe FME '96*, Volume 1051 of Springer-Verlag *Lecture Notes in Computer Science*, pages 662–681, Oxford, UK, March 1996.

[13] Ravi Hosabettu, Mandayam Srivas, and Ganesh Gopalakrishnan. Proof of correctness of a processor with reorder buffer using the completion functions approach. In Halbwachs and Peled [11], pages 47–59.
[14] Shmuel Katz, Pat Lincoln, and John Rushby. Low-overhead time-triggered group membership. In Marios Mavronicolas and Philippas Tsigas, editors, *11th International Workshop on Distributed Algorithms (WDAG '97)*, Volume 1320 of Springer-Verlag *Lecture Notes in Computer Science*, pages 155–169, Saarbrücken Germany, September 1997.
[15] Hermann Kopetz and Günter Grünsteidl. TTP—a protocol for fault-tolerant real-time systems. *IEEE Computer*, 27(1):14–23, January 1994.
[16] Zohar Manna, Anca Browne, Henny B. Sipma, and Tomás E. Uribe. Visual abstractions for temporal verification. In Armando M. Haeberer, editor, *Algebraic Methodology and Software Technology, AMAST'98*, Volume 1548 of Springer-Verlag *Lecture Notes in Computer Science*, pages 28–41, Amazonia, Brazil, January 1999.
[17] Zohar Manna and Amir Pnueli. Temporal verification diagrams. In M. Hagiya and J.C. Mitchell, editors, *International Symposium on Theoretical Aspects of Computer Software: TACS'94*, Volume 789 of Springer-Verlag *Lecture Notes in Computer Science*, pages 726–765, Sendai, Japan, April 1994.
[18] Zohar Manna and The STeP Group. STeP: Deductive-algorithmic verification of reactive and real-time systems. In Alur and Henzinger [2], pages 415–418.
[19] Sam Owre, John Rushby, Natarajan Shankar, and Friedrich von Henke. Formal verification for fault-tolerant architectures: Prolegomena to the design of PVS. *IEEE Transactions on Software Engineering*, 21(2):107–125, February 1995.
[20] Seungjoon Park and David L. Dill. Verification of cache coherence protocols by aggregation of distributed transactions. *Theory of Computing Systems*, 31(4):355–376, 1998.
[21] Holger Pfeifer. Formal verification of the TTA group membership algorithm, 2000. Submitted for publication.
[22] A. W. Roscoe. *The Theory and Practice of Concurrency*. Prentice Hall International Series in Computer Science. Prentice Hall, Hemel Hempstead, UK, 1998.
[23] John Rushby. Formal verification of a low-overhead group membership algorithm, 2000. In preparation.
[24] Hassen Saïdi and Susanne Graf. Construction of abstract state graphs with PVS. In Orna Grumberg, editor, *Computer-Aided Verification, CAV '97*, Volume 1254 of Springer-Verlag *Lecture Notes in Computer Science*, pages 72–83, Haifa, Israel, June 1997.
[25] Hassen Saïdi and N. Shankar. Abstract and model check while you prove. In Halbwachs and Peled [11], pages 443–454.

Verifying Advanced Microarchitectures that Support Speculation and Exceptions *

Ravi Hosabettu[1], Ganesh Gopalakrishnan[1], and Mandayam Srivas[2]

[1] Department of Computer Science, University of Utah, Salt Lake City, UT 84112,
hosabett,ganesh@cs.utah.edu
[2] Computer Science Laboratory, SRI International, Menlo Park, CA 94025,
srivas@csl.sri.com

Abstract. In this paper, we discuss the verification of a microprocessor involving a reorder buffer, a store buffer, speculative execution and exceptions at the microarchitectural level. We extend the earlier proposed *Completion Functions Approach* [HSG98] in a uniform manner to handle the verification of such microarchitectures. The key extension to our previous work was in systematically extending the abstraction map to accommodate the possibility of all the pending instructions being squashed. An interesting detail that arises in doing so is how the commutativity obligation for the program counter is proved despite the program counter being updated by both the instruction fetch stage (when a speculative branch may be entertained) and the retirement stage (when the speculation may be discovered to be incorrect). Another interesting detail pertains to how store buffers are handled. We highlight a new type of invariant in this work—one which keeps correspondence between store buffer pointers and reorder buffer pointers. All these results, taken together with the features handled using the completion functions approach in our earlier published work [HSG98,HSG99,HGS99], demonstrates that the approach is uniformly applicable to a wide variety of pipelined designs.

1 Introduction

Formal Verification of pipelined processor implementations against instruction set architecture (ISA) specifications is a problem of growing importance. A significant number of processors being sold today employ advanced features such as out-of-order execution, store buffers, exceptions that cause pending uncommitted instructions to be squashed, and speculative execution. Recently a number of different approaches [HSG99,McM98,PA98] have been used to verify simple out-of-order designs. To the best of our knowledge, no single formal verification

---

* The first and second authors were supported in part by NSF Grant No. CCR-9800928. The third author was supported in part by ARPA contract F30602-96-C-0204 and NASA contract NASI-20334. The first author was also supported by a University of Utah Graduate Fellowship.

technique has been shown to be capable of verifying processor designs that support all of these features and also apply to other processors such as those that perform out-of-order retirement. In this paper, we report our successful application of the *Completion Functions Approach* to verify an out-of-order execution design with a reorder buffer, a store buffer, exceptions and speculation, using the PVS [ORSvH95] theorem-prover, taking only a modest amount of time for the overall proof. This result, taken together with the earlier published applications of the completion functions approach [HSG98,HSG99,HGS99], demonstrates that the approach is uniformly applicable to a wide variety of pipelined designs.

One of the challenges posed in verifying a combination of the above mentioned advanced features is that the resulting complex interaction between data and control usually overwhelms most automatic methods, whether based on model checking or decision procedures. One of the main contributions of this work is that we develop a way of cleanly decomposing the squashing of instructions from normal execution. These decomposition ideas are applicable to theorem proving or model checking or combined methods.

Our basic approach is one of showing that any program run on the specification and the implementation machines returns identical results. This verification is, in turn, achieved by identifying an abstraction map ABS that relates implementation states to corresponding specification states. The key to make the above technique work efficiently in practice is a proper definition of ABS. As we showed, in our earlier work [HSG98], one should ideally choose an approach to constructing ABS that is not only simple and natural to carry out, but also derives other advantages, the main ones being *modular verification* that helps localize errors, and *verification reuse* that allows lemmas proved about certain pipeline stages to be used as rewrite rules in proving other stages. In [HSG98], we introduced such a technique to define ABS called the *Completion Functions Approach*. In subsequent work [HSG99,HGS99,Hos99], we demonstrated that the completion functions approach can be applied uniformly to a wide variety of examples that include various advanced pipelining features. An open question in our previous work was whether combining out-of-order execution with exceptions and speculation would make the task of defining completion functions cumbersome and the approach impractical.

In this paper, we demonstrate that the completion functions approach is robust enough to be used effectively for such processors, that is, (i) the specification of completion functions are still natural, amounting to expressing knowledge that the designer already has; (ii) verification proceeds incrementally, facilitating debugging and error localization; (iii) mistakes made in specifying completion functions never lead to false positives; and (iv) verification conditions and most of the supporting lemmas needed to finish a proof can be generated systematically, if not automatically. They can also be discharged with a high degree of automation using strategies based on decision procedures and rewriting. These observations are supported by our final result: a processor design supporting superscalar execution, store buffers, exceptions, speculative branch prediction, and user and supervisor modes could be fully verified in 265 person hours. This, we believe, is a modest investment in return for the significant benefits of design verification.

Some of the highlights of the work we report are as follows. Given that our correctness criterion is one of showing a commutativity obligation between implementation states and specification states, the abstraction map used in the process must somehow accommodate the possibility of instructions being squashed. We show how this is accomplished. This leads us to a verification condition with two parts, one pertaining to the processor states being related before and after an implementation transition, and the other relating to the squashing predicate itself. Next, we show how the commutativity obligation for the program counter is obtained despite the program counter being updated by both the instruction fetch stage (when a speculative branch may be entertained) and the retirement stage (when the speculation may be discovered to be incorrect). We also show how the store buffer is handled in our proof. We detail a new type of invariant in this work, which was not needed in our earlier works. This invariant keeps correspondence between store buffer pointers and reorder buffer pointers.

2 Processor Model

At the specification level, the state of the processor is represented by a register file, a special register file accessed only by privileged/special instructions, a data memory, a mode flag, a program counter and an instruction memory. The processor operating mode (one of user/supervisory) is maintained in the mode flag. User mode instructions are an `alu` instruction for performing arithmetic and logical operations, `load` and `store` instructions for accessing the data memory, and a `beq` instruction for performing conditional branches. Three additional privileged instructions are allowed in the supervisory mode: `rfeh` instruction for returning from an exception handler, and `mfsr` and `mtsr` instructions for moving data from and to the special register file. Three types of exceptions are possible: arithmetic exception raised by an `alu` instruction, data access exception raised by `load` and `store` instructions when the memory address is outside legal bounds (two special registers maintain the legal bounds, and this is checked only in user mode), and an illegal instruction exception. When an exception is raised, the processor saves the address of the faulting instruction in a special register and jumps to an exception handler assuming supervisory mode in the process. After processing a raised exception, the processor returns to user mode via the `rfeh` instruction.

An implementation model of this processor is shown in Figure 1. A reorder buffer, implemented as a circular FIFO queue with its tail pointing to the earliest issued instruction and head pointing to the first free location in the buffer, is used to maintain program order, to permit instructions to be committed in that order. Register translation tables (regular and special) provide the identity of the latest pending instruction writing a particular register. "Alu/Branch/Special Instr. Unit" (referred to as ABS Unit) executes `alu`, `beq` and all the special instructions. The reservation stations hold the instructions sent to this unit

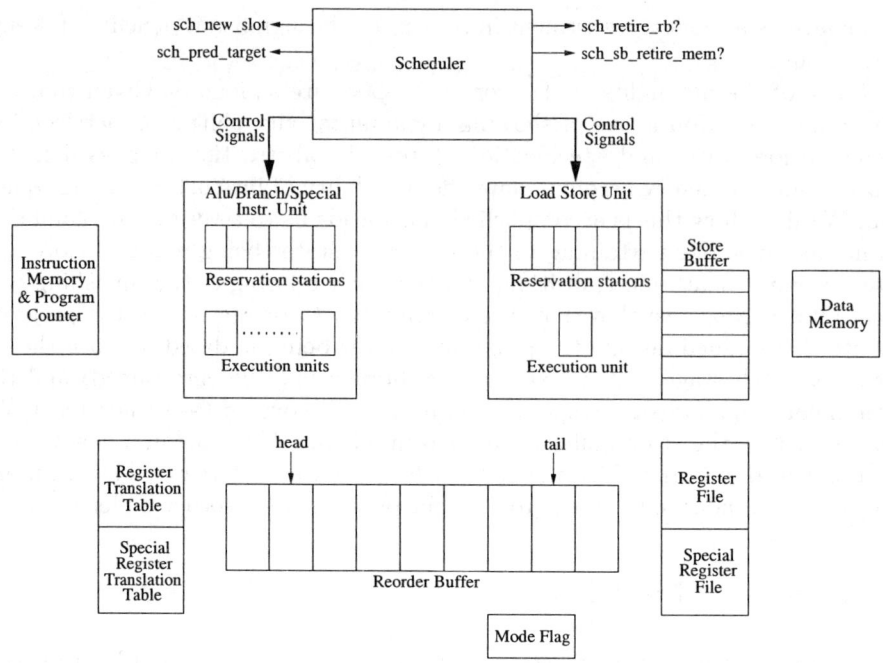

Fig. 1. The block diagram model of our implementation

until they are ready to be dispatched onto an appropriate execution unit. These instructions are executed out of program order by the multiple execution units present in the ABS Unit. Instructions `load` and `store` are issued to the "Load Store Unit" (referred to as LS Unit) where the reservation stations form a circular FIFO queue storing the instructions in their program order. (Again, tail points to the earliest instruction and head points to the first free reservation station.) These instructions are executed in their program order by the single execution unit present in the LS Unit. For a `store` instruction, the memory address and the value to be stored are recorded in an entry in the *store buffer*, and the value is later written into the data memory. The store buffer is again implemented as a circular FIFO queue, with head and tail pointers, keeping the instructions to be written to the data memory in their program order. When two store buffer entries refer to the same memory address, the latest one has a flag set. A `load` instruction first attempts an associative search in the store buffer using the memory address. If multiple store buffer entries have the same address, the search returns the value of the latest entry. If the search does not find a matching entry, the data for that address is returned from the data memory. A scheduler controls the movement of the instructions through the execution pipeline (such as being dispatched, executed etc.) and its behavior is modeled by axioms (to allow us to concentrate on the processor "core"). Instructions are fetched from the instruction memory using a program counter; and the implementation also takes a no_op input, which suppresses an instruction fetch when asserted.

An instruction is *issued* by allocating an entry for it at the head of the reorder buffer and (depending on the instruction type) either a free reservation station (sch_new_slot) in the ABS Unit or a free reservation station at the head of the queue of reservation stations in the LS Unit. If the instruction being issued is a branch instruction, then the program counter is modified according to a *predicted* branch target address (sch_pred_target, an unconstrained arbitrary value), and in the next cycle the new instruction is fetched from this address. No instruction is issued if there are no free reservation stations/reorder buffer entries or if no_op is asserted or if the processor is being restarted (for reasons detailed later). The RTT entry corresponding to the destination of the instruction is updated to reflect the fact that the instruction being issued is the latest one to write that register. If the source operands are not being written by previously issued pending instructions (checked using the RTT) then their values are obtained from the register file, otherwise the reorder buffer indices of the instructions providing the source operands are maintained (in the reservation station). Issued instructions wait for their source operands to become ready, monitoring all the execution units if they produce the values they are waiting for. An instruction can be *dispatched* when its source operands are ready and a free execution unit is available [1]. In case of the LS Unit, only the instruction at the tail of the queue of reservation stations is dispatched. As soon as an instruction is dispatched, its reservation station is freed. The dispatched instructions are *executed* and the results are *written back* to their respective reorder buffer entries as well as forwarded to those instructions waiting for this result. If an exception is raised by any of the executing instructions, then a flag is set in the reorder buffer entry to indicate that fact. In case of a store instruction, the memory address and the value to be stored are written into a store buffer entry instead of the reorder buffer entry when the store instruction does not raise an exception (other information such as the "ready" status etc. are all written into the reorder buffer entry). The control signals from the scheduler determine the timings of this movement of the instructions in the execution pipeline.

The instruction at the tail of the reorder buffer is committed to the architecturally visible components, when it is done executing (at a time determined by sch_retire_rb?). If it is a store instruction, then the corresponding store buffer entry is marked *committed* and later written into the data memory (at a time determined by sch_sb_retire_mem?). Also, if the RTT entry for the destination of the instruction being retired is pointing to the tail of the reorder buffer, then that RTT entry is updated to reflect the fact that the value of that register is in the appropriate register file. If the instruction at the tail of the reorder buffer has raised an exception or if it is a mis-predicted branch or if it is a rfeh in-

---

[1] Multiple instructions can be simultaneously dispatched, executed and written back in one clock cycle. However, for simplicity, we do not allow multiple instruction issue or retirement in a single clock cycle.

struction, then the rest of the instructions in the reorder buffer are squashed and the processor is restarted by resetting all of its internal (non-observable) state.

3 The Completion Functions Approach

The key idea in proving the correctness of pipelined microprocessors is to discover a formal correspondence between the execution of the implementation and the specification machines. The completion functions approach suggests a way of constructing this abstraction in a manner that leads to an elegant decomposition of the proof. In the first subsection, we briefly discuss the correctness criterion we use. In the second subsection, we describe the different steps in constructing a suitable abstraction function for the example under consideration. In the third subsection, we discuss how to decompose the proof into verification conditions, the proof strategies used in discharging these obligations, and the invariants needed in our approach. The PVS specifications and the proofs can be found at [Hos99].

3.1 Correctness Criterion

We assume that the pipelined implementation and the ISA-level specification are provided in the form of transition functions, denoted by I_step and A_step respectively. The specification machine state is made up of certain components chosen from the implementation machine called the observables. The function projection extracts these observables given an implementation machine state. The state where the pipelined machine has no partially executed instructions is called a *flushed* state.

We regard a pipelined processor implementation to be *correct* if the behavior of the processor starting in a flushed state, executing a program, and terminating in a flushed state is matched by the ISA level specification machine whose starting and terminating states are in direct correspondence with those of the implementation processor through projection. This criterion is shown in Figure 2(a) where n is the number of implementation machine transitions in a run of the pipelined machine and m corresponds to the number of instructions executed in the specification machine by this run. An additional correctness criterion is to show that the implementation machine is able to execute programs of all lengths, that is, it does not get into a state where it refuses to accept any more new instructions. In this paper, we concentrate on proving the correctness criterion expressed in Figure 2(a) only.

The criterion shown in Figure 2(a) spanning an entire sequential execution can be established with the help of induction once a more basic *commutativity obligation* shown in Figure 2(b) is established on a single implementation machine transition. This criterion states that if the implementation machine starts in an arbitrary state q and the specification machine starts in a corresponding specification state (given by an abstraction function ABS), then after executing a transition their new states correspond. A_step_new stands for zero or more applications of A_step. The number of instructions executed by the specification machine corresponding to an implementation transition is given by a user defined *synchronization* function. Our method further verifies that the ABS function chosen corresponds to projection on flushed states, that is, ABS(fs) = projection(fs) holds on flushed states, thus helping debug ABS. The user may also need to discover invariants to restrict the set of implementation states considered in the proof of the commutativity obligation and prove that it is closed under I_step.

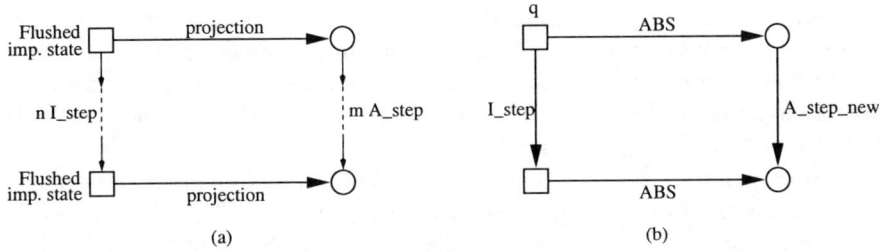

Fig. 2. Pipelined microprocessor correctness criterion

The crux of the problem here is to define a suitable abstraction function relating an implementation state to a specification state. The completion functions approach suggests a way of doing this in a manner that leads to an elegant decomposition of the proof. We now detail how this is achieved for our example processor.

3.2 Compositional Construction of the Abstraction Function

The first step in defining the abstraction function is to identify all the unfinished instructions in the processor and their program order. In this implementation, the processor (when working correctly) stores all the currently executing instructions in their program order in the reorder buffer. We identify an instruction in the processor with its reorder buffer index, that is, we refer to instruction at reorder buffer index rbi as just instruction rbi[2]. In addition to these, the store buffer has certain committed store instructions yet to be written into the data memory, recorded in their program order. These store instructions are not associated with any reorder buffer entry and occur earlier in the program order than all the instructions in the reorder buffer.

---

[2] Brief explanation of some of the notation used throughout rest of the paper: q refers to an arbitrary implementation state, s the scheduler output, i the processor input, I_step(q,s,i) the next state after an implementation transition. We sometimes refer to predicates and functions defined without explicitly mentioning their arguments, when this causes no confusion.

Having determined the program order of the unfinished instructions, the second step is to define a completion function for every unfinished instruction in the pipeline. Each completion function specifies the *desired effect* on the observables of completing a particular unfinished instruction assuming those that are ahead of it (in the program order) are completed. The completion functions, which map an implementation state to an implementation state, leave all non-observable state components unchanged. However not every instruction in the pipeline gets executed completely and updates the observables. If an instruction raises an exception or if the target address is mis-predicted for a branch instruction, then the instructions following it must be squashed. To specify this behavior, we define a squashing predicate for every unfinished instruction that is true exactly when the unfinished instruction can cause the subsequent instructions (in the program order) to be squashed. The completion function for a given instruction updates the observables only if the instruction is not squashed by any of the instructions preceding it.

We now elaborate on specifying the completion functions and the squashing predicates for the example under consideration. An unfinished instruction rbi in the processor can be in one of the following seven phases of execution: Issued to ABS Unit or to LS Unit (*issued_abs* or *issued_lsu*), dispatched in either of these units (*dispatched_abs* or *dispatched_lsu*), executed in either of these units (*executed_abs* or *executed_lsu*) or written back to the reorder buffer (*writtenback*). A given unfinished instruction is in one of these phases at any given time and the information about this instruction (the source values, destination register etc) is held in the various implementation components. For each instruction phase "ph", we define a predicate "Instr_ph?" that is true when a given instruction is in phase "ph", a function "Action_ph" that specifies what ought to be the effect of completing an instruction in that phase, and a predicate "Squash_rest?_ph" that specifies the conditions under which an instruction in that phase can squash all the subsequent instructions. We then define a single parameterized completion function and squashing predicate (applicable to all the unfinished instructions in the reorder buffer) as shown in [1]. We similarly define (a parameterized) completion function for the committed store instructions in the store buffer. These store instructions can only be in a single phase, that is, *committed*, and they do not cause the subsequent instructions to be squashed. (A store instruction that raises an exception is not entered into the store buffer.)

```
% state_I: impl. state type. rbindex: reorder buffer index type.      1
Complete_instr(q:state_I, rbi:rbindex, kill?:bool): state_I =
  IF kill? THEN q
  ELSIF Instr_writtenback?(q,rbi) THEN Action_writtenback(q,rbi)
  ELSIF Instr_executed_lsu?(q,rbi) THEN Action_executed_lsu(q,rbi)
  ELSIF ... Similarly for other phases ... ENDIF

Squash_rest?_instr(q:state_I, rbi:rbindex): bool =
  IF Instr_writtenback?(q,rbi) THEN Squash_rest?_writtenback(q,rbi)
  ELSIF Instr_executed_lsu?(q,rbi) THEN Squash_rest?_executed_lsu(q,rbi)
  ELSIF ... Similarly for other phases ... ENDIF
```

In this implementation, when an instruction is in the *writtenback* phase, its reorder buffer entry has the result value and destination of the instruction, and also enough information to determine whether it has raised any exceptions or has turned out to be a mis-predicted branch. Action_writtenback and Squash_rest?_writtenback are then defined using this information about the instruction. Similarly, we define the "Action"s and the "Squash_rest?"s for the other phases. When an instruction is in an execution phase where it has not yet read its operands, the completion function obtains the operands by simply reading them from the observables. The justification is that the completion functions are composed in their program order in constructing the abstraction function (described below), and so we talk of completing a given instruction in a context where the instructions ahead of it are completed.

```
% Complete_Squash_rest?_till returns a tuple.                              2
% proj_1 and proj_2 extracts the first and the second components.
% rbindex_p is type ranging from 0 to the size of the reorder buffer.
Complete_Squash_rest?_till(q:state_I,rbi_ms:rbindex_p):
                                            RECURSIVE [state_I,bool] =
 IF rbi_ms = 0 THEN (q,FALSE)
 ELSE LET t = Complete_Squash_rest?_till(q,rbi_ms-1),
          x = proj_1(t), y = proj_2(t) IN
    (Complete_instr(x,measure_fn_rbi(q,rbi_ms),y), %% 1st component.
     Squash_rest?_instr(x,measure_fn_rbi(q,rbi_ms)) OR y) %% 2nd one.
 ENDIF
 MEASURE rbi_ms

Complete_till(q:state_I,rbi_ms:rbindex_p): state_I =
 proj_1(Complete_Squash_rest?_till(Complete_committed_in_sb_till(
                            q,lsu_sb_commit_count(q)),rbi_ms))

Squash_rest?_till(q:state_I,rbi_ms:rbindex_p): bool =
 proj_2(Complete_Squash_rest?_till(Complete_committed_in_sb_till(
                            q,lsu_sb_commit_count(q)),rbi_ms))

% state_A is the specification state type.
ABS(q: state_I): state_A = projection(Complete_till(q,rb_count(q)))
```

The final step is to construct the abstraction function (that has the cumulative effect of flushing the pipeline) by completing all the unfinished instructions in their program order. A given instruction is to be killed, that is, the kill? argument of Complete_instr is true, when the squashing predicate is true for any of the instructions ahead of that given instruction. In order to define an ordering among the instructions, we define a measure function rbi_measure_fn that associates a measure with every instruction in the reorder buffer such that the tail has measure one and successive instructions have a measure one greater than the previous instruction. So the instructions with lower measures occur earlier in the program order than instructions with higher measures. The function measure_fn_rbi returns the reorder buffer index of the instruction with the given measure. To define the abstraction function, we first define a recursive function

`Complete_Squash_rest?_till` that completes the instructions and computes the disjunction of the squashing predicates from the tail of the reorder buffer till a given unfinished instruction, as shown in 2 . `Complete_committed_in_sb_till` is a similar recursive function that completes all the committed `store` instructions in the store buffer. We can then define the abstraction function by first completing all the committed instructions in the store buffer (they are earlier in the program order that any instruction in the reorder buffer) and then completing all the instructions in the reorder buffer. So we define `Complete_till` and `Squash_rest?_till` as shown in 2 , and then in constructing the abstraction function ABS, we instantiate the `Complete_till` definition with the measure of the latest instruction in the reorder buffer. The implementation variable `rb_count` maintains the number of instructions in the reorder buffer, and hence corresponds to the measure of the latest instruction.

3.3 Decomposing the Proof

The proof of the commutativity obligation is split into different cases based on the structure of the synchronization function. In this example, the synchronization function returns zero when the processor is restarted or if the squashing predicate evaluates to true for any of the instructions in the reorder buffer (i.e., `Squash_rest?_till(q,rb_count(q))` is true) or if no new instruction is issued. Otherwise it returns one, and we consider each of these cases separately. We discuss proving the commutativity obligation for register file `rf` and program counter `pc` only. The proofs for the special register file, mode flag and data memory are similar to that `rf`, though in the case of data memory, one needs to take into account the additional details regarding the committed instructions in the store buffer. The proof for instruction memory is straight-forward as it does not change at all.

We first consider an easy case in the proof of the commutativity obligation (for `rf`), that is, when the processor is being restarted in the current cycle (`restart_proc` is true).

- The processor discards all the executing instructions in the reorder buffer, and sets `rb_count` and `lsu_sb_commit_count` to zeros. So `Complete_till` will be vacuous on the implementation side of the commutativity obligation (the side on which `I_step(q,s,i)` occurs), and the expression on the implementation side simplifies to `rf(I_step(q,s,i))`.
- Whenever the processor is being restarted, the instruction at the tail of the reorder buffer is causing the rest of the instructions to be squashed, so `Squash_rest?_till(q,1)` ought to be true. (Recall that the tail of the reorder buffer has measure one.) We prove this, and then from the definition of `Complete_Squash_rest?_till` in 2 , it follows that the `kill?` argument is true for all the remaining instructions in the reorder buffer, and hence these do not affect `rf`. Also, the synchronization function returns zero when the processor is being restarted. So the expression on the specification side of the commutativity obligation simplifies to `rf(Complete_till(q,1))`.

- We show that the rf(I_step(q,s,i)) and rf(Complete_till(q,1)) are indeed equal by expanding the definitions occurring in them and simplifying.

Now assume that restart_proc is false. We first postulate certain verification conditions, prove them, and then use them in proving the commutativity obligation. Consider an arbitrary instruction rbi. Though the processor executes the instructions in an out-of-order manner, it commits the instructions to the observables only in their program order. This suggests that the effect on rf of completing all the instructions till rbi is the same in the states q and I_step(q,s,i). Similarly, the truth value of the disjunction of the squashing predicates till rbi is the same in the states q and I_step(q,s,i). This verification condition Complete_Squash_rest?_till_VC is shown in $\boxed{3}$. This is proved by an induction on rbi_ms[3] (the measure corresponding to instruction rbi).

```
% valid_rb_entry? predicate tests whether rbi is within the         3
% reorder buffer bounds.
Complete_Squash_rest?_till_VC: LEMMA
FORALL(rbi_ms:rbindex): LET rbi = measure_fn_rbi(q,rbi_ms) IN
((valid_rb_entry?(q,rbi) AND NOT restart_proc?(q,s,i)) IMPLIES (
rf(Complete_till(q,rbi_ms)) = rf(Complete_till(I_step(q,s,i),rbi_ms)) AND
Squash_rest?_till(q,rbi_ms) = Squash_rest?_till(I_step(q,s,i),rbi_ms)))
```

As in the earlier proofs based on completion functions approach [HSG99,HSG98], we decompose the proof of Complete_Squash_rest?_till_VC into different cases based on how an instruction makes a transition from its present phase to its next phase. Figure 3 shows the phase transitions for an instruction rbi in the reorder buffer (when the processor is not restarted) where the predicates labeling the arcs define the conditions under which those transitions take place. The Figure also shows the three transitions for a new instruction entering the processor pipeline. Having identified these predicates, we prove that those transitions indeed take place in the implementation machine. For example, we prove that an instruction rbi in phase *dispatched_lsu* (D_lsu in the Figure) goes to *executed_lsu* phase in I_step(q,s,i) if Execute_lsu? predicate is true, otherwise it remains in *dispatched_lsu* phase.

We now return to the proof of Complete_Squash_rest?_till_VC and consider the induction argument (i.e., rbi_ms is not equal to 1). The proof outline is as follows:

- Expand the Complete_till and the Squash_rest?_till definitions on both sides of Complete_Squash_rest?_till_VC and unroll the recursive definition of Complete_Squash_rest?_till once.
- Consider the first conjunct (i.e., one corresponding to rf). The kill? argument to Complete_instr is Squash_rest?_till(q,rbi_ms-1) on the left

---

[3] Since the measure function is dependent on the tail of the reorder buffer, and since the tail can change during an implementation transition, the measure needs to be adjusted on the right hand side of Complete_Squash_rest?_till_VC to refer to the same instruction. This is a detail which we ignore in this paper for the ease of explanation, and use just rbi_ms.

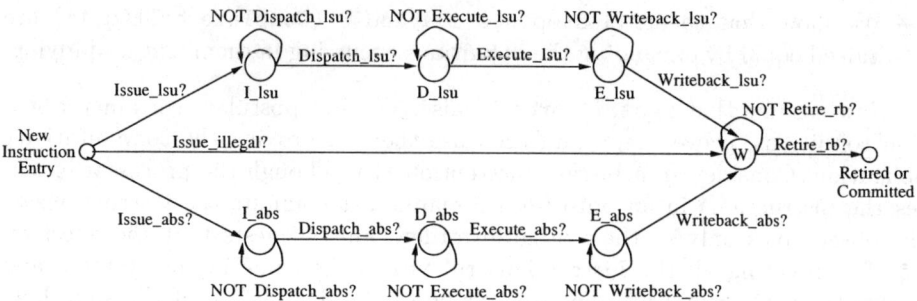

Fig. 3. The various phases an instruction can be in and transitions between them (when the processor is not being restarted). Also, the three transitions for an instruction entering the processor are shown.

hand side and `Squash_rest?_till(I_step(q,s,i),rbi_ms-1)` on the right hand side, and these have the same truth value by the induction hypothesis. When it is true, the left hand side reduces to

$$\texttt{rf(Complete\_till(q,rbi\_ms}-1))$$

and the right hand side to

$$\texttt{rf(Complete\_till(I\_step(q,s,i),rbi\_ms}-1))$$

which are equal by the induction hypothesis. When it is false, the proof proceeds as in our earlier work [HSG99]. We consider the possible phases `rbi` can be in and whether or not, it makes a transition to its next phase. Assume `rbi` is in *dispatched_abs* phase and the predicate `Execute_abs?` is true. Then, in `I_step(q,s,i)`, `rbi` is in *executed_abs* phase. By the definition of `Complete_instr`, the left hand side of the verification condition simplifies to `rf(Action_dispatched_abs(Complete_till(q,rbi_ms-1),rbi_ms))` and the right hand side reduces to `rf(Action_executed_abs(Complete_till(I_step(q,s,i),rbi_ms-1),rbi_ms))`. The proof now proceeds by expanding these "Action" function definitions, using the necessary invariant properties and simplifying. The induction hypothesis will be used to infer that the register file contents in the two states `Complete_till(q,rbi_ms-1)` and `Complete_till(I_step(q,s,i),rbi_ms-1)` are equal, as those two terms appear when the "Action" definitions are expanded. Overall, the proof decomposes into 14 cases for the seven phases `rbi` can be in.
- Consider the second conjunct of `Complete_Squash_rest?_till_VC`. Using the induction hypothesis, this reduces to showing that the two predicates `Squash_rest?_instr(Complete_till(q,rbi_ms-1),rbi_ms)` and `Squash_rest?_instr(Complete_till(I_step(q,s,i),rbi_ms-1),rbi_ms)` have the same truth value. This proof again proceeds as before by a case analysis on the possible phases `rbi` can be in and whether or not, it makes a transition

to its next phase. The proof again decomposes into 14 cases for the seven phases rbi can be in.

For the program counter, however, it is not possible to relate its value in states q and I_step(q,s,i) by considering the effect of instructions *one at a time in their program order* as was done for rf. This is because I_step updates pc if a new instruction is fetched, either by incrementing it or by updating it according to the speculated branch target address, but this new instruction is the latest one in the program order. However, if the squashing predicate is true for any of the executing instructions in the reorder buffer, then completing that instruction modifies the pc with a higher precedence, and the pc ought to be modified in the same way in both q and I_step(q,s,i). This observation suggests a verification condition on pc, shown in $\boxed{4}$. This verification condition is again proved by an induction on rbi_ms, and its proof is decomposed into 14 cases based on the instruction phase transitions as in the earlier proofs.

---
pc_remains_same_VC: LEMMA   4
FORALL(rbi_ms:rbindex): LET rbi = measure_fn_rbi(q,rbi_ms) IN
  (valid_rb_entry?(q,rbi) AND NOT restart_proc?(q,s,i) AND
       Squash_rest?_till(q,rbi_ms)) IMPLIES
  pc(Complete_till(q,rbi_ms)) = pc(Complete_till(I_step(q,s,i),rbi_ms))

Now we come to the proof of the commutativity obligation, where we use the above lemmas after instantiating them with rb_count. We consider the different remaining cases in the definition of the synchronization function in order—Squash_rest?_till(q,rb_count(q)) is true, no new instruction is issued or the three transitions corresponding to a new instruction being issued as shown in Figure 3.

– When Squash_rest?_till(q,rb_count(q)) is true, the kill? argument for the new instruction fetched (if any) will be true in I_step(q,s,i) since Squash_rest?_till has the same truth value in states q and I_step(q,s,i). Hence on the implementation side of the commutativity obligation, there is no new instruction executed. On the specification side, the synchronization function returns zero, so A_step_new is vacuous. The proof can then be accomplished using Complete_Squash_rest?_till_VC (for the register file) and pc_remains_same_VC (for the program counter).
– The proof when no new instruction is issued or when one is issued is similar to the proof in our earlier work [HSG99]. For example, if the issued instruction is in *issued_lsu* phase in I_step(q,s,i), then we have to prove that completing this instruction according to Action_issued_lsu has the same effect on the observables as executing a specification machine transition.

Correctness of the feedback logic: Whenever there are data dependencies among the executing instructions, the implementation keeps track of them and forwards the results of the execution to all the waiting instructions. The correctness of this feedback logic, both for the register file and the data memory, is expressed in a similar form as in our earlier work [HSG99]. For example, a load instruction obtains the value from the store buffer if there is an entry with the matching address (using associative search), otherwise it reads the value from the data memory. Consider the value obtained when all the instructions ahead of the `load` instruction are completed, and then the data memory is read. This value and the value returned by the feedback logic ought to be equal. The verification condition for the correctness of the feedback logic for data memory is based on the above observation. It will be used in the proof of the commutativity obligation and the proof of this verification condition itself is based on certain invariants.

Invariants needed: Many of the invariants needed like the exclusiveness and the exhaustiveness of instruction phases, and the invariants on the feedback logic for the register file and data memory are similar to the ones needed in our earlier work [HSG99]. We describe below one invariant that was not needed in the earlier work.

The LS Unit executes the `load` and `store` instructions in their program order. These instructions are stored in their program order in the reservation stations in the LS Unit and in the store buffer. It was necessary to use these facts during the proof and it was expressed as follows (for the reservation stations in LS Unit): Let `rsi1` and `rsi2` be two instructions in the reservation stations in the LS Unit. `rsi1_ptr` and `rsi2_ptr` point to the reorder buffer entries corresponding to these instructions respectively. Let `lsu_rsi_measure_fn` be a measure function defined on the LS Unit reservation station queue similar to `rbi_measure_fn`. If `rsi1` has a lower/higher measure than `rsi2` according to `lsu_rsi_measure_fn`, then `rsi1_ptr` has a lower/higher measure than `rsi2_ptr` according to a `rbi_measure_fn`.

PVS proof effort organization: This exercise was carried out in four phases. In the first phase, we "extrapolated" certain invariants and properties from the earlier work, and this took 27 person hours. In the second phase, we formulated and proved the invariants and certain other properties on the store buffer, and this took 54 person hours. In the third phase, we formulated and proved all the verification conditions about the observables and the commutativity obligation, and this took 131 person hours. In the fourth phase, we proved the necessary invariants about the feedback logic and its correctness, and this took 53 person hours. So the entire proof was accomplished in 265 person hours.

Related work: There is one other reported work on formally verifying the correctness of a pipelined processor of comparable complexity. In [SH99], Sawada and Hunt construct an explicit intermediate abstraction in the form of a table called MAETT, express invariant properties on this and prove the final correctness from these invariants. They report taking 15 person months. Also, their approach is applicable to fixed size instantiations of the design only. Various other approaches have been proposed to verify out-of-order execution processors recently [McM98,PA98,JSD98,BBCZ98,CLMK99,BGV99], but none of these have been so far demonstrated on examples with a similar set of features as we have handled.

4 Experimental Results and Concluding Remarks

Example verified	Effort spent doing the proof
EX1.1 and EX1.2	2 person months
EX3.1	13 person days
EX2.1	19 person days
EX3.2	7 person days
EX2.2	34 person days

Table 1. Examples verified and the effort needed.

We have applied our methodology to verify six example processors exhibiting a wide variety of implementation issues, and implemented our methodology in PVS [ORSvH95]. Our results to date are summarized in Table 1. This table summarizes the manual effort spent on each of the examples, listing them in the order we verified them. The first entry includes the time to learn PVS[4]. Each verification effort built on the earlier efforts, and reused some the ideas and the proof machinery.

The processor described in this paper is listed as EX2.2. In contrast, EX1.1 is a five stage pipeline implementing a subset of the DLX architecture, EX1.2 is a dual-issue version of the same architecture, and EX2.1 is a processor with a reorder buffer and only arithmetic instructions. We also considered two examples that allowed out-of-order completion of instructions: EX3.1 allowed certain arithmetic instructions to bypass certain other arithmetic instructions when their destinations were different, and EX3.2 implemented Tomasulo's algorithm without a reorder buffer and with arithmetic instructions only.

In conclusion, the completion functions approach can be used effectively to verify a wide range of processors against their ISA-level specifications. We have articulated a systematic procedure by which a designer can formulate a very intuitive set of completion functions that help define the abstraction function, and then showed how such a construction of the abstraction function leads to decomposition of the proof of the commutativity obligation. We have also presented how the designer can systematically address details such as exceptions and feedback logic. Design iterations are also greatly facilitated by the completion functions approach due to the incremental nature of the verification, as changes to a pipeline stage do not cause ripple-effects of changes across the whole specification; global re-verification can be avoided because of the layered

---

[4] By the first author who did all the verification work.

nature of the verification conditions. Our future work will be directed at overcoming the current limitations of the completion functions approach, by seeking ways to automate invariant discovery, especially pertaining to the control logic of processors.

References

[BBCZ98] Sergey Berezin, Armin Biere, Edmund Clarke, and Yunshan Zu. Combining symbolic model checking with uninterpreted functions for out-of-order processor verification. In Gopalakrishnan and Windley [GW98], pages 369–386.

[BGV99] Randal Bryant, Steven German, and Miroslav Velev. Exploiting positive equality in a logic of equality with uninterpreted functions. In Halbwachs and Peled [HP99], pages 470–482.

[CLMK99] Byron Cook, John Launchbury, John Matthews, and Dick Kieburtz. Formal verification of explicitly parallel microprocessors. In Pierre and Kropf [PK99], pages 23–36.

[GW98] Ganesh Gopalakrishnan and Phillip Windley, editors. *Formal Methods in Computer-Aided Design, FMCAD '98*, volume 1522 of *Lecture Notes in Computer Science*, Palo Alto, CA, USA, November 1998. Springer-Verlag.

[HGS99] Ravi Hosabettu, Ganesh Gopalakrishnan, and Mandayam Srivas. A proof of correctness of a processor implementing Tomasulo's algorithm without a reorder buffer. In Pierre and Kropf [PK99], pages 8–22.

[Hos99] Ravi Hosabettu. The Completion Functions Approach homepage, 1999. At address http://www.cs.utah.edu/~hosabett/cfa.html.

[HP99] Nicolas Halbwachs and Doron Peled, editors. *Computer-Aided Verification, CAV '99*, volume 1633 of *Lecture Notes in Computer Science*, Trento, Italy, July 1999. Springer-Verlag.

[HSG98] Ravi Hosabettu, Mandayam Srivas, and Ganesh Gopalakrishnan. Decomposing the proof of correctness of pipelined microprocessors. In Hu and Vardi [HV98], pages 122–134.

[HSG99] Ravi Hosabettu, Mandayam Srivas, and Ganesh Gopalakrishnan. Proof of correctness of a processor with reorder buffer using the completion functions approach. In Halbwachs and Peled [HP99], pages 47–59.

[HV98] Alan J. Hu and Moshe Y. Vardi, editors. *Computer-Aided Verification, CAV '98*, volume 1427 of *Lecture Notes in Computer Science*, Vancouver, BC, Canada, June/July 1998. Springer-Verlag.

[JSD98] Robert Jones, Jens Skakkebaek, and David Dill. Reducing manual abstraction in formal verification of out-of-order execution. In Gopalakrishnan and Windley [GW98], pages 2–17.

[McM98] Ken McMillan. Verification of an implementation of Tomasulo's algorithm by compositional model checking. In Hu and Vardi [HV98], pages 110–121.

[ORSvH95] Sam Owre, John Rushby, Natarajan Shankar, and Friedrich von Henke. Formal verification for fault-tolerant architectures: Prolegomena to the design of PVS. *IEEE Transactions on Software Engineering*, 21(2):107–125, February 1995.

[PA98]   Amir Pnueli and Tamarah Arons. Verification of data-insensitive circuits: An in-order-retirement case study. In Gopalakrishnan and Windley [GW98], pages 351–368.
[PK99]   Laurence Pierre and Thomas Kropf, editors. *Correct Hardware Design and Verification Method, CHARME '99*, volume 1703 of *Lecture Notes in Computer Science*, Bad Herrenalb, Germany, September 1999. Springer-Verlag.
[SH99]   J. Sawada and W.A. Hunt, Jr. Results of the verification of a comples pipelined machine model. In Pierre and Kropf [PK99], pages 313–316.

FoCs - Automatic Generation of Simulation Checkers from Formal Specifications

Yael Abarbanel, Ilan Beer, Leonid Gluhovsky,
Sharon Keidar, and Yaron Wolfsthal

IBM Haifa Research Laboratory, Israel
{yaell,beer,leonid,sharon,wolfstal}@il.ibm.com

1 Introduction and Motivation

For the foreseeable future, industrial hardware design will continue to use both simulation and model checking in the design verification process. To date, these techniques are applied in isolation using different tools and methodologies, and different formulations of the problem. This results in cumulative high cost and little (if any) cross-leverage of the individual advantages of simulation and formal verification.

With the goal of effectively and advantageously exploiting the co-existence of simulation and model checking, we have developed a tool called **FoCs** ("**Formal Checkers**"). FoCs, implemented as an independent component of the RuleBase toolset, takes RCTL[1] properties as input and translates them into VHDL programs ("checkers") which are integrated into the simulation environment and monitor simulation on a cycle-by-cycle basis for violations of the property.

Checkers, also called Functional Checkers, are not a new concept: manually-written checkers are a traditional part of simulation environments (cf. [GB+99]). Checkers facilitate massive random testing, because they automate test results analysis. Moreover, checkers facilitate the analysis of intermediate results, and therefore save debugging effort by identifying problems directly - "as they happen", and by pointing more accurately to the source of the problems.

However, the manual writing and maintenance of checkers is a notoriously high-cost and labor-intensive effort, especially if the properties to be verified are complex temporal ones. For instance, in the case of a checker for a design with overlapping transactions (explained in Section 3), writing a checker manually is an excruciating error-prone effort.

Observing the inefficient process of manual checker writing in ongoing IBM projects has inspired the development of FoCs, as a means for automatically generating checkers from formal specifications. For each property of the specification, represented as an RCTL formula, FoCs generates a checker for simulation. This checker essentially implements a state machine which will enter an error

---

[1] RCTL includes a rich and useful set of CTL safety formulas and regular expressions, see [BBL98]

state in a simulation run if the formula fails to hold in this run. The next section will describe the checker generation process in more detail.

Experience with FoCs in multiple projects has been very favorable in terms of verification cost and quality. Verification effort is reduced by leveraging the same formal rules for model checking of small design blocks as well as for simulation analysis across all higher simulation levels. An equally important benefit of FoCs is the conciseness and expressiveness of RCTL formulas. Formulas consisting of just a few lines can efficiently represent complex and subtle cases, which would require many lines of code if described in a language such as VHDL. This makes maintenance, debugging, porting and reuse of specifications and checkers highly cost-effective.

2 Tool Architecture and Implementation

Figure 1 shows the overall environment in which FoCs operates. The user provides a design to be verified, as well as formal specifications and a set of test programs generated either manually or automatically. FoCs translates the formal specification into checkers, which are then linked to the design and simulated with it. During simulation, the checker produces indications of property violations. It is up to the user to decide what action to take: fix the design, the property, or the simulation environment.

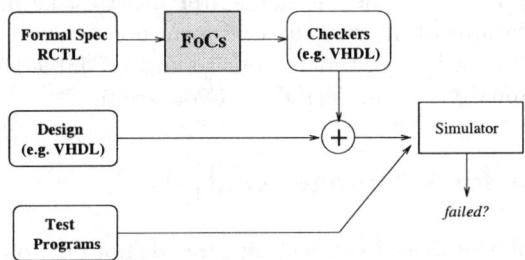

Fig. 1. FoCs Environment

FoCs translates RCTL into VHDL as follows: First, each property is translated into a non-deterministic finite automaton (NFA) and a simple $AG(p)$ formula, where p is a Boolean expression. The NFA has a set of distinguished error states, and the formula specifies that the NFA will never enter an error state (entering an error state means that the design does not adhere to the specification under the test conditions). The translation details are described in [BBL98].

Since contemporary simulators do not support non-determinism, the NFA has to be converted into a deterministic automaton (DFA). The DFA, in turn, is translated into a VHDL process - the FoCs checker. The $AG(p)$ formula is translated into a VHDL $Assert(p)$ statement that prints a message when the VHDL process reaches a state where the underlying property is violated, and possibly stops simulation.

The number of states of the DFA may be exponential in the number of states of the NFA, but simulation is sensitive to the size of the representation (the number of VHDL lines) rather than to the number of states. The number of VHDL lines in the resulting VHDL checker is at most quadratic in the size of the property. Practically, it is almost always linear because of the types of properties that people tend to write.

The above translation process is implemented within the RuleBase model checker [BBEL96].

3 Example

The following example will demonstrate the conciseness and ease of use of RCTL for checker writing and the advantage of automatic checker generation. Assume that the following property is part of the specification: **If a transaction that starts with tag t has to send k bytes, then at the end of the transaction k bytes have been sent.** The user can formulate this property in RCTL as follows:

forall k: [2]

$\{*, start$ & $start\_tag=t$ & $to\_send=k, !end*, end$ & $end\_tag=t\} \rightarrow \{sent=k\}$

Manual writing of a checker for this property may become complicated if transactions may overlap, which means that a new transaction may start while previous transactions are still active. The checker writer has to take into consideration all possible combinations of intervals and perform non-trivial bookkeeping. The RCTL formula is evidently much more concise and readable than the resulting VHDL file or a manually written VHDL or C program.

4 Using FoCs for Coverage Analysis

The quality of simulation-based verification depends not only on thorough checking of results, but also on the quality of the tests used (a.k.a. input patterns or test vectors) [KN96]. FoCs checkers can serve to enhance the quality of tests by providing a means for measuring *test coverage*. Test coverage measurement is the process of recording if certain user-defined events occurred during simulation of a set of tests. When used for coverage purposes, the FoCs checkers will evaluate the quality of the test suite by discovering events, or scenarios, that never happen during simulation. This feedback will guide the user which further tests are needed in order to cover scenarios that have not been exercised.

The implementation of coverage checkers is similar to that of functional checkers. The only difference is that instead of reporting an error, a coverage checker provides a positive indication when covering the relevant scenario. An

---

[2] The semantics of *forall* are intuitive. The implementation, however, is not trivial. It involves spawning a new automaton whenever a new value of k is encountered. Neither the formal semantics nor the implementation are included here due to lack of space.

example of a scenario to cover is: **a snoop event happens twice between read and write**, which can be formulated in RCTL as follows:

$$\{*,\ read,\ \{!snoop*,\ snoop,\ !snoop*,\ snoop\}\ \&\ \{!write*\}\ \} \rightarrow \{cover\}$$

A special case of coverage analysis is detection of *simulation vacuity*. While vacuity in model checking is defined as a failure of a subformula to influence the model checking results [BBER97], simulation vacuity refers to the failure of a set of tests to trigger a functional checker, which means that the checker did not influence simulation results. To detect simulation vacuity, FoCs attaches a coverage checker to each functional checker it generates; the coverage checker indicates whether the functional checker was triggered in at least one simulation run.

5 Experience

The FoCs toolset has been deployed in several projects in IBM, notably in the GigaHertz processor development effort in Austin and in the IBM Haifa ASIC development laboratory. FoCs has also been successfully used by the formal verification team of Galileo Technology, Inc. The experience with FoCs in these projects has been very favorable in terms of verification cost and quality. Using FoCs, verification effort was reduced - reportedly by up to 50% - by using the same formal rules for model checking at the unit level and for simulation analysis in the subsystem and system levels. This reduction was achieved despite the fact that the addition of checkers increases simulation time considerably (up to a factor of two). Thousands of FoCs checkers were written so far by virtue of the great ease of writing RCTL specifications and translating them to FoCs checkers.

6 Related Work

In a previous work, Kaufmann et al [KMP98] described an approach to verification in which all specifications and assumptions have the form $AG(p)$, where p is a Boolean formula. Both specifications and assumptions of this form can be used in simulation, with specification being translated into simple checkers, and assumptions being translated into testbench code which avoids leading the simulation into undesired states.

Canfield et al [CES97] describe a platform called Sherlock, aiming to serve both model checking (through translation to CTL) and simulation. Sherlock includes a high level language for specifying reactive behavior, while we use RCTL - a regular expression based language. While Sherlock postprocesses simulation traces, our method works during simulation. No experience has been described in [CES97]. Our own experience has demonstrated that the simple, concise syntax and semantics of RCTL, coupled with online simulation checking, is highly useful to the verification teams with whom we work.

Finally, in [SB+97], Schlipf et al describe a methodology and tool that inspired our work. They unify formal verification and simulation efforts by automatically translating state machines which represent the environment specification either to simulation behavioral models or to input for a model checker. Boolean assertions attached to the state machines serve as $AG(p)$ formulas in model checking or $Assert(p)$ in simulation. In contrast, our solution represents the specification as temporal logic formulas rather than state machines, for the sake of conciseness and readability.

7 Future Plans

Although focused on checker generation for functional testing and coverage analysis, we view FoCs as a step towards a full methodology of "Formal Specification, Design and Verification". We intend to provide a set of integrated, complementary tools that will facilitate the use of formal specification for multiple purposes. Once written, the formal specification will:
- Serve as an executable specification; architects can experiment with it while defining the specification
- Be used as a golden model to resolve ambiguities and misunderstandings during the implementation stage
- Be translated into temporal formulas for model checking
- Be translated into simulation checkers
- Be used for derivation of coverage criteria
- Provide hints for automatic test generation

We believe that such a methodology, once supported by the appropriate tools, will significantly contribute to the quality and efficiency of the design process.

References

[BBEL96] I. Beer, S. Ben-David, C. Eisner, A. Landver, "RuleBase: an Industry-Oriented Formal Verification Tool", Proc. DAC'96, pp. 655-660.
[BBER97] I. Beer, S. Ben-David, C. Eisner, Y. Rodeh, "Efficient Detection of Vacuity in ACTL Formulas", CAV'97, LNCS 1254, pp. 279-290.
[BBL98] I. Beer, S. Ben-David, A. Landver, "On-The-Fly Model Checking of RCTL Formulas", CAV'98, LNCS 1427, pp. 184-194.
[CES97] W. Canfield, E.A. Emerson, A. Saha, "Checking Formal Specifications under Simulations" Proc. ICCD'97.
[GB+99] D. Geist, G. Biran, T. Arons, Y. Nustov, M. Slavkin, M. Farkash, K. Holtz, A. Long, D. King, S. Barret, "A Methodology for Verification of a System on Chip", Proc. DAC'99.
[KN96] M. Kantrowitz, L. M. Noack, "I'm Done Simulating; Now What? Verification Coverage Analysis and Correctness ", Proc. DAC'96.
[KMP98] M. Kaufmann, A. Martin, C. Pixley, "Design Constraints in Symbolic Model Checking", CAV '98, LNCS 1427, pp. 477-487.
[SB+97] T. Schlipf, T. Buechner, R. Fritz, M. Helms and J. Koehl, "Formal verification Made Easy", IBM Journal of R&D, Vol. 41, No. 4/5 , 1997.

IF: A Validation Environment for Timed Asynchronous Systems

Marius Bozga[1], Jean-Claude Fernandez[2], Lucian Ghirvu[1]*, Susanne Graf[1], Jean-Pierre Krimm[1], and Laurent Mounier[1]

[1] VERIMAG, Centre Equation, 2 avenue de Vignate, F-38610 Gières
[2] LSR/IMAG, BP 82, F-38402 Saint Martin d'Hères Cedex

1 Introduction

Formal validation of distributed systems relies on several specification formalisms (such as the international standards LOTOS [15] or SDL [16]), and it requires different kinds of tools to cover the whole development process. Presently, a wide range of tools are available, either commercial or academic ones, but none of them fulfills in itself all the practical needs.

Commercial tools (like *Object*GEODE [20], SDT [1], STATEMATE [14],*etc.*) provide several development facilities, like editing, code generation and testing. However, they are usually restricted to basic verification techniques (exhaustive simulation, deadlock detection, *etc*) and are "closed" in the sense that there are only limited possibilities to interface them with others. On the other hand, there exist many academic tools (like SMV [19], HYTECH [12], KRONOS [22], UPPAAL [18], SPIN [13], INVEST [2], *etc.*) offering a broad spectrum of quite efficient verification facilities (symbolic verification, on-the-fly verification, abstraction techniques, *etc.*), but often supporting only low-level input languages. This may restrict their use at an industrial scale.

This situation motivated the development of IF, an intermediate representation for timed asynchronous systems together with an open validation environment. This environment fulfills several requirements. First of all, it is able to support *different validation techniques*, from interactive simulation to automatic property checking, together with test case and executable code generation. Indeed, all these functionalities cannot be embodied in a single tool and only tool integration facilities can provide all of them. For a sake of efficiency, this environment supports *several levels of program representations*. For instance it is well-known that model-checking verification of real life case studies usually needs to combine different optimization techniques to overcome the state explosion problem. In particular, some of these techniques rely on a syntactic level representation (like static analysis and computations of abstractions) whereas others techniques operate on the underlying semantic level. Another important feature is to keep this environment *open* and *evolutive*. Therefore, tool connections are performed by sharing either input/output formats, or libraries of components. For this purpose several well-defined application programming interfaces (APIs) are provided.

---
* Work partially supported by Région Rhône-Alpes, France

2 Architecture

The IF validation environment relies on three levels of program representation: the *specification level*, the IF *intermediate level*, and the LTS *semantic model level*. Figure 1 describes the overall architecture and the connections between the toolbox components.

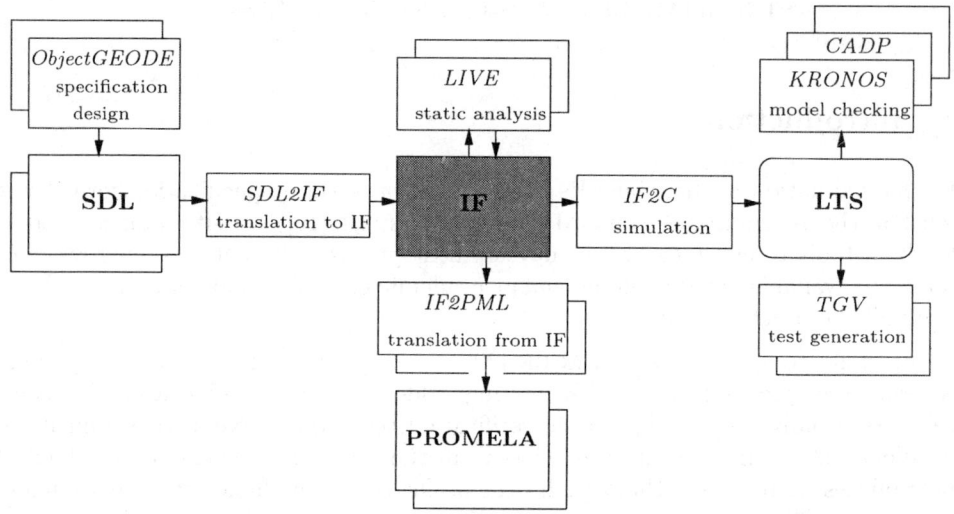

Fig. 1. An open validation environment for IF

The **specification level** is the initial program description, expressed for instance using an existing language. To be processed, this description is (automatically) translated into its IF representation. Currently the main input specification formalism we consider is SDL, but connections with other languages such as LOTOS or PROMELA could also be possible.

The **intermediate level** corresponds to the IF representation [7]. In IF, a system is expressed by a set of parallel processes communicating either asynchronously through a set of buffers, or synchronously through a set of gates. Processes are based on timed automata with deadlines [3], extended with discrete variables. Process transitions are guarded commands consisting of synchronous/asynchronous inputs and outputs, variable assignments, and clock settings. Buffers have various queuing policies (fifo, stack, bag, *etc.*), can be bounded or unbounded, and reliable or lossy.

A well-defined API allows to consult and modify the abstract tree of the IF representation. Since all the variables, clocks, buffers and the communication structure are still explicit, high-level transformations based on static analysis (such as *live variables* computation) or program abstraction can be applied. Moreover, this API is also well suited to implement translators from IF to other specification formalisms.

The **semantic model level** gives access to the LTS representing the behaviour of
the IF program. Depending on the application considered, three kinds of API are
proposed:

- The *implicit enumerative representation* consists in a set of C functions and
  data structures allowing to compute on demand the successors of a given state
  (following the OPEN-CAESAR [11] philosophy). This piece of C code is generated
  by the IF2C compiler, and it can be linked with a "generic" exploration program
  performing *on-the-fly* analysis.
- In the *symbolic representation* sets of states and transitions of the LTS are expressed by their characteristic predicates over a set of finite variables. These predicates are implemented using decision diagrams (BDDs). Existing applications
  based on this API are symbolic model-checking and minimal model generation.
- Finally, the *explicit enumerative representation* simply consists in an LTS file
  with an associated access library. Although such an explicit representation is
  not suitable for handling large systems globally, it is still useful in practice to
  minimize some of its abstractions with respect to bisimulation based relations.

3 Components Description

We briefly present here the main components of the environment, together with
some external tools for which a strong connection exists.

The specification level components. *Object*GEODE [20] is a commercial toolset
developed by TTT supporting SDL, MSC and OMT. In particular, this toolset provides an API to access the abstract tree generated from an SDL specification. We
have used this API to implement the SDL2IF translator, which generates operationally equivalent IF specifications from SDL ones. Given the static nature of IF, this
translation does not cover the dynamical features of SDL (e.g., process instances
creation).

The intermediate level components. LIVE [5] implements several algorithms
based on static analysis to transform an IF specification. A first transformation
concerns *dead variable resetting* (a variable is dead at some control point if its value
is not used before being redefined). This optimisation can be also applied to buffer
contents (a message parameter is dead if its value is not used when the message is
consumed). Although very simple, such optimisation is particularly efficient for state
space generation (reductions up to a factor 100 were frequently observed), while
preserving the exact behaviour of the original specification. A second transformation
is based on the *slicing* technique [21]. It allows to automatically abstract a given
specification by eliminating some irrelevant parts w.r.t. a given property or test
purpose [6].

IF2PML [4] is a tool developed at Eindhoven TU to translate IF specifications into
PROMELA.

The semantic model level components. CADP [9] is a toolset for the verification
of LOTOS specifications. It is developed by the VASY team of INRIA Rhône-Alpes
and VERIMAG. Two of its model-checkers are connected to the IF environment:
ALDEBARAN (bisimulation based), and EVALUATOR (alternating-free μ-calculus).

For both tools, diagnostic sequences are computed on the LTS level and they can be translated back into MSC to be observed at the specification level.

KRONOS [22] is a model-checker for symbolic verification of TCTL formulae on communicating timed automata. The current connection with the IF environment is as follows: control states and discrete variables are expressed using the implicit enumerative representation, whereas clocks are expressed using a symbolic representation (particular polyhedra).

TGV [10] is a test sequence generator for conformance testing of distributed systems (joint work between VERIMAG and the PAMPA project of IRISA). Test cases are computed during the exploration of the model and they are selected by means of *test purposes*.

4 Results and Perspectives

The IF environment has already been used to analyze some representative SDL specifications, like SSCOP, an ATM signalisation layer protocol [8], and MASCARA, an ATM wireless transport protocol. It is currently used in several on going industrial case-studies, including the real-time multicast protocol PGM, and the control part of the ARIANE 5 launcher flight sequencer. The benefits of combining several techniques, working at different program level, were clearly demonstrated. In particular, traditional model-checking techniques (as provided by *Object*GEODE) were not sufficient to complete on these large size examples.

Several directions can be investigated to improve this environment.

First of all, other formalisms than SDL could be connected to IF. In particular, the translation from a subset of UML is envisaged. To this purpose new features will be added to handle *dynamic process creation* and *parametrized network specifications*.

From the verification point of view, the results obtained using the currently implemented static analysis techniques are very encouraging. We now plan to experiment some more sophisticated algorithms implemented in the INVEST tool [2], such as *structural invariant generation* and general *abstraction computation techniques* for infinite space systems.

Another promising approach to verify large systems consists in generating their underlying model in a *compositional* way: each sub-system is generated in isolation, and the resulting LTSs are minimized before being composed with each other. The IF environment offers all the required components to experiment it in an asynchronous framework [17].

The IF package can be downloaded at http://www-verimag.imag.fr/DIST_SYS/IF.

References

[1] Telelogic AB. *SDT Reference Manual.* http://www.telelogic.se.
[2] S. Bensalem, Y. Lakhnech, and S. Owre. Computing Abstractions of Infinite State Systems Compositionally and Automatically. In *Proceedings of CAV'98*, vol. 1427 of *LNCS*, p. 319–331. Springer, June 1998.

[3] S. Bornot, J. Sifakis, and S. Tripakis. Modeling Urgency in Timed Systems. In *International Symposium: Compositionality - The Significant Difference*, vol. 1536 of *LNCS*. Springer, September 1997.
[4] D. Bošnački, D. Dams, L. Holenderski, and N. Sidorova. Model Checking SDL with Spin. In *Proceedings of TACAS'2000*, vol. 1785 of *LNCS*, p. 363–377. March 2000.
[5] M. Bozga, J.Cl. Fernandez, and L. Ghirvu. State Space Reduction based on Live Variables Analysis. In *Proceedings of SAS'99*, vol. 1694 of *LNCS*, p. 164–178. Springer, September 1999.
[6] M. Bozga, J.Cl. Fernandez, and L. Ghirvu. Using Static Analysis to Improve Automatic Test Generation. In *Proceedings of TACAS'00*, vol. 1785 in LNCS, p. 235–250. March 2000.
[7] M. Bozga, J.Cl. Fernandez, L. Ghirvu, S. Graf, J.P. Krimm, and L. Mounier. IF: An Intermediate Representation and Validation Environment for Timed Asynchronous Systems. In *Proceedings of FM'99*, vol. 1708 of *LNCS*, p. 307–327. September 1999.
[8] M. Bozga, J.Cl. Fernandez, L. Ghirvu, C. Jard, T. Jéron, A. Kerbrat, P. Morel, and L. Mounier. Verification and Test Generation for the SSCOP Protocol. *Journal of Science of Computer Programming, Special Isssue on Formal Methods in Industry*, 36(1):27–52, January 2000.
[9] J.Cl. Fernandez, H. Garavel, A. Kerbrat, R. Mateescu, L. Mounier, and M. Sighireanu. CADP: A Protocol Validation and Verification Toolbox. In *Proceedings of CAV'96*, vol. 1102 of *LNCS*, p. 437–440. Springer, August 1996.
[10] J.Cl. Fernandez, C. Jard, T. Jéron, and C. Viho. An Experiment in Automatic Generation of Test Suites for Protocols with Verification Technology. *Science of Computer Programming*, 29, 1997.
[11] H. Garavel. OPEN/CÆSAR: An Open Software Architecture for Verification, Simulation, and Testing. In *Proceedings of TACAS'98*, vol. 1384 of *LNCS*, p. 68–84. March 1998.
[12] T.H. Henzinger, P.-H. Ho, and H. Wong-Toi. HyTech : A Model Checker for Hybrid Systems. In *Proceedings of CAV'97*, vol. 1254 of *LNCS*, p. 460–463. June 1997.
[13] Gerard J. Holzmann. *Design and Validation of Computer Protocols*. Prentice Hall Software Series, 1991.
[14] I-Logix. *StateMate.* http://www.ilogix.com/.
[15] ISO/IEC. LOTOS — A Formal Description Technique Based on the Temporal Ordering of Observational Behaviour. Technical Report 8807, ISO/OSI, 1988.
[16] ITU-T. Recommendation Z.100. Specification and Description Language (SDL). Technical Report Z-100, International Telecommunication Union – Standardization Sector, Genève, 1994.
[17] J.P. Krimm and L. Mounier. Compositional State Space Generation with Partial Order Reductions for Asynchronous Communicating Systems. In *Proceedings of TACAS'2000*, vol. 1785 of *LNCS*, p. 266–282. March 2000.
[18] K.G. Larsen, P. Petterson, and W. Yi. UPPAAL: Status & Developments. In *Proceedings of CAV'97*, vol. 1254 of *LNCS*, p. 456–459. June 1997.
[19] K.L. McMillan. *Symbolic Model Checking: an Approach to the State Explosion Problem*. Kluwer Academic Publisher, 1993.
[20] Verilog. *ObjectGEODE Reference Manual.* http://www.verilogusa.com/.
[21] M. Weiser. Program Slicing. *IEEE Transactions on Software Engineering*, SE-10(4), July 1984.
[22] S. Yovine. KRONOS: A Verification Tool for Real-Time Systems. *Software Tools for Technology Transfer*, 1(1+2):123–133, December 1997.

Integrating WS1S with PVS*

Sam Owre and Harald Rueß

Computer Science Laboratory
SRI International
333 Ravenswood Ave
Menlo Park, CA 94025, USA
{owre, ruess}@csl.sri.com

There is a growing trend to integrate theorem proving systems with specialized decision procedures and model checking systems. The proving capabilities of the PVS theorem prover, for example, have been improved considerably by extending it with new proof tactics based on a BDD package, a μ-calculus model-checker [4], and a polyhedral library. In this way, a theorem proving system like PVS provides a common front-end and specification language for a variety of specialized tools. This makes it possible to use a whole arsenal of verification and validation methods in a seamless way, combine them using a strategy language, and provide development chain analysis.

Here we describe a novel PVS tactic for deciding an interesting fragment of PVS that corresponds to the *Weak Second-order Theory of 1 Successor*, WS1S. This logic may not only be viewed as a highly succinct alternative to the use of regular expressions, but can also be used to encode Presburger arithmetic or quantified boolean logic. The decidability of WS1S is based on the fact that regular languages may be characterized by logics. However, this automata-theoretic procedure is of staggering complexity, namely non-elementary.

Although this logic-automaton connection has been known for more than 40 years, it was only through the recent work at BRICS that it become possible to make effective use of automata-based decision procedures for logics like WS1S. Their tool, called MONA [2], acts as a decision procedure and as a translator to finite-state automata. It is based on new algorithms for minimizing finite-state automata using binary decision diagrams (BDDs) to represent transition functions in compressed form. Various applications of MONA—including hardware verification, validation of software design constraints, and establishing safety and liveness conditions for distributed systems—are mentioned in [2].

We are using the efficient automata-construction capabilities of MONA for building a tactic that decides a fragment of the PVS specification language. This fragment includes boolean expressions, arithmetic on the natural numbers restricted to addition/subtraction with/from a constant, and operations on finite sets over the naturals like union, intersection, set difference, addition and removal of a natural. Predicates include arithmetic comparisons, equality, disequality, the subset relation, and membership in the form of function application P(i).

---

* This research was funded by DARPA AO D855 under US Air Force Rome Laboratory contract F30602-96-C-0204 and by the National Science Foundation Contract No. CCR-9712383.

Moreover, there is quantification over the booleans, the natural numbers, finite sets of naturals, and predicate subtypes of the aforementioned types built from WS1S formulas. Finite sets of natural numbers may also be described using the choice operator the. In this way, ripple-carry addition may be defined as follows.

```
+(P, Q: finite_set[nat]): finite_set[nat] =                                    1
  the({R | EXISTS (C: finite_set[nat]): NOT(C(0)) AND
          FORALL (t: nat):
            (C(t+1) = ((P(t)&Q(t)) OR (P(t)&C(t)) OR (Q(t)&C(t)))) &
            (R(t) = P(t) = Q(t) = C(t))});
```

Here a natural number k is mapped to a set of indices corresponding to 1's in the binary representation of k; e.g., 10 is represented as {1,3}. Usually, functions are encoded in a relational style in WS1S, but the inclusion of the choice operator allows one to provide functional representation. Notice that the carry vector C is hidden by means of second-order quantification.

This fragment of the PVS language is being decided by associating an automata with every formula. This translation proceeds in two steps. First, definitions are unfolded to transform formulas into the language of WS1S. In this step, the full arsenal of theorem proving capabilities of PVS, including decision procedures, rewriting, and lemma application, may be used to simplify the resulting formula. The second step of the translation traverses this formula and recursively builds up a corresponding automata that recognizes the language of interpretations of the PVS formula. Here we use foreign function calls to directly call the C functions of the MONA library [2] from the Lisp implementation of PVS.

Moreover, we use facilities provided by the Allegro Lisp garbage collector to also take the automaton and BDD data structures of MONA into account. In this way, we create a transparent and functional view of the MONA capabilities. This makes it possible, for example, to memoize the translation process. In addition, the translation of PVS formulas to deterministic finite automata includes abstraction. Whenever the translator encounters a PVS expression outside the scope of WS1S, it creates a new variable—of type nat, bool, or finite_set[nat], depending on the type of the expression—and replaces the original expression with this variable throughout the formula. This abstraction increases the scope of our proof procedure. When the expression to be abstracted away includes bound variables, however, the translator gives up. Abstraction has been found particularly useful in the analysis of state machines, where the state usually consists of a record of state components and the specification includes accesses to these components that can easily be abstracted. This translation has been packaged as a new PVS tactic.

```
stamps: LEMMA                                                                  2
    FORALL (i: finite_set[nat]): i >= [| 8 |] =>
      EXISTS (j, k: finite_set[nat]): i = 3 * j + 5 * k
```

```
ltl: THEORY
BEGIN
   time : TYPE = nat;
   tpred: TYPE = finite_set[time]

   t, t1  : VAR time
   P, Q, R: VAR tpred

   [](P)(t): boolean = FORALL (t1: upfrom[t]): P(t1);
   <>(P)(t): boolean = EXISTS (t1: upfrom[t]): P(t1);

   |=(P): boolean = P(0);           % Validity

   WF(A, EA, I: tpred): tpred = ([]<>(A & NOT(I))) OR []<>(NOT(EA));
   SF(A, EA, I: tpred): tpred = ([]<>(A & NOT(I))) OR <>[](NOT(EA));
END ltl
```

Fig. 1. Encoding of a Linear Temporal Logic

Consider, for example, the Presburger formula stamps, where ∗ is defined by iterating addition as defined above, and [| k |] is a recursively defined function for computing a finite set that represents the unsigned representation of k.[1]
This inductive property is shown to be valid by simply calling the (ws1s) tactic within the PVS prover, since, after unfolding and unwinding all definitions, including the recursive ones, the associated automata recognizes the full language of interpretations. Most proof attempts, however, fail.

```
   (EXISTS (x: nat): x = 100 & P!1(x))
 & (EXISTS (x: nat): x = 111 & P!1(x))
 & (FORALL (i: nat): i /= 100 & i /= 111 => NOT P!1(i))
```

This formula is neither valid nor unsatisfiable. Thus, the tactic (ws1s) returns with a counterexample (P!1 = emptyset[nat]) and a witness (P!1 = add(111, add(100, emptyset[nat]))) for the free variable P!1.

Using the approach outlined above we have encoded various theories in WS1S: Presburger arithmetic, lossy queues, regular expressions, a restricted linear temporal logic (LTL), and fixed-sized bitvectors. The complete encoding of a LTL, including definitions for weak and strong fairness is shown in Figure 1. Boolean connectives do not have to be defined explicitly for this logic, since the conversion mechanism of PVS [3] automatically lifts the built-in logic connectors to the type tpred. Regular expressions are represented by means of a datatype, and a recursively defined meaning function associates the WS1S defined set of

---

[1] Notice that [| k |] is not a WS1S arithmetic relation, because otherwise one could define addition directly on the natural numbers; but this is outside the scope of WS1S.

words recognized by this regular expression; hereby, a word is of type `[below[N] -> finite_set[nat]]`, where `N` specifies an alphabet of size `expt(2,N)`.

Notice that we automatically have a decision procedure for the combination of the encoded theories mentioned above, since all encodings are definitional extensions of the base language of WS1S. Moreover, the list of encoded theories is open-ended.

Among other applications we have been using the (`ws1s`) tactic for discharging verification conditions that have been generated using the abstraction method described in [1]. These examples usually involve a combination of the lossy queue theory and regular expressions. Also, quantifier reasoning and Skolemization has to be used to transform the formulas under consideration into the fragment supported by the translation process. For example, universal-strength quantification over words needs Skolemization, since words are elements of a third-order type (see above). After preprocessing and unfolding the definitions, verification conditions are typically proved within a fraction of a second.

Altogether, the WS1S decision procedures enrich PVS by providing new automated proving capabilities, an alternative approach for combining decision procedures, and a method for generating counterexamples from failed proof attempts. On the other hand, this integration provides an appealing frontend and input language for the MONA tool, and permits using automata-theoretic decision procedures in conjunction with both traditional theorem proving techniques and specialized symbolic analysis like abstraction. This connection, however, needs further exploration.

The WS1S decision procedure has been integrated with PVS 2.3, which has been released in fall '99. PVS 2.3 is freely available at `pvs.csl.sri.com`.

Acknowledgements. We would like to thank A. Møller for clarifying discussions about MONA internals, M. Sorea for comments on this paper, and S. Bensalem for providing interesting test cases.

References

[1] P.A. Abdulla, A. Annichini, S. Bensalem, A. Bouajjani, P. Habermehl, and Y. Lakhnech. Verification of infinite-state systems by combining abstraction and reachability analysis. volume 1633 of *Lecture Notes in Computer Science*, pages 146–159, Trento, Italy, July 1999. Springer-Verlag.

[2] N. Klarlund and A. Møller. *MONA Version 1.3 User Manual.* BRICS Notes Series NS-98-3, Dept. of Computer Science, University of Aarhus, October 1998.

[3] S. Owre, N. Shankar, J. M. Rushby, and D. W. J. Stringer-Calvert. *PVS Language Reference.* Computer Science Laboratory, SRI International, Menlo Park, CA, September 1999.

[4] S. Rajan, N. Shankar, and M.K. Srivas. An integration of model-checking with automated proof checking. In Pierre Wolper, editor, *Computer-Aided Verification, CAV '95*, volume 939 of *Lecture Notes in Computer Science*, pages 84–97, Liege, Belgium, June 1995. Springer-Verlag.

PET: An Interactive Software Testing Tool

Elsa Gunter, Robert Kurshan, and Doron Peled

Bell Laboratories
600 Mountain Ave.
Murray Hill, NJ 07974

Abstract. We describe here the PET (standing for *path exploration tool*) system, developed in Bell Labs. This new tool allows an interactive testing of sequential or concurrent programs, using techniques taken from deductive program verification. It automatically generates and displays a graphical representation of the flow graph, and links the visual representation to the code. Testing is done by selecting execution paths, or, in the case of concurrent programs, interleaved sequences of code. The PET system calculates the exact condition to execute path being selected, in terms of the program variables. It also calculates (when possible) whether this condition is vacuous (never satisfied) or universal (always satisfied). The user can then edit the path and select variants of it by either extending it, truncating it, or switching the order of appearance of concurrent events. This testing approach is not limited to finite state systems, and hence can be used in cases where a completely automatic verification cannot be applied.

1 Introduction

Software testing is the most commonly used method for enhancing the quality of computer software. Testing is done usually in a rather informal way, such as by walking through the code or inspecting the various potential pitfalls of the program [1]. Methods that are more formal, such as model checking or deductive theorem proving, which have been used very successfully for hardware verification, have not succeeded to gain superiority in the area of software reliability. Deductive verification of actual software systems is very time consuming, while model checking suffers from the state space explosion problem, and is, in most cases, restricted to the handling finite state systems.

Concurrent programs may exhibit complicated interactions that can make debugging and testing them a difficult task. We describe here a tool that helps the user to test sequential or concurrent software using a graphical interface. It allows the user to walk through the code by selecting execution paths from the flow graph of the program. The most general relation between the program variables that is necessary in order to execute the selected path is calculated and reported back to the user. An attempt is made to decide using the path condition whether the path is at all executable. The user can edit the execution paths by adding, truncating and exchanging (in case of a concurrent program) the order of the transitions.

The PET tool is based on symbolic computation ideas taken from program verification. It allows more general ways of debugging programs than simulating one execution of the checked code at a time, as each path of the flow graph corresponds to all the executions that are consistent with it.

The input language to current implementation of PET is Pascal, extended with communication and synchronization constructs for concurrent programming. However, Pascal is just one possible choice. The main principles, on which this tool is based, can be used with other formalisms. In fact, it is quite easy to change the input language from Pascal to, e.g., C, SDL or VHDL.

Part of the problem in software testing and verification is coping with scalability. The PET tool also contains an abstraction algorithm, which can be applied during the compilation of the code. The algorithm attempts to abstract out certain variables and presents a *projection* of the program. That is, the obtained program is a simplified version in which some of the variables are abstracted away. This produces a simplified version of the program, allowing the user to better understand certain aspects of the code.

2 PET: Path Exploration Tool

A flow graph is a visual representation of a program. In the PET system [2], a node in a flow graph is one of the following: *begin, end, predicate, random, wait, assign, send* or *receive*. The *begin* and *end* nodes appear as ovals, the *predicate, wait* and *random* nodes appear as diamonds, labeled by a condition, or the word *random*, in the latter case. All other nodes appear as boxes labeled by the assignment, send or receive statement.

Each node, together with its output edge constitutes a *transition*, i.e., an atomic operation of the program, which can depend on some condition (e.g., the current program counter, an *if-then-else* or a while *condition* in the node, the nonemptiness of a communication queue) and make some changes to the program variables (including message queues and program counters). Notice that a *predicate* node corresponds to a pair of transitions: one with the predicate holding (corresponding to the 'yes' outedge), and one with the predicate not holding (corresponding to the 'no' outedge).

Unit testing [1] is based on examining paths. Different *coverage techniques* suggest criteria for the appropriate coverage of a program by different paths. Our tool leaves the choice of the paths to the user (a future version will allow a semi-automatic choice of the paths which uses various coverage algorithm in order to suggest the path selection, e.g., based on the coverage techniques in [1, 4]). The user can choose a path by clicking on the appropriate nodes on the flow graph.

In order to make the connection between the code, the flow chart and the selected path clearer, sensitive highlighting is used. For example, when the cursor points at some predicate node in the flow graph window, the corresponding text is highlighted in the process window. The code corresponding to a predicate node can be, e.g., an *if-then-else* or a *while* condition.

Once a path is fixed, the condition to execute it is calculated, based on repeated symbolic calculation of preconditions, as in program verification [3]. The condition is calculated backwards, starting with *true*. Thus, we proceed from a *postcondition* of a transition, in order to calculate its *precondition*. In order to calculate the precondition given the transition and the postcondition, we apply various transformations to the current condition, until we arrive to the beginning of the paths. For a transition that consists of a predicate p with the 'yes' outedge, we transform the current condition from c to $c \wedge p$. The same predicate with the 'no' outedge, results in $c \wedge \neg p$. For an assignment of the form $x := e$, we replace in p every (free) occurrence of the variable x in the postcondition c by the expression e. We start the calculation with the postcondition *true* at the end of the selected path. Other kinds of transitions will be discussed later.

PET then allows altering the path by removing nodes from the end, in reversed order to their prior selection, or by appending new nodes. This allows, for example, the selection of an alternative choice for a condition (after the nodes that were chosen past that predicate nodes are removed). Another way to alter a path is to use the same transitions but allow a different interleaving of them. When dealing with concurrent programs, the way the execution of transitions from different nodes are interleaved is perhaps the foremost source of errors. The PET tool allows the user to flip the order of adjacent transitions on the path, when they belong to different processes.

The most important information that is provided by PET is the condition to execute a selected path. The meaning of the calculated path condition is different for sequential and concurrent or nondeterministic programs. In a sequential deterministic program, the condition expresses exactly the possible assignments that would *ensure* executing the selected path, starting from the first selected node. When concurrency or nondeterminism are allowed, because of possible alternative interleavings of the transitions or alternative nondeterministic choices, the condition expresses the assignments that would make the execution of the selected path *possible*. The path condition obtained in this process is simplified using rewriting rules, based on arithmetic. Subexpressions that contain only integer arithmetic without multiplication (Pressburger arithmetic) are further simplified using decision procedures (see [2]). In this case, we can also check algorithmically whether the path condition is equivalent to *false* (meaning that this path can never be executed), or to *true*.

In order to allow testing of communication protocols, one needs to add *send* and *receive* communication operations. Our choice is that of *asynchronous* communication, as its use seems to be more frequently used. The syntax of Pascal is then extended with two types of transitions:

ch!exp The calculated value of the expression exp is added to the end of the communication queue ch. (we will henceforce assume the queues are not limited to any particular capacity).

ch?var The first item of the communication queue ch is removed and assigned to the variable var. This transition cannot be executed if the queue ch is empty.

Typical communication protocols would allow a concurrent process to wait for the first communication arriving from one out of multiple available communications. The *random* construct represents nondeterministic choice and can be used for that. An example for a choice of one out of three communications is as follows:

```
if random then
    if random then ch7?x
              else ch2?z
    else ch3?t
```

For the communication constraints, the translation algorithm scans the path in the forward direction. Whenever a *send* transition of the form `ch!exp` occurs, it introduces a new temporary variable, say `temp`, and replaces the transition by the assignment `temp:=exp`. It also adds `temp` to a queue, named as the communication channel `ch`. When a *receive* transition `ch?var` occurs, the oldest element `temp` in the queue `ch` is removed, and the *receive* transition is replaced by `var:=temp`. This translation produces a path that is equivalent to the original one in the case that all the queues were empty prior to the execution of the path. We can easily generalize this to allow the case where there are values already in the queues when the execution of the path begins.

Transition	queue	transformed	condition
P1:x:=3	ch=⟨⟩		*false*
P1:ch1!x+y	ch=⟨temp1⟩	temp1:=x+y	$x > 3$
P1:ch1!x	ch=⟨temp1, temp2⟩	temp2:=x	$x > 3$
P1:x:=4	ch=⟨temp1, temp2⟩		$temp2 > 3$
P2: ch1?t	ch=⟨temp2⟩	t:=temp1	$temp2 > 3$
P2: ch1?z	ch=⟨⟩	z:=temp2	$temp2 > 3$
P2: z>3	ch=⟨⟩		$z > 3$
P2: z:=z+1	ch=⟨⟩		*true*

Fig. 1. A path with its calculated condition

In Figure 1, the replacement is applied to a path with communication transitions. The first column describes the path. The second column denotes the (single in this example) queue used to facilitate the translation. The third column denotes the translated transitions (it is left empty in the cases where the translation maintain the original transition). The last column gives the calculated path condition (calculated backwards).

The user can select to project out a set of program variables. PET checks if there are assignments to other variables that use any of the projected variables. If there are, it reports to the user which additional variables need to be projected out. The projection algorithm removes the assignments to the projected variables and replaces predicates that use them by a nondeterministic choice.

References

[1] G.J. Myers, The Art of Software Testing, John Wiley and Sons, 1979.
[2] E.L. Gunter, D. Peled, Path Exploration Tool, to appear in Tools and Algorithms for the Construction and Analysis of Systems (TACAS), Amsterdam, 1999.
[3] C.A.R. Hoare, An axiomatic basis for computer programming, Communication of the ACM 12, 1969, 576-580.
[4] S. Rapps, E.J. Weyuker, Selecting Software Test Data Using Data Flow Information, Transactions on Software Engineering 11(4): 367-375 (1985).

A Proof-Carrying Code Architecture for Java

Christopher Colby, Peter Lee, and George C. Necula

Cedilla Systems Incorporated
4616 Henry Street
Pittsburgh, Pennsylvania 15213
Hackers@CedillaSystems.com

1 Introduction

In earlier work, Necula and Lee developed *proof-carrying code* (PCC) [3,5], which is a mechanism for ensuring the safe behavior of programs. In PCC, a program contains both the code and an encoding of an easy-to-check proof. The validity of the proof, which can be automatically determined by a simple proof-checking program, implies that the code, when executed, will behave safely according to a user-supplied formal definition of safe behavior. Later, Necula and Lee demonstrated the concept of a *certifying compiler* [6,7]. Certifying compilers promise to make PCC more practical by compiling high-level source programs into optimized PCC binaries completely automatically, as opposed to depending on semi-automatic theorem-proving techniques. Taken together, PCC and certifying compilers provide a possible solution to the code safety problem, even in applications involving mobile code [4].

In this paper we describe a PCC architecture comprising two tools:

- A thin PCC layer implemented in C that protects a host system from unsafe software. The host system can be anything from a desktop computer down to a smartcard. The administrator of the host system specifies a safety policy in a variant of the Edinburgh Logical Framework (LF) [1]. This layer loads PCC binaries, which are Intel x86 object files that contain a .lf section providing a binary encoding of a safety proof, and checks them against the safety policy before installing the software.
- A software-development tool that produces x86 PCC binaries from Java .class files. It is implemented in Objective Caml [2]. From a developer's perspective, this tool works just like any other compiler, with an interface similar to javac or gcc. Behind the scenes, the tool produces x86 machine code along with a proof of type safety according to the Java typing rules.

The demonstration will use a small graphics program to show that this architecture delivers Java safety guarantees without sacrificing the performance of native compilation.

2 Architecture

Figure 1 shows the architecture of our PCC system. The right side of the figure shows the software-development process, and the left side shows the secure host system. VC stands for "verification condition".

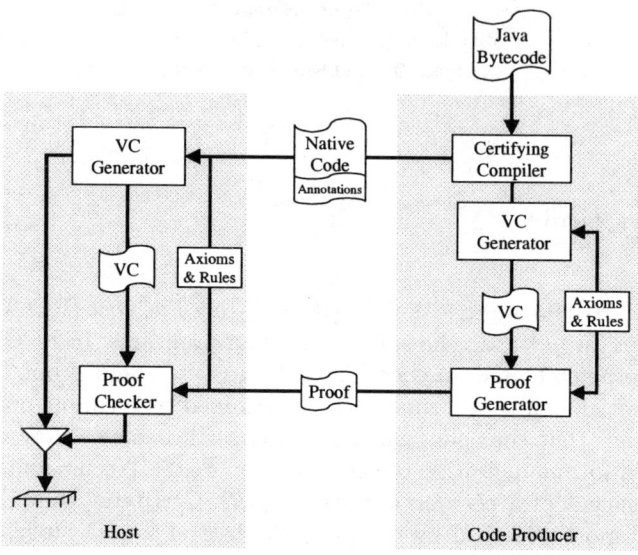

Fig. 1. The architecture of our PCC implementation.

The right side of Figure 1 is a code-production tool that the user runs offline to generate Intel x86 PCC binaries from Java bytecode. First, a compiler generates x86 native code from a Java .class file. This compiler is largely conventional except that it attaches some logical annotations to the resulting binary. These annotations are "hints" that help the rest of the system understand how the native code output corresponds to the bytecode input. These annotations are easy for the compiler to generate from the bytecode, but would be difficult for the rest of the system to "reverse engineer" from unannotated native code.

The annotated x86 binary is then analyzed by a tool called a verification-condition generator, or *VC generator*. The VC generator is parameterized by a set of axioms and rules, specified in the Edinburgh Logical Framework (LF), that describe the safety policy against which the binary must be proven. The VC generator outputs a logical predicate, also expressed in LF, that describes a precondition that, if true, would imply that any possible execution of the binary is safe. Intuitively speaking, it performs this task by scanning each native-code instruction and emitting safety conditions as they arise. The result is called the verification condition, or *VC*.

Finally, the VC is sent to an automated theorem prover, which, using the same axioms and rules, attempts to prove the VC and, if successful, outputs the resulting logical proof in binary form. The annotations and proof are added to the binary as an .lf segment, thus producing a PCC binary. This object file can be loaded and linked with existing tools just like any other object file, in which case the .lf section is ignored. Currently, proofs are 10–40% of the code size, but preliminary results with a new proof-representation technology indicate that this can be decreased to 5–10% [8].

Now we turn to the host on the left side of Figure 1. The host runs a thin PCC layer that loads PCC binaries and verifies them. The host first separates the annotated binary from the proof. In Figure 1, these are shown already separated. It then runs a VC generator on the annotated binary to produce a VC from a safety policy specified by the same set of rules and axioms.[1] Lastly, it checks the proof to make sure that it is indeed a valid proof under the safety policy. If it checks out, then the unannotated binary is installed on the host system. The annotations and the proof are discarded.

The PCC layer on the host illustrates another key engineering point that makes the PCC architecture viable—checking a proof is usually much faster and simpler than generating a proof. It is important that it is *fast* because it is happening dynamically, as software is downloaded into the host. It is important that it is *simple* because the trusted computing base (TCB) on the host must be bug-free. Furthermore, some of our current applications involve small embedded systems that lack memory resources to run large programs. For these reasons, it is unacceptable to run a complex verifier on the host system.

In contrast, PCC development tools such as the code producer on the right side of Figure 1 can be slow and buggy without compromising the soundness of the basic architecture that we are proposing in this demonstration. For instance, the compiler is free to perform aggressive optimizations, even though that might present difficult and time-consuming problems for the proof generator, because proof generation is done offline. Technically, this result is provided by a soundness theorem [6]. This result is not specific to any particular code-production tool, to Java, or to any particular safety policy, but rather is a property of the PCC architecture itself.

3 Demonstration

We have implemented prototypes of both sides of Figure 1 for the Intel x86 architecture. The certifying compiler performs register allocation and some global optimizations, including a form of partial redundancy elimination. The VC generator and proof checker are quite complete and have been stable for several months. The compiler and proof generator, on the other hand, are still under heavy development. At present, the compiler handles a large subset of the Java

---

[1] The system that we demonstrate shares the same VC generator between the two sides of the architecture, and this is often a convenient approach. Conceptually, however, the host's module is part of the TCB and thus must be bug-free, while the code producer's module is not trusted, and so bugs will simply produce incorrect binaries that will be caught by the host before installation.

features, including objects, exceptions, and floating-point arithmetic. However, there are several key features that have yet to be implemented, including threads and dynamic class loading. Also, a number of important optimizations are not yet finished, including the elimination of null-pointer and array-bounds checks, and the stack allocation of non-escaping objects.

The demonstration will use a small graphics program to show that this architecture delivers Java safety guarantees without sacrificing the performance of native compilation. The demonstration will compare three different approaches to transmitting untrusted code to a secure host:

1. Java bytecode, verified and run by a JVM on the host (safe but slow)
2. x86 native code produced by a C compiler, run via the Java Native Interface (JNI) on the host (fast but unsafe)
3. x86 native code produced by our certifying compiler, run via JNI on the host (fast and safe)

We demonstrate the safety of our approach (3) by showing that various forms of tampering with the PCC binary cause the host to reject the binary as potentially unsafe.

In future work, we plan to release our current system for public use. Also of great interest is to extend the safety policy to go beyond Java type safety, in particular to allow enforcement of some constraints on the use of resources such as execution time and memory.

References

[1] Robert Harper, Furio Honsell, and Gordon Plotkin. A framework for defining logics. *Journal of the Association for Computing Machinery*, 40(1):143–184, January 1993.
[2] Xavier Leroy. The ZINC experiment, an economical implementation of the ML language. Technical Report 117, INRIA, 1990.
[3] George Necula and Peter Lee. Safe kernel extensions without run-time checking. In *Second Symposium on Operating Systems Design and Implementation*, pages 229–243, Seattle, October 1996.
[4] George Necula and Peter Lee. Safe, untrusted agents using proof-carrying code. In *Special Issue on Mobile Agent Security*, volume 1419 of *Lecture Notes in Computer Science*. Springer-Verlag, October 1997.
[5] George C. Necula. Proof-carrying code. In Neil D. Jones, editor, *Conference Record of the 24th Symposium on Principles of Programming Languages (POPL'97)*, pages 106–119, Paris, France, January 1997. ACM Press.
[6] George C. Necula. *Compiling with Proofs*. PhD thesis, Carnegie Mellon University, October 1998. Available as Technical Report CMU-CS-98-154.
[7] George C. Necula and Peter Lee. The design and implementation of a certifying compiler. In Keith D. Cooper, editor, *Proceedings of the Conference on Programming Language Design and Implementation (PLDI'98)*, pages 333–344, Montreal, Canada, June 1998. ACM Press.
[8] George C. Necula and Shree P. Rahul. Oracle-based checking of untrusted software. Submitted to Programming Language Design and Implementation, PLDI'00, November 1999.

The STATEMATE Verification Environment
Making It Real

Tom Bienmüller[1], Werner Damm[2], and Hartmut Wittke[2]

[1] Carl von Ossietzky University, 26111 Oldenburg, Germany
Bienmueller@Informatik.Uni-Oldenburg.DE
[2] OFFIS, Escherweg 2, 26121 Oldenburg, Germany
{Damm, Wittke}@OFFIS.DE

Abstract. The STATEMATE Verification Environment supports requirement analysis and specification development of embedded controllers as part of the STATEMATE product offering of I-Logix, Inc. This paper discusses key enhancements of the prototype tool reported in [2,5] in order to enable full scale industrial usage of the tool-set. It thus reports on a successfully completed technology transfer from a prototype tool-set to a commercial offering. The discussed enhancements are substantiated with performance results all taken from real industrial applications of leading companies in automotive and avionics.

1 Introduction

This paper reports on a successful technology transfer, taking a prototype verification system for STATEMATE [2,5] to a version available as commercial product offering. It is only through the significant improvements reported in this paper that key companies are now taking up this technology in an industrial setting. In particular, other approaches such as [15,14], though similar in overall goal, did as of today not reach a comparable level neither in quality of handling nor degree of captured complexity.

The leading players in automotive and avionics base their product developments on well established and highly matured process models, typically variations of the well known V-model originally introduced as a standard for military avionics applications. E.g. [16] reports on the development process and process improvements of Aerospatiale, documenting the benefits of a model based development process. Overall product quality is critically dependent on the familiarity of system and software designers with the established process, and any change, in particular the introduction of a technology completely novel to designers, can potentially cause significant process degradation, thus leading to quality reduction rather than quality enhancements. It is thus essential to tune layout and handling to use-cases well understood and easily appreciated by designers. Particular causes of concern identified in numerous discussions with industrial partners are:

- *scariness of formal methods*: With a typical background in mechanical or electrical engineering, it is prohibitive to expose any of the underlying mathematical machinery to designers. We tried to maintain as much of the "look and feel" of the simulation capabilities of the tool-set, offering in particular pure push button analysis techniques described in Section 2, which completely hide the underlying

verification technology. We spent a significant effort in providing a tight integration with STATEMATE for all verification related activities, as described in Section 4.
- *relation to testing*: A standard topic of discussion is the relation to testing, which typically causes confusion. The techniques are complementary, but model-checking can take over a significant part traditionally handled by testing. In terms of the V-diagram, the so-called virtual V supports model based integration of components of subsystems, and model-checking based verification can replace all model-based testing (if clear interface specifications are given), as well as capture a large share of errors typically detected today in integration testing. We found that test engineers not only accept but appreciate a transition, in which the traditional activity of designing test sequences for properties captured only informally or even mentally is replaced by the process of capturing these in forms of requirement patterns (provided as library), leaving construction of test-sequences to the model-checker.
- *user models*: Test engineers constitute only one out of a number of identified classes of users. While there are differences in company cultures, we feel that a second prominent use-case of model-checking rests in its capabilities as a powerful debugging tool, simply reducing the number of iterations until stable models are achieved, and thus reducing development costs.

Of slightly different nature, though similar in spirit, is the introduction of a methodology for supporting successive refinements of abstractions. We allow to selectively "degrade" accuracy, with which the model-checker tracks computations on selected objects within the cone-of-influence for a given property. In particular, all tests dependent on floats are over approximated, while for objects with finite domain a more refined view of computations can be maintained (see Section 3). This technique is complemented by a symbolic evaluation engine, whose underlying machinery rests on a simplified, but restricted version of the first-order model-checking algorithm documented in [1]—see [1] for a description of the use of these enhancement on automotive applications.

While the prototype system reported in [2,5] was based on the SVE system [10], the current version rests on a tight integration with the VIS model-checker [11] and the CUDD BDD package [17], yielding in average a five time performance boost for model-generation times and a 50% speed-up for model-checking.

Acknowledgments. The development of the STATEMATE verification environment has been a collaborative effort of our research team. We gratefully acknowledge the excellent cooperation with Jürgen Bohn, Udo Brockmeyer, Claus Eßmann, Martin Fränzle, Hans Jürgen Holberg, Hardi Hungar, Bernhard Josko, Jochen Klose, Karsten Lüth, Ingo Schinz and Rainer Schlör, with Peter Jansen (BMW), Joachim Hofmann and Andreas Nägele (DaimlerChrysler – DC), and Geoffrey Clements (British Aerospace – BAe), with the VIS Group, in particular Roderick Bloem, for supporting the integration, Fabio Somenzi for the CUDD BDD package and I-Logix, in particular Moshe Cohen.

2 Model Analysis

The STATEMATE semantics [12] contains modeling techniques which enables simultaneous activation of conflicting transitions or nondeterministic resolution of multiple write accesses to data-items. Even if these mechanisms are captured by the STATEMATE semantics, such properties prove to be errors in later design processes, where the design is mapped to more concrete levels of abstraction, for instance, by using code-generation facilities.

The current version of the verification environment has been extended by *push-button* analysis for STATEMATE designs to be able to verify if some robustness properties are fulfilled by the system under design. These debugging facilities cover

a) simultaneous activation of conflicting transitions,
b) several write accesses to a single data-item in the same step[1], and
c) parallel read- and write-accesses to the same object.

Besides these robustness checks, which are completely automated, the verification environment offers simple reachability mechanisms to drive the simulation to some user provided state or property, for example, a state where some specific atomic proposition holds. Such analysis can be used to verify, for instance, that states indicating fatal errors are not reachable. In the context of testing, reachability related analysis can be used for achieving simulation prefixes.

These use cases require—in contrast to verification activities related to quality acceptance gates for complete Electronic Control Units (ECUs) or subsystems—a white box view of the underlying model, allowing to refer to states and transitions of the model, typically asking for state-invariants.

Implementation and Results. Model analysis is performed using symbolic model-checking as described in Section 1. In order to use model-checking for model analysis, the finite state machine describing the model's behavior is extended automatically by *observers*, which allow to specify robustness properties as atomic propositions p. These propositions are then checked using simple $\mathbf{AG}(p)$ formulae, stating that nothing bad ever happens. If there is a path leading to some state σ with $\sigma \models \neg p$, then that path is a witness for erroneous modeling. This path can be used to drive the STATEMATE simulator as described in [2,4].

Model analysis has been successfully applied to industrial sized applications like a central locking system (BMW; c.f. [7]), a main component of a stores management system of an aircraft (BAe; c.f. [2]), and an application of another leading european car manufacturer. Each application consists of up to 300 state-variables and 80 input-bits. In every model, all types of robustness failures were detected, consuming 300 seconds of analysis time in average on an UltraSparc II, 277MHz, equipped with 1GB of RAM. Note that these results have been achieved on top level designs. If these facilities will—as intended—be used while developing a design, model analysis will be performed much faster as it will be applied mainly to subcomponents of a complete system.

---

[1] Within STATEMATE, W/W-races are reported disregarding the values to be written simultaneously. Besides such an analysis, the verification environment also provides an enhanced W/W-race detection, also taking into account the values to be assigned, since designers often considered W/W-races wrt. equal values to be not harmful.

3 Propositional Abstraction

Several different approaches have been proposed in the literature to overcome the state explosion problem, which is inherent even to symbolic model checking. Besides techniques for compositional reasoning, the current version of the STATEMATE verification environment provides a simple but powerful abstraction technique, which is offered to the user as special verification method for component proofs. This abstraction method improves the approach described in [2].

State of the art model checkers like VIS [11] compute the cone-of-influence (COI) of a model $\mathcal{M}$ regarding a requirement ϕ before verification is initiated. The COI of $\mathcal{M}$ contains those variables of $\mathcal{M}$, which may influence the truth value of ϕ. As the COI preserves the exact behavior of $\mathcal{M}$ regarding ϕ, it potentially still contains very complex computations for its variables—this complexity often remains too high for successful verification. On the other hand, the COI provides useful information about dependencies of objects within $\mathcal{M}$ when verifying ϕ.

Even if the COI contains all variables which may influence requirement ϕ, some of them can safely be omitted if ϕ must hold for *any* value of these variables. If the exact valuation for some variable x is not required to verify ϕ, also all computations for its concrete representation can be omitted. The propositional abstraction supported in the STATEMATE verification environment provides a mechanism to automatically compute an over-approximation $\mathcal{M}_a$ of $\mathcal{M}$ wrt. a user selected set of variables from within the COI. Every computation required to build $\mathcal{M}_a$ is performed on a higher level language SMI [3], which serves as intermediate format in the STATEMATE verification environment. Note that also the COI can be calculated on that level. Since it is not required to build $\mathcal{M}$ to obtain $\mathcal{M}_a$, the abstraction technique becomes suitable also for models containing infinite objects. Abstracted variables are eliminated and only their influence on other objects is maintained in $\mathcal{M}_a$.

Let x be a variable to be abstracted. Then, each condition b occurring in $\mathcal{M}$ is replaced by $\exists x.b$.[1] Assignments to x are eliminated, and if x is referenced in a right hand side of an assignment $y := t(\ldots, x, \ldots)$, the assignment is replaced by $y := y\_inp$, where y_inp is a fresh input ranging over the domain of y.[2] The model checking problem becomes simpler on the abstract model, as any computations regarding x are not further in use.

The verification environment offers an application methodology for propositional abstraction, which is based upon an iterative scheme:

1) compute cone-of-influence of $\mathcal{M}$ regarding ϕ,
2) select set of variables to be abstracted from $\mathcal{M}$ and compute $\mathcal{M}_a$,
   a) if $\mathcal{M}_a \models \phi$, the requirement also holds for $\mathcal{M}$,
   b) if verification fails due to complexity or a (user defined) timeout occurs for $\mathcal{M}_a$, set $\mathcal{M} := \mathcal{M}_a$ and go to 1),
   c) otherwise, analyze error-path to identify needed increase of accuracy.

---

[1] Since SMI does not provide existential quantification, this is approximated by replacing positive occurrences of propositions referring to x by *true*, while negative ones are replaced by *false*.

[2] [2] reports other possible types of computations for $\mathcal{M}_a$ These types differ in the remaining degree of information about some abstract variable x in $\mathcal{M}_a$.

Results. The abstraction technique and its application methodology have been completely integrated into the verification environment. The abstraction technique itself proves to be powerful for industrial applications. Verification of some non-trivial safety requirements regarding a BAe application (stores management system) with up to 1200 state-bits became possible using this type of abstraction within a couple of seconds. The number of state-bits dropped to 160 in the abstract model. Propositional abstraction has also been successfully applied to a DC application [13], which originally contained four 32-Bit integer and two real variables. The automatically abstracted version used only 80 state-bits and 7800 BDD nodes and model-checking some relevant safety properties was performed successfully within 60 seconds.

4 Integration

The tool-set for STATEMATE verification is enhanced with a graphical interface which significantly eases its use. All verification related activities can be performed by graphical operations. Compiling the design to the internal representation for the verification [4] as well as model analysis described in Section 2 can be initiated directly from appropriate icons.

The verification environment provides a behavioral view for each activity of the STATEMATE design. This allows to apply model analysis on each activity separately. Results are recorded in a report. Witness paths found by the analysis operations are translated into simulation control programs [4], which can be used to drive the STATEMATE simulator.

Verification of specific properties of the design under consideration is supported by a graphical specification formalism integrated in the user interface. For each activity of the design the user can state requirements using predefined specification patterns, which can also be employed to express assumptions about the environment of an activity. Typical properties for verification are offered as a library of patterns, which can easily be instantiated in customized specifications.

The user interface ensures automatic translation of requirements into temporal logic formulae [9], while assumptions about the environment of an activity are compiled into observer automata. Verification is done by adding the observers for the assumptions plus fairness constraints to the model [6] and performing regular model checking using the CTL model checker VIS. This process is managed by the user interface, hiding all control aspects from the user.

Creation of proof obligations and execution of proof tasks is integrated in the user interface. The interface keeps track of verification results. Proof-results are automatically invalidated by changes in the design or modifications of the specification. A fine granular dependency management ensures minimal invalidation. Proofs can be established again wrt. the changes by re-executing the affected proof tasks. Witness sequences are collected and managed by the environment. The user can easily animate runs of the activity violating requirements by using the STATEMATE simulator. Additionally, a violation can be displayed as set of waveforms.

The user interface offers propositional abstraction for each proof task. The abstraction iterations discussed in Section 3 are recorded and automatically reapplied when the proof task needs to be re-executed, for example, if some changes are made to the model.

Compositional reasoning is guided by the user interface as described in [2]. Specifications of sub-components can be used hierarchically to derive specifications of composed activities of the design. Such structural implications are maintained wrt. the verification results for the sub-activities.

5 Conclusion

We have described key enhancements taking a prototype verification system for STATE-MATE to a verification environment now available as commercial offering from I-Logix. As part of the ongoing cooperation, further extensions of the technology are under development, including in particular support for industrially relevant classes of hybrid controller models and support for a recently developed extension of Message Sequence Charts called Live Sequence Charts [8]. Within the SafeAir project, the same verification technology is linked to other modeling tools used by our partners Aerospatiale, DASA, Israeli Aircraft Industries, and SNECMA. In cooperation with BMW and DC we are integrating further modeling tools.

References

[1] Tom Bienmüller, Jürgen Bohn, Henning Brinkmann, Udo Brockmeyer, Werner Damm, Hardi Hungar, and Peter Jansen. Verification of automotive control units. In Ernst-Rüdiger Olderog and Bernd Steffen, editors, *Correct System Design*, number 1710 in LNCS, pages 319–341. Springer Verlag, 1999.

[2] Tom Bienmüller, Udo Brockmeyer, Werner Damm, Gert Döhmen, Claus Eßmann, Hans-Jürgen Holberg, Hardi Hungar, Bernhard Josko, Rainer Schlör, Gunnar Wittich, Hartmut Wittke, Geoffrey Clements, John Rowlands, and Eric Sefton. Formal Verification of an Avionics Application using Abstraction and Symbolic Model Checking. In Felix Redmill and Tom Anderson, editors, *Towards System Safety – Proceedings of the Seventh Safety-critical Systems Symposium, Huntingdon, UK*, pages 150–173. Safety-Critical Systems Club, Springer Verlag, 1999.

[3] Jürgen Bohn, Udo Brockmeyer, Claus Essmann, and Hardi Hungar. SMI – system modelling interface, draft version 0.1. Technical report, Kuratorium OFFIS, e.V., Oldenburg, 1999.

[4] Udo Brockmeyer. *Verifikation von STATEMATE Designs*. PhD thesis, Carl von Ossietzky Universität Oldenburg, December 1999.

[5] Udo Brockmeyer and Gunnar Wittich. Tamagotchis Need Not Die – Verification of STATEMATE Designs. In *Tools and Algorithms for the Construction and Analysis of Systems*, number 1384 in LNCS, pages 217–231. Springer Verlag, 1998.

[6] E. Clarke, O. Grumberg, and K. Hamaguchi. Another Look at LTL Model Checking. *Formal Methods in System Design*, 10(1):47–71, February 1997.

[7] W. Damm, U. Brockmeyer, H.-J. Holberg, G. Wittich, and M. Eckrich. Einsatz formaler Methoden zur Erhöhung der Sicherheit eingebetteter Systeme im KFZ, 1997. VDI/VW Gemeinschaftstagung.

[8] W. Damm and D. Harel. LSCs: Breathing Life into Message Sequence Charts. In *FMOODS'99 IFIP TC6/WG6.1 Third International Conference on Formal Methods for Open Object-Based Distributed Systems*, 1999.

[9] Konrad Feyerabend and Bernhard Josko. A visual formalism for real time requirement specifications. In *Proceedings of the 4th International AMAST Workshop on Real-Time Systems and Concurrentand Distributed Software, ARTS'97, Lecture Notes in Computer Science 1231*, pages 156–168, 1997.

[10] Thomas Filkorn. Applications on Formal Verification in Industrial Automation and Telecommunication, April 1997. *Workshop on Formal Design of Safety Critical Embedded Systems.*

[11] The VIS Group. VIS : A System for Verification and Synthesis. In *8th international Conference on Computer Aided Verification*, number 1102 in LNCS, 1996. VIS 1.3 is available from the VIS home-page: http://www-cad.eecs.Berkeley.EDU/~vis.

[12] D. Harel and A. Naamad. The STATEMATE semantics of statecharts. Technical Report CS95-31, The Weizmann Institute of Science, Rehovot, 1995.

[13] Joachim Hoffmann, Hans-Jürgen Holberg, and Rainer Schlör. Industrieller Einsatz formaler Verifikationsmethoden, February 2000. to appear in ITG/GI/GMM-Workshop *Methoden und Beschreibungssprachen zur Modellierung und Verifikation von Schaltungen und Systemen*, Frankfurt/Main.

[14] E. Mikk, Y. Lakhnech, and M. Siegel. Hierarchical automata as model for statecharts. In *Asian Computing Conference (ASIAN'97)*, number 1345 in LNCS. Springer Verlag, 1997.

[15] E. Mikk, Y. Lakhnech, and M. Siegel. Towards Efficient Modelchecking Statecharts: A Statecharts to Promela Compiler, April 1997.

[16] Francois Pilarski. Cost effectiveness of formal methods in the development of avionics systems at Aerospatiale. In *17th Digital Avionics Systems Conference, Seattle, WA*. Springer Verlag, 1998.

[17] Fabio Somenzi. CU Decision Diagram Package, 1998. CUDD 2.3.0 is available from http://vlsi.Colorado.EDU/~fabio.

TAPS: A First-Order Verifier for Cryptographic Protocols

Ernie Cohen

Telcordia Technologies
ernie@research.telcordia.com

1 Introduction

In recent years, a number of cryptographic protocols have been mechanically verified using a variety of inductive methods (e.g., [4,3,5]). These proofs typically require defining a number of recursive sets of messages, and require deep insight into why the protocol is correct. As a result, these proofs often require days to weeks of expert effort.

We have developed an automatic verifier, TAPS, that seems to overcome these problems for many cryptographic protocols. TAPS uses the protocol text to construct a number of first-order invariants; the proof obligations justifying these invariants, along with any user-specified protocol properties (e.g. message authentication), are proved from the invariants with a resolution theorem prover. The only flexibility in constructing these invariants is to guess, for each type of nonce[1] and encryption generated by the protocol, a formula capturing conditions necessary for that nonce/encryption to be published (i.e., sent in the clear). TAPS chooses these formulas heuristically, attempting to match the designer's intent as expressed in traditional protocol notations (for example, the choice can be influenced by the formally irrelevant use of the same variable name in different transitions). When necessary, the user can override these choices, but TAPS usually needs these hints only for recursive protocols and certain types of nested encryptions. Justifying the invariants usually requires substantial protocol reasoning; proving the invariants in a single simultaneous induction is critical to making the proofs work.

TAPS has verified properties of about 60 protocols, including (variants of) all but 3 protocols from the Clark & Jacob survey [1]. 90% of these protocols require no hints from the user; the remainder an average about 40 bytes of user input (usually a single formula). The average verification time for these protocols is under 4 seconds (on a 266MHz PC), and TAPS verifications seem to require about an order of magnitude less user time than equivalent Isabelle verifications. Although TAPS cannot generate counterexamples, it can quickly verify many protocols without the artificial limitations on protocol or state space required by model checking approaches.

For a more complete description of TAPS, see [2].

---

[1] We use "nonce" to describe any freshly generated unguessable value (e.g. including session keys).

```
Protocol NeedhamSchroederLowe       /* 0.7 sec */
  /* k(X) =  X's public key,   dk(k(X)) <=> X has been compromised */
  Definitions {
    m0 = {A,Na}_k(B)    m1 = {B,Na,Nb}_k(A)    m2 = {Nb}_k(B)
  }
  Transitions {
    /* A->B   */   Na: pub(A) /\ pub(B)        -p0-> m0
    /* B->A   */   Nb: pub(B) /\ pub(m0)       -p1-> m1
    /* A->B   */       p0 /\ pub(m1)           -p2-> m2
    /* B      */       p1 /\ pub(m2)           -p3-> {}
    /* oopsNa */       p0 /\ dk(k(A))          -oopsNa-> Na
    /* oopsNb */       p1 /\ dk(k(B))          -oopsNb-> Nb
  }
  Axioms { k injective }
  Goals { /* If either A or B has executed his last step and neither is
             compromised, then his partner has executed the preceding
             step, with agreement on A,B,Na,Nb                         */
    p2 => p1 \/ dk(k(A)) \/ dk(k(B))
    p3 => p2 \/ dk(k(A)) \/ dk(k(B))
  }
```

Fig. 1. TAPS input for the Needham-Schroeder-Lowe protocol

2 The Protocol Model

Figure 1 shows TAPS input for the Needham-Schroeder-Lowe (NSL) protocol. Each protocol makes use of an underlying set of *messages* whose structure is given by a first-order theory. Identifiers starting with uppercase letters ($A, B, Na, \ldots$) are first-order variables, ranging over messages; the remainder are first-order functions (k), first-order predicates, history predicates ($p0, p1, p2, p3$), and the unary predicate *pub*. The message theory includes the list constructors *nil* and *cons*, *enc* (encryption), and the predicates *atom* (unary) and d ($d(X, Y)$ means that messages encrypted using X can be decrypted using Y), as well as any functions mentioned in the protocol (like k in the example). The first-order theory says that *nil*, *cons*, and *enc* are injective, with disjoint ranges, and do not yield atoms. The user can provide arbitrary first-order axioms in the Axioms section. Lists in braces are right-associated *cons* lists, and _ is infix encryption (e.g., {Nb}_k(B) abbreviates $enc(k(B), cons(Nb, nil))$).

Each protocol defines an (infinite state) transition system. The state of the system is given by interpretations assigned to the history predicates and *pub*. These interpretations grow monotonically, so any positive formula (one in which history predicates and *pub* occur only with positive polarity) is guaranteed to be stable (once true, it remains true). The abbreviation $dk(X)$ ("X is a decryptable key") is defined by $dk(X) \Leftrightarrow (\exists Y : d(X, Y) \wedge pub(Y))$.

The transitions of the protocol are each of the form

$$nv_p : g_p \xrightarrow{p} M_p$$

where p is a history predicate, $\mathsf{nv_p}$ is an optional list of variables (the *nonce variables* of p), $\mathsf{g_p}$ is a positive formula, and $\mathsf{M_p}$ is a message term. For each p, TAPS generates a minimal signature (list of distinct variables) Σ_p that includes all the free variables in $\mathsf{nv_p}$, $\mathsf{g_p}$, and $\mathsf{M_p}$; used as a predicate, p abbreviates $\mathsf{p}(\Sigma_\mathsf{p})$[2]. For example, in NSL, $\Sigma_{p0} = \Sigma_{oopsNa} = A, B, Na$, and $\Sigma_{p1} = \Sigma_{p2} = \Sigma_{p3} = \Sigma_{oopsNb} = A, B, Na, Nb$.

A transition describes two separate atomic actions. In the first action, the system (1) chooses arbitrary values for all variables in Σ_p, such that variables in $\mathsf{nv_p}$ are assigned fresh, distinct atoms; (2) checks that $\mathsf{g_p}$ holds in the current state; (3) adds the tuple $\langle\Sigma_\mathsf{p}\rangle$ to the interpretation of p, and (4) checks that all the axioms hold. In the second action, the system (1) chooses an arbitrary tuple from the interpretation of p, (2) publishes the corresponding message $\mathsf{M_p}$, and (3) checks that the axioms hold. Execution starts in the state where all history predicates have the empty interpretation, no messages are published, and all the axioms hold.

In addition, each protocol implicitly includes transitions modeling the ability of the spy to generate (and publish) new messages; these transitions generate fresh atoms, tuple, untuple, and encrypt previously published messages, and decrypt previously published messages encrypted under decryptable keys.

3 Generating the Invariants

To generate the invariants, TAPS has to choose a formula $\mathsf{L_v}$ for each nonce variable v (giving conditions under which a freshly generated v atom might be published) and a formula for each encryption subterm of each $\mathsf{M_p}$ (giving conditions under which the subterm might be published). The user can influence these choices by providing formulas for some of the $\mathsf{L_v}$'s or providing explicit labels for some of the subterms of the $\mathsf{M_p}$'s. TAPS calculates these formulas as follows. Let S initially be the set of all formulas $\mathsf{p}(\Sigma_\mathsf{p}) \Rightarrow ok(\mathsf{M_p})$, and let T initially be the empty set; TAPS repeatedly

– replaces a formula $\mathsf{f} \Rightarrow ok(cons(\mathsf{X}, \mathsf{Y}))$ in S with $\mathsf{f} \Rightarrow ok(\mathsf{X})$ and $\mathsf{f} \Rightarrow ok(\mathsf{Y})$;
– removes a formula $\mathsf{f} \Rightarrow ok(nil)$ from S;
– replaces a formula $\mathsf{f} \Rightarrow ok(\mathsf{X})$ in S, where X is explicitly labeled by the user with the formula g, with $\mathsf{f} \Rightarrow \mathsf{g}$ and $\mathsf{g} \Rightarrow ok(\mathsf{X})$;
– replaces a formula $\mathsf{f} \Rightarrow ok(enc(\mathsf{X},\mathsf{Y}))$ in S with $\mathsf{f} \wedge dk(\mathsf{X}) \Rightarrow ok(\mathsf{Y})$ and adds $\mathsf{f} \Rightarrow primeEnc(enc(\mathsf{X},\mathsf{Y}))$ to T.

For example, applying this procedure to the $p2$ transition of NSL has the net effect of adding the formula $p2 \wedge dk(k(B)) \Rightarrow ok(Nb)$ to S and adding the formula $p2 \Rightarrow primeEnc(m2)$ to T.

When this process has terminated, TAPS defines $\mathsf{L_v}$ to be the disjunction of all formulas f for which $\mathsf{f} \Rightarrow ok(\mathsf{v})$ is a formula of S (unless the user has defined

---
[2] TAPS provides an explicit substitution operator to allow history predicates to take arbitrary arguments. Default arguments make large protocols much easier to read and modify.

L_v explicitly), and defines *primeEnc* to be the strongest predicate satisfying the formulas of T (universally quantified). For example, for NSL, TAPS defines

$$L_{Na} \Leftrightarrow (p0 \wedge dk(k(B))) \vee (p1 \wedge dk(k(A))) \vee oopsNa$$
$$L_{Nb} \Leftrightarrow (p1 \wedge dk(k(A))) \vee (p2 \wedge dk(k(B))) \vee oopsNb$$
$$primeEnc(X) \Leftrightarrow$$
$$(\exists A, B, Na, Nb : (X = m0 \wedge p0) \vee (X = m1 \wedge p1) \vee (X = m2 \wedge p2))$$

TAPS then proposes the following invariants (in addition to the axioms of the underlying first-order theory, and any axioms specified in the `Axioms` section):

(1) $\quad\quad\quad\quad\quad\quad p(\Sigma_p) \Rightarrow g_p \wedge (\forall v : v \in nv_p : atom(v))$

(2) $\quad p(\Sigma_p) \wedge p(\Sigma_p') \wedge v = v' \Rightarrow \Sigma_p = \Sigma_p'$

(3) $\quad\quad\quad\quad p(\Sigma_p) \wedge q(\Sigma_q) \Rightarrow v \neq w$ for distinct $v \in \Sigma_p, w \in \Sigma_q$

(4) $\quad\quad\quad\quad\quad\quad\quad pub(X) \Rightarrow ok(X)$

(5) $\quad\quad\quad\quad\quad\quad\quad\quad ok(nil)$

(6) $\quad\quad\quad ok(cons(X,Y)) \Leftrightarrow ok(X) \wedge ok(Y)$

(7) $\quad\quad\quad ok(enc(X,Y)) \Leftrightarrow primeEnc(enc(X,Y)) \vee (pub(X) \wedge pub(Y))$

(8) $\quad\quad\quad\quad\quad\quad p(\Sigma_p) \Rightarrow (ok(v) \Leftrightarrow (\exists V : L_v))$ for $v \in nv_p$

where V is the set of free variables of L_v not in Σ_p

These formulas say (1) each history predicate implies its corresponding guard, and nonce variables are instantiated to atoms; (2)-(3) no atom is used more that once as the instantiation of a nonce variable; (4) all published messages are *ok*; (5)-(6) a tuple is *ok* iff each of its components is *ok*; (7) an encryption is *ok* iff it is either a *primeEnc* or the encryption of published messages; and (8) an atom used to instantiate a nonce variable v is *ok* iff L_v holds.

The remaining formulas of S (universally quantified) are left as proof obligations; if these formulas follow from the invariants, then the invariants hold in all reachable states. The invariants are then used to prove the goals.

References

[1] J. Clark and J. Jacob. A survey of the authentication protocol literature, version 1.0. Unpublished Monograph, 1997.
[2] Ernie Cohen. TAPS: A first-order verifier for cryptographic protocols. In *Computer Security Foundations Workshop XIII*. IEEE Computer Society Press, 2000.
[3] C. Meadows. The NRL Protocol Analyzer: An overview. In *2nd Intl. Conf. on Practical Applications of Prolog*, 1993.
[4] L. Paulson. The inductive approach to verifying cryptographic protocols. *Journal of Computer Security*, 6, 1998.
[5] S. Schneider. Verifying authentication protocols with CSP. In *Computer Security Foundations Workshop X*. IEEE Computer Society Press, 1997.

VINAS-P: A Tool for Trace Theoretic Verification of Timed Asynchronous Circuits

Tomohiro Yoneda

Tokyo Institute of Technology
2-12-1 O-okayama Meguro-ku Tokyo 152-8552, Japan
yoneda@cs.titech.ac.jp

1 Introduction

Asynchronous circuit design can probably avoid the occurrence of various problems which arise in designing large synchronous circuits, such as clock skews and high power consumption. On the other hand, the cost of the verification of asynchronous circuits is usually much higher than that of synchronous circuits. This is because every change of wires should be taken into account in order to capture the behavior of asynchronous circuits unlike in the case of synchronous circuits. Furthermore, asynchronous circuit designers have recently preferred to use timed circuits for implementing fast and compact circuits. This trend increases the cost of verification, and at the same time increases the demands for formal verification tools. VINAS-P is our newest formal verification tool for timed asynchronous circuits using the techniques proposed in [1]. The main idea in these techniques is the partial order reduction based on the timed version [2] of the Stubborn set method [3].

This short paper mainly introduces what VINAS-P can verify and how we use it. We are planning to release VINAS-P on our web site soon.

2 What Can VINAS-P Verify?

In order to formally verify timed circuits, VINAS-P uses the timed version [1] of the trace theoretic verification method [4], and as its internal model, time Petri nets are used. Thus, its implementation and specification are both modeled by time Petri nets, and it produces the result whether the implementation conforms to the specification or not. Since the time Petri nets for an implementation are automatically generated from a Verilog-like description and the VINAS-P gate library, users must usually handle a time Petri net only for the specification. The properties to be verified by the current version of VINAS-P are safety properties. That is, it checks whether a failure state where the circuit produces an output that the specification does not expect (i.e., the specification is not ready for accepting the output) is reachable or not. Any causality relation between input and output wires can be expressed in the specifications. Checking liveness properties (e.g., that some output is actually produced) will be supported in the future.

Here, we will demonstrate verification using VINAS-P with a simple example. Consider the circuit shown in Figure 1(a), which is a two-stage asynchronous FIFO. The gate with a "C" symbol is actually implemented as shown in (b). To describe this circuit, we prepare a Verilog-like description as shown in (c). We do not have to describe primitive gates such as ANDs or ORs, because they

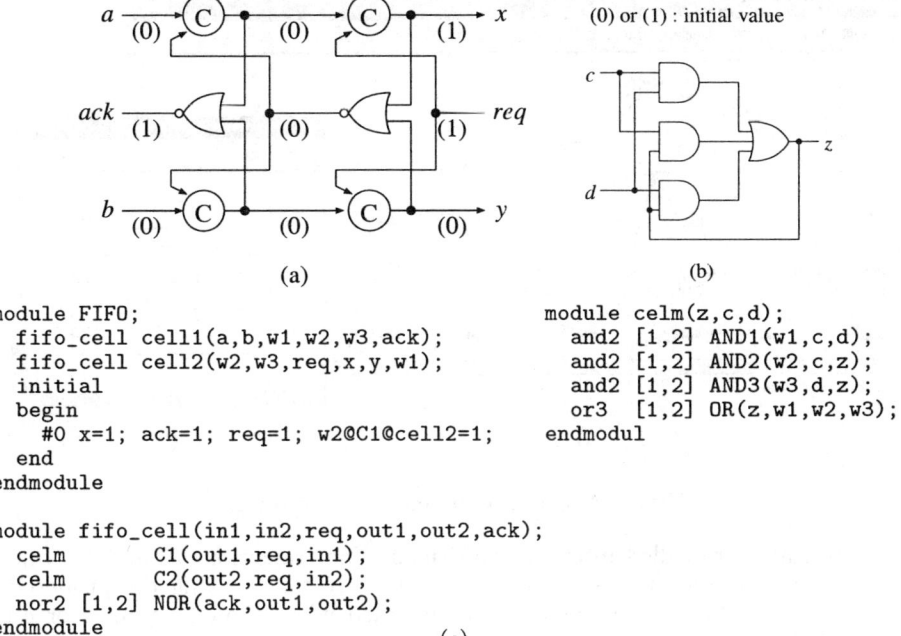

Fig. 1. A circuit to be verified.

are included in the gate library. A module celm is for the "C" gate. This gate produces the value v only when v is given to both inputs, otherwise, it holds the previous value. The delay values (e.g., [1,2]) are specified for each primitive gate. VINAS-P assumes the bounded delay model, and these delay values represent the minimal and maximal delays.

Suppose that this circuit is used in the following environment. Either (0,1) or (1,0) and then (0,0) is given to (a, b) periodically, say, every 12 time units. However, due to clock skew, up to one time unit inaccuracy can occur. For req, 0 is given when (0,1) or (1,0) is given to (a,b), and 1 for (0,0). What we want to verify is that this FIFO never causes overflow, that is, that ack is always activated (i.e., 0 for (0,1) or (1,0), and 1 for (0,0)) before the next data is given to (a,b). In order to describe both the environment and this property, we prepare a time Petri net as shown in Figure 2(a). Some transitions have timing information like $[p, q]$. It means that the transition must have been enabled for p time units or more before its firing, and that it must fire before q time units have passed unless it is disabled. Thus, the transitions labeled $t0$ and $t1$ fire exactly every 12 time units. $[0,1]$ in some transitions models the effect of the clock skew. The transitions which are related to the input wires of the circuit are labeled "(in)", and the transitions related to the output wires are labeled "(out)". The names of these transitions end with "+" or "−". The firings of "+" ("−") transitions correspond to $0 \to 1$ ($1 \to 0$) signal transitions. The firings of these transitions are synchronized with the changes of the corresponding wires of the circuit. Since the output wires are controlled by the circuit, the specification cannot specify any timing information to those transitions. It is assumed that they have $[0, \infty]$. The transitions without "(in)" or "(out)" are not related to

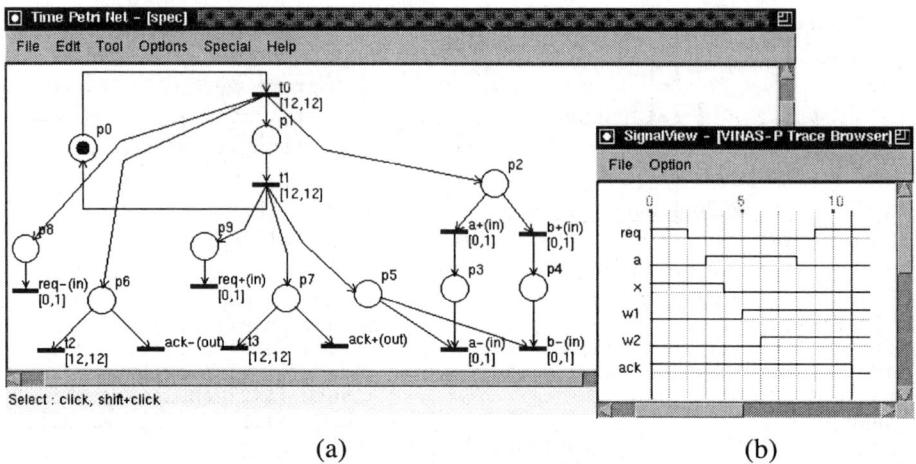

Fig. 2. A specification and a failure trace.

any wires, and are called internal transitions. The transitions $t2$ and $t3$ which conflict with the transitions for $ack-$ or $ack+$ are for checking the properties to be verified. These transitions become enabled when the change of a or b is triggered. If the circuit changes the ack before the firings of these transitions, then it is the correct behavior of the circuit (no overflow occurs). On the other hand, if the ack is not changed for 12 time units, it means that the overflow can be caused by the next data. In this case, $t2$ (or $t3$) fires and the transitions for the ack become disabled. Thus, when the circuit eventually produces ack, the situation in which the circuit produces an output that the specification does not expect occurs. VINAS-P detects this as a failure. It is straightforward to see that this time Petri net expresses both the behavior of the environment of the circuit and the expected behavior of the circuit itself. All we should do for this verification is to push the "verify" button and see the results. If the circuit does not conform to the specification (actually it does not), the failure trace shown in Figure 2(b) is displayed.

The major advantage of VINAS-P is that verification can be performed without traversing the entire state space of the given system. This is possible by the partial order reduction technique, and it often reduces the verification cost dramatically. For example, an abstracted TITAC2 instruction cache subsystem which contains around 200 gates (modeled by over 1500 places and 1500 transitions) was verified in about 15 minutes, using less than 20 MBytes of memory [5]. No conventional methods can complete this verification.

The most closely related work is probably ATACS developed at the University of Utah. It also uses some kind of partial order reduction [6]. However, since ATACS only uses restricted information relating to the concurrency between events, VINAS-P is expected to be faster in many cases. On the other hand, the expressibility of the ATACS modeling language is superior to that of VINAS-P.

3 User Interface

The verifier core of VINAS-P written in C is almost stable, and the graphical user interface written in Java is being improved. It can select circuit files and specification Petri net files, and launch editors for them. The Petri net editor (see view in Figure 2(a)) recognizes Petri net objects such as transitions, places, and arcs, and is designed so that the creation or modification of Petri nets can be easily done. Information of the Petri net objects created by this editor is also used when browsing failure traces.

When VINAS-P detects a failure state, it shows a trace which leads the system from the initial state to the failure state as shown in Figure 2 (This trace is obtained simply from the recursion stack, and thus there is no timing information in it). The user can select a set of wires to be shown. When this failure trace is displayed, the specification net is also shown, and by moving the vertical cursor on the failure trace, the corresponding marking of the specification net is displayed by an animation. This function of VINAS-P helps users tremendously in debugging circuits.

For early stages of debugging circuits, VINAS-P also provides a function which we call "guided simulation". It allows users to easily specify input sequences for simulation and to browse the output traces.

4 Future Works

¿From some experimental results [7], we feel that the approach based on compressing and thinning out the visited state information is more effective in reducing the memory usage than symbolic approaches based on decision diagrams especially for the partial order reduction technique of timed systems. We are currently implementing this idea in VINAS-P.

At present, we are also designing a specification description language for VINAS-P in order to easily handle large specifications. Although CCS, CSP, and their extensions can be used for this purpose, we do not think that it is easy for nonexperts to use them. Instead, we have designed a Java-like language, and are now checking its expressibility in comparison with Petri nets.

Acknowledgment

We would like to thank Yoshinori Tomita for helping with the development of the Petri net editor and Trace browser of VINAS-P.

References

[1] T. Yoneda and H. Ryu. Timed trace theoretic verification using partial order reduction. *Proc. of Fifth International Symposium on Advanced Research in Asynchronous Circuits and Systems*, pages 108–121, 1999.
[2] T. Yoneda and H. Schlingloff. Efficient verification of parallel real–time systems. *Formal Method in System Design*, pages 187–215, 1997.
[3] A. Valmari. Stubborn sets for reduced state space generation. *LNCS 483 Advances in Petri Nets*, pages 491–515, 1990.
[4] D. L. Dill. *Trace Theory for Automatic Hierarchical Verification of Speed-Independent Circuits*. MIT press, 1988.
[5] T. Yoneda. Verification of abstracted instruction cache of titac2. *VLSI: Systems on a chip (Kluwer Academic Publishers)*, pages 373–384, 1999.
[6] W. Belluomini and C. Myers. Verification of timed systems using POSETs. *LNCS 1427 Computer Aided Verification*, pages 403–415, 1998.
[7] K. Oikawa, K. Kitamura, and T. Yoneda. Saving memory for verification of asynchronous circuits. *IEICE Technical Report (in Japanese)*, FTS99(11):37–44, 1999.

XMC: A Logic-Programming-Based Verification Toolset*

C.R. Ramakrishnan, I.V. Ramakrishnan, Scott A. Smolka
with
Yifei Dong, Xiaoqun Du, Abhik Roychoudhury, and V.N. Venkatakrishnan

Department of Computer Science, SUNY at Stony Brook
Stony Brook, NY 11794-4400, USA

1 Introduction

XMC is a toolset for specifying and verifying concurrent systems.[1] Its main mode of verification is temporal-logic model checking [CES86], although equivalence checkers have also been implemented. In its current form, temporal properties are specified in the alternation-free fragment of the modal mu-calculus [Koz83], and system models are specified in XL, a value-passing language based on CCS [Mil89]. The core computational components of the XMC system, such as those for compiling the specification language, model checking, etc., are built on top of the XSB tabled logic-programming system [XSB99].

A distinguishing aspect of XMC is that model checking is carried out as *query evaluation*, by building proof trees using tabled resolution. The main advantage to making proof-tree construction central to XMC is the resultant flexibility and extensibility of the system. For example, XMC provides the foundation for the XMC-RT [DRS99] model checker for real-time systems, and for XMC-PS [RKR+00], a verification technique for parameterized systems. Secondly, it paves the way for building an effective and uniform interface, called the *justifier*, for debugging branching-time properties.

The main features of the XMC system are as follows.

- The specification language, XL, extends value-passing CCS with parameterized processes, first-class channels, logical variables and computations, and supports SML-like polymorphic types.
- XL specifications are compiled into efficient automata representations using techniques described in [DR99]. XMC implements an efficient, local model checker that operates over these automata representations. The optimization techniques in the compiler make the model checker comparable, in terms of performance, to SPIN [HP96] and Murphi [Dil96].
- The model checker is declaratively written in under 200 lines of XSB tabled Prolog code [RRR+97]. XSB's tabled-resolution mechanism automatically

---

* Research supported in part by NSF grants EIA-9705998, CCR-9711386, CCR-9805735, and CCR-9876242.
[1] See http://www.cs.sunysb.edu/~lmc for details on obtaining a copy of the system.

yields an on-the-fly, local model checker. Moreover, state representation using Prolog terms yields a form of data-independence [Wol86], permitting model checking of certain infinite-state systems.
- The model checker saves "lemmas", i.e. intermediate steps in the proof of a property. The XMC justifier extracts a proof tree from these lemmas and permits the user to interactively navigate through the proof tree.

The XMC system has been successfully used for specifying and verifying different protocols and algorithms such as Rether [CV95], an Ethernet-based protocol supporting real-time traffic; the Java meta locking algorithm [ADG$^+$99, BSW00], a low-overhead mutual exclusion algorithm used by Java threads; and the SET protocol [SET97], an e-commerce protocol developed for Visa/Master-Card.

Below we describe the salient features of the XMC system.

2 XL: The Specification Language

XL is a language for specifying asynchronous concurrent systems. It inherits the parallel composition (written as '|'), and choice operators ('#'), the notion of channels, input ('!') and output ('?') actions, and synchronization from Milner's value-passing calculus. XL also has a sequential composition (';'), generalizing CCS's prefix operation, and a builtin conditional construct ('if'). XL's support of parameterized processes fills the roles of CCS-style restriction and relabeling.

Complex processes may be defined starting from the elementary actions using these composition operations. Process definitions may be recursive; in fact, as in CCS, recursion is the sole mechanism for defining iterative processes. Processes take zero or more parameters. Process invocations bind these parameters to values: data or channel names.

Data values may be constructed out of primitive types (integers and boolean), predefined types such as lists (written as [Hd|Tl] and [] for empty list) or arbitrary user-defined (possibly recursive) types. XL provides primitives for manipulating arithmetic values; user-defined computation may be specified directly in XL, or using inlined Prolog predicates. The specification of a FIFO channel having an unbounded buffer given in Figure 1 illustrates some of these features.

Type declarations are not always necessary, as the example illustrates. XMC's type-inference module automatically infers the most general types for the different entities in the specification.

3 The XMC Compiler and Model Checker

The XMC system incorporates an optimizing compiler that translates high-level XL specifications into *rules* representing the global transition relation of the underlying automaton. The transitions can be computed from these rules in unit time (modulo indexing) during verification. The compiler incorporates several

```
chan(Read, Write, Buf) ::=
    receive(Read, Write, Buf) # {Buf \== []; send(Read, Write, Buf)}.
receive(Read, Write, Buf) ::=
    Read?Msg; chan(Read, Write, [Msg|Buf]).
send(Read, Write, Buf) ::=
    strip_from_end(Buf, Msg, NBuf); Write!Msg; chan(Read, Write, NBuf).
{*                          % Inlined Prolog code appears between braces
strip_from_end([X], X, []).
strip_from_end([X,Y|Ys], Z, [X|Zs]) :- strip_from_end([Y|Ys], Z, Zs).*}
```

Fig. 1. Example Specification in XL

optimizations to reduce the state space of the generated automaton. One optimization combines computation steps across boundaries of basic blocks, which cannot be done based on user annotations alone, and has been shown as particularly effective [DR99].

The mu-calculus model checker in XMC is encoded using a predicate `models` which verifies whether a state represented by a process term models a given modal mu-calculus formula. This predicate directly encodes the natural semantics of the modal mu-calculus [RRR+97]. The encoding reduces model checking to logic-program query evaluation; the goal-directed evaluation mechanism of XSB ensures that the resultant model checker is local.

Various statistics regarding a model-checking run, such as the memory usage, may be directly obtained using primitives provided by the underlying XSB system. In addition, certain higher-level statistics, such as the total number of states in the system, are provided by the XMC system.

4 Justifier

Tabled resolution of logic programs proceeds by recording subgoals ("lemmas") and their provable instances in tables. Thus, after a goal is resolved, the relevant parts of the proof tree can be reconstructed by inspecting the tables themselves. In XMC, model checking is done by resolving a query to the `models` predicate. The justifier inspects the tables after a model-checking run to create a *justification* tree: a representation of the proof tree or the set of all failed proof paths, depending on whether the verification succeeded or failed, respectively.

The justification tree is usually too large for manual inspection. Hence XMC provides an interactive proof-tree navigator which permits the user to expand or truncate subtrees of the proof. Each node in the proof tree corresponds to computing a single-step transition or a subgoal to the `models` predicate; at each node the justifier interface shows the values of the program counters and other variables of each local process corresponding to the current global state.

5 Future Work

Work to extend the XMC system is proceeding in several directions. First, we are adding a local LTL model checker to the system. Secondly, we are expanding the class of systems that can be verified by incorporating a model checker for real-time systems, XMC-RT [DRS99] built by adding a constraint library to XSB. Thirdly, we plan to include deductive capabilities to XMC by incorporating our recent work in automatically constructing induction proofs for verifying parameterized systems [RKR+00]. Finally, we are enhancing the proof-tree navigator by integrating message sequence charts for better system visualization.

References

[ADG+99] O. Agesen, D. Detlefs, A. Garthwaite, R. Knippel, Y. S. Ramakrishna, and D. White. An efficient meta-lock for implementing ubiquitous synchronization. In *Proc. of OOPSLA '99*, 1999.

[AH96] R. Alur and T. A. Henzinger, editors. *Computer Aided Verification (CAV '96)*, volume 1102 of *LNCS*. Springer Verlag, 1996.

[BSW00] S. Basu, S. A. Smolka, and O. R. Ward. Model checking the Java Meta-Locking algorithm. In *Proc. of 7th IEEE Intl. Conference and Workshop on the Engineering of Computer Based Systems (ECBS 2000)*, 2000.

[CES86] E. M. Clarke, E. A. Emerson, and A. P. Sistla. Automatic verification of finite-state concurrent systems using temporal logic specifications. *ACM TOPLAS*, 8(2), 1986.

[CV95] T. Chiueh and C. Venkatramani. The design, implementation and evaluation of a software-based real-time ethernet protocol. In *Proc. of ACM SIGCPMM'95*, pages 27–37, 1995.

[Dil96] D. L. Dill. The Murφ verification system. In Alur and Henzinger [AH96], pages 390–393.

[DR99] Y. Dong and C. R. Ramakrishnan. An optimizing compiler for efficient model checking. In *Proc. of FORTE/PSTV '99*, 1999.

[DRS99] X. Du, C. R. Ramakrishnan, and S. A. Smolka. Tabled resolution + constraints: A recipe for model checking real-time systems. Technical report, Dept. of Computer Science, SUNY, Stony Brook, 1999. URL: http://www.cs.sunysb.edu/~cram/papers/manuscripts/rtlmc.

[HP96] G. J. Holzmann and D. Peled. The state of SPIN. In Alur and Henzinger [AH96], pages 385–389.

[Koz83] D. Kozen. Results on the propositional μ-calculus. *Theoretical Computer Science*, 27:333–354, 1983.

[Mil89] R. Milner. *Communication and Concurrency*. International Series in Computer Science. Prentice Hall, 1989.

[RKR+00] A. Roychoudhury, K. Narayan Kumar, C.R. Ramakrishnan, I.V. Ramakrishnan, and S.A. Smolka. Verification of parameterized systems using logic-program transformations. In *Proc. of TACAS 2000*. Springer Verlag, 2000.

[RRR+97] Y. S. Ramakrishna, C. R. Ramakrishnan, I. V. Ramakrishnan, S. A. Smolka, T. W. Swift, and D. S. Warren. Efficient model checking using tabled resolution. In *Proc. of CAV'97*, 1997.

[SET97]   SET Secure Electronic Transaction LLC. *The SET Standard Specification*, May 1997. URL: http://www.setco.org/set_specifications.html.
[Wol86]   P. Wolper. Expressing interesting properties of programs in propositional temporal logic. In *ACM POPL*, pages 184–192, 1986.
[XSB99]   The XSB Group. The XSB logic programming system v2.1, 1999. Available from http://www.cs.sunysb.edu/~sbprolog.

Author Index

Abarbanel, Yael, 538
Abdulla, Parosh Aziz, 4, 495
de Alfaro, Luca, 186
Alur, R., 280
Andersen, Flemming, 5
Annichini, Aurore, 419
Asarin, Eugene, 419
Ayari, Abdelwaheb, 99, 170
Aziz, Adnan, 5

Baier, Christel, 358
Basin, David, 99, 170
Baumgartner, Jason, 5
Beer, Ilan, 538
Behrmann, Gerd, 216
Bienmüller, Tom, 561
Biere, Armin, 124
Bloem, Roderick, 248
Bouajjani, Ahmed, 403, 419
Bouyer, Patricia, 464
Bozga, Marius, 543
Bryant, Randal E., 85
Bultan, Tevfik, 69

Cassez, Franck, 373
Chan, William, 450
Clarke, Edmund M., 124, 154
Cohen, Ernie, 568
Colby, Christopher, 557

Damm, Werner, 561
Dang, Zhe, 69
Delzanno, Giorgio, 53
Dong, Yifei, 576
Du, Xiaoqun, 576
Dufourd, Catherine, 464

Esparza, Javier, 232

Fernandez, Jean-Claude, 543
Fix, Limor, 389
Fleury, Emmanuel, 464
Fraer, Ranan, 389

Geist, Danny, 20
Ghirvu, Lucian, 543

Gluhovsky, Leonid, 538
Gopalakrishnan, Ganesh, 521
Graf, Susanne, 543
Grosu, R., 280
Grumberg, Orna, 20, 154
Gunter, Elsa, 552
Gupta, Anubhav, 124

Hansel, David, 232
Haverkort, Boudewijn, 358
Henzinger, Thomas A., 186
Hermanns, Holger, 358
Heyman, Tamir, 20
Hosabettu, Ravi, 521
Hune, Thomas, 216

Ibarra, Oscar H., 69
Iyer, S. Purushothaman, 495

Jha, Somesh, 154
Jonsson, Bengt, 4, 403
Jurdziński, Marcin, 202

Kamhi, Gila, 389
Katoen, Joost-Pieter, 358
Keidar, Sharon, 538
Kemmerer, Richard A., 69
Klaedtke, Felix, 170
Klay, Francis, 344
Krimm, Jean-Pierre, 543
Kukula, James H., 113
Kupferman, Orna, 36
Kurshan, Robert P., 435, 552

Laroussinie, François, 373
Lee, Peter, 557
Liu, Yanhong A., 264
Lu, Yuan, 154

Mang, Freddy Y.C., 186
Marques-Silva, João, 3
McDougall, M., 280
McMillan, Kenneth L., 312
Meadows, Catherine, 2
Mounier, Laurent, 543

Author Index

Namjoshi, Kedar S., 139, 435
Necula, George C., 557
Nilsson, Marcus, 403
Nylén, Aletta, 495

Owre, Sam, 548

Peled, Doron, 552
Petit, Antoine, 464
Pnueli, Amir, 1, 328

Qadeer, Shaz, 312

Ramakrishnan, C.R., 576
Ramakrishnan, I.V., 576
Rossmanith, Peter, 232
Roychoudhury, Abhik, 576
Rueß, Harald, 548
Rushby, John, 508
Rusinowitch, Michaël, 344

Sakallah, Karem, 3
Saxe, James B., 312
Schuster, Assaf, 20
Schwoon, Stefan, 232
Shahar, Elad, 328
Shiple, Thomas R., 113
Shtrichman, Ofer, 480

Singhal, Vigyan, 5
Smolka, Scott A., 576
Somenzi, Fabio, 248
Srivas, Mandayam, 521
Stoller, Scott D., 264
Stratulat, Sorin, 344
Su, Jianwen, 69

Touili, Tayssir, 403
Trefler, Richard J., 139
Tripp, Anson, 5

Unnikrishnan, Leena, 264

Vaandrager, Frits, 216
Vardi, Moshe Y., 36, 389
Veith, Helmut, 154
Velev, Miroslav N., 85, 296
Venkatakrishnan, V.N., 576
Vöge, Jens, 202

Williams, Poul F., 124
Wittke, Hartmut, 561
Wolfsthal, Yaron, 538

Yoneda, Tomohiro, 572

Ziv, Barukh, 389

Lecture Notes in Computer Science

For information about Vols. 1–1760
please contact your bookseller or Springer-Verlag

Vol. 1761: R. Caferra, G. Salzer (Eds.), Automated Deduction in Classical and Non-Classical Logics. Proceedings. VIII, 299 pages. 2000. (Subseries LNAI).

Vol. 1762: K.-D. Schewe, B. Thalheim (Eds.), Foundations of Information and Knowledge Systems. Proceedings, 2000. X, 305 pages. 2000.

Vol. 1763: J. Akiyama, M. Kano, M. Urabe (Eds.), Discrete and Computational Geometry. Proceedings, 1998. VIII, 333 pages. 2000.

Vol. 1764: H. Ehrig, G. Engels, H.-J. Kreowski, G. Rozenberg (Eds.), Theory and Application of Graph Transformations. Proceedings, 1998. IX, 490 pages. 2000.

Vol. 1765: T. Ishida, K. Isbister (Eds.), Digital Cities. IX, 444 pages. 2000.

Vol. 1767: G. Bongiovanni, G. Gambosi, R. Petreschi (Eds.), Algorithms and Complexity. Proceedings, 2000. VIII, 317 pages. 2000.

Vol. 1768: A. Pfitzmann (Ed.), Information Hiding. Proceedings, 1999. IX, 492 pages. 2000.

Vol. 1769: G. Haring, C. Lindemann, M. Reiser (Eds.), Performance Evaluation: Origins and Directions. X, 529 pages. 2000.

Vol. 1770: H. Reichel, S. Tison (Eds.), STACS 2000. Proceedings, 2000. XIV, 662 pages. 2000.

Vol. 1771: P. Lambrix, Part-Whole Reasoning in an Object-Centered Framework. XII, 195 pages. 2000. (Subseries LNAI).

Vol. 1772: M. Beetz, Concurrent Ractive Plans. XVI, 213 pages. 2000. (Subseries LNAI).

Vol. 1773: G. Saake, K. Schwarz, C. Türker (Eds.), Transactions and Database Dynamics. Proceedings, 1999. VIII, 247 pages. 2000.

Vol. 1774: J. Delgado, G.D. Stamoulis, A. Mullery, D. Prevedourou, K. Start (Eds.), Telecommunications and IT Convergence Towards Service E-volution. Proceedings, 2000. XIII, 350 pages. 2000.

Vol. 1775: M. Thielscher, Challenges for Action Theories. XIII, 138 pages. 2000. (Subseries LNAI).

Vol. 1776: G.H. Gonnet, D. Panario, A. Viola (Eds.), LATIN 2000: Theoretical Informatics. Proceedings, 2000. XIV, 484 pages. 2000.

Vol. 1777: C. Zaniolo, P.C. Lockemann, M.H. Scholl, T. Grust (Eds.), Advances in Database Technology – EDBT 2000. Proceedings, 2000. XII, 540 pages. 2000.

Vol. 1778: S. Wermter, R. Sun (Eds.), Hybrid Neural Systems. IX, 403 pages. 2000. (Subseries LNAI).

Vol. 1779: M. Nagl, A. Schürr, M. Münch (Eds.), Application of Graph Transformations with Industrial Relevance. Proceedings, 1999. XV, 496 pages. 2000.

Vol. 1780: R. Conradi (Ed.), Software Process Technology. Proceedings, 2000. IX, 249 pages. 2000.

Vol. 1781: D.A. Watt (Ed.), Compiler Construction. Proceedings, 2000. X, 295 pages. 2000.

Vol. 1782: G. Smolka (Ed.), Programming Languages and Systems. Proceedings, 2000. XIII, 429 pages. 2000.

Vol. 1783: T. Maibaum (Ed.), Fundamental Approaches to Software Engineering. Proceedings, 2000. XIII, 375 pages. 2000.

Vol. 1784: J. Tiuryn (Ed.), Foundations of Software Science and Computation Structures. Proceedings, 2000. X, 391 pages. 2000.

Vol. 1785: S. Graf, M. Schwartzbach (Eds.), Tools and Algorithms for the Construction and Analysis of Systems. Proceedings, 2000. XIV, 552 pages. 2000.

Vol. 1786: B.H. Haverkort, H.C. Bohnenkamp, C.U. Smith (Eds.), Computer Performance Evaluation. Proceedings, 2000. XIV, 383 pages. 2000.

Vol. 1787: J. Song (Ed.), Information Security and Cryptology – ICISC'99. Proceedings, 1999. XI, 279 pages. 2000.

Vol. 1789: B. Wangler. L. Bergman (Eds.), Advanced Information Systems Engineering. Proceedings, 2000. XII, 524 pages. 2000.

Vol. 1790: N. Lynch, B.H. Krogh (Eds.), Hybrid Systems: Computation and Control. Proceedings, 2000. XII, 465 pages. 2000.

Vol. 1792: E. Lamma, P. Mello (Eds.), AI*IA 99: Advances in Artificial Intelligence. Proceedings, 1999. XI, 392 pages. 2000. (Subseries LNAI).

Vol. 1793: O. Cairo, L.E. Sucar, F.J. Cantu (Eds.), MICAI 2000: Advances in Artificial Intelligence. Proceedings, 2000. XIV, 750 pages. 2000. (Subseries LNAI).

Vol. 1795: J. Sventek, G. Coulson (Eds.), Middleware 2000. Proceedings, 2000. XI, 436 pages. 2000.

Vol. 1794: H. Kirchner, C. Ringeissen (Eds.), Frontiers of Combining Systems. Proceedings, 2000. X, 291 pages. 2000. (Subseries LNAI).

Vol. 1796: B. Christianson, B. Crispo, J.A. Malcolm, M. Roe (Eds.), Security Protocols. Proceedings, 1999. XII, 229 pages. 2000.

Vol. 1800: J. Rolim et al. (Eds.), Parallel and Distributed Processing. Proceedings, 2000. XXIII, 1311 pages. 2000.

Vol. 1801: J. Miller, A. Thompson, P. Thomson, T.C. Fogarty (Eds.), Evolvable Systems: From Biology to Hardware. Proceedings, 2000. X, 286 pages. 2000.

Vol. 1802: R. Poli, W. Banzhaf, W.B. Langdon, J. Miller, P. Nordin, T.C. Fogarty (Eds.), Genetic Programming. Proceedings, 2000. X, 361 pages. 2000.

Vol. 1803: S. Cagnoni et al. (Eds.), Real-World Applications and Evolutionary Computing. Proceedings, 2000. XII, 396 pages. 2000.

Vol. 1805: T. Terano, H. Liu, A.L.P. Chen (Eds.), Knowledge Discovery and Data Mining. Proceedings, 2000. XIV, 460 pages. 2000. (Subseries LNAI).

Vol. 1806: W. van der Aalst, J. Desel, A. Oberweis (Eds.), Business Process Management. VIII, 391 pages. 2000.

Vol. 1807: B. Preneel (Ed.), Advances in Cryptology – EUROCRYPT 2000. Proceedings, 2000. XVIII, 608 pages. 2000.

Vol. 1810: R.López de Mántaras, E. Plaza (Eds.), Machine Learning: ECML 2000. Proceedings, 2000. XII, 460 pages. 2000. (Subseries LNAI).

Vol. 1811: S.W. Lee, H.. Bülthoff, T. Poggio (Eds.), Biologically Motivated Computer Vision. Proceedings, 2000. XIV, 656 pages. 2000.

Vol. 1813: P.L. Lanzi, W. Stolzmann, S.W. Wilson (Eds.), Learning Classifier Systems. X, 349 pages. 2000. (Subseries LNAI).

Vol. 1815: G. Pujolle, H. Perros, S. Fdida, U. Körner, I. Stavrakakis (Eds.), Networking 2000 – Broadband Communications, High Performance Networking, and Performance of Communication Networks. Proceedings, 2000. XX, 981 pages. 2000.

Vol. 1816: T. Rus (Ed.), Algebraic Methodology and Software Technology. Proceedings, 2000. XI, 545 pages. 2000.

Vol. 1817: A. Bossi (Ed.), Logic-Based Program Synthesis and Transformation. Proceedings, 1999. VIII, 313 pages. 2000.

Vol. 1818: C.G. Omidyar (Ed.), Mobile and Wireless Communications Networks. Proceedings, 2000. VIII, 187 pages. 2000.

Vol. 1819: W. Jonker (Ed.), Databases in Telecommunications. Proceedings, 1999. X, 208 pages. 2000.

Vol. 1821: R. Loganantharaj, G. Palm, M. Ali (Eds.), Intelligent Problem Solving. Proceedings, 2000. XVII, 751 pages. 2000. (Subseries LNAI).

Vol. 1822: H.H. Hamilton, Advances in Artificial Intelligence. Proceedings, 2000. XII, 450 pages. 2000. (Subseries LNAI).

Vol. 1823: M. Bubak, H. Afsarmanesh, R. Williams, B. Hertzberger (Eds.), High Performance Computing and Networking. Proceedings, 2000. XVIII, 719 pages. 2000.

Vol. 1824: J. Palsberg (Ed.), Static Analysis. Proceedings, 2000. VIII, 433 pages. 2000.

Vol. 1825: M. Nielsen, D. Simpson (Eds.), Application and Theory of Petri Nets 2000. Proceedings, 2000. XI, 485 pages. 2000.

Vol. 1826: W. Cazzola, R.J. Stroud, F. Tisato (Eds.), Reflection and Software Engineering. X, 229 pages. 2000.

Vol. 1830: P. Kropf, G. Babin, J. Plaice, H. Unger (Eds.), Distributed Communities on the Web. Proceedings, 2000. X, 203 pages. 2000.

Vol. 1831: D. McAllester (Ed.), Automated Deduction – CADE-17. Proceedings, 2000. XIII, 519 pages. 2000. (Subseries LNAI).

Vol. 1832: B. Lings, K. Jeffery (Eds.), Advances in Databases. Proceedings, 2000. X, 227 pages. 2000.

Vol. 1833: L. Bachmair (Ed.), Rewriting Techniques and Applications. Proceedings, 2000. X, 275 pages. 2000.

Vol. 1834: J.-C. Heudin (Ed.), Virtual Worlds. Proceedings, 2000. XI, 314 pages. 2000. (Subseries LNAI).

Vol. 1835: D. N. Christodoulakis (Ed.), Natural Language Processing – NLP 2000. Proceedings, 2000. XII, 438 pages. 2000. (Subseries LNAI).

Vol. 1837: R. Backhouse, J. Nuno Oliveira (Eds.), Mathematics of Program Construction. Proceedings, 2000. IX, 257 pages. 2000.

Vol. 1838: W. Bosma (Ed.), Algorithmic Number Theory. Proceedings, 2000. IX, 615 pages. 2000.

Vol. 1839: G. Gauthier, C. Frasson, K. VanLehn (Eds.), Intelligent Tutoring Systems. Proceedings, 2000. XIX, 675 pages. 2000.

Vol. 1840: F. Bomarius, M. Oivo (Eds.), Product Focused Software Process Improvement. Proceedings, 2000. XI, 426 pages. 2000.

Vol. 1841: E. Dawson, A. Clark, C. Boyd (Eds.), Information Security and Privacy. Proceedings, 2000. XII, 488 pages. 2000.

Vol. 1842: D. Vernon (Ed.), Computer Vision – ECCV 2000. Part I. Proceedings, 2000. XVIII, 953 pages. 2000.

Vol. 1843: D. Vernon (Ed.), Computer Vision – ECCV 2000. Part II. Proceedings, 2000. XVIII, 881 pages. 2000.

Vol. 1844: W.B. Frakes (Ed.), Software Reuse: Advances in Software Reusability. Proceedings, 2000. XI, 450 pages. 2000.

Vol. 1845: H.B. Keller, E. Plöderer (Eds.), Reliable Software Technologies Ada-Europe 2000. Proceedings, 2000. XIII, 304 pages. 2000.

Vol. 1846: H. Lu, A. Zhou (Eds.), Web-Age Information Management. Proceedings, 2000. XIII, 462 pages. 2000.

Vol. 1847: R. Dyckhoff (Ed.), Automated Reasoning with Analytic Tableaux and Related Methods. Proceedings, 2000. X, 441 pages. 2000. (Subseries LNAI).

Vol. 1848: R. Giancarlo, D. Sankoff (Eds.), Combinatorial Pattern Matching. Proceedings, 2000. XI, 423 pages. 2000.

Vol. 1849: C. Freksa, W. Brauer, C. Habel, K.F. Wender (Eds.), Spatial Cognition II. XI, 420 pages. 2000. (Subseries LNAI).

Vol. 1850: E. Bertino (Ed.), ECOOP 2000 – Object-Oriented Programming. Proceedings, 2000. XIII, 493 pages. 2000.

Vol. 1851: M.M. Halldórsson (Ed.), Algorithm Theory – SWAT 2000. Proceedings, 2000. XI, 564 pages. 2000.

Vol. 1853: U. Montanari, J.D.P. Rolim, E. Welzl (Eds.), Automata, Languages and Programming. Proceedings, 2000. XVI, 941 pages. 2000.

Vol. 1855: E.A. Emerson, A.P. Sistla (Eds.), Computer Aided Verification. Proceedings, 2000. X, 582 pages. 2000.

Vol. 1857: J. Kittler, F. Roli (Eds.), Multiple Classifier Systems. Proceedings, 2000. XII, 404 pages. 2000.

Vol. 1860: M. Klusch, L. Kerschberg (Eds.), Cooperative Information Agents IV. Proceedings, 2000. XI, 285 pages. 2000. (Subseries LNAI).